MPLS in the SDN Era

Antonio Sánchez-Monge &
Krzysztof Grzegorz Szarkowicz

Beijing · Boston · Farnham · Sebastopol · Tokyo

MPLS in the SDN Era

by Antonio Sánchez-Monge and Krzysztof Grzegorz Szarkowicz

Printed in the United States of America.

Published by O'Reilly Media, Inc., 1005 Gravenstein Highway North, Sebastopol, CA 95472.

O'Reilly books may be purchased for educational, business, or sales promotional use. Online editions are also available for most titles (*http://safaribooksonline.com*). For more information, contact our corporate/ institutional sales department: 800-998-9938 or *corporate@oreilly.com*.

Editors: Brian Anderson and Courtney Allen	**Indexer:** WordCo Indexing Services
Production Editor: Nicole Shelby	**Interior Designer:** David Futato
Copyeditor: Octal Publishing	**Cover Designer:** Ellie Volckhausen
Proofreader: Jasmine Kwityn	**Illustrator:** Rebecca Demarest

December 2015:   First Edition

Revision History for the First Edition
2015-12-08:   First Release

See *http://oreilly.com/catalog/errata.csp?isbn=9781491905456* for release details.

978-1-491-90545-6

[LSI]

Table of Contents

Preface

About This Book

There are many Multiprotocol Label Switching (MPLS) books available on the market. In particular, we have been very much influenced in the recent past by these two great books:

- *MPLS-Enabled Applications: Emerging Developments and New Technologies, Third Edition* by Ina Minei and Julian Lucek (Wiley, 2010).
- *MPLS and VPN Architectures* by Ivan Pepelnjak and Jim Guichard (Cisco Press, 2010).

What is the point in releasing another book about MPLS? In two words: interoperability and Software-Defined Networking (SDN).

Interoperability

Although this first edition is published in late 2015, the initial idea dates from mid-2012. This book was initially conceived to describe real MPLS interoperability.

Over the past decade, we have heard this sentence from many customers: "You vendors keep speaking about what you do better than your competitors, but you never tell us what you can do *with* them on a multivendor network." Clearly, the answer, "We try to comply to the standards—ask the other vendors to do the same and it should be fine," is not satisfactory enough for large feature sets. This book attempts to break that taboo by describing, for the first time in networking history, how a large portfolio of *multivendor* MPLS services can be deployed on real networks, down to the configuration level. We'll look at what interoperates and what does not interoperate yet.

The two chosen network operating systems are Juniper's Junos and Cisco's IOS XR. Although there are other relevant MPLS vendors, a basic combinatory analysis shows that achieving interoperability among four vendors is six times as costly as doing it for two vendors.

MPLS in the SDN Era

In the early 2010s, some people claimed that Softwared-Defined Netwroking (SDN), specifically, OpenFlow would replace MPLS. However, after realizing the many challenges of the first OpenFlow version, SDN was redefined into a paradigm (SDN 2.0) that shares many of the principles that have made MPLS a very successful service provider technology for decades.

Looking at SDN and MPLS as competing technologies is fundamentally wrong. MPLS is a key SDN enabler. This statement holds particularly true if you look at MPLS as an architectural paradigm (not as an encapsulation). In a nutshell, this is the MPLS model:

- Decoupling control plane from forwarding plane.
- Decoupling service from transport.
- Decoupling overlay from underlay.
- Layered architecture with a feature-rich edge and a fast transport core. This approach can be applied to the WAN, to data centers, and so on.
- Building overlay networks at the edge in order to support multitenancy and multiservice.
- Minimizing the forwarding state on the core.
- Advanced packet steering by either signaling forwarding paths and/or by stacking instructions on packet headers.

It is hard to imagine a scalable network that does not follow these principles. The implementation details (and the actual encapsulation is one of these details) are secondary. For example, this book considers Ethernet VPN (EVPN) with Virtual eXtensible LAN (VXLAN) transport as a genuine MPLS technology. Even if it does not make use of MPLS labels, this solution is truly based on the MPLS paradigm. Looking at the details, VXLAN does not implement instruction stacking and it uses an IP-based encapsulation whose header overhead is 10 times bigger than that of MPLS.

On the other hand, there is a fast-growing MPLS trend at large-scale data centers, especially for cloud providers. New data center solutions use the Border Gateway Protocol (BGP) and MPLS technologies in a similar way to what WAN service providers have done for decades. This trend not only includes the MPLS paradigm, but more and more, the MPLS encapsulation, too.

One of the proofs that MPLS is more relevant in the SDN era than ever is the exploding amount and variety of MPLS features that networking vendors are developing to meet the requirements of a fast-changing market. This book tries to reflect this reality by including technologies and use cases that are in their earliest life stage.

MPLS is a flexible technology that is not complex, per se. As any modular technology, it can become as complex as you want (or rather, as complex as the requirements are).

Live Book

This book is very practical, and the authors want to keep it alive after publication. Here are some additional resources that you can use:

- For a better reading experience and for space reasons, this book only shows the configuration that is relevant for each section but not the full configurations. In the months following this book's publication, the authors will start to upload some full configurations to this book's blog at *http://www.mplsinthesdnera.net*.

- The authors kept some interop scenarios in the cellar and they will post them periodically on this book's blog at *http://www.mplsinthesdnera.net*.

- You can write directly to the authors at *mplsinthesdnera@gmail.com*. Please keep it fair. Feedback, suggestions for new blog posts, or clarification queries are very welcome. Consultancy requests will not be answered.

Contents of This Book

This book is written so that you can read it in a linear fashion, from its first page to the last one, which is the approach that we recommend. However, if you are only interested in certain chapters, the following list alerts you to the interchapter dependencies. For example, the dependencies for Chapter 9 are Chapter 1, Chapter 2, and Chapter 3. This means that in order to read Chapter 9 you need to master the concepts explained in the first three chapters but you can skip Chapter 4 through Chapter 8 if you'd like.

Chapter 1, Introduction to MPLS and SDN lays the foundation for the rest of the book by introducing basic MPLS and SDN concepts and by providing a static LSP example. There are no chapter dependencies.

Chapter 2, The Four MPLS Builders covers the four methods for signaling dynamic MPLS LSPs: LDP, RSVP-TE, IGP (IS-IS, OSPF) SPRING, and BGP. Chapter dependencies: 1.

Chapter 3, Layer 3 Unicast MPLS Services explains 6PE (IPv6 transport over an IPv4/ MPLS core) and BGP/MPLS IP VPNs (also known as L3VPNs). Chapter dependencies: 1, 2.

Chapter 4, Internet Multicast Over MPLS provides an IP multicast introduction and describes one interoperable method to transport global (non-VPN) IP multicast traffic over MPLS. Chapter dependencies: 1, 2, 3.

Chapter 5, Multicast VPN extensively covers most if not all of the interoperable flavors of BGP MVPN, previously known as next-gen MVPN. Chapter dependencies: 1, 2, 3, 4.

Chapter 6, Point-to-Point Layer 2 VPNs is all about pseudowires. The LDP-based and BGP-based flavors are both discussed. Chapter dependencies: 1, 2, and the first L3VPN sections of 3 (RD and RT concepts).

Chapter 7, Virtual Private LAN Service describes multipoint L2VPNs whose MAC learning is implemented at the forwarding plane. Chapter dependencies: 1, 2, 6.

Chapter 8, Ethernet VPN describes multipoint L2VPNs whose MAC learning is implemented at the control plane. Several flavors are discussed: EVPN with MPLS transport, EVPN with VXLAN transport, and PBB EVPN. Chapter dependencies: 1, 2, 6.

Chapter 9, Inter-Domain MPLS Services focuses on BGP/MPLS IP VPN Inter-AS options A, B, and C. Chapter dependencies: 1, 2, 3.

Chapter 10, Underlay and Overlay Architectures explores the myth of control-plane and forwarding-plane separation by presenting architectures that are very similar despite being used for quite different purposes: multiforwarder devices, fabrics, and virtualization overlays. Chapter dependencies: 1.

Chapter 11, Network Virtualization Overlays is the first genuine SDN chapter in this book. It describes how you can use the MPLS paradigm to interconnect VMs with one another and with subscribers. Dependencies: 1, 3, 8, 9 (option B), 10.

Chapter 12, Network Function Virtualization explains how to build Service Function Chains in order to steer traffic through virtualized network appliances. Chapter dependencies: 1, 10, 11.

Chapter 13, Introduction to Traffic Engineering explains how explicit paths can be dynamically computed upon static constraints such as metric, colors, and Shared-Risk Link Groups. The main focus is on RSVP-TE and there is also a scenario based on BGP-LU for Egress Peer Engineering (EPE). Chapter dependencies: 1, 2.

Chapter 14, TE Bandwidth Reservations shows how to reserve bandwidth with RSVP-TE, both statically and dynamically (auto-bandwidth). It also describes container LSPs applied to RSVP-TE load balancing. Chapter dependencies: 1, 2.

Chapter 15, Centralized Traffic Engineering introduces a model in which LSP path computation is performed by a central controller that communicates to network devices via PCEP. Chapter dependencies: 1, 2, 13.

Chapter 16, Scaling MPLS Transport and Seamless MPLS covers IGP and RSVP-TE scaling best practices and many flavors of LSP hierarchy with applications for service providers and data centers, with or without controllers. Chapter dependencies: 1, 2, 3, 9 (option C).

Chapter 17, Scaling MPLS Services describes common strategies to reduce the control plane load on low-scale devices. The focus is on L3VPN services. Chapter dependencies: 1, 2, 3.

Chapter 18, Transit Fast Restoration Based on the IGP explains how to achieve sub-50 ms convergence upon failure of transit links/nodes with IGP (OSPF, IS-IS) mechanisms, some of them tactically combined with RSVP-TE. It covers technologies like LFA, RLFA, TI-LFA, TI-FRR, and MRT. Chapter dependencies: 1, 2.

Chapter 19, Transit Fast Restoration Based on the RSVP-TE explains how to achieve sub-50 ms convergence upon failure of transit links/nodes by exclusively using RSVP-TE. Two models of path protection are described: facility protection and one-to-one protection. Chapter dependencies: 1, 2.

Chapter 20, FIB Optimization for Fast Restoration is a very vendor-specific chapter that explains how both Junos and IOS XR enhance their FIB structures to meet fast restoration requirements. Chapter dependencies: 1, 2, 3.

Chapter 21, Egress Service Fast Restoration explains how to achieve sub-50 ms convergence upon failure of transit egress links/nodes. It includes technologies like BGP PIC, tail-end protection and EPE protection. Chapter dependencies: 1, 2, 3, 6, 20.

Disclaimer

The honest intention of the two authors has been to show working interoperable scenarios, focusing on the successful scenarios rather than criticizing any implementations. We have made every effort to remain neutral, despite both being Juniper Networks employees when we were writing this. If you spot any kind of favoritism, we can assure you that it was not intentional.

This book exclusively reflects the opinion of the authors and *not* the company for which they work. It does not contain any corporate message from Juniper Networks or any other vendors.

Every statement you see in this book is a conclusion drawn from personal research and lab testing. Let's use the example of statements that are worded as follows: "vendor X supports, or implements, or does not support, or behaves, or interoperates, etc." The actual meaning of this type of sentence is: "*after some unofficial research and lab testing, these book authors came to the personal conclusion that vendor X seems to support, or seems to implement, or seems not to support, or seems to behave, or seems to interoperate, and so on.*"

This book is *not* a vendor official document.

Please also be aware of the following:

- Some scenarios have been built with alpha prototypes. It is possible that at the time of publication some of the features and commands were not yet generally available. Vendors are not committed to releasing any of the features that are described in this book and have not yet been released. There is a good side: this book opens a window to the real state of the art and you have the opportunity to spy on the things that *may* be coming.
- It is possible that some of the commands used in this book will change or become obsolete in the future. Syntax accuracy is not guaranteed.

Finally, for space and brevity reasons, the authors took the liberty to edit the command output examples by removing lines, columns, or characters. For this reason, this book's examples do not have guaranteed accuracy either.

Conventions Used in This Book

The following typographical conventions are used in this book:

Italic
: Indicates new terms, URLs, standards, drafts, email addresses, filenames, and file extensions.

`Constant width`
: Used for device configuration, operation commands and their output, as well as protocol captures.

This element signifies a tip or suggestion.

This element signifies a general note.

This element indicates a warning or caution.

Safari® Books Online

 *Safari Books Online* is an on-demand digital library that delivers expert content in both book and video form from the world's leading authors in technology and business.

Technology professionals, software developers, web designers, and business and creative professionals use Safari Books Online as their primary resource for research, problem solving, learning, and certification training.

Safari Books Online offers a range of plans and pricing for enterprise, government, education, and individuals.

Members have access to thousands of books, training videos, and prepublication manuscripts in one fully searchable database from publishers like O'Reilly Media, Prentice Hall Professional, Addison-Wesley Professional, Microsoft Press, Sams, Que, Peachpit Press, Focal Press, Cisco Press, John Wiley & Sons, Syngress, Morgan Kaufmann, IBM Redbooks, Packt, Adobe Press, FT Press, Apress, Manning, New Riders, McGraw-Hill, Jones & Bartlett, Course Technology, and hundreds more. For more information about Safari Books Online, please visit us online.

How to Contact Us

Please address comments and questions concerning this book to the publisher:

O'Reilly Media, Inc.
1005 Gravenstein Highway North
Sebastopol, CA 95472
800-998-9938 (in the United States or Canada)
707-829-0515 (international or local)
707-829-0104 (fax)

We have a web page for this book, where we list errata, examples, and any additional information. You can access this page at *http://bit.ly/mpls-sdn-era*.

To comment or ask technical questions about this book, send email to *bookquestions@oreilly.com*.

For more information about our books, courses, conferences, and news, see our website at *http://www.oreilly.com*.

Find us on Facebook: *http://facebook.com/oreilly*

Follow us on Twitter: *http://twitter.com/oreillymedia*

Watch us on YouTube: *http://www.youtube.com/oreillymedia*

Acknowledgments

MPLS in the SDN Era has two authors and four key contributors (Harold Ritter, Javier Antich, Gonzalo Gómez, and David Roy), who are further credited at the end of the book, together with Raghu Subramanian.

The first thing a book requires is time to write. The authors would like to thank their families for an outstanding level of patience, support, and understanding. Also to Pablo Mosteiro, Jos Bazelmans, and higher management for tactically freeing up time so the authors could write.

Then, it requires an editor and a publisher. Patrick Ames has helped in every phase of this 18-month project since its early scoping, and the authors could not have been in better hands. He took care of everything so they could focus exclusively on writing. O'Reilly has proven their excellence with a great flexibility, respect for the writers' work, and top-notch editing (special thanks to Nicole Shelby, Courtney Allen, Octal Publishing and to The Book Analyst) and execution.

Minto Jeyananth, the main inventor of tail-end protection, helped countless times and produced a handful of interoperability fixes while displaying a mix of brightness and humility. In terms of innovation, the authors were also very lucky to count on the strong, bright, and humble support of several other inventors (in alphabetical order: Bruno Decraene, Hannes Gredler, Kaliraj Vairavakkalai, Nischal Sheth, Nitin Singh, Pushpasis Sarkar, Santosh Esale, Wen Lin, and more mentioned in the list that follows) who are helping to drive many of the latest developments explained in this book.

Writing about MPLS in the SDN era needs the guidance of people who have a 360-degree technological vision, like Bruno Rijsman, Pravin Bhandarkar, and Stuart Mackie. The authors also had the priviledge of interacting with two essential creators of MPLS and SDN: Kireeti Kompella and Yakov Rekhter.

This is a practical book and it would be nothing without labs. Many people helped but three of them were absolutely key. Manuel Cornejo spent several days developing a homemade solution to interconnect vMX with IOS XRv virtual machines, allowing for arbitrary interop topologies (something unimaginable just a short time ago). Sree Lakshmi Sarva and the Contrail Solutions Engineering team kindly designed, built and shared a set of latest and greatest SDN scenarios. Mohammed Khan and his team built physical ASR9K and MX topologies, which were essential for some feature sets that were not still supported by one or both of the two virtual network OSs.

Ato and Krzysztof are overwhelmed by so much help from many other great people who performed technical reviews, concept clarifications, hands-on lab tasks, or copy-editing; and who provided access to valuable prototypes, fixed interop issues, wrote helpful blog posts, or simply freed up time so the authors could write.

Among the many valuable technical reviews, those conducted by Alejandro Tovar, Camilo Cardona, and Péter Maros covered many chapters and were exceptionally thorough.

It would take a full chapter to explain who did what. In strict alphabetical order, this is the (probably incomplete) list of additional key contributors:

Ahmed Guetari, Alvaro de las Heras, Ambrose Kwong, Andrea Di Donato, Andy Ingram, Anil Lohiya, Ankur Singla, Anshu Verma, Antoine Sibout, Anton Bernal, Antonio Huete, Antonio Sanchez-Benavente, Aravind Srikumar, Ashish Ranjan, Balaji Rajagopalan, Bill Dicks, Bill Twibill, Bob Russell, Brian Anderson, Carlos Durán, Chandrasekar Ramachandran, Chris Bowers, Chris Hellberg, Colby Barth, Colleen Lobner, Cressida Downing, Cyril Margaria, Damien Garros, Dan Fauxsmith, David Delgado, David Lobo, Dianne Russell, Didier Bousser, Dilip Sundarraj, Diogo Montagner, Disha Chopra, Domiciano Alonso, Doug Hanks, Efraín González, Erdem Sener, Evgeny Bugakov, Fawad Shaikh, Fernando (Fertxo) Muñoz Macaya, Francisco Sánchez, Guilhem Tesseyre, Guy Davies, Harish Sitaraman, Harshad Nakil, Hartmut Schroeder, Hassan Hosseini, Iria Varela, Ivan Pepelnjak, Ivan Tomić, Javier Campos, Jeetendra Lulla, Jeff Haas, Jeffrey Fry (Fryguy), Jeffrey (Zhaohui) Zhang, José Cid, José Luis Perez, José Miguel Huertas, Joseph Li, Julian Lucek, Julie Wider, Kapil Arora, Kevin F Wang, Kishore Tiruveedhula, Kostas Anagnopoulos, Mahesh Narayanan, Manish Gupta, Manoj Sharma, Manuel Delgado, Marco Rodrigues, María Caraballo, Matthew Jones, Michael Henkel, Michael Langdon, Michael Pergament, Michał Styszyński, Miguel Barreiros, Miguel Cros, Nacho Martín, Oleg Karlashchuk, Oscar Carnicero, Oscar Santiago, Pablo Sagrera, Parantap Lahiri, Paul Jarvis, Paul Obsitnik, Pedro Marques, Ping Wang, Pierre François, Pooja Mangla, Praveen Karadakal, Qasim Arham, Rafał Jan Szarecki, Rahul Kasralikar, Rakesh Manocha, Ramdas Machat, Ramesh Yakkala, Ranjini Rajendran, Raveendra Torvi, Ravi Singh, Rendo Wibawa, René Triana, Robert Kebler, Rocío Benavente, Rodny Molina, Sachin Natu, Sanju Abraham, Sean Clarke, Selvakumar Sivaraj, Shraddha Hegde, Sreedhevi Sankar,

Steve Kensil, Sudharsana Venkataraman, Sue Oliva, Suman Dara, Suneel Pentala, Sunesh Rustagi, Sunil Malali, Tao (Tony) Liu, Tapraj Singh, Thomas Murray, Tom Adams, Usman Latif, Vallinayakam Somasundaram, Vasu Venkatraman, Victor Ganjian, Víctor Rodríguez, Vinay K Nallamothu, Vishal Nagaonkar, Vivek Shenoy, Walter Goralski, Xander Thuijs, Yimin Shen, and Zeeshan Sabri.

## CHAPTER 1

Introduction to MPLS and SDN

This chapter introduces the basic Multiprotocol Label Switching (MPLS) and Software-Defined Networking (SDN) concepts. These technologies were born for a reason, and a very good way to put them in the proper context is to understand their history. For example, although MPLS has countless applications and use cases today, it was originally conceived to solve a very specific problem in the Internet.

The Internet

The Internet is a collection of *autonomous systems* (*ASs*). Each AS is a network operated by a single organization and has routing connections to one or more neighboring ASs.

AS numbers ranging from 64512 to 65534 are reserved for private use. Although the examples in this book use AS numbers from this range, in real life, Internet Service Providers (ISPs) use public AS numbers to peer with their neighboring ASs.

Traditionally, AS numbers were 16 bits (2-byte) long, but newer protocol implementations support AS numbers that are 32 bits (4-byte) in length, too.

Figure 1-1 provides a very simplified view of the Internet. Here, we're going to take a look at Annika, a random Internet user. She lives in Europe, has a wireline Internet connection at home, and works in a big enterprise that is also connected to the Internet. The company that employs Annika happens to have its own AS number (65001)—this is *not* a requirement for corporate Internet access. Coincidentally, this company is connected to the Internet through the same ISP (AS 65000) that Annika uses for her residential access.

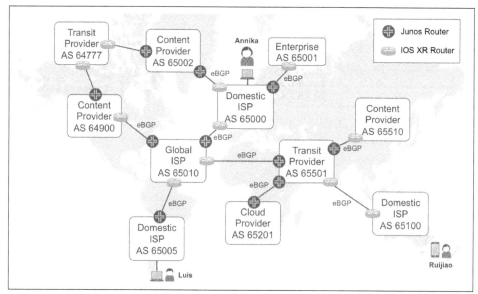

Figure 1-1. The Internet—one day in the life of Annika

As shown in the figure, Annika has two friends who are also ISP subscribers:

- Ruijiao lives in Oceania and connects with her mobile phone to AS 65100.
- Luis lives in South America and connects with his laptop to AS 65005.

Annika also uses the public-cloud services of a provider in Africa (65201) and consumes content from different providers in Asia (AS 65510), Europe (AS 65002), and North America (AS 64900).

Figure 1-1 shows different types of providers. The list that follows describes each:

Domestic ISPs

In this example, Annika's residential and corporate Internet connections go through a *domestic ISP* (AS 65000) that provides Internet access in a particular country, state, or region. Likewise, Ruijiao and Luis are also connected to the Internet through domestic ISPs (AS 65100 and AS 65005, respectively).

Global ISPs

101.230The domestic ISP's to which Annika (AS 65000) and Luis (AS 65005) are connected belong to the same global ISP group, which has presence in several countries in Europe and America. This global ISP uses a specific network (AS 65010) to interconnect all of the domestic ISPs of the group with one another. In addition, global ISPs also connect their domestic ISPs to the rest of the world.

Content and cloud providers
> These service providers (SPs) do not generate revenue by charging the subscribers for Internet *access*. Instead, they provide other types of services to users around the world. For example, they offer multimedia, hosting, cloud services, and so on.

Transit providers
> These are typically large Tier-1 networks that comprise the Internet skeleton. Their customers are other SPs. If two SPs are not directly connected, they typically reach one another through one or more transit providers.

In practice, this classification is a bit fuzzy. Most SPs try to diversify their portfolios by getting a share from more than one of these markets.

There is yet one more key piece of information in Figure 1-1: the links that interconnect ASs have routers at their endpoints. Pay attention to the icons used for Junos and IOS XR because this convention is used throughout this book.

A router that is placed at the border of an AS and which connects to one or more external ASs is called an *AS Border Router* (ASBR). Internet ASBRs speak to one another using the Border Gateway Protocol (BGP), described in RFC 4271. BGP runs on top of Transmission Control Protocol (TCP); it is called *external BGP* (eBGP) if the session's endpoints are in different ASs. Internet eBGP is responsible for distributing the global IPv4 and IPv6 routing tables. The former already contains more than half a million prefixes and is continually growing.

And this is the Internet some bricks (ASs), links, and a protocol (eBGP) that distributes routing information worldwide. Figure 1-1 is a simplistic representation of the Internet; in reality, it looks more like Figure 1-2.

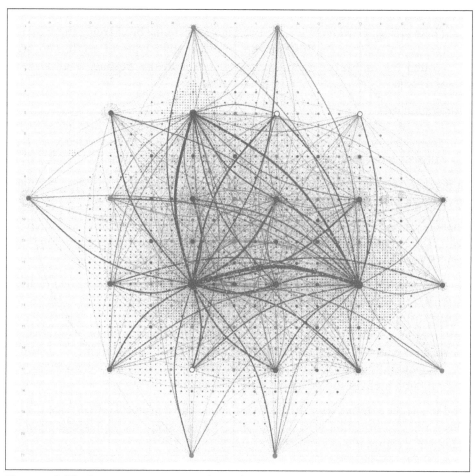

Figure 1-2. The Internet in 2011—topology of autonomous systems (copyright © Peer1 Hosting; used with permission)

This great picture, provided by its owner, Peer1 Hosting, represents ASs as nodes. Peer1's description of the image is as follows:

> This image depicts a graph of 19,869 AS nodes joined by 44,344 connections. The sizing and layout of the ASs is based on their eigenvector centrality, which is a measure of how central to the network each AS is—an AS is central if it is connected to other ASs that are central. This is the same graph-theoretical concept that forms the basis of Google's PageRank algorithm.

> The graph layout begins with the most central nodes and proceeds to the least, positioning them on a grid that subdivides after each order of magnitude of centrality. Within the constraints of the current subdivision level, nodes are placed as near as possible to previously placed nodes that they are connected to.

So far, this description of the Internet is unrelated to MPLS. To understand the original motivation for MPLS, you need to look *inside* an AS.

Let's take the time to understand the topology that will be used in the first eight chapters of this book. It is a worthwhile investment of time.

ISP Example Topology

This topology builds on the previous example. Annika is working, and her laptop is **H1**. At some point, she realizes that she needs to retrieve some data from the provider (more specifically from H3).

For the moment, let's forget about Network Address Translation (NAT) and imagine that all the addresses are actually public.

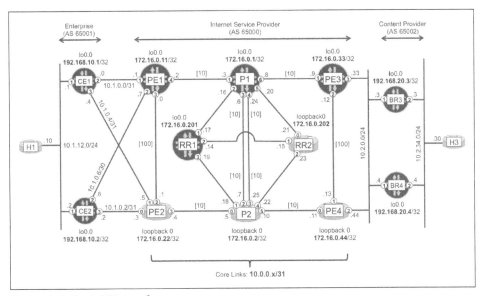

Figure 1-3. Basic ISP topology

More than half of the lab scenarios built for this book run on a single server. The hypervisor spawned virtual machines (VMs) running Junos or IOS XR, which were internally connected through a vSwitch/vRouter.

Around each router, you can see numbers in circles. These are the network interface numbers. For example, if the number inside the circle is <#>, the actual port number is as follows:

- On devices running Junos, ge-2/0/<#>
- On devices running IOS XR, Gi 0/0/0/<#>

This convention is used throughout the book.

All the inter-router links are point-to-point (/31), except for the multipoint connection 10.2.0.0/24. Although the latter topology can be found in the WAN access, it is progressively being considered as legacy. For the moment, let's think of these LANs as classical /24 IPv4 subnets and ignore how they are actually instantiated.

The ISP in this example runs a single Level 2 IS-IS domain with point-to-point interfaces. The PE1-PE2 and PE3-PE4 links are configured with symmetrical IS-IS metric 100, and the remaining core links (PE-P and P-P) are left with the default IS-IS metric 10. These metrics are represented inside square brackets in Figure 1-3.

 Ensure that the RRs are configured with the IS-IS overload bit or with Open Shortest-Path First (OSPF) high metrics so that they do not attract transit traffic.

Router Types in a Service Provider

Although at first sight they look similar, the Enterprise (AS 65001) and the Content Provider (AS 65002) play a different role from the perspective of the ISP (AS 65000):

- The Enterprise is a corporate customer that pays the ISP for Internet access. It can be dual-homed to more than one ISP for redundancy, but overall the relationship between the Enterprise and the ISP is that of traditional customer-to-provider.
- The Content Provider has a peering relationship to several ISPs, including AS 65000, AS 64777, and others. The business model is more complex and there is no clear customer-provider relationship: the SPs reach agreements on how to bill for traffic.

The devices in Figure 1-3 play different roles *from the perspective of AS 65000*, which we'll explore in the sections that follow.

Customer equipment

CE1 and CE2 in Figure 1-3 are *Customer-Premises Equipment* (CPE), also known as *customer equipment* (CE). Traditionally, they are physically located on the customer's facilities. In the SDN era, it is also possible to virtualize some of their functions and run them on the SP network: this solution is called *virtual CPE* or *vCPE*.

For the moment, let's think of traditional CEs that are on a customer's network. The operation and management of the CE might be the responsibility of the ISP or the customer, or both. We can classify CEs as follows:

Residential
> These can be DSL modems, FTTH ONTs, and so on. They don't run any routing protocols and they are seen by the IP layer of the ISP as *directly connected*.

Mobile
> These are smartphones, tablets, and so forth. They also don't run any routing protocols and are seen by the IP layer of the ISP as *directly connected*.

Organizational
> These are dedicated physical or virtual routers that might (or might not) implement an additional set of value-added network functions. They typically have static or dynamic routing to the ISP. eBGP is the most commonly used—and the most scalable—dynamic protocol. If the organization is multihomed to several ISPs, eBGP is simply the only reasonable option.

 The organization might be an external enterprise, an internal ISP department, a government institution, a campus, an NGO, and so on.

Now, let's look at the different functions performed by the core (backbone) routers of the ISP (AS 65000): PE1, PE2, P1, P2, PE3, and PE4.

The core—provider edge

Provider edge (PE) is an *edge function* performed by ISP-owned core network devices that have both external connections to CEs and internal connections to other core routers. PE1 and PE2 in Figure 1-3 perform the PE role when they forward traffic between CEs and other core routers.

The core—provider

Provider (P) is a *core function* performed by ISP-owned core routers that have internal backbone connections to more than one other core router. P1 and P2 are pure P-routers because they do not have any connections to external providers or to customers. As for PE1, PE2, PE3, and PE4, they might perform the P role when they forward traffic between two core interfaces. For example, if PE1 receives a packet on ge-2/0/3 and sends it out of ge-2/0/4, it is acting as a P-router.

The border—ASBR

ASBR is an *edge function* performed by ISP-owned core routers that establish external eBGP peering to other SPs. Although PE1 and PE2 can establish eBGP sessions to CE1 and CE2, they are not considered ASBRs, because the remote peer is a customer, not an SP.

On the other hand, PE3, PE4, BR1, and BR2 are ASBRs, and they perform that function when they forward traffic between external and internal interfaces. For example, if PE3 receives a packet on ge-2/0/1 and sends it out to ge-2/0/3, it is behaving as an ASBR.

The Content Provider (AS 65002) in Figure 1-3 has an overly simplified network. This is fine given that the focus here is on the ISP (AS 65000).

Hosts

The purpose of hosts (H) H1 and H3 in this example is to run ping and traceroute, so their OS is not very relevant. In this example, these hosts are VMs that happen to be running IOS XR; hence, the router icon for a host.

H1 belongs to the customer intranet, and H3 is connected to the content provider core. Neither H1 nor H3 run any routing protocols.

Route Reflectors

Route Reflectors (RR) RR1 and RR2 do not forward user traffic. They have a pure control-plane mission: reflecting BGP routes.

BGP Configuration

Intermediate System–to–Intermediate System (IS-IS) provides loopback-to-loopback connectivity inside the ISP, which is required to establish the multihop *internal BGP* (iBGP) sessions.

Figure 1-4 shows the BGP sessions and their endpoints: loopback addresses for iBGP, and *link* addresses on the border (eBGP).

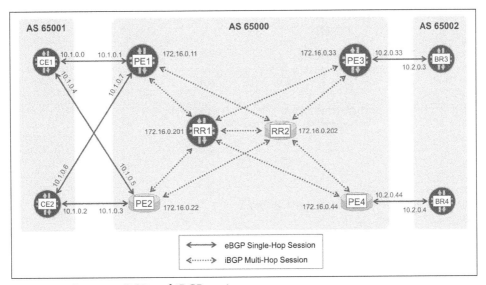

Figure 1-4. Internet eBGP and iBGP sessions

BGP configuration—PEs and ASBRs running Junos

Example 1-1 shows the BGP configuration at PE1.

Example 1-1. BGP configuration at PE1 (Junos)

```
1    routing-options {
2        autonomous-system 65000;
3    }
4    protocols {
5        bgp {
6            group iBGP-RR {
7                type internal;
8                local-address 172.16.0.11;
9                family inet {
10                   unicast {
11                       add-path {
12                           receive;
13                           send {
14                               path-count 6;
15                           }
16                       }
17                   }
18               }
19               export PL-iBGP-RR-OUT;
20               neighbor 172.16.0.201;
21               neighbor 172.16.0.202;
22           }
23           group eBGP-65001 {
```

```
24              family inet {
25                  unicast;
26              }
27              peer-as 65001;
28              neighbor 10.1.0.0 {
29                  export PL-eBGP-65001-CE1-OUT;
30              }
31              neighbor 10.1.0.6 {
32                  export PL-eBGP-65001-CE2-OUT;
33              }
34          }
35      }
36  }
37  policy-options {
38      policy-statement PL-iBGP-RR-OUT {
39          term NHS {
40              from family inet;
41              then {
42                  next-hop self;
43              }
44          }
45      }
46      policy-statement PL-eBGP-65001-CE1-OUT {
47          term BGP {
48              then {
49                  metric 100;
50              }
51          }
52      }
53      policy-statement PL-eBGP-65001-CE2-OUT {
54          term BGP {
55              then {
56                  metric 200;
57              }
58          }
59      }
60  }
```

PE1 and PE3 have a similar configuration. The different business relationship to the peering providers does not change the fact that the protocol is the same: eBGP.

Lines 6 through 22 contain the loopback-to-loopback configuration for the PE1-RR1 and PE1-RR2 iBGP sessions. The Add-Path functionality (lines 11 through 16) will be explained later.

When a router readvertises a prefix into iBGP, it does not change the original BGP *next hop* attribute by default. So, if PE1 advertises the 10.1.12.0/24 route to the RRs, the BGP next hop of the route is 10.1.0.0. This next hop is not reachable from inside the ISP—for example, from PE3 and PE4—making the BGP route useless. The cleanest solution is to make PE1 rewrite the BGP next-hop attribute to its own loopback (lines 19, and lines 38 through 45) before advertising the route via iBGP.

Lines 23 through 34 contain the single-hop PE1-CE1 and PE1-CE2 eBGP configuration. The eBGP route policies (lines 29, 32, and 46 through 59) will be explained soon.

BGP configuration—RRs running Junos

This BGP configuration at RR1 is very similar to PE1's, but it has one key difference, as demonstrated in Example 1-2, for which the neighbors are omitted for brevity.

Example 1-2. BGP configuration at RR1 (Junos)

```
1    protocols {
2        bgp {
3            group iBGP-CLIENTS {
4                cluster 172.16.0.201;
5    }}}
```

What makes RR1 a Route Reflector is line 4; without it, the default iBGP rule—iBGP routes must not be readvertised via iBGP—would apply.

The peering with the other RR (RR2) is configured as a neighbor on a different group that does *not* contain the cluster statement.

BGP Configuration—PEs and ASBRs running IOS XR

PE2 and PE4 have a similar configuration. Example 1-3 presents that of PE2.

Example 1-3. BGP configuration at PE2 (IOS XR)

```
1     router bgp 65000
2      address-family ipv4 unicast
3       additional-paths receive
4       additional-paths send
5      !
6      neighbor-group RR
7       remote-as 65000
8       update-source Loopback0
9       address-family ipv4 unicast
10       route-policy PL-iBGP-RR-OUT out
11      !
12     neighbor 10.1.0.2
13      remote-as 65001
14      address-family ipv4 unicast
15       route-policy PL-eBGP-65001-IN in
16       route-policy PL-eBGP-CE2-OUT out
17      !
18     neighbor 10.1.0.4
19      remote-as 65001
20      address-family ipv4 unicast
```

```
21        route-policy PL-eBGP-65001-IN in
22        route-policy PL-eBGP-CE1-OUT out
23      !
24    neighbor 172.16.0.201
25     use neighbor-group RR
26     !
27    neighbor 172.16.0.202
28     use neighbor-group RR
29     !
30    !
31   route-policy PL-iBGP-RR-OUT
32      set next-hop self
33   end-policy
34   !
35   route-policy PL-eBGP-CE1-OUT
36      set med 200
37      pass
38   end-policy
39   !
40   route-policy PL-eBGP-CE2-OUT
41      set med 100
42      pass
43   end-policy
44   !
45   route-policy PL-eBGP-65001-IN
46      pass
47   end-policy
```

The syntax is different, but the principles are very similar to Junos. The Add-Path functionality (lines 3 through 4) will be explained later.

A remarkable difference between the BGP implementation of Junos and IOS XR is that IOS XR by default blocks the reception and advertisement of routes via eBGP. There are two alternative ways to change this default behavior:

- Explicitly configure input and output policies (lines 15 through 16, 21 through 22, and 35 through 47) in order to allow IOS XR to signal eBGP routes.

- Configure `router bgp 65000 bgp unsafe-ebgp-policy`. This is a shortcut that you can use for quick configuration which is especially useful *in the lab*. This command automatically creates and attaches the "pass all" policies

Due to the constraints of space, from this point forward, Junos and IOS XR configuration examples may be represented with merged lines.

BGP configuration—RRs running IOS XR

The BGP configuration at RR2 shown in Example 1-4 is very similar to that of PE2, but it has some differences.

Example 1-4. BGP configuration at RR2 (IOS XR)

```
1     router bgp 65000
2      address-family ipv4 unicast
3       additional-paths receive
4       additional-paths send
5      !
6      neighbor-group iBGP-CLIENTS
7       cluster-id 172.16.0.202
8       address-family ipv4 unicast
9        route-reflector-client
10    !
```

What makes RR2 a Route Reflector are lines 7 and 9; without them, the default iBGP rule—iBGP routes must not be readvertised via iBGP—would apply.

The peering with the other RR (RR1) is *not* configured through this `neighbor-group`.

BGP Route Signaling and Redundancy

This book considers three BGP redundancy models—Nonredundant, Active-Backup, and Active-Active—and they are all supported by the topology in Figure 1-3.

Nonredundant BGP Routes

In this example, CEs and BRs advertise their own loopacks to one single eBGP peer:

- CE1 advertises 192.168.10.1/32 to PE1 only.
- CE2 advertises 192.168.10.2/32 to PE2 only.
- BR3 advertises 192.168.20.3/32 to PE3 only.
- BR4 advertises 192.168.20.4/32 to PE4 only.

If an eBGP session fails, the loopback of the affected CE or BR is no longer reachable via AS 65000. This scenario is frequent in single-homed access topologies. In this example, it is simulated by selectively blocking the local loopback advertisement from CE1 and CE2 (eBGP export policies), and by only configuring one eBGP session at each BR.

Figure 1-5 shows CE1's loopback route signaling process.

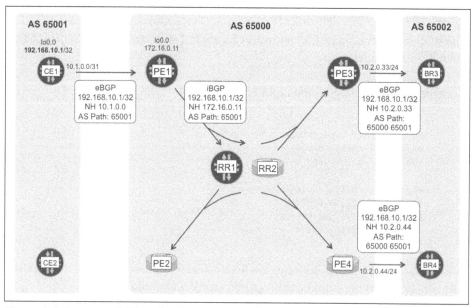

Figure 1-5. Internet eBGP and iBGP route signaling—CE1 loopback

CE1's loopback is single-homed to PE1, so a packet that any device in AS 65002 sends to CE1's loopback should go via PE1 at some point.

The RRs do not change the value of the BGP next hop and AS path attributes when they reflect the route to PE2, PE3, and PE4.

On the other hand, PE2 does not advertise the route to CE2, because it would result in an AS loop. This behavior, which you can change by using the `as-override` configuration command, is further discussed in Chapter 3.

Figure 1-6 shows BR4's loopback route signaling process.

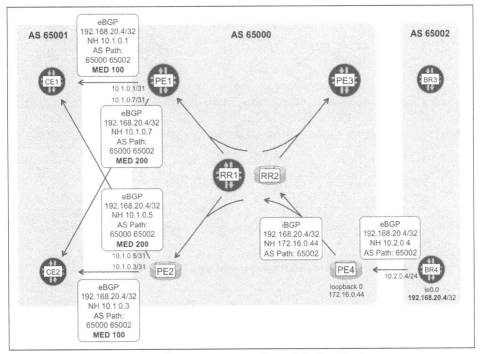

Figure 1-6. Internet eBGP and iBGP route signaling—BR4 loopback

BR4's loopback is single-homed to PE4, so a packet that any device in AS 65001 sends to BR4's loopback should go via PE4 at some point.

There is an additional redundancy level on the left side of Figure 1-6. CE1 prefers to reach BR4 via PE1 (Multi Exit Discriminator [MED] 100 is better than MED 200), but if the CE1-PE1 eBGP session fails, it can still fail-over to PE2.

In the absence of access link failures:

- Inter-loopback ping and traceroute between CE1 and BR3 go via PE1 and PE3. In this book, this is called *the Junos plane*.

- Inter-loopback ping and traceroute between CE2 and BR4 go via PE2 and PE4. In this book, this is called *the IOS XR plane*.

Active-Backup BGP routes

As you can see in Figure 1-7, BR3 and BR4 both advertise the 10.2.34.0/24 route, but they do it with a different MED. As a result, PE1 and PE2 prefer to reach BR4 via PE4. If, for whatever reason, PE4 no longer advertises the 10.2.34.0/24 route (or if the route is in an invalid state), then PE1 and PE2 can fail-over to PE3.

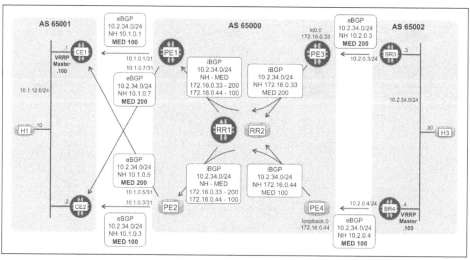

Figure 1-7. Internet eBGP and iBGP route signaling—H3's subnet

H1 has a default route pointing to the virtual IPv4 address 10.1.12.100. CE1 and CE2 run Virtual Router Redundancy Protocol (VRRP) on the host LAN, and in the absence of failures CE1 is the VRRP master that holds the 10.1.12.100 address. On the other hand, VRRP route tracking is configured so that if CE1 does not have a route to reach H3 and CE2 does, CE2 becomes the VRRP master. The mechanism is very similar between BR3 and BR4, except in this case BR4 is the nominal VRRP master.

Finally, the MED scheme configured on PE1's and PE2's eBGP export policies is such that CE1 prefers to reach H3 via PE1 rather than via PE2. With all the links and sessions up, the path followed by H1→H3 (10.1.12.10→10.2.34.30) packets is CE1-PE1-PE4-BR4. VRRP mastership on the first hop, and then MED on the remaining hops, are the tie-breaking mechanisms to choose the best path.

Active-Active BGP routes

PE1 and PE2 both have an eBGP route to 10.1.12.0/24 with MED 100, so both advertise the route with MED 100 to the RRs, as you can see in Figure 1-8.

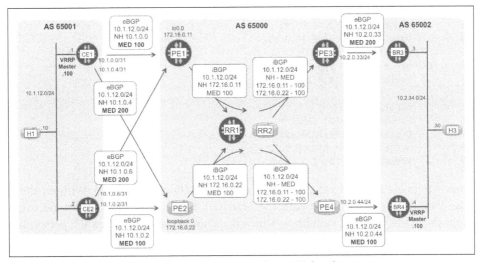

Figure 1-8. Internet eBGP and iBGP route signaling—H1's subnet

The path followed by H3→H1 packets is BR4-PE4-PE2-CE2. PE4 prefers PE2 because the MED value is 100 for both BGP next hops (PE1 and PE2) and the IGP metric of the shortest internal path PE4→PE2 is lower than the IGP metric of PE4→PE1. Likewise, PE3 prefers PE1, but BR4 is the VRRP master, so PE3 is not in the nominal H3→H1 path.

The end result is asymmetrical but *optimal* forwarding of H1→H3 and H3→H1 flows. It is optimal because the RRs are reflecting all the routes, not just those that they consider to be the best, as shown in Example 1-5.

Example 1-5. iBGP Route Reflection with Add-Path—RR1 (Junos)

```
1    juniper@RR1> show route advertising-protocol bgp 172.16.0.44
2            10.1.12.10
3
4    inet.0: 33 destinations, 38 routes (33 active, ...)
5      Prefix            Nexthop         MED     Lclpref    AS path
6    * 10.1.12.0/24      172.16.0.11     100     100        65001 I
7                        172.16.0.22     100     100        65001 I
8
9    juniper@RR1> show route advertising-protocol bgp 172.16.0.44
10            10.1.12.0/24 detail
11
12   inet.0: 33 destinations, 38 routes (33 active, ...)
13   * 10.1.12.0/24 (3 entries, 2 announced)
14     BGP group CLIENTS type Internal
15         Nexthop: 172.16.0.11
16         MED: 100
17         Localpref: 100
```

```
18          AS path: [65000] 65001 I
19          Cluster ID: 172.16.0.201
20          Originator ID: 172.16.0.11
21          Addpath Path ID: 1
22       BGP group CLIENTS type Internal
23          Nexthop: 172.16.0.22
24          MED: 100
25          Localpref: 100
26          AS path: [65000] 65001 I
27          Cluster ID: 172.16.0.201
28          Originator ID: 172.16.0.22
29          Addpath Path ID: 2
```

This is possible thanks to the Add-Path extensions (lines 21 and 29). Without them, RR1 would choose the route with the best IGP metric from its own perspective— from the RR to the BGP next hop—which does not necessarily match the perspective from PE4.

In summary, policies are configured in such a way that the MED or BGP metric is symmetrically set. Following are the results:

- CE1 prefers reaching H3 via PE1 rather than via PE2.
- CE2 prefers reaching H3 via PE2 rather than via PE1.
- PE1 prefers reaching H1 via CE1 rather than via CE2.
- PE2 prefers reaching H1 via CE2 rather than via CE1.
- PE1 and PE2 prefer reaching H3 via PE4 rather than via PE3.
- PE3 and PE4 prefer reaching H1 via PE1 and PE2, respectively.

Packet Forwarding in a BGP-Less Core

Everything is fine so far, except for one major detail: H1 and H3 cannot communicate to each other. Let's take the example of an IPv4 packet with source H1 and destination H3. PE1 decides to forward the packet via PE4, but PE1 and PE4 are *not* directly connected to each other. The shortest path from PE1 to PE4 is PE1-P1-P2-PE4. Thus, PE1 sends the packet to its next hop, P1. Here is the problem: P1 does not speak BGP, so it does not have a route to the destination H3. As a result, P1 drops the packet.

How about establishing iBGP sessions between P1 and the RRs? This is a relatively common practice in large SPs with high-end core devices. In the real Internet there are more than half a million routes, and it keeps growing. Although route summarization is possible, it still requires a significant control-plane load for P1 to program all the necessary BGP routes. P1 would also lose agility upon network topology changes because it would need to reprogram many routes on the forwarding plane.

P1 and P2 are internal core routers (they do not have any eBGP peerings), and their role is to take packets as fast and reliably as possible between edge routers such as PE1, PE2, PE3, and PE4. This is possible if PE1 adds to the H1→H3 IPv4 packet an extra header—or set of headers—with the following instruction: *take me to PE4*.

One option is to use IP tunneling. By encapsulating the H1→H3 IPv4 packet inside another IPv4 header with source and destination PE1→PE4, the packet reaches PE4. Then, PE4 removes the tunneling headers and successfully performs an IPv4 lookup on the original H1→H3 packet. There are several IP tunneling technologies available such as GRE, IP-in-IP, and VXLAN. However, this approach has several problems when it comes to forwarding terabits per second or petabits per second, or more.

The most immediate of these problems was cost, given that IP tunneling used to be expensive:

- First, an IPv4 header alone comprises 20 bytes. Add the extra adaptation headers, and the overhead becomes significant, not to mention the effort that is required to create and destroy headers with many dynamic fields.

- Second, performing an IPv4 lookup has traditionally been expensive. Although modern platforms have dramatically reduced its differential cost, in the 1990s IPv4 forwarding resulted in a much worse performance than label switching.

There is another technology that is better in terms of overhead (4 bytes per header) and forwarding efficiency. This technology is natively integrated with BGP and brings a large portfolio of features that are of paramount importance to SPs. You might have guessed already that its name is *MPLS*, or *Multiprotocol Label Switching*. In the SDN era, forwarding cost is no longer the main driver to deploy MPLS: its architecture and flexibility are.

MPLS

MPLS was invented in the late 1990s, at a time when *Asynchronous Transfer Mode* (ATM) was a widespread WAN technology.

ATM had some virtues: multiservice, asynchronous transport, class of service, reduced forwarding state, predictability, and so on. But it had at least as many defects: no tolerance to data loss or reordering, a forwarding overhead that made it unsuitable to high speeds, no decent multipoint, lack of a native integration with IP, and so forth.

MPLS learned from the instructive ATM experience, taking advantage of its virtues while solving its defects. Modern MPLS is an asynchronous packet-based forwarding technology. In that sense, it is similar to IP, but MPLS has a much lighter forwarding plane and it greatly reduces the amount of state that needs to be signaled and pro-grammed on the devices.

MPLS in Action

Probably the best way to understand MPLS is by looking at a real example, such as that shown in Figure 1-9.

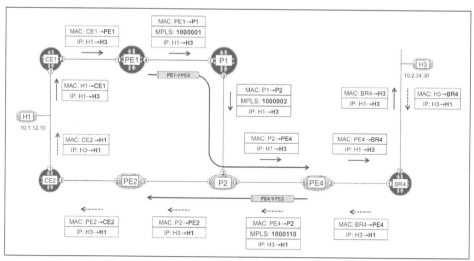

Figure 1-9. MPLS in action

Figure 1-9 shows two unidirectional MPLS *Label-Switched Paths* (LSPs) named PE1→PE4 and PE4→PE2. Let's begin with the first one. An IPv4 H1→H3 (10.1.12.10→10.2.34.30) packet arrives at PE1, which leads to the following:

1. H3 is reachable through PE4, so PE1 places the packet in the PE1→PE4 LSP. It does so by inserting a new MPLS header between the IPv4 and the Ethernet headers of the H1→H3 packet. This header contains MPLS label 1000001, which is locally significant to P1. In MPLS terminology, this operation is a label *push*. Finally, PE1 sends the packet to P1.

2. P1 receives the packet and inspects and removes the original MPLS header. Then, P1 adds a new MPLS header with label 1000002, which is locally significant to P2, and sends the packet to P2. This MPLS operation is called a label *swap*.

3. P2 receives the packet, inspects and removes the MPLS header, and then sends the plain IPv4 packet to PE4. This MPLS operation is called a label *pop*.

4. PE4 receives the IPv4 packet without any MPLS headers. This is fine because PE4 speaks BGP and is aware of all the IPv4 routes, so it knows how to forward the packet toward its destination.

The H3→H1 packet travels from PE4 to PE2 in a shorter LSP where only two MPLS operations take place: label push at PE4 and label pop at P2. There is no label swap.

These LSPs *happen to* follow the shortest IGP path between their endpoints. This is not mandatory and it is often not the case.

Is This IPv4-Over-MPLS or MPLS-Over-IPv4?

This is a trickier question than it seems. It is *IPv4-over-MPLS*. The IPv4 packet is encapsulated *behind* an MPLS header. On the other hand, in this book's diagrams, you will always see the MPLS header over the IPv4 header—the other way around.

Packets in this book are shown in the same way that a sniffer would decode them. The most external headers are on top. When we talk about MPLS labels, outer means upper, and inner means lower.

This is actually the natural way to visualize MPLS packets. MPLS headers are stackable and the topmost label is the most external one.

Router roles in a LSP

Looking back at Figure 1-9, the PE1→PE4 LSP starts at PE1, traverses P1 and P2, and ends... at P2 or at PE4? Let's see. By placing the packet in the LSP, PE1 is basically sending it to PE4. Indeed, when P2 receives a packet with label 1000002, the forwarding instruction is clear: pop the label and send the packet out of the interface Gi 0/0/0/5. So *the LSP ends at PE4*.

The H1→H3 packet arrives unlabeled to PE4 by virtue of a mechanism called *Penultimate Hop Popping* (PHP) executed by P2.

Following are the different router roles from the point of view of the PE1→PE4 LSP. For each of these roles, there are many terms and acronyms:

- PE1 **Ingress PE**, Ingress Label Edge Router (LER), LSP Head-End, LSP Upstream Endpoint. The term *ingress* comes from the fact that user packets like H1→H3 enter the LSP at PE1, which acts as an entrance or ingress point.

- P1 (or P2) **Transit P**, P-Router, Label Switching Router (LSR), or simply P.

- PE4 **Egress PE**, Egress Label Edge Router (LER), LSP Tail-End, LSP Downstream Endpoint. The term *egress* comes from the fact that user packets such as H1→H3 exit the LSP at this PE.

The MPLS Header

Paraphrasing Ivan Pepelnjak, technical director of NIL Data Communications, in his www.ipspace.net blog:

> MPLS is not tunneling, it's a virtual-circuits-based technology, and the difference between the two is a major one. You can talk about tunneling when a protocol that should be lower in the protocol stack gets encapsulated in a protocol that you'd usually find above or next to it. MAC-in-IP, IPv6-in-IPv4, IP-over-GRE-over-IP... these are tunnels. IP-over-MPLS-over-Ethernet is not tunneling.
>
> It is true, however, that MPLS uses virtual circuits, but they are not identical to tunnels. Just because all packets between two endpoints follow the same path and the switches in the middle don't inspect their IP headers, doesn't mean you use a tunneling technology.

MPLS headers are elegantly inserted in the packets. Their size is only 4 bytes. Example 1-6 presents a capture of the H1→H3 packet as it traverses the P1-P2 link.

Example 1-6. MPLS packet on-the-wire

```
1    Ethernet II, Src: MAC_P1_ge-2/0/3, Dst: MAC_P2_gi0/0/0/2
2        Type: MPLS label switched packet (0x8847)
3    MultiProtocol Label Switching Header
4        1111 0100 0010 0100 0010 .... .... .... = Label: 1000002
5        .... .... .... .... .... 000. .... .... = Traffic Class: 0
6        .... .... .... .... .... ...0 .... .... = Bottom of Stack: 1
7        .... .... .... .... .... .... 1111 1100 = MPLS TTL: 252
8    Internet Protocol Version 4, Src: 10.1.12.10, Dst: 10.2.34.30
9        Version: 4
10       Header Length: 20 bytes
11       Differentiated Services Field: 0x00
12       # IPv4 Packet Header Details and IPv4 Packet Payload
```

Here is a description of the 32 bits that compose an MPLS header:

1. The first 20 bits (line 4) are the MPLS label.

2. The next 3 bits (line 5) are the *Traffic Class*. In the past, they were called the experimental bits. This field is semantically similar to the first 3 bits of the IPv4 header's Differentiated Services Code Point (DSCP) field (line 11).

3. The next 1 bit (line 6) is the *Bottom of Stack* (BoS) bit. It is set to value 1 only if this is the MPLS header in contact with the next protocol (in this case, IPv4) header. Otherwise, it is set to zero. This bit is important because the MPLS

header does not have a type field, so it needs the BoS bit to indicate that it is the last header before the MPLS payload.

4. The next 8 bits (line 7) are the MPLS Time-to-Live (TTL). Like the IP TTL, the MPLS TTL implements a mechanism to discard packets in the event of a forwarding loop. Typically the ingress PE decrements the IP TTL by one and then copies its value into the MPLS TTL. Transit P-routers decrement the MPLS TTL by one at each hop. Finally, the egress PE copies the MPLS TTL into the IP TTL and then decrements its value by one. You can tune this default implementation in both Junos and IOS XR.

Figure 1-10 shows two other label operations that have not been described so far:

- The first incoming packet has a two-label stack. You can see the usage of the BoS bit. The swap operation only affects the topmost (outermost) label.

- The second incoming packet initially has a one-label stack, and it is processed by a composite label operation: swap and push. The result is a two-label stack.

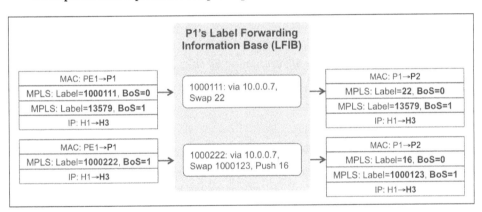

Figure 1-10. Other MPLS operations

MPLS Configuration and Forwarding Plane

MPLS interface configuration

The first step is to enable MPLS on the interfaces on which you want to forward MPLS packets. Example 1-7 shows the Junos configuration of one interface at PE1.

Example 1-7. MPLS interface configuration—PE1 (Junos)

```
1    interfaces {
2        ge-2/0/4 {
3            unit 0 {
4                family mpls;
```

```
5    }}}
6    protocols {
7        mpls {
8            interface ge-2/0/4.0;
9    }}
```

Lines 1 through 4 enable the MPLS encapsulation on the interface, and lines 6 through 8 enable the interface for MPLS protocols. Strictly speaking, the latter configuration block is not always needed, but it is a good practice to systematically add it.

 Throughout this book, it is assumed that every MPLS-enabled interface in Junos has at least the configuration from Example 1-7.

In IOS XR, there is no generic MPLS configuration. You need to enable the interface for each of the MPLS flavors that you need to use. This chapter features the simplest of all the MPLS flavors: static MPLS. Example 1-8 presents the configuration of one interface at PE4.

Example 1-8. MPLS interface configuration—PE4 (IOS XR)

```
mpls static
 interface GigabitEthernet0/0/0/0
 !
```

Label-switched path PE1→PE4—configuration

Remember that H1→H3 packets go through PE1 and PE4. You need an LSP that takes these packets from PE1 to PE4. Let's make the LSP follow the path PE1-P1-P2-PE4 that we saw in Figure 1-9.

 This example is based on *static* LSPs, which are not scalable because they require manual label assignments at each hop of the path. Beginning in Chapter 2, the focus is on the much more scalable *dynamic* LSPs.

Example 1-9 gives the full configuration along the path.

Example 1-9. LSP PE1→PE4 configuration—Junos and IOS XR

```
#PE1 (Junos)

protocols {
    mpls {
```

```
        static-label-switched-path PE1--->PE4 {
            ingress {
                next-hop 10.0.0.3;
                to 172.16.0.44;
                push 1000001;
}}}}
```

#P1 (Junos)

```
protocols {
    mpls {
        icmp-tunneling;
        static-label-switched-path PE1--->PE4 {
            transit 1000001 {
                next-hop 10.0.0.7;
                swap 1000002;
}}}}
```

#P2 (IOS XR)

```
mpls static
 address-family ipv4 unicast
  local-label 1000002 allocate
   forward
    path 1 nexthop GigabitEthernet0/0/0/5 10.0.0.11 out-label pop
!
```

PE4 receives plain IPv4 packets from P2, so it does not require any LSP-specific configuration.

Labels 1000001 and 1000002 are locally significant to P1 and P2, respectively. Their numerical values could have been identical and they would still correspond to different instructions because they are not interpreted by the same LSR.

LSP PE1→PE4—forwarding plane

It's time to inspect the forwarding instructions that steer the H1→H3 IPv4 packet through the PE1→PE4 LSP. Let's begin at PE1, which is shown in Example 1-10.

Example 1-10. Routing and forwarding state at the ingress PE—PE1 (Junos)

```
1    juniper@PE1> show route receive-protocol bgp 172.16.0.201
2                10.2.34.30 active-path
3
4    inet.0: 36 destinations, 45 routes (36 active, ...)
5      Prefix          Nexthop       MED    Lclpref    AS path
6    * 10.2.34.0/24    172.16.0.44   100    100        65002 I
7
8    juniper@PE1> show route 172.16.0.44
9
10   inet.0: 36 destinations, 45 routes (36 active, ...)
```

```
11    + = Active Route, - = Last Active, * = Both
12
13    172.16.0.44/32      *[IS-IS/18] 1d 11:22:00, metric 30
14                         > to 10.0.0.3 via ge-2/0/4.0
15
16    inet.3: 1 destinations, 1 routes (1 active, ...)
17    + = Active Route, - = Last Active, * = Both
18
19    172.16.0.44/32       *[MPLS/6/1] 05:00:00, metric 0
20                          > to 10.0.0.3 via ge-2/0/4.0, Push 1000001
21
22    juniper@PE1> show route 10.2.34.30 active-path
23
24    inet.0: 36 destinations, 45 routes (36 active...)
25    + = Active Route, - = Last Active, * = Both
26
27    10.2.34.0/24    *[BGP/170] 06:37:28, MED 100, localpref 100,
28                         from 172.16.0.201, AS path: 65002 I
29                      > to 10.0.0.3 via ge-2/0/4.0, Push 1000001
30
31    juniper@PE1> show route forwarding-table destination 10.2.34.30
32    Routing table: default.inet
33    Internet:
34    Destination    Next hop           Type  Index   NhRef Netif
35    10.2.34.0/24                       indr  1048575   3
36                   10.0.0.3 Push 1000001          513   2 ge-2/0/4.0
37
38    juniper@PE1> show mpls static-lsp statistics name PE1--->PE4
39    Ingress LSPs:
40    LSPname      To            State   Packets     Bytes
41    PE1--->PE4   172.16.0.44   Up        27694   2768320
```

The best BGP route to the destination 10.2.34.30 (H3) has a BGP next-hop attribute (line 6) equal to 172.16.0.44. There are two routes toward 172.16.0.44 (PE4's loopback):

- An IS-IS route in the global IPv4 routing table inet.0 (lines 10 through 14).

- A MPLS route in the inet.3 auxiliary table (lines 16 through 20). The static LSP configured in Example 1-9 automatically installs this MPLS route.

The goal of the inet.3 auxiliary table is to resolve BGP next hops (line 6) into forwarding next hops (line 20). Indeed, the BGP route 10.2.34.0/24 is installed in inet.0 with a labeled forwarding next hop (line 29) that is copied from inet.3 (line 20). Finally, the BGP route is installed in the forwarding table (lines 31 through 36) and pushed to the forwarding engines.

The fact that Junos has an auxiliary table (inet.3) to resolve BGP next hops is quite relevant. Keep in mind that Junos uses inet.0 and not inet.3 to program the forwarding table. For this reason, PE1's default behavior is *not* to push any labels on the packets that it sends to internal (non-BGP) destinations such as PE4's loopback, as demonstrated in Example 1-11.

Example 1-11. Unlabeled traceroute to a non-BGP destination—PE1 (Junos)

```
juniper@PE1> traceroute 172.16.0.44
traceroute to 172.16.0.44
 1  P1 (10.0.0.3)  42.820 ms  11.081 ms  4.016 ms
 2  P2 (10.0.0.25)  6.440 ms P2 (10.0.0.7)  3.426 ms  *
 3  PE4 (10.0.0.11)  9.139 ms  *  78.770 ms
```

Let's get back to the PE1→PE4 LSP and move on to P1, the first LSR on the path.

Example 1-12. Routing and forwarding state at a transit P—P1 (Junos)

```
juniper@P1> show route table mpls.0 label 1000001

mpls.0: 5 destinations, 5 routes (5 active, 0 holddown, 0 hidden)
+ = Active Route, - = Last Active, * = Both

1000001    *[MPLS/6] 07:23:19, metric 1
            > to 10.0.0.7 via ge-2/0/3.0, Swap 1000002
```

The mpls.0 table stores label instructions. For example, if P1 receives a packet with label 1000001, the instruction says: swap the label for 1000002 and send the packet out of ge-2/0/3 to P2. This instruction set is known as the *Label Forwarding Information Base* (LFIB). The mpls.0 table is *not* auxiliary: it populates the forwarding table.

Finally, let's look at P2's LFIB in Example 1-13.

Example 1-13. Routing and forwarding state at a transit P—P2 (IOS XR)

```
RP/0/0/CPU0:P2#show mpls forwarding labels 1000002
Local  Outgoing   Outgoing      Next Hop         Bytes
Label  Label      Interface                      Switched
------ ---------- ------------- ---------------- -----------
1000002 Pop       Gi0/0/0/5     10.0.0.11        8212650
```

There is no point in looking at PE4, which behaves like a pure IP router with respect to the H1→H3 packets.

LSP PE4→PE2—Configuration

For completeness, Example 1-14 presents the full configuration of the PE4→PE2 LSP.

Example 1-14. LSP PE4→PE2 configuration—IOS XR

```
#PE4 (IOS XR)
mpls static
 address-family ipv4 unicast
  local-label 1000200 allocate per-prefix 172.16.0.22/32
   forward
    path 1 nexthop GigabitEthernet0/0/0/0 10.0.0.10 out-label 1000110
 !

#P2 (IOS XR)
mpls static
 address-family ipv4 unicast
  local-label 1000110 allocate
   forward
    path 1 nexthop GigabitEthernet0/0/0/0 10.0.0.4 out-label pop
 !
```

The key syntax at PE4 is per-prefix: this says that in order to place a packet on an LSP whose tail end is PE2 (172.16.0.22), *push label 1000110 and send it to P2.*

The first label value (1000200) from Example 1-14 is not really part of the PE4→PE2 LSP. It means that if it receives an MPLS packet with the outermost label 1000200, PE4 puts the packet on the PE4→PE2 LSP by swapping the label for 1000110. This logic is not very relevant to the current example, where H3→H1 packets arrive unlabeled to PE4.

Example 1-15 demonstrates the routing and forwarding state at the ingress PE (PE4).

Example 1-15. Routing and forwarding state at the ingress PE—PE4 (IOS XR)

```
RP/0/0/CPU0:PE4#show bgp 10.1.12.0/24 brief
[...]
   Network        Next Hop      Metric LocPrf Weight Path
* i10.1.12.0/24   172.16.0.11     100    100      0 65001 i
*>i               172.16.0.22     100    100      0 65001 i

RP/0/0/CPU0:PE4#show cef 10.1.12.10
[...]
 local adjacency 10.0.0.10
   via 172.16.0.22, 2 dependencies, recursive [flags 0x6000]
    path-idx 0 NHID 0x0 [0xa137dd74 0x0]
    next hop 172.16.0.22 via 172.16.0.22/32

RP/0/0/CPU0:PE4#show cef 172.16.0.22
[...]
 local adjacency 10.0.0.10
   via 10.0.0.10, GigabitEthernet0/0/0/0, 4 dependencies, [...]
    next hop 10.0.0.10
    local adjacency
     local label 1000200        labels imposed {1000110}
```

```
RP/0/0/CPU0:PE4#show mpls forwarding labels 1000200
Local  Outgoing Prefix          Outgoing  Next Hop  Bytes
Label  Label    or ID           Interface           Switched
------ -------- --------------- ---------- --------- --------
1000200 1000110 172.16.0.22/32 Gi0/0/0/0  10.0.0.10 10410052
```

The logic in IOS XR is very similar, except that in this case there are no auxiliary tables. As a result, PE4's default behavior is to push labels on the packets that it sends to internal (non-BGP) destinations that are more than a hop away, like PE2's loopback shown in Example 1-16.

Example 1-16. Labeled traceroute to a non-BGP destination—PE4 (IOS XR)

```
RP/0/0/CPU0:PE4#traceroute 172.16.0.22

1  p2 (10.0.0.10) [MPLS: Label 1000110 Exp 0] 9 msec ...
2  pe2 (10.0.0.4) 0 msec ...
```

End-to-end user traffic

After the PE1→PE4 and the PE4→PE2 LSPs are up, end-to-end connectivity is fine.

Example 1-17. End-to-end user traceroute through an MPLS network

```
RP/0/0/CPU0:H1#traceroute vrf H1 10.2.34.30

1  ce1 (10.1.12.1) 0 msec ...
2  pe1 (10.1.0.1) 0 msec ...
3  p1 (10.0.0.3) [MPLS: Label 1000001 Exp 0] 9 msec ...
4  p2 (10.0.0.7) [MPLS: Label 1000002 Exp 0] 9 msec ...
5  pe4 (10.0.0.11) 9 msec ...
6  br4 (10.2.0.4) 9 msec ...
7  h3 (10.2.34.30) 9 msec ...
```

As expected, traceroute shows the forward path with the PE1→PE4 LSP's labels.

You might wonder how P1 can send an Internet Control Message Protocol (ICMP) Time Exceeded message to H1, taking into account that it does not even have a route to reach H1. What happens is the following:

1. P1 receives a UDP packet with MPLS label 1000001 and MPLS TTL =1.

2. P1 decrements the TTL, detects that it expired, and encapsulates the original UDP packet with MPLS label 1000001 inside an ICMP Time Exceeded packet, which is in turn encapsulated with MPLS label 1000002. This packet has TTL=255.

3. P1 sends the MPLS-encapsulated ICMP Time Exceeded packet to P2, which pops the label and sends the packet to PE4.

4. PE4 looks at the destination of the ICMP Time Exceeded packet, which is H1. According to a regular IPv4 lookup, PE4 sends this packet through the PE4→PE2 LSP, and this is how it gets to H1.

This mechanism works by default in IOS XR, but you must explicitly activate it in Junos by using the command `set protocols mpls icmp-tunneling`.

Forwarding Equivalence Class

The previous example focused on the communication between two hosts, H1 and H3. Let's take one step back and think of the global Internet. Imagine that PE1 chooses PE4 as the BGP next hop for 100,000 routes. Think twice: all of these 100,000 routes have the same BGP next hop. This means that PE1 can send all the packets toward any of these 100,000 prefixes through the same LSP. Of course, this can raise concerns with regard to load balancing and redundancy, but these topics are fully covered in this book.

Every packet that PE1 maps to the PE1→PE4 LSP belongs to a single *Forwarding Equivalence Class* (FEC). The transit LSRs only need to know how to forward in the context of this FEC: basically, just one entry in the LFIB. Thus, trillions of flows can be successfully forwarded with just one forwarding entry.

Forwarding state aggregation is one of the first immediate benefits of MPLS.

Again, What Is MPLS?

MPLS is *not* an encapsulation. It is an architectural framework that *decouples transport from services*. In this case, the service is Internet access (IPv4 unicast) and the transport is performed by MPLS LSPs.

This decoupling is achieved by encoding instructions in packet headers. Whether the encapsulation is MPLS or something else, the MPLS paradigm remains.

The Internet is living proof of how MPLS is a cornerstone of network service scalability. Every second that our user, Annika, is in a video conference with her friend Ruijiao, more than 1,000 MPLS labels are pushed, swapped, or popped to make it happen. The core devices that do these label operations have no visibility of the public IP addresses that Annika's and Ruijiao's terminals use to connect to the Internet.

Another important aspect of MPLS is instruction stacking. Whether these instructions are in the form of labels or something else, being able to stack them is equivalent to providing a sequence of instructions. For network services that go beyond simple connectivity, this is a *key* enabler.

As discussed later in Chapter 10, scalable network architectures have a North-South and an East-West direction. Instruction stacking introduces another dimension: Up-Down.

 MPLS is a natural fit for architectures with a feature-rich network edge combined with a fast and resilient backbone.

MPLS was born for the Internet. It started small and continues to grow. The initial goal of MPLS was to solve a very specific challenge, but now it keeps evolving to meet many other requirements in terms of service, transport, class of service, performance, resilience, and so on.

OpenFlow

The SDN era started with an experimental protocol that created a high level of expectation: *OpenFlow*.

OpenFlow enables flow-based programmability of a forwarding engine. Its initial version (v1.0) is basically a network switch abstraction. Over time, different versions of OpenFlow have incorporated more functionality, the details of which are beyond the scope of this book. You can find all the definitions and specifications at the Open Networking Forum (*https://www.opennetworking.org/sdn-resources/openflow*).

Figure 1-11 shows OpenFlow v1.0 at work. OpenFlow assumes that there is a central controller software running as a virtual machine (VM), or as a container, or directly on the host OS of a server. The controller must have IP connectivity to the switches by using either of the following:

- An out-of-band network that is *not* under the command of the controller
- An in-band network connection that relies on some preexisting forwarding state

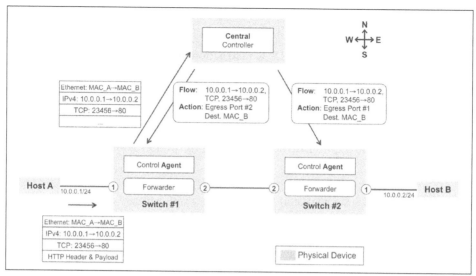

Figure 1-11. Openflow in action

Switches have a lightweight control plane and a comparatively more powerful forwarding engine. The most important piece of state on an OpenFlow-controlled switch is its flow table. The switches' control plane is connected to the central controller via an OpenFlow TCP session, whose purpose is to exchange OpenFlow messages.

Figure 1-11 shows Host A sending the first packet of a user TCP flow to Host B. When the packet arrives to port 1, Switch #1 realizes that this flow is not programmed on its flow table, so its control agent "punts" the packet to the controller. The controller had previously learned where Host B is, and with this information it is able to program the new flow on the switches. At this point, the switches are able to forward this flow's packets to the destination.

OpenFlow—Flow-Based Forwarding

One fundamental architectural attribute of OpenFlow is its per-flow programmability, offering a fine granularity when it comes to defining flows and their associated actions. This results in a flow-based forwarding model. For decades, the industry has produced a wide variety of both *flow-based forwarding* and *packet-based forwarding* solutions. Which model is better? Neither—both are. It really depends on the use case.

There are parts of the network where even thinking about flow-based forwarding is out of the question, like in the core and most of the broadband edge functions, because it would not scale and there is no need for it. The Internet requires state aggregation (FECs) instead of state expansion (flows). Keeping state for flows is inherently more expensive and complex than doing packet-based forwarding. However, there are other network functions, such as firewalling, DPI, and CGNAT, among others, that *need* to be flow-based due to the nature of the function they execute.

The same principles by which the industry has naturally selected which parts of the network should be flow-based and which should not are still completely valid. The fact that there is a new protocol to program flows on a network does not make flow-based forwarding either a better or worse idea.

New developments in forwarding technology, memory, and costs, could shift things in one direction or the other. For this reason, it is wise to decouple the existence of the OpenFlow protocol from the debate of whether flow-based forwarding is a good idea or not. In fact, OpenFlow, as such, does not mandate nor specify the granularity of the flows to be programmed.

When deciding to use one model or the other, the first question to answer is *do you need flow-based forwarding?* If not, it's better to use packet-based forwarding. Data center fabrics (described in Chapter 10) are a good example of the risks involved in blindly moving to a flow-based forwarding paradigm. At first glance, it looks like a good fit, but a deeper analysis proves that it really depends on the primary use of the data center.

Ivan Pepelnjak wrote an enlightening article called "OpenFlow and Fermi Estimates," which is included in his book, *SDN and OpenFlow—The Hype and the Harsh Reality* (self-published, 2014, *http://www.ipspace.net/Books*). You might have realized that your web browser automatically establishes connections to many URLs that you had no intention to visit. For example, when you read your favorite online newspaper, a wide variety of content—such as advertisements, multimedia, and stats—are automatically loaded from external sites. Every piece of content is retrieved via an individual short-lived connection. It is this short-lived characteristic of many Internet flows that makes flow programming a very intensive task. This is particularly true for high-speed data center switches, which have a comparatively weak control plane. Pepelnjak's Fermi estimate shows that the forwarding capacity of a typical data center switch is reduced by several orders of magnitude when it must perform flow-based forwarding of HTTP flows. The control plane becomes the bottleneck in this case, so most of the bandwidth cannot be used. If your network transports short-lived flows, use OpenFlow carefully.

OpenFlow—Openness and P4

OpenFlow is an open protocol and P4 (a newer high-level language—*programming protocol-independent packet processors*—thus four Ps) takes it one step further, from a protocol to a programming language. Despite the definitions, not everyone agrees on whether OpenFlow and P4 are actually high level or low level.

No wonder, openness is cool. On the other hand, implementing fine-grained edge features is complex. There is no way around it. Regardless of whether the complexity is on the application-specific integrated circuits (ASICs), or on the low-level micro-code, or on high-level instructions, it must be somewhere, and not every approach is equally efficient or flexible. Standardizing a high-level language hides complexity, which is great, but for many features, developers need to go down to the lower levels.

There is value in low-level languages because they provide flexibility due to how close they are to the actual hardware. They are, and must be, inherently specific, and if they want to be generic, they will precisely lose that specificity. Hardware has differences that must be exposed because there is a lot of innovation that vendors are adding to their ASICs to differentiate them from one another. If they are exposed, the language becomes specific. If they are not exposed, the innovation is lost, and the system becomes a disincentive to innovation.

At a certain low level, the relationship between hardware and the software that programs it is very intimate. Trying to insert a layer between, even an industry-defined layer, is not guaranteed to boost innovation. Only time will tell whether standardizing the way that a network device is programmed brings innovation or slows down the new feature implementations. It will certainly be an interesting story to watch or in which to at least play a role.

Another important characteristic of the OpenFlow model is the decoupling of the control and forwarding planes. Let's discuss this topic in the broader context of SDN.

SDN

This book does not attempt to redefine the SDN concept itself: this is up to the inventors of the acronym. What this book takes the liberty of describing is the *SDN era*. Let's first discuss the *official* definition of SDN and then later move on to the SDN era.

SDN has been defined by Open Networking Forum (*https://www.opennetworking.org*) (*https://www.opennetworking.org*) as follows:

> The physical separation of the network control plane from the forwarding plane, and where a control plane controls several devices.

Following this definition, it states:

> Software-Defined Networking (SDN) is an emerging architecture that is dynamic, manageable, cost-effective, and adaptable, making it ideal for the high-bandwidth, dynamic nature of today's applications. This architecture decouples the network control and forwarding functions enabling the network control to become directly programmable and the underlying infrastructure to be abstracted for applications and network services. The OpenFlow™ protocol is a foundational element for building SDN solutions.

Separation of the Control and Forwarding Planes

The process of decoupling the control and the forwarding planes is presented as a key element that drives SDN adoption; however, some engineers contend that such separation has existed for many years on their own networks. For example, both Juniper and Cisco routers clearly separated the control and forwarding planes in the 1990s. The fact that they were running on the same physical chassis did not negate such separation, which was, in fact, fundamental to enable growth on the Internet. When Juniper introduced such separation, along with ASIC-based forwarding, it triggered an era of unprecedented capacity growth. And with hindsight, it was required to sustain the unprecedented traffic growth that lay ahead.

Since the early 2000s—a few years before OpenFlow was proposed—networking vendors have implemented and shipped solutions that instantiate the control plane on an external physical device. This is essentially a controller that programs the so-called "line card chassis."

It is therefore fair to note that the fundamental architectural attribute associated with SDN, separating the control and forwarding planes, is not essentially new, and is widely used already on the networks. Anyway, new or not, this attribute is valuable.

Another fundamental architectural ingredient of SDN is centralization. Sometimes it is *logical centralization*, because physical centralization is not always feasible. If you assume that the control plane of your network is physically decoupled from the forwarding plane, it leads to an interesting set of challenges:

- You need a network to connect both functions (the control and forwarding planes). If such a network fails, how does the solution work?
- There are latency constraints for proper interworking between the control and forwarding planes. Latency is important for resiliency, response to network events, telemetry, and so on. How far can the controller be from the forwarding elements?

It is not trivial to generalize, for any network, a way that these principles can be applied. SDN's principles are better analyzed in the context of specific use cases. You can then see if an architecture that adheres to these principles is feasible or not.

Separating the control and forwarding planes—data center overlays

A paradigmatic use case for which SDN principles fit well is the overlay architecture at data centers, assuming the following:

- There is an underlay fabric that provides resilient connectivity between the overlay's forwarding plane (usually a vRouter or a vSwitch on a server) and the control plane (central controller).

- The latency is contained within specific working limits.

Separating the control and forwarding planes—WAN IP/MPLS

Let's now analyze the applicability of the SDN architectural principles to the WAN IP/MPLS network on any ISP. Although there are certain control plane functions that we can centralize, it is unfeasible to achieve a full centralization. Indeed, if you place the entire control plane hundreds or thousands of kilometers (and N network hops) away from the forwarding plane, it is not possible to guarantee the interaction between both planes in a reliable and responsive way. For this reason, the SDN concept can only be applied to the WAN environment in a tactical manner.

Having *some* centralized network-wide control intelligence can lead to more accurate calculations, which is very useful for cases such as Traffic Engineering. In this case, the *distributed* control plane is *enhanced* by an additional centralized intelligence. This is fully explained in Chapter 15.

These examples show that SDN can have different levels of applicability for each scenario (no one-size-fits-all). Network vendors have applied this design principle over the years to many technology and architecture designs: *centralize what you can, distribute what you must.* If something can be centralized, and there are no physical or functional constraints, centralize it; otherwise, it should be left distributed.

SDN and the Protocols

It is fair to claim that OpenFlow was a spark that caused a mind shift in the industry, triggering a healthy debate that has acted as a catalyzer for the SDN era.

That having been said, there is some controversy about the technical relevance of OpenFlow. Whereas some engineers believe that OpenFlow is the cornerstone of SDN, others believe that it does not propose anything fundamentally new. In all fairness, as with any other protocol or technology, OpenFlow is evolving through its different versions. Whether it will really enable a fundamental benefit in the future or not, only time will tell.

In parallel with the continual development of OpenFlow, other industry forums such as IETF have also been developing similar concepts. In fact, two of the IETF's crown jewels, BGP and MPLS, are gaining momentum as SDN-enabler protocols.

It is not surprising to find BGP in the SDN era, because it is the most scalable networking protocol that ever has been designed and implemented. On the other hand, the MPLS paradigm (decoupling service from transport, placing instructions on packet headers) is gaining an ever-growing relevance in the development and deployment of scalable SDN solutions. This paradigm has indeed been renamed by the OpenFlow community as SDN 2.0.

Remember that the MPLS paradigm is *not* an encapsulation.

Chapter 11 and Chapter 12 describe production-ready SDN solutions mainly based on BGP—and its derivatives—in combination with the MPLS paradigm.

In practice, OpenFlow is an *optional* element of the SDN-like architectures. Many modern SDN-like solutions do not rely on OpenFlow and are not even inspired by it. Others do: of course, OpenFlow belongs to the SDN era.

Some parallel IETF projects concentrate on standardizing the way to program and configure the network elements' behavior (e.g., PCEP, BGP Flowspec, NETCONF/YANG/OpenConfig, I2RS, and ForCES). Although some have not been widely adopted, others are gaining momentum and they also belong to the SDN era. Chapter 15 covers PCEP in detail.

Regardless of the terminology debate and the protocol choice, one thing is certain: the industry will continue exploring and implementing new architectures that are certainly changing the way we see and use networking.

The SDN Era

If you look at all the SDN-like implementations and technologies, you'll find two elements in common that reveal what was missing at the beginning of the century in our industry:

Automation
    Creating the conditions to automate actions on the networks (configuration, provisioning, operation, troubleshooting, etc.)

Abstraction
    Achieving North-South communication by surpassing the vendor-specific barriers and complexities that customers had to adapt to, or avoid

If you look at how the industry has adopted two protocols such as OpenFlow or Netconf, the focus has typically been on the "how": *how to program* low-level flows or *how to configure* a device. However, what the industry really needs is a focus on the "what": *what is the intent*. It is going high level, going abstract, which enables defining intents and automating actions around those intents. In other words: "*Say what you want, not how you want it.*" Then make the network intelligent enough to decide the best "how" possible.

In summary, what is common across the myriad SDN terms and cross initiatives, industry wide, is automation and abstraction. This is the real essence of what this book considers the SDN era and that we, as an industry, should probably care about. Let's briefly look at a few specific use cases of new technologies that seem to provide concrete added value to real customer challenges through automation and abstraction.

SDN-Era Use Cases

If we step away from the term SDN and its many interpretations, there are in fact new solutions and technologies developed for specific use cases that involve both an architectural change, and a response to a real problem. The following is a list of representative scenarios that are part of the new thinking in the SDN era. Some use tested technologies in a practical, often brilliant, way.

Data center

The data center requirements have grown by orders of magnitude in many dimensions, and very rapidly. Data centers have suffered a rapid transition from being mere dense LANs into hyperscale infrastructures with very strict requirements not only in performance but also in latency, scale, multitenancy, and security. And associated with all of that is the need for improved manageability.

Some proposed data center switching infrastructures are based on OpenFlow with a central controller programming flows along the path, but the industry has also looked at other architectures and technologies that have proven to deliver on the same requirements at scale. You do not need to look far to find them: the Internet itself. The suite of protocols and architectures used to build the Internet and the ISP IP networks have become the best mirror to look at to build the next generation data centers that do the following:

- Decouple transport from services (the architectural principle of MPLS)
- Build a stable, service-agnostic transport infrastructure (fabrics)
- Provision services only at the edge, and use scalable protocols for the control plane (BGP)

This ISP architecture has been adapted to data centers in several ways. First, the underlay's forwarding plane is optimized to the specific requirements of data centers, which include very low latency among the end systems (servers) and very high transport capacity with almost no restriction.

The ISP's edge is replaced with the data center's overlay-capable edge forwarders, typically instantiated by the vRouter/vSwitch on server hypervisors or eventually the Top-of-Rack (ToR) switch.

This provides a good opportunity to use a central controller that is capable of programming the edge forwarders as if they were the packet forwarding engines or the line cards of a multicomponent physical network device. You can see this model in detail throughout Chapter 11.

WAN

The ISP WAN—the internal ISP backbone—is another specific use case for which there are new challenges that need to be addressed. Bandwidth resources are scarcer than ever, and CAPEX control levels make it impossible to deploy as much capacity as in the past. However, traffic continues to grow, and a growing variety of services flow across the WAN infrastructure, raising the need for mechanisms that are capable of managing these resources more efficiently and dynamically. MPLS Traffic Engineering has existed for many years, but the distributed nature of the Traffic Engineering decisions led to inefficiencies.

Now, with the broader availability and implementations of protocols such as PCEP, it is possible to enable centralized intelligent controllers that *complement* the distributed control plane of the network, by adding a network-wide vision and decision process. The ISP WAN can now take advantage of implementations that offer intelligent management of resources and automation for tasks that previously could only be done in a limited fashion and to some extent manually, or were simply not done, because there was enough capacity. The resource scarcity and the business requirements now mandate a different way of doing it, and this is another example and use case of new implementations that employ long-standing concepts, such as the PCE Client-Server architecture. This model is detailed in Chapter 15.

Packet-optical convergence

Packet-based and circuit-based switching are two fundamentally different paradigms, and they both have reasons to exist. Traditionally they have been separate layers, most of the time with the circuit-switching network as the server layer for the packet-switching network (the client). This role is sometimes reversed; for example—with TDM emulated circuits over MPLS in Mobile backhaul scenarios, briefly discussed in Chapter 6.

Optical networks are the most common circuit-switched technology. They provide optical circuits that packet-based networks use for point-to-point communication among the different packet-switching nodes (routers, switches, etc.).

In the SDN era, the vast majority of the traffic is becoming IP—even mobile voice with technologies such as VoLTE. It is already a fact that the main (if not only) purpose of the optical network is to transport the IP network. For this reason, the tight coordination and optimization of the optical and IP networks becomes business critical. Any inefficiency on such integration immediately becomes a large source of extra CAPEX and OPEX.

Therefore, here's another area where ISPs face a strong challenge that requires specific solutions. The need for resource coordination, automation, and optimization is addressed by doing the following:

- Exposing resources in a normalized way (abstraction)
- Having the ability to automate the right resource allocation decisions (set up paths, optimize paths, search for backup resources, etc.) while considering both the optical layer and the packet layer

Again, the role of a centralized controller is paramount. The model described in Chapter 15 is also targeting this use case.

IP peering

IP peering provides another opportunity to enhance and optimize the existing mechanisms. So far, the IP peering points' behavior has been exclusively governed by BGP protocol rules. BGP implements a decision algorithm that searches for the best loop-free path—loop-free in the sense that the AS path does not contain the same AS twice. Although many tools such as BGP attributes can be used to influence the decision process, it still remains a built-in algorithm that is based on certain predefined rules. Such rules may not take into account business-related aspects that a provider could need to consider in order to make the best routing decisions.

Some of these business aspects are the price of the peering connection (it might be a transit link), the actual latency to the destination (shorter AS paths do not necessarily imply lower latency), link occupation, and maybe others. As business conditions become stricter in our industry, network decisions need to factor in more variables.

ISPs often use ad hoc tunneling overlays (based on IP or MPLS) to bypass the default forwarding decisions, but this approach does not scale: ISPs deserve a better solution.

A controller-based solution that addresses this opportunity needs to have detailed visibility of all the BGP routing state in the SP. The BGP Monitoring Protocol (BMP), implemented in both Junos and IOS XR, accommodates retrieving from a given router:

The Adj-RIB-in
    These are the prefixes that the polled router has received from a peer, prior to the application of import routing policies.

The Adj-RIB-out
    These are the prefixes that the polled router has advertised to a peer, after the application of export routing policies.

Additionally, enhanced telemetry mechanisms are being implemented to retrieve significant traffic statistics. Putting all together, such a solution is definitely feasible in the mid-term future.

This is another example of a real customer challenge that can be solved in the SDN era by a partial centralization of the decision process through incremental intelligence. And it's another case of automation and abstraction.

The branch office

The services offered at the branch office have been substantially static. SPs are looking at ways to offer more dynamic services that the customer might even self-provision. These services can reduce operating expenses by delegating some tasks to the customer, and at the same time help increase the revenue through a faster service adoption (point-and-click customer service-provisioning) and new business models (try-and-buy).

This is an old aspiration from SPs and has been the object of traditional technologies such as policy servers, PCRF, Radius/CoA, and the like. For example, the so-called Turbo Button, with which the customer can increase the bandwidth temporarily of its broadband connection, or the self-provisioning portals that enable it, among other possibilities, have existed in the industry for many years. However, the market and business is now rising and more SPs are interested in actively offering these options.

Today, in the SDN era, the business pressure threatens sustainability, so increasing top-line revenue becomes a must through offering more flexible services. This is an opportunity for new emerging solutions based on centralized controllers that implement flexible and automated services configuration.

Although these scenarios use existing technologies and do not represent any radical architectural shift, all of these use cases represent a clever combination of one or more of the following attributes:

- Automation and abstraction
- Complementing the intelligence of the existing infrastructure
- Making the network decisions more dynamic
- Decoupling overlay from underlay in order to scale

These attributes are what the authors intend to apply to the book's many chapters on MPLS, making it fundamentally a key tool in the SDN era.

## CHAPTER 2

The Four MPLS Builders

Depending on the function of a Multiprotocol Label Switching (MPLS) label, it can receive many names: transport label, service label, VPN label, entropy label, and so on. This chapter focuses on the original and primary function of MPLS labels: *the transport of data packets through a labeled tunnel.*

Chapter 1 describes how MPLS tunnels are provisioned by using a static label-mapping technique. However, this approach is limited in terms of scalability, operability, failure detection, and redundancy. There is fortunately a classic solution at hand: signaling the tunnels with protocols that create MPLS paths in a dynamic manner. What protocols? There are actually a few of them, each with their pros and cons.

This chapter covers the following alternatives:

- Two pure MPLS signaling protocols: Label Distribution Protocol (LDP) and Resource Reservation Protocol with Traffic Engineering (RSVP-TE)
- The modern MPLS extensions of classic IP routing protocols: Border Gateway Protocol (BGP), Intermediate System–to–Intermediate System (IS-IS), and Open Shortest-Path First (OSPF)

BGP has had MPLS extensions since the early times, and they keep evolving. As for IS-IS and OSPF, their MPLS extensions have come more recently with a technology called SPRING or Segment Routing. SPRING, which was still in IETF draft state at the time of the publication of this book, also has extensions for BGP.

The four MPLS Builders are therefore: LDP, RSVP-TE, BGP, and the Interior Gateway Protocol (IGP). LDP was already proposed in the 1990s, so why are there so many other MPLS signaling protocols? First, LDP did not cover the Traffic Engineering use case, so RSVP-TE was soon proposed for that purpose. And because neither LDP nor RSVP-TE nicely solved the interdomain use case, new BGP extensions were defined to achieve it. Some scenarios are a good fit for LDP, or for RSVP-TE, or for BGP, or for a combination of them. As for SPRING, most of its use cases can be covered by a combination of other protocols (LDP, RSVP-TE, and BGP), but it is a recent technology whose applications are diversifying, it brings deterministic labels to the table, and it is very interesting to see how you can use the IGP to build MPLS LSPs.

Let's begin with LDP, probably the most classic and widespread of them all. The baseline topology is borrowed from Chapter 1. For convenience, it is also displayed here in Figure 2-1.

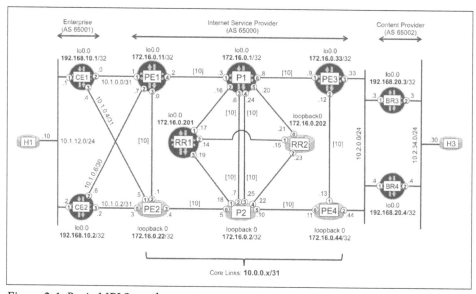

Figure 2-1. Basic MPLS topology

In this chapter, all the IGP core link IS-IS metrics are set to the default value (10). This makes internal load-balancing scenarios more interesting.

LDP

Despite its simple appearance, LDP (RFC 5036) is not that easy to understand. Indeed, LDP can signal three types of transport Label-Switched Paths (LSPs): multipoint-to-point (MP2P), point-to-multipoint (P2MP), and multipoint-to-multipoint (MP2MP). Unlike its fellow RSVP-TE, LDP does not signal the LSP type that happens to be the most intuitive of them all: point-to-point (P2P) LSPs. This chapter focuses on unicast traffic, which in the context of LDP is transported in

MP2P LSPs. These go from any ingress provider edge (PE) to a given egress PE. Last but not least, LDP does not implement Traffic Engineering.

So, why is LDP such a popular MPLS transport protocol? Several characteristics make it highly scalable and operationally attractive. First, label signaling takes place on TCP connections, achieving reliable delivery with minimal refresh. Second, MP2P LSPs involve a significant state reduction. And finally, when it comes to configuring transport LSPs, LDP is plug-and-play. You just enable LDP on the core interfaces, and the magic is done.

Example 2-1. LDP configuration at PE1 (Junos)

```
protocols {
    ldp {
        track-igp-metric;
        interface ge-0/0/3.0;
        interface ge-0/0/4.0;
}}
```

The `track-igp-metric` knob couples LDP to the IGP and it is a best practice for loop avoidance. Remember that throughout this entire book, it is assumed that all the MPLS interfaces are declared under [edit protocols mpls] and have family mpls enabled, as in Chapter 1.

Following is a basic LDP configuration in IOS XR.

Example 2-2. LDP configuration at PE2 (IOS XR)

```
mpls ldp
 interface GigabitEthernet0/0/0/3
 interface GigabitEthernet0/0/0/4
```

> In IOS XR, MPLS often relies on LDP to be globally enabled. If the network runs a different MPLS label signaling protocol, you don't need to configure any interfaces under mpls ldp, but the global statement is typically needed.

LDP Discovery and LDP Sessions

As soon as LDP is enabled on an interface, a process called *basic discovery* begins. The LSR begins to send and receive LDP hello messages on each of the configured interfaces. Let's focus on the message exchange between P1 and P2, which is illustrated in Figure 2-2.

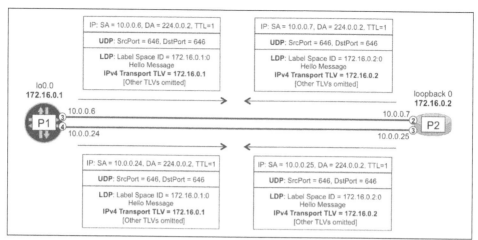

Figure 2-2. LDP hello messages

In the basic discovery process, LDP hello messages are encapsulated as follows:

- First, in a UDP header, with source and destination port 646
- Then, in an IPv4 header with TTL=1 and destination address 224.0.0.2, the all-routers link-local multicast address

These packets are not routable, and their purpose is to establish adjacencies between directly connected neighbors only. Note that there is another method called *extended discovery*, also known as *targeted LDP*, whereby the LDP hellos are unicast and multi-hop (TTL>1). This is described later in this chapter.

The basic discovery process builds LDP hello adjacencies. There is one per LDP-enabled interface, so P1 and P2 establish two hello adjacencies.

Example 2-3. LDP hello adjacencies at P1 (Junos)

```
juniper@P1> show ldp neighbor
Address          Interface       Label space ID      Hold time
10.0.0.2         ge-2/0/1.0      172.16.0.11:0          13
10.0.0.7         ge-2/0/3.0      172.16.0.2:0           12
10.0.0.25        ge-2/0/4.0      172.16.0.2:0           12
10.0.0.9         ge-2/0/6.0      172.16.0.33:0          14
```

Example 2-4. LDP hello adjacencies at P2 (IOS XR)

```
RP/0/0/CPU0:P2#show mpls ldp discovery brief

Local LDP Identifier: 172.16.0.2:0

Discovery Source   VRF Name      Peer LDP Id      Holdtime Session
```

```
------------------    --------------   ---------------   --------  -------
Gi0/0/0/0          default        172.16.0.22:0     15       Y
Gi0/0/0/2          default        172.16.0.1:0      15       Y
Gi0/0/0/3          default        172.16.0.1:0      15       Y
Gi0/0/0/5          default        172.16.0.44:0     15       Y
```

The LDP hello messages originated by P1 have two key pieces of information:

- The *label space* 172.16.0.1:0, whose format is *<LSR ID>:<label space ID>*. The *<LSR ID>* is simply P1's router ID.
- The IPv4 *transport address*, which is also P1's router ID.

But, what do the label space and the transport address stand for?

Let's begin with the transport address. LDP discovery triggers the establishment of one LDP-over-TCP session between each pair of neighboring LSRs. The endpoints of these multihop TCP sessions are precisely the *transport addresses* encoded in the UDP-based hellos, as shown in Example 2-5.

Example 2-5. LDP over TCP session (CE1)

```
juniper@P1> show system connections | match "proto|646"
Proto Recv-Q Send-Q  Local Address    Foreign Address      (state)
tcp4      0      0   172.16.0.1.646   172.16.0.2.51596     ESTABLISHED
tcp4      0      0   172.16.0.1.646   172.16.0.33.50368    ESTABLISHED
tcp4      0      0   172.16.0.1.646   172.16.0.11.49804    ESTABLISHED
tcp4      0      0   *.646            *.*                  LISTEN
udp4      0      0   *.646            *.*
```

It is important to configure the router ID to the same value as a reachable loopback address; otherwise, the LDP session cannot be established.

Even though P1 and P2 have more than one LDP hello adjacency, they only establish one LDP session, from loopback to loopback.

After they establish the TCP connection via the classic three-way handshake, P1 and P2 exchange LDP initialization messages and finally the label information. Let's have a look at the LDP sessions.

Example 2-6. LDP sessions at P1 (Junos)

```
juniper@P1> show ldp session
  Address        State      Connection    Hold time  Adv. Mode
172.16.0.2       Operational Open            24         DU
```

```
172.16.0.11      Operational  Open                    21          DU
172.16.0.33      Operational  Open                    20          DU
```

Example 2-7. LDP Sessions at P2 (IOS XR)

```
RP/0/0/CPU0:P2#show mpls ldp neighbor brief

Peer              GR  NSR  Up Time   Discovery  Address  IPv4 Label
----------------  --  ---  --------  ---------  -------  ----------
172.16.0.22:0     N   N    1d04h         1         6         25
172.16.0.44:0     N   N    1d04h         1         5         23
172.16.0.1:0      N   N    00:02:02      2         6         10
```

The terminology becomes a bit confusing across vendors, so we've summarized the concepts. This book uses the RFC terms.

Table 2-1. LDP neighbor terminology

RFC 5036	LDP hello adjacencies (UDP)	LDP sessions (TCP)
Junos	`show ldp neighbor`	`show ldp session`
IOS XR	`show mpls ldp discovery`	`show mpls ldp neighbor`

There are two types of heartbeat mechanisms in LDP:

- LDP-over-UDP Hello messages to maintain LDP Hello Adjacencies
- LDP-over-TCP keepalives to maintain LDP Sessions (TCP already provides a keepalive mechanism, but LDP keepalives are more frequent and hence more robust)

LDP Label Mapping

As soon as two neighbors establish an LDP session, they begin to exchange label mapping messages that associate IPv4 prefixes to MPLS labels. These label mappings make up a Label Information Base (LIB).

IPv4 prefixes are one example of Forwarding Equivalence Class (FEC) elements. According to RFC 5036, "The FEC associated with an LSP specifies which packets are 'mapped' to that LSP."

Translated to this chapter's example topology, PE1 needs an LSP terminated at PE3 in order to send packets beyond PE3. And the FEC associated to that LSP is represented by 172.16.0.33/32, PE3's loopback address. Although it is not the most precise expression, you could say that *172.16.0.33/32 is a FEC*. The ingress PE (in this example, PE1) does not necessarily tunnel traffic destined to the FEC itself. Most typically, the packet matches a route at PE1 whose BGP next hop is 172.16.0.33. This is the association between the packet and the FEC. Good old MPLS logic!

Probably the best way to understand LDP is to see it at work. Let's focus on one IPv4 prefix or FEC: the loopback address of PE3 (172.16.0.33/32).

In Figure 2-3, you can see that *all* of the core routers in the network advertise a label mapping for this prefix. This is a bit surprising because PE3 receives from its neighbors label mappings for its own loopback address! As its name implies, LDP is just that, a label distribution protocol, not a routing protocol. It simply distributes label mappings and does not care about whether these announcements make topological sense.

Looking carefully at Figure 2-3, you can see that each router advertises the same label mapping on every LDP session. For example, P1 advertises the mapping [FEC element 172.16.0.33/32, label 300000] to all its neighbors. This is a local label binding at P1. Indeed, P1 locally binds the label 300000 to 172.16.0.33/32, and it's telling its LDP peers: *if you want me to tunnel a packet toward PE3, send it to me with a topmost MPLS header containing label 300000.*

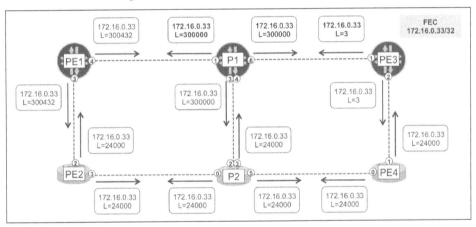

Figure 2-3. LDP label mapping messages for 172.16.0.33

This assignment has only local significance and must be interpreted in the context of *label space* 172.16.0.1:0. How is the label space decoded? The first field is P1's router ID, and the second field (zero) translates to a *platform* label space. What does this mean? Label lookup takes place in P1 *regardless of the interface* on which the MPLS packet arrives. If P1 receives a packet whose outer MPLS label is 300000, no matter the input interface, P1 will place it on a LSP toward PE3. The mapping (172.16.0.33/32, 3000000) has platform-wide significance within P1.

Both Junos and IOS XR use a platform label space.

RFC 3031 also defines per-interface label spaces, wherein each input interface has its own LIB: an incoming MPLS packet's label is interpreted in the context of the input interface. Although per-interface label spaces are *not* implemented, Chapter 21 covers a more generic concept: context-specific label spaces, defined in RFC 5331.

Back to Figure 2-3. Because MPLS labels have local significance, each router typically advertises a different label mapping for a given FEC. However, there is no rule that enforces the labels to be different. For example, PE2, P2, and PE4 happen to all be advertising the same label for 172.16.0.33/32. This is completely fine because each label belongs to a different platform (LSR) label space. It's a simple coincidence.

LDP label mappings are dynamic and *may* change upon route flap.

LDP signaling and MPLS forwarding in the Junos plane

Example 2-8 gives us a chance to look at a live demonstration; in this case, a loopback-to-loopback traceroute from CE1 to BR3 traversing the Junos plane (PE1, P1, PE3).

Example 2-8. Traceroute through the Junos LDP plane

```
juniper@CE1> traceroute 192.168.20.3 source 192.168.10.1
traceroute to 192.168.20.3 (192.168.20.3) from 192.168.10.1 [...]
 1  PE1 (10.1.0.1)  7.962 ms  4.506 ms  5.145 ms
 2  P1 (10.0.0.3)  16.347 ms  10.390 ms  10.131 ms
    MPLS Label=300000 CoS=0 TTL=1 S=1
 3  PE3 (10.0.0.9)  9.755 ms  7.490 ms  7.409 ms
 4  BR3 (192.168.20.3)  8.266 ms  10.196 ms  6.466 ms
```

Let's interpret the output step by step. As you saw in Chapter 1, PE1 has a BGP route toward BR3's loopback, and the BGP next hop of this route is PE3. Then, PE1 resolves this BGP next hop by looking at the inet.3 auxiliary table, and this is how the Internet route (to BR3) gets a labeled forwarding next hop.

If an IPv4 BGP route does not have a BGP next hop in inet.3, Junos tries to find it in inet.0. You can disable this second lookup and make inet.3 the only resolution Routing Information Base (RIB) for IPv4 routes by using this command: `set routing-options resolution rib inet.0 resolution-ribs inet.3`

Let's see the BGP next-hop resolution process in detail.

Example 2-9. MPLS forwarding at ingress PE1 (Junos)

```
juniper@PE1> show route 192.168.20.3 active-path detail
[...]
                Protocol next hop: 172.16.0.33

juniper@PE1> show route table inet.3 172.16.0.33

inet.3: 9 destinations, 9 routes (9 active, 0 holddown, 0 hidden)
+ = Active Route, - = Last Active, * = Both

172.16.0.33/32     *[LDP/9] 11:00:49, metric 20
                    > to 10.0.0.3 via ge-2/0/4.0, Push 300000

juniper@PE1> show route forwarding-table destination 192.168.20.3
Routing table: default.inet
Internet:
Destination     Type Next hop  Type      Index  NhRef Netif
192.168.20.3/32 user           indr    1048574  3
                     10.0.0.3  Push 300000  593  2     ge-2/0/4.0
```

This double table lookup takes place only at the control plane. Transit packets are processed according to the forwarding table, which already has the resolved forwarding next hop.

PE1 pushes an MPLS header with label 300000 and sends the packet to the forwarding next hop P1. Why label 300000? The answer is in Figure 2-3 and in Example 2-10. This is the label that P1 maps to FEC 172.16.0.33/32.

Example 2-10. Label Mappings at ingress PE1 (Junos)

```
juniper@PE1> show ldp database | match "put|172.16.0.33"
Input label database, 172.16.0.11:0--172.16.0.1:0
 300000     172.16.0.33/32
Output label database, 172.16.0.11:0--172.16.0.1:0
 300432     172.16.0.33/32
Input label database, 172.16.0.11:0--172.16.0.22:0
  24000     172.16.0.33/32
```

```
Output label database, 172.16.0.11:0--172.16.0.22:0
 300432     172.16.0.33/32
```

This is an interesting command. It lets you know the label mappings that PE1 is learning (Input label database) and advertising (Output label database). This usage of the input and output keywords is sometimes a bit confusing:

- The Input label database contains MPLS labels that PE1 must add to a packet when sending it out to a neighbor. This is input for the control or signaling plane (LDP), but output for the forwarding (MPLS) plane.

- The Output label database contains MPLS labels that PE1 expects to receive from its neighbors. This is output for the control or signaling plane (LDP), but it's input for the forwarding (MPLS) plane.

After this point is clarified, let's answer the most important question of this LDP section. If PE1 learns label 300000 from space 172.16.0.1:0, and label 24000 from space 172.16.0.22:0, why is it choosing the first mapping to program the forwarding plane? The answer is on the IGP. Although most of the example topologies in this book use IS-IS, OSPF is an equally valid option and (unless specified otherwise), every statement henceforth applies to IS-IS and OSPF indistinctly.

The shortest path to go from PE1 to PE3 is via P1, so among the several label mappings available for 172.16.0.33/32, PE1 chooses the one advertised by P1. This tight coupling with the IGP is the conceptual key to understanding LDP.

Let's move on to P1, a pure LSR or P-router.

Example 2-11. LDP signaling and MPLS forwarding at P1 (Junos)

```
juniper@P1> show ldp database | match "put|172.16.0.33"
Input label database, 172.16.0.1:0--172.16.0.2:0
 24000      172.16.0.33/32
Output label database, 172.16.0.1:0--172.16.0.2:0
 300000     172.16.0.33/32
Input label database, 172.16.0.1:0--172.16.0.11:0
 300432     172.16.0.33/32
Output label database, 172.16.0.1:0--172.16.0.11:0
 300000     172.16.0.33/32
Input label database, 172.16.0.1:0--172.16.0.33:0
    3       172.16.0.33/32
Output label database, 172.16.0.1:0--172.16.0.33:0
 300000     172.16.0.33/32

juniper@P1> show route table mpls.0 label 300000

mpls.0: 12 destinations, 12 routes (12 active, 0 holddown, 0 hidden)
+ = Active Route, - = Last Active, * = Both
```

```
300000                  *[LDP/9] 00:47:20, metric 10
                        > to 10.0.0.9 via ge-2/0/6.0, Pop
300000(S=0)             *[LDP/9] 00:47:20, metric 10
                        > to 10.0.0.9 via ge-2/0/6.0, Pop

juniper@P1> show route forwarding-table label 300000 table default
Routing table: default.mpls
MPLS:
Destination  Type RtRef Next hop       Index  NhRef Netif
300000       user    0 10.0.0.9  Pop    605     2   ge-2/0/6.0
300000(S=0)  user    0 10.0.0.9  Pop    614     2   ge-2/0/6.0
```

The IGP tells P1 that the next router in the path toward PE3 is PE3 itself. Naturally! And PE3 maps label 3 to FEC 172.16.0.33/32, its own loopback. This is a reserved label value called *implicit null*. It is not a real label, but a forwarding instruction that translates to *pop the label*. In other words, an MPLS packet never carries the label value 3, which is simply a signaling artifact. So, the IPv4 packet arrives unlabeled to PE3, and PE3 has the BGP route to reach BR3. The traceroute trip finishes here. This behavior is called Penultimate Hop Popping (PHP).

There is no label swap operation in a two-hop LSP with PHP. For a longer LSP such as PE1-P1A-P1B-PE3, P1A would perform a label swap.

 You can disable PHP and configure explicit null (value 0 for IPv4, value 2 for IPv6), therefore making a real transport MPLS header arrive at the egress PE. One of the applications of explicit null is to keep independent class of service policies for IP and MPLS.

So, is this an LSP? Yes, it is Label-Switched Path; there are MPLS labels after all. But it is signaled in a particular way. The Label Mapping messages depicted in Figure 2-3 allow any router in the network to send MPLS-labeled traffic toward PE3. This is a many-to-one or, in other words, an MP2P LSP.

Let's finish with a useful toolset described in RFC 4379: MPLS ping and traceroute. These tools don't require any specific configuration in Junos and they inject UDP-over-IPv4 data packets in an LSP. In that sense, they are very useful to test an LSP's forwarding plane. The destination IPv4 address of these packets is in the range 127/8, which is reserved for loopback use and is not routable. The appropriate MPLS labels are pushed in order to reach the destination PE, in this case 172.16.0.33. Following is an MPLS traceroute.

Example 2-12. MPLS LDP traceroute (Junos)

```
juniper@PE1> traceroute mpls ldp 172.16.0.33
  Probe options: ttl 64, retries 3, wait 10, paths 16, exp 7[...]
```

```
ttl    Label  Protocol   Address      Previous Hop   Probe Status
  1    300000 LDP        10.0.0.3     (null)         Success
FEC-Stack-Sent: LDP
ttl    Label  Protocol   Address      Previous Hop   Probe Status
  2         3 LDP        10.0.0.9     10.0.0.3       Egress
FEC-Stack-Sent: LDP

Path 1 via ge-2/0/4.0 destination 127.0.0.64
```

LDP signaling and MPLS forwarding in the IOS XR plane

Figure 2-4 presents a similar example, this time focusing on the IOS XR plane (PE2, P2, PE4). The logic is practically identical.

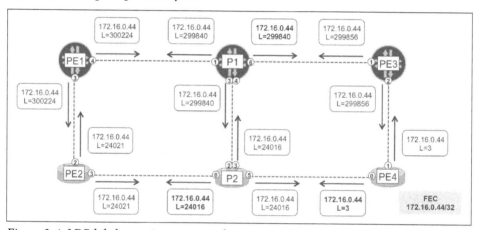

Figure 2-4. LDP label mapping messages for 172.16.0.44

Following is an IPv4 (non MPLS) traceroute from CE2 to BR4.

Example 2-13. Traceroute through the IOS XR Plane

```
juniper@CE2> traceroute 192.168.20.4 source 192.168.10.2
traceroute to 192.168.20.4 (192.168.20.4) from 192.168.10.2 [...]
 1  PE2 (10.1.0.3)  4.358 ms  2.560 ms  5.822 ms
 2  P2 (10.0.0.5)  9.627 ms  8.049 ms  9.261 ms
    MPLS Label=24016 CoS=0 TTL=1 S=1
 3  PE4 (10.0.0.11)  8.869 ms  7.833 ms  9.193 ms
 4  BR4 (192.168.20.4)  10.627 ms  11.592 ms  11.593 ms
```

PE2 has a BGP route toward BR4's loopback, and the BGP next hop of this route is PE4. As is expained in Chapter 1, IOS XR does not have an auxiliary table such as inet.3 in Junos. The actual forwarding is ruled by the Cisco Express Forwarding (CEF) entry for 172.16.0.44/32.

Example 2-14. MPLS forwarding at ingress PE2 (IOS XR)

```
RP/0/0/CPU0:PE2#show route 192.168.20.4

Routing entry for 192.168.20.4/32
  Known via "bgp 65000", distance 200, metric 0
  Tag 65002, type internal
  Installed Nov 17 08:32:32.941 for 00:30:58
  Routing Descriptor Blocks
    172.16.0.44, from 172.16.0.201
      Route metric is 0
  No advertising protos.

RP/0/0/CPU0:PE2#show cef 172.16.0.44
172.16.0.44/32, version 91, internal [...]
 local adjacency 10.0.0.5
 Prefix Len 32, traffic index 0, precedence n/a, priority 3
   via 10.0.0.5, GigabitEthernet0/0/0/3, 6 dependencies [...]
   path-idx 0 NHID 0x0 [0xa0eb34a4 0x0]
   next hop 10.0.0.5
   local adjacency
   local label 24021        labels imposed {24016}
```

PE2 pushes an MPLS header with label 24016 and sends the packet to the forwarding
next hop P2. Why label 24016? As you can see in Figure 2-4 and in Example 2-15, this
is the label that P2 maps to FEC 172.16.0.44/32.

Example 2-15. Label mappings at ingress PE2 (IOS XR)

```
RP/0/0/CPU0:PE2# show mpls ldp bindings 172.16.0.44/32
172.16.0.44/32, rev 85
        Local binding: label: 24021
        Remote bindings: (2 peers)
            Peer                 Label
            ----------------     ---------
            172.16.0.2:0         24016
            172.16.0.11:0        300224
```

Now, let's see the LDP signaling and the forwarding state on P2, the next hop LSR.

Example 2-16. LDP signaling and MPLS forwarding at P2 (IOS XR)

```
RP/0/0/CPU0:P2# show mpls ldp bindings 172.16.0.44/32
172.16.0.44/32, rev 36
        Local binding: label: 24016
        Remote bindings: (3 peers)
            Peer                 Label
            ----------------     ---------
            172.16.0.1:0         299840
            172.16.0.22:0        24021
```

```
         172.16.0.44:0      ImpNull
```

```
RP/0/0/CPU0:P2#show mpls forwarding labels 24016
Local  Outgoing  Prefix         Outgoing     Next Hop      Bytes
Label  Label     or ID          Interface                  Switched
------ --------- -------------- ---------- ------------ ----------
24016  Pop       172.16.0.44/32 Gi0/0/0/5  10.0.0.11    379266
```

Unlike Junos, IOS XR uses MPLS forwarding to reach internal IPv4 prefixes. So, a plain IPv4 traceroute from PE2 to PE4 shows the label, too (although it provides less information than MPLS traceroute).

Example 2-17. IPv4 Traceroute from PE2 to PE4 (IOS XR)

```
RP/0/0/CPU0:PE2#traceroute ipv4 172.16.0.44
[...]
 1  p2 (10.0.0.5) [MPLS: Label 24016 Exp 0] 9 msec   0 msec   0 msec
 2  pe4 (10.0.0.11) 0 msec   *  0 msec
```

LDP and Equal-Cost Multipath

According to the IGP metric, there is no single shortest path from PE1 to PE4. Instead, there are four possible equal-cost paths: PE1-PE2-P2-PE4, PE1-P1-PE3-PE4, and two times PE1-P1-P2-PE4 (there are two parallel links between P1 and P2). This condition is called Equal-Cost Multipath (ECMP). With ECMP, each next hop is distinct from a Layer 3 (L3) perspective.

Similarly, a popular technology called Link Aggregation Group (LAG), or Link Bundling, also results in several equal-cost paths. Some common LAG variants are Aggregated Ethernet (AE) and Aggregated SONET (AS). In this case, a single L3 interface can span several physical links that are bundled together. Finally, you can achieve complex equal-cost topologies by combining ECMP and LAG together (e.g., one of the P1-P2 connections could be a LAG).

As soon as there are equal-cost paths to a destination, a natural question arises: which path do the packets follow? Well, they are load balanced, according to a certain logic that is explained later in this section.

Let's step back for a moment and revisit LDP. Because LDP is coupled to the IGP, it implements ECMP natively. You can check this easily by using MPLS traceroute from PE1 to PE4 (different 127/8 destination IPv4 addresses are automatically used to trigger load balancing); see Example 2-18.

Example 2-18. LDP ECMP (Junos)

```
juniper@PE1> traceroute mpls ldp 172.16.0.44/32
  Probe options: ttl 64, retries 3, wait 10, paths 16, exp 7 [...]
```

```
ttl    Label  Protocol  Address      Previous Hop  Probe Status
  1    24021  LDP       10.0.0.1     (null)        Success
FEC-Stack-Sent: LDP
ttl    Label  Protocol  Address      Previous Hop  Probe Status
  2    24016  Unknown   10.0.0.5     10.0.0.1      Success
FEC-Stack-Sent: LDP
ttl    Label  Protocol  Address      Previous Hop  Probe Status
  3        3  Unknown   10.0.0.11    10.0.0.5      Egress
FEC-Stack-Sent: LDP
```

Path 1 via ge-2/0/3.0 destination **127.0.0.64**

```
ttl    Label   Protocol  Address      Previous Hop  Probe Status
  1    299840  LDP       10.0.0.3     (null)        Success
FEC-Stack-Sent: LDP
ttl    Label   Protocol  Address      Previous Hop  Probe Status
  2    299856  LDP       10.0.0.9     10.0.0.3      Success
FEC-Stack-Sent: LDP
ttl    Label   Protocol  Address      Previous Hop  Probe Status
  3         3  LDP       10.0.0.13    10.0.0.9      Egress
FEC-Stack-Sent: LDP
```

Path 2 via ge-2/0/4.0 destination **127.0.1.64**

```
ttl    Label  Protocol  Address      Previous Hop  Probe Status
  2    24016  LDP       10.0.0.25    10.0.0.3      Success
FEC-Stack-Sent: LDP
ttl    Label  Protocol  Address      Previous Hop  Probe Status
  3        3  Unknown   10.0.0.11    10.0.0.25     Egress
FEC-Stack-Sent: LDP
```

Path 3 via ge-2/0/4.0 destination **127.0.1.65**

```
ttl    Label  Protocol  Address      Previous Hop  Probe Status
  2    24016  LDP       10.0.0.7     10.0.0.3      Success
FEC-Stack-Sent: LDP
ttl    Label  Protocol  Address      Previous Hop  Probe Status
  3        3  Unknown   10.0.0.11    10.0.0.7      Egress
FEC-Stack-Sent: LDP
```

Path 4 via ge-2/0/4.0 destination **127.0.1.69**

 You must explicitly enable MPLS Operations, Administration and Management (OAM) in IOS XR by using the global configuration command mpls oam.

The LSP from PE1 to PE4 has four possible equal-cost paths. So, not only the LDP LSPs are MP2P, they are also ECMP-aware. This makes it more challenging to perform fault isolation on very meshed LDP networks.

Here's what happens from the point of view of a given LSR:

- *When a packet arrives* at a specific interface and with a given MPLS label, is it easy to determine the interface to which the LSR will switch the packet out? If there is just one shortest path to the egress PE, it's easy. But if there is ECMP toward the destination FEC, only advanced vendor-specific tools (beyond the scope of this book) can help to predict the result of the load-balancing decision.

- *When the LSR switches a packet out* of an interface with a given MPLS label, it is not easy to guess the previous history of that packet. Which ingress PE did inject it in the MPLS core? At which interface did the packet arrive to the LSR? It is tricky to answer these questions because these LSPs are MP2P and the LDP label space is per platform.

Note that in the previous example, TTL=1 entry for paths 3 and 4 is the same as in path 2; therefore, in the interest of brevity, Junos does not display it. All of these paths traverse P-routers at both planes: Junos (P1) and IOS XR (P2). With the software versions used in this book, MPLS OAM has an interoperability issue that causes the Pro tocol to be displayed as Unknown. This issue is specific of MPLS OAM only: as far as plain transport LDP is concerned, interoperability is perfect.

In practice, load balancing in LDP networks takes place on a hop-by-hop basis. PE1 has two equal-cost next hops to reach PE4: P1 and PE2. In turn, P1 has three equal-cost next hops to reach PE4: PE3 and twice P2. And so on.

Load-balancing hash algorithm

Load balancing is a complex topic that is intimately related to the hardware implementation of each platform. The good news is that Junos and IOS XR are both capable of doing per-flow load balancing of IP and MPLS traffic. Unlike stateful firewalls, LSRs perform packet-based (not flow-based) forwarding, so what is a flow in the context of a LSR?

A flow is a set of packets with common values in their headers. For example, all the packets of a TCP connection from a client to a server (or of a voice stream between two endpoints), have several fields in common: source and destination address, transport protocol, source and destination ports, and so on. To guarantee that all the packets of a given flow arrive to the destination in the correct order, they should all follow exactly the same path; indirectly, this means that they share respectively the same MPLS label values, hop by hop.

The set of fields that are selected from the packet headers depends on the platform and on the configuration. These fine-tuning details are beyond the scope of this book.

On the other hand, different flows should be evenly distributed across equal-cost next hops such as ECMP, LAG, and so on. Otherwise, some links would not be utilized and others would quickly saturate. This phenomenon is commonly called *traffic polarization*.

Let's see how routers achieve per-flow load balancing. For every single packet, the router selects some header fields (plus a fixed local randomization seed) and applies a mathematical algorithm to them called a *hash*. This algorithm is very sensitive to small variations of its input values. The hash result determines (modulus the number of equal-cost next hops) the actual forwarding next hop to which the packet is mapped. All the packets of a given flow receive the same hash value and are hence forwarded out to the same next hop.

Basic per-flow load balancing is enabled by default in IOS XR, but it requires explicit configuration in Junos, which performs per-destination route hashing by default.

Example 2-19. Enabling per-flow load balancing in Junos

```
policy-options {
    policy-statement PL-LB {
        then load-balance per-packet;
}}
routing-options {
  forwarding-table export PL-LB;
}
```

The per-packet syntax remains for historical reasons, but the way it is implemented in modern Junos versions is per-flow (hash based).

Let's forget for a moment that the topology has two vendor-specific planes. This is a vendor-agnostic analysis of an IP flow from CE1 to BR4:

- The ingress PE1 receives plain IPv4 packets from CE1 and applies a hash to them. Because all the packets belong to the same flow, the result of the hash is the same and they are all forwarded to the same next hop: P1 or P2. If the next hop is PE2, there is only one shortest path remaining and the load-balancing discussion stops here.

- Let's suppose that the next hop is P1. So, P1 receives MPLS packets and applies a hash to them. This hash takes into account the MPLS label value(s) and it might also consider the inner (e.g., IPv4) headers. As a result, all the packets of this flow are sent out to one and only one of the available next hops: PE3, P2-link1, or P2-link2.

MPLS hash and Entropy Labels

Many LSRs in the industry are able to include MPLS packet payload fields (like IP addresses, TCP/UDP ports) into the load-balancing hash algorithm. But some low-end (or old) platforms from different vendors cannot do that. This can be an issue if the number of active FECs is low. For example, in a domestic Internet Service Provider (ISP) that sends all the upstream traffic up to only two big Internet gateways, most of the packets carry either label L1 (mapped to FEC gateway_1) or label L2 (mapped to FEC gateway_2). Two different label values are clearly not enough to spread traffic across multiple equal-cost paths.

To ensure that there is enough randomness to achieve good load balancing on these devices, RFC 6790 introduces the concept of *Entropy Labels*. These labels have a per-flow random value and do not have any forwarding significance. In other words, they are not mapped to any FEC. Their goal is just to ensure smooth load balancing along the available equal cost paths. You can read more about Entropy Labels in Chapter 6.

There is a similar technology called Flow-Aware Transport (FAT, RFC 6391), but it is specific of Layer 2 (L2) services. Chapter 6 also covers this in greater detail.

LDP Implementation Details

Although Junos and IOS XR have behaved similarly in the examples so far, their LDP implementation is actually quite different. Let's follow the LDP advertising flow, starting at the egress PE.

Local FEC label binding/allocation

As shown earlier, PE3 and PE4 both advertise their own loopback mapped to the implicit null label. The following command shows all of the local (or egress) FECs that PE3 and PE4 advertise.

Example 2-20. Default label bindings for local routes (Junos, IOS XR)

```
juniper@PE3> show ldp database session 172.16.0.44 | match "put| 3"
Input label database, 172.16.0.33:0--172.16.0.44:0
        3       10.0.0.10/31
        3       10.0.0.12/31
        3       10.2.0.0/24
        3       10.255.0.0/16
```

```
     3      172.16.0.44/32
Output label database, 172.16.0.33:0--172.16.0.44:0
     3      172.16.0.33/32
```

The only local FEC that PE3 (Junos) advertises via LDP is its primary lo0.0 address. This is a default behavior that you can change by applying an egress-policy at the [edit protocols ldp] hierarchy. A common use case covered in Chapter 3 is the advertisement of nonprimary lo0.0 IP addresses. Additionally, LDP export policies provide granular per-neighbor FEC advertisement.

On the other hand, PE4 (IOS XR) advertises label mappings for all its directly connected routes by default. Most services use LSPs whose endpoints are loopback addresses, though. In that sense, you can configure IOS XR to do the following:

- Only advertise /32 FECs by using mpls ldp address-family ipv4 label local allocate for host-routes

- Granular label binding and advertisement with policies applied at mpls ldp address-family ipv4 label.

The benefit is a lower amount of state to be kept and exchanged in the LIBs.

What about remote (nonlocal) FECs? By default, both Junos and IOS XR advertise label mappings for IGP routes, regardless of their mask. Again, the previously listed knobs make it possible to change this default behavior.

Label advertisement modes

Figure 2-3 and Figure 2-4 illustrate the Downstream Unsolicited (DU) LDP label advertisement (or distribution) mode that both Junos and IOS XR use by default. This elicits two questions:

- Why downstream? When it advertises label mapping (300000, 172.16.0.33/32), P1 is telling its neighbors: *if you want to use me as a downstream LSR to reach 172.16.0.33/32, send me the packets with this label.* So, P1 becomes a potential downstream LSR for that FEC.

- Why unsolicited? P1's neighbors do not request any label mappings from P1; however, P1 sends the messages.

Chapter 16 briefly mentions another label distribution method called Downstream on Demand (DoD), which is also used by RSVP-TE.

Label distribution control modes

There are two label distribution control modes: ordered and independent. Junos implements the ordered mode, whereas IOS XR implements the independent mode.

In the ordered mode, the following sequence takes place in strict chronological sequence (see Figure 2-3):

1. PE3 advertises the label mapping (172.16.0.33/32, 3) to its neighbors.

2. P1 receives this label mapping from PE3, the *egress LSR*, and the *shortest-path* next hop from P1 to 172.16.0.33 is precisely the direct link P1→PE3.

3. P1 binds label 300000 to this FEC, installs the forwarding entry (300000→ *pop* to 10.0.0.9) in its Label Forwarding Information Base (LFIB) and advertises the Label Mapping (172.16.0.33/32, 300000) to its neighbors.

4. PE1 receives the label mapping from P1, and the *shortest path* next hop from PE1 to 172.16.0.33 is precisely P1.

5. PE1 binds label 300432 to the FEC, installs the forwarding entry (300432→ *swap 300000* to 10.0.0.3) in its LFIB and advertises the label mapping (172.16.0.33/32, 300432) to its neighbors.

In a nutshell, before binding a label to a remote FEC, Junos LSRs first need to receive a label mapping from the shortest-path downstream LSR en route to the FEC. Likewise, if it loses the *downstream* labeled state to the FEC (due to an LDP event or to a topology change), after some time the Junos LSR removes the label binding and sends a Label Withdraw message out to its neighbors.

The ordered mode guarantees a strong consistency between the control and the forwarding plane; on the other hand, it requires a potentially higher time to establish the LSPs.

How about independent mode? P2 (IOS XR) binds and announces label mappings regardless of the FEC's downstream label state.

Suppose that P2 has not established any LDP session yet. Nevertheless, P2 binds labels to local and remote FECs. Then, suppose that the LDP session between P2 and PE2 (and only this session) comes up. At this point, P2 advertises all the label mappings to PE2. These mappings include (172.16.0.33/32, 24000) and (172.16.0.44/32, 24016). As you can see in Example 2-21, the resulting LFIB entries at P2 are marked as Unlabelled.

Example 2-21. Unlabeled bindings in independent mode (IOS XR)

```
RP/0/0/CPU0:P2#show mpls forwarding
Local  Outgoing    Prefix           Outgoing    Next Hop    Bytes
Label  Label       or ID            Interface               Switched
------ ----------- ---------------- ----------- ----------- ---------
[...]
24000  Unlabelled  172.16.0.33/32   Gi0/0/0/2   10.0.0.6    25110
       Unlabelled  172.16.0.33/32   Gi0/0/0/3   10.0.0.24   2664
       Unlabelled  172.16.0.33/32   Gi0/0/0/5   10.0.0.11   2664
```

```
24016  Unlabelled  172.16.0.44/32  Gi0/0/0/5  10.0.0.11  134
[...]
```

What if P2 receives a packet whose outer MPLS label is 24000? The `Unlabelled` instruction means *pop all the labels and forward to the next hop(s) in the LFIB*. This is different from the `Pop` instruction, which just pops the outer label.

The outcome depends on the traffic flows:

- Internet traffic from CE2 to BR4 successfully reaches its destination.
- Internet traffic from CE2 to BR3 is forwarded by P2 across three equal-cost next hops. Two of them point to P1, which has no route toward the destination and thus drops the packets.
- VPN traffic with several labels in the stack might be mapped to the master routing instance (and likely discarded) by the next hop.

When all the LDP sessions come up and P2 receives all the label mapping messages from its neighbors, P2's LFIB is programmed with the appropriate `Swap` (to a given label) and `Pop` instructions.

Example 2-22. Labeled bindings in independent mode (IOS XR)

```
RP/0/0/CPU0:P2#show mpls forwarding
Local   Outgoing    Prefix          Outgoing    Next Hop    Bytes
Label   Label       or ID           Interface               Switched
------  ----------  --------------  ----------  ----------  ---------
[...]
24000   300000      172.16.0.33/32  Gi0/0/0/2   10.0.0.6    25110
        300000      172.16.0.33/32  Gi0/0/0/3   10.0.0.24   2664
        24000       172.16.0.33/32  Gi0/0/0/5   10.0.0.11   2664
24016   Pop         172.16.0.44/32  Gi0/0/0/5   10.0.0.11   134
[...]
```

The ordered and independent label distribution control modes are radically different and each has its pros and cons in terms of control and delay. The final state after LDP converges is the same, regardless of the implemented mode.

Label retention modes

Both Junos and IOS XR implement Liberal Label Retention Mode (as opposed to Conservative) by default, meaning that the LSRs accept and store all the incoming label mapping messages. For example, PE1 receives label mappings for FEC 172.16.0.33/32 from both P1 and PE2. Even though the forwarding next hop is P1, PE1 decides to store both label mappings. Why? Potentially, a topology change in the future might turn PE2 into the next hop. Therefore, PE1 keeps all the states, just in case.

FEC aggregation

Looking back at Example 2-20, PE4 advertises five different local FECs to PE3, all of them mapped to the implicit null label. Let's focus on two of them: 172.16.0.44/32 and 10.0.0.10/31. By default, PE3 advertises them with the same label to P1.

This default behavior in Junos is called *FEC aggregation*, and you can disable it by configuring `set protocols ldp deaggregate`. Here is the outcome:

Example 2-23. Default FEC aggregation (Junos)

```
juniper@PE3> show ldp database | match "put|172.16.0.44|10.0.0.10"
[...]
Output label database, 172.16.0.33:0--172.16.0.1:0
 299856      10.0.0.10/31
 299856      172.16.0.44/32
Input label database, 172.16.0.33:0--172.16.0.44:0
     3       10.0.0.10/31
     3       172.16.0.44/32
```

Example 2-24. FEC de-aggregation (Junos)

```
juniper@PE3> show ldp database | match "put|172.16.0.44|10.0.0.10"
[...]
Output label database, 172.16.0.33:0--172.16.0.1:0
 299920      10.0.0.10/31
 299856      172.16.0.44/32
Input label database, 172.16.0.33:0--172.16.0.44:0
     3       10.0.0.10/31
     3       172.16.0.44/32
```

IOS XR does *not* perform FEC aggregation by default. In other words, it performs FEC de-aggregation by default.

LDP Inter-Area

Looking back at Figure 2-1, let's suppose the following:

- PE1 and PE2 are **L2**-only IS-IS routers in Area 49.0001.
- PE3 and PE4 are **L1**-only IS-IS routers in Area 49.0002.
- P1 and P2 are IS-IS L1-L2 routers, present in both Areas.

In this scenario, PE3 and PE4 only have a default route to reach PE1 and PE2. And the same would happen with OSPF stub areas. A default route is not specific enough for PE3 and PE4 to process the LDP label mappings for 172.16.0.11/32 and 172.16.0.22/32. This breaks MPLS forwarding.

RFC 5283 proposes a clean solution to this problem, but it is not implemented yet. Is there a workaround? Yes: selective IS-IS L2-to-L1 route leaking, or non-stub OSPF areas. However, this approach has an impact on routing scalability. Chapter 16 covers a clean solution to this challenge, called *Seamless MPLS*.

Protecting LDP Networks from Traffic Blackholing

Because it is tightly coupled to the IGP but it is *not* the IGP, plain LDP builds fragile MPLS networks that can easily cause traffic *blackholing*. Let's see why, and how to make it more robust.

LDP IGP Synchronization (RFC 5443)

What happens if PE1 and P1 bring up an IS-IS adjacency together, but for whatever reason (routing/filtering issue, misconfiguration, etc.), they do not establish an LDP session to each other? From the point of view of PE1, the shortest path to PE3 is still PE1-P1-PE3. Unfortunately, this path is unlabeled, so P1 discards the customer traffic. In other words, CE1 can no longer ping BR3.

The LDP IGP Synchronization feature increases the IGP metric of a link if LDP is down on it. This way, the network dynamically skips unlabeled links and restores the service. Following is the syntax for IS-IS, which is very similar to the one for OSPF.

Example 2-25. LDP IGP Synchronization in Junos and IOS XR

```
/* Junos sample configuration */
protocols {
  isis {
     interface ge-0/0/4.0 ldp-synchronization;
 }}

/* IOS XR sample configuration */
router isis mycore
 interface GigabitEthernet0/0/0/3
  address-family ipv4 unicast
   mpls ldp sync
```

In the following example, the LDP IGP Synchronization feature is turned on for all the network core links, and all the LDP sessions are up except for the one between PE1 and P1. The customer traffic finds its way through a longer yet labeled path. So the end-to-end service is fine.

Example 2-26. LDP IGP Synchronization in action

```
juniper@PE1> show isis database level 2 PE1.00-00 extensive
[...]
    IS extended neighbor: P1.00, Metric: default 16777214
    IS extended neighbor: PE2.00, Metric: default 10
[...]

juniper@PE1> show isis database level 2 P1.00-00 extensive
[...]
    IS extended neighbor: PE1.00, Metric: default 16777214
    IS extended neighbor: P2.00, Metric: default 10
    IS extended neighbor: P2.00, Metric: default 10
    IS extended neighbor: PE3.00, Metric: default 10
[...]

juniper@CE1> traceroute 192.168.20.3 source 192.168.10.1
traceroute to 192.168.20.3 (192.168.20.3) from 192.168.10.1 [...]
 1  PE1 (10.1.0.1)  7.577 ms  3.113 ms  3.478 ms
 2  PE2 (10.0.0.1)  14.778 ms  13.087 ms  11.303 ms
    MPLS Label=24000 CoS=0 TTL=1 S=1
 3  P2 (10.0.0.5)  11.723 ms  12.630 ms  14.843 ms
    MPLS Label=24000 CoS=0 TTL=1 S=1
 4  P1 (10.0.0.24)  14.599 ms  15.018 ms  23.803 ms
    MPLS Label=300032 CoS=0 TTL=1 S=1
 5  PE3 (10.0.0.9)  13.564 ms  20.615 ms  25.406 ms
 6  BR3 (192.168.20.3)  18.587 ms  15.589 ms  19.322 ms
```

Both Junos and IOS XR support this feature on IGP interfaces configured as point-to-point, which is the recommended mode for core links. In addition, IOS XR also supports it on broadcast links.

LDP Session Protection

Session Protection is another LDP robustness enhancement, based on the Targeted Hello functionality that is defined on RFC 5036. With this feature, two directly connected LDP peers exchange two kinds of *LDP-over-UDP* Hello packets:

LDP Link Hellos
> Single-hop (TTL=1) multicast packets sourced at the link address, destined to 224.0.0.2 and sent independently on each link. These packets achieve basic discovery (see Figure 2-2).

LDP Targeted Hellos
> Multihop (TTL>1) loopback-to-loopback unicast packets, enabled by using the Session Protection feature.

LDP-over-UDP Targeted Hellos are not the same thing as LDP-over-TCP keepalive messages; they coexist.

LDP Session Protection, as it name implies, maintains the LDP session up upon a link flap. Even if the direct PE1-P1 link goes down, the LDP-over-TCP session and the LDP-over-UDP targeted hello adjacency are both multihop. These packets are routed across the alternate PE1-PE2-P2-P1 path, and in this way the LDP session and the LDP hello adjacency between PE1 and P1 both remain up. The routers keep all the LDP label mappings, which adds forwarding plane robustness to the network.

Let's look at the configuration and its outcome in Junos:

Example 2-27. LDP Session Protection in Junos (PE1)

```
protocols {
    ldp {
        interface lo0.0;
        session-protection;
}}

juniper@PE1> show ldp session
  Address          State        Connection  Hold time  Adv. Mode
  172.16.0.1       Operational  Open            26         DU
  172.16.0.22      Operational  Open            29         DU

juniper@PE1> show ldp neighbor
Address            Interface        Label space ID    Hold time
10.0.0.1           ge-2/0/3.0       172.16.0.22:0         13
10.0.0.3           ge-2/0/4.0       172.16.0.1:0          14
172.16.0.1         lo0.0            172.16.0.1:0          44
172.16.0.22        lo0.0            172.16.0.22:0         41
```

PE1 does not have parallel links to any neighboring router. So, there are two hello adjacencies to each peer (identified by a common Label space ID): the link hello and the targeted hello adjacency.

Finally, let's see it on IOS XR:

Example 2-28. LDP Session Protection in IOS XR (PE2)

```
mpls ldp
 session protection

RP/0/0/CPU0:PE2#show mpls ldp discovery brief

Local LDP Identifier: 172.16.0.22:0
```

Discovery Source	VRF Name	Peer LDP Id	Holdtime	Session
Gi0/0/0/2	default	172.16.0.11:0	15	Y
Gi0/0/0/3	default	172.16.0.2:0	15	Y
Tgt:172.16.0.2	default	172.16.0.2:0	90	Y
Tgt:172.16.0.11	default	172.16.0.11:0	45	Y

RSVP-TE

RSVP was initially defined in RFC 2205 as a protocol to make resource reservations along paths in the Internet. Although this original specification did not have much success in terms of industry adoption and real deployments, RSVP was further evolved into the popular RSVP-TE (RFC 3209, *Extensions to RSVP for LSP Tunnels*), the most flexible and powerful of all the MPLS signaling protocols—which requires more state in the network. Although the *TE* in the acronym RSVP-TE stands for *Traffic Engineering*, RSVP-TE has its own place in the MPLS world, and it is a valid deployment choice even for scenarios in which TE is not required. This section covers basic RSVP-TE, and leaves Traffic Engineering to Chapter 13, Chapter 14, and Chapter 15. Very often, this book refers to RSVP-TE simply as RSVP.

RSVP-TE is easier to understand than LDP. It builds two types of LSPs: P2P and P2MP. IP unicast traffic is tunneled in P2P LSPs. Unlike the MP2P LSPs (from-any-to-one) signaled with LDP, RSVP-TE P2P LSPs (from-one-to-one) have a clear head-end. Conceptually, they are very similar to the static LSPs of Chapter 1, except that this time they are dynamically signaled with a protocol: RSVP-TE.

On the other hand, RSVP-TE is not as plug-and-play as LDP. The first necessary (but not sufficient) step is to enable Traffic Engineering in the IGP (IS-IS, in this example) and to configure RSVP on the core interfaces, except for the links to the RRs.

Example 2-29. RSVP-TE configuration at PE1 (Junos)

```
protocols {
    isis {
        level 2 wide-metrics-only;
    }
    rsvp {
        interface ge-0/0/3.0;
        interface ge-0/0/4.0;
    }
}}
```

In Junos, IS-IS Traffic Engineering extensions are turned on by default. OSPF TE extensions require explicit configuration by using the set protocols ospf traffic-engineering command.

Example 2-30. RSVP-TE configuration at PE2 (IOS XR)

```
1    router isis mycore
2     address-family ipv4 unicast
3      metric-style wide
4      mpls traffic-eng level-2-only
5      mpls traffic-eng router-id Loopback0
6    !
7    rsvp
8     interface GigabitEthernet0/0/0/3
9     interface GigabitEthernet0/0/0/4
10   !
11   mpls traffic-eng
12    interface GigabitEthernet0/0/0/3
13    interface GigabitEthernet0/0/0/4
```

 Lines 7 through 9 are actually not needed for basic RSVP-TE operation, but it is a good practice to add them.

The configuration in Example 2-29 and Example 2-30 does not bring up any RSVP-TE neighbors or LSPs. As you can see in Example 2-31, it just enables the RSVP protocol on the interfaces.

Example 2-31. RSVP-TE baseline state at PE1 and PE2

```
juniper@PE1> show rsvp neighbor
RSVP neighbor: 0 learned

juniper@PE1> show rsvp interface
RSVP interface: 2 active
               Active Subscr- Static  Available Reserved[...]
Interface   State resv  iption BW       BW        BW     [...]
ge-2/0/3.0  Up       0   100%  1000Mbps 1000Mbps  0bps   [...]
ge-2/0/4.0  Up       0   100%  1000Mbps 1000Mbps  0bps   [...]

RP/0/0/CPU0:PE2#show rsvp neighbors
RP/0/0/CPU0:PE2#show rsvp interface

RDM: Default I/F B/W %: 75% [default] (max resv/bc0), 0% [default]

Interface   MaxBW (bps)  MaxFlow (bps) Allocated (bps) MaxSub (bps)
----------- ------------ ------------- --------------- ------------
Gi0/0/0/2            0              0        0 (  0%)            0
Gi0/0/0/3            0              0        0 (  0%)            0
```

The lack of neighbors is expected. Unlike LDP and IGPs, the role of hello packets in RSVP-TE is quite secondary. RSVP-TE LSPs have their own refresh mechanism and it is not mandatory to have hello adjacencies on the interfaces. RSVP hello adjacencies are typically established when at least one RSVP-TE LSP traverses the link.

RSVP-TE LSP Fundamentals

Unless you use a central controller (see Chapter 15), you need to configure RSVP LSPs explicitly at the ingress PE. There are basically two ways of doing it: defining LSPs one by one, or enabling a certain level of endpoint autodiscovery. Let's begin with the first approach, which has the advantage of providing more control and flexibility for each individual LSP. Despite its power, the need for manual LSP configuration is one of the reasons why *some* designers prefer LDP to RSVP, and reserve RSVP for scenarios in which Traffic Engineering is required.

RSVP-TE Tunnels, LSPs, and Sessions

Table 2-2 summarizes the different terminology used by RFC 3209, Junos, and IOS XR.

Table 2-2. RSVP-TE terminology

RFC 3209	Tunnel	LSP
Junos	LSP	Session
IOS XR	Tunnel	Path, Session

In the terms of RFC 3209, you configure *tunnels* on the ingress PE. A tunnel is incarnated through one or more LSPs. There are several reasons why you may have more than one LSP per tunnel, for example:

- A tunnel has a primary LSP protected by a standby LSP. This topic is discussed in Chapter 19. This type of tunnel has two *persistent* LSPs.

- A tunnel has only one primary LSP but it is being resignaled upon failure, reoptimization, or a change in TE constraints such as bandwidth. In these cases, the tunnel may *transitorily* have more than one LSP.

You can view an LSP as an incarnation of a tunnel. Two LSPs that belong to the same tunnel share the Tunnel ID value and have a different LSP ID that differentiates them.

In this book, the different vendor terminologies are used and you might see the words tunnel and LSP used in a relatively relaxed and interchangeable manner. This chapter uses the Junos terminology.

RSVP-TE LSP configuration

RSVP-TE LSPs are configured at the head-end (ingress) PE. This makes sense for P2P LSPs, because MPLS LSPs in general—with the exception of MP2MP—are unidirectional. So, even with no specific LSP configuration at PE3 and PE4, Example 2-32 and Example 2-33 are enough to signal the following LSPs.

From PE1 (Junos) to: PE2, PE3, and PE4.

Example 2-32. RSVP-TE LSP configuration at PE1 (Junos)

```
1     groups {
2        GR-LSP {
3           protocols {
4              mpls label-switched-path <*> adaptive;
5     }}}
6     protocols {
7        mpls {
8           apply-groups GR-LSP;
9           label-switched-path PE1--->PE2 to 172.16.0.22;
10          label-switched-path PE1--->PE3 to 172.16.0.33;
11          label-switched-path PE1--->PE4 to 172.16.0.44;
12    }}
```

From PE2 (IOS XR) to: PE1, PE3, and PE4.

Example 2-33. RSVP-TE LSP configuration at PE2 (IOS XR)

```
group GR-LSP
 interface 'tunnel-te.*'
  ipv4 unnumbered Loopback0
  autoroute announce
  record-route
  path-option 1 dynamic
end-group
!
interface tunnel-te11
 apply-group GR-LSP
 signalled-name PE2--->PE1
 destination 172.16.0.11
!
interface tunnel-te33
 apply-group GR-LSP
 signalled-name PE2--->PE3
 destination 172.16.0.33
!
interface tunnel-te44
 apply-group GR-LSP
 signalled-name PE2--->PE4
 destination 172.16.0.44
```

Bidirectional end-to-end traffic (such as a successful ping between CE1 and BR3) also requires right-to-left LSPs for the return traffic. As a result, unless another MPLS flavor such as LDP or SPRING is enabled in the core, you also need to configure RSVP-TE LSPs rooted from PE3 and from PE4.

In this way, the network has a full mesh of PE→PE RSVP LSPs.

In "RSVP-TE in Action" on page 78, you will see that PE1 (Junos) automatically installs 172.16.0.33/32 in the `inet.3` auxiliary table, pointing to LSP PE1--->PE3. On the other hand, PE2 (IOS XR) needs the `autoroute announce` command to make the CEF entry 172.16.0.44/32 point to interface tunnel-te44 (LSP PE2--->PE4). But this command has more implications, as you can see at the end of Chapter 3.

The Traffic Engineering Database

What happens directly after you configure a RSVP-TE LSP? By default, the ingress PE doesn't leave anything to fate. It decides in advance the LSP's exact itinerary by building an ordered list of the hops that the LSP should go through. This list is encoded in an Explicit Route Object (ERO). But where does the ingress PE find the information to compute the ERO? It finds it in the *Traffic Engineering Database (TED)*.

Let's have a sneak peek on a Junos router's TED.

Example 2-34. TED at PE1 (Junos)

```
juniper@PE1> show ted database PE1.00
TED database: 7 ISIS nodes 7 INET nodes
ID                          Type Age(s) LnkIn LnkOut Protocol
PE1.00(172.16.0.11)         Rtr    198    2      2 IS-IS(2)
   To: P1.00(172.16.0.1), Local: 10.0.0.2, Remote: 10.0.0.3
   To: PE2.00(172.16.0.22), Local: 10.0.0.0, Remote: 10.0.0.1

juniper@PE1> show ted database P1.00
TED database: 7 ISIS nodes 7 INET nodes
ID                          Type Age(s) LnkIn LnkOut Protocol
P1.00(172.16.0.1)           Rtr     92    4      4 IS-IS(2)
   To: PE1.00(172.16.0.11), Local: 10.0.0.3, Remote: 10.0.0.2
   To: PE3.00(172.16.0.33), Local: 10.0.0.8, Remote: 10.0.0.9
   To: P2.00(172.16.0.2), Local: 10.0.0.6, Remote: 10.0.0.7
   To: P2.00(172.16.0.2), Local: 10.0.0.24, Remote: 10.0.0.25

juniper@PE1> show ted database PE3.00
TED database: 7 ISIS nodes 7 INET nodes
ID                          Type Age(s) LnkIn LnkOut Protocol
PE3.00(172.16.0.33)         Rtr    133    2      2 IS-IS(2)
   To: P1.00(172.16.0.1), Local: 10.0.0.9, Remote: 10.0.0.8
   To: PE4.00(172.16.0.44), Local: 10.0.0.12, Remote: 10.0.0.13
```

Similarly, PE2 (IOS XR) also has a TED (Example 2-35).

Example 2-35. TED at PE2 (IOS XR)

```
RP/0/0/CPU0:PE2#show mpls traffic-eng topology brief 172.16.0.22
[...]
IGP Id: 1720.1600.0022.00, MPLS TE Id: 172.16.0.22 Router Node
  (IS-IS mycore level-2)
  Link[0]:Point-to-Point, Nbr IGP Id:1720.1600.0002.00 [...]
  Link[1]:Point-to-Point, Nbr IGP Id:1720.1600.0011.00 [...]

RP/0/0/CPU0:PE2#show mpls traffic-eng topology brief 172.16.0.2
[...]
IGP Id: 1720.1600.0002.00, MPLS TE Id: 172.16.0.2 Router Node
  (IS-IS mycore level-2)
  Link[0]:Point-to-Point, Nbr IGP Id:1720.1600.0022.00 [...]
  Link[1]:Point-to-Point, Nbr IGP Id:1720.1600.0001.00 [...]
  Link[2]:Point-to-Point, Nbr IGP Id:1720.1600.0001.00 [...]
  Link[3]:Point-to-Point, Nbr IGP Id:1720.1600.0044.00 [...]

RP/0/0/CPU0:PE2#show mpls traffic-eng topology brief 172.16.0.44
[...]
IGP Id: 1720.1600.0044.00, MPLS TE Id: 172.16.0.44 Router Node
  (IS-IS mycore level-2)
  Link[0]:Point-to-Point, Nbr IGP Id:1720.1600.0002.00 [...]
  Link[1]:Point-to-Point, Nbr IGP Id:1720.1600.0033.00 [...]
```

 Although not shown due to the restrictions of space, the TEDs for PE1 and PE2 also contain the nodes from the other vendor's plane.

The TED looks very much like a Link State Database (LSDB). Indeed, protocols such as IS-IS or OSPF feed the information to build the TED. In addition, both the LSDB and the TED contain per-link Traffic Engineering information that you can see by using the extensive keyword.

Here are the main differences between the IS-IS (or OSPF) LSDB and the TED:

- The TED is protocol agnostic. It can be populated by IS-IS, OSPF, or even BGP (with a special address family).
- The TED is unique and there is one separate LSDB per IGP (OSPF, IS-IS) instance or process.
- The IS-IS (or OSPF) LSDB has information about MPLS and non-MPLS interfaces, whereas the TED only contains MPLS interfaces.

And how can you tell from the LSDB whether a link has MPLS turned on? Let's temporarily remove family mpls from PE1's interface ge-2/0/4 (connected to P1). Or, alternatively, delete ge-2/0/4 from protocols rsvp | mpls. Example 2-36 shows PE1's Link State Packet.

Example 2-36. Link State Packet with MPLS and non-MPLS interfaces (Junos)

```
juniper@PE1> show isis database PE1 extensive
[...]
  TLVs:
    IS extended neighbor: PE2.00, Metric: default 10
      IP address: 10.0.0.0
      Neighbor's IP address: 10.0.0.1
      Local interface index: 336, Remote interface index: 0
      Current reservable bandwidth:
        Priority 0 : 1000Mbps
        Priority 1 : 1000Mbps
        Priority 2 : 1000Mbps
        Priority 3 : 1000Mbps
        Priority 4 : 1000Mbps
        Priority 5 : 1000Mbps
        Priority 6 : 1000Mbps
        Priority 7 : 1000Mbps
      Maximum reservable bandwidth: 1000Mbps
      Maximum bandwidth: 1000Mbps
      Administrative groups:  0 <none>
    IS extended neighbor: P1.00, Metric: default 10
      IP address: 10.0.0.2
      Neighbor's IP address: 10.0.0.3
      Local interface index: 337, Remote interface index: 0

juniper@PE1> show ted database PE1
TED database: 11 ISIS nodes 7 INET nodes
ID                        Type Age(s) LnkIn LnkOut Protocol
PE1.00(172.16.0.11)        Rtr   601     2      1 IS-IS(2)
    To: PE2.00(172.16.0.22), Local: 10.0.0.0, Remote: 10.0.0.1
      Local interface index: 336, Remote interface index: 0
```

 The acronym LSP can stand for Label-Switched Path or for Link State Packet. In this book, it typically has the first meaning.

Only the MPLS link (PE1-PE2) contains Traffic Engineering sub–Type Length Value (sub-TLVs), and as a result this is the only interface at PE1 that makes it to the TED. Let's enable MPLS and RSVP on PE1-P1 interface again and move on.

Both Junos and IOS XR ensure that all the interfaces included in the TED are fully operational at the MPLS and RSVP levels. And because it is computed from the TED, the path that a RSVP-TE LSP follows is always labeled.

Constrained Shortest-Path First

To compute the ERO for the PE1→PE3 LSP, PE1 runs an algorithm called *Constrained Shortest-Path First* (CSPF), which finds the best path to PE3 in the TED. Although this book does explore a wide variety of TE constraints later on in Chapter 13 through Chapter 15, the LSPs in Example 2-32 and Example 2-33 are so simple that they impose no constraints at all. And without constraints, CSPF looks very much like the traditional Shortest-Path First (SPF). Here is the outcome of the CSPF calculation that preceded PE1→PE3 LSP's signaling from PE1:

Example 2-37. CSPF computation for PE1→PE3 LSP (Junos)

```
juniper@PE1> show rsvp session name PE1--->PE3 detail
[...]
  Explct route: 10.0.0.1 10.0.0.5 10.0.0.24 10.0.0.9
```

Surprise! The PE1→PE3 LSP is now signaled via PE2, and it has four hops instead of two. Why? Remember that MPLS was temporarily disabled on the PE1→P1 link. This brought down the RSVP-TE LSP and triggered a CSPF computation through a longer alternate path. Yet, now that PE1→P1 is fine again from the point of view of MPLS, why is the LSP still following a longer path?

In both Junos and IOS XR, simple RSVP-TE LSPs tend to avoid flapping links. When they are signaled, RSVP LSPs can remain indefinitely on their current path. If there is a failure (e.g., in one of the path's links or nodes), the ingress PE runs CSPF again and resignals the LSP.

Thus, the PE1→PE3 LSP has a suboptimal ERO. How can you reoptimize this LSP, or in other words, how can you trigger a CSPF recalculation? Manually flapping a link is not a good idea. There are better ways.

First, you can manually reoptimize an LSP by executing the following operational commands:

- Junos: `clear mpls lsp name PE1--->PE3 optimize`
- IOS XR: `mpls traffic-eng reoptimize 44 (tunnel-te 44)`

However, this is not scalable from an operational perspective. In both Junos and IOS XR, it is recommended that you configure a reoptimization timer. When the timer expires, the ingress PE runs CSPF again, and if the result is better than the current path, the LSP is resignaled.

 If the network service requirements (latency, bandwidth, etc.) allow it, try to use high timer values. Staying on stable links is a good thing!

You can configure reoptimization timers in Junos either globally or on a per-LSP basis, and they are global in IOS XR. Let's call this timer *T1* (in seconds):

- Junos: `protocols mpls [label-switched-path <name>] optimize-timer <T1>`

- IOS XR: `mpls traffic-eng reoptimize <T1>`

LSP optimization takes place in a make-before-break fashion. Before tearing down the original path, PE1 signals a new PE1→PE3 path and gracefully switches the traffic to it. In that sense, the change is not disruptive and does not cause any transit packet loss. In scaled environments, it is wise to delay this switchover, allowing time for the LSP's forwarding plane to be ready before the routes point to the new path. Let's call this timer *T2* (in seconds):

- Junos: `protocols mpls optimize-switchover-delay <T2>`

- IOS XR: `mpls traffic-eng optimize timers delay installation <T2>`

How do T1 and T2 relate to each other? Let's see an example, by using the Junos terminology from Table 2-2.

The PE1→PE3 LSP is initially mapped to RSVP *session A*, which follows the shortest IGP path PE1-P1-PE3. Then, the PE1-P1 link experiences a short flap (up→down→up).

Directly after the up→down transition, RSVP *session A* goes down, and PE1 signals a new RSVP *session B* through a (longer) available path—for example, PE1-PE2-P2-PE4-PE3. PE1 quickly activates the LSP on RSVP *session B* and starts timer T1. At this point, the user traffic is restored.

While T1 is ticking down, the link comes back up and IS-IS converges. That's orthogonal to T1, which just keeps ticking down. When T1 expires, PE1 signals a new RSVP *session C* through the shortest path PE1-P1-PE3, and starts timer T2.

While T2 is ticking down, PE1 keeps both RSVP *sessions B and C* up, but the LSP and the user traffic are still on *session B*. Only when T2 expires, PE1 switches the LSP and the user traffic to *session C*.

RSVP-TE messages

After the ingress PE computes the ERO, it begins to signal the LSP. Let's focus on the PE1→PE3 example. As shown in Figure 2-5, the ingress PE (PE1) sends *Path* messages and the egress PE (PE3) answers with *Resv* messages. These RSVP messages are encapsulated directly on top of IP (RSVP = IPv4 protocol 46).

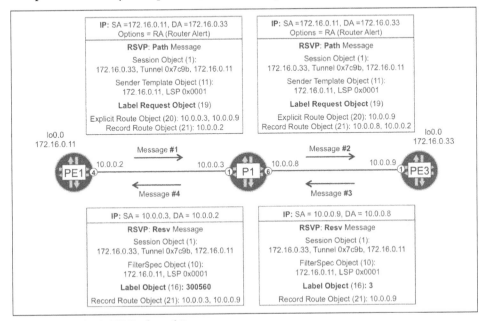

Figure 2-5. RSVP-TE Path and Resv messages

In addition to the ERO, a Path message contains several objects, including the Record Route Object (RRO). The ERO and the RRO have symmetrical roles: whereas the ERO shrinks hop by hop (as there are less hops to go), the RRO grows hop by hop (as there are more hops left behind).

Try to spot the Tunnel ID and the LSP ID in Figure 2-5. When the LSP is resignaled (upon failure, reoptimization, or a change in TE requirements), the Tunnel ID remains the same and the LSP ID is incremented.

RSVP Path messages have a destination IPv4 address equal to the egress PE's loopback (and not to the transit LSR). For this reason, the ingress PE sets the Router Alert (RA) option in the IPv4 header. This allows the transit LSRs (P1) to intercept and process the Path messages at the control plane, thereby creating dynamic local LSP state and updating both the ERO and the RRO on a hop-by-hop basis.

The Resv messages flow in the opposite direction (upstream) and contain label information. First, the egress PE (PE3) signals the implicit null label; then, the upstream LSRs assign a locally unique label bound to the LSP.

 In RSVP-TE, a label is locally bound to an LSP, not to an FEC. If PE1 signals 1,000 LSPs toward PE3 with the same ERO, P1 assigns 1,000 different MPLS labels, one per LSP.

Because Resv messages are triggered by Path messages, RSVP-TE label distribution method is DoD, as compared to the default LDP mode (DU).

RSVP-TE LSPs are maintained by periodic Path/Resv message refresh. This per-LSP message exchange is often called an *RSVP session*. You can view an RSVP session as a control plane incarnation of an LSP. This is a subtle nuance, so in the RSVP world, the terms *LSP* and *session* are often used interchangeably (see Table 2-3).

After it is configured to do so, PE3 also signals a PE3→PE1 LSP by sending Path messages to PE1 and receiving Resv messages from PE1. This enables bidirectional end-to-end traffic.

LSRs send Path and Resv messages periodically in order to keep the RSVP-TE sessions alive. Chapter 16 covers some possible optimizations.

There is also a set of messages (PathErr, PathTear, ResvErr, and ResvTear) that signal LSP error conditions or tear down RSVP-TE LSPs.

RSVP-TE in Action

Let's see two end-to-end traffic examples, first on the Junos plane (LSP PE1→PE3) and then on the IOS XR plane (PE2→PE4). Figure 2-6 illustrates the RSVP signaling involved in both examples.

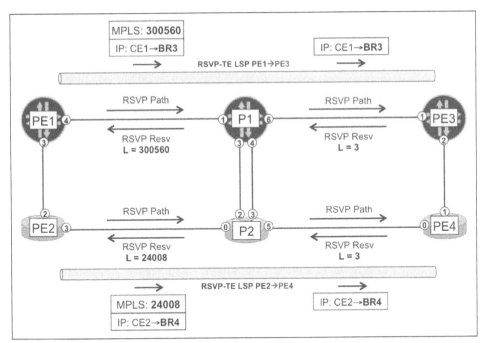

Figure 2-6. RSVP-TE LSPs on Junos and IOS XR planes

RSVP-TE signaling and MPLS forwarding in the Junos plane

The first example (Example 2-38) is a loopback-to-loopback traceroute from CE1 to BR3 traversing the Junos plane (PE1, P1, PE3).

Example 2-38. Traceroute through the Junos plane

```
juniper@CE1> traceroute 192.168.20.3 source 192.168.10.1
traceroute to 192.168.20.3 (192.168.20.3) from 192.168.10.1 [...]
 1  PE1 (10.1.0.1)  21.468 ms  8.833 ms  4.311 ms
 2  P1 (10.0.0.3)  20.169 ms  33.771 ms  137.208 ms
    MPLS Label=300560 CoS=0 TTL=1 S=1
 3  PE3 (10.0.0.9)  14.305 ms  13.516 ms  12.845 ms
 4  BR3 (192.168.20.3)  23.651 ms  10.378 ms  11.674 ms
```

Let's interpret the output step by step. As you saw in Chapter 1, PE1 has a BGP route toward BR3's loopback, and the BGP next hop of this route is PE3. Then, PE1 resolves this BGP next hop by looking at the inet.3 auxiliary table, and this is how the Internet route (to BR3) gets a labeled forwarding next hop.

Example 2-39. MPLS forwarding at ingress PE1 (Junos)

```
juniper@PE1> show route 192.168.20.3 active-path detail
[...]
```

```
        Protocol next hop: 172.16.0.33

juniper@PE1> show route table inet.3 172.16.0.33

inet.3: 3 destinations, 3 routes (3 active, 0 holddown, 0 hidden)
+ = Active Route, - = Last Active, * = Both

172.16.0.33/32    *[RSVP/7/1] 05:01:26, metric 20
          > to 10.0.0.3 via ge-2/0/4.0, label-switched-path PE1--->PE3

juniper@PE1> show route forwarding-table destination 192.168.20.3
Routing table: default.inet
Internet:
Destination      Type Next hop  Type      Index  NhRef Netif
192.168.20.3/32  user           indr    1048576  2
                      10.0.0.3   Push 300560  595  2     ge-2/0/4.0
```

PE1 pushes an MPLS header with label 300560 and sends the packet to the forwarding next hop P1. Why label 300560? The answer is in Figure 2-5, Figure 2-6, and Example 2-40: because this is the label that P1 maps to the LSP PE1→PE3.

Example 2-40. RSVP sessions at PE1 (Junos)

```
juniper@PE1> show rsvp session
Ingress RSVP: 3 sessions
To          From        State Style Labelin Labelout LSPname
172.16.0.22 172.16.0.11 Up      SE    -         3 PE1--->PE2
172.16.0.33 172.16.0.11 Up      FF    -    300560 PE1--->PE3
172.16.0.44 172.16.0.11 Up      SE    -    300256 PE1--->PE4
Total 3 displayed, Up 3, Down 0

Egress RSVP: 3 sessions
To          From        State Style Labelin Labelout LSPname
172.16.0.11 172.16.0.22 Up      SE    3         - PE2--->PE1
172.16.0.11 172.16.0.44 Up      SE    3         - PE4--->PE1
172.16.0.11 172.16.0.33 Up      FF    3         - PE3--->PE1
Total 3 displayed, Up 3, Down 0

Transit RSVP: 2 sessions
To          From        State Style Labelin Labelout LSPname
172.16.0.22 172.16.0.33 Up      SE  299952       3 PE3--->PE2
172.16.0.33 172.16.0.22 Up      SE  299968  300144 PE2--->PE3
Total 2 displayed, Up 2, Down 0

juniper@PE1> show rsvp session name PE1--->PE3 detail
[...]
  PATH sentto: 10.0.0.3 (ge-2/0/4.0) 4226 pkts
  RESV rcvfrom: 10.0.0.3 (ge-2/0/4.0) 4235 pkts[...]
  Explct route: 10.0.0.3 10.0.0.9
  Record route: <self> 10.0.0.3 10.0.0.9
```

The two first columns in the previous output are To and From. The order is important: first comes the tail-end of the LSP and then the head-end. It's not always intuitive because the LSPs are signaled the other way around.

From the perspective of PE1, there are three types of RSVP sessions:

- Ingress RSVP sessions correspond to LSPs originated at PE1 (head-end). They have PE1's router ID in the second column (From).
- Egress RSVP sessions correspond to LSPs that terminate at PE1 (tail-end). They have PE1's router ID in the first column (To).
- Transit RSVP sessions correspond to LSPs that go through PE1, but whose two endpoints are both outside PE1.

The Style column can show two different values: Shared Explicit (SE) and Fixed Filter (FF). SE is the recommended mode because it makes sure that bandwidth reservations (if any) are not double counted. It is the default in IOS XR and requires explicit configuration in Junos, as you can see in Example 2-32, line 4 (adaptive keyword).

Now, let's see how to interpret the Labelin and Labelout columns:

- If PE1 needs to *send* a packet through LSP PE1→PE3, PE1 pushes label 300560 to the packet before sending it out to the next hop.
- If PE1 *receives* an incoming packet with outermost label 299968, PE1 maps the packet to LSP PE2→PE3 and swaps its label to 300144.
- If PE1 *receives* an incoming packet with outermost label 299952, PE1 maps the packet to LSP PE3→PE2 and pops the label.

As you can see, RSVP's Labelin and Labelout are forwarding-plane concepts. MPLS data packets are received by using Labelin and sent by using Labelout. In this sense, show rsvp session and show ldp database have an opposite interpretation of what input and output mean. Indeed, LDP's input and output label database contain labels learned and advertised, respectively. But MPLS packets flow in the reverse direction!

Back to RSVP: let's compare two similar (but not identical) commands in Junos.

Example 2-41. RSVP session versus MPLS LSP (Junos)

```
juniper@PE1> show rsvp session ingress name PE1--->PE3
Ingress RSVP: 3 sessions
To          From       State Style Labelin Labelout LSPname
172.16.0.33 172.16.0.11 Up    FF      -      300560 PE1--->PE3
```

```
juniper@PE1> show mpls lsp ingress name PE1--->PE3
Ingress LSP: 3 sessions
To           From         State  P    ActivePath  LSPname
172.16.0.33  172.16.0.11  Up     *                PE1--->PE3
Total 1 displayed, Up 1, Down 0
```

If the LSP is up and stable, the first command provides more information (namely, the labels). But, the second command is very useful in other situations: for example, if the LSP cannot be established due to a CSPF failure (no RSVP session), or if the LSP is being reoptimized or it has path protection (two RSVP sessions for the same LSP). These two commands are complementary.

 You can see the Tunnel ID by looking at the port number in the show rsvp session extensive output.

Let's move on to P1, a pure LSR or P-router (Example 2-42).

Example 2-42. RSVP signaling and MPLS forwarding at P1 (Junos)

```
juniper@PE1> show rsvp session transit name PE1--->PE3
Transit RSVP: 6 sessions
To           From         State Style  Labelin Labelout LSPname
172.16.0.33  172.16.0.11  Up    FF     300560        3 PE1--->PE3

juniper@P1> show route forwarding-table label 300560 table default
Routing table: default.mpls
MPLS:
Destination  Type RtRef Next hop       Index  NhRef Netif
300560       user     0 10.0.0.9  Pop    586    2     ge-2/0/6.0
300560(S=0)  user     0 10.0.0.9  Pop    588    2     ge-2/0/6.0
```

The forwarding table has two routes for label 300560, one for each value of the Bottom of Stack (BoS) bit in the external MPLS header. Which one is relevant for the CE1-to-BR3 traceroute packets? These arrive to P1 with just one MPLS label. In single-label stacks, the Top of Stack (ToS) label is at the same time the BoS label, so the BoS bit is set to 1 (S=1) and the first route applies.

As you saw in the LDP section, label 3 is a reserved label value called *implicit null* and it translates to *pop the label*. So, the IPv4 packet arrives unlabeled to PE3, and PE3 has the BGP route to reach BR3.

Let's wrap up by looking at an RSVP-TE LSP traceroute.

Example 2-43. MPLS RSVP-TE traceroute from PE1 to PE3 (Junos)

```
juniper@PE1> traceroute mpls rsvp PE1--->PE3
  Probe options: retries 3, exp 7

  ttl   Label  Protocol  Address   Previous Hop  Probe Status
   1    300560 RSVP-TE   10.0.0.3  (null)        Success
  FEC-Stack-Sent: RSVP
  ttl   Label  Protocol  Address   Previous Hop  Probe Status
   2        3  RSVP-TE   10.0.0.9  10.0.0.3      Egress
  FEC-Stack-Sent: RSVP


  Path 1 via ge-2/0/4.0 destination 127.0.0.64
```

RSVP-TE signaling and MPLS forwarding in the IOS XR plane

Example 2-44 is an end-to-end traceroute from CE2 to BR4 that goes through the IOS XR plane (PE2, P2, PE4).

Example 2-44. Traceroute through the IOS XR plane

```
juniper@CE2> traceroute 192.168.20.4 source 192.168.10.2
traceroute to 192.168.20.4 (192.168.20.4) from 192.168.10.2 [...]
 1  PE2 (10.1.0.3)  2.833 ms  3.041 ms  2.441 ms
 2  P2 (10.0.0.5)  10.465 ms  8.480 ms  9.311 ms
    MPLS Label=24008 CoS=0 TTL=1 S=1
 3  PE4 (10.0.0.11)  8.461 ms  8.757 ms  7.982 ms
 4  BR4 (192.168.20.4)  9.109 ms  10.427 ms  9.248 ms
```

PE2 has a BGP route toward BR4's loopback, and the BGP next hop of this route is PE4. The key here is the CEF entry for 172.16.0.44/32. Let's have a look at it.

Example 2-45. MPLS forwarding at ingress PE2 (IOS XR)

```
1    RP/0/0/CPU0:PE2#show cef 172.16.0.44
2    172.16.0.44/32, version 91, internal [...]
3      local adjacency 10.0.0.5
4      Prefix Len 32, traffic index 0, precedence n/a, priority 1
5        via 172.16.0.44, tunnel-te44, 4 dependencies [...]
6        path-idx 0 NHID 0x0 [0xa0db3250 0x0]
7        next hop 172.16.0.44
8        local adjacency
9          local label 24016     labels imposed {ImplNull}
```

The label operation for this LSP is as follows: push a *real* label, not implicit null. The real label does not show in line 9. Actually, seeing ImplNull there is a sign that everything is OK.

What is `tunnel-te44`? This is an explicitly configured interface, and it pushes an MPLS label with a value (24008) that matches traceroute's output, as shown in Example 2-44 and in Example 2-46 (line 7):

Example 2-46. RSVP-TE LSP at PE2 (IOS XR)

```
1    RP/0/0/CPU0:PE2#show mpls traffic-eng tunnels name tunnel-te44 detail
2    Name: tunnel-te44  Destination: 172.16.0.44  Ifhandle:0x580
3      Signalled-Name: PE2--->PE4
4      Status:
5        Admin:    up Oper:   up  Path:  valid   Signalling: connected
6    [...]
7        Outgoing Interface: GigabitEthernet0/0/0/3, Outgoing Label: 24008
8        Path Info:
9          Outgoing:
10           Explicit Route:
11             Strict, 10.0.0.5
12             Strict, 10.0.0.11
13             Strict, 172.16.0.44
14         Resv Info:
15           Record Route:
16             IPv4 10.0.0.5, flags 0x0
17             IPv4 10.0.0.11, flags 0x0
18
19   RP/0/0/CPU0:PE2#show rsvp session tunnel-name PE2--->PE4
20   Type Destination Add DPort  Proto/ExtTunID  PSBs  RSBs  Reqs
21   ---- --------------- ----- --------------- ----- ----- -----
22   LSP4    172.16.0.44    44      172.16.0.22    1     1     0
```

Now, let's look at the RSVP-TE session and forwarding entries on P2, the next hop LSR.

Example 2-47. RSVP signaling and MPLS forwarding at P2 (IOS XR)

```
RP/0/0/CPU0:P2#show rsvp session tunnel-name PE2--->PE4 detail
SESSION: IPv4-LSP Addr: 172.16.0.44, TunID: 44, ExtID: 172.16.0.22
 Tunnel Name: PE2--->PE4 [...]
  RSVP Path Info:
   InLabel: GigabitEthernet0/0/0/0, 24008
   Incoming Address: 10.0.0.5
   Explicit Route:
     Strict, 10.0.0.5/32
     Strict, 10.0.0.11/32
     Strict, 172.16.0.44/32
   Record Route:
     IPv4 10.0.0.4, flags 0x0
   Tspec: avg rate=0, burst=1K, peak rate=0
  RSVP Resv Info:
   OutLabel: GigabitEthernet0/0/0/5, 3
   FRR OutLabel: No intf, No label
```

```
   Record Route:
     IPv4 10.0.0.11, flags 0x0

RP/0/0/CPU0:P2#show mpls forwarding labels 24008
Wed Nov 26 10:58:09.822 UTC
Local  Outgoing    Prefix      Outgoing     Next Hop    Bytes
Label  Label       or ID       Interface                Switched
------ ----------- ----------- ------------ ----------- --------
24008  Pop         44          Gi0/0/0/5    10.0.0.11   192900
```

And finally, following is an example of RSVP-TE LSP traceroute in IOS XR.

Example 2-48. MPLS RSVP-TE traceroute from PE2 to PE4 (IOS XR)

```
RP/0/0/CPU0:PE2#traceroute mpls traffic-eng tunnel-te 44

[...]
  0 10.0.0.4 MRU 1500 [Labels: 24008 Exp: 0]
L 1 10.0.0.5 MRU 1500 [Labels: implicit-null Exp: 0] 0 ms
! 2 10.0.0.11 1 ms    IPv4 10.0.0.4, flags 0x0
```

Remember that MPLS OAM requires explicit configuration in IOS XR.

RSVP-Constrained Paths and ECMP

RSVP-TE EROs determine the path of an LSP univocally. There is no load balancing inside an LSP: after it is established, the LSP follows one—and only one—path until the LSP is resignaled and moves to another *single* path. This makes RSVP-TE less ECMP-aware than LDP. Let's see how to achieve load balancing with plain RSVP-TE LSPs: you basically need several LSPs between the same head and tail.

Following is a Junos configuration with three RSVP-TE LSPs from PE1 to PE4.

Example 2-49. Three RSVP-TE LSPs from PE1 to PE4 (Junos)

```
protocols {
    mpls {
        label-switched-path PE1--->PE4 to 172.16.0.44;
        label-switched-path PE1--->PE4-A {
            to 172.16.0.44;
            primary PE4-A;
        }
        label-switched-path PE1--->PE4-B {
            to 172.16.0.44;
            primary PE4-B;
```

```
        }
        path PE4-A {
            10.0.0.3 strict;
            10.0.0.7 strict;
            10.0.0.11 strict;
        }
        path PE4-B {
            172.16.0.22 loose;
}}}
```

This configuration brings up three LSPs:

- PE1→PE4 does not have any CSPF constraints. PE1 chooses an ERO among the four available equal-cost paths to PE4, and the result is not deterministic.

- PE1→PE4-A has strict CSPF constraints: an ordered list of forwarding next hops. This is actually a manually configured ERO and it leaves CSPF with only one option. Hence, the path is deterministic.

- PE1→PE4-B has a loose CSPF constraint: *go via PE2*. It is loose because it does not specify how to enter or exit PE2. However, there is only one possible path that meets the constraint in this topology.

PE1 load balances across the three LSPs, regardless of their path.

Example 2-50. RSVP-TE ECMP from PE1 to PE4 (Junos)

```
1    juniper@PE1> show rsvp session ingress name PE1--->PE4* extensive
2    [...]
3      LSPname: PE1--->PE4, LSPpath: Primary
4      Resv style: 1 SE, Label in: -, Label out: 300576
5      Explct route: 10.0.0.3 10.0.0.9 10.0.0.13
6    [...]
7      LSPname: PE1--->PE4-A, LSPpath: Primary
8      Resv style: 1 SE, Label in: -, Label out: 300560
9      Explct route: 10.0.0.3 10.0.0.7 10.0.0.11
10   [...]
11     LSPname: PE1--->PE4-B, LSPpath: Primary
12     Resv style: 1 SE, Label in: -, Label out: 24003
13     Explct route: 10.0.0.1 10.0.0.5 10.0.0.11
14
15   juniper@PE1> show route table inet.3 172.16.0.44
16
17   inet.3: 3 destinations, 3 routes (3 active, 0 holddown, 0 hidden)
18   + = Active Route, - = Last Active, * = Both
19
20   172.16.0.44/32    *[RSVP/7/1] 11:44:37, metric 30
21      > to 10.0.0.3 via ge-2/0/4.0, label-switched-path PE1--->PE4
22        to 10.0.0.3 via ge-2/0/4.0, label-switched-path PE1--->PE4-A
23        to 10.0.0.1 via ge-2/0/3.0, label-switched-path PE1--->PE4-B
24
```

```
25    juniper@PE1> show route forwarding-table destination 192.168.20.4
26    Routing table: default.inet
27    Internet:
28    Destination        Type Next hop        Type  Index    Netif
29    192.168.20.4/32    user                 indr  1048577
30                                            ulst  1048581
31                        10.0.0.3 Push 300576         596   ge-2/0/4.0
32                        10.0.0.3 Push 300560         599   ge-2/0/4.0
33                        10.0.0.1 Push 24003          597   ge-2/0/3.0
```

As you can see, the ingress PE actually expands the 172.16.0.22 loose next hop into a list of strict next hops (lines 5, 9, and 13). In this case, *loose* and *strict* are local properties, only meaningful in the context of CSPF. The resulting ERO has a simpler structure: it's just a list of IPv4 next hops.

 In some cases, the RSVP-TE Path messages *may* actually include loose next hops. This is the case of inter-area scenarios where the ingress PE signals a loose next hop and the ABR expands it into a list of strict next hops.

If the manually defined path is not valid or it has loops, CSPF fails and the ingress PE does not signal the LSP. In addition, RSVP-TE has a mechanism (based on the RRO) to detect loops in transit during LSP establishment.

Load balancing is achieved with a unilist next hop (line 30). Although not shown in Example 2-50, all the unicast next hops (lines 31 through 33) have weight 0x1. This topic is fully explained in Chapter 20.

Note that after a packet enters a given RSVP-TE LSP, there is just one possible path ahead. All of the load balancing is performed at the head-end, unlike LDP LSPs for which ECMP happens in a hop-by-hop basis.

The load-balancing scheme illustrated in Example 2-50 and in Figure 2-7 is imperfect: one of the P1-P2 links is not utilized and the PE1-P1 link is loaded two more times than the PE1-PE2 link. As the network grows more complex, it's virtually impossible to achieve decent load balancing with this manual approach. Fortunately, this challenge can be addressed with container LSPs (Chapter 14) and/or external controllers (Chapter 15).

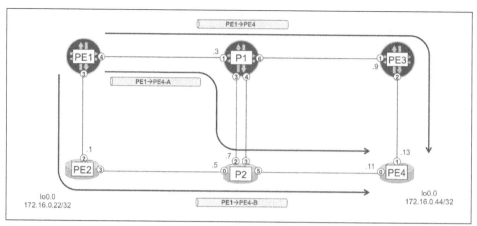

Figure 2-7. Three RSVP-TE LSPs from PE1 to PE4

What if a transit link fails? If the currently active path of PE1→PE4 were affected, the LSP would be resignaled successfully through a different path. But PE1→PE4-A (like PE1→PE4-B) does not have this flexibility and it would fail—see the fast restoration (Chapter 18 through Chapter 21) for protection features.

Now let's discuss a different example. Suppose that PE1 has two LSPs toward PE3 (not PE4). These two LSPs follow the paths (PE1, P1, PE3) and (PE1, PE2, P2, PE4, PE3), respectively. Obviously, the second path is longer and has a higher cumulative metric. However, PE1 load-balances flows across the two LSPs. Why?

 By default in Junos and IOS XR, the metric of a RSVP-TE LSP is equal to the IGP shortest-path metric to the destination. This is regardless of the actual path followed by the LSP: only the end-points matter.

Let's finish up the ECMP discussion by looking at Example 2-51, which is based on IOS XR. In this case, PE2 signals several LSPs toward PE3.

Example 2-51. Two RSVP-TE LSPs from PE2 to PE3 (IOS XR)

```
group GR-LSP-NO-PATH
 interface 'tunnel-te.*'
  ipv4 unnumbered Loopback0
  autoroute announce
  record-route
end-group
!
interface tunnel-te33
 apply-group GR-LSP-NO-PATH
 signalled-name PE2--->PE3
```

```
  destination 172.16.0.33
  path-option 1 dynamic
!
interface tunnel-te330
  apply-group GR-LSP-NO-PATH
  signalled-name PE2--->PE3-A
  destination 172.16.0.33
  path-option 1 explicit name PE3-A
!
explicit-path name PE3-A
  index 10 next-address strict ipv4 unicast 10.0.0.5
  index 20 next-address loose ipv4 unicast 172.16.0.44
```

As expected, the PE2→PE3-A path follows the path specified, and PE2 load-balances PE2-to-PE3 traffic between the two LSPs (Example 2-52).

Example 2-52. RSVP-TE ECMP from PE2 to PE3 (IOS XR)

```
RP/0/0/CPU0:PE2#show rsvp session tunnel-name PE2--->PE3 detail
[...]
   Explicit Route:
     Strict, 10.0.0.0/32
     Strict, 10.0.0.3/32
     Strict, 10.0.0.9/32
     Strict, 172.16.0.33/32

RP/0/0/CPU0:PE2#show rsvp session tunnel-name PE2--->PE3-A detail
[...]
   Explicit Route:
     Strict, 10.0.0.5/32
     Strict, 10.0.0.11/32
     Strict, 172.16.0.44/32

RP/0/0/CPU0:PE2#show cef 172.16.0.33
172.16.0.33/32, version 829, internal [...]
 Updated Nov 29 10:35:04.150
 Prefix Len 32, traffic index 0, precedence n/a, priority 1
   via 172.16.0.33, tunnel-te33, 4 dependencies [...]
   path-idx 0 NHID 0x0 [0xa0db3638 0x0]
   next hop 172.16.0.33
   local adjacency
   via 172.16.0.33, tunnel-te330, 4 dependencies [...]
   path-idx 1 NHID 0x0 [0xa0db3250 0x0]
   next hop 172.16.0.33
   local adjacency
```

Like Junos, IOS XR decouples the load-balancing decision from the actual path followed by the LSP. If PE2 has several paths to PE4, for example (PE2, P2, PE4) and (PE2, PE1, P1, PE3, PE4), PE2 spreads traffic flows between both LSPs, even if one path is much longer than the other.

Inter-Area RSVP-TE LSPs

RFC 4105 defines a set of requirements on inter-area RSVP-TE LSPs.

Looking back at Figure 2-1, let's suppose the following:

- PE1 and PE2 are **L2**-only IS-IS routers in Area 49.0001
- PE3 and PE4 are **L1**-only IS-IS routers in Area 49.0002
- P1 and P2 are IS-IS L1-L2 routers, present in both Areas

In this scenario, the link-state information is fragmented so that only P1 and P2 have a complete TED. On the other hand, a PE's TED only contains links of the local area. This makes it impossible for PE1 or PE2 to compute an ERO to reach PE3 or PE4, and vice versa. And a similar situation would occur with OSPF, too.

Route redistribution (such as IS-IS L2-to-L1 route leaking) does not propagate topology information, so it doesn't solve the issue. There are two clean solutions:

- BGP-LS (covered in Chapter 15) solves the issue by propagating interdomain topology information.
- Segmented and Hierarchical LSPs (Chapter 9 and Chapter 16) relax the need for inter-area RSVP-TE LSPs.

Let's now see a quick but limited approach to get the inter-area RSVP-TE LSPs up and running. It's the third (and less preferred) solution.

Although by default Junos and IOS XR compute a complete ERO and include it in Path messages, in reality this is not mandatory. The ERO is an optional object, and CSPF is optional, too. If you configure the PE3→PE1 LSP with the `no-cspf` option in Junos, PE3 simply looks for the best IGP route to PE1. It sends the Path message with no ERO to the next-hop LSR and waits for a Resv message. This actually works fine, but PE3 has no control on the path beyond the first next hop, which is clearly a challenge if you want to use Traffic Engineering constraints.

As an administrator, you can actually influence the LSP's itinerary within the local area of the ingress PE. For example, PE3 can choose the path that PE3→PE1 takes within area 49.0002. This can be useful to select the path toward the ABR, but there is no control beyond the ABR because there is no end-to-end visibility of the TED.

Likewise, the following IOS XR configuration results in an inter-area PE4→PE1 LSP successfully signaled end to end.

Example 2-53. Inter-area RSVP-TE LSP signaled from PE4 (IOS XR)

```
group GR-LSP-PATH
 interface 'tunnel-te.*'
```

```
  ipv4 unnumbered Loopback0
  record-route
 end-group
 !
 interface tunnel-te11
  apply-group GR-LSP-PATH
  signalled-name PE4--->PE1
  destination 172.16.0.11
  path-option 1 explicit name PE1-A
 !
 explicit-path name PE1-A
  index 10 next-address loose ipv4 unicast 172.16.0.2
 !
 router static
  address-family ipv4 unicast
   172.16.0.11/32 tunnel-te11
```

The static route is necessary because IOS XR only supports autoroute announce in single-domain LSPs. You must configure it so that the CEF entry for 172.16.0.11/32 points to the tunnel interface.

RSVP Auto Tunnel

When it comes to RSVP-TE LSPs, there is much confusion around the words *static* and *dynamic*. In this book, *RSVP-TE is always considered to be dynamic*. Chapter 1 presents an example of static (protocol-less) LSPs. But RSVP-TE is a dynamic protocol that signals LSPs end to end, detects and reacts upon failures, and so on. This remains true even if the LSP has a statically configured ERO.

RSVP Auto Tunnel (or Dynamic Tunnels) brings endpoint autodiscovery to the table. Instead of having to explicitly configure LSPs one by one, you let the ingress PE do the job of discovering remote PEs and automatically building LSPs toward them. It is still possible to apply Traffic Engineering constraints to these LSPs via a template, but you can no longer specify strict or loose IPv4 paths. So, RSVP Auto Tunnel is a time saver, but it has a cost: less control and less granularity.

The following example presents RSVP Auto Tunnel in Junos (PE1).

Example 2-54. RSVP-TE Auto Tunnel at PE1 (Junos)

```
routing-options {
    dynamic-tunnels {
        TN-PE1 {
            rsvp-te LOOPBACKS {
                label-switched-path-template default-template;
                destination-networks 172.16.0.0/16;
}}}}

juniper@PE1> show rsvp session ingress
```

```
Ingress RSVP: 3 sessions
To              From            State Labelout LSPname
172.16.0.22   172.16.0.11    Up           3 172.16.0.22:dt-rsvp-TN-PE1
172.16.0.33   172.16.0.11    Up      300512 172.16.0.33:dt-rsvp-TN-PE1
172.16.0.44   172.16.0.11    Up      300608 172.16.0.44:dt-rsvp-TN-PE1
Total 3 displayed, Up 3, Down 0
```

There is no LSP toward P1 and P2. So, why does PE1 only signal LSPs toward the PEs? The P-routers are not advertising any BGP route, so PE1 does not need to resolve the BGP next hops 172.16.0.1 and 172.16.0.2. This is a resource-saving strategy: PE1 signals only the LSPs it needs.

Finally, let's see the Auto Tunnel feature in IOS XR (PE2).

Example 2-55. RSVP-TE Auto Tunnel at PE2 (IOS XR)

```
ipv4 unnumbered mpls traffic-eng Loopback0
!
ipv4 prefix-list PR-TUNNEL
 10 deny 172.16.0.0/30 eq 32          # No tunnels to P1 and P2
 20 permit 172.16.0.0/26 eq 32
!
mpls traffic-eng
  auto-tunnel mesh
    group 1
      attribute-set AT-MESH
      destination-list PR-TUNNEL
    tunnel-id min 10 max 20
  attribute-set auto-mesh AT-MESH
    autoroute announce

RP/0/0/CPU0:PE2# show mpls traffic-eng tunnels brief

          TUNNEL NAME       DESTINATION    STATUS STATE
          +tunnel-te10      172.16.0.11       up  up
          +tunnel-te11      172.16.0.33       up  up
          +tunnel-te12      172.16.0.44       up  up
    autom_PE4_t12_mg1       172.16.0.22       up  up
  172.16.0.22:dt-rsv       172.16.0.22       up  up
  172.16.0.22:dt-rsv       172.16.0.22       up  up
+ = automatically created mesh tunnel
```

The Auto Tunnel LSPs signaled to PE2 from PE1, PE3 and PE4 are: 172.16.0.22:dt-rsvp-TN-PE1, 172.16.0.22:dt-rsvp-TN-PE3 and autom_PE4_t12_mg1, respectively.

IGP and SPRING

Source Packet Routing in Networking (SPRING), also known as *Segment Routing* (SR), is a recent network routing paradigm covered by several complementary IETF drafts at the time of publication of this book. The most fundamental are *draft-ietf-spring-segment-routing*, *draft-ietf-spring-segment-routing-mpls*, *draft-ietf-isis-segment-routing-extensions*, and *draft-ietf-ospf-segment-routing-extensions*.

SPRING is proposed as an alternative to LDP and/or RSVP-TE:

- As an LDP alternative, SPRING is natively implemented by the IGP (IS-IS or OSPF), so it reduces the number of protocols running in the network.

- As an RSVP-TE alternative, SPRING natively supports ECMP and implements a more scalable control plane because it does not need to keep per-LSP state in the network. On the other hand, SPRING does not have bandwidth reservation mechanisms, so if this function is required, you can achieve it only with the help of a central controller.

SPRING initial use cases are Traffic Engineering (see Chapter 16) and fast restoration (see Chapter 18), but new applications are being defined.

You might be venturing a guess that SPRING uses source routing as a means to transport packets from one PE to another PE across the core. However, this is *not* always the case. Strikingly, the SPRING technology applied to this chapter's basic transport scenario can be explained without invoking the source routing concept at all. Indeed, this first example's SPRING LSP's are MP2P and have only *one segment*. This chapter later explains what the "Source Packet Routing" in SPRING and the "Segment" in SR actually stand for.

For the moment, you can think of a segment as an instruction. On the wire, a segment is either encoded into a MPLS header or into something else (the alternatives are explained later in this section). Following is a first classification of segments, assuming that the forwarding plane is MPLS-based. Unlike labels, which are always local (see RFC 3031), segments can either be local or global.

- **Local segments**

The router that originates and advertises a local segment is the only one that assigns a label to the segment and installs that label in its LFIB.

- **Global segments**

Typically every router in the domain assigns a (local) label to a (global) segment and installs that label in its LFIB.

SPRING in Action

One of the most important components of SPRING is its ability to advertise *MPLS label information in the IGP*, in the form of IS-IS sub-TLVs or new opaque OSPF LSAs. Let's see it in detail for IS-IS.

This is a basic SPRING configuration in Junos (PE1).

Example 2-56. SPRING configuration at PE1 (Junos)

```
protocols {
    isis {
        source-packet-routing {
            node-segment ipv4-index 11;
```

And here it is in IOS XR (PE2).

Example 2-57. SPRING configuration at PE2 (IOS XR)

```
router isis mycore
 address-family ipv4 unicast
  segment-routing mpls
 !
 interface Loopback0
  address-family ipv4 unicast
   prefix-sid index 22
```

This configuration leads to the automatic creation of MP2P LSPs (any-to-PE1 and any-to-PE2), topologically identical to the ones signaled by LDP. SPRING is easier to understand when the LSPs have at least two hops on each (Junos, IOS XR) plane. The links PE1-P1 and P2-PE4 are temporarily disabled to achieve the forwarding path shown in Example 2-58 and in Figure 2-8.

Example 2-58. Traceroute from CE1 to BR4

```
juniper@CE1> traceroute 192.168.20.4 source 192.168.10.1
traceroute to 192.168.20.4 (192.168.20.4) from 192.168.10.1 [...]
 1  PE1 (10.1.0.1)  33.591 ms  9.484 ms  3.845 ms
 2  PE2 (10.0.0.1)  45.782 ms  11.524 ms  16.886 ms
    MPLS Label=16044 CoS=0 TTL=1 S=1
 3  P2 (10.0.0.5)  11.891 ms  11.991 ms  13.639 ms
    MPLS Label=16044 CoS=0 TTL=1 S=1
 4  10.0.0.24 (10.0.0.24)  13.205 ms  15.812 ms  16.886 ms
    MPLS Label=800044 CoS=0 TTL=1 S=1
 5  PE3 (10.0.0.9)  21.226 ms  15.272 ms  18.900 ms
    MPLS Label=800044 CoS=0 TTL=1 S=1
 6  PE4 (10.0.0.13)  19.875 ms  15.498 ms  21.145 ms
 7  BR4 (192.168.20.4)  15.067 ms  21.923 ms  21.952 ms
```

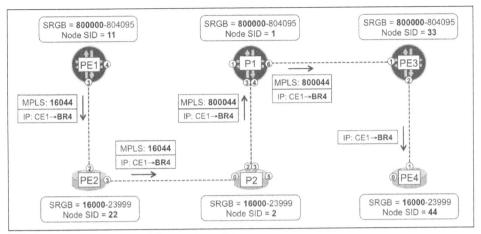

Figure 2-8. SPRING tunnel from PE1 to PE4

Interestingly, all the labels end in 44, the Node Segment Identifier (Node SID) of PE4. And, there are only two different label values in the flow: 16044 and 800044. Actually, if the path had 10 times more next hops, there would still be only two label values (one for Junos, one for IOS XR). This is totally different from LDP and RSVP, whose labels are not deterministic and often change to a different value over time and on a hop-by-hop basis.

But, where do these labels come from? Every LSR in the path adds new sub-TLVs to their own IS-IS node Link State Packet.

Example 2-59. SPRING sub-TLVs in IS-IS Link State Packets

```
RP/0/0/CPU0:PE2# show isis database verbose

IS-IS mycore (Level-2) Link State Database
LSPID           LSP Seq Num  LSP Checksum  LSP Holdtime  ATT/P/OL
P1.00-00        0x00000645   0xdde2        472           0/0/0
  Router Cap:   172.16.0.1, D:0, S:1
    Segment Routing: I:1 V:1, SRGB Base: 800000 Range: 4096
  Metric: 0           IP-Extended 172.16.0.1/32
    Prefix-SID Index: 1, R:0 N:1 P:0 E:0 V:0 L:0
[...]
P2.00-00        0x000005e2   0x3a06        942           0/0/0
  Router Cap:   172.16.0.2, D:0, S:0
    Segment Routing: I:1 V:0, SRGB Base: 16000 Range: 8000
  Metric: 0           IP-Extended 172.16.0.2/32
    Prefix-SID Index: 2, R:0 N:1 P:0 E:0 V:0 L:0
[...]
PE1.00-00       0x0000065e   0x8515        1151          0/0/0
  Router Cap:   172.16.0.11, D:0, S:1
    Segment Routing: I:1 V:1, SRGB Base: 800000 Range: 4096
```

```
    Metric: 0              IP-Extended 172.16.0.11/32
      Prefix-SID Index: 11, R:0 N:1 P:0 E:0 V:0 L:0
[...]
PE2.00-00       * 0x00000591   0x1254        1057            0/0/0
   Router Cap:    172.16.0.22, D:0, S:0
      Segment Routing: I:1 V:0, SRGB Base: 16000 Range: 8000
   Metric: 0              IP-Extended 172.16.0.22/32
      Prefix-SID Index: 22, R:0 N:1 P:0 E:0 V:0 L:0
[...]
PE3.00-00         0x00000055   0x573f         900            0/0/0
   Router Cap:    172.16.0.33, D:0, S:1
      Segment Routing: I:1 V:1, SRGB Base: 800000 Range: 4096
   Metric: 0              IP-Extended 172.16.0.33/32
      Prefix-SID Index: 33, R:0 N:1 P:0 E:0 V:0 L:0
[...]
PE4.00-00         0x00000049   0xea9c         749            0/0/0
   Router Cap:    172.16.0.44, D:0, S:0
      Segment Routing: I:1 V:0, SRGB Base: 16000 Range: 8000
   Metric: 0              IP-Extended 172.16.0.44/32
      Prefix-SID Index: 44, R:0 N:1 P:0 E:0 V:0 L:0
[...]
```

Following is the way these sub-TLVs are displayed in Junos CLI.

Example 2-60. SPRING sub-TLVs in IS-IS Link State Packets (Junos)

```
juniper@PE1> show isis database extensive
[...]
PE2.00-00 Sequence: 0x643, Checksum: 0xe1e0, Lifetime: 910 secs
 Router Capability:  Router ID 172.16.0.22, Flags: 0x01
   SPRING Capability - Flags: 0x80, Range: 8000, SID-Label: 16000
 IP extended prefix: 172.16.0.22/32 metric 0 up
   Node SID, Flags: 0x40, Algo: SPF(0), Value: 22
[...]
```

When a Prefix SID has the N-Flag (0x40), it becomes a Node SID. Node segments are global because every prefix segment is global. On the other hand, MPLS labels are locally significant by definition (RFC 3031).

SRGB stands for *Segment Routing Global Block*, and it's a *locally significant* MPLS label block that each LSR allocates to SPRING global segments. Using the terms "local" and "global" in the same sentence might sound like a contradiction, but it will become clearer as you keep reading this section. The SRGB is encoded as a *Base* (displayed as SID-Label in Junos) and a *Range*. The lowest and highest label values of the block are Base, and Base+Range–1, respectively.

Earlier SPRING drafts hoped that all the vendors would agree on a common label block. But it turned out that every vendor had its own way to partition the platform label space; hence, the introduction of the per-platform SRGB concept.

In addition, you need to allocate, configure, and associate a Prefix Segment Identifier (SID) to the LSR's loopback IP address (see Example 2-56 and Example 2-57). A Prefix SID is a *globally significant* number linked to an address FEC.

 Prefix (and Node) SIDs are global, so they must remain unique across the entire routing domain. A good practice is to define a deterministic mathematical rule that maps local Router IDs to Node SID values.

Going back to the LDP case study, each LSR dynamically allocated a local label for each remote FEC. This is also true for SPRING, except that these *local label mappings are deterministic and not explicity advertised.*

Let's suppose that PE2 needs to map a local label to FEC 172.16.0.44/32 (PE4's loopback). PE2 adds its own *local* SRGB Base (16000) to the *global* Node SID (44), and the result is the local label mapping (172.16.0.44/32, 16044) at PE2. This label is *locally unique* (local to PE2, and unique because the Node SID value uniquely identifies PE4). It is a *classic* downstream-allocated label: if an MPLS packet arrives with label 16044, PE2 knows that the packet must be sent along the LSP toward PE4.

Let's see how the LSP is built in the forwarding plane. It all begins at the Ingress PE (PE1).

Example 2-61. MPLS forwarding at ingress PE1 (Junos)

```
juniper@PE1> show route 192.168.20.4 active-path detail
[...]
                Protocol next hop: 172.16.0.44

juniper@PE1> show route 172.16.0.44 table inet.3

inet.3: 5 destinations, 5 routes (5 active, 0 holddown, 0 hidden)
+ = Active Route, - = Last Active, * = Both

172.16.0.44/32    *[L-IS-IS/14] 00:04:49, metric 50
                  > to 10.0.0.1 via ge-2/0/3.0, Push 16044

juniper@PE1> show route forwarding-table destination 192.168.20.4
Routing table: default.inet
Internet:
Destination     Type Next hop     Type      Index  NhRef Netif
```

```
192.168.20.4/32  user            indr    1048577    2
                 10.0.0.1 Push 16044      588       2 ge-2/0/3.0
```

The next hop is PE2 because it's the only available path to PE4 from the IGP perspective (remember the PE1-P1 link is down). Label 16044 is calculated as follows: PE2's SRGB Base (16000) plus 172.16.0.44's global Node SID (44): 16000 + 44 = 16044.

Let's move on to the first transit LSR (PE2).

Example 2-62. MPLS forwarding at transit PE2 (IOS XR)

```
RP/0/0/CPU0:PE2#show mpls forwarding labels 16044
Local  Outgoing  Prefix   Outgoing     Next Hop    Bytes
Label  Label     or ID    Interface                Switched
------ --------- -------- ------------ ----------- ---------
16044  16044     No ID    Gi0/0/0/3    10.0.0.5    7524
```

The next hop is P2, and label 16044 is calculated as follows: P2's SRGB Base (16000) plus 172.16.0.44's global Node SID (44).

Let's look at the next transit LSR (P2).

Example 2-63. MPLS forwarding at transit P2 (IOS XR)

```
RP/0/0/CPU0:P2#show mpls forwarding labels 16044
Local  Outgoing  Prefix   Outgoing     Next Hop    Bytes
Label  Label     or ID    Interface                Switched
------ --------- -------- ------------ ----------- ---------
16044  800044    No ID    Gi0/0/0/2    10.0.0.6    102318
       800044    No ID    Gi0/0/0/3    10.0.0.24   3324
```

The next hop is P1 and traffic is load-balanced across the two parallel P1-P2 links. Good!

 Remember that LDP is natively ECMP-aware because it is coupled to the IGP. Well, SPRING is also natively ECMP-aware because *it is actually a part of the IGP!*

The outgoing label 800044 is calculated as follows: P1's SRGB Base (800000) plus 172.16.0.44's global Node SID (44).

Let's look at the next transit LSR (P1).

Example 2-64. MPLS forwarding at transit P1 (Junos)

```
juniper@P1> show route forwarding-table label 800044
Routing table: default.mpls
MPLS:
Destination  Type  Next hop              Index  NhRef  Netif
800044       user  10.0.0.9 Swap 800044  603    2      ge-2/0/6.0
```

The next hop is PE3, and the outgoing label 800044 is calculated as follows: PE3's SRGB Base (800000) plus 172.16.0.44's global Node SID (44).

PE3, the penultimate hop LSR. PE3 realizes that the Node SID (44) is attached to the neighboring router PE4. Furthermore, the 172.16.0.44/32 SID (see Example 2-59) does not have the P flag set (P:0). This is the no-PHP flag, and because it is not set, *there is PHP*. As a result, PE3 simply pops the label.

Example 2-65. MPLS forwarding at transit PE3 (Junos)

```
juniper@PE3> show route forwarding-table label 800044
Routing table: default.mpls
MPLS:
Destination   Type  Next hop        Index  NhRef  Netif
800044        user  10.0.0.13  Pop  595    2      ge-2/0/2.0
800044(S=0)   user  10.0.0.13  Pop  596    2      ge-2/0/2.0
```

Finally, as an exercise, you can decipher the traceroute output (from BR4 to CE1) in Example 2-66 with the help of Figure 2-8. Note that there is ECMP between P1 and P2 (although only one of the paths is displayed).

Example 2-66. Traceroute from BR4 to CE1

```
juniper@BR4> traceroute 192.168.10.1 source 192.168.20.4
traceroute to 192.168.10.1 (192.168.10.1) from 192.168.20.4 [...]
 1  PE4 (10.2.0.44)  3.543 ms  2.339 ms  2.941 ms
 2  PE3 (10.0.0.12)  15.954 ms  14.377 ms  12.769 ms
    MPLS Label=800011 CoS=0 TTL=1 S=1
 3  P1 (10.0.0.8)  17.500 ms  12.640 ms  12.053 ms
    MPLS Label=800011 CoS=0 TTL=1 S=1
 4  P2 (10.0.0.25)  14.233 ms  11.790 ms  P2 (10.0.0.7)  12.726 ms
    MPLS Label=16011 CoS=0 TTL=1 S=1
 5  PE2 (10.0.0.4)  12.302 ms  52.934 ms  182.355 ms
    MPLS Label=16011 CoS=0 TTL=1 S=1
 6  PE1 (10.0.0.0)  13.430 ms  12.928 ms  12.125 ms
 7  CE1 (192.168.10.1)  16.963 ms  18.107 ms  15.797 ms
```

SPRING Concepts

The previous examples illustrated a simple SPRING scenario because it only involves one segment, namely PE4's (or PE1's) Node SID.

Figure 2-9 illustrates a more complex scenario with four segments pushed on the packets, from top to bottom: a node segment (for TE), an adjacency segment (for TE), another node segment (the egress PE), and a service segment (see Chapters Chapter 3 through Chapter 8 for examples of this).

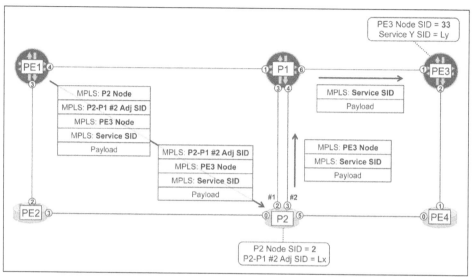

Figure 2-9. Node, adjacency, and service segments

Before sending the packet into the core, PE1 pushes four MPLS headers, each with one label. They are, from top to bottom (remember that all of these labels are locally-significant):

P2's Node (Global Segment)
The outermost label takes the packet from PE1 to P2 in an ECMP-aware manner. PE1 has two equal-cost next hops to reach P2: P1 and PE2. Depending on whether PE1 decides to go via P1 or PE2, the label would be 800002 or 16002, respectively. This is due to the different SRGB Base at P1 and PE2. Then, P1 or PE2 pops the outer header from the packet on its way to P2.

P2-P1 #2 Adjacency (Local Segment)
P2 receives the packet with a three-label stack. The outer label, Lx, represents a local segment, and it identifies an IGP adjacency. This is a new type of segment and it means: *pop the label and send the packet over the P2-P1 link #2*. This time it is an internal core link, but it could have been an external peering link or even a RSVP-TE LSP beginning at P2.

PE3's Node (Global Segment)

P1 receives the packet with a two-label stack. The outer label is 800033, and it is P1's SRGB Base plus PE3's Node SID. P1 pops this label before sending the packet to PE3.

Service Y (Local Segment)

PE3 receives the packet with just one MPLS header. The label Ly is a local segment that identifies a service. This new type of segment means: *pop the label and map the packet to Service Y.*

You can view segments as *instructions*. When PE1 pushes four headers, it is giving four consecutive instructions to the LSRs in the path: first take the packet to P2, then send it over link P2-P1 #2, then take it to PE3, and then when it arrives at PE3, map it to Service Y. A global instruction can actually require multiple hops to be completed (Node Segments are a good example of this).

PE1 codes a sequence of routing instructions directly in the data packet. This time the instructions are coded as MPLS labels, but SPRING also supports IPv6 (with extension headers) forwarding plane. The key concept here is that the source (PE1) not only decides the next hop, but also the subsequent forwarding decisions. This model is traditionally called Source Routing and this is how the SPRING acronym becomes meaningful.

Back to RSVP-TE, the ingress PE also decided the path. Is that Source Routing, too? Let's see:

- You can see back in Figure 2-5 that the RSVP-TE Path messages are actually source-routed. Thanks to the ERO, the ingress PE can decide the exact path of the LSP. Conversely, the data packets typically have one MPLS label only, which is mapped to the LSP. In SPRING terminology, an RSVP-TE LSP is just one *segment*. So, in the RSVP-TE world, the control plane relies on Source Routing but the forwarding plane does not.

- SPRING is a totally different paradigm: the control plane is not even routed (IGP packets are flooded hop-by-hop), and the forwarding plane may be source-routed.

Let's examine each segment type in more detail.

Node Segments are actually a particular subcase (N-flag=1) of Prefix Segments. They are routed along the IGP's ECMP shortest path and may be rerouted if the IGP topology changes. In that sense, Node Segments are *loose* next hops. Their Segment IDs must be unique because they have global significance. After they're shifted by the SRGB Base, the resulting, locally significant, labels are present in the LFIBs of all the LSRs: this is what a *global segment* stands for.

Adjacency Segments are local segments, which are only installed in the LFIB of the LSR advertising them. Said differently, two LSRs can advertise the same label value for totally different adjacencies. Adjacency Segments can be interpreted as *strict* next hops. For example, by pushing five MPLS headers, the ingress PE can send a packet into an LSP consisting of five strict next hops.

Service Segments are mapped to a service. What is a service? The following chapters cover several L2 and L3 services in detail. For the time being, it is worth noting that stacking a service label below a transport label (and, more generally, stacking *any* kind of labels) is a standard MPLS technique, *not* a new contribution from SPRING.

SPRING Adjacency Segments

Both Junos and IOS XR advertise an Adjacency SID by default for each of its IGP adjacencies.

Following is how the Adjacency SIDs look in Junos and IOS XR CLI.

Example 2-67. SPRING Adjacency SIDs in Junos and IOS XR CLI

```
juniper@PE1> show isis database PE1.00 extensive
[...]
    IS extended neighbor: PE2.00, Metric: default 10
      IP address: 10.0.0.0
      Neighbor's IP address: 10.0.0.1
      P2P IPV4 Adj-SID - Flags:0x30, Weight:0, Label: 299904
    IS extended neighbor: P1.00, Metric: default 10
      IP address: 10.0.0.2
      Neighbor's IP address: 10.0.0.3
      P2P IPV4 Adj-SID - Flags:0x30, Weight:0, Label: 299920

RP/0/0/CPU0:P2#show isis database verbose PE1.00
[...]
  Metric: 10        IS-Extended PE2.00
    Interface IP Address: 10.0.0.0
    Neighbor IP Address: 10.0.0.1
    ADJ-SID: F:0 B:0 V:1 L:1 S:0 weight:0 Adjacency-sid:299904
  Metric: 10        IS-Extended P1.00
    Interface IP Address: 10.0.0.2
    Neighbor IP Address: 10.0.0.3
    ADJ-SID: F:0 B:0 V:1 L:1 S:0 weight:0 Adjacency-sid:299920
```

Following is the local meaning of label 299904 at PE1:

- If PE1 receives a packet with outer MPLS label 299904, it pops the label and sends the packet to PE2 over the link whose remote IPv4 address is 10.0.0.1.

It is worthwhile to have a look at PE1's Label Forwarding Information Base (LFIB) and look for the Node and Adjacency SIDs in it.

Example 2-68. LFIB at PE1 (Junos)

```
juniper@PE1> show route table mpls.0
[...]
299904             *[L-ISIS/14] 00:05:27, metric 0
                    > to 10.0.0.1 via ge-2/0/3.0, Pop
299904(S=0)        *[L-ISIS/14] 00:01:10, metric 0
                    > to 10.0.0.1 via ge-2/0/3.0, Pop
299920             *[L-ISIS/14] 00:01:29, metric 0
                    > to 10.0.0.3 via ge-2/0/4.0, Pop
299920(S=0)        *[L-ISIS/14] 00:01:10, metric 0
                    > to 10.0.0.3 via ge-2/0/4.0, Pop
800001             *[L-ISIS/14] 00:01:20, metric 10
                    > to 10.0.0.3 via ge-2/0/4.0, Pop
800001(S=0)        *[L-ISIS/14] 00:01:10, metric 10
                    > to 10.0.0.3 via ge-2/0/4.0, Pop
800002             *[L-ISIS/14] 00:01:20, metric 20
                      to 10.0.0.1 via ge-2/0/3.0, Swap 16002
                    > to 10.0.0.3 via ge-2/0/4.0, Swap 800002
800022             *[L-ISIS/14] 19:49:26, metric 10
                    > to 10.0.0.1 via ge-2/0/3.0, Pop
800022(S=0)        *[L-ISIS/14] 00:01:10, metric 10
                    > to 10.0.0.1 via ge-2/0/3.0, Pop
800033             *[L-ISIS/14] 00:01:20, metric 20
                    > to 10.0.0.3 via ge-2/0/4.0, Swap 800033
800044             *[L-ISIS/14] 00:01:10, metric 30
                      to 10.0.0.1 via ge-2/0/3.0, Swap 16044
                    > to 10.0.0.3 via ge-2/0/4.0, Swap 800044
```

As you can see, PE1's LFIB contains all the Node labels (global Node SID + local→remote SRGB Base), and only the local Adjacency SID labels.

Another interesting case is the double P1-P2 link. Depending on the implementation, LSRs may advertise one different Adjacency SID for each link and/or advertise one single Adjacency SID representing both links. As a result, the head-end LER may have the possibility to choose either ECMP or a specific link. The authors did not verify these implementation details in the lab.

A Comparison of LDP, RSVP-TE, and SPRING

So far, this chapter has covered three protocols (or actually four, if you consider SPRING both over IS-IS and OSPF) that are capable of signaling MPLS LSPs. Which one is better? It depends!

MPLS is a flexible technology and depending on the application, the topology, the requirements, and more in some cases, the best fit can be RSVP-TE, or SPRING, or

LDP. It really depends on the relative importance of each factor. Table 2-2 summarizes the pros and cons of each of these great technologies.

Table 2-3. Comparison of internal MPLS signaling protocols

Technology	LDP	RSVP-TE	SPRING
Supports Traffic Engineering	No	Yes	With label stacking, no BW reservation.
Natively supported by the IGP	No	No	Yes
Supports P2MP LSPs	Yes	Yes	Not yet
Simple configuration	Yes	With Auto Tunnel	SID provisioning
Control plane load	Low	Per-LSP state	Null
Deterministic labels	No	No	For global segments

Deterministic labels have benefits in terms of forwarding plane stability and provide easier troubleshooting. On the other hand, networking devices can simultaneously push a limited number of MPLS labels, which is a factor to consider for SPRING-based TE deployments.

BGP-Labeled Unicast

All of the examples in this chapter rely on BGP to propagate IPv4 unicast routes between different Autonomous Systems (65000, 65001, and 65002). Advertising plain IPv4 prefixes is actually the original application of BGP as described in RFC 4271. This classic BGP flavor is commonly called *vanilla BGP*, and it is the cornerstone of the IPv4 Internet.

Although the BGP protocol is extremely scalable and flexible, vanilla BGP is only capable of advertising IPv4 unicast prefixes. This is where BGP multiprotocol extensions (RFC 4760) come into play. The word *multiprotocol* is actually an understatement: with these extensions, BGP can advertise virtually *anything*. It can be routes, but also MAC addresses, or multicast subscriptions, or security filters, or even label mappings!

In the same way as vanilla BGP exchanges IPv4 routes, multiprotocol BGP exchanges more generic objects called Network Layer Reachability Information (NLRI). Again, there is a wide variety of information that can be encoded in an NLRI, and many times this information has nothing to do with the *network layer* concept. However, the NLRI acronym remains very popular and it refers to an object (or prefix) announced via multiprotocol BGP.

How can different types of NLRI be identified? Every NLRI has an AFI, SAFI pair. (*AFI* stands for *Address Family Identifier*, and *SAFI* is an acronym for *Subsequent Address Family Identifier*.) For example, IPv4 unicast is (AFI=1, SAFI=1) and IPv6 unicast is (AFI=2, SAFI=1). You can get the full list of AFI and SAFI here:

- *http://www.iana.org/assignments/address-family-numbers/address-family-numbers.xhtml*
- *http://www.iana.org/assignments/safi-namespace/safi-namespace.xhtml*

This chapter covers (AFI=1, SAFI=4), an NLRI that contains label mappings, very similar to LDP's. This flavor of BGP is described in RFC 3107, and its familiar name is Labeled Unicast or simply BGP-LU.

BGP-LU has numerous applications such as interprovider VPN, MPLS in the data center or Seamless MPLS. Chapter 9 and Chapter 16 cover these use cases, many of which are hierarchical. Let's examine a simple example now.

IGP-Free Large-Scale Data Centers

Fabric Clos topologies have become the de facto underlay architecture in modern data centers. Depending on whether they are MPLS-enabled or not, they are called *MPLS fabrics* or *IP fabrics*. Due to its unparalleled scalability, many large-scale data centers use BGP as the *only* routing protocol inside their fabrics.

Data center underlay terminology (Clos, fabric, stage, leaf, spine, tier) and concepts are fully explained in Chapter 10. For the moment, you can view the fabric as a classic MPLS topology with PEs and Ps.

External BGP (eBGP) is preferred over internal BGP (iBGP) due to its better multi-path and loop-detection capabilities.

Most typically, a controller programs the MPLS labels on the server's FIB. In this case, MPLS-capable servers do *not* run BGP-LU; only the fabric LSRs do that. Anyway, let's keep the BGP-everywhere example in this chapter and leave the more realistic scenario for Chapter 16.

Figure 2-10 shows a minimal three-stage fabric topology.

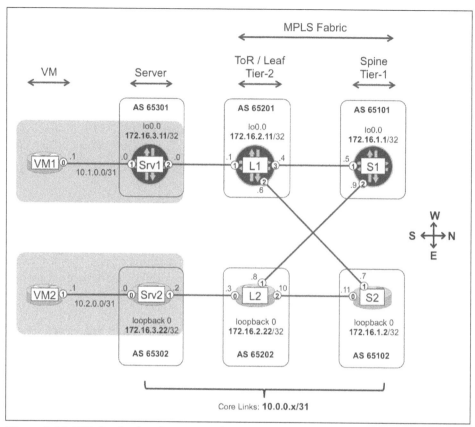

Figure 2-10. IGP-free leaf-and-spine topology

Following are descriptions of the components in Figure 2-10:

- Virtual machines (VMs) are like CEs: they do not have a MPLS stack.
- Servers or hypervisors hosting the VMs (or containers) have an MPLS stack. In this example, Junos and IOS XR routers emulate the role of the MPLS-enabled servers. They are lightweight PEs.
- Top-of-Rack (ToR) or leaf IP/MPLS switches—Tier-2 in this topology—implement Clos fabric stages #1 and #3. They are P-routers.
- Spine IP/MPLS switches—Tier-1 in this topology—implement Clos fabric stage #2. They are P-routers and, in this example, also service route reflectors.

Large-scale data centers typically have a more complex (5-stage) topology.

Like all the examples in this chapter, Figure 2-10's scenario provides a global IPv4 unicast service (AFI=1, SAFI=1) with vanilla BGP. Instead of Internet access, this service interconnects VMs in the data center. And for that to be possible, the infrastructure LSPs must be signaled between MPLS-enabled servers; and that is the goal of BGP-LU.

Figure 2-11 illustrates the role of the two types of BGP sessions: vanilla BGP for service, and BGP-LU for transport. All of the MPLS-enabled devices establish single-hop external BGP-LU sessions with all their adjacent neighbors. For example, L1's eBGP-LU peers are Srv1, S1, and S2. You can view these sessions as a combination of IGP and LDP: they encode infrastructure IPv4 addresses mapped to MPLS labels. Although eBGP-LU does not convey topology information, *draft-ietf-rtgwg-bgp-routing-large-dc* explains why it remains a great option for large-scale data centers.

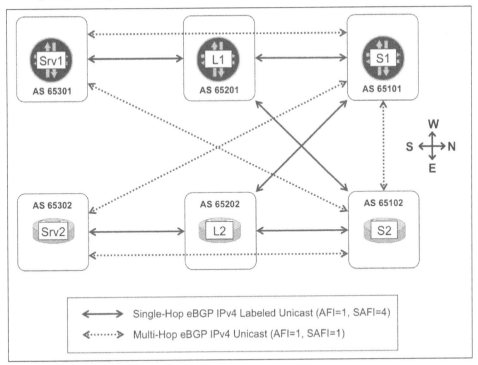

Figure 2-11. BGP sessions in IGP-free leaf-and-spine topology

Although not shown in this example, it is recommended to use 4-byte AS numbering. Otherwise, the AS:device 1:1 mapping might result in the exhaustion of the AS space.

BGP-LU—policy and community scheme

Let's clarify the usage of BGP communities in this example before jumping into the configuration details:

Servers

Advertise their own loopback addresses 172.16.3.11 and 172.16.3.22, respectively, as eBGP-LU routes with standard community CM-SERVER (65000:3).
Advertise the VM addresses 10.1.0.0/31 and 10.2.0.0/31, respectively, as vanilla eBGP routes with standard community CM-VM (65000:100).
Do *not* readvertise any eBGP route at all.

Leaf LSRs

Readvertise all of the eBGP-LU routes. Although they might advertise their local loopback, it is not required for the solution to work.

Spine LSRs

Advertise their own loopback addresses 172.16.1.1 and 172.16.1.2, respectively, as eBGP-LU routes with standard community CM-RR (65000:1).
Readvertise only those vanilla eBGP routes with community CM-VM.
Readvertise only those eBGP-LU routes with community CM-SERVER.

This careful community scheme is due to the fact that IOS XR keeps labeled and unlabeled IP routes in the same global table, so it is important not to readvertise labeled routes as unlabeled routes, or vice versa. Said differently, you need to pay special attention so that the SAFI=1 and SAFI=4 worlds remain independent.

As you can see, communities CM-VM and CM-SERVER play a key role in the route advertising flow. Conversely, the community CM-RR plays a subtler role that we'll look at a bit later.

BGP-LU Configuration

In general, IOS XR treats the label as an additional property of the IP unicast route. On the other hand, Junos treats labeled unicast and unlabeled unicast routes as different entities, keeping them in different tables by default.

Junos—copying interface routes from `inet.0` to `inet.3`

The role of the `inet.0` and `inet.3` routing tables in Junos has already been explained. Nonetheless, here's a quick refresher:

- `inet.0` is the global IPv4 routing table that populates the FIB and is typically populated by IP routing protocols (IGP, vanilla BGP, etc.).
- `inet.3` is an auxiliary table for BGP next-hop resolution and is typically populated by MPLS signaling protocols (LDP, RSVP, SPRING-enabled IGP, etc.)

But is BGP-LU an IP routing protocol or an MPLS signaling protocol? Actually, it's both. In Junos, you can configure it in two modes:

- BGP-LU installs prefixes in `inet.0` and picks prefixes from `inet.0` for further advertising. Optionally, explicit configuration might copy all (or a selection of) the prefixes into the `inet.3` table, enabling BGP next-hop resolution for MPLS services.
- BGP-LU installs prefixes in `inet.3` and picks prefixes from `inet.3` for further advertising. Optionally, explicit configuration might copy all (or a selection of) the prefixes into the `inet.0` table, enabling IPv4 forwarding with labeled next hop toward these prefixes.

This book uses the second method because it provides more flexibility. For example, with this model, a single BGP session can exchange prefixes from plain unicast and labeled unicast address families. Also, it is a good choice in terms of scalability because BGP-LU prefixes are not automatically installed in the FIB, relaxing the FIB load on low-end devices. The configuration is slightly more complex, though.

OK, let's make BGP-LU work on the `inet.3` routing table. The first step at Srv1 is to copy the local loopback address from `inet.0` (where it resides by default) to `inet.3`, so BGP-LU can advertise it in later steps.

Example 2-69. Copying an interface route from inet.0 to inet.3 at Srv1 (Junos)

```
1    policy-options {
2        policy-statement PL-LOCAL-LOOPBACK {
3            term LOCAL-LOOPBACK {
4                from interface lo0.0;
5                then {
6                    metric 0;
7                    origin incomplete;
8                    community add CM-SERVER;
9                    accept;
10               }
11           }
12           term DIRECT {
13               from protocol direct;
14               then reject;
15           }
16       }
```

```
17          community CM-SERVER members 65000:3;
18      }
19      routing-options {
20          interface-routes {
21              rib-group inet RG-LOCAL-LOOPBACK;
22          }
23          rib-groups {
24              RG-LOCAL-LOOPBACK {
25                  import-rib [ inet.0 inet.3 ];
26                  import-policy PL-LOCAL-LOOPBACK;
27      }}}
```

A similar configuration is required on S1, just with a different community: CM-RR. The usage and relevance of all these communities is explained later. The service does not require L1's loopback to be advertised; hence, this configuration is optional for L1 (you can use another community such as 65000:2 for L1 and L2 loopbacks).

A rib-group is like a template. It contains an ordered list of RIBs (line 25). The list begins with a single primary RIB (inet.0 here) where the to-be-copied prefixes originally reside, and then it lists one or more secondary RIBs (only inet.3 here) to which the prefixes must be copied. The rib-group is then applied to a protocol, or in this case, to the interface routes (lines 20 and 21) because the local loopback is one of them. As a result, the route 172.16.3.11/32 is copied from inet.0 to inet.3.

If no policy were specified, all the interface routes would be now in both inet.0 and inet.3. The policy (PL-LOCAL-LOOPBACK) performs a selective copy of the local loopback route only. Also, to provide consistency between Junos and IOS XR, the policy changes two route attributes:

- By default, there is no Multi Exit Discriminator (MED) in Junos, and in IOS XR it is set to zero. The policy sets the MED to zero for consistency across vendors.

- By default, the origin in Junos and IOS XR is igp and incomplete, respectively. The policy sets it to incomplete.

 It is a good practice to also add a geographical or location community that will eventually help to filter the prefixes based on where the prefix is originally injected.

Note that the policy can only select or modify the routes installed in the secondary RIBs; it has no effect on the primary RIB. Also, if there were several secondary RIBs, the to rib knob makes the action specific to a subset of the secondary RIBs only.

Now that the configuration is applied, let's have a look at the local loopback route.

Example 2-70. Effect of copying the Local Loopback Route—Srv1 (Junos)

```
juniper@Srv1> show route 172.16.3.11/32 detail

inet.0: 11 destinations, 12 routes (11 active, 0 holddown, 0 hidden)
172.16.3.11/32 (1 entry, 0 announced)
(...)
                Secondary Tables: inet.3

inet.3: 12 destinations, 12 routes (12 active, 0 holddown, 0 hidden)
172.16.3.11/32 (1 entry, 1 announced)
(...)
                Communities: 65000:3
                Primary Routing Table inet.0
```

The loopback IPv4 address is copied to `inet.3` (secondary table), and the copied route has a new community. A similar check on other local link address (e.g., 10.0.10.8/31) only shows the route in `inet.0`, due to the policy constraints at the `rib-group`.

Junos—BGP-LU configuration

The next step is to assign a label to the route and advertise it with BGP-LU.

Example 2-71. eBGP-LU configuration—Srv1 (Junos)

```
protocols {
    bgp {
        group eBGP-LU-65201 {
            family inet {
                labeled-unicast {
                    per-prefix-label;
                    rib {
                        inet.3;
                    }
                }
            }
            export PL-LOCAL-LOOPBACK;
            peer-as 65201;
            neighbor 10.0.0.1;
}}}
```

BGP-LU's `per-prefix-label` knob is equivalent to LDP's `deaggregate`. It is recommended in BGP-LU to improve convergence times. However, because it raises the scalability requirements on the peers, it is not recommended for other BGP address families. Chapter 3 discusses this topic more in detail.

A similar configuration is required on S1. As for L1, it does not need any export policies, because Junos readvertises eBGP prefixes by default.

With the previous configuration (Example 2-71), Srv1 advertises its labeled loopback to L1, as you can see in the following example.

Example 2-72. Local loopack advertisement via BGP-LU—Srv1 (Junos)

```
juniper@Srv1> show route advertising-protocol bgp 10.0.0.1
              172.16.3.11 detail

inet.3: 12 destinations, 12 routes (12 active, 0 holddown, ...)
* 172.16.3.11/32 (1 entry, 1 announced)
 BGP group eBGP-LU-65201 type External
     Route Label: 3
     Nexthop: Self
     Flags: Nexthop Change
     AS path: [65301] I
     Communities: 65000:3
     Entropy label capable
```

As expected, Srv1 assigns the implicit null label to enable PHP.

IOS XR—BGP-LU configuration

Following is the IOS XR configuration at Srv2.

Example 2-73. eBGP-LU configuration—Srv2 (IOS XR)

```
1     route-policy PL-LOCAL-INTERFACES
2       if destination in (172.16.3.22/32) then
3         set community CM-SERVER
4         pass
5       endif
6     end-policy
7     !
8     route-policy PL-LOCAL-LOOPBACK
9       if community matches-any CM-SERVER then
10        pass
11      else
12        drop
13      endif
14    end-policy
15    !
16    route-policy PL-ALL
17      pass
18    end-policy
19    !
20    community-set CM-SERVER
21      65000:3
```

```
22    end-set
23    !
24    router bgp 65302
25     mpls activate
26      interface GigabitEthernet0/0/0/1
27     !
28     address-family ipv4 unicast
29      redistribute connected route-policy PL-LOCAL-INTERFACES
30      allocate-label all
31     !
32     neighbor 10.0.0.3
33      remote-as 65202
34      address-family ipv4 labeled-unicast
35       send-community-ebgp
36       route-policy PL-LOCAL-LOOPBACK out
37       route-policy PL-ALL in
38     !
39    router static
40     address-family ipv4 unicast
41      10.0.0.3/32 GigabitEthernet0/0/0/1
```

The local loopback is labeled and announced via eBGP-LU with the following actions:

- Redistribute the local loopback (lines 1 through 6, and 29) into BGP. The PL-LOCAL-INTERFACES policy is later extended during vanilla BGP configuration.

- Allocate labels to the unicast routes (line 30). It is recommended to apply a policy here in order to select the routes that require label allocation.

- Attach (line 36) a BGP outbound policy (lines 8 through 14) to only advertise the local loopback with the appropriate community. In this case, this community is set during route redistribution but it could have been set during route announcement, too.

A similar configuration is required on L2 and S2, just with different policies, as detailed in "BGP-LU—policy and community scheme" on page 108.

Sending communities over eBGP is turned on by default on Junos; you need to turn it on explicitly for IOS XR (line 35).

 Beware of the else drop action in line 12. This is fine for servers, which only need to advertise their own loopback. Leaf-and-spine LSRs, however, need to allow the readvertisement of eBGP-LU routes, too. Their policies need to be less restrictive.

Furthermore, in IOS XR there is a default "reject all" inbound and outbound route policy applied to eBGP sessions. Explicit policies are required to accept and advertise eBGP routes (lines 16 through 18, 36 and 37).

When the previous configuration (Example 2-73) is applied, Srv2 advertises its loopback via eBGP-LU, as demonstrated in Example 2-74.

Example 2-74. Local loopack advertisement via BGP-LU—Srv2 (IOS XR)

```
RP/0/0/CPU0:Srv2#show bgp ipv4 labeled-unicast advertised

172.16.3.22/32 is advertised to 10.0.0.3
[...]
  Attributes after outbound policy was applied:
    next hop: 10.0.0.2
    MET ORG AS COMM
    origin: incomplete  metric: 0
    aspath: 65302
    community: 65000:3
```

 Incomplete configurations may cause the learned eBGP-LU routes to remain unresolved. You can check that by using the IOS XR command show cef unresolved. A similar and very useful Junos command is show route hidden.

This is why a static route toward L1's peer interface is configured (Example 2-73, lines 39 through 41). Thanks to that, Srv2 can resolve the eBGP-LU routes. Let's see it.

Example 2-75. Inter-server labeled reachability—Srv2 (IOS XR)

```
RP/0/0/CPU0:Srv2#show cef 172.16.3.11
172.16.3.11/32, version 159, internal 0x1000001 [...]
 Prefix Len 32, traffic index 0, precedence n/a, priority 4
   via 10.0.0.3, 6 dependencies, recursive, bgp-ext [flags 0x6020]
     path-idx 0 NHID 0x0 [0xa1558774 0x0]
     recursion-via-/32
     next hop 10.0.0.3 via 24006/0/21
       local label 24004
       next hop 10.0.0.3/32 Gi0/0/0/1 labels imposed {ImplNull 24005}
```

Service Configuration in an IGP-Less Topology

Now that the LSP signaling infrastructure is in place, it is time to signal the service routes corresponding to the VMs. For that to happen, Srv1 and Srv2 need to establish vanilla multihop eBGP sessions with the service route reflectors S1 and S2.

Nothing special is required in IOS XR, but Junos needs to get the remote loopbacks—previously learned via single-hop eBGP-LU—copied from inet.3 to inet.0 so that multihop vanilla eBGP sessions can be established.

Junos—copying eBGP-LU routes from `inet.3` to `inet.0`

Back in Example 2-69 and Example 2-70, the local loopback route was copied from `inet.0` to `inet.3`—this was so it could be advertised via eBGP-LU. Now, the process is the reverse: certain routes learned via eBGP-LU need to be copied from `inet.3` to `inet.0`—so that they are reachable from a pure IPv4 forwarding perspective. The following example illustrates how to achieve it.

Example 2-76. Copying eBGP-LU routes from inet.3 to inet.0—Srv1 (Junos)

```
policy-options {
    policy-statement PL-RR-INET {
        term RR {
            from community CM-RR;
            then accept;
        }
        then reject;
    }
    community CM-RR members 65000:1;
}
routing-options {
    rib-groups {
        RG-RR-INET {
            import-rib [ inet.3 inet.0 ];
            import-policy PL-RR-INET;
        }
    }
}
protocols {
    bgp {
        group eBGP-LU-65201 {
            family inet {
                labeled-unicast {
                    rib-group RG-RR-INET;
}}}}}
```

As mentioned earlier, S1 and S2 are advertising their local loopback routes with community CM-RR. As a result of the copy in Example 2-76, these routes are installed in both `inet.3` and `inet.0` at Srv1, as shown in Example 2-77.

Example 2-77. Effect of copying an eBGP-LU route—Srv1 (Junos)

```
juniper@Srv1> show route 172.16.1.1/32 detail

inet.0: 11 destinations, 12 routes (11 active, 0 holddown, 0 hidden)
172.16.1.1/32 (1 entry, 0 announced)
(...)
                Communities: 65000:1
                Primary Routing Table inet.3
```

```
inet.3: 12 destinations, 12 routes (12 active, 0 holddown, 0 hidden)
172.16.3.11/32 (1 entry, 1 announced)
(...)
                        Communities: 65000:1
                        Secondary Tables: inet.0
```

Likewise, S1 is configured to copy all the routes with community CM-SERVER from
inet.3 to inet.0. Here is a summary of the use of communities so far:

- Srv1 and Srv2 announce their loopbacks with community CM-SERVER.
- S1 and S2 announce their loopbacks with community CM-RR.
- Srv1 copies eBGP-LU routes with community CM-RR from inet.3 to inet.0.
- S1 copies eBGP-LU routes with community CM-SERVER from inet.3 to inet.
  0.
- Srv2 and S2 run IOS XR, which does not have a resolution RIB, so no route copy
  is needed.

At this point, IPv4 connectivity between PEs (Srv1, Srv2) and RRs (S1, S2) is guaranteed and multihop vanilla eBGP sessions can be established as in Figure 2-11's dotted
lines.

Junos—Vanilla eBGP configuration in IGP-less topology

Following is the service configuration at Srv1.

Example 2-78. Vanilla BGP configuration in IGP-less topology—Srv1 (Junos)

```
policy-options {
    policy-statement PL-eBGP-INET-OUT {
        term VM-INTERFACE {
            from interface ge-2/0/1.0;
            then {
                community add CM-VM;
                accept;
            }
        }
        then reject;
    }
    community CM-VM members 65000:100;
}
protocols {
    bgp {
        group eBGP-INET {
            multihop;
            local-address 172.16.3.11;
            export PL-eBGP-INET-OUT;
            neighbor 172.16.1.1 { peer-as 65101; }
```

```
                neighbor 172.16.1.2 { peer-as 65102; }
}}}
```

And Example 2-79 shows the service configuration at S1.

Example 2-79. Vanilla BGP configuration in IGP-less topology—S1 (Junos)

```
1    policy-options {
2        policy-statement PL-eBGP-INET-OUT {
3            term VM {
4                from community CM-VM;
5                then accept;
6            }
7            then reject;
8        }
9    }
10   protocols {
11       bgp {
12           group eBGP-INET {
13               multihop {
14                   no-nexthop-change;
15               }
16               local-address 172.16.1.1;
17               export PL-eBGP-INET-OUT;
18               neighbor 172.16.3.11 { peer-as 65301; }
19               neighbor 172.16.3.22 { peer-as 65302; }
20   }}}
```

Here is the logic behind this configuration: MPLS-enabled servers advertise the VM prefixes with community CM-VM. Service RRs—S1 and S2, which in this example happen to be spine LSRs, too—only reflect routes with the community CM-VM. This prevents any unexpected leaking between labeled and unlabeled routes. A very important piece of configuration is in line 14. By default, announcing a prefix to a different AS triggers a BGP next-hop attribute rewrite. This is not desired for service route reflection, and this is why no-nexthop-change is configured.

IOS XR—vanilla eBGP configuration in IGP-less topology

Following is the service configuration at Srv2.

Example 2-80. Vanilla BGP configuration in IGP-less topology—Srv2 (IOS XR)

```
route-policy PL-LOCAL-INTERFACES
  if destination in (172.16.3.22/32) then
    set community CM-SERVER
    pass
  endif
  if destination in (10.2.0.0/31) then
    set community CM-VM
```

```
      pass
   endif
end-policy
!
route-policy PL-eBGP-INET
  if community matches-any CM-VM then
     pass
  else
     drop
  endif
end-policy
!
community-set CM-VM
  65000:100
end-set
!
router bgp 65302
 neighbor-group eBGP-INET
  ebgp-multihop 255
  update-source Loopback0
  address-family ipv4 unicast
   send-community-ebgp
   redistribute connected route-policy PL-LOCAL-INTERFACES
   route-policy PL-eBGP-INET out
   route-policy PL-eBGP-INET in
  !
 neighbor 172.16.1.1
  remote-as 65101
  use neighbor-group eBGP-INET
 !
 neighbor 172.16.1.2
  remote-as 65102
  use neighbor-group eBGP-INET
```

The logic is similar to Junos. Only the VM routes, flagged with community CM-VM, are advertised as unlabeled IPv4 prefixes toward the service RRs.

Remember that the PL-LOCAL-INTERFACES policy is in control of the redistribution of interface routes into BGP (Example 2-73, line 29). The local loopback and the VM route are flagged with community CM-SERVER and CM-VM, respectively. With this entire configuration in place, the local loopback is only distributed via eBGP-LU, whereas the VM route is only distributed via vanilla BGP.

The configuration at S2 is similar, with two differences. First, it reflects only remote VM routes, so it does not have any local VM route to announce. Second, it must not change the BGP next-hop attribute, so the extra configuration is required.

Example 2-81. Vanilla BGP configuration in IGP-less topology—S2 (IOS XR)

```
router bgp 65302
 neighbor-group eBGP-INET
  address-family ipv4 unicast
   next-hop-unchanged
```

BGP-LU—Signaling and Forwarding Plane

Figure 2-12 puts it all together by showing the end-to-end signaling and forwarding in detail.

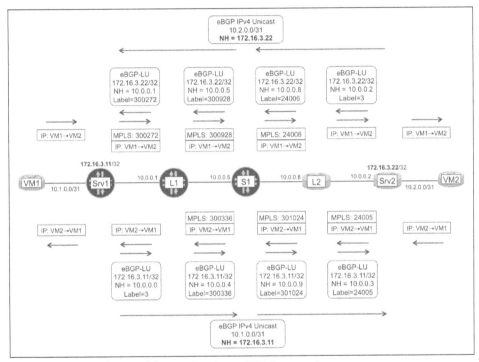

Figure 2-12. Signaling and forwarding in an IGP-free topology

Although only one path is shown, you can definitely configure multipath in eBGP-LU so that traffic can also transit S2.

Let's have a look at the traceroute between VM1 and VM2.

Example 2-82. Traceroute from VM1 to VM2

```
RP/0/0/CPU0:VM#traceroute vrf VM1 10.2.0.1
[...]

 1  10.1.0.0 0 msec  0 msec  0 msec
```

```
   2  10.0.0.1 [MPLS: Label 300272 Exp 0] 0 msec  0 msec  9 msec
   3  10.0.0.5 [MPLS: Label 300928 Exp 0] 0 msec  0 msec  0 msec
   4  10.0.0.8 [MPLS: Label 24006 Exp 0] 0 msec  0 msec  0 msec
   5  10.0.0.2 0 msec  0 msec  0 msec
   6  10.2.0.1 0 msec  *  39 msec
```

Let's see how the LSPs are signaled. Each PE has three BGP sessions in total: one BGP-LU session (single-hop to the adjacent P) and two vanilla BGP sessions to the RRs.

The routing and forwarding state at the Junos ingress PE is shown in Example 2-83.

Example 2-83. Signaling and MPLS forwarding at ingress PE—Srv1 (Junos)

```
juniper@Srv1> show route 10.2.0.1
              receive-protocol bgp 172.16.1.1 detail

inet.0: 11 destinations, 12 routes (11 active, 0 holddown, [...])
* 10.2.0.0/31 (2 entries, 1 announced)
     Accepted
     Nexthop: 172.16.3.22
     AS path: 65101 65302 ?
     Communities: 65000:100

juniper@Srv1> show route 172.16.3.22 table inet.3
              receive-protocol bgp 10.0.0.1 detail

inet.3: 12 destinations, 12 routes (12 active, 0 holddown, [...])
* 172.16.3.22/32 (1 entry, 1 announced)
     Accepted
     Route Label: 300272
     Nexthop: 10.0.0.1
     AS path: 65201 65101 65202 65302 ?
     Communities: 65000:3

juniper@Srv1> show route 172.16.3.22 table inet.3

inet.3: 12 destinations, 12 routes (12 active, 0 holddown, 0 hidden)
+ = Active Route, - = Last Active, * = Both

172.16.3.22/32    *[BGP/170] 06:18:31, localpref 100
                    AS path: 65201 65101 65202 65302 ? [...]
                  > to 10.0.0.1 via ge-2/0/2.0, Push 300272

juniper@Srv1> show route forwarding-table destination 10.2.0.1
Routing table: default.inet
Internet:
Destination       Type Next hop  Type       Index Nhref Netif
10.2.0.1/31       user           indr     1048576   2
                       10.0.0.1  Push 300272  588   2       ge-2/0/2.0
```

Srv1 pushes an MPLS header and sends the packet to the forwarding next hop, L1, with label 300272. This is the label that L1 advertises for 172.16.3.22 via eBGP-LU. L1 swaps the label for 300928, sends the packet to S1, and so on.

Finally, if you look at the reverse flow (VM2→VM1) shown in Figure 2-12 and Example 2-84, Srv2 acts as an ingress PE.

Example 2-84. Vanilla BGP routing state at ingress PE—Srv2 (IOS XR)

```
RP/0/0/CPU0:Srv2#show route 10.1.0.1

Routing entry for 10.1.0.0/31
  Known via "bgp 65302", distance 20, metric 0
  Tag 65101, type external
  Routing Descriptor Blocks
    172.16.3.11, from 172.16.1.1, BGP external
      Route metric is 0
  No advertising protos.
```

You can combine Example 2-75 (Srv2# show cef 172.16.3.11/32, next hop 10.0.0.3, labels imposed {ImplNull 24005}) with Example 2-84 and obtain the packet sent by Srv2 to L2 in Figure 2-12.

Forwarding at the transit Ps has been skipped here for the sake of brevity. It follows the same principles as the other protocols. Simply, the protocol changes; for example, there are BGP routes in mpls.0.

BGP-LU—SPRING Extensions

Deterministic labels require manual provisioning and have several advantages:

- They improve resiliency by reducing the likelihood of events that require reprogramming the label stacks on the FIB. This is especially important in large-scale data centers whose devices might need to store a high amount of label forwarding state.
- They ease the integration with external controllers that are able to program a label stack on MPLS-capable servers. This becomes relevant if the servers do not speak BGP-LU or other MPLS protocols with the fabric. In addition, by programming stacks of labels, this architecture enables explicit routing à la SPRING.
- They provide easier operation and troubleshooting.

As described in *draft-ietf-idr-bgp-prefix-sid*, it is possible to use the SPRING paradigm with BGP thanks to the *BGP-Prefix-SID Label Index* attribute.

Let's see how it works with the help of Figure 2-13

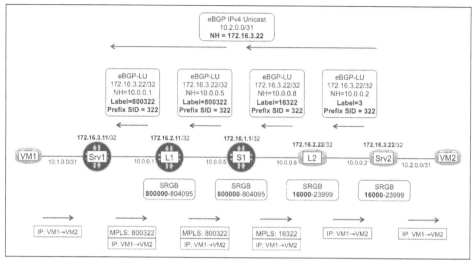

Figure 2-13. BGP-LU with SPRING extensions

Here is the sequence on the control plane:

1. Srv2 has a policy that assigns the Prefix SID value 322 to the prefix 172.16.3.22/32. This time it is Srv2's local loopback but it could be any other pre-fix—used as BGP next hop—referenced by the policy; hence, the name Prefix SID and not Node SID. This value must be unique in the domain and assigned by a central administration entity, as it is also the case for IGP-based SPRING.

2. Srv2 sends the eBGP-LU route 172.16.3.22/32 with an implicit null label and the locally configured Prefix SID.

3. L2 receives the route and allocates a label for the prefix 172.16.3.22/32. This new label is locally significant to L2 but its value is not arbitrary: L2 calculates it by adding its local SRGB to the received Prefix SID: 16000 + 322 = 16322. After it allocates the label, L2 advertises it with a regular eBGP-LU update, but this time it adds also the Prefix SID, allowing S1 to repeat the logic.

The same process is repeated on S1 and L1, which have a different SRGB from L2.

Here are a couple of interesting differences between IGP-based SPRING and BGP-based SPRING:

- IGP-based SPRING does *not* advertise labels.
- BGP-based SPRING does advertise labels because it is based on BGP-LU. In addi-tion, the BGP updates also contain the SID and the SRGB (the latter is not shown in Figure 2-13).

As of this writing, this feature is under development for Junos and IOS XR. The authors had access to a Junos prototype and this is how the eBGP-LU export policy can be modified in order for Srv1 to assign and announce a prefix SID for its local loopback.

Example 2-85. Assigning a prefix SID—Srv1 (Junos)

```
policy-options {
    policy-statement PL-LOCAL-LOOPBACK {
        term LOCAL-LOOPBACK {
            then {
                prefix-segment-index 311;
}}}}
```

SPRING Anycast

Anycast segments allow sharing the same SID (for a given so-called *anycast* prefix) among a group of devices. Several drafts cover two possible scenarios: if all of the anycast nodes advertising a given SID use the same SRGB, or if they use different SRGBs. Further details are beyond the scope of this book.

A related technology called Egress Peer Engineering (EPE) is discussed in Chapter 13.

## CHAPTER 3

Layer 3 Unicast MPLS Services

So far, this book has illustrated the primary role of MPLS: building tunnels (LSPs) across the service provider (SP) or the data center core in order to transport packets. In previous examples, the ingress PE performs a *route lookup* on each IPv4 packet before placing it on an LSP. This route lookup process takes into account *Layer 3* (L3) fields contained in the IPv4 header; and the user packets are unicast—destined to a single host. Putting it all together, IPv4 Internet Transit over MPLS is an L3 Unicast MPLS Service. It is, historically speaking, the first MPLS service and in terms of volume it also remains the most widely used.

IPv4 Internet over MPLS is an *unlabeled* service, in the sense that packets typically have no MPLS label when they arrive to the egress (service) PE. While in the LSP, packets only carry *transport* labels, but no *service* labels. What is a service label? It is simply an MPLS label that identifies a service. At first glance, it is impossible to distinguish transport labels from service labels: they look the same. The difference lies in the way Label Switch Routers (LSRs) and Label Edge Routers (LERs) interpret them, as determined by the signaling process: when an LSR/LER advertises a label, it is also mapping it to *something* with a precise meaning.

If an MPLS service is *labeled*, the ingress PE typically pushes a stack of two MPLS headers—as long as the egress PE is more than one hop away. The outer and the inner headers contain a transport and a service label, respectively. Later in the path, the penultimate LSR pops the transport label and exposes the service label to the egress PE. Don't worry if you are struggling to visualize it, the examples that follow will help.

What other L3 Unicast MPLS services are there? Here are some popular examples:

- Transport of Internet IPv6 packets over an IPv4/MPLS core—a service popularly known as *6PE*. The ingress PE performs a route lookup on its *global* IPv6 table.

- L3 Virtual Private Networks (L3VPNs). The ingress PE performs a route lookup on a *private* table that is dedicated to a specific customer or tenant.

A tenant typically can be either an external customer or an internal department, but it can also be an application. The term *multitenancy* refers to the capability of a service to keep traffic and routing information isolated between tenants.

In all of the examples in this chapter, PEs translate routing state from one NLRI to another—the AFI/SAFI values change. This automatically triggers a next-hop-self (NHS) action at the PE.

6PE: IPv6 Transport in an IPv4/MPLS Core

The 6PE solution shown in Figure 3-1 and described in RFC 4798 allows transporting IPv6 unicast packets through an IPv4/MPLS backbone whose P-routers are totally unaware of IPv6. Taking into account that native Label Distribution Protocol (LDP) over IPv6 is *not* implemented as of this writing, 6PE is the de facto technology that carriers use to transport IPv6 in the Internet core.

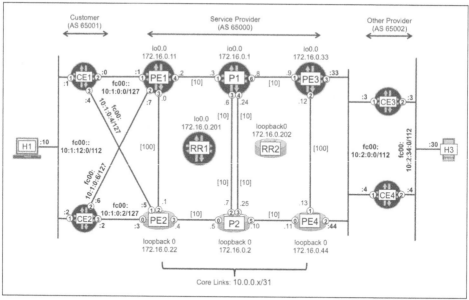

Figure 3-1. 6PE Topology

From now on, in Chapter 3 through Chapter 9, the PE1-PE2 and PE3-PE4 links have Intermediate System–to–Intermediate System (IS-IS) metric 100. So, the preferred path from PE1 to PE4 is PE1-P1=P2-PE4, and vice versa.

The hosts, CEs, and PEs, are dual-stack devices that support both IPv4 and IPv6. To make the example easy to follow, IPv6 addressing looks very similar to IPv4. For example, H1 has IPv4 and IPv6 addresses **10.1.12.10**/24 and fc00:0:0:0:**10:1:12:10**/112, respectively. Shortened with the "::" construct—which means *all zeros* and can only appear at most once in an IPv6 prefix—thus, H1's IPv6 address becomes fc00::10:1:12:10/112. Although the addresses *look* similar, the IPv4 and IPv6 prefixes are in decimal and hexadecimal format, respectively. So, this addressing choice is more cosmetic rather than a real translation of the bits from IPv4 to IPv6. And the example's IPv6 mask /112 provides twice as many host bits than the IPv4 mask /24.

H1 has a default IPv6 route (0::0/0) pointing to fc00::10:**1:12**:100, a Virtual Router Redundancy Protocol (VRRP) group address whose default master is CE1. VRRP route tracking is in place, so if CE1 does not have visibility of the fc00::10:**2:34**:0/112 remote route but CE2 does, CE2 becomes the VRRP master.

Similarly, H3 has a default IPv6 route pointing to fc00::10:**2:134**:100, a VRRP group address whose master is CE4, provided that it has visibility of the fc00::10:**1:12**:0/112 remote route.

How about the IPv6 route exchange all the way between CE1 and CE4? Let's go step by step, starting with the iBGP sessions between PEs and Route Reflectors (RRs).

6PE—Backbone Configuration at the PEs

Let's see the configuration in Junos and IOS XR.

6PE—backbone configuration at Junos PEs

Example 3-1 shows the relevant core-facing configuration at PE1.

Example 3-1. 6PE—core-facing configuration at PE1 (Junos)

```
1    protocols {
2        mpls {
3            ipv6-tunneling;
4        }
5        bgp {
6            group iBGP-RR {
7                family inet6 {
8                    labeled-unicast;
9    }}}}
```

So it looks like IPv6 packets are to be tunneled in MPLS (line 3). The internal BGP (iBGP) sessions convey IPv6 Labeled Unicast (AFI=2, SAFI=4) prefixes, instead of *unlabeled* IPv6 Unicast (AFI=2, SAFI=1) ones. You'll see more about this in the signaling section.

6PE—backbone configuration at IOS XR PEs

Here is the relevant core-facing configuration at PE2:

Example 3-2. 6PE—core-facing configuration at PE2 (IOS XR)

```
1   router bgp 65000
2    address-family ipv6 unicast
3     allocate-label all
4    !
5    neighbor-group RR
6     address-family ipv6 labeled-unicast
7    !
```

The principle is the same as in Junos. PE2 assigns MPLS labels to IPv6 prefixes, and this information is sent via iBGP to the RRs. In addition, PEs exchange *unlabeled* prefixes with CEs via eBGP. Later in the chapter, see Example 3-8, line 10.

6PE—RR Configuration

This is the additional configuration at RR1:

Example 3-3. 6PE—RR configuration at RR1 (Junos)

```
1   protocols {
2       bgp {
3           group CLIENTS {
4               family inet6 labeled-unicast;
5   }}}
6   routing-options {
7       rib inet6.0 static route 0::0/0 discard;
8   }
```

An IPv6 (AFI=2) BGP route carries a BGP next-hop attribute with IPv6 format. But RR1 is not running any IPv6 routing protocols, so it cannot resolve the BGP next hop. This is why a default IPv6 route is configured in lines 6 through 7.

Example 3-4 shows the additional configuration at RR2.

Example 3-4. 6PE—RR configuration at RR2 (IOS XR)

```
router bgp 65000
 address-family ipv6 unicast
```

```
!
neighbor-group CLIENTS
 address-family ipv6 labeled-unicast
  route-reflector-client
!
```

IOS XR does not require any extra configuration to resolve the BGP next hop.

6PE—Access Configuration at the PEs

Let's now focus on the CE-PE routing. The most scalable protocol is BGP, and there are two configuration options for the PE1-CE1 connection:

- The first option requires two eBGP sessions. One eBGP session is established between the IPv4 endpoints (10.1.0.0-1) and exchanges IPv4 unicast (AFI=1, SAFI=1) prefixes; the other session is established between the IPv6 endpoints (fc00::10:1:0:0-1) and exchanges IPv6 unicast (AFI=2, SAFI=1) prefixes.

- The second option relies on a *single* eBGP session established between the IPv4 endpoints (10.1.0.0-1). This multiprotocol eBGP session is able to signal both IPv4 unicast (AFI=1, SAFI=1) and IPv6 unicast (AFI=2, SAFI=1) prefixes.

Both options are valid, but the second one is more scalable; hence, it is used here.

6PE—access configuration at Junos PEs

Example 3-5 shows the access configuration at PE1. The only logical interface and eBGP session displayed correspond to the PE1-CE1 link.

Example 3-5. 6PE—access configuration at PE1 (Junos)

```
1    interfaces {
2        ge-2/0/1 {
3            unit 1001 {
4                vlan-id 1001;
5                family inet address 10.1.0.1/31;
6                family inet6 address fc00::10:1:0:1/127;
7    }}}
8    protocols {
9        bgp {
10           group eBGP-65001 {
11               family inet unicast;
12               family inet6 unicast;
13               peer-as 65001;
14               neighbor 10.1.0.0 export PL-eBGP-CE1-OUT;
15   }}}
16   policy-options {
17       policy-statement PL-eBGP-CE1-OUT {
18           term BGP {
```

```
19                    from protocol bgp;
20                    then metric 100;
21                }
22            term IPv6 {
23                    from family inet6;
24                    then next-hop fc00::10:1:0:1;
25    }}}
```

As you can see, the logical interface is dual-stacked (lines 5 and 6). Both IPv4 and IPv6 unicast (lines 11 and 12) prefixes can be exchanged on top of one single eBGP session (line 14).

The BGP next-hop rewrite in line 24 is essential. Without it, PE1 would advertise IPv6 routes to CE1 in the format shown in Example 3-6.

Example 3-6. 6PE—IPv4-mapped IPv6 BGP next hop

```
juniper@PE1> show route advertising-protocol bgp 10.1.0.0 detail
            table inet6.0

* fc00::10:2:34:0/112 (2 entries, 1 announced)
    [...]
    Nexthop: ::ffff:10.1.0.1
```

In classical IPv6 notation, ::ffff:10.1.0.1 is ::ffff:0a01:0001. This is an IPv4-mapped IPv6 address, automatically derived from 10.1.0.1. But, the PE1-CE1 link is configured with IPv6 network fc00::10:1:0:0, which is totally different—watch out for hex colon versus decimal dot. Hence, the need for a BGP next-hop rewrite: without it, CE1 would not be able to resolve the BGP next hop. The same technique must be applied for prefixes announced by CE1 to PE1. Following is the next hop after the policy is applied.

Example 3-7. 6PE—rewritten IPv6 BGP next hop

```
juniper@PE1> show route advertising-protocol bgp 10.1.0.0 detail table inet6.0

* fc00::10:2:34:0/112 (2 entries, 1 announced)
    [...]
    Nexthop: fc00::10:1:0:1
```

As a more complex alternative, you can install the ::ffff:10.1.0.1/128 route into inet6.3, which is the auxiliary table to resolve BGP next hops in IPv6 format. This technique is illustrated in Chapter 9.

In the remainder of this section, dual-stack is assumed. Even if not shown, all of the BGP sessions are also configured with `family inet unicast` (address-family ipv4 unicast).

6PE—access configuration at IOS XR PEs

Following is the access configuration at PE2. The only logical interface and eBGP session displayed correspond to the PE2-CE2 link.

Example 3-8. 6PE—access configuration at PE2 (IOS XR)

```
1     interface GigabitEthernet0/0/0/0.1001
2      ipv4 address 10.1.0.3 255.255.255.254
3      ipv6 address fc00::10:1:0:3/127
4      encapsulation dot1q 1001
5     !
6     router bgp 65000
7      address-family ipv6 unicast
8      neighbor 10.1.0.2
9       remote-as 65001
10      address-family ipv6 unicast
11       route-policy PL-eBGP-65001-IN in
12       route-policy PL-eBGP-CE2-OUT out
13     !
```

The principle is very similar to Junos, except that IOS XR PE2 automatically performs the BGP next-hop rewrite (to fc00::10:1:0:3) on its IPv6 advertisements to CE2.

The eBGP route policies (lines 11 and 12) basically *pass all* the prefixes (see Chapter 1).

6PE—Signaling

Figure 3-2 illustrates the entire signaling and forwarding logic. The labeled IPv6 route signaling always relies on BGP. As for the transport mechanism, you have the same flexibility as with any other MPLS service: it can be based either on IP tunnels or, better, on MPLS LSPs (static, LDP, RSVP, BGP IPv4-LU, or SPRING). This example uses LDP, but any other option is valid.

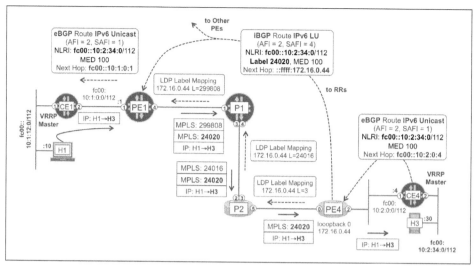

Figure 3-2. 6PE in action

Refer back to Chapter 1 for an explanation as to why, in this multi-homing scenario, the packet follows the path H1→CE1→PE1→...→PE4→CE4→H3.

Let's first see the signaling flow. First, PE4 receives an IPv6 Unicast (AFI=2, SAFI=1) route from CE4, as shown in the following example:

Example 3-9. 6PE—IPv6 Labeled Unicast route

```
RP/0/0/CPU0:PE4# show bgp ipv6 unicast fc00::10:2:34:0/112
[...]
   Network     Next Hop        Metric LocPrf Weight Path
*> fc00::10:2:34:0/112
               fc00::10:2:0:4    100              0 65002 i
```

Then, PE4 allocates an MPLS label to the prefix and advertises it to the RRs. Example 3-10 shows how the IPv6 Labeled Unicast route advertised by PE4 looks from the perspective of RR1.

Example 3-10. 6PE—IPv6 Labeled Unicast route

```
1    juniper@RR1> show route receive-protocol bgp 172.16.0.44 detail table inet6.0
2
3    inet6.0: 3 destinations, 6 routes (...)
4    * fc00::10:2:34:0/112 (2 entries, 1 announced)
5         Accepted
```

```
6          Route Label: 24020
7          Nexthop: ::ffff:172.16.0.44
8          MED: 100
9        Localpref: 100
10         AS path: 65002 I
```

 RRs do *not* change the BGP next hop, and as a consequence they do not change the label encoded in the Network Layer Reachability Information (NLRI) either: the label is meaningful to the egress PE only.

You can refer to Example 3-7 to partially see the route advertised from PE1 to CE1.

6PE—Forwarding Plane

Let's examine the forwarding bits illustrated in Figure 3-2 step by step. First, H1 sends the packet via its default gateway CE1, which holds the VRRP group's virtual IPv6 and MAC addresses.

Next, CE1 must choose between two routes to the same destination: one from PE1 (with Multi Exit Discriminator [MED] 100), and another one from PE2 (with MED 200). CE1 chooses the best route, which is via PE1.

Then, PE1 looks at the BGP next hop of the Labeled Unicast route (Example 3-10, line 7), which is ::ffff:172.16.0.44. What does it mean? It is the IPv4-mapped IPv6 address derived from PE4's IPv4 loopback address: 172.16.0.44.

Example 3-11. 6PE—BGP next-hop resolution at ingress PE—PE1 (Junos)

```
juniper@PE1> show route table inet6.3 ::ffff:172.16.0.44/128
[...]
::ffff:172.16.0.44/128
                    *[LDP/9] 2d 20:39:37, metric 30
                    > to 10.0.0.3 via ge-2/0/4.0, Push 299808
```

If you look back at Figure 3-2, you can see that P1 only advertises an LDP label mapping for the IPv4 FEC 172.16.0.44, *not* for ::ffff:172.16.0.44. Indeed, only the PEs are assumed to be IPv6-aware, and LDP only signals IPv4 FECs. In other words, there is no change at the LDP level when the 6PE service is turned on.

As you can see in Example 3-12, and in Figure 3-2, PE1 pushes two MPLS labels before sending the packet to P1.

Example 3-12. 6PE—Double MPLS label push at the ingress PE—PE1 (Junos)

```
1    juniper@PE1> show route forwarding-table destination fc00::10:2:34:0
2    [...]
```

```
3    Destination        Next hop    Type   Index    NhRef
4    fc00::10:2:34:0/112             indr  1048574     2
5                        10.0.0.3   Push 24020, Push 299808(top) ge-2/0/4.0
```

This is the first time that this book shows a double MPLS label push operation. There are several use cases for MPLS label stacking, and this is one of the most common: a *bottom service label* (24020 in line 5) and a *top transport label* (299808 in line 5). The transport label typically changes hop by hop, and in this example, it is eventually popped at the penultimate hop. On the other hand, the service label travels intact down to the egress PE, in this case PE4. And PE4 is the router that in the first instance had allocated that service label to the IPv6 prefix, so it knows how to interpret it.

Example 3-13. 6PE—MPLS label pop at the egress PE—PE4 (IOS XR)

```
1    RP/0/0/CPU0:PE4#show mpls forwarding
2    Local  Outgoing     Prefix
3    Label  Label        or ID
4    ------ -----------  ------------------
5    24020  Unlabelled   fc00::10:2:34:0/112
6
7    Outgoing          Next                            Bytes
8    Interface         Hop                             Switched
9    --------------    ----------------------          --------
10   Gi0/0/0/2.1001    fe80::205:8603:e971:f501        32576
```

When PE4 receives a packet with label 24020, it pops all the labels and sends the packet out toward CE4. How do you check that this strange IPv6 address in line 10 actually belongs to CE4? Let's see how by taking a look at Example 3-14.

Example 3-14. 6PE—IPv6 link-local address

```
juniper@CE4> show interfaces ge-0/0/1.1001 terse
Interface       Admin Link Proto   Local
ge-0/0/1.1001   up    up   inet    10.2.0.4/24
                           inet6   fc00::10:2:0:4/112
                                   fe80::205:8603:e971:f501/64
```

Indeed, CE4 computes a link-local IPv6 address from the link's MAC address.

6PE—why is there a service label?

PE4 pops the service label and maps the packet to the Internet Global IPv6 Routing Table. Does PE4 really *need* the service label? Not really. If PE4 had received a native IPv6 packet on its core uplink Gi 0/0/0/0, it would still have mapped the packet to the global routing table. And it would know that it is an IPv6 packet due to the Layer 2 (L2) header's Ethertype, not to mention that the first nibble (four bits) of the packet is 6.

So, why is there a service MPLS label? The main reason is PHP. The 6PE model was developed assuming that no LSR (including the penultimate one) supports IPv6 on its core uplinks. If PE1 had only pushed the transport MPLS label, this would be the Bottom of Stack (BoS) label. After popping it, P2 inspects the resulting packet and finds a first nibble with value 6. This is definitely not an IPv4 packet, whose first nibble would be 4. So far, no problem: P2 should be able to send the packet to the egress PE (PE4), as dictated by the LSP. But there is one snag: after all this popping, the packet has no L2 header.

In IPv4, the solution is easy: P2 builds an L2 header with Ethertype 0x0800 (IPv4) and a destination MAC address corresponding to PE4—and resolved via Address Resolution Protocol (ARP) by asking *who has 10.0.0.11*.

Now, in IPv6, P2 needs to push an L2 header with Ethertype 0x86DD (IPv6), but to which destination MAC address? ARP is an IPv4 thing! In IPv6 you need Neighbor Discovery (ND), an ICMPv6 mechanism that relies on IPv6 forwarding. And this is not possible if P2 does not support or is not configured for IPv6.

By using a service label, things are made easier for P2 because there is still an MPLS label after popping the transport label. P2 builds the L2 header with Ethertype 0x8847 (MPLS) and the destination MAC address is the one resolved via ARP for 10.0.0.11.

OK, this is why there is a service label. But how important is its value if the egress PE is going to pop it anyway? This is where it becomes more interesting.

6PE—service label allocation

There are three service label allocation modes at the egress PEs:

Per-prefix mode
> This is the default mode in IOS XR for routes learned from (or pointing to) CEs. Every different service prefix (in this case, IPv6 route) has a different label. This mode is illustrated in Figure 3-2.

Per-CE
> Also called per-NH (next hop) mode. This is the default mode in Junos. Let's illustrate it with an example. Imagine PE3 has 1,000 IPv6 routes pointing to CE3, and 500 IPv6 routes pointing to CE4. PE3 assigns two labels: L1 to the first 1,000 routes, and L2 to the other 500 routes.

Per-table
> Also called per-VRF (even if strictly speaking in the 6PE case there is no VRF). An egress PE assigns the same label to all the prefixes in the same table.

The most scalable model is per-table, followed by per-CE. Why? Because the lower the number of labels, the lower the number of forwarding next hops that the remote ingress PEs need to store and update.

However, using a high number of labels has an advantage if the backbone is composed of LSRs that do not have the capability of extracting fields from the IPv6 payload to compute the load-balancing hash. Most of the modern platforms are capable of doing it; hence, the trend is toward reducing the number of labels.

Following is the procedure to tune IOS XR in order to use per-CE or per-VRF mode.

Example 3-15. 6PE—changing the label allocation mode in IOS XR

```
RP/0/0/CPU0:PE4#configure
RP/0/0/CPU0:PE4(config)#router bgp 65000
RP/0/0/CPU0:PE4(config-bgp)#address-family ipv6 unicast
RP/0/0/CPU0:PE4(config-bgp-af)#label mode ?
  per-ce       Set per CE label mode
  per-vrf      Set per VRF label mode
  route-policy Use a route policy to select prefixes ...
```

The per-vrf mode is very interesting. The assigned label to all the global IPv6 prefixes is number 2 or, in other words, the IPv6 Explicit Null label. For this reason, it is recommended to turn on this mode in Junos, as follows:

Example 3-16. 6PE—per-table label allocation mode in Junos

```
protocols {
    bgp {
        group iBGP-RR {
            family inet6 labeled-unicast explicit-null;
}}}
```

Using one label mode or another is a purely local decision. It is possible to have an interoperable network with PEs using different modes.

The choice of a label allocation mode has additional implications. The following statements hold true for Junos and might apply to IOS XR, too:

- With per-prefix and per-CE modes, the egress PE performs an MPLS lookup on the packet, and as a result, the forwarding next hop is already determined. The egress PE is actually performing packet switching, in MPLS terms.

- With per-table mode, the egress PE performs an IPv4 lookup on the packet after the MPLS label is popped. This results in a richer functionality set.

Now consider the PE-CE subnet fc00::10:2:0:0/112, which is local from the perspective of PE3. If PE3 is using per-CE mode for the 6PE service, what CE is actually linked to that prefix? Is it CE3 or CE4? Actually it's neither. This is why, in per-CE mode, the local multipoint subnets are not advertised in Junos. You can still advertise CE3 (fc00::10:2:0:3/128) and CE4 (fc00::10:2:0:4/128) host routes if you locally configure a static route to the host.

6PE—traceroute

Here is a working traceroute from H1 (a host running IOS XR) to H3. You can compare the following example to Figure 3-2.

Example 3-17. 6PE—traceroute

```
RP/0/0/CPU0:H#traceroute fc00::10:2:34:30

1  fc00::10:1:12:1 0 msec 0 msec 0 msec               # CE1
2  fc00::10:1:0:1 59 msec 9 msec 0 msec               # PE1
3  fc00::10:0:0:3 [MPLS: Labels 299808/24020 Exp 0] ...   # P1
4  ::ffff:172.16.0.2 [MPLS: Labels 24016/24020 Exp 0] ... # P2
5  fc00::10:2:0:44 0 msec 0 msec 39 msec              # PE4
6  fc00::10:2:0:4 39 msec 0 msec 0 msec               # CE4
7  fc00::10:2:34:30 0 msec 0 msec 9 msec              # H4
```

The traceroute mechanism in an MPLS core is the same as the one described in Chapter 1 for IPv4 over MPLS packets. When an IPv6 packet's Time-to-Live (TTL) expires at a transit LSR, such as P1 or P2, the LSR generates an ICMPv6 time exceeded toward the original source (H1). The resulting ICMPv6 message is then encapsulated on the original LSP (→PE4), so the egress PE (PE4) can IPv6-route it toward the source (H1) The egress PE (PE4) is configured in per-VRF label allocation mode, so it does not include the service label in the time exceeded message.

But how can a non-IPv6 LSR generate an ICMPv6 packet? IOS XR does it automatically by sourcing the packet from the IPv6 address that is mapped from its own loopback IPv4 address (line 4). As for Junos, it requires that you configure `icmp-tunneling`, and *also* some IPv6 addressing in place. The common practice is to configure IPv6 addresses on all the core links, and not to advertise them in the Interior Gateway Protocol (IGP)— in IS-IS, `protocols isis no-ipv6-routing`.

BGP/MPLS IP Virtual Private Networks

BGP/MPLS IP Virtual Private Networks (VPNs), often called *L3VPNs*, are the most popular application of MPLS. If someone enters a room full of network engineers and asks them to write down the first MPLS application that comes to mind, most will put L3VPN. That having been said, L3VPNs are not the leading MPLS service in terms of traffic. Instead, the classic Internet over MPLS service (Global IPv4 over MPLS) described in Chapter 1 transports the majority of the data and multimedia traffic in the world.

So why are L3VPNs so recognizable?

- L3VPNs make it possible for customers to interconnect their headquarters, branch offices, and mobile users in a very simple manner. The Enterprises can keep their original private IP addressing, while the SP maintains the routing and traffic separate among tenants. In this way, connectivity and security needs are all addressed at the same time.
- SPs achieve higher revenue per user (and per bit) compared to residential IP services.

True, there are other popular VPN technologies such as Secure VPNs based on IPsec or on SSL/TLS. These deal with similar business requirements and can even work over a plain Internet connection. But the flexibility, scalability, manageability, and simplicity of BGP/MPLS IP VPNs, both from the point of view of the tenant and of the SP, are unparalleled. BGP/MPLS IP VPNs remain an undeniably fundamental piece of the VPN portfolio in the world.

BGP/MPLS IP VPNs were originally described in RFC 2547, which was later obsoleted by RFC 4364. You can find a great description of this technology in the RFC itself:

> This method uses a "peer model," in which the customers' edge (CE) routers send their routes to the Service Provider's edge (PE) routers [...] Routes from different VPNs remain distinct and separate, even if two VPNs have an overlapping address space [...]. The CE routers do not peer with each other; hence, the "overlay" is not visible to the VPN's routing algorithm [...].

In this book, the terms BGP/MPLS IP VPN and L3VPN are used interchangeably. This is not totally accurate because L3VPN also includes non-IP services such as OSI VPNs. However, for the sake of simplicity and readability we will use the term *L3VPN*. This section focuses on a dual stack (IPv4 and IPv6) scenario.

Attachment Circuits and Access Virtualization

Multiplexing at L2 is one of the primary forms of virtualization. For example, it is perfectly possible for one single CE-facing physical interface (such as PE1's ge-2/0/1) to have several logical interfaces, each with its own VLAN/802.1q identifier. Each VLAN ID identifies a separate *attachment circuit* (AC), using the terminology of RFC 4364. An AC connects a PE either to a single CE or to a multipoint access network—such as an Ethernet Metropolitan Area Network (MAN).

The terminology can be a bit confusing across vendors. If you have some hands-on experience with Juniper and Cisco, you should certainly have noticed that an untagged Ethernet interface is *directly* configured in IOS XR, whereas in Junos it is done via unit 0. The reason lies in the following implementation difference:

- In Junos, a physical interface (IFD: Interface Device) can have several logical interfaces (IFL: Interface Logical or unit), thanks to L2 multiplexing techniques such as VLAN tagging. On the other hand, if the IFD has a native encapsulation with no multiplexing, only one IFL is supported and it must be unit 0. In all cases, *an AC in Junos is a CE-facing IFL.*

- In IOS XR, there are two options: an AC can be either a native (nonmultiplexed) physical interface, or if there is L2 multiplexing, a subinterface (similar to an IFL).

 Junos ACs are typically IFLs, whereas in IOS XR an AC can be a subinterface or an interface—depending on the encapsulation.

An AC is a *logical* concept. In L3 services, the AC is where service L3 parameters such as IP addresses are configured at the PE.

An AC is typically associated with a single service at the PE. Let's use an example wherein PE1's ge-2/0/1 has four IFLs with VLAN ID 1001, 1002, 1003, and 1004, respectively. The per-IFL unit number may match the VLAN ID or not—for simplicity, let's suppose that it does match. It is perfectly possible to map IFL 1001 to a global Internet service, IFL 1002 to L3VPN A, IFL 1003 to L3VPN B, and IFL 1004 to an L2VPN.

On the other hand, one service can have several ACs at a given PE. For example, a PE can have several ACs connected to different CEs in such a way that all these ACs are associated to a global Internet service, or all of them to the same VPN.

AC classification—per technology

One of the most common AC types is VLAN-tagged Ethernet. One VLAN/802.1q header contains a 12-bit VLAN ID field, so its maximum value is 4,095. It's also possible to stack two VLAN/802.1q headers inside the original MAC header, overcoming the limit of 4,096 VLANs in one LAN. This is a popular technique that has different names: *stacked VLAN, Q-in-Q, SVLAN/CVLAN* (where S stands for *Service* and C for *Customer*), and so on. VXLAN is a different technology, and it is discussed in Chapter 8.

In addition to the classic AC types (*native Ethernet, VLAN-tagged Ethernet, ATM, Frame Relay*, etc.), there are many other flavors. For example, an AC can actually be totally virtual, such as a VLAN transported in a locally terminated MPLS Pseudowire (see PWHE at Chapter 6), or a PPPoE session, or an L2TP session, or a dynamic interface created upon the headers of incoming IP traffic (IP demux), and so forth. Even an IPsec tunnel coming from the Internet can be terminated at the PE, itself becoming an AC of a BGP/MPLS IP VPN. Not all these access flavors are covered here, but there is an important concept to keep in mind: *any connection with an endpoint at the PE can be a valid attachment circuit.*

Going back to the classic ACs (such as basic Ethernet with or without VLANs), in many real-life scenarios the connection between CE and PE is not direct. An L2 service provider is typically in the middle, transporting the frames between CE and PE in a transparent manner—via either a point-to-point or a multipoint mechanism. In that case, the L2 carrier provides an overlay: the CEs and PEs are the only IP endpoints of the circuit connection. So, if the AC is Ethernet-based and the service is a BGP/MPLS IPv4 VPN, CE1 and PE1 can resolve each other's IPv4 addresses by using ARP.

L3VPN in a Nutshell

In the examples that follow, the topology and IPv4/IPv6 addressing scheme remain the same as in Figure 1-1 and Figure 3-1, with the following differences:

- The VLAN ID of the ACs is 1002 instead of 1001.
- At the PEs, the ACs do not belong to the global routing instance, but to private instances called Virtual Routing and Forwarding (VRFs).
- The PEs are the same, but a new set of CEs is used, one per site and VPN. For example, on the lefthand side, there is CE1-A and CE2-A for VPN A.
- This is an Intranet VPN service, so CE3 (BR3) and CE4 (BR4) are replaced with CE3-A and CE4-A, respectively. The righthand AS is 65001, matching the lefthand AS number.

The primary goal of an MPLS VPN is to provide connectivity between tenant CEs that are attached to different PEs. The VPN concept is global, whereas a VRF is a local instance at a specific PE.

For the time being, you can think of a VRF as the local representation of one (*and only one*) VPN. This will change later on in this chapter.

Many routing flavors and protocols (static routes, Routing Information Protocol [RIP], OSPF, IS-IS, eBGP) can run between CE and PE. We use eBGP in this book because it's the most scalable protocol:

- PE-CE eBGP sessions are used to exchange IP Unicast (SAFI=1) prefixes.
- PE-RR iBGP sessions convey IP Unicast VPN (SAFI=128) prefixes.

How about the AFI? It's 1 for IPv4; 2 for IPv6. So, for example, IPv6 VPN Unicast corresponds to [AFI=2, SAFI=128].

 IPv6 Unicast VPN is commonly called 6vPE

IP VPN prefixes have one thing in common with the Labeled Unicast (LU) prefixes used in the 6PE solution: they both encode a label in the NLRI. However, IP VPN is more complex because it also must provide information about the private context. This is achieved with the help of Route Distinguishers and Route Targets.

Given this, it's only logical that L3VPN configurations are longer than 6PE's. So let's see L3VPN signaling and forwarding first; then, when the service is understood, move on to the configurations.

L3VPN—Signaling

Figure 3-3 illustrates the entire signaling and forwarding flow for IPv4 Unicast VPN. The IP VPN route signaling always relies on BGP. As for the transport mechanism, you have the same flexibility as with any other MPLS service: it can be based either on IP tunnels or, better, on MPLS LSPs (static, LDP, RSVP, BGP IPv4-LU, or SPRING). This example uses LDP, but any other option is valid.

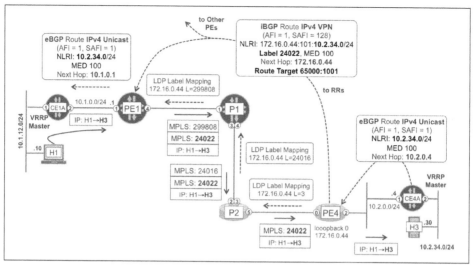

Figure 3-3. IPv4 VPN Unicast in action

 Go to Chapter 1 for an explanation as to why, in this multihoming scenario, the packet follows the path H1→CE1A→PE1→...→PE4→CE4A→H3.

Let's analyze the signaling flow for IPv4 and IPv6 prefixes. First, PE4 receives IPv4 Unicast and IPv6 Unicast routes from CE4-A.

Example 3-18. eBGP IPv4 and IPv6 Unicast routes

```
RP/0/0/CPU0:PE4# show bgp vrf VRF-A ipv4 unicast
[...]
   Network      Next Hop        Metric LocPrf Weight Path
*> 10.2.34.0/24
                10.2.0.4        100             0 65001 i

RP/0/0/CPU0:PE4# show bgp vrf VRF-A ipv6 unicast
[...]
   Network      Next Hop        Metric LocPrf Weight Path
*> fc00::10:2:34:0/112
                fc00::10:2:0:4  100             0 65001 i
```

Then, PE4 allocates an MPLS label to each prefix and advertises them to the RRs. Example 3-19 shows how the IPv4 Unicast VPN and IPv6 Unicast VPN routes advertised by PE4 look, from the perspective of RR1.

Example 3-19. L3VPN—IPv4 and IPv6 Unicast VPN routes (Junos)

```
1    juniper@RR1> show route receive-protocol bgp 172.16.0.44 detail
2                    table bgp.l3vpn
3
4    bgp.l3vpn.0: 6 destinations, 12 routes [...]
5    * 172.16.0.44:101:10.2.34.0/24 [...]
6        Accepted
7        Route Distinguisher: 172.16.0.44:101
8        VPN Label: 24022
9        Nexthop: 172.16.0.44
10       MED: 100
11       Localpref: 100
12       AS path: 65001 I
13       Communities: target:65000:1001
14
15   bgp.l3vpn-inet6.0: 6 destinations, 12 routes [...]
16
17   * 172.16.0.44:101:fc00::10:2:34:0/112 [...]
18       Accepted
19       Route Distinguisher: 172.16.0.44:101
20       VPN Label: 24023
21       Nexthop: ::ffff:172.16.0.44
22       MED: 100
23       Localpref: 100
24       AS path: 65001 I
25       Communities: target:65000:1001
```

 Remember that RRs do not change the BGP next-hop attribute by default. For this reason, they do not change the VPN label, either.

Example 3-20 shows these same routes from the perspective of PE4 itself.

Example 3-20. L3VPN—IPv4 and IPv6 Unicast VPN routes (IOS XR)

```
RP/0/0/CPU0:PE4#show bgp vpnv4 unicast advertised
Route Distinguisher: 172.16.0.44:101
10.2.34.0/24 is advertised to 172.16.0.201 [...]
  Attributes after outbound policy was applied:
    next hop: 172.16.0.44
    MET ORG AS EXTCOMM
    origin: IGP  neighbor as: 65001  metric: 100
    aspath: 65001
    extended community: RT:65000:1001
    /* Same route advertised to RR2 (omitted) */

RP/0/0/CPU0:PE4#show bgp vpnv6 unicast advertised
Route Distinguisher: 172.16.0.44:101
```

```
fc00::10:2:34:0/112 is advertised to 172.16.0.201 [...]
  Attributes after outbound policy was applied:
    next hop: 172.16.0.44
    MET ORG AS EXTCOMM
    origin: IGP  neighbor as: 65001  metric: 100
    aspath: 65001
    extended community: RT:65000:1001
    /* Same route advertised to RR2 (omitted) */
```

Example 3-19 and Example 3-20 also introduced three key L3VPN concepts: Route Distinguisher, VPN Label, and Route Target.

Route Distinguisher

Route Distinguisher (RD) is a very accurate name. An RD does precisely what the term implies: it distinguishes routes. PE4 may have the route 10.2.34.0/24 in different VRFs. The host 10.2.34.30 may be a server in a multinational enterprise (VRF-A), and at the same time a mobile terminal in a university (VRF-B). VPNs provide independent addressing spaces, so prefixes from different VRFs can overlap with no collision.

The prefixes exchanged over PE-CE eBGP sessions are IP Unicast (SAFI=1) and they do not contain any RDs. Indeed, from the point of view of the PE, each eBGP session is bound to one single VRF, so there is no need to distinguish the prefixes. On the other hand, CEs have no VPN awareness: from the perspective of the CE, a PE is just an IPv4/IPv6 router.

Now, one single PE-RR (or PE-PE) iBGP session can signal prefixes from multiple VPNs. For example, PE4 may advertise the 10.2.34.0/24 route from VRF-A and VRF-B. The 10.2.34.0/24 prefix represents a different reality in each of the VRFs, and this is where an RD comes in handy. The actual prefixes that PE4 announces to the RRs are *<RD1>*:10.2.34.0/24 and *<RD2>*:10.2.34.0/24. These prefixes are different as long as *<RD1>* is different from *<RD2>*.

In a given PE, you must configure each VRF with a different RD. It is also possible to configure a router so that it automatically generates a distinct RD for each VRF.

Back in Figure 3-3, the RD is 172.16.0.44:101. There are several ways to encode RDs, as regulated by IANA. This book discusses two types: 0 and 1. These formats are *<AS>*:*<VPN_ID>* and *<ROUTER_ID>*:*<VPN_ID>*, respectively.

In an Active-Backup redundancy scheme, CE3-A and CE4-A advertise the 10.2.34.0/24 prefix with a different MED: 200 to PE3 and 100 to PE4, respectively. This makes PE3 prefer the iBGP route over the eBGP route; as a result, PE4 does not advertise it to the RRs. In this model, the RD choice is not very important.

In an Active-Active redundancy scheme, CE3-A and CE4-A would advertise the 10.2.34.0/24 with the same MED, so both PE3 and PE4 would in turn advertise it to the RRs. In this case, the RD choice is critical. Let's consider the case of VRF-A:

- If the RD format is *<AS>:<VPN_ID>*, unless each PE assigns a different *<VPN_ID>* to the VRF—which would result in a virtually unmanageable numbering scheme—both PE3 and PE4 advertise the 65000:101:10.2.34.0/24 prefix. The RR selects the best route (from its point of view) and reflects it. This results in information loss and suboptimal routing. Not only that, it also causes a delay in failure recovery. The RRs must detect that the primary route is not valid before they can advertise the backup route to the ingress PEs. Typically, RRs have many peers, so this process usually takes time, and RRs act as a control-plane bottleneck. In the Internet service, BGP Add-Path extensions were required to address this challenge, but not necessarily in IP VPN, where there is a native solution!

- If the RD format is *<ROUTER_ID>:<VPN_ID>*, PE3 and PE4 advertise two different prefixes: 172.16.0.33:101:10.2.34.0/24 and 172.16.0.44:101:10.2.34.0/24, respectively. These are two different NLRI prefixes, and RRs reflect both of them. This guarantees that all of the PEs have all the information, achieving optimal routing and improved convergence. This is the scheme we use in this book. Note that in this case the *<VPN_ID>* value is the same (101) on both PEs, but this is not mandatory.

It is possible to have iBGP multihoming with unequal-cost multipath—see Chapter 20 for more details. The ingress PE can load-balance traffic between several egress PEs, even if these are not at the same IGP distance.

VPN label

The VPN label is an MPLS label that is locally significant to the egress PE. It is a service label by which the egress PE can map the downstream (from the core) user packets to the appropriate VRF (or CE). Like in 6PE, there are different label allocation schemes, which we'll discuss later.

Although the VPN label is encoded in the IP Unicast VPN (SAFI=128) NLRI, routers in general—and RRs in particular—consider it more like a route attribute rather than as part of the NLRI. In other words, two identical RD:route prefixes are considered to be the same even if the VPN label is different. Thus, the RRs only reflect one of them.

 RRs do *not* change the BGP next hop, and as a consequence they do not change the label encoded in the NLRI either: the label is meaningful to the egress PE only.

Route Target

The Route Target (RT) concept is probably the one that makes BGP/MPLS VPNs so powerful. RTs are one type of BGP extended community.

 You can see an exhaustive list of standard Extended Communities in RFC 7153 and at *http://www.iana.org/assignments/bgp-extended-communities/bgp-extended-communities.txt*.

Every BGP VPN route carries at least one RT. RTs control the distribution of VPN routes. How? Locally at a PE, a VRF has the following export and import policies:

- An *export* policy influences the transition of (local and CE-pointing) VRF routes from IP Unicast to IP Unicast VPN, before these routes are advertised to the RRs or other PEs. The export policy can filter prefixes and change their attributes; its most important task is to *add* RTs to the IP Unicast VPN routes.

- An *import* policy influences the installation of remote IP Unicast VPN routes into the local VRFs. The import policy can filter prefixes and change their attributes; its most important task is to *look* at the incoming routes' RTs and make a decision as to whether to install the route on the VRF where the import policy is applied.

You could view RTs as door keys. When a PE advertises a VPN route, it adds a key chain to the route. When the route arrives to other PEs, the route's keys (RTs) can open one or more doors (import policies) at the target PE. These doors give access to rooms (VRFs) where the route is installed after stripping the RD.

For example, you can configure VRF-A on all PEs to export RT 65000:1001 and to also import RT 65000:1001. This symmetrical policy—with the same import and export RT—results in a full-mesh topology in which all the CEs are reachable from one another. In this sense, you can easily identify VPN A routes: they all carry RT 65000:1001.

But there are many other ways to configure RT policies (hub-and-spoke, service chaining, etc.). Indeed, RTs are a fundamental concept that will be discussed quite a few times in this book. Let's move on.

L3VPN—Forwarding Plane

This section takes a look at the forwarding bits back in Figure 3-3, step by step. The text will describe what happens to an IPv4 packet, but the command output also shows the IPv6 variant.

First, H1 sends the packet via its default gateway CE1-A, which holds the VRRP group's virtual IPv4 and MAC addresses.

Next, CE1-A must choose between two routes to the same destination: one from PE1 (with MED 100) and another one from PE2 (with MED 200). CE1-A chooses the best route, which is via PE1.

Prior to forwarding the packet, PE1 must have installed the route to the destination in its forwarding table. To do that, PE1 first looks at the BGP next hop of the labeled unicast route (Example 3-19, line 9), which is 172.16.0.44. This BGP next hop is present in PE1's inet.3 table, with a forwarding next hop that says *push 299808 label, send to P1*. PE1 combines this instruction with the VPN label (Example 3-19, line 8), so it pushes two MPLS labels before sending the packet to P1.

Example 3-21. L3VPN—double MPLS label push at ingress—PE1 (Junos)

```
1    juniper@PE1> show route forwarding-table destination 10.2.34.30
2                 table VRF-A
3    [...]
4    Destination      Next hop     Type   Index     NhRef
5    10.2.34.0/24                  indr   1048587      2
6                     10.0.0.3     Push 24022, Push 299808(top) ge-2/0/4.0
7
8    juniper@PE1> show route forwarding-table destination fc00::10:2:34:0
9                 table VRF-A
10   [...]
11   Destination      Next hop     Type   Index     NhRef
12   fc00::10:2:34:0/112           indr   1048584      2
13                    10.0.0.3     Push 24023, Push 299808(top) ge-2/0/4.0
```

In Junos, 6vPE (like 6PE) routes get their BGP next hop resolved in the auxillary table inet6.3.

There is a *bottom service label* (24022 in line 6) and a *top transport label* (299808 in line 6). The transport label typically changes hop by hop—in this example, it is popped at the penultimate hop. Conversely, the service label travels intact down to the egress PE—in this case PE4. And because PE4 is the router that in the first instance had allocated the service label to the IPv4 VPN prefix, it therefore knows how to interpret it fully.

Example 3-22. L3VPN—MPLS label pop at the egress PE—PE4 (IOS XR)

```
RP/0/0/CPU0:PE4#show mpls forwarding vrf VRF-A
Local  Outgoing    Prefix              Outgoing        Next   Bytes
Label  Label       or ID               Interface       Hop    Switched
------ ----------- ------------------- --------------- -----  -------
24022  Unlabelled  10.2.34.0/24[V]     Gi0/0/0/2.1001  10.2.0.4

Local  Outgoing    Prefix
Label  Label       or ID
------ ----------- ------------------
24023  Unlabelled  fc00::10:2:34:0/112[V]

Outgoing        Next                    Bytes
Interface       Hop                     Switched
--------------  ----------------------  --------
Gi0/0/0/2.1001  fe80::205:8603:e971:f501  0
```

Finally, it is interesting to see how the return route (to 10.1.12.0/24) looks from the perspective of PE4—acting as an ingress PE.

Example 3-23. L3VPN—double MPLS label push at ingress—PE4 (IOS XR)

```
RP/0/0/CPU0:PE4#show cef vrf VRF-A 10.1.12.0/24
10.1.12.0/24 [...]
  via 172.16.0.22, 5 dependencies, recursive [flags 0x6000]
   recursion-via-/32
   next hop VRF - 'default', table - 0xe0000000
   next hop 172.16.0.22 via 24005/0/21
    next hop 10.0.0.10/32 Gi0/0/0/0 labels imposed {24002 24019}
```

You can use the same command for IPv6 prefixes. In that case, ensure that you introduce the keyword ipv6 between the VRF name and the prefix.

L3VPN—why is there a service label?

The answer is quite straightforward: the VPN label is essential for the egress PE to know to which VRF the downstream (from the core) packet belongs. The service label allocation models are similar to those of 6PE, and they are further described later.

L3VPN—Backbone Configuration at the PEs

Let's take a look at the backbone configuration in Junos and IOS XR.

L3VPN—backbone configuration at Junos PEs

Example 3-24 shows the relevant core-facing configuration at PE1.

Example 3-24. L3VPN—core-facing configuration at PE1 (Junos)

```
protocols {
    bgp {
        group iBGP-RR {
            family inet-vpn unicast;
            family inet6-vpn unicast;
}}}
```

As expected, two new address families are added: IPv4 Unicast VPN (AFI=1, SAFI=128) and IPv6 Unicast VPN (AFI=2, SAFI=128).

You must also configure IPv6 tunneling as shown in Example 3-1, line 3. This is needed in order to install IPv4-mapped addresses in the inet6.3 auxiliary table.

L3VPN—backbone configuration at IOS XR PEs

Here is the relevant core-facing configuration at PE2:

Example 3-25. L3VPN—core-facing configuration at PE2 (IOS XR)

```
router bgp 65000
 address-family vpnv4 unicast
 address-family vpnv6 unicast
 !
 neighbor-group iBGP-RR
  address-family vpnv4 unicast
  address-family vpnv6 unicast
!
```

Regardless of the transport LSP technology you use, don't forget to globally configure mpls ldp. Otherwise, IP VPN prefixes will remain unresolved in the Cisco Express Forwarding (CEF). If you do not really need LDP as a protocol, just configure mpls ldp without any interfaces below.

L3VPN—RR Configuration

Example 3-26 lays out the additional configuration at RR1.

Example 3-26. L3VPN—RR configuration at RR1 (Junos)

```
1    protocols {
2        bgp {
3            group CLIENTS {
```

```
4                    family inet-vpn unicast;
5                    family inet6-vpn unicast;
6      }}}
7      routing-options {
8          rib inet.3 static route 0/0 discard;
9          rib inet6.3 static route 0::0/0 discard;
10     }
```

 In the examples in this chapter, MPLS is fully functional and LDP is active at all the PE-PE, PE-P, and P-P links. However, the RRs have no MPLS configuration in place.

An IP VPN Unicast (SAFI=128) BGP route has a private context. Indeed, transit P-routers do not keep any IP VPN routing state. For this reason, packets matching such route must be transported to the egress PE via an IP tunnel or an MPLS LSP.

In Junos, the tables in which BGP next hops can be resolved into labeled paths are inet.3 (for IPv4) and inet6.3 (for IPv6). Because this example's RRs do not run any MPLS protocol, they need static routes (lines 8 and 9) to perform BGP next-hop resolution and reflect IP VPN routes.

Following is the additional configuration at RR2:

Example 3-27. L3VPN—RR configuration at RR2 (IOS XR)

```
1      router bgp 65000
2       address-family vpnv4 unicast
3       address-family vpnv6 unicast
4       !
5       neighbor-group CLIENTS
6        address-family vpnv4 unicast
7         route-reflector-client
8        !
9        address-family vpnv6 unicast
10        route-reflector-client
11     !
```

IOS XR does not require any extra configuration to resolve the BGP next hop.

L3VPN—VRF Configuration at the PEs

Now, let's take a look at the VRF configuration in Junos and IOS XR.

L3VPN—VRF configuration at Junos PEs

Example 3-28 presents the access configuration at PE1. The only logical interface and eBGP session displayed correspond to the PE1-CE1 link.

Example 3-28. L3VPN—VRF configuration at PE1 (Junos)

```
1    interfaces {
2        ge-2/0/1 {
3            unit 1002 {
4                vlan-id 1002;
5                family inet address 10.1.0.1/31;
6                family inet6 address fc00::10:1:0:1/127;
7    }}}
8    routing-instances {
9        VRF-A {
10           instance-type vrf;
11           interface ge-2/0/1.1002;
12           route-distinguisher 172.16.0.11:101;
13           vrf-export PL-VRF-A-EXP;
14           vrf-import PL-VRF-A-IMP;
15           protocols {
16               bgp {
17                   group eBGP-65001 {
18                       family inet unicast;
19                       family inet6 unicast;
20                       peer-as 65001;
21                       as-override;
22                       neighbor 10.1.0.0 {
23                           export PL-VRF-A-eBGP-CE1A-OUT;
24                       }
25   }}}}}
26   policy-options {
27       policy-statement PL-VRF-A-eBGP-CE1A-OUT {
28           term BGP {
29               from protocol bgp;
30               then {
31                   metric 100;
32                   community delete RT-ALL;
33               }
34           }
35           term IPv6 {
36               from family inet6;
37               then {
38                   next-hop fc00::10:1:0:1;
39               }
40       }}
41       policy-statement PL-VRF-A-EXP {
42           term eBGP {
43               from protocol bgp;
44               then {
45                   community add RT-VPN-A;
46                   accept;
47               }
48       }}
49       policy-statement PL-VRF-A-IMP {
50           term VPN-A {
```

```
51                from community RT-VPN-A;
52                then accept;
53            }
54        }
55        community RT-ALL members target:*:*;
56        community RT-VPN-A members target:65000:1001;
57    }
```

The AC configuration (lines 1 through 6) has nothing special: just a dual-stack IFL.

The VRF export (lines 13, and 41 through 46) and VRF import (lines 14, and 49 through 52) are very simple, to the point that they would not need to be defined. You could replace lines 13 and 14 with `vrf-target target:65000:1001`. But this shortcut is compatible only with full-mesh VPN topologies, and it does not allow filtering or modifying prefixes. For this reason, it's a good practice to use the syntax in Example 3-28.

The `as-override` configuration in line 21 is not specific to L3VPNs. In fact, it is required for *any* BGP-based design that requires connecting two islands with the same AS (65001 in this case). Otherwise, the AS-loop detection logic would drop the prefixes at some point. There are other techniques to achieve the same result, but this one is simple.

Unlike IOS XR, when Junos readvertises an IP Unicast VPN route—after converting it to IP Unicast format—it keeps all the communities, including the RTs. It is a good practice to strip the RTs before sending the route to a plain CE (line 32).

As for the IPv6 next-hop rewrite in line 38, it is due to the fact that there is a single eBGP session used for IPv4 and IPv6 prefixes. The rationale is the same as explained previously in the 6PE section. (See the full discussion with respect to Example 3-6.)

L3VPN—VRF configuration at IOS XR PEs

Example 3-29 contains the access configuration at PE4. The only logical interface and eBGP session displayed correspond to the PE4-CE4A link.

Example 3-29. L3VPN—VRF configuration at PE4 (IOS XR)

```
1     interface GigabitEthernet0/0/0/2.1002
2      vrf VRF-A
3      ipv4 address 10.2.0.44 255.255.255.0
4      ipv6 address fc00::10:2:0:44/112
5      encapsulation dot1q 1002
6     !
7     router bgp 65000
8      vrf VRF-A
9       rd 172.16.0.44:101
10      address-family ipv4 unicast
11      address-family ipv6 unicast
```

```
12      !
13      neighbor 10.2.0.4
14       remote-as 65001
15       address-family ipv4 unicast
16        route-policy PL-VRF-A-eBGP-CE4A-IN in
17        route-policy PL-VRF-A-eBGP-CE4A-OUT out
18        as-override
19       !
20       address-family ipv6 unicast
21        route-policy PL-VRF-A-eBGP-CE4A-IN in
22        route-policy PL-VRF-A-eBGP-CE4A-OUT out
23        as-override
24      !
25      vrf VRF-A
26       address-family ipv4 unicast
27        import route-target
28         65000:1001
29        export route-target
30         65000:1001
31       !
32       address-family ipv6 unicast
33        import route-target
34         65000:1001
35        export route-target
36         65000:1001
37       !
38      route-policy PL-VRF-A-eBGP-CE4A-IN
39        pass
40      end-policy
41      !
42      route-policy PL-VRF-A-eBGP-CE4A-OUT
43        pass
44      end-policy
```

See the discussion about eBGP policies in Chapter 1. It explains
why eBGP pass policies are required in IOS XR but not in Junos.

As a side note, there is one significant configuration difference in the way non-BGP
prefixes can be announced via BGP. In Junos, you need to modify the VRF export
policy. Here is the syntax in IOS XR: router bgp <AS> vrf <VRF> address-family
<AF> redistribute [...].

L3VPN—Routing Tables in Junos

You have already seen a few auxiliary tables: `inet.3` and `inet6.3` are used to resolve BGP IPv4 and IPv6 next hops, respectively. Their routes never make it to the forwarding table.

On the other hand, the `bgp.l3vpn.0` and `bgp.l3vpn-inet6.0` tables store the received RD:IPv4 and RD:IPv6 prefixes, respectively. Only the prefixes that match a local VRF's import policy—typically, because the route's RTs matches the import policy's RTs—are stored. The other prefixes are simply discarded by default.

There are several exceptions to this *discard-if-no-match* rule. First, is PEs with the `keep all` knob configured. Second, certain routers readvertise IP Unicast VPN routes in IP Unicast VPN (SAFI=128) format:

- RRs readvertise IP VPN iBGP routes as IP VPN iBGP routes.
- Inter-AS Option B ASBRs (a concept discussed in Chapter 9) readvertise IP VPN iBGP routes as IP VPN eBGP routes, and vice versa.
- A variant of the latter involves eiBGP (confederations) instead of eBGP.

In all of these exceptions, the device installs all the incoming IP VPN routes in the `bgp.l3vpn[-inet6].0` auxiliary tables.

Let's forget for the moment about these exceptions and think of a regular PE that receives a matching route. After the RD is stripped from it, the IP prefix is copied—as a secondary route—to the VRFs with a matching import policy. Yes, there can be several matching VRFs, and that will be discussed later. In the case of VRF-A, IPv4 and IPv6 prefixes are stored in `VRF-A.inet.0` and `VRF-A.inet6.0` routing tables, respectively.

Defining a VRF as a table has been cautiously avoided. In fact, a VRF is an instance that can have *several* tables, one for each route type.

As you can see in Figure 3-4, the export logic is a bit different from that of the import. In Junos, by default, IP Unicast VPN routes are advertised directly from the VRF, not from L3VPN auxiliary tables.

However, if a device reflects IP VPN prefixes (like RR1), or if you configure the `advertise-from-main-vpn-tables` knob, all the IP VPN routes are advertised from the `bgp.l3vpn[-inet6].0` table. Let's call it the main IP VPN table. Now suppose that RR1 is also a PE and it has a local VRF connected to CE10. RR1 installs IP VPN prefixes learned from CE10 into the VRF (primary RIB) and copies them into the main

IP VPN table (secondary RIB). In this case, which is not shown in Figure 3-4, RR1 advertises all the prefixes (either reflected or originated in the VRF) from the main IP VPN table.

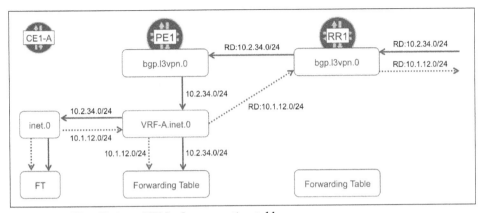

Figure 3-4. IPv4 Unicast VPN—Junos routing tables

Do you really need to worry about from which table the routes are exported? If, for whatever reason, a PE advertises IP Unicast VPN prefixes from the main IP VPN table, the BGP next hop of these routes cannot be changed with VRF export policies; you can do it only with the global export policy applied to the iBGP group. On a separate note, if the primary RIB of an advertised prefix is the local VRF, the global export policy applies to this prefix only if you configure `vpn-apply-export` under the group.

Virtual routers

The idea of having a private routing instance is very attractive, and not only in the context of an L3VPN service. For example, a physical CE can be turned into a set of virtual CEs, each with its own upstream circuits and routing table(s).

In Junos, this is called *virtual router* (VR, a.k.a., VRF Lite), and you can configure it as shown in Example 3-28, with the following differences:

- The `instance-type` in line 10 is `virtual-router`.
- Lines 12 through 14 must be removed, and line 32 is not necessary.

Graphically, if you disconnect `VRF-A.inet.0` from `bgp.l3vpn.0` in Figure 3-4, VRF-A becomes a VR.

You cannot further virtualize virtual routers. Conversely, Junos Logical Systems can in turn contain their own VRFs and VRs.

The Cisco term for this same concept is VRF Lite. You can turn VRF-A into a VRF Lite by suppressing lines 27 through 30, and 33 through 36 from Example 3-29. Note that eBGP configuration in VRF Lite requires that you configure an RD, even if it is not actually signaled.

L3VPN—Service Label Allocation

The three different label allocation modes are already described in the context of 6PE. The concepts are the same with L3VPN.

The default label allocation mode in IOS XR is per-prefix, but you can change it to per-CE or per-VRF mode, as demonstrated in the following example:

Example 3-30. L3VPN—changing the label allocation mode in IOS XR

```
RP/0/0/CPU0:PE4#configure
RP/0/0/CPU0:PE4(config)#router bgp 65000
RP/0/0/CPU0:PE4(config-bgp)#vrf VRF-A
RP/0/0/CPU0:PE4(config-bgp-vrf)#address-family ipv4 unicast
RP/0/0/CPU0:PE4(config-bgp-vrf-af)#label mode ?
  per-ce        Set per CE label mode
  per-vrf       Set per VRF label mode
  route-policy  Use a route policy to select prefixes ...
```

IOS XR per-prefix mode is the default for routes learned from (or pointing to) CEs. Other VRF prefixes (directly connected, static to Null0, aggregate) are all advertised with the same label by default.

It is possible to do the same tuning for address-family ipv6 unicast. In any case, a label that is bound to an IPv4 prefix is never bound to an IPv6 prefix in IOS XR: different label sets are kept for each address family.

This is different in Junos, for which per VRF label allocation mode associates the same label to all the prefixes in a VRF, regardless of whether they are IPv4 or IPv6.

The default label allocation mode in Junos is per-CE, but you can change it to per-VRF in two different ways. Let's look at the first one:

Example 3-31. 6PE—per-table label allocation mode in Junos (I)

```
routing-instances VRF-A vrf-table-label;
```

This configuration creates a Label-Switched Interface (LSI), which is a global virtual IFL that is associated to one single MPLS label and to one single VRF. This LSI processes all the downstream (from the core) packets with that MPLS label: the label is popped and the packet is mapped to the correct VRF.

Example 3-32 depicts the second method, which is mutually exclusive to the first one.

Example 3-32. 6PE—per-table label allocation mode in Junos (II)

```
1    chassis {
2        fpc 2 pic 0 tunnel-services bandwidth 10g;
3    }
4    interfaces {
5        vt-2/0/0 unit 101 family inet;
6    }
7    routing-instances {
1        VRF-A interface vt-2/0/0.101;
2    }
```

The result is similar to an LSI, but this time the virtual IFL is anchored to a specific Packet Forwarding Engine (PFE) in the PE. This results in lower resource consumption because the IFL (Virtual Tunnel or vt-) is only instantiated in one PFE. On the other hand, the placement of the tunnel resources must be carefully planned to achieve an optimal forwarding path inside the router. Finally, it is possible to provision redundant vt- interfaces for a higher resiliency.

In both Junos and IOS XR, it is possible to change the label allocation method in a granular manner with policies. You can select different methods for different VRFs, and even for different prefix sets inside the same VRF.

L3VPN—Topologies

Symmetric VRF import and export policies using one single (and distinct) RT per VRF results in a full-mesh routing topology. Any site can reach any other site in the VPN, but you can tune RT policies to create arbitrary routing topologies. This is not only true for L3VPN: it also applies to any BGP-based service.

L3VPN—hub-and-spoke VPN

The lefthand scenario in Figure 3-5 shows a classic hub-and-spoke L3VPN. PE1 and PE2 are the hub PEs, connected to the corporate headquarters' data center. PE3 and PE4 are spoke PEs, connected to small offices, home offices, or mobile users.

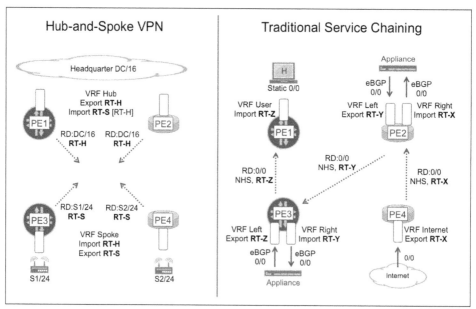

Figure 3-5. L3VPN Topology Samples

The remote sites do not need to communicate with one another.

With these connectivity requirements, hub-and-spoke PEs use complementary policies in the context of the same VPN:

- Spoke PEs export routes with route target RT-S, so hub PEs import them.
- Hub PEs export routes with route target RT-H, so spoke PEs import them.
- Spoke PEs do not import routes from other spoke PEs.
- Hub PEs *may* import routes from other hub PEs, if their import policies are configured to also accept routes with RT-H. This adds an extra level of redundancy.

The following example shows a typical asymmetrical RT configuration in Junos.

Example 3-33. L3VPN—hub VPN policy configuration (Junos)

```
1    policy-options {
2        policy-statement PL-VRF-A-HUB-EXP {
3            term eBGP {
4                from protocol bgp;
5                then {
6                    community add RT-VPN-A-HUB;
7                    accept;
8                }
9        }}
```

```
10      policy-statement PL-VRF-A-HUB-IMP {
11          term VPN-A {
12              from community [ RT-VPN-A-SPOKE RT-VPN-A-HUB ];
13              then accept;
14          }
15      }
16      community RT-VPN-A-HUB members target:65000:2001;
17      community RT-VPN-A-SPOKE members target:65000:3001;
18  }
```

Junos applies the following logical operators:

[OR]

> This operator is applied if several communities are listed in a `from community` statement. It is enough for the route to contain *any* of the communities in order to match the term.

[AND]

> This operator is applied if several communities are listed in `members`. The route must contain *all* the communities in order to match the community.

Following is an IOS XR sample.

Example 3-34. L3VPN—hub VPN configuration (IOS XR)

```
1   vrf VRF-A-HUB
2     address-family ipv4 unicast
3       import route-target
4         65000:2001
5         65000:3001
6       !
7       export route-target
8         65000:2001
9   !
```

L3VPN—management VPN

The righthand scenario in Figure 3-5 is explained later. Let's see a simpler example first. Very frequently, SPs manage all or a subset of the tenant CEs—just the first routing device, not necessarily the tenant network behind it.

Imagine 10 fully meshed customer VPNs called VPN-*n* (VPN-1 through VPN-10). These are instantiated on each PE as a VRF-*n* (VRF-1 through VRF-10), and each VPN has its own and different RT-*n* (RT-1 through RT-10).

In addition, the SP has a management VPN (VPN-M). This VPN is instantiated at PE1 and PE2 as VRF-M and the ACs are connected to the SP's management network.

The SP's management servers need to communicate to the customer VPN CEs, but *not* to the tenant's end hosts. Here is how you can meet the connectivity requirement:

- PEs' VRF-*n* export policies tag *all* the exported prefixes with at least RT-*n*.

- PEs' VRF-M export policies tag the management server's prefixes with RT-M.

- The SP assigns a globally unique loopback IP address to each CE in a VPN-*n*. PEs' VRF-*n* export policies advertise these prefixes with RT-*n* and RT-CE-LO.

- PEs' VRF-*n* import policies accept prefixes containing its RT-*n* and/or RT-M.

- PEs' VRF-M import policies accept prefixes containing RT-CE-LO and/or RT-M.

- CEs must not advertise management prefixes to the tenants' internal networks.

Management VPNs are examples of a broader solution called *extranet*. In an extranet, VPNs are no longer isolated, because they can exchange prefixes with one another. This process is controlled by policies.

The same RT techniques used in Example 3-33 and Example 3-34 apply here, but this time it is necessary to do something more granular on the CE loopback prefixes.

Let's assume that the CEs are advertising their own loopback to the PEs with standard community 65000:1234. In this way, PE3 can easily recognize CE3-A's loopback. Then, PE3 adds RT-CE-LO to the prefix before announcing it via iBGP to the RRs.

Example 3-35. L3VPN—granular RT setting at PE1 (Junos)

```
1    policy-options {
2        policy-statement PL-VRF-A-EXP {
3            term CE-LO {
4                from community CM-CE-LO;
5                then community add RT-CE-LO;
6            }
7            term eBGP {
8                from protocol bgp;
9                then {
10                   community add RT-VPN-A;
11                   accept;
12               }
13           }
14       }
15       community CM-CE-LO members 65001:1234;
16       community RT-CE-LO members target:65000:1234;
17       community RT-VPN-A members target:65000:1001;
18   }
```

The resulting route 172.16.0.33:101:<CE-LO>/32 has the three communities in lines 15 through 17, because it is evaluated by both terms in the policy. The original community 65001:1234 is kept because the action in line 5 is community **add**. If it had been community **set**, the original community would have been stripped.

The following example illustrates how RTs can be granularly set in IOS XR:

Example 3-36. L3VPN—granular RT Setting at PE4 (IOS XR)

```
vrf VRF-A
 address-family ipv4 unicast
  export route-policy PL-VRF-A-EXP
!
route-policy PL-VRF-A-EXP
  if community matches-any CM-LO-CE then
    set extcommunity rt (65000:1001, 65000:1234)
  endif
end-policy
!
community-set CM-LO-CE
  65000:1234
end-set
!
```

Again, the resulting IPv4 Unicast VPN prefix has three communities in total: one standard (65000:1234) and two extended (target:65000:1001 and target:65000:1234) communities. Hence, IOS XR differs from Junos in that the **set** keyword is additive.

As for the generic RT configuration in IOS XR Example 3-29 (lines 25 through 36), it still applies to prefixes that do not match the configured VRF export and import policies.

L3VPN—extranet

The previous example illustrated a generic technique known as *extranet*. In an extranet, a set of tenants is no longer isolated from one another and they can exchange prefixes. How much connectivity and which type of connectivity the VPNs have with each other is totally at the discretion of the configured routing policies.

There are two types of prefixes from the point of view of a VRF: remote and local. Remote prefixes are received from the RRs and/or from remote PEs. Conversely, local prefixes belong to the *access* side: these are typically routes learned from directly connected CEs, or they can also be static routes, directly connected ACs, local VRF loopbacks at the PE, and so on.

When a PE receives a remote IP Unicast VPN prefix, typically the RTs and other attributes determine the VRFs (it can be none, one or several) in which the prefix is imported. How about the local prefixes? The logic is the same. RT policies are evaluated, so two VRFs in a given PE may exchange local prefixes if their VRF policies match. This is known as *route leaking*.

A very common use case here is a tenant merger. Imagine VRF-A and VRF-B used to belong to different corporations but the two are merging into a bigger company. Provided that the IP addressing scheme is carefully analyzed and there is no overlap, the two VPNs can be merged into one by just importing each other's RTs in their respective VRFs. As a final step after the extranet interim period, the two VRFs are then merged into one single VRF.

 Route leaking between local VRFs in Junos requires the `routing-instances <VRF> routing-options auto-export` knob at both the donor (primary) and receiver (secondary) VRF.

Route leaking is a very rich topic, and for further reading about this and other topics, we highly recommend the *#TheRoutingChurn blog (http://forums.juniper.net/t5/TheR outingChurn/bg-p/RoutingChurn)* at *http://forums.juniper.net/*.

L3VPN—Service Chaining

Service Chaining or Service Function Chaining (SFC) is one of the most rapidly evolving solutions these days. As is detailed in Chapter 12, some network virtualization solutions go beyond the RT concept in order to achieve modern SFC.

In the late 1990s, well before the SDN era, the earliest flavor of SFC already existed in traditional L3VPN services. Let's examine how SFC looked at that time, not only for historical reasons, but because it is still a common practice in carriers.

Imagine that an SP wants to provide added value services such as NAT, firewall, DDoS protection, deep-packet inspection, IDS/IDP, traffic big-data analytics, and so on to its high-touch customers. One expensive option is to implement all of these services at the CE—which can be particularly challenging for mobile users. In contrast, the most scalable and convenient option is to steer the traffic to service nodes that perform these added value tasks. These service nodes can be all in the same location or distributed in different sites.

RT policies can steer traffic through routing-aware appliances distributed in different data centers, each on a different VPN site. Indeed, this is possible even in classical BGP VPN setups, like the one on the righthand side of Figure 3-5. Each appliance performs an added-value function on top of the baseline Internet access service. The diagram shows the routes required to steer upstream traffic from the tenant's host to the Internet, through the different (physical or virtual) appliances.

A similar routing scheme (not shown) would be required for downstream traffic, too. This is a bit more complex—but definitely feasible—when NAT is in the picture. Very often, the NAT function is performed directly on the PEs so the Left/Right VRFs are stitched locally at the PE through the NAT service interfaces.

Another challenge is redundancy, because many services (NAT, stateful firewalling, etc.) typically require symmetrical traffic. When there are several appliances in a redundancy pool, it is important that upstream and downstream packets from the same flow are all handled by the same appliance. Again, you can solve this challenge by carefully defining the policies.

It's not theoretical: as mentioned, this approach has been used for decades in many SPs. This traditional SFC concept has evolved in the more recent years:

- Virtualizing the appliances
- Decoupling the PE's control/signaling from the routing/forwarding functions into different entities
- Introducing flexible BGP next-hop manipulation and enhanced forwarding intelligence at the programmable PEs
- Natively implementing scalable security functions in the forwarding logic
- Automating the service provisioning, configuration, resiliency, and monitoring

Chapter 12 shows how the BGP VPN technology, which has always supported service chaining at some extent, recently evolved into a flexible, scalable, and modern SFC solution.

L3VPN—Loop Avoidance

Multihoming brings redundancy, at the expense of introducing the possibility of incurring routing loops. Luckily, in L3 services, you can count on the TTL field that is present in IPv4, IPv6, and MPLS packet headers; and thanks to TTL, packets cannot loop forever. For this reason, the impact of an L3 forwarding loop is much less scary than the one caused by an L2 loop. Regardless, L3 routing loops are not desirable and it is important to avoid them.

When eBGP is the PE-CE protocol, most deployments rely on another extended community called Site of Origin (SoO). As it name implies, a route's SoO informs about the site where the route originated.

What sites are there in this example? CE1-A and CE2-A have a backdoor link to each other, as do CE3-A and CE4-A. So, there are two sites in total, one on the left and one on the right. The following SoO values are globally assigned to the sites in VPN A:

- 65000:10112 to the lefthand site (CE1-A and CE2-A). This SoO value is set on the prefixes that either PE1 or PE2 learn from CE1-A or CE2-A.
- 65000:10134 to the righthand site (CE3-A and CE4-A). This SoO value is set on the prefixes that either PE3 or PE4 learn from CE3-A or CE4-A.

Using the SoO prevents intrasite traffic from transiting the service provider. How? Simply, PEs do not readvertise routes learned from a given site into the same site. For example, when the SoO is correctly configured and PE1 receives a route from CE1-A:

- PE1 does not readvertise the route to CE2-A.
- PE1 advertises the route with SoO:65000:10112 to the RRs, which in turn reflects it to all the PEs. PE2 would never readvertise this route to CE1-A or CE2-A.

Here is how the route looks when PE1 advertises it to the RRs.

Example 3-37. L3VPN—Site of Origin Advertisement (Junos)

```
juniper@PE1> show route advertising-protocol bgp 172.16.0.201
             table VRF-A
[...]
    Communities: target:65000:1001 origin:65000:10112
```

The same communities are displayed as follows in IOS XR: Extended community: RT:65000:1001 SoO:65000:10112.

This mechanism is especially useful when same-site CEs run a routing protocol with each other. For example, CE1-A and CE2-A might well establish an iBGP (SAFI=1) session with NHS if the tenant network is more complex than just a backdoor link.

In addition, SoO is handy for operators to manually check where a route originated.

The following example presents the Junos configuration for the PE1-CE1 session, assuming that the -OUT and -IN policies are applied to the 10.1.0.0 neighbor as export and import, respectively.

Example 3-38. L3VPN—site of origin configuration for PE1-CE1 (Junos)

```
policy-options {
    policy-statement PL-VRF-A-eBGP-CE1A-OUT {
        term SOO {
            from community SOO-VPN-A-SITE-12;
            then reject;
        }
        term BGP { ... }
    }
    policy-statement PL-VRF-A-eBGP-CE1A-IN {
        term SOO then community add SOO-VPN-A-SITE-12;
    }
    community SOO-VPN-A-SITE-12 members origin:65000:10112;
}
```

Example 3-39 shows the equivalent syntax in IOS XR.

Example 3-39. L3VPN—SoO configuration for PE2-CE2 (IOS XR)

```
router bgp 65000
 vrf VRF-A
  neighbor 10.1.0.2
   address-family ipv4 unicast
    site-of-origin 65000:10112
    !
   address-family ipv6 unicast
    site-of-origin 65000:10112
!
```

The loop avoidance logic is more complex when the PE-CE protocol is link-state, like OSPF and IS-IS, especially when multi-area and route redistribution are in the game. Although OSPF as a PE-CE protocol was tested successfully in this book's interoperable setup, it falls outside the scope of the current edition.

Internet Access from a VRF

Providing Internet services to L3VPN tenants is a wide and relatively complex topic that this book just touches on very briefly. There are many options to achieve it. The key is whether upstream Internet traffic is sourced from public or private IP addresses at the CE→PE link. Or, to put it in a different way, whether downstream Internet traffic is destined to public or private IP addresses at the PE→CE link.

Let's focus on upstream traffic. If the PE receives Internet packets from the CE with *public* source IP addresses, there are several options. Probably the cleanest approach is to use a different attachment circuit for each service: one for Internet, and one for intranet (L3VPN). In this case, the CE has at least two service-specific logical connections to the PE. And ACs are associated to different routing instances—global routing and a tenant VRF, respectively.

There is no mandate to provide Internet service on the global routing table. It is perfectly possible to have an Internet VPN and establish eBGP peerings to other providers in the context of the Internet VRF.

Other options include classifying packets based on their source and destination IP address, and then using one or more of the following tools:

- Hairpin connecting the tenant VRF and the global routing instance. It can be an external back-to-back connection or an internal link such as a Junos logical tunnel.

- Filter-Based Forwarding (FBF), also known as ACL-Based Forwarding (ABF). This is the name used for modern Policy-Based Routing (PBR).

- Route leaking between the global routing table and the VRF.
- Routes pointing from one table to another.

If, on the other hand, the PE receives Internet packets from the CE with *private* source IP addresses, a NAT function is necessary on the PE or further upstream:

- If the PE performs the NAT function, typically the NAT service provides two logical interfaces: an internal one belonging to the tenant VRF, and an external one at the global routing table (or Internet VRF). The public (post-NAT) tenant IP addresses are advertised from the public instance.

- If the NAT function is performed by a different entity further upstream—such as a physical or virtual appliance—upstream traffic needs to be conveniently steered from the PE toward the NAT. Typically, a dynamic default route advertised from the NAT inside function does the trick.

Route Target Constraint

Imagine an SP network with 1,000 VPNs. Most PEs only have a subset of VPNs locally instantiated as VRFs.

A new PE called PE5 is now configured with just VRF-A and symmetrical RT policies that set and match RT 65000:1001. When the iBGP session comes up, by default the RRs send to PE5 *all* the IP Unicast VPN routes for the 1,000 VPNs. Then, PE5 only stores the small fraction of routes containing RT 65000:1001 and (by default) silently discards the rest. Every time there is a new routing change, the RRs propagate it to PE5, regardless of whether the change affects VRF-A.

Now a new VRF called VRF-B—with a new RT 65000:1002—is configured on PE5, which sends a BGP refresh message to the RRs. These in turn send all the IP Unicast VPN routes to PE5 again. And so on.

Fortunately, this mechanism can be greatly optimized, as described in RFC 4684: *Constrained Route Distribution for BGP/MPLS IP VPNs*. This solution is commonly called *Route Target Constraint* (RTC). It relies on an additional NLRI called Route Target Membership (AFI=1, SAFI=132), or simply RT.

The format of this NLRI is simply *<AS>:<Route Target>*.

RTC—Signaling

When all the iBGP sessions in the SP network negotiate the RT address family, the first thing the peers do is to exchange RT prefixes:

- RRs advertise an RT default prefix 0:0:0/0, which simply means: *send me all your VPN routes.*

- PEs walk through their VRF import policies and, for each matching RT, they send to the RRs a specific RT prefix (e.g., AS:65000:1001), which means: *if you have a VPN route with this RT (65000:1001), send the route to me.*

Example 3-40 shows the RT prefix exchange between PE1 and RR1, illustrated in the left half of Figure 3-6. PE1 has two VRFs locally configured: VRF-A (with RT 65000:1001) and VRF-B (with RT 65000:1002).

Example 3-40. RTC—prefix exchange (Junos)

```
juniper@PE1> show route receive-protocol bgp 172.16.0.201 table bgp.rtarget.0

bgp.rtarget.0: 3 destinations, 4 routes [...]
  Prefix         Nexthop        MED   Lclpref   AS path
* 0:0:0/0        172.16.0.201         100       I

juniper@PE1> show route advertising-protocol bgp 172.16.0.201 table bgp.rtarget.0

bgp.rtarget.0: 3 destinations, 4 routes [...]
  Prefix               Nexthop   MED   Lclpref   AS path
* 65000:65000:1001/96  Self      100     I
* 65000:65000:1002/96  Self      100     I
```

 RT routes are *not* readvertised, so RRs do not reflect them.

Then, the PEs send all their VPN routes to the RRs. Junos PEs only do it if they have previously received a matching RT prefix (which can be 0:0:0/0) from the BGP peer. Conversely, IOS XR PEs do it spontaneously. So the default RT route—advertised by the RRs—is particularly important for Junos PEs, but not so much for IOS XR PEs.

The *VPN* routes are distributed in a conservative manner. Why do RRs reflect the 172.16.0.44:10.2.34.0/24 route to PE1? Because PE1 had previously expressed its interest to receive VPN routes with RT 65000:1001.

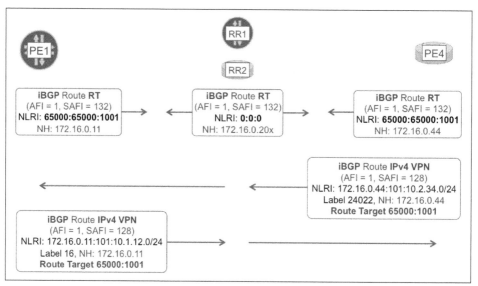

Figure 3-6. Route Target Constraint

This mechanism ensures that PEs only receive the VPN routes that they are interested in: nothing more, nothing less. Also, every time a VRF is added, removed, or modified at PE1, its RT routes are updated accordingly, potentially triggering tailored VPN route updates from the RRs. There is no need for a full route refresh anymore. And the same reasoning applies to PE2, too.

Note that the term VPN (and not L3VPN) has been used intentionally. RT routes are not bound to any particular type of VPN NLRI. Indeed, RTC is a conceptually universal mechanism. In Junos, every VPN NLRI supports RTC. In IOS XR, as of this writing, IPv4 and IPv6 Unicast VPN (SAFI=128) NLRIs support RTC.

RTC—RR Configuration

Following is the Junos RR additional configuration:

Example 3-41. RTC configuration at RR1 (Junos)

```
protocols {
    bgp {
        group CLIENTS {
            family route-target advertise-default;
}}}
```

Here is the equivalent for IOS XR PE:

Example 3-42. RTC configuration at RR2 (IOS XR)

```
router bgp 65000
 address-family ipv4 rt-filter
 !
 neighbor-group CLIENTS
  address-family ipv4 rt-filter
   default-originate
!
```

The `ipv4` notation is due to the fact that RT NLRI has AFI=1. But RT prefixes also determine the distribution of non-IPv4 VPN routes such as IPv6 Unicast VPN.

Remember that RT prefixes are not reflected. Also, there is no need to negotiate the RT NLRI on the inter-RR iBGP sessions.

RTC—PE Configuration

The following example provides the Junos PE additional configuration:

Example 3-43. RTC configuration at PE1 (Junos)

```
1    protocols {
2        bgp group iBGP-RR family route-target;
3    }
4    routing-options {
5        rib inet.3 {
6            static {
7                route 172.16.0.201/32 discard;
8                route 172.16.0.202/32 discard;
9    }}}
```

RRs advertise an RT default prefix whose BGP next hop equals the RR's local loopback (172.16.0.201 or 172.16.0.202). In this example, the RRs do not run any MPLS protocols, so their loopbacks are missing from the PE1's inet.3 routing table. Without the static routes in lines 4 through 8, the RT prefixes would be hidden at PE1—effectively disrupting the L3VPN service.

Alternatively, you can configure: `set routing-options resolution rib bgp.rtarget.0 resolution-ribs [ inet.3 inet.0 ]`.

Finally, Example 3-44 shows here is the additional configuration at an IOS XR PE.

Example 3-44. RTC configuration at PE2 (IOS XR)

```
router bgp 65000
 address-family ipv4 rt-filter
 !
 neighbor-group RR
```

```
address-family ipv4 rt-filter
!
```

 The RT static route concept is explored in Chapter 9.

Coupling MPLS Services to Transport Planes

Every MPLS service has its own requirements. Let's suppose that you want to do the following:

- Transport high-volume Internet traffic through a set (#1) of core RSVP-TE LSPs that take the available bandwidth and the actual link utilization into account. In this way (fully covered in Chapter 14) you can minimize packet loss by avoiding situations in which some links are underutilized, whereas others are saturated.

- Transport low-volume VPN traffic by following the IGP. This traffic does not contribute to link bandwidth significantly, and the shortest path is preferred. For this service, LDP or node-SID SPRING are perfectly fine transport alternatives.

- Transport the traffic from critical VPNs—or specific flows within these VPNs—with a new set (#2) of RSVP-TE LSPs that have fast restoration paths; and you don't want the Internet traffic to use these LSPs.

The solution is to define three loopback addresses on every LSR and LER:

- Loopback address A is reachable through RSVP-TE LSPs named with suffix PLANE_A. Internet BGP routes have their iBGP next hop set to this address.

- Loopback address B is advertised as a FEC in LDP. Most VPN routes have their iBGP next hop set to this address.

- Loopback address C is reachable through RSVP-TE LSPs named with suffix PLANE_C. Certain VPN routes have their iBGP next hop set to this address.

Let's see how to configure several global loopback addresses, how to bind them to RSVP-TE LSPs or LDP FECs, and how to change the iBGP next hop.

Configuring Several Loopbacks in the Default Instance

Junos supports a maximum of one loopback IFL per instance. You can configure several IPv4 addresses on the same unit as follows:

Example 3-45. Multiple global loopback address—PE1 (Junos)

```
interfaces {
    lo0 {
        family inet {
            address 172.16.0.11/32 primary;
            address 172.16.1.11/32;
            address 172.16.2.11/32;
}}}
```

These are loopback addresses A, B, and C mentioned previously. The router ID is better set explicitly to the primary loopback address A.

IOS XR provides two options: either configuring several loopback interfaces, or configuring several addresses on the same interface. Let's look at the first option:

Example 3-46. Multiple global loopback address—PE4 (Junos)

```
interface Loopback0
 ipv4 address 172.16.0.44 255.255.255.255
 ipv4 address 172.16.1.44 255.255.255.255 secondary
 ipv4 address 172.16.2.44 255.255.255.255 secondary
 !
```

Signaling LSPs to Different Loopback Addresses

Let's carry on with the example, this time focusing on the signaling and forwarding between PE1 and PE4. From PE1's perspective, the remote PE is PE4, and vice versa.

Plane A—RSVP-TE LSPs to the remote PE's router ID

These are the two RSVP-TE LSPs signaled on plane A: PE1→PE4_PLANE-A and PE4→PE1_PLANE-A. They have as a destination the remote PE's loopback address A.

By default, Junos only installs a route to the RSVP-TE LSP destination (to address) in the inet.3 routing table. This is exactly what we want in this case.

Example 3-47. RSVP-TE LSP plane A, rooted at PE1 (Junos)

```
protocols {
    mpls {
        label-switched-path PE1--->PE4_PLANE-A {
            to 172.16.0.44;
}}}
```

As for IOS XR, by default there is no prefix bound to a RSVP-TE LSP. Indeed, auto route is not turned on by default; you must configure it explicitly.

Now, the autoroute announce feature automatically uses the RSVP-TE LSPs as a next hop for all the destinations that are at or *behind* the tail end. So, PE4's CEF sees the three PE1's loopback IP addresses as reachable via the PE4→PE1_PLANE_A LSP. This is not what you want in this scenario, and the solution is not to use autoroute announce. There are several alternative methods for coupling prefixes to a LSP. One option is to use static routes, but it is much better to use a dynamic method that takes the IGP metric into account: this is the autoroute **destination** feature.

Example 3-48. RSVP-TE LSP plane A, rooted at PE4 (IOS XR)

```
1    interface tunnel-te1101
2    ipv4 unnumbered Loopback 0
3    signalled-name PE4--->PE1_PLANE-A
4    autoroute destination 172.16.0.11
5    !
6    destination 172.16.0.11
7    record-route
8    path-option 1 dynamic
9    !
```

It is line 4, not line 6, that determines what is installed at PE4's CEF. In this case, PE4 sees only one prefix as reachable via PE4→PE1_PLANE_A: 172.16.0.11.

 The IOS XR autoroute announce feature is equivalent to Junos' shortcuts, which are briefly described in Chapter 16.

Plane B—controlling LDP label bindings

The two vendors covered by this book have a different default behavior:

- Junos PE1 only advertises a label mapping for one local FEC: its primary loopback address (A). As for remote FECs, it uses the *ordered* label distribution control mode, which means that it only advertises label mappings for those remote FECs for which it has already received label mappings from the downstream LSR.

- IOS XR advertises a label mapping for all the local and remote (IGP) FECs in independent mode. This means that PE2, P2, and PE4 advertise a label mapping for all the loopback addresses (A, B, and C) of all the PEs, including PE1 and PE4.

Is the default implementation a valid one in this scenario? Let's focus on plane A first.

In both Junos and IOS XR, if a remote FEC is reachable via a RSVP-TE LSP and via LDP label mappings, RSVP-TE is preferred. So RSVP-TE LSPs PE1→PE4_PLANE_A and PE4→PE1_PLANE_A take precedence over LDP. Only if the RSVP-TE LSPs cannot be signaled, for whatever reason, does LDP act as a fallback mechanism.

But this might not be your preferred option. Suppose that all the LSRs in the network are capable of IP routing Internet packets in the global instance. Although this scenario deviates from the first classical MPLS use case, it is a common practice in international carriers because it provides hop-by-hop control. In this case, you might prefer the fallback mechanism in plane A—dedicated in this example to the Internet service—*not* to be LDP, but hop-by-hop classical (unlabeled) IP routing. In this case, it is necessary to filter loopback address A out of LDP advertisements.

As for plane B, Junos P1 only advertises a label mapping for PE1's loopback address B if it has previously received the corresponding label mapping from PE1.

Finally, let's assume that LDP is a desirable fallback mechanism for plane C. Putting this all together, LDP must advertise label mappings for planes B and C, but not for plane A.

Following is the required configuration at Junos PE1:

Example 3-49. Controlling LDP label bindings for Local FECs—PE1 (Junos)

```
1      protocols {
2          ldp egress-policy PL-LDP-EGRESS;
3      }
4      policy-options {
5          policy-statement PL-LDP-EGRESS {
6              term LOOPBACK-B-C {
7                  from {
8                      route-filter 172.16.1.11/32;
9                      route-filter 172.16.2.11/32;
10                 }
11                 then accept;
12             }
13             term REST {
14                 then reject;
15     }}}
```

Junos PE3 needs a similar configuration—just by adapting lines 8 and 9 to its local addressing—and P1 does not require any additional changes.

The required configuration on *all* the IOS XR core routers (PE2, P2, and PE4) is shown in Example 3-50.

Example 3-50. Controlling LDP label bindings—IOS XR

```
mpls ldp
 address-family ipv4
  label
```

```
    local
      allocate for ALL-LOCAL-PLANE-B-C
 !
ipv4 access-list AL-LOCAL-PLANE-B-C
 10 permit ipv4 172.16.1.0 0.0.0.255 any
 20 permit ipv4 172.16.2.0 0.0.0.255 any
 30 deny ipv4 any any
 !
```

Plane C—RSVP-TE LSPs to a secondary loopback address

These are the two RSVP-TE LSPs signaled on plane C: PE1→PE4_PLANE-C and PE4→PE1_PLANE-C. They are coupled to the remote PE's loopback address C.

 In both Junos and IOS XR, by default a RSVP-TE LSP must be targeted to the tail end's router ID. In this scenario, this is loopback address A. You can relax this requirement in Junos with the inter-domain knob.

Taking into account this boundary condition, here is the configuration at PE1:

Example 3-51. RSVP-TE LSP plane C, rooted at PE1 (Junos)

```
1     protocols {
2         mpls {
3             label-switched-path PE1--->PE4_PLANE-C {
4                 to 172.16.0.44;
5                 no-install-to-address;
6                 install 172.16.2.44;
7     }}}
```

With the previous configuration, the LSP is a next hop for the 172.16.2.44/32 route (line 6) at PE1's inet.3 table. But it is not a next hop for 172.16.0.44/32 (line 5).

Here is the IOS XR configuration at PE4.

Example 3-52. RSVP-TE LSP plane C, rooted at PE4 (IOS XR)

```
1     interface tunnel-te1103
2      ipv4 unnumbered Loopback 0
3      signalled-name PE4--->PE1_PLANE-C
4      autoroute destination 172.16.2.11
5      !
6      destination 172.16.0.11
7      record-route
8      path-option 1 dynamic
9      !
```

It is line 4, not line 6, that determines what is installed at PE4's CEF. In this case, PE4 sees only one prefix as reachable via PE4→PE1_PLANE_C: 172.16.2.11.

There is an interesting implementation difference between Junos install and IOS XR autoroute destination. Junos calculates the 172.16.2.44/32 FEC metric as the shortest IGP path to the LSP's tail end (172.16.0.44). IOS XR, on the other hand, calculates it as the shortest IGP path to the FEC itself (172.16.2.11, not 172.16.0.11).

In this example, there is no difference because the FEC is local to the LSP's tail end. But there are other use cases of this technique—mainly Traffic Engineering—for which the LSP's tail end may be en route to the FEC; however, the FEC is still one or more hops beyond. In this case, the previous implementation difference is relevant. There is a way to make Junos use the FEC metric—based on LDP tunneling and LDP policies—but it is beyond the scope of this book.

Changing the Service Routes' BGP Next Hop

Now that there are three transport planes, let's couple the services to them according to the previously stated requirements. No change is required on plane A, because the BGP next-hop self (NHS) action automatically picks the primary loopback address (A).

Let's see plane B in Junos:

- If PE1 advertises IP VPN prefixes directly from the VRF (this topic was further discussed earlier in this chapter), the way to go is making the VRF export policy execute a then next-hop 172.16.1.11 action.

- If PE1 advertises IP VPN prefixes from the main IP VPN table, the then next-hop 172.16.1.11 action must be applied at the iBGP-RR group export policy, where you can also match the RTs in order to achieve a good granularity. Don't forget in this case to configure vpn-apply-export under the group, too.

Example 3-53 shows the procedure in IOS XR.

Example 3-53. Changing BGP next hop for L3VPN routes—PE4 (IOS XR)

```
1    router bgp 65000
2     neighbor-group RR
3      address-family vpnv4 unicast
4       route-policy PL-VRF-NH-CHANGE out
5      !
6      address-family vpnv6 unicast
7       route-policy PL-VRF-A-NH-CHANGE out
8     !
9    route-policy PL-VRF-NH-CHANGE
10     if extcommunity rt matches-any RT-VPN-A then
```

```
11        set next-hop 172.16.1.44
12      endif
13      pass
14    end-policy
15    !
16    extcommunity-set rt RT-VPN-A
17      65000:1001
18    end-set
19    !
```

For IPv6 Unicast VPN prefixes (line 6), the next hop changes to ::ffff:172.16.1.44 even if it's configured to be 172.16.1.44. Good!

The approach for plane C is identical, except that further per-prefix granularity may be configured in the policies.

## CHAPTER 4

Internet Multicast Over MPLS

This chapter describes Global Internet Multicast, as opposed to Chapter 5, which focuses on Multicast VPN. Let's begin with a basic multicast introduction that should also help for a better understanding of Chapter 5.

Multicast packets flow from a given source (S) to a group (G) of receivers, as compared to unicast packets, which are destined to a single receiver. The forwarding path used to transport multicast is typically modeled as a tree, with the source being the root and the receivers sitting at the leaves. In a *multicast tree*, the routers replicate the traffic at the branching points. The traffic flows from the root to the leaves, like sap in a tree. In that sense, the terms upstream and downstream defy gravity: take a picture of a tree and turn it upside down, with the root on top and the leaves at the bottom, and let the traffic flow down. With this image in mind it's easier to understand why, in multicast land, upstream means toward the root (source) and downstream is toward the leaves (receivers). Multicast packets flow downstream in a point-to-multipoint manner.

Let's get back to reality after this short imagination twister. In a nutshell, multicast technologies make it possible for a network to replicate one single packet to multiple destinations. A popular and typical multicast application is IP Television (IPTV), whereby many residential and mobile users can be watching the same live channel at the same time. If the source had to replicate and produce thousands or millions of copies for each packet, the requirements in terms of processing power and network bandwidth at the source site would be huge, not to mention the impact on latency. Fortunately, the IPTV source is typically a server (or a cluster) that sends only one copy of the multicast stream out of its network interface. But, how can this stream reach all the receivers? Multicast solves the challenge: the service provider (SP) network builds a tree that replicates the original packet, ensuring that each receiver gets one and only one copy of it. This tree performs an efficient replication at the branching points; so only one copy of each packet traverses a given network link.

There are many other multicast applications, each with different requirements. Some of them have low bit rates and strict low latency (e.g., stock-ticker data real-time distribution to trading companies, or radar signal transmission to air control operators.) Other multicast applications move high traffic volumes and have varied latency requirements, like videoconferencing, or software and media distribution to repositories and caches.

This chapter covers IPv4 multicast distribution across a MPLS core for two types of service: Internet Multicast (in the Global Routing Table) and Multicast IP VPN. Although IPv6 is not covered in depth, the configuration and mechanics are very similar.

But, before diving into the services, let's first brush up on the very basics of IP Multicast.

IP Multicast

An IP multicast flow is often represented as (S, G), where S and G are the source and destination IP addresses of the data packets, respectively:

S

> This is a *unicast* IP (v4 or v6) address, representing a single host. This host (S) is the *source* of the multicast stream.

G

> This is a *multicast* IP address, representing a *group* of hosts (receivers) interested in receiving the traffic.

What is the difference between a unicast and a multicast IP address? They both look similar, but there are well-known address ranges that are reserved for multicast:

- IPv4 multicast address range is 224/4, or 224.0.0.0 through 239.255.255.255
- IPv6 multicast address range is ff00::/8

Not all the multicast IP addresses are routable across domains. Any addresses in the 224/24 and ff02::/16 ranges are link-local and therefore are not routable. Just to provide one example, nontargeted LDP hello packets have destination IP address 224.0.0.2. For a complete list of multicast address ranges reserved for different purposes, refer to the IPv4 and IPv6 *Multicast Address Space Registry* at the IANA website.

In Ethernet Layer 2 (L2) domains, IP Multicast packets are encapsulated inside an Ethernet header. The network interface card that introduces the frame into the L2 domain simply copies its own MAC address into the Source MAC address field of the frame's Ethernet header; that's Ethernet business as usual. The destination MAC address is special, though:

IPv4 Multicast

> Address Resolution Protocol (ARP) plays no role here. The last 23 bits of the IPv4 Multicast address are appended to the 01:00:5e MAC prefix in order to make up a destination MAC address. For example, IPv4 packets destined to 232.1.2.3 are encapsulated in an Ethernet header with destination MAC address 01:00:5e:01:02:03.

IPv6 Multicast

> Neighbor Discovery (ND) plays no role here. The last 32 bits of the IPv6 Multicast address are appended to the 33:33 MAC prefix. For example, IPv6 packets destined to ff3e::0001:0203 have destination MAC address 33:33:00:01:02:03.

There is actually something in common between the 01:00:5e and 33:33 prefixes. The last bit of the first octet is set to 1 in both cases. In Ethernet, any frame with that bit set to 1 is considered to be a (not necessarily IP) *multicast frame*. Many non-IP protocols use such destination MAC addresses. For example, Intermediate System–to–Intermediate System (IS-IS) point-to-point and LAN hellos are sent to 09:00:2b: 00:00:05 and 01:80:c2:00:00:15 MAC addresses, respectively.

Likewise, in *unicast frames* the destination MAC address has the last bit of the first octet set to 0. Typically, a unicast MAC address is *dynamically* resolved via ARP (in IPv4) or ND (in IPv6); unlike multicast MAC addresses, which are *statically* calculated with the mathematical rule explained in the previous paragraphs.

IP Multicast Protocols

Multicast sources are stateless. They just send the packets out of a network interface into a local network segment. This segment might contain local receivers, and more important, also a multicast-capable router(s) called First Hop Router (FHR).

In contrast, end receivers are stateful and signal their multicast subscriptions by using a link-local protocol: *Internet Group Management Protocol* (IGMP) for IPv4 groups, and *Multicast Listener Discovery* (MLD) for IPv6 groups. Hopefully, there is a multicast-capable router locally connected to the same segment as the receivers. Such device is called a Last Hop Router (LHR), and it processes the local IGMP and MLD messages.

What if an FHR and an LHR are several hops away from each other? Well, a multicast tree must connect the FHR to the LHR, such that all the segments with local receivers can get the multicast packets. And how is such a tree signaled? This is the principal role of the *Protocol Independent Multicast* (PIM) protocol.

PIM has additional functions such as multicast source discovery, and it also provides a redundancy mechanism in topologies with several FHRs (or several LHRs) in the same segment.

IP Multicast Modes

PIM can operate in two main modes:

Sparse Mode
   In Sparse Mode (RFC 4601, standards track), receivers trigger the signaling of the multicast tree. In other words, a multicast flow is natively forwarded if, and only if, there are downstream receivers for that flow. This results in an efficient utilization of bandwidth resources.

Dense Mode
   In Dense Mode (RFC 3973, experimental track), traffic is flooded first down all the possible paths, *in case* there are receivers. Later, if there are no receivers down a given path, that branch is pruned from the multicast tree. This mode is seldom used, because it is not scalable in terms of bandwidth and signaling. Therefore, it is not covered in this book.

Inside PIM sparse mode, there are three submodes: Any Source Multicast (ASM), Source-Specific Multicast (SSM), and Bidirectional (BIDIR).

Cisco documentation often uses the Sparse Mode term to refer to ASM only. Strictly speaking, Sparse Mode is actually a superset that includes ASM, SSM, and BIDIR. This book uses the standard terminology.

Some receivers simply subscribe to a group G if they are interested in receiving all the traffic destined to the group address G, regardless of what sources are active for that group. These receivers generate a (*, G), or ASM subscription via IGMP or MLD.

Other receivers also specify the source S from which they want to receive multicast traffic. These receivers generate a (S, G), or SSM subscription via IGMP or MLD. RFC 4607 lists all the IP multicast addresses reserved for SSM usage. In the case of IPv4, the default SSM address range is 232/8, or 232.0.0.0 to 232.255.255.255. You can also configure the network to use addresses outside this range for SSM.

There is no solid border line between ASM and SSM. Even if a receiver sends an ASM (*, G) message, at some point the network might end up signaling SSM (S, G) state directly toward the source (upstream). There are several scenarios in which this happens, and you will see them later in this chapter.

Both ASM and SSM have pros and cons. Although ASM is simpler for the receiver, SSM is simpler for the network. Routers find it much easier to build a multicast tree if the sources are known beforehand than if they must discover the sources from scratch. For this reason, ASM is left for the end of Chapter 5.

In ASM and SSM, multicast trees are unidirectional: they transport traffic from sources to receivers. On the other hand, BIDIR (RFC 5015) covers a special use case for which sources can also be receivers, and vice versa. For these applications, it makes sense to build a bidirectional tree.

 This book focuses on ASM and SSM, the most common modes.

Multicast in general and PIM in particular have a lot of terminology. Instead of reviewing it all from scratch, let's introduce it gradually as the examples move along.

Classic Internet Multicast

Internet Multicast stands for the transport of global IP Multicast traffic across an SP core. The provider edges (PEs) forward the packets in the context of the Global Routing Table (GRT). In other words, there is no VPN involved in this service. On the other hand, *Classical* implies MPLS-free: the starting point is hence very similar to that of Chapter 1, and the need for MPLS (or IP tunneling) will naturally show up.

Starting Multicast Sources and Receivers

Figure 4-1 shows this chapter's topology. The IS-IS metrics are initially configured as follows: value 15 for the PE1-PE2 and PE3-PE4 links, and the default value (10) on the remaining links (PE-P and P-P). This topology also has Route Reflectors (RRs) even if they are not displayed in Figure 4-1.

H1 and H2 are actively generate traffic toward SSM groups 232.1.1.1 and 232.2.2.2, respectively. Multicast receivers for both groups are spread all over the network, and they will subscribe one by one, so you can see how the multicast tree is created.

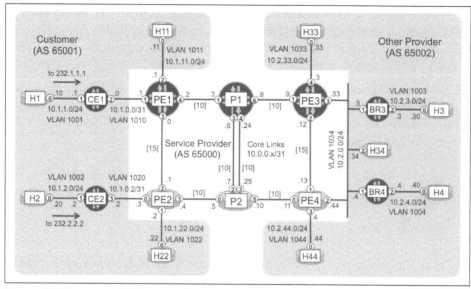

Figure 4-1. Internet Multicast topology

All the hosts are simulated within a single IOS XR device or virtual machine (VM) called H. More specifically, each host is a VRF–lite inside H.

A simple ping is enough to generate multicast traffic. Let's make host H1 send one packet per second toward 232.1.1.1, as shown in the following example:

Example 4-1. Generating IP Multicast traffic by using ping (IOS XR)

```
RP/0/0/CPU0:H#ping vrf H1 232.1.1.1 source 10.1.1.10
               count 100000 timeout 1
Type escape sequence to abort.
Sending 100000, 100-byte ICMP Echos to 232.1.1.1, timeout is 0s:
.............[...]
```

If you generate multicast packets from a Junos device, ensure that you use the bypass-routing, interface, and ttl ping options.

The previous ping fails. That's expected given that there are no receivers yet: just let the ping run continuously in the background.

Next, let's turn some hosts into dynamic multicast receivers. Here is a sample configuration for receiving host H11 at device H:

Example 4-2. Multicast receiver at H11 (IOS XR)

```
router igmp
 vrf H11
  interface GigabitEthernet0/0/0/0.1011
   join-group 232.1.1.1 10.1.1.10
!
```

This makes H11 begin to send dynamic IGMP Report messages, effectively subscribing to the (S, G) = (10.1.1.10, 232.1.1.1) flow. Let's assume that H3, H4, H22, H33, H34, and H44 (in other words, every host except for H2) also subscribe to the same (S, G) flow.

Strictly speaking, the previous example is incomplete. For IOS XR to simulate a multicast end receiver, the interface must be turned on at the `multicast-routing` level first, and this has some implications.

> In Junos, this dynamic receiver emulation feature is only available in the ASM mode (`protocols sap listen <group>`). Additionally, both Junos and IOS XR support *static* subscriptions—ASM and SSM—at the receiver-facing interface of an LHR.

Signaling the Multicast Tree

After multicast sources and receivers are active, it's time to signal the multicast tree. And for that, CEs and PEs need to run the multicast protocols shown here:

Example 4-3. Multicast routing configuration at PE1 (Junos)

```
protocols {
    igmp {
        interface ge-2/0/2.1011 version 3;
    pim {
        interface ge-2/0/2.1011;
        interface ge-2/0/1.1010;
}}
```

A similar configuration is applied to PE3, CE1, CE2, BR3, and BR4. For the moment, only the access (PE-H, PE-CE, and CE-H) interfaces are configured.

By default in Junos, an interface configured for PIM automatically runs IGMP on it, too. The default IGMP version is 2, and IGMP version 3 is required to process (S, G) Reports.

PIM is a router-to-router protocol, so strictly speaking the receiver-facing interface ge-2/0/2.1011 does not really need PIM. IGMP is enough on the last-hop interface. However, H11 might become a multicast sender at some point. Furthermore, as you will see soon in this chapter, enabling PIM on all of the router's IP multicast access interfaces is considered a good practice for potential redundancy and loop detection.

The multicast traffic now flows end to end, thanks to the protocol exchange illustrated in Figure 4-2.

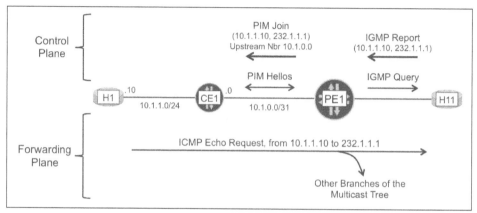

Figure 4-2. IGMP and PIM in action (SSM model)

Let's look at the multicast routing configuration in IOS XR:

Example 4-4. Multicast routing configuration at PE2 (IOS XR)

```
multicast-routing
 address-family ipv4
  interface GigabitEthernet0/0/0/0.1020
   enable
  interface GigabitEthernet0/0/0/1.1022
   enable
```

The previous configuration actually enables PIM and IGMP on the specified PE-CE and PE-H interfaces.

IGMP signaling

The multicast tree is signaled in the upstream direction, from the receivers to the source. Let's begin with the tree branch whose leaf is H11. The following capture, taken at PE1, shows the IGMP packet exchange between PE1 and H11.

Example 4-5. IGMP query (from PE1) and report (from H11)

```
juniper@PE1> monitor traffic interface ge-2/0/2.1011 no-resolve
              size 2000 extensive matching igmp
<timestamp> Out
  -----original packet-----
  00:50:56:8b:32:4a > 01:00:5e:00:00:01, ethertype 802.1Q (0x8100),
  length 54: vlan 1011, p 6, ethertype IPv4, (tos 0xc0, ttl 1,
  id 20138, offset 0, flags [none], proto: IGMP (2), length: 36,
  optlength: 4 ( RA )) 10.1.11.1 > 224.0.0.1: igmp query v3

<timestamp> In
  -----original packet-----
  IP (tos 0xc0, ttl 1, id 2772, offset 0, flags [none], proto: IGMP (2), length: 76,
  optlength: 4 ( RA )) 10.1.11.11 > 224.0.0.22: igmp v3 report [...]
  [gaddr 232.1.1.1 is_in { 10.1.1.10 }]
```

PE1 sends the IGMP Query to 224.0.0.1, the *all-hosts* link-local multicast address. H11 replies with an IGMP Report destined to 224.0.0.22, the *all-IGMPv3-routers* address. The information about the (S, G) subscriptions is in the payload of the IGMP Report.

Reverse Path Forwarding

PE1 further processes the IGMP Report by looking at the S address (10.1.1.10) and performing a unicast IP route lookup. This process of looking up the source is called *Reverse Path Forwarding* (RPF) and it's a central concept in the multicast world.

Example 4-6. RPF at PE1 (Junos)

```
juniper@PE1> show route active-path 10.1.1.10

inet.0: 44 destinations, 53 routes (44 active, 0 holddown, 0 hidden)
+ = Active Route, - = Last Active, * = Both

10.1.1.0/24        *[BGP/170] 02:32:51, MED 100, localpref 100
                      AS path: 65001 I, validation-state: unverified
                    > to 10.1.0.0 via ge-2/0/1.1010

juniper@PE1> show multicast rpf 10.1.1.10
Multicast RPF table: inet.0 , 44 entries

10.1.1.0/24
    Protocol: BGP
    Interface: ge-2/0/1.1010
    Neighbor: 10.1.0.0
```

In a nutshell, multicast packets that arrive at the non-RPF interface are discarded.

By default, the unicast IP route lookup and the RPF lookup provide exactly the same result. The unicast and multicast topologies are then said to be *congruent*. If you want to make the unicast and multicast traffic follow different paths, it is also possible to make the topologies *noncongruent*. This is further discussed at the end of Chapter 5.

PIM signaling

CE1 and PE1 exchange PIM hello packets destined to 224.0.0.13, the *all-PIM-routers* link-local multicast address. Through that exchange, they become PIM neighbors.

Example 4-7. PIM neighbors at PE1 (Junos)

```
juniper@PE1> show pim neighbors
B = Bidirectional Capable, G = Generation Identifier
H = Hello Option Holdtime, L = Hello Option LAN Prune Delay,
P = Hello Option DR Priority, T = Tracking Bit

Instance: PIM.master
Interface         IP V Mode  Option   Uptime   Neighbor addr
ge-2/0/1.1010      4 2       HPLGT    02:40:25 10.1.0.0
```

From the perspective of PE1, the PIM neighbor CE1 is also the RPF upstream neighbor *en route* to the source. So, PE1 sends a PIM (S, G) Join message upstream to CE1:

Example 4-8. PIM (S, G) Join state from PE1 to CE1 (Junos)

```
juniper@PE1> show pim join inet detail
Instance: PIM.master Family: INET
R = Rendezvous Point Tree, S = Sparse, W = Wildcard

Group: 232.1.1.1
    Source: 10.1.1.10
    Flags: sparse,spt
    Upstream interface: ge-2/0/1.1010
    Downstream neighbors:
        Interface: ge-2/0/2.1011
```

The PIM (S, G) Join is actually a PIM Join/Prune packet. These messages contain a Join (*add a branch*) list, and a Prune (*cut a branch*) list. In this example, the receiver is turned on, so PE1 sends the Join/Prune packet with an empty Prune list. Such a PIM Join/Prune packet is commonly called a PIM Join. Example 4-9 shows the packet in detail.

Example 4-9. PIM (S, G) Join Packet from PE1 to CE1 (Junos)

```
juniper@PE1> monitor traffic interface ge-2/0/1.1010 no-resolve
             size 2000 detail matching pim
<timestamp> Out IP (tos 0xc0, ttl 1, id 36704, offset 0, no flags,
```

```
proto: PIM (103), length: 54) 10.1.0.1 > 224.0.0.13
  Join / Prune, cksum 0xd6dc (correct), upstream-neighbor: 10.1.0.0
    1 group(s), holdtime: 3m30s
      group #1: 232.1.1.1, joined sources: 1, pruned sources: 0
        joined source #1: 10.1.1.10(S)
```

IGMP and PIM are hence *soft-state* protocols. In the IP Multicast world, all of the protocol messages (IGMP Query and Report, PIM Hello and Join/Prune, etc.) are refreshed periodically. By default, PIM Hello and Join/Prune are refreshed every 10 and 60 seconds, respectively.

As you can see, PIM messages are encapsulated as IP packets with protocol #103 and destination IP address 224.0.0.13. Because it is a link-local multicast IPv4 address, all of the PIM routers in the same VLAN would also process the packet. PE1 only has one neighbor in VLAN 1010, but what if there were more neighbors in the broadcast domain? How can PE1 indicate that the message is actually targeted to CE1? It does this via the *upstream neighbor* field in the PIM payload.

But, why is the PIM Join message sent to 224.0.0.13 if it's targeted to CE1 only? PIM in a LAN is a complex topic and in some cases it is important that all the neighboring PIM routers LAN have full visibility of all the message exchanges. This prevents undesired traffic blackouts and duplication.

Multicast forwarding

Finally, CE1 is the FHR and after receiving the PIM Join/Prune packet, it just needs to forward the multicast traffic down to PE1, as shown in the following example:

Example 4-10. Multicast forwarding state at CE1 (Junos)

```
juniper@CE1> show multicast route inet detail
Instance: master Family: INET

Group: 232.1.1.1
    Source: 10.1.1.10/32
    Upstream interface: ge-0/0/1.1001
    Downstream interface list:
        ge-0/0/2.1010
    Session description: Source specific multicast
    Statistics: 0 kBps, 1 pps, 6064 packets
[...]
```

This multicast route is not really a *route*. It is more accurately viewed as a forwarding cache entry.

Now that the source (H1) and the receiver (H11) are connected via the multicast tree, the multicast ping is successful: every echo request sent from H1 to 232.1.1.1 has one reply back, coming from H11 (10.1.11.11). If you don't see the replies, you might be facing a corner-case condition in the dynamic receiver implementation: try to restart it by deleting and applying again the `router igmp vrf H11` configuration at H (in two commits).

Classic Internet Multicast—Connecting Multicast Islands Across the Core

The tree now has one root (H1), one leaf (H11), and one single branch connecting them.

One-hop transit through the core (PE1-PE2)

Let's add two more leaves to the tree:

- H22 sends an IGMP (S, G) Report to PE2.
- H2 sends an IGMP (S, G) Report to CE2, which sends a PIM (S, G) Join to PE2.

As a result, PE2 has the multicast (S, G) state depicted in the following example:

Example 4-11. Multicast RIB (IOS XR)

```
RP/0/0/CPU0:PE2#show mrib route 232.1.1.1
[...]
IP Multicast Routing Information Base
(10.1.1.10,232.1.1.1) RPF nbr: 0.0.0.0 Flags: RPF
  Up: 01:26:05
  Outgoing Interface List
    GigabitEthernet0/0/0/0.1020 Flags: F NS, Up: 01:26:00
    GigabitEthernet0/0/0/1.1022 Flags: F NS LI, Up: 01:26:05
```

The (S, G) entry is installed in PE2's Multicast RIB (MRIB), but unfortunately the RPF neighbor is 0.0.0.0. In other words, RPF has failed. as shown in Example 4-12.

Example 4-12. Failed RPF at PE2 (IOS XR)

```
RP/0/0/CPU0:PE2#show pim rpf

Table: IPv4-Unicast-default
* 10.1.1.10/32 [200/100]
    via Null with rpf neighbor 0.0.0.0
```

Actually, PE2 has a valid BGP route toward 10.1.1.10, and its BGP next hop (172.16.0.11) is reachable via interface Gi 0/0/0/2. Why does RPF fail? Because PIM is not enabled in the core, so PE1 and PE2 are not PIM neighbors of each other.

In this classic MPLS-free example, the next step is enabling PIM on the core interfaces. When this is done, the new receivers are successfully connected to the source.

Example 4-13. Successful RPF at PE2 (IOS XR)

```
RP/0/0/CPU0:PE2#show pim neighbor GigabitEthernet 0/0/0/2
[...]
Neighbor Address  Interface              Uptime    Expires  DR pri

10.0.0.0          GigabitEthernet0/0/0/2 00:00:20  00:01:25 1
10.0.0.1*         GigabitEthernet0/0/0/2 00:00:20  00:01:26 1 (DR)

RP/0/0/CPU0:PE2#show pim rpf

Table: IPv4-Unicast-default
* 10.1.1.10/32 [200/100]
    via GigabitEthernet0/0/0/2 with rpf neighbor 10.0.0.0

RP/0/0/CPU0:PE2#show mrib route 232.1.1.1
[...]
(10.1.1.10,232.1.1.1) RPF nbr: 10.0.0.0 Flags: RPF
  Up: 01:50:26
  Incoming Interface List
    GigabitEthernet0/0/0/2 Flags: A, Up: 00:01:13
  Outgoing Interface List
    GigabitEthernet0/0/0/0.1020 Flags: F NS, Up: 01:50:21
    GigabitEthernet0/0/0/1.1022 Flags: F NS LI, Up: 01:50:26
```

At this point, the multicast tree has three leaves (H11, H22, and H2) connected to the root (H1), so the multicast ping receives three replies per request, as shown in Example 4-14.

Example 4-14. Successful multicast ping with three receivers

```
RP/0/0/CPU0:H#ping vrf H1 232.1.1.1 source 10.1.1.10 count 100000
Type escape sequence to abort.
Sending 100000, 100-byte ICMP Echos to 232.1.1.1, timeout is 2s:

Reply to request 0 from 10.1.11.11, 1 ms
Reply to request 0 from 10.1.2.20, 1 ms
Reply to request 0 from 10.1.22.22, 1 ms
Reply to request 1 from 10.1.11.11, 9 ms
Reply to request 1 from 10.1.2.20, 9 ms
Reply to request 1 from 10.1.22.22, 1 ms
[...]
```

One single copy of each packet traverses each link, including the PE1→PE2 connection. There are two replication stages: one at PE1, and another one at PE2.

With respect to the (10.1.1.10, 232.1.1.1) flow, PE1 and PE2 are popularly called *sender PE* and *receiver PE*, respectively. This is a per-flow role: one given PE can be a source PE for some flows, and a receiver PE for others. PE1 is not considered as a receiver PE even if it has a local receiver (H11), because the flow is not arriving from the core.

 In this chapter and in Chapter 5, the following terms are equivalent: root PE, ingress PE, and sender PE. Similarly, these terms are also synonyms: leaf PE, egress PE, and receiver PE.

Two-hop transit through the core (PE1-P1-PE3)

Let's add one more leaf: H33. The LHR is now PE3, which as a PE has complete visibility of the customer BGP routes. Thanks to that, PE3 successfully performs an RPF lookup toward the source (10.1.1.10) and sends a PIM (S, G) Join to its upstream PIM neighbor: P1. So far, so good. However, P1 as a pure P-router does not have visibility of the BGP routes, so it fails to perform RPF toward the multicast source:

Example 4-15. Failed RPF at P1 (Junos)

```
juniper@P1> show route 10.1.1.10

inet.0: 33 destinations, 33 routes (33 active, 0 holddown, 0 hidden)
+ = Active Route, - = Last Active, * = Both

0.0.0.0/0          *[Static/5] 2w2d 05:08:19
                        Discard

juniper@P1> show pim join inet
Instance: PIM.master Family: INET
R = Rendezvous Point Tree, S = Sparse, W = Wildcard

Group: 232.1.1.1
    Source: 10.1.1.10
    Flags: sparse,spt
    Upstream interface: unknown (no neighbor)
```

But, how did the H2 and H22 receivers manage to join the multicast tree rooted at H1? Because the multicast branches that connects the root to H2 and H22 do not traverse any P-routers. Conversely, connecting H1 and H33 can be done only through a P-router; hence, the failure to signal the multicast branch end-to-end for H33.

How can you solve this problem? Actually, there are many ways—probably too many! Let's see the different qualitative approaches to this challenge.

Signaling Join State Between Remote PEs

RPF failure in a transit router is a very similar problem to the classical one that motivated MPLS in Chapter 1. Now, it does not impact the forwarding of unicast data packets, but the propagation of PIM (S, G) Join states. The source S is an *external* unicast prefix that belongs to a different AS and is not reachable through the IGP. Chapter 1 proposed several ways to solve the unicast forwarding problem (without redistributing the external routes into the IGP), and all of them consisted of tunneling the user data packets. But here in the multicast case, it is the PIM (S, G) Join (a *control* packet), not the user data traffic, that needs to be tunneled. This opens the door to a more diverse set of design choices. Following are some possible strategies to *signal Join state between remote PEs.*

This section focuses on the ways to solve RPF failures on transit routers. The discussion is independent of the service, which can be either Global Internet Multicast or Multicast VPN (MVPN). In practice, some of the approaches that follow are only implemented for MVPN.

Carrier IP Multicast Flavors

So let's move from Classical IP Multicast to Carrier IP Multicast, which has tunneling capabilities in order to solve the multihop core challenge.

Table 4-1 lists six of the many dimensions that the multicast universe has.

Table 4-1. Carrier Multicast Flavors

Service	Global Internet Multicast (S1), Multicast VPN (S2)
C-Multicast Architecture	None (A0), Direct Inter-PE (A1), Hop-by-Hop Inter-PE (A2), Out-of-Band (A3)
C-Multicast Inter-PE Signaling Protocol	None (C0), PIM (C1), LDP (C2), BGP (C3)
P-Tunnel Encapsulation	None (E0), GRE over IP Unicast (E1), GRE over IP Multicast (E2), MPLS (E3)
P-Tunnel Signaling Protocol	None (T0), PIM (T1), LDP (T2), RSVP-TE (T3), Routing Protocol with MPLS Extensions (T4)
P-Tunnel Layout	None (Y0), P2P (Y1), MP2P (Y2), P2MP (Y3), MP2MP (Y4)

The C- and P- prefixes stand for customer and provider, respectively. The classic IP Multicast model is purely C-Multicast. Conversely, Carrier IP Multicast models also have P- dimensions.

Every carrier multicast flavor has at least one element from each dimension. As you can imagine, not all the combinations make sense and each vendor supports only a subset of them. Although this book focuses on the combinations supported both by Junos and IOS XR, for completeness, noninteroperable combinations are also briefly discussed.

Print a copy of Table 4-1 and keep it as a reference as you read this book's multicast chapters.

There are two types of *service*, depending on whether the multicast routing is performed on the global routing table or on a VRF. This chapter focuses on global services but it tactically borrows some examples that are only implemented for Multicast VPN.

This book considers three C-Multicast *architectures*:

- In the Direct Inter-PE (A1) model, PE1 and PE3 establish a C-PIM adjacency through a bi-directional tunnel. This tunnel transports control and data C-Multicast packets.
- In the Hop-by-Hop (A2) model, PE3 converts the upstream C-PIM Join state into a *different* message that P1 can process and send to PE1, which in turn converts it into C-PIM Join state. This architecture is also known as In-Band, or Proxy.
- In the Out-of-Band (A3) model, PE3 signals the C-Join state to PE1 with a non-tunneled IP protocol. Like in the A1 model, P1 does not take any role in the C-Multicast control plane.

Don't worry if these definitions do not make much sense yet. Keep them as a reference and they should be much clearer as you continue reading.

In the terms of Table 4-1, the classic IP multicast model is: S1, A2, C1, E0, T0, Y0.

Direct Inter-PE Model—PE-to-PE PIM Adjacencies over Unicast IP Tunnels

In the terms of Table 4-1, this model is A1, C1, E1, T0, Y1. It is implemented by both Junos and IOS XR for S1 and S2.

This approach requires a unicast IP tunnel (e.g., GRE-based) between each pair of PEs. There is one PIM instance and it is running on the PEs only. This PIM context is often called C-PIM.

Let's focus on the following tunnels: PE1→PE3 and PE3→PE1. PE1 and PE3 see this pair of GRE tunnels as a point-to-point interface that interconnects the two IP Multicast islands in a transparent manner. PE1 and PE3 exchange two types of multicast traffic over the GRE tunnels:

- *Control* packets such as PIM Hello or (S, G) Join are destined to 224.0.0.13, a multicast (even if link-local, where the link is the GRE tunnel) address
- *Data* packets of the active multicast user stream (10.1.1.10→232.1.1.1)

From the point of view of the GRE tunnels, there is no distinction between Control and Data. If PE1 needs to send a (Control or Data) multicast packet to PE3 over the PE1→PE3 GRE tunnel, it adds the following headers:

- GRE header with Protocol Type = 0x0800 (IPv4).
- IPv4 header with (Source, Destination) = (172.16.0.11, 172.16.0.33). In other words, the GRE tunnel's endpoints are the primary loopback addresses of PE1 and PE3.

After receiving the tunneled packets, PE3 strips these two headers. The result is the original (Control or Data) multicast packet that PE1 had initially put into the tunnel. And the same logic applies to the packets that travel in the reverse direction: from PE3 to PE1.

How good is this model? Although you can use it in a tactical manner for limited or temporary deployments, you cannot consider it as a modern and scalable approach, for the same reasons why the Internet does not run over IP tunnels. The model is also affected by the following multicast-specific limitations:

- If PE1 has two core uplink interfaces but it needs to send a multicast data packet to 1,000 remote PEs, PE1 must replicate the packet 999 times and send each one of the 1,000 copies into a different unicast GRE tunnel. This technique is called *Ingress Replication*, and it causes inefficient bandwidth consumption. When the multicast data packets are sent into the core, the main advantage of multicast (efficient replication tree) is simply lost.
- The PEs establish PIM adjacencies through the GRE tunnels. The soft-state nature of PIM causes a periodic refresh of all the PIM packets (Hello, Join/Prune, etc.) at least once per minute. This background noise loads the control plane unnecessarily. Think for a moment on how the PEs exchange unicast routes: one BGP update through a reliable TCP connection, and that's it (no periodic route

refresh is required). In that sense, the multicast PE-to-PE protocol (PIM) is less scalable than the unicast protocol (BGP).

Whenever unicast GRE tunnels come into the multicast game, it is important to ensure that *only* the customer multicast traffic goes through them. The customer unicast traffic should travel in MPLS. This requirement for *noncongruency* is analyzed further at the end of Chapter 5.

Direct Inter-PE Model—PE-to-PE PIM Adjacencies over Multicast IP Tunnels

In the terms of Table 4-1, this model is A1, C1, E2, T1, [Y3, Y4]. It is implemented by both Junos and IOS XR for S2 only.

It is described in historic RFC 6037 - *Cisco Systems' Solution for Multicast in BGP/MPLS IP VPNs*. Most people call it *draft Rosen* because *draft-rosen-vpn-mcast* was the precursor to RFC 6037.

In draft Rosen—implemented only for IP VPNs—each PE (e.g., PE1) is the root of at least one multicast GRE tunnel per VPN, called *Multicast Distribution Tree* (MDT). Why *at least* one and not *just* one? Let's skip this question just for a moment, and think of each PE as the root of one MDT called the *default MDT*.

This model requires two different instances of PIM: C-PIM (where *C* stands for *Customer*) and P-PIM (where *P* stands for *Provider*). Note that C- and P- just represent different contexts. PIM is actually implemented in the same way—it is the same protocol after all:

- C-PIM is the *service instance* of PIM and it runs at the edge: PE-to-CE, and PE-to-PE (the latter, through the GRE tunnels). It is used to signal the end-user multicast trees, in this example (10.1.1.10→232.1.1.1). So far, the PIM context used throughout this chapter has always been C-PIM. From the point of view of C-PIM, the core is just a LAN interface that interconnects all of the PEs. The PEs simply establish PIM adjacencies over the core, as they would do over any other interface.

- P-PIM is the *transport instance* of PIM and runs on the core links only. It is used to build the Multicast GRE Provider Tunnels or P-Tunnels. The most popular P-PIM mode is SSM. One of the advantages of SSM here is that it makes Provider Group (P-G) assignment much simpler. Let's suppose that PE1 and PE3 are the roots of P-Tunnels (172.16.0.11→P-G1) and (172.16.0.33→P-G3), respectively. P-G1 and P-G3 can be different, but they could also be the same. With SSM, as long as the sources are different, the multicast trees remain distinct even if G1 equals G3. This is especially important for data MDTs, discussed later in this section.

P-PIM runs on the global routing instance (default VRF), whereas C-PIM runs on a (nondefault) VRF. So, the service is provided in the context of a VPN. And it can be the Internet Multicast service as long as it is provided within an Internet VPN.

Looking back at Table 4-1, P-PIM SSM corresponds to Y3 and P-PIM ASM to Y4.

Let's suppose that each of the PEs in the core is the root of a P-Tunnel whose SSM P-Group is 232.0.0.100—the same one for simplicity, although it could be a different P-Group per root, too. PE1 receives the following P-PIM (S1, G) Joins from its P-PIM neighbors, where S1 = 172.16.0.11 and G = 232.0.0.1:

- PE2 sends an (S1, G) Join directly to PE1.
- PE3 sends an (S1, G) Join to P1 and then P1 sends an (S1, G) Join packets to PE1.
- PE4 sends an (S1, G) Join to P2, then P2 sends an (S1, G) Join to P1, which is already sending (S1, G) Join packets to PE1.

In this way, PE1 is the root of a default MDT whose leaves are PE2, PE3, and PE4.

Likewise, PE1 is also a leaf of the remote PEs' default MDTs. Indeed, PE1 *sends* the following P-PIM Joins: (172.16.0.22, 232.0.0.100) to PE2, (172.16.0.33, 232.0.0.100) to P1 en route to PE3, and (172.16.0.44, 232.0.0.100) to P1 en route to PE4.

This process ends up establishing an all-to-all LAN-like overlay that interconnects all the PEs with one another. PEs exchange two types of C-Multicast traffic over the default MDT:

- *Control* packets like C-PIM Hello or C-PIM (S, G) Join are destined to 224.0.0.13, a multicast (even if link-local) address
- *Data* packets of the active C-Multicast user stream (10.1.1.10→232.1.1.1)

From the point of view of the default MDT, there is no distinction between Control and Data. If PE1 needs to send a (Control or Data) C-Multicast packet to its neighbors over the default MDT, PE1 adds the following headers:

- GRE header with Protocol Type = 0x0800 (IPv4)
- IPv4 header with (Source, Destination) = (172.16.0.11, 232.0.0.100)

The tunneled packets arrive at all the other PEs, which strip the two headers. The result is the original (Control or Data) C-Multicast packet that PE1 had initially put into the default MDT.

PE1 is the root of its default MDT, and can optionally be the root of one or more data MDTs. What is a *data MDT*? Suppose that PE1 is the sender PE of a high-bandwidth

C-Multicast (C-S, C-G) stream, and out of 1,000 remote PEs, only 10 of them have downstream receivers for (C-S, C-G). For bandwidth efficiency, it makes sense to signal a new MDT that is dedicated to transport that particular (C-S, C-G) only. This data MDT would only have 10 leaves: the 10 receiver PEs interested in receiving the flow.

Default and Data MDTs are often called *Inclusive* and *Selective Trees*, respectively. Inclusive Trees *include* all the possible leaves, and Selective Trees *select* a specific leaf subset.

Note that the protocols described so far (C-PIM, P-PIM SSM, and GRE) are typically not enough to auto-discover the leaves of each MDT. Additional protocols are required and deployed to achieve this autodiscovery (AD) function. Which protocols? The answer varies depending on the implementation flavor. Using Cisco terminology (as of this writing):

Rosen GRE

Default MDT with P-PIM Any Source Multicast (ASM) does not require any extra protocols, because the P-Source AD function is performed by P-PIM (source discovery in PIM ASM is discussed in Chapter 15). As for Data MDTs, they are signaled with User Datagram Protocol (UDP) packets that are exchanged in the Default MDT.

Rosen GRE with BGP AD

Default MDT with P-PIM SSM requires a new multiprotocol BGP address family for (P-S, P-G) AD. As for Data MDTs, they can be signaled either by using BGP or UDP.

Cisco documentation associates each carrier multicast flavor with a profile number. For example, Rosen GRE is MVPN Profile 0, and Rosen GRE with BGP AD is MVPN Profile 3.

Further details of Rosen GRE implementation and interoperability are beyond the scope of this book, as we're focusing on MPLS and not GRE. Let's be fair: draft Rosen has been the de facto L3 Multicast VPN technology for two decades, and it has solved the business requirements of many customers. But, as time moves on, it is being replaced by next-generation models.

Wrapping up, let's take a look at the pros and cons of this model:

- Pro: an MDT is actually a (provider) multicast tree that facilitates the efficient replication of multicast data. If PE1 has two core uplink interfaces and it needs to send a multicast data packet to 1,000 remote PEs, PE1 replicates the packet at most once and sends at most one copy of the packet out of each core uplink. Also, this model implements data MDT for an even more efficient distribution.

- Con: C-PIM in a LAN is complex and noisy. If PE3 sends a C-PIM Join to PE1, all of the other PEs in the VPN receive it and look into it. As you have seen previously, PIM Join/Prune messages are sent to 224.0.0.13 and are periodically refreshed. This makes the solution less scalable and robust in the control plane.

- Finally, this model does not provide total forwarding-plane flexibility. There are two P-Tunnel types available: PIM/GRE and MP2MP mLDP (coming next). None of them can benefit from MPLS features such as Traffic Engineering.

 Before moving on, let's first remove PIM from all of the core links because P-PIM is not needed anymore. From now on, the core is MPLS territory!

Direct Inter-PE Model—PE-PE PIM Adjacencies over MPLS Label-Switched Paths

In the terms of Table 4-1, this model is A1, C2, E3, T2, Y4. It is implemented only by IOS XR and for S2 only.

PIM is designed for bidirectional links. When R1 sends a PIM Join to R2 over link L, the multicast traffic must flow from R2 to R1 over the same link L. However, MPLS Label-Switched Paths (LSPs) are unidirectional—or are they? Actually, there is one type of LSP that is bi-directional. It is called *Multipoint-to-Multipoint LSP* (MP2MP LSP) and it's one of the two LSP types described in RFC 6388 - *Label Distribution Protocol Extensions for Point-to-Multipoint and Multipoint-to-Multipoint Label Switched Paths*. With any of these (P2MP or MP2MP) extensions, LDP is often referred to as Multipoint LDP (mLDP). Paraphrasing the RFC:

> An MP2MP LSP [...] consists of a single root node, zero or more transit nodes, and one or more Leaf LSRs acting equally as an ingress or egress LSR.

In a nutshell, MP2MP LSPs have a central (so-called *root*) LSR, where all the branches meet. The PEs sit at the leaves and exchange with their LDP neighbors two types of multipoint (MP) FEC Label Mappings: *up*, for user traffic flowing from a leaf to the root, and *down*, for user traffic flowing from the root to a leaf. From a service perspective, the MP2MP LSP emulates a bidirectional LAN interconnecting the PEs, and with no learning mechanism to reduce flooding. Any packet put in an MP2MP LSP reaches all of the leaves. In that sense, the MP2MP LSP is a Default MDT or Inclusive Tree.

As of this writing, Cisco calls this model *Rosen mLDP*, as it has many similarities to Rosen GRE. Cisco documentation uses the name *Rosen* to tag a wide variety of MVPN profiles. Some of them are similar to draft Rosen (*draft-rosen-vpn-mcast*), whereas others are not. So, this tag does not really provide a hint with respect to the underlying technology.

In both Rosen GRE and Rosen mLDP, the PEs build C-PIM adjacencies over the Default MDT. Therefore, they both rely on the implementation of *C-PIM on a LAN*. Last but not least, they both require additional mechanisms to auto-discover the leaves of Default and/or Data MDTs.

 Data MDTs are P2MP, unlike the Default MDT, which is MP2MP.

The main difference between Rosen GRE and Rosen mLDP lies in the way the C-PIM messages and C-Multicast packets are exchanged over the Default MDT: through IP or MPLS tunnels, respectively. In Rosen mLDP, C-PIM Joins are encapsulated in MPLS, and they flow in the opposite direction to C-Multicast traffic. You can compare Rosen GRE to Rosen mLDP by replacing P-PIM with LDP, and GRE with MPLS.

Neither Rosen GRE nor Rosen mLDP are further covered in this book. The first is not based on MPLS, and the second is not interoperable as of today. Both models rely on establishing PE-PE C-PIM adjacencies across the core.

Beyond the Direct Inter-PE Model—Not Establishing PE-PE PIM Adjacencies

Previous models' assessment shows that tunneling C-PIM between PEs is not particularly scalable. In the early 2000s, Juniper and Cisco began to define new frameworks to signal and transport multicast traffic across an MPLS backbone. At the time, this new set of paradigms was called Next-Generation or NG, but right now it is simply state-of-the-art technology. Although many people continue to call it NG, this book does not.

These modern frameworks leave PIM running on PE-CE and PE-Host links only. However, the PEs no longer establish C-PIM adjacencies with one another. Instead, a scalable carrier-class protocol signals inter-PE C-Multicast information. There are basically two such protocols: BGP and LDP. Both of them are capable of encoding C-Multicast state.

Out-of-Band Model

When BGP is used to signal C-Multicast Join state, the *service* and the *transport* planes are loosely coupled. Thanks to certain techniques that are described in Chapter 5, BGP virtually supports all of the dynamic P-Tunnel technologies listed in Table 4-1.

Let's consider the particular case in which LDP is the P-Tunnel signaling protocol. In the terms of Table 4-1, this model is A3, C3, E3, T2, [Y2, Y3, Y4]. The role of LDP in this case is to build the LSPs that *transport* the multicast data. BGP fully takes care of the PE-to-PE *service* C-Multicast signaling. In that sense, the service plane (BGP) is not tightly coupled to the transport plane (LDP here). BGP performs *Out-of-Band* C-Multicast signaling. This model provides great flexibility in the P-Tunnel choice, and it relies on a rich signaling mechanism, which is covered later in Chapter 5.

Hop-by-Hop Inter-PE model

When LDP is used (instead of BGP) to signal C-Multicast Join state, the *service* and the *transport* planes are tightly coupled: LDP signals both at the same time, thanks to special FEC types. This is *In-Band* C-Multicast signaling, which means that the service and the transport planes are blended.

This model is less flexible and scalable than the out-of-band architecture, but also simpler to understand, so let's use it for the first Multicast over MPLS illustrated example in this book. Finally!

Internet Multicast over MPLS with In-Band Multipoint LDP Signaling

This section illustrates the P2MP part of RFC 6826 - *Multipoint LDP In-Band Signaling for Point-to-Multipoint and Multipoint-to-Multipoint Label Switched Paths*.

In the terms of Table 4-1, this model is S1, A2, C2, E3, T2, Y3. In Cisco documentation, it is called Global Inband. It is the simplest way to deploy *dynamic* Multicast over MPLS. Although it brings easy operation and deployment, this carrier multicast flavor also has some limitations:

- It creates C-Multicast label state at the core LSRs, breaking one of the main benefits of MPLS: reducing the state by not propagating customer routes to the P-routers.
- It does not have P-Tunnel flexibility (it is restricted to LDP only).
- It does not yet support Inclusive Tunnels (default MDTs).

Multipoint LDP

Multipoint LDP (mLDP) is *not* a new protocol; rather, it is a set of LDP extensions and procedures. PE1 and PE2 establish one single LDP session, and they use it to exchange label mappings for all the FEC elements. These include good old IPv4 prefixes (as in *plain* LDP) and, in addition, the Multipoint FEC elements; all advertised in the same LDP session.

 Use the policy framework in Junos and IOS XR to select which FECs you want to advertise over the LDP session. For example, you might want to use LDP only for P2MP FECs, not for IPv4 Unicast FECs.

LDP is called mLDP if the neighbors negotiate special MP capabilities. More specifically, a neighbor supporting the P2MP capability (0x0508) can signal P2MP FEC elements over a (m)LDP session.

Let's begin with a scenario in which LDP is configured on all the interfaces (see Chapter 2). Example 4-16 shows the incremental mLDP configuration in Junos.

Example 4-16. mLDP configuration (Junos)

```
protocols {
    ldp p2mp;
}
```

Example 4-17 presents the configuration in IOS XR.

Example 4-17. mLDP configuration (IOS XR)

```
mpls ldp
 mldp
```

 It is a good practice in both Junos and IOS XR to configure mLDP make-before-break in order to minimize traffic loss upon link recovery. The details are outside the scope of this book.

As a result of this configuration, LDP peers negotiate the P2MP capability. Let's see the negotiation between PE1 (Junos) and PE2 (IOS XR): they both have in common the P2MP capability:

Example 4-18. LDP capability negotiation (Junos and IOS XR)

```
juniper@PE1> show ldp session 172.16.0.22 detail
[...]
  Capabilities advertised: p2mp, make-before-break
  Capabilities received: p2mp

RP/0/0/CPU0:PE2#show mpls ldp neighbor 172.16.0.11:0 detail
[...]
  Capabilities:
    Sent:
      0x508  (MP: Point-to-Multipoint (P2MP))
      0x509  (MP: Multipoint-to-Multipoint (MP2MP))
      0x50b  (Typed Wildcard FEC)
    Received:
      0x508  (MP: Point-to-Multipoint (P2MP))
```

For now, the LDP session only signals the classic IPv4 prefix FEC elements. For the moment, no P2MP FEC elements are being advertised on the LDP sessions because there is no service requiring a multipoint LSP yet. This is about to change.

You need to configure mLDP on all the LSRs and LERs.

In-Band Signaling

At this point, PE2, PE3, and PE4 have upstream PIM Join state pointing to PE1, but RPF is failing because PIM has been removed from the core links. In C- and P- terminology, P-PIM is no longer running and C-PIM needs to rely on mLDP in order to extend the multicast tree through the core. However, C-PIM does not *know* that it can rely on mLDP. Yet.

Later in this chapter, you will see the configuration (see Example 4-19 and Example 4-26) that allows the automatic conversion of C-PIM Join state into LDP P2MP FECs. This triggers the creation of a P2MP LSP rooted at PE1 and with three leaves (PE2, PE3, and PE4). The P2MP LSP is built by mLDP, and the signaling actually goes in the upstream direction: from the leaves toward the root (PE1). In contrast, the C-Multicast data is tunneled downstream, from the root to the leaves.

You can use Figure 4-3 as a guide for the following mLDP walkthrough.

For the remainder of this chapter, the links PE1-PE2 and PE3-PE4 have their IS-IS metrics raised to 100. So, in the absence of link failures, all the inter-PE shortest paths go through P-routers.

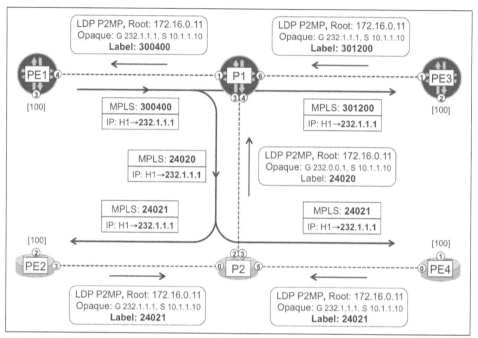

Figure 4-3. mLDP P2MP LSPs—In-Band signaling and forwarding

Assume that all the hosts back in Figure 4-1, with the exception of source H1, are subscribed to the (10.1.1.10, 232.1.1.1) multicast flow. In other words: H2, H3, H4, H22, H33, H34, and H44 are all C-Multicast receivers.

Signaling Join state from an egress PE that runs Junos

The folowing Junos configuration links C-PIM to mLDP at the Junos PEs:

Example 4-19. mLDP In-Band configuration at the PEs (Junos)

```
protocols {
    pim mldp-inband-signalling;
}
```

This configuration is only needed on the (ingress and egress) PEs. Pure P-routers such as P1 and P2 do not need it, because they do not even run PIM.

After clearing the C-PIM Join state at PE3—by using the command clear pim join—the multicast ping from H1 to 232.1.1.1 begins to receive replies from H3, H4, and H33.

Use the clear pim join command with caution. This command is typically disruptive for the established multicast flows. Try to be specific with respect to the particular (S, G) that you want to clear.

Letl's see how this PE1→PE3 *branch* of the multicast tree is signaled through the core. The egress PE (PE3) knows that the C-Multicast source 10.1.1.10 is beyond PE1.

Example 4-20. RPF resolution at egress PE—PE3 (Junos)

```
juniper@PE3> show route 10.1.1.10 detail active-path
[...]
          Protocol next hop: 172.16.0.11

juniper@PE3> show pim source inet
Instance: PIM.master Family: INET

Source 10.1.1.10
    Prefix 10.1.1.0/24
    Upstream protocol MLDP
    Upstream interface Pseudo MLDP
    Upstream neighbor MLDP LSP root <172.16.0.11>
```

Thanks to the configuration just applied, PE3's upstream C-PIM Join state can be resolved via Multicast Label Distribution Protocol (mLDP), as shown in Example 4-21.

Example 4-21. Upstream C-PIM Join state at egress PE—PE3 (Junos)

```
juniper@PE3> show pim join inet detail
Instance: PIM.master Family: INET
R = Rendezvous Point Tree, S = Sparse, W = Wildcard

Group: 232.1.1.1
    Source: 10.1.1.10
    Flags: sparse,spt
    Upstream protocol: MLDP
```

```
    Upstream interface: Pseudo MLDP
  Downstream neighbors:
      Interface: ge-2/0/3.1034
      Interface: ge-2/0/4.1033
```

From the forwarding plane perspective, the (downstream) path is PE1→PE3, but it must be signaled the other way around: from PE3 to PE1. In other words, signaling takes place upstream from the leaf to the root. PE3 is not directly connected to PE1, so PE3 (the egress PE) needs to find the RPF neighbor toward PE1 (the root).

Example 4-22. RPF lookup at egress PE—PE3 (Junos)

```
juniper@PE3> show route 172.16.0.11 table inet.0

inet.0: 43 destinations, 51 routes (43 active, 0 holddown, 0 hidden)
+ = Active Route, - = Last Active, * = Both

172.16.0.11/32      *[IS-IS/18] 04:37:38, metric 20
                    > to 10.0.0.8 via ge-2/0/1.0
```

Now, PE3 builds a P2MP FEC element, maps a label to it, and advertises the Label Mapping *only* to P1. Why P1? Because it is the RPF neighbor—and LDP neighbor—toward the root (PE1). This targeted advertisement is totally different from the *promiscuous* Label Mapping distribution of IPv4 Prefix FEC elements, depicted in Figure 2-3 and Figure 2-4. In the P2MP case, the downstream LSR performs a route lookup before advertising the Label Mapping, and as a result, only the RPF neighbor receives it.

Example 4-23. P2MP FEC signaling from egress PE—PE3 (Junos)

```
juniper@PE3> show ldp p2mp fec
LDP P2MP FECs:
 P2MP root-addr 172.16.0.11, grp: 232.1.1.1, src: 10.1.1.10
  Fec type: Egress (Active)
  Label: 301200

juniper@PE3> show ldp database p2mp
Input label database, 172.16.0.33:0--172.16.0.1:0
Labels received: 8

Output label database, 172.16.0.33:0--172.16.0.1:0
Labels advertised: 19
  Label    Prefix
 301200    P2MP root-addr 172.16.0.11, grp: 232.1.1.1, src: 10.1.1.10

Input label database, 172.16.0.33:0--172.16.0.44:0
Labels received: 19
```

```
Output label database, 172.16.0.33:0--172.16.0.44:0
Labels advertised: 18
```

Let's interpret the new FEC element. The format of MP (P2MP and MP2MP) FEC elements is described in RFC 6388 - *LDP Extensions for Point-to-Multipoint and Multipoint-to-Multipoint Label Switched Paths*, which we paraphrase here:

> The P2MP FEC Element consists of the address of the root of the P2MP LSP and an opaque value. [...] The opaque value is unique within the context of the root node. The combination of (Root Node Address type, Root Node Address, Opaque Value) uniquely identifies a P2MP LSP within the MPLS network.

Back to the example, the P2MP Root Address is 172.16.0.11 (PE1's loopback address) and the Opaque Value is: group 232.1.1.1, source 10.1.1.10. As you can see, the FEC element used to build this P2MP LSP also contains C-Multicast information, namely the C-Group and the C-Source. This is precisely what In-Band means. But this information is encoded in an *opaque value*, which means that the transit LSRs do not need to understand it: only the root does.

When P1 receives this P2MP FEC element, it *only* looks at its root address (172.16.0.11) and, of course, at the label. P1 performs an RPF check, allocates a new label, and sends a P2MP Label Mapping to its RPF neighbor toward the root, PE1.

Example 4-24. mLDP P2MP FEC signaling from transit P—P1 (Junos)

```
juniper@P1> show ldp p2mp fec
LDP P2MP FECs:
 P2MP root-addr 172.16.0.11, grp: 232.1.1.1, src: 10.1.1.10
  Fec type: Transit (Active)
  Label: 300400

juniper@P1> show ldp database session 172.16.0.11 p2mp
Input label database, 172.16.0.1:0--172.16.0.11:0
Labels received: 9

Output label database, 172.16.0.1:0--172.16.0.11:0
Labels advertised: 7
  Label  Prefix
 300400    P2MP root-addr 172.16.0.11, grp: 232.1.1.1, src: 10.1.1.10
```

Unlike P1, the ingress PE (PE1) is the root, so it looks into the MP opaque value, which contains C-Multicast state. Indeed, PE1 converts the downstream mLDP FEC into upstream C-PIM Join state. The latter already exists due to the local receiver H11, so the mLDP FEC simply triggers an update of the outgoing interface list.

Example 4-25. Upstream C-PIM Join state at ingress PE—PE1 (Junos)

```
juniper@PE1> show pim join inet detail
Instance: PIM.master Family: INET
```

```
R = Rendezvous Point Tree, S = Sparse, W = Wildcard

Group: 232.1.1.1
    Source: 10.1.1.10
    Flags: sparse,spt
    Upstream interface: ge-2/0/1.1010
    Downstream neighbors:
        Interface: ge-2/0/2.1011
        Interface: Pseudo-MLDP
```

 As of this writing, mLDP In-Band signaling builds Selective Trees (data MDTs) only. Each P2MP LSP transports one single (C-S, C-G) flow to the receiver PEs that have downstream (C-S, C-G) Join state.

Signaling Join state from an egress PE that runs IOS XR

The IOS XR configuration that links C-PIM to mLDP at PE2 is shown in Example 4-26.

Example 4-26. mLDP In-Band Configuration at PE2 (IOS XR)

```
prefix-set PR-REMOTE-SOURCES
  10.1.1.0/24 eq 32,
  10.2.0.0/16 eq 32
end-set
!
route-policy PL-MLDP-INBAND
  if source in PR-REMOTE-SOURCES then
    set core-tree mldp-inband
  else
    pass
  endif
end-policy
!
router pim
 address-family ipv4
  rpf topology route-policy PL-MLDP-INBAND
!
multicast-routing
 address-family ipv4
  mdt mldp in-band-signaling ipv4
!
```

PE4 is configured in a similar way, with just some adjustments in the `prefix-set`. Like in Junos, this configuration is only required at the PEs, not at the Ps. After clearing the C-PIM Join state at PE2 and PE4—by using the command `clear pim ipv4 topology`—the multicast ping from H1 to 232.1.1.1 begins to receive replies from H2, H22, and H44.

Use the `clear pim ipv4 topology` command with caution. This command is typically disruptive for the established multicast flows. Try to be specific with respect to the particular (S, G) that you want to clear.

Let's see how these *branches* of the multicast tree are signaled through the core. Actually, one of the egress PEs (PE2) acts as a branching point, so the H1→H2 and H1→H22 paths actually share the same subpath (PE1→PE2) in the core.

Following is the C-PIM upstream Join state at PE2. Remember that the PE1-PE2 link has a high IS-IS metric value, so the shortest PE2→PE1 path goes via P2 and P1.

Example 4-27. Upstream C-PIM Join at egress PE—PE2 (IOS XR)

```
RP/0/0/CPU0:PE2#show mrib route 232.1.1.1

IP Multicast Routing Information Base
[...]
(10.1.1.10,232.1.1.1) RPF nbr: 10.0.0.5 Flags: RPF
  Up: 01:00:38
  Incoming Interface List
    Imdtdefault Flags: A LMI, Up: 01:00:38
  Outgoing Interface List
    GigabitEthernet0/0/0/0.1020 Flags: F NS, Up: 01:00:38
    GigabitEthernet0/0/0/1.1022 Flags: F NS LI, Up: 01:00:38
```

The `imdtdefault` interface is the internal "glue" between the C-PIM and the mLDP domains at PE2. Don't be confused by the name: this mLDP LSP is a data MDT (selective tree). Now, the C-PIM upstream Join state triggers the creation and signaling of a P2MP FEC label mapping that PE2 sends up to P2.

Example 4-28. P2MP FEC signaling from egress PE—PE2 (IOS XR)

```
RP/0/0/CPU0:PE2#show mpls mldp database
mLDP database
LSM-ID: 0x00001   Type: P2MP   Uptime: 01:08:29
  FEC Root           : 172.16.0.11
  Opaque decoded     : [ipv4 10.1.1.10 232.1.1.1]
  Upstream neighbor(s) :
    172.16.0.2:0 [Active] Uptime: 00:12:26
      Local Label (D) : 24021
  Downstream client(s):
    PIM MDT           Uptime: 01:08:29
      Egress intf   : Imdtdefault
      Table ID      : IPv4: 0xe0000000
      RPF ID        : 3
```

P2 receives P2MP FEC label mappings from PE2 and PE4, which are then aggregated into one single label mapping that P2 signals upstream to P1.

Example 4-29. P2MP FEC signaling at Transit P—P2 (IOS XR)

```
RP/0/0/CPU0:P2#show mpls mldp database
mLDP database
LSM-ID: 0x00003   Type: P2MP   Uptime: 00:39:07
  FEC Root          : 172.16.0.11
  Opaque decoded    : [ipv4 10.1.1.10 232.1.1.1]
  Upstream neighbor(s) :
    172.16.0.1:0 [Active] Uptime: 00:39:07
      Local Label (D) : 24020
  Downstream  client(s):
    LDP 172.16.0.22:0  Uptime: 00:39:07
      Next Hop        : 10.0.0.4
      Interface       : GigabitEthernet0/0/0/0
      Remote label (D) : 24021
    LDP 172.16.0.44:0  Uptime: 00:37:55
      Next Hop        : 10.0.0.11
      Interface       : GigabitEthernet0/0/0/5
      Remote label (D) : 24021
```

 In Example 4-29, the remote label value 24021 happens to be the same in both of the downstream branches. This is just a *typical MPLS* coincidence; the labels also could have had different values.

This is the control-plane view of a branching point: two downstream branches (P2→PE2 and P2→PE4) are merged into a single upstream branch (P1→P2). In the forwarding plane, the process is the opposite: a packet arriving on P2 from P1 is replicated toward PE2 and PE4. Let's examine the life of a C-Multicast packet.

Life of a C-Multicast Packet in an mLDP P2MP LSP

After analyzing the control plane, let's focus on the forwarding plane.

Ingress PE

PE1 replicates each incoming (10.1.1.10, 232.1.1.1) C-Multicast packet and sends one copy down to the directly connected receiver H11, and one more copy—encapsulated in MPLS—down the PE1-P1 core link, as shown in Example 4-30.

Example 4-30. mLDP P2MP LSP forwarding at the ingress PE—PE1 (Junos)

```
1    juniper@PE1> show multicast route detail
2    Instance: master Family: INET
```

```
3
4     Group: 232.1.1.1
5         Source: 10.1.1.10/32
6         Upstream interface: ge-2/0/1.1010
7         Downstream interface list:
8             ge-2/0/4.0 ge-2/0/2.1011
9         Session description: Source specific multicast
10        Statistics: 0 kBps, 1 pps, 8567 packets
11        Next-hop ID: 1048581
12        Upstream protocol: PIM
13
14    juniper@PE1> show route table inet.1 match-prefix "232.1.1.1*"
15
16    inet.1: 4 destinations, 4 routes (4 active, 0 holddown, 0 hidden)
17    + = Active Route, - = Last Active, * = Both
18
19    232.1.1.1,10.1.1.10/64*[PIM/105] 07:08:35
20                        to 10.0.0.3 via ge-2/0/4.0, Push 300400
21                        via ge-2/0/2.1011
22
23    juniper@PE1> show route forwarding-table destination 232.1.1.1
24            table default extensive
25    Destination:  232.1.1.1.10.1.1.10/64
26      Route type: user
27      Route reference: 0                    Route interface-index: 332
28      Multicast RPF nh index: 0
29      Flags: cached, check incoming interface, [...]
30      Next-hop type: indirect      Index: 1048581  Reference: 2
31      Nexthop:
32      Next-hop type: composite     Index: 595      Reference: 1
33      # Now comes the list of core (MPLS) next hops
34      Next-hop type: indirect      Index: 1048577  Reference: 2
35      Nexthop:
36      Next-hop type: composite     Index: 592      Reference: 1
37      Nexthop: 10.0.0.3
38      Next-hop type: Push 300400   Index: 637      Reference: 2
39      Load Balance Label: None
40      Next-hop interface: ge-2/0/4.0
41      # Now comes the list of access (IPv4) next hops
42      Next-hop type: indirect      Index: 1048591  Reference: 2
43      Nexthop:
44      Next-hop type: composite     Index: 633      Reference: 1
45      Next-hop type: unicast       Index: 1048574  Reference: 3
46      Next-hop interface: ge-2/0/2.1011
```

All of the previous commands simply show different stages of a multicast forwarding cache entry. The inet.1 auxiliary Routing Information Base (RIB) is actually a multicast cache whose entries populate the forwarding table (the Forwarding Information Base [FIB]). There is a deep level of indirection in the Junos next-hop structures. In practice, you can think of the composite next hop as an action. In the case of multicast routes, this action is *replicate*. You can find a full discussion about composite next hops applied to unicast in Chapter 20.

Look at line 37 in Example 4-30. One copy of the C-Multicast packet is encapsulated in MPLS and then into Ethernet. The destination MAC address of the Ethernet frame is the unicast MAC address associated to 10.0.0.3 (P1), typically resolved via ARP.

> Multicast over MPLS over Ethernet is transported in *unicast* frames.

This is an important advantage for scenarios in which the core link, despite being logically point-to-point, transits an underlying multipoint infrastructure. For example, AS 65000 may buy multipoint L2VPN services to an external SP and use this L2 overlay to implement its own *core* links. From the perspective of AS 65000, these are point-to-point core links, but behind the scenes multicast Ethernet frames are flooded through the multipoint L2VPN at the transport provider network. This reasoning highlights the advantage of encapsulating the C-Multicast packets in *unicast* MPLS-over-Ethernet frames. L2VPN services are further discussed in Chapters Chapter 6, Chapter 7 and Chapter 8.

Finally, you can ignore the term `unicast` in Example 4-30, line 45. Its meaning is fully explained in Chapter 20 and it has nothing to do with the classical notion of unicast.

Due to the currently configured IGP metric scheme—inter-PE links have a higher metric (100)—PE1 only sends one copy of the C-Multicast packet into the core. If the IGP metrics were set back to the default values, PE1 would send one copy to P1 and another copy to PE2. In other words, nothing prevents an ingress PE from being a replication point of a P2MP LSP if the topology requires it.

> In this example, the ingress PE (PE1) runs Junos. If the multicast ping is sourced from H2, the ingress PE (PE2) runs IOS XR, and the results are successful and symmetrical to those shown here.

Transit P-router running Junos

When it arrives to P1, the MPLS packet is further replicated in two copies: one goes to PE3, and another one to P2, as shown in Example 4-31.

Example 4-31. mLDP P2MP LSP forwarding at a transit PE—P1 (Junos)

```
juniper@P1> show ldp p2mp path
P2MP path type: Transit/Egress
  Output Session (label): 172.16.0.11:0 (300400) (Primary)
  Input Session (label): 172.16.0.33:0 (301200)
                         172.16.0.2:0 (24020)
  Attached FECs:  P2MP root-addr 172.16.0.11,
                  grp: 232.1.1.1, src: 10.1.1.10 (Active)


juniper@P1> show route forwarding-table label 300400 extensive
Routing table: default.mpls [Index 0]
MPLS:


Destination:  300400
  Route type: user
  Route reference: 0                Route interface-index: 0
  Multicast RPF nh index: 0
  Flags: sent to PFE
  Next-hop type: indirect           Index: 1048582  Reference: 2
  Nexthop:
  Next-hop type: composite          Index: 602      Reference: 1
  # Now comes the replication towards PE3
  Nexthop: 10.0.0.9
  Next-hop type: Swap 301200        Index: 594      Reference: 2
  Load Balance Label: None
  Next-hop interface: ge-2/0/6.0
  # Now comes the replication towards P2
  Next-hop type: unilist            Index: 1048581  Reference: 2
  # Now comes the first P1-P2 link for load balancing
  Nexthop: 10.0.0.7
  Next-hop type: Swap 24020         Index: 596      Reference: 1
  Load Balance Label: None
  Next-hop interface: ge-2/0/3.0  Weight: 0x1
  # Now comes the second P1-P2 link for load balancing
  Nexthop: 10.0.0.25
  Next-hop type: Swap 24020         Index: 597      Reference: 1
  Load Balance Label: None
  Next-hop interface: ge-2/0/4.0  Weight: 0x1
```

If you look carefully at Example 4-31, there is a new type of next hop called `unilist`. It means that the *single* copy of the packet that is sent down to P2 needs to be load balanced—not replicated—across the two P1-P2 links. This single copy is sent down the first or down the second link, depending on the results of the packet hash computation (see "LDP and Equal-Cost Multipath" on page 56 if this language does not sound familiar to you). The fact that the Weight is 0x1 in both links means that they are both available for load balancing. Hence, in Junos, mLDP natively supports Equal-Cost Multipath (ECMP) across parallel links.

Transit P-router running IOS XR

P2 further replicates the packet down to PE2 and PE4, as illustrated in the folowing example:

Example 4-32. mLDP P2MP LSP forwarding at a transit PE—P2 (IOS XR)

```
RP/0/0/CPU0:P2#show mpls forwarding labels 24020
Local  Outgoing  Prefix          Outgoing   Next Hop    Bytes
Label  Label     or ID           Interface              Switched
------ -------   ---------------  ---------  ----------  --------
24020  24021     MLDP: 0x00003    Gi0/0/0/0  10.0.0.4    2170
       24021     MLDP: 0x00003    Gi0/0/0/5  10.0.0.11   2170
```

Egress PE running Junos

PE3 pops the MPLS label and replicates the resulting IPv4 multicast packets toward the two receiver ACs, as you can see in Example 4-33.

 There is no Penultimate Hop Popping (PHP) for P2MP LSPs. In this chapter's Global Internet Multicast case, this is important because the core links should not transport native user multicast packets. As for the Multicast VPN case, it is also important but for a different reason, which is discussed in Chapter 5.

Example 4-33. mLDP P2MP LSP forwarding at an egress PE—PE3 (Junos)

```
juniper@PE3> show route forwarding-table label 301200 extensive
Routing table: default.mpls [Index 0]
MPLS:

Destination:  301200
  Route type: user
  Route reference: 0                      Route interface-index: 0
  Multicast RPF nh index: 0
  Flags: sent to PFE
  Next-hop type: indirect                 Index: 1048577  Reference: 2
  Nexthop:
  Next-hop type: composite                Index: 601      Reference: 1
  # Now comes the replication towards VLAN 1034 [...]
  Next-hop type: Pop                       Index: 597      Reference: 2
  Load Balance Label: None
  Next-hop interface: ge-2/0/3.1034
  # Now comes the replication towards H33 [...]
  Next-hop type: Pop                       Index: 600      Reference: 2
  Load Balance Label: None
  Next-hop interface: ge-2/0/4.1033
```

Unicast next hops have been stripped from Example 4-33 because they are misleading: multicast MAC addresses are calculated with a mathematical rule; they are not resolved via ARP.

Egress PE running IOS XR

Let's see how PE4 pops the MPLS label and sends the IPv4 multicast packet to H44 *only*.

Example 4-34. mLDP P2MP LSP Forwarding at an egress PE–PE4 (IOS XR)

```
RP/0/0/CPU0:PE4#show mrib route 10.1.1.10 232.1.1.1

IP Multicast Routing Information Base
[...]
(10.1.1.10,232.1.1.1) RPF nbr: 10.0.0.10 Flags: RPF
  Up: 09:45:39
  Incoming Interface List
    Imdtdefault Flags: A LMI, Up: 03:17:05
  Outgoing Interface List
    GigabitEthernet0/0/0/2.1034 Flags: LI, Up: 12:40:38
    GigabitEthernet0/0/0/3.1044 Flags: F NS LI, Up: 09:01:24
```

In this book's tests, H44 only receives the C-Multicast flow if PE4's *unicast* CEF entry for 172.16.0.11 resolves to an LDP label. If PE4's RPF to PE1 resolves to a (P2P) RSVP tunnel, PE4 does not forward the traffic to H44. In other words, as of this writing, IOS XR implementation of mLDP does not coexist with *unicast* RSVP-TE. This boundary condition was not observed in Junos PE3.

The key point of the previous output is the flag F – Forward. The interface toward H44 has the flag set, but the other interface (VLAN 1034) does not. However, if you stop the source and wait for a few minutes, the F flag is set again on both entries. Let's see why.

CE Multihoming

It is essential that each host receives one, *and only one*, copy of each multicast packet. H2, H11, H22, H33, and H44 have no access redundancy, so they do *not* receive multiple copies of each packet sent by H1. Conversely, H3, H4, and H34 are (directly or indirectly) multihomed to PE3 and PE4. Let's discuss this case more in detail.

Egress PE redundancy

The following discussion is quite generic in IP Multicast and *not* specific of the mLDP In-Band model. VLAN 1034 topology (Figure 4-1) is a classic example of PE Redundancy. Three devices (BR3, BR4, and H34) are connected to the SP (AS 65000) on a VLAN that is multihomed to both PE3 and PE4. There are two EBGP sessions established: PE3-BR3 and PE4-BR4. Furthermore, all the routers in VLAN 1034 are PIM neighbors. Here is the specific PIM configuration of the devices:

- PE3: `protocols pim interface ge-2/0/3.1034` **priority 200**
- PE4: Default configuration (PIM **priority 1**)
- BR3, BR4: `protocols pim interface ge-0/0/1.1034` **priority 0**
- H34: `router pim [vrf H34] address-family ipv4 interface GigabitEthernet0/0/0.1034` **dr-priority 0**

With this configuration, PE3 is the Designated Router (DR), which you can verify by using the `show pim interfaces` command on PE3, or `show pim neighbor` on PE4. The DR is responsible for processing the IGMP Reports from the directly connected hosts (in this case, H34).

Figure 4-4 illustrates the C-Multicast convergence process on VLAN 1034, in two steps.

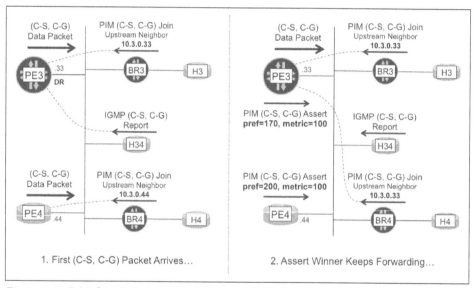

Figure 4-4. C-Multicast—egress PE redundancy and C-PIM Assert

Initially, both PE3 and PE4 are ready to forward the (10.1.1.10, 232.1.1.1) traffic to VLAN 1034. Here is why:

- PE3 is the DR and is processing the IGMP Reports from H34.
- PE3 is the Upstream Neighbor of a PIM (10.1.1.10, 232.1.1.1) Join sent by BR3, because BR3 only has an eBGP session with PE3.

- PE4 is the Upstream Neighbor of a PIM (10.1.1.10, 232.1.1.1) Join sent by BR4, because BR4 only has an eBGP session with PE4.

When H1 sends the first C-Multicast packet to 232.1.1.1, both PE3 and PE4 forward it to VLAN 1034. This causes C-Multicast packet duplication in VLAN 1034, which you can verify in the first set of ping replies.

Example 4-35. mLDP P2MP LSP forwarding at a transit PE—P2 (IOS XR)

```
1   RP/0/0/CPU0:H# ping vrf H1 232.1.1.1 source 10.1.1.10 count 1
2   Reply to request 0 from 10.1.11.11, 1 ms
3   Reply to request 0 from 10.1.22.22, 9 ms
4   Reply to request 0 from 10.2.33.33, 9 ms
5   Reply to request 0 from 10.2.44.44, 9 ms
6   Reply to request 0 from 10.2.3.30, 9 ms
7   Reply to request 0 from 10.2.0.34, 9 ms
8   Reply to request 0 from 10.2.4.40, 9 ms
9   Reply to request 0 from 10.2.3.30, 19 ms
10  Reply to request 0 from 10.2.0.34, 19 ms
11  Reply to request 0 from 10.2.4.40, 19 ms
```

ICMP echo request #0 receives duplicate replies from H3, H34, and H4. From a service perspective, this is strongly undesirable. For most multicast applications, receiving a duplicate or multiplied copy of the original data stream can be as bad as not receiving it at all. For that reason, when PE3 and PE4 detect this packet duplication, they start a competition called PIM Assert, based on their route to the 10.1.1.10 multicast source.

Example 4-36. Egress PE redundancy—Unicast Route to the C-Source

```
1   juniper@PE3> show route active-path 10.1.1.10
2
3   inet.0: 44 destinations, 53 routes (44 active, 0 holddown, 0 hidden)
4
5   10.1.1.0/24   *[BGP/170] 1d 12:04:09, MED 100, localpref 100,
6                   from 172.16.0.201, AS path: 65001 I [...]
7                   > to 10.0.0.8 via ge-2/0/1.0, Push 300368
8
9   RP/0/0/CPU0:PE4#show route 10.1.1.10
10
11  Routing entry for 10.1.1.0/24
12    Known via "bgp 65000", distance 200, metric 100
13    Tag 65001, type internal
14    Installed Jan  6 06:11:52.147 for 15:19:12
15    Routing Descriptor Blocks
16      172.16.0.11, from 172.16.0.201
17        Route metric is 100
18    No advertising protos.
```

Although the MED attribute of the route is 100 in both cases, the default administrative distance of the BGP protocol is 170 on PE3 (line 5, Junos), as opposed to 200 on PE4 (line 12, IOS XR). The lowest administrative distance wins, so PE3 becomes the C-PIM (10.1.1.10, 232.1.1.1) Assert winner. At this point, PE4 stops injecting the flow on VLAN 1034. Also, because PIM Assert packets are sent to the 224.0.0.13 address, BR4 sees the Assert competition and redirects its PIM (C-S, C-G) Join Upstream Neighbor to PE3. Overall, the packet duplication in VLAN 1034 is fixed and PE3 becomes the single forwarder.

 There is no assert in VLAN 1044. So the fact that PE3 is the Assert winner in VLAN 1034 does not prevent PE4 from forwarding the packets to H44.

As you would expect with PIM, Assert packets are refreshed periodically. In other words, Assert, like Join/Prune, has *soft state*. Some minutes after the C-Source stops sending traffic, Assert times-out and the initial condition resumes (the F flag appears for VLAN 1034 in Example 4-34). So, even in a model with PIM SSM, there are scenarios in which the signaling of the multicast tree is data driven.

Ingress PE redundancy

Now, suppose that an active C-Multicast source is multihomed to PE1 and PE2, and that this source is sending traffic to (C-S, C-G). Now, both H33 and H44 send an IGMP Report subscribing to that flow. How is the P2MP LSP signaled? There are two cases:

- Both PE3 and PE4 choose the same Upstream PE (either PE1 or PE2) as the root for the P2MP FEC. In this case, a single P2MP LSP is created, with one root and two leaves: PE3 and PE4.

- PE3 and PE4 choose different Upstream PEs. For example, PE3 selects PE1 and PE4 selects PE2. In this case, there are two P2MP LSPs, one rooted at PE1 and the other rooted at PE2. Each of these P2MP LSPs has a single (and different) leaf.

There is no risk of data duplication in any of these cases: each egress PE signals the P2MP FEC toward a single ingress PE. This is a general advantage of Selective Trees.

mLDP In-Band and PIM ASM

As of this writing, the vendor implementations support only PIM SSM in combination with mLDP In-Band. The efforts to bring support of PIM ASM are polarized in two RFCs:

- RFC 7438 - *mLDP In-Band Signaling with Wildcards*
- RFC 7442 - *Carrying PIM-SM in ASM Mode Trees over mLDP*

Other Internet Multicast over MPLS Flavors

There are some additional Global Internet Multicast (S1) flavors. Here is a non-exhaustive list.

Static RSVP-TE P2MP LSPs

There is one more interoperable model to signal and transport Internet Multicast between Junos and IOS XR PEs. In Cisco documentation, it is called Global P2MP-TE. In the terms of Table 4-1, it is S1, A0, C0, E3, T3, Y3.

It relies on using static routes to place IP Multicast traffic into RSVP-TE P2MP LSPs. The network administrator manually configures the leaves of each LSP. Although you can successfully apply this model to relatively static environments such as traditional IPTV, it is not particularly appealing for the purposes of this book.

BGP Internet Multicast

Junos supports one type of routing instance called `mpls-internet-multicast`, which applies BGP Multicast VPN techniques to the signaling and transport of Internet Multicast traffic. In the terms of Table 4-1, it is S1, A3, C3, [E1, E2, E3], [T0, T1, T2, T3, T4], [Y1, Y2, Y3, Y4]. Not all the combinations are supported, though.

Although IOS XR does not implement this approach, you can configure the IOS XR PEs with Internet VRFs running BGP Multicast VPN. That being said, from an interoperability perspective it is more interesting to focus on the genuine BGP Multicast VPN, with VRFs on both PE types (Junos and IOS XR). Let's go for it in Chapter 5!

## CHAPTER 5

Multicast VPN

After exploring Internet Multicast over MPLS, let's see Multicast VPN (MVPN) over MPLS. The three implemented models in growing scalability order, are:

- Rosen mLDP, already discussed in Chapter 4 and only implemented in IOS XR. In the terms of Table 4-1, it is S2, **A1**, C2, E3, T2, Y4.

- VRF In-Band mLDP, only implemented in IOS XR. In the terms of Table 4-1, this model is S2, **A2**, C2, E3, T2, Y3. It is nearly identical to the one discussed for Internet Multicast in Chapter 4, but it also encodes VPN-specific information (the RD of the S unicast route) in the LDP opaque value.

- BGP Multicast VPN, formerly known as Next-Generation MVPN or NG-MVPN. It is implemented by both Junos and IOS XR. In the terms of Table 4-1, this model is S2, **A3**, C3, [E1, E2, E3], [T0, T1, T2, T3, T4], [Y1, Y2, Y3, Y4]. Not all the combinations make sense and/or are supported, though.

As of this writing, the only interoperable solution is BGP MVPN. Fortunately, it is the most flexible and scalable flavor of them all. Table 4-1 lists the different C-Multicast Architectures: Out-of-band (A3) is more scalable than Hop-by-Hop Inter-PE (A2), which in turn is more scalable than Direct Inter-PE (A1). The only implemented solution that is compatible with the A3 model is precisely BGP MVPN.

MVPN is a multidimensional universe, whose richest galaxy is BGP MVPN. Its Out-of-Band signaling approach, which decouples service from transport, makes BGP MVPN flavors and use cases quite extensive. As a technology it requires more time to fully understand and master than In-Band signaling, but it's worth the effort.

BGP MVPN architectural and functional aspects are described in RFC 6513 - *Multicast in MPLS/BGP IP VPNs*. This RFC is the result of a multivendor effort to achieve a common specification for Multicast VPN in the industry. It provides a big framework that supports two totally different C-Multicast signaling paradigms:

- PE-PE C-PIM peering: Rosen GRE and Rosen mLDP. These models rely on the Direct Inter-PE (A1) architecture and are discussed in Chapter 4.
- PE-PE BGP peering: BGP MVPN. This model relies on the Out-of-Band (A3) architecture.

 In-Band MVPN signaling is not covered in this RFC. Refer back to Chapter 4 for more details on this model, which relies on the Hop-by-Hop Inter-PE (A2) architecture.

BGP Multicast VPN with mLDP Transport

This chapter is based on the same topology as Chapter 4 (see Figure 4-1).

 In this chapter, Figure 4-1 needs to be modified so that the right-hand AS is 65001, the BRs are replaced with CEs, and the inter-PE links have IS-IS metric 100.

Let's discuss BGP MVPN in detail. In the terms of Table 4-1, the following scenario is S2, A3, C3, **E3, T2, Y3**.

MVPN Address Family

The first step when configuring any BGP MVPN flavor is enabling a new BGP address family. Multiprotocol BGP routes can encode virtually anything. Yes, also C-Multicast state: neighbors, joins, prunes and registers. How? With a new Multiprotocol BGP Network Layer Reachability Information (NLRI), called MCAST-VPN. This NLRI is commonly called the *MVPN address family* (IPv4: AFI=1, SAFI=5; IPv6: AFI=2, SAFI=5), and it supports different route types. These are described in RFC 6514 - *BGP Encodings and Procedures for Multicast in MPLS/BGP IP VPNs*. The first scenario illustrated in this chapter involves three of these route types. Let's first look at the full picture, and then we'll examine each step in detail.

MVPN route types

Table 5-1 can serve as a reference for all the upcoming Layer 3 (L3) MVPN scenarios, here and in subsequent chapters. All of these routes will be fully explained as the scenarios evolve. For the moment, here is a quick acronym list: *AD* is *Autodiscovery*, *I* is *Inclusive*, *S* is *Selective*, and *PMSI* is *Provider Multicast Service Interface*.

Table 5-1. MCAST-MVPN (SAFI=5) route types

Type	Route name	C-PIM analogy	Has C- information?
1	Intra-AS I-PMSI AD (a.k.a., Site AD)	Hello Packet	No
2	Inter-AS I-PMSI AD	Hello Packet	No
3	S-PMSI AD	N/A	Yes
4	Leaf AD	N/A	Yes
5	Source Active AD	Register-Start	Yes
6	C-Multicast (C-S, C-G) Source Tree Join	(S, G) Join	Yes
7	C-Multicast (*, C-G) Shared Tree Join	(*, G) Join	Yes

The following pages are dedicated to exploring the signaling in detail. For a first impression, have a look at Figure 5-1, which illustrates how one C-Receiver in one site pulls C-Multicast traffic from a C-Source in a remote site. The lower part of Figure 5-1 shows the signaling of one of the Provider Tunnel branches. You can easily add and merge more branches into the tree by using similar (but not identical) LDP P2MP mechanisms to those discussed in Chapter 4.

You can use the Figure 5-1 as a reference, but don't worry if it doesn't make sense yet. As this section progresses, the different pieces will fit together.

The main difference between AD and non-AD routes lies in the Route Target (RT):

- AD routes have a static configurable RT that is typically imported by all the remote PEs in the MVPN—or, by playing with RT export and import policies, just by a subset of the PEs.

- Non-AD routes (Types 6 and 7) have a dynamic RT that is imported only by one provider edge (PE): namely, by the sender PE to which the C-Multicast Join is targeted.

Let's now see a BGP MVPN scenario in detail, step by step.

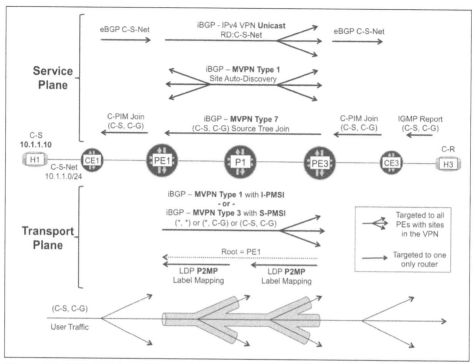

Figure 5-1. BGP Multicast VPN with mLDP transport—the full picture

MVPN address family configuration

First, the PE-RR BGP sessions need to support the new NLRI.

Multicast relies on a healthy unicast service. The configuration examples that follow assume that the IPv4 VPN address family (inet-vpn unicast or vpnv4 unicast) is already configured.

This is the additional configuration in a Junos PE (it would be inet6-mvpn for IPv6):

Example 5-1. MVPN address family configuration—PE1 (Junos)

```
protocols {
    bgp {
        group iBGP-RR {
            family inet-mvpn signaling;
            mvpn-iana-rt-import;
}}}
```

Adding this configuration to all of the BGP groups also does the trick on Junos RRs. The `mvpn-iana-rt-import` command ensures that a very important extended community has the correct format to interoperate with other vendors.

Here is the additional configuration on IOS XR PEs (it would be `ipv6 mvpn` for IPv6):

Example 5-2. MVPN address family configuration—PE2 (IOS XR)

```
router bgp 65000
address-family ipv4 mvpn
 !
 neighbor-group RR
  address-family ipv4 mvpn
!
```

 On RRs running IOS XR, you also need to add the **route-reflector-client** knob under each `neighbor[-group]` `adddress-family`.

With this configuration in place, the new address family is successfully negotiated, as shown in Example 5-3. No MVPN routes are exchanged yet, though.

Example 5-3. BGP MVPN address family—PE1 (Junos) and PE2 (IOS XR)

```
juniper@PE1> show bgp summary instance master
[...]
Peer             AS     State|#Active/Received/Accepted/Damped...
172.16.0.201   65000   Establ
  inet.0: 0/0/0/0
  bgp.l3vpn.0: 12/12/12/0
  bgp.mvpn.0: 0/0/0/0
  VRF-A.inet.0: 12/12/12/0
172.16.0.202   65000   Establ
  inet.0: 0/0/0/0
  bgp.l3vpn.0: 0/12/12/0
  bgp.mvpn.0: 0/0/0/0
  VRF-A.inet.0: 0/12/12/0


RP/0/0/CPU0:PE2#show bgp ipv4 mvpn summary
[...]
Neighbor         AS MsgRcvd MsgSent  InQ OutQ Up/Down  St/PfxRcd
172.16.0.201   65000       9       7    0    0 00:00:07         0
172.16.0.202   65000      11       7   80    0 00:00:11         0
```

Configuring BGP MVPN

What is an MVPN? It is *not* a new type of VPN; rather, it is an extension of a BGP/MPLS IP VPN. The starting point is a classic VRF, with unicast routing up and running. On this very same VRF, you turn on multicast services: this is how you make an MVPN.

Junos basic configuration

The initial VRF-A configuration is similar to the L3VPN baseline of Chapter 3 (Example 3-24, Example 3-28, and Example 3-32). There are minor differences, mainly at the access interface configuration level (VLANs and IPv4 addresses).

The additional configuration at PE1 makes its VRF-A part of a MVPN:

Example 5-4. Multicast VPN configuration at VRF-A—PE1 (Junos)

```
1    interfaces {
2        vt-2/0/0 unit 101 family inet;
3    }
4    policy-options {
5        policy-statement PL-VRF-A-EXP {
6            # Other terms #
7            term MULTICAST {
8                from family inet-mvpn;
9                then {
10                    community add RT-VPN-A;
11                   accept;
12    }}}}
13   routing-instances {
14       VRF-A {
15           interface vt-2/0/0.101 multicast;
16           vrf-table-label;
17           protocols {
18               pim {
19                   interface ge-2/0/1.1010;
20                   interface ge-2/0/2.1011;
21               }
22               mvpn;
23   }}}
```

Chapter 3 explains the vrf-table-label and vt- concepts. With this configuration, the VRF behaves in vrf-table-label mode for unicast services while it relies on a vt- interface for multicast. Although strictly speaking a vt- interface is not mandatory for Multicast VPN to work, it becomes necessary if a given LSR behaves as a Bud LSR—simultaneously acting as an egress PE and Transit P for a given flow. Because in most topologies PEs can potentially be Bud LSRs, the vt- interface is a de facto requirement for MVPN in Junos. Not a big deal in modern platforms, which implement vt- directly on the Packet Forwarding Engines. Another specific feature that requires vt- interfaces in Junos is MVPN Extranet.

As you can see, the access interfaces and the PIM configuration have simply been moved from the global routing table to the VRF. This makes the VRF exchange Protocol Independent Multicast (PIM) and Internet Group Management Protocol (IGMP) packets with the connected CEs and hosts. Finally, MVPN (line 22) is not really a protocol; it is the "glue" between C-PIM and BGP. With protocols mvpn, the VRF is no longer isolated from the multicast point of view. PEs can become MVPN neighbors of each other and exchange C-Multicast information, all by using BGP.

IOS XR basic configuration

Again, the initial VRF-A configuration presented in the following example builds on top of a L3VPN baseline that is very similar to that of Chapter 3 (Examples Example 3-25 and Example 3-29). There are minor differences, mainly at the access interface configuration level (VLANs and IPv4 addresses). Example 5-5 shows the additional configuration required to make PE4's VRF-A part of a MVPN.

 To bring MVPN neighbors up, IOS XR requires information about P-Tunnels. For this reason, the following example includes references to mLDP P2MP and MDT. Just ignore them for the moment.

Example 5-5. Multicast VPN configuration at VRF-A—PE2 (IOS XR)

```
1     router bgp 65000
2      vrf VRF-A
3      address-family ipv4 mvpn
4     !
5     multicast-routing
6      address-family ipv4
7       interface Loopback0
8        enable
9       !
10      mdt source Loopback0
11     !
12     vrf VRF-A
13      address-family ipv4
14       interface GigabitEthernet0/0/0/0.1020
15        enable
16       !
17       interface GigabitEthernet0/0/0/1.1022
18        enable
19       !
20       bgp auto-discovery mldp
21       mdt default mldp p2mp
```

```
22    !
23    mpls ldp
24      mldp
```

MVPN Site AD

With the previous configuration, PEs become the following:

- C-PIM neighbors of the directly connected CEs
- MVPN neighbors of the remote PEs

Example 5-6. C-PIM and MVPN neighbors—PE1 (Junos)

```
juniper@PE1> show pim neighbors instance VRF-A

Instance: PIM.VRF-A
Interface       IP V Mode   Option      Uptime Neighbor addr
ge-2/0/1.1010    4 2        HPLGT    1d 01:52:51 10.1.0.0

juniper@PE1> show mvpn neighbor inet instance-name VRF-A

Instance : VRF-A
  MVPN Mode : SPT-ONLY
  Neighbor                    Inclusive Provider Tunnel
  172.16.0.22
  172.16.0.33
  172.16.0.44
```

How do the PEs become MVPN neighbors of each other in VRF-A? They do it by
exchanging a new BGP route. The MCAST-VPN address family defines seven route
types. Out of them, *Type 1* routes perform Site AD. They are functionally similar to
PIM hellos, except that they are only signaled once, not periodically.

The official name of Type 1 routes is Intra-AS I-PMSI AD, because they *may* carry a
BGP attribute called PMSI. This is a mandatory attribute for some route types, but it
is totally optional for Type 1. This book sometimes refers to Type 1 routes as *Site* AD.

MVPN Site AD in PEs running Junos

Following is the Intra-AS Site AD route advertised by PE1 (Junos):

Example 5-7. MVPN Type 1: intra-AS site AD route—PE1 (Junos)

```
juniper@PE1> show route advertising-protocol bgp 172.16.0.201
            match-prefix "1:*" detail
[...]
bgp.mvpn.0: 6 destinations, 9 routes (6 active, ..., 0 hidden)
* 1:172.16.0.11:101:172.16.0.11/240 (1 entry, 1 announced)
```

```
BGP group iBGP-RR type Internal
    Nexthop: Self
    Flags: Nexthop Change
    Localpref: 100
    AS path: [65000] I
    Communities: target:65000:1001

VRF-A.mvpn.0: 6 destinations, 9 routes (6 active, ..., 0 hidden)
# Same route here - omitted for brevity
```

The format of the prefix is **1:<RD>:<ADVERTISING_PE_ROUTER_ID>**. The /240 mask is internal in Junos and not advertised via iBGP: you can simply ignore it.

As is detailed in Chapter 3, the Route Distinguisher (RD) format can be <ROUTER_ID>:<VPN_ID> or <AS>:<VPN_ID>. In this chapter, the format chosen is <ROUTER_ID>:<VPN_ID>. The MVPN multihoming section explains its advantages.

The route target is 65000:1001, exactly the same as in unicast routes. Consequently, the resulting MVPN topology is a full PE-PE mesh. This is actually chosen by configuration (Example 5-4, line 10), and you can modify it to achieve arbitrary MVPN topologies. This can make sense, for example, if the set of sender PEs is clearly identified and you don't want the sender PEs to become neighbors of each other. The same logic would apply to receiver PEs. BGP with its flexibility makes that possible. Finally, note that this route doesn't carry a PMSI attribute (at least yet).

Junos—even on pure PEs with no route reflection enabled—advertises MVPN routes from the bgp.mvpn.0 table. The routes are first copied from VRF-A.mvpn.0 to bgp.mvpn.0, and then advertised to other PEs via iBGP. This implementation is different from unicast IP VPN routes, which are advertised by default from the VRF tables on pure PEs (you can find more details in Chapter 3).

MVPN Site AD in PEs running IOS XR

Here is the Intra-AS Site AD route advertised by PE2 (IOS XR):

Example 5-8. MVPN Type 1: intra-AS site AD route—PE2 (IOS XR)

```
RP/0/0/CPU0:PE2#show bgp ipv4 mvpn vrf VRF-A advertised

Route Distinguisher: 172.16.0.22:101
[1][172.16.0.22]/40 is advertised to 172.16.0.202
[...]
  Attributes after outbound policy was applied:
    next hop: 172.16.0.22
    ORG AS COMM EXTCOMM
    origin: IGP
    aspath:
    community: no-export
```

```
        extended community: RT:65000:1001
[...]
```

Although the format looks a bit different, Junos and IOS XR advertise the NLRI exactly with the same format on the wire (only the BGP attributes may differ).

 The BGP next hop is a mandatory BGP attribute but in MCAST-VPN routes it is typically irrelevant: the meat is in the NLRI and in the extended communities.

Signaling C-Multicast (S, G) Join State with BGP

This example is based on Source-Specific Multicast (SSM) mode. Any Source Multicast (ASM) is covered later.

In SSM mode, the sources are known beforehand, so the forwarding state is created independently of the multicast traffic. If the sources begin to send multicast traffic before there is any receiver, the First Hop Router (FHR)—let it be a PE or a CE—simply drops the traffic. Indeed, in SSM (unlike ASM) the sources play no role in building the multicast tree. The receivers, with their IGMP (S, G) Reports, are the ones that trigger the multicast tree signaling.

Let's start the following receivers of the (10.1.1.10, 232.1.1.1) flow: H3, H4, H33, H34, and H44 (see Figure 4-1). The C-Multicast source is H1, so PE1 is the sender PE.

Receiver PE configuration

There are two receiver PEs in this example, PE3 and PE4, which run Junos and IOS XR, respectively. They both get IGMP (S, G) Reports from the directly connected hosts (H33, H34, and H44) and C-PIM Joins from their downstream CEs (CE3 and CE4). Any of these messages—IGMP Report *or* PIM Join—is enough for the receiver PEs to generate a (C-S, C-G) Join state pointing to the upstream C-Source. Let's see how PE3 and PE4 perform Reverse Path Forwarding (RPF) toward a C-Source that is beyond a remote PE (PE1).

Junos receiver PEs just require the basic MVPN AD configuration (Example 5-4). With it in place, PE3 performs RPF successfully toward the C-Source, as demonstrated here:

Example 5-9. Successful RPF at receiver PE—PE3 (Junos)

```
juniper@PE3> show pim join inet instance VRF-A
Instance: PIM.VRF-A Family: INET
R = Rendezvous Point Tree, S = Sparse, W = Wildcard
```

```
Group: 232.1.1.1
    Source: 10.1.1.10
    Flags: sparse,spt
    Upstream protocol: BGP
    Upstream interface: Through BGP
```

Then, PE3 converts this downstream Join state into a BGP route. But how can PE3 make sure that the new route is targeted only to PE1, the Source PE? This logic and the format of the new route are unveiled in the next few pages.

Before that, let's see how PE4 performs RPF toward the remote C-Source. To perform Site Auto-Discovery, IOS XR receiver PEs require P-Tunnel specific information (see Example 5-5, lines 20 and 21).

However, that configuration is still incomplete, so RPF fails:

Example 5-10. Failed RPF at receiver PE—PE4 (IOS XR)

```
RP/0/0/CPU0:PE4#show mrib vrf VRF-A route 232.1.1.1
[...]
(10.1.1.10,232.1.1.1) RPF nbr: 0.0.0.0 Flags: RPF
  Up: 2d00h
  Outgoing Interface List
    GigabitEthernet0/0/0/2.1034 Flags: LI, Up: 00:05:51
    GigabitEthernet0/0/0/3.1044 Flags: F NS LI, Up: 2d00h
```

Example 5-11 provides the additional configuration, which will allow IOS XR PE4 to do a successful RPF lookup and signal the C-Multicast Join state via BGP.

Example 5-11. RPF policy at receiver PE—PE4 (IOS XR)

```
route-policy PL-BGP-MVPN-LDP-P2MP
  set core-tree mldp-default
end-policy
!
router pim
 vrf VRF-A
  address-family ipv4
   rpf topology route-policy PL-BGP-MVPN-LDP-P2MP
   mdt c-multicast-routing bgp
!
```

After this configuration is applied, PE4 performs a successful RPF lookup:

Example 5-12. Successful RPF at receiver PE—PE4 (IOS XR)

```
RP/0/0/CPU0:PE4#show mrib vrf VRF-A route 232.1.1.1
[...]
(10.1.1.10,232.1.1.1) RPF nbr: 172.16.0.11 Flags: RPF
```

```
    Up: 2d00h
    Incoming Interface List
      LmdtVRF-A Flags: A LMI, Up: 00:00:07
    Outgoing Interface List
      GigabitEthernet0/0/0/2.1034 Flags: LI, Up: 00:00:04
      GigabitEthernet0/0/0/3.1044 Flags: F NS LI, Up: 2d00h
```

It's time to see how the BGP Joins are built and targeted.

Route Import—a new extended community

First, let's have a look at PE1 (the sender PE) and forget for a moment about multicast. PE1 advertises the unicast route toward the source (10.1.1.10):

Example 5-13. Unicast C-S route, advertised from sender PE—PE1 (Junos)

```
juniper@PE1> show route advertising-protocol bgp 172.16.0.201
            10.1.1.10 detail

VRF-A.inet.0: 22 destinations, 30 routes (22 active, ..., 0 hidden)
* 10.1.1.0/24 (1 entry, 1 announced)
 BGP group iBGP-RR type Internal
      Route Distinguisher: 172.16.0.11:101
      VPN Label: 16
      Nexthop: Self
      Flags: Nexthop Change
      MED: 100
      Localpref: 100
      AS path: [65000] 65001 I
      Communities: target:65000:1001 src-as:65000:0
                   rt-import:172.16.0.11:8
```

This unicast route has the following communities:

- RT 65000:1001, the *full mesh* RT of VPN A, so the unicast route is installed in all the PEs of the VPN.

- Source AS 65000:0, matching the locally configured AS at PE1 and PE3.

- Route Import 172.16.0.11:8. It contains the router ID of PE1 (its global loopback address) and 8, a number that is *locally generated* by PE1.

> Chapter 3 discussed the *<IP>:<number>* format. But that format was associated with RDs, which have nothing to do with communities.

PE1 adds these two new communities (Source AS and Route Import) to the VPN IP unicast routes, simply because MVPN is enabled at VRF-A and all the unicast subnets might potentially contain C-Sources. But what is the purpose of Route Imports? Route Import communities are C-Multicast Join *attractors*.

Now, if number 8 is locally generated by PE1, it must mean something to PE1.

Example 5-14. Internal policies at sender PE—PE1 (Junos)

```
juniper@PE1> show policy __vrf-mvpn-export-inet-VRF-A-internal__
Policy __vrf-mvpn-export-inet-VRF-A-internal:
 Term unnamed:
   then community
          + __vrf-mvpn-community-rt_[rt-import:172.16.0.11:8]
          + __vrf-mvpn-community-src_[src-as:65000:0]
       accept

juniper@PE1> show policy __vrf-mvpn-import-cmcast-VRF-A-internal__
Policy __vrf-mvpn-import-cmcast-VRF-A-internal:
 Term unnamed:
   from community
          __vrf-mvpn-community-rt_[target:172.16.0.11:8]
   then accept
```

Nobody configured these policies, at least directly. They were dynamically created after applying the set routing-instances VRF-A protocols mvpn statement. The **export-inet** policy explains why the unicast routes now carry two additional communities. The **import-cmcast** policy is even more interesting: if a C-Multicast— whatever that means—BGP route arrives with RT 172.16.0.11:8, it is imported in VRF-A. In other words, number 8 locally represents VRF-A at PE1.

Route Import and RT are symmetrical or reverse concepts:

- PE1 sets RT 65000:1001, hoping that its prefix will be imported in the VRFs of the *remote* PEs. RTs are like keys that open others' homes.

- PE1 sets Route Import 172.16.0.11:8, telling remote PEs what RT value they must set in order for *their* routes to be imported in PE1's *local* VRF. Sending a Route Import is like telling your friend a code to enter your *own* home.

So, if a PE adds a Route Import community to a prefix, it is basically instructing the remote PEs to *put this value in your prefixes' RT, and they will be installed on my VRF.*

Stripping extended communities from PE→CE eBGP updates

It is a good practice to keep extended communities internal to the local AS. To achieve that, you can remove them with eBGP export policies, as illustrated here:

Example 5-15. Stripping extended communities—PE3 (Junos)

```
policy-options {
    policy-statement PL-VRF-A-eBGP-65001-OUT {
        term BGP {
            from protocol bgp;
            then {
                community delete RT-ALL;
                community delete RI-ALL;
                community delete SRC-AS-ALL;
            }
        } # Other terms omitted
    }
    community RT-ALL members target:*:*;
    community RI-ALL members rt-import:*:*;
    community SRC-AS-ALL members src-as:*:*;
}
```

As discussed earlier in Chapter 3, IOS XR does not require this explicit configuration.

MVPN Source Tree Join routes

OK, let's get back to multicast. PE3 converts its downstream C-PIM Join state into a BGP route called (C-S, C-G) Source Tree Join. This is the *Type 7* route of the MCAST-VPN NLRI, and it is the BGP equivalent of a (C-S, C-G) PIM Join; see Example 5-16.

Example 5-16. Type 7—(C-S, C-G) Source-Tree Join—PE3 (Junos)

```
juniper@PE3> show route advertising-protocol bgp 172.16.0.201
                match-prefix "7:*" detail
[...]
bgp.mvpn.0: 7 destinations, 10 routes (7 active, ..., 0 hidden)
* 7:172.16.0.11:101:65000:32:10.1.1.10:32:232.1.1.1/240
 BGP group iBGP-RR type Internal
     Nexthop: Self
     Flags: Nexthop Change
     Localpref: 100
     AS path: [65000] I
     Communities: target:172.16.0.11:8

VRF-A.mvpn.0: 7 destinations, 10 routes (7 active, ..., 0 hidden)
# Same route here - omitted for brevity
```

The format of a Type 7 route is **7:<ROOT_RD>:<AS>:**<C-S_LENGTH>**:<C-S_ADDRESS>:<C-G_LENGTH>:<C_G_GROUP>**. The <ROOT_RD> field is the RD of VRF-A at the Root PE (PE1).

The prefix does not contain any information about the receiver PE addresses. Imagine 100 receiver PEs have downstream subscribers for the (10.1.1.10, 232.1.1.1) flow.

In this case, the RR gets 100 identical (C-S, C-G) Source Tree Join prefixes, one from each receiver PE. Then, the RR selects one of the 100 routes and reflects it. This is totally fine, because at this C-Multicast stage the sender PE only needs to know whether it needs to add the core to the outgoing interface list; in other words, whether there are receiver PEs for the flow. As for the number and identity of the receiver PEs, it simply does not matter from the perspective of C-Multicast. It is definitely relevant later, when the P-Tunnel is selected and signaled, but that takes place in the Provider context and the sender PE finds the information elsewhere, not in the Source Tree Join routes.

The meat is in the RT—**target:172.16.0.11:8**—which identifies the Source PE at which the BGP route is targeted. Functionally, this RT is equivalent to the Upstream Neighbor field of a PIM Join packet. So, the route is targeted to PE1 (172.16.0.11), the sender PE. But what does number **8** stand for? If you go back to Example 5-13, you can see that **172.16.0.11:8** is precisely the Route Import carried in the *unicast* route toward the C-Source. Figure 5-2 illustrates this mechanism.

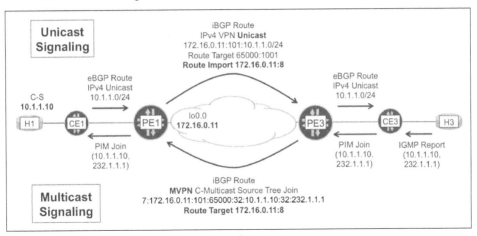

Figure 5-2. C-Multicast Source Tree Join and Route Import

It all comes from the RPF lookup at PE3, the receiver PE. The unicast route toward the C-Source has Route Import **172.16.0.11:8**, and this value is literally copied into the RT of PE3's Source Tree Join BGP route. In this way, PE3 targets the (C-S, C-G) *BGP Join* to PE1, its RPF upstream PE. This route is only imported in PE1's VRF-A.

Receiver PE4, which runs IOS XR, also generates a (C-S, C-G) Source Tree Join route:

Example 5-17. Type 7—(C-S, C-G) Source-Tree Join—PE4 (IOS XR)

```
RP/0/0/CPU0:PE4#show bgp ipv4 mvpn advertised
[...]
Route Distinguisher: 172.16.0.44:101  /* This is the local RD */
```

```
[7][172.16.0.11:101][65000][32][10.1.1.10][32][232.1.1.1]/184
[...]
  Attributes after outbound policy was applied:
    next hop: 172.16.0.44
    ORG AS EXTCOMM
    origin: IGP
    aspath:
    extended community: RT:172.16.0.11:8
```

As you can see, the NLRI in Example 5-16 and Example 5-17 are identical. Indeed, the NLRI does not contain information of the receiver PE.

Let's get back to the (10.1.1.10, 232.1.1.1) flow. At this point, the Root PE (PE1) still doesn't forward the C-Multicast traffic into any P-Tunnel; see Example 5-18.

Example 5-18. Discarding C-Multicast traffic at ingress PE—PE1 (Junos)

```
juniper@PE1> show route forwarding-table multicast table VRF-A detail
[...]
Destination        Type RtRef Next hop   Type Index   NhRef Netif
232.1.1.1.10.1.1.10/64
                   user   0               mdsc  28170    3
```

The mdsc next hop stands for *multicast discard*.

Why is the traffic discarded? Simply, there is no P-Tunnel yet. Let's take care of that.

Signaling Provider Tunnels—BGP and the PMSI Attribute

Let's move from the customer (C-) to the provider (P-) context.

Provider tunnels and PMSIs

RFC 6513 classifies the PEs depending on their role in each Multicast VPN:

Sender Sites set
> PEs in the Sender Sites set can send C-Multicast traffic to other PEs by using P-Tunnels. (In this book, we use the terms "sender PE", "ingress PE," and "root PE" interchangeably.)

Receiver Sites set
> PEs in the Receiver Sites set can receive C-Multicast traffic from P-Tunnels rooted on other (sender) PEs. (In this book, we use the terms "receiver PE," "egress PE," and "leaf PE" interchangeably.)

One PE can be both sender and receiver in the same VPN. Every time you read the words "sender," "receiver," "ingress," "egress," "root," or "leaf", keep in mind that they are used in the context of one specific VPN and even one C-Multicast flow. It is perfectly possible for one PE to be sender for VPN A, receiver for VPN B, and both sender and receiver for VPN C.

RFC 6513 also defines the general concept of PMSI (P-Multicast Service Interface) as the virtual interface that a sender PE uses to put C-Multicast traffic into a P-Tunnel. The P-Tunnel is functionally point-to-multipoint (even if it might be implemented differently) and takes the traffic to a set of receiver PEs. It is very common to refer to the P-Tunnel as a tree, where the sender PE is the root and the receiver PEs are the leaves. The P-Tunnel provides an overlay to the C-Multicast tree: from the point of view of the C-Multicast tree, the P-Tunnel is just one hop.

There are basically three criteria to classify P-Tunnels:

- Whether the P-Tunnel can be shared by different VPNs: Aggregate and Non-Aggregate, respectively.
- How the P-Tunnel's *leaf set* is chosen: Inclusive or Selective.
- The underlying tunnel technology: Ingress Replication, RSVP-TE P2MP, LDP P2MP, LDP MP2MP, and multipoint GRE.

For the first classification, let's consider two VRFs (A and B) and one P-Tunnel. *Typically*, the P-Tunnel is dedicated to one VPN only; either VRF A or B can use it, but not both. There are two exceptions to this rule:

- In *current vendor implementations*, two VPNs can share a given P-Tunnel only if they leak unicast prefixes with each other. In other words, two VPNs that are isolated from each other cannot share a P-Tunnel.
- RFC 6513 also defines the concept of an Aggregate Tunnel, where MPLS label stacking allows two distinct (isolated from each other) VRFs to use the same P-Tunnel. As of this writing, neither Junos nor IOS XR implements Aggregate Tunnels.

In current vendor implementations, and therefore in all of this book's examples, there is a 1:1 relationship between each PMSI and each P-Tunnel. In other words, only one PMSI can point to a given Non-Aggregate P-Tunnel.

Provider tunnel classification—based on the leaf set

In Figure 5-3, PE1 is the sender PE of C-Multicast flow (S1, G1) and it has four MVPN neighbors in VRF-A: PE2, PE3, PE4, and PE5. Clearly, PE2 has a high likelihood to be a receiver PE because it has downstream receivers precisely for (S1, G1). But, what about the other PEs? It depends on the P-Tunnel type:

- An Inclusive Tree (P-Tunnel) goes from the sender PE to *all* of its MVPN neighbors, regardless of their C-PIM Join state. In this example, only PE2 has downstream receivers for (S1, G1). As for the other PEs, they simply drop the packets locally, unless the topology makes them act as transit LSRs for other downstream PEs.

- Selective Trees only reach the receiver PEs with downstream C-Multicast receivers. C-Multicast flows are mapped to Selective PMSIs (S-PMSIs) in different manners. Out of the three S-PMSI examples in Figure 5-3, the first two of them are of type *wildcard*: (*, *) S-PMSI points to a tree that reaches all of the PEs with downstream receivers for *any* flow; (*, G1) S-PMSI points to the PEs with downstream receivers for any (S, G1) flow, where S may be equal to or different from S1. Finally, the (S1, G1) S-PMSI points to the PEs with downstream receivers for (S1, G1).

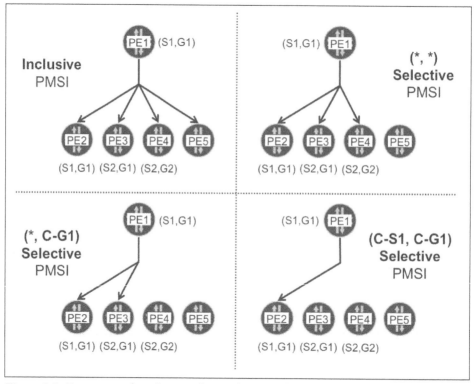

Figure 5-3. Four types of single-rooted provider tunnels

 In a unicast analogy, you can see PMSIs as if they were routes. An Inclusive PMSI (I-PMSI) is like a *static default* route; (*, *) S-PMSI is like a *dynamic default* route; (*, G1) S-PMSI is like a more specific route; and (S1, G1) S-PMSI is like a host /32 route.

It is important to note that the appearance of wildcards does not mean that the scenario moved into ASM mode. Indeed, wildcard S-PMSIs are just a method to map C-Multicast flows to P-Tunnels. This concept is *orthogonal* to C-PIM SSM versus ASM: the model used in the core might or might not match the C-Multicast flavor.

In BGP MVPN, Inclusive Tunnels are advertised inside Type 1 (Intra-AS I-PMSI AD) routes, by using their *optional* PMSI attribute. As for Selective Tunnels, they are advertised inside the *mandatory* PMSI attribute of the MCAST-VPN route *Type 3*: Selective PMSI Auto-Discovery (S-PMSI AD).

In the multicast world, it is not possible to achieve bandwidth efficiency and signaling efficiency at the same time; it is one or the other. (S, G) and (*, G) Selective Tunnels are the most efficient in terms of bandwidth, at the expense of a higher load on the control plane. Inclusive Tunnels and (*, *) Selective Tunnels, on the other hand, have a very efficient signaling, but they often result in a waste of bandwidth resources.

For a good compromise between bandwidth and signaling efficiency, it is a good practice to set a data threshold for the signaling of Selective Tunnels. In this way, low-bitrate flows stay in Inclusive Tunnels, whereas high-bitrate flows are transported in Selective Tunnels.

Inclusive PMSI

Junos MVPN PEs are by default pure receiver PEs. They need explicit P-Tunnel configuration to act as sender PEs. In the following example, PE1 becomes—in the context of VRF-A—the root of an Inclusive P-Tunnel that is to be signaled with mLDP P2MP:

Example 5-19. Inclusive Tunnel based on mLDP P2MP—PE1 (Junos)

```
routing-instances {
    VRF-A {
        provider-tunnel ldp-p2mp;
}}
```

Now, at this point, PE1 readvertises its Type 1 route (now, properly called I-PMSI AD) with a new attribute called PMSI:

Example 5-20. Type 1 route with mLDP P2MP I-PMSI—PE1 (Junos)

```
juniper@PE1> show route advertising-protocol bgp 172.16.0.201
            match-prefix "1:*" detail
[...]
bgp.mvpn.0: 7 destinations, 11 routes (7 active, ..., 0 hidden)
* 1:172.16.0.11:101:172.16.0.11/240 (1 entry, 1 announced)
```

```
[...]
    Communities: target:65000:1001
    PMSI: Flags 0x0: Label 0: LDP-P2MP: Root 172.16.0.11, lsp-id 16777226

VRF-A.mvpn.0: 7 destinations, 11 routes (7 active, ..., 0 hidden)
# Same route here - omitted
```

Thanks to the PMSI attribute, PE1 tells all its MVPN neighbors about the new P-Tunnel: it is based on LDP P2MP, the root is PE1 itself, and there is an opaque value (displayed as lsp-id). These are mLDP root and opaque values, two concepts that were previously explained in the context of mLDP Inband Signaling. Now, in the BGP MVPN case, the mLDP opaque value no longer contains C-Multicast information; it is simply a number, locally significant to PE1, which is the *root* PE that advertises the PMSI.

Are you wondering about the label field? It is mandatory in the PMSI attribute, and it is zero in this case because the sender PE does not choose the label value.

Let's focus on PE2, a sender PE running IOS XR. Site Auto-Discovery in IOS XR—unlike in Junos—requires some P-Tunnel configuration to take place. In other words, an auto-discoverable MVPN PE running IOS XR can potentially be a sender PE by default. Let's pick the key lines from Example 5-5, in the context of the *Inclusive* P-Tunnel that is rooted at PE2 and bound to VRF-A.

Example 5-21. Inclusive Tunnel based on mLDP P2MP—PE2 (IOS XR)

```
multicast-routing
 vrf VRF-A
  address-family ipv4
   bgp auto-discovery mldp
   mdt default mldp p2mp
!
```

With this configuration, PE2 sends the MCAST-VPN Type 1—Intra-AS I-PMSI—route with the PMSI attribute, as you can see from the perspective of the Junos RR.

Example 5-22. Type 1 route with mLDP P2MP I-PMSI—PE2 (IOS XR)

```
juniper@RR1> show route receive-protocol bgp 172.16.0.22
           match-prefix "1:*" detail table bgp.mvpn
[...]
* 1:172.16.0.22:101:172.16.0.22/240 (1 entry, 1 announced)
[...]
   Communities: no-export target:65000:1001
   PMSI: Flags 0x0: Label 0: LDP-P2MP: Root 172.16.0.22, lsp-id 2
```

It is possible to remove the PMSI attribute from the Type 1 route by using `multicast-routing vrf VRF-A address-family ipv4 bgp auto-discovery mldp receiver-site`.

Before moving on to how the actual mLDP tunnel is built, let's explore a bit more about the PMSI attribute's signaling with BGP, this time in the context of Selective Tunnels.

(S, G) Selective PMSI

With the configuration shown in Example 5-23, the Junos sender PE (PE1) creates a specific (S, G) S-PMSI that points to a Selective P-Tunnel, also built with mLDP P2MP.

Example 5-23. (C-S, C-G) S-PMSI based on mLDP P2MP—PE1 (Junos)

```
routing-instances {
    VRF-A {
        provider-tunnel {
            selective {
                group 232.0.0.0/8 {
                    source 0.0.0.0/0 {
                        ldp-p2mp;
                        threshold-rate <kbps>;  # Optional
}}}}}}
```

The (10.1.1.10, 232.1.1.1) Source Tree Join BGP route—sent by remote PEs and targeted to PE1—matches the rule (S, G) = (0/0, 232/8), so PE1 does the following:

- If there is no `threshold-rate`, or if the (C-S, C-G) bit rate exceeds the configured value, PE1 advertises a (C-S, C-G) S-PMSI AD route. Later, PE1 switches this flow's C-Multicast packets to the new (C-S, C-G) Selective Tunnel.

- If there is a `threshold-rate`, but the actual (C-S, C-G) bit rate is below the configured value, PE1 does *not* advertise any (C-S, C-G) S-PMSI AD route. And if it had previously advertised one such route, PE1 withdraws it. Then, PE1 switches this flow's C-Multicast packets into the Inclusive Tunnel, if any. This switchover can be further tuned with timers.

 If you specify a `threshold-rate` and there is no Inclusive PMSI, PE1 cannot forward the low-bitrate flows and discards the packets. For this reason, it is essential to configure an Inclusive PMSI as a fallback whenever a flow does not reach the configured `threshold-rate`.

Example 5-24 shows the newly generated (S, G) S-PMSI MVPN Type 3 route.

Example 5-24. Type 3—(C-S, C-G) S-PMSI AD route—PE1 (Junos)

```
juniper@PE1> show route advertising-protocol bgp 172.16.0.201
            match-prefix "3:*" detail
[...]
bgp.mvpn.0: 8 destinations, 12 routes (8 active, ..., 0 hidden)
* 3:172.16.0.11:101:32:10.1.1.10:32:232.1.1.1:172.16.0.11/240
 BGP group iBGP-RR type Internal
      Nexthop: Self
      Flags: Nexthop Change
      Localpref: 100
      AS path: [65000] I
      Communities: target:65000:1001
      PMSI: Flags 0x0: Label 0: LDP-P2MP: Root 172.16.0.11 ,
                          lsp-id 17004996

VRF-A.mvpn.0: 8 destinations, 12 routes (8 active, ..., 0 hidden)
# Same route here - omitted
```

The format of this (S, G) S-PMSI AD route is `3:<ROOT_RD>:<C-S_LENGTH>:<C-S_ADDRESS>:<C-G_LENGTH>:<C_G_GROUP>:<SENDER_PE_ROUTER_ID>`. The prefix contains a mix of C-Multicast and Provider information.

Note that the IPv4 address length can either be 0 (for wildcard) or 32 (for specific). In other words, there is no subnetting concept here.

Now, let's consider the flow (10.1.2.20, 232.1.1.1), whose sender PE is PE2 and it runs IOS XR. Here again, the receivers are: H3, H4, H33, H34, and H44.

Following is the IOS XR configuration required to signal (S, G) Selective PMSIs:

Example 5-25. (C-S, C-G) S-PMSI based on mLDP P2MP—PE2 (IOS XR)

```
multicast-routing
 vrf VRF-A address-family ipv4
   mdt data mldp <max-number-of-tunnels> threshold <kbps>
!
```

The `threshold` is 1 kbps by default, and you can configure `immediate-switch` if you do not want to set a threshold at all. The latter is the IOS XR's equivalent to not configuring any `threshold-rate` in Junos.

Like in Junos, in IOS XR the (C-S, C-G) flow uses the Inclusive Tunnel until it exceeds the bitrate threshold. Then, PE2 advertises a (C-S, C-G) S-PMSI and switches the traffic to the new (C-S, C-G) Selective Tunnel.

Example 5-26. Type 3—(C-S, C-G) S-PMSI AD route—PE2 (IOS XR)

```
juniper@RR1> show route receive-protocol bgp 172.16.0.22
            match-prefix "3:*" detail table bgp.mvpn
[...]
* 3:172.16.0.22:101:32:10.1.2.20:32:232.1.1.1:172.16.0.22/240
[...]
  Communities: no-export target:65000:1001
  PMSI: Flags 0x0: Label 0: LDP-P2MP: Root 172.16.0.22 , lsp-id 3
```

Junos and IOS XR behave in the same manner for (S, G) S-PMSI AD routes: they both require a matching (S, G) Source Tree Join targeted at the local PE.

Signaling Provider Tunnels—Multipoint LDP for Transport

Inclusive and Selective Tunnels differ in the way they are signaled in BGP—Type 1 versus Type 3 routes—and, of course, in the leaf set. Let's focus on the (C-S, C-G) = (10.1.1.10, 232.1.1.1) C-Multicast flow, whose sender PE is PE1. Suppose that PE1 is the root of an Inclusive Tunnel and of a (C-S, C-G) Selective Tunnel:

- The Inclusive Tree has leaves PE2, PE3, and PE4. This matches the list of PE1's MVPN neighbors.
- The (C-S, C-G) Selective Tree has leaves PE3 and PE4. This is indeed the list of PEs with downstream receivers for (C-S, C-G).

When it receives an I-PMSI AD route, a receiver PE looks for a PMSI attribute. If it finds one—remember it is optional—and its type is LDP P2MP, the receiver PE *immediately* begins to signal an LSP branch toward the root. This happens regardless of the actual C-Multicast state. In the context of a given VRF, a receiver PE must become a leaf of *all* the I-PMSI's rooted at its MVPN neighbors, even if the receiver PE is not connected to any C-Multicast receivers whatsoever.

The logic is different for Selective Trees. After receiving an S-PMSI AD route, the receiver PE looks at the PMSI attribute. Then, it checks if there are downstream C-Multicast receivers in the VRF matching the (C-S, C-G) or (*, C-G) or (*, *) information encoded in the NLRI. *Only if there is a best-match*—in the sense that there is no other NLRI that matches the downstream C-Multicast state in a more specific manner—the receiver PE becomes a leaf of the Selective Tree.

These are the differences. But what do Inclusive and Selective P-Tunnels have in common? If the P-Tunnels are based on LDP P2MP, their Multipoint LDP (mLDP) signaling logic is identical. Although each PMSI has a different [`root address, opaque value`] pair and it has a different leaf set, there is no clue inside the mLDP FECs about the Inclusive or Selective nature of the tree. Let's pick as an example a Selective Tree rooted at PE1 and dedicated to the (10.1.1.10, 232.1.1.1) flow. You can compare

Figure 5-4 to Example 5-24 and verify that the BGP PMSI attribute matches the mLDP P2MP FEC value.

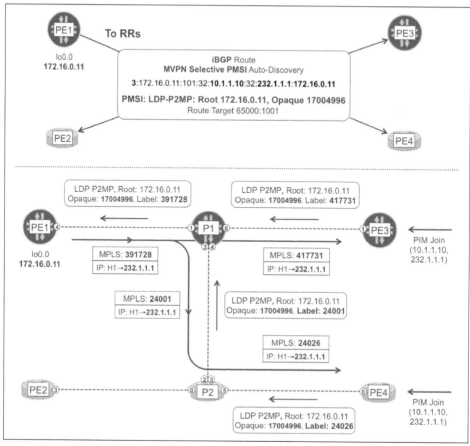

Figure 5-4. MVPN Selective P-Tunnel—signaled with mLDP P2MP

mLDP signaling begins at the receiver PEs

Remember, in the LDP world, signaling typically begins from the tail end. The following example demonstrates how Junos receiver PE3 proclaims itself a leaf of the new LDP P2MP, and it informs P1 (its RPF neighbor toward the root):

Example 5-27. mLDP P2MP FEC signaling from egress PE—PE3 (Junos)

```
juniper@PE3> show ldp database p2mp
Input label database, 172.16.0.33:0--172.16.0.1:0
Labels received: 8

Output label database, 172.16.0.33:0--172.16.0.1:0
Labels advertised: 16
```

```
  Label     Prefix
  417731      P2MP root-addr 172.16.0.11, lsp-id 17004996 [...]
[...]
```

In parallel, IOS XR PE4 also informs P2 (its RPF neighbor toward the root) that it intends to become a leaf of the new LDP P2MP tunnel, as shown here in Example 5-28.

Example 5-28. mLDP P2MP FEC signaling from egress PE—PE4 (IOS XR)

```
RP/0/0/CPU0:PE4# show mpls mldp database root 172.16.0.11
mLDP database
LSM-ID: 0x00015   Type: P2MP   Uptime: 01:53:57
  FEC Root         : 172.16.0.11
  Opaque decoded   : [global-id 17004996]
  Upstream neighbor(s) :
    172.16.0.2:0 [Active] Uptime: 01:53:57
      Local Label (D) : 24026
  Downstream  client(s):
    PIM MDT          Uptime: 01:53:57
      Egress intf    : LmdtVRF-A [...]
```

There are two things in common between Example 5-27 and Example 5-28: the root 172.16.0.11, and the opaque value 17004996. These are identical to the values encoded in the S-PMSI AD route's PMSI attribute back in Example 5-24. The label may differ between PE3 and PE4, though: MPLS business as usual.

mLDP signaling continues at the Transit Ps

To review the LDP P2MP signaling and forwarding in detail, refer back to "In-Band Signaling" on page 201. The mechanics are almost identical here, except for one difference. In the BGP MVPN service, the mLDP Opaque field no longer contains C-Multicast information; instead, it is just a number, which is locally significant to PE1 because PE1 previously encoded it inside the PMSI attribute.

As the LDP P2MP FEC signaling progresses toward the root, the (root, opaque) values remain unchanged. P2 generates another LDP P2MP label mapping that it sends to P1 the branch point of the LSP. And P1 sends a single Label Mapping to PE1.

Following is the view from P1's perspective:

Example 5-29. mLDP P2MP FEC signaling at Transit P—P1 (Junos)

```
juniper@P1> show ldp database p2mp
Input label database, 172.16.0.1:0--172.16.0.2:0
  Label     Prefix
  24001       P2MP root-addr 172.16.0.11, lsp-id 17004996

Output label database, 172.16.0.1:0--172.16.0.2:0
```

```
Input label database, 172.16.0.1:0--172.16.0.11:0

Output label database, 172.16.0.1:0--172.16.0.11:0
Label     Prefix
 391728      P2MP root-addr 172.16.0.11, lsp-id 17004996

Input label database, 172.16.0.1:0--172.16.0.33:0
 Label     Prefix
 417731      P2MP root-addr 172.16.0.11, lsp-id 17004996

Output label database, 172.16.0.1:0--172.16.0.33:0
```

mLDP signaling arrives at the sender PE

When PE1 receives the label mapping from P1, the opaque value 17004996 makes full
sense. Indeed, as you can see back in Example 5-24, PE1 had generated that number
dynamically! As shown in Example 5-30, there is a useful command that binds C-
Multicast state to P-Tunnels.

Example 5-30. C-Multicast state at ingress PE—PE1 (Junos)

```
juniper@PE1> show mvpn c-multicast inet instance-name VRF-A
[...]
Instance : VRF-A
  MVPN Mode : RPT-SPT
  C-mcast IPv4 (S:G)          Provider Tunnel                       St
    10.1.1.10/32:232.1.1.1/32   S-LDP-P2MP:172.16.0.11, lsp-id 17004996  RM
```

The RM flag means that the original Source Tree Join was received from a remote PE
(as compared to being generated by the local PE). Remember, while keeping in mind
Figure 5-1: a Source Tree Join triggered the S-PMSI AD route, which in turn triggered the mLDP signaling from the leaves.

 All the signaling described so far is fully driven by the control plane
(except when S-PMSI data thresholds are in place). This is one key
advantage of BGP MVPN over establishing C-PIM PE-PE adjacencies.

Forwarding plane: from the Junos root PE to the leaves

After the P2MP LSP is completely signaled, the C-Multicast traffic flows nicely to all
the receivers. Here is the forwarding state at the sender PE:

Example 5-31. Forwarding state at ingress PE—PE1 (Junos)

```
juniper@PE1> show route table VRF-A.inet.1 active-path
            match-prefix "232.1.1.1,*"

VRF-A.inet.1: 4 destinations, 5 routes (4 active, ..., 0 hidden)
+ = Active Route, - = Last Active, * = Both

232.1.1.1,10.1.1.10/64*[MVPN/70] 00:10:00
                      > to 10.0.0.3 via ge-2/0/4.0, Push 391728
```

 In both Junos and IOS XR, when *any* service uses a P2MP LSP for the transport of C-Multicast packets, the ingress PE only pushes one MPLS label. There is no label stacking because the P2MP LSP only transports packets of a single VPN (if the tunnel is non-aggregate). In other words, the P2MP LSP label has a combined service + transport significance.

The forwarding state in the transit LSRs is very similar to the one already shown for mLDP In-Band Signaling, so it is omitted.

Let's have a look at PE3, a Junos receiver PE (see Example 5-32).

Example 5-32. Forwarding state at an egress PE—PE3 (Junos)

```
juniper@PE3> show route label 417731

mpls.0: 16 destinations, 16 routes (16 active, 0 holddown, 0 hidden)
+ = Active Route, - = Last Active, * = Both

417731             *[LDP/9] 00:03:47, metric 1
                   > via vt-2/0/0.101, Pop
```

The C-Multicast packets get their MPLS header removed at the vt- interface. Then, PE3 performs an IPv4 lookup in the context of VRF-A and replicates the packet toward the two access interfaces with downstream receivers.

Likewise, the IOS XR receiver PE4 also pops the label and processes the packet in the context of VRF-A, as illustrated in Example 5-33.

Example 5-33. Forwarding state at egress PE—PE4 (IOS XR)

```
RP/0/0/CPU0:PE4#show mpls mldp forwarding label 24026
mLDP MPLS forwarding database

24026  LSM-ID: 0x00023 HLI: 0x00001 flags: None
   LmdtVRF-A, RPF-ID: 3, TIDv4: E0000011, TIDv6: E0800011
```

In this book's tests, H44 only receives the C-Multicast flow if PE4's *unicast* CEF entry for 172.16.0.11 resolves to a LDP label. If it resolves to a RSVP tunnel, the traffic is not forwarded to H44. This restriction was not observed in Junos PE3. Chapter 4 covers this topic in more detail.

 Remember that there is no Penultimate Hop Popping (PHP) for P2MP LSPs! There is one MPLS label, end to end. Thanks to this label, receiver PEs know to which VRF the C-Multicast packets belong.

Root PE running IOS XR

Let's focus for a moment on the (10.1.2.20, 232.1.1.1) flow, whose sender PE is PE2. The lsp-id in Example 5-26 corresponds to the Opaque value locally assigned by PE2.

Example 5-34. mLDP P2MP FEC at the ingress PE—PE2 (IOS XR)

```
RP/0/0/CPU0:PE2#show mpls mldp database root 172.16.0.22
mLDP database
LSM-ID: 0x0002E   Type: P2MP   Uptime: 1w1d
  FEC Root            : 172.16.0.22 (we are the root)
  Opaque decoded      : [global-id 3]
  Upstream neighbor(s) :
    None
  Downstream client(s):
    LDP 172.16.0.2:0  Uptime: 23:05:14
      Next Hop        : 10.0.0.5
      Interface       : GigabitEthernet0/0/0/3
      Remote label (D) : 24002
    PIM MDT           Uptime: 1w1d
      Egress intf     : LmdtVRF-A
[...]
```

By combining the two commands in Example 5-35, you can see how PE2 forwards the (10.1.2.20, 232.1.1.1) packets in the context of VRF-A.

Example 5-35. Forwarding state at ingress PE—PE2 (IOS XR)

```
RP/0/0/CPU0:PE2#show mrib vrf VRF-A route 232.1.1.1 10.1.2.20 detail
[...]
(10.1.2.20,232.1.1.1) Ver: 0x4313 RPF nbr: 10.1.22.0 Flags: RPF EID
[...]
  Incoming Interface List
    GigabitEthernet0/0/0/0 Flags: A, Up: 01:05:50
  Outgoing Interface List
    LmdtVRF-A Flags: F LMI, Up: 01:05:50, Head LSM-ID: 0x0002E
  [...]
```

```
RP/0/0/CPU0:PE2# show mrib mpls forwarding
LSP information (MLDP) :
    LSM ID: 0x0002E Role: Head [...]
    HEAD LSM ID: 0x0002E
[...]
      Outsegment Info #1 [H/Push]:
        Outgoing Label: 24002
        Outgoing  IF: GigabitEthernet0/0/0/3 (P) Nexthop: 10.0.0.5
```

The key is to link the LSM ID of both commands' output (LSM stands for *Label-Switched Multicast*). This method applies to Multicast MPLS in general and is not specific of mLDP.

BGP Multicast VPN with RSVP-TE P2MP Transport

The main advantage of BGP Multicast VPN is the way it decouples C-Multicast from P-Tunnel signaling. The very flexible PMSI attribute is the glue between both worlds. So far, you saw PMSIs encoding LDP P2MP information, but many other P-Tunnel technologies are available. Keep in mind that the sender PE is the one responsible for choosing the P-Tunnel. And each sender PE makes its own choice, which may be even different for each C-Multicast flow. It is up to the receiver PEs to tune and join the P-Tunnels signaled by the sender PEs. This flexible logic is allowed by the protocol and currently implemented by Junos.

In both Junos and IOS XR, it is possible to transport C-Unicast traffic on LDP P2MP LSPs while C-Multicast traffic travels on RSVP-TE P2MP LSPs. The reverse combination (C-Unicast with RSVP-TE P2MP, and C-Multicast with mLDP) is also supported in Junos. The P-Tunnel choices for C-Unicast and C-Multicast are generally independent from each other.

In the interest of brevity, this section skips the Site AD and C-Multicast signaling, which is orthogonal to the P-Tunnel flavor chosen. The goal is to illustrate how you can signal P2MP LSPs by using RSVP-TE and the role that BGP takes on it. You can already guess that the PMSI attribute is of fundamental importance.

In the terms of Table 4-1, the following scenario is S2, A3, C3, E3, **T3, Y3**.

The baseline RSVP-TE configuration is very simple:

- Junos PEs and Ps have core links configured under [edit protocols rsvp].
- IOS XR PEs and Ps have core links configured under mpls traffic-eng (and optionally rsvp).

Advertising the Inclusive PMSI—RSVP-TE P2MP

Sender PE running Junos

PE1 can be the root of only one Inclusive P-Tunnel at VRF-A. If instead of using mLDP (Example 5-19) you choose to build the P-Tunnel with RSVP-TE P2MP, the following example shows you how to do it:

Example 5-36. Inclusive Tunnel based on RSVP-TE P2MP—PE1 (Junos)

```
routing-instances {
    VRF-A {
        provider-tunnel {
            rsvp-te {
                label-switched-path-template {
                    default-template;
}}}}}
```

The `default-template` exists by default, and it means no Traffic Engineering (TE) constraints. It is also possible to explicitly configure named templates that define the TE constraints of the new LSPs. This is indeed one of the unique advantages of RSVP-TE, and it applies to P2MP LSPs, as well. With the previous configuration, PE1 readvertises the Type 1 (I-PMSI AD) BGP route with a new PMSI value.

Example 5-37. Type 1 route with RSVP-TE P2MP I-PMSI—PE1 (Junos)

```
juniper@PE1> show route advertising-protocol bgp 172.16.0.201
            match-prefix "1:*" detail
[...]
* 1:172.16.0.11:101:172.16.0.11/240 (1 entry, 1 announced)
[...]
    Communities: target:65000:1001
    PMSI: Flags 0x0: Label 0: RSVP-TE: Session_13[172.16.0.11:0:19208:172.16.0.11]
[...]
```

The PMSI format is already familiar: a protocol (RSVP-TE), a root (172.16.0.11 = PE1), and a number that is locally significant to the root. If you are thinking that this number will be present in RSVP-TE protocol messages, you made a good guess! Indeed, it's the RSVP-TE Tunnel ID.

The RSVP-TE messages used to establish a P2MP LSP contain an object called P2MP LSP Tunnel IPv4 Session. This object is defined in RFC 4875 - *Extensions to RSVP-TE for Point-to-Multipoint TE Label Switched Paths (LSPs)*. Its format is <*Extended Tunnel ID, Reserved, Tunnel ID, P2MP ID*> and must be globally unique. And, it is globally unique because it contains the loopback address for PE1 and a number that is locally generated by PE1 in order to identify the P-Tunnel.

Sender PE running IOS XR

PE2 can be the root of only one Inclusive P-Tunnel at VRF-A, right now configured with mLDP (Example 5-21). Example 5-38 contains the syntax to make it based on RSVP-TE P2MP instead.

Example 5-38. Inclusive Tunnel based on RSVP-TE P2MP—PE1 (Junos)

```
ipv4 unnumbered mpls traffic-eng Loopback0
!
multicast-routing
 vrf VRF-A
  address-family ipv4
   bgp auto-discovery p2mp-te
   mdt default p2mp-te
!
mpls traffic-eng
 auto-tunnel p2mp
  tunnel-id min 1000 max 1050
!
```

PE2 now sends the MCAST-VPN Type 1—Intra-AS I-PMSI—route with a different PMSI attribute, as you can see from the perspective of the Junos RR.

Example 5-39. Type 1 route with RSVP-TE P2MP I-PMSI—PE2 (IOS XR)

```
juniper@RR1> show route receive-protocol bgp 172.16.0.22
            match-prefix "1:*" detail table bgp.mvpn
[...]
* 1:172.16.0.22:101:172.16.0.22/240 (1 entry, 1 announced)
[...]
    Communities: no-export target:65000:1001
    PMSI: Flags 0x0: Label 0: RSVP-TE: Session_13[0.0.3.238:0:1006:172.16.0.22]
```

The format is slightly different from that of Junos because the Extended Tunnel ID is no longer equal to the P2MP ID; instead, it is equal to the Tunnel ID: 0.0.3.238 = 3 x 256 + 238 = 1006. It is still globally unique, though, and more important, interoperable with Junos.

Receiver PEs running Junos

Junos receiver PEs such as PE3 look into the received MCAST-VPN routes and dynamically adapt to the P-Tunnel encoded in the PMSI, which can be a MPLS flavor or P-PIM/GRE. In other words, as an administrator you can change the PMSI configuration on the (Junos or IOS XR) sender PEs without having to adapt the configuration on Junos receiver PEs. The latter dynamically determine what to do and no configuration is required.

Receiver PEs running IOS XR

Both Junos and IOS XR support the coexistence of P-PIM/GRE and MPLS P-Tunnels to migrate an existent P-PIM/GRE transport to MPLS. In contrast, as of this writing, IOS XR supports up to one P-Tunnel *MPLS* technology per VRF, which can be mLDP P2MP, RSVP-TE P2MP, and so on. After the choice is made, the PE uses this one technology for all the MPLS P-Tunnels in the VRF. This happens regardless of the role (root or leaf) that the PE plays in each P-Tunnel. In other words, it is generally assumed that all of the PEs in the VPN are configured with the same P-Tunnel type.

The configuration of a receiver PE is a combination of Example 5-38 and Example 5-40.

Example 5-40. RPF Policy at receiver PE—PE4 (IOS XR)

```
route-policy PL-BGP-MVPN-RSVP-TE-P2MP
  set core-tree p2mp-te-default
end-policy
!
router pim
 vrf VRF-A
  address-family ipv4
   rpf topology route-policy PL-BGP-MVPN-RSVP-TE-P2MP
   mdt c-multicast-routing bgp
!
```

Advertising Selective PMSIs—RSVP-TE P2MP

You can also base Selective P-Tunnels on RSVP-TE P2MP. Suppose that H1 starts to generate a new flow (10.1.1.10, **232.2.2.2**), and you decide to transport it on a P2MP LSP signaled with RSVP-TE. You can turn Example 5-23 from mLDP into RSVP-TE, but it would also affect (10.1.1.10, **232.1.1.1**), the other active flow sent by H1. So, let's leave that configuration block in place *as is* and add a more specific one for the new flow. Junos uses a best-match logic to map a C-Multicast flow to a PMSI.

The following additional configuration at PE1 meets the requirements:

Example 5-41. (C-S, C-G) S-PMSI based on RSVP-TE P2MP—PE1 (Junos)

```
routing-instances {
    VRF-A {
        provider-tunnel {
            selective {
                group 232.2.0.0/16 {
                    source 0.0.0.0/0 {
                        rsvp-te {
                            label-switched-path-template {
                                default-template;
                            }
```

```
                        }
                        threshold-rate <kbps>;  # Optional
}}}}}}
```

By playing with (C-S, C-G) addresses and masks, Junos sender PEs can use different P-Tunnel protocols for different C-Multicast flows. Example 5-42 illustrates how the (C-S, C-G) S-PMSI AD route looks like after the configuration is applied and all the conditions to signal a S-PMSI are met (see the details in the previous section about BGP MVPN with mLDP).

Example 5-42. Type 3—(C-S, C-G) S-PMSI AD route—PE1 (Junos)

```
juniper@PE1> show route advertising-protocol bgp 172.16.0.201
            match-prefix "3:*" detail
[...]
bgp.mvpn.0: 9 destinations, 14 routes (9 active, ..., 0 hidden)
* 3:172.16.0.11:101:32:10.1.1.10:32:232.2.2.2:172.16.0.11/240
[...]
   Communities: target:65000:1001
   PMSI: Flags 0x1: Label 0: RSVP-TE: Session_13[172.16.0.11:0:58476:172.16.0.11]

VRF-A.mvpn.0: 9 destinations, 14 routes (9 active, ..., 0 hidden)
# Same route here - omitted for brevity
```

Note the flag 0x1. It stands for *Leaf Information Required*. In other words, PE1 is instructing its neighbors to *send me a leaf AD route if you want to become a leaf for this S-PMSI*. This flag was not set for mLDP-based P-Tunnels.

Following is the IOS XR syntax to configure Selective Tunnels based on RSVP-TE P2MP:

Example 5-43. (C-S, C-G) S-PMSI based on RSVP-TE P2MP—PE2 (IOS XR)

```
ipv4 unnumbered mpls traffic-eng Loopback0
!
multicast-routing
 vrf VRF-A
  address-family ipv4
   mdt data p2mp-te <max-number-of-tunnels> threshold <kbps>
!
mpls traffic-eng
 auto-tunnel p2mp
  tunnel-id min 1000 max 1050
!
```

As of this writing, the MPLS PMSIs rooted or terminated at the same VRF on a given IOS XR PE, must all rely on the same P-Tunnel technology.

Signaling P- Tunnels with RSVP-TE P2MP

RSVP-TE and LDP have many differences, and one of them is the *direction* in which LSPs are signaled. This has important implications:

- LDP LSP signaling begins from downstream (tail-end). In P2MP terms, LDP P2MP LSPs are signaled from the leaves. This means that the leaves must know in advance what the root is. And they do know it easily, because the root address is part of the PMSI attribute included in the I-PMSI and S-PMSI AD routes.

- RSVP-TE LSP signaling begins from upstream (head-end). In P2MP terms, RSVP-TE P2MP LSPs are signaled from the root. This means that the root must know in advance what the leaves are. This is trickier because the PMSI is advertised from the root to the leaves, not the other way around.

So, how does a sender PE know what the set of receiver PEs is?

For the Inclusive PMSI, it is easy: by definition, every neighbor in the MVPN is a leaf of the Inclusive Tree. So PE1 signals a RSVP-TE P2MP LSP with leaves PE2, PE3, and PE4. Likewise, PE2 signals an LSP toward PE1, PE3, and PE4.

For Selective PMSIs, the mechanism is a bit more complex. There must be a way for the receiver PEs to signal that they want to be a leaf of a certain Selective Tree. They achieve that with a new BGP MCAST-VPN **Type 4 – Leaf AD** route, which they target to the sender PE.

Let's examine the following example: an S-PMSI rooted at PE1 and transporting the (10.1.1.10, 232.2.2.2) C-Multicast flow. Note that the RSVP-TE P2MP LSP signaling mechanism is the same, regardless of the Inclusive or Selective nature of the Tree, but the S-PMSI example involves more BGP signaling and therefore it is more interesting to illustrate.

Figure 5-5 illustrates the entire signaling (BGP and RSVP-TE). As you can see, a field is common to the S-PMSI AD BGP route (the PMSI attribute) and to the RSVP-TE messages. The value of this field is 172.16.0.11:0:58476:172.16.0.11, and it is the P2MP LSP Tunnel IPv4 Session. You can think of it as a globally unique P2MP LSP identifier.

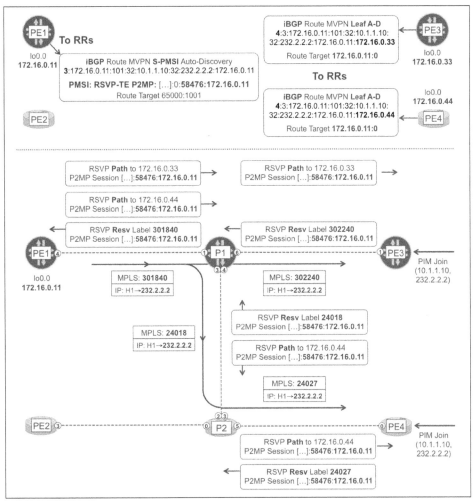

Figure 5-5. MVPN Selective P-Tunnel—signaled with RSVP P2MP

One RSVP-TE P2MP LSP is actually a set of sub-LSPs—in this case, two sub-LSPs: PE1→PE3 and PE1→PE4. The ingress PE (PE1) signals each sub-LSP independently, so there are two different Path messages from PE1 to P1. On the way back, P1 realizes that the P2MP LSP identifier is the same in both sub-LSPs and sends one single Resv message up to P1. This is very similar to the way LDP P2MP works at the branch LSRs.

One common way to call these sub-LSPs is Source to Leaf (S2L).

Finally, the leaf PEs (PE3 and PE4) receive RSVP-TE Path messages whose P2MP LSP Tunnel IPv4 Session has a value that perfectly matches the PMSI attribute of the BGP route. This is how the leaf PE binds the RSVP-TE P2MP sub-LSP to VRF-A.

Leaf AD routes

Let's have a look at the leaf AD route sent by Junos PE3:

Example 5-44. Type 4—leaf AD route—PE3 (Junos)

```
juniper@PE3> show route advertising-protocol bgp 172.16.0.201
            match-prefix "4:*" detail
[...]
bgp.mvpn.0: 9 destinations, 14 routes (9 active, ..., 0 hidden)
* 4:3:172.16.0.11:101:32:10.1.1.10:32:232.2.2.2:172.16.0.11:172.16.0.33/240
[...]
   Communities: target:172.16.0.11:0

VRF-A.mvpn.0: 9 destinations, 14 routes (9 active, ..., 0 hidden)
# Same route here - omitted for brevity
```

The NLRI format is **4:<S-PMSI-A-D_NLRI>:<RECEIVER_PE_ROUTER_ID>**. Type 4 (leaf AD) routes are sent as a response to Type 3 (S-PMSI AD) routes. Their meaning is *I want to become a leaf of this S-PMSI that you advertised*. So, the receiver PE simply takes the prefix of the S-PMSI AD route to which it is replying, and inserts it in the leaf AD route prefix.

As for the route target, it contains the router ID of PE1—the sender PE that originated the S-PMSI AD route—and *always* number zero. PE1 automatically creates a *global* policy (one common policy for all the VRFs) to import routes with this route target.

Example 5-45. Internal policy at sender PE—PE1 (Junos)

```
juniper@PE1> show policy
                    __vrf-mvpn-import-cmcast-leafAD-global-internal__
Policy __vrf-mvpn-import-cmcast-leafAD-global-internal__:
   Term unnamed:
       from community
          __vrf-mvpn-community-rt_import-target-global-internal__
                                    [target:172.16.0.11:0]
       then accept
   Term unnamed:
       then reject
```

This RT is slightly different from the one used in Type 7 (Source Tree Join) routes, which contained a non-zero VRF identifier. So, how does PE1 find the VRF to which the leaf AD route belongs? When PE3 copies the original S-PMSI AD route into the leaf AD prefix, it is basically mirroring a NLRI that *PE1 had locally assigned* to VRF-A. Thus, the RT does not require any extra information apart from PE1's router ID.

Let's have a look at the leaf AD route sent by IOS XR PE4, shown in Example 5-46.

Example 5-46. Type 4—leaf AD route—PE4 (IOS XR)

```
RP/0/0/CPU0:PE4#show bgp ipv4 mvpn advertised
[...]
Route Distinguisher: 172.16.0.44:101    /* This is the local RD */
[4][3][172.16.0.11:101][32][10.1.1.10][32][232.2.2.2][172.16.0.11]
                                                 [172.16.0.44]/224
[...]
  Attributes after outbound policy was applied:
[...]
     extended community: RT:172.16.0.11:0 SEG-NH:172.16.0.44:0
```

RSVP-TE P2MP state at the sender PEs

As the following example demonstrates, the sender PE maintains one RSVP-TE session per sub-LSP:

Example 5-47. RSVP-TE P2MP LSP at the ingress PE—PE1 (Junos)

```
juniper@PE1> show rsvp session p2mp ingress
Ingress RSVP: 2 sessions
P2MP name: 172.16.0.11:101:mv1:VRF-A, P2MP branch count: 2
To          From        State Style Labelin Labelout LSPname
172.16.0.33 172.16.0.11 Up    SE    -       301840
                        172.16.0.33:172.16.0.11:101:mv1:VRF-A

172.16.0.44 172.16.0.11 Up    SE    -       301840
                        172.16.0.44:172.16.0.11:101:mv1:VRF-A
Total 2 displayed, Up 2, Down 0
```

The sub-LSPs are linked together into one single P2MP LSP, thanks to the common P2MP LSP Tunnel IPv4 Session object, whose Tunnel ID is displayed as port here:

Example 5-48. P2MP Session object at the ingress PE—PE1 (Junos)

```
juniper@PE1> show rsvp session p2mp detail
            name 172.16.0.11:101:mv1:VRF-A
[...]
  Port number: sender 1 receiver 58476 protocol 0
[...]
  Port number: sender 1 receiver 58476 protocol 0
```

As a result, PE1 does not need to replicate the packet. One single copy of the packet is pushed out to P1, as illustrated in Example 5-49.

Example 5-49. Forwarding state at the ingress PE—PE1 (Junos)

```
juniper@PE1> show route table VRF-A.inet.1 match-prefix "232.2.2.2*"

VRF-A.inet.1: 5 destinations, 5 routes (5 active, ...)
```

```
+ = Active Route, - = Last Active, * = Both

232.2.2.2,10.1.1.10/64*[MVPN/70] 01:12:14
                   > to 10.0.0.3 via ge-2/0/4.0, Push 301840
```

The mechanics are the same in IOS XR sender PEs. The format of the LSP dynamic names is different, though, as you can see here:

Example 5-50. RSVP-TE P2MP LSP at the ingress PE—PE2 (IOS XR)

```
RP/0/CPU0:PE2#show mpls traffic-eng tunnels auto-tunnel brief

           TUNNEL NAME          DESTINATION      STATUS  STATE
        ^tunnel-mte1009         172.16.0.11        up    up
        ^tunnel-mte1009         172.16.0.33        up    up
        ^tunnel-mte1009         172.16.0.44        up    up
        ^tunnel-mte1011         172.16.0.33        up    up
        ^tunnel-mte1011         172.16.0.44        up    up
^ = automatically created P2MP tunnel [...]
```

In Example 5-50, ^tunnel-mte1009 is the Inclusive Tunnel rooted at PE2, whereas ^tunnel-mte1011 is a Selective Tunnel also rooted at PE2.

RSVP-TE P2MP state at the Transit LSRs

P1 is a branching point for the Selective Tree that carries the (10.1.1.10, 232.2.2.2) flow.

Example 5-51. RSVP-TE P2MP LSP at the Transit P—P1 (Junos)

```
juniper@P1> show rsvp session transit p2mp
[...]
P2MP name: 172.16.0.11:101:mv1:VRF-A, P2MP branch count: 2
To              From         State  Style  Labelin Labelout LSPname
172.16.0.33     172.16.0.11  Up        SE   301840   302240
                             172.16.0.33:172.16.0.11:101:mv1:VRF-A

172.16.0.44     172.16.0.11  Up        SE   301840    24018
                             172.16.0.44:172.16.0.11:101:mv1:VRF-A
[...]
```

P1 is replicating the packets toward PE3 and P2. Finally, P2 is not a branching point and therefore only displays one branch for this Selective Tree rooted at PE1.

Example 5-52. RSVP-TE P2MP LSP at the Transit P—P2 (IOS XR)

```
RP/0/CPU0:P2# show mpls forwarding labels 24018
Local  Outgoing  Prefix          Outgoing    Next Hop     Bytes
Label  Label     or ID           Interface                Switched
------ --------- --------------- ----------- ------------ --------
24018  24027     P2MP TE: 58476  Gi0/0/0/5   10.0.0.11     2170
```

RSVP-TE P2MP state at the receiver PEs

Because there is no PHP for P2MP LSPs, the receiver PEs pop the MPLS label and replicate the packet toward their C-Multicast interfaces with receiver state for the (10.1.1.10, 232.2.2.2) flow.

BGP Multicast VPN with Ingress Replication

Multicast was invented as a method to efficiently replicate traffic in a network. Ingress Replication (IR) is at the opposite end: the sender PE (ingress PE) sends one different copy of each C-Multicast packet to each of the remote receiver PEs. Each packet copy is targeted to one receiver PE and it travels in a P2P (or MP2P, in the case of LDP) LSP.

Imagine a sender PE with just one core uplink interface and 1,000 receiver PEs. With P2MP LSPs, the sender/ingress PE just needs to send one copy of each C-Multicast packet out of the core uplink. With IR, however, it needs to send 1,000 copies!

Despite its extreme inefficiency in the forwarding plane, IR has a use case. Because you can use the same LSPs for transporting the C-Unicast and the C-Multicast packets, from a signaling perspective, IR can be totally transparent for the transit LSRs. This facilitates deploying an MVPN service without having to touch the configuration of the P-routers. For fast, ad hoc deployments or in multivendor networks with legacy implementations that do not support P2MP LSPs in an interoperable manner, this can be an advantage.

In the terms of Table 4-1, there are many IR flavors depending on the *-to-point* tunneling technology used. Here is the list:

- For GRE Unicast, it is S2, A3, C3, **E3 over E1**, **T0**, **Y1**. This is MPLS-over-GRE-over-IP Unicast, and it is beyond the scope of this book.

- For LDP, it is S2, A3, C3, **E3**, **T2**, **Y2**.

- For RSVP-TE, it is S2, A3, C3, **E3**, **T3**, **Y1**.

- For regular node-segment SPRING, it is S2, A3, C3, **E3**, **T4**, **Y2**.

- For traffic-engineered SPRING, it is S2, A3, C3, **E3**, **T4**, **Y1**.

The good news is that the MVPN configuration and signaling are the same for all of these different flavors.

Inclusive PMSI—IR

Let's begin with Inclusive PMSIs and then move on to Selective PMSIs.

IR I-PMSI configuration

Following is the Junos configuration of an IR Inclusive Tunnel rooted at PE1:

Example 5-53. Inclusive Tunnel based on IR—PE1 (Junos)

```
routing-instances {
    VRF-A {
        provider-tunnel {
            ingress-replication label-switched-path;
}}}
```

This configuration reuses the existing *-to-point* LSPs without signaling any new LSPs. If you want to signal new *-to-point* LSPs, which are dedicated to this service, you can also specify a template (this option is available for RSVP-TE P2P only).

Here is the IOS XR configuration of an IR Inclusive Tunnel rooted at PE2:

Example 5-54. Inclusive Tunnel based on IR—PE2 (IOS XR)

```
1     multicast-routing
2      vrf VRF-A
3       address-family ipv4
4        bgp auto-discovery ingress-replication
5        mdt default ingress-replication
6      !
```

The configuration of IR Selective Trees is left as an exercise for the reader.

IR I-PMSI signaling

Figure 5-6 illustrates the IR Inclusive Tree rooted at PE1. Note that the label value advertised by PE1 is irrelevant for this P-Tunnel; it would be relevant for the Inclusive Trees rooted at other PEs. As for the LDP-PEx labels, they are mapped, hop by hop, to the IPv4 unicast FEC 172.16.0.xx/32 (refer back to Figure 2-3 and Figure 2-4).

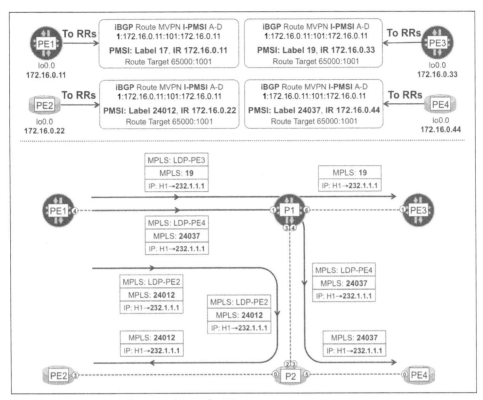

Figure 5-6. MVPN Inclusive P-Tunnel—IR

The forwarding mechanism for each packet is similar to IPv4 VPN Unicast: double push at the ingress PE, and PHP of the transport label. In this example, the MPLS transport protocol is LDP, but it could be a different one, as well.

In Junos, each sender PE can freely choose the P-Tunnel technology of its own rooted PMSIs. There is one exception to this rule: *Inclusive* IR P-Tunnels.

Looking back at Figure 5-6, PE1 knows what service MPLS label to push by looking at the Intra-AS PMSI AD route of the remote PEs. In other words, the IR Inclusive Tree rooted at PE1 requires the remote PEs (PE2, PE3, and PE4) to *also* be themselves the root of an IR Inclusive Tree.

Selective PMSI—IR

IR Selective Trees are *not* affected by this restriction. They are signaled with a similar albeit slightly different strategy:

- S-PMSI AD routes carry PMSI attribute with Label 0 and Tunnel Type IR.

- Leaf AD routes carry a PMSI attribute with non-zero Label and Tunnel Type IR.

Unlike Figure 5-6, in which the leaf router advertises the downstream service label via the I-PMSI AD route, in the Selective PMSI, the label is signaled in a separate leaf AD route. This makes it possible for a Junos PE to be the root of an I-PMSI based on mLDP or on RSVP-TE P2MP while being a leaf of an IR S-PMSI.

BGP Multicast VPN with Other P- Tunnel Flavors

The Tunnel Type encoded in the PMSI attribute can also be PIM, and all of the PIM modes (SSM, ASM, and BIDIR) are defined in RFCs 6513 and 6514. In the terms of Table 4-1, this model is S2, A3, C3, E2, T1, [Y3 for SSM, Y4 for ASM and BIDIR].

PIM signals the P-Tunnels, which are based on multipoint GRE. Although this model is very similar to *draft Rosen* at the transport level (P-PIM and GRE), C-Multicast signaling is the responsibility of BGP and not C-PIM, so it is genuinely BGP Multicast VPN. In the terms of Table 4-1, draft Rosen is A1, C1 (not A3, C3).

Finally, mLDP MP2MP is also an available option (S2, A3, C3, E3, T2, Y4), but as of this writing it is only implemented on IOS XR.

CE Multihoming in BGP Multicast VPN

Egress PE Redundancy

When C-Receivers are multihomed to several PEs, the same mechanisms discussed around Figure 4-4 apply. There is nothing specific to BGP MVPN in that respect.

Ingress PE Redundancy

Let's suppose that H2 (10.1.2.20) is multihomed in an active-active model. CE1 and CE2 advertise the 10.1.2.0/24 IPv4 route with the same attributes—Local Preference, MED, and AS Path—to PE1 and PE2, respectively. The Root PEs do not change these attributes, so they prefer the eBGP route to the iBGP route. With these conditions, both PE1 and PE2 advertise an RD:10.1.2.0/24 route to the RRs.

Now, both PE3 and PE4 have downstream C-Multicast receivers of (10.1.2.20, 232.1.1.1) at VRF-A. Do they target the Source Tree Join route to PE1 or to PE2? If this is the first time you ask yourself this question, you might find the answer somewhat surprising.

This is called the Upstream Multicast Hop (UMH) selection process. According to RFC 6513: "the default procedure [...] is to select the route whose corresponding Upstream PE address is numerically highest." This is actually the default implementation in Junos. It means that PE3 targets its Source Tree Join to PE2, regardless of the

IGP metric toward the Upstream PEs. In other words, Unicast and UMH are not congruent when it comes to selecting the Upstream PE for C-Multicast traffic.

During this book's tests, it was observed that the default implementation of IOS XR and Junos differ. PE4 also targets its Source Tree Join to PE2, but for a different reason: PE4's best unicast route toward the source is via PE2, due to the lower IGP metric. In other words, Unicast and UMH are congruent by default in IOS XR. You can achieve this behavior in Junos by using the configuration command `set routing-instances VRF-A protocols mvpn unicast-umh-election`.

Aligning Unicast to UMH has some risks, and it is good to know them well so that you can work around them. In this example, PE1 and PE2 both advertise the *unicast* IPv4 VPN route RD:10.1.2.0/24. With the IGP metric as a tie-breaker, the preferred BGP next hop toward 10.1.2.0/24 in VRF-A is 172.16.0.11 for PE3, and 172.16.0.22 for PE4. So, PE3 and PE4 target the Source Tree Join to PE1 and PE2, respectively. What is the impact?

- If the C-Multicast flow is transported in (S, G) Selective Trees, PE3 is a leaf of PE1's S-PMSI only, and PE4 is a leaf of PE2's S-PMSI only. As a result, there is no traffic duplication at the receivers and the service is fine. This cannot be guaranteed for Wildcard (*, G) or (*, *) S-PMSI, though.

- If the C-Multicast flow is transported in Inclusive Trees, the Source Tree Join that PE3 sends to PE1 is enough for PE4 to receive the C-Multicast traffic tunneled by PE1. Likewise, the Source Tree Join that PE4 sends to PE2 is enough for PE3 to receive the C-Multicast traffic tunneled by PE2. The result is traffic duplication at PE3 and PE4. But, does that affect the service?

PE3 and PE4 may implement an RPF mechanism to discard the traffic arriving from the wrong Upstream PE. This is possible if each P2MP LSP has a different egress MPLS label, which is always the case in IOS XR and it requires vt- interfaces in Junos (like in Example 5-4). The different label value makes it possible for the receiver PE to determine what sender PE injected the C-Multicast packet in the network. This is one key advantage of *not* doing PHP.

This *label RPF* behavior is implemented by default in IOS XR. As for Junos, it requires explicit configuration: `set routing-instances <VRF_NAME> protocols mvpn sender-based-rpf`. As of this writing, this knob is supported for RSVP-TE P2MP only.

This mechanism cannot work with IR Inclusive Tunnels in any of the vendors. Looking back at Figure 5-6, PE3 advertises one single I-PMSI AD route with one single service label to all the PEs. Thus, both PE1 and PE2 would push the same inner label toward PE3. This behavior, combined with the fact that IR relies on PHP, makes it impossible for PE3 to determine whether a C-Multicast packet is coming from PE1 or

PE2. For this reason, IR with Inclusive Tunnels requires an active-backup unicast scheme in which all the egress PEs select the same Upstream PE.

Choosing the Best RD Scheme

The RD scheme choice is critical from the perspective of convergence. Let's keep analyzing the scenario where the C-S (H2) is multihomed in an active-active manner.

With per-VPN RDs (`<AS>:<VPN_ID>`) format, the RR selects the best (from its point of view) IPv4 VPN unicast route to C-S and reflects it. As you saw in Chapter 3, this introduces a delay in unicast convergence. How about multicast? First, multicast RPF is based on unicast, and the MVPN Source Tree Join route's RT is copied from the IPv4 VPN C-S unicast route's RI. For this reason, multicast is equally affected by this delay. This issue is cleanly fixed with a `<ROUTER_ID>:<VPN_ID>` RD scheme, which brings both IPv4 VPN C-S unicast routes to the receiver PEs.

How about the MVPN routes? Source Tree Join prefixes contain the `<ROOT_RD>`, which is VRF's RD at the Root PE. Imagine PE3 and PE4 target their (10.1.2.20, 232.1.1.1) joins to PE1 and PE2, respectively. With the `<AS>:<VPN_ID>` RD format, the Source Tree Join routes are identical and the only difference is in the RT. The RR selects one of the routes only and reflects it. That route contains just one RT, so only one of the two PEs (PE1 or PE2) receive a Source Tree Join targeted to itself. This is typically service-disruptive for the receiver PE whose Source Tree Join is not reflected. On the other hand, with the `<ROUTER_ID>:<VPN_ID>` RD scheme, the Source Tree Join prefixes—which contain the `<ROOT_RD>`—are different and the RR reflects both of them. Again, per-PE-and-VPN RDs prove more advantageous.

Now, let's consider a pure active-backup scenario with PE1 and PE2 as primary and secondary Root PEs, respectively. There are 1,000 receiver PEs—PE3 to PE1002—for (10.1.2.20. 232.1.1), and the VRFs are configured with the `<AS>:<VPN_ID>` RD format. Now, imagine that the RR choses PE1002's as the best Source Tree Join prefix. If PE1 fails, the Leaf PEs update their self-originated (10.1.2.20, 232.1.1.1) Source Tree Join routes so that the RT points to PE2. But only one of these 1,000 updates has an effect: the one coming from PE1002. This means that fast-updating Leaf PEs would need to wait for PE1002 before they can receive the flow from PE2. Again, the solution to this challenge is using a `<ROUTER_ID>:<VPN_ID>` RD scheme.

On a parallel note, during this book's tests, RTC has been proven to be an efficient manner to limit the distribution of MVPN routes while maintaining the service in an interoperable manner. RTC is fully discussed in Chapter 3. As of this writing, RTC for MVPN is supported in Junos only. The design implications of this fact in a multivendor network are discussed in Chapter 6 for the L2VPN NLRI (same reasoning is applicable to the MPVN NLRI).

The most scalable, responsive, and efficient MVPNs are obtained by combining per-PE-and-VPN RDs with Route Target Constraint (RTC).

BGP Multicast VPN with C-PIM ASM

After discussing the different P-Tunnel options, let's briefly explore the C-Multicast world beyond SSM. By default, the multicast groups 232.0.0.0–232.255.255.255 (shortly stated, 232/8) are reserved for SSM mode.

If you want multicast groups outside the 232/8 range to also behave in SSM mode, you need to do the following:

- In Junos, declare them explicitly. For example: `set routing-instances VRF-A routing-options multicast ssm-groups 226/8`.
- In IOS XR, it just works. An equivalent command exists, but it is not required in this book's tests.

ASM Mode

In ASM mode, multicast receivers send an IGMP (*, G) Report and rely on the network to discover the C-Sources and bring the C-Multicast flow down. It's easier said than done: for the network, the complexity of the task is much higher!

A special router called Rendezvous Point (RP) performs source discovery and converts (*, G) into (S, G) join state. *Rendezvous* is French for *meeting*, and it is a nice metaphorical way of saying that the RP brings multicast sources and receivers together.

On one hand, the FHR encapsulates (S, G) multicast data packets into *unicast* PIM packets called Register-Start or simply Register. PIM Registers are sent unicast to the RP, and this is how the RP learns about the active (S, G) flows. At this point, the RP sends a Register-Stop to the FHR, so the FHR stops encapsulating every single (C-S, C-G) packet toward the RP.

On the other hand, Last Hop Routers (LHRs) process the IGMP (*, G) Reports and send PIM (*, G) Joins to their RPF neighbors en route to the RP—the LHR does not know about the source S yet. This (*, G) Join state is propagated up to the RP.

After it has information about active (S, G) flows and also downstream (*, G) receivers, the RP sends PIM (S, G) Join packets to its RPF neighbor en route to the source S. This is how the RP Tree (RPT), also known as Shared Tree, connects sources to receivers. Initially, C-Multicast traffic flows down the RPT. As soon as a LHR receives the first (S, G) data packet, it discovers the source S. At this point, the LHR can (and does by default) signal a branch of the Shortest Path Tree (SPT), also known as Source Tree, and prunes its branch from the RPT. This process is called SPT switch-over.

The RP is a critical element in multicast networks and it is often redundant. In IP Multicast, the most scalable RP redundancy technique is MSDP Anycast (RFC 4611). In this model, RPs have two loopback IPv4 addresses:

- Each RP has a *different primary* loopback IPv4 address, which they use to establish MSDP sessions with other RPs. MSDP (RFC 3618) is a soft-state TCP-based protocol that is capable of exchanging (S, G) Source Active messages.

- All of the RPs have the *same secondary* loopback IPv4 address. All of the routers in the network consider it as the RP address, where the Registers and the (*, G) Joins go.

 All of the following models account for C-RP redundancy. They all rely on the loopback addressing strategy just described.

IPv4 Multicast in general and PIM in particular are complex technologies. Therefore, let's keep the MPLS focus and see how to solve the ASM challenge in the context of the BGP Multicast VPN service.

Figure 5-7 shows four different solutions to the same challenge.

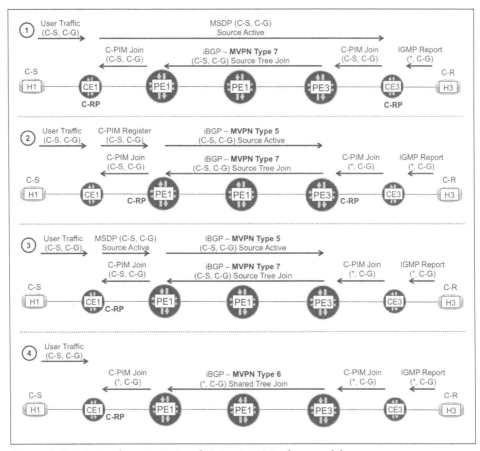

Figure 5-7. BGP Multicast VPN and C-PIM ASM—four models

Let's take a closer look at each of them:

Solution 1

The Customer RPs (C-RPs) are all based on CE devices. The C-RPs exchange Source Active messages over a full mesh of MSDP sessions. A big drawback of this model is that every site in the MVPN must have a local CE acting as a C-RP: this imposes an administrative overhead to the service provider's customer, not to mention the need to maintain an MSDP full mesh. Conversely, it is totally transparent for the SP, unless it manages the CEs.

Solution 2

More than one (for redundancy) PE in the MVPN has a loopback interface in the VRF acting as C-RP. The advantage of this model is that the SP's customer only needs to point to the (same) C-RP address and completely rely on the SP to perform the C-RP role. The administrative overhead is low because there are no

MSDP sessions to configure, and the extra BGP signaling is light and simple. On the down side, the customer is totally dependent on the SP even for intra-site multicast.

Solution 3

More than one (for redundancy) CE act as C-RPs. The C-RPs maintain a full MSDP mesh and also *more than one* MSDP session between a CE and the VRF loopback of a PE in the MVPN. Redundancy is ensured if there are at least two CE-PE MSDP sessions, whose CE *and* PE are both different. This solution makes it possible for the SP's customer to keep the control of their C-RPs. This is a better solution than Solution 1 because it relaxes the requirement to have a CE configured as C-RP on every site. On the downside, like Solution 1 it also requires a protocol (MSDP) with manual provisioning to work.

Solution 4

More than one (for redundancy) CE act as C-RPs. The C-RPs maintain a full MSDP mesh, but they do not peer via MSDP with any PE. This is a simple solution for the SP's customer, but it brings a significant complexity to the SP. From a C-Multicast perspective, this is the only model where not only the SPT, but also the Rendezvous Point Tree RPT (or Shared Tree) are signaled across the core. Then, comes the SPT switchover and many design considerations regarding the C-RP placement. What if the C-Source, the C-Receiver and the C-RP are in three different sites? It works, but the signaling is quite complex and it is beyond the scope of this book.

As of this writing, the authors have not exhaustively tested each of these options in a multivendor lab setup. However, past Junos deployment experiences rank Solution 2 as the most scalable and the less complex of them all, especially when *all* of the PEs in the MVPN are configured as a local C-RP. Solutions 1, 2, and 3 are supported in mvpn-mode spt-only (the default), whereas Solution 4 is supported in mvpn-mode rpt-spt.

C-Rendezvous Point—PE and CE Configuration

Let's pick Solution 2 and provide some configuration and signaling examples.

Here is the additional configuration on a Junos CE, pointing to an external C-RP:

Example 5-55. C-RP static configuration at a CE—CE1 (Junos)

```
protocols {
    pim rp static address 10.10.10.10;
}
```

Let's have a look at a Junos PE locally configured as a C-RP in VRF-A.

Example 5-56. C-RP local configuration at a PE—PE1 (Junos)

```
interfaces {
    lo0 {
        unit 1 {
            family inet {
                address 192.168.10.11/32 primary;
                address 10.10.10.10/32;
}}}}
routing-instances {
    VRF-A {
        interface lo0.1;
        protocols {
            pim {
                rp local address 10.10.10.10;
}}}}
```

 Watch local versus static. It really makes a difference.

And, finally, here is an IOS XR PE locally configured as a C-RP in VRF-A:

Example 5-57. C-RP local configuration at a PE—PE4 (IOS XR)

```
interface Loopback1
 vrf VRF-A
 ipv4 address 192.168.20.44 255.255.255.255
 ipv4 address 10.10.10.10 255.255.255.255 secondary
!
router pim
 vrf VRF-A
  address-family ipv4
   rp-address 10.10.10.10
!
```

C-Multicast Signaling—ASM Mode with C-RP at the PEs

Let's suppose that H1 is sending C-Multicast packets (10.1.1.10, 225.0.0.1). By default, 225.0.0.1 is an ASM C-G address.

PE3 and PE4 receive C-PIM (*, 225.0.0.1) Joins and/or IGMP (*, 225.0.0.1) Reports at their downstream interfaces. But, they cannot originate a (C-S, 225.0.0.1) Source Tree Join BGP route until they learn at least one C-S (in this case, 10.1.1.10).

PE1 has that information because it received (C-S, C-G) C-PIM Registers from CE1. Then, PE1 sends a new MCAST-VPN route: Type 5—(S, G) Source-Active AD.

Example 5-58. Type 5—(C-S, C-G) Source-Active AD route—PE1 (Junos)

```
juniper@PE1> show pim statistics instance VRF-A

PIM Message type        Received      Sent  Rx errors
V2 Register                 2667         0          0
V2 Register Stop               0        50          0


juniper@PE1> show route advertising-protocol bgp 172.16.0.201
             match-prefix "5:*" detail
[...]
bgp.mvpn.0: 9 destinations, 16 routes (9 active, ..., 0 hidden)
* 5:172.16.0.11:101:32:10.1.1.10:32:225.0.0.1/240 (1 entry...)
 BGP group iBGP-RR type Internal
     Nexthop: Self
     Flags: Nexthop Change
     Localpref: 100
     AS path: [65000] I
     Communities: target:65000:1001

VRF-A.mvpn.0: 9 destinations, 16 routes (9 active, ..., 0 hidden)
# Same route here - omitted
```

The format of this (S, G) Source-Active AD route is **5:<RD>**:**<C-S_LENGTH>**:**<C-S_ADDRESS>**:**<C-G_LENGTH>**:**<C_G_GROUP>**. The prefix only contains C-Multicast information.

The Source-Active AD route is targeted to all of the PEs in the MVPN. As soon as PE3 and PE4 receive it, they can signal (C-S, C-G) Source Tree Join routes and the rest of the story is the same as in the SSM examples.

The interoperability of this Solution 2 was successfully tested.

Noncongruent C-Unicast and C-Multicast

Long before BGP Multicast VPN was proposed, there was one thing called *Multicast BGP*. It is first mentioned in the precursor of RFC 4760 - *Multiprotocol Extensions for BGP-4* as *Network Layer Reachability Information used for multicast forwarding*.

Interestingly, it is a set of *unicast* address families, which you can see in Table 5-2.

Table 5-2. BGP Address families for noncongruent RPF

AFI	SAFI	Junos family	Junos tables	IOS XR family
1	2	inet multicast	inet.2	ipv4 multicast
1	129	inet-vpn multicast	bgp.l3vpn.2 and <vrf-name>.inet.2	vpnv4 multicast
2	2	inet6 multicast	inet6.2	ipv6 multicast

AFI	SAFI	Junos family	Junos tables	IOS XR family
2	129	inet6-vpn multicast	bgp.l3vpn-inet6.2 and <vrf-name>.inet6.2	vpnv6 multicast

What is the purpose of these address families? PIM (S, G) Join and BGP (S, G) Source Tree Join are targeted to the RPF neighbors en route to the multicast Source. Similarly, PIM (*, G) Join and BGP (*, G) Source Tree Join are targeted to the RPF neighbors en route to the Rendezvous Point.

Multicast RPF is tightly coupled to unicast routing. This usually elicits two questions: *what is my RPF neighbor en route to the source (or the RP)?* and *what is the next hop if I want to send unicast packets to the source (or the RP)?* Typically, they have the same answer. This is the default behavior, and it can be changed. Actually, sometimes it makes sense to decouple RPF from unicast routing. And this is when these address families become handy.

Figure 5-8 illustrates a use case. The CE-PE connections are not straight; instead, there is an L2 (Ethernet) transport provider in the middle. These connections do not support the transport of multicast Ethernet frames. As a result, the only way to transport multicast packets between CE1 and PE1, or between CE3 and PE3, is by encapsulating them within unicast frames. There are basically two options: extending MPLS to the CEs, or using GRE-over-IP unicast tunnels as PE-CE access interfaces at the VRF (in other words, as ACs). The first model is nice and scalable, but it requires a significant architectural change. The second model, with all its limitations, can fit into a quick deployment and it is used by some SPs.

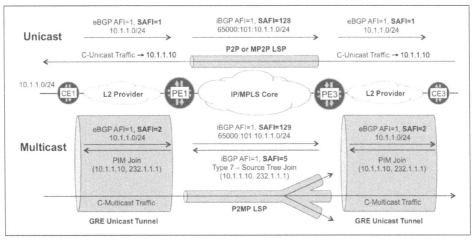

Figure 5-8. Incongruent Unicast and Multicast topology—use case

In this case, it is important that you use the GRE tunnels *only* to transport the multicast packets. On the other hand, you can transport unicast packets natively. This is a motivation to keep two separate *unicast* topologies or RIBs: one for unicast forwarding, and another one for multicast source RPF.

 To achieve interoperability, Junos routers require the `rfc6514-compliant-safi129` knob on all the BGP neighbors supporting SAFI 129.

If you look back at Table 5-1 and Figure 5-1, they should make more sense now than they might have when you first saw them. It's time to move on from L3 multicast services, and explore another universe: L2VPN.

## CHAPTER 6

Point-to-Point Layer 2 VPNs

In all of the MPLS services discussed in previous chapters, the entire service provider (SP) network acts like a *distributed router* from the perspective of the SP's customer. These are Layer 3 (L3) MPLS services. The Ingress PE removes the original Layer 2 (L2) header and looks at the packet's L3+ information. On its way out to the destination CE, the Egress PE pushes a new L2 header. Both the ingress and the egress PE have L3 addresses on the attachment circuits, which might rely on different L2 technologies.

On the other hand, in L2 services, the SP acts like a *distributed switch*, whose ports are the PEs' attachment circuits. And there is no L2 global public service equivalent to the Internet, so all the L2 MPLS services are actually VPNs.

L2VPN in a Nutshell

Figure 6-1 has outer headers on top, and it compares the forwarding plane of L3 and L2 VPNs (with P1 performing PHP). This is an all-Ethernet example—both on the access circuits and on the underlying core links—so it does not provide the full picture. It conveys the main idea, though: *the customer frame's L2 information is preserved*. This is not a hard statement: in reality, the user frame's L2 header can actually change. For example, in Ethernet L2VPNs, it is a frequent practice to manipulate the frame's VLAN tags at the Label Edge Routers (LERs); but key information like the source or destination MAC address is typically preserved—although it can be tunneled in certain L2VPN flavors.

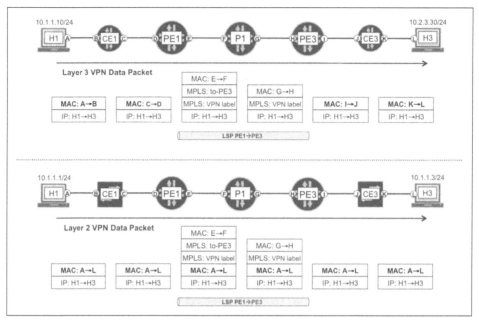

Figure 6-1. L3 and L2VPNs—forwarding plane

L2VPN Use Cases

Among the many use cases for L2VPN, two of them are especially relevant.

Corporate WAN and data centers

Like L3VPN, L2VPN can be a service that a traditional SP offers to its customers. These customers can be enterprises or small cloud providers that have a couple of things in common:

- They cannot afford or do not want to pay for their own WAN infrastructure.
- They need an L2 overlay to stretch their L2 domains among physically distant sites.

Data centers are a powerful example. Traditionally, data center architectures relied on flat L2 connectivity. As data centers scale with more traffic and virtual machines (VMs), while they also become geographically distributed, legacy L2 bridging is no longer an option.

Let's look at the data center WAN use case. This is a popular application often called Data Center Interconnect (DCI). Many enterprises and cloud providers place gateways at the edge of each data center. These act as L2VPN PEs interconnected through a central IP/MPLS core. From the perspective of a data center gateway, the local data center network infrastructure plays the role of a CE or a set of CEs. And the IP/MPLS core interconnects the different data centers. L2VPN not only helps to scale, it also provides virtualization so different tenants or end customers can share the same data center—or set of data centers.

This virtualization capability is also the reason why L2VPN has another powerful use case: inside each data center for scalable server and application connectivity. In this scenario, though, most often the intra–data center L2VPN PEs are interconnected via an IP fabric (or an MPLS fabric) rather than a classic IP/MPLS core. We will explore this topic in Chapter 10; for the moment, let's get back to MPLS.

DCI is not the only reason why an organization might purchase L2VPN services from an SP. For example, some customers build their own WAN links by purchasing L2VPN services from SPs. The SP becomes a pure transport provider and the customer uses the L2VPN as if it were an L2 link that interconnects two of the customer's core devices. Why do that? In this way, the customer could build its own MPLS core! Although this MPLS over L2 over MPLS architecture might sound like science fiction, it is a common practice: many small and medium-sized organizations already use this nested overlay approach (although they do not really have visibility of the inner MPLS layer, which is transparently implemented by the transport provider).

Backhauling—L2VPN as a transport

Although L2VPN is definitely a popular commercial service offered to customers for many applications (e.g., DCI or WAN emulation), SPs also use internal L2VPNs as part of their own infrastructure: L2VPN *as a transport* in aggregation networks. This is a common approach to backhaul both mobile and wireline traffic.

Figure 6-2 represents a classic architecture. Note that the Customer and Service VLAN are optional: it is also possible to backhaul with one or zero VLAN tags. Using both tags is great for multiplexing, though.

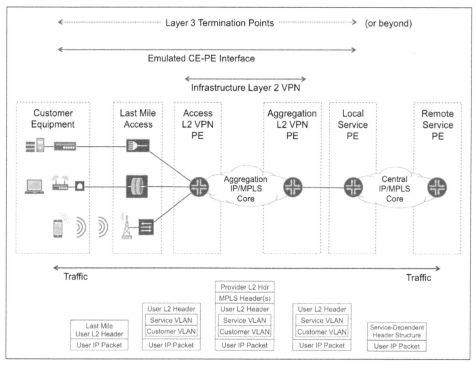

Figure 6-2. *Backhauling—L2VPN as a transport*

The Metro Ethernet Forum (MEF) has defined some standards and mechanisms (such as OAM) necessary to achieve carrier-class behavior in a Carrier Ethernet network.

The last-mile access device is typically a translational L2 bridge whose customer-facing interfaces might or might not be *pure* Ethernet. On the left side of Figure 6-2, you can see the following:

- A corporate customer with a DSL connection that transports Ethernet over ATM
- A residential customer with a native Ethernet FTTH (Fiber to the Home) connection
- A 4G mobile user with a non-Ethernet microwave connection

These are just a few examples to illustrate the variety of access technologies. The last-mile access device hides all this complexity by translating CE→PE customer frames or cells into Ethernet frames and forwarding them up to the aggregation network. Likewise, PE→CE Ethernet frames are translated into the appropriate L2 format and sent down to the customer device. The manipulation of the original L2 headers can range from no action (such as in some FTTx implementations) to a significant translation logic. But it remains L2 bridging.

The Local Service PE may in turn provide an L3 service (Internet, IP VPN, etc.). In this case, the access L3 endpoints are the CE and the Local Service PE.

Or, the Local Service PE may provide an L2VPN Service; this is why in Figure 6-2 the right-side L3 Termination Point is labeled *or beyond*. In this case, the concepts of L2VPN as a Transport and L2VPN Service are totally orthogonal to each other. L2VPN as a Transport relates to *how* the SP transports L2 frames from CE to Local Service PE, and this should be transparent for the customer. On the other side, the L2VPN Service is *what* the customer purchases: L2 connectivity between its sites. In Figure 6-2, the Local Service PE sees the CE-PE interface as an L2 *straight* attachment circuit. How the L2 frames are actually transported inside the aggregation network is quite transparent to the Local Service PE. In that sense, the Infrastructure (Transport) L2VPN is just an overlay.

In more modern architectures, some of the functions depicted in Figure 6-2 are collapsed as follows:

- The same device can perform the last-mile access and Access L2VPN PE functions. This is just an internal implementation at the last-mile access device, which gets promoted from a L2 bridge to a L2VPN PE.

- The same device may perform the Aggregation L2VPN PE and Local Service PE functions. This interesting dimension (called PWHE) is explored later in this chapter.

 L2VPN—regardless of its application—is a *bidirectional* service that provides an overlay to transport L2 frames. The actual underlay is composed of *unidirectional* transport LSPs, a.k.a., PSN Tunnels.

L2VPN Topological Classification

L2VPNs can be Point-to-Point (P2P) or Multipoint-to-Multipoint (MP2MP). This concept is service-centric, not transport-centric, and it refers to the number of sites that a given L2VPN can have:

- P2P L2VPNs can have only two sites, which may be redundant or protected. These L2VPNs are commonly called Pseudowire Edge-to-Edge Emulation (PWE3), or Virtual Private Wire Service (VPWS), or E-Line, or Virtual Leased Line (VLL).

- MP2MP L2VPNs can have more than two sites. Depending on the topology, they are called E-Tree or E-LAN. Other popular terms such as Virtual Private LAN Service (VPLS) or Ethernet VPN (EVPN) are specific to certain flavors and do not represent the MP2MP L2VPN technology as a whole.

Another important concept is that of a pseudowire (PW). Paraphrasing RFC 6624, "the entity that connects two attachment circuits across the SP network is called a pseudowire." In the context of the previous service classification, P2P L2VPNs rely on a single PW, and some flavors of MP2MP L2VPNs rely on a *set* of PWs.

Ethernet frames can be forwarded in the context of any of these two L2VPN topologies. Indeed, Ethernet is a multiaccess technology and it supports both. An MP2MP Ethernet L2VPN service behaves like a distributed switch with more than two ports, so it performs MAC learning. Conversely, P2P Ethernet L2VPNs do not require MAC learning because they are like a distributed *hub* with two ports (like a *pipe*): whatever the ingress PE receives on port #1, the egress PE simply sends it out of port #2, and vice versa.

Non-Ethernet L2 technologies are typically P2P in nature, so these can only be transported by using P2P L2VPNs.

L2VPN Signaling and Transport

Like L3VPNs, modern L2VPNs decouple the service from the transport by using MPLS label stacking: the outer label takes the tunneled packets to the egress PE, and the inner label identifies the VPN service.

> In L2VPN literature, a Transport LSP is often called a Packet-Switched Network (PSN) Tunnel. We use both terms in this book interchangeably. But is a PSN Tunnel a Pseudowire? No! Actually, a Pseudowire is a bidirectional *service* element that uses at least two unidirectional PSN Tunnels (maybe more if redundancy is required) for *transport*.

Two protocols are capable of signaling the service labels: Multiprotocol BGP and Targeted LDP. In general, you can choose one or the other, after you've evaluated the pros and cons, with one exception: the latest L2VPN flavor (EVPN) is only supported in BGP.

As for the PSN Tunnels, they are simply MPLS LSPs so all of the options discussed in Chapter 2 apply here, too: LDP, RSVP-TE, BGP-LU, and SPRING.

P2P L2VPN—Varied Access Technologies

The mechanisms to *signal* a P2P L2VPN are quite agnostic of the L2 technology that needs to be transported. After you have chosen the signaling protocol (BGP or Targeted LDP), the message exchange required to establish an Ethernet or a non-Ethernet P2P L2VPN are practically identical. The only difference lies in a protocol attribute that encodes the L2 technology type for the VPN. This attribute is either an extended community (BGP) or a TLV (Targeted LDP).

As for the forwarding plane, L2 frames or cells are encapsulated in MPLS by using a collection of methods that are specific to each technology:

- Ethernet L2VPN forwarding is covered in RFC 4448 - *Encapsulation Methods for Transport of Ethernet over MPLS Networks.*

- There are equivalent RFCs for other L2 technologies: HDLC/PPP over MPLS (RFC 4618), Frame Relay over MPLS (RFC 4619), and ATM over MPLS (RFC 4717).

These forwarding plane RFCs belong to a collection of standards that are frequently referred to as *Martini encapsulation*, for Luca Martini. They explain how to encapsulate L2 frames or cells in MPLS. Actually, it is possible to go even one step further and simulate leased lines by encapsulating Time Division Multiplexing (TDM) data in packets over MPLS. This technology is commonly called Circuit Emulation Services (CES), and it has several flavors. For traditional Digital Signal (DS): Structure-*Agnostic* TDM over Packet (SAToP, RFC 4553) and Structure-*Aware* TDM Circuit Emulation Service over Packet Switched Network (CESoPSN, RFC 5086). These are implemented and widely deployed in a variety of physical interfaces such as E1/T1, OC3/STM1, and OC12/STM4. As for mapping native SONET/SDH frames into packets, the model is described in RFC 4842, but the authors are unaware of any production-ready implementation.

CES is very important in mobile backhaul legacy applications such as 2G and 3G requiring TDM transport. The TDM circuits begin at the base stations and are terminated on the BSC (Base Station Controller) or the RNC (Radio Network Controller). Timing and packet order requirements are typically quite strict for TDM, which motivates the usage of a *control word*. This concept is presented later in this chapter and can also be used in other L2VPNs services like Ethernet.

L2VPN versus L1VPN

L2VPNs and **L3** (*three*) VPNs have many things in common: tunneling and transporting data between CE-facing attachment circuits, label stacking, and so on.

On the other hand, the L2VPN and **L1** (*one*) VPN concepts are *completely different.* L2VPN is a service that uses the IP/MPLS core as an overlay, whereas L1VPN is a technology aimed to *build* the core underlay. L1VPN and Generalized MPLS (GMPLS) are widely deployed technologies, but they fall outside the scope of this book.

The IP/MPLS core underlay can be based on Ethernet, on TDM, or on any other L2 technology. Figure 6-1 shows an Ethernet L2VPN service and also an Ethernet underlay, but this is just a coincidence; the L2VPN service flavor is totally independent from the underlying L2 technology used at the IP/MPLS core links.

CES is an L2VPN service; its concept is the reverse of L1VPN.

L2.5 VPN

An interesting variation is L2.5 VPN, where each attachment circuit is based on a different L2 technology—for example, Ethernet on one endpoint and ATM on the other endpoint. The L2.5 VPN service automatically performs frame/cell conversion while leaving the payload (e.g., the IPv4 packet with its IPv4 header) untouched. The L2.5 term comes from the fact that there is L2 media conversion—a traditional function of routers—but no L3 lookup.

Circuit Cross-Connect and Translational Cross-Connect

For many years, Junos has supported an L2VPN flavor called Circuit Cross-Connect (CCC), which does not require any service signaling (no BGP, no Targeted LDP). Indeed, with CCC the service and the transport are *not* decoupled and each transport LSP (or PSN tunnel) is dedicated to one service: linking two remote attachment circuits via the IP/MPLS core. CCC signals exclusive RSVP-TE LSPs that cannot be shared with other services. This service-to-transport 1:1 relationship allows bringing up the L2VPN without the intervention of any service signaling protocol (BGP or LDP). On the downside, no autodiscovery is available for CCC and coupling the service to transport is less scalable.

Translational Cross-Connect (TCC) is CCC applied to L2.5VPN. This book does *not* cover CCC and TCC in detail. You will often see the CCC acronym, though: the interface encapsulation used for L2VPN is [vlan-]ccc. Indeed, the forwarding plane is the same for CCC and for modern L2VPN.

L2VPN Flavors Covered in This Book

This book covers L2VPNs whose service and transport are decoupled. This means that regardless of the protocol used to signal the service (BGP or LDP), the transport

LSP can be signaled with any of the available protocols: LDP, RSVP-TE, BGP-LU, or SPRING.

Although this L2VPN *set* fully supports the transport of Ethernet frames, the P2P flavors also support the transport of other data in a wide variety of formats: frames, cells, and CES. Looking forward, all of this chapter's examples feature the transport of Ethernet frames. Not a hard constraint: the variety of solutions is still overwhelming! Table 6-1 lists the Ethernet L2VPN flavors addressed in this book.

Table 6-1. Ethernet L2VPN flavors

Flavor	Topology	Signaling protocol	RFC	MAC learning
VPWS	Point-to-point	BGP	6624	N/A
VPWS	Point-to-point	Targeted LDP	4447	N/A
VPLS	Multipoint	BGP	4761	Forwarding plane
VPLS	Multipoint	Targeted LDP	4762	Forwarding plane
EVPN	Multipoint	BGP	7432	Control plane

A recent acronym for BGP-based L2 Services is *BESS*, which stands for *BGP-Enabled Services*.

All of these Ethernet L2VPN flavors rely on the same forwarding-plane encapsulation, as defined in RFC 4448 - *Encapsulation Methods for Transport of Ethernet over MPLS Networks*. The differences are in the signaling plane. When referring to Martini, it is important to differentiate between Martini encapsulation (RFC 4448 in the case of Ethernet) and Martini transport or signaling (RFC 4447, LDP VPWS). The latter is just one of the several L2VPN flavors that rely on the Martini encapsulation.

There are also L2VPN flavors based on a different encapsulation called Provider Backbone Bridging (PBB) or MAC-in-MAC on the AC side. This requires some extensions for VPLS (VPLS-PBB, RFC 7041) and for EVPN (EVPN-PBB, RFC 7623). The latter is briefly discussed in Chapter 8.

For the moment, let's stick to the classic Martini encapsulation.

This chapter focuses on L2VPN with MPLS forwarding plane in the core. Non-MPLS encapsulations such as VXLAN are discussed in Chapter 8, Chapter 10, and Chapter 11.

VPWS Signaled with BGP

BGP VPWS is commonly known as *Kompella* L2VPN, because *draft-kompella-l2vpn-l2vpn* was the precursor to RFC 6624. As of this writing, Kireeti Kompella, who keeps making important contributions to both MPLS and SDN, is the CTO of Juniper's Development and Innovation team. The forwarding plane of BGP VPWS is based on Martini encapsulation (RFC 4448).

Probably the best way to understand BGP VPWS technology is to see it at work. In Figure 6-3, the CEs are no longer L3 routers but L2 switches. Initially, the following links are administratively down in order to prevent L2 loops: CE1-PE2, CE2-PE1, CE3-PE4, and CE4-PE3.

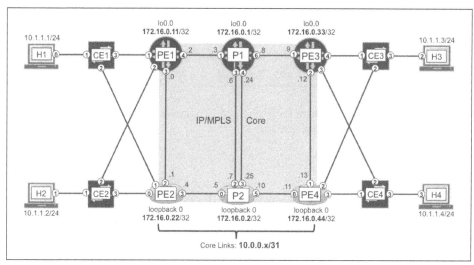

Figure 6-3. L2VPN—physical topology

As in the previous chapter, inter-PE links PE1-PE2 and PE3-PE4 have a high IGP metric, so they are not used for transit in the absence of core link failures.

Let's bring up a BGP VPWS service, and later explore CE multihoming in depth. The L2 service goes like this: CE1—PE1—PE4—CE4. When it is correctly provisioned, H1 and H4 can resolve each other's MAC addresses (via ARP) successfully, so ping between H1 and H4 succeeds.

BGP L2VPN Address Family

BGP VPWS and BGP VPLS both use the same multiprotocol BGP address family: AFI=25, SAFI=65. Let's call it the L2VPN address family.

Here is the additional configuration at a Junos PE:

Example 6-1. L2VPN address family configuration—PE1 (Junos)

```
protocols {
    bgp {
        group iBGP-RR {
            family l2vpn signaling;
}}}
```

Adding this configuration to all the BGP groups also does the trick on Junos RRs.

The additional configuration on IOS XR PEs is shown in Example 6-2.

Example 6-2. L2VPN address family configuration—PE2 (IOS XR)

```
router bgp 65000
 address-family l2vpn vpls-vpws
 !
 neighbor-group RR
  address-family l2vpn vpls-vpws
 !
```

 On RRs running IOS XR, you also need to add the **route-reflector-client** knob under each neighbor[-group] adddress-family.

BGP VPWS Configuration at the PEs

Let's begin with the simplest VPWS example, featuring a PW that interconnects these two ACs: PE1's ge-2/0/1 and PE4's GigabitEthernet0/0/0/3. All of the Ethernet frames entering one of these *physical* ports exits unchanged from the remote AC. As you can see, this PW is somehow stretching a physical wire between two CEs. Other, more flexible, models are described later.

The original frames can be untagged or VLAN-tagged. In the latter case, the VLAN tags are transported end to end because they are considered as part of the payload.

Example 6-3 the configuration of the PE1—PE4 PW at the Junos PE1 side.

Example 6-3. BGP VPWS configuration with physical AC—PE1 (Junos)

```
1    interfaces {
2        ge-2/0/1 {
3            mtu 2000;
4            encapsulation ethernet-ccc;
5            unit 0;
6        }
7    }
```

```
8      routing-instances {
9          L2VPN-A {
10             instance-type l2vpn;
11             interface ge-2/0/1.0;
12             route-distinguisher 172.16.0.11:1010;
13             vrf-target target:65000:1010;
14             protocols {
15                 l2vpn {
16                     encapsulation-type ethernet;
17                     interface ge-2/0/1.0;
18                     site CE1-A {
19                         site-identifier 1;
20                         ignore-mtu-mismatch;
21                         interface ge-2/0/1.0 {
22                             remote-site-id 4;
23     }}}}}}
```

As with any BGP-based VPN service, the Route Distinguisher (RD, line 12) format can be *<IP>:<#>* or *<AS>:<#>*. But we strongly recommend using the *<IP>:<#>* format for L2VPN prefixes, especially in CE multihoming topologies.

Note that the configuration does *not* include the remote PE address. BGP takes care of the autodiscovery!

The local and remote sites (lines 19 and 22, respectively) are L2VPN CE-IDs. They are numbered here according to the CE to which the attachment circuit is connected.

Let's take care of the maximum transmission unit (MTU) now. One of the stickiest L2VPN interoperability challenges between Junos and IOS XR is setting and negotiating the PW MTU. When the negotiated MTU is not the same at both ends of a PW, typically the PW does not come up due to MTU mismatch.

There are two options to overcome this challenge:

Configuring the endpoints to ignore MTU mismatch
    This is achieved both in Junos and IOS XR by using the knob ignore-mtu-mismatch. Actually, in IOS XR there are two knobs: ignore-mtu-mismatch for LDP-based L2VPNs, and ignore-mtu-mismatch-ad for BGP-based L2VPNs. The latter is hidden, so it does not autocomplete and does not show up in the running configuration even if it's set.

Configuring a matching MTU on both ends
    This has the advantage of providing more control, but both vendors have implementation gaps. Setting an explicit MTU is only available for some of the L2VPN flavors; and this flavor subset is different for each vendor.

A negotiated MTU is *not* really enforced on the traffic. The actual PW's MTU is determined by the MTU of the local and remote ACs as well as the core links. L2 traffic cannot be fragmented, so it is very important to set the AC physical links' MTU large enough to account for a standard IP packet (1,500 bytes), plus the Ethernet and VLAN headers. Furthermore, core links need to account for RFC 4448 encapsulation and for MPLS headers, too. In this book's examples, it is assumed that all of the access interfaces are configured with a physical MTU of 2,000 bytes (line 3), and the core links with a MTU of at least 2,100 bytes.

In both Junos and IOS XR, sometimes a configuration change on the PW MTU does not have an immediate effect, and the PW needs to be deleted and added again or deactivated/activated in order for the change to take effect.

The approach used in this book is to ignore MTU mismatches (line 20). In addition, one more Junos knob might help to work around negotiation mismatch issues: ignore-encapsulation-mismatch.

Example 6-4 the configuration for the PE1—PE4 PW at the IOS XR PE4 side.

Example 6-4. BGP VPWS configuration with physical AC—PE4 (IOS XR)

```
1     interface GigabitEthernet0/0/0/3
2      mtu 2000
3      l2transport
4     !
5     l2vpn
6      ignore-mtu-mismatch-ad
7      xconnect group myL2VPN
8       mp2mp L2VPN-A
9        vpn-id 123456789
10       mtu 1986
11       l2-encapsulation vlan
12       autodiscovery bgp
13         rd 172.16.0.44:1010
14         route-target 65000:1010
15         signaling-protocol bgp
16           ce-id 4
17            interface GigabitEthernet0/0/0/3 remote-ce-id 1
18    !
```

Strictly speaking, a physical mtu 2000 does not necessarily mean the same on Junos and on IOS XR. Whether the Ethernet header is taken into account or not depends on the implementation.

The IOS XR configuration hierarchy in line 8 (mp2mp) supports a collection of BGP VPWS services, each with a different [local ce-id, remote ce-id] pair. VPWS is actually P2P, and it does *not* perform proper Ethernet bridging or MAC learning. So despite the `mp2mp` term, you can think point to point.

The `vpn-id` (line 9) is mandatory but its value is arbitrary because it is not signaled with BGP. Its value is only relevant when targeted LDP (and not BGP) is the protocol responsible for signaling the service.

How about the MTU? In some L2VPN flavors, IOS XR performs two MTU checks:

- The local PW's MTU must match the MTU advertised by the remote end.
- The local AC's MTU must match the locally configured PW's MTU.

The `ignore-mtu-mismatch-ad` knob (line 6) helps to bypass the first check in BGP L2VPN, whereas the second check—if present—needs a little more work.

Why is the PW's MTU (line 10) different from the AC's MTU (line 2)? If you take line 10 off Example 6-4, the PW goes down (see Example 6-5).

Example 6-5. Automatic AC MTU computation—PE4 (IOS XR)

```
RP/0/0/CPU0:PE4#show l2vpn xconnect group myL2VPN detail | i MTU
        AC MTU Mismatch
    MTU 1986; XC ID 0x3881ef5; interworking none
```

The value in line 3 is dynamically computed from the physical MTU and must be configured explicitly on the PW (Example 6-4, line 10). This extra step is only required on a minority of the L2VPN flavors.

This is the MTU Toolbox. Many of the upcoming examples require playing with the previous knobs and/or setting the PW's MTU.

BGP VPWS Signaling

After they're configured, PE1 and PE4 advertise one L2VPN BGP route each.

Example 6-6 the BGP L2VPN route advertised by Junos PE1.

Example 6-6. L2VPN route advertised by PE1 (Junos)

```
1    juniper@PE1> show route advertising-protocol bgp 172.16.0.201
2                    table L2VPN-A.l2vpn.0 detail
3
4    L2VPN-A.l2vpn.0: 2 destinations, 3 routes (2 active, ...)
5    *  172.16.0.11:1010:1:3/96 (1 entry, 1 announced)
6      BGP group iBGP-RR type Internal
```

```
7        Route Distinguisher: 172.16.0.11:1010
8        Label-base: 800012, range: 2, offset: 3, status-vector: 0x0
9        Nexthop: Self
10       Flags: Nexthop Change
11       Localpref: 100
12       AS path: [65000] I
13       Communities: target:65000:1010
14                    Layer2-info: encaps: ETHERNET, control flags:[0x2]
15                                 Control-Word, mtu: 0
16                                 site preference: 100
```

The /96 mask is internal in Junos and not advertised via iBGP: you can safely ignore it.

The NLRI in line 5 contains the RD, the advertised local CE-ID (1) and the lowest numbered remote CE-ID (3) to which this advertisement applies. This value is equal to the offset in line 8.

Line 8 contains the MPLS label information. PE1 is allocating two labels (range: 2). The mathematical rule to calculate the label is as follows:

- Label = Label base + (Remote CE-ID – offset)
- Frames from remote CE-ID 3 (CE-ID = offset = 3) should arrive to PE1 with MPLS label 800012 (Label base + 0 = 800012).
- Frames from remote CE-ID 4 (CE-ID = offset + 1 = 4) should arrive to PE1 with MPLS label 800013 (Label base + 1 = 800013).

In this P2P L2VPN, there is just one remote CE from the perspective of PE1 and its CE-ID is 4. This is why you can see label 800013 in Figure 6-4, but not label 800012. Out of the two labels (800012 and 800013), only one is used in this P2P L2VPN. So what's the point of advertising a label block?

This is not the first appearance of a label block in this book. You might remember the SRGB concept from Chapter 2. In SPRING, each *destination* SID is reachable with one different label. In BGP L2VPN, each *source* CE-ID can be identified by one different label.

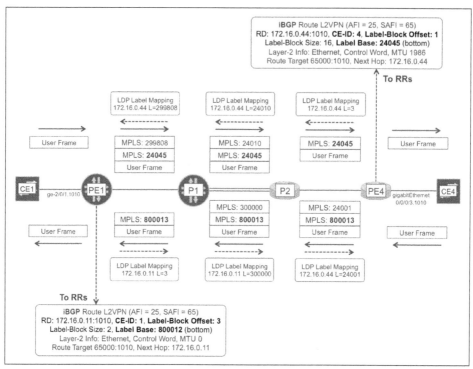

Figure 6-4. BGP VPWS signaling with LDP-based PSN Tunnel

Not only can you define several sites inside the same L2VPN instance, you can also declare several interfaces under the *same* site. For example, imagine there are two logical interfaces connecting CE1 to PE1—which might be on the same or in different physical links. In this case, you can connect (CE-ID 1, interface A) to remote CE-ID 3, and also connect (CE-ID 1, interface B) to remote CE-ID 4. This is still a VPWS service that connects each link from CE1 to one and only one remote CE. One single label block would be enough to achieve the two *parallel* VPWS services.

On the other hand, the L2VPN NLRI is also used for MP2MP L2VPN, where more labels are required for MAC learning purposes—see Chapter 7. Instead of defining two different L2VPN NLRIs, one for P2P and one for MP2MP, there is just one NLRI for both purposes, and that is another reason why you see a label block here.

The Layer2 Info extended community (lines 14 and 15) contains all the information about the attachment circuit and the way frames must be encapsulated in the MPLS core. This community must be consistent on both ends for the PW to come up.

Example 6-7 shows the L2VPN route advertised by IOS XR PE4, as seen from Junos RR1.

Example 6-7. L2VPN route advertised by PE4 (IOS XR)

```
1    juniper@RR1> show route receive-protocol bgp 172.16.0.44
2                 table bgp.l2vpn.0 detail
3
4    bgp.l2vpn.0: 2 destinations, 4 routes (...)
5      172.16.0.44:1010:4:1/96 (2 entries, 1 announced)
6        Accepted
7        Route Distinguisher: 172.16.0.44:1010
8        Label-base: 24045, range: 16, offset: 1, status-vector: 0x7F 0xFF
9        Nexthop: 172.16.0.44
10       Localpref: 100
11       AS path: I
12       Communities: target:65000:1010
13                   Layer2-info: encaps: ETHERNET, control flags:[0x2]
14                           Control-Word, mtu: 1986
```

Line 8 contains the MPLS label information. PE4 is allocating 16 labels (range: 16).
Following is what the lowest and highest numbered labels are for:

- Frames from remote CE-ID 1 (CE-ID = offset = 1) should arrive to PE4 with
  MPLS label 24045 (Label base + 0 = 24045).

- Frames from remote CE-ID 16 (CE-ID = offset + 15 = 16) should arrive to
  PE1 with MPLS label 24060 (Label base + 15 = 24060).

In this P2P L2VPN, there is just one remote CE from the perspective of PE4 and it is
CE-ID is 1. This is why you can see label 24045 in Figure 6-4, but not the other labels
in the block (24046 up to 24060).

At this point, the PW is correctly established:

Example 6-8. PW established between PE1 (Junos) and PE4 (IOS XR)

```
juniper@PE1> show l2vpn connections instance L2VPN-A
[...]
Instance: L2VPN-A
Edge protection: Not-Primary
  Local site: CE1-A (1)
    connection-site      Type  St    [...] # Up trans
    4                    rmt   Up    [...] 1
      Remote PE: 172.16.0.44, Negotiated control-word: Yes
      Incoming label: 800013, Outgoing label: 24045
      Local interface: ge-2/0/1.0
      Status: Up, Encapsulation: ETHERNET

RP/0/0/CPU0:PE4#show l2vpn xconnect group myL2VPN detail

Group myL2VPN, XC L2VPN-A.4:1, state is up; Interworking none
  Local CE ID: 4, Remote CE ID: 1, Discovery State: Advertised
```

```
AC: GigabitEthernet0/0/0/3, state is up
  Type VLAN; Num Ranges: 1
  Outer Tag: 1010
  VLAN ranges: [123, 123]
  MTU 1994; XC ID 0x1; interworking none
[...]
PW: neighbor 172.16.0.11, PW ID 262145, state is up (established)
    MPLS          Local             Remote
    ------------  ----------------  ----------------
    Label         24045             800013
    MTU           1986              unknown
    Control word  enabled           enabled
    PW type       Ethernet          Ethernet
    CE-ID         4                 1
    ------------  ----------------  ----------------
[...]
```

Route Target Constraint and L2VPN

One drawback of BGP P2P L2VPN is the fact that RRs reflect a L2VPN route to all
the PEs, even though there is only one remote PE at the other end of the P2P L2VPN.
So, all the PEs receive the route, but only one PE imports it. Chapter 3 describes the
solution to this efficiency challenge: Route Target Constrain (RTC).

Junos supports BGP L2VPN in combination with RTC. As of this writing, IOS XR
allows both address families to coexist; but the distribution of L2VPN NLRI is not
constrained. This means that IOS XR does not advertise specific RTC routes for the
RTs configured in local L2VPNs.

Here are the possible scenarios when the L2VPN and RTC address families are both
advertised on the same Multiprotocol-BGP (MP-BGP) session:

MP-BGP session between two Junos routers
> In this case, L3VPN and L2VPN prefixes are distributed successfully in a con-
> strained and efficient manner.

MP-BGP session between two IOS XR routers
> In this case, L3VPN prefixes are distributed in a constrained and efficient man-
> ner; on the other hand, L2VPN prefixes are flooded as if RTC was not config-
> ured. In any case, the services work fine.

MP-BGP session between a Junos router and an IOS XR router
> In one sense, the IOS XR router floods all of the L2VPN prefixes toward the
> Junos router; although this is not perfectly efficient, it keeps the L2VPN service
> up. In the other sense, the Junos router only sends the L2VPN prefixes toward
> the IOS XR router if the latter advertises a matching RTC route—this can only be
> a default RTC route. If the IOS XR router is a pure RR, it should be configured to
> advertise the default RTC route anyway: business as usual. But, if the IOS XR

router is a PE, advertising the default RTC route means receiving *all* the L3VPN prefixes, too: this has a cost in efficiency, but it does make it possible to keep the L2VPN service up and running.

 Complex, isn't it? Try to avoid mixing the BGP L2VPN and RTC address families in the same multivendor Junos-IOS XR BGP session. If you really need to, there is a potential workaround: defining *fake* L3VPNs on the IOS XR side with the same RT as the one used by the L2VPN.

L2VPN Forwarding Plane

Junos computes L2VPN forwarding entries by using a new set of RIBs. Let's review the Junos routing tables used by all the MPLS services described so far in this book.

Junos routing tables

Several routing tables are worth examining in the context of Junos L2VPN instances. Table 6-2 shows the equivalence between tables of different VPN services.

Table 6-2. Junos routing tables for MPLS VPN services

Service	Global auxiliary: raw NLRIs	Instance-specific: raw NLRIs	Instance-specific: processed NLRIs
IPv4 Unicast VPN	bgp.l3vpn.0		<VRF>.inet.0
IPv6 Unicast VPN	bgp.l3vpn-inet6.0		<VRF>.inet6.0
IPv4 Multicast VPN	bgp.mvpn.0	<VRF>.mvpn.0	
IPv6 Multicast VPN	bgp.mvpn-inet6.0	<VRF>.mvpn-inet6.0	
BGP L2VPN	bgp.l2vpn.0	<L2VPN>.l2vpn.0	<L2VPN>.l2id.0

The <L2VPN> tag represents the actual name of the L2VPN instance—in this example, *L2VPN-A*. And the <L2VPN>.l2id table contains the resolved local and remote CE IDs: 1, 4, and so on. However, the most useful table from the forwarding perspective is actually mpls.0, which contains the routes that are later pushed to the forwarding table.

Example 6-9. L2VPN forwarding entries at PE1 (Junos)

```
juniper@PE1> show route table mpls.0 protocol l2vpn

mpls.0: 15 destinations, 15 routes (15 active, ...)
+ = Active Route, - = Last Active, * = Both

800013          *[L2VPN/7] 1d 11:58:41
                 > via ge-2/0/1.0, Pop [...]
ge-2/0/1.0      *[L2VPN/7] 1d 09:11:58, metric2 4
```

```
        > to 10.0.0.3 via ge-2/0/4.0,
          Push 24045, Push 299808(top) [...]
```

If a packet arrives with MPLS label 800013, PE1 pops the MPLS header and sends the resulting frame out of ge-2/0/1.0. Likewise, if PE1 receives a frame on ge-2/0/1.0, it pushes the MPLS service label 24045 and puts the packet on an LSP toward PE4.

L2 frame encapsulation in MPLS is a bit more complex than what you can see back in Figure 6-4. H1 sends the frame untagged to CE1, and CE1 pushes two VLAN tags (outer 1010, inner 123). As discussed, the L2VPN service transports by default the VLAN tags in a transparent manner. Following is an L2 frame from H1 to H4 as it transits the link PE1→P1.

Example 6-10. Ethernet L2VPN forwarding plane

```
Ethernet II, Src: MAC_PE1_ge-2/0/4, Dst: MAC P1_ge-2/0/3
MPLS Header, Label: 299808, Exp: 0, S: 0, TTL: 255
MPLS Header, Label: 24045, Exp: 0, S: 1, TTL: 255
PW Ethernet Control Word, Sequence Number: 0
Ethernet II, Src: MAC H1_Gi0/0/0/0, Dst: MAC H2_Gi0/0/0/2
    Type: 802.1Q Virtual LAN (0x8100)
# Outer VLAN header #
802.1Q Virtual LAN, PRI: 0, CFI: 0, ID: 1010
    Type: 802.1Q Virtual LAN (0x8100)
# Inner VLAN header #
802.1Q Virtual LAN, PRI: 0, CFI: 0, ID: 123
    Type: IP (0x0800)
Internet Protocol Version 4, Src: 10.1.1.1, Dst: 10.1.1.4
Internet Control Message Protocol
    Type: 8 (Echo (ping) request) [...]
```

Control Word

There is an extra header, called Control Word (CW), inserted between the inner MPLS header and the transported L2 frame. Its usage is described in RFC 4385 - *Pseudowire Emulation Edge-to-Edge (PWE3) Control Word for Use over an MPLS PSN*. As discussed in Chapter 2, label switching routers (LSRs) perform load balancing by applying a hash to certain packet fields. To know what fields to take into account for the hash, it is essential to know the packet type. But MPLS headers do not have any protocol field, so LSRs must play a guessing game:

- IP packets have the IP version number encoded in the first nibble (four bits) of their header. Consequently, if a MPLS packet has a payload whose first nibble is number four, the LSR assumes that the MPLS payload is an IPv4 packet, without any L2 headers.

- If the first nibble of the MPLS payload is six, the LSR assumes that it is an IPv6 packet.

Let's suppose that the payload is an Ethernet frame whose destination MAC address' first nibble equals four. In this case, the hash (assuming that the hardware and the configuration support hashing at the MPLS payload level) is computed as if it were an IPv4 packet. Now suppose that the fourth byte of the source MAC address—which is the tenth byte in the frame—is six, the IPv4 protocol number for TCP. The way the LSR interprets it is *this is a TCP-over-IPv4 L3 packet*. Which is wrong: the MPLS payload is an L2 Ethernet frame, which might in turn contain an IPv4 packet—or not! Then, the LSR looks for the source and destination TCP ports at a certain byte offset inside the frame. What the LSR interprets as TCP ports are actually certain bytes within the Ethernet payload, whose value may differ between several packets of the same flow. These packets can be load-balanced across different paths and potentially arrive to the egress PE out of order. For certain applications requiring a strict packet order, this can be a big issue. And if you think about CES, it would simply break the service.

The CW is a four-byte header whose first nibble is zero. In this way, it is guaranteed that LSRs do not load-balance two frames belonging to the same flow across different equal-cost next hops. The two ends of the PW must agree on whether they use the CW, otherwise the PW is not successfully established.

There is another use case of the CW, described in RFC 5885 - *Bidirectional Forwarding Detection (BFD) for the Pseudowire Virtual Circuit Connectivity Verification (VCCV)*. VCCV establishes a BFD session between the two endpoints of a PW. One of the available VCCV options uses the CW as a header that precedes a raw (no IP header, no UDP header) BFD packet.

BGP VPWS—CE Multihoming to Several PEs

Imagine an L2 frame circulating in the following manner (see Figure 6-3): H3→CE3→PE3→PE1→CE1→PE2→PE1→CE1, and so on, looping in a triangle with vertices CE1, PE1 and PE2. In general, L2 frames do not have a Time-to-Live (TTL) field in the L2 header, so a frame can be looping forever. Such an L2 loop scenario typically causes broadcast storms and connectivity loss, thus it is extremely undesirable. This is why redundancy is one of the touchiest aspects of L2 services in general.

Strictly speaking, there is one only clean solution to this problem: moving to L3! In L3, every time a packet traverses a device, the TTL field is decremented and when it expires the packet is dropped, which limits the impact of forwarding loops. This is not always an option for applications and services, so let's see what alternatives are available to prevent, detect, and mitigate L2 loops.

In traditional LANs, L2 loops are prevented with Spanning Tree protocols (STP, RSTP, MSTP, etc.). If a loop takes place, it can be handled with a series of techniques: MAC move detection, broadcast storm control and mitigation, policing, automatic port disabling, and so on. Still, L2 loops do sometimes happen in L2 bridging networks, no matter how many protection measures are in place.

Now moving to L2VPN, it is possible to keep these measures in place, but just for the sake of extra protection. The L2VPN design (assuming that there are no backdoor links) should guarantee a loop-free protection even without Spanning Tree. You may add Spanning Tree on top only as an extra protection layer.

 Transporting Spanning Tree frames in the L2VPN (between sites) is only a reasonable option for P2P L2VPN. It does not make sense in MP2MP L2VPN flavors where Bridge PDUs (BPDUs) would be flooded to several remote sites.

There are several multihoming options in L2VPN, and the most robust are based on Link Aggregation Group (LAG). LAGs with Link Aggregation Control Protocol (LACP) are stateful, and a CE does not switch frames between two members of a LAG, which is a great built-in way to avoid L2 loops. Here are some common approaches:

- The CE may control the multihomed AC redundancy. For example, CE1 may group its two uplinks in a standard LAG. PE1 and PE2 both have a standard one-link LAG toward CE1, and their local System ID is different. Due to this System ID discrepancy, CE1 only activates one of the LAG's links. If the chosen link is CE1-PE1, CE1 changes the flags of its LACP packets to PE2 to inform it that the link is not active in the LAG. The result is that PE1 flags its AC up, whereas PE2 flags its AC down. Although this solution relies on a LAG that goes to different chassis (PE1 and PE2), it is *not* what the industry calls a Multichassis LAG (MC-LAG).

- The solution may be implemented on the SP, and this is a preferred option for the SP because it can take control over the critical L2 redundancy decisions. CE1 groups its two uplinks in a standard LAG, and this time PE1 and PE2 are configured with the same System ID, so CE1 sees both links as if they were connected to the same chassis. PE1 and PE2 communicate to each other over the SP core by using Inter-Chassis Communication Protocol (ICCP) and decide on whether to keep both links active or only one of them. In the all-active case—only supported in EVPN—CE1 sees both links as part of the LAG and load-balances the frames between both uplinks. In the single-active case, then if PE2 assumes the standby role—according to the ICCP negotiation—it changes the flags of its LACP packets to CE1 in order to inform it that the link is not active in the LAG. As a result,

CE1 only activates its link toward PE1. This *is* MC-LAG. A downgraded MC-LAG without ICCP is also possible and operational (it works), but this latter model does not benefit from the possibility of having a decision point at the multi-PE side.

How about not aggregating the uplinks? This is a bad idea. Allowing a CE to switch traffic between its uplinks is opening the door to L2 loops!

If either PE1 or PE2 has its local AC down—or not active in the LAG—it must signal this state accordingly to the remote PEs. Otherwise, the remote PEs might send traffic to a PE that is not able to forward the traffic to the AC, which results in *traffic black-holing*. Let's see how the AC status is signaled in BGP VPWS.

BGP VPWS—PW status vector

By looking carefully at Example 6-6 and Example 6-7, you can see that PE1 (Junos) and PE4 (IOS XR) advertise a status vector as part of the NLRI. Its value is 0x0000 and 0x7FFF for PE1 and PE4, respectively. Very different!

The status vector bit length and the label block size are exactly the same. Each bit in the status vector corresponds to a label in the label block (first bit to first label, second bit to second label, etc.). Let's see how to interpret the 0x0000 and 0x7FFF values:

- PE4 advertises the following prefix: *RD 172.16.0.44:1010, CE-ID 4, Label-Block Offset 1, Label-Block Size 16, Label Base 24045, Status Vector 0x7F 0xFF*. It corresponds to local CE-ID 4, which is connected to remote CE-ID 1. The offset is precisely 1, which means that the only meaningful label for VPWS is the first one of the block (24045). And the only relevant bit of the status vector is the first one, too. In binary: 0x7F 0xFF = 01111111 11111111. The first bit is zero and it means that the local attachment circuit is up from the perspective of PE4.

- Now, PE1 advertises the following prefix: *RD 172.16.0.11:1010, CE-ID 1, Label-Block Offset 3, Label-Block Size 2, Label Base 800012, Status Vector 0x00*. It corresponds to local CE-ID 1, which is connected to remote CE-ID 4. The offset is 3 and not 4, which means that the only meaningful label is the second one of the block (800013). And the only relevant bit of the status vector is the second one, too. The second bit of 0x00 is obviously zero, and it means that the local attachment circuit is up from the perspective of PE1.

Despite the different way to code the unused bits of the status vector (zero in Junos, one in IOS XR) there is no interoperability issue because the meaningful bits are set accordingly: zero = up; one = down.

What happens if the attachment circuit at PE4 (interface Gi 0/0/0/3.1010) is down? In that case, PE4 advertises the L2VPN BGP route with status vector 0xFF 0xFF. All bits are set to 1, including the meaningful bit. At this point, PE1 detects the failure.

Example 6-11. PW status reflecting the received status vector—PE1 (Junos)

```
juniper@PE1> show l2vpn connections
[...]
Instance: L2VPN-A
Edge protection: Not-Primary
  Local site: CE1-A (1)
    connection-site        Type  St    Time last up
    4                      rmt   VC-Dn  -----
[...]
```

If the attachment circuit at PE1 (interface ge-2/0/1.1010) is down, PE1 advertises the L2VPN BGP route with status vector 0x40 = 01000000. Remember that the offset is 3 and the remote CE-ID is 4, so the second bit of the status vector is the meaningful one, and it is set to 1. At this point, PE4 detects the failure.

Example 6-12. PW status reflecting the received status vector—PE4 (IOS XR)

```
RP/0/0/CPU0:PE4#show l2vpn xconnect
XConnect                Segment 1              Segment 2
Group Name       ST     Description     ST     Description     ST
-------------------     ------------------     -----------------
L2VPN-A.4:1      DN     Gi0/0/0/3       UP     172.16.0.11     DN
```

Junos and IOS XR PEs both update the status vector to reflect the state of its local attachment circuits. In addition, Junos PEs *also* change the Layer2 Info extended community when all the local interfaces toward a given CE are down.

Example 6-13. Down "D" bit in Layer2-info extended community—PE1 (Junos)

```
juniper@PE1> show route advertising-protocol bgp 172.16.0.201
             table L2VPN-A.l2vpn.0 detail

L2VPN-A.l2vpn.0: 2 destinations, 3 routes (3 active, ...)
* 172.16.0.11:1010:1:3/96 (1 entry, 1 announced)
 BGP group iBGP-RR type Internal
    Route Distinguisher: 172.16.0.11:1010
    Label-base: 800004, range: 2, status-vector: 0x40, offset: 3
```

```
[..]Communities: target:65000:1010
               Layer2-info: encaps: ETHERNET, control flags:[0x82]
                            Control-Word Site-Down, mtu: 0
                            site preference: 100
```

This detail is relevant for CE multihoming scenarios.

> The AC status is propagated to the PW status, but the reverse is not
> necessarily true. As a general design rule, try *not* to assume that
> when a PW is down, the PE notifies the CE via LACP or Ethernet
> OAM.

BGP VPWS multihoming at work

After understanding how the AC status is signaled with BGP, it's time to see BGP
VPWS multihoming in action. Junos supports *draft-ietf-bess-vpls-multihoming*, which
describes BGP L2VPN active-backup multihoming scenarios such as in Figure 6-5.
As of this writing, IOS XR does not support multihoming with BGP VPWS; however,
it supports multihoming with LDP VPWS, as you will see later in this chapter.

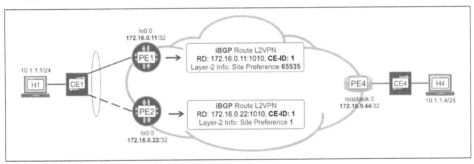

Figure 6-5. BGP VPWS—CE Multihoming

The dashed line in Figure 6-5 means that PE2 is not forwarding traffic from/to the
AC. This is typically the case if the LAG is in single-active mode (the AC is logically
down on PE2). But, before uplink LAGs became popular, the CE uplinks were often
not aggregated, and then the standby PE (PE2) saw the AC up but did not forward
traffic. BGP VPWS multihoming takes care of both scenarios, but remember that
LAG uplink is a good practice whenever possible.

With BGP VPWS multihoming, one, and only one, PE is chosen as a Designated Forwarder (DF) for CE1. How? PE1 and PE2 have a CE-ID (or Site ID) assigned to their
CE1-facing attachment circuits. The key is that *you must configure the same CE-ID
value on both PEs*. Why? Because they are connected to the same CE!

The `site-identifier` assignment is therefore critical:

- PE1 and PE2 both have local CE ID = 1 and remote CE ID = 4. The same local CE ID ensures that either PE1 or PE2—only one of them—is a DF.

- PE3 and PE4 both have local CE ID = 4 and remote CE ID = 1. The same local CE ID ensures that either PE3 or PE4—only one of them—is a DF.

The election of the DF for each L2VPN site is deterministic: every PE in the network chooses the same DF for each L2VPN site. The preferred way to control the outcome of this election is to configure a site preference:

Example 6-14. BGP VPWS—site preference—PE1 (Junos)

```
routing-instances {
    L2VPN-A {
        protocols {
            l2vpn {
                site CE1-A {
                    site-identifier 1;
                    site-preference primary;
}}}}}
```

Alternatively, you can configure `site-preference backup`. Junos automatically sets the preference numerical values accordingly (65,535 for primary and 1 for backup).

Looking back at Figure 6-5, PE1 has a higher site preference, so it becomes the DF for CE1. Junos automatically copies the site preference—which is a numeric field in the Layer2 Info extended community—to the well-known BGP Local Preference attribute. This ensures that all of the PEs in the network—those that support *draft-ietf-bess-vpls-multihoming*—choose PE1 as the Designated Forwarder for CE1.

What happens if the PE1-CE1 attachment circuit goes down? PE1 advertises its L2VPN route with a modified status vector in the NLRI and, more important, with the Down "D" bit in the Layer2 Info extended community flags. Thanks to this "D" bit, all the other PEs learn that PE1 can no longer be a DF for CE1. At this point, PE2 becomes the DF for CE1, and all the PEs agree on that. Last but not least, PE1 sets the Local Preference of its L2VPN route to zero.

Note that PE1 does not withdraw its route upon PE1-CE1 failure, it only changes its attributes.

 It is recommended to use a *<ROUTER_ID>:<VPN_ID>* RD scheme in BGP VPWS scenarios with CEs multihomed to several PEs.

What if CE1 and CE4 are *also* connected via a direct backdoor link without the intervention of the MPLS/IP backbone? In that case, which is strongly undesirable, they would need to run a loop prevention mechanism such as Spanning Tree, both on the L2VPN and on the backdoor link. This is only an option for P2P L2VPN.

Ethernet OAM (802.3ah, 802.1ag)

Looking back at Figure 6-2, there are many reasons why the CE might lose connectivity to the Service PE, and many of them do *not* involve a physical link failure on the Service PE side.

If the attachment circuit on the Service PE side is L3-capable, it can run a routing or a keepalive end-to-end protocol (such as BFD) and keep track of the PE1-CE's connection health. However, this is not always possible, especially if the Service PE provides an L2VPN service to the end customer, in which case the attachment circuit is not L3-capable.

The CE and the PE can also run LACP, even in non-multihomed scenarios (one-link LAG). Although this approach works and is gaining traction in real deployments, this is not what LACP was designed for in the first instance.

Ethernet OAM was designed for this purpose and it comes to the rescue with the following L2 tools:

Link Fault Management (IEEE 802.3ah)
> This provides, among other things, a link-local keepalive that is exchanged between L2-capable adjacent devices.

Connectivity Fault Management (IEEE 802.1ag)
> This provides, among other things, a hierarchical end-to-end keepalive between two remote endpoints that are not necessarily adjacent to each other.

This book does not cover Ethernet OAM interoperability but here are some notes based on the authors' deployment experience, particulary on Junos.

You can couple an Ethernet OAM `action-profile` to an interface. These profiles monitor events such as `[link-]adjacency-loss` (no longer receiving Ethernet OAM PDUs) or `[interface|port]-status-tlv` (receiving a *down* status TLV in an incoming Ethernet OAM PDU). As a result of one of these events, the attachment circuit can be considered to be logically *down* even if the physical interface is up. If that happens, the local PE updates the L2VPN status vector and notifies the remote PE.

However, the remote PE does *not* notify its CE by changing the `[interface|port]-status-tlv` of its Ethernet OAM PDUs. Why? This is intentional and the goal is to avoid a deadlock where CEs prevent one another from coming up.

On a side note, an Ethernet OAM `action-profile` that checks for `[link-]adjacency-loss` is event-driven. To bring an attachment circuit logically down, the PE must *stop* receiving keepalives. But if keepalives have never been received on the interface, the `action-profile` is not executed.

BGP VPWS—VLAN Tag Multiplexing

The basic PW configured in Example 6-3 and Example 6-4 can transport native Ethernet as well as VLAN-tagged frames. There is no restriction about the number of VLAN tags, or about the outer VLAN tag's value. However, this approach has a big drawback: the entire AC physical interface is dedicated to a single PW; or, in other words, it is dedicated to a single remote PE. The model does not allow mapping different frames to different PWs in a per-VLAN basis; and it does not allow associating certain VLANs to other services such as L3VPN. Let's consider a more flexible model!

If you look back to Figure 6-2, the last-mile access device inserts two VLAN tags in the user frame. What are these? It is very common to refer to the outer and inner tags as Service VLAN (S-VLAN) and Customer VLAN (C-VLAN), respectively.

Typically, the S-VLAN identifies one last-mile access device. Being the outer tag, this is the *only* VLAN that the aggregation network cares about. The mapping is not always 1:1, and there *may* be several S-VLANs handled by the same last-mile access device.

The C-VLAN typically identifies one customer circuit. Imagine that the last-mile access device receives—from the upstream aggregation network—a frame whose outer VLAN tag matches one of the S-VLANs for which it is responsible. The last-mile access device (which is a bridge, not a PE) determines, according to the combination of S-VLAN and C-VLAN, the actual end customer interface to which the frame must be forwarded. In that sense, C-VLANs act as pure multiplexers.

What if you want to map one S-VLAN to one PW? Example 6-15 shows how you can do it in Junos.

Example 6-15. BGP VPWS Configuration with SVLAN AC—PE1 (Junos)

```
1    interfaces {
2        ge-2/0/1 {
3            mtu 2000;
4            flexible-vlan-tagging;
5            encapsulation flexible-ethernet-services;
6            unit 1010 {
7                encapsulation vlan-ccc;
8                vlan-id 1010;
9        }}}
10   routing-instances {
11       L2VPN-A {
```

```
12          instance-type l2vpn;
13          interface ge-2/0/1.1010;
14          route-distinguisher 172.16.0.11:1010;
15          vrf-target target:65000:1010;
16          protocols {
17              l2vpn {
18                  encapsulation-type ethernet-vlan;
19                  interface ge-2/0/1.1010;
20                  site CE1-A {
21                      site-identifier 1;
22                      ignore-mtu-mismatch;
23                      interface ge-2/0/1.1010 {
24                          remote-site-id 4;
25  }}}}}}
```

VLAN tags are just a multiplexing field in the VPWS world. They do *not* identify a bridge domain, because there is simply no intelligent bridging in VPWS. Indeed, a VPWS service is just a cross-connect between an AC and a PW.

A single VLAN tag is specified on line 8. As a result, all the following frames are transported by the VPWS service:

- Frames with single VLAN tag 1010.
- Frames with double VLAN tag, being 1010 the outer (SVLAN) tag. In this case, the CVLAN header is considered as part of the payload and it is preserved.

If you want to be more selective, you can use the syntax `vlan-tags outer 1010 inner[-list] <CVLAN(s)>`, specifying the CVLAN(s) that are mapped to the PW.

For easier reading, this chapter's examples use the same numbering for the VLAN, RT, and RD (in this case, 1010). This is arbitrary: the three numbers could just as well be all different.

Example 6-16 shows the configuration to map one S-VLAN to one PW in IOS XR.

Example 6-16. BGP VPWS Configuration with SVLAN AC—PE4 (IOS XR)

```
1   interface GigabitEthernet0/0/0/3
2    mtu 2000
3    !
4   interface GigabitEthernet0/0/0/3.1010 l2transport
5    encapsulation dot1q 1010
6    !
7   l2vpn
8    xconnect group myL2VPN
9     mp2mp L2VPN-A
```

```
10        vpn-id 123456789
11        l2-encapsulation vlan
12        autodiscovery bgp
13          rd 172.16.0.44:1010
14          route-target 65000:1010
15          signaling-protocol bgp
16          ce-id 4
17            interface GigabitEthernet0/0/0/3.1010 remote-ce-id 1
18      !
```

The handling of additional VLAN tags is the same as in Junos. If you want to be more selective, you can use the syntax encapsulation dot1q 1010 second-dot1q <CVLAN>, specifying the CVLAN that is mapped to the PW.

The two previous examples are interoperable between both vendors.

Finally, it is also possible to specify a list of S-VLANs that are mapped to a PW. Here are the changes that you would need to apply:

- In Junos, let's use Example 6-15 as a reference. First, replace vlan-id (line 8) with, for example, vlan-id-list [1001-1019 2001-2009]. Then, set the encapsulation-type (line 18) to ethernet.
- In IOS XR, simply configure the list on the AC itself. In Example 6-16, line 5, use the syntax encapsulation dot1q 1010-1019.

This *S-VLAN list* scenario works fine in single-vendor scenarios, but, as of this writing, it does not interoperate between Junos and IOS XR. This is because Junos and IOS XR signal Ethernet and VLAN encapsulation, respectively. Neither Junos nor IOS XR allows changing the encapsulation successfully in this case, and the ignore-encapsulation-mismatch knob is only available in Junos.

There is one way to achieve interoperability, though. If the entire physical interface is reserved in the IOS XR device (Example 6-4), it interoperates successfully with Junos vlan-id-list.

 This interoperability issue is specific to the *current* BGP VPWS implementation; it does not affect LDP VPWS or BGP/LDP VPLS.

BGP VPWS—VLAN Tag Translation and Manipulation

Now, put a mirror on Figure 6-2. Place it in the middle of the right-side cloud (labeled *Central IP/MPLS Core*) and look from the left so that you can see the same picture twice in a nice symmetrical manner. Imagine that two end customers—one on the far left and one on the far right—need to communicate to each other. The Service PEs can provide an L3 Service or an L2 Service to achieve that:

- If they provide an L3 Service, the ingress PE strips the Ethernet header—including the VLAN tags—from the user frame, as you can see at the top of Figure 6-1.

- In the L2 Service case, the Ethernet header—including its VLAN tags—is preserved. Now, the VLAN tags must match on the left and on the right. That is a tough provisioning challenge, and its workaround is VLAN tag translation.

 In the remainder of the BGP VPWS section, all the configuration examples are incomplete for the sake of brevity. To complete them, you can mix and match with Example 6-3 and Example 6-4.

In the following example, a frame with (SVLAN, CVLAN) = (1010, 123) in the PE-CE interface would have (SVLAN, CVLAN) = (2020, 123) in the PW. And if the frame has only one VLAN tag equal to 1010 on the AC, the tag would be 2020 on the PW.

Example 6-17. Rewriting the SVLAN tag in the PW—Junos, IOS XR

```
# PE1 (Junos)

interfaces {
    ge-2/0/1 {
        unit 1010 {
            encapsulation vlan-ccc;
            vlan-id 1010;
            input-vlan-map {
                swap;
                vlan-id 2020;
            }
            output-vlan-map swap;
}}}

juniper@PE1> show interfaces ge-2/0/1.1010 | match vlan
    VLAN-Tag [ 0x8100.1010 ]
        In(swap-swap .2020) Out(swap-swap .1010)
    Encapsulation: VLAN-CCC

# PE4 (IOS XR)

interface GigabitEthernet0/0/0/3.1010 l2transport
 encapsulation dot1q 1010
 rewrite ingress tag translate 1-to-1 dot1q 2020 symmetric
!
```

This technique resolves mismatched SVLAN/CVLAN values at the PW's endpoints. Indeed, Example 6-17 interoperates fine, regardless of the AC's VLANs.

Finally, in Example 6-18, a frame with (SVLAN, CVLAN) = (1010, 123) in the AC would have single VLAN = 123 in the PW. And if the frame has only one VLAN tag equal to 1010 on the AC, it travels with no VLAN tag through the PW.

Example 6-18. Removing SVLAN tag in the PW—Junos and IOS XR

```
1    # PE1 (Junos)
2
3    interfaces {
4        ge-2/0/1 {
5            unit 1010 {
6                encapsulation vlan-ccc;
7                vlan-id 1010;
8                input-vlan-map pop;
9                output-vlan-map push;
10    }}}
11   routing-instances {
12       L2VPN-A {
13           protocols {
14               l2vpn {
15                   encapsulation-type ethernet;
16   }}}}
17
18   # PE4 (IOS XR)
19
20   interface GigabitEthernet0/0/0/3.1010 l2transport
21    encapsulation dot1q 1010
22    rewrite ingress tag pop 1 symmetric
23    !
```

Several combinations of the pop, push, and swap actions are available and the flexibility is so nice that there is often more than one solution to each challenge.

Just note that the SVLAN-pop scenario in Example 6-18 works fine in single-vendor scenarios, but as of this writing, it does not interoperate between Junos and IOS XR. The reason is the encapsulation mismatch discussed in the context of vlan-id-list, and it is specific to the current BGP VPWS multivendor implementation.

What if the AC is configured with two VLAN tags? In that case, you can apply the pop/push actions as in Example 6-18 (lines 8 and 9) and keep encapsulation ethernet-vlan on the PW. With these settings, interoperability is successful. However, the encapsulation mismatch issue is hit if there is a double pop/push instead of a single one, for exactly the same reasons discussed earlier.

BGP VPWS—PW Head-End (PWHE)

The traditional *L2VPN as a transport* architecture depicted back in Figure 6-2 offers a pair of possibilities to optimize provisioning and service delivery:

- Merging the functions of the last-mile access device and the Access L2VPN PE into a converged Access Node. This is a local implementation matter.
- Merging the functions of the Aggregation L2VPN PE and the Local Service PE in one single Service Node device, as in Figure 6-6.

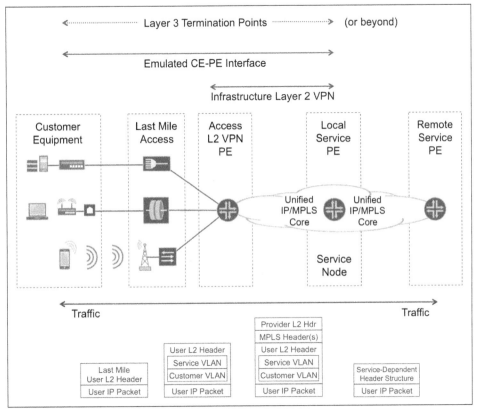

Figure 6-6. Aggregation L2VPN and Local Service PE in one device

The second evolution brings the possibility of having one unified IP/MPLS backbone. The core can be flat from the IGP perspective or, for better scaling, it can be partitioned if the Local Service PE acts as an Area Border Router (ABR) or Autonomous System Border Router (ASBR), and you can find further details in Chapter 16.

This Local Service PE may be offering different services:

L3 Services (Internet or L3VPN)

In this case, the Local Service PE is an L3 Endpoint: you can ignore the mention *or beyond* in Figure 6-6. Each VLAN or SVLAN/CVLAN transported in the PW gets mapped to a different L3 logical interface. In turn, each such L3 interface can belong to the master routing table (Internet service) or to a L3VPN.

P2P L2VPN

The Infrastructure PW is *stitched* to the Service PW. PW stitching is not discussed in detail in this book.

MP2MP L2VPN

There is more about this option in Chapter 7.

Let's discuss the first use case. It is called Pseudowire Head-End (PWHE or PWH), also known as Pseudowire Head-End Termination (PWHT or PHT). Among all the acronyms, this book picks PWHE.

We are in VLAN (de)multiplexing mode: the traffic from all the customers that share the same pair (last-mile access device, Local Service PE) are grouped into one single PW. Let's focus on just one such PW.

Back in Figure 6-2, the Aggregation L2VPN PE has one AC pointing to the right, toward the Local Service PE. Similarly, the Local Service PE has one AC per VLAN(s) pointing to the left, toward the Aggregation L2VPN PE.

Now, in Figure 6-6 both functions are collapsed into the same device, labeled as Local Service PE: let's call it Head-End PE from now on.

Conceptually, PWHE is simply VLAN (de)multiplexing on the same PW. The only difference is that the Head-End PE—converged Aggregation L2VPN PE + Local Service PE—terminates the L2 emulated circuit, *instead of* switching traffic between PW and external L2 ACs.

As of this writing, both IOS XR and Junos support PWHE with LDP VPWS, but only Junos supports PWHE with BGP VPWS. The following example uses BGP VPWS, but because the Head-End role (PWHE function) is implemented on a Junos PE, the end result is interoperable. The Access L2VPN PE, which runs IOS XR, simply sees a regular L2VPN, but it has no L3 visibility of the PWHE.

The IOS XR configuration is *exactly* the same as in Example 6-4. The only difference is on the Head-End PE side, running Junos (see Example 6-19).

Example 6-19. BGP VPWS—PW Head-End termination—PE1 (Junos)

```
1    chassis {
2        pseudowire-service device-count 10;
3        fpc 0 pic 0 tunnel-services bandwidth 10g;
4    }
```

```
5    interfaces {
6        ps1 {
7            anchor-point lt-0/0/0;
8            flexible-vlan-tagging;
9            mtu 9192;
10           unit 0 {
11               encapsulation ethernet-ccc;
12           }
13           unit 1010 {
14               vlan-tags outer 1010 inner 123;
15               family inet address 10.1.1.100/24;
16   }}}
17   routing-instances {
18       L2VPN-A {
19           instance-type l2vpn;
20           interface ps1.0;
21           route-distinguisher 172.16.0.1:111;
22           vrf-target target:65000:111;
23           protocols {
24               l2vpn {
25                   encapsulation-type ethernet;
26                   interface ps1.0;
27                   site CE1-A {
28                       site-identifier 1;
29                       mtu 2000;
30                       interface ps1.0 remote-site-id 4;
31   }}}}}}
```

You can view each ps interface as the local termination of a PW coming from one single last-mile access device. With the previous configuration (line 2), you can define up to 10 psX interfaces (ps0 through ps9), each mapped to/from one PW. These interfaces are anchored (line 7) to an lt interface (line 3). Anchoring instantiates the psX interface in a Packet Forwarding Engine (PFE) inside the router. This makes the service actually work by associating bandwidth resources and also enabling Quality of Service (QoS).

Now, the psX.0 logical interface (lines 10 through 12) is special in that it represents the PW's AC inside the Head-End PE (lines 20, 26, and 30). VLANs are then used as (de)multiplexers and *many* non-zero units (lines 13 through 15) can be created: these are the service endpoints. In this case, the service is L3 but it could be in theory L2 (not implemented yet), as well.

The L3 endpoint units such as ps1.1010 can have single or dual VLAN tags. They can be kept in the master routing table or declared in a VRF. Although as of this writing the latter is not officially supported yet, the authors' lab testing was successful.

The logical interface ps1.1010 is static. But it is also possible to create dynamic interfaces by using VLAN autosensing, which opens the door to a very flexible broadband access and subscriber management model. The classical BNG (Broadband Network Gateway) is replaced with a Service PE that can be anywhere in the MPLS core.

BGP VPWS—Load Balancing

As you saw before, the CW is required to ensure that all the L2VPN frames of the same flow are forwarded on the same path so that they do not arrive to the destination out of order. The downside of the CW is that all the packets of the same PW may follow the same path. For some applications, this is a poor load-balancing scheme that can easily lead to traffic polarization in the core network. There are two solutions to this challenge:

RFC 6790 - The Use of Entropy Labels in MPLS Forwarding
It is applicable to MPLS in general (not only L2VPN) and it relies on inserting two MPLS labels just below the transport label: the Entropy Label Indicator (ELI), which is a reserved fixed label with value 7, and the *entropy label* itself. The full MPLS label stack from top to bottom would be: the transport label, the ELI, the entropy label, and the VPN label (if any).

RFC 6391 - Flow-Aware Transport (FAT) of Pseudowires over a MPLS Packet Switched Network
This is only available for L2VPN and it relies on inserting an MPLS label—a so-called *flow label*—at the bottom of the stack. This label lies between the L2VPN label and the Control Word.

The principle of both approaches is quite simple: entropy (or flow) labels have pseudo-random values and are *not* interpreted by any routers. By inserting such label(s), the ingress PE is actually adding a variable seed for load-balancing hash computation when the packet arrives to transit LSRs. The ingress PE assigns the same entropy (or flow) label value to every packet of a given flow, so packet order is guaranteed. As a result of the entropy (or flow) label, different flows in the same PW can be mapped to different equal-cost paths.

Here is what happens when the packet reaches the egress PE:

- In the entropy label case, due to PHP the ELI is exposed (although the penultimate LSR may decide to also pop the ELI and entropy label). If needed, the egress PE removes the ELI and the entropy label, exposing the service label (if any). The packet is then mapped to the appropriate service—for example, to an L2VPN AC.

- In the FAT scenario, due to PHP the L2VPN label is exposed. The egress PE maps the packet to the appropriate L2VPN AC, and then it pops all the remaining labels (VPN and flow label) without any further processing.

As of this writing, entropy labels were supported by Junos, but not by IOS XR. On the other hand, this book's tests provided interoperable PW with FAT and LDP VPWS.

As for BGP VPWS, flow labels can be enabled in IOS XR but not in Junos. The result is interoperable, in the sense that PE4 pushes the flow label and PE1 is able to pop it and forward the frame successfully. In the other direction, PE1 does not push the flow label, but that is fine for PE4, too.

Example 6-20 shows the IOS XR configuration.

Example 6-20. BGP VPWS—FAT configuration—PE4 (IOS XR)

```
l2vpn
 xconnect group myL2VPN
  mp2mp L2VPN-A
   autodiscovery bgp
    signaling-protocol bgp
     load-balancing flow-label both static
!
```

VPWS Signaled with LDP

LDP VPWS is commonly known as Martini transport and, like BGP VPWS (Kompella), it relies on Martini encapsulation (RFC 4788). It is also called L2 Circuit or L2CKT.

In Chapter 2 and Chapter 4 you saw two applications of LDP: building MP2P and P2MP LSPs with IPv4 and P2MP FECs, respectively. These FECs are typically exchanged over *direct* LDP sessions, whose endpoints are the loopback interfaces of two directly connected neighbors. These LDP sessions are therefore *not* targeted.

LDP VPWS, on the other hand, requires PE-PE *targeted* LDP sessions:

- If the PEs are directly connected to each other, and they already have a LDP session established to exchange other FEC types (e.g., IPv4), there is no need to signal any more LDP sessions: the existing one is used to exchange L2VPN FECs. Note that sometimes you might need to selectively filter the FECs that you want to advertise or receive: for example, the network design might rely on a given session to exchange L2VPN FECs but not IPv4 FECs, or vice versa.

- If the PEs are several hops away from each other, a new LDP session must be established between the two PEs.

LDP VPWS Configuration at the PEs

Let's begin with a scenario in which a physical AC is mapped to a PW. The AC configuration is skipped because it is similar to BGP VPWS (see Example 6-3, lines 1 through 7 and Example 6-4, lines 1 through 4).

Example 6-21 shows the PE1—PE4 PW configuration at Junos PE1.

Example 6-21. LDP VPWS configuration with physical AC—PE1 (Junos)

```
1    protocols {
2        ldp {
3            interface lo0.0;
4        }
5        l2circuit {
6            neighbor 172.16.0.44 {
7                interface ge-2/0/1.0 {
8                    virtual-circuit-id 13579;
9                    encapsulation-type ethernet;
10                   ignore-mtu-mismatch;
11                   pseudowire-status-tlv;
12   }}}}
```

One key aspect of LDP VPWS is its lack of a native autodiscovery mechanism. You must configure neighbors (line 6) explicitly. Later you will see how this limitation is overcome by using BGP AD.

The service is identified by a VC ID (line 8) that must match on both ends of the PW.

The `pseudowire-status-tlv` usage is explained later.

Following is the PE1—PE4 PW configuration at PE4, which runs IOS XR:

Example 6-22. LDP VPWS configuration with physical AC—PE4 (IOS XR)

```
l2vpn
 ignore-mtu-mismatch
 pw-class PW-L2CKT-UNTAGGED
  encapsulation mpls
   protocol ldp
   control-word
   transport-mode ethernet
 !
 xconnect group myL2CKT
  p2p L2CKT-A
   interface GigabitEthernet0/0/0/3
   neighbor ipv4 172.16.0.11 pw-id 13579
    pw-class PW-L2CKT-UNTAGGED
 !
```

LDP VPWS Signaling and Forwarding Planes

With the previous configuration, the PW comes up. Let's verify that.

Example 6-23. Established LDP VPWS—Junos and IOS XR

```
# PE1 (Junos)

juniper@PE1> show l2circuit connections interface ge-2/0/1.0
[...]
Neighbor: 172.16.0.44
 Interface                   Type  St    # Up trans
 ge-2/0/1.0(vc 13579)    rmt   Up     1
   Remote PE: 172.16.0.44, Negotiated control-word: No
   Incoming label: 299776, Outgoing label: 16080
   Negotiated PW status TLV: Yes
   Local PW status code: 0x0000, Neighbor PW status code: 0x0000
   Local interface: ge-2/0/1.0, Status: Up, Encapsulation: ETHERNET
   Flow Label Transmit: No, Flow Label Receive: No


# PE4 (IOS XR)

RP/0/0/CPU0:PE4#show l2vpn xconnect group myL2CKT
XConnect                 Segment 1          Segment 2
Group    Name    ST  Description   ST  Description            ST
-------------------  ------------------  ----------------------
myL2CKT  L2CKT-A  UP   Gi0/0/0/3       UP  172.16.0.11  13579  UP
-------------------------------------------------------------
```

In IOS XR, you can use the show l2vpn xconnect **detail** option in order to see the local and remote PW status TLV values. The following couple of tips can help you to interpret the output of both Junos and IOS XR commands:

- Local PW Status in Junos means the same as Outgoing PW Status in IOS XR: the advertised PW Status TLV value.

- Neighbor PW Status in Junos means the same as Incoming Status in IOS XR: the received PW Status TLV.

Figure 6-7 shows an example in which the transport LSP is signaled by using LDP. This is just one option and all the other transport protocols are also available. Indeed, LDP-based L2VPNs can also be transported with RSVP-TE, BGP-LU, and SPRING-signaled LSPs, as well as with IP (e.g., GRE) tunnels.

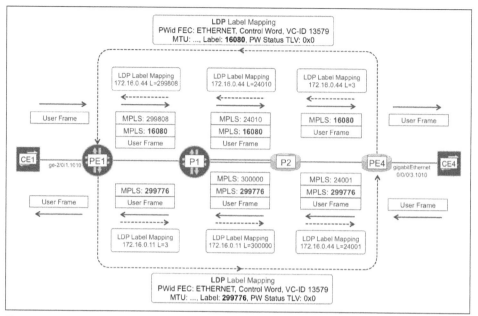

Figure 6-7. LDP VPWS signaling with LDP-based PSN Tunnel

 LDP PWid FEC has type 0x80 = 128. It is popularly called FEC 128 or Martini FEC.

The forwarding plane is the same as in BGP VPWS. Just one note about the CW: by default, an LDP VPWS whose endpoints run Junos negotiate to use the CW, whereas two IOS XR PEs negotiate *not* to use it. As a result, in a multivendor PW with one PE running Junos and the other running IOS XR, there is no CW unless the IOS XR PE is explicitly instructed to use it (Example 6-22).

LDP VPWS—CE Multihoming and PW Redundancy

The concepts were already discussed in the context of BGP VPWS. With the FEC 129 model, discussed in Chapter 7, it is possible to deploy the same multihoming mechanisms as in BGP VPWS, but let's see what can be done with plain FEC 128.

LDP VPWS—PW Status TLV

Back in BGP VPWS, there was a Status Vector that accounted potentially for several VPWS connections to different local CEs. In the LDP VPWS case, each PW only connects two CEs, so there is no need to have a vector. However, the PW Status TLV that optionally accompanies each PWid FEC is actually a vector. This time, the bits do *not* represent several remote CEs, but different aspects of the status of a single PW. This makes it possible to provide richer information than just the up/down state. A *perfect* PW Status TLV has all bits set to zero, and any non-zero bits reflect an exceptional condition whose interpretation is ruled by the following standards:

- RFC 4446 - *IANA allocations for PWE3*, defines the following values: PW forwarding (clear all failures) (0x0), PW not forwarding (0x01), local AC receive fault (0x02), local AC transmit fault (0x04), local PSN-facing PW receive fault (0x08), and local PSN-facing PW transmit fault (0x10).
- RFC 6870 - *Pseudowire Preferential Forwarding Status Bit*, defines the following values: PW forwarding standby (0x20), and PW request switchover (0x40). These values are quite relevant for PW redundancy solutions.

The PW Status TLV is advertised in two types of LDP messages: in LDP Label Mapping during PW establishment, and in LDP Notification messages when there is a status change.

The usage of these bits is not unified across vendors. For example, if an AC is down from the point of view of LACP (on an active-backup LAG), Junos signals 0x01 (PW not forwarding) and IOS XR signals 0x06 (local AC receive and transmit faults). The reaction on the remote end is the same, though: considering the PW as down from a forwarding-plane perspective.

LDP VPWS—PW redundancy configuration

Let's suppose that PE1 signals a VPWS service and both PE3 and PE4 are two valid endpoints. For example, both PE3 and PE4 are connected to the same CE, or they both provide L3 PWHE, or they both can stitch PWs (PE1-PE3 or PE1-PE4) to the next L2VPN hierarchy level.

Unlike BGP VPWS, traditional (FEC 128) LDP VPWS has no native autodiscovery so if PE1 needs to have PW redundancy toward both PE3 and PE4, you need to configure these PWs manually. In the configuration shown in Example 6-24 Junos PE1 chooses PE4 as primary and PE3 as standby.

Example 6-24. Active-Standby LDP VPWS configuration—PE1 (Junos)

```
protocols {
    l2circuit {
        neighbor 172.16.0.44 {
            interface ge-2/0/1.0 {
                virtual-circuit-id 13579;
                pseudowire-status-tlv;
                backup-neighbor 172.16.0.33 {
                    virtual-circuit-id 13579;
```

```
        [hot-]standby;
}}}}}
```

The `hot-standby` knob allows faster convergence than that of the `standby` by doing the following:

- Allowing frames received from the backup (and, of course, the primary) neighbor. PE1 signals status TLV 0x20 (backup) and 0x00 to PE3 and PE4, respectively. Therefore, by default, PE3 does not send frames to PE1. You can change this default behavior by configuring PE3 with the hot-standby-vc-on knob, which has the downside of causing BUM frame duplication.

- Using the backup neighbor as a *preprogrammed* backup forwarding next hop. This idea is further explained in Chapter 21.

And here is the PW redundancy configuration for IOS XR PE4, which chooses PE1 as primary and PE2 as standby:

Example 6-25. Active-Standby LDP VPWS configuration—PE4 (IOS XR)

```
l2vpn
 xconnect group myL2CKT
  p2p L2CKT-A
   interface GigabitEthernet0/0/0/3
   neighbor ipv4 172.16.0.11 pw-id 13579
    pw-class PW-L2CKT-UNTAGGED
   backup neighbor 172.16.0.22 pw-id 13579
    pw-class PW-L2CKT-UNTAGGED
 !
```

 During this book's tests, PW redundancy interoperability between Junos and IOS XR proved to be tricky. The details will be covered in a blog post at *http://mplsinthesdnera.net*.

LDP VPWS—VLAN Tag Multiplexing

As with BGP VPWS, you can map one or more S-VLANs to a PW in LDP VPWS. Example 6-26 builds on top of the AC configuration in Example 6-15 (lines 1 through 9), except that the unit and VLAN IDs are 1020 instead of 1010 now.

Example 6-26. LDP VPWS configuration with SVLAN AC—PE1 (Junos)

```
protocols {
    l2circuit {
        neighbor 172.16.0.44 {
            interface ge-2/0/1.1020 {
```

```
        virtual-circuit-id 13579;
        ignore-mtu-mismatch;
        pseudowire-status-tlv;
}}}}
```

Likewise, the following example builds on top of the AC configuration in
Example 6-16 (line 1 through 6), after replacing 1010 with 1020:

Example 6-27. LDP VPWS Configuration with SVLAN AC—PE4 (IOS XR)

```
l2vpn
 ignore-mtu-mismatch
 pw-class PW-L2CKT-TAGGED
  encapsulation mpls
   protocol ldp
   control-word
   transport-mode vlan passthrough
 !
 xconnect group myL2CKT
  p2p L2CKT-A
   interface GigabitEthernet0/0/0/3.1020
   neighbor ipv4 172.16.0.11 pw-id 13579
    pw-class PW-L2CKT-TAGGED
 !
```

To transport all the frame's VLAN tags on the PW, IOS XR needs the vlan pass
through knob. This is the default in Junos.

The strategy to map an SVLAN and one or more CVLAN(s) to a PW is the same as in
BGP VPWS, and the AC configuration is identical, so it is skipped here.

As for the possibility to map a list of SVLANs to a PW, the AC configuration remains
the same as in BGP VPWS (vlan-id-list, etc.), and you can achieve interoperability
by using the following Junos configuration:

Example 6-28. Adjustment for S-VLAN List PW Interop—PE1 (Junos)

```
protocols {
    l2circuit {
        neighbor 172.16.0.44 {
            interface ge-2/0/1.1020 {
                encapsulation-type ethernet-vlan;
}}}}
```

So, multiplexing several SVLANs in the same PW fully interoperates without having
to reserve a physical interface on any PE. This is an advantage of LDP VPWS over
BGP VPWS that has nothing to do with the protocols; it has to do with the current
implementation in both vendors.

LDP VPWS—VLAN Tag Translation and Manipulation

Again, the concepts are the same as in BGP VPWS. The techniques are already illustrated in Example 6-17 and Example 6-18 (just ignore lines 11 through 16 in the latter). And the good news with the current LDP VPWS implementation is that all of the scenarios—not just a subset—are fully interoperable.

The BGP VPWS interoperability issue happens if all the VLAN tags (one or two) configured on the AC are popped at the PW's ingress—and pushed at egress. Junos and IOS XR considered the resulting encapsulation to be Ethernet and VLAN, respectively. Now, in LDP VPWS it is possible to tune the encapsulation on the Junos side, achieving interoperability. As of this writing, the difference is due exclusively to the implementation in both vendors; it has nothing to do with the protocols.

The adjustment required on the Junos PE side in order to achieve full interoperability with IOS XR is already shown in Example 6-28.

LDP VPWS—PWHE

Once again, the concepts are the same as in BGP VPWS. And for the same implementation reasons just discussed, in LDP VPWS it is not necessary to dedicate a physical interface on any PE to achieve interoperability between IOS XR and Junos.

Following is an interoperable PWHE configuration in Junos:

Example 6-29. LDP VPWS—PWHE termination—PE1 (Junos)

```
1     protocols {
2         ldp {
3             interface lo0.0;
4         }
5         l2circuit {
6             neighbor 172.16.0.44 {
7                 interface ps2.0 {
8                     virtual-circuit-id 13579;
9                     ignore-mtu-mismatch;
10                    control-word;
11                    encapsulation-type ethernet-vlan;
12                    pseudowire-status-tlv;
13     }}}}
```

The configuration of the `ps2` interface follows the same principle as Example 6-19, lines 1 through 16: `ps2.0` binds to the PW, and `ps2.<X>` are the L3 multiplexed interfaces.

As of this writing, Junos PWHE requires the CW to be negotiated in the PW. This requires explicit configuration on the IOS XR side, as shown earlier in Example 6-22.

In Example 6-29, PE1 is acting as the PWHE, and PE4 as a plain L2VPN PE.

In Example 6-30, we'll reverse the roles, and make IOS XR PE4 the PWHE.

Example 6-30. LDP VPWS—PWHE termination—PE4 (IOS XR)

```
1    generic-interface-list GIL-CORE
2     interface GigabitEthernet0/0/0/0
3     interface GigabitEthernet0/0/0/1
4    !
5    interface PW-Ether100
6     attach generic-interface-list GIL-CORE
7    !
8    interface PW-Ether100.1020
9     ipv4 address 10.2.2.200 255.255.255.0
10    encapsulation dot1q 1020 second-dot1q 123
11   !
12   l2vpn
13    ignore-mtu-mismatch
14    xconnect group myL2CKT
15     p2p L2CKT-A
16      interface PW-Ether1020
17      neighbor ipv4 172.16.0.11 pw-id 13579
18       pw-class PW-L2CKT-TAGGED
19   !
```

PW-Ether interfaces in IOS XR are anchored on physical interfaces. The best practice is to include all the core-facing links in the generic-interface-list (lines 1 through 3). The pw-class PW-L2CKT-TAGGED configuration is the same as in Example 6-27.

LDP VPWS—FAT

The concept is already discussed in "BGP VPWS Signaling" on page 284. This book's tests provided interoperable LDP VPWS with FAT by using the configuration shown in Example 6-31.

Example 6-31. LDP VPWS—FAT interoperability—Junos and IOS XR

```
# PE1 (Junos)

protocols {
    l2circuit {
        neighbor 172.16.0.44 {
```

```
            interface ge-2/0/1.1020 {
                flow-label-transmit-static;
                flow-label-receive-static;
}}}}

# PE4 (IOS XR)

l2vpn
 pw-class PW-L2CKT     ! This pw-class is applied to the PW
  encapsulation mpls
   load-balancing
    flow-label both static
 !
```

The usage of flow labels can also be negotiated during LDP VPWS establishment, but it did not provide successfully interoperable results in this book's tests. On the other hand, when FAT was statically configured as in Example 6-31, interoperability was successful.

## CHAPTER 7

Virtual Private LAN Service

Using a rough analogy, you can view a Virtual Private LAN Service (VPLS) instance like a Layer 2 (L2) VRF. Following are two important differences with respect to L3 VRFs:

- A real (L3) VRF provides virtualized routing, and VPLS provides virtualized switching.
- PEs advertise L3 (e.g., IP VPN) routes, but they do *not* advertise VPLS MAC routes to remote PEs.

VPLS just provides Multipoint-to-Multipoint (MP2MP) L2 connectivity between sites; MAC learning is performed in the forwarding plane—unlike IP routes, which are advertised in the control plane. It is very likely that in the following years Ethernet VPN (EVPN) takes over VPLS progressively, but as of this writing, the installed base of VPLS is big, so it deserves its own chapter.

Introduction to VPLS

VPLS is a virtual LAN switching instance with two types of interfaces: traditional Attachment Circuits (ACs) and Pseudowires (PWs). VPLS is a natural extension of Virtual Private Wire Service (VPWS). In a nutshell, here are differences:

- VPWS can support many L2 technologies; VPLS supports only Ethernet.
- VPWS is Point-to-Point (P2P), and VPLS is truly MP2MP. Actually, the topology can be quite arbitrary (full-mesh E-LAN, hub-and-spoke E-TREE, etc.) because both the usage of RTs in BGP VPLS and the manual definition of targeted neighbors in LDP VPLS provide that topological flexibility.

- VPWS does not perform MAC learning (it is not needed), and VPLS does it in the forwarding plane.

The entire VPLS service behaves like a big switch with distributed MAC learning intelligence implemented on each PE. In the context of a given VPLS instance, a PE can have one or more local ACs, and one or more PWs toward remote PEs.

Remember that all the PWs between the same two PEs can share the same pair (one in each direction) of LSPs, which are also known as Packet-Switched Network (PSN) Tunnels, for transport.

For the moment and for the sake of simplicity, let's use a VPLS example with one VLAN only. In Figure 7-1, all of the PEs are interconnected with a full mesh of bidirectional P2P PWs: PE1—PE2, PE1—PE3, PE1—PE4, PE2—PE3, PE2—PE4, and PE3—PE4.

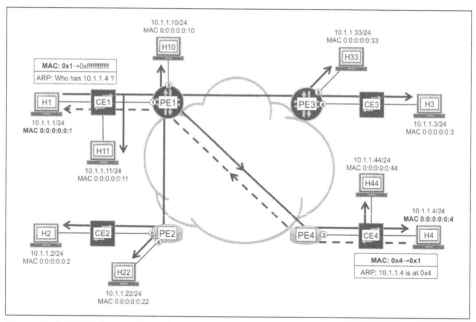

Figure 7-1. VPLS forwarding plane

The service just started, and the very first frame is an ARP request sent by H1. An ARP request is a broadcast frame, which means that its destination MAC address is ff:ff:ff:ff:ff:ff. This is the all-ones or broadcast MAC address, and it represents all the hosts in the bridging domain.

This frame arrives to all the hosts with the MAC addresses unchanged. First, CE1 replicates the frame and sends one copy of the frame to H11 and another copy to PE1. This replication process is known as *L2 flooding*. Then, PE1 sends one copy to H10—local switching between ACs—and one additional copy over each of the PWs toward PE2, PE3, and PE4. Thus, PE1 sends in total four copies of the original frame. The process continues until all of the hosts receive the ARP request.

During this flooding process, every switching device in the path (the CEs and the VPLS instances on the PEs) also inspects the *source* MAC address of the frame. In this way, they learn on which interface, or on which PW, the unicast MAC address 00:00:00:00:00:01 can be reached: PE1 learns that MAC 0x1 is reachable over its interface to CE1, and PE4 learns that MAC 0x1 is reachable over its PW to PE1. This process is one of the essential functions of a bridge, and it is known as *MAC learning*. As a result of MAC learning, bridges populate a MAC table in which they keep track of the interface (or PW) where each unicast MAC is reachable.

When H4 replies to the ARP request, it does so with a unicast Ethernet frame. Its destination MAC address is 0x1, which has already been learned by the network. CE4 knows that it must send this frame on its port toward PE4; in turn, PE4 sends it only over the PW to PE1; and so on. Because the destination MAC address (0x1) has already been learned, the frame is classified as *known unicast*: it is not replicated and it is forwarded point-to-point until it reaches the destination host H1. In parallel, all the bridges in the path (CE4, PE4, PE1, and CE1) learn the MAC address of H4, 00:00:00:00:00:04.

Figure 7-1 represents a bridge domain, often called a broadcast domain: a broadcast frame is flooded to all the elements in the domain. According to its destination MAC address, a frame can be classified as follows:

- Broadcast frames have destination MAC address ff:ff:ff:ff:ff:ff.
- Multicast frames have a destination MAC address whose first octet has its last bit set to one—for example, 01:00:5e:11:22:33 (see Chapter 4) or ff:ff:ff:ff:ff:ff. Strictly speaking, broadcast is a specific case of multicast.
- Unicast frames have a destination MAC address whose first octet has its last bit set to zero.

What packets are *not flooded* in a broadcast domain? Unicast frames whose destination MAC address is known—that is, the address is present in the MAC tables—are forwarded point-to-point to the destination host. All of the other frames are flooded, and these are collectively referred to as BUM, or Broadcast, Unknown unicast, and Multicast.

Bridges keep an idle timer for each of the MAC table (cache) entries. If, for a certain amount of time (typically minutes), there is no traffic from a given *source* MAC address, that particular MAC entry expires and is deleted from the table. Later, if the bridge needs to forward a frame *destined* to that MAC address, the frame is flooded: known unicast became unknown unicast! So, the known/unknown characteristic of L2 unicast frames depends on the actual traffic patterns.

Then what is the function of VPLS? Simply put, it interconnects the different sites, acting as a "glue" that binds together the PWs and the ACs in a distributed bridge domain. You already saw how PWs are signaled and how traffic is forwarded in a PW. VPLS relies exactly on the same BGP or LDP mechanisms, so this section is shorter.

A very important aspect of VPLS implementation is *split horizon*. A frame received on a PW is *never* sent back on the same PW: this is an elementary property of Ethernet bridges. In addition, by default, a frame received on a PW is not forwarded on any other PW, either. Without this precaution, L2 loops would be easily created.

 You can tactically change this default behavior in some cases (such as Hierarchical VPLS, discussed later in this chapter).

VPLS Signaled with BGP

BGP VPLS has many points in common with BGP VPWS.

BGP VPLS Configuration

In Junos, you can configure VPLS with two different routing instance types: `vpls` and `virtual-switch`. The pros and cons of each approach will be discussed in the context of LDP VPLS. Example 7-1 shows the configuration of a `vpls` instance at Junos PE1.

Example 7-1. BGP VPLS configuration—PE1 (Junos)

```
1   interfaces {
2       ge-2/0/1 {
3           flexible-vlan-tagging;
4           encapsulation flexible-ethernet-services;
5           unit 2010 {
6               encapsulation vlan-vpls;
7               vlan-id 2010;
8   }}}
9   routing-instances {
10      VPLS-A {
11          instance-type vpls;
12          vlan-id 2010;
13          interface ge-2/0/1.2010;
14          route-distinguisher 172.16.0.11:2010;
```

```
15              vrf-target target:65000:2010;
16              protocols {
17                  vpls {
18                      control-word;
19                      interface ge-2/0/1.2010;
20                      no-tunnel-services;
21                      site CE1-A {
22                          site-identifier 1;
23                          interface ge-2/0/1.2010;
24      }}}}}
```

This VPLS instance just has one AC, but it could have several ACs, as is demonstrated in Figure 7-1. How many PWs does it have? Any number, starting from zero. Unlike LDP VPLS, in BGP VPLS, PWs are *not* explicitly configured and they are not explicitly signaled, either. As you saw in Chapter 6, there is an autodiscovery mechanism relying on CE numbering and label blocks.

For the configuration, you can refer to the explanations between Examples Example 6-3 and Example 6-4. In Example 7-1, a single VLAN tag is specified in the AC, but it could be two (or none), as well.

Line 20 (`no-tunnel-services`) is optional but recommended for VPLS. It is further explained after Example 7-4.

As for the MTU, Junos does not take it into account in BGP VPLS implementation, but IOS XR does. The only way to achieve interoperability is to configure IOS XR to ignore the MTU mismatch. Example 7-2 shows the configuration at IOS XR PE4.

Example 7-2. BGP VPLS configuration—PE4 (IOS XR)

```
1       interface GigabitEthernet0/0/0/3.2010 l2transport
2        encapsulation dot1q 2010
3        !
4       l2vpn
5        ignore-mtu-mismatch-ad
6        bridge-group myVPLS
7         bridge-domain VPLS-A
8          interface GigabitEthernet0/0/0/3.2010
9          !
10         vfi CE4-A
11          vpn-id 1234567
12          autodiscovery bgp
13           rd 172.16.0.44:2010
14           route-target 65000:2010
15           signaling-protocol bgp
16           ve-id 4
17           control-word
18        !
```

In line 10, *VFI* stands for *Virtual Forwarding Instance*. In line 16, *VE* stands for *VPLS Edge*. In Junos terminology, a VE is a *site*: a collection of ACs identified by a number (Example 7-1, line 22; and Example 7-2, line 16) that is globally unique in the context of the VPLS.

BGP VPLS Signaling

A very important advantage of BGP VPLS over LDP VPLS is autodiscovery. There is no need to manually specify the remote PEs because RTs dynamically do the trick.

RTs make it possible to build topologies different from a full mesh, exactly like in L3VPN. Although you can achieve the same level of control in LDP VPLS by manually configuring the desired PW topology, using RTs is more dynamic and efficient.

Let's assume a single-homing topology with the following connections: CE1—PE1, CE2—PE2, CE3—PE3, and CE4—PE4.

The signaling of BGP VPLS is very similar to BGP VPWS. Indeed, it is the same NLRI. This is the autodiscovery route advertised by PE1 for VPLS-A's site CE1-A.

Example 7-3. L2VPN route advertised for a VPLS service—PE1 (Junos)

```
juniper@PE1> show route advertising-protocol bgp 172.16.0.201
            table VPLS-A.l2vpn.0 detail

VPLS-A.l2vpn.0: 4 destinations, 7 routes (4 active, ...)
*  172.16.0.11:2010:1:1/96 (1 entry, 1 announced)
 BGP group iBGP-RR type Internal
    Route Distinguisher: 172.16.0.11:2010
    Label-base: 2049, range: 8, offset: 1
    Nexthop: Self
    Flags: Nexthop Change
    Localpref: 100
    AS path: [65000] I
    Communities: target:65000:2010
                 Layer2-info: encaps: VPLS, control flags:[0x2]
                              Control-Word, mtu: 0
                              site preference: 100
```

Here are the differences between the routes for BGP VPWS and BGP VPLS:

- The encapsulation signaled in the Layer2 Info community is VPLS for BGP VPLS, versus Ethernet or VLAN for BGP VPWS.

- There is no Status Vector in BGP VPLS. In BGP *VPWS*, each local AC is linked to a remote AC in a one-to-one basis, composing a collection of P2P services that could be represented with a vector. In BGP *VPLS*, any local AC can communicate to any remote AC: this is a communication matrix, not a vector. The decision is not to include the vector in the BGP VPLS NLRI.

The BGP L2VPN NLRI already allocates a label block, so it is prepared for multisite.

Example 7-4. PWs in BGP VPLS instance—PE1 (Junos)

```
juniper@PE1> show vpls connections instance VPLS-A
            table VPLS-A.l2vpn.0 detail

Instance: VPLS-A
  Local site: CE1-A (1)
    connection-site   Type  St     # Up trans
    2                 rmt   Up     1
      Remote PE: 172.16.0.22, Negotiated control-word: Yes (Null)
      Incoming label: 2050, Outgoing label: 24000
      Local interface: lsi.1048834, Status: Up, Encapsulation: VPLS
    3                 rmt   Up     1
      Remote PE: 172.16.0.33, Negotiated control-word: Yes (Null)
      Incoming label: 2051, Outgoing label: 800256
      Local interface: lsi.1048832, Status: Up, Encapsulation: VPLS
    4                 rmt   Up     1
      Remote PE: 172.16.0.44, Negotiated control-word: Yes (Null)
      Incoming label: 2052, Outgoing label: 24000
      Local interface: lsi.1048833, Status: Up, Encapsulation: VPLS
```

Here is what each service MPLS label signifies when PE1 receives them:

2049

The labeled frame is coming from site 1, so it must be dropped because site 1 is local to PE1.

2050

The labeled frame is coming from site 2, and therefore on the PW from PE2.

2051

The labeled frame is coming from site 3, and therefore on the PW from PE3.

2052

The labeled frame is coming from site 4, and therefore on the PW from PE4.

Knowing which PW each frame is received on is essential to perform MAC learning and to avoid flooding of known unicast traffic.

After its MPLS labels are removed, the L2 frame is forwarded according to the destination MAC address and the VPLS instance's forwarding table.

By default, Junos automatically creates one vt- logical interface per remote site; in other words, one for each value of the incoming service MPLS label. When the egress PE receives a L2VPN packet from the core, it pops the service label and maps the packet to a label-specific vt- interface for MAC learning. If the no-tunnel-services knob is configured, there is a Label Switched Interface (lsi)—instead of a vt-interface—per remote site. The vt- and lsi concepts are discussed in more detail in Chapter 3.

BGP VPLS implements a MAC flush mechanism. When a site goes down, the local PE readvertises the site, this time setting the "F" bit in the Layer2 Info control flags. With the "F" flag, the local PE is telling the remote PEs the following: *if you have a MAC entry pointing to me for this site, remove it from your MAC table*.

The "F" bit is also used in Active-Backup multihoming architectures like the one discussed around Figure 6-5 for BGP VPWS. In normal conditions, the Designated Forwarder in a given site does *not* set the "F" bit. On the other hand, non-DF PEs set the "F" bit in order to trigger MAC flush on remote PEs that might have MAC entries pointing to them.

 VLAN manipulation techniques for instance-type vpls are very similar to those already discussed for VPWS in Chapter 6.

BGP VPLS—Efficient BUM Replication

Both Junos and IOS XR perform Ingress Replication (IR) by default. Therefore, if PE1 receives a BUM frame from an AC, it creates three copies of the original frame and sends one such copy to each of the remote PEs: PE2, PE3, and PE4. Each copy typically has two MPLS labels (inner service label and outer transport label), except for PHP, and travels through a P2P or MP2P LSP.

As discussed in Chapter 5, IR is not particularly efficient as compared to using P2MP LSPs. If configured to do so, both Junos and IOS XR can flood BUM traffic by using single-labeled RSVP-TE Point-to-Multipoint (P2MP) LSPs. This mechanism was already explored in the context of BGP MVPN, which was formerly known as NG-MVPN. In analogy, VPLS with P2MP LSPs for BUM flooding is sometimes called Next Generation VPLS or NG-VPLS.

As of this writing, both Junos and IOS XR support NG-VPLS with RSVP-TE P2MP LSPs. Neither of the two vendors implement it yet for Multipoint LDP (mLDP).

VPLS with P2MP LSPs—Junos configuration

The principle is the same as in BGP Multicast VPN. With the following configuration, PE1 becomes the root of a P2MP RSVP-TE LSP that it uses for BUM flooding in the context of VPLS-A:

Example 7-5. RSVP-TE P2MP LSPs for BUM transport—PE1 (Junos)

```
routing-instances {
    VPLS-A {
        provider-tunnel {
            rsvp-te {
                label-switched-path-template {
                    default-template;    # Or a custom template
}}}}}
```

If you have read Chapter 5, this configuration should look familiar.

VPLS with P2MP LSPs—IOS XR configuration

The following configuration achieves similar results in IOS XR:

Example 7-6. RSVP-TE P2MP LSPs for BUM transport—PE4 (IOS XR)

```
l2vpn
 bridge group myVPLS
  bridge-domain VPLS-A
   vfi CE4-A
    multicast p2mp
     signaling-protocol bgp
     transport rsvp-te
!
```

VPLS with P2MP LSPs—signaling

When configured as in the two previous examples, the PE updates its BGP L2VPN autodiscovery routes by adding a Provider Multicast Service Interface (PMSI) attribute:

Example 7-7. PMSI attribute in a BGP L2VPN route—PE1 (Junos)

```
juniper@PE1> show route advertising-protocol bgp 172.16.0.201
            table VPLS-A.l2vpn.0 detail

VPLS-A.l2vpn.0: 3 destinations, 5 routes (3 active, ...)
*  172.16.0.11:2010:1:1/96 (1 entry, 1 announced)
[...]
    PMSI: Flags 0x0: Label 0:
          RSVP-TE: Session_13[172.16.0.11:0:58496:172.16.0.11]
```

In multicast terms (see Chapter 5), this is an *Inclusive PMSI*, so all the remote PEs in VPLS-A become leaves of the P2MP LSP.

The rest of the signaling is exactly the same as described in Chapter 5. The leaf PEs receive RSVP-TE path messages whose *P2MP LSP Tunnel IPv4 Session* is `172.16.0.11:0:58496:172.16.0.11`. This value matches the PMSI attribute and that is how the leaf PE binds the RSVP-TE P2MP sub-LSP to the VPLS-A instance.

Likewise, because all of the RSVP-TE P2MP sub-LSPs belonging to the same LSP share the same *P2MP LSP Tunnel IPv4 Session* value, a transit LSR advertises the same label for all of these sub-LSPs to the upstream LSR. This is how the transit LSRs act as branching points, achieving efficient replication of BUM frames.

VPLS Signaled with LDP

LDP VPLS has many points in common with LDP VPWS.

LDP VPLS Configuration

As already mentioned, there are two instance types in Junos that support VPLS: VPLS instances and Virtual Switches. Which one is better? There is no simple answer. Let's begin by looking at a configuration example for each instance type and leave the feature comparison for "VLANs and Learning Domains in VPLS" on page 332.

LDP VPLS—Junos VPLS instances

Example 7-8 shows a configuration example in Junos featuring a VPLS instance with just one AC (it could be more than one) and three PWs.

Example 7-8. LDP VPLS with VPLS instance—PE1 (Junos)

```
1     interfaces {
2         ge-2/0/1 {
3             flexible-vlan-tagging;
4             encapsulation flexible-ethernet-services;
5             unit 2010 {
6                 encapsulation vlan-vpls;
7                 vlan-id 2010;
8     }}}
9     routing-instances {
10        VPLS-B {
11            instance-type vpls;
12            vlan-id 2010;
13            interface ge-2/0/1.2010;
14            protocols {
15                vpls {
16                    no-tunnel-services;
17                    vpls-id 24680;
```

```
18              mtu 1900;
19                  neighbor 172.16.0.22;
20                  neighbor 172.16.0.33;
21                  neighbor 172.16.0.44;
22  }}}}
```

The vpls-id (line 17) value must match on both endpoints, and it is equivalent to the virtual-circuit-id from Example 6-21. Indeed, it is the value of the Martini FEC's VC-ID.

LDP VPLS—Junos Virtual Switches

Example 7-9 shows the equivalent configuration on a Virtual Switch instead of a VPLS instance.

Example 7-9. LDP VPLS with Virtual Switch—PE1 (Junos)

```
1    interfaces {
2        ge-2/0/1 {
3            flexible-vlan-tagging;
4            encapsulation flexible-ethernet-services;
5            unit 2010 {
6                encapsulation vlan-bridge;
7                vlan-id 2010;
8    }}}
9    routing-instances {
10       VS-B {
11           instance-type virtual-switch;
12           interface ge-2/0/1.2010;
13           protocols {
14               vpls {
15                   no-tunnel-services;
16                   vpls-id 24680;
17                   mtu 1900;
18                   neighbor 172.16.0.22;
19                   neighbor 172.16.0.33;
20                   neighbor 172.16.0.44;
21               }
22           }
23           bridge-domains {
24               BR-2010 {
25                   vlan-id 2010;
26                   interface ge-2/0/1.2010;
27    }}}}
```

LDP VPLS—IOS XR configuration

IOS XR has one way to configure LDP VPLS, on a bridge-domain (see Example 7-10).

Example 7-10. LDP VPLS configuration—PE4 (IOS XR)

```
interface GigabitEthernet0/0/0/3.2010 l2transport
 encapsulation dot1q 2010
!
l2vpn
 brige-group myVPLS
  bridge-domain VPLS-B
   mtu 1900
   interface GigabitEthernet0/0/0/3.2010
   !
   vfi CE4-B
    vpn-id 654321   ! This number is irrelevant (not signaled)
    neighbor 172.16.0.11 pw-id 24680
    neighbor 172.16.0.22 pw-id 24680
    neighbor 172.16.0.33 pw-id 24680
!
```

LDP VPLS Signaling

LDP VPLS and LDP VPWS signaling are virtually identical, to the point that a PW between PE1 and PE4 may be associated to a LDP VPWS at PE1, and to an LDP VPLS instance at PE4, or vice versa (VPLS at PE1 and VPWS at PE4). Interoperability is perfect and you need only ensure that MTU and encapsulation at both ends of the PW match—the Junos `ignore-mtu-mismatch` and `ignore-encapsulation-mismatch` knobs are helpful, too.

Due to the multipoint nature of VPLS, there is no AC:PW 1:1 mapping; that's why you don't see the AC in the Example 7-11 (as compared to Example 6-23 for VPWS).

Example 7-11. Established LDP VPLS—Junos and IOS XR

```
# PE1 (Junos)

juniper@PE1> show vpls connections instance VPLS-B
[...]
Instance: VPLS-B
  VPLS-id: 24680
    Neighbor                  Type  St    # Up trans
    172.16.0.22(vpls-id 24680) rmt   Up     1
      Remote PE: 172.16.0.22, Negotiated control-word: No
      Incoming label: 2305, Outgoing label: 24141
      Negotiated PW status TLV: No
      Local interface: lsi.1049614, Status: Up,
                      Encapsulation: ETHERNET
    172.16.0.33(vpls-id 24680) rmt   Up     1
      Remote PE: 172.16.0.33, Negotiated control-word: No
      Incoming label: 2306, Outgoing label: 2405
      Negotiated PW status TLV: No
      Local interface: lsi.1049615, Status: Up,
```

```
                   Encapsulation: ETHERNET
    172.16.0.44(vpls-id 24680) rmt  Up      1
      Remote PE: 172.16.0.44, Negotiated control-word: No
      Incoming label: 2307, Outgoing label: 24367
      Negotiated PW status TLV: No
      Local interface: lsi.1049616, Status: Up,
                   Encapsulation: ETHERNET

# PE4 (IOS XR)

RP/0/0/CPU0:PE4#show l2vpn bridge-domain bd-name VPLS-B
[...]
  List of VFIs:
    VFI CE2-B (up)
      Neighbor 172.16.0.11 pw-id 24680, state: up, [...]
      Neighbor 172.16.0.22 pw-id 24680, state: up, [...]
      Neighbor 172.16.0.33 pw-id 24680, state: up, [...]
```

Here is what each service MPLS label signifies when PE1 receives a labeled packet:

2305

> The labeled frame is coming from PE2, and it is processed at lsi.1049614.

2306

> The labeled frame is coming from PE3, and it is processed at lsi.1049615.

2307

> The labeled frame is coming from PE4, and it is processed at lsi.1049616.

As discussed many times before, an alternative to lsi is vt- interfaces. The key, regardless of the choice, is that depending on what PE the frame is coming from, it is processed via a different logical interface inside the router. This is essential for the MAC learning process in Junos.

After its MPLS labels are removed, the L2 frame is forwarded according to the destination MAC address and the VPLS instance's forwarding table.

The command to show the MAC table associated to a given VPLS service in Junos is show vpls mac-table for VPLS instances, and show bridge mac-table for Virtual Switches, as shown in Example 7-12.

Example 7-12. Virtual Switch MAC table—PE1 (Junos)

```
juniper@PE1> show bridge mac-table instance VS-B

Routing instance : VS-B
 Bridging domain : BR-2010, VLAN : 2010
   MAC              MAC    Logical      NH    RTR
   address          flags  interface    Index ID
```

```
6c:9c:ed:37:8a:df   D       xe-0/0/0.2001
80:71:1f:c0:e9:00   D       lsi.1049904
```

During this book's tests, Junos and IOS XR interoperability was successful.

LDP VPLS—Autodiscovery via BGP

If you look back to BGP VPLS configuration (Example 7-1 and Example 7-2), you can see that the administrator does not need to manually specify the remote PE addresses. The magic of BGP and RTs does the trick.

However, LDP VPLS does not have this autodiscovery capability, and you must manually configure the targeted LDP sessions on both ends of each PW. This is the FEC 128 model, and its name comes from the fact that Martini LDP FEC is #128.

Although for VPWS this does not look like a big issue, in LDP VPLS each instance can have many PWs, and manually configuring all of them is quite an overhead and hard to manage. The solution comes with BGP.

Instead of manually configuring the neighbors like in Example 7-8, Example 7-9, and Example 7-10, it is possible to let BGP autodiscover them. When the endpoints are known, the PEs use targeted LDP to signal the PW. This mixed BGP+LDP solution is commonly called FEC 129, because that FEC type is ultimately signaled in the LDP session. Let's see how it works.

LDP VPLS—FEC 129—BGP configuration

The same L2VPN address family (AFI=25, SAFI=65) is used as for BGP VPWS/VPLS.

IOS XR works fine with the configuration on Example 6-2. As for Junos, it requires the extra configuration shown here:

Example 7-13. L2VPN address family for FEC 129—PE1 (Junos)

```
protocols {
    bgp {
        group iBGP-RR {
            family l2vpn {
                auto-discovery-only;
}}}}
```

LDP VPLS—FEC 129—Junos service configuration

FEC 129 works fine in Junos VPLS instances, and as of this writing it is not implemented on Virtual Switches. To transition to FEC 129, you can take the configuration from Example 7-8, remove the neighbors, delete the vpls-id, and then add the following lines:

Example 7-14. LDP VPLS with FEC 129—PE1 (Junos)

```
1    routing-instances {
2        VPLS-B {
3            route-distinguisher 172.16.0.11:2010;
4            l2vpn-id l2vpn-id:65000:24680;
5            vrf-target target:65000:2010;
6    }}
```

LDP VPLS—FEC 129—IOS XR service configuration

To transition to FEC 129, you can take the configuration on Example 7-10, remove the neighbors, and then add the lines shown in Example 7-15.

Example 7-15. LDP VPLS configuration—PE4 (IOS XR)

```
1    l2vpn
2      brige-group myVPLS
3        bridge-domain VPLS-B
4          vfi CE4-B
5            autodiscovery bgp
6              rd 172.16.0.22:2010
7              route-target 65000:2010
8              signaling-protocol ldp
9                vpls-id 65000:24680
10   !
```

LDP VPLS—FEC 129 signaling

You might have guessed from Example 7-14 (line 4) and Example 7-15 (line 9) that there is a new BGP community that identifies the PW service and must match on both ends. Let's have a look at it:

Example 7-16. L2VPN FEC 129 route advertised by PE1 (Junos)

```
juniper@PE1> show route advertising-protocol bgp 172.16.0.201
             table VPLS-B.l2vpn.0 detail

VPLS-B.l2vpn.0: 4 destinations, 5 routes (4 active, ...)
*  172.16.0.11:2010:172.16.0.11/96 (1 entry, 1 announced)
 BGP group iBGP-RR type Internal
     Route Distinguisher: 172.16.0.11:2001
     Autodiscovery for mesh-group: __ves__
     Nexthop: Self
     Flags: Nexthop Change
     Localpref: 100
     AS path: [65000] I
     Communities: target:65000:2010 l2vpn-id:65000:24680
```

The route advertised by IOS XR looks similar. Thanks to the two communities, the PEs discover each other in the context of this VPLS service.

Now it's time to signal the PWs themselves:

Example 7-17. LDP FEC 129 exchanged between Junos and IOS XR

```
juniper@PE1> show ldp database session 172.16.0.44

Input label database, 172.16.0.11:0--172.16.0.44:0
  Label     Prefix
  24011       FEC129 NoCtrlWord ETHERNET
              000afde8:00006068 ac10002c ac10000b

Output label database, 172.16.0.11:0--172.16.0.44:0
  Label     Prefix
   2305       FEC129 NoCtrlWord ETHERNET
              000afde8:00006068 ac10000b ac10002c
```

The hexadecimal pattern contains 0x6068 = 24680, which nicely matches the L2VPN ID community value. If you look carefully, you can also see the loopback addresses of PE1 and PE4. This completes the signaling of the PW's service label.

Like BGP VPLS, FEC 129 brings to LDP VPLS the possibility to have an Active-Backup multihoming mechanism and implements the "F" bit.

As for PW Status TLV, it is not that useful in VPLS, because there is no longer an AC:PW coupling. In general, the redundancy story of VPLS is not very compelling, and that is one of the main reasons why EVPN is gaining traction.

LDP VPLS—efficient BUM replication

As of this writing, IOS XR supports RSVP-TE P2MP LSPs for BUM forwarding in the FEC 129 model. The mechanism is based on the BGP Provider Multicast Service Interface (PMSI) attribute, exactly as described in the BGP VPLS section.

Neither Junos nor IOS XR support it in the FEC 128 model.

VLANs and Learning Domains in VPLS

In the old days of enterprise LANs, virtual LANs (VLANs) were introduced as a way to segment traffic. The VLAN ID can be interpreted in two different manners: it is a 12-bit tag carried on the wire, and also a bridge domain identifier. What is a bridge (or broadcast) domain? Basically, it is a set of (logical) links and hosts such that an L2 frame sent by one host can reach the other hosts without any L3 routing action. Typically, a bridge domain is a full-mesh E-LAN, but with VPLS it is possible to create other topologies such as a hub-and-spoke E-Tree.

VLANs bring virtualization in the forwarding plane as well as in the control plane, in the sense that a different MAC table is kept for each VLAN. In the same way that one IP route can be present in different VRFs and represent a separate network, the same MAC address can be present in different MAC tables or learning domains.

 Although the concepts are not strictly equivalent, for simplicity this book uses the terms "learning domain," "bridge domain," and "broadcast domain" interchangeably.

Keeping in mind that the VLAN ID on-the-wire is not necessarily identical to the VLAN ID identifying the bridge domain, let's see the different options.

For brevity, let's consider ACs configured with one VLAN tag only. In this case, if a frame has two VLAN tags, only the outer one is taken into account for bridging: the internal tag is left untouched and it's considered as part of the payload.

Suppose that each PE has four ACs locally attached to the VPLS service:

- AC-A and AC-B—connected to CE-A and CE-B, respectively—are both configured with VLAN 2010.
- AC-C—connected to CE-C—is configured with VLAN 2011.
- AC-D—connected to CE-D—is configured with VLAN 2222.

Each PE has four CEs attached, which adds up to 16 CEs in total.

VLANs 2010, 2011, and 2222 are the on-the-wire VLAN tags. The frames sent and received on the ACs have these values set in the outer (maybe the only) VLAN header.

VPLS in default VLAN mode

The default behavior in both IOS XR VFIs and Junos VPLS instances is the same (Virtual Switches are discussed later). There is only one learning domain associated with the instance, which is VLAN-agnostic. After it receives a frame from an AC, the PE preserves the original VLAN tag(s). If the frame needs to be sent out to one or more PWs, it also travels with the original VLAN tag(s). Here is the result:

- CE-A can communicate to the local CE-B, and to remote PEs' CE-A and CE-B.
- CE-B can communicate to the local CE-A, and to remote PEs' CE-A and CE-B.
- CE-C can communicate to the remote PEs' CE-C.
- CE-D can communicate to the remote PEs' CE-D.

If you want all the CEs to communicate to one another, you need to use VLAN translation techniques such as those shown in Example 6-17.

In this default implementation, the VLAN tag is considered as a property of the frame: it does *not* identify the bridge domain. In Junos, this is achieved when the `vlan-id` is *not* set on the VPLS instance (Example 7-8, line 12).

In Junos VPLS instances, it is recommended that you set the `vlan-id`.

Junos VPLS Instances—Normalized VLAN Mode

Let's see the implementation when the `vlan-id` is set to a specific number on a VPLS instance. In this case, the on-the-wire VLAN tag is replaced inside the router with a different value, called the *normalized* tag. This tag is kept when the frame is flooded or forwarded to a PW.

If you set `vlan-id 2222` (for example) on the VPLS instance, the VLAN tags for incoming frames are swapped to the normalized tag: 2222. And the outgoing frames whose VLAN tag is 2222 get their tag swapped to the AC's on-the-wire VLAN tag. For example, if CE-A sends a BUM frame, it is flooded:

- To the local CE-B with VLAN tag 2010.
- To the local CE-C with VLAN tag 2011.
- To the local CE-D and into the PWs with VLAN tag 2222.

Before the frame is sent out of AC-B and AC-C, it actually has VLAN tag 2222 inside the router, but this tag is swapped as the frame is sent out of the AC.

The end result is a single bridge domain where local switching between the ACs is successful, regardless of whether the on-the-wire VLAN tags match the in-box tag. This ensures communication among all the CEs and is called VLAN *normalization*, shown in Example 7-18.

Example 7-18. VLAN normalization in a VPLS instance—PE1 (Junos)

```
interfaces {
    ge-2/0/1 unit 2010 vlan-id 2010;
}
routing-instances {
    VPLS-B vlan-id 2222;
}
```

```
juniper@PE1> show interfaces ge-2/0/1.2010 | match vlan-tag
    VLAN-Tag [ 0x8100.2010 ] In(swap .2222) Out(swap .2010)
```

What about the remote CEs that are reachable via the PWs? The remote PEs' VPLS instance must know what to do with frames whose VLAN tag is 2222:

- If it is a Junos VPLS instance with vlan-id 2222, it works fine.
- If it is a Junos VPLS instance with a different vlan-id, it does not work.
- If it is an IOS XR VFI or a Junos VPLS instance in the default mode, it works fine if either the AC is configured with on-the-wire tag 2222 or it has a translation rule (vlan-map in Junos language) applied that handles the translation from/to the normalized tag 2222 to the AC-specific tag on-the-wire.

> It is possible to normalize both SVLAN and CVLAN. In this case, use vlan-tags on the VPLS instance and on the ACs. These values don't need to match: normalization takes care of the translation!

Junos VPLS Instances—VLAN-Free Mode

Let's see the implementation when the vlan-id is set to none. In this case, the outer on-the-wire VLAN tag is popped when the frame enters the router. It is pushed when the frame is sent out of the AC.

For example, if CE-A sends a BUM frame, it is flooded:

- To the local CE-B with VLAN tag 2010.
- To the local CE-C with VLAN tag 2011.
- To the local CE-D with VLAN tag 2222.
- With no VLAN tag into the PWs, unless the CE sent dual-tagged frames, in which case the original inner tag is preserved.

Before the frame is sent out of AC-B, AC-C, and AC-D, it actually has no VLAN tag (unless the original frame was dual-tagged) inside the router. The AC-specific VLAN tag is pushed as the frame is sent out of the AC.

The end result is a single bridge domain where local switching between the ACs is successful, regardless of the on-the-wire VLAN tag value.

What about the remote CEs that are reachable via the PWs? The remote PEs' VPLS instance must know what to do with tag-less Ethernet frames:

- If it is a Junos VPLS instance with vlan-id none, it works fine.

- If it is a Junos VPLS instance with a different `vlan-id <value>`, it does not work, unless the original frame sent by the CE was dual-tagged and its inner VLAN tag matched `<value>`.
- If it is an IOS XR VFI or a Junos VPLS instance in the default mode, either the AC is a physical port with no VLAN tag, or the AC has applied an in-pop out-push translation rule (`vlan-map` in Junos language), such as that shown in Example 6-18, or the original frame sent by the CE was dual-tagged and its inner tag matches the AC's VLAN ID.

Junos VPLS Instances—VLAN-Aware Mode

Let's see the implementation when the `vlan-id` is set to `all`. In this case, the PE auto-detects the VLAN tag of a frame as it enters the router. When an incoming frame has a VLAN tag that does not match any existing bridge domain, Junos creates a new bridge domain for the new (VPLS instance, VLAN tag) pair. Therefore, flooding is VLAN-aware. You can check that by using the command `show vpls mac-table`, which displays one domain per VLAN with active traffic and MAC entries.

For example, if CE-A sends a BUM frame, it is flooded:

- To the local CE-B with VLAN tag 2010.
- With the original VLAN tag 2010 into the PWs.

Let's go back to the BUM frame sent by CE-A. The remote PEs' VPLS instance must know what to do with a frame with VLAN ID 2010:

- If it is a Junos VPLS instance with `vlan-id all` or `vlan-id 2010`, it works fine.
- If it is a Junos VPLS instance with a different `vlan-id <value>`, or none, end-to-end connectivity fails.
- If it is an IOS XR VFI or a Junos VPLS instance in the default mode, either the AC is configured with on-the-wire tag 2010, or it has a translation rule (`vlan-map` in Junos language) applied that handles the translation from/to the 2010 tag to the specific AC-specific tag on-the-wire.

Junos Virtual Switches

Virtual Switches have the greatest granularity because they support per-VLAN bridge domains, and these implement automatic normalization. If you look back at Example 7-9, you can define several bridge domains such as BR-2010 in the same Virtual Switch; each bridge domain can have one or more associated ACs.

The scenario becomes even more interesting when the AC on-the-wire VLAN tag is different from the learning VLAN tag. This is VLAN normalization:

Example 7-19. VLAN normalization in a bridge domain—PE1 (Junos)

```
interfaces {
    ge-2/0/1 unit 2010 vlan-id 2010;
}
routing-instances {
    VS-B {
        bridge-domains {
            BR-2222 {
                vlan-id 2222;
                interface ge-2/0/1.2010;
}}}}

juniper@PE1> show interfaces ge-2/0/1.2010 | match vlan
    VLAN-Tag [ 0x8100.2010 ] In(swap .2222) Out(swap .2010)
    Encapsulation: VLAN-Bridge
```

The concept is identical to VLAN normalization in VPLS instances, with the advantage that here you can associate one different learning VLAN to each bridge domain in the Virtual Switch.

As you know, a Virtual Switch supports one or more bridge domains, which can be displayed by using the show bridge domain and show bridge mac-table commands.

The end result is similar to a *set* of VPLS instances in normalized VLAN mode, with several advantages. First, Virtual Switches can use the same set of PWs to transport frames for several *feature-rich* bridge domains. True, VPLS instances with vlan-id all can also multiplex the PWs and dynamically create per-VLAN bridge domains, but these domains are not feature-rich. But what does feature-rich mean? Each of the bridge domains in a Virtual Switch can have its own normalization VLAN and its own IRB interface. Now, let's see what IRB stands for.

 As an alternative to IRB in instances with vlan-id all, you can define a pair of lt- units per VLAN: one unit on the VPLS instance, and its peer unit with family inet and/or family inet6, acting like an IP gateway.

Integrated Routing and Bridging in VPLS

The Integrated Routing and Bridging (IRB) concept was conceived in enterprise LANs, where so-called L3 switches implement inter-VLAN routing. Every bridge domain or VLAN has a default gateway that is implemented in an IRB interface. Suppose that an L2 switch has four VLANs: 2001 through 2004. Each VLAN spans many access (untagged) and trunk (VLAN-tagged) ports on the switch. A pure L2 switch does not need to have any IP address on the VLANs: it just bridges frames on each domain separately. But that results in four isolated domains.

If you want to interconnect the four VLANs at the L3 level, you can do either of the following:

- Use a traditional L3 router on-a-stick.
- Enhance the L2 switch with L3 capabilities so that it becomes an L3 switch.

In the latter case, the L3 switch has four virtual IP interfaces, each linked to one VLAN. These IP interfaces are called IRB in Junos and Bridge Virtual Interface (BVI) in IOS XR. The hosts in each VLAN typically use the IRB/BVI address as the default gateway—Virtual Router Redundancy Protocol (VRRP) is discussed later. The L3 switch performs inter-VLAN routing and also routing between a VLAN and the WAN.

VPLS with IRB/BVI provides an L3 switching service. IRB is especially important in Data Center Interconnect scenarios. As for L2VPN as a Transport, IRB is not that relevant: PWHE is.

IRB Configuration in Junos VPLS Instances

Junos VPLS instances only support one IRB interface. This makes IRB suitable for normalized VLAN Mode (vlan-id *<number>* or vlan-tags) and for VLAN-free mode (vlan-id none). Example 7-20 shows an IRB configuration.

Example 7-20. IRB on a VPLS Instance—PE1 (Junos)

```
1    interfaces {
2        irb {
3            unit 2010 {
4                family inet address 10.1.1.101/24;
5                mac 00:00:01:00:20:10;
6    }}}
7    routing-instances {
8        VPLS-B {
9            routing-interface irb.2010;
10    }}
```

 The IRB unit ID (line 3) does not need to match the VPLS vlan-id.

Now, the `irb.2010` interface is like any L3 interface. It can be either left in the global routing table, or assigned to a VRF (`set routing-instances <VRF> interface irb.2010`). How is inter-VLAN routing possible? Just take several VPLS instances, each with its own IRB logical interface, and ensure that all these IRB interfaces belong to the same L3 routing instance. The latter can also have L3 WAN interfaces and then our PE becomes a full-blown data center gateway (DC GW).

The MAC address configuration (line 5) is critical. In VPLS, it is important that every host in the domain can send frames to—and receive frames from—the IRB MAC address of every PE in an independent manner. This is guaranteed only if each PE uses a *different* MAC address on the IRB. Otherwise, a PE can intercept frames packets targeted to (or sourced from) another PE. The MAC address must be unicast, so the last bit of the first octet must be zero. It must also be unique; in the example, it is made of the PE number and the VLAN ID, but you can use any other numbering schemes.

The IRB interface is untagged, and the ACs are typically tagged. Junos automatically handles this discrepancy; not only in VLAN-free mode, but also in normalized VLAN mode. Suppose that PE1 receives on ge-2/0/1.2010 (or on a PW) a frame tagged with VLAN 2010 and with destination MAC address 00:00:01:00:20:10 (or the broadcast address). In that case, PE1 automatically pops the VLAN tag before handing the frame to the IRB. Likewise, when the IRB originates an untagged frame, PE1 pushes the VLAN tag before sending the frame out of the AC (or the PW). However, if the incoming traffic has two VLAN tags and the AC's configuration has only one VLAN tag, forwarding breaks: Junos IRB relies on the actual traffic matching the AC's settings.

IRB Configuration in Junos Virtual Switches

One advantage of Virtual Switches over VPLS instances is that it supports one IRB per bridge domain. Example 7-21 shows how to bind an IRB logical interface to a Virtual Switch.

Example 7-21. IRB on a Virtual Switch's bridge domain—PE1 (Junos)

```
routing-instances {
    VS-B {
        bridge-domains BR-2010 routing-interface irb.2010;
}}
```

IRB Configuration in IOS XR

The following example shows the configuration of an IRB (BVI) interface in IOS XR:

Example 7-22. IRB on a bridge domain—PE4 (IOS XR)

```
interface BVI2010
 ipv4 address 10.1.1.104 255.255.255.0
 mac-address 0000.0400.2010
!
l2vpn
 bridge group myVPLS
  bridge-domain VPLS-B
   routed interface BVI2010
!
```

This BVI interface is shared by all of the ACs and PWs in the bridge domain VPLS-B, regardless of their VLAN tag. As in Junos IRB, the BVI interface is untagged. But unlike Junos, VLAN tag pop/push for IRB/BVI is not automatic in IOS XR. As a result, any frame destined to the BVI unicast MAC address (or to the broadcast address) from an AC or a PW must be explicitly stripped from any VLAN tags. This is critical for interoperability: it is not only PE4 that must be locally configured with this in mind; the remote PEs—and some of them run Junos—also need to send and receive untagged frames over the PWs they establish with PE4.

Now, if the ACs are VLAN tagged, you need to use the following techniques:

- Manually stripping VLAN tags from the ACs, such as in Example 6-18, so that the frames arrive untagged to the BVI. This works fine in IOS XR and also in Junos VPLS instances running in legacy mode (no `vlan-id` on the instance).

- Junos VPLS instances running in VLAN-free mode (`vlan-id none`). This is the recommended approach in Junos for interoperating with IOS XR.

VPLS—IRB Redundancy and Traffic Tromboning

Let's take the example of a data center with four L2 switches: CE1, CE2, CE3, and CE4. Each CE has different hosts attached, distributed in broadcast domains, as outlined in Figure 7-2.

The topology is single-homed with the following VLAN-tagged links: CE1-PE1, CE2-PE2, CE3-PE3, and CE4-PE4. Every link transports two different VLAN tags (2001 and 2002). Each VLAN is associated to a different broadcast domain in the data center, to a bridge domain (or VPLS instance) at the PEs, and to a different IPv4 subnet (10.1.1.0/24 and 10.1.2.0/24, respectively). More specifically:

- PE1 and PE3 have two VPLS instances configured with `vlan-id none`. The logical ACs with `vlan-id 2001` and 2002 are attached to the VPLS-1 and VPLS-2 instances, respectively. Each VPLS instance has its own IRB interface: irb.2001 and irb.2002.

- PE2 and PE4 have two bridge domains. The logical ACs with `encapsulation dot1q` 2001 and 2002 are attached to the VPLS-1 and VPLS-2 instances, respectively. Each VPLS instance has its own IRB interface: BVI2001 and BVI2002.

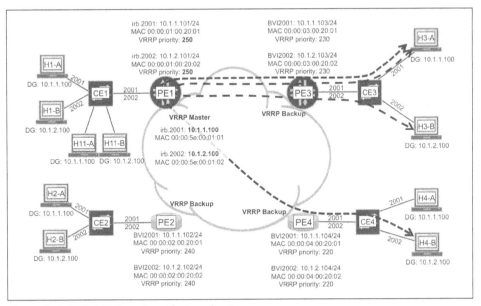

Figure 7-2. VPLS IRB and traffic tromboning

The IRBs' primary IPv4 and MAC addresses are unique in the entire data center domain. In other words, each [PE, IRB] pair has a *different primary* IPv4 address and a *different primary* MAC address. Why different MAC *and* IPv4 addresses? Duplicate MAC addresses might result in a segmented bridge domain because a PE would block transit traffic sourced from its own IRB MAC address. And non-unique IPv4 addresses might result in unpredictable ARP resolution.

> Thanks to its more powerful control plane, EVPN supports having the same IRB IPv4 and MAC addresses in different PEs. You will see that in Chapter 8.

Now, on each PE, the three IRB/BVI interfaces are all grouped in the same VRF. So, there is one single L3VPN for the entire data center. This makes inter-VLAN routing possible.

Let's assume that each host has a default gateway configuration pointing to the IPv4 address configured on the *closest* PE's `irb.<vlan>` or `BVI<vlan>` interface.

H1-A and H4-B are two hosts in the data center. H1-A is connected to CE1 and it belongs to VLAN 2001. H4-B is connected to CE4 and it belongs to VLAN 2002. Packets from H1-A to H4-B are routed by PE1, and packets from H4-B to H1-A are routed by PE4. This results in an asymmetrical routing scheme, but it is perfectly fine.

VPLS and VRRP

The previously described architecture has a couple of issues:

- First, if the CE1-PE1 uplink fails, the hosts connected to CE1 become isolated.
- Second, each site must be configured with a different default gateway address. This is not only very complex to manage, it also breaks modern applications such as VM mobility across the data center.

VPLS can solve the first challenge with Active-Backup CE multihoming—because VPLS does not support Active-Active. When multihomed, CE1 has an Active-Backup Link Aggregate Group with two links: one to PE1, and one to PE2.

The second challenge is addressed by VRRP. For each VRRP group—and the common practice is to define one group per bridge domain—all the routers share a *common secondary* IPv4 address and a *common secondary* MAC address. But, for each group, only one PE (so-called the VRRP master) has these addresses in an active state on its IRB interface. The VRRP master is the only router in each group that does the following:

- Periodically sends VRRP hellos sourced from the group MAC address.
- Sends ARP replies (and gratuitous ARP requests) mapping the group IPv4 address to the group MAC address.

All the hosts in a given VLAN configure the group IPv4 address as their default gateway, and resolve via ARP this IPv4 address to the group MAC address. Back to our example, PE1's IRB interfaces are VRRP masters on their respective bridge domains. The virtual (MAC, IPv4) addresses for each bridge domain are (00:00:5e:00:01:01, 10.1.1.100) and (00:00:5e:00:01:02, 10.1.2.100), respectively. The VRRP master is elected according to the configured priorities and a tie-breaking mechanism based on the primary IPv4 address numerical value.

Now, what are the challenges of this solution?

First, suppose that there is one more PE that provides connectivity between the data center and the rest of the world (or the rest of the L3VPN). This Gateway PE advertises IPv4 VPN routes that the data center PEs (PE1, PE2, PE3, and PE4) import in their own data center VRF. Now, it's important that a PE does not become a VRRP master if it does not have the full routing picture. Otherwise, such a PE would attract upstream traffic that it cannot route, which ultimately results in *traffic blackholing*.

One way to handle this is by making the VRRP priority a dynamic value which is automatically decreased if certain routes are missing from the local VRF. Still, this solution is far from clean as compared to the elegant way that EVPN addresses this very same challenge, as you will see soon.

In addition, if the gateway PE needs to send a packet to one of the hosts in the data center, it will send it to one of the data center PEs. Which one? Well, they all advertise the /24 addresses, so one of them will be considered as the best (based on the BGP route-selection process), but it might not necessarily be the PE that is local to the host. This results in suboptimal forwarding that you can fix in two ways: activating the VPLS service at the gateway PE, or replacing VPLS with EVPN.

On a separate note, in VPNs in general and VPLS/EVPN in particular, it is considered a good practice to configure a delay between the time an AC goes up and the time when the control and forwarding planes consider the AC to be active. In this way, you give time for the core protocols to converge before enabling the ACs, reducing the likelihood of traffic blackholes.

> As a general rule on interfaces with L2 ACs, set hold-time up (Junos) or carrier-delay up (IOS XR) to at least one minute.

Traffic tromboning

Here is one more issue illustrated in Figure 7-2. H3-A and H3-B are two hosts connected to CE3 and belonging to VLAN 2001 and 2002, respectively. PE1 is the VRRP master for VLAN 2001. If H3-A sends an IP packet to H3-B, it must send it to its default gateway: PE1's irb.2001.

As a result, H3-A to H3-B inter-VLAN routing follows this path: H3-A→CE3→ PE3→PE1→PE3→CE3→H3-B. Thus, packets originated and destined to the same data center site are actually forwarded via a remote data center site. This phenomenon is called traffic *tromboning* (inspired by the shape of a trombone) and is also elegantly solved by EVPN.

Hierarchical VPLS

To enhance the scalability or security of a VPLS design, you can implement hierarchical VPLS (H-VPLS) models. Depending on the VPLS signaling protocol, you can deploy three different models:

LDP signaling
    H-VPLS model based on PWs (VPWS service) initiated on Spoke devices and terminated inside a VPLS instance on Hub devices

BGP signaling
    H-VPLS based on Route Target (RT) filtering

BGP signaling
    H-VPLS based on site ID (site-range) filtering

 Due to space constraints, this book presents only a short description of each hierarchical VPLS model.

H-VPLS Model with LDP Signaling

VPLS scaling with LDP signaling, as defined in RFC 4762, Section 10, looks at how to minimize the number of required PWs. As discussed earlier in this chapter, VPLS in its typical form requires a full mesh of PWs established between all participating devices. As the network grows, and more and more VPLS Edge (VE) devices are added, the number of required PWs might grow considerably—significantly enough, in fact, that it can cause scaling problems on some low-end VE devices.

The problem is somehow similar to the iBGP session full-mesh problem. In the case of iBGP, to overcome session full-mesh scaling limitation, you can deploy Route Reflectors (very frequently used) or confederations (used sometimes, as well). The basic idea of all these solutions is to break the session full-mesh requirement and allow iBGP neighbors to peer to one another only in a partial-mesh fashion—full mesh is no longer required.

Looking from very high level, you can apply the basic idea introduced to solve iBGP session full-mesh problem to solving the PW full-mesh problem between VPLS edge devices. The significant difference, however, is that the iBGP problem is a pure control-plane one, whereas in LDP-based VPLS, control and forwarding planes are more coupled together.

To relax the requirement for PW full-mesh, the H-VPLS model is defined in RFC 4762, Section 10. There are a couple of variations of the H-VPLS model outlined in the RFC. On the hub side (referenced in RFC as *PE-rs*, meaning a PE device that can perform global routing and private switching), the variations do not differ—in each of those variations PWs from a spoke device terminate in a VPLS instance on V-hubs.

The basic H-VPLS variation (Section 10.1.3 in the RFC) assumes that the spoke device (referenced in the RFC as *PE-r*) is not capable of providing bridging capability among multiple interfaces. In this variation, the spoke is only capable of establishing a PW and transporting frames from the local interface (AC) over such PW, and vice versa.

A more advanced H-VPLS variation (Section 10.1.1 in the RFC) and its redundant option (Section 10.2 in the RFC) assumes that you can configure bridging instances on the spokes (referred to *MTU-s* in the RFC).

The H-VPLS model is conceptually similar to the hierarchical L3VPN model based on PWHE architecture (see Chapter 17). However, there are, of course, some differences that you typically see in H-VPLS architectures:

- PWs used in the H-VPLS architecture can be terminated on the hub device directly (natively) inside a VPLS instance without the need for *ps* (Junos) or *PW-Ether* (IOS XR) auxiliary interfaces. However, the integration of VPLS with the L3 world relies on IRB interfaces, which do not implement the same feature set as PWHE interfaces.
- Because H-VPLS operates in principle on L2, you can use L2-capable spoke devices to provide local bridging for locally connected CEs. In the PWHE-based H-L3VPN model, traffic between two CEs connected to the same spoke device typically goes via the hub, as only the hub provides L3 (routing) capabilities required to route the traffic between two CEs.

Depending on the configuration of the hub device, L2 forwarding between two spokes with PWs terminated on the same hub can be allowed (classic H-VPLS with spoke-to-spoke forwarding) or prevented (H-VPLS without spoke-to-spoke forwarding, called as well *Hub-and-Spoke* VPLS).

H-VPLS Models with BGP for Autodiscovery and Signaling

In BGP VPLS, you can deploy two models for hierarchical VPLS, as briefly described in the following sections.

Model A: RT filtering

This model is exactly the same one as the hub-and-spoke L3VPN discussed in Chapter 3. Described simply, you allocate one RT (RT-H) to VPLS hub sites, and another RT (RT-S) to VPLS spoke sites. Spoke sites export RT-S but import RT-H only, whereas hub sites export RT-H and import RT-S (plus eventually import RT-H, if two-way connectivity between VPLS hub sites is required).

As the result of such RT deployment, VPLS spokes import only information from hub site(s) but not from other spoke site(s). Hub sites, on the other hand, have full visibility. Therefore, PWs are established only between spoke and hub sites (and optionally between hub sites), but not between spoke sites.

With this model, apart from reducing the overall number of PWs (PWs between spoke sites are not established), you also limit the possible connectivity. As opposed to H-VPLS with LDP signaling, for which the hub could be configured to allow or prevent frame forwarding between PWs from different spokes, here forwarding between spokes is always blocked.

Model B: Site-ID (Site-Range) filtering

Hub-and-spoke VPLS Model A unfortunately has certain limitations—namely, it doesn't support multihomed VPLS spoke sites based on *draft-ietf-bess-vpls-multihoming*. As already discussed in Chapter 6, two PEs connected to the same CE site perform *Designated Forwarded* (*DF*) election process. The DF election process is based on the comparison of BGP local preference values advertised by PEs attached to the same multihomed CE site.

However, in hub-and-spoke VPLS Model A, BGP prefixes carrying VPLS information (and other BGP attributes, like, for example, local preference) are not exchanged between spokes. Therefore, two PEs connected to a given VPLS spoke site do not see each other, which can cause L2 loops. A hub-and-spoke VPLS architecture with multihomed spoke sites must fulfill two requirements:

- Prefixes between spoke PEs must be exchanged so that visibility of the local preference BGP attribute advertised by multiple PEs connected to the same VPLS spoke site (multihomed spoke) is not restricted (required for DF election).
- PWs between spoke sites must not be established (hub-and-spoke VPLS design requirement).

Therefore, in hub-and-spoke VPLS Model B, RTs are no longer filtered. A single RT used for both hub-and-spoke sites provides full-mesh site visibility. On the other hand, site ID numbering requires more attention. If hub sites are numbered with site-ID numbers from a low range (e.g., 1 to 15), and spoke sites are numbered with site-ID numbers from a high range (e.g., 16 to 127), two distinct site-ID ranges are defined. This makes it possible to enforce PW establishment restrictions. Namely, you can configure spoke PEs to allow PW establishment toward sites with IDs from range 1 to 15 only (hub sites).

## CHAPTER 8

Ethernet VPN

Ethernet VPN (EVPN) is *not* Virtual Private LAN Service (VPLS). It is a more recent technology that aims to overcome some of the challenges that have arisen during more than a decade of VPLS live deployments.

EVPN with MPLS Transport

EVPN, formerly called MAC VPN, is described in RFC 7432 - *BGP MPLS-Based Ethernet VPN*.

EVPN Versus VPLS

If there was already a multipoint L2VPN solution (VPLS), why has another one been defined and implemented? Let's compare both technologies.

EVPN versus VPLS—signaling protocols

VPLS has two possible signaling protocols, LDP and BGP, of which only BGP supports autodiscovery. EVPN takes good note of that by deprecating Targeted LDP and adopting BGP as the one and only service signaling protocol.

EVPN versus VPLS—MAC address learning

VPLS has only data-plane MAC learning, which can easily lead to stale forwarding state.

Indeed, if a local Attachment Circuit (AC) goes down, it is important to flush the associated MAC entries from the bridge table. You must do this on the local PE, and *also* on the remote PEs. The PW Status TLV is not a valid option, due to the lack of an AC:PW deterministic mapping in VPLS. True, VPLS has the concept of a MAC

Flush flag (BGP VPLS) or TLV (LDP VPLS), but it is more like a patch than a robust solution.

Although EVPN also performs data-plane MAC learning on its local ACs, it relies on control-plane MAC learning between PEs. In fact, it uses BGP to exchange MAC address routes. This greatly reduces unknown unicast flooding and, more important, it natively implements a flush mechanism in BGP by withdrawing the BGP routes.

EVPN versus VPLS—CE Multihoming

EVPN natively implements two CE multihoming solutions: single-active (one active, N standby) and all-active (with known unicast per-flow load balancing).

True, the mechanism is complex as it involves a few route types, the election of a BUM Designated Forwarder, and so on. But it represents a breakthrough with respect to VPLS, which only implements single-active solutions. Actually, in the VPLS world, the flavors that implement a genuine albeit single-active multihoming solution are all BGP-based: BGP VPLS and LDP VPLS with BGP autodiscovery (FEC 129).

EVPN versus VPLS—Layer 2 to Layer 3 coupling

In VPLS, the Integrated Routing and Bridging (IRB) or BVI interface acts like an anchor into the Layer 3 (L3) world. But the Layer 2 (L2) and L3 worlds are quite decoupled from a state perspective. Last but not least, VPLS gateway redundancy typically relies on VRRP, which brings together some undesired effects: risk of *traffic blackholing* (mitigated with VRRP route or interface tracking, together with a rich set of VRRP and interface timers), *traffic tromboning*, complex operation, and difficult troubleshooting.

EVPN natively implements several L2-L3 hooks, as you are about to discover; this brings a native way to handle active virtual machine (VM) moves across different servers in the same data center.

EVPN Implementations

As of this writing, there are implementations of EVPN with MPLS transport, Provider Backbone Bridging[PBB]-EVPN with MPLS transport, and EVPN with Virtual eXtensible LAN (VXLAN) transport. Some of them are publicly made available at the same time as this book, so the only flavor that the authors could test in an interoperable manner is PBB-EVPN with MPLS transport. This book also includes Junos examples of the two other flavors. Stay tuned to the blog http://mplsinthesdnera.net for EVPN interoperability posts.

PBB-EVPN is more complex than EVPN, so let's begin with EVPN. Hence, this first scenario is Junos-only (except for the BGP address family, which is shown for both vendors).

EVPN—This Book's Topology

This book's EVPN example focuses on the Data Center Interconnect (DCI) application. The technology remains the same for different applications, though.

In the initial topology depicted in Figure 8-1, the CE1-PE2 and CE3-PE4 links are administratively down. They will be brought up later, in the multihoming section. So, the CE1-PE1 and CE3-PE3 connections are single-link LAGs.

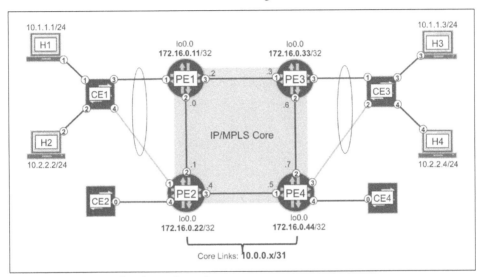

Figure 8-1. EVPN—the physical topology

H1 and H3 are connected via access (untagged) interfaces to the CEs, and they belong to VLAN 2100. Likewise, H2 and H4 belong to VLAN 2200. As for the PE-CE ACs, they are trunk (VLAN-tagged) interfaces that transport VLANs 2100 and 2200.

Although not shown in the picture, there are two Route Reflectors (RRs) with loopback addresses 172.16.0.201 and 172.16.0.202, respectively.

BGP EVPN Address Family

BGP EVPN use Multiprotocol-BGP (MP-BGP) address family: AFI=25, SAFI=70.

Example 8-1 shows how to configure the EVPN address family at a Junos PE.

Example 8-1. EVPN address family configuration—PE1 (Junos)

```
protocols {
    bgp {
        group iBGP-RR {
```

```
        family evpn signaling;
}}}
```

Adding this configuration to all the BGP groups also does the trick on Junos RRs.

Like for other BGP VPN flavors, Junos uses different RIBs for EVPN. In the language of Table 6-2, bgp.evpn.0 and <instance_name>.evpn.0 are *Global Auxiliary: Raw NLRI* and *Instance-Specific: Raw NLRI*, respectively.

Although this EVPN scenario is Junos-only, at the end of this chapter you will see an interoperable PBB-EVPN example. EVPN and PBB-EVPN use the same BGP address family. Here is the additional configuration on IOS XR PEs:

Example 8-2. EVPN address family configuration—PE2 (IOS XR)

```
router bgp 65000
 address-family l2vpn evpn
 !
 neighbor-group RR
  address-family l2vpn evpn
!
```

 On RRs running IOS XR, you also need to add the **route-reflector-client** knob under each neighbor[-group] adddress-family.

EVPN with MPLS Transport—Junos Configuration

As with VPLS, Junos has two types of routing instances that both support EVPN:

- EVPN instances (EVIs) are more suitable for models with one single bridge domain. RFC 7432 calls these models *VLAN-based*.
- Virtual Switches are the best fit for services where each VLAN must have its own bridge table and its own IRB interface. This model, called *VLAN-aware bundle* in RFC 7432, is the one chosen for this book's example.

Example 8-3 shows PE1's EVPN configuration. PE1 has one AC that is a Link Aggregation Group (LAG). Note that the Inter-Chassis Communication Protocol (ICCP) and Multichassis LAG (MC-LAG) specific commands are skipped here for brevity.

Example 8-3. EVPN MPLS on a Virtual Switch—PE1 (Junos)

```
1    chassis {
2        aggregated-devices ethernet device-count 20;
3    }
```

```
4     interfaces {
5         ge-2/0/1 {
6             gigether-options 802.3ad ae10;
7         }
8         ae10 {
9             flexible-vlan-tagging;
10            encapsulation flexible-ethernet-services;
11            aggregated-ether-options lacp active;
12            unit 2100 {
13                encapsulation vlan-bridge;
14                vlan-id 2100;
15            }
16            unit 2200 {
17                encapsulation vlan-bridge;
18                vlan-id 2200;
19    }}}
20    routing-instances {
21        EVPN-A {
22            instance-type virtual-switch;
23            route-distinguisher 172.16.0.11:2000;
24            vrf-target target:65000:2000;
25            protocols {
26                evpn {
27                    extended-vlan-list [ 2100 2200 ];
28                }
29            }
30            bridge-domains {
31                BR-2100 {
32                    vlan-id 2100;
33                    interface ae10.2100;
34                }
35                BR-2200 {
36                    vlan-id 2200;
37                    interface ae10.2200;
38    }}}}
```

Lines 23 and 24 are BGP business as usual: RDs to distinguish routes belonging to different VPNs, and RTs to control route distribution at the PEs. As for the configuration of the AC and the Virtual Switch, it follows the same principles as Example 7-9.

EVPN MPLS—Inclusive Tunnel and Autodiscovery

The Inclusive Tunnel and Provider Multicast Service Interface (PMSI) concepts have already been illustrated in the context of BGP MVPN and VPLS. In a VLAN-aware bundle EVPN service, every PE is the root of a VLAN-specific Inclusive Tunnel. This tunnel is used to send BUM traffic to all the remote PEs that also have sites in the same EVPN:VLAN.

In BGP MVPN, Inclusive Tunnels were signaled with MVPN Route Type 1. On the other hand, EVPN uses Route Type 3 for this same purpose. Indeed, EVPN uses a totally different Route Type numbering as compared to MVPN. Table 8-1 lists these route types.

Table 8-1. EVPN (AFI=25, SAFI=70) route types

Type	Route Name
1	Ethernet autodiscovery (AD) route
2	MAC/IP advertisement route
3	Inclusive multicast Ethernet tag route
4	Ethernet segment (ES) route
5	IP prefix route

 This book does *not* cover EVPN IP Prefix (Type 5) routes. For more information, see *draft-ietf-bess-evpn-prefix-advertisement*.

Example 8-4 shows the EVPN Type 3 routes advertised by PE1, one per VLAN.

Example 8-4. EVPN Type 3: inclusive multicast route—PE1 (Junos)

```
1    juniper@PE1> show route advertising-protocol bgp 172.16.0.201
2                 table EVPN-A.evpn.0 match-prefix "3:*" detail
3    [...]
4    * 3:172.16.0.11:2000::2100::172.16.0.11/304 (1 entry, 1 announced)
5     BGP group IBGP type Internal
6         Route Distinguisher: 172.16.0.11:2000
7         Nexthop: Self
8         Localpref: 100
9         AS path: [65000] I
10        Communities: target:65000:2000
11        PMSI: Flags 0x0: Label 299840:
12            Type INGRESS-REPLICATION 172.16.0.11
13
14   * 3:172.16.0.11:2000::2200::172.16.0.11/304 (1 entry, 1 announced)
15    BGP group IBGP type Internal
16        Route Distinguisher: 172.16.0.11:2000
17        Nexthop: Self
18        Localpref: 100
19        AS path: [65000] I
20        Communities: target:65000:2000
21        PMSI: Flags 0x0: Label 299856:
22            Type INGRESS-REPLICATION 172.16.0.11
```

So, PE1 is advertising two Type 3 routes: one for each VLAN (2100 and 2200).

These routes are called *Inclusive Multicast Ethernet Tag* because they provide information about the Inclusive Tunnel; they are used for BUM and they contain the VLAN ID or Tag.

The prefix format **3:<RD>:<VLAN_ID>:**<ROUTER_ID_LENGTH>:**<ROUTER_ID>** (lines 4 and 14) is partially displayed in the previous example. Indeed, as of this writing, Junos displays everything except for the <ROUTER_ID_LENGTH>, which is invariably 32 for IPv4. The /304 mask is internal in Junos and not advertised via iBGP: you can simply ignore it. As you will see soon, Type 2 routes can also include IP information.

The BGP next hop is irrelevant for Type 3 routes: it's there simply because it is a mandatory BGP attribute.

As of this writing, Ingress Replication (IR) is the only PMSI type implemented for EVPN. Consequently, to flood a BUM frame, the ingress PE (PE1) replicates the frame and sends one individual copy to each of the remote PEs individually. How? By using the same set of *to-point* (Point-to-Point [P2P] or Multipoint-to-Point [MP2P]) LSPs that are used for *unicast* services. The MPLS label encoded in the PMSI attribute (lines 11 and 21) is the VPN label, which is stacked below the transport label.

One important aspect of the MPLS labels included in the PMSI attribute (lines 11 and 21) is that they are downstream-allocated labels. Exactly as in BGP MVPN with IR transport, PE1 uses the PMSI attribute to specify that:

- As a *root PE*, PE1 uses an Inclusive Tunnel based on IR to send frames to remote PEs—pushing the service labels specified by the remote PEs.
- As a *leaf PE*, PE1 expects to receive frames with the MPLS label value included in the PMSI attribute that it generates: in the example, label 299840 for VLAN 2100, and label 299856 for VLAN 2200.

Figure 5-6 illustrates the IR mechanism for BGP MVPN, similar to the EVPN one except that the *to-point* tunnels transport L3 packets instead of L2 frames.

EVPN with MPLS Transport—Advertising MACs

EVPN was once called MAC VPN because it implements MAC route advertising. One important aspect of MAC addresses, as compared to IP, is that MAC addresses do not support any subnetting. Two hosts connected to the same L2 switch and in the same VLAN can have completely different MAC addresses; to the point that the first bytes of a MAC address identify the network adapter's vendor.

This means that EVPN advertises one MAC route per host: there is no possibility to aggregate them. PBB EVPN changes this rule a bit, as you will see later.

Every bridge domain in the EVPN instance performs independent MAC learning. As soon as a new source MAC address is learned on an AC, the PE advertises a MAC route. These are EVPN Type 2 routes, corresponding to H1's MAC address:

Example 8-5. EVPN Type 2: MAC Advertisement route—PE1 (Junos)

```
1    juniper@PE1> show route advertising-protocol bgp 172.16.0.201
2              table EVPN-A.evpn.0 match-prefix "2:*" detail
3    [...]
4    * 2:172.16.0.11:2000::2100::5c:5e:ab:0a:c3:92/304 (1 entry, ...)
5    BGP group IBGP type Internal
6        Route Distinguisher: 172.16.0.11:2000
7        Route Label: 299776
8        ESI: 00:00:00:00:00:00:00:00:00:00
9        Nexthop: Self
10       Localpref: 100
11       AS path: [65000] I
12       Communities: target:65000:2000
13   /* Other routes omitted */
```

The prefix format is **2:<RD>:<VLAN_ID>:<MAC_LENGTH>:<MAC_ADDRESS>** (line 4). Junos does not display the <MAC_LENGTH>, which is invariably 48. The /304 mask is internal in Junos and not advertised via IBGP: you can simply ignore it.

With the Route Label 299776, PE1 is telling the remote PEs *if you receive a frame from a local AC in EVPN-A, and the bridge domain is associated to VLAN 2100, and the destination MAC address is 5c:5e:ab:0a:c3:92, send it to me with VPN label 299776.*

Because PE1 learned H1's MAC address through a frame received from a single-homed CE, the Ethernet Segment Identifier (ESI) is set to 0x0 (line 8). PEs map to ESI #0 all the ACs connected to either single-homed CEs or *single-active* multihomed CEs.

Only MAC addresses learned on *all-active* multihomed CEs have a non-zero ESI value. How do PEs realize whether the CE is single-homed or multihomed? Actually, they don't. It is up to the network administrator or an external software to configure a non-zero ESI on each AC that is connected to an all-active multihomed CE. EVPN ESIs and VPLS CE-IDs have points in common, but also differences, as explained later on.

EVPN with MPLS Transport—Intra-VLAN Bridging

The two previously described EVPN route types are enough to enable bridging among hosts in the same VLAN. The full sequence is illustrated in Figure 8-2. Read it from top to bottom. In this chapter, the control-plane signaling is shown with round corners, and the forwarding-plane units are shown with sharp corners. The outer-

---

most headers are displayed on top, and the external Ethernet headers at the core links are omitted.

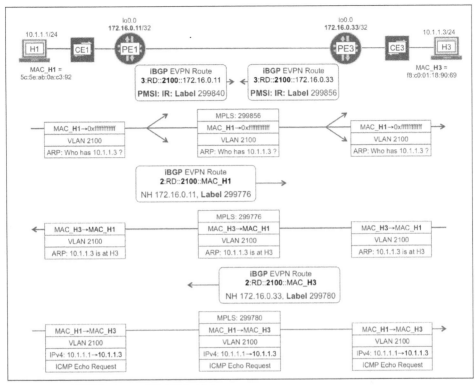

Figure 8-2. EVPN—intra-VLAN bridging

You can check that MAC learning takes place thanks to EVPN MAC Advertisement (Type 2) routes. This is an important difference as compared to VPLS, and it allows a PE to advertise *the same label to all the remote PEs*. Because MAC learning takes place in the control plane, in EVPN it is no longer necessary to know from which remote PE the frame arrives.

This example has no transport label because the PEs are directly connected to each other. Otherwise, label stacking would take place and the transport label would be the top of the stack, and then removed at the penultimate hop: MPLS VPN + PHP business as usual.

The broadcast frame (ARP request sent from H1) uses the Inclusive Tunnel, so it is flooded to all the remote PEs. On the other hand, unicast frames (ARP reply and ICMP echo request) are only sent to one remote PE, thanks to MAC learning. Note that EVPN Type 3 (Inclusive Multicast) and Type 2 (MAC Advertisement) use different MPLS label values, and so does BUM versus known unicast traffic.

Like in VPLS, there is a default split horizon rule in EVPN: a tunneled frame received from the core is not forwarded back to the core (to any PE). This is essential to prevent L2 loops.

Finally, there is a strong coupling between a bridge domain's MAC table and the EVPN Type 2 (MAC Advertisement) routes. If the H1 entry in PE1's MAC table expires due to traffic inactivity, or if it is manually cleared, PE1 withdraws H1's MAC Advertisement route. This triggers a MAC table entry flush in the remote PEs. MAC Advertisement routes synchronize all the PEs' MAC tables. It is the BGP way to program a distributed switch.

The MAC tables can be checked with the commands show evpn mac-table (for EVPN instances) or show bridge mac-table (for Virtual Switches).

EVPN with MPLS Transport—Inter-VLAN Forwarding

One of the key advantages of EVPN over VPLS lies on the integration of the L2 and L3 worlds. Let's see that in detail.

EVPN IRB—Junos configuration

It's time to allow H1 and H3 (VLAN 2100) to communicate to H2 and H4 (VLAN 2200). IRB in VPLS and IRB in EVPN are configured in a similar way. However, if we look closely, the implementation is very different, making EVPN a superior solution.

Typically, the IRB interfaces are placed in an L3 VRF. Unlike VPLS, the EVPN instance is tightly coupled to the L3 VRF(s) where its IRBs are placed. Example 8-6 shows the configuration at PE1, where this tight coupling is not obvious yet.

Example 8-6. EVPN IRB configuration—PE1 (Junos)

```
1    interfaces {
2        irb {
3            unit 2100 {
4                family inet address 10.1.1.100/24;
5                mac 00:00:0a:01:01:64;
6            }
7            unit 2200 {
8                family inet address 10.2.2.200/24;
9                mac 00:00:0a:02:02:c8;
10       }}}
11   routing-instances {
12       VRF-A {
13           instance-type vrf;
14           interface irb.2100;
15           interface irb.2200;
```

```
16            route-distinguisher 172.16.0.11:1234;
17            vrf-target target:65000:1234;
18            vrf-table-label;
19        }
20    EVPN-A {
21        protocols {
22            evpn {
23                default-gateway advertise;
24        }}
25        bridge-domains {
26            BR-2100 {
27                routing-interface irb.2100;
28            }
29            BR-2200 {
30                routing-interface irb.2200;
31    }}}}
```

The new L3 VRF has different RD (line 16) and RT (line 17), with respect to the EVPN Virtual Switch instance (Example 8-3, lines 23 and 24).

A very important aspect of the previous example is the fact that the IRB MAC addresses are manually derived from the IPv4 address. This is a method to ensure that if two PEs have the same IRB IPv4 address on a given bridge domain, they also have the same IRB MAC address on that domain. Why do this? Imagine that, for a given VLAN, you set the same IRB IPv4 and MAC addresses on all the PEs. This makes it possible to seamlessly move an active VM from one site to another or even from one data center to another. The VM would keep its original ARP entry pointing to its default gateway, remaining valid! On the down side, it is not possible to ping the individual IRB interfaces in a precise manner, and the solution to this challenge is briefly mentioned later.

Strictly speaking, it would even be possible to set the same MAC address on all the IRBs of all the bridge domains; but keeping a per-VLAN unique MAC is typically enough.

VPLS *cannot* use the same trick. You will see why in a few pages.

Just one more implementation detail: modern Junos releases enable chained-composite-next-hop for EVPN by default. You need to confirm that this is the case in your Junos PEs; otherwise, you need to configure it explicitly. Indeed, it is required by the L2 rewrites that take place during inter-VLAN forwarding at the ingress PE.

Example 8-7. EVPN chained composite next hop—PE1 (Junos)

```
juniper@PE1> show configuration groups junos-defaults routing-options
forwarding-table {
    export evpn-pplb;
    chained-composite-next-hop ingress evpn;
}
```

EVPN IRB—new routes advertised

The previous configuration triggers a series of new routes. First, the new L3 VRF locally connected routes 172.16.0.11:1234:**10.1.1.0/24** and 172.16.0.11:1234: **10.2.2.0/24**. These routes are exported with RT 65000:1234 and imported in the matching L3 VRF of the remote PEs. Nothing special: just L3 VPN business as usual.

Second, for every logical IRB interface there are *two* new MAC/IP Advertisement routes exchanged in the context of the EVPN instance.

Example 8-8. EVPN Type 2: gateway MAC/IP Advertisement—PE1 (Junos)

```
juniper@PE1> show route advertising-protocol bgp 172.16.0.201
            table EVPN-A.evpn.0 match-prefix "2:*" detail
[...]
* 2:172.16.0.11:2000::2100::00:00:0a:01:01:64/304 (1 entry, ...)
     Route Label: 299776
     ESI: 00:00:00:00:00:00:00:00:00:00
     Communities: target:65000:2000 evpn-default-gateway
[...]
* 2:172.16.0.11:2000::2200::00:00:0a:02:02:c8/304 (1 entry, ...)
     Route Label: 299776
     ESI: 00:00:00:00:00:00:00:00:00:00
     Communities: target:65000:2000 evpn-default-gateway
[...]
* 2:172.16.0.11:2000::2100::00:00:0a:01:01:64::10.1.1.100/304
     Route Label: 299776
     ESI: 00:00:00:00:00:00:00:00:00:00
     Communities: target:65000:2000 evpn-default-gateway
[...]
* 2:172.16.0.11:2000::2200::00:00:0a:02:02:c8::10.2.2.200/304
     Route Label: 299776
     ESI: 00:00:00:00:00:00:00:00:00:00
     Communities: target:65000:2000 evpn-default-gateway
[...]
```

Indeed, for each IRB (2100 and 2200), there are two EVPN Type 2 routes:

- A good old MAC Advertisement route, which just the IRB's MAC in the NLRI.

- A juicier MAC/IP Advertisement route (also Type 2), which contains both the IRB's MAC and IPv4 address in the NLRI.

Why two routes and not just one? Actually, a MAC route belongs to a pure L2 context and it is linked to the EVPN bridge domain's MAC table. On the other hand, a MAC/IP route has an L3 side and it is linked to the L3 VRF ARP table!

Let's learn more about this, and leave the default-gateway community for a bit later.

EVPN IRB—strong L2 to L3 coupling

Here comes one of the most interesting aspects of EVPN.

 EVPN PEs with IRB synchronize their ARP state with each other.

When PE1 resolves the MAC addresses of H1 (or H2) via ARP, it does two things:

- Advertises an EVPN MAC/IP route with ARP-like mappings to the remote PEs.
- Advertises an IPv4 VPN route with the host's /32 address to the remote PEs.

Let's see that for H1 (Example 8-9).

Example 8-9. EVPN Type 2: host MAC/IP Advertisement—PE1 (Junos)

```
1    juniper@PE1> show arp vpn VRF-A hostname 10.1.1.1
2    [...]
3    MAC Address       Address   Name      Interface     Flags
4    5c:5e:ab:0a:c3:92 10.1.1.1  10.1.1.1  ae10.2000     none
5
6    juniper@PE1> show route advertising-protocol bgp 172.16.0.201
7              evpn-mac-address 5c:5e:ab:0a:c3:92 detail
8
9    EVPN-A.evpn.0: 24 destinations, 24 routes (24 active, ...)
10   * 2:172.16.0.11:2000::2100::5c:5e:ab:0a:c3:92/304 (1 entry, ...)
11       Route Label: 299776
12       ESI: 00:00:00:00:00:00:00:00:00:00
13       Communities: target:65000:2000
14   [...]
15   * 2:172.16.0.11:2000::2100::5c:5e:ab:0a:c3:92::10.1.1.1/304
16       Route Label: 299776
17       ESI: 00:00:00:00:00:00:00:00:00:00
18       Communities: target:65000:2000
19   [...]
20
21   juniper@PE1> show route advertising-protocol bgp 172.16.0.201
22              table VRF-A.inet.0 10.1.1.1/32 detail
23
24   VRF-A.inet.0: 7 destinations, 13 routes (7 active, ...)
25   * 10.1.1.1/32 (1 entry, 1 announced)
26   [...]
27       VPN Label: 16
28       Communities: target:65000:1234
```

The EVPN MAC route (lines 10 through 13) has a pure L2 meaning, therefore it is not really related to ARP. The EVPN MAC/IP route (lines 15 through 18) is aimed to synchronize the remote PEs' ARP bindings. Finally, the IPv4 VPN host route (lines 25 through 28) ensures that the traffic forwarding is fully optimized.

Imagine a remote IPv4 VPN PE—let's call it PE100—that is providing access from the data center's IPv4 VPN to different external services. PE100 might not be connected to any of the data center sites. Now let's make it more interesting: PE100 could have no local EVPN instance at all! But thanks to the dynamically generated host /32 routes, PE100 knows exactly where to forward downstream packets. Is it PE1, or PE2, or PE3, or PE4? PE100 makes the right choice! This is a breakthrough advantage over VPLS.

Now, other PEs in the EVPN receive both the EVPN MAC/IP route and the IPv4 VPN host route for H1. Which one takes preference? By default in Junos, the EVPN MAC/IP route takes preference, so it is programmed in the forwarding table.

Example 8-10. Choosing between EVPN MAC/IP and IP VPN route—PE3 (Junos)

```
juniper@PE3> show route table VRF-A 10.1.1.1

VRF-A.inet.0: 7 destinations, 13 routes (7 active, ...)
+ = Active Route, - = Last Active, * = Both

10.1.1.1/32     *[EVPN/7] 00:52:41
                 > to 10.0.0.2 via ge-2/0/1.0, Push 299776
                 [BGP/170] 00:52:42, localpref 100, from 172.16.0.201
                   AS path: I, validation-state: unverified
                 > to 10.0.0.2 via ge-2/0/1.0, Push 16
```

EVPN IRB in action

Let's see how H1 in VLAN 2100 can send an IPv4 packet to H4 in VLAN 2200. For a complete learning experience, let's take the less favorable case: for whatever reason, the PEs have not yet learned about H4's MAC/IP mapping. PE3 not only populates its local ARP table with H4's MAC address, it also advertises the MAC/IP mapping to all the PEs, including PE1. End of the story: now PE1 knows H4's MAC address and the original IPv4 H1→H4 packet can reach its destination.

Figure 8-3 shows the sequence.

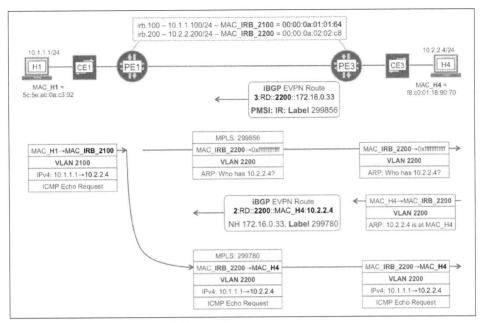

Figure 8-3. EVPN—Inter-VLAN forwarding

Here's what's happening in Figure 8-3:

1. H1 is configured with 10.1.1.100 as its default gateway. H1 resolves this address via ARP (not shown in the illustration) into MAC address 00:00:0a:01:01:64. H1 sends the frame with that destination MAC address.

2. PE1 receives the frame in the bridge domain BR-2100 and sees that the destination MAC address matches its own `irb.2100` interface. PE1 removes the L2 header and performs an L3 route lookup for which the result is this: the destination is directly connected via `irb.2200`.

3. PE1 does not know the MAC address of H4, so it sources an ARP request from its `irb.2200` interface (source MAC = 00:00:0a:02:02:c8) and floods it in bridge domain BR-2200.

4. H4 replies to the ARP request with an ARP reply whose destination is 00:00:0a: 02:02:c8, PE1's `irb.2200` MAC address. But it's also PE3's `irb.2200` MAC address! If this was VPLS instead of EVPN, the flow would break here. This is one of the reasons why in VPLS it is not an option to use the same MAC address in different PEs. But this is EVPN, so let's continue!

5. PE3 advertises H4's MAC/IP route to all the PEs in the EVPN, including PE1. At this point, PE1 knows H4's MAC address, and it can forward the original frame.

So, what is the `default-gateway` community in Example 8-8? It is just another type of extended community. Its value is irrelevant: all that matters is whether it is present. The EVPN MAC/IP routes for the IRB addresses carry this community in order to inform the remote PEs that these addresses belong to default gateways. This mechanism is called *default gateway synchronization*, and in this book's example it is not really needed. Indeed, the default gateways are already *manually* synchronized because all of the PEs have the same IRB IPv4 and MAC addresses configured.

The use case of automatic default gateway synchronization is a scenario in which the IRB MAC (and IPv4) addresses for a given VLAN are set to different values at each PE. If an active VM is moved by the hypervisor from one site to another, the VM still has the old ARP entry for the default gateway. The new gateway processes the frames coming from this VM because it knows that the destination MAC address actually corresponds to a default gateway somewhere in the EVPN. Although this alternative approach allows to ping the individual IRB interfaces in a precise manner, it is still a better practice to configure the same IRB IP and MAC address on every PE because it is cleaner from a forwarding perspective. An even better option is the virtual gateway functionality, which is discussed later.

EVPN—VM mobility

It is possible to move a VM *live* from one data center site to another by using hypervisor features such as VMware's vMotion. The ARP cache of the VM is still valid, even the entry for the default gateway, if the IRB's MAC/IP is the same on all PEs. This is enough to get outbound (leaving the DC site toward the core) traffic seamlessly flowing without any significant interruption.

As for inbound traffic (arriving from the core), it relies on the VM to send at least one frame so that the [EVI, VLAN] MAC table is refreshed on all the PEs. As soon as the *new* PE advertises a MAC/IP route for the VM, the *old* PE withdraws it. At this point, inbound traffic is correctly attracted to the new VM location. You can apply the same logic to each of the VM's virtual Network Interface Cards (NICs).

Although not implemented at the time of this writing, RFC 7432 describes the MAC Mobility extended community. This new community is *not* strictly necessary for VM mobility, but it keeps track of MAC moves with a sequence number. If this sequence number grows abnormally fast, it is an indication of a potential L2 loop.

EVPN with MPLS Transport—All-Active Multihoming

All-active multihoming is one of the main advantages of EVPN over VPLS.

EVPN all-active—Junos configuration

As mentioned before, an EVPN AC has an ESI that is set to zero by default. This is fine for single-homed, or single-active multihomed CEs.

To guarantee correct forwarding state, it is essential to assign a unique non-zero ESI to each CE that is all-active multihomed to more than one PE. The ESI is configured on the PE ACs, not on the CE; and its value must be the same on all the ACs connected to a given multihomed CE. An ESI is to an Active-Active multihomed CE in EVPN, as a CE-ID is to any CE (multihomed or not) in VPLS.

The CE3-PE4 link, initially down in Figure 8-1, is now brought up, so CE3 becomes multihomed to PE3 and PE4.

The very same AC configuration needs to be applied on both PE3 and PE4:

Example 8-11. EVPN: CE multihoming—PE3 and PE4 (Junos)

```
1    interfaces {
2        ae10 {
3            esi {
4                00:11:00:11:00:11:00:11:00:11;
5                all-active;
6            }
7            aggregated-ether-options {
8                lacp system-id 00:11:22:33:44:55;
9    }}}
```

The ESI is a property of the physical interface. For this reason, EVIs can have logical ACs on the same ES. Conversely, a VPLS CE-ID is a property of the logical AC. Another difference is the following: the ESI is set to zero if the physical AC is connected to a single-homed (or single-active multihomed) CE, unlike the CE-ID, which has a globally unique non-zero number for every connected CE.

A real MC-LAG has a larger configuration. For CE3 to *believe* that it has just one device in front, PE3 and PE4 must send the same system-id (line 8) in their Link Aggregation Control Protocol (LACP) packets to CE3. In addition, PE3 and PE4 must also send the same LACP key. The key is typically a dynamic value, and you can set it to a deterministic value in Junos only if you apply a complete MC-LAG configuration, which in the interest of brevity, is not shown here.

From CE3's point of view, there is no such thing as a MC-LAG: thanks to the common system-id and key received on both links, it believes to have a LAG to one single device (see Example 8–12).

Example 8-12. MC-LAG from the perspective of CE3 (Junos)

```
juniper@CE3> show lacp interfaces ae0
Aggregated interface: ae0
[...]
LACP protocol:  Rx State   Tx State       Mux State
  ge-2/0/1      Current    Fast periodic  Collecting distributing
  ge-2/0/2      Current    Fast periodic  Collecting distributing
```

Let's focus on the traffic flows H3→H1 and H1→H3. From the perspective of the data center site on the right (PE3, PE4), the H3→H1 and H1→H3 flows are outbound and inbound, respectively. In data center terminology, outbound traffic goes out of the data center (CE→PE) and inbound traffic goes into the data center (PE→CE).

The transition to an all-active multihoming scenario has an immediate effect on *outbound* traffic: CE3 load-balances the traffic, sending some flows via PE3 and other flows via PE4. It is possible that due to hashing at CE3, some outbound flows that originated from H3 might go via CE3→PE3 and others via CE3→PE4. For this reason, H3's MAC and MAC/IP routes can be generated either by PE3, or by PE4, or by both of them. As you are about to see, this detail is not that relevant as long as there is at least one PE advertising the routes, which happens if H3 remains actively sending outbound traffic and CE forwards it over at least one member link in the LAG.

If both PE3 and PE4 advertise H3's MAC, it is not considered as a MAC move, because the ESI is non-zero and has the same value in both routes.

EVPN all-active—change to existing routes

H3's MAC and MAC/IP routes get their ESI changed from zero to the configured value, as show in Example 8-13.

Example 8-13. EVPN Type 2: non-zero ESI—PE3 or PE4 (Junos)

```
juniper@PE3> show route advertising-protocol bgp 172.16.0.201
            evpn-mac-address f8:c0:01:18:90:69 detail

EVPN-A.evpn.0: 25 destinations, 25 routes (25 active, ...)
* 2:172.16.0.33:2000::2100::f8:c0:01:18:90:69/304 (1 entry, ...)
     Route Label: 299780
     ESI: 00:11:00:11:00:11:00:11:00:11
     Communities: target:65000:2000
[...]
* 2:172.16.0.33:2000::2100::f8:c0:01:18:90:69::10.2.2.4/304
     Route Label: 299780
     ESI: 00:11:00:11:00:11:00:11:00:11
     Communities: target:65000:2000
[...]
```

For a proper active-active behavior, it is important that all of the PEs know to which ESI each MAC/IP route belongs. That's why the ESI is included in the MAC/IP route.

IRB interfaces are not associated with any AC, so they are still advertised with an ESI set to zero. MACs learned from local single-homed (or single-active multihomed) CEs also remain with ESI set to zero.

EVPN all-active—new routes

PE3 and PE4 advertise three new routes each. Example 8-14 shows the new routes from PE3.

Example 8-14. EVPN Types 1 & 4: Ethernet AD and ES Routes—PE3 (Junos)

```
1    juniper@PE3> show route advertising-protocol bgp 172.16.0.201
2                     evpn-esi-value 00:11:00:11:00:11:00:11:00:11 detail
3
4    EVPN-A.evpn.0: 31 destinations, 31 routes (31 active, ...)
5    * 1:172.16.0.33:2000::110011001100110011::0/304
6      BGP group IBGP type Internal
7          Route Distinguisher: 172.16.0.33:2000
8          Route Label: 299780
9          Nexthop: Self
10         Localpref: 100
11         AS path: [65000] I
12         Communities: target:65000:2000
13
14   default_evpn__.evpn.0: 3 destinations, 3 routes (3 active, ...)
15
16   * 1:172.16.0.33:0::110011001100110011::FFFF:FFFF/304
17     BGP group IBGP type Internal
18         Route Distinguisher: 172.16.0.33:0
19         Nexthop: Self
20         Localpref: 100
21         AS path: [65000] I
22         Communities: target:65000:2000
23                      esi-label:all-active (label 299872)
24
25   * 4:172.16.0.33:0::110011001100110011:172.16.0.33/304
26     BGP group IBGP type Internal
27         Route Distinguisher: 172.16.0.33:0
28         Nexthop: Self
29         Localpref: 100
30         AS path: [65000] I
31         Communities: es-import-target:0-11-0-11-0-1
```

These are new EVPN route types: per-EVI Ethernet AD (Type 1), per-ESI Ethernet AD (Type 1, too), and Ethernet Segment (Type 4).

The additional routes from PE4 are nearly identical, as shown next.

Example 8-15. EVPN Types 1 and 4: Ethernet AD and ES routes—PE4 (Junos)

```
1    juniper@PE4> show route advertising-protocol bgp 172.16.0.201
2                    evpn-esi-value 00:11:00:11:00:11:00:11:00:11 detail
3
4    EVPN-A.evpn.0: 31 destinations, 31 routes (31 active, ...)
5    * 1:172.16.0.44:2000::110011001100110011::0/304
6        Route Label: 300000
7        Communities: target:65000:2000
8    [...]
9    default_evpn__.evpn.0: 3 destinations, 3 routes (3 active, ...)
10
11   * 1:172.16.0.44:0::110011001100110011::FFFF:FFFF/304
12       Communities: target:65000:2000
13                    esi-label:all-active (label 299876)
14   [...]
15   * 4:172.16.0.44:0::110011001100110011:172.16.0.44/304
16       Communities: es-import-target:0-11-0-11-0-11
```

The advertised MPLS labels—which have local significance—are different in PE4 versus PE3. There are actually two label types:

- Aliasing label: Example 8-14, line 8; and Example 8-15, line 6.
- Split horizon label: Example 8-14, line 23;and Example 8-15, line 13.

Let's see each of the three routes per PE in detail, before discussing the purpose of the two label types.

Per-EVI Ethernet AD routes carry both the EVI's RD and RT. Conversely, per-ESI Ethernet AD routes are slightly more tricky. Indeed, their RD is generic (not EVI-specific), but they carry the RTs of all the EVIs that have ACs on this particular ES. As a result, the receiving PEs import the per-ESI AD route on all their matching EVI tables. You will soon see that this speeds up convergence upon link failure on the ES.

Ethernet Segment (Type 4) routes don't have a traditional RT. Instead, they carry a new extended community called ES-Import Route Target, which contains the ESI's six most significant bytes. This ensures that only PE3 and PE4—but neither PE1 nor PE2 —import the route, because they are the only PEs with a local AC matching that ESI prefix.

What if PE1 happens to have a local AC whose ESI is 00:11:00:11:00:11:22:33:44:55? PE1 imports the Type 4 route because its ES-Import Route Target matches the six most significant bytes of a local ESI. But the NLRI (Example 8-15, line 15) contains the entire ESI, so PE1 simply ignores the route after it's imported. The end result is a higher memory consumption on PE1, but the ES redundancy logic is not fooled.

EVPN all-active—aliasing label

The per-EVI Ethernet AD route in Example 8-14 (lines 5 through 12) is a Type 1 EVPN route whose NLRI contains the ESI 00:11:00:11:00:11:00:11:00:11. Both PE3 and PE4 advertise one such route, which is imported by all the PEs in the EVPN. These routes carry the aliasing label for the advertised ESI.

The per-ESI Ethernet AD route in Example 8-14 (lines 16 through 23) also provides information for ESI 00:11:00:11:00:11:00:11:00:11, and it is also imported by all of the PEs in the EVPN. Have a look at the new ESI Label extended community. Let's ignore for the moment the encoded label value and pay attention to the `all-active` part—it is a result of the configuration in Example 8-11, line 5. Thus, if they are equally configured, both PE3 and PE4 advertise the ESI as an `all-active` one.

Now, if hashing at CE3 makes all the outbound frames from H3 go via PE3, only PE3 advertises H3's Type 2 MAC/IP routes (Example 8-13). That's fine; let's move on.

As for the H1→H3 frames, PE1 distributes them in a per-flow basis between PE3 and PE4. But, how can PE1 send a H1→H3 frame to PE4 if PE4 is not announcing H3's MAC/IP route? PE1 knows that H3's MAC is at ESI 00:11:00:11:00:11:00:11:00:11. And PE4 is advertising an aliasing label for that ESI. So, PE1 just pushes the aliasing label as if it were a MAC label.

You can see the process in Figure 8-4, which is *almost* complete. Actually, the PE1→PE4 LSP is two-hop, so there is also an outer transport label at the first hop. Also, the MAC and aliasing labels advertised by PE3 happen to be the same on the current Junos implementation.

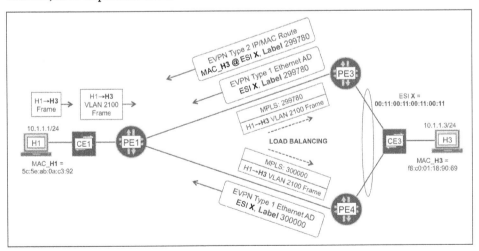

Figure 8-4. EVPN—Aliasing in all-active multihoming

In Figure 8-4, PE3 advertises the same values for the MAC label and for the aliasing label. This is valid but *not* mandatory. PE3 might have also advertised different values. Conversely, the split horizon label *must* be different.

There is one additional advantage of using Ethernet AD routes. Imagine that PE3 is advertising 1,000 MAC/IP routes for ESI 00:11:00:11:00:11:00:11:00:11, and its link to CE3 fails or LACP times-out. In this case, by withdrawing the Ethernet AD routes (before withdrawing 1,000 MAC/IP routes), PE3 signals to PE1 that it must flush or update the 1,000 MAC addresses in its bridge table. This speeds up convergence. Furthermore, the single per-ESI Ethernet AD route is very helpful when there is a large number of EVIs.

EVPN all-active—split horizon label

The H1→H3 flow is known unicast, because PE3 has previously learned and advertised H3's MAC. But, what about BUM traffic? The answer depends on whether the traffic is inbound or outbound with respect to the multihomed ES.

Let's begin with inbound frames. By virtue of IR, PE1 sends the following:

- One copy to PE3, after pushing the label that PE3 advertised in its Inclusive Multicast route for [EVPN-A, VLAN 2100]
- One copy to PE4, after pushing the label that PE4 advertised in its Inclusive Multicast route for [EVPN-A, VLAN 2100]

If both PE3 and PE4 forward the frame to CE3, the end result would be frame duplication toward H3; which is quite undesirable. For this reason, there is a Designated Forwarder (DF) election between PE3 and PE4. Both PEs execute an algorithm to choose the DF. Although this algorithm is locally executed, it must be deterministic in the sense that both PEs choose the *same* DF for a given [ES, VLAN] pair.

 The algorithm is described in RFC 7432, Section 8.5. A different DF may be elected for each VLAN: this is known as *service carving*.

In this particular example, PE3 is the DF and it is the only one that forwards inbound BUM traffic from VLAN 2100 toward CE3.

What about outbound BUM frames? CE3 performs hash-based load balancing:

- If a BUM frame in VLAN 2100 goes from CE3 via PE3, PE3 performs IR toward all the other PEs in the EVPN, including PE4. The mechanism is exactly the same as in single-homed ES. PE4 does *not* forward the frame back to CE3, because it is not the DF.

- If a BUM frame in VLAN 2100 goes from CE3 via PE4, the mechanism is slightly different because PE4 is *not the DF*. Although PE4 sends the frame to PE1 and PE2 using the standard IR mechanism, it also sends the frame to PE3 in a very special manner. Indeed, *before* pushing PE3's Inclusive Multicast label for VLAN 2100 (see label 299856 in Figure 8-2), PE4 pushes at the bottom of the stack the *split horizon label* previously advertised by PE3 (Example 8-14, line 23).

When PE3 receives a MPLS-labeled BUM frame from PE4, it first pops the Inclusive Multicast label and maps the frame to [EVPN-A, VLAN 2100]. Then, PE3 looks at the next label and sees the split horizon label that it had previously announced. The key role of the Split Horizon label is to prevent L2 loops: PE3 realizes that the frame comes from ES 00:11:00:11:00:11:00:11:00:11, so it does *not* forward the frame back to CE3.

But why does PE4 send the frame to PE3 in the first place? Because PE3 might have *other* local Ethernet Segments to which the frame must be flooded.

EVPN virtual gateway

Setting the same IRB IP+MAC across PEs—for a specific [EVI, VLAN] pair—is enough to achieve all-active load balancing *as long as every PE has such an IRB interface*. Now, let's consider an all-active topology in which CE1 is multihomed to PE1 and PE2, whereas CE3 is multihomed to PE3 and PE4. By combining the concepts illustrated in Figure 8-3 and Figure 8-4 for known unicast, you can infer the following:

- CE1 applies a local hash to distribute outbound H1→H4 frames between its two LAG member interfaces, toward PE1 or PE2, respectively.
- PE1 (or PE2) receives the packets on its local `irb.2100` interface, strips the L2 header, performs an L3 lookup that yields output interface `irb.2200`, pushes a new L2 header, and then tunnels the frame toward PE3 or PE4. The frame is encapsulated under a service MPLS label, which can be either a MAC label or an aliasing label.

But, what if PE1 and PE2 do *not* have a local IRB interface? In this case, they need to bridge the frame in the context of bridge domain BR-2100 toward the remote IRB, which is in PE3 or PE4. Is there all-active load-balancing from the ingress PE to the two egress PEs? Not really: the ingress PE chooses either PE3 or PE4 because there is no aliasing for the IRB (`irb.2100`) MAC. Unless you dynamically associate an ESI to the IRB interface: in this case, all-active load-balancing is possible. This virtual gateway functionality is implemented with EVPN Type 1 (Ethernet Segment AD), the details for which are beyond the scope of this book. As of this writing, the Virtual Gateway functionality is implemented in Junos for EVPN with VXLAN transport.

 As the authors will document in the blog http://mplsinthesd-nera.net, the Virtual Gateway feature supports VM mobility while allowing to ping each of the PEs' IRB interfaces in a deterministic manner.

Ethernet VPN with VXLAN Transport

Ethernet VPN is a powerful technology that supports several encapsulation types. VXLAN is one of the available transport options in those typically small-scale and medium-scale data centers whose network does not support (or is not configured for) the transport of MPLS packets.

Data Center Challenges

Although Chapter 10 discusses data center challenges and architectures in greater detail, let's do a very brief introduction of the use case for VXLAN here.

Data center transport challenge

Data centers are growing exponentially in terms of traffic, services, and geographical distribution. With its many limitations—flooding, L2 loops, and so on—a legacy L2 underlay is no longer an acceptable option. What are the options to build a scalable transport overlay?

In the early 2000s, MPLS was considered to be a pure service provider (SP) (carrier) technology. This has changed now: MPLS is being progressively accepted and deployed as a powerful technology for Data Center Interconnection (DCI) at the WAN edge.

What about server connectivity *inside* of each data center? As of this writing, not all of the hypervisors support native MPLS yet, so many modern data centers run with an IPv4 overlay. This approach—popularly called *IP fabric*—supports the transport of servers' L3 traffic. But that's not all: it can also transport L2 frames by *somehow* encapsulating them within an IPv4 packet at the edge of the fabric.

Regardless of the specific flavor chosen, an IPv4 overlay is similar to an IP core network that transparently tunnels customer traffic between edge devices. The edge devices in the data center can be either traditional network PEs (data center gateways) or the networking logic in modern hypervisors, or Top-of-Rack (ToR) switches.

Let's expand this powerful analogy a bit more:

- The L2 tunneling overlay is to the data center as an L2 VPN is to an SP.
- IP is to an IP fabric as IP+MPLS is to an SP core.

Data center multitenancy challenge

Now add the requirement to separate traffic in different virtual instances or *tenants*. What is a tenant? You can view it as a data center customer or service (it can even be an application). The concept is pretty similar to that of a MPLS VPN in the SP world.

The legacy way to separate tenants in a data center is VLANs. But this approach has many drawbacks, for example:

- It is a pure L2 technology, with no intelligence to build a scalable overlay.
- The VLAN ID is a 12-bit value, limiting the number of VLANs (or SVLANs) in a data center to a maximum of 4,095.

Now think of SPs: how was the multitenant problem solved several decades ago? By pushing a (MPLS) label to the packets. This label only *lives* inside the core and is stripped from the packet before sending it to the customer device.

How is this challenge solved in a data center having an IP overlay? With the very same idea: by encoding something such as a *service label* over IP. As you can see in Chapter 10's Figure 10-5, this "something" can be an MPLS label—for example, using MPLS over Generic Routing Encapsulation (GRE) or MPLS over User Datagram Protocol (UDP)—or it can also be a VXLAN Network Identifier (VNI). But what is VXLAN?

VXLAN

Recall from earlier in the chapter that *VXLAN* stands for *Virtual eXtensible Local Area Network*. It is defined in RFC 7348 and is basically an L2VPN technology that does *not* rely on MPLS for transport or service multiplexing. VXLAN was initially proposed with a MAC learning paradigm that was based on the forwarding plane. Because this mechanism does not scale well, control planes came to the rescue and one of them is EVPN.

VXLAN transport tunnels are IP-based. Indeed, VXLAN runs on top of UDP destination port 4789, and its payload is an Ethernet frame—which can be either native or VLAN-tagged. IP tunnels are less optimized than MPLS from the point of view of resiliency and forwarding-plane lookup resources. On the other hand, as of this writing, many intra-data center deployments rely on IP transport—as an evolution from pure legacy L2 VLAN. So let's explore VXLAN in more detail.

How can we distinguish tenants in the VXLAN world? The VXLAN header has a 24-bit field called segment ID or VXLAN Network Identifier (VNI). And, like an MPLS service label, the VNI acts as a multiplexing field. There is an important implementation difference when comparing a VNI to a service MPLS label: a VNI typically has global significance among the VXLAN Tunnel End Points (VTEPs) in the data center network, whereas a service MPLS label typically has a local significance to the egress PE only.

Figure 8-5 shows a typical architecture with two data centers (one on top, one at the bottom). VXLAN tunnels span inside a single data center, and VXLAN packets are exchanged between VTEPs.

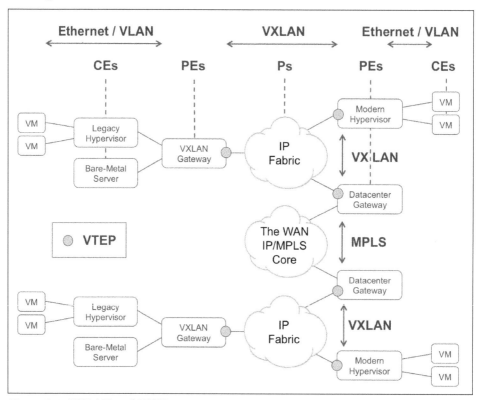

Figure 8-5. VXLAN and VTEPs

Let's view Figure 8-5 in analogy to MPLS L2 VPN:

- A VM or a bare-metal server is like a CE. These do *not* speak VXLAN. They just send and receive untagged or VLAN-tagged Ethernet frames. Traditional hypervisor vSwitches, which are plain VLAN-aware Ethernet bridges, are also considered like (L2) CEs.

- VTEPs are like PEs. They have (physical or virtual) CE-facing interfaces where they exchange plain native or VLAN-tagged Ethernet frames. And they also have core-facing interfaces where they exchange VXLAN packets.
- The IP fabric is like an MPLS/IP core. In the same way that MPLS P routers typically do not look at the MPLS service labels, the IP fabric nodes do not look at the packets' VNI.

There are more than 16 million possible VNI values, overcoming the 4,000 VLAN limitation. Conceptually, though, a VXLAN is closer to an MPLS label than to a VLAN.

You can implement the VTEP function in the software of modern hypervisors and host operating systems. VMs and containers still act as CEs, so they don't implement VXLAN.

What about bare-metal servers or hypervisors without VXLAN support? You need to connect them as CEs to a VXLAN gateway that performs the VTEP function.

Finally, a data center gateway is a (physical or logical) network device that acts as a VTEP toward the local data center, and as a L2 VPN PE toward the WAN IP/MPLS core.

Nothing prevents you from grouping these functions (hypervisor, VXLAN gateway, and data center gateway) into the same physical device(s).

It's time to paraphrase RFC 7348.

> *VXLAN runs over the existing networking infrastructure and provides a means to stretch an L2 network. In short, VXLAN is an L2 overlay scheme on an L3 network. Each overlay is termed a VXLAN segment. Only VMs within the same VXLAN segment can communicate with each other. Each VXLAN segment is identified through a 24-bit segment ID [...] (VNI).*

Finishing the analogy, a VXLAN *segment* is equivalent to a VPN in the MPLS world.

 Beyond the 16 million versus 4,000 identifier space, the main advantage of VXLAN over legacy VLAN switching in the data center is L3 itself. When hypervisors perform IP tunneling and the infrastructure is natively L3, the risk of L2 loops is drastically reduced.

EVPN with VXLAN Transport—Motivation

As of this writing, EVPN VXLAN is described in IETF *draft-ietf-bess-evpn-overlay*. It is in the standards track, so it might be an RFC by the time you read these lines.

One of the most important use cases of EVPN is DCI: interconnecting several data centers across a MPLS/IP core. This is popularly called the *WAN* application and it is a natural fit for EVPN MPLS. But EVPN also has a use case *within* each data center.

How about EVPN VXLAN? If, for whatever reason, a data center does not support the transport of MPLS packets, there are several multitenant IP tunneling options available, and one of them is VXLAN. Strictly speaking, simple VXLAN is already VPN-aware (via the VNI) and has a transport method (IP). VXLAN even implements a native IP Multicast mechanism for VTEP autodiscovery and BUM flooding. Then, what is the point of running EVPN with VXLAN transport?

Using EVPN as the VXLAN's control plane has many advantages over plain VXLAN:

- MAC learning implemented by the control plane. VM mobility assisted by the control plane. Unnecessary flooding is reduced.
- Robust autodiscovery based on BGP, as compared to IP Multicast.
- Native integration between the L2 and L3 worlds. Strong IRB solution.
- All-Active multihoming.
- Arbitrary E-LAN, E-LINE, E-TREE topologies, thanks to RT policies. Use RT policies with care because they may break CE multihoming solutions.

As of this writing, there is one disadvantage of EVPN: plain VXLAN uses IP multicast trees for BUM flooding, which provide a higher forwarding-plane efficiency than IR, the currently implemented mechanism for EVPN VXLAN. That having been said, EVPN is a technology designed to reduce unicast flooding to the minimum. You can also have a look at the Assisted Replication model defined in draft-rabadan-bess-evpn-optimized-ir.

EVPN with VXLAN Transport—Forwarding Plane

Here's what happens when a bridge domain has a learning `vlan-id` configured:

- In both VPLS and EVPN MPLS, the learning VLAN travels within the MPLS-encapsulated frame. Why? An egress PE may allocate the same MPLS label for different bridge domains in a given EVI. To de-multiplex inbound traffic correctly and map it to the right bridge domain, the egress PE expects a VLAN tag.
- In EVPN VXLAN, *by default* the VLAN tag is stripped before encapsulating the frame in VXLAN. Why? Every bridge domain has a different VNI, so the VNI acts as a multiplexer. There is typically no need to carry VLAN tags on the core.

You can configure EVPN VXLAN to carry the VLAN tags on the core with two knobs: `encapsulate-inner-vlan` and `decapsulate-accept-inner-vlan`.

Example 8-16 shows an H3→H1 frame—an ICMP echo request—encapsulated in VXLAN, assuming that the two previous knobs are configured.

Example 8-16. VXLAN encapsulation (Junos)

```
Ethernet II, Src: MAC_PE3_ge-0/0/1, Dst: MAC_PE1_ge-0/0/3
Internet Protocol Version 4, Src: 172.16.0.33 , Dst: 172.16.0.11
User Datagram Protocol, Src Port: 55468, Dst Port: 4789
Virtual eXtensible Local Area Network
    Flags: 0x08
        0... .... = Reserved(R): False
        .0.. .... = Reserved(R): False
        ..0. .... = Reserved(R): False
        ...0 .... = Reserved(R): False
        .... 1... = VXLAN Network ID(VNI): Present
        ...0 .... = Reserved(R): False
        ...0 .... = Reserved(R): False
        ...0 .... = Reserved(R): False
    Reserved: 0x000000
    VXLAN Network Identifier (VNI): 5100
    Reserved: 0
Ethernet II, Src: H3 (f8:c0:01:18:90:69), Dst: H1 (5c:5e:ab:0a:c3:92)
802.1Q Virtual LAN, PRI: 0, CFI: 0, ID: 2100
Internet Protocol Version 4, Src: 10.1.1.3, Dst: 10.1.1.1
Internet Control Message Protocol
    Type: 8 (Echo (ping) request)
    Code: 0
```

You can see the original frame encapsulated in VXLAN, which is in turn encapsulated in UDP. The destination UDP port for VXLAN is 4789.

EVPN with VXLAN Transport—Junos Configuration

EVPN VXLAN was released (in Junos and IOS XR) just before this book's publication, so the authors did not have time to build multivendor scenarios. However, there was an interoperability proof-of-concept executed and published by the European Advanced Networking Test Center (EANTC).

In the interest of brevity, the following Junos configuration only includes one bridge domain and it has neither IRB nor multihoming. You can refer to Examples Example 8-3 and Example 8-6 for AC and IRB configuration, respectively.

Example 8-17. EVPN VXLAN on a Virtual Switch—PE1 (Junos)

```
1    routing-instances {
2        EVPN-A {
3            instance-type virtual-switch;
4            vtep-source-interface lo0.0;
5            route-distinguisher 172.16.0.11:2000;
```

```
6                vrf-target target:65000:2000;
7                protocols {
8                    evpn {
9                        encapsulation vxlan;
10                       extended-vni-list 5100;
11                   }
12               }
13               bridge-domains {
14                   BR-2100 {
15                       vlan-id none;
16                       interface ae10.2100;
17                       vxlan {
18                           vni 5100;
19                           ingress-node-replication;
20   }}}}}
```

 The encapsulate-inner-vlan and decapsulate-accept-inner-vlan knobs are configurable under the vxlan hierarchy (line 17).

The bridge domain's vlan-id (line 15) is actually the normalization or learning VLAN. The on-the-wire VLAN tag may be different in a per-AC basis, as shown in Example 7-19. And the normalization VLAN is mapped to a VNI. In this case, it is set to none—even if it had a specific value it would be stripped by default.

Multitenancy is possible because a VNI has twice as many bits as a VLAN ID. Imagine 1,000 different tenants, each with its own VLAN ID space (1–4,095). Each [tenant, VLAN] pair can be mapped to a different VNI.

EVPN with VXLAN Transport—Signaling

The signaling is very similar to EVPN with MPLS transport, except for certain details. Here is the Inclusive Multicast route advertised by PE1, one per VNI:

Example 8-18. EVPN VXLAN—Inclusive Multicast route—PE1 (Junos)

```
1    juniper@PE1> show route advertising-protocol bgp 172.16.0.201
2                table EVPN-A.evpn.0 match-prefix "3:*" detail
3    [...]
4    * 3:172.16.0.11:2000::5100::172.16.0.11/304 (1 entry, 1 announced)
5      BGP group IBGP type Internal
6          Route Distinguisher: 172.16.0.11:2000
7          Nexthop: Self
8          Localpref: 100
9          AS path: [65000] I
10         Communities: target:65000:2000
```

```
11        PMSI: Flags 0x0: Label 5100:
12              Type INGRESS-REPLICATION 172.16.0.11
```

The NLRI now contains the VNI instead of the VLAN ID. And the label encoded in the PMSI attribute is no longer a MPLS label: it is the VNI!

As shown in the following example, the MAC/IP route's NLRI also contains the VNI:

Example 8-19. EVPN VXLAN—MAC route—PE1 (Junos)

```
1     juniper@PE1> show route advertising-protocol bgp 172.16.0.201
2                 table EVPN-A.evpn.0 match-prefix "2:*" detail
3     [...]
4     * 2:172.16.0.11:2000::5100::5c:5e:ab:0a:c3:92/304 (1 entry, 1 announced)
5      BGP group IBGP type Internal
6         Route Distinguisher: 172.16.0.11:2000
7         Nexthop: Self
8         Localpref: 100
9         AS path: [65000] I
10        Communities: target:65000:2000 encapsulation:vxlan
```

Back to EVPN MPLS, MAC/IP routes included a MPLS label. Here in EVPN VXLAN, the NLRI includes a VNI. As expected!

The VNI is the same for BUM traffic (Example 8-18, lines 4 and 11) and known unicast traffic (Example 8-19, line 4). This is another subtle difference with respect to EVPN MPLS. Another difference is the way in which all-active multihoming works. Since there is no way of using a split-horizon label with VXLAN, the external IP header of the VXLAN packet is inspected in order to determine which PE a BUM frame is arriving from.

Provider Backbone Bridging EVPN

Provider Backbone Bridging (PBB) EVPN is an EVPN variant that can also run either over MPLS or over VXLAN. In a nutshell, PBB EVPN inserts an extra encapsulation between the original Ethernet frame and the transport (MPLS or VXLAN) header. The goal of PBB EVPN is to achieve a higher scalability than native EVPN in the control plane. Let's see how, after the following analogy.

Introduction to PBB

As of this writing, the Internet IPv4 Full Routing comprises more than a half million prefixes: this is the number of routes that an Internet ASBR typically learns from its transit eBGP peers. Are all of these routes needed? Not really, there is a lot of inefficiency there. However, it could be much worse! Indeed, it is estimated that there are more than ten *billion* active devices in the Internet of Things (IoT), and many of them have their own public IPv4 address. On average, each single IPv4 public route represents thousands of active hosts. This aggregation—made possible thanks to subnetting and summarization—is one of the reasons why the Internet can scale worldwide. Imagine that every single host resulted in one IPv4 public route: the Internet control plane would be unmanageable!

Now, think about a big data center, with up to millions of MAC addresses, typically corresponding to VMs. Wouldn't it be great to create *MAC group* prefixes so that each such prefix could represent thousands of MAC addresses? Unfortunately, this is not implemented in Ethernet. The most significant bytes of a MAC address compose the vendor code of the network interface; so MAC summarization is not an option these days.

How can you scale the L2 service? The best option is to make it L3! It sounds trivial, but it *is* the best option. On the other hand, some legacy apps require L2 flat connectivity, so the data center infrastructure usually keeps the L2 service in place. What scaling options are there? One of them is PBB, also known as MAC-in-MAC.

PBB is defined in IEEE 802.1ah-2008. It is different from IEEE 802.1ad (Q-in-Q):

- Q-in-Q or VLAN stacking leaves the original MAC header in place and *inserts* an extra 4-byte VLAN header—with 3 bytes or 12 bits composing the VLAN tag.
- PBB *encapsulates* the original Customer MAC (C-MAC) frame inside a new set of headers including a 24-bit tag called I-SID, and a Backbone MAC (B-MAC) header.

Effectively, this increases the multiplexing space from 4,000 (VLAN) to 16 million (I-SID) values. This achievement is similar to VXLAN's but, unlike VXLAN, PBB adds a new MAC header. These technologies are very different: VXLAN is L2 over L3, whereas PBB is L2 over L2 (and PBB EVPN is L2 over L2 over L3).

When combined with EVPN, VXLAN and PBB cover two different use cases. VXLAN resolves the challenge of transporting Ethernet frames through an IP fabric; on the other hand, PBB tries to provide a higher scalability by hiding *many* different C-MACs behind a much more reduced number of B-MACs.

PBB itself does not provide a solution to transport L2 over an IP fabric or an IP/MPLS core. Indeed, PBB EVPN needs to run over VXLAN *or* MPLS. For this reason, the VXLAN and PBB technologies are *not* comparable like *apples and apples*: they fulfill a completely orthogonal purpose.

PBB is a generic technology that has been applied to VPLS, as well: RFC 7041 - *Extensions to the Virtual Private LAN Service (VPLS) Provider Edge (PE) Model for Provider Backbone Bridging*. PBB VPLS is not covered in this book.

PBB EVPN in a Nutshell

PBB EVPN is described in RFC 7623. This is how it compares to EVPN:

- There is no concept of B-MAC in EVPN. Each PE advertises all the C-MACs that it locally learns (on its ACs) via EVPN MAC/IP routes. Synchronizing the PEs' bridge tables via the control plane (BGP) minimizes unicast frame flooding. And customer MAC/IP routes provide a native L2-L3 hook that brings robustness while avoiding undesired behavior like traffic tromboning. On the downside, when C-MACs are in the order of many thousands or even millions, advertising every single C-MAC stresses the control plane—and this is the only motivation for PBB EVPN.

- PBB EVPN maintains control-plane MAC learning for B-MACs, but it leaves C-MAC address learning exclusively to the forwarding plane (like in VPLS). PEs still need to maintain huge C-MAC bridge tables, and the only benefit brought by PBB EVPN is a reduction in the number of BGP routes. What are the disadvantages?

> PBB EVPN dramatically reduces the control-plane load, at the expense of much more flooding and complexity. As for the nice L3 hooks in EVPN, the PBB layer hides them, so they are no longer available.

PBB EVPN finds its natural application in the WAN (DCI, provider transport, etc.), where the highest number of MAC addresses is expected.

After comparing PBB EVPN to EVPN, let's now compare PBB EVPN to VPLS. Both technologies rely on the forwarding plane for customer MAC learning, so what are the advantages of PBB EVPN over VPLS? Two specific advantages are all-active multihoming and its better B-MAC flush mechanism.

PBB EVPN Implementations

As of this writing, both Junos and IOS XR support PBB EVPN with MPLS transport.

How about PBB EVPN with VXLAN transport? Neither vendor supports it in generally available (GA) releases as of this writing, but IOS XR had a working prototype at EANTC in 2015.

PBB EVPN in Action

Many examples in this book begin with the configuration and then move on to the signaling and forwarding details. But PBB EVPN is such a tricky technology that it is very difficult to make any sense of the configuration without seeing it in action first.

This book's PBB EVPN tests achieved Junos and IOS XR interoperability, so the reference topology is the multivendor one in Figure 6-3.

PBB EVPN—IM signaling and BUM traffic forwarding

Figure 8-6 provides a view of how a PBB EVPN service transports an ARP request initially sent from H1 (remember that EVPN route type 3 is Inclusive Multicast). The logic inside PE4 is similar to PE1's.

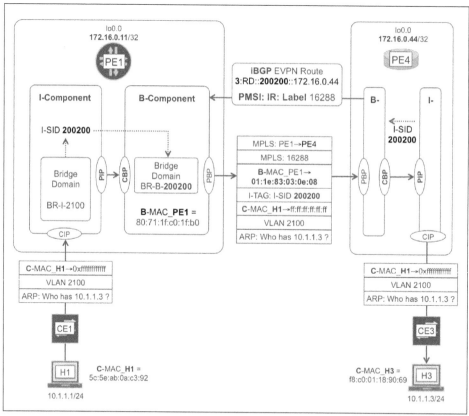

Figure 8-6. PBB EVPN—BUM intra-VLAN bridging

PBB is MAC-in-MAC, and it requires two components on each service endpoint:

The I-Component (where "I" stands for "Instance")

This component is customer facing and bridges frames according to the C-MAC. This C- concept is *different* from C- in C-VLAN. Indeed, PE1 receives (on its AC) Ethernet frames that can be non-tagged, single-tagged or double-tagged. How PE1 maps these frames to a bridge domain in the I-Component is just virtual switch/bridge domain business as usual (see the VPLS section for more details). In the following examples, the ACs and bridge domains are actually configured with one single vlan-id, so it is an SVLAN model. Still, from the PBB perspective, the frame's MAC header is considered to be C-MAC.

The B-Component (where "B" stands for "Backbone")

This component is core-facing and it bridges frames according to the B-MAC. The B-MAC is in an outer MAC header as compared to the C-MAC.

The core links in this example are based on Ethernet, so there is yet a third Ethernet header in order to transport the packet from one LER/LSR to its downstream neighbor LSR/LER. This outermost header is not shown in Figure 8-6, but you can find it in Example 8-20, line 1.

The original PBB standard allows for the I-Component and B-Component to be in different devices, but in PBB EVPN, they are assumed to be both in the same PE.

The following interfaces are defined in the PBB model:

- Customer Instance Port (CIP), at the I-Component and pointing to the ACs
- Provider Instance Port (PIP), at the I-Component, pointing to the B-Component
- Customer Backbone Port (CBP), at the B-Component, pointing to the I-Component
- Provider Backbone Port (PBP), at the B-Component and pointing to the SP core

Let's assume that each bridge domain only has one (S-)VLAN assigned to it, so there is a 1:1 VLAN:BD mapping. The following N:1 mappings are defined on each PE:

- N x VLANs to one I-SID
- N x I-SIDs to one I-Component
- N x I-Components to one B-Component
- N x B-Components in one PE; each B-Component is an EVPN Instance.

The N number is arbitrary and it can have a different value for each of these mappings—of course, it can be 1, as well. The *I-SID* stands for *Backbone Service Instance Identifier*, and it is the "glue" that binds an I-Component to its peer B-Component.

So there are several levels of N:1 multiplexing. How can de-multiplexing work at all? As you can see in Figure 8-6, the customer frames get some more headers added, including the VLAN tag, the I-SID, and the Inclusive Multicast MPLS label that identifies the B-Component on the egress PE (PE4).

Looking at the B-MAC header in Figure 8-6, the source B-MAC is the local B-MAC assigned to ESI #0 at PE1's B-Component. This MAC address is locally generated by PE1 in a dynamic manner, and it needs to have a *different* value on each PE. If PE1 has thousands of C-MACs on ESI #0—remember this is the ESI for all the single-homed and single-active multi-homed sites—all of these C-MACs are hidden behind one single B-MAC. Additionally, it is possible to reuse the same B-MAC in several B-Components on the same PE, because the B-MAC is *not* a multiplexing field.

How about the destination B-MAC address 01:1e:83:03:0e:08? It is composed of two parts: a fixed 01:1e:83 prefix, and 0x030e08 = 200200, the I-SID value! The following capture shows the Ethernet frame represented earlier in Figure 8-6. As expected, it is encapsulated over PBB-over-MPLS (although, in the capture, *over* becomes *under*).

Example 8-20. PBB-over-MPLS encapsulation

```
1    Ethernet II, Src: MAC_PE1_ge-0/0/4, Dst: MAC_P1_ge-0/0/1
2    MPLS Header, Label: <Transport to-PE4 Label>, Exp: 0, S: 0, TTL: 255
3    MPLS Header, Label: 16288, Exp: 0, S: 1, TTL: 255
4    PW Ethernet Control Word, Sequence Number: 0
5    Ethernet II, Src: 80:71:1f:c0:1f:b0, Dst: 01:1e:83:03:0e:08
6        Type: 802.1ah Provider Backbone Bridge (mac-in-mac) (0x88e7)
7    IEEE 802.1ah
8        I-TAG, I-SID: 200200
9        C-Src: H1_MAC (5c:5e:ab:0a:c3:92)
10       C-Dst: Broadcast (ff:ff:ff:ff:ff:ff)
11       Type: 802.1Q Virtual LAN (0x8100)
12   802.1Q Virtual LAN, PRI: 0, CFI: 0, ID: 2100
13   ARP Request, who is 10.1.1.3, tell 10.1.1.1
```

Here are the three Ethernet headers:

- Line 1: Outermost header to take the packet from PE1 to its neighbor P1.
- Line 5: Source B-MAC dynamically assigned by PE1, and Destination B-MAC computed for BUM in the context of I-SID 200200.
- Lines 9 through 10: Embedded in the IEEE 802.1ah header, the unicast C-MAC associated to H1 and the broadcast C-MAC address.

When PE4 receives the packet, it first pops the service MPLS label (line 3) and maps the packet to the appropriate B-Component. Then, by looking at the I-SID, PE4 maps the packet to the corresponding I-Component. And the I-Component delivers the customer frame (lines 9 through 13) out of the local ACs. Note that the Source B-MAC is useful for Source C-MAC learning (see Example 8-22).

Complex, isn't it? Well, there is still known unicast to come, not to mention multi-homing. This complexity is the result of one of the most repeated mantras in networking:

> Simplicity is never a free lunch. If application developers assume the network is flat, reliable and with zero latency, network designers and engineers need to implement incredibly complex solutions.

In modern times, application development should take the network into account and assume L3 (not L2) connectivity at the very least. A really network-respectful application should also rely on intelligent transport mechanisms that are load-balancing aware. Paraphrasing a blog post (*http://blog.ipspace.net/2011/03/open-networking-foundation-fabric.html*) from Ivan Pepelnjak on ipspace.net:

> In a world with scale-out applications, you don't need fancy combinations of routing, bridging, and whatever else; you just need fast L3 transport between endpoints.

In a world with really modern applications, a solution such as PBB EVPN should not be needed.

PBB EVPN—B-MAC signaling and known unicast traffic forwarding

Figure 8-7 illustrates how a PBB EVPN service transports the unicast ARP reply from H3 to H1. This is a known unicast packet because of the following:

- PE4's I-Component already learned H1's C-MAC address on its forwarding plane.
- PE4's B-Component already learned PE1's B-MAC address on its control plane.

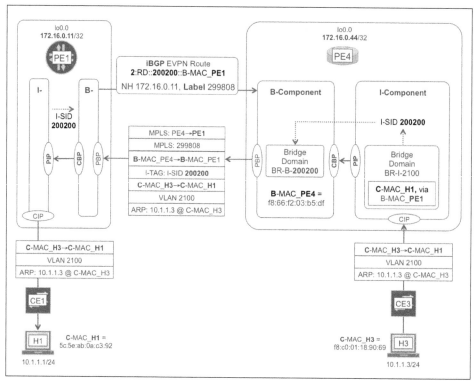

Figure 8-7. PBB EVPN—known unicast intra-VLAN bridging

As you can see, the C_MAC_H1 to B_MAC_PE1 mapping is held at PE4's I-Component. It is the result of a more-complex-than-usual MAC learning process that was triggered by H1's ARP request in Figure 8-6. PE4 created this state while processing and removing the ARP request's B-MAC and I-TAG headers (Example 8-20).

Remember that EVPN Type 2 is MAC/IP. In this case, it is B-MAC.

PBB EVPN Configuration

Now that we can spell PBB EVPN, let's see an interoperable configuration example.

PBB EVPN—Junos configuration

The AC is configured as is shown in Example 7-9, lines 1 through 8 (just replace 2010 with 2100). Example 8-21 shows a PBB EVPN configuration with just one VLAN and one I-SID.

Example 8-21. PBB EVPN configuration—PE1 (Junos)

```
1    # I-COMPONENT
2
3    interfaces {
4        pip0 {
5            unit 2000 {
6                family bridge {
7                    interface-mode trunk;
8                    bridge-domain-type svlan;
9                    isid-list all-service-groups;
10   }}}}
11   routing-instances {
12       EVPN-I-COMPONENT-A {
13           instance-type virtual-switch;
14           interface pip0.2000;
15           bridge-domains {
16               BR-I-2100 {
17                   vlan-id 2100;
18                   interface ge-2/0/1.2100;
19               }
20           }
21           pbb-options {
22               peer-instance EVPN-B-COMPONENT-A;
23           }
24           service-groups {
25               SG-A {
26                   service-type elan;
27                   pbb-service-options {
28                       isid 200200 vlan-id-list 2100;
29   }}}}}
30
31   # B-COMPONENT
32
33   interfaces {
34       cbp0 {
35           unit 2000 {
36               family bridge {
37                   interface-mode trunk;
38                   bridge-domain-type bvlan;
39                   isid-list all;
40   }}}}
41   routing-instances {
42       EVPN-B-COMPONENT-A {
43           instance-type virtual-switch;
44           interface cbp0.2000;
45           route-distinguisher 172.16.0.11:2000;
46           vrf-target target:65000:2000;
47           protocols {
48               evpn {
49                   control-word;
50                   pbb-evpn-core;
```

```
51                  extended-isid-list 200200;
52              }
53          }
54          bridge-domains {
55              BR-B-200200 {
56                  vlan-id 1234;
57                  isid-list 200200;
58                  vlan-id-scope-local;
59      }}}}
```

As shown in Figure 8-6 and Figure 8-7 the PIP (lines 3 through 10) and CBP (lines 33 through 40) interconnect the I-Component to the B-Component, respectively. The actual I-to-B mapping is performed on line 22. VLAN 2100 is mapped to I-SID 200200 on line 28. And I-SID 200200 is mapped to the B-Component on lines 51 and 57.

As for the B-Component bridge domain's VLAN ID (line 56), it must be set, but its value is not very relevant, because it is never sent on the wire.

 The B-Component is an EVPN-capable instance but the I-Component is not.

Example 8-22 shows the result of the configuration.

Example 8-22. PBB EVPN—MAC table—PE1 (Junos)

```
1       juniper@PE1> show brige mac-table
2
3       MAC flags       (D -dynamic MAC, C -Control MAC)
4
5       Routing instance : EVPN-B-COMPONENT-A
6        Bridging domain : BR-B-200200, VLAN : 1234
7          MAC                 MAC      Logical    NH       RTR
8          address             flags    interface  Index    ID
9          01:1e:83:03:0e:08   DC                  1048575 0
10         f8:66:f2:03:b5:df   DC                  1048576 1048576
11
12      Routing instance : EVPN-I-COMPONENT-A
13       Bridging domain : BR-I-2100, ISID : 200200, VLAN : 2100
14         MAC                 MAC      Logical    Remote
15         address             flags    interface  BEB address
16         5c:5e:ab:0a:c3:92   D        ge-2/0/1.2100
17         f8:c0:01:18:90:69   D        rbeb.32768  f8:66:f2:03:b5:df
```

By looking carefully at Figure 8-6 and Figure 8-7, you can identify all of the MAC addresses displayed in the previous example:

- Line 9: Multicast B-MAC address used for BUM in the context of I-SID 200200
- Line 10: B-MAC address locally assigned by PE4
- Lines 16 and 17: H1's and H3's C-MAC addresses, respectively

The `Remote BEB address` column (*BEB* stands for *Backbone Edge Bridge*) shows, from the perspective of PE1, how H3's C-MAC is mapped to PE4's B-MAC. This mapping allows PE1 to successfully process unicast frames destined to H3.

PBB EVPN—IOS XR configuration

IOS XR implicitly creates the PIP and CBP interfaces, so the configuration is shorter:

Example 8-23. PBB EVPN configuration—PE4 (IOS XR)

```
1    # I-COMPONENT
2
3    interface GigabitEthernet0/0/0/3.2100 l2transport
4     encapsulation dot1q 2100
5    !
6    l2vpn
7     bridge group I-COMPONENTS
8      bridge-domain BR-I-2100
9       interface GigabitEthernet0/0/0/3.2100
10      !
11      pbb edge i-sid 200200 core-bridge BR-B-200200
12   !
13
14   # B-COMPONENT
15
16    bridge group B-COMPONENTS
17     bridge-domain BR-B-200200
18      pbb core
19       evpn evi 2000
20   !
```

The I-SID clearly acts as a glue from the I-Component to the B-Component (line 11). Where are the EVPN instance's RD and RT? They are automatically calculated from `evpn evi 2000` (line 19):

- The RD is calculated as *<Router ID>:<EVI>*, so it is 172.16.0.44:2000.
- The RT is calculated as *<AS>:<EVI>*, so it is 65000:2000.

PBB EVPN Signaling

PBB EVPN and EVPN signaling are very similar, but not identical. Here are some differences.

First, PBB EVPN signals B-MACs, whereas EVPN signals C-MACs. Obvious!

There is no L3 hook on the B-Component, so PBB EVPN's Type 2 routes are only MAC—and not IP/MAC—routes. The NLRI contains the I-SID instead of the VLAN (see the NLRI format shown in Example 8-5 and replace 2100 with 200200).

The trickier difference comes with all-active multihoming. In EVPN, all the ACs connected to the same Ethernet Segment are identified with a common ESI. In PBB EVPN, the implementation is very different. Let's see it in detail.

First, the administrator or external software manually configures the ES's B-MAC address. For example, in Junos: `set interfaces ae10 esi source-bmac 00:11:22:33:44:55`. The ACs connected to a given all-active ES must all have the same B-MAC address, regardless of which PE they are on. So, taking as a reference the topology in Figure 8-1, PE3 and PE4 both have the same B-MAC value configured on the right-facing LAG. The EVPN MAC route looks like the following example:

Example 8-24. EVPN Type 2 MAC route: non-zero ESI—PE3 (Junos)

```
juniper@PE3> show route advertising-protocol bgp 172.16.0.201
              evpn-mac-address 00:11:22:33:44:55 detail

EVPN-B-COMPONENT-A.evpn.0: [...]
* 2:172.16.0.33:2000::200200::00:11:22:33:44:55/304 (1 entry, ...)
    Route Label: 300776
    ESI: ff:ff:ff:ff:ff:ff:ff:ff:ff:ff
    Communities: target:65000:2000
[...]
```

Regardless of the configured ESI, the B-MAC route has the ESI attribute set to the all-ones binary value. The key is the B-MAC, which must match on all the PEs connected to a given all-active Ethernet Segment.

There are no Ethernet AD (Type 1) routes in PBB EVPN, simply because there is no need for aliasing. Both PE3 and PE4 advertise the single B-MAC associated to a given ES in a *permanent* manner (there is no B-MAC aging), so the ingress PEs just need to look up the MPLS label that the egress PEs are advertising for that single B-MAC.

Ethernet Segment (Type 4) routes are present in both EVPN and PBB EVPN, as they are needed for the BUM DF election in all-active ES.

## CHAPTER 9

Inter-Domain MPLS Services

Inter-domain MPLS services is such a vast topic that it could fill a book on its own. This chapter focuses on an inter-domain type (Inter-AS) and a service type (IP VPN). Although this is just one piece of the entire picture, it is enough to get an idea of the challenges and techniques that are typically seen in inter-domain MPLS services.

But, before diving into Inter-AS IP VPN, let's get an overview of what the different inter-domain MPLS services are and how they can be classified.

Inter-Domain Architectures

Given two domains, D1 and D2, there are two ways to design the border:

Inter-AS
Each domain is a different AS: D1 = AS1, D2 = AS2. The border is composed of two devices, each belonging to a single domain. These are AS Border Routers (ASBRs). One ASBR belongs to D1 and the other one belongs to D2. They both peer with each other through a neutral inter-domain link.

Inter-area
Each IGP area is one domain: D1 = Area X, D2 = Area Y. One single device is enough to instantiate the border. Such a border device is typically called a Border Node (BN) or Area Border Router (ABR). It has some interfaces in D1 and other interfaces in D2. Actually, it can also connect to D3, D4, and so on.

 Two ASs are connected through a link with one device at each end, whereas two areas are connected through a network device.

This chapter focuses on Inter-AS. Chapter 16 and Chapter 17 also feature inter-area scenarios.

In classic networking, an AS and an IGP area are two completely different concepts: an AS represents an organization and an IGP area is just one region within a larger network. This interpretation is outdated. True, each service provider typically has one or more public ASs in order to become part of the Internet. But this is just one application of the AS concept. Any public or private network can be segmented in multiple—typically private—ASs or in multiple areas, or in a combination of both. ASs and areas are just elements of the network designer toolbox. For example, the last example of Chapter 2 is a single data-center network that is composed of many different private ASs, one per device.

It is assumed that the IGP prefixes of one domain are *not* leaked in the IGP of the other domain. MPLS needs to work with this constraint.

This Chapter's Example Topology

Let's take the following example as a reference to discuss all the models:

- There are three IP VPNs. These correspond to three VRFs that are instantiated at PE1, PE2, PE3, and PE4. The VRF names are: VRF-BLUE, VRF-GREEN, and VRF-RED. Each VRF has its own Route Target (RT) that it uses for importing and exporting prefixes. The RT policies are symmetrical (full mesh).

- Each CE device in Figure 9-1 in fact represents three CEs. The topology has the following CEs: CE<#>-BLUE, CE<#>-GREEN, and CE<#>-RED, where <#> is a number that can take the values 1, 2, 3, or 4. Each *colored* CE is connected to the adjacent PE through a separate AC. For a given PE, all the ACs share the same physical interface and reuse the same IP addresses. ACs remain different because each of them uses a different VLAN tag.

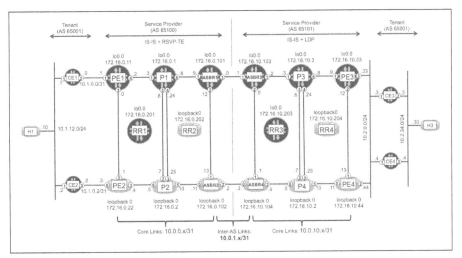

Figure 9-1. Inter-AS example topology

- Likewise, each H device represents three hosts: H<#>-BLUE, H<#>-GREEN, and H<#>-RED, where <#> is a number that can take the values 1 or 3. Again, the physical interfaces and the IP addressing remain the same and VLAN tags act as multiplexers.

- The challenge is to connect H1-BLUE to H3-BLUE; H1-GREEN to H3-GREEN; and H1-RED to H3-RED.

Although they are not shown in the Figure 9-1, this chapter illustrates both IPv4 VPN and IPv6 VPN. All the access and inter-AS links are dual-tagged so every IPv4 address 10.x.y.z coexists with an IPv6 address fc00::10:x:y:z. The MPLS/IP core networks in each AS are IPv4-only.

Inter-AS Flavors

RFC 4364 - *BGP/MPLS IP VPNs*, section 10, lists three options to provide IP VPN services to tenants that have sites in different ASs. These options are listed in the RFC as: (a), (b), and (c). For these reason, these three models are known in the industry as inter-AS Options A, B, and C, respectively.

Figure 9-2 shows an additional model, referred to in this book as Option X.

The gray shadow next to certain MPLS Transport headers represents *implicit null*. In other words, a MPLS transport label is signaled but its control-plane value is 3, so there is no associated MPLS header.

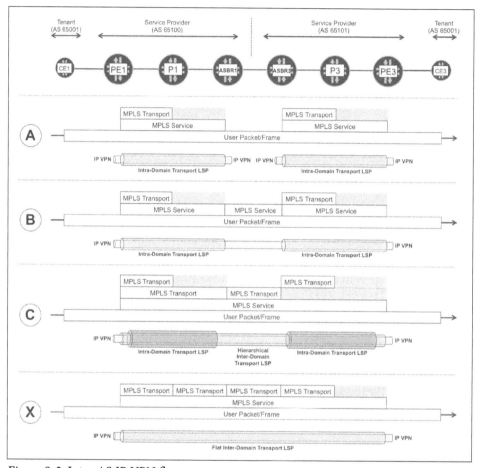

Figure 9-2. Inter-AS IP VPN flavors

For the purposes of simplicity, let's assume in this illustration that VRRP priorities on H-CE links—and MEDs on CE-PE sessions—are set so that the preferred path is via PE1 and PE3.

This chapter's goal is to make Figure 9-2 meaningful to you—keep reading and it will become clearer.

Inter-AS Option A

Inter-AS Option A, illustrated in Figure 9-3, requires the VRFs to be instantiated in the ASBRs. You can enable VLAN tagging on the inter-AS link and define three different logical interfaces on each ASBR:

- ASBR1's VRF-BLUE: ge-2/0/3.1001. ASBR3's VRF-BLUE: ge-2/0/1.1001
- ASBR1's VRF-GREEN: ge-2/0/3.1002. ASBR3's VRF-GREEN: ge-2/0/1.1002
- ASBR1's VRF-RED: ge-2/0/3.1003. ASBR3's VRF-RED: ge-2/0/1.1003

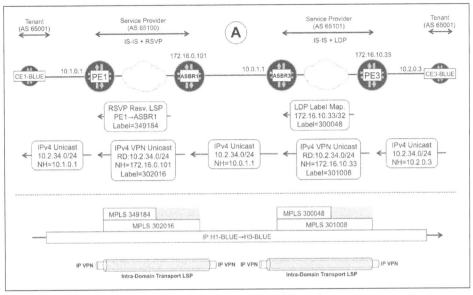

Figure 9-3. Inter-AS VPN Option A—signaling and forwarding

This technique relies on stitching the ACs of the two ASBRs. ASBR1 sees ASBR3 as a CE, and vice versa. These inter-AS ACs are like PE-CE ACs in all respects. You can run any routing protocol or even static routing over these ACs.

As you might expect, eBGP (SAFI=1) is the most popular choice due to its scalability. So to extend 10K VPNs across the two ASs, the two ASBRs need to establish 10K eBGP sessions with each other. This has an effect on scalability.

Option A is the simplest model, but also *the least scalable* of them all.

Looking back at Figure 9-2, every AS has its own MPLS protocol. It is perfectly possible to run RSVP-TE on AS 65100 and LDP on AS 65101. Let's assume that this is the case.

Following is the "imaginary" life of the packet as it goes from CE1-BLUE to CE3-BLUE. It is imaginary because in reality the forwarding table is precomputed with all the instructions, so the control plane has already executed the complex recursive logic. Also, let's assume that the VPN label allocation mode is per-CE.

1. CE1 sends the IP packet to PE1, which receives it on the VRF-BLUE's AC.

2. PE1 looks for a route in VRF-BLUE to the destination. It finds an IP VPN (SAFI=128) route with an MPLS service label S1 (302016) and a BGP next hop equal to ASBR1's loopback address 172.16.0.101. This next hop resolves into a RSVP-TE LSP, whose first-hop transport label is T1 (349184). This LSP terminates at ASBR1. PE1 sends the packet to P1 with two labels: S1 at the bottom, and T1 on top.

3. P1 pops the T1 label and sends the packet to ASBR1.

4. ASBR1 looks at the S1 label, pops it, and sends the plain IP packet to ASBR3. From the perspective of ASBR1, ASBR3 is a CE.

5. ASBR3 receives the packet and processes it in the context of VRF-BLUE. It finds a route to the destination with an MPLS service label S2 (301008) and a BGP next hop equal to PE3's loopback address 172.16.10.33. This next hop resolves into an LDP LSP, whose first-hop transport label is T2 (300048). This LSP terminates at PE3. ASBR3 sends the packet to P3 with two labels: S2 at the bottom, and T2 on top.

6. P3 pops the T2 label and sends the packet to PE3.

7. PE3 looks at the S2 label, pops it, and sends the packet to CE3-BLUE.

Remember that an MPLS service label, which is sometimes called a service MPLS label, or simply a service label, is just an MPLS label. On the wire, it cannot be distinguished from a transport label. What makes it a service label is the way in which the receiver interprets it.

Option A is a model in which the inter-AS link is *not* MPLS-enabled. Strictly speaking, in Option A the MPLS service is not extended; it is terminated by each AS. The extension takes place as a non-MPLS service.

The service BGP route undergoes several transformations:

1. From PE3 to ASBR3, it is an IP VPN route (SAFI=128) with BGP next hop PE3 (172.16.10.33).

2. From ASBR3 to ASBR1, it is a plain IP route (SAFI=1) with BGP next hop ASBR3 (10.0.1.1).

3. From ASBR1 to PE1, it is an IP VPN route (SAFI=128) with BGP next hop ASBR1 (172.16.0.101).

Each ASBR behaves like a traditional PE, so all the techniques described in Chapter 3 apply here, too. You might remember from Chapter 3 that Junos, by default, does not strip the extended communities from eBGP updates. In inter-AS Option A scenarios, it is especially important to remove these communities by using the appropriate eBGP policies. Otherwise, the prefix might be mistakenly imported into the wrong VRFs at the receiver AS, based on the RT(s) attached by the sender AS.

Inter-AS Option B

In this model, VPN packets that traverse the link ASBR1→ASBR3 all egress ASBR1 through the same *logical* interface. In this case, it is no longer possible to use the VLAN tag as a sort of VPN identifier in the inter-AS link. Another multiplexing technique comes to the rescue: MPLS!

ASBR1 and ASBR3 establish one single eBGP session with each other. This session exchanges IP VPN (SAFI=128) prefixes, essentially extending the VPN in an MPLS-aware manner. This has an immediate scaling benefit: one eBGP session shared by all VPNs, instead of one eBGP session for each VPN. However, ASBRs still need to keep all the routes for every extended VPN.

> In a pure Option B model, ASBRs do not have any local VRFs. They act like transit LSRs and perform MPLS label operations.

Inter-AS Option B—Signaling and Forwarding

Looking back at Figure 9-2, every AS has its own MPLS protocol. Again, let's assume that AS 65100 runs RSVP-TE, and AS 65101 uses LDP.

Inter-AS Option B—signaling and forwarding—Junos plane

Figure 9-4 illustrates inter-AS Option B signaling and forwarding planes.

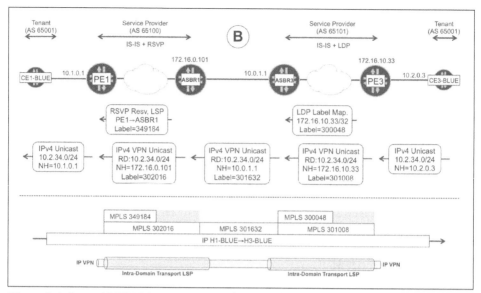

Figure 9-4. Inter-AS VPN Option B—signaling and forwarding

Let's inspect the H1-BLUE→H3-BLUE packet, assuming for simplicity that the forwarding path flows through a single-vendor plane (Junos in this case).

Example 9-1. Inter-AS Option B forwarding—Junos plane

```
RP/0/0/CPU0:H#traceroute vrf H1-BLUE 10.2.34.30

Type escape sequence to abort.
Tracing the route to 10.2.34.30

1  10.1.12.1 0 msec  0 msec  0 msec
2  10.1.0.1 0 msec  0 msec  0 msec
3  10.0.0.3 [MPLS: Labels 349184/302016 Exp 0] 0 msec  [...]
4  10.0.0.9 [MPLS: Label 302016 Exp 0] 79 msec  19 msec  [...]
5  10.0.1.1 [MPLS: Label 301632 Exp 0] 9 msec  9 msec  [...]
6  10.0.10.3 [MPLS: Labels 300048/301008 Exp 0] 19 msec  [...]
7  10.0.10.9 [MPLS: Label 301008 Exp 0] 0 msec  [...]
8  10.2.0.3 9 msec  0 msec  0 msec
9  10.2.34.30 9 msec
```

Following is the "imaginary" life of the packet as it goes from CE1-BLUE to CE3-BLUE. It is imaginary because in reality the forwarding table is precomputed with all of the instructions, so the control plane has already executed the complex recursive logic. Also, let's assume that PE3's VPN label allocation mode is per-CE.

1. CE1-BLUE sends the packet to PE1, which receives it on one of VRF-BLUE's ACs.

2. PE1 looks for a BGP IP VPN route in VRF-BLUE to the destination. It finds a route with a MPLS service label S1 (302016) and a BGP next hop equal to ASBR1's loopback address 172.16.0.101. This next hop resolves into a RSVP-TE LSP, whose first-hop transport label is T1 (349184). This LSP terminates at ASBR1. PE1 sends the packet to P1 with two labels: S1 at the bottom, and T1 on top.

3. P1 pops the T1 label and sends the packet to ASBR1.

4. ASBR1 looks at the S1 label, swaps it for S2 (301632), and sends the packet out of its ge-2/0/3.1001 interface toward ASBR3.

5. ASBR3 receives the packet, looks at the S2 label, swaps it for S3 (301008), and pushes transport label T2 (300048). This label corresponds to an LDP LSP that terminates at PE3.

6. P3 pops the T2 label and sends the packet to PE3.

7. PE3 looks at the S3 label, pops it, and sends the packet to CE3-BLUE.

As you can see, the ASBRs no longer perform an IP lookup. It is pure MPLS forwarding. This is possible due to the way that the service BGP route is transformed at the border:

1. From PE3 to ASBR3, it is an IP VPN route (SAFI=128) with BGP next hop PE3 (172.16.10.33).

2. From ASBR3 to ASBR1, it is an IP VPN route (SAFI=128) with BGP next hop ASBR3 (10.0.1.1).

3. From ASBR1 to PE1, it is an IP VPN route (SAFI=128) with BGP next hop ASBR1 (172.16.0.101).

This route transformation is practically identical to the one described in Option A. But it has a very important difference: between the ASBRs, the route is IP VPN (SAFI=128) instead of IP (SAFI=1). ASBRs must have iBGP export policies that change the BGP next-hop attribute of the reflected IP VPN routes to *self*. This next-hop rewrite operation triggers a new MPLS label allocation, which further modifies the IP VPN routes:

- The Option A example features *two* different service label values: S1 from PE1 to ASBR1, and S2 from ASBR3 to PE3. These S1 and S2 labels are locally meaningful to ASBR1 and PE3, respectively.

- The Option B example features *three* different service label values: S1 from PE1 to ASBR1, S2 from ASBR1 to ASBR3, and S3 from ASBR3 to PE3. These S1, S2, and S3 labels are locally meaningful to ASBR1, ASBR3, and PE3, respectively.

When allocating a new service label, ASBR3 is programming a new entry in its LFIB.

MPLS service label S2 is the only and topmost (outermost) label in the inter-AS link. This label is advertised in IP VPN (SAFI=128) eBGP routes. So, is it a service or a transport label? Functionally, it acts more like a transport than a service label!

Most of the Junos-specific commands are already explained in Chapter 3. Let's focus on the MPLS forwarding state created at ASBR3 (see Example 9-2).

Example 9-2. Inter-AS Option B signaling and forwarding—ASBR3 (Junos)

```
1    juniper@ASBR3> show route receive-protocol bgp 172.16.10.203
2                   table bgp.l3vpn.0 community target:65000:1001
3                   match-prefix "*10.2.34.*" detail
4
5    bgp.l3vpn.0: 8 destinations, 16 routes (8 active, 0 holddown, ...)
6    * 172.16.10.33:101:10.2.34.0/24 (2 entries, 1 announced)
7        Accepted
8        Route Distinguisher: 172.16.10.33:101
9        VPN Label: 301008
10       Nexthop: 172.16.10.33
11       MED: 100
12       Localpref: 100
13       AS path: 65001 I (Originator)
14       Cluster list:  172.16.10.203
15       Originator ID: 172.16.10.33
16       Communities: target:65000:1001
17
18   juniper@ASBR3> show route table inet.3 172.16.10.33
19
20   inet.3: 11 destinations, 11 routes (11 active, 0 holddown, ...)
21   + = Active Route, - = Last Active, * = Both
22
23   172.16.10.33/32    *[LDP/9] 2d 00:37:33, metric 30
24                        > to 10.0.10.3 via ge-2/0/3.0, Push 300048
25
26   juniper@ASBR3> show route advertising-protocol bgp 10.0.1.0
27                   table bgp.l3vpn.0 community target:65000:1001
28                   match-prefix "*10.2.34.*" detail
29
30   bgp.l3vpn.0: 8 destinations, 16 routes (8 active, 0 holddown, ...)
31   * 172.16.10.33:101:10.2.34.0/24 (2 entries, 1 announced)
32    BGP group eBGP-VPN type External
33       Route Distinguisher: 172.16.10.33:101
34       VPN Label: 301632
35       Nexthop: Self
36       Flags: Nexthop Change
37       AS path: [65101] 65001 I
38       Communities: target:65000:1001
39
40   juniper@ASBR3> show route label 301632
```

```
41
42    mpls.0: 14 destinations, 14 routes (14 active, 0 holddown, ...)
43    + = Active Route, - = Last Active, * = Both
44
45    301632  *[VPN/170] 00:17:32, metric2 30, from 172.16.10.203
46              > to 10.0.10.3 via ge-2/0/3.0, Swap 301008, Push 300048(top)
```

ASBR3 receives the IP VPN route (lines 1 through 16) with BGP next hop
172.16.10.33 and MPLS service label 301008 (S3). Next, it looks at the inet.3 table
and realizes that the BGP next hop 172.16.10.33 is resolved via LDP (lines 18 through
24), being the first-hop label equal to 300048 (T2). Then, ASBR3 associates the new
MPLS service label 301632 (S2) to every single received IP VPN route with original
BGP next hop 172.16.10.33 and original MPLS service label 301008.

ASBR3 then programs the LFIB accordingly (lines 40 through 46): upon reception of
a packet with topmost label S2 (301632), swap it for S3 (301008) and push T2
(300048). Finally, ASBR3 advertises the IP VPN route (lines 26 through 38) with the
new MPLS service label S2 (301632) and the new BGP next hop 10.0.1.1.

The BGP next-hop change operation at ASBR3 is crucial: it is this
operation that makes ASBR3 generate a new MPLS service label.
Remember this in the rest of the book. *A device that changes the
BGP next hop of a labeled BGP route also allocates a new MPLS
label.*

Inter-AS Option B—forwarding—IOS XR plane

The signaling mechanisms in Junos and IOS XR are very similar. Let's have a brief
look at the forwarding plane in IOS XR, focusing on the MPLS service label that
ASBR4 allocates for RD:10.2.34.0/24 (see Example 9-3).

Example 9-3. Inter-AS Option B forwarding—ASBR4 (IOS XR)

```
1     RP/0/0/CPU0:ASBR4# show mpls forwarding labels 24023
2     Sun Jul 26 12:59:30.533 UTC
3     Local  Outgoing   Prefix                    Outgoing
4     Label  Label      or ID                     Interface
5     ------ ---------- ------------------        ----------
6     24023  24029      172.16.10.44:101:10.2.34.0/24
7
8     Next Hop        Bytes
9                     Switched
10    -------------- -----------
11    172.16.10.44    317400
12
13    RP/0/0/CPU0:ASBR4# show cef 172.16.10.44
14    [...]
15      local adjacency 10.0.10.5
```

```
16      Prefix Len 32, traffic index 0, precedence n/a, priority 3
17        via 10.0.10.5, GigabitEthernet0/0/0/2, 5 dependencies, ...
18        path-idx 0 NHID 0x0 [0xa1044bd4 0x0]
19        next hop 10.0.10.5
20        local adjacency
21          local label 24002       labels imposed {24009}
```

ASBR4 assigns label 24023 (S2) to the IP VPN prefix 172.16.10.44:101:10.2.34.0/24 (line 6). In the LFIB, ASBR4 swaps S2 (24023) for S3 (24029) and pushes T2 (24009). This conclusion results from combining lines 6 and 21 in Example 9-3.

You can see this label operation in the traceroute lines for TTL=5 and TTL=6 shown in Example 9-4.

Example 9-4. Inter-AS Option B forwarding—IOS XR plane

```
RP/0/0/CPU0:H#traceroute vrf H1-BLUE 10.2.34.30

Type escape sequence to abort.
Tracing the route to 10.2.34.30

 1  10.1.12.1 0 msec   0 msec   0 msec
 2  10.1.0.5 0 msec   0 msec   0 msec
 3  10.0.0.5 [MPLS: Labels 24000/24031 Exp 0] 9 msec   [...]
 4  10.0.0.11 [MPLS: Label 24031 Exp 0] 59 msec   [....]
 5  10.0.1.3 [MPLS: Label 24023 Exp 0] 79 msec   [...]
 6  10.0.10.5 [MPLS: Labels 24009/24029 Exp 0] 9 msec   [...]
 7  10.0.10.11 9 msec   9 msec   9 msec
 8  10.2.0.4 9 msec   9 msec   9 msec
 9  10.2.34.30 9 msec   [...]
```

Inter-AS Option B—Junos Configuration

PE1 and PE3 are configured the same as they are in Chapter 3, except for the AS number and the IP addressing. For PEs, inter-AS or intra-AS only results in a minor difference: the AS path. All the rest is identical.

An ASBR's configuration is also similar to a PE's, except that it has *no* local VRFs. The configuration of the iBGP sessions toward the Route Reflector (RR) must include an export policy with next-hop self. Let's look at the eBGP configuration for an ASBR, shown in Example 9-5.

Example 9-5. Inter-AS Option B configuration—ASBR3 (Junos)

```
protocols {
    bgp {
        group eBGP-VPN {
            family inet-vpn unicast;
            family inet6-vpn unicast;
```

```
            export eBGP-65100-OUT;
            peer-as 65100;
            neighbor 10.0.1.0;
}}}
policy-options {
    policy-statement eBGP-65100-OUT {
        term IPv6 {
            from family inet6-vpn;
            then next-hop fc00::10:0:1:1;
}}}
```

Nothing special is required for IPv4 VPN prefixes. As for IPv6 VPN, the IPv6 next-hop rewrite is essential. Otherwise—like you saw in Chapter 3—the BGP next hop is set to ::ffff:10.0.1.1, and ASBR1 cannot resolve it.

Inter-AS Option B—Junos and IOS XR interoperability

The IPv6 next-hop requirement just discussed has interoperability implications. Although in Figure 9-1 all the inter-AS links are single-vendor, the authors also successfully tested multivendor inter-AS Option B.

The first attempt was similar to the aforementioned IPv6 BGP next-hop rewrite, but the authors did not find how to achieve it in IOS XR. Thus, IOS XR uses an IPv4-mapped address as BGP next hop, and the Junos device cannot resolve it. The good news is that there are two ways to get around it and achieve next-hop resolution at the Junos ASBR.

One method is to split the eBGP session in two:

- One eBGP session between the IPv4 endpoints (10.0.1.x), used to exchange IPv4 VPN (AFI=1, SAFI=128) prefixes.
- One eBGP session between the IPv6 endpoints (fc00::10:0:1:x), used to exchange IPv6 VPN (AFI=2, SAFI=128) prefixes.

The second method is compatible with having one single eBGP session for both address families, and it requires an additional trick on the Junos ASBR (see Example 9-6).

Example 9-6. Installing IPv4-mapped routes in inet6.3—ASBR1 (Junos)

```
routing-options {
    rib-groups {
        RG-STATIC-IPv6 {
            import-rib [ inet.0 inet6.3 ];
            import-policy PL-ASBR-LINKS;
        }
    }
    static {
```

```
        rib-group RG-STATIC-IPv6;
        route 10.0.1.1/32 {
            next-hop 10.0.1.1;
            community 65000:12345;
}}}
policy-options {
    policy-statement PL-ASBR-LINKS {
        term ASBR-LINKS {
            from {
                protocol static;
                community CM-ASBR-LINKS;
            }
            then accept;
        }
        then reject;
    }
    community CM-ASBR-LINKS members 65000:12345;
}
```

This technique consists of creating a static route on the Junos ASBR's inet.0 table toward the remote ASBR peering address (10.0.1.x/32). This route is then leaked into inet6.3 with RIB groups, so the Junos ASBR automatically coverts it and installs a ::ffff:10.0.1.x/128 route on its inet6.3 table.

Example 9-7. IPv4-Mapped Route in inet6.3—ASBR1 (Junos)

juniper@ASBR1> show route ::ffff:10.0.1.1 table inet6.3

```
inet6.3: 2 destinations, 2 routes (2 active, 0 holddown, 0 hidden)
+ = Active Route, - = Last Active, * = Both
```

::ffff:10.0.1.1/128
```
                  *[Static/5] 00:26:38
                  > to 10.0.1.1 via ge-0/0/3.0
```

Thanks to this route, ASBR1 can resolve IPv4-mapped IPv6 next hops. After it is configured, interoperability is successful. Even in a Junos-to-Junos eBGP session, the next-hop rewrite shown in Example 9-5 is no longer necessary.

Inter-AS Option B—optimizing the control plane

By default, ASBRs establish iBGP sessions toward the RRs and pull *all* of the IP VPN routes from them. This is a waste of resources. Ideally, ASBRs should pull only the IP VPN routes for those VPNs that are extended across the AS border. This is typically a subset of all the VPNs provisioned in the local AS.

The solution is to use the RT address family (SAFI=132), but there is a challenge. Pure Option B ASBRs do not have local VRFs. They need a way to know in which RTs they are interested. This need is fulfilled in Junos by RT static routes.

Example 9-8. Inter-AS Option B and RTC—ASBR1 and ASBR3 (Junos)

```
protocols {
    bgp {
        group iBGP-RR family route-target;
        group eBGP-VPN family route-target;
}}
routing-options {
    rib bgp.rtarget.0 {
        static {
            route-target-filter 65000:1001/64 group [iBGP-RR eBGP-VPN];
            route-target-filter 65000:1002/64 group [iBGP-RR eBGP-VPN];
            route-target-filter 65000:1003/64 group [iBGP-RR eBGP-VPN];
}}}
```

RTs 65000:1001, 65000:1002, and 65000:1003 are the global route targets of VPNs BLUE, GREEN, and RED, respectively.

Inter-AS Option B—IOS XR Configuration

PE2 and PE4 are configured the same as in Chapter 3, except for the AS number and the IP addressing. Let's look at the relevant configuration at ASBR4, shown in Example 9-9.

Example 9-9. Inter-AS Option B configuration—ASBR4 (IOS XR)

```
1    router bgp 65101
2     mpls activate
3      interface GigabitEthernet0/0/0/0
4      !
5     neighbor-group RR
6      remote-as 65101
7      update-source Loopback0
8      address-family vpnv4 unicast
9       next-hop-self
10     !
11      address-family vpnv6 unicast
12       next-hop-self
13     !
14     neighbor 10.0.1.2
15      remote-as 65100
16      update-source GigabitEthernet0/0/0/0
17      address-family vpnv4 unicast
18       route-policy PL-ALL in
19       route-policy PL-ALL out
20      !
21      address-family vpnv6 unicast
22       route-policy PL-ALL in
23       route-policy PL-ALL out
24      !
```

```
25      neighbor 172.16.10.203
26        use neighbor-group RR
27      !
28      neighbor 172.16.10.204
29        use neighbor-group RR
30      !
31      route-policy PL-ALL
32        pass
33      end-policy
34      !
35      router static
36      address-family ipv4 unicast
37        10.0.1.2/32 GigabitEthernet0/0/0/0
38      !
```

The next-hop-self knob (lines 9 and 12) in the sessions toward the RRs is an essential piece to make the solution work, and it was not present in the PE configuration.

Another significant piece of configuration is the static route in lines 35 through 37. Without it, the IP VPN routes stay unresolved in the CEF (show cef unresolved). This trick is similar to the Junos one in Example 9-6, except that IOS XR does not have auxiliary tables like inet.3 and inet6.3 in Junos, so the route copy is not an option.

Inter-AS Option B with Local VRF

Nothing prevents an Option B ASBR from being a PE itself and having its own local ACs. Actually, an ASBR can act in four different manners with respect to a given VPN:

- The VPN is extended to the remote AS and does not have local presence at the ASBR. This is the pure inter-AS Option B scenario that has been discussed so far in this chapter. The ASBR does *not* need to provision the corresponding VRF.

- The VPN is extended to the remote AS and also has local presence at the ASBR. The ASBR locally provisions the VRF and may have local ACs connected to CEs. The device acts like an ASBR/PE.

- The VPN is *not* extended to the remote AS. This VPN is instantiated in VRFs at different PEs of the local AS. The list of PEs includes the local ASBR, which behaves like a classical PE—not really an ASBR—with respect to this VPN.

- The VPN is neither locally present nor extended to the remote AS.

The suboption described in the second bullet item receives different names in the literature, depending on the vendor and the particular flavor: AB, AB+, A+B, D, E, and so on. This book uses the term "Option B with local VRF".

There are reasons to define a local VRF in the ASBR, even if there are no local CEs to connect. For example, a local VRF allows for route summarization.

Route summarization with local VRF—Junos

In the following example, a local VRF in ASBR3 is not connected to any CEs, but it is defined in order to summarize the 10.2.x.0/24 prefixes into 10.2.0.0/16. With the configuration shown in Example 9-10, only the summary route is advertised to ASBR1.

Example 9-10. Inter-AS Option B prefix aggregation—ASBR3 (Junos)

```
protocols {
    bgp {
        group iBGP-RR vpn-apply-export;
        group eBGP-VPN vpn-apply-export;
}}
routing-instances {
    VRF-BLUE {
        instance-type vrf;
        interface lo0.1001;
        route-distinguisher 172.16.10.103:101;
        vrf-target target:65000:1001;
        vrf-table-label;
        routing-options {
            aggregate route 10.2.0.0/16;
}}}
policy-options {
    policy-statement eBGP-65100-OUT {
        term VRF-BLUE-AGGREGATE {
            from {
                protocol aggregate;
                community RT-VPN-BLUE;
            }
            then accept;
        }
        term VRF-BLUE-IPv4-SPECIFIC {
            from {
                community RT-VPN-BLUE;
                route-filter 10.2.0.0/0 prefix-length-range /17-/32;
            }
            then reject;
        }
    }
    community RT-VPN-BLUE members [ target:65000:1001 ];
}
```

As discussed in Chapter 3, inter-AS Option B ASBRs behave as IP VPN RRs between iBGP and eBGP. When local VRFs are configured, don't forget the `vpn-apply-export` knob.

Some configuration bits have been skipped for brevity:

- The interface lo0.1001 configuration just contains an IPv4 address.
- The eBGP-65100-OUT policy may also have an additional term that you can find in Example 9-5.
- A policy to prevent the advertisement of the aggregate to RR3 and RR4 is needed. This is the reason why the iBGP-RR also has the `vpn-apply-export` knob.

Route summarization with local VRF—IOS XR

Example 9-11 achieves a similar result in ASBR4.

Example 9-11. Inter-AS Option B prefix aggregation—ASBR4 (IOS XR)

```
router bgp 65101
 vrf VRF-BLUE
  rd 172.16.0.104:101
  address-family ipv4 unicast
   aggregate-address 10.2.0.0/16
!
```

Again, some configuration bits have been skipped for brevity:

- The VRF-BLUE VRF and the loopback 1001 interface configuration.
- Two policies are needed: one to prevent the advertisement of more specific routes to ASBR2, and one more to filter out the aggregate toward RR3 and RR4.

Inter-AS Option B with local VRF—implementation details

In both Junos and IOS XR, when an Option B ASBR readvertises an IP VPN route, the original Route Distinguisher (RD) is maintained. There is no RD rewrite.

The same Route Target (RT) is typically used for every single site of a given VPN, regardless of the actual AS where the sites are.

In Junos, the same VPN label allocation mechanisms that were described in Chapter 3 apply here, too:

- The default mode is per-CE and it includes both local-AS and remote-AS CEs.

- When per-table (per-VRF) label allocation is selected, the same label is allocated to both locally originated and reflected prefixes. This triggers an IP lookup on the VRF for certain transit packets that otherwise would have been MPLS-switched. If, for certain non-aggregated prefixes, you wish to revert to MPLS forwarding of inter-AS transit traffic, you can use label allocation policies so that the IP lookup is only performed, for example, on local VRF destinations and aggregate routes.

 This book does not cover label allocation details in Option B ASBRs running IOS XR. These details are explained in Chapter 3 for regular PEs.

Finally, as far as routing tables in Junos are concerned, the internal implementation in RRs and in Option B ASBRs is very similar. At the end, the latter also perform service route reflection between eBGP and iBGP. Chapter 3 contains all the details.

Inter-AS Option C

As in Option B, Option C just requires one logical interface on each inter-AS link. However, the topmost MPLS label as the packet traverses the inter-AS link does not contain any VPN information. It is a pure transport label.

In Option C, ASBRs no longer need to keep IP VPN routing state—except for those VPNs where the ASBR acts like a local PE. This is a huge advantage in terms of scalability because the ASBR can act like a transit LSR with a smaller forwarding table.

If the ASBRs do not keep IP VPN routes, how are these advertised between ASs? The RRs of AS 65100 establish multihop eBGP sessions to the RRs of AS 65101 in order to exchange IP VPN prefixes. This means that certain IGP prefixes of one AS need to be reachable from the other AS. For example, the RR loopbacks need to be visible in both ASs, otherwise the inter-AS multihop eBGP sessions cannot be established.

Furthermore, the IP VPN routes keep the original BGP next-hop attribute and VPN label. There is no next-hop rewrite operation as there is in Option B. As a result, PEs must be able to resolve BGP next hops corresponding to the loopbacks of PEs in the remote AS. Again, this requires inter-AS visibility of PEs' loopback addresses.

There is a clean solution to achieve inter-AS loopback prefix visibility: BGP Labeled Unicast (BGP-LU). This protocol and its configuration are fully covered in Chapter 2.

The internal addresses of AS 65100 are not redistributed in AS 65101's IGP, and vice versa. All the inter-domain information is kept in BGP.

BGP Sessions in Inter-AS Option C

Figure 9-5 shows a first classification of the BGP flavors that are involved in this solution. The RRs in a box are actually a way to avoid too many arrows in the illustration. An arrow between PE1 and the box containing RR1 and RR2 actually represents two BGP sessions: PE1-RR1 and PE1-RR2. Inside each box, there is one session: RR1-RR2 on one box, and RR3-RR4 on the other. As for the arrow connecting the two boxes, it represents up to four BGP sessions: RR1-RR3, RR1-RR4, RR2-RR3, and RR2-RR4.

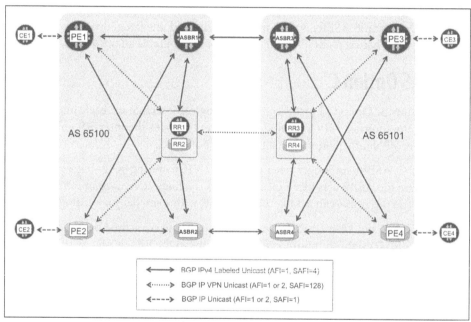

Figure 9-5. Inter-AS VPN Option C—BGP flavors

The RRs do *not* reflect BGP-LU prefixes. The only reason why they negotiate the IPv4-LU address family is for inter-AS RR reachability.

Here is the role of each address family in the solution:

IPv4 Labeled Unicast (AFI=1, SAFI=4)

BGP-LU is an infrastructure protocol. Indeed, its goal is to signal end-to-end LSPs. There are two types of BGP-LU sessions in this example: iBGP multihop (ASBR-RR and ASBR-PE) and eBGP single-hop (ASBR-ASBR). These sessions propagate labeled internal prefixes; namely, the loopback addresses of PEs and RRs. Due to the session layout, only ASBRs readvertise these routes. When they do so, ASBRs change the routes' BGP next hop: this triggers a new label allocation at the ASBR. A new set of LSPs is forming!

IPv4 or IPv6 VPN Unicast (AFI=1 or 2, SAFI=128)

In this context, BGP is a service signaling protocol. There are two types of BGP sessions that propagate IP VPN prefixes: iBGP multihop (PE-RR) and eBGP multihop (RR-RR). In this solution, the BGP next hop of the IP VPN routes is untouched. A route originated by PE3 and advertised all the way to PE1 keeps the original BGP next hop and VPN label values.

IPv4 or IPv6 Unicast (AFI=1 or 2, SAFI=1)

This is the BGP service protocol incarnation outside the MPLS world. These sessions are eBGP single-hop.

Inter-AS Option C—Signaling and Forwarding

Looking back at Figure 9-2, every AS has its own MPLS protocol. Again, let's assume that AS 65100 runs RSVP-TE and AS 65101 uses LDP.

Inter-AS Option C—signaling and forwarding—Junos plane

Figure 9-6 illustrates the life of a H1-BLUE→H3-BLUE packet as it traverses the two ASs in an inter-AS Option C solution.

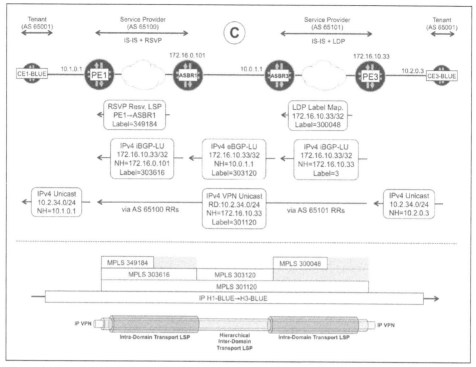

Figure 9-6. Inter-AS VPN Option C—signaling and forwarding

You can match the label values in Figure 9-6 with those in Example 9-12.

Example 9-12. Inter-AS Option C forwarding—Junos plane

```
RP/0/0/CPU0:H#traceroute vrf H1-BLUE 10.2.34.30

Type escape sequence to abort.
Tracing the route to 10.2.34.30

  1  10.1.12.1 0 msec  0 msec  0 msec
  2  10.1.0.1 0 msec  0 msec  0 msec
  3  10.0.0.3 [MPLS: Labels 349184/303616/301120 Exp 0] 29 msec [...]
  4  10.0.0.9 [MPLS: Labels 303616/301120 Exp 0] 19 msec [...]
  5  10.0.1.1 [MPLS: Labels 303120/301120 Exp 0] 9 msec [...]
  6  10.0.10.3 [MPLS: Labels 300048/301120 Exp 0] 209 msec [...]
  7  10.0.10.9 [MPLS: Label 301120 Exp 0] 149 msec [...]
  8  10.2.0.3 19 msec [...]
  9  10.2.34.30 19 msec [...]
```

Again, here is the "imaginary" life of the packet as it goes from CE1-BLUE to CE3-BLUE. It is imaginary because in reality the forwarding table is precomputed with all the instructions, so the control plane has already executed the complex recursive logic:

1. CE1-BLUE sends the packet to PE1, which receives it on VRF-BLUE's AC.

2. PE1 looks for a BGP IP VPN route in VRF-BLUE to the destination. It finds a route with a MPLS service label S0 (301120) and a BGP next hop equal to PE3's loopback address 172.16.10.33. This next hop cannot be resolved through a plain LSP.

3. PE1 tries to resolve the address 172.16.10.33 into a labeled path. It finds a BGP-LU prefix 172.16.10.33/32 with the following properties: BGP next hop 172.16.0.101 and label L1 (303616).

4. PE1 resolves 172.16.0.101 into a RSVP-TE LSP, whose first-hop transport label is T1 (349184). This LSP terminates at ASBR1.

5. PE1 pushes three labels, S0, L1, and T1, and sends the packet to P1.

6. P1 pops the T1 label and sends the packet to ASBR1.

7. ASBR1 looks at the L1 label, swaps it for L2 (303120), and sends the packet out of its ge-2/0/3.0 interface toward ASBR3.

8. ASBR3 receives the packet, looks at the L2 label, pops it, and pushes transport label T2 (300048). This label corresponds to a LDP LSP that terminates at PE3. ASBR3 programs the *pop-push* label operation as a simple *swap* instruction in the LFIB. ASBR3 sends the packet to P3.

9. P3 pops the T2 label and sends the packet to PE3.

10. PE3 looks at the S0 label, pops it, and sends the IP packet to CE3-BLUE.

As you can see, all of the elements in the path except for the ingress PE are plain LSRs. A hierarchical LSP takes the packet from PE1 to PE3, and only MPLS label operations take place at each hop.

Let's focus on the recursive next-hop logic that takes place at the ingress PE, shown in Example 9-13.

Example 9-13. Inter-AS Option C at ingress PE—PE1 (Junos)

```
1    juniper@PE1> show route receive-protocol bgp 172.16.0.201
2               table VRF-BLUE 10.2.34.0/24 detail
3
4    VRF-BLUE.inet.0: 6 destinations, 10 routes (6 active, ...)
5    * 10.2.34.0/24 (2 entries, 1 announced)
6        Import Accepted
7        Route Distinguisher: 172.16.10.33:101
8        VPN Label: 301120
9        Nexthop: 172.16.10.33
```

```
10          Localpref: 100
11          AS path: 65101 65001 I
12          Communities: target:65000:1001
13
1    juniper@PE1> show route receive-protocol bgp 172.16.0.101
2                172.16.10.33/32 detail
3
4    inet.3: 13 destinations, 15 routes (13 active, ...)
5    * 172.16.10.33/32 (1 entry, 1 announced)
6          Accepted
7          Route Label: 303616
8          Nexthop: 172.16.0.101
9          Localpref: 100
10         AS path: 65101 ?
11
12   juniper@PE1> show route table inet.3 172.16.0.101
13
14   inet.3: 13 destinations, 15 routes (13 active, ...)
15   + = Active Route, - = Last Active, * = Both
16
17   172.16.0.101/32    *[RSVP/7/1] 14:05:16, metric 20
18                       > to 10.0.0.3 via ge-2/0/4.0,
19                         label-switched-path PE1-->ASBR1
20
21   juniper@PE1> show rsvp session name PE1-->ASBR1
22   Ingress RSVP: 2 sessions
23   To              From          State    Labelout LSPname
24   172.16.0.101    172.16.0.11   Up         349184 PE1-->ASBR1
25
1    juniper@PE1> show route forwarding-table destination 10.2.34.0/24
2                table VRF-BLUE
3    Routing table: VRF-BLUE.inet
4    Internet:
5    Destination    Next hop
6    10.2.34.0/24   10.0.0.3  Push 301120, Push 303616, Push 349184(top)
7                   ge-2/0/4.0
```

As you can see, the control-plane logic is complex, but the forwarding-plane entry is very simple: just push three labels and send out of the ge-2/0/4.0 interface.

Inter-AS Option C—signaling and forwarding—IOS XR plane

The mechanics in IOS XR are very similar, so we will skip them here, for brevity. You can find examples of the relevant operational commands in Chapter 2 and Chapter 3.

Inter-AS Option C—Configuration

Inter-AS Option C is an intelligent combination of IP VPN and BGP-LU. These technologies have already been illustrated with configuration examples in Chapters Chapter 3 and Chapter 2, respectively. Rather than presenting the full configurations (which are quite long) the focus here is on the particularities of inter-AS Option C configuration with respect to the previous examples featuring IP VPN and BGP-LU.

Inter-AS Option C—P-router configuration

In this example, P-routers are totally unaware of BGP-LU and IP VPN. They just implement the intra-AS LSPs—based on LDP and RSVP-TE here. Therefore, inter-AS Option C does not require any special configuration on the P-routers. This is actually true for all the inter-AS flavors.

Inter-AS Option C—PE configuration

No special configuration is required in either Junos or IOS XR.

The BGP-LU example in Chapter 2 required a relatively complex community scheme to prevent labeled routes from being redistributed as unlabeled routes, and vice versa. This was due to the fact that IOS XR treats an IP prefix as one entity, regardless of whether it is encoded as IP Unicast (SAFI=1) or IP Labeled Unicast (SAFI=4). In that scenario, the service was global IP routing (SAFI=1).

Here, in inter-AS VPN, the service is IP VPN (SAFI=128). There is no risk of mixing BGP-LU (SAFI=4) with IP VPN (SAFI=128) routes, so the special community scheme from Chapter 2 is not required in this inter-AS Option C example.

iBGP is multihop by default, so no special care is required in that respect for iBGP-LU.

As for the iBGP sessions toward the RRs, they are IP VPN business as usual.

Just one note for Junos PEs: to resolve the BGP next hop of the IPv6 VPN routes, it is important to copy BGP-LU routes from `inet.3` to `inet6.3`, as demonstrated in Example 9-14.

Example 9-14. Copying routes from inet.3 to other tables—PE1 (Junos)

```
routing-options {
    rib-groups]
        RG-REMOTE-LOOPBACKS {
            import-rib [ inet.3 inet.0 inet6.3 ];
        }
}}
protocols {
    bgp {
        group iBGP-LU {
            family inet {
                labeled-unicast {
                    rib-group RG-REMOTE-LOOPBACKS;
                    rib inet.3;
}}}}}
```

With the previous configuration, the BGP-LU loopback routes are copied to two secondary tables:

`inet.0`

> This is optional because it is not required for the service to work. However, it is a good practice because it enables PE-to-PE IPv4 reachability and this is interesting from an operational perspective. Who doesn't want to run ping?

`inet6.3`

> This is essential for the IPv6 VPN service to work. For example, the prefix 172.16.10.33/32 from `inet.3` becomes ::ffff:172.16.10.33/128 when copied to `inet6.3`. This is precisely the next hop of the IPv6 VPN routes advertised by PE3.

Inter-AS Option C—RR configuration

In all of the previous IP VPN examples, RRs did not have MPLS enabled. They did not need MPLS, because they could establish iBGP sessions by exchanging plain IP packets.

Inter-AS Option C is different: RRs in different ASs can only reach each other through a hierarchical LSP, as shown in Figure 9-7.

You can match the label values in Figure 9-7 with those in Example 9-15.

Example 9-15. Inter-AS Option C—inter-RR reachability

```
juniper@RR1> traceroute 172.16.10.203 source 172.16.0.201

 1  10.0.0.16 (10.0.0.16)  59.155 ms  98.086 ms  91.264 ms
    MPLS Label=349264 CoS=0 TTL=1 S=0
    MPLS Label=303664 CoS=0 TTL=1 S=1
 2  10.0.0.9 (10.0.0.9)  89.668 ms  411.857 ms  11.368 ms
    MPLS Label=303664 CoS=0 TTL=1 S=1
 3  10.0.1.1 (10.0.1.1)  45.761 ms  90.310 ms  122.391 ms
    MPLS Label=303152 CoS=0 TTL=1 S=1
 4  10.0.10.3 (10.0.10.3)  9.407 ms  12.204 ms  11.089 ms
    MPLS Label=300128 CoS=0 TTL=1 S=1
 5  172.16.10.203 (172.16.10.203)  12.576 ms  13.402 ms  6.773 ms
```

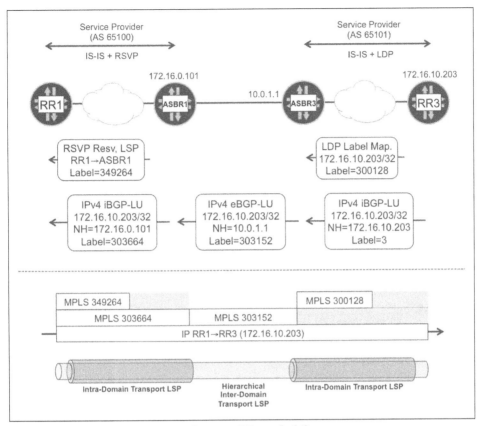

Figure 9-7. Inter-AS VPN Option C—inter-RR reachability

This means that the RRs need to be fully integrated with the intra-domain MPLS protocols (LDP, RSVP-TE, etc.). As long as the IS-IS overload bit—or very high metrics in OSPF—is set on the RRs, there is no risk of attracting transit traffic toward them.

Let's suppose that the RRs only reflect VPN routes and they do not need reflect Internet (IP Unicast, SAFI=1) routes. Because RRs must not forward actual transit traffic, they do not require BGP-LU routes in `inet.3` table, which is used for next-hop resolution of BGP labeled services. For this reason, it is perfectly fine to install iBGP-LU routes only into the `inet.0` routing table at the Junos RRs. You can achieve that by configuring the iBGP-LU group with `family inet labeled-unicast` and no explicit RIB. In this way, there is no need to leak routes between `inet.0` and `inet.3` at the Junos RRs.

This solution is not valid if the RRs also reflect Internet routes. Check Chapter 2 for the full story.

As for IP VPN itself, here are some tips to configure (at the local AS' RRs) the BGP group containing the remote AS' RRs:

- In Junos RRs, configure `multihop no-nexthop-change`.
- Configure RRs running IOS XR according to Example 9-16.

Example 9-16. eBGP multihop configuration—RR2 (IOS XR)

```
route-policy PL-ALL
 pass
end-policy
!
router bgp 65100
 neighbor-group eBGP-RR-65101
  remote-as 65101
  ebgp-multihop 255
  update-source Loopback0
  address-family vpnv4 unicast
   route-policy PL-ALL in
   route-policy PL-ALL out
   next-hop-unchanged
  !
  address-family vpnv6 unicast
   route-policy PL-ALL in
   route-policy PL-ALL out
   next-hop-unchanged
!
```

Inter-AS Option C—ASBR configuration

Option C ASBRs do not handle IP VPN routes, so you only need to take care of BGP-LU.

In Junos, the `family inet labeled-unicast rib inet.3` is specified in both the iBGP-LU and the eBGP-LU group configuration, as expected.

In IOS XR, remember that you need to do the following:

- Configure static host routes on the inter-AS link; this is to avoid unresolved CEF entries.

- Under the iBGP-LU neighbor group configuration, set `address-family ipv4 labeled-unicast next-hop-self`.
- Manually apply permissive import (in) and export (out) policies to the eBGP-LU group or use `unsafe-ebgp-policy` to apply dynamically created policies allowing everything.

Carrier Supporting Carrier

Is MPLS a complex technology? It really depends on how far you want to stretch it. Carrier Supporting Carrier (CsC), also known as Carrier-of-Carriers, is quite a stretch.

The previous inter-AS options consider each AS equally important. AS 65100 and AS 65101 peer with each other without any hierarchical relationship. On the other hand, CsC defines a hierarchical relationship between the involved ASs.

When a service provider (or an enterprise) wants to provision its own MPLS VPN services, it needs an MPLS backbone. Now, suppose that it does not have a WAN. This SP needs to purchase transport services to yet another SP or carrier.

 In this section, the *SP* term is kept for the company in need for a WAN. The WAN infrastructure provider is referred to as a Transport Provider.

Nowadays, SPs in need of a WAN typically request L2 services to the Transport Provider: *just give me a transparent wire and I will pass my MPLS frames through it.*

However, this is not always an option, so the SP might need to purchase L3 services to the Transport Provider. Unless the SP establishes IP tunnels between its remote PEs—which is a non-scalable approach—a solution such as CsC is required (see Figure 9-8). Some people consider CsC as MPLS at its best. However, it is complex and this book does not cover it in detail.

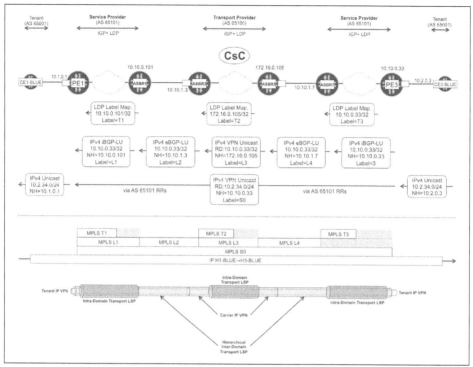

Figure 9-8. Carrier Supporting Carrier (CsC)

If you *really* want to understand Figure 9-8, keep in mind the following:

- From the point of view of the Transport Provider, the SP is just a customer. The Transport Provider uses a VRF to peer with the SP's global routing.

- The P-routers of the Transport Provider core have no awareness of the SP's infrastructure addresses.

- ASBR3 and ASBR5 have a dual ASBR/PE role: they are PEs from the point of view of the Transport Provider, and ASBRs from the point of view of the SP.

- ASBR1 and ASBR7 have a dual ASBR/CE role: they are CEs from the point of view of the Transport Provider, and Option C ASBRs from the point of view of the SP.

- PE1 and PE3 are PEs from the point of view of the SP. For the Transport Provider, they are simply *behind the CEs*.

- eBGP-LU is the PE-CE protocol on the Transport Provider VRF. For that reason, the SP's eBGP-LU labels are stitched to the Transport Provider's IP VPN labels.

Inter-Domain RSVP-TE LSPs

Let's get back to inter-AS—no hierarchy between ASs—and look at Figure 9-2:

- The inter-AS Option C model establishes hierarchical LSPs. This is a great option if you do *not* want to leak AS1's IGP prefixes into AS2's IGP, or vice versa. Actually, reciprocal IGP prefix leaking is a very bad idea. Inter-AS Option C is the most scalable of all the inter-AS models because it does not rely on such leaking and also relieves the ASBRs from keeping VPN routes.

- In contrast, the inter-AS model that Figure 9-2 calls Option X establishes flat LSPs. What for? There is one application for that: establishing inter-domain RSVP-TE LSPs, which are not fully covered in this book.

Inter-area RSVP-TE is briefly discussed in Chapter 2. The challenges in inter-AS topologies are very similar. In general, inter-domain RSVP-TE is a good fit for a new BGP address family, called BGP-LS (Link State) or BGP-TE (Traffic Engineering). However, the main application of this address family is different: propagating the Traffic Engineering Database, or TED, to a northbound external controller. This topic is fully covered in Chapter 15.

## CHAPTER 10

Underlay and Overlay Architectures

Software-Defined Networking (SDN) is an umbrella concept that means many things —probably, too many things. Depending on whom you ask, you will hear a completely different definition of what SDN is. Every new solution is wrapped with the SDN-ready mention and every new project is immediately overvalued when one says *we will do it with SDN*.

To separate hype from reality, it is very important to know precisely what we are talking about. Two key ideas, *overlay* and *underlay*, are at the center of the discussion and are often treated very lightly. They happen to be very complex concepts, with many derivatives, gray areas, and nuances. And, most important, they have a long history. Paraphrasing Martin Luther King Jr.: *history is a great teacher*. Ignoring it is a sure recipe for reinventing the wheel or, even worse, resurrecting architectures that have already been seen to fail repeatedly in the past.

The centralized and distributed control-plane dilemma is an old one. Phrases such as "centralize what you can, distribute what you must" have been told so many times and belong to the culture of good-old network engineers.

Here is the structure of this chapter:

- Introduction to the overlay and underlay concepts
- Architecture of multiforwarder network devices
- Discussion of the challenges of legacy data center networking and the need for an overlay
- Architecture of IP fabrics, with a distributed or centralized control plane
- Architecture of overlays in the data center

This chapter's conductive wire is analogy. If you understand well how a *big* network device is built inside, you will easily understand the architectural challenges of designing a data center underlay and overlay. If it sounds strange, keep reading.

Overlays and Underlays

If you are a networking professional, you might have already encountered some difficulties in explaining your job to people outside the industry. For them, the Internet *just works*. Their laptops or mobile phones simply exchange IP packets with other end devices, which are typically very, very far away. These packets go hop by hop through an amazing series of transformations—light through fibers, electrical signals on wires, microwaves through the air—but this *underlay* is completely transparent for the user.

The Internet is the most archetypical example of an *overlay*, and its magic is in the IP header. If a group of bytes generated by an application gets an IP header on top, suddenly the resulting data unit—an *IP packet*—is placed in an overlay that seamlessly takes it to the destination. Headers can act as "tickets" to enter an overlay network.

VPNs are also a classic family of overlays. As discussed in Chapter 3 through Chapter 8, Layer 2 VPN (L2VPN) and Layer 3 VPN (L3VPN) look from the point of view of the end customer like an L2 bridge or a L3 router, respectively. The hop-by-hop and multiheader encapsulations are transparent to the end customer devices, which might not have any visibility of the underlying signaling and transport mechanisms.

Overlay and Underlay Are Relative Concepts

Let's step back from data centers for a moment and discuss a quite baroque example that illustrates the relativity of overlay and underlay concepts.

Imagine a customer that builds a private WAN by connecting its geographically distant sites with a set of Virtual Private Wire Service (VPWS) purchased from a service provider (SP). These VPWS emulate WAN links, which the customer can use in turn to build its own MPLS core. Then, on top of this MPLS core, the customer runs its own L3VPN services.

If you sniff one such packet transiting an SP link, you might see something as *nested* as the following: IP over MPLS over MPLS over Ethernet over MPLS over MPLS over Ethernet! So many headers actually compose a stack where the *up* and *down* concepts are relative to one another. Although this is quite a complex example, CEs connected to the customer's PEs use an L3VPN overlay, whose underlay is the customer's MPLS core. In turn, each customer's MPLS core link actually uses an overlay (VPWS) whose underlay is the multihop SP core.

Not to mention the additional tunneling that packets undergo *inside* network devices.

Fortunately, a typical data center scenario is not that nested. But its actual complexity is not very far from that example. Beware of *it just works because it's an overlay* explanations. If it works, there is a reason and, most important, an underlying mechanism.

Other Fundamental Concepts

Here are some additional terms that are very common, so it's good to define them at least once in this book.

First, there are two ways to scale a network infrastructure:

Scale up
> Deploying *more powerful* network devices and raising the throughput of network links (e.g., from 10M Ethernet to 100G Ethernet or beyond).

Scale out
> Deploying *more devices* and network links.

Changing topics, in the figures that follow you will see a compass with its four points:

- In the *control plane*, North and South determine hierarchical relationships: typically, an element in the North has control over an element in the South. Conversely, East and West are relationships between equals (e.g., an eBGP session).
- In the *forwarding plane*, North and South typically indicate a bandwidth hierarchy. Elements in the South are closer to the edge, have lower bandwidth, and implement customer-facing features. They rely on the higher-capacity elements in the North to exchange traffic with each other; and to reach the rest of the world.

Now, let's mix both concepts: when you scale-out an infrastructure (control or forwarding), the growth direction is West-East. This is *horizontal* scaling.

Multiforwarder Network Devices

Let's have a look at the inside of a physical high-end single-chassis network device.

A given multicomponent router such as a Juniper MX/PTX or a Cisco ASR/CRS, just to name a few examples, is actually *a network on its own*. Or, more strictly, two networks: the forwarding plane and the control plane. You can view the different functional components (CPUs, ASICs) in a physical router as different devices interconnected to one another. They just are *packaged together* with some degree of modularity. Like parts of a body, they don't live independently; they are different interconnected entities.

Single-Chassis Network Devices—Forwarding Plane

Figure 10-1 provides a simplified view of the forwarding plane *inside* a multicomponent router, or switch, or firewall, and so on.

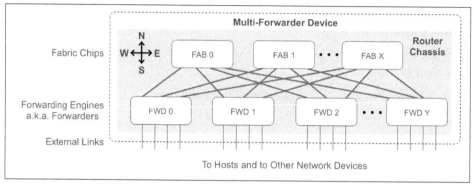

Figure 10-1. Single-chassis multiforwarder network device—forwarding plane

The forwarding plane of a multicomponent network device is composed of three types of elements:

Forwarding engines

These handle traffic coming from and going out to the outside world. They are responsible for route/label/flow lookup and for all the externally visible forwarding-plane features: packet header manipulation, classification, scheduling, policing, rewrite, replication, filtering, accounting, fine-grained traffic steering, mirroring, sampling, unicast and multicast RPF checks, class-based forwarding, and many others. A line card typically contains one or more forwarders, which in turn are composed of one or more application-specific integrated circuits (ASICs) and/or network processors. The generic term *forwarding engine* is like an umbrella for many different vendor-specific terms. For example, Juniper calls it a Packet Forwarding Engine (PFE), and Cisco uses different names for each platform: CRS have Packet Switching Engines (PSE) and ASR has Network Processing Units (NPU). Actually, the latter name is also used by Juniper for certain packet processors, too. For simplicity, let's use the shorter term *forwarder* to designate a forwarding engine.

The fabric

A network device can scale up by using more powerful forwarders, which are typically shipped in newer generation line cards. It also can scale out by having *more* forwarders. When a device has multiple forwarders, it needs a fabric to interconnect them. Fabrics are much simpler than forwarders: they just know how to move data units from an ingress/source forwarder to an egress/destination forwarder. Conceptually, fabric chips are similar to Asynchronous Transfer

Mode (ATM)—or, why not, MPLS—switches that implement a full mesh of virtual circuits among all the forwarders in a given device; their forwarding state contains just a few destinations.

Links

Like in any network, the device's components are linked together. In this example, the physical connections are instantiated via high-speed links at the midplane: don't look for the cables!

What does this have to do with *real* networks and with data centers? Well, this internal network has feature-rich edge components (the forwarding engines) and simple core components (the fabric). Now we are talking! Let's move on with the analogy.

Suppose that the forwarder FWD_0 in Figure 10-1 receives a packet from the outside world. FWD_0 looks at the packet headers and performs a lookup whose result is: *send the packet out of port X that is anchored to FWD_2*. FWD_0 adds a new header to the packet—which may be previously fragmented, but that's another story. This header simply says, *take me to FWD_2*. Then, it sends the packet to the fabric, using a load-balancing algorithm to distribute the data across the fabric chips (FAB_0, FAB_1 up to FAB_X).

Thanks to this extra (tunnel) header, the fabric can switch the packet to FWD_2 without looking at the packet's content. When it receives the packet from the fabric, FWD_2 removes the extra header and forwards the packet out of port X toward its destination.

Wait, isn't this tunneling? Indeed, it *is* tunneling inside the router! True, this tunneling is transparent to the outside world. But packets can flow inside a multicomponent network device, simply because the edge components (forwarders) use an overlay based on a tunneling header that steers the packets through the fabric underlay.

Forwarding engines inside a network device use an overlay to exchange packets with one another. The fabric acts like a *dummy* underlay. Fabric chips are not capable of doing a real forwarding lookup: they need a header that points to a destination forwarder.

Single-Chassis Network Devices—Control Plane

As in the case of the forwarding plane, let's use the powerful analogy between a multicomponent single-chassis network device and a multidevice network.

Remember that there are two networks inside a network device: the forwarding plane and the control plane. It's time to have a look inside the control plane.

Although the general architecture is similar for all vendors, the details of the following example are inspired on a Juniper MX—for example, not all vendors use a TCP/IP stack for the internal control plane.

Figure 10-2 represents one single MX chassis. Rectangular components act like hosts from the point of view of the control plane's internal network. The Ethernet Bridges, represented with rounded corners, switch internal and external control packets as described here:

- Internal control packets are *natively* exchanged between internal hosts through the internal Ethernet Bridges.

- External control packets are actually coming from, or destined to, the outside world. When a Controller processes external control packets, these are *tunneled* through the Ethernet Bridges between the Controller and the Control Agent(s).

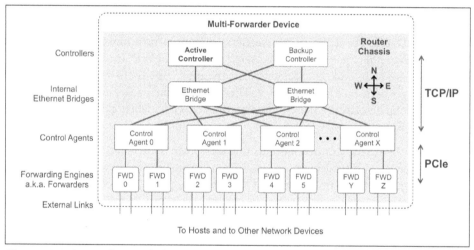

Figure 10-2. Internal control plane in a Juniper MX

At first sight, this topology might remind you of a fabric, but it is not. The topmost elements in a fabric are (spine) switches. Here, they are hosts. And control-plane links have a lower bandwidth than fabric links.

Controller is a generic term for the *software* that computes all the forwarding rules of the device. This software typically runs on a pair of boards—active and backup—with varied vendor-specific names such as Juniper Routing Engine (RE), Cisco CRS Route Processor (RP), or Cisco ASR Route Switch Processor (RSP). These boards contain multipurpose CPUs that execute the Controller code. Among their many tasks, Controllers are responsible for pushing a forwarding table to Control Agents.

Junos uses the term Master as an equivalent to Active in an Active-Backup control plane. This is a horizontal relationship. In this book, the term Master is reserved for a different concept: a hierarchical relationship between two Controllers.

Control Agents are also pieces of software that run in less powerful CPUs, typically located in line cards. These are responsible, among other tasks, for translating the high-level instructions received from Controllers into low-level hardware-specific instructions that are optimized and adapted to forwarding ASICs.

Software? Yes, this type of (internal) Networking is *also* Software-Defined!

Single-chassis network devices—internal control traffic

For the Controllers to send instructions to Control Agents, and for the Control Agents to report events and statistics to Controllers, they need a communication infrastructure: indeed, internal Ethernet Bridges that physically interconnect them.

Every internal host has a MAC address (derived from its physical location) and an IPv4 address. For example, in Junos, the master RE has IPv4 address 128.0.0.1 and line cards have IPv4 address 128.0.0.16+<slot_number>. These addresses reside in a hidden private routing table called __juniper_private1__, whose purpose is to exchange data between Controllers and Control Agents (and also between the Active and Backup Controllers). These addresses are not visible from the outside.

When a Control Agent boots, it gets from the Active Controller via BOOTP (over UDP) both an IPv4 address and the name of the software image, and then it gets the image itself via TFTP (over UDP). After booting, Control Agents establish TCP sessions with Controllers. Controllers use these sessions to send a forwarding table, filter attachments and definitions, class of service structures, and so on to the Control Agents. On the other hand, Control Agents send events and statistics to Controllers via these TCP sessions, too.

Finally, Control Agents adapt the forwarding instruction set to a format that is understandable by the Forwarding Engine ASICs. This is typically a complex layered process with two main stages: a hardware-agnostic stage called Hardware Adaptation Layer (HAL) in Junos, and a hardware-specific layer that depends on the actual chipset in the Forwarding Engine. The resulting microcode instructions and structures are programmed into the ASICs by using a mechanism such as Peripheral Component Interconnect Express (PCIe). Chapter 12 compares this architecture—based on purpose-built ASICs that have a special instruction set used for networking—with the multipurpose x86 architecture, for which only the software (OS or controller) knows that this is a networking device, but the hardware is "dumb."

Single-chassis multiforwarder devices—external control traffic

So far, we have very briefly seen how the internal control plane works. But a network device needs to exchange control packets with the outside world, too. If a router does not learn routes from the outside, it cannot even compute a useful forwarding table!

Figure 10-3 shows how two adjacent MX routers (CE1 and PE1) exchange an eBGP update. The gray header fields only live in the internal control network, so they cannot be captured with an inline sniffer at the CE1-PE1 link. As for the external MAC header MAC_A→MAC_B, it is surrounded by a dotted line in the internal path because it is not always present. For example, in MX, CE1's Active Controller builds the packet with that header, which goes on the wire, and PE1 strips the header before sending the packet up to its local Active Controller.

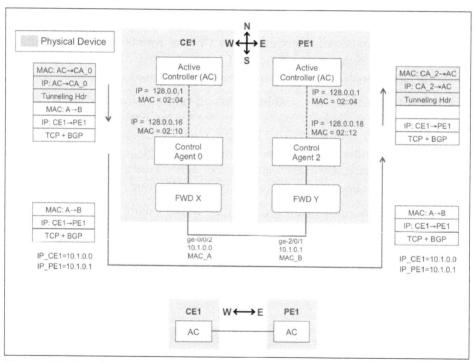

Figure 10-3. Distributed control plane between two Juniper MX devices

It is important to note that the control plane relies on the forwarding plane. Let's focus on the most interesting aspect: the ingress path at PE1. When the packet arrives to FWD_Y at PE1, a route lookup occurs. The result of this lookup is: *the destination is a local IPv4 address; send it up to the control plane.* So, the Forwarding Engine hands the packet to the Control Agent on which it depends. The Control Agent adds a Generic Routing Encapsulation (GRE)-like header (the actual protocol used in Juniper devices is called TTP, but it is very similar to GRE).

The resulting packet has two IPv4 headers:

- An external IPv4 header, from the Control Agent at line card slot #2 (128.0.0.18 = 128.0.0.16+<*slot_number*>) to the Active Controller (128.0.0.1). Thanks to this header, the packet arrives to PE1's Active Controller, which removes the tunneling headers and processes the original BGP (CE1→PE1) packet.

- An internal IPv4 header with the configured—externally visible—addresses at the CE1-PE1 link (10.1.0.0 → 10.1.0.1).

The model represented in Figure 10-3 also applies to the exchange of other one-hop control packets like those used by link-state protocols (OSPF, IS-IS, etc.).

Things become a bit more interesting when the control packet follows an external multihop path, such as that shown in Figure 10-4. Although the examples in previous chapters included a Route Reflector (RR), this implies a hierarchy that makes things more confusing for an initial multihop example. So let's consider a flat multihop iBGP session between PE1 and PE3 loopback addresses. The original physical interfaces started with ge-2/0/x, so they all belonged to the same forwarder. These numbers have been changed in order to make the example more interesting.

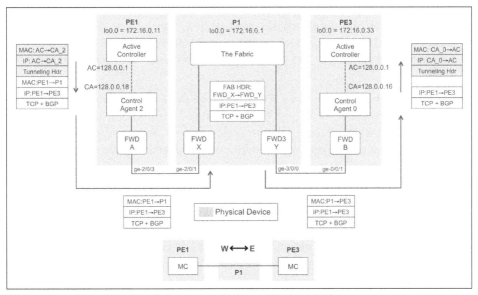

Figure 10-4. Distributed multihop control plane—Juniper MX

From the point of view of P1, the PE1→PE3 iBGP update is *not* a control packet; it is a transit packet. This raises an important paradigm of modern networking:

- The control plane does not process the vast majority of the packets that transit a network device. Instead, transit traffic typically uses the high-speed links of the forwarding plane.
- Only control and exception packets (e.g., IPv4 packets with an expired Time-to-Live [TTL], or with options in their headers) are "punted" to the control plane, bypassing the fabric. The gates between both worlds are the medium-speed links between Control Agents and Forwarders.

 Even if an internal Ethernet Bridge may coexist in the same physical cards with Fabric Chips, they are all different functional components. Internal Ethernet Bridges are *not* part of the fabric.

When P1 receives the BGP update, it does not find anything exceptional: TTL is fine, no IP options, and the destination is out of FWD_Y. So, the packet bypasses the control plane. There are at least a couple of scenarios in which things would have been different:

- If the packet had TTL expired due to IP forwarding. After passing a hierarchical anti-DDoS rate limiter, the packet reaches the Control Agent. This, in turn, generates an ICMP message back to the original packet's source informing of the TTL expired condition. The Controller is not bothered for simple tasks like this one.
- If the packet had IP Options. This would be the case of a non-bundled RSVP PE1→PE3 packet. Even though the destination IP address of such packets is the remote PE, they need to be fully processed, hop by hop, involving all the Active Controllers in the path. As a result, these packets typically do not transit the fabric.

As you can see, a simple PE1→PE3 BGP packet actually undergoes three stages of tunneling: two at internal control-plane networks (PE1 and PE3) and one at a forwarding-plane internal network (P1). This example is adequate to illustrate the relativity of the overlay and underlay concepts. P1 is an underlay from the point of view of the PE1→PE3 BGP update. But P1's forwarding plane is an overlay built over its underlying fabric.

A very important piece of Figure 10-4 is the simplified diagram at the bottom. Despite all the internal complexity, PE1 and PE3 establish a West-East control peering for which all the internal and external forwarding components are simply an underlay. Many of this chapter's figures use such an abstraction. Although it is essential to understand the details, there is no need to recall them over and over.

Multichassis Network Devices

One way to scale the forwarding plane of a network device is to use a single control plane to manage several chassis at the same time. The result is often called a *virtual chassis*. It is virtualization by fusion (several physical devices become one virtual device) rather than fission (one physical server runs several virtual machines [VMs], or one router instantiates several VRFs).

Here is one possible coarse classification of virtual-chassis architectures, from the point of view of the forwarding plane:

- The fabric is implemented by certain physical devices whose forwarding plane only performs this function. These are dedicated chassis with fabric-only links. They look different and, in fact, are different from the line-card chassis that contain both the forwarding engines and the external facing interfaces. This architecture is beyond the scope of this book.

- The fabric is implemented by physical devices that could be used as standalone network devices, as well. This architecture will be discussed later.

Let's zoom out for a moment and take a broader look at data centers. The analogy between multiforwarder (or multichassis) devices and data center networks will naturally unfold.

Legacy Data Center Networking

The previous discussion provides very powerful analogies to data center networking. But it's important to provide some context before explaining the analogies.

The Challenges of L2 Bridged Networks

In the early days of the Internet, public and private data centers consisted of physical servers connected to legacy L2 bridged networks. And this is still the case in many small and medium-sized data centers and countless private enterprise networks.

Over time, compute virtualization has become more and more popular with the universal adoption of applications running on VMs or containers. There's no doubt: virtualization is cool, but in the legacy L2 connectivity model, hypervisors are still connected via VLAN trunks to the physical underlay. This takes a huge toll.

Revolution against the VLAN tyranny

In a legacy L2 bridged network, traffic segmentation is achieved by VLANs. Every time that a new server is deployed, its Network Interface Cards (NICs) typically obtain static or dynamic IP addresses. These addresses cannot be freely assigned; they belong to IP subnets, which in turn are rigidly coupled to VLANs. These VLANs must be *provisioned all the way* from the server (or hypervisor) through the broadcast domain—spanning L2 bridges—to all the host and router interfaces in the VLAN. The result is a monolithic paradigm in which the service and the applications are intimately associated to the network underlay. Despite all the possible attempts to automate and orchestrate this process, in practice the IT staff must coordinate service deployment with the network team; this clearly interferes with business agility.

VLANs were initially proposed as a broadcast containment mechanism. The NICs for end systems are in promiscuous mode for broadcast, so the system performance would be much more affected by broadcasts without VLANs.

Then, the VLAN became a service delimiter mechanism: department isolation, service A versus service B, or customer 1, 2, 3.

As a result, the VLAN tag has two interpretations:

- It is a (multipoint) circuit identifier at the L2 network infrastructure level.
- It is a multiplexer for edge devices (hosts, hypervisors, and routers); at the edge, a VLAN is conceptually linked to an L3 network, and it acts like a tenant or a service identifier.

Divide and conquer is a general rule for workable solutions, and a VLAN means too many things. In contrast, modern data center architectures completely decouple the service from the transport; regardless of whether the multiplexing object is an MPLS service label, or a Virtual eXtensible LAN (VXLAN) Network Identifier (VNI), or something else, it is only meaningful for edge devices.

> Edge devices in a modern data center must use a multiplexing technique that is *decoupled* from the underlying infrastructure. In other words, they must use an overlay.

One additional limitation imposed by VLANs is the creation of deployment silos. Imagine that the data center network is composed of an L3 core interconnecting L2 islands. If a legacy application requires L2 connectivity, the application is constrained to just one island. The introduction of an overlay breaks this barrier by allowing any-to-any connectivity.

Oh, yes, and the VLAN ID is just a 12-bit field, so only 4,095 values are available. This is often mentioned as the main reason to use an overlay instead of VLANs. Although it is an important point indeed, there are more compelling reasons to move away from VLANs.

Bandwidth scaling

As mentioned earlier, there are two ways to grow a network: scale up and scale out.

The scale-up approach is limited and very often must be combined with scale out. On the other hand, more network devices and links typically results in a meshed topology full of loops. With an L2 bridged underlay, this is a no-go: Spanning Tree would block most of the redundant links, resulting in a degraded topology. This is one of the main reasons why the underlay in a modern data center must be L3.

Control-plane scaling

L2 bridges typically have a limit on the number of MAC addresses that they can learn—when this limit is reached, the bridge floods frames destined for the new MAC addresses. Core bridges need to learn all the MACs, and this creates a serious scalability issue.

If in order to ease provisioning you configure all the VLANs on hypervisor ports, broadcast significantly loads the control plane in the hypervisor stack.

Network stability and resiliency

Redundant topologies are always looped and, if the underlay is L2 Ethernet, loop avoidance relies on Spanning Tree, which is probably the scariest and most fragile control protocol suite. The broadcast storm beast has been responsible for so many network meltdowns throughout networking history. Simply stated, a broadcast domain is a single point of failure. This is probably the most important reason to claim that *L2 bridging is legacy*.

Underlays in Modern Data Centers

In a data center, the underlay is a set of interconnected network devices that provide data transport between (physical or virtual) computing systems. You can view this underlay as a core inconnecting edge devices. These edge devices—called here *edge forwarders* or *VPN forwarders*—are functionally equivalent to PEs and are responsible for implementing the overlay.

Due to the numerous challenges that L2 bridged networks face, an underlay in a modern data center *must* be based on L3, pretty much like an SP core underlay.

Oh, some applications require L2 connectivity? In reality, the majority of the applications work perfectly well over L3 (in multihop connections). Technologies such as

VM mobility, which traditionally relied on L2, are beginning to support L3, as well. However, many data centers still run applications that require L2 connectivity. Sometimes, data center administrators might not know what particular application has this requirement, but still they decide to prepare their infrastructure for that eventuality. Anyway, when L2 connectivity is needed, it is handled by the overlay. The underlay can definitely remain L3:

- Network devices build an IP core that is typically modeled as an IP fabric (soon to be explained). IP control plane provides great resiliency and multipath capabilities.

- In large-scale data centers, the underlay core typically supports *native* MPLS transport, because MPLS is the only technology that provides the required level of scaling and features required by the most demanding and scalable data centers. Over time, MPLS may be progressively adopted by lower-scale data centers, too.

Overlays in Modern Data Centers

Depending on the logic implemented by an edge device, the overlay can be L3 or L2 (see Figure 10-5). In an analogy to the concepts already covered in previous chapters, these overlays are similar to L3VPNs or L2VPNs.

	L3 Overlays			L2 Overlays			
Underlay One-Hop L2	Ethernet	Ethernet	Ethernet	Ethernet	Ethernet	Ethernet	Ethernet
Underlay Multi-Hop L3	IP	IP	MPLS	IP	IP	IP	MPLS
Overlay Tunnel	GRE	UDP		UDP	GRE	UDP	
Overlay Multiplexer	MPLS	MPLS	MPLS	VXLAN	MPLS	MPLS	MPLS
Encapsulated Tenant Data	IP	IP	IP	Ethernet	Ethernet	Ethernet	Ethernet
	L4-L7	L4-L7	L4-L7	L3-L7	L3-L7	L3-L7	L3-L7
	MPLSoGRE	MPLSoUDP	MPLSoMPLS	VXLAN	MPLSoGRE	MPLSoUDP	MPLSoMPLS

Figure 10-5. L3 and L2 overlays

Remember that this book represents frames following the MPLS convention: the upper label is also the outer label. In X over Y, X is actually represented below Y. The wire is on top of the representation.

There are many types of overlay encapsulations available and implemented.

First, here are three MPLS-over-*X* flavors that are capable of encapsulating both L2 and L3:

- MPLS-over-GRE encodes a MPLS packet inside the GRE payload.

- MPLS-over-UDP encodes a MPLS packet inside the UDP payload. The variable values of the source and destination ports in the UDP header makes it a more suitable solution for hashing and load balancing than the less feature-rich original GRE header. However, as of this writing, most network devices do not yet support it.

- MPLS-over-MPLS is just MPLS VPN as usual. It requires an MPLS-capable underlay.

Next, here are some examples of IP-over-IP tunnels with a multiplexing header:

- VXLAN is similar to MPLS-over-UDP except that the MPLS label is replaced with a field that gets a different name (VXLAN Network Identifier [VNI]). As of this writing, it is only capable of encapsulating L2 frames because it lacks a control plane for L3.

- Network Virtualization using GRE (NVGRE) is similar to VXLAN, just that it uses an enhanced GRE header with a multiplexing key instead of VXLAN over UDP. The principle is the same. This is not covered in this book.

- STT (Stateless Transport Tunneling) uses a TCP-like header but it does *not* use the TCP logic: it is stateless. The only advantage is the possibility to reuse the TCP offload implementations in host operating system (OS) kernels. This, too, is not covered in this book.

- Other encapsulations such as Geneve, IEEE 802.1BR, and the next one round the corner.

The actual encapsulation is an implementation detail. What matters are the structural model, the control plane, and the possibility of *stacking*. From an efficiency perspective, nothing beats a 4-byte stackable header like MPLS. Other overlay encapsulations are available if, for whatever reasons (be they technical or not), MPLS is not desired. Anyway, even if the on-the-wire packet does not have any MPLS headers, the structural model of any overlay is still MPLS-like. This is the spinal chord of the MPLS paradigm. Deep innovation comes with new structural models and not with new encapsulations.

Except for MPLS-over-MPLS, all the listed encapsulations work perfectly well over plain IP networks. VXLAN is a widely adopted L2 overlay in small to medium-sized data centers. Conversely, large-scale data centers typically rely on a native MPLS encapsulation with an MPLS-capable kernel network stack at the servers' OS.

Remember that VXLAN implements the overlay by embedding a VNI in a transport IP tunnel. The VNI is a multiplexer and its role is similar to a service MPLS label.

Chapter 8 already covers VXLAN, including its forwarding plane and an example of a control plane (Ethernet VPN [EVPN]).

Multiplexer fields such as MPLS service labels and VNIs are only significant to edge forwarders. They do not create any state in core or IP fabric devices.

Let's add a cautionary note about L2 overlays: if an application requires L2 connectivity between end systems in geographically distant data centers, it is possible to stretch the L2 overlay across the WAN. This service is known as Data Center Interconnection (DCI), and you can read more about it in Chapter 8. True, stretching L2 overlays across geographical boundaries might be required by legacy applications, but this does not make it a good practice: it is a remedy. The good practice is to reduce as much as possible the scope of L2 broadcast domains. Even L2 overlays have the risk of loops.

Data Center Underlays—Fabrics

IP fabrics (and MPLS fabrics) have become a de facto underlay in modern data centers. These fabrics are typically composed of many network devices. There is a powerful analogy between a multicomponent device and a multidevice network. Many of the challenges (and solutions) proposed for modern multidevice data center underlays were already addressed, in the context of multicomponent devices, by networking vendors. Of course, the momentum created by the evolution of data center networking has certainly opened new horizons and accelerated the development of more powerful paradigms. But the foundations were already there for decades.

High-scale data centers are evolving toward MPLS fabrics. Indeed, their servers implement a lightweight MPLS stack. The architectural IP fabric concepts discussed in this chapter also apply to MPLS fabrics. You can find some simple examples of the latter in Chapter 2 and Chapter 16.

Traffic in data centers has evolved from a model in which the North-South (client-to-server) traffic pattern was dominant into one in which horizontal (West-East) traffic is very relevant. For example, imagine a video provider with a frontend web application that needs to talk to file services and many other applications—like advertising—inside the same data center. Horizontal traffic appears more and more in the full picture.

IP Fabrics—Forwarding Plane

An IP fabric is simply an IP network with a special physical topology that is very adequate to scale out and to accommodate a growing West-East traffic pattern.

Let's discuss Figure 10-6, in which all the unshaded boxes are separate physical devices. Beginning at the South, there are VMs, containers (labeled CT), bare-metal servers (labeled BM), and legacy hypervisors. These elements are either not capable or not configured to implement an overlay over an IP network.

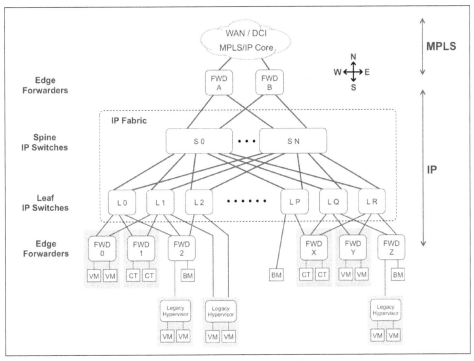

Figure 10-6. Leaf-and-spine architecture—three-stage fabric

Edge forwarders

Edge forwarders (labeled FWD) implement an overlay through the IP Fabric. They are responsible for encapsulating packets or frames coming from their clients—VMs, bare-metal servers, legacy hypervisors, and systems beyond the WAN—into IP tunnels that can be transported through the IP fabric. Likewise, they decapsulate the traffic received from the IP fabric and deliver the resulting data to their clients. Conceptually, they play the same role as do PEs in an SP core.

Don't look for the term "edge forwarders" in the existing literature. It is a generic term proposed ad hoc in this book to describe that function.

Although this overlay function is typically performed by a dedicated edge forwarder device, optionally it can be performed by a leaf switch, provided that the latter has one or more directly connected hosts that are not overlay-capable.

There are three types of edge forwarders:

- Modern hypervisors (and host OSs) that implement an overlay stack. In Figure 10-6, these are FWD_0, FWD_1, FWD_X, and FWD_Y. The overlay headers are handled by the forwarder component inside the hypervisor (or host OS). VMs just send and receive plain Ethernet frames: they have no overlay/ underlay awareness.

- Top of the Rack (ToR) switches with an overlay stack, providing connectivity to legacy bare-metal servers and legacy hypervisors which lack an overlay stack. In Figure 10-6, FWD_2 and FWD_Z are dedicated to this function, whereas L_1, L_2, and L_P perform it in combination with their underlay function.

- PE routers (data center gateways) implementing an overlay stack (FWD_A and FWD_B in Figure 10-6). These gateways typically interconnect the local data center to other data centers (DCI service) and/or to the outside world, represented as the WAN.

Edge forwarders implement an overlay by using an additional set of packet headers, including at least one header that is only meaningful to edge forwarders.

Leaf-and-spine IP switches

The IP fabric spans leaf-and-spine IP switches. These are basically IP routers that transport tunneled traffic, similar to what P-routers do in an IP/MPLS core. The encapsulation in an IP fabric is, obviously, IP! IP switches in a fabric forward the IP packets that are produced by an overlay encapsulation. As for the necessary IP routing logic, it is discussed later in the context of the control plane.

In Figure 10-6, edge forwarders FWD_0, FWD_1, and FWD_2 are multihomed to one or more of these leaf switches: L_0, L_1, and L_2. However, it is not a perfect mesh; for example, FWD_0 and FWD_1 are not connected to L_2. The single bare-metal server connected to L_P is only connected to L_P. The bottom line is that south of the leaf IP switches, there is no connectivity mandate.

Only within the fabric is there such a mandate: each leaf IP switch is connected to every spine IP switch.

Three-stage IP fabrics

In 1952, Charles Clos designed a model for multistage telephone switching systems. Today, this model is still the de facto reference for scale out, nonblocking architectures (you can find more information on Wikipedia). Paraphrasing Yakov Rekhter, one of the fathers of MPLS:

> Do not assume that being innovative, or being a technology leader, requires inventing new technologies. To the contrary, one can be quite innovative by simply combining creative use and packaging with high-quality implementation of existing technologies.

The Clos model is being applied over and over to different use cases, always in a very successful manner. Some of them are covered in this chapter.

In Clos terminology:

- Leaf IP Switches implement fabric stages #1 and #3.
- Spine IP Switches implement fabric stage #2.

Another frequently used term is *Tier*. In this topology, spine IP switches are Tier-1, and leaf IP switches are Tier-2. The lower the Tier, the higher is the relevance.

Back to Figure 10-6, let's suppose that FWD_0 places a user packet inside an IP overlay header whose destination is FWD_Y. Because there is no leaf device connecting FWD_0 to FWD_Y, the packet must go through three stages:

- Stage 1 via one of the leaf switches connected to FWD_0: L_0 or L_1
- Stage 2 via one of the spine switches: S_0, S_1, ..., S_N
- Stage 3 via one of the leaf switches connected to FWD_Y: L_Q or L_R

From the point of view of a packet that flows in the reverse direction, Stage 1 would be on L_Q or L_R, and Stage 3 on L_0 or L_1.

The Clos architecture is a perfect paradigm for optimal bandwidth utilization and, most important, it is typically nonblocking. This means that if you activate two unused ports at Stages 1 and 3, a switching path can be established between them with no impact on the existing paths. In practice, the traffic between a pair of [source forwarder, destination forwarder] can affect the traffic flowing between another pair of forwarders if the links or devices are congested. *Of course!* However, this congestion is more unlikely with this architecture than with any other. Clos architectures are the best for horizontal scaling.

Five-stage IP fabrics

You can scale-up an IP fabric by making it five-stage. This model is sometimes referred to as multistage (although, strictly speaking, three-stage fabrics are also multistage).

Figure 10-7 illustrates two five-stage fabric topologies in which all the shaded circles are separate physical devices. The Point of Delivery (POD) model is optimized for connect more PODs, in other words, to connect more sites and devices. As for the Performance model, it is perfect for nonblocking scale out. Adding more leaves and more spines efficiently increases the capacity without a major network redesign.

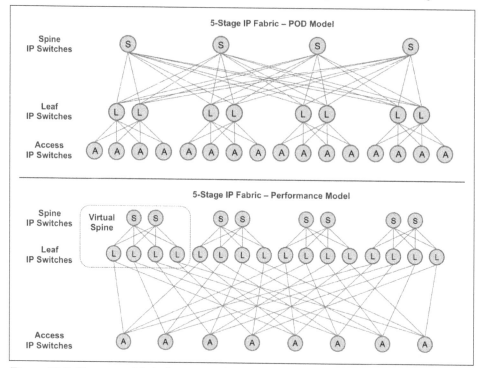

Figure 10-7. Five-stage fabric (courtesy of Doug Hanks)

There is a practical limit on the number of devices that you can add to any architecture while maintaining the nonblocking property.

Here is the translation from Tier to Stage terminology in the context of five-stage fabrics:

- Access IP switches are in fabric stages 1 and 5, and are considered Tier-3 devices.
- Leaf IP switches on Stages 2 and 4 are considered Tier-2 devices.
- Spine IP switches on Stage 3 are considered Tier-1 devices.

In the POD model, these roles are usually called leaf (stages 1 and 5), spine (stages 2 and 4), and fabric (stage 3).

Another scaling option is to connect IP fabrics with one another on the West-East direction, but this is complex and beyond the scope of this document.

OK, it's time to talk about the control plane.

IP Fabrics with Distributed-Only Control Plane

For simplicity, let's discuss a three-stage IP fabric. The concepts for a five-stage IP fabric are exactly the same: just the topology changes.

An IP fabric is composed of network devices that have a forwarding plane. For this reason, Figure 10-8 shows a forwarder component inside each physical device. In this context, the forwarding plane has the role of taking control and transit packets from one device to another. Although not shown for graphical reasons, these packets also traverse the forwarding plane of the leaf IP switches.

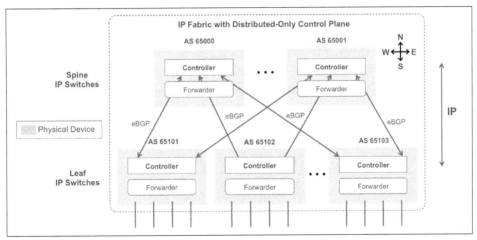

Figure 10-8. IP fabric—distributed-only control plane

You can run any routing protocol between the IP switches, from that of a link-state, to eBGP. A trend in medium and high-scale data centers is to use eBGP because it is simply the most scalable protocol and it has great multipath capabilities. And when the overlay supports native MPLS, this is actually eBGP Labeled Unicast (eBGP-LU), as discussed in Chapter 2 and Chapter 16.

And there is no control plane hierarchy apart from the one imposed by eBGP—spine IP switches readvertise routes from one leaf to another. Nothing fancy in this distributed control plane model: just good-old IP routing as usual.

Figure 10-9 illustrates the forwarding plane in this architecture (for an L3 overlay).

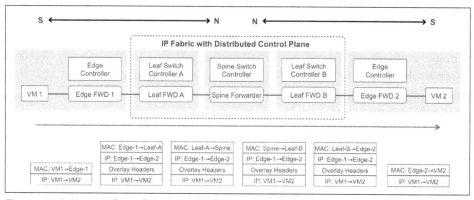

Figure 10-9. Forwarding plane of an IP Fabric with a centralized-only control plane

IP Fabrics with Hybrid Control Plane

It is also possible to have an IP fabric with a hybrid control plane (see Figure 10-10):

- To perform topology autodiscovery, there is a *distributed* control plane based on IP routing like the one just described. It is typically a link-state protocol. The goal is to build an internal IP underlay that is able to transport packets between any pair of devices in the fabric.

- After the topology is discovered, devices can exchange *further* internal control packets. Through this packet exchange, a spine switch is elected as the active controller of a *centralized* control plane. Leaf switch controllers are demoted to control agents. Very much like in a multiforwarder single-chassis device, control agents get their forwarding instruction set from the central controller.

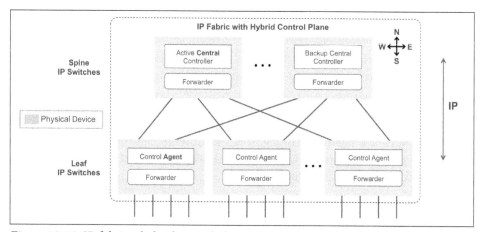

Figure 10-10. IP fabric—hybrid control plane

The result is one single virtual device, spanning several physical devices: an *enveloped* IP fabric. This virtual device is composed of devices that can also run in standalone mode.

IP fabrics have two port types: *fabric ports* interconnect two IP switches in the fabric, and *network ports* connect the fabric to the outside world. In a nutshell, the distributed control plane *runs* on the fabric ports, whereas the centralized control plane *programs* the network ports.

Having a centralized control plane is useful to program—inside the IP fabric—certain advanced forwarding rules. Enforcing these rules requires acting upon several devices according to a global topology view. For example, the central controller can create automatic link-aggregates at two different levels (next-hop and remote destination), and also build optimized, resilient replication trees for Broadcast, Unknown unicast, and Multicast (BUM).

A centralized IP fabric logic is simple enough to be implemented in the processor of a network device. As an alternative, this logic can also run as an application on an external server or VM.

When its control plane is hybrid, the IP fabric looks like one single device, and as a result, an extra header—the fabric header—steers packets from one leaf to another. The central parts of Figure 10-4 and Figure 10-11 are strictly analogous. In that sense, a leaf IP switch integrated in the IP fabric behaves like a line card, with its control agent and its forwarding engine(s). Figure 10-11 illustrates a L3 overlay example.

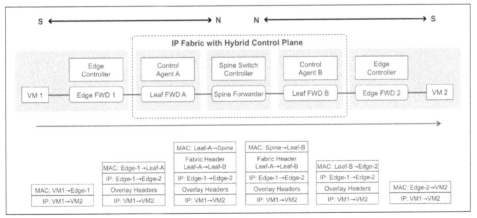

Figure 10-11. Forwarding plane of an IP fabric with a hybrid control plane

Network Virtualization Overlay

As you have just seen, centralizing the control plane of an IP fabric underlay is an interesting option. How about the overlay? At the edge, requirements become more complex: multitenancy, policies, services, and so on. Centralizing the control plane becomes the strongly preferred way to automate the provisioning, evolution, and operation of virtual overlay networks. This is especially true taking into account that there are several types of edge forwarder, and sometimes it is necessary to coordinate all of them to deploy a service. Remember, they can be classified as follows:

- Hypervisor or Host OS implementing an overlay stack. The overlay header is handled by the forwarder component in the kernel. If the system is virtualized, then VMs or containers just send and receive plain (may be VLAN-tagged) Ethernet frames: they have no awareness of the overlay implementation.

- ToR switches with an overlay stack, providing connectivity to legacy bare metal servers and hypervisors which lack an overlay stack. These ToR switches act like gateways between the legacy and the overlay worlds.

- PE routers (data center gateways) implementing an overlay stack.

Modern overlay architectures such as Network Virtualization Overlay (NVO), shown in Figure 10-12, typically have an active-active central control plane that programs the networking stack of overlay-capable hypervisors and host OSs. The resulting architecture is very similar to those in Figure 10-2 and Figure 10-8. Although they need to be interpreted in totally different contexts—a network device, an underlay, and an overlay—they have a common denominator. All of them provide a centralized control plane. There is one way to shape a wheel: round!

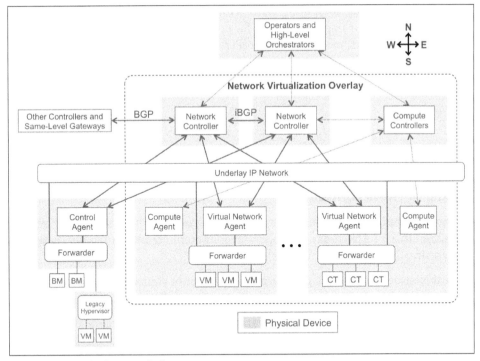

Figure 10-12. NVO control plane

Compute Controllers

To scale-out a virtual compute deployment, it is essential to have a cluster of central-ized controllers in charge of defining, instantiating, and moving the virtual comput-ing entities that run on different physical servers.

There are roughly two types of virtual computing entities:

Virtual machines
> These have their own OS, applications, and libraries. You can see a VM as a full OS with its own kernel running on top a hypervisor. One single hypervisor can run many VMs and provides emulated hardware resources to each VM. Type 1 hypervisors are embedded in the host OS, and Type 2 hypervisors are basically an application that runs on top of yet another host OS. Type 1 hypervisors are more efficient since they involve one less computing layer.

Containers
> These do *not* have their own OS. A container is a bundle of applications and dependencies that runs as an isolated process in host OS' user space. All of the containers running on a given host share the kernel of the host OS.

Both flavors of virtual computing architectures exist in the industry, and there are many different vendor implementations for each of them. As soon as you start adding more physical servers, centralized controllers become handy. Here is an ultra-short list of popular central compute controller examples (there are many more):

- In the VM world, two different solid references are VMware vCenter and Openstack.

- In the Container world, Kubernetes (as a centralized controller) and Docker (as a server-local agent and container engine) are popular examples.

Virtual Network Controllers

In legacy compute networking, every virtual interface card in a VM or container is connected to a VLAN. Today, in modern overlay architectures virtual interfaces connect to virtual networks (not VLANs).

Virtual Network Controllers provide a central point of control to define and operate virtual networks together with their policies and forwarding rules.

These controllers typically implement various protocols and programmatic interfaces:

To the North

Controllers expose a programmatic northbound interface that an external orchestrator can use to provide an additional level of customized automation to the entire overlay builder solution.

East-West internal

Two controllers that belong to the same overlay builder talk to each other through a series of protocols that allow them to synchronize their configuration, state, analytics data, and so on. Among these protocols, there is a special one that performs the function of synchronizing the network overlay routing information. To avoid reinventing the wheel, this protocol can definitely be BGP.

East-West external

Controllers can federate to other external controllers via BGP. This provides a good scale-out option by deploying overlay builders in parallel. BGP is also the de facto protocol that controllers use to peer to network gateways.

To the South

Controllers send a dynamic forwarding instruction set (networks, policies, etc.) to Control Agents or Virtual Network Agents. Two popular options are XMPP—conceptually, similar to BGP—and OVSDB. These protocols are described later in this book.

Because controllers are the brain that centralizes network signaling, they are also the main entry point for operators and external applications. For this reason, controllers typically expose a GUI, a CLI, a northbound programmatic interface, and so on.

NVO—Transport of Control Packets

Internal Ethernet Bridges in Figure 10-2 are similar to the Underlay IP Network in Figure 10-12, with two main differences:

- In Figure 10-2, the underlay is L2, whereas in Figure 10-12 it is L3.
- In Figure 10-2, there is a dedicated control network, whereas in Figure 10-12 control plane packets use the same underlay network that transports transit traffic from the tenants' applications. This is the typical architecture, although an Out-of-Band control network is an option, too.

NVO—Agents

Virtual Network Agents and Control Agents are responsible for converting the high-level instruction set received from the Controllers into low-level instructions that are adapted and optimized for the forwarders. The name Control Agent is reserved for traditional network devices, whereas Virtual Network Agents run on hypervisors. But they play the same role in the architecture.

In the same way as line cards in a multiforwarder network device, hypervisors are slave entities and they typically implement a very basic user interface as compared to the comprehensive ones offered by the controllers.

## CHAPTER 11

Network Virtualization Overlays

This chapter discusses one of the most important incarnations of Software-Defined Networking (SDN) for clouds and data centers: Network Virtualization Overlay (NVO).

Chapter 10 introduced the Edge Forwarder concept in detail. Now, let's have another look at it from a functional and service-centric perspective. In the context of NVO, Edge Forwarders support multitenancy by implementing flexible network policies that rely on an overlay transport mechanism. You should know that this is basically the definition of a VPN; thus in this chapter, Edge Forwarders are actually VPN Forwarders.

One type of VPN Forwarder, network devices that implement L3 VPNs and L2 VPNs, has already been the subject of many pages in the first part of this book. These PE routers can run in dedicated physical platforms, or virtualized in a container, or as a VM in a hypervisor, or even directly on a bare-metal server. Anyway, physical or virtual, they perform the same function—of course, performance differs.

This chapter focuses on two *other* VPN Forwarder types:

- Host operating system (OS) that implements virtual networks (VNs) while acting at the same time as a Hypervisor or as a Container Engine. As you are about to see, this is *not* the same as a network OS running on a virtual machine (VM). From the computing perspective, it is lower in the stack and hence more *native*. But these approaches are not mutually exclusive; actually, they combine nicely in Network Functions Virtualization (NFV), which is covered in Chapter 12.

- Top-of-Rack (ToR) switches with overlay capabilities.

Let's begin with the first type of VPN Forwarders in this short list. They are at the heart of SDN. Depending on the actual implementation, they are called vRouters or vSwitches. Both perform a similar function but not all vSwitches are overlay-capable.

Several vendors have developed products that create overlay virtual networks in order to achieve connectivity between VMs, containers, and the physical world. As of this writing, it is an emerging market. This book's SDN chapter block (10, 11, 12, and 15) focuses on illustrating the technology, not product comparisons. In the end, concepts are quite universal and network solutions are meant to interoperate.

As of this writing, there are several NVO production-ready solutions on the market, and one of them is OpenContrail. Here are the reasons why OpenContrail was chosen for this book's NVO examples:

- It happens to be a solution that the authors know well. Resources are limited in every project, and this book is no exception. A choice had to be made. If you enjoy this book, a future second edition would likely cover other vendors' SDN solutions and multivendor interoperability.

- OpenContrail is a deployed, production-ready SDN solution with a comprehensive feature set in all the key areas, including network policy and network service architecture, providing a wide range of overlay flavors from which to choose.

- Like Open vSwitch (OVS), OpenContrail is an open source project.

- Unlike OVS, OpenContrail was *inspired* since day one by BGP and MPLS service architecture. It clearly decouples overlay from underlay, and control plane from forwarding plane. After policies are centrally defined, distributed vRouters are empowered to locally create flows with no intervention from the controller—which later gets information about the flows for analytics purposes. Having this architecture since its conception, OpenContrail vRouter has better scalability, performance, and robustness than current OVS implementations, which are influenced by OpenFlow's initial design approach.

As for Network Virtualization Controllers (NVCs), OpenContrail is also kept as a main reference for the same reasons. For the record, other popular solutions include OpenDaylight (ODL), Nuage, and VMware's NSX.

OpenContrail in a Nutshell

Chapter 10 explains the generic architecture of cloud SDN solutions. This chapter's Figure 11-1 is similar to Figure 10-12, except that now we are actually using Open-Contrail terms (such as vRouter) and actual protocols between the different functions.

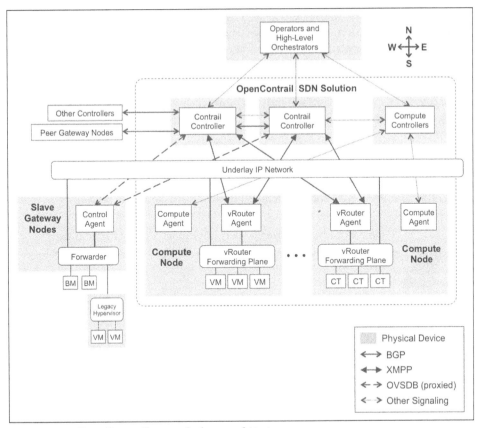

Figure 11-1. OpenContrail control-plane architecture

OpenContrail Controllers

Although in Figure 11-1 each OpenContrail Controller is represented as a single box, it is actually the combination of at least four different software components or *nodes*.

 Beware of the term *node*: here, it is just software running on general-purpose x86 processors. Each of these nodes can run on the same or on different physical servers—and on the same or on different VMs.

The following description is from the OpenContrail book in Juniper's *Day One* library:

> All nodes of a given type run in an active-active configuration, so no single node is a bottleneck. This scale-out design provides both redundancy and horizontal scalability.

Configuration nodes, which are responsible for translating the high-level data model into a lower-level form suitable for interacting with network elements.

Control nodes, which are responsible for propagating this low-level state to and from network elements and peer systems in an eventually consistent way.

Analytics nodes, which are responsible for capturing real-time data from network elements, abstracting it, and presenting it in a form suitable for applications to consume.

In more recent OpenContrail versions, controllers also have *database nodes*.

From a networking perspective, the control node is the most interesting because it's the one performing all the network protocol signaling that is required to build overlay networks. Control nodes speak BGP in the West-East direction, and eXtensible Messaging and Presence Protocol (XMPP) in the North-South direction.

 ToR Service Nodes (covered later) implement a proxy function that translates XMPP messages from and to Open vSwitch Database Management (OVSDB).

Compute, Gateway, and Service Nodes

The other node types have a more physical meaning:

- *Compute nodes* are an intrinsic part of OpenContrail.
- *Gateway and service nodes* are external and interact with OpenContrail.

Again, paraphrasing the OpenContrail *Day One* book:

Compute nodes are general-purpose virtualized servers that host VMs. These VMs may be tenant running general applications, or these VMs may be service VMs running network services such as a virtual load balancer or virtual firewall. Each compute node contains a vRouter that implements the forwarding plane and the distributed part of the control plane.

Gateway nodes are physical gateway routers or switches that connect the tenant virtual networks to physical networks such as the Internet, a customer VPN, another data center, or to non-virtualized servers.

Service nodes are physical network elements providing network services such as Deep Packet Inspection (DPI), Intrusion Detection (IDP), Intrusion Prevention (IPS), WAN optimization, Network Address Translation (NAT) and load balancing. Service chains can contain a mixture of virtual services (implemented as VMs on compute nodes) and physical services (hosted on service nodes).

Gateway nodes can also run as a VM, and the service function can definitely be virtualized. Anyway, all these node terms (Compute, Gateway, Service, and ToR service) typically refer to a physical host or device.

Compute nodes

Like other SDN solutions, OpenContrail is a networking product. To avoid reinventing the wheel, OpenContrail integrates with existing compute virtualization solutions that are responsible for managing, instantiating, and moving VMs or containers:

- If OpenStack is used as the Compute Controller + Agent, there are two virtualization options: Linux KVM (Kernel-based Virtual Machine) and Docker. The first is a VM-based hypervisor; the second is a container engine.

- OpenContrail can also integrate with VMware vCenter as the Compute Controller + Agent, using VMware ESXi as the hypervisor. This requires interconnecting OpenContrail's vRouter to VMware's vSwitch, and dynamically mapping vSwitch's VLANs to vRouter's Virtual Networks.

- As of this writing, there is ongoing work to evaluate a possible integration with Kubernetes as the Compute Controller + Agent, using Docker as the container engine; however, it is not yet implemented.

In an analogy to a multiforwarder network device:

- A compute node is like a line card.

- A vRouter agent runs in user space and is analogous to a control agent in a line card.

- The vRouter's forwarding plane runs in the kernel and is analogous to a forwarding engine.

Gateway nodes

Figure 11-1 shows that there are actually two types of gateway nodes:

- Peer gateway nodes are capable of building their own overlays. They are typically PEs and establish iBGP sessions to the control nodes.

- Slave gateway nodes can build overlays as instructed by the control node.

Strictly speaking, nothing prevents a gateway node from running in a VM or container.

Service nodes

Chapter 12 provides more detail on the topic. Service nodes have nothing to do with ToR service nodes.

ToR service nodes

OpenContrail controllers are also capable of extending overlay networks to ToR switches that connect legacy hosts and hypervisors. This overlay extension is performed by ToR service nodes, which have *nothing to do* with the aforementioned service nodes. ToR service nodes implement the intelligence to act as a control-plane proxy between control nodes and ToR devices.

Case Study: A Private Cloud

One of the most powerful applications of SDN solutions like OpenContrail is subscriber access to a private cloud, as illustrated in Figure 11-2. Service providers (SPs) can offer this access in the context of Infrastructure as a Service (IaaS), Platform as a Service (PaaS), or Software as a Service (SaaS). Or, put all together, XaaS.

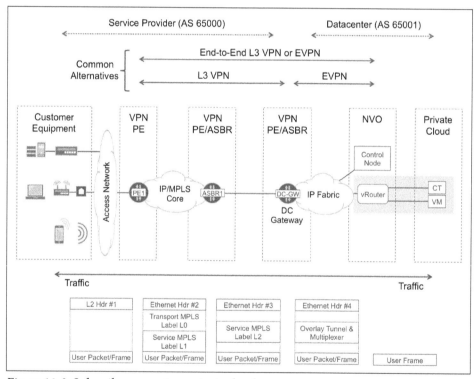

Figure 11-2. Subscriber access to a private cloud

As soon as you associate a VM—or a container—interface to a Virtual Network with OpenContrail, the VM is immediately reachable by the subscribers, and vice versa. This is a very cool example of a natural integration between SDN and BGP/MPLS services.

Security is implicit because it is a VPN service: subscribers do not need to establish IPSec or Secure Socket Layers (SSL) tunnels toward their private cloud.

Let's discuss the contents of Figure 11-2, moving *from right to left*:

- VMs and containers are like CEs. They are totally unaware of the overlay, and simply send and receive Ethernet frames—which are typically untagged.
- vRouters are like PEs. They can perform the role of either an Ethernet VPN (EVPN) or an IP VPN PE.
- Like ASBR1, the data center gateway is an Option B Autonomous System Border Router (ASBR). Alternatively, you can merge the two ASBRs into one Area Border Router (ABR). In any case, the data center gateway changes (into a local address) the BGP next hop of the VPN routes that it reflects; as Chapter 9 details, this triggers a new service label allocation. Although it is completely optional to instantiate a local VRF and/or EVPN instance at the data center gateway, doing so can be advantageous because it allows performing route summarization and applying advanced routing policies.
- Further to the left, it is a classic SP network.

At the bottom of Figure 11-2, notice the User Packet/Frame box. Indeed, it can be an L3 packet or an L2 frame depending on whether the service is EVPN or IP VPN. Thanks to EVPN's hooks into the L3 world, it is possible to combine EVPN for intrasubnet traffic with IP VPN for intersubnet traffic (this combination is known in OpenContrail as L2_L3 mode). Extending EVPN end-to-end to the subscriber is technically feasible, but it is a bad practice in general to stretch L2 domains.

Although it is not shown in Figure 11-2, OpenContrail also provides communication inside the data center. This makes it possible for VMs running in the same or different vRouters—and for applications running outside OpenContrail—to communicate with one another inside the data center network.

Let's look at the case study in detail. The focus is on SDN because BGP/MPLS VPNs in physical PEs are already covered in earlier chapters.

For simplicity, Figure 11-3 shows all of the controller functions in the same physical server. Anyway, the focus is on the control node. OpenContrail supports two forwarding modes: pure L3 and mixed L2_L3. The simplest one is pure L3, so let's begin with it.

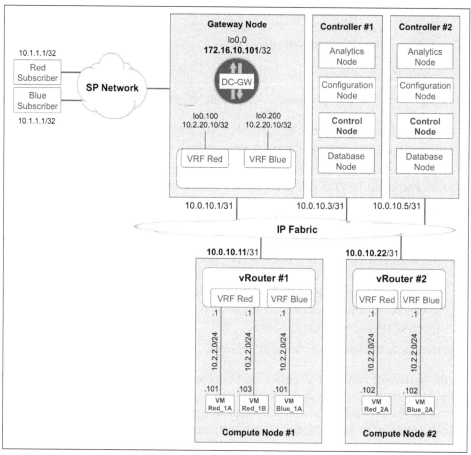

Figure 11-3. Infrastructure and VPN addressing—L3 mode

You can see two types of addressing:

- Infrastructure IPv4 addresses (10.0.10.x/31), which reside in the global routing table and provide underlay connectivity through the IP fabric.

- VPN overlay addresses (10.1.1.1/32, 10.2.20.10/32, 10.2.2.0/24). These correspond to subscribers, the data center gateway loopback, and VMs, respectively. The same address scheme is used for VPNs Red and Blue. This is fine: they are VPNs after all!

Let's go through the entire signaling process that enables a private cloud service, step by step.

vRouter-VM Link Addressing

This book focuses on technology and does *not* include an OpenContrail user guide. Very brief GUI pointers are provided so you can easily match the concepts to the actual configuration hierarchies in OpenContrail.

 In general, anything that OpenContrail GUI can do, you can also do by using OpenContrail's northbound RESTful API.

Although other options are available, the following Virtual Machine Manager GUI pointers (steps 1 and 3 below) assume that the Compute Controller and Agents are based on OpenStack:

1. The first administrative step in VM addressing is to create a project within Open-Stack Horizon GUI: Admin→Identity Panel→Projects. This book's examples use a project named *mpls-in-the-sdn-era*. A project is typically associated to a tenant, and it supports one or more VNs.

2. In the context of the new project, define the VNs (Red, Blue) in OpenContrail GUI: Configure→Networking→Networks. You can think of a VN as a set of IP subnets with some additional properties: zero or more route targets (RTs), optionally a VXLAN Network Identifier (VNI), and so on. Each of these IP subnets can be broken into /32 addresses that are assigned to the endpoints of VM-vRouter (CE-PE) links.

3. VMs are defined and instantiated through the OpenStack Horizon GUI: Project→ Instances→Launch Instance. Each VM typically has one or more VN interfaces (vNICs), and each vNIC is connected to a vRouter's *tap* interface.

A vNIC and a tap interface are the two ends of a CE—PE point-to-point link. Both interfaces are internally linked together, and they are dynamically created as soon as a new VM is spawned. A given tap interface in a vRouter belongs to one and only one VN, and it is connected to a single VM.

Is a VN like a VRF? Almost! Strictly speaking, the OpenContrail term for a VRF is Routing Instance (RI). RIs are implicitly configured through their parent VNs, not directly. By default, there is only one VRF for each VN. On the other hand, Chapter 3 explains the extranet concept, in which VRF:VPN mappings are *N*:1 instead of 1:1. Similarly, the VRF:VN mappings are N:1. For the moment, in simple scenarios such as that presented in Figure 11-3, *VN Red only has one VRF called Red:Red*. Note that it is sometimes represented as VRF Red for graphical reasons.

As in a physical PE, a VRF can have local and remote routes. In addition, remember that a CE can have several uplinks, each connected to a different (or the same) VRF at the PE. Likewise, a VM can have several vNICs, each connected to a different VRF at the vRouter. In this first example, each VM has only one vNIC.

One of the most striking aspects of Figure 11-3 is the fact that the 10.2.2.1 address is present multiple times in the same VRF—on the vRouter side. Let's focus on VRF Red. The first and second host addresses—in this case, 10.2.2.1 and 10.2.2.2—are automatically reserved for the VM's default gateway and DNS server, respectively. Both of these functions are provided by the vRouters. Their tap interfaces all have the same MAC address 00:00:5e:00:01:00.

Having a deterministic IP and MAC address on the vRouter tap interfaces provides perfect conditions for VM mobility in L3 architectures. Chapter 8 discusses a similar scenario, in which all the IRBs in a given subnet were configured with the same IP and MAC addresses.

The 10.2.2.0/24 network is not advertised by the control node, only the /32 routes assigned to the VMs are. Now, suppose that VM Red_1A sends an ARP request to resolve 10.2.2.102 (at Red_2A) or 10.2.2.103 (at Red_1B). If vRouter_1 knows the corresponding /32 L3 route, vRouter_1 sends an ARP reply to VM Red_1A, providing the well-known MAC address that it uses on all the vRouter-VM links (00:00:5e:00:01:00). This is an intelligent ARP proxy process where the destination VM does not receive any (original or proxied) ARP request packets originated by other VMs.

In L3 mode, the vRouter acts like an L3 router, as opposed to a vSwitch. In L2_L3 mode, the vRouter acts like an L2/L3 switch from the perspective of the VMs.

vNICs get IPv4/IPv6 and MAC addresses from the control node. Figure 11-3 shows five VMs, with one vNIC each—some in VRF Red and others in VRF Blue. As you might expect in a VPN, vNICs in VRF Red can communicate with one another, but not with vNICs in VRF Blue (by default). When you create a new VM, the Compute Controller—in this example, OpenStack—communicates the configured vNIC-to-VN mappings to the OpenContrail controller. Based on this information, the latter assigns IPv4/IPv6 and MAC addresses to each vNIC.

Initializing vNICs—XMPP as a DHCP-Like Protocol

XMPP, formerly known as *Jabber*, is a communications protocol for message-oriented middleware based on eXtensible Markup Language (XML). It implements a series of functions such as Subscribe, Publish, and Update that make it suitable for the communication between the centralized control plane (control node) and the control agents (vRouter agents).

One of the primary functions that XMPP performs in OpenContrail is the assignment of all the network attributes of a vNIC, including the VRF to which it belongs, its IP and MAC addresses, security, policies, and so on. This information makes it possible for the vRouter to act as a DHCP server in the context of VM addressing, as shown in Figure 11-4.

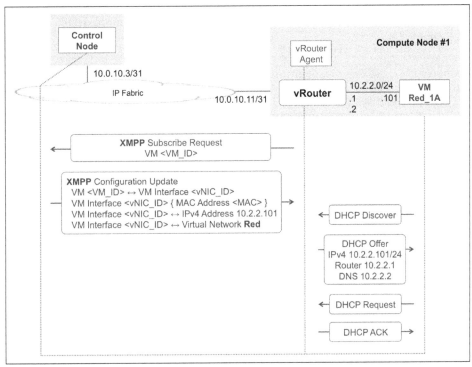

Figure 11-4. VM addressing—XMPP and DHCP

XMPP Subscribe Request messages are very simple, as demonstrated in Example 11-1.

Example 11-1. XMPP—vRouter agent sends Subscribe Request for a VM

```
1    <?xml version="1.0"?>
2    <iq type="set" from="vrouter_1"
3        to="network-control@contrailsystems.com/config">
4        <pubsub xmlns="http://jabber.org/protocol/pubsub">
5        <subscribe node="virtual-machine:
6                    9747613d-a93a-43f9-b5aa-de747fc96d44"/>
```

```
7        </pubsub>
8     </iq>
```

This message goes from the control agent at vRouter_1 to the control node (lines 2 and 3). It is triggered by the creation of VM Red_1A in the context of the Compute Controller and Agent (in this case, OpenStack Nova). These compute control elements had already communicated the vNIC-to-VN mappings (in this case, eth0:Red) to OpenContrail.

The internal VM ID (line 6) is different from the VM's user-friendly name (Red_1A).

Let's see the XMPP configuration update from Figure 11-4 in more detail, as shown in Example 11-2.

Example 11-2. XMPP—Configuration Update to a vRouter Agent

```
1     <?xml version="1.0"?>
2     <iq type="set" from="network-control@contrailsystems.com"
3        to="default-global-system-config:vrouter_1/config">
4       <config>
5         <update>
6           <node type="virtual-machine">
7             <name>9747613d-a93a-43f9-b5aa-de747fc96d44</name>
8           </node>
9           <link>
10            <node type="virtual-router">
11              <name>default-global-system-config:vrouter_1</name>
12            </node>
13            <node type="virtual-machine">
14              <name>9747613d-a93a-43f9-b5aa-de747fc96d44</name>
15            </node>
16            <metadata type="virtual-router-virtual-machine" />
17          </link>
18          <node type="virtual-machine-interface">
19            <name>default-domain:mpls-in-the-sdn-era:
20                  75fa145a-07c6-4c84-98b7-3e793fc540b4</name>
21            <virtual-machine-interface-mac-addresses>
22              <mac-address>02:75:fa:14:5a:07</mac-address>
23            </virtual-machine-interface-mac-addresses>
24          </node>
25          <link>
26            <node type="virtual-machine-interface">
27              <name>default-domain:mpls-in-the-sdn-era:
28                    75fa145a-07c6-4c84-98b7-3e793fc540b4</name>
29            </node>
30            <node type="virtual-machine">
31              <name>9747613d-a93a-43f9-b5aa-de747fc96d44</name>
32            </node>
33            <metadata type="virtual-machine-interface-virtual-machine"/>
34          </link>
35          <link>
```

```
36            <node type="virtual-machine-interface">
37              <name>default-domain:mpls-in-the-sdn-era:
38                    75fa145a-07c6-4c84-98b7-3e793fc540b4</name>
39            </node>
40            <node type="virtual-network">
41              <name>default-domain:mpls-in-the-sdn-era:Red</name>
42            </node>
43            <metadata type="virtual-machine-interface-virtual-network"/>
44          </link>
45          <node type="instance-ip">
46            <name>d8ba77df-df69-450b-b4d5-daeb53163655</name>
47            <instance-ip-address>10.2.2.101</instance-ip-address>
48            <instance-ip-family>v4</instance-ip-family>
49          </node>
50          <link>
51            <node type="instance-ip">
52              <name>d8ba77df-df69-450b-b4d5-daeb53163655</name>
53            </node>
54            <node type="virtual-machine-interface">
55              <name>default-domain:mpls-in-the-sdn-era:
56                    75fa145a-07c6-4c84-98b7-3e793fc540b4</name>
57            </node>
58            <metadata type="instance-ip-virtual-machine-interface"/>
59          </link>
60        </update>
61      </config>
62    </iq>
```

XMPP Configuration Update messages contain a graph structure with nodes and links between nodes. This structure is like a network, but its nodes are not necessarily network nodes: they can be virtually anything. Unlike relationships between objects in relational databases, which are strictly unidirectional, these links can be interpreted as bidirectional.

 The concept of *node* in an XMPP configuration update message has absolutely nothing to do with OpenContrail's architectural elements, which are also called nodes (control node, compute node, etc.).

The message in Example 11-2 goes from a control node to the control agent at vRouter_1 (lines 2 and 3). It contains the following nodes:

- Virtual Machine <*VM_ID*> (lines 6 through 8). This ID matches Example 11-1, line 6, and it is different from the VM's user-friendly name (Red_1A).

- VM Interface <*vNIC_ID*> (lines 18 through 24). The most important property of this node is a MAC address assigned by the control node.

- Instance IP (lines 45 through 49). Its most important element is an IP address (10.2.2.101).

The rest of the message is a series of links between pairs of nodes that are either defined in this XMPP configuration update message or in previous ones:

- VM <*VM_ID*> is linked to the vRouter named vrouter_1 (lines 9 through 17).
- VM Interface <*vNIC_ID*> is linked to VM <*VM_ID*> (lines 25 through 34).
- VM Interface <*vNIC_ID*> is linked to VN Red (lines 35 through 44).
- Instance IP 10.2.2.101 is linked to VM Interface <*vNIC_ID*> (lines 50 through 59).

 For brevity, some data has been omitted from Example 11-2, such as the vNIC-to-security group link, or the routing instance (Red:Red) information. Chapter 12 discusses the latter topic further.

From the perspective of VM Red_1A, vRouter_1 acts as a DHCP server, as an IPv4 default gateway, and as a DNS server. Now that VM Red_1A has an interface with an IPv4 address, it can communicate with the outside world. But, can vRouter_1? Let's see how a vRouter communicates with other vRouters and with gateway nodes.

Interconnecting VMs—XMPP as a BGP-Like Protocol

In the context of SDN, probably the most important function of XMPP is its ability to perform the same function as Multiprotocol BGP (MP-BGP) in signaling overlay networks. XMPP is as powerful and scalable as BGP and it has the same extensibility as XML. Unlike BGP, which is mainly a West-East protocol, XMPP has its application as a southbound protocol. This routing application of XMPP is defined in *draft-ietf-l3vpn-end-system*: BGP-signaled end-system IP/VPNs. As you will soon see, you can easily extend XMPP to also signal EVPNs.

Let's suppose that the 10.2.2.0/24 subnet in VN Red has been configured with the following range of IPs that can be assigned to VMs: 10.2.2.101–10.2.2.200. Let's further suppose that VMs with a vNIC in Red VN are started in the following order: Red_1A, Red_2A, and Red_1B.

vRouter subscribes to a VRF

Figure 11-5 illustrates how vRouter_1 and vRouter_2 first subscribe to the routing instance Red:Red, and then exchange VM host routes through the control node.

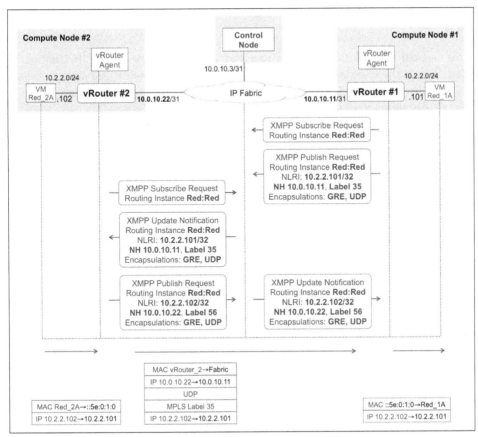

Figure 11-5. XMPP routing and inter-vRouter forwarding—L3 mode

As soon as it starts its first VM with a link in Red, vRouter_1 becomes interested in receiving routing updates for Red:Red. So it sends the Subscribe Request message shown in Example 11-3 to the control node (you can match Figure 11-5 to Example 11-3).

Example 11-3. XMPP—VN Subscribe Request

```
<?xml version="1.0"?>
<iq type="set" from="vrouter_1"
            to="network-control@contrailsystems.com/bgp-peer"
            id="subscribe779">
  <pubsub xmlns="http://jabber.org/protocol/pubsub">
    <subscribe node="default-domain:mpls-in-the-sdn-era:Red:Red">
      <options>
        <instance-id>1</instance-id>
      </options>
    </subscribe>
```

```
    </pubsub>
</iq>
```

This message is semantically similar to a BGP RT prefix (look for RTC in Chapter 3). Here is what the vRouter agent is telling the control node: *Now that I have to provide connectivity to VMs with vNICs in Red:Red, I need to know all the existing routes in that routing instance, so please send them to me.*

If this is the very first vNIC in VN Red that comes up in the cloud, and subscribers did not come up yet, the control node has no routes to send to vRouter Agent #1.

vRouter advertises VM's host IP route to the control nodes

vRouter_1 has a virtual tap interface that is connected to VM Red_1A. vRouter_1's agent assigns a locally significant MPLS label to this tap interface, following a per-CE label allocation model.

Is a vRouter like a PE or like a line card? Functionally, it is more like a line card because it plays a slave role in the control plane; and XMPP is a southbound protocol. On the other hand, a vRouter is able to allocate an MPLS label—in multiforwarder PEs with per-platform label space, this is typically a centralized task. So, it is fair to say that a vRouter is like a line card that has been promoted to allocate its own MPLS labels.

After it assigns an MPLS label to the tap interface facing VM Red_1A, vRouter_1's agent advertises prefix 10.2.2.101 plus the label in an XMPP Publish Request message, as demonstrated in Figure 11-5 and Example 11-4. This message goes to the control node and is equivalent to a BGP update.

Example 11-4. XMPP Publish Request—VM's vNIC /32 route

```
1    <?xml version="1.0"?>
2    <iq type="set" from="vrouter_1"
3        to="network-control@contrailsystems.com/bgp-peer" id="pubsub20">
4      <pubsub xmlns="http://jabber.org/protocol/pubsub">
5        <publish node="1/1/default-domain:mpls-in-the-sdn-era:
6                  Red:Red/10.2.2.101">
7          <item>
8            <entry>
9              <nlri>
10               <af>1</af>
11               <safi>1</safi>
12               <address>10.2.2.101/32</address>
13             </nlri>
14             <next-hops>
15               <next-hop>
16                 <af>1</af>
17                 <address>10.0.10.11</address>
18                 <label>35</label>
```

```
19                  <tunnel-encapsulation-list>
20                    <tunnel-encapsulation>gre</tunnel-encapsulation>
21                    <tunnel-encapsulation>udp</tunnel-encapsulation>
22                  </tunnel-encapsulation-list>
23                </next-hop>
24              </next-hops>
25              <virtual-network>default-domain:mpls-in-the-sdn-era:Red
26              </virtual-network>
27              <sequence-number>0</sequence-number>
28              <local-preference>100</local-preference>
29            </entry>
30          </item>
31        </publish>
32      </pubsub>
33    </iq>
34    <iq type="set" from="vrouter_1"
35        to="network-control@contrailsystems.com/bgp-peer"
36        id="collection20">
37      <pubsub xmlns="http://jabber.org/protocol/pubsub">
38        <collection node="default-domain:mpls-in-the-sdn-era:
39                          Red:Red">
40          <associate node="1/1/default-domain:mpls-in-the-sdn-era:
41                          Red:Red/10.2.2.101" />
42        </collection>
43      </pubsub>
44    </iq>
```

This message is sent by vRouter_1's agent to the control node (lines 2 and 3) and is very similar to a BGP update from both a semantic and a structural point of view (the security group information has been omitted for brevity). Despite being an IP VPN prefix, it is encoded as [AFI=1, SAFI=1] because it does not carry a Route Distinguisher (RD). And it does not have any RTs, either. Indeed, the VRF information is explicitly encoded in the message, so there is no need for an RD or for RTs. This message is for internal consumption within the OpenContrail ecosystem and the control node knows precisely how to distribute this routing information.

There is a little nuance here. For the moment (lines 1 through 33), the route is bound to a VN (Red) but not to a VRF. One more XMPP message (lines 34 through 44) binds the route to its VRF (Red:Red).

Control nodes reflect VM's route to other vRouters

Control nodes act like Route Reflectors (RRs): they centralize the route signaling, but they do not forward any user traffic. As a result, this route is sent to vRouter_2 in the form of a XMPP Update Notification. XMPP Publish Requests and Update Notifications both look like BGP update messages, and they receive a different name depending on the direction they flow. Publish Requests flow toward the North (vRouter→controller), and Update Notifications flow toward the South (controller→vRouter).

Example 11-5 presents the resulting XMPP Update Notification, which you can also match to Figure 11-5.

Example 11-5. XMPP Update Notification—VM's vNIC /32 route

```
<?xml version="1.0"?>
  <message from="network-control@contrailsystems.com"
         to="vrouter_2/bgp-peer">
    <event xmlns="http://jabber.org/protocol/pubsub">
      <items node="1/1/default-domain:mpls-in-the-sdn-era:Red:Red">
        <item id="10.2.2.101/32">
          <entry> *route at Example 11-4, lines #8-#29* </entry>
        </item>
      </items>
    </event>
  </messages>
</iq>
```

Although it is not shown for brevity, the `<entry>` in Example 11-5 looks exactly the same as the one in Example 11-4, lines 8 through 29. This behavior, illustrated in Figure 11-5, matches what you might expect from an RR (no next-hop change). The BGP next hop is still vRouter_1's infrastructure address (10.0.10.11), the MPLS label is also the same, and the list of encapsulations remains Generic Routing Encapsulation (GRE) (MPLSoGRE) and User Datagram Protocol (UDP) (MPLSoUDP). This is an *unordered* list and the final encapsulation choice is made by the ingress PE (in this case, by vRouter_2). When VM Red_2A comes up, a similar message exchange results in the route 10.2.2.102 learned by vRouter1. At the bottom of Figure 11-5, you can see an IP packet sent all the way from VM Red_2A to Red_1A.

By default, OpenContrail vRouters prefer MPLSoUDP over MPLSoGRE. This is because IP switch implementations typically perform a much better load balancing of UDP packets than GRE packets. You can tune this encapsulation preference order at the OpenContrail GUI: Configure→Infrastructure→Global Config.

What if VMs Red_1A and Red_1B send IP packets to each other? They are both at vRouter_1, so there is no tunneling involved. IP packets are routed from one tap interface to another tap interface, locally at vRouter_1. This is similar to a PE that is forwarding IP traffic between different locally connected CEs.

Interconnecting Subscribers to Cloud VMs

The magic of this cloud SDN solution is that as soon as a VM comes up in the data center, or a subscriber connects to its access SP, they have end-to-end IP reachability. No network device needs to get any additional configuration: overlay networking combined with intelligent protocols like BGP do the trick.

ASBR1 is connected to the SP core and is supposed to have iBGP sessions established to the core RRs. The rest of the signaling is depicted in Figure 11-6. OpenContrail control nodes act like *multiprotocol* RRs. They speak XMPP to the vRouter agents and iBGP to the data center gateway node (DC-GW) converting the routes between both formats as appropriate.

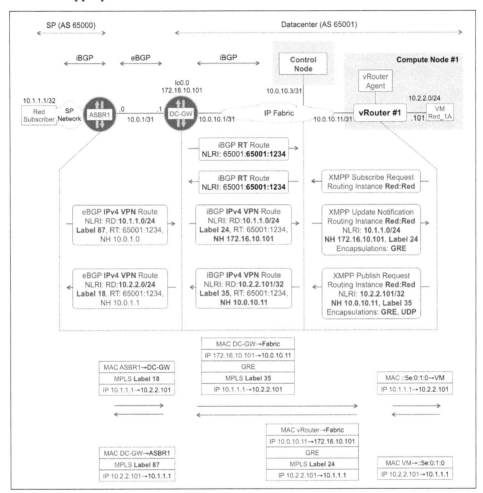

Figure 11-6. XMPP and BGP—L3 overlay at gateway and vRouter

BGP prefixes originated by OpenContrail have an automatically generated RD in the format <*ROUTER_ID*>:<*VPN_ID*>, so it supports load balancing of inbound traffic between different vRouters.

OpenContrail advertises its L3 prefixes by listing both GRE (MPLSoGRE) and UDP (MPLSoUDP) as available encapsulations. This information is encoded in the BGP *encapsulation* extended community.

For detailed coverage of the extended communities that OpenContrail adds to BGP prefixes, search in GitHub for an article on the topic.

In contrast, DC-GW does not include the encapsulation extended community, so OpenContrail assumes that the gateway supports only GRE (MPLSoGRE).

This is a least common denominator decision: MPLSoGRE is used, simply because it is the only encapsulation that *both* the gateway and OpenContrail (in L3 mode) support.

DC-GW configuration—MPLS-over-GRE

The Junos MPLS-over-GRE tunneling configuration is provided in Example 11-6.

Example 11-6. Dynamic GRE tunnel configuration—DC-GW (Junos)

```
1    routing-options {
2        dynamic-tunnels {
3            OVERLAY-TUNNELS {
4                source-address 172.16.10.101;
5                gre;
6                destination-networks 10.0.10.0/24;
7    }}}
```

With this configuration, the local PE (in this case, DC-GW) creates a dynamic GRE interface for each remote address <A> that meets the following two conditions:

- A received BGP VPN route has as remote BGP next hop <A>.
- <A> is within the address range specified in line 6.

Let's look at a dynamic GRE interface, which is pointing to vRouter_1 (Example 11-7).

Example 11-7. Dynamic GRE tunnel—DC-GW (Junos)

```
user@DC-GW> show route table inet.3 10.0.10.11
inet.3: 4 destinations, 4 routes (4 active, 0 holddown, 0 hidden)

+ = Active Route, - = Last Active, * = Both
10.0.10.11/32      *[Tunnel/300] 3d 15:31:10
                   > via gr-0/0/0.32769

user@DC-GW> show interfaces gr-0/0/0.32769
  Logical interface gr-0/0/0.32769 (Index 376) (SNMP ifIndex 579)
    Flags: Up Point-To-Point SNMP-Traps 0x0
```

```
IP-Header 10.0.10.11:172.16.10.101:47:df:64:0000080000000000
Encapsulation: GRE-NULL
Protocol inet, MTU: 1576
Protocol mpls, MTU: 1564, Maximum labels: 3
```

```
user@DC-GW> show route table VRF-Red.inet.0
```

```
10.2.2.101/32  *[BGP/170] 09:18:20, localpref 200, from 10.0.10.3
                  AS path: ?, validation-state: unverified
                > via gr-0/0/0.32769, Push 35
```

There is an interoperability example with IOS XE in the OpenContrail web page (*http://www.opencontrail.org/how-to-setup-opencontrail-gateway-juniper-mx-cisco-asr-and-software-gw/*).

Communication Between Virtual Networks

Inter-VN connectivity requirements are frequent. For example, the Red subscribers in the upper-left corner of Figure 11-3 might require access to the Blue VMs (Blue_1A and Blue_2A). Or Red VMs might need to communicate to Blue VMs.

Here is a nonexhaustive list on how to address these requirements:

- Add a new vNIC to the Blue VMs and place the vNIC in the Red VN. This approach solves the connectivity problem, but it's not very secure. Communication from Blue VMs toward the Red VMs becomes unrestricted.

- Add a new common RT to both VN Red and Blue in OpenContrail. This automatically leaks prefixes between both VNs. If the policies are conveniently updated in the DC-GW, the VNs are functionally blended into one VN. Again, the connectivity problem is solved, but it is not the best approach in terms of security.

- Define an OpenContrail policy (Configure→Networking→Policies) that allows traffic between both VNs. This policy is then explicitly applied to both VNs (Configure→Networking→Networks). After it is applied, prefixes are automatically leaked between VN Red and Blue inside OpenContrail. However, RTs are not modified. For this reason, it is necessary to explicitly configure the extranet (see Chapter 3) at the DC-GW to make this leaking effective up to the subscribers. But this has security implications, mind you.

Let's step back for a moment and briefly talk about policies in OpenContrail. Depending on the security requirements, policies can have a set of unidirectional and/or bidirectional terms. Suppose, for example, that you apply a policy that allows TCP traffic from the Red VN toward the Blue VN. As a result, vRouters become stateful firewalls and they support the creation of flows from Red to Blue but not from Blue to Red.

Control nodes retrieve flow information from vRouter agents for analytics purposes. However, vRouters are empowered to create flows with no intervention from the control nodes. This is very important from the perspective of performance: flow creation is distributed.

Last but not least, the most powerful and secure approach to allow inter-VN communication is to configure Service Function Chains (SFC). This is an SDN best-in-breed approach that lies at the heart of the NFV concept. One of its breakthrough advantages is that you can define SFCs without touching the configuration of the DC-GW. Chapter 12 covers NFV in detail.

Network Virtualization Overlay: L2_L3 Mode

After discussing OpenContrail's L3 mode, let's now focus on the L2_L3 mode. Unlike classical PEs, which keep the L3 VRF in a different instance with respect to the L2 EVI, an OpenContrail's VRF have a dual mode and integrate the L2 and L3 functionalities.

VXLAN Refresher

Chapter 8 introduces the Virtual eXtensible LAN (VXLAN) basic concepts, including its forwarding plane and an example of the control plane (EVPN). Let's quickly refresh the basics. Any VXLAN Tunnel Endpoint (VTEP) is an edge forwarder (functionally, like a PE). There are basically three types of VTEPs:

- Hypervisors implementing a VXLAN stack. The VXLAN header is handled by the forwarder component within the hypervisor. VMs just send and receive plain Ethernet frames: they have no VXLAN awareness.

- ToR switches with a VXLAN stack, providing connectivity to legacy switches, bare-metal servers, and hypervisors, which lack overlay capabilities.

- PE routers (data center gateways) implementing a VXLAN stack.

As of this writing, VXLAN has three alternative solutions to achieve MAC learning between VTEPs: EVPN, OVSDB, and BUM flooding over IP Multicast. This book considers the last approach as legacy so it only covers EVPN and OVSDB.

VXLAN use cases

VXLAN in SDN cloud architectures is typically used to provide an L2 overlay inside a data center that has an L3 underlay. ToR switches with VXLAN capabilities can also integrate legacy equipment (bare-metal servers, hypervisors, and switches that lack overlay capabilities) into the L2 overlay. Another use case is L2 Data Center Interconnection (DCI). If an application requires L2 connectivity between end systems in geo-graphically distant data centers, it is possible to stretch the L2 overlay across the WAN by using VXLAN.

> MPLS-over-X (where X can be MPLS, or UDP, or GRE), also addresses these very same use cases successfully.

Stretching L2 overlays across geographical boundaries is not necessarily a good idea. The best practice is to reduce as much as possible the scope of L2 broadcast domains. Even L2 overlays have a loop risk.

There are several ways to implement DCI, and probably the most popular is depicted in Figure 11-7. In this case, the data center gateway implements EVPN VXLAN toward the local data center, and EVPN MPLS toward the WAN. These two services are stitched at the same L2 instance in the DC-GW.

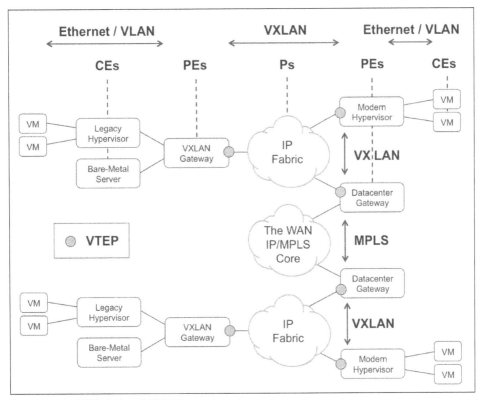

Figure 11-7. VXLAN and VTEPs

Intrasubnet (L2) and Intersubnet (L3) Traffic

In L3-only mode, OpenContrail supports two overlay encapsulations (GRE and UDP) and two address families (RT and IP VPN). Moving to L2_L3 mode, one more encapsulation (VXLAN) and one more BGP address family (EVPN) are added to the list. But these are only applicable to intrasubnet traffic.

In L2_L3 mode, there are two types of traffic: *intrasubnet* and *intersubnet*. Remember that a VN is a set of subnets, so intra-VN traffic can either be intrasubnet or intersubnet. For example, if VN Red consists of 10.2.2.0/24 and 10.3.3.0/24:

- A packet from 10.2.2.101 to 10.2.2.103 is intrasubnet.
- A packet from 10.2.2.101 to 10.3.3.101 is intersubnet.

Intersubnet traffic follows the same rules that have just been described for L3-only mode. The mechanisms shown in Figure 11-5 and Figure 11-6 are applicable to this case. So let's focus on *intrasubnet* traffic. The current specification for EVPN as an NVO (*draft-ietf-bess-evpn-overlay*) does not allow for a given EVPN MAC/IP route to advertise both a MPLS label and a VNI. It is one or the other. For this reason, Open-Contrail advertises EVPN routes that have the following:

- MPLS label if VXLAN is not the locally preferred encapsulation
- VNI if VXLAN is the locally preferred encapsulation

Thus, the following examples assume that VXLAN is set as the top preferred encapsulation in OpenContrail configuration. Note that Figure 11-8 provides the network architecture and addressing for the upcoming examples.

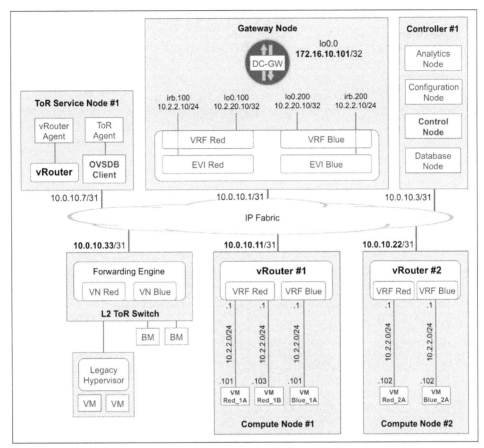

Figure 11-8. Infrastructure and VPN addressing—L2_L3 mode

Interconnecting VMs—IntraSubnet Traffic with VXLAN

The L2_L3 signaling process is shown in Figure 11-9, and it is very similar to the L3 illustration in Figure 11-5, but there are some differences. In L2_L3 mode, three routes are advertised for each vNIC address:

- IP VPN host address with encapsulation communities GRE and UDP. This is exactly the same route that is advertised in L3 mode (Figure 11-5).

- EVPN IP/MAC route with encapsulation VXLAN and a VNI (5100, in this example). This is the only route shown in Figure 11-9.

- EVPN MAC route with encapsulation VXLAN and a VNI (5100, in this example).

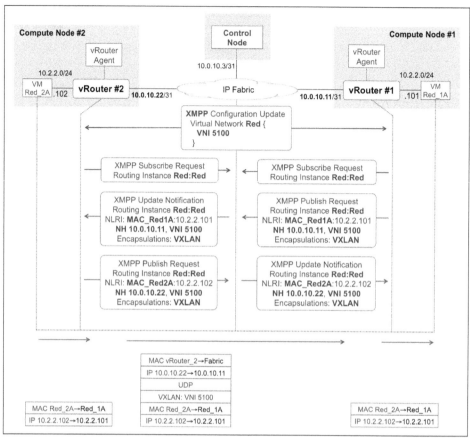

Figure 11-9. XMPP and VXLAN—L2_L3 intrasubnet mode

Remember that EVPN IP/MAC and MAC routes are conceptually similar to ARP and bridge entries—they are just distributed through the control plane. The most relevant information element for intrasubnet traffic forwarding is the EVPN MAC route.

MPLS labels are locally assigned by a vRouter. On the other hand, VNIs are typically configured to the same value on all VTEPs. In OpenContrail, the VNI is a property of the VN, and this is why the control node sends the message shown in Example 11-8 to all the vRouters with at least one tap interface in VN Red.

Example 11-8. XMPP—Configuration update with VN-VNI mapping

```
<?xml version="1.0"?>
<iq type="set" from="network-control@contrailsystems.com"
    to="default-global-system-config:vrouter_1/config">
  <config>
```

```
<update>
  <node type="virtual-network">
    <name>default-domain:mpls-in-the-sdn-era:Red</name>
    <virtual-network-properties>
      <vxlan-network-identifier>5100</vxlan-network-identifier>
      <forwarding-mode>l2_l3</forwarding-mode>
      <rpf></rpf>
    </virtual-network-properties>
  </node>
</update>
</config>
</iq>
```

The format of the remaining XMPP messages—Subscribe Request, Publish Request,
and Update Notification—is very similar to those shown in L3-only mode.
Example 11-9 presents an example of how an EVPN MAC/IP route is encoded in
XMPP.

Example 11-9. XMPP Publish Request—VM's vNIC MAC/IP route

```
<?xml version="1.0"?>
<iq type="set" from="vrouter_1"
    to="network-control@contrailsystems.com/bgp-peer" id="pubsub12">
  <pubsub xmlns="http://jabber.org/protocol/pubsub">
    <publish node="25/242/02:4e:a3:72:02:87,10.2.2.101/32">
      <item>
        <entry>
          <nlri>
            <af>25</af>
            <safi>242</safi>
            <ethernet-tag>5100</ethernet-tag>
            <mac>02:4e:a3:72:02:87</mac>
            <address>10.2.2.101/32</address>
          </nlri>
          <next-hops>
            <next-hop>
              <af>1</af>
              <address>10.0.10.11</address>
              <label>5100</label>
              <tunnel-encapsulation-list>
                <tunnel-encapsulation>vxlan</tunnel-encapsulation>
              </tunnel-encapsulation-list>
            </next-hop>
          </next-hops>
          <sequence-number>0</sequence-number>
          <local-preference>100</local-preference>
        </entry>
      </item>
    </publish>
  </pubsub>
</iq>
```

```
<iq type="set" from="vrouter_1"
    to="network-control@contrailsystems.com/bgp-peer"
    id="collection20">
  <pubsub xmlns="http://jabber.org/protocol/pubsub">
    <collection node="default-domain:mpls-in-the-sdn-era:
                      Red:Red">
      <associate node="25/242/02:4e:a3:72:02:87,10.2.2.101/32"/>
    </collection>
  </pubsub>
</iq>
```

The VNI is encoded as a `<label>`. Not surprising: it plays the same role! SAFI 242 is reserved for private use. Because XMPP is used only between control nodes and vRouter agents, using a reserved SAFI is fine. The proper EVPN SAFI (70) is used in the iBGP updates: this is all that matters for interoperability purposes.

BUM traffic flooding

As of this writing, a vRouter (as a VTEP) floods BUM traffic by using an Ingress Replication (IR) mechanism. See the EVPN sections in Chapter 8 for more details. Translated to XMPP, these routes contain `<mac>ff:ff:ff:ff:ff:ff</mac>`.

VMs take care of ARP resolution. In L2_L3 mode, unlike L3-only mode, vRouters do not perform any proxy-like ARP function for intrasubnet IP addresses. This is the current implementation, but it might change in the future.

vRouter and Gateway Nodes—L2_L3 Mode

Again, as you can see in Figure 11-10, control nodes translate XMPP messages to BGP messages, and vice versa.

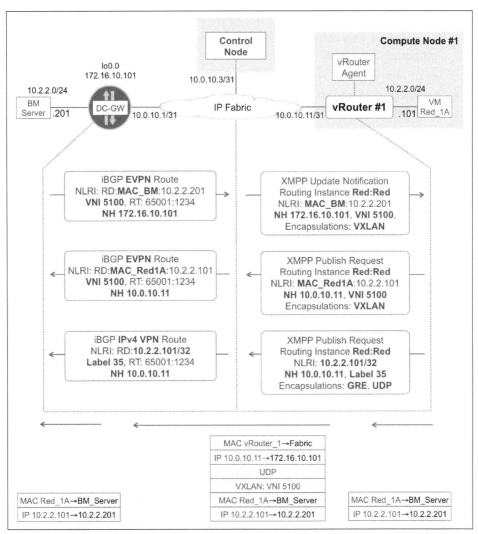

Figure 11-10. XMPP and BGP—L2 overlay at gateway and vRouter

DC-GW can act either as an L2 or an L3 gateway. With regard to the bare-metal (BM) server on the left in Figure 11-10, DC-GW plays the role of an L2 gateway because BM and VM Red_1A are in the same subnet. So, as you might expect from an L2 overlay solution, the original MAC headers are preserved end-to-end.

What if the BM server was in a different subnet than the VM? In this case (*not* shown in Figure 11-10), DC-GW acts as an L3 gateway, and it should be configured with two different bridge domains:

- One bridge domain that includes the local Attachment Circuit (AC) connected to the BM server: you can optionally stretch this bridge domain beyond DC-GW by configuring a VXLAN VNI on it, but this VNI must be different from 5100 in this particular example.

- One bridge domain that is configured with VNI 5100 and therefore is L2 overlay-connected to the VM Red_1A.

Now, DC-GW has two Integrated Routing and Bridging (IRB) interfaces, one linked to each bridge domain. These IRB interfaces make it possible for DC-GW to perform L3 forwarding, the mechanics of which are fully discussed in Chapter 8. This is inter-subnet traffic and the original L2 headers are stripped before sending the packets through the overlay tunnel. From a routing perspective, the IP VPN routes for the BM's and VM's host prefixes are the ones taken into account. Therefore, for intersub-net traffic, DC-GW is an L3 gateway, and the transport is MPLS-over-GRE (not VXLAN).

As of this writing, the implementation in OpenContrail and in a Junos DC-GW is symmetrical:

L2_L3 intrasubnet
 EVPN as the control plane and VXLAN as the overlay tunnel; original L2 headers are preserved.

L2_L3 intersubnet is similar to L3
 IP VPN as the control plane and MPLS-over-GRE as the overlay tunnel (or MPLS over UDP for vRouter-to-vRouter); original L2 headers are stripped.

This symmetry rule has a very specific exception. Imagine an intrasubnet IP flow between a VM and an IRB interface at DC-GW. For example, ping between 10.2.2.101 and 10.2.2.10 (this is DC-GW's IRB address, as illustrated in Figure 11-8). One IP endpoint of this flow is the IRB interface itself—in other words, it is host traffic from the point of view of DC-GW. In this very specific case, OpenContrail vRouter uses an L2 mechanism (like L2_L3 intrasubnet in the preceding list) while a Junos DC-GW uses a L3 mechanism (like L2_L3 intersubnet in the preceding list). The implementation in IOS XR was not explored.

Integrating Legacy L2 World into the NVO

NVOs are great, but not every OS supports them. As a result, some legacy servers, hypervisors, and switches are not overlay-capable. These legacy devices typically support VLANs only; therefore, they need a gateway to become part of the NVO.

L2 Gateways and OVSDB

There are basically two options for such a legacy device:

- Connecting the device to an L3 gateway that provides IP termination and assigns the AC to an IP VPN or to the global IP routing table. This is a classic approach.
- Connecting the device to an L2 gateway that stitches the AC into an overlay L2 VPN—such as VXLAN. Typically, an external service node is also required to handle broadcast traffic like ARP and DHCP.

The first option is IP VPN business as usual. Let's explore the second option. VXLAN is a common L2 overlay in IP fabrics. Among the different control-plane options available for VXLAN, EVPN is the most scalable and flexible one. However, not every L2 gateway (and not every NVO controller) supports it.

As of this writing, EVPN often coexists with a different control-plane protocol. This protocol is OVSDB. It is a TCP-based protocol defined in RFC 7047, and like EVPN, can propagate MAC learning state through the control plane. The vast majority of NVO solutions in the industry, including OpenContrail, support OVSDB.

OVSDB is very different from BGP (and XMPP). It is easy to see that this protocol comes from the IT world. The controller has a centralized relational database, and each agent has a subset of this database. Both the controller and the agents must be able to modify this database, and the changes must be synchronized.

Figure 11-11 shows BM, a bare-metal server that is connected to an L2 gateway—labeled as L2 ToR. The L2 ToR is a VTEP and also implements an OVSDB server.

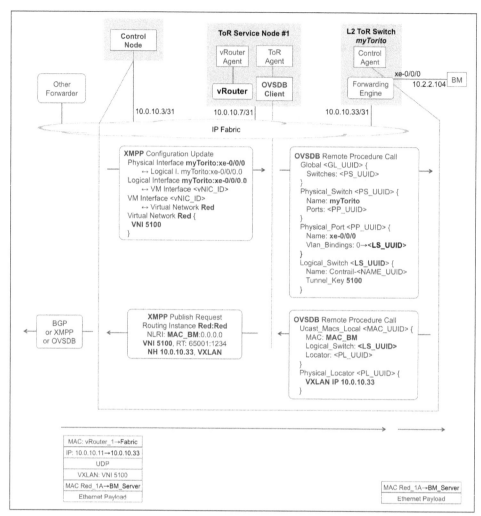

Figure 11-11. XMPP and OVSDB—Extending L2 overlay to BM server

ToR Service Nodes

ToR service nodes (TSN) are part of OpenContrail and they perform two functions through their different software components:

Control Plane Proxy

The TSN instantiates one *ToR agent* for every L2 ToR gateway that supports OVSDB but not EVPN. Each ToR agent speaks XMPP with the control node and implements an OVSDB client that interacts with the L2 ToR device. ToR agents at a TSN basically implement a selective translation function between XMPP and OVSDB.

Control Packet Proxy

The TSN also runs one *vRouter*, but this does not connect VMs. Instead, the vRouter acts as a VTEP that exchanges certain VXLAN-encapsulated control traffic (ARP, DHCP, DNS) with the L2 ToR devices. The vRouter agent at the TSN implements a proxy function. It generates control packets based on the information that it receives from the control node. For example, suppose that the TSN vRouter receives a DHCP discover message—originated by a BM server and VXLAN-tunneled by the L2 ToR toward the TSN's vRouter. In this case, the vRouter can send the DHCP offer back, based on the information that it has previously received from the control node via XMPP.

From the perspective of both the control node and the vRouter, and regardless of whether the latter is VM-facing or TSN-based, the mechanism to assign an IP to a VM or to a BM server, respectively, is exactly the same. The control node centralizes this information and provides it to the vRouter agent via XMPP.

It is possible to provide TSN active-active redundancy by making the control nodes advertise a floating IP and redirect OVSDB over TCP sessions to the appropriate TSN.

Binding a Bare-Metal Server to the Overlay

If an L2 ToR device supports EVPN, it just needs to establish BGP sessions to the control nodes. Things become more complex if the L2 ToR supports OVSDB but not EVPN. Figure 11-11 shows how OpenContrail integrates—into the VNO—a BM server that is connected to such an L2 ToR.

XMPP signaling

After the ToR-BM link is added on the OpenContrail GUI (Configure→Physical Devices) or on the north-bound RESTful API, control nodes start the signaling.

Example 11-10. XMPP—Configuration update to a TSN vRouter agent

```
1    <?xml version="1.0"?>
2    <iq type="set" from="network-control@contrailsystems.com"
3        to="default-global-system-config:tsn_1/config">
4    <config>
5      <update>
6        <node type="physical-interface">
7          <name>default-global-system-config:myTorito:xe-0/0/0</name>
8        </node>
9        <node type="logical-interface">
10         <name>default-global-system-config:myTorito:
11               xe-0/0/0:xe-0/0/0.0</name>
12       </node>
13       <link>
```

```
14          <node type="physical-interface">
15            <name>default-global-system-config:myTorito:xe-0/0/0</name>
16          </node>
17          <node type="logical-interface">
18            <name>default-global-system-config:myTorito:
19                  xe-0/0/0:xe-0/0/0.0 </name>
20          </node>
21          <metadata type="physical-interface-logical-interface" />
22        </link>
23        <node type="virtual-machine-interface">
24          <name>default-domain:mpls-in-the-sdn-era:
25                e20af8cd-ef70-4608-a3ec-f34eb5018410</name>
26        </node>
27        <link>
28          <node type="logical-interface">
29            <name>default-global-system-config:myTorito:
30                  xe-0/0/0:xe-0/0/0.0</name>
31          </node>
32          <node type="virtual-machine-interface">
33            <name>default-domain:mpls-in-the-sdn-era:
34                  e20af8cd-ef70-4608-a3ec-f34eb5018410
35              </name>
36          </node>
37          <metadata type="logical-interface-virtual-machine-interface">
38        </link>
39      </update>
40    </config>
41  </iq>
```

The Configuration Update in Example 11-10 is not complete. A selection is shown to illustrate the key idea: OpenContrail internally maps the ToR-BM interface to a VM interface or virtual-machine-interface object (lines 27 through 38). This is very important because the XMPP encoding used for VM interfaces is reused for ToR-BM interfaces.

Let's see how. Back in Example 11-2 (lines 35 through 59), a genuine VM interface was linked to a VN, an IP address, and a VRF. It's possible to do exactly the same thing for the VM interface that is associated to a BM server. Following is the additional information that the control node sends to the TSN:

- The VN that the ToR-BM interface belongs to (*Red*): this VN is in L2_L3 mode and it has a VNI associated, so the VXLAN encapsulation is known.

- The VRF that the ToR-BM interface belongs to (Red:Red).

- The IP address that is preassigned to the BM server. Thus, the TSN knows what IP to offer when the BM sends a DHCP discover packet—and the L2 ToR device encapsulates it in VXLAN toward the TSN.

OVSDB signaling

As its name implies, OVSDB is a protocol used to transfer and synchronize a database between different systems. OVSDB is based on JavaScript Object Notation (JSON). The schema of the *hardware_vtep* database is documented, and you can easily find it in the OVS (Open vSwitch) website at *http://www.openvswitch.org*.

You might wonder why OpenContrail internally uses XMPP instead of OVSDB. The reasons are flexibility and performance, especially when a DC-GW is present: XMPP and BGP follow the same structural principles.

In the MPLS analogy, an L2 ToR is seen as a PE, BM servers as CEs, and ToR's access interfaces as ACs. With the information shown in Example 11-11, the L2 ToR switch called myTorito knows how to integrate its untagged access interface xe-0/0/0.0 into a VXLAN overlay with VNI 5100.

Example 11-11. OVSDB—Integrating a ToR-BM Port in the Overlay

```
1    "Global":{
2      "587dc36b-09dd-411b-b0e3-44300800d6b9":{
3        "new":{
4          "switches":
5            ["uuid","3841501b-71a6-4f84-97f4-b8aa72ea1723"]
6        }
7      }
8    }
9    "Physical_Switch":{
10     "3841501b-71a6-4f84-97f4-b8aa72ea1723":{
11       "new":{
12         "name":"myTorito",
13         "tunnel_ips":"10.0.10.33",
14         "ports":[
15           "set",[
16             ["uuid","37e69f8a-4c29-413a-b641-a9b420c1548b"],
17           ]
18         ]
19       }
20     }
21   }
22   "Physical_Port":{
23     "37e69f8a-4c29-413a-b641-a9b420c1548b":{
24       "new":{
25         "name":"xe-0/0/0",
26         "vlan_bindings":[
27           "map",[
28             [0,["uuid","26aeb04f-89c7-4c5b-a0d7-c4c9b16aff5c"]]
29           ]
30         ]
31       }
32     }
```

```
33    }
34    "Logical_Switch":{
35      "26aeb04f-89c7-4c5b-a0d7-c4c9b16aff5c":{
36        "new":{
37          "name":"Contrail-fd2f3fd7-db4f-4f0a-a5ab-f3800f5348a0",
38          "tunnel_key":5100
39        }
40      }
41    }
```

Let's analyze this example from a database perspective. The Global table contains the list of physical L2 ToR devices. More specifically, it contains the list of the Universally Unique Identifier (UUID) of each device. The TSN has the full database, but it only exchanges with a given ToR the section that corresponds to that ToR. In this example, there is only one ToR, whose UUID identifies one entry in the Physical_Switch table (lines 5 and 10 match).

The Physical_Switch table has one entry per physical L2 ToR. Lines 10 through 20 display one single entry, with the following fields:

name
    States the L2 ToR's hostname (myTorito).

tunnel_ips
    Specifies the L2 ToR's VTEP address.

port
    Lists the UUIDs of all the access ports that the L2 ToR integrates in the overlay. Each UUID references one entry in the Physical_Port table: lines 16 and 23 match.

The Physical_Port table has one entry per port. Lines 23 through 32 display one single entry, with the following fields:

name
    This is the access port in L2 ToR's vendor-specific terminology. In this example, the L2 ToR is a device running Junos, hence the xe-0/0/0 format. Of course, the format needs to be adapted to the L2 ToR specific vendor, as appropriate.

vlan_bindings
    This is a map between per-port access VLANs and logical switches. You can see a logical switch like a separate bridge domain at a given L2 ToR. In this example, the BM port is untagged so there is only VLAN zero and it is mapped to the UUID of an entry in the Logical_Switch table (lines 28 and 35 match).

The Logical_Switch table has one entry per bridge domain. Lines 35 through 40 display one single entry, with the following fields:

name
 This is the name of the bridge domain as it has to be configured on the L2 ToR.

tunnel_key
 This is the VNI of the bridge domain.

Putting it all together, the OVSDB message in Example 11-11 triggers a configuration change on the L2 ToR. The latter is responsible for translating the standard OVSDB message into a vendor-specific configuration. For example, Example 11-12 shows the resulting change if the L2 ToR device is a QFX Series running Junos.

Example 11-12. Configuration change triggered by an OVSDB message—Junos

```
1    [edit interfaces]
2    +   xe-0/0/0 {
3    +       encapsulation ethernet-bridge;
4    +       unit 0;
5    +   }
6    [edit vlans]
7    +   Contrail-fd2f3fd7-db4f-4f0a-a5ab-f3800f5348a0 {
8    +       interface xe-0/0/0.0;
9    +       vxlan {
10   +           vni 5100;
11   +       }
12   +   }
```

The VLAN configured in lines 6 through 12 is actually a bridge domain: it does not even have a vlan-id! Note that Example 11-11 (line 37) and Example 11-12 (line 7) match.

Access ports can also be VLAN tagged. In this case, there could be several entries in the vlan_bindings map.

MAC Learning with OVSDB

As shown in Example 11-13 a new entry in a bridge domain's MAC table is simply a new entry in a certain table inside the *hardware_vtep* database. As soon as the L2 ToR learns the MAC address of the BM server, it adds a new row to the Ucast_Macs_Local table and propagates the change toward the TSN.

Example 11-13. MAC table entry in an OVSDB message

```
1    "Ucast_Macs_Local":{
2        "935afb18-23b8-42b2-8691-41342cf56c07":{
```

```
 3          "new":{
 4            "ipaddr":"0.0.0.0",
 5            "logical_switch":["uuid",
 6                              "26aeb04f-89c7-4c5b-a0d7-c4c9b16aff5c"],
 7            "MAC":"00:21:59:c4:1c:ee",
 8            "locator":["uuid","0d42b081-e569-4cec-91e3-ff4e92813e9f"]
 9          }
10        }
11      }
12      "Physical_Locator":{
13        "0d42b081-e569-4cec-91e3-ff4e92813e9f":{
14          "new":{
15            "dst_ip":"10.0.10.33",
16            "encapsulation_type":"vxlan_over_ipv4"
17          }
18        }
19      }
```

Putting it all together again, the L2 ToR switch is telling the TSN that the BM server's MAC address (line 7) is reachable at the ToR's VTEP address (line 15) via VXLAN (line 16). And, according to the Logical_Switch table in Example 11-11, with VNI 5100.

Let's reread the message from a database perspective.

The Ucast_Macs_Local table has one entry for each MAC address of a device that is locally connected on an access port. Lines 2 through 9 display one single entry, with the following fields:

logical_switch
    This is the UUID of the logical switch (or bridge domain). Example 11-13 (line 6) matches the logical switch in Example 11-11 (lines 35 through 40). This is a VXLAN domain with VNI 5100.

locator
    This is the UUID of an entry in the Physical_Locator table.

The Physical_Locator table has one entry for each local or remote VTEP. Lines 13 through 18 display one single entry, with the following columns:

dst_ip
    This is L2 ToR myTorito's local VTEP address.

encapsulation_type
    This is (surprise!) VXLAN-over-IPv4.

As you can see, lines 8 and 13 in Example 11-13 match.

There is another table called Umacs_Macs_Remote for the MAC addresses that the L2 ToR learns from the TSN. Logically, a MAC that is *local* from the perspective of an

L2 ToR device is by definition remote *from* the perspective of another L2 ToR device. So, these entries are moved around between tables depending on the L2 ToR to which the TSN is talking.

Example 11-14 demonstrates how the resulting MAC table looks in a QFX Series running Junos.

Example 11-14. MAC table with local and remote (OVSDB) entries—Junos

```
1    root@QFX> show ethernet-switching table
2
3    MAC flags (S - static MAC, D - dynamic MAC, O - ovsdb MAC)
4
5    Ethernet switching table : 3 entries, 1 learned
6    Routing instance : default-switch
7       Vlan          MAC              MAC      Age    Logical
8       name          address          flags           interface
9       Contrail-fd2f3fd7-db4f-4f0a-a5ab-f3800f5348a0
10                    00:21:59:c4:1c:ee   D       -      xe-0/0/0.0
11      Contrail-fd2f3fd7-db4f-4f0a-a5ab-f3800f5348a0
12                    02:75:fa:14:5a:07   SO      -      vtep.32769
13      Contrail-fd2f3fd7-db4f-4f0a-a5ab-f3800f5348a0
14                    02:1d:1e:10:74:ad   SO      -      vtep.32770
```

Lines 9 through 10 show the entry associated to the local BM server's MAC address. It corresponds to a row in the Umacs_Macs_Local table (Example 11-13, line 7).

The following two MAC entries correspond to entries in the Umacs_Macs_Remote table:

- Lines 11 and 12 show the MAC address of VM Red_1A, which is reachable through vRouter_1 acting as a VTEP.

- Lines 13 and 14 show the MAC address of the remote BM server that is connected to the DC-GW (see Figure 11-10, in the upper-left corner). Remember that in this case, the DC-GW is acting as a VTEP, but its control plane is EVPN and not OVSDB.

As you can see, the `vtep.<#>` tunneling interface is different on each of the two remote entries. Indeed, the overlay tunneling headers differ because the remote VTEPs are not the same: vRouter_1 versus DC-GW.

Bare-Metal Servers and OVSDB—the Forwarding Plane

Intrasubnet known unicast traffic is forwarded as shown at the bottom of Figure 11-11. Traffic is directly exchanged between the VTEPs by using standard VXLAN encapsulation. The TSN stays *off* the forwarding path.

Although the control plane is complex, with several protocols involved, the forwarding plane is very similar: VXLAN everywhere.

How about intersubnet known unicast traffic? The BM servers need to have a default gateway or static route pointing to the DC-GW. The latter performs intersubnet routing through its IRB interfaces, the details of which are simply beyond the scope of this book.

Unknown unicast traffic is regulated by the OpenContrail VN configuration: it can either be dropped or flooded. In the latter case, the information about remote VTEPs is kept in the table Mcast_Macs_Remote. The corresponding entries have MAC "unknown-dst". Because flooding typically involves IR toward several remote VTEPs, this table has a `locator_set` rather than a single locator.

Finally, broadcast traffic in OVSDB environments relies on the TSN to perform the replication. This is especially important for ARP and DHCP, as discussed earlier in this chapter. On the other hand, IR of broadcast frames is definitely an option for L2 gateways that support EVPN.

 Multicast in NVO is not covered in this book.

## CHAPTER 12

Network Function Virtualization

Chapter 11—which is dedicated to Network Virtualization Overlays (NVO)—described a modern paradigm for the integration of virtual machines (VMs), containers, and bare-metal servers in a (private, public, or telco) cloud. The resulting overlay provides connectivity between subscribers and VMs, or between different VMs. The latter are typically servers, which behave like IP endpoints. Subscribers also behave like IP endpoints, therefore a typical service example would be a TCP session between a subscriber client and a VM acting as a database server (or a web server) in the cloud.

Network Function Virtualization (NFV) takes advantage of NVO by allowing VMs (or containers) to actually perform a *network service* function. These VMs are typically in-line and instead of acting as communication endpoints, they are transit devices, with a left and a right interface. There are many examples of such network service functions: stateful firewalling, Network Address Translation (NAT), load balancing, Distributed Denial-of-Service (DDoS) detection and mitigation, Deep Packet Inspection (DPI), Intrusion Detection and Prevention (IDS/IDP), IPSec/TLS tunnel termination, proxy functions, and so on.

 Throughout this chapter, every time you see the term *VM*, you can think of either a VM or a container. Network functions can be implemented on any of these virtual compute entities (and on *physical* devices, too).

Depending on the actual service provided by the Virtual Network Function (VNF), a VM may act as follows:

As an IP endpoint
> For example, a VM can establish TCP sessions, becoming a TCP client or server for both left-facing and right-facing sessions. An archetypical use case is a web proxy. From a network architecture perspective, this model is similar to a plain NVO in which the VM has two interfaces—one left-facing and one right-facing. The NVO does not need to perform any fancy traffic steering, because the IP endpoints are at the VM itself.

As a transit element in the IP communications
> In this case, the VM acts upon packets, and the IP endpoints are outside the VM. For example, a TCP session might transit this VM in such a way that the VM is neither the client nor the server of that session. This is a genuine network function and it's the main focus of this chapter.

NFV in the Software-Defined Networking Era

NFV was initially proposed as a paradigm to implement network functions over Intel x86–based architectures. Its natural applicability to cloud infrastructures makes NFV interesting, attractive, and timely. Before diving into the details, let's step back for a moment and analyze NFV from a broader business perspective.

A first motivation for NFV is the perceived ability to reduce capital expenditures (CAPEX), assuming that x86-based commodity servers can be cheaper than vendor-specific hardware and application-specific integrated circuits (ASICs). And they are. Commodity servers are much cheaper than, for example, a router, by quite a substantial factor. But that is comparing apples to oranges because the biggest source of cost in our industry is software development, not hardware or hardware development. If there are no hardware sales to amortize the software R&D, software needs to be priced based on its development costs, and summed up to the x86 commodity servers. In addition to the various software components, there's also the operating system (OS), the virtualization layer, and the orchestration layer, which all come with any new NFV components or elements.

Virtual or Physical?

Anyway, let's take the software costs out of the discussion and imagine a hypothetical world where all the network service applications were open source, supported, and reliable. Does NFV replace the need for physical network devices? Not always. It all depends on the actual requirements. Let's answer this question after a brief technical introduction.

In the NFV world, the term *virtual* is used somewhat in a misleading manner. For many people, something is virtual if it is executed in general-purpose processors based on the Intel x86 architecture. This is actually a very narrow definition. This book is full of virtual things; for example, VPNs are virtual, but they are orthogonal to x86.

Software is ubiquitous and is not only restricted to general-purpose processors. For example, network device ASICs typically execute microcode. Although this microcode used to be very limited in the past, in recent years it has dramatically increased in flexibility and richness. One good example is Juniper's Trio architecture, whose microcode programmability makes it possible to implement any new encapsulation with software.

Table 12-1 provides a comparison between the three available platforms to execute network function software.

Table 12-1. Platform comparison

	Function flexibility	Network performance	Power efficiency	Platform portability
Intel x86	High	Low	Low	High
Custom Silicon	High	High	High	Medium[a]
Merchant Silicon	Low	High	Medium	Low

[a] *For both Junos and IOS XR, the control plane has always run on general-purpose processors. However, until very recently the low-level microcode instructions that execute on custom ASICs were not portable to x86. With Juniper virtual MX—and soon Cisco virtual ASR—a fully x86-compatible OS emulates both the control-plane and the forwarding-engine ASICs. In this way, the software that runs on custom silicon is portable to x86.

Faithful ASIC emulations over x86 typically have a lower performance for two reasons: the interplatform adaptation layers, and the intrinsic limitations of the x86 architecture. There is no free lunch.

Intel x86 processors

The x86 architecture is specialized for complex computation tasks and provides the best environment in which to program, test, and deploy new applications. That is where it excels over any other technology. But, because it is general purpose, it can perform many functions and not all at the same level of efficiency. Packet-forwarding functions do not require complex computation steps (with the exception of encryption/decryption) but instead need fast context switching and memory lookup. The key aspect for efficiency when it comes to packet forwarding is the ability to parallelize. Certainly x86 can do packet forwarding, but at the expense of efficiency, and that (if you are looking for scale) means higher power consumption, higher space, higher cooling requirements, and ultimately, potentially higher total cost of ownership (TCO).

The barriers preventing the Intel x86 architecture from achieving better forwarding performance are well known: clock frequency limits, challenges to increase number of cores, chipset size constraints, number of pins, and so on. All these constraints have set a slow pace of incremental improvement. Unless something very innovative is discovered, the ability to substantially grow packet-forwarding capacity for Intel x86 CPUs is questionable.

Intel x86 remains a great platform for many use cases. Indeed, if the required packet-processing performance is low, Intel x86 is the best way to go. As mentioned earlier, several networking vendors have *virtual*—or rather, x86-adapted—images of their network OSs. And the possibility of deploying new innovative services on x86 is bound only by the imagination.

Custom ASICs

Custom ASICs are designed by networking vendors and have the richest and most flexible packet plus flow-processing features. If the target packet-processing performance is medium or high while the processing logic required is somewhat complex, custom silicon provides the lowest TCO—despite having a higher cost per unit.

Merchant ASICs

Merchant ASICs are designed and produced by chip vendors. Networking vendors write the software for the ASICs and ship them in self-branded network devices. As a result, the very same ASIC may be present in the equipment sold by different vendors. These chips typically have a very efficient pipeline, which is adapted to simple straight-line code, but as soon as the code has branching and looping—as is typically required for the sophisticated features in the network edge—these ASICs are neither efficient nor even capable of fulfilling the functionality requirements.

The bottom line is that there are several available architectures to execute network software functions, and they are all valid but not equivalent. Each has its own pros. The network designer must carefully choose among the options for *each* use case.

Applicability of NFV to Service Providers

After the technical foundations are laid, let's pursue the market analysis. Traffic growth on networks is still at 40%–50%, or even more, year on year. The network capacity required to sustain such demand growth must be at least at that level. The only way for the ecosystem to be sustainable is to have the following capacity growth characteristics:

- It is larger than the demand growth.

- It is at the same or lower cost, because demand growth does not necessarily drive revenue growth.

Such capacity growth is ultimately sustained on edge routers, core routers, security systems, and switching systems that increase their forwarding density at such pace. This hardware also keeps improving its footprint in terms of space, power consumption, cooling requirements, and so on.

As for the x86 architecture, it improves its packet-forwarding capacity on average 10% per year. A generalized shift of the networking industry toward NFV would lead to a capacity growth below the demand growth. Such a difference would need to be paid in number of units deployed, with the associated increase in CAPEX and OPEX.

Taking all of these factors into account, NFV has its best use case on the low-traffic regime. Does it make it irrelevant? No, not at all. NFV is a key enabler of *network agility*. If there is any single challenge that service providers (SPs) face, it is agility: introducing new services and new capabilities on their infrastructure, changing network behavior, and ultimately, reacting faster and with lower costs to new requirements. In one sentence: quickly adapting to the present and future demands of the market. And with traffic growth at 40%–50% year on year, there's a strong business reason why network agility is more important than ever.

Traditionally, the ISP business model has focused on large-scale services such as residential or mobile access, assuming that statistical gain drives the economics into the green zone. But these services are now commoditized: the revenue associated with them has already reached a plateau, if not decreased due to competition. Being able to provide new services in an agile manner is paramount.

On the other hand, shifting from a business model with one single service for ten million subscribers to another with one thousand services—and ten thousand subscribers for each service—is a major challenge. What if the service does not attain market traction? And if the validation cycle is so long that the service is already obsolete by the time it is finally launched?

Here is where NFV comes into play. The key factor is *uncertainty*. The more uncertainty there is about a service or about the demand, the more convenient it will be to approach it with NFV. And the more *certainty* there is about a service or demand (expected number of subscribers, traffic patterns, etc.), the more suitable a hardware technology will be.

Any new service or new function deployed on the network, mainly at the edge, starts with a lot of uncertainty. It is hard to predict how much traffic it will consume, how many subscribers are needed for the service to be profitable, how successful it will be, how fast the demand will grow, and so on. It is at this stage where an NFV-based deployment provides agility, lower entry costs, and a faster time to market. As demand grows, stabilizes, or becomes more predictable, uncertainties transform into knowledge. Then, cost efficiency per service unit likely becomes a priority, and only ASICs offer the capacity required to address the next phases of the service deployment.

On the other hand, NFV can play a major role in trying out new services with the guarantee that you can shut it down without a major upfront investment. In conclusion, NFV is a key tool for SPs to address many new small opportunities, each one characterized by a high uncertainty.

So, it's not a black-and-white decision between going virtual or going physical. Both have key roles at different phases of network growth and viability. They can definitely *coexist on a network infrastructure*, be connected to one another, and with the right tools also be seamlessly operated. This is what we go on to discuss in this chapter: how VNFs can be interconnected (chained) using technologies, such as MPLS, that can be naturally extended to hardware elements. In short, MPLS in the SDN era!

NFV Practical Use Case

Figure 12-1 shows a common NFV use case that will serve as this chapter's reference example. In it, subscribers access the Internet through a Service Function Chain (SFC)—frequently just called *Service Chain*—that consists of three VMs: SI_A, SI_B, and SI_C. The acronym *SI* stands for *service instance*, and here it is basically a VM that performs a network function. Being a VM, the function is virtualized by definition, so it is an NFV.

Each service instance performs a different network function and these are executed in sequence. For the moment, let's assume that none of these functions is NAT. In other words, the original IP source and destination addresses are maintained throughout the entire packet life—represented in Figure 12-1 as a snake-like double-arrowed solid line.

Similar to the NVO chapter and for exactly the same reasons, the examples in this NFV chapter are based on OpenContrail and the main challenge is finding a way to steer the traffic through the entire service function chain.

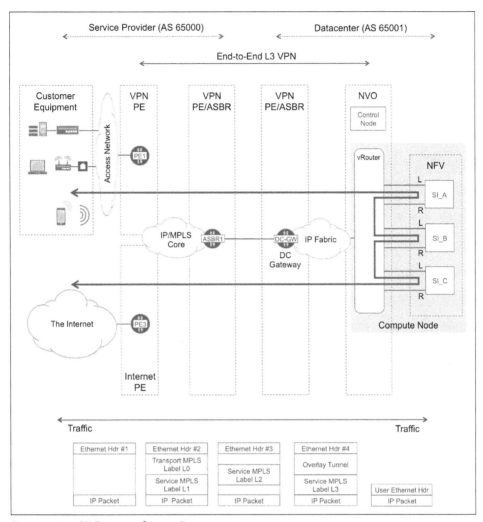

Figure 12-1. SFC inserted in an Internet access

 NFV is typically *intersubnet*. For simplicity, let's assume that the Virtual Networks (VNs) are in L3 mode.

Let's get into the heart of NFV and its forwarding and control planes.

NFV Forwarding Plane

As compared to its control plane, NFV's forwarding plane is quite simple, because it is just a combination of features that have already been described in this book. The signaling and forwarding in Figure 12-2 should look familiar if you have thoroughly read all the previous chapters.

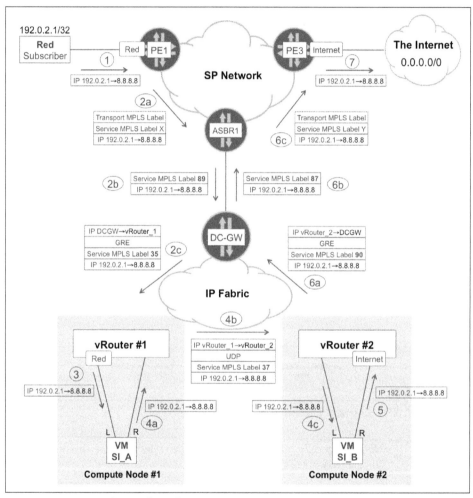

Figure 12-2. NFV—forwarding plane

Let's review a short description of the signaling.

PE3 injects the 0/0 prefix into the VPN Internet. This route is propagated in IP VPN format via BGP, reaching the NVO control nodes—not shown in the picture—after several session hops. Control nodes convey this information to the vRouter agents via

XMPP. Then, some magic route leaking takes place inside the NVO; as a result, the control nodes advertise the same 0/0 route into VPN Red, up to the data center gateway (DC-GW). This advertisement reaches PE1 after several BGP session hops.

 This chapter focuses on left-to-right or subscriber-to-Internet traffic. The reverse path is strictly symmetrical—with reversed source and destination IP addresses, and different MPLS labels. The subscriber's address 192.0.2.1 is reachable from VPN Internet through the NVO and, finally, VPN Red.

Figure 12-2 also illustrates a service chain with two service instances (for simplicity, the external one-hop L2 headers are not shown). Although it is perfectly possible to run both service instances on the *same* compute node, this example features them in *different* compute nodes in order to again illustrate the overlay connection between vRouters.

Here is the sequence for left-to-right packets that go from the subscriber to the Internet (note that the number sequence is also represented in Figure 12-2):

1. The Red subscriber, as a CE, sends a plain IP packet to PE1.

2. This part of the forwarding path takes place in the context of IP VPN Red. PE1 and vRouter_1 are the ingress and egress PE, respectively. PE1 processes the packet in VRF Red—strictly speaking, the VRF name is *Red:Red*. The MPLS service label changes twice, once at each of the Option B ASBRs (ASBR1 and DC-GW), which perform a next-hop-self operation on the BGP control plane.

3. vRouter_1, as an egress IP VPN PE, pops the MPLS service label. This label is associated to a CE: the VM interface (vNIC) connected to the left interface of VM SI_A.

4. The magic of the service function chain takes place and the remainder of the chapter unveils the magic. For the moment, just note that inside each vRouter the packet is plain IP, whereas it requires an overlay encapsulation to jump between vRouters.

5. The VM SI_B acts like a CE and sends the packet out of its right interface.

6. This next part of the forwarding path takes place in the context of IP VPN Internet. vRouter_2 and PE3 are the ingress and egress PEs, respectively. vRouter_2 processes the packet in the context of VRF Internet—strictly speaking, the VRF name is *Internet:Internet*. The MPLS service label changes twice, once at each of the Option B ASBRs (DC-GW and ASBR1), which perform a next-hop-self operation on the BGP control plane. As discussed in Chapter 3, it is possible to establish eBGP sessions from a VRF to connect to the Internet.

7. Finally, PE3 pops the last MPLS label and sends the packet out to the Internet.

There are several missing pieces in the puzzle, like the packet processing and forwarding inside the service instance VMs, or the service-chain implementation.

Regarding the VMs, let's assume for the moment that they implement interface-based forwarding: if a VM receives a packet on the left interface and the packet is not dropped (and it is not destined for the VM itself), the VM sends it out of the right interface. Conversely, what arrives on the right is forwarded out of the left interface. This topic is discussed at the end of this chapter.

Let's now focus on how OpenContrail builds the service chain by linking the service instances, and how the traffic is steered through the chain.

NFV—VRF Layout Models

Let's review sequence 4a in Figure 12-2. When the packet arrives to vRouter_1 from SI_A's right interface, it must be processed in the context of a VRF. But, which one?

- If it is VRF Red:Red, the next hop would be the vNIC connected to the left interface of VM SI_A. This would create a forwarding loop, so it is not an option.
- If it is VRF Internet:Internet, the next hop would be the DC-GW and the packet would escape the service chain without being processed by VM SI_B. Again, this is not an option.

So, this reasoning highlights that more auxiliary VRFs are needed to instantiate a service function chain.

If you look back at Figure 3-5, service chaining is not a new concept; in fact, it has existed for decades in SP networks. However, that asymmetrical route target (RT) chaining strategy is not particularly efficient—especially for long chains—and it is not easy to automate and operate.

OpenContrail supports the two alternative mechanisms to build SFCs depicted in Figure 12-3 and listed here:

- The transit VN model, referenced in *draft-fm-bess-service-chaining* as "Service Function Instances Connected by Virtual Networks".
- The two-VN model, referenced in *draft-fm-bess-service-chaining* as "Logical Service Functions Connected in a Chain"

Although not explicitly shown in this particular figure, you can definitely distribute service instances across different compute nodes.

Remember that OpenContrail allows creating VNs, whereas VRFs are automatically instantiated from VNs. By default, VN Red is linked to one single VRF called *Red:Red*.

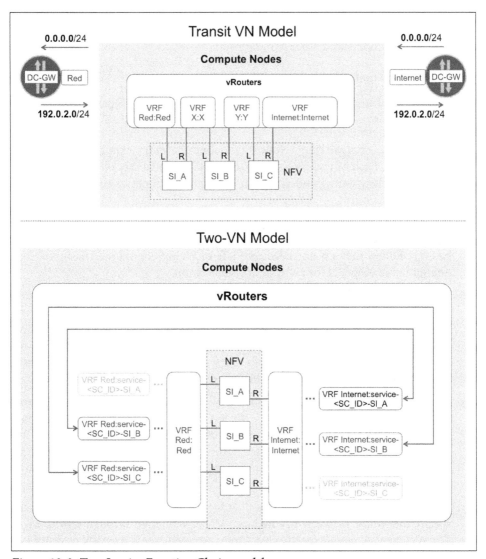

Figure 12-3. Two Service Function Chain models

Legacy VRF Layout—Transit VN Model

This *legacy* model requires N-1 transit VNs (named X and Y in Figure 12-3) for an SFC consisting of *N* service instances. The only purpose of these transit VNs is to build the chain. Although the following statement is not strictly accurate, you can view this model as functionally based on a 1:1 VN:VRF mapping. It is worthwhile to quickly review this model because it establishes a valuable conceptual foundation that you will need to understand other paradigms.

Transit VN model—configuration

Here are the steps to configure an SFC with transit VRFs using OpenContrail GUI—there are equivalent methods using the CLI and the north-bound API, too:

1. At Configure→Networking→Networks, define the entry-exit VNs, namely *Red* and *Internet*. Each of these VNs requires an RT that matches on the corresponding VRF at the gateway nodes. Assign at least one subnet to each VN for vNIC address allocation.

2. At Configure→Networking→Networks, define the transit VNs, namely X and Y. These VNs are flagged *Allowed Transit* and, because they are not propagated to gateway nodes, they do not need any RTs explicitly configured. Assign at least one subnet to each VN for vNIC address allocation.

3. At Configure→Services→Service Templates, define one template for each different network function. Typically, for a three-instance chain you need three templates. These specify the VM image to use and the interfaces that it will have. Typically, you need left, right, and management interfaces—the latter is not shown in the figures, because it does not participate on the SFC. (You can read more about templates at the end of this chapter.)

4. At Configure→Services→Service Instances, launch SI_A, SI_B, and SI_C from their corresponding templates. Place the left and right interfaces of each instance into the appropriate VN according to the upper part of Figure 12-3. Note that unlike *regular* VMs, which are defined at the compute controller, network service VMs or instances are defined at the NVO controller (OpenContrail), which in turn talks to the compute controller for the VM instantiation.

5. At Configure→Networking→Policies, define three policies. The first one should specify that traffic between VN Red and VN X should go through service SI_A. The second one should specify that traffic between VN X and VN Y should go through service SI_B. And the third policy should specify that traffic between VN Y and VN Internet should go through service SI_C.

6. At Configure→Networking→Networks, assign the previously created policies to the appropriate networks: first policy to VN Red and VN X; second policy to VN X and VN Y; and, third policy to VN Y and VN Internet.

This policy assignment automatically leaks the routes between the VNs, taking care of next hops in order to achieve the desired traffic steering.

Transit VN model—routes and next hops

Let's keep our focus on the top of Figure 12-3. Taking left-to-right (upstream) traffic as an example, the leaking process for the default 0/0 route goes as follows:

1. OpenContrail learns the 0/0 route from DC-GW and installs it on VRF *Internet:Internet*, setting DC-GW as the (MPLS-labeled) next hop.

2. OpenContrail leaks the 0/0 route into VRF Y:Y, setting the next hop to the left (L) interface of VM SI_C.

3. OpenContrail leaks the 0/0 route into VRF X:X, setting the next hop to the left (L) interface of VM SI_B.

4. OpenContrail leaks the 0/0 route into VRF *Red:Red*, setting the next hop to the left (L) interface of VM SI_A.

5. OpenContrail advertises the 0/0 route to the DC-GW in the context of VRF *Red:Red*, setting the vRouter—at the compute node where SI_A is running—as the (labeled) next hop.

A similar (reverse) mechanism applies to right-to-left (downstream) traffic. It relies on left-to-right leaking of the 192.0.2.0/24 prefix, setting the right-facing interfaces of the service instance VMs as the next hops throughout the chain.

NFV relies on the BGP and XMPP mechanisms already discussed in the NVO chapter. At this point, it is assumed that you know how routes are learned, advertised, and programmed in OpenContrail.

Modern VRF Layout—Two-VN Model

Let's make a first interpretation of the center-down area of Figure 12-3. In a nutshell, VRF *Red:Red* has a default route 0/0 that points to the left interface of SI_A. After receiving a packet on its left interface, SI_A performs interface-based forwarding and sends the packet out of its right interface. The vRouter receives the packet from SI_A's right interface and forwards it according to VRF *Internet:service-<SC_ID>_SI_A*, which is linked to VRF *Red:service-<SC_ID>_SI_B*, whose default route points to the left interface of SI_B. In this way, the packet flows through the chain until it exits

SI_C's right interface. At this point, the vRouter forwards the packet according to the VRF *Internet:Internet* table, which has a default route pointing to the outside world (DC-GW).

This alternative and modern approach for defining an SFC in OpenContrail simply relies on just two VNs: the left VN and the right VN. It will take several pages to fully describe this model so that we can make sense of it. Keep reading.

Of course, as many VNs as you like can play the left or right VN role; but within a given SFC, there is only one VN pair [left, right]. In this example, these are VNs Red and Internet, respectively. The left interface of all of the service instances are assigned to the left VN on the vRouter. Likewise, all the right interfaces are assigned to the right VN.

Let's begin with the configuration details because they will cement the foundation to understand the actual implementation.

Two-VN model—configuration

Here are the steps to configure an SFC with transit VRFs in OpenContrail's GUI— there are equivalent methods using the CLI and the north-bound API:

1. At Configure→Networking→Networks, define the entry-exit VNs, namely *Red* and *Internet*. Each of these VNs requires an RT that matches on the corresponding VRF at the gateway nodes. Assign at least one subnet to each VN for vNIC address allocation. No transit VNs need to be defined.

2. At Configure→Services→Service Templates, define one template for each different network function.

3. At Configure→Services→Service Instances, launch SI_A, SI_B, and SI_C from their corresponding templates. Place the left and right interfaces of each instance into the appropriate VN: *left on Red, right on Internet*.

4. At Configure→Networking→Policies, define *one single policy*. The policy states that traffic between VN Red and VN Internet should go through the following service instances *in sequence*: SI_A, SI_B, and SI_C.

5. At Configure→Networking→Networks, assign the previously created policy to VN Red and VN Internet.

This policy assignment automatically leaks the routes between the VNs, taking care of next hops so as to achieve the desired traffic steering. This model has a much simpler configuration scheme, given that you don't need to define transit VNs. The complex magic happens behind the curtains.

In L3VPN terms, this magic is a combination of the following three features implemented at the vRouter (this list is dedicated to those readers who come from the SP routing and MPLS worlds—if this is not the case for you, feel free to skip it):

- Interface leaking between VRFs so that different VRFs can resolve routes toward the same vRouter-VM interface.
- Per-CE MPLS labels so that packets arriving from the overlay are MPLS-switched (by executing a pop operation) toward a VM, without an IPv4 lookup.
- Filter-based forwarding (FBF), formerly known as policy-based routing (PBR), so that packets arriving from a VM are steered to a different next hop from the one dictated by the normal routing path.

 Here's what mapping label X to a vRouter-VM interface means: if a packet is received with MPLS label X from an overlay tunnel, pop the label and then send the packet out of that vRouter-VM interface.

Two-VN model—routes and next hops

The two-VN model relies on a 1:*N* VN:VRF relationship. The administrator only creates two VNs, but these are cloned in several VRFs with different content. For example, the Red VN is linked to four VRFs—*Red:Red*, *Red:service-<SC_ID>_SI_A*, *Red:service-<SC_ID>_SI_B*, and *Red:service-<SC_ID>_SI_C*. Out of these, three are especially relevant for this chain, whereas the leftmost one is grayed-out in Figure 12-3. It could become relevant if the SFC is further extended through an additional service instance to the left.

Taking left-to-right traffic as an example (in Figure 12-3, it goes up→down), the 0/0 default route has the following next hops in the relevant VRFs at the NVO:

1. At VRF Internet:Internet, the (labeled) next hop is DC-GW.
2. At VRFs Red:service-<SC_ID>_SI_C and Internet:service-<SC_ID>_SI_B, which are linked together, the next hop is the left interface of SI_C.
3. At VRFs Red:service-<SC_ID>_SI_B and Internet:service-<SC_ID>_SI_A, which are linked together, the next hop is the left interface of SI_B.
4. At VRF Red:Red, the next hop is the left interface of SI_A.

The two-VN model will be used for the remainder of this chapter. If you don't fully understand it yet, that's normal. Keep reading.

NFV—Long Version of the Life of a Packet

For simplicity, let's move back to a scenario with just two service instances in the chain, rather than three. And for completeness, let's place the two service instances at two different compute nodes. You might remember that Figure 12-2 was followed by a list of steps describing the life of a left-to-right packet, and that step 4 in that list began with a mysterious note: *the magic of the service function chain takes place.*

It's time to unveil the magic. This is the life of a packet inside the SFC as illustrated in Figure 12-4:

1. The packet arrives to vRouter_1 as MPLS-over-GRE with label 35. This label corresponds to PE-CE interface tapX, so vRouter_1 pops the label and sends the packet to the left interface of VM SI_A. There is no IP lookup in this step.

2. VM SI_A performs per-interface forwarding and, after processing the packet, sends it out of its right interface. The remote endpoint of this internal link is interface tapY.

3. Although tapY belongs to VRF *Internet:Internet*, OpenContrail dynamically applies a VRF mapping table to the interface. This table basically says: if the incoming packet's source IP address is VM SI_A's right interface (10.3.3.111), map the packet to VRF *Internet:Internet*; otherwise, it is supposed to be a transit packet for VM SI_A, so map it to *Internet:service-<SC_ID>_SI_A*. The *<SC_ID>* field is a service chain identifier dynamically generated by the control node. In routing terms, this is FBF (or PBR).

4. VRF *Internet:service-<SC_ID>_SI_A* at vRouter_1 has a 0/0 route whose next hop is vRouter_2, MPLS-over-UDP, label 37.

5. The packet arrives to vRouter_2 with MPLS label 37. This label corresponds to PE-CE interface tapZ, so vRouter_2 pops the label and sends the packet to the left interface of VM SI_B. There is no IP lookup in this step.

6. VM SI_B performs per-interface forwarding, and after processing the packet, sends it out of its right interface. The remote endpoint of this internal link is interface tapT.

7. Interface tapT belongs to VRF *Internet:Internet*, and being the rightmost end of the SFC, there is no policy-based routing. The route in that VRF is honored and

vRouter_2 sends the packet to DC-GW with MPLS service label 90. After that, it's IP VPN with Inter-AS Option B business as usual (see Figure 12-2).

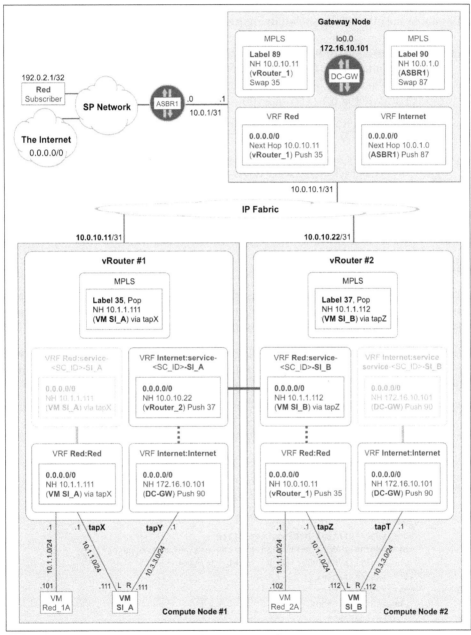

Figure 12-4. NFV routing state for left-to-right traffic

In this example, the following tables at the NVO are relevant to forwarding: MPLS table at vRouter_1, VRF *Internet:service-<SC_ID>_SI_A* at vRouter_1, MPLS table at vRouter_2 and VRF *Internet:Internet* at vRouter_2.

How about the other tables shown in Figure 12-4? They are relevant for other flows:

- A packet traveling from the Internet to the Red subscriber is processed by: MPLS table at vRouter_2, VRF *Red:service-<SC_ID>_SI_B* at vRouter_2, MPLS table at vRouter_1, and VRF *Red:Red* at vRouter_1. Of course, the relevant route is 192.0.2.0/24 or 192.0.2.1/32—not 0/0—and the MPLS labels are different.

- VRF *Red:Red* at vRouter_1 is relevant for packets sourced from VM Red_1A.

 Look back at the center-down area of Figure 12-3. This illustration should be easier to understand now.

NFV Control Plane

After reading Chapter 11, programming and signaling routes on the NVO should no longer be a mystery. Control nodes implement all the logic and signal it conveniently via BGP or XMPP, depending on whether the peer is a gateway node or a vRouter.

On the other hand, there are a few new logical constructs specific to NFV, like service templates, service chains, Access Control Lists (ACLs), VRF mapping tables, or links between routing instances. To illustrate this, Example 12-1 shows how the control node instructs a vRouter to assign a VRF mapping table to a tap interface.

Example 12-1. XMPP—VRF mapping table on a VM interface

```
1    <?xml version="1.0"?>
2    <iq type="set" from="network-control@contrailsystems.com"
3       to="default-global-system-config:vrouter_1/config">
4     <config>
5      <update>
6       <node type="virtual-machine-interface">
7        <name>default-domain:mpls-in-the-sdn-era:default-domain
8            mpls-in-sdn-era__SI_A__right__2</name>
9        <vrf-assign-table>
10        <vrf-assign-rule>
11         <match-condition>
12          <src-address>
13           <subnet>
14            <ip-prefix>10.3.3.111</ip-prefix>
15            <ip-prefix-len>32</ip-prefix-len>
```

```
16          </subnet>
17        </src-address>
18      </match-condition>
19      <routing-instance>default-domain:mpls-in-the-sdn-era:
20                      Internet:Internet</routing-instance>
21    </vrf-assign-rule>
22    <vrf-assign-rule>
23      <match-condition></match-condition>
24      <routing-instance>default-domain:mpls-in-the-sdn-era:
25                      Internet:service-71b49d3d-b710-477a-9fb9-
26                      5bc571579cfb-default-domain_mpls-in-the-
27                      sdn-era_SI_A</routing-instance>
28    </vrf-assign-rule>
29    </vrf-assign-table>
30   </node>
31  </update>
32  </config>
33 </iq>
```

You can see the SI_A__right__2 interface (line 8) is nothing but the right interface of VM SI_A. The numeral *2* comes from the fact that it is the right interface (left interface is 1). As for the VRF mapping table, it is applied at the vRouter side—in other words, on the interface tapY in Figure 12-4. This table applies to packets received by the vRouter from the VM.

The long identifier `71b49d3d-b710-477a-9fb9-5bc571579cfb` (lines 24 and 25) is nothing but the dynamically generated service chain identifier or *<SC_ID>*.

The construct in Example 12-1 is the cornerstone of traffic steering through the chain. VRF *Internet:Internet* is only relevant for packets that are *originated* from SI_A. All the packets that *traverse* SI_A (like those going from the subscriber to the Internet) are processed in the context of VRF *Internet:service-<SC_ID>_SI_A*. This FBF (or PBR) mechanism is essential for the SFC to work as expected.

If, instead, a transit packet entering vRouter_1 at tapY was assigned to VRF *Internet:Internet*, it would exit the SFC prematurely and go to the DC-GW without being processed by SI_B.

Example 12-2 shows another interesting XMPP construct: a link between routing instances.

Example 12-2. XMPP—Link between routing instances

```
<?xml version="1.0"?>
<iq type="set" from="network-control@contrailsystems.com"
    to="default-global-system-config:vrouter_1/config">
 <config>
  <update>
   <link>
```

```
<node type="routing-instance">
  <name>default-domain:mpls-in-the-sdn-era:Internet:service-
        71b49d3d-b710-477a-9fb9-5bc571579cfb-default-domain_
        mpls-in-the-sdn-era_SI_A</name>
</node>
<node type="routing-instance">
  <name>default-domain:mpls-in-the-sdn-era:Red:service-
        71b49d3d-b710-477a-9fb9-5bc571579cfb-default-domain_
        mpls-in-the-sdn-era_SI_B</name>
</node>
<metadata type="connection" />
    </link>
  </update>
 </config>
</iq>
```

The full signaling involved in SFC creation is beyond the scope of this book on MPLS, but these brief appearances should give you a feeling for how it works.

NFV Scaling and Redundancy

The SFC examples discussed so far include one single VM at each stage. This might not be sufficient from the point of view of scaling and redundancy, so Figure 12-5 shows you how to address these concerns.

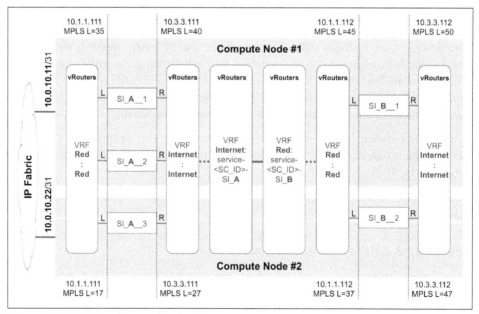

Figure 12-5. NFV scaling and redundancy

In OpenContrail configuration terms, you should check the scaling box on the Service Template configuration, and then define a new service instance with a number of instances greater than one. In this example, two service instances are defined:

- SI_A, with a number of instances equal to three.
- SI_B, with a number of instances equal to two.

The SI_A__# and SI_B__# VMs are dynamically created upon the previous configuration. From a functional point of view, this SFC is very similar to a simple SFC; it just has more than one VM per stage. The result is more horsepower and a higher level of resiliency. Here are some key observations from Figure 12-5:

- VMs are distributed across compute nodes.
- Shared IP addressing is supported. For example, all the left interfaces of SI_A instances have IP address 10.1.1.111. And they also get the same MAC address in this flavor of service instance.
- MPLS labels are locally assigned by each vRouter, so they do not necessarily have the same value on different compute nodes. For example, if vRouter_1 receives an MPLS packet with label 45, it pops the label and sends the packet to the left interface of one of its SI_B instances. And there is only one such instance in compute node 1, namely SI_B__1. The outcome on vRouter_2 would be different, again due to the local significance of MPLS labels.

NFV Scaling and Redundancy—Load Balancing

OK, so MPLS labels are different across vRouters. On the other hand, vRouter_1 maps the same MPLS label (35) to the left interfaces of both SI_A__1 and SI_A__2. And it also maps MPLS label 40 to the right interfaces of the same VMs. The reason: these VMs belong to a common scaled service instance.

In Example 12-3, we can see these routes from the point of view of the gateway node.

Example 12-3. Route pointing to an SFC—Junos (DC-GW)

```
1    juniper@DC-GW> show route receive-protocol bgp 10.0.10.3
2                        table Red 0/0 exact
3
4    [...]
5    * 0.0.0.0/0 (1 entry, 1 announced)
6         Route Distinguisher: 10.0.10.11:15
7         VPN Label: 35
8         Nexthop: 10.0.10.11
9    [...]
10        Route Distinguisher: 10.0.10.22:15
```

```
11        VPN Label: 17
12        Nexthop: 10.0.10.22
```

The IP address of the control node is 10.0.10.3 (line 1), whereas the vRouter addresses are 10.0.10.11 (lines 6 and 8) and 10.0.10.22 (lines 10 and 12).

Because OpenContrail uses a *<ROUTER_ID>:<VPN_ID>* Route Distinguisher (RD) format, the gateway node considers the two IP VPN routes 10.0.0.11:15:**0/0** and 10.0.0.22:15:**0/0** as different. Thanks to that, the gateway node can load-balance the traffic across the two available next hops: vRouter_1 label 35 and vRouter_2 label 17.

Let's look at how vRouter_1 effectively load-balances flows between the left interfaces of SI_A__1 and SI_A__2 (Example 12-4).

Example 12-4. Load balancing across service instances—OpenContrail (vRouter_1)

```
1     root@compute_node_1:~# mpls --get 35
2     MPLS Input Label Map
3        Label     NextHop
4        ------------------
5          35         58
6
7     root@compute_node_1:~# nh --get 58
8     Id:58  Type:Composite  Fmly: AF_INET
9     Flags:Valid, Policy, Ecmp, Rid:0  Ref_cnt:2 Vrf:3
10               Sub NH(label): 41(22) 57(41)
11
12    root@compute_node_1:~# nh --get 41
13    Id:41  Type:Encap  Fmly: AF_INET  Flags:Valid, Rid:0 Ref_cnt:4 Vrf:3
14               EncapFmly:0806 Oif:7 Len:14
15               Data:02 8a 40 57 28 43 00 00 5e 00 01 00 08 00
16
17    root@compute_node_1:~# nh --get 57
18    Id:57  Type:Encap  Fmly: AF_INET  Flags:Valid, Rid:0 Ref_cnt:4 Vrf:3
19               EncapFmly:0806 Oif:5 Len:14
20               Data:02 8a 40 57 28 43 00 00 5e 00 01 00 08 00
```

This is a sample of the commands available on the vRouter command-line interface (CLI). These are plain commands that you can run on the host OS shell, and they are further documented on the OpenContrail website. But back to the example, incoming packets with MPLS label 35 are processed with an Equal-Cost Multipath (ECMP) next hop (line 9) containing two sub next hops. These have different outgoing interfaces (lines 14 and 19), as can be expected, because they point to two different VMs: SI_A__1 and SI_A__2. Conversely, they have the same encapsulation. Lines 15 and 20 can be decoded as shown here:

- Destination MAC address 02:8a:40:57:28:43, shared by both VMs' left interfaces
- Source MAC address 00:00:5e:00:01:00, on the vRouter side

- Ethertype 0x0800 (IPv4)

NFV—load-balancing assessment

Load balancing is great because it makes it possible to distribute different left-to-right packets across all of the six available paths. Indeed, a given left-to-right packet stream can traverse SI_A__X and SI_B__Y, where X has three possible values (1, 2, 3) and Y has two possible values (1, 2). In total, there are six possible combinations.

Likewise, right-to-left packets also have six possible paths. And here comes the challenge. Many network services—actually, the majority of them—require flow symmetry. If the upstream half-flow traverses SI_A__1 and SI_B__2, return packets must traverse SI_B__2 and SI_A__1. Otherwise, the flow is either disrupted or the appropriate services are not applied to it.

OpenContrail vRouters have flow awareness, and they can redirect packets appropriately. This topic is a complex one and OpenContrail website has interesting articles about it that you can read at *http://www.opencontrail.org*.

Service Instance Flavors

Until now, all of this chapter's examples feature service instances cloned from a service template that, in OpenContrail technology, is of type *[In-Network, Firewall]*.

The term *Firewall* refers here to a VM with left and right interface, as compared to a VM with just one service interface (Analyzer). The VM itself does not need to be a firewall—or to implement a firewall service—for that, at all.

In-Network Service Instances

The term *In-Network* is a much more interesting concept. In-Network means that the service instances (VMs) have IP capability on their left and right interfaces. In other words, they provide L2 termination and they process packets at L3. So VMs need some kind of L3 forwarding intelligence to avoid disrupting the chain's forwarding plane. The following alternatives are available for In-Network service instances:

- Make the VMs run in interface-based forwarding mode. A packet that enters the VM on one service interface (left, right) must exit—unless it is discarded by the VM—via the other (right, left) service interface. Of course, this imposes a requirement on the forwarding logic implemented by the VM. That being said, from a pure NFV perspective, it is the best practice.

- Bring routing awareness to the VM. One option is to let OpenContrail include route prefixes in its DHCP offer, as described in RFC 3442 - *The Classless Static*

Route Option for DHCP version 4. In this way, a service instance can learn how to reach certain destination networks through its left or right interface.

- Letting the VM run dynamic routing protocols with other elements in the same tenant; although not a trivial operation, it is also an option.

Apart from In-Network, there are two other service instance types in OpenContrail.

In-Network-NAT Service Instances

This service instance flavor is similar to In-Network, with one big difference: the left VN prefixes are not leaked into the right VN. Back to the original example in Figure 12-2, the subscriber prefix 192.0.2.0/24 would not be leaked to the Internet VRF. This is perfectly fine if the service instance is performing a NAT function: there is no need to expose the inner (left) private address to the (right) public network domain.

To achieve end-to-end connectivity, the right VN must have the appropriate routes toward the public NAT pool. These routes must be installed at—and advertised by—the NVO. They should point to the NAT service instance's right-facing interface. This is definitely possible in OpenContrail but beyond the scope of this MPLS book.

Transparent Service Instances

The best practice is L3. In that sense, it is preferred to run service VMs in the In-Network mode. But if a given service VM performs L2 bridging on transit packets, the service instance must be defined as transparent. One immediate implication is that MAC addresses are no longer shared.

When a service instance runs in transparent mode, the vRouter-VM link is VLAN-tagged allowing for the same service instance to be used in different SFCs, each with its own VLAN tag. Thus, the VM must be aware that traffic can arrive tagged with any VLAN tag and that tag must be preserved when switching frames between the left and the right interface. Back to Example 12-4, if the service instances were transparent you would see ethertype 0x8100 and additional bytes to encode the VLAN tags on lines 15 and 20.

Network Service Function Outside a VM or Container

VMs and containers in the NVO do not necessarily implement all the Network Service Functions (NSFs). Here are some other frequent alternatives:

- Implementing the network function at the vRouter. The feature set of vRouters and vSwitches in different NVO solutions keeps growing. Sometimes, the NVO infrastructure can implement a service directly instead of relying on a VM for that.

- Using an external device or appliance, which is called a Service Node in Open-Contrail terminology. Very frequently, a data center may have physical network or security elements that need to be integrated in the SFC.

This book does not cover the integration of these two types of network service functions with VM-based SFCs like the one illustrated throughout this chapter.

## CHAPTER 13

Introduction to Traffic Engineering

Traffic Engineering (TE), simply speaking, is the possibility to send traffic from source to destination on a path that differs from the lowest-cost path calculated by routing protocols. There could be multiple reasons for using TE, such as the following:

- The lowest-cost path to the destination is congested, so you can offload that path by redirecting (part of) the traffic over a different (longer) path.

- The lowest-cost path has a high latency, so you redirect delay-sensitive traffic over a different path with lower latency while keeping the traffic that is not sensitive to delays over the lowest-cost path.

- The lowest-cost path uses insecure (easy to eavesdrop) transmission media, so you redirect traffic requiring the highest security over different (more difficult to eavesdrop) path. Typically, optical transmission is considered more secure than transmission over microwave or copper links.

- Certain applications might require multiple disjoint paths to a single destination for proper application-level redundancy failover. So, you can create multiple traffic-engineered paths for such applications. Potentially, these paths, or at least some of them, do not follow the lowest path to the destination.

Those are just a few examples of potential deployment scenarios for TE. But, there could be many more. Each service provider (SP) will have its own view of what traffic should be forwarded over paths that differ from the lowest-cost path.

TE can also be implemented in different provisioning models:

- The operator manually configures an explicit path on the router and enforces various traffic flows to follow that path.

- The operator manually configures TE link attributes (e.g., different attributes for optical, copper, and microwave links) and leaves it to the router to dynamically calculate the path that fulfills certain constraints (e.g., use optical or copper links, but do not use microwave links). Next, various traffic flows use said path.

- External *Path Computation Element* (*PCE*) collects information from the network and calculates paths based on various criteria. Next, PCE instructs routers in the network to use the calculated paths.

Chapter 2 covers the first method (manual path specification for RSVP-TE). This chapter covers the second method in detail, and Chapter 15 describes the PCE method.

TE Protocols

TE requires two types of protocols:

TED Builders
One or more protocols that distribute link information, enabling every router in the network to build a local Traffic Engineering Database (TED). The two classic examples are IS-IS and OSPF with their TE extensions. BGP can also distribute TE information, as described in Chapter 15.

LSP Builders
These are protocols that use the information contained in the TED to *build* LSPs that satisfy a set of TE constraints. The term *build* (and not *signal*) has been carefully chosen. You are about to see why.

TE LSP Types

There are three types of TE LSPs in the SDN era:

Stateful TE LSPs
These LSPs are only defined at the ingress PE, but they have a state that is *signaled* and maintained end to end. The only protocol with this capability is RSVP-TE. Each LSP is an RSVP-TE session, and the ingress PE typically pushes the *one* label that it learns through the session's Resv messages.

Stateless TE LSPs
These LSPs are only defined at the ingress PE. Furthermore, only the ingress PE keeps state for these LSPs, which are *not signaled* end to end. The ingress PE pushes a label *stack* that steers the packet through the chosen network path. In this model, the ingress PE often needs to know the label values allocated by remote routers that are two or more hops away. This can only work if the label

values are signaled explicitly (see the BGP section at the end of this chapter) or implicitly (with SPRING).

Static LSPs

According to this book's definition of TE, static LSPs like those described in Chapter 2 are also TE LSPs. Indeed, they can follow a custom path, regardless of the IGP metrics. However, they do not take into account the TED. Finally, they require provisioning hop-by-hop on all the LSRs in the path, not just on the ingress PE.

The decision to build any TE LSP, regardless of its type, can be driven by the router's configuration, by an external controller, or by a combination of both.

Back to the *signal* versus *build* dilemma, all these TE LSP types are built, but only RSVP-TE LSPs are actually signaled through the path.

Bandwidth reservations can only be signaled with stateful TE LSPs. RSVP-TE is the only protocol with this capability. Unless the entire bandwidth policy is offloaded to a central controller, you can perform TE bandwidth management only by using RSVP-TE.

These protocols are the LSP builders: RSVP-TE, all the SPRING-capable protocols (IS-IS, OSPF, BGP), and as you will see at the end of this chapter, BGP-LU, too. In addition, you can consider protocols such as Path Computation Element (PCE) Communication Protocol (PCEP), by which central controllers and routers can exchange TE instructions, as LSP builders (you can see this architecture in Chapter 15).

This chapter's examples focus primarily on RSVP-TE. However, the path decision logic for SPRING is exactly the same: both protocols match the TED to a set of local constraints. Of course, the configuration syntax at the LSP head-end and the PCEP extensions are different.

As of this writing, SPRING TE LSP configuration syntax and PCEP extensions are under development, so they are not covered here.

TE Information Distribution

Normally, link-state routing protocols such as OSPF or IS-IS use *Shortest-Path First* (SPF) algorithms to calculate paths (next hops). These algorithms take into account IGP link costs (metrics) to determine the path with the lowest accumulated cost. TE extends the basic SPF algorithm so that in addition to (or apart from) IGP link metrics, some other criteria (constraints) are taken into account during path calculation. Such an extended algorithm is called *Constrained Shortest-Path First* (CSPF).

Before going into details about the CSPF algorithm itself, let's first discuss how you can signal and distribute the additional information used during CSPF calculations. In addition to the usual IGP link metrics, TE uses further link attributes. These link attributes are distributed via additional sub-TLVs in Link TLV Type 2 (OSPF) or Extended IS Reachability TLV Type 22 (IS-IS). You can view the complete list of link attributes distributed via OSPF or IS-IS in sub-TLV at the following locations:

- *http://www.iana.org/assignments/ospf-traffic-eng-tlvs/ospf-traffic-eng-tlvs.xhtml*
- *http://www.iana.org/assignments/isis-tlv-codepoints/isis-tlv-codepoints.xhtml*, section Sub-TLVs for TLVs 22, 23, 141, 222, and 223

Some of these attributes are known under multiple names, for example:

- Traffic Engineering Metric: Admin Metric, Admin Weight.
- Administrative Group: Admin Group, Affinity Bits, Attribute Flags, Color, Resource Class Affinity.

TE Distribution via OSPF

The TE extension to OSPFv2 was initially defined in RFC 3630. After this initial RFC, further OSPF TE capabilities were covered in several other RFCs.

OSPF uses opaque Link-State Advertisement (LSA) Type 10 (area-local scope) to flood TE information, and in this chapter we use the network topology presented in Figure 13-1.

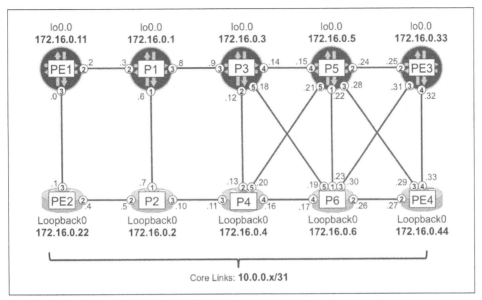

Figure 13-1. Network topology for TE discussion

Both Junos and IOS XR require explicit configuration to enable TE extensions for OSPF, as shown in Example 13-1 and Example 13-2, respectively.

Example 13-1. Enabling OSPF TE extensions—PE1 (Junos)

```
1    routing-options {
2        router-id 172.16.0.11;
3    }
4    protocols {
5        ospf {
6            traffic-engineering;
7    }}
```

Example 13-2. Enabling OSPF TE Extensions in IOS XR

```
1    router ospf core
2     area 0
3      mpls traffic-eng
4     !
5     mpls traffic-eng router-id Loopback0
6    !
7    mpls traffic-eng
8     interface GigabitEthernet0/0/0/2
9     interface GigabitEthernet0/0/0/3
```

OSPF Router ID

First, you need to configure the *TE Router ID* (line 2 in Example 13-1, line 5 in Example 13-2). The TE Router ID (referred to as *Router Address* in RFC 3630) specifies a stable IP address of the advertising router, and is used to uniquely identify the router in the TED. The TED can be populated by multiple protocols (OSPF, IS-IS and BGP, for example). In this context, the TE Router ID is used to determine if the TE information received from different protocols is, indeed, from a single router.

In Junos, there is no separate configuration knob for the TE Router ID. Simply, the `router-id` knob applies to all the protocols and contexts (OSPF, BGP, TE, etc.). In IOS XR, however, you can configure per-protocol and TE Router IDs: unless you have a very good reason not to do it, ensure that you set them to the same value.

OSPF TE Extensions

Next, in Junos you simply need to enable TE extensions (line 6 in Example 13-1) to start advertising complete TE information for all the MPLS-enabled interfaces—those with `family mpls` and listed under the `protocols mpls` stanza.

In IOS XR, apart from enabling TE extensions in OSPF (line 3 in Example 13-2), you also need to explicitly list the interfaces (lines 7 through 9) for which TE information should be flooded. This configuration automatically enables RSVP-TE on the referenced interfaces.

OSPF TE Opaque LSAs

Good. Let's now check what new information is flooded in the OSPF database (see Example 13-3).

Example 13-3. Opaque LSAs generated by PE1 and P2

```
1    juniper@PE1> show ospf database | match "16.0.2 |16.0.11|Type"
2    Type      ID            Adv Rtr       Seq         Age   Opt  Cksum  Len
3    Router    172.16.0.2    172.16.0.2    0x80000045  582   0x22 0x3dc9 108
4    Router   *172.16.0.11   172.16.0.11   0x80000036  937   0x22 0x3dc1 84
5    OpaqArea 1.0.0.0        172.16.0.2    0x80000039  1589  0x20 0x92e9 28
6    OpaqArea*1.0.0.1        172.16.0.11   0x8000002b  187   0x22 0xaaca 28
7    OpaqArea*1.0.0.3        172.16.0.11   0x80000030  350   0x22 0x5c55 136
8    OpaqArea 1.0.0.4        172.16.0.2    0x80000007  582   0x20 0x894a 168
9    OpaqArea*1.0.0.4        172.16.0.11   0x80000001  348   0x22 0xfef2 136
10   OpaqArea 1.0.0.5        172.16.0.2    0x80000007  582   0x20 0xc6fa 168
11   OpaqArea 1.0.0.6        172.16.0.2    0x80000039  1589  0x20 0x3985 168
```

You can see that both routers (PE1 and P2) flood standard Router LSAs (lines 3 and 4). Additionally, PE1 floods three Opaque LSAs (lines 6, 7, and 9), while P2 floods four Opaque LSAs (lines 5, 8, 10, and 11). Why this difference? Let's look at a couple of Opaque LSAs in more detail to see why (see Example 13-4).

Example 13-4. TE attributes in OSPF generated by PE1 (Junos)

```
1    juniper@PE1> show ospf database opaque-area advertising-router
2                172.16.0.11 lsa-id 1.0.0.1 detail
3        OSPF database, Area 0.0.0.0
4    Type       ID         Adv Rtr        Seq      Age  Opt  Cksum  Len
5    OpaqArea*1.0.0.1   172.16.0.11  0x8000002b  2561  0x22 0xaaca  28
6      Area-opaque TE LSA
7      RtrAddr (1), length 4: 172.16.0.11
8
9    juniper@PE1> show ospf database opaque-area advertising-router
10               172.16.0.11 lsa-id 1.0.0.3 detail
11       OSPF database, Area 0.0.0.0
12   Type       ID         Adv Rtr        Seq      Age  Opt  Cksum  Len
13   OpaqArea*1.0.0.3   172.16.0.11   0x80000031  988  0x22 0x5a56 136
14     Area-opaque TE LSA
15     Link (2), length 112:
16       Linktype (1), length 1:
17         1
18       LinkID (2), length 4:
19         172.16.0.22
20       LocIfAdr (3), length 4:
21         10.0.0.0
22       RemIfAdr (4), length 4:
23         10.0.0.1
24       TEMetric (5), length 4:
25         1000
26       MaxBW (6), length 4:
27         1000Mbps
28       MaxRsvBW (7), length 4:
29         1000Mbps
30       UnRsvBW (8), length 32:
31           Priority 0, 1000Mbps
32           Priority 1, 1000Mbps
33           Priority 2, 1000Mbps
34           Priority 3, 1000Mbps
35           Priority 4, 1000Mbps
36           Priority 5, 1000Mbps
37           Priority 6, 1000Mbps
38           Priority 7, 1000Mbps
39       LinkLocalRemoteIdentifier (11), length 8:
40         Local 338, Remote 0
41       Color (9), length 4:
42         0
```

Each Opaque LSA represents either a router's global TE information or link specific TE attributes:

- PE1's Opaque LSA with ID 1.0.0.1 (lines 5 through 7) advertises the Router Address (TE Router ID, TLV Type 1) in line 7.

- PE1's Opaque LSA with ID 1.0.0.3 (lines 13 through 42) contains link parameters (TLV Type 2, line 15). These are TE attributes for a single link only: PE1→PE2.
- PE1's Opaque LSA with ID 1.0.0.4, also contains TE attributes for another single link: PE1→P1 (not shown for brevity).

Thus, each router generates $N+1$ Opaque LSAs: one for global TE parameters, and one for each link. Therefore, PE1 and P2 generate three and four Opaque LSAs, respectively.

Opaque LSA IDs themselves (e.g., 1.0.0.3) have no special meaning. The pair [Advertising Router, LSA ID] must be unique. The first 8 bits (first octet) encode the type (1 = TE LSA; see lines 6 and 14), whereas the remaining 24 bits (3 octets) are used to uniquely distinguish the Opaque LSAs generated by the same router.

Verifying the content of the TE LSA with link parameters (lines 13 through 42), you'll recognize the following TE link attributes:

- Link Type (sub-TLV 1): point-to-point (value 1), lines 16 and 17.
- Link ID (sub-TLV 2): 172.16.0.22 (neighbor's router ID), lines 18 and 19.
- Local Interface IP Address (sub-TLV 3): 10.0.0.0, lines 20 and 21. And so on.

Junos refers to *Administrative Group* (sub-TLV 9) as *Color* (lines 41 and 42). Otherwise, the displayed names are self-explanatory. There is a default set of TE link attributes (and values) that is generated right after enabling TE extensions. These default values might be different for each operating system (OS). For example, *by default*:

- Junos allows bandwidth reservations up to the full link bandwidth.
- IOS XR does not allow any bandwidth reservations (reservable bandwidth is zero).

There is also a difference in the *default* way that these OSs encode the link metrics:

- Both OSs advertise the IGP metric in the standard (not opaque) Router LSAs.
- Both OSs advertise the TE metric in the opaque LSA with link attributes.
- Only IOS XR advertises the IGP metric in the opaque LSA with link attributes.

One more difference: IOS XR advertises the *Extended Administrative Groups* by default.

The use cases for all these attributes will be discussed later in this chapter.

The default values of link attributes such as TE Metric, Bandwidth, or Administrative Group can, of course, be modified via configuration commands; and you can add additional attributes such as SRLG, too. These options are explored later on in this chapter.

The equivalent command in IOS XR to verify the content of Opaque LSAs is show ospf database opaque-area. The output is similar, but the bandwidth values are expressed in bytes/sec, not bits/sec.

TE Distribution via IS-IS

Another IGP that you can use for TE information distribution is IS-IS. In Junos, IS-IS TE extensions are enabled by default. In IOS XR, you need to explicitly enable TE extensions (Example 13-5), and like in OSPF, list the interfaces (Example 13-2, lines 7 through 9) for which TE information should be flooded.

Example 13-5. Enabling IS-IS TE extensions in IOS XR

```
1    router isis core
2     address-family ipv4 unicast
3      metric-style wide
4      mpls traffic-eng level-2-only
5      mpls traffic-eng router-id Loopback0
```

Similar to OSPF, IS-IS distributes TE attributes via new sub-TLVs. However, this time, no new LSA or rather LSP (Link-State PDU, not to be confused with LSP as in Label-Switched Path) is required. IS-IS was designed to be easily extensible from its early days. Therefore, the *Extended IS Reachability* TLVs (Type 22) of the node's LSP are simply enhanced with additional sub-TLVs describing the TE link attributes, as you can see in Example 13-6.

Example 13-6. TE Attributes in IS-IS LSP generated by PE1 (Junos)

```
1    juniper@PE1> show isis database PE1 extensive | find TLVs
2     TLVs:
3       Area address: 49.0000 (3)
4       LSP Buffer Size: 1492
5       Speaks: IP
6       IP router id: 172.16.0.11
7       IP address: 172.16.0.11
8       Hostname: PE1
9       IS extended neighbor: P1.00, Metric: default 1000
10        IP address: 10.0.0.2
11        Neighbor's IP address: 10.0.0.3
12        Local interface index: 337, Remote interface index: 335
13        Current reservable bandwidth:
14          Priority 0 : 1000Mbps
15          Priority 1 : 1000Mbps
16          Priority 2 : 1000Mbps
17          Priority 3 : 1000Mbps
```

```
18              Priority 4 : 1000Mbps
19              Priority 5 : 1000Mbps
20              Priority 6 : 1000Mbps
21              Priority 7 : 1000Mbps
22           Maximum reservable bandwidth: 1000Mbps
23           Maximum bandwidth: 1000Mbps
24           Administrative groups:  0 <none>
25    (...)
```

You can see the MPLS TE ID (line 6), the local and neighbor's link addresses (lines 10 and 11), the local and neighbor's interface indexes (line 12), the bandwidth parameters (lines 13 through 23), as well as the administrative groups (line 24). The MPLS TE metric is not advertised by IS-IS if not configured explicitly.

Let's now take a look at the LSP generated from an IOS XR router, this time using IOS XR CLI.

Example 13-7. TE attributes in IS-IS LSP generated by P2 (IOS XR)

```
1    RP/0/0/CPU0:P2#show isis database P2 verbose
2
3    IS-IS core (Level-2) Link State Database
4    LSPID          LSP Seq Num  LSP Checksum  LSP Holdtime  ATT/P/OL
5    P2.00-00  *    0x0000000d   0x4c4d          39137          0/0/0
6     Auth:         Algorithm HMAC-MD5, Length: 17
7     Area Address: 49.0000
8     NLPID:        0xcc
9     Hostname:     P2
10    IP Address:   172.16.0.2
11    Router ID:    172.16.0.2
12    Metric: 1000      IS-Extended PE2.00
13      Affinity: 0x00000000
14      Interface IP Address: 10.0.0.5
15      Neighbor IP Address: 10.0.0.4
16      Physical BW: 1000000 kbits/sec
17      Reservable Global pool BW: 0 kbits/sec
18      Global Pool BW Unreserved:
19        [0]: 0        kbits/sec       [1]: 0      kbits/sec
20        [2]: 0        kbits/sec       [3]: 0      kbits/sec
21        [4]: 0        kbits/sec       [5]: 0      kbits/sec
22        [6]: 0        kbits/sec       [7]: 0      kbits/sec
23      Admin. Weight: 1000
24      Ext Admin Group: Length: 32
25        0x00000000    0x00000000
26        0x00000000    0x00000000
27        0x00000000    0x00000000
28        0x00000000    0x00000000
29    (...)
```

IOS XR advertises a similar set of TE attributes: the MPLS TE ID (line 11), the administrative groups called *Affinity* (line 13), the local and neighbor's link addresses (lines 14 and 15), the bandwidth parameters (lines 16 through 22). Unlike Junos, the default maximum reservable bandwidth in IOS XR is zero, both for OSPF and IS-IS.

IOS XR displays the IS-IS link bandwidth parameters differently for each protocol: in bits/sec for IS-IS and in bytes/sec for OSPF.

By default, IOS XR advertises more link attributes than Junos: for example, the MPLS TE metric called *Admin. Weight* (line 23) and the Extended Administrative Groups (lines 24 through 28).

The TED

TE information, distributed by any protocol (OSPF, IS-IS, or even BGP) is collected in a single database called: TED. CSPF actually uses TED as input when performing TE paths calculations. (Chapter 2 shows some examples.)

In certain network deployments, TE information about the same links might be provided by different routing protocols (IS-IS, OSPF, BGP). Indeed, the topology in Figure 13-1 might run two IGPs in parallel: IS-IS and OSPF. This is common in protocol migrations.

When multiple protocols feed TE information about the same link, some TE attributes can actually differ. Therefore, there is a need for a preference order between protocols. In Junos, this preference order is called *TE credibility protocol preference*, which is different from normal protocol preference. Example 13-8 shows the default values.

Example 13-8. TE credibility protocol preference (Junos)

```
juniper@PE3> show ted protocol
Protocol name        Credibility  Self node
IS-IS(2)             2            PE3.00(172.16.0.33)
IS-IS(1)             1
OSPF(0)              0            PE3.00(172.16.0.33)
```

When CSPF selects information in the TED, Junos prefers by default IS-IS level 2 over IS-IS level 1 over OSPF. IOS XR, however, sets the preferences in the TED according to the protocols' administrative distances: the higher the administrative distance, the less preferred the protocol is both for routing and for the TED.

Therefore, Junos and IOS XR defaults are different: Junos prefers the TED collected by IS-IS, whereas IOS XR prefers the TED collected by OSPF. So in multi-IGP deployments, you need to make manual adjustments to have consistency between Junos and IOS XR.

In Junos, there is no way to directly change TE credibility values, but you can do it indirectly, as outlined in Example 13-9. On a per-protocol basis, you can switch off the default TE credibility and generate new TE credibility values inherited from the standard protocol preference values according to this formula:

```
512 - protocol-preference
```

Example 13-9. TE credibility adjustments (Junos)

```
protocols {
    isis traffic-engineering credibility-protocol-preference;
    ospf traffic-engineering credibility-protocol-preference;
}

juniper@PE3> show ted protocol
Protocol name       Credibility  Self node
OSPF(0)                  502      PE3.00(172.16.0.33)
IS-IS(1)                 497
IS-IS(2)                 494      PE3.00(172.16.0.33)
```

The credibility values are derived from the default protocol preferences: 10 (OSPF), 15 (IS-IS Level 1), and 18 (IS-IS Level 2). So, OSPF becomes the most credible protocol.

TE Static Constraints

Thus far, the first few pages of this chapter have clarified how OSPF and IS-IS distribute the TE information, the selection process between OSPF and IS-IS, and how to influence it.

Now let's actually begin to use TE in use cases that include different link attributes in the TE constraints. The examples that follow use IS-IS as the only protocol. In the end, TE link attributes have the same meaning in both protocols.

TE Metric

The *TE Metric* attribute was introduced with the initial TE extensions in OSPF and IS-IS. This attribute is called *Admin Metric* in IOS XR's OSPF, and *Admin Weight* in IOS XR's IS-IS. You can manipulate the TE metric and make it different from the IGP metric. In this way, you define different metric schemes for CSPF versus SPF calculations. The TE module uses the results of CSPF calculations to build TE paths, whereas SPF calculation results are used to install next-hops for prefixes not reachable over TE LSPs.

For example, let's explicitly set TE metrics to 3000 on all four cross-links, as shown in Figure 13-2, and configured in Example 13-10 and Example 13-11. The standard IGP metric is configured to 1000 on all links in the topology.

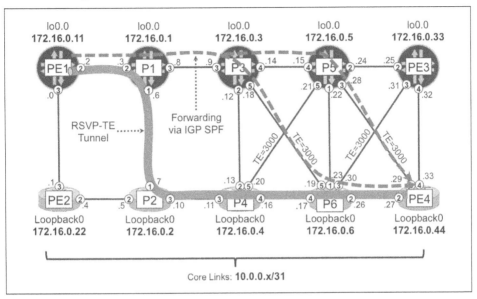

Figure 13-2. TE metric constraint

Example 13-10. TE metric setting on P3 (Junos)

```
protocols {
    isis interface ge-2/0/5.0 level 2 te-metric 3000;
}
```

Example 13-11. TE metric setting on P4 (IOS XR)

```
mpls traffic-eng
  interface GigabitEthernet0/0/0/5
    admin-weight 3000
```

As you can see, the TE metric of an interface is set globally in IOS XR, and it can be configured on a per-protocol basis in Junos.

Now, for testing purposes, let's create two RSVP-TE tunnels: PE1→PE4 and PE2→PE3 (shown in Example 13-12 and Example 13-13), respectively. PE3 and PE4 have secondary loopback addresses (172.17.0.33 and 172.17.0.44, respectively), and only these addresses should be reachable through the new LSPs.

Example 13-12. PE1→PE4 RSVP-TE tunnel on PE1 (Junos)

```
1      protocols mpls label-switched-path PE1--->PE4 {
2          no-install-to-address;
3          to 172.16.0.44;
4          install 172.17.0.44/32 active;
5      }
```

Example 13-13. PE2→PE3 RSVP-TE tunnel on PE2 (IOS XR)

```
1      interface tunnel-te33
2      ipv4 unnumbered Loopback0
3      signalled-name PE2--->PE3
4      destination 172.16.0.33
5      record-route
6      path-option 1 dynamic
7      !
8      router static
9      address-family ipv4 unicast
10      172.17.0.33/32 tunnel-te33
```

There are some small differences between Junos and IOS XR. By default, Junos installs the destination address of the RSVP-TE tunnel in the routing table. In IOS XR, you need to specify autoroute [announce|destination] to install routes downstream of the LSP, including the tunnel endpoint, as discussed in Chapter 3.

This is the first time that this book uses the Junos *active* knob (Example 13-12, line 4). Without it, the route is only installed in inet.3. With it, it is *also* installed in inet.0.

Now, you can reach the primary loopbacks of PE3 and PE4 via IS-IS (using SPF), and their secondary loopbacks via RSVP-TE tunnels (using CSPF); see Example 13-14.

Example 13-14. Remote primary and secondary loopbacks reachability

```
1      juniper@PE1> show route table inet.0 172.16.0.44/32
2      (...)
3      172.16.0.44/32     *[IS-IS/18] 00:57:08, metric 4000
4                          > to 10.0.0.3 via ge-2/0/2.0
5
6      juniper@PE1> show route table inet.0 172.17.0.44/32
7      (...)
8      172.17.0.44/32     *[RSVP/7/1] 00:46:35, metric 4000
9                          > to 10.0.0.3 via ge-2/0/2.0, lsp PE1--->PE4
10      .
11      juniper@PE1> show mpls lsp name PE1--->PE4 detail | match metric
12          Computed ERO (S [L] strict [loose] hops): (CSPF metric: 5000)
13
14      RP/0/0/CPU0:PE2#show route 172.16.0.33/32 | include via
15        Known via "isis core", distance 115, metric 4000, type level-2
16          10.0.0.5, from 172.16.0.33, via GigabitEthernet0/0/0/2
```

```
17
18    RP/0/0/CPU0:PE2#show route 172.17.0.33/32 | include via
19      Known via "static", distance 1, metric 0 (connected)
20        directly connected, via tunnel-te33
21
22    RP/0/0/CPU0:PE2#show mpls traffic-eng tunnels 33 | include weight
23        path option 1, type dynamic (Basis for Setup, path weight 5000)
```

Remember that both in Junos and IOS XR, the metric of a prefix using LSP as a next hop equals the lowest IGP metric to the destination (the primary loopback), regardless of the actual path followed by the LSP. The shortest PE1→PE4 IGP paths are shown with dashed lines in Figure 13-2, and they have IGP metric 4000. The same logic applies to PE2→PE3.

On the other hand, the actual PE1→PE4 LSP is signaled through the solid line in Figure 13-2 because that is the path with the lowest cumulative TE metric: 5000. In other words, the LSP (CSPF) is skipping the cross-links with high TE metric and prefers to take a path that from the point of view of the IGP (SPF) is suboptimal.

In IOS XR, static routes pointing to RSVP-TE LSPs have metric 0. The autoroute destination feature, discussed in Chapter 3, inherits the IGP metric to the destination.

As shown in Example 13-15, the actual paths to the primary and secondary loopbacks can be verified with traceroute.

Example 13-15. Verification of SPF and CSPF paths

```
juniper@PE1> traceroute 172.16.0.44
traceroute to 172.16.0.44 (172.16.0.44)
 1  P1 (10.0.0.3)  3.015 ms  2.511 ms  2.795 ms
 2  P3 (10.0.0.9)  4.094 ms  5.989 ms  5.773 ms
 3  P5 (10.0.0.15)  6.233 ms P6 (10.0.0.19)  3.750 ms  4.271 ms
 4  PE4 (10.0.0.27)  5.538 ms PE4 (10.0.0.29)  6.500 ms *

juniper@PE1> traceroute 172.17.0.44
traceroute to 172.17.0.44 (172.17.0.44)
 1  P1 (10.0.0.3)  22.592 ms  106.019 ms  10.758 ms
    MPLS Label=362784 CoS=0 TTL=1 S=1
 2  P2 (10.0.0.7)  11.303 ms  7.543 ms  8.318 ms
    MPLS Label=24039 CoS=0 TTL=1 S=1
 3  P4 (10.0.0.11)  10.365 ms  7.818 ms  7.692 ms
    MPLS Label=24041 CoS=0 TTL=1 S=1
 4  P6 (10.0.0.17)  8.589 ms  10.847 ms  9.510 ms
    MPLS Label=24027 CoS=0 TTL=1 S=1
 5  PE4 (10.0.0.27)  10.384 ms 10.291 ms

RP/0/0/CPU0:PE2#traceroute 172.16.0.33
(...)
 1  p2 (10.0.0.5) 0 msec  0 msec  0 msec
```

```
    2  p4 (10.0.0.11) 0 msec   0 msec   0 msec
    3  p5 (10.0.0.21) 0 msec   0 msec   0 msec
    4  pe3 (172.16.0.33) 0 msec   19 msec   0 msec

RP/0/0/CPU0:PE2#traceroute 172.17.0.33
(...)
    1  pe1 (10.0.0.0) [MPLS: Label 332608 Exp 0] 9 msec
    2  p1 (10.0.0.3) [MPLS: Label 362640 Exp 0] 0 msec
    3  p3 (10.0.0.9) [MPLS: Label 360208 Exp 0] 29 msec
    4  p5 (10.0.0.15) [MPLS: Label 304304 Exp 0] 0 msec
    5  172.17.0.33 0 msec   0 msec   0 msec
```

As you can see, paths calculated by SPF (traceroute to primary loopbacks 172.16.0.xx)
and CSPF (traceroute to secondary loopbacks 172.17.0.xx) differ. This confirms that
CSPF uses the TE metric, and not the IGP metric, for path calculation. On links for
which the TE metric is not explicitly configured, the TE metric inherits its value from
the IGP metric. By manipulating TE metrics, you can influence the path taken by
RSVP-TE tunnels and deviate it from the IGP shortest path.

A typical use case is associating the IGP metric to the link bandwidth (the lower the
bandwidth, the higher the IGP metric), while tuning the TE metric according to the
link delay (the higher the delay, the higher the TE metric). In this way, RSVP-TE tunnels follow the path with the smallest accumulated delay, whereas native forwarding
prefers links with the largest bandwidth. The ingress PE can deploy a traffic forwarding policy, as in Chapter 3, to inject delay-sensitive traffic into RSVP-TE tunnels
while keeping the remaining bulk of the traffic over IGP paths.

Link Coloring—Administrative Group

The second TE link attribute to be explored is the *Administrative Group* (AG), again
introduced with the initial TE extensions in OSPF and IS-IS. Depending on the vendor and protocol, the actual terminology differs from the one used in the RFCs. In
show commands, IOS XR calls it *Affinity Bits* (in OSPF) or simply *Affinity* (in IS-IS),
whereas Junos uses the term *Color* (in OSPF) or *Administrative Groups* (in IS-IS).
When it comes to the configuration, in IOS XR you can configure *Attribute Flags*, and
in Junos *Admin Groups*. And in some earlier RFCs (like 2702) it was also called
Resource Class Affinity.

Confused? Don't be! All these terms refer to the same TE link attribute: AG in RFC
3630 and RFC 5305. The term AG will be used in this book for consistency.

So what actually is AG? The AG TE link attribute is a set of 32 flags (bits) distributed
in OSPF or IS-IS via the appropriate sub-TLV. Each flag (bit) corresponds to one AG
or color assigned to the interface. A link can belong to multiple groups, if multiple
flags (bits) are set to 1—in this case, the link has several colors at the same time. By

convention, the least significant bit is referred to as *group 0*, and the most significant bit is referred to as *group 31*.

 The TED, like IGP databases, contains half-links. When you set an AG on a link on one router only, you are actually coloring it in one direction only.

Figure 13-3 illustrates an example in which the network administrator has *symmetrically* configured AGs on some of the links.

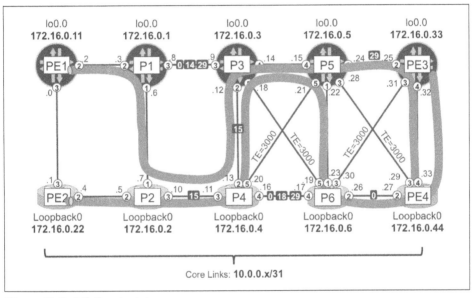

Figure 13-3. AG Constraint

Here are the AG configurations:

- Link P1-P3: AG 0, 14 and 29
- Link P2-P4: AG 15
- Link P4-P6: AG 0, 18 and 29
- Link P5-PE3: AG 29
- Link P6-PE4: AG 0

You can influence path selection by specifying which links can be used, or cannot be used, based on the specific AGs assigned to each link.

The first step is to color the links by assigning AGs to them. Let's examine the configuration of P3 (Junos; see Example 13-16) and P4 (IOS XR; see Example 13-17).

Example 13-16. AG link configuration on P3 (Junos)

```
1       protocols mpls {
2           admin-groups {
3               AG-0 0;
4               AG-14 14;
5               AG-15 15;
6               AG-29 29;
7           }
8           interface ge-2/0/2.0 {
9               admin-group AG-15;
10          }
11          interface ge-2/0/3.0 {
12              admin-group [ AG-0 AG-14 AG-29 ];
13      }}
```

The configuration is pretty easy. First, assign custom names to bit positions (lines 2 through 6). Then, set the appropriate AGs (bits) on the interfaces (lines 8 through 12). Example 13-17 shows the equivalent configuration in IOS XR.

Example 13-17. AG link configuration on P4 (IOS XR)

```
mpls traffic-eng
 interface GigabitEthernet0/0/0/2
  attribute-names AG-15
 !
 interface GigabitEthernet0/0/0/3
  attribute-names AG-15
 !
 interface GigabitEthernet0/0/0/4
  attribute-names AG-0 AG-18 AG-29
 !
 affinity-map AG-0 bit-position 0
 affinity-map AG-15 bit-position 15
 affinity-map AG-18 bit-position 18
 affinity-map AG-29 bit-position 29
```

As a result, IS-IS starts to advertise the configured AGs for these links and installs the appropriate information in the TED (see Example 13-18).

Example 13-18. AG distribution

```
1       juniper@P3> show isis database P4 extensive
2       (...)
3           IS extended neighbor: P6.00, Metric: default 1000
4               Administrative groups:  0x20040001 AG-29 18 AG-0
```

```
5
6    juniper@P3> show ted database 172.16.0.4 extensive
7    (...)
8        To: P6.00(172.16.0.6), Local: 10.0.0.16, Remote: 10.0.0.17
9        Color: 0x20040001 AG-29 18 AG-0
10
11   RP/0/0/CPU0:P4#show isis database P3 verbose
12
13     Metric: 1000        IS-Extended P1.00
14       Affinity: 0x20004001
15
16   RP/0/0/CPU0:P4#show mpls traffic-eng topology 172.16.0.3
17   (...)
18     Link[2]:PtP, Nbr IGP Id:1720.1600.0001.00, Nbr Node Id:15
19       Attribute Flags: 0x20004001
20       Attribute Names: AG-0(0) AG-29(29)
21       Unnamed bits   : 14
```

Junos—in both the IS-IS database and the TED—displays AGs in hexadecimal format (eight digits, each representing four bits), and additionally, explicitly lists the bits set to 1 (lines 4 and 9). For those AGs (bits) that do not have a locally defined name, the numerical bit position (check 18 in lines 4 and 9) is displayed, instead.

In IOS XR, you can find only hexadecimal formats in the IS-IS database display (line 14). Consequently, during troubleshooting, you need to decipher the actual AGs (bit positions) that are set. Or, you can look at the TED, in which apart from hexadecimal format (line 19), AG names (line 20) and unnamed bit positions (line 21) are also displayed.

OK some AGs were configured, so now it's time to put additional constraints on your LSPs to actually make use of the AGs.

Example 13-19. AG constraint for PE1→PE4 LSP (Junos)

```
protocols mpls {
    label-switched-path PE1--->PE4 admin-group exclude AG-0;
}
```

Example 13-20. AG constraint for PE2→PE3 LSP (IOS XR)

```
interface tunnel-te33
 affinity exclude AG-29
```

Here, you simply state that your PE1→PE4 LSP is not allowed to use links marked with AG 0, whereas PE2→PE3 LSP must not use links marked with AG 29. Now, after LSP reoptimization, let's check the path taken by these LSPs.

Example 13-21. Path Taken for LSPs Constrained by Administrative Groups

```
juniper@PE1> show rsvp session name PE1--->PE4 detail
[...]  Record route: <self> 10.0.0.3 10.0.0.7 10.0.0.11 10.0.0.12
                     10.0.0.15 10.0.0.25 10.0.0.33

RP/0/0/CPU0:PE2#show mpls traffic-eng tunnels 33
[...]
  Path info (IS-IS core level-2):
  Node hop count: 7
  Hop0: 10.0.0.5
  Hop1: 10.0.0.11
  Hop2: 10.0.0.12
  Hop3: 10.0.0.15
  Hop4: 10.0.0.23
  Hop5: 10.0.0.27
  Hop6: 10.0.0.32
  Hop7: 172.16.0.33
```

Analyzing Record route objects you will find the following paths:

- PE1→PE4 LSP takes PE1→P1→P2→P4→P3→P5→PE3→PE4 path
- PE2→PE3 LSP takes PE2→P2→P4→P3→P5→P6→PE4→PE3 path

The paths are different from the paths observed previously in Example 13-15, and the new paths do not take any prohibited links. This confirms that the configured AG constraints are properly taken into account by CSPF calculations.

There is an important aspect of IOS XR implementation that you need to take into account. When an RSVP-TE LSP does not have any configured AG constraints, in fact there is a default AG constraint encoded as 0x0/0xffff—or to use its full format, 0x00000000/0x0000ffff. What does this mean? Well, the first numeral is the 32-bit flag register representing 32 AGs. The second numeral is the 32-bit mask. If in the mask the bit is set to 1, it is a significant bit, and according to the first numeral its value must be zero. So, every link with one or more of the 0–15 AG bit positions set is automatically excluded by CSPF calculations for such RSVP-TE LSPs.

So, what does 0x00000000/0x0000ffff finally mean? It means that, for example, for the PE2→PE4 tunnel (using default IOS XR AG constraint) only links with no AGs from range 0–15 can be taken into account (AGs from range 16–31 are not checked, because corresponding mask bits are set to 0). And this is the problem. Links P1-P3, P2-P4, and P3-P4 all have some AGs from range 0–15, thus PE2→PE4 tunnel initiated with the IOS XR default AG constraints, cannot use these links.

Example 13-22. Status of LSP toward PE4 on PE2 (IOS XR)

```
1    RP/0/0/CPU0:PE2#show mpls traffic-eng tunnels 44
2    (...)
3       Last PCALC Error: Wed Jun  3 12:58:26 2015
4         Info: No path to destination, 172.16.0.44 (affinity)
5    (...)
6      Config Parameters:
7        Bandwidth:  0 kbps (CT0) Priority: 7 7 Affinity: 0x0/0xffff
8        Metric Type: TE (default)
9    (...)
```

The equivalent default AG constraint in Junos is 0x0/0x0; in other words, Junos by default does not take AGs into account for CSPF calculations.

The example that follows demonstrates how you can change IOS XR behavior to ignore all AGs for tunnels without explicit AG constraints. This enforces consistency across vendors in the network.

Example 13-23. Ignoring AGs on RSVP-TE Tunnels (IOS XR)

```
interface tunnel-te44
 affinity ignore
```

After the changes outlined in Example 13-23 are implemented on all RSVP-TE tunnels without explicit AG constraints, all the RSVP-TE LSPs are in the up state.

Extended Administrative Groups

The standard AG attribute, introduced via RFC 3630 (OSPF) and RFC 5305 (IS-IS), includes 32 groups (bits). In some deployment scenarios, this might be too low number, and more AGs are required. For example, an administrator might use different AGs to constrain traffic within specific topological regions of the network, and a large network may well have far more than 32 geographic regions.

Therefore, RFC 7308 introduces *Extended Administrative Groups* (EAGs) in OSPF (sub-TLV Type 26) and IS-IS (TLV Type 14). Using this attribute, multiple 32-bit group series can be advertised. In the RFC, the number of EAGs has no fixed limit. It is constrained only by protocol-specific restrictions such as LSA in OSPF, Link State PDU (LSP) in IS-IS, or maximum transmission unit (MTU) sizes.

Following is the EAG configuration syntax in Junos and IOS XR, respectively.

Example 13-24. EAG configuration on PE1 (Junos)

```
routing-options {
    admin-groups-extended-range {
        minimum 32;
```

```
        maximum 95;
    }
    admin-groups-extended {
        EAG-39 group-value 39;
    }
}
protocols mpls {
    interface ge-2/0/3.0 admin-group-extended EAG-39;
}
```

Example 13-25. EAG configuration on PE2 (IOS XR)

```
mpls traffic-eng
 interface GigabitEthernet0/0/0/3
  attribute-names AG-39
  !
 affinity-map AG-39 bit-position 39
```

Unfortunately, as of this writing, neither IOS XR nor Junos implementations were compliant with the RFC 7308 specification. Both vendors used different pre-RFC7308 implementations, which were incompatible with each other.

To propagate EAG, Junos used TLV Type 138 reserved by IANA for the SRLG attribute (discussed in the following section). IOS XR, on the other hand, used sub-TLV Type 252, reserved by IANA for Cisco proprietary extensions. So interoperability is not successful and therefore not further explored in this book.

Shared Risk Link Group

The *Shared Risk Link Group* (SRLG) is the next MPLS TE link attribute introduced via RFC 4202 - *Routing Extensions in Support of Generalized Multi-Protocol Label Switching (GMPLS)*, and specifically for OSPF via RFC 4203 - *OSPF Extensions in Support of GMPLS*, and for IS-IS via RFC 5307 - *IS-IS Extensions in Support of GMPLS*.

SRLG is conceptually similar to AG or EAG, in so much as you can configure SRLG on links and later specify some constraints based on SRLGs for your LSPs. There are, however, several main differences between AG/EAG and SRLG:

AG or EAG always represents hard (strict) constraints.
> For example, if you configure an LSP to exclude links with a certain AG or EAG, when a path fulfilling this criterion cannot be found, the LSP is not established. You can use SRLG, however, for *soft (loose)* constraints, so you could specify that an LSP should avoid links with a certain SRLG, but if there is no other choice, it can use such links as a last resort.

You must always manually define AG or EAG constraints
> For example, the configuration that says *RSVP-TE LSP X must not use links with AG/EAG Y* must be manually specified. Conversely, you can use SRLG in deploy-

ments with automatic SRLG constraints such as, *path X and path Y should not use links with the same SRLG*, but you don't need to specify the exact SRLG value that should be avoided.

AG and SRLG are both 32-bit fields

AG is interpreted as a *single* vector with 32 bit positions. On the other hand, an SRLG value is interpreted as a 32-bit *number*: a given link can have several 32-bit SRLG attributes assigned. Two SRLG values are considered different if they are different. Of course!

Typically, you should configure router links that share resources (e.g., two fibers in the same cable, or two Dense Wavelength Division Multiplexing (DWDM) lambdas in the same fiber) with the same SRLG value, because such links share the risk. If a common (shared) resource fails (e.g., a fiber cable cut), all the affected router links fail at the same time.

Therefore, SRLGs are typically used in protection scenarios. You can build two LSPs to protect each other. If one LSP fails, traffic can be redirected over the presignaled second LSP. Obviously, it makes sense that both LSPs use links that do not share risk. Chapter 19 provides more insight into MPLS protection, but for now, let's configure two basic scenarios for SRLG deployment here.

SRLG use case 1—Path Protection

First, let's configure SRLGs in the network, as presented in Figure 13-4.

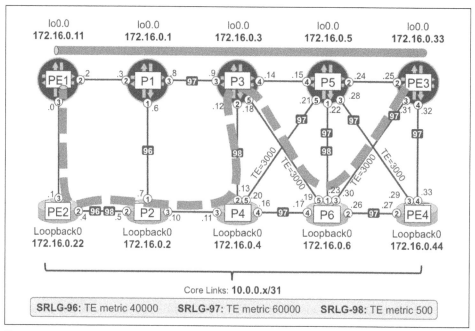

Figure 13-4. SRLG constraint use case 1

Each SRLG is associated with two characteristics:

SRLG value

A 32-bit value exchanged via IGP TE Extensions (Sub-TLV 16 in OSPF, TLV 138 in IS-IS). Figure 13-4 shows SRLG values *symmetrically* configured on specific links.

SRLG metric

An incremental TE link metric used in CSPF calculations for links with SRLG configured. This information is local to the router and never exchanged between the routers. It means, theoretically, that for the same SRLG value *X*, one router can be configured to use incremental TE metric 1000, whereas another router can be configured to use a different incremental metric 2000. In typical deployments, though, for a given SRLG value the same incremental TE metric is configured on all routers for consistency.

Following is the Junos SRLG configuration of P5:

Example 13-26. SRLG configuration on P5 (Junos)

```
1    routing-options {
2        srlg {
3            SRLG-96 {
```

```
4              srlg-value 96;
5              srlg-cost 40000;
6          }
7          SRLG-97 {
8              srlg-value 97;
9              srlg-cost 60000;
10         }
11         SRLG-98 {
12             srlg-value 98;
13             srlg-cost 500;
14     }}}
15     protocols {
16         mpls {
17             interface ge-2/0/1.0 srlg [ SRLG-97 SRLG-98 ];
18             interface ge-2/0/3.0 srlg SRLG-97;
19             interface ge-2/0/5.0 srlg SRLG-97;
20     }}
```

And here is an IOS XR example (P2):

Example 13-27. SRLG configuration on P2 (IOS XR)

```
1      srlg
2       interface GigabitEthernet0/0/0/1
3        name SRLG-96
4       !
5       interface GigabitEthernet0/0/0/2
6        name SRLG-96
7        name SRLG-98
8       !
9       name SRLG-96 value 96
10      name SRLG-97 value 97
11      name SRLG-98 value 98
12     !
13     mpls traffic-eng
14      srlg
15       value 96 admin-weight 40000
16       value 97 admin-weight 60000
17       value 98 admin-weight 500
```

You can check how the SRLG configuration is actually translated into the TED by using the following commands:

- Junos: show ted link detail
- IOS XR: show mpls traffic-eng topology detail

Now, in the first SRLG scenario, you will deploy two presignaled paths for the PE3→PE1 tunnel. This concept, called *Path Protection*, is described in detail in Chapter 19. For the moment, let's concentrate only on SRLG usage. The goal is that the secondary path avoids links with the same SRLG values as links used by the primary path.

Example 13-28. Two presignaled paths configuration for PE3→PE1 tunnel

```
1     protocols {
2         mpls {
3             label-switched-path PE3--->PE1 {
4                 to 172.16.0.11;
5                 primary PRIMARY;
6                 secondary SECONDARY standby;
7             }
8             path PRIMARY;
9             path SECONDARY;
10    }}
```

The configuration is pretty basic. The primary and secondary paths without explicit IP addresses (lines 8 and 9), referenced in the LSP configuration (lines 5 and 6), cause two dynamically computed paths to be established. The primary path has no specific imposed constraints; therefore it finds its way through the lowest accumulated TE metric.

Similarly, the secondary path has no explicit constraints, either. However, Junos imposes two default constraints on the secondary path:

- The secondary path should avoid links used by primary path.

- The secondary path should avoid links with the same SRLG value as links used by primary path.

These two constraints are automatic, so no specific configuration is required, but let's check how the paths are established.

Example 13-29. Two presignaled paths for PE3→PE1 tunnel

```
1     juniper@PE3> show mpls lsp name PE3--->PE1 detail
2     (...)
3     *Primary   PRIMARY          State: Up
4     (...)
5       SRLG: SRLG-97
6       Computed ERO (S [L] strict [loose] hops): (CSPF metric: 4000)
7       10.0.0.24 S 10.0.0.14 S 10.0.0.8 S 10.0.0.2 S
8     (...)
9     Standby   SECONDARY        State: Up
10    (...)
11      SRLG: SRLG-96 SRLG-97 SRLG-98
12      Computed ERO (S [L] strict [loose] hops): (CSPF metric: 70000)
13      10.0.0.30 S 10.0.0.18 S 10.0.0.13 S 10.0.0.10 S
```

```
14      10.0.0.4 S 10.0.0.0 S
15      (...)
```

The two paths are up (lines 3 and 9). The primary path follows the lowest TE metric path to the destination via PE3→P5→P3→P1→PE1 (line 7) with total accumulated TE metric 4000 (line 6), which is correct, because each link on the path has TE metric 1000. You can also see that at least one of the links used by the primary path has SRLG-97 (line 5). In this case, it is link P3→P1, as is visible in Figure 13-4.

More interesting is the secondary path. It uses the PE3→P6→P3→P4→P2→PE2→PE1 route (lines 13 and 14), instead of the shorter route: PE3→P6→P4→P2→PE2→PE1, which has a lower cumulative TE metric.

So what's happening here? Well, Junos temporarily increases the TE metric for certain links when performing CSPF calculation for the secondary path. The primary path uses a link with SRLG-97 (line 5), therefore Junos temporarily increases the TE metric on *all* the links with SLRG-97 before doing the computation of the secondary path. The value is specified in the local configuration on PE3 (see line 9 in Example 13-26 for a similar configuration on P5). Therefore, for the secondary path computation CSPF considers links with SRLG-97 with TE metric 61000 (where the original TE metric was 1000) or 63000 (where the original TE metric was 3000).

Now CSPF performs the calculation for the secondary path, which avoids the links from the primary path. The lowest TE metric route is the route mentioned in lines 13 and 14 from Example 13-29. The total accumulated metric (70000) is correct, as well:

- PE3→P6: 3000 (explicit TE metric) + 60000 (SRLG-97)
- P6→P3: 3000 (explicit TE metric)
- P3→P4: 1000 (implicit TE metric)
- P4→P2: 1000 (implicit TE metric)
- P2→PE2: 1000 (implicit TE metric)
- P22→PE1: 1000 (implicit TE metric)

This path completely avoids links used by the primary path. Additionally, it minimizes the usage of links with common SRLG values (97, in the example) on the primary and secondary paths. Depending on the network topology and the SRLG configuration, it is not always possible to avoid such links. Therefore, the secondary path now uses one link with SRLG-97 (link PE3→P6), compared to two, or even three such links, if only IGP or TE metrics were taken into account.

Note that, the TE metric on links with SLRG different from SRLG 97 (e.g., P3→P4 with SRLG 98 or P2→PE2 with SRLGs 96 and 98) is not increased. SRLG 96 and 98 are not present on links used by the primary path, so there is no requirement to avoid such links in the secondary path.

As of this writing, IOS XR didn't support this SRLG application for calculating secondary standby paths in Path Protection scenarios.

SRLG use case 2—Facility (link) Protection

The second use case for SRLG, similar to Path Protection, is related again to protection—this time to *Facility (link) Protection*. Although details of facility protection are discussed in Chapter 19, let's concentrate only on SRLG.

The goal here is to establish a bypass tunnel that reroutes the traffic around certain links during link failure. Looking at the topology from Figure 13-5, let's create such a bypass tunnel for the link P2→PE2.

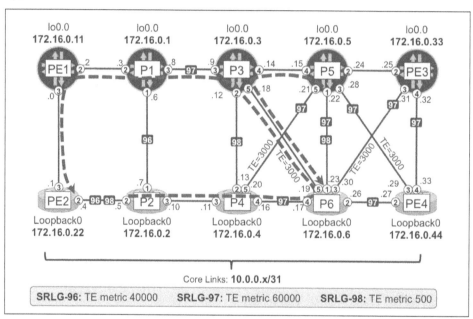

Figure 13-5. SRLG constraint use case 2

As Figure 13-5 illustrates, this link has two SRLGs: 96 and 98. Therefore, it is advisable that the bypass tunnel avoids links with these SRLGs. Otherwise, if the link being protected and some links used for the bypass tunnel share the risk, one single network failure could bring down the primary link and the bypass tunnel.

Example 13-30. Configuration of link bypass with SRLG constraint—P2 (IOS XR)

```
1    mpls traffic-eng
2      interface GigabitEthernet0/0/0/2
```

```
3      auto-tunnel backup
4        exclude srlg
5        attribute-set AS-AFFINITY-IGNORE
6    !
7    attribute-set auto-backup AS-AFFINITY-IGNORE
8      affinity-ignore
```

The basic configuration is, again, pretty easy. For interface Gi0/0/0/2, an automatically established bypass tunnel (line 3) should be established. Additionally, on this bypass tunnel, the SRLG constraints should be enforced (line 4). Furthermore, similar to the case described already in Example 13-23, you need to disable the AG constraints (lines 5, 7, and 8) if you want to allow that bypass tunnel to use links with AGs 0–15.

 Refer to Chapter 19 for a detailed coverage of Facility Protection.

Again, let's check how the tunnel is established (see Example 13-31).

Example 13-31. Link bypass with SRLG constraint on P2 (IOS XR)

```
1    RP/0/0/CPU0:P2#show mpls traffic-eng tunnels 103
2    (...)
3    Name: tunnel-te103  Destination: 172.16.0.22  (auto-tunnel backup)
4        path option 10,  type explicit (autob_nhop_srlg_te103)
5                          (Basis for Setup, path weight 8000)
6        SRLGs Excluded: SRLG-96(96), SRLG-98(98)
7    (...)
8      Auto Backup:
9        Protected i/f: Gi0/0/0/2
10       Attribute-set: AS-AFFINITY-IGNORE
11       Protection: NHOP+SRLG (SRLG strict)
12   (...)
13     Path info (IS-IS core level-2):
14     Node hop count: 6
15     Hop0: 10.0.0.11
16     Hop1: 10.0.0.17
17     Hop2: 10.0.0.18
18     Hop3: 10.0.0.8
19     Hop4: 10.0.0.2
20     Hop5: 10.0.0.1
21     Hop6: 172.16.0.22
```

You can see the automatic bypass tunnel (line 3) to protect Gi0/0/0/2 interface (line 9). The path for this bypass tunnel strictly avoids (line 11) links with SRLG 96 or 98 (line 6). Other AGs are not taken into account as constraints (line 10). The path automatically calculated by CSPF is P2→P4→P6→P3→P1→PE1→P2 (lines 14 through 21), with the accumulated TE metric 8000 (line 5).

It is certainly not the shortest path to avoid the P2→PE2 link. If you look at the topology in Figure 13-5, you can see that links P2→P1, P4→P3, and P6→P5 have either SRLG 96 or 98. Therefore, because *strict* SRLG constraint is enforced, the bypass tunnel cannot use these links. Thus, CSPF properly selected the lowest accumulated TE metric path that avoids links with SRLG 96 or 98.

Apart from strict SRLG constraint, IOS XR supports *weighted* (configured by using `exclude srlg weighted`) or *preferred* (configured by using `exclude srlg preferred`) SRLG constraints. Weighted constraint is equivalent to the default SRLG constraint in Junos, discussed previously, whereas you can configure *strict* SRLG constraint in Junos by using the `exclude-srlg` keyword. Due to limited space in this book, these SRLG constraint methods are not discussed, but you are encouraged to further explore these methods.

For the sake of completeness, the Junos configuration for bypass tunnel with strict SRLG constrains is presented in the following example:

Example 13-32. Link bypass configuration with strict SRLG constraint—P5 (Junos)

```
1    protocols {
2        rsvp {
3            interface ge-2/0/1.0 {
4                link-protection {
5                    bypass BP-P5-P6 {
6                        to 172.16.0.6;
7                        bandwidth 0;
8                        exclude-srlg;
9    }}}}}
```

By default, Junos uses *weighted* SRLG constraints, so if you remove lines 5 through 9 from the configuration, bypass will be established based on *weighted* constraints, and no longer on *strict* SRLG constraints. Refer to Chapter 19 for detailed discussion about the protection mechanisms in RSVP-TE.

Egress Peer Engineering

Egress Peer Engineering (EPE) is a classic TE requirement that has gained momentum in the context of high-scaled data centers and is also perfectly applicable to IP peering environments such as that depicted in Figure 13-6. The challenge is this: how can PE2 choose the external inter-domain link that a packet should use to get out of the local domain? PE2 needs to push two labels: one that takes the packet to PE3 (a classic PE2→PE3 transport LSP), and one more that is *locally significant to PE3* and uniquely determines the interdomain link.

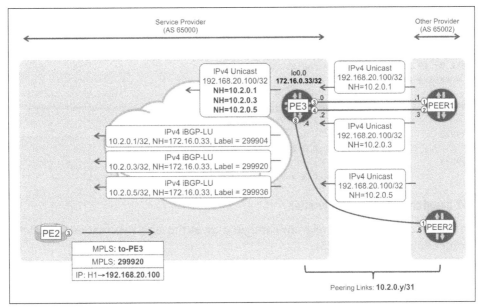

Figure 13-6. EPE with BGP-LU

If you remember the different SPRING SID types from Chapter 2, the Adjacency SID automatically comes to mind. Indeed, *draft-ietf-idr-bgpls-segment-routing-epe* defines a protocol ID that can be used to encode this type of information in the BGP-LS NLRI. BGP-LS is discussed in Chapter 15.

EPE Based on BGP-LU

Alternatively, good old BGP-LU is also capable of encoding this type of information, as you can see in Figure 13-6. This model, described in *draft-gredler-idr-bgplu-epe*, does not require any protocol extensions and simply relies on a clever manipulation of the BGP next-hop attribute:

- No BGP next hop change for the service route, relying on Add-Path extensions in order to advertise all the possible peering next hops. In this example, the service route is IPv4 Unicast 192.168.20.100/32, but it could be a different address family, too.

- Allocating a *different* label to each peering next hop and announcing it via internal BGP-LU to the Route Reflectors (RRs).

The MPLS label 299920 (see Example 13-33) is an instruction (a segment in SPRING terminology) that PE3 interprets as: *pop the label and send the packet out to PEER1 through the bottom link.*

Example 13-33. EPE based on BGP-LU—LFIB at PE3 (Junos)

```
user@PE3> show route table mpls.0 protocol VPN

mpls.0: 19 destinations, 19 routes (19 active, ...)
+ = Active Route, - = Last Active, * = Both

299904              *[VPN/170] 1d 07:32:02
                     > to 10.2.0.1 via ge-2/0/3.0, Pop
299920              *[VPN/170] 1d 07:32:02
                     > to 10.2.0.3 via ge-2/0/4.0, Pop
299936              *[VPN/170] 1d 07:32:02
                     > to 10.2.0.5 via ge-2/0/8.0, Pop
```

EPE based on BGP-LU—configuration

Example 13-34 shows the relevant configuration at the egress Autonomous Systems Border Router (ASBR) (PE3).

Example 13-34. EPE based on BGP-LU—configuration at PE3 (Junos)

```
1    protocols bgp {
2        group eBGP-PEER1-UPPER-LINK {
3            family inet unicast;
4            egress-te;
5            neighbor 10.2.0.1 peer-as 65002;
6        }
7        group eBGP-PEER1-BOTTOM-LINK {
8            family inet unicast;
9            egress-te;
10           neighbor 10.2.0.3 peer-as 65002;
11       }
12       group eBGP-PEER2 {
13           family inet unicast;
14           egress-te;
15           neighbor 10.2.0.5 peer-as 65002;
16       }
17       group iBGP-RR {
18           type internal;
19           family inet {
20               unicast {
21                   add-path {
22                       receive;
23                       send path-count 6;
24                   }
25               }
26               labeled-unicast rib inet.3;
27           }
28           export iBGP-RR-OUT;
29           neighbor 172.16.0.201;
30           neighbor 172.16.0.202;
```

```
31          }
32      }
33      policy-options {
34          policy-statement iBGP-RR-OUT {
35              term eBGP-PEERS {
36                  from {
37                      protocol arp;
38                      rib inet.3;
39                  }
40                  then {
41                      next-hop self;
42                      accept;
43      }}}}
```

Remember that BGP policies accept BGP prefixes that do not match any terms. The egress-te knob (lines 4, 9, and 14) automatically creates a so-called ARP route for each eBGP peer in inet.3.

Example 13-35. ARP Routes in inet.3—PE3 (Junos)

```
user@PE3> show route table inet.3 10.2.0.0/24

inet.3: 9 destinations, 9 routes (9 active, ...)
+ = Active Route, - = Last Active, * = Both

10.2.0.1/32        *[ARP/170] 1d 07:32:02
                    > to 10.2.0.1 via ge-2/0/3.0, Pop
10.2.0.3/32        *[ARP/170] 1d 07:32:02
                    > to 10.2.0.3 via ge-2/0/4.0, Pop
10.2.0.5/32        *[ARP/170] 1d 07:32:02
                    > to 10.2.0.5 via ge-2/0/8.0, Pop
```

These are the routes that PE3 later advertises via iBGP-LU thanks to the configured policies (Example 13-33, lines 28, and 34 through 42).

Let's move on to Chapter 14, which discusses advanced TE constraints.

## CHAPTER 14

TE Bandwidth Reservations

Bandwidth reservations are an essential tool that you can use to do the following:

- Avoid link congestion in networks with high-volume traffic, such as ISP back-bones.
- Ensure that the most critical applications have their bandwidth resources available.

This chapter covers the control plane required to perform bandwidth reservations. To date, the only protocol that is capable of actually reserving bandwidth in a network is RSVP-TE. Most forwarding plane details—in particular, fine-grained mapping of certain traffic to certain LSPs—are specific to each platform and beyond the scope of this book.

 This book does not cover DiffServ-TE. It is not widely deployed.

The Traffic Engineering (TE) link constraints that are discussed in Chapter 13 are very simple, and are represented by single numbers. In this chapter, you will discover more complex TE use cases, with composite TE link attributes such as bandwidth.

TE Static Bandwidth Constraints

The next TE link characteristic is *bandwidth*. Bandwidth is a little bit special. It is no longer a single attribute, but a *set* of attributes that you can find in the IGP's link-state databases, in the Traffic Engineering Database (TED) and in the RSVP-TE messages.

TE Bandwidth Attributes

Let's have a look at the different attributes that comprise the TE bandwidth.

Maximum bandwidth (4 octets)

This is the physical interface bandwidth (e.g., 1.25 GByte/s for a 10GE interface). Typically, this parameter is inherited from the interface bandwidth, but you can also set it manually. This parameter is not used in TE calculations and is purely informational.

Maximum reservable bandwidth (4 octets)

This is the bandwidth that RSVP-TE is allowed to reserve. It can be bigger than the Maximum Bandwidth (if you allow RSVP-TE oversubscription), equal to the Maximum Bandwidth (if all the interface bandwidth can be taken by RSVP-TE) or smaller than the Maximum Bandwidth (if you don't allow RSVP-TE to take the full interface bandwidth). Typically, this parameter is manually configured. If not explicitly configured, the default value in Junos is the full interface bandwidth, whereas in IOS XR, it is zero.

Unreserved bandwidth per priority level (8 x 4 octets)

This is the set of eight counters that keep track of the available bandwidth for each RSVP-TE priority (priority will be discussed later in this chapter). Although the previous two parameters are rather stable (after you start the IGP, the same values are advertised continuously), unreserved bandwidth changes dynamically. Each time a new LSP with bandwidth reservation is established, or existing LSPs with bandwidth reservation are torn down, or they change their bandwidth reservations, the value of this parameter is adjusted and flooded via the IGP. Actually, typical IGP implementations set some thresholds to suppress flooding when bandwidth changes are not significant.

Putting it all together, IGP distributes bandwidth information using 40 octets (4 + 4 + 32), plus normal TLV headers. All the bandwidth values are in bytes/s (not bits/s). Bandwidth was introduced with the initial TE extensions in OSPF and in IS-IS.

Default TE Interface Bandwidth

After this small bit of theory, let's get into the lab. First, the default behavior of Junos and IOS XR is completely different. As mentioned previously, without any explicit RSVP-TE bandwidth configuration, Junos allows RSVP-TE to utilize the full interface bandwidth, whereas IOS XR does not allow RSVP-TE to reserve any bandwidth.

Example 14-1. RSVP interface status with default bandwidth on PE1 (Junos)

```
juniper@PE1> show rsvp interface
RSVP interface: 2 active
              Active Subscr- Static  Available Reserved Highwater
Interface  St resv  iption BW       BW        BW       mark
ge-2/0/2.0 Up     8    100%  1000Mbps 1000Mbps  0bps     0bps
ge-2/0/3.0 Up     4    100%  1000Mbps 1000Mbps  0bps     0bps
```

Example 14-2. RSVP interface status with default bandwidth on PE2 (IOS XR)

```
RP/0/0/CPU0:PE2#show rsvp interface
(...)
Interface  MaxBW (bps)  MaxFlow (bps) Allocated (bps) MaxSub (bps)
---------- ------------ ------------- --------------- ------------
Gi0/0/0/2            0             0         0 (  0%)            0
Gi0/0/0/3            0             0         0 (  0%)            0
```

Basic RSVP-TE Bandwidth Reservation

Figure 14-1 shows three LSPs: PE1→PE3, PE2→PE4, and PE2→P5. Initially, only the two first LSPs are configured, and this time an explicit bandwidth reservation is included.

Let's request 500 kbps for PE1→PE3 and 700 kbps for PE2→PE4, as shown in Figure 14-1 and presented in Example 14-3 and Example 14-4. Note that, in IOS XR, you specify bandwidth in *kbps*, whereas in Junos it's *bps*.

Example 14-3. RSVP-TE bandwidth request on PE1 (Junos)

```
protocols {
    mpls label-switched-path PE1--->PE3 bandwidth 500k;
}
```

Example 14-4. RSVP-TE bandwidth request on PE2 (IOS XR)

```
interface tunnel-te44
 signalled-bandwidth 700
```

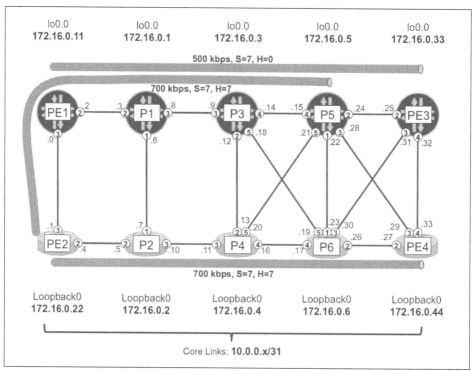

Figure 14-1. TE with bandwidth constraints

RSVP-TE tries to signal the tunnel, but now CSPF verifies if the additional constraint (bandwidth) is fulfilled. That is, the LSP is established only if all the links on the path have at least 500 (or 700) kbps *free* bandwidth. *Free* in this context means bandwidth that can be reserved by RSVP-TE, and for the moment, has nothing to do with the bandwidth utilized by actual traffic.

Example 14-5. RSVP-TE LSP status on PE1 and PE2

```
1    juniper@PE1> show mpls lsp name PE1--->PE3 detail | match <pattern>
2      From: 172.16.0.11, State: Up, ActiveRoute: 0, LSPname: PE1--->PE3
3        Bandwidth: 500kbps
4
5    RP/0/0/CPU0:PE2#show mpls traffic-eng tunnels 44 | include <pattern>
6        Admin:    up Oper: down    Path: not valid    Signalling: Down
7          Info: No path to destination, 172.16.0.44 (bw)
8        Bandwidth Requested: 700 kbps  CT0
```

The PE1→PE3 tunnel is up (line 2), whereas the PE2→PE4 tunnel is down (line 6). Apparently, between PE2 and PE4 there is no path for which at least 700 kbps are free (meaning *reservable* by RSVP-TE).

Explicit TE interface reservable bandwidth

So, as shown in Example 14-6 and Example 14-7, let's configure consistent bandwidth reservations through the network and allow 10 Mbps for RSVP-TE on each link in the network. You can simply enhance existing GR-RSVP configuration groups to include the new bandwidth parameters.

Example 14-6. RSVP-TE link bandwidth configuration (Junos)

```
1    groups {
2        GR-RSVP {
3            protocols rsvp interface "<*[es]*>" subscription 1;
4    }}}
5    protocols rsvp apply-groups GR-RSVP;
```

Example 14-7. RSVP-TE link bandwidth configuration (IOS XR)

```
1    group GR-RSVP
2      rsvp
3       interface 'GigabitEthernet.*'
4         bandwidth 10000
5      !
6    rsvp apply-group GR-RSVP
7      !
```

In Junos, you can specify the percentage of interface bandwidth (line 3 in Example 14-6) that can be used for RSVP-TE reservations, or set explicit limits in bps—1% of 1 Gbps is 10 Mbps, so the result is the same. However, in IOS XR, you simply specify the limit in kbps (line 4 in Example 14-7).

With this configuration in place, the PE2→PE4 LSP is now up.

Example 14-8. Tunnel status on PE2 (IOS XR)

```
RP/0/0/CPU0:PE2#show mpls traffic-eng tunnels 44 | include <pattern>
    Admin:    up Oper:   up   Path:  valid   Signalling: connected
    Bandwidth Requested: 700 kbps   CT0
```

Because there are 10 Mbps available to reserve on every link by RSVP-TE, you can establish the tunnel with the 700 kbps requirement without any problems, and routers update the link bandwidth reservations accordingly.

Example 14-9. RSVP interface status with explicit bandwidth

```
juniper@PE1> show rsvp interface
RSVP interface: 2 active
              Active Subscr- Static  Available Reserved Highwater
Interface   ST resv  iption BW       BW        BW       mark
```

```
ge-2/0/2.0  Up     8    1%  1000Mbps 9.5Mbps  500kbps  500kbps
ge-2/0/3.0  Up     3    1%  1000Mbps 10Mbps   0bps     0bps

RP/0/0/CPU0:PE2#show rsvp interface
(...)
Interface MaxBW (bps) MaxFlow (bps) Allocated (bps) MaxSub (bps)
--------- ----------- ------------- --------------- ------------
Gi0/0/0/2      10M          10M       700K ( 7%)         0
Gi0/0/0/3      10M          10M         0 ( 0%)          0
```

You can see that now the *Maximum Reservable Bandwidth* is 10 Mbps on each link (Junos: `AvailableBW` + `ReservedBW`; IOS XR: `MaxBW`). Also, you can see the currently reserved bandwidth on each interface (Junos: `ReservedBW`; IOS XR: `Allocated`). This information is distributed via the IGP, as demonstrated in Example 14-10.

Example 14-10. TE bandwidth announcements in IS-IS

```
1    juniper@PE1> show isis database PE1 extensive
2    (...)
3        IS extended neighbor: P1.00, Metric: default 1000
4          IP address: 10.0.0.2
5          Neighbor's IP address: 10.0.0.3
6          Local interface index: 337, Remote interface index: 335
7          Current reservable bandwidth:
8            Priority 0 : 9.5Mbps
9            Priority 1 : 9.5Mbps
10           Priority 2 : 9.5Mbps
11           Priority 3 : 9.5Mbps
12           Priority 4 : 9.5Mbps
13           Priority 5 : 9.5Mbps
14           Priority 6 : 9.5Mbps
15           Priority 7 : 9.5Mbps
16         Maximum reservable bandwidth: 10Mbps
17         Maximum bandwidth: 1000Mbps
18         Administrative groups:  0 <none>
19
20   RP/0/0/CPU0:PE2#show isis database PE2 verbose
21   (...)
22     Metric: 1000        IS-Extended P2.00
23       Affinity: 0x00000000
24       Interface IP Address: 10.0.0.4
25       Neighbor IP Address: 10.0.0.5
26       Physical BW: 1000000 kbits/sec
27       Reservable Global pool BW: 10000 kbits/sec
28       Global Pool BW Unreserved:
29         [0]: 10000    kbits/sec      [1]: 10000    kbits/sec
30         [2]: 10000    kbits/sec      [3]: 10000    kbits/sec
31         [4]: 10000    kbits/sec      [5]: 10000    kbits/sec
32         [6]: 10000    kbits/sec      [7]: 9300     kbits/sec
33   (...)
```

Both PE1 and PE2 advertise 10 Mbps as the links' maximum reservable bandwidth (lines 16 and 27). Conversely, there are some differences when you look for the bandwidth available at each priority level. For the PE1→P1 link, the announced bandwidth for each priority is 9.5 Mbps (lines 8 through 15), whereas for the PE2→P2 link it is 10 Mbps for priority 0–6 (lines 29 through 32), and 9.3 Mbps for priority 7 only (line 32). This is yet another difference in the default implementation of Junos and IOS XR; let's see its meaning after introducing some new concepts.

LSP Priorities and Preemption

If you now configure PE2→P5 (the remaining LSP from Figure 14-1) with a 700 kbps reservation, it has several available paths to choose. Let's suppose that it uses the PE2→PE1 link and that completes all the LSPs shown in Figure 14-1.

Now, suppose that you configure yet another new PE2→P6 tunnel (not shown in Figure 14-1) with 9400 kbps bandwidth reservation. As you can see by looking at the bandwidth reservations on Figure 14-1, the new LSP's setup would fail because there is no path with 9400 kbps of available bandwidth on all links. Specifically, all links adjacent to PE2 have available bandwidth less than 9400 kbps.

You can fix the problem by moving one of the small bandwidth LSPs to another link. For example, if you move the PE2→P5 LSP from the PE2→PE1 to the PE2→P2 link, the PE2→PE1 link would have 10 Mbps free bandwidth. This is enough for the new LSP requiring 9.4 Mbps to fit, at least on this link.

How can you achieve this? Well, one option is to manually reroute the PE2→P5 LSP, by setting an explicit path. However, in large networks with many LSPs in place, setting explicit paths everywhere can be a challenging task.

Therefore, let's consider another approach: *LSP preemption*. With LSP preemption, you can designate some LSPs as more important, and other LSPs as less important. More-important LSPs can preempt (kick-out or remove: choose your verb) existing less-important LSPs. Let's suppose that you designate the high-bandwidth PE2→P6 LSP to be more important that the PE2→P5 LSP. In this case, the PE2→P6 LSP preempts the PE2→P5 LSP. As a result of this preemption, the PE2→P5 LSP is removed from the PE2→PE1 link. When the PE2→P5 LSP is calculated again, PE2 signals it over a different path. As you can see in Figure 14-2, in the end every configured LSP successfully comes up.

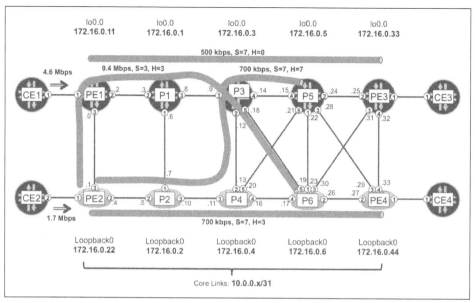

Figure 14-2. TE with bandwidth constraints and preemption

Setup and Hold priorities

Now, how can you configure the importance of an LSP? In TE, there is a concept of *Setup* and *Hold* priority. Numerically lower priority is better. Thus, when a new LSP is being signaled, in case of resource conflict (e.g., not enough bandwidth on a certain link) the *Setup* priority of the new LSP is compared to the *Hold* priority of the existing LSP. If it is numerically lower, the new LSP can preempt the existing LSP.

As shown next, the default settings for Setup and Hold priority are different in Junos and IOS XR.

Example 14-11. Default Setup and Hold priorities

```
juniper@PE1> show mpls lsp name PE1--->PE3 detail | match Priorities
    Priorities: 7 0

RP/0/0/CPU0:PE2#show mpls traffic-eng tunnels 44 | include Priority
    Bandwidth:      700 kbps (CT0) Priority:  7  7
```

What is the difference? In Junos, it is 7 (Setup) and 0 (Hold), whereas in IOS XR it is 7 for *both* Setup and Hold. It means that the LSPs signaled by Junos are by default *rock-solid*: after they are established, no other LSP can preempt them. Why? The Hold priority of Junos-signaled LSPs is 0, so it is not possible for another LSP to have a numerically lower Setup priority. IOS XR is just the opposite: the Hold priority is 7, so any LSP with Setup priority 0 through 6 can preempt such an LSP.

If you go back to Example 14-10, you will now understand why Junos and IOS XR advertised different free bandwidths. IOS XR advertised the full bandwidth (10 Mbps) available at priority level 0 through 6, meaning that any LSP with a Setup priority level 0 through 6 can take full bandwidth on the advertised link.

With that behind us, let's configure a better (numerically lower) hold priority for PE2→PE4 LSP. This will make it more resistant to preemption by other LSPs.

Example 14-12. PE2→PE4 LSP priority configuration on PE2 (IOS XR)

```
interface tunnel-te44
 priority 7 3
```

With this configuration, the lines 29 through 32 from Example 14-10 would change to the following:

- Priorities [0] to [2]: reservable bandwidth 10000 kbps
- Priorities [3] to [7]: reservable bandwidth 9300 kbps

Now, let's configure the PE2→PE6 tunnel, which is requesting 9.4 Mbps bandwidth, with Setup priority 3, as demonstrated in Figure 14-2 and in Example 14-13.

Example 14-13. PE2→P6 LSP priority configuration on PE2 (IOS XR)

```
interface tunnel-te6
 priority 3 3
```

To maintain LSP stability, the Hold priority cannot be worse (numerically higher) than the Setup priority. This is enforced by a commit check, on both IOS XR and Junos platforms. Therefore, 3 was configured for both Setup and Hold priorities.

Results of LSP preemption and resignaling

With its new Setup priority, the PE2→PE6 LSP will be able to preempt the PE2→P5 tunnel (Hold priority 7), but not the PE2→PE4 tunnel (Hold priority 3). Let's check that.

Example 14-14. RSVP interface status after preemption on PE2 (IOS XR)

```
1   RP/0/0/CPU0:PE2#show rsvp interface
2   (...)
3   Interface   MaxBW (bps)  MaxFlow (bps) Allocated (bps) MaxSub (bps)
4   ----------  -----------  ------------- --------------- ------------
5   Gi0/0/0/2          10M           10M   1400K ( 14%)             0
6   Gi0/0/0/3          10M           10M   9400K ( 94%)             0
```

The RSVP bandwidth reservations reported on the interfaces confirm that now all four of the LSPs in question, three of them initiated at PE2, are established. You can see the global LSP placement in Figure 14-2.

In Junos, you also can configure RSVP-TE LSP priorities by using the `priority <SETUP> <HOLD>` keyword, this time under the `mpls label-switched-path <NAME>` stanza. The logic is similar to IOS XR, we'll skip it for brevity.

> You can achieve an enhanced LSP distribution logic with the help of a central controller. See Chapter 15 for more details.

Traffic Metering and Policing

Now, let's push some traffic through the PE1→PE3 and PE2→PE4 LSPs. Suppose that the actual utilization of both PE1's and PE2's uplinks exceed the reserved LSP bandwidth (500 and 700 kbps, respectively). If you want to know what LSPs are contributing to the overall traffic rate, there are at least two handy operational commands that you can use:

- For Junos: `show mpls lsp statistics`
- For IOS XR: `show mpls forwarding`

Although these commands are great, they do not really integrate with the TE logic of PE1 and PE2. If you really want to make TE traffic-aware, you need at the very least to add some configuration to collect traffic statistics on a per-LSP basis.

Example 14-15. LSP bandwidth monitoring on PE1 (Junos)

```
1    protocols mpls {
2        statistics {
3            file mpls.stat size 100m files 10;
4            interval 120;
5            auto-bandwidth;
6        }
7        label-switched-path PE1--->PE3 {
8            auto-bandwidth monitor-bandwidth;
9    }}
```

Example 14-16. LSP bandwidth monitoring on PE2 (IOS XR)

```
1    interface tunnel-te44
2      auto-bw
3       collect-bw-only
```

```
4    !
5    mpls traffic-eng
6      auto-bw collect frequency 2
```

This configuration enables the collection of average bandwidth samples every 120 seconds (Example 14-15), or in other words, every 2 minutes (Example 14-16). As a result, the TE logic is aware of the bandwidth that is actually used by the LSP.

Example 14-17. LSP bandwidth utilization

```
juniper@PE1> show mpls lsp name PE1--->PE3 detail | match <pattern>
  Max AvgBW util: 4.65488Mbps
..
RP/0/0/CPU0:PE2#show mpls traffic-eng tunnels 44 | include <pattern>
      Highest BW: 1738 kbps    Underflow BW: 0 kbps
```

Your LSPs are consuming much more bandwidth than the requested 500 (or 700) kbps! This simple example shows that there is no admission control for traffic entering TE tunnels. TE bandwidth is simply an accounting term, but it is not coupled with any policing by default. It is like requesting 700 tickets for a football game, and subsequently sending 1,738 people, hoping that there aren't any ticket checks at the entrance to the stadium. And, in the case of RSVP-TE, there aren't!

Therefore you need to take additional measures, and you basically have two options to ensure that the traffic demand and bandwidth accounting (TE bandwidth reservations) are aligned:

- Limit the traffic entering TE tunnels (comparable to using football game ticket checks) to match the requested bandwidth.
- Adjust TE tunnels bandwidth reservations to match the traffic demand (comparable to allocating more tickets for the football game).

This chapter will soon dive deep into the second model. Regarding the first model, as of this writing, it is implemented by Junos but not by IOS XR. Here is the Junos syntax:

Example 14-18. Automatic LSP policing configuration on PE1 (Junos)

```
protocols {
    mpls auto-policing class all drop;
}
```

This feature assigns policers to LSPs that automatically match each of the LSPs' reserved bandwidth.

TE Auto-Bandwidth

So far in this chapter, all of the examples have relied on static bandwidth constraints. However, traffic patterns and bandwidth utilization are extremely dynamic. The rest of this chapter looks at ways to adapt the LSP layout based on the actual traffic.

Introduction to Auto-Bandwidth

As already mentioned, it is possible to adapt bandwidth reservations to the actual traffic demand. This is obviously gentler to traffic than admission control.

Doing it manually is not an option for large networks with thousands of LSPs, oscillating traffic patterns, and changing service demands. Therefore, it's better to use automation for implementing adjustments. Two building blocks are required:

- Traffic rate measurements per LSP (already described).
- Periodic adjustments of RSVP-TE bandwidth reservations based on the measured traffic rates. This feature is called *auto-bandwidth*.

If a bandwidth adjustment is needed, the ingress PE takes into account the new bandwidth and runs CSPF again. If CSPF succeeds, the ingress PE resignals the LSP according to new path computation.

> Auto-bandwidth is an asynchronous process. Ingress Label Edge Routers (LERs) are distributed across the network and typically perform their own calculations and bandwidth adjustments, at their own timing.

If LER-1 performs a bandwidth adjustment, it can influence the next adjustment performed by LER-2. There is even a risk of "collision" when the two LERs try to simultaneously reserve resources on the same link. Although real experience in large providers shows that auto-bandwidth is robust and converges fine, it is also an opportunity for a central controller to bring synchrony to this process.

Both Junos and IOS XR support auto-bandwidth, but as usual, the terminology and the implementation details are different. The following subsections list the most important auto-bandwidth parameters for both vendors. Take the time to carefully read this short "user guide" because these concepts are mandatory to understand the practical example.

Collection (sampling) interval

Junos

```
set protocols mpls statistics interval <seconds>
```

IOS XR

```
mpls traffic-eng auto-bw collect frequency <minutes>
```

This timer controls how often the router collects traffic rates for every LSP that has the auto-bandwidth feature turned on. These measurements, called *bandwidth samples*, are traffic averages calculated for the collection interval. They are stored in an internal database for MPLS statistics (in Junos, it is a logfile whose properties you can tune).

Application (adjustment) interval

Junos

```
set protocols mpls label-switched-path <name> auto-bandwidth adjust-
interval <seconds>
```

IOS XR

```
interface tunnel-te<id> auto-bw application <minutes>
```

Typically, the adjustment interval is a multiple of the sampling interval; so several samples are collected for the LSP within each adjustment interval. When the adjustment timer expires, there is an adjustment event. The router looks at all of the samples that have been collected within the last adjustment interval and chooses the one with a *maximum* value: the *maximum bandwidth sample*. This value is compared to the currently signaled LSP bandwidth and this comparison *may* cause the RSVP-TE LSP to be resignaled in order to update the reserved bandwidth. Whether this update takes place depends on whether the bandwidth has changed enough (see the following parameter).

Application (adjustment) threshold

Junos

```
set protocols mpls label-switched-path <name> auto-bandwidth adjust-
threshold <percent>
```

IOS XR

```
interface tunnel-te<id> auto-bw adjustment-threshold <percent> min
<kbps>
```

This is defined as a percentage of the current tunnel's reserved bandwidth. In IOS XR, optionally, you also can specify an absolute bandwidth difference.

At the end of each adjustment interval, the router compares the following two values:

- The currently reserved LSP bandwidth
- The maximum bandwidth sample from the expired adjustment interval

If the difference is larger than the configured thresholds, the LSP is resignaled with a new bandwidth value that equals the maximum bandwidth sample.

 It is assumed that you understand the connection between application and adjustment, and collection and sampling, from this point on.

Overflow detection

Junos

```
set protocols mpls label-switched-path <name> auto-bandwidth adjust-
threshold-overflow-limit <number>
```

IOS XR

```
interface tunnel-te<id> auto-bw overflow threshold <percent> min
<kpbs> limit <number>
```

If the rate of the traffic entering an LSP drastically increases, the LSP bandwidth should be resized quickly, without having to wait for the expiry of an adjustment interval.

At the end of each sampling interval, the router compares the following two values:

- The currently reserved LSP bandwidth.
- The average bandwidth sample from the expired sampling interval.

If the difference is larger than the configured thresholds, the current sample is considered an *overflow sample*. After a configurable number of consecutive overflow samples, the adjustment interval prematurely ends. An adjustment event takes place and the router resignals the LSP with a new bandwidth value that equals the maximum bandwidth sample. This configurable number of consecutive overflow samples is called an *overflow limit*.

For overflow detection, Junos reuses the threshold parameter (percentage) specified for adjustment thresholds, whereas with IOS XR, you can specify separate parameters.

Underflow detection

Junos

```
set protocols mpls label-switched-path <name> auto-bandwidth adjust-
threshold-underflow-limit <number>
```

IOS XR
```
interface tunnel-te<id> auto-bw underflow threshold <percent> min
<kpbs> limit <number>
```

This is similar to overflow detection, but it works in the opposite direction. When the traffic rate entering the tunnel significantly lowers within the current adjustment interval, the tunnel bandwidth can be decreased automatically without waiting for the current adjustment interval to expire.

Requested bandwidth minimum and maximum limits

Junos
```
set protocols mpls label-switched-path <name> auto-bandwidth
minimum-bandwidth <bps> maximum-bandwidth <bps>
```

IOS XR
```
interface tunnel-te<id> auto-bw bw-limit min <kbps> max <kbps>
```

The auto-bandwidth feature can dynamically change LSP bandwidth reservations within certain limits. These commands set the limits.

Auto-Bandwidth in Action

The meaning of all these auto-bandwidth parameters might be difficult to understand at first glance, so let's discuss the example presented in Figure 14-3.

Let's assume the following parameters:

- Collection (sampling) interval: 2 minutes (120 seconds)
- Application (adjustment) interval: 20 minutes (1200 seconds) → 10 times the collection (sampling) interval
- Requested minimum and maximum bandwidth: 1 kbps and 10 Mbps
- Adjustment threshold: 10%, minimum 0.1 Mbps
- Overflow threshold: 10%, minimum 0.1 Mbps
- Overflow limit: 3

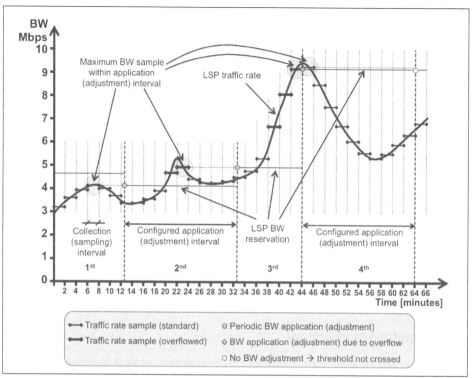

Figure 14-3. Auto-bandwidth in action

These timers are set quite aggressively for testing purposes, but they are not suitable for a scaled production environment.

Also, let's assume that the tunnel has already been established for some time, so there are some traffic rate samples collected before (not shown in the Figure 14-3). There is some (around 4.7 Mbps) existing bandwidth reservation already in place.

Figure 14-3 begins with the six last traffic rate samples from the first application interval. Each sample is collected every 2 minutes, so here you see the last 12 minutes (out of 20) from this application interval. Each collected sample is an average rate of traffic entering the monitored LSP. The average is calculated over the sampling interval (2 minutes).

Now, the sample at T=8 is the highest, with around 4.0 Mbps (let's assume that the not-visible four samples from the first adjustment interval are below 4.0 Mbps, too). The first application interval expires slightly after T=12. The bandwidth difference between the current bandwidth reservation (around 4.7 Mbps) and the maximum bandwidth sample (around 4.0 Mbps) is higher than the configured adjustment threshold (10% and 0.1 Mbps). Further, 4.7 Mbps is within the configured minimum and maximum (1 and 10 Mbps) limits. Therefore the router resignals the LSP, requesting around 4.0 Mbps bandwidth reservation only.

In the second application interval, the 10 bandwidth samples are collected again. Note that samples at T=22 (BW≈4.7) and T=24 (BW≈5.0) are above these two values:

- 4.1 x 110% = **4.4**, the current bandwidth reservation adjusted to the 10% threshold.

- 4.0 + 0.1 = the current bandwidth reservation plus the minimum overflow difference.

These two samples are therefore considered as *overflow* samples.

However, the next sample (BW≈4.3), at T=26, is back below the overflow threshold. Therefore it is a standard sample. Because the configured overflow limit requires three consecutive overflow samples, the overflow-based bandwidth adjustment is not triggered. The bandwidth is adjusted based on the highest sample (T=24, BW≈5.0) only after T=32, when the configured application interval ends.

In the third application interval, the sample at T=38 is higher (BW≈5.3) than the current bandwidth reservation (BW≈5.0). However, it doesn't cross the 10% overflow threshold; thus, it is not high enough to be considered as an overflow sample. The next three samples (T=40, T=42, and T=44), however, are well above the overflow threshold. Because three consecutive overflow samples are collected, the router doesn't wait for the application timer to expire (after T=52). Instead, it prematurely expires the timer, resignals the bandwidth (based on the highest sample: T=44, BW≈9.0) reservation, and starts the new application interval immediately. Therefore, the rapid increase in bandwidth demand can be quickly addressed with bandwidth reservation resignaling, without the need to wait for the application interval to finish. Note, in this case, that if the bandwidth sample at T=44 were more than 10 Mbps, only 10 Mbps would be resignaled, due to the configured maximum bandwidth limit of 10 Mbps.

In the fourth application interval, only the first sample (T=46) is (slightly) higher than the current bandwidth reservation. All other samples are lower. However, because the difference between the first (maximum) sample and the current bandwidth reservation is small (less than the configured adjustment interval, which is 10%), when the application interval ends, the bandwidth is not resignaled. This helps to keep the RSVP-TE signaling load low, as the unimportant bandwidth changes don't trigger the signaling.

It is worth noting that in the fourth application period you can see rapid bandwidth decreases of traffic flowing through the monitored LSP. However, this doesn't trigger any bandwidth resignaling, because the underflow detection (similar to overflow detection) is not configured. If underflow detection had been configured with similar parameters to those used for overflow, the bandwidth would have been resignaled after T=54, following three consecutive underflow samples (T=50, T=52, T=54).

Auto-Bandwidth Configuration

That's enough for the extended theory—let's get into the lab now to configure automatic bandwidth adjustments in the network for all LSPs. Example 14-19 and Example 14-20 assume that the entire configuration discussed in this chapter (bandwidth reservations, LSP statistics, and LSP policing) is already removed before proceeding.

Example 14-19. Auto-bandwidth configuration on PE1 (Junos)

```
1     groups GR-LSP {
2         protocols mpls label-switched-path <*> {
3             auto-bandwidth {
4                 adjust-interval 1200;
5                 adjust-threshold 10;
6                 minimum-bandwidth 1k;
7                 maximum-bandwidth 10m;
8                 adjust-threshold-overflow-limit 3;
9                 resignal-minimum-bandwidth;
10    }}}
11    protocols mpls {
12        apply-groups GR-LSP;
13        statistics {
14            file mpls.stat size 100m files 10;
15            interval 120;
16            auto-bandwidth;
17    }}
```

Example 14-20. Auto-bandwidth configuration on PE2 (IOS XR)

```
1     group GR-LSP
2      interface 'tunnel-te.*'
3       auto-bw
4        bw-limit min 1 max 10000
5        overflow threshold 10 min 100 limit 3
6        adjustment-threshold 10 min 100
7        application 20
8      end-group
9      !
10    apply-group GR-LSP
11    !
12    mpls traffic-eng
13     auto-bw collect frequency 2
```

You can check that this configuration matches the parameters listed before Figure 14-3.

This book's tests successfully achieved Junos and IOS XR interoperable auto-bandwidth.

Auto-Bandwidth Deployment Considerations

Both Junos and IOS XR use similar algorithms for automatic, periodic adjustments in bandwidth reservations. In the case of significant changes in detected traffic volume, both support very similar overflow and underflow detection mechanisms, to prematurely adjust reserved bandwidth without the need to wait for the application interval to end.

But in what scenarios is auto-bandwidth deployed? In many cases, auto-bandwidth is deployed in combination with preemption. You mark some LSPs (e.g., carrying voice or IPTV traffic) as *important* (numerically lower-priority values) and some other LSPs (e.g., carrying best-effort Internet traffic) as *less important* (numerically higher-priority values). For each LSP, you measure and periodically adjust the bandwidth reservation by using auto-bandwidth.

Now, CSPF tries to establish each LSP based on the TE metrics (shortest path to the destination), but it takes into account the bandwidth constraints enforced by auto-bandwidth. If there is enough unreserved bandwidth available on all the links on the shortest path, all of the LSPs will follow the shortest path. If there is not enough unreserved bandwidth, some LSPs will be placed over longer paths to the destination, where bandwidth is available. Which ones? Less-important LSPs. This all happens dynamically, without the need for user intervention. If bandwidth for some of the important LSPs increases, these LSPs will be able to kick-out (thanks to the configured priority levels) less-important LSPs from the shortest path. Less-important LSPs will be rerouted elsewhere in the network. And the reverse is also true. When the bandwidth used by important LSPs decreases, less-important LSPs might be placed back on the shortest path.

Another application of auto-bandwidth is load-balancing over equal or unequal-cost multipaths. For example, suppose that you might have multiple (not necessarily equal cost) paths available between PE-X and PE-Y, each path with a capacity of 10G, and you want to transport 15G worth of traffic between PE-X and PE-Y. You cannot transport it by using a single LSP, but you can create multiple LSPs and the ingress PE (PE-X) can perform load-balancing of traffic between the multiple LSPs. The auto-bandwidth feature will ensure that these multiple LSPs will be spread across multiple available paths if the bandwidth on a single path is not sufficient.

You can do load balancing, combined with auto-bandwidth, manually, so you define how many LSPs should be established between PE-X and PE-Y in the configuration.

However, in large networks, with dynamically changing traffic patterns, this would be difficult from both a design and operation perspective. Therefore, Junos offers the next level of automation here; you not only measure and adjust LSP bandwidth reservations automatically, but you also increase or decrease the number of LSPs between two endpoints automatically. Let's move on to this feature, which is called *Dynamic Ingress LSP Splitting/Merging*, which we'll see in the next section.

 As of this writing, IOS XR didn't support the Dynamic Ingress LSP Splitting/Merging feature yet, so the examples only feature Junos.

Dynamic Ingress LSP Splitting/Merging

Dynamic Ingress LSP Splitting/Merging is based on RSVP-TE extensions defined in *draft-kompella-mpls-rsvp-ecmp: Multi-path Label Switched Paths Signaled Using RSVP-TE*. This draft introduces the new RSVP *Association Object*, which allows associating multiple child LSPs, called *member LSPs*, with a single parent LSP, called a *container LSP*. These are all Point-to-Point (P2P) LSPs: there is load balancing and not replication.

Figure 14-4 illustrates this concept. It is similar to Ethernet Link Aggregation Groups (LAG, IEEE 802.3ad), for which multiple physical Ethernet links are bundled together to make a single, aggregated Ethernet interface, consisting of multiple Ethernet link members. Now, members are LSPs, and the bundle is a container LSP.

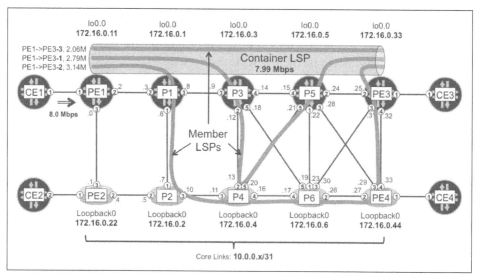

Figure 14-4. RSVP-TE multipath

As in Ethernet LAG, the ingress PE can load-balance the traffic across multiple member LSPs. Also like in Ethernet LAG, traffic is not always perfectly distributed between the members: this is an inherent limitation of hashing and load balancing.

You can place member LSPs over different paths across the network, so the traffic load between two endpoints (PE1 and PE3, in the example) can be spread across different links in the network. In the example topology presented in Figure 14-4, only the PE1→P1 link carries all three member LSPs. Some of the links carry two member LSPs, whereas most of the links carry only single member LSPs. The distribution of member LSPs is automatic, and greatly depends on the requested bandwidth of each LSP, and the bandwidth available for RSVP reservations on each link.

Dynamic Ingress LSP Splitting/Merging—Configuration

That's the theory. Now let's again get into the lab and remove the current PE1→PE3 LSP configuration from PE1, and then configure PE1 to use a container LSP, instead (see Example 14-21).

Example 14-21. PE1→PE3 container LSP configuration (Junos)

```
1    protocols mpls {
2        label-switched-path LSP-TEMPLATE {
3            template;
4            least-fill;
5            adaptive;
6            auto-bandwidth {
7                adjust-interval 600;
8                adjust-threshold 10;
9                minimum-bandwidth 1k;
10               maximum-bandwidth 10m;
11               adjust-threshold-overflow-limit 3;
12               resignal-minimum-bandwidth;
13           }
14       }
15       container-label-switched-path PE1--->PE3 {
16           label-switched-path-template LSP-TEMPLATE;
17           to 172.16.0.33;
18           splitting-merging {
19               maximum-member-lsps 4;
20               minimum-member-lsps 1;
21               splitting-bandwidth 4m;
22               merging-bandwidth 2m;
23               normalization normalize-interval 1200;
24   }}}
```

Notice that instead of label-switched-path PE1--->PE3, you now have container-label-switched-path PE1--->PE3 (line 15). Likewise, the operational commands begin with show mpls container-lsp.

You can create templates for container LSPs (lines 2 through 14) describing common LSP characteristics, including auto-bandwidth parameters or other TE constraints. LSP-TEMPLATE is not a standard LSP definition: it includes the keyword `template` (line 3) instead of the keyword `to`. The template can be used later under the container LSP configuration stanza (line 16) so that the dynamically created member LSPs can inherit the parameters from the template.

Dynamic Ingress LSP Splitting/Merging in Action

Figure 14-4 shows a real lab test performed during this book's writing. The traffic generator was sending an average of 8.0 Mbps, but this value was fluctuating a bit. At the time the picture was taken, the container LSP PE1→PE3 was transporting a total 7.99 Mbps of traffic, distributed across its member LSPs. Each of these member LSPs actually transported a different traffic rate due to the intrinsic imperfection of load balancing. So if the instantaneous bandwidth was 7.99 Mbps, why are there three member LSPs? Let's answer this question fully.

Example 14-21 contains a completely new configuration stanza that controls the LSP splitting/merging behavior (lines 18 through 23):

- Minimum (1) and maximum (4) number of member LSPs within a container LSP (lines 19 and 20)
- Minimum (`merging-bandwidth 2m`) and maximum (`splitting-bandwidth 4m`) bandwidth of a single member LSP (lines 21 and 22) enforced during each normalization event
- Normalization interval duration in seconds (line 23): 1200 seconds or 20 minutes.

At the end of each normalization interval, the system decides if the existing member LSPs should be merged or split. Figure 14-5 provides a correlation between the various intervals (auto-bandwidth sampling interval, auto-bandwidth adjustment interval, and LSP splitting/merging normalization interval) used in this dynamic process.

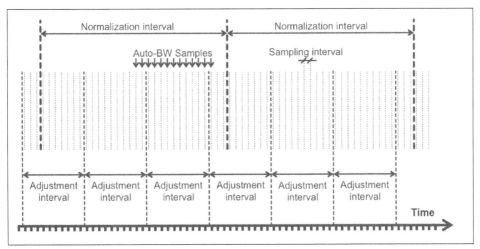

Figure 14-5. Interval correlations in dynamic LSP splitting/merging

Given the parameters from Example 14-21, and with a current aggregate bandwidth of 7.99 Mbps, there are two options:

- 3 (member LSPs) x 2.66 Mbps (each member LSP) approximately
- 2 (member LSPs) x 3.99 Mbps (each member LSP) approximately

Both options are valid (the number of member LSPs is between 1 and 4, and the member LSP's bandwidth is between 2 and 4 Mbps). Here, the second option would normally be preferred because it requires the lowest number of member LSPs. However, there are three member LSPs. Why? Because the traffic generator was sending 8 Mbps on average, and one of the bandwidth samples collected during the last adjustment interval resulted in an aggregate of 8.01 Mbps.

Dynamic bandwidth calculations for splitting/merging are made according to the *maximum bandwidth samples* collected during the last normalization interval. With the parameters in Example 14-21, the only way to distribute 8.01 Mbps is to have three member LSPs.

Now imagine that the traffic generator brings down the traffic rate from 8 Mbps to 7.5 Mbps. After the *next* normalization interval (2 minutes) fully expires, the maximum bandwidth sample is around 7.5 Mbps and there are two options to distribute this traffic:

- 3 (member LSPs) x 2.50 Mbps (each member LSP)
- 2 (member LSPs) x 3.75 Mbps (each member LSP)

Both options are valid, but the second option will be used because this is the option with the lowest number of member LSPs. At this point, the container LSP brings one member LSP down and resignals the two other member LSPs with 3.75 Mbps.

Now imagine that the average bandwidth goes up to 15 Mbps. In this case, one simple LSP would never be able to reserve all the bandwidth because the links' maximum reservable bandwidth is 10 Mbps. Only a container LSP with four member LSPs would satisfy the requirements. This is a key benefit of the new model.

Dynamic Ingress LSP Splitting/Merging and Auto-Bandwidth

Normalization (splitting or merging) starts assuming perfect load balancing; thus, the bandwidth initially requested during the normalization event is equal on all member LSPs. Then, standard auto-bandwidth mechanisms can further adjust the bandwidth reservation on each member LSP, based on the traffic statistics collected separately for each member LSP. As already discussed in "TE Auto-Bandwidth" on page 560 this automatic adjustment can be:

- A periodic bandwidth adjustment, which is separately tracked for each member LSP.
- An ad hoc bandwidth adjustment, if traffic volume inside the member LSP significantly changes and overflow/underflow detection is enabled.

As of this writing, overflow/underflow detection mechanisms for the LSP splitting/merging feature were not implemented in Junos. Therefore, LSP normalization (splitting or merging) occurred only at scheduled intervals, without the possibility for faster reaction in case of significant changes in traffic volumes. However, you can definitely adjust member LSPs' bandwidth upon an overflow/underflow condition.

## CHAPTER 15

Centralized Traffic Engineering

All the TE models discussed so far are distributed. In Chapter 13 and Chapter 14, Label Edge Routers (LERs) signal Label-Switched Paths (LSPs) by matching the Traffic Engineering Database (TED) against a set of locally defined constraints.

This chapter explores a totally different paradigm. Although LERs are still allowed to define LSPs on their own, the central controller is also capable of defining LSPs. A basic requirement for such a controller is to have an accurate and up-to-date view of the link-state database. To get that view, the controller establishes BGP sessions to one or more LSR/LER devices. Through these sessions, it receives link-state prefixes (BGP-LS NLRI). This is good due to the scalable and multihop nature of BGP.

> LERs always compute the TED locally and according to the distributed link-state database. This task is not (and should not be) centralized.

As soon as it has the TED view, the controller can perform path computations and ask the different LERs of the network to signal, resignal, or tear down LSPs in a precise manner. The controller could do that by accessing the LER configuration via Netconf or other similar mechanism, but this is a heavy approach. Using a protocol abstraction to signal LSPs on the fly is a more scalable strategy. Such a protocol exists and it's called Path Computation Element Protocol (PCEP).

This model might remind you of OpenFlow, but there are some key differences. First, an LSP can easily transport millions or billions of flows. Using a centralized programming approach for entities such as LSPs, which are very efficient forwarding aggregators, is more than viable. Second, this is a pure control-plane solution: there is no "punting" of transit traffic from the LERs to the controller.

BGP Link-State

BGP Link-State (BGP-LS), also known as BGP-TE (for Traffic Engineering), is a new BGP address family whose main usage is described in *draft-ietf-idr-ls-distribution: North-Bound Distribution of Link-State and TE Information using BGP*. It is supported both in Junos and IOS XR and it is encoded as: AFI=16388, SAFI=71.

 This book describes only the Junos implementation of BGP-LS.

In Example 15-1, P1 establishes a BGP-LS session to a northbound controller. The IGP that runs in the network is IS-IS and it has the TE extensions turned on by default.

Example 15-1. BGP link-state configuration—P1 (Junos)

```
1    protocols {
2        bgp {
3            group NORTH-CONTROLLER {
4                type internal;
5                local-address 10.255.11.1;
6                family traffic-engineering {
7                    unicast;
8            }}
9            export PL-ANNOUNCE-TED;
10           neighbor 10.255.10.2;
11       }
12       mpls traffic-engineering database import policy PL-ACQUIRE-TED;
13   }}
14   policy-options {
15       policy-statement PL-ANNOUNCE-TED {
16           term ISIS {
17               from {
18                   protocol isis;
19                   family traffic-engineering;
20               }
21               then accept;
22           }
23       }
24       policy-statement PL-ACQUIRE-TED {
25           term ISIS {
26               from protocol isis;
27               then accept;
28   }}}
```

Example 15-2 shows how the topology from Figure 15-1 (presented later, in "PCE Implementations" on page 576) is encoded in BGP-LS NLRI.

Example 15-2. BGP link-state NLRI—P1 (Junos)

```
1    juniper@P1> show route advertising-protocol bgp 10.255.10.2
2
3    lsdist.0: 36 destinations, 36 routes (36 active, ...)
4
5    NODE { AS:65000 ISO:1720.1600.0001.00 ISIS-L2:0 }/1152
6    NODE { AS:65000 ISO:1720.1600.0002.00 ISIS-L2:0 }/1152
7    NODE { AS:65000 ISO:1720.1600.0003.00 ISIS-L2:0 }/1152
8    NODE { AS:65000 ISO:1720.1600.0004.00 ISIS-L2:0 }/1152
9    NODE { AS:65000 ISO:1720.1600.0011.00 ISIS-L2:0 }/1152
10   NODE { AS:65000 ISO:1720.1600.0022.00 ISIS-L2:0 }/1152
11   LINK { Local { AS:65000 ISO:1720.1600.0001.00 }.{ IPv4:10.0.0.1 }
12        Remote { AS:65000 ISO:1720.1600.0011.00 }.{ IPv4:10.0.0.0 }
13        ISIS-L2:0 }/1152
14   LINK { Local { AS:65000 ISO:1720.1600.0011.00 }.{ IPv4:10.0.0.0 }
15        Remote { AS:65000 ISO:1720.1600.0001.00 }.{ IPv4:10.0.0.1 }
16        ISIS-L2:0 }/1152
17
18   /* 28 more links skipped */
```

The two links in lines 11 through 16 are actually unidirectional half-links. They are the two directions of the first P1-PE1 link: P1→PE1 and PE1→P1. IGPs and the TED also encode half-links, so everything is consistent.

Now that the controller is aware of the topology, let's see how it can actually control TE LSPs.

PCEP

RFC 5440 defines the PCEP. It runs over TCP server port 4189. PCEP is a hierarchical protocol with two roles:

Path Computation Element (PCE)
    (Also known as Path Computation Server [PCS]) At the North. Typically a stand-alone software controller that runs in a (virtualized or not) x86 architecture. It acts like a server from the perspective of PCEP. The PCE uses its global view of the topology and the network resources to centralize path computation and to globally apply traffic engineering policies. Typically, PCEs are in a cluster for redundancy.

Path Computation Client (PCC)
    At the South. Network devices that are capable of acting like a head-end LER—in other words, like an ingress PE. PCCs are the ones that actually signal the LSPs in

the network. They do so by merging the instructions they receive from the PCE with some optional local configuration.

PCE Implementations

As of this writing, there are several production-ready PCE solutions. Probably the two most relevant among them are Juniper's Northstar and Cisco Open SDN Controller—the latter is based on OpenDaylight. These solutions have evolved from two previous company acquisitions: Wandl by Juniper, and Cariden by Cisco Systems.

Again, this book is a project and every project has limited resources. One controller choice must be made for the examples, and for our purposes it is Northstar. However, this book focuses on technology and there is just one protocol here: PCEP. All vendors, including Juniper and Cisco, are making sure that they implement PCEP in an interoperable manner.

Figure 15-1 illustrates this chapter's topology. There is one PCE and two PCCs: PE1 and PE2 running Junos and IOS XR, respectively. In Northstar, topology discovery via BGP-LS is performed by a VM that is nested into the Northstar image. This is why you can see two addresses on the server: 10.255.10.1 for PCEP, and 10.255.10.2 for BGP.

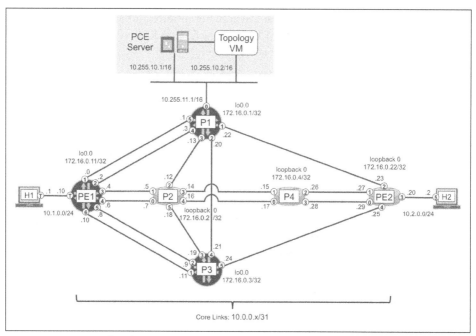

Figure 15-1. Centralized TE topology

In this book's tests, interoperability was successful between North-star as a PCE and two PCC operating systems: Junos and IOS XR.

Interaction Between PCE and PCC

Actually, the original definitions of PCE and PCC in RFC 5440 are completely differ-ent from those in this book. RFC 5440 describes a model in which the PCC first *requests* a path computation from the PCE. The PCE returns the computation results to the PCC; if the results are positive, the PCC signals the path through the network.

Although RFC 5440 covers a possible paradigm, typical real-life scenarios are differ-ent. The operational logic in a service provider is more aligned with the following two complementary IETF drafts in the standards track:

- *draft-ietf-pce-stateful-pce*: PCEP Extensions for Stateful PCE.
- *draft-ietf-pce-pce-initiated-lsp*: PCEP Extensions for PCE-initiated LSP Setup in a Stateful PCE Model.

These drafts introduce new PCEP messages that enable the two most common use cases:

- The PCE initiates (on its own) the computation of a path and sends the results to the PCC, which in turn signals the LSP. In this case, the PCC does not request anything to the PCE, which takes the initiative in the entire process. This is a *PCE-initiated* LSP—even if the actual LSP signaling is ultimately performed by the PCC.
- The PCC has a locally configured LSP. This is a *PCC-initiated* LSP. The PCC sends the LSP details to the PCE. This is important because the PCE needs to have a global view of every path in the network in order to perform accurate computations. *Optionally*, the PCC might decide to delegate the control of these paths to the PCE.

Both PCC types (Junos and IOS XR) can successfully act as a PCC for PCE-initiated LSPs, and of course, for PCC-initiated LSPs, too.

PCE-Initiated RSVP-TE LSPs

Figure 15-2 illustrates the early life of a RSVP-TE LSP that is initiated by the PCE.

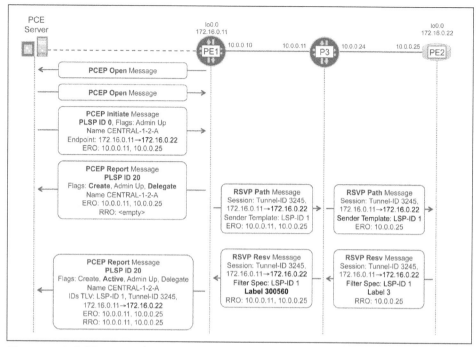

Figure 15-2. PCE-initiated RSVP-TE LSPs

If the PCEP session is not established yet, the PCC initiates and completes a TCP three-way handshake (not shown in Figure 15-2 and Figure 15-3) before exchanging PCEP Open messages. The purpose of these Open messages is to exchange capabilities. In this respect, PCEP and BGP are very similar.

When the administrator or the orchestrator defines a new LSP on the PCE, the PCE calculates an Explicit Route Object (ERO). This ERO is one of the objects included in the PCEP Initiate message that the PCE sends to the PCC.

In addition to the ERO, the PCEP Initiate message also contains other objects. The LSP object is particularly important because it contains the PCEP-specific LSP ID (PLSP-ID), whose non-zero value is assigned by the PCC. The pair [PCC Address, PLSP-ID] globally identifies an LSP in all PCEP communication.

> PCEP PLSP-ID, RSVP-TE Tunnel-ID and RSVP-TE LSP-ID are totally different concepts. The two latter are fully explained in Chapter 2 and Chapter 19, especially around Example 19-16. After successfully signaling a RSVP-TE tunnel, the PCC passes these IDs (among other RSVP-TE objects) to the PCE via PCEP Report Messages.

Paraphrasing (with minor rewording) *draft-ietf-pce-stateful-pce*:

> Note that the PLSP-ID is a value that is constant for the lifetime of the PCEP session, during which time there might be different RSVP identifiers (LSP-id, tunnel-id) allocated to the RSVP-signaled LSP.

Some objects are shown in Figure 15-2, but not all of them are. Here is a more exhaustive list:

- The *LSP Object* includes: an initially null PLSP-ID, certain state flags, and optional TLVs. These TLVs convey varied information such as the LSP symbolic name (in Figure 15-2, this name is CENTRAL-1-2-A), or RSVP information and state such as RSVP IDs, RSVP Errors, LSP Errors, and so on.

- The *Endpoint Object* simply lists the addresses of the LSP's head-end and tail-end.

- The *Stateful PCE Request Parameters (SRP) Object* consists of a sequence number that is incremented every time the PCE decides to change the properties of the LSP. It is crucial for statefulness.

- The *LSPA Object*, where *A* stands for *Attributes*, contains administrative group vectors—exclude any, include any, and include all—as well as the LSP's Setup and Hold priorities.

- The *Metric Object* and the *Bandwidth Object* are self-explanatory.

Therefore, PCEP Initiate messages include a set of TE constraints combined with the path computation outcome (the ERO). This is all the information that the PCC needs to signal the RSVP-TE LSP.

 Some PCEP objects have strictly equivalent RSVP objects that are simply copied into the RSVP Path messages.

After receiving a PCEP Initiate message, the PCC sends a PCEP Report message to the PCE. This message contains the LSP Object, updated with the following:

- A non-zero (20, in this example) PLSP-ID assigned by the PCC.

- Additional flags. The D (Delegate) flag is especially important. By setting it, the PCC is informing the PCE: *you are in full control of this LSP.*

The PCEP Report message also contains an SRP Object, whose value is identical to the one set by the PCE in the Initiate message. At this point, RSVP-TE signaling starts; the interpretation of the remainder of Figure 15-2 is left as an exercise for you to do.

PCCs send PCEP Report messages periodically. By updating the LSP object, a PCC can report LSP or RSVP errors to the PCE.

On the other hand, if the PCE needs to dynamically change the properties of an LSP, it sends a PCEP Update Request to the PCC. All the PCEP messages discussed so far (Initiate, Report, Update) were defined *after* RFC 5440 was published. They are defined in the drafts mentioned earlier in this chapter.

PCC-Initiated RSVP-TE LSPs

Figure 15-3 illustrates the early life of a RSVP-TE LSP that is initiated by the PCC.

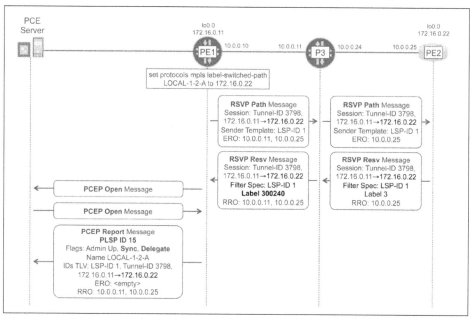

Figure 15-3. PCC-initiated RSVP-TE LSPs

The Sync flag is only set in the first set of Report messages. After the PCC has transmitted all the local LSP information to the PCE, this flag is cleared.

The Delegate flag is optional:

- If it is not set, the PCE has no control of the LSP.
- If it is set, the PCE can change the TE properties of the PCC-initiated LSP, but it has no way to delete it. The closest thing to deletion that PCE can do is setting the LSP's bandwidth to zero.

PCC Label-Switched Path Signaling

PCEP runs between the controller and the PEs. But at some point the PEs (PCCs) need to signal and maintain an LSP. Obviously, only those MPLS control plane flavors that support traffic engineering are available. If you need to refresh basic RSVP-TE and SPRING concepts, have a look at Chapter 2.

RSVP-TE LSPs

As of this writing, RSVP-TE is the only protocol that is already integrated with PCEP in shipping code. This protocol truly signals LSPs throughout the network. Indeed, RSVP-TE maintains hop-by-hop session state for each LSP by periodically sending Path and Resv messages along the path. Each LSP has its own dynamically learned label, which typically changes at each hop. As discussed in Chapter 14, RSVP-TE can reserve bandwidth resources in the network.

SPRING (IGP) TE LSPs

From a TE perspective, SPRING is quite stateless. The ingress PE is the only network device that is aware of the existence of SPRING-TE LSPs. By stacking several—node, adjacency—labels, the ingress PE enforces the forwarding path of a traffic-engineered LSP. Transit LSRs do not keep any per-LSP state.

 Whenever you read in this chapter that *the PCC signals the path*, assume it is RSVP-TE's way of thinking. In the SPRING case, the PCC just locally *programs* the path: there is no LSP signaling.

Although this has an immediate benefit in terms of control-plane scaling, *someone* needs to program the LSP's labels on the ingress PE. Basically, an additional *logic* is required; this logic can be implemented either on the PCC or on the PCE:

On the PCC
SPRING is based on the IGP and both IS-IS and OSPF have TE extensions. Actually, both SPRING and RSVP-TE look at the same TED. CSPF is protocol-agnostic and therefore it is identical for both protocols. Conversely, part of the power of RSVP-TE resides in its capacity to reserve resources along the path. Because SPRING TE does not create any state on the LSRs, the PCC is not able to reserve bandwidth. And it cannot signal Setup and Hold priorities, either. This is where a PCE with a global view becomes handy.

On the PCE
Having a centralized controller that is capable of deciding which LSPs must be signaled in the network in order to meet TE policies is very powerful in general.

But in SPRING, it is almost essential. With SPRING, PCCs are unable to reserve or prioritize network resources and therefore the PCE role becomes more important than in the RSVP-TE case.

 This is an emerging feature set that might still being developed as you read these lines. Check the vendor documentation for the latest status.

BGP LSPs

There are several emerging applications that are a good potential fit for centralized BGP-signaled LSPs. Here are some examples where it would make sense to have a controller:

Single-hop eBGP in large-scale data centers
Every device in the fabric is configured with a different AS. This approach, which was discussed in Chapter 2, is especially powerful when BGP also advertises a transport label (BGP-LU) and the servers are MPLS-capable. These servers are typically able to deal with MPLS encapsulation but they do not implement a full MPLS control plane yet; hence, the need for a controller.

BGP for Egress Peer Engineering (EPE)
This use case is discussed in Chapter 13. There are basically two different flavors: one based on eBGP-LU, and the other based on BGP SPRING extensions. In combination with a controller, it would allow the centralized logic to choose the egress hop out of the local AS.

This is a fast-evolving domain that will likely produce several different prototypes until it converges into mainstream-accepted solutions and ultimately in shipping code.

PCC Configuration

The baseline PCC configuration is very simple.

Example 15-3 shows the Junos configuration at PE1.

Example 15-3. PCC baseline configuration—PE1 (Junos)

```
1    protocols {
2        pcep {
3            pce myPCE {
4                local-address 172.16.0.11;
5                destination-ipv4-address 10.255.10.1;
```

```
6                    destination-port 4189;
7                    pce-type active stateful;
8                    lsp-provisioning;
9                }
10          }
11          mpls {
12              lsp-external-controller pccd;
13          }
14      }
```

These commands are only available if the JUNOS SDN Software Suite is installed, which you can verify by using the command show version. The name pccd in line 12 is not arbitrary: it is the name of the Junos daemon that implements the PCC logic.

You can check at any time the status of the PCEP connection by using the Junos operational command show path-computation-client active-pce.

And here is the IOS XR configuration at PE2:

Example 15-4. PCC baseline configuration—PE2 (IOS XR)

```
1       ipv4 unnumbered mpls traffic-eng Loopback0
2       !
3       mpls traffic-eng
4        pce
5         peer source ipv4 172.16.0.22
6         peer ipv4 10.255.10.1
7         !
8         stateful-client
9          instantiation
10         report
11        !
12       !
13       auto-tunnel pcc
14        tunnel-id min 1 max 99
15       !
16      !
```

With this configuration, PE2 can signal PCE-initiated LSPs (line 9) and report PCC-initiated LSPs (line 10) to the PCE.

You can check at any time the status of the PCEP connection by using the IOS XR operational command show mpls traffic-eng pce peer.

PCC Templates for PCE-Initiated LSPs

PCCs signal PCE-initiated LSPs according to:

- The ERO and other properties decided by the PCE.

- Additional properties determined by the local configuration of the PCC.

Merging the PCE instructions with the PCC local configuration can result in a conflict. For example, the PCE and the PCC might *want* to reserve 1 Mbps and 10 Mbps bandwidth, respectively. In this case, the PCE takes precedence, so the PCC signals a RSVP-TE LSP with 1 Mbps of bandwidth reservation.

Now suppose that the PCE does not specify a given property of the LSP. That property can be set by the PCC's local configuration successfully because there is no conflict.

Example 15-5 shows how to do this in Junos.

Example 15-5. PCC templates for PCE-initiated LSPs—PE1 (Junos)

```
1    protocols {
2        mpls {
3            lsp-external-controller pccd {
4                label-switched-path-template {
5                    PCC-DEFAULT-TEMPLATE;
6                }
7                pce-controlled-lsp PCS-AUTOBW-* {
8                    label-switched-path-template {
9                        AUTOBW-TEMPLATE;
10                   }
11               }
12           }
13           label-switched-path PCC-DEFAULT-TEMPLATE {
14               template;
15               link-protection;
16           }
17           label-switched-path AUTOBW-TEMPLATE {
18               template;
19               link-protection;
20               auto-bandwidth {
21                   adjust-interval 300;
22                   adjust-threshold 0;
23                   minimum-bandwidth 100k;
24                   maximum-bandwidth 500k;
25    }}}}
```

When it receives a PCEP Initiate message, the PCC looks at the LSP name, and according to the previous configuration, it does the following:

- If the LSP name begins with the pattern PCS-AUTOBW-, it adds two properties to the LSP: link-protection (explained in Chapter 19) and auto-bandwidth (discussed in Chapter 14). This is according to lines 7 through 10 and 17 through 25 in Example 15-3.

- If the LSP name does not match any named template configuration, like in line 7, the default template is executed and the LSP only gets the additional `link-protection` property. This is according to lines 4 through 6 and 13 through 16.

 Lines 13 through 25 define templates, not real LSPs. The `template` and the `to <address>` statements are mutually exclusive under a given `label-switched-path` configuration.

Delegating PCC-Initiated LSPs to the PCE

Every PCC sends PCEP Report messages to the PCE including both of the following:

- The PCE-Initiated LSPs whose head-end is the local PCC. These have the D-flag set.
- The PCC-Initiated LSPs whose head-end is the local PCC. These are locally configured and by default do *not* have the D-flag set, so they are not delegated.

This is how you can delegate a locally initiated LSP in Junos.

Example 15-6. Delegation of a PCC-Initiated LSP—PE1 (Junos)

```
1    protocols {
2        mpls {
3            label-switched-path LOCAL-1-2-A {
4                to 172.16.0.22;
5                lsp-external-controller pccd;
6            }
7        }
8    }
```

With this configuration, the D-flag is set as shown in Figure 15-3.

The following example presents the equivalent configuration in IOS XR:

Example 15-7. Delegation of a PCC-initiated LSP—PE2 (IOS XR)

```
1    interface tunnel-te11
2    ipv4 unnumbered Loopback0
3    signalled-name LOCAL-2-1-A
4    autoroute announce
5    !
6    destination 172.16.0.11
7    record-route
8    path-option 1 dynamic
9    pce
```

```
10      delegation
11    !
12    !
```

PCE Use Cases

You could claim that one advantage of having a PCE is that it has a global view of the topology and its resources. Well, every PCC does, as well! The main power of the PCE is that it can *act* in a centralized manner upon every single PCC in the network. Vendors are implementing powerful statistic collection mechanisms that shall soon allow for centralized auto-bandwidth. How cool is that? Instead of having every PCC taking independent auto-bandwidth decisions, one single entity can take control over the entire network and avoid the *exponentially damped oscillation* behavior that you might observe in distributed auto-bandwidth. But before this cool feature is available, let's see some other use cases that are implemented by centralized PCEs.

Extending the Link Attributes Palette

IGP TE extensions basically encode per-priority bandwidth reservation and availability, link coloring (administrative groups), and Shared Risk Link Group (SRLG). This is very powerful, but what if you want to add more properties to a link? That would require implementing the corresponding extensions in IS-IS and OSPF. New standards and implementations: a long cycle before the extensions are available in production networks.

Now suppose that you add a PCE to the network and it discovers the entire topology via BGP-LS. The PCE has visibility of all the link attributes encoded by the routing protocols, but in addition it can define its own attributes. Indeed, the PCE is already the central entity responsible for path computation: whenever it binds a new attribute to a link, this attribute remains local to the PCE database and does *not* need to be advertised to the rest of the network. The boss has all the info.

In Figure 15-4, all the links have the same IGP metric: 10. On the other hand, they have a different *cost* associated (1, 50, 300). The link cost is just an example of PCE-local link attribute. It represents the economic price of using a given link, assuming that the transport provider responsible for the link is charging for bandwidth utilization. This link attribute is local to the PCE database and is *not* part of the distributed TED.

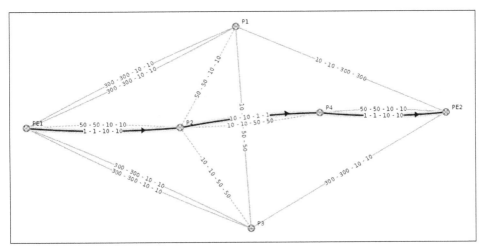

Figure 15-4. Maximum cost constraint—Northstar

The LSP is configured in Northstar with the following constraints: from PE1 to PE2, maximum cost 5. There is only one path that satisfies the constraints and it is the one highlighted in Figure 15-4. As soon as the computation is performed, the PCE instructs the PCC (PE1, in this case) to signal the LSP, as demonstrated here:

Example 15-8. PCE-initiated LSP—PE1 (Junos)

```
1    juniper@PE1> show mpls lsp externally-provisioned
2    Ingress LSP: 1 sessions
3    To              From          State      LSPname
4    172.16.0.22     172.16.0.11   Up         PE1-PE2-MaxCost-5
5    Total 1 displayed, Up 1, Down 0
```

The equivalent command in IOS XR is show mpls traffic-eng pce tunnels.

Other link attributes

Another useful PCE-local attribute is the link delay. You could also add different delay values to each link and come up with composite constraints such as maximum delay 700, maximum cost 50, maximum hop count 2. Take a look at Figure 15-4 again: there are no delays defined yet, but suppose that they are all set to 100. Would any path satisfy all the requirements? The answer is no, and the reasoning is left as an exercise for you to do.

Let us consider a situation in which multiple paths meet all the constraints: the PCE must choose one of them. By default, the cumulative *IGP metric* is the tiebreaker. But you can configure the PCE to use the minimum-path delay—or other conditions—as a tiebreaker, too.

Enhanced LSP Preemption Logic

Let's look back at Figure 14-1. Suppose that three low-bandwidth LSPs were initially signaled with different bandwidth reservations:

- PE1→PE3 with a reserved bandwidth of 500 kbps.
- PE2→PE4 with a reserved bandwidth of 700 kbps.
- PE2→P5 with a reserved bandwidth of 700 kbps.

Then, a higher-bandwidth LSP PE2→P6 tries to reserve 9.5 Mbps, but it cannot due to the way that the three preexisting LSPs are *already* laid out. Chapter 14 proposed to give a better setup priority to the PE2→P6 LSP, but as the number of LSPs increases it is not easy to come up with a policy that fulfills all the needs.

 Container LSPs, described in Chapter 14, also provide a good solution for this challenge.

Is this a priority-related problem? Not really. In this case, there is *space for everyone*. All of the LSPs should have the same priority if the type of traffic that they transport is, regardless of the volume, equally important.

The new LSP could be signaled if the preexisting LSPs were rearranged or resignaled to different paths. It is not easy to implement this logic on PCCs: what if several PCCs decide to rearrange LSPs at the same time? They could come up with conflicting decisions, and the churn that would be generated is only bound by imagination. The solution might require a central point of decision, and that is the PCE.

Diverse Paths

PCEs can easily define an LSP whose primary and secondary (standby) paths are diverse. There are two possible definitions of *diverse*:

- The paths have no link in common.
- The paths have no LSR in common. This definition is more demanding, and, if the topology allows it, results in two paths with just the endpoints (ingress and egress PE) in common.

You can achieve this at a PCC, too, but it requires playing with administrative groups, SRLG, or even EROs. With the PCE, it is much more straightforward: the administrator or the orchestrator requests diverse paths, and the PCE just finds its way.

Figure 15-5 shows the outcome of the computation of an LSP with diverse primary and secondary (standby) paths. Because no specific constraint is specified, the two paths are chosen according to the lowest cumulative IGP metric.

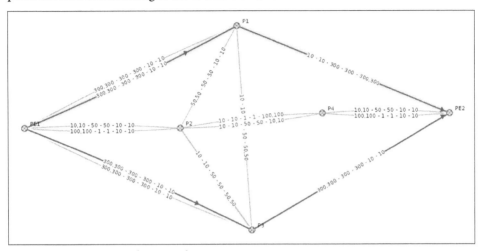

Figure 15-5. Diverse paths—Northstar

One variant of this use case is defining two LSPs such that:

- The primary paths of LSP #1 and #2 are diverse from each other.
- The primary and secondary paths of LSP #1 are diverse from each other.
- The primary and secondary paths of LSP #2 are diverse from each other.

The use cases explained in this chapter are just a small sample of what we can do today, and a tiny sample of what will be feasible in the near future.

## CHAPTER 16

Scaling MPLS Transport and Seamless MPLS

Today, our industry is experiencing a paradigm shift in service provider (SP) networking: network applications are becoming independent from the transport layers. Modern, cloud-based SP applications need flexible, intelligent overlay network services and are not well-served by legacy, static, low-layer data transmission.

This trend is driven by many factors:

- Increased demand to bring the service delivery point closer to the user. IP devices are progressively replacing legacy Layer 2 (L2) network elements, hence partitioning the L2 domains.

- More "intelligent" features for fast protection available at the IP/MPLS layer that could replace the corresponding fast protection features of optical networks.

- Shifting of mobile traffic—traditionally delivered over TDM circuits—toward Ethernet, and subsequently toward IP in 3G (e.g., Universal Mobile Telecommunications System [UMTS]), or 4G (e.g., Long-Term Evolution [LTE]), or small-cells networks.

- High-scale data centers shifting to MPLS fabrics and MPLS-enabled servers.

To cope with this demand, increasing the capacity of existing core (or spine) devices is necessary but not sufficient. The required presence of service endpoints in many small-range sites also relies on increasing the overall number of MPLS-enabled devices in the networks.

As a result of bringing the L3 edge closer to the end user, networks are witnessing the introduction of many *small* devices:

- In the *edge*, routers with a relatively small capacity, albeit rich IP/MPLS feature set, some of them targeted as small universal access or cell site access devices.

- In high-scale *data centers*, servers and hypervisors with a basic MPLS stack.

The universal edge model provides great flexibility in deploying a service. The edge concept dilutes, and the service termination points can be anywhere in the network. The provider edge (PE) function is distributed in service endpoints, or service termination points. Any device that has a VRF, or that terminates a pseudowire (PW), and so on links the service with the MPLS transport and becomes a service endpoint. In some sense, the function is decoupled from the actual location and type of connectivity of the device.

As for high-scale data centers, implementing MPLS on the servers might end up creating a network with the order of 100,000 MPLS-enabled devices.

Although this MPLS-everywhere approach has many advantages, the introduction of a large number of devices can be challenging. This is especially true if these devices are limited by the amount of state that they can handle and program on their forwarding plane. Segmentation, hierarchy, and state reduction become key properties of the designs and mechanisms that can achieve the required control-plane scalability.

Thus, the Software-Defined Networking (SDN) era networks need to be designed carefully and take into account the control-plane and forwarding-plane scaling capacity of the devices involved.

This chapter discusses several architectural approaches:

- IP/MPLS scaling with flat LSPs in a single IGP domain (intradomain scaling)
- IP/MPLS scaling with hierarchical LSPs in a single IGP domain
- IP/MPLS scaling with hierarchical LSPs in a network split into multiple IGP domains (inter-domain scaling)
- IP/MPLS scaling with hierarchical LSPs in an IGP-less network

Scaling an IGP Domain

The maximum size of a single IGP domain with MPLS used for transport depends mainly on the control-plane capacity of the weakest router participating in the domain as well as the MPLS transport mechanisms used in the domain. Let's begin with the IGP.

 In this section, the word *domain* stands for a single OSPF or IS-IS area inside an Autonomous System (AS).

To scale an IGP to potentially the highest possible number of routers in a single IGP domain, you need to follow five major design principles:

- *The IGP should only advertise transport addresses.*

  — Preferably only the loopback addresses from the local IGP domain should be injected into the IGP database.

  — In addition, link addresses from the local IGP domain can eventually be injected into the IGP database. In IS-IS backbones where all the core routers speak BGP, it is a common practice to advertise the link addresses via BGP instead of IS-IS. However, OSPF lacks this flexibility, as there is no way to suppress the advertisement of link addresses with OSPF.

- *You should avoid redistribution of external prefixes into the IGP.*

  — Preferably—apart from the prefixes mentioned previously—no other prefixes should be distributed via the IGP. For example, customer routes should be carried via BGP, which is designed for a much higher scalability than IGPs.

  — In some cases, a limited number of external prefixes (e.g., a default route, routes to a management network, or some summary routes) may be redistributed in the IGP. This situation, however, should be considered as an exception, rather than as rule.

- *Prefixes announced via the IGP should be suppressed during flapping. In other words, the prefix should only be advertised if it is stable. This applies to the following prefixes:*

  — Prefixes that are inherited from the interface where the IGP is configured. The interface prefix is not advertised until the interface has stabilized (as determined by a fixed hold timer or by an exponential damping algorithm).

  — Prefixes that are eventually redistributed (not recommended, as mentioned previously) from external protocols (e.g., from BGP, or static). The suppression of such prefixes is often questionable and difficult to achieve. Very often, the network administrator responsible of the redistribution point has no authority to influence the configuration (in order to implement some sort of flapping suppression) at the source router where the prefix is originally introduced.

- *IGP packets (both Hello packets and packets distributing link state information) should be protected with cryptographic authentication (HMAC-MD5, or newer types of authentication such as different types of HMAC-SHA) to reliably and quickly detect packet corruption and thus improve IGP stability. Standard IS-IS checksum, for example, doesn't cover LSP ID or Sequence Number fields at all.*

- *IGP interfaces should run in Point-to-Point (P2P) mode, whenever possible (the default for Ethernet interfaces is broadcast mode), for more efficient protocol operation and an optimized resource usage at the control-plane level.*

With these basic design principles, the number of prefixes carried by the IGP is controlled. All prefixes carried by the IGP are suppressed during flapping; efficient (P2P) operation mode is in place; and IGP packet corruption is detected quickly and reliably. These design principles greatly contribute to IGP scalability and stability during network failures.

Another topic, as outlined in the following sections, is the scaling comparison between OSPF and IS-IS. Although both protocols are link-state, there are some small differences that make IS-IS more stable in very large IGP domains.

Scaling an IGP—OSPF

The Link-State Advertisement (LSA) refresh timer (as specified in RFC 2328, Section B) has a fixed, non-configurable value of 30 minutes (1,800 seconds). Thus, LSAs cause flooding and Shortest-Path First (SPF) calculations relatively often in large networks.

For example, in a stable network with 600 LSAs, every 3 seconds, on average one LSA is reflooded. During network instability, these flooding events are even more frequent.

Junos' implementation of OSPF uses, by default, 50 minutes (instead of 30 minutes specified in RFC 2328, Section B) of *LSARefreshTime* for increased network stability. This default can be changed by using the `set protocols ospf lsa-refresh-interval` command to conform to RFC 2328, if required.

Scaling an IGP—IS-IS

The LSP MaxAge can be approximately 18 times bigger compared to OSPF LSA MaxAge timer (1 hour, according to RFC 2328, Section B.), because in IS-IS this timer is no longer fixed (as described in original specification ISO 10589, Section 7.3.21); it is configurable (RFC 3719, Section 2.1) up to 65,535 seconds (18.2 hours).

RFC 3719, Section 2.1, further specifies that LSPs must be refreshed at least 300 seconds before LSP MaxAge timer expires. In Junos, the LSP refresh timer is not configurable, but is always 317 seconds less than the (configurable) LSP MaxAge timer.

In IOS XR, on the other hand, you can explicitly configure both LSP MaxAge and LSP refresh timer. It is up to the responsibility of the network administrator to configure timers that comply with RFC 3719.

Now, for example, in a network with 600 LSPs, when configuring 65,535 seconds for LSP MaxAge (and 65,218 seconds for LSP refresh) there is on average re-flooding of one LSP every ~109 seconds, which is ~36 times less frequent than in the corresponding OSPF case.

Conversely, the ISO 10589 standard describes the periodic retransmission of Complete Sequence Number PDU (CSNP) packets, which contain the headers (ID, sequence number, lifetime, and checksum) of all the LSPs in the local IS-IS link database. Although the standard only mandates this periodic retransmission over LAN links, Junos additionally performs it over P2P links. This improves the overall network stability thanks to more robust database synchronization, especially when the IS-IS LSP distribution graphs are sparse.

The Junos implementation of IS-IS performs a SPF recalculation at least every 15 minutes for increased reliability.

Increasing the LSP refresh time increases the amount of time that an undetected link-state database corruption can persist. Thus, it is important to enable cryptographic authentication to minimize the risk of corrupting the link-state database.

Scaling an IGP—MPLS Protocols

Inside an IGP domain, the following techniques are available: Source Packet Routing in Networking (SPRING), Label Distribution Protocol (LDP), Resource Reservation Protocol (RSVP), or a combination of them.

Scaling an IP/MPLS network within a single IGP domain can depend on the MPLS transport method used. With SPRING or LDP, the scaling limits are dictated by IGP itself, rather than by the MPLS transport protocol. So, before reaching any scaling limits related to SPRING or LDP, you would reach IGP limits that would require dividing the single IGP domain into several domains (areas, ASs). Such MPLS scaling architectures based on multiple IGP domains are discussed later in this chapter.

If you use RSVP for MPLS transport (to benefit from a wide range of different protection and traffic engineering features), the network scaling limits may be dictated by RSVP scalability, and not any longer by the IGP. Let's analyze that in more detail.

Scaling RSVP-TE

The topology illustrated in Figure 16-1 has three layers of routers:

- Edge (PE) layer: PE1, PE2, PE3, and PE4
- Aggregation (combined PE/P) layer: P1, P2, P5, and P6
- Core (P) layer: P3 and P4

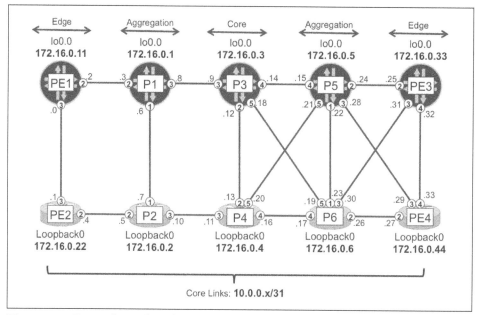

Figure 16-1. Example topology for intra-domain scaling

To provide MPLS-based services (e.g., L3VPN), MPLS transport needs to be established between each pair of routers of the outer (edge or aggregation) layers.

Let's suppose that RSVP-TE is the *only* MPLS transport signaling protocol enabled in the network. PE1 signals LSPs toward all of these routers: PE2, P1, P2, P5, P6, PE3, and PE4. This is basically a $O(n^2)$ scaling problem, as the number of RSVP LSPs in the network is proportional to the square of the number of endpoints (PE and PE/P layer, in our example). Based on the example topology, the number of RSVP LSPs that need to be established is 8*(8 − 1) = 56. Despite the fact that not all LSPs are traversing all the routers, a proper design needs to take into account possible network failures, which would eventually cause more concentration of LSPs after LSP rerouting. From a scaling perspective, the most affected routers are closer to the center of the core, because they typically concentrate a high number of transit LSPs.

However, RSVP-TE is a unique protocol, and it can do things that no other protocol can do; for example, reserving bandwidth for LSPs. This makes it *the* core MPLS protocol for big Internet Service Providers (ISPs). Actually, although these core networks typically have very powerful Label Edge Routers (LERs)/Label Switch Routers (LSRs), the actual number of devices is not extremely high. It is high, but it's nothing compared to universal edge and high-scale data center environments, for which there are many more devices, and these devices have a relatively weaker control plane. That said, ISPs typically prefer not to have a full RSVP mesh due to the $O(n^2)$ scaling problem.

There are basically two ways to scale RSVP: on the protocol itself, and with hierarchical designs. RSVP is a stateful protocol, and there are tools to optimize the amount of state and signaling that it can create in large networks with a high number of LSPs.

RSVP-TE Protocol Best Practices

Before discussing hierarchical designs, let's touch upon basic RSVP features to enhance scaling (and stability) mechanisms, as described in RFC 2961 - *RSVP Refresh Overhead Reduction Extensions* and RFC 2747 - *RSVP Cryptographic Authentication*. A well-designed network should use these extensions:

- Refresh Overhead Reduction Extensions (RFC 2961):
  — Message bundling (aggregation)
  — Reliable message delivery: acknowledgments and retransmissions
  — Summary refresh
- RSVP cryptographic authentication (RFC 2747, RFC 3097)

Without RFC 2961 RSVP generates separate messages for every LSP; as you can imagine, there could be quite a considerable number in very large networks. In addition, the delivery of the RSVP message is not acknowledged by the recipient, which requires a constant refresh of the RSVP state by resending the messages quite frequently.

RFC 2961 addresses this problem in several manners:

Bundling or aggregating the messages
   Standard Path/Resv RSVP messages are bundled into one large message.

Introducing the Summary Refresh concept
   Multiple LSP states can be refreshed with a single RSVP message.

Reliable delivery mechanism
   ACK, NACK, and retransmissions with exponential timers. These mechanisms are similar to the reliable delivery used, for example, in OSPF or IS-IS.

Further steps to increase RSVP's overall stability can also increase its potential scalability; for example, with the introduction of cryptographic checksums (RFC 2747 and RFC 3097), which improve the reliability in detecting RSVP message corruption.

All these features are supported in both Junos and IOS XR, and example configurations from routers P1 and P2 (Example 16-1 and Example 16-2) are provided for reference. Refresh reduction is enabled by default on IOS XR, whereas you need explicitly enable it on Junos. You need to manually enable cryptographic checksum in both cases.

Example 16-1. RSVP scaling enhancements on P1 (Junos)

```
groups {
    GR-RSVP {
        protocols {
            rsvp {
                interface <ge-*> {
                    authentication-key "$9$OyXSIhyM87s2alK2aZU.mO1R";
                    aggregate;
                    reliable;
}}}}}
protocols {
    rsvp {
        apply-groups GR-RSVP;
        interface ge-0/0/2.0;
        interface ge-0/0/3.0;
        interface ge-0/0/4.0;
}}
```

Example 16-2. RSVP scaling enhancements on P2 (IOS XR)

```
group GR-RSVP
 rsvp
  interface 'GigabitEthernet.*'
   authentication
    key-source key-chain KC-RSVP
 !
end-group
!
key chain KC-RSVP
 key 0
  accept-lifetime 00:00:00 january 01 1993 infinite
  key-string password 002E06080D4B0E14
  send-lifetime 00:00:00 january 01 1993 infinite
  cryptographic-algorithm HMAC-MD5
!
rsvp
 apply-group GR-RSVP
 interface GigabitEthernet0/0/0/1
 interface GigabitEthernet0/0/0/2
 interface GigabitEthernet0/0/0/3
 !
```

As of this writing, new Junos versions with additional and significant RSVP scaling enhancements have just been released. This book does not describe them for timing reasons.

Intradomain LSP Hierarchy

Suppose that you need to satisfy the following four requirements at the same time:

- You need to fully mesh MPLS transport from any PE to any other PE.
- You want to use RSVP-TE due to its unique feature set.
- You do *not* want to face the $O(n^2)$ scaling problem associated to establishing the full mesh with RSVP-TE LSPs only.
- You do *not* want to split the IGP domain.

In certain network topologies, it is possible to define an innermost core layer within the IGP domain—and without splitting the domain. This layer is typically composed of the most powerful devices in the network and they are a lower number of devices, thereby easing the $O(n^2)$ challenge.

For the Internet service, some ISPs run only RSVP-TE on the innermost core layer and they tactically perform IP lookups at the edge of this layer. In other words, the Internet service is only MPLS-aware at the inner core. This can be done with the Internet service because it is an *unlabeled* one. For labeled services such as L3VPN or L2VPN, it is essential to have end-to-end MPLS on the entire domain.

The solution to this challenge is using LSP hierarchy:

- The external core devices establish a full mesh of *edge* LSPs, which *may* include the internal core devices (as *endpoints*), too. This edge LSP layer can naturally be built with LDP or SPRING, and with some tricks, also with RSVP-TE (this will be discussed soon).
- The internal core devices establish a full mesh of *core* LSPs based on RSVP-TE.
- The edge LSPs are tunneled inside the core LSPs.

You can view the edge and core LSPs as client and server LSPs, respectively.

Let's look at the different options available to achieve this kind of LSP hierarchy. These options can coexist. Remember that you can configure several global loopback addresses on the PEs and create different service planes, each with its own MPLS transport technology (for more details, go to Chapter 3). Additionally, you can still signal flat (nonhierarchical) RSVP-LSPs between two edge devices in a tactical manner, because you need it for a given service and not for full-mesh connectivity requirements.

Tunneling RSVP-TE LSPs Inside RSVP-TE LSPs

Pure RSVP-TE LSP hierarchy concepts are described in RFC 4206. Figure 16-2 illustrates the idea with two LSPs:

- A core P1→P5 LSP with two hops: P1→P3 and P3→P5
- An edge PE1→PE3 LSP with three hops *only*: PE1→P1, P1→P5 and P5→PE3

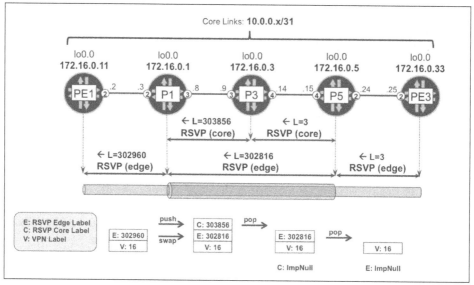

Figure 16-2. Tunneling RSVP-TE LSPs inside RSVP-TE LSPs

Because P1 and P5 are not directly connected, the core LSP is responsible for tunneling the edge LSP, so the P1→P5 path looks like one hop. The inner LSR (P3) is totally unaware of the edge LSP, reducing the state and signaling that P3 needs to handle. As for P1 and P5, they keep some edge LSP state, but only for their geographical region.

As of this writing, this model is not supported in IOS XR, and in Junos it is only implemented for networks using OSPF as the IGP. For this reason, this book does not cover it in detail.

Tunneling LDP LSPs Inside RSVP-TE LSPs

This model, commonly called *LDP tunneling*, covers a slightly different case. Although this time the network design still requires RSVP-based traffic engineering features in the core, these features are no longer required in the edge.

Based on the sample topology presented in Figure 16-3, Example 16-3 and Example 16-4 contain the basic configuration required to implement LDP tunneling in Junos (P1) and IOS XR (P2) devices. A similar configuration needs to be deployed on P5 and P6 routers, too. LDP tunneling is currently supported for IS-IS and OSPF in both operating systems. This example uses IS-IS and the metrics are left to the default value (10) except on the PE1-PE2 and PE3-PE4 links, where it is set to 100.

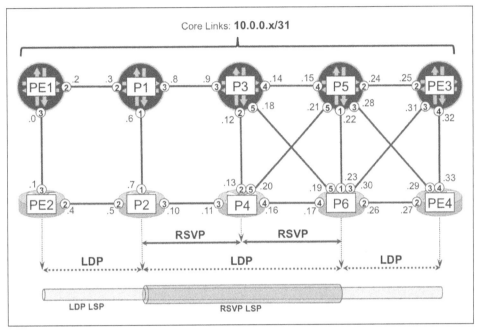

Figure 16-3. LDP Tunneling topology

Example 16-3. LDP tunneling configuration at P1 (Junos)

```
groups {
    GR-LSP {
        protocols {
            mpls {
                label-switched-path <*> {
                    ldp-tunneling;
                }
}}}}
protocols {
    rsvp {
        interface ge-0/0/1.0;
        interface ge-0/0/3.0;
    }
    mpls {
        apply-groups GR-LSP;
        label-switched-path P1--->P2 to 172.16.0.2;
```

```
        label-switched-path P1--->P5 to 172.16.0.5;
        label-switched-path P1--->P6 to 172.16.0.6;
        interface ge-0/0/1.0;
        interface ge-0/0/2.0;
        interface ge-0/0/3.0;
    }
    ldp {
        interface ge-0/0/2.0;
        interface lo0.0;
}}
```

Example 16-4. LDP tunneling configuration at P2 (IOS XR)

```
interface tunnel-te1
 signalled-name P2--->P1
 destination 172.16.0.1
 !
interface tunnel-te5
 signalled-name P2--->P5
 destination 172.16.0.5
 !
interface tunnel-te6
 signalled-name P2--->P6
 destination 172.16.0.6
 !
rsvp
 interface GigabitEthernet0/0/0/1
 interface GigabitEthernet0/0/0/3
 !
mpls traffic-eng
 interface GigabitEthernet0/0/0/1
 interface GigabitEthernet0/0/0/3
 !
mpls ldp
 interface tunnel-te1
  address-family ipv4
  !
 interface tunnel-te5
  address-family ipv4
  !
 interface tunnel-te6
  address-family ipv4
  !
 interface GigabitEthernet0/0/0/2
  address-family ipv4
 !
```

The following major configuration elements can be emphasized from this example:

- RSVP is enabled only on the interfaces toward the core (P routers), and is no longer enabled on interfaces toward the edge (PE routers).

- LDP is enabled on the interface toward edge (PE routers) as well as over the RSVP tunnels. In Junos, you need to explicitly enable LDP on the loopback interface.

 As a best practice, you can also enable LDP on all the IS-IS interfaces, providing a backup MPLS transport mechanism.

When LDP tunneling is enabled, the aggregation routers establish LDP sessions that are targeted to the remote end of the P→P RSVP LSPs, as visible in Example 16-5 and Example 16-6. The word "targeted" here means *not necessarily between directly connected neighbors*. These sessions make it possible for the routers to exchange the LDP labels required to establish end-to-end forwarding paths.

Example 16-5. Targeted LDP session on P1 (Junos)

```
juniper@P1> show ldp session
  Address       State        Connection    Hold time   Adv. Mode
  172.16.0.11   Operational  Open              26         DU
  172.16.0.2    Operational  Open              25         DU
  172.16.0.5    Operational  Open              27         DU
  172.16.0.6    Operational  Open              22         DU
```

Example 16-6. Targeted LDP session on P2 (IOS XR)

```
RP/0/0/CPU0:P2#show mpls ldp neighbor brief
Peer                Up Time     Discovery   Address   IPv4 Label
----------------    ----------  ---------   -------   ----------
172.16.0.22:0       1d01h           2          4          10
172.16.0.1:0        1d01h           1          2           9
172.16.0.5:0        00:38:41        1          3           8
172.16.0.6:0        00:38:44        1          7          10
```

The targeted LDP sessions exchange LDP bindings for the access PEs (PE1, PE2, PE3, and PE4). A targeted LDP session, viewed as one piece of the LDP end-to-end LSP, exchanges label bindings to "glue" together other LDP LSP segments. These other segments are signaled with hop-by-hop LDP sessions outside the RSVP domain.

LDP tunneling in action

Let's suppose that an IP VPN service is provisioned on all the PEs and, according to the BGP next hop, a user packet needs to be label-switched from PE1 to PE4.

The key piece is the following label exchange. P1 learns from P6 the label value 16022 to reach the loopback of PE4 (172.16.0.44).

Example 16-7. FEC binding over targeted LDP on P1 (Junos)

```
juniper@P1> show ldp database session 172.16.0.6 | match <pattern>

Input label database, 172.16.0.1:0--172.16.0.6:0
  16022      172.16.0.44/32
Output label database, 172.16.0.1:0--172.16.0.6:0
  299808     172.16.0.44/32
```

As a result of this signaling, P1 installs the entry shown in Example 16-8 in its LFIB.

Example 16-8. LDP tunneling—forwarding plane on P1 (Junos)

```
1    juniper@P1> show route label 299808 table mpls.0
2
3    299808  *[LDP/9] 00:00:20, metric 30
4               > to 10.0.0.9 via ge-2/0/3.0, label-switched-path P1-->P5
5               > to 10.0.0.9 via ge-2/0/3.0, label-switched-path P1-->P6
6
7    juniper@P1> show route forwarding-table label 299808
8
9    Routing table: default.mpls
10   MPLS:
11   Destination  Type RtRef  Type Index    NhRef
12   299808       user     0  ulst 1048579    2
13   Next hop                           Index  NhRef Netif
14   10.0.0.9  Swap 300016, Push 300112(top)    556    1  ge-2/0/3.0
15   10.0.0.9  Swap 16022, Push 301104(top)     563    1  ge-2/0/3.0
```

Due to the classical Equal-Cost Multipath (ECMP)–awareness of LDP, the traffic is load-balanced between the following equal-cost paths:

- PE1→P1→P3→P5→PE4 (lines 4 and 14).
- PE1→P1→P3→P6→PE4 (lines 5 and 15).

Figure 16-4 shows the signaling and forwarding-plane details for an L3VPN user packet that flows through the second path: PE1→P1→P3→P6→PE4.

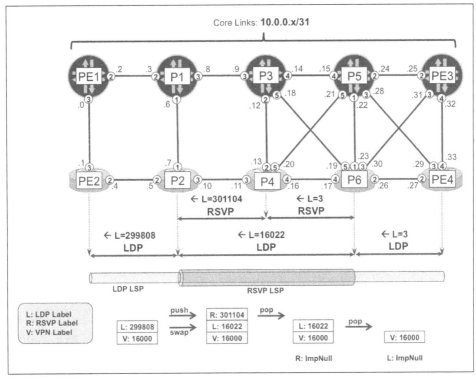

Figure 16-4. Tunneling to-PE4 LDP LSP in P1→P6 RSVP-TE LSP

The label stack in the core now has three labels, from top to bottom: the RSVP label, the LDP label, and the VPN label.

Tunneling SPRING LSPs Inside RSVP-TE LSPs

This model is very similar to LDP tunneling, with one important difference: it does not require any extra signaling. There is no strict equivalent to the targeted LDP session. As you know, IGP-based SPRING encodes segment information in the Link State Packets, and LERs/LSRs automatically translate these segments into MPLS labels. This solution is therefore operationally simpler than LDP tunneling.

Like LDP, SPRING is natively ECMP-aware, so there are several possible paths. This example focuses on the PE1→P1→P3→P6→PE4 path, as shown in Figure 16-5.

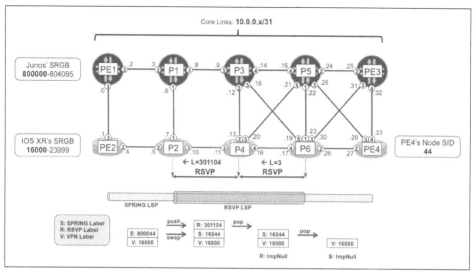

Figure 16-5. Tunneling to-PE4 SPRING LSP in P1→P6 RSVP-TE LSP

This is the path followed by a user packet that is label-switched from PE1 to PE4:

- PE1 pushes the VPN label and the SPRING label calculated from P1's Segment Routing Global Block (SRGB) and PE4's node SID, and then sends the packet to P1.

- P1 swaps the incoming SPRING label for the SPRING label calculated from P6's SRGB and PE4's node SID. Then, it pushes the transport label associated to the RSVP-TE LSP P1→P6 and sends the packet to P3.

- P3 pops the RSVP label and sends the packet to P6.

- P6 pops the SPRING label and sends the packet to PE4.

Let's have a look at the forwarding state at P1.

Example 16-9. SPRING shortcuts on P1 (Junos)

```
juniper@P1> show route label 800044 table mpls.0

800044  *[L-ISIS/14] 00:00:21, metric 30
         > to 10.0.0.9 via ge-2/0/3.0, label-switched-path P1-->P5
         > to 10.0.0.9 via ge-2/0/3.0, label-switched-path P1-->P6

juniper@P1> show route forwarding-table label 800044

Routing table: default.mpls
MPLS:
Destination  Type RtRef  Type Index    NhRef
```

```
800044       user    0 ulst 1048596      2
Next hop                             Index  NhRef Netif
10.0.0.9  Swap 800044, Push 300112(top)    576     1  ge-2/0/3.0
10.0.0.9  Swap 16044, Push 301104(top)    593     1  ge-2/0/3.0
```

This tunneling mechanism is enabled in Junos with the following syntax, assuming that the IGP is IS-IS:

Example 16-10. Configuring TE shortcuts on P1 (Junos)

```
protocols {
    isis {
        traffic-engineering {
            family inet {
                shortcuts;
}}}}
```

This configuration basically installs the RSVP-TE LSP as a next hop for all the destinations that are at or *behind* the tail end.

You can achieve the same behavior in IOS XR by using the `autoroute announce` command.

Interdomain Transport Scaling

As a network grows, it might no longer be possible to keep a single IGP domain. The network is often divided into multiple IGP domains to cope with the increased scale requirements. This is especially important when low-end devices with limited scalability are deployed. Depending on the actual design requirements, the division can be based on different IGP areas, different (sub)ASs, or a combination of the two.

 In this chapter, splitting the network in different domains has a scaling purpose. The context is therefore different from that of Chapter 9, where each AS really represented one single administrative domain.

From the MPLS perspective, multidomain transport architectures add additional challenges. To provide end-to-end services (e.g., L3VPN) across multiple domains, you can consider two high-level approaches:

Nonsegmented tunnels
   End-to-end transport LSPs established across domains and service provisioning only takes place at the LSP endpoints. This model is conceptually aligned to inter-AS Option C, and it typically relies on LSP hierarchy. The next-hop attributes *for the service* BGP routes are *not* changed at the boundaries.

Segmented tunnels

Transport LSPs span only a local domain and service-aware "stitching" takes place at the domain boundaries (Area Border Router [ABR], Autonomous System Border Router [ASBR]). This model is conceptually aligned to inter-AS Option B, and in it, next-hop attributes for the *service* BGP routes typically are changed at the domain boundaries.

Both approaches have their advantages and disadvantages. Depending on the scaling capabilities of the devices deployed in the network, functional elements of both architectural solutions can be found in most typical large-scale IP/MPLS designs.

Let's begin the discussion covering the options to provide nonsegmented, end-to-end transport LSPs across a divided network; we'll leaving the *service stitching* concepts for the Chapter 17, which focuses on service scaling. Nonsegmented tunnels can be further classified as Nonhierarchical and Hierarchical. Let's look at each of them in detail.

Nonhierarchical Interdomain Tunnels

To provide end-to-end transport LSPs across domains, you can use different techniques:

- Redistribution of /32 loopback addresses between IGP domains, to enable end-to-end LDP-based LSPs between IGP domains. This is in conformance with LDP specification (RFC 5036), which requires an exact match between routing table prefixes and the FECs to which labels are mapped.

- Redistribution of summary routes (loopback address ranges) between IGP domains. This is in conformance with LDP inter-area (RFC 5283), which relaxes the requirements of RFC 5036 by allowing nonexact matches. It also relaxes the stress on the IP routing tables in very-large-scale networks. Now, FEC label bindings can still be processed if they match a less-specific prefix (e.g., a default route), even if the exact /32 route is not present in the routing table.

- RSVP inter-area LSP, based on RFC 4105.

 Inter-area SPRING has not been explored in this book's tests.

The real benefit of the LDP-based or SPRING-based interdomain solutions is their simplicity.

The first option (loopback redistribution) can still suffer from IGP/LDP scalability problems, especially on low-end devices. The size of the IGP database, the IP Forwarding Information Base (FIB) and the MPLS FIB might still be too big.

The second option (loopback summary redistribution) relaxes the scaling issue associated with the IGP and IP FIB size, but still might cause MPLS FIB scalability problems. Indeed, LDP bindings for all the loopbacks are still exchanged among IGP domains.

One way to mitigate this problem is to apply LDP policies at the IGP domain boundary, in such a way that redistribution takes place only for *selected* FECs. Another option is to deploy LDP Downstream on Demand (DoD) in access domains. Unlike the default label distribution method in LDP (downstream unsolicited), DoD makes it possible for low-scale devices to request labels for *selected* FECs only.

In many cases, the operational challenge lies on the definition of a set of *selected* FECs. If the low-scale access PEs provide only L2 PWs, the selection is quite obvious: only labels for the remote endpoints of L2 PWs are required. If, however, multipoint services such as L3VPNs are implemented, as well, the definition of *selected* FECs is no longer straightforward, unless there is a limited number of hub-and-spoke–style L3VPNs only. Another method to mitigate the problem is a service design that removes the requirement to have label bindings for remote loopbacks, which is discussed in detail in the Chapter 17.

Many network operators rely on traffic engineering (TE) techniques, so RSVP becomes their preferred protocol. Although inter-area RSVP is an option, its scalability is limited. There is a conceptual conflict between dividing the network in smaller pieces (domains) while maintaining an end-to-end RSVP LSP full mesh. Therefore, although you can use inter-area end-to-end RSVP LSPs tactically in some scoped scenarios, they are not a generic strategy to fully mesh all the PE routers in large-scale networks.

Hierarchical Interdomain Tunnels (Seamless MPLS)

Let's discuss the most robust scaling architecture that is available for ISPs.

Seamless MPLS overview

Scaling and BGP often go hand in hand. In this approach, whereas the MPLS transport inside each IGP domain is provided by LDP, RSVP, or SPRING (or by a combination of these), end-to-end LSPs between domains are provided by BGP. The architecture is relatively new, and it is defined in *draft-ietf-mpls-seamless-mpls*. In reality, this model is based on a mature protocol (BGP labeled unicast: RFC 3107). What's new is how this protocol is used to provide a very scalable MPLS architecture, supporting up to 100,000 routers.

At a high level, Seamless MPLS is similar to the aforementioned LSP Hierarchy concept. Each IGP domain establishes *standard* intradomain LSPs by using LDP, RSVP, or SPRING. Tunneled inside these intradomain LSPs, there are other—*inter*domain— LSPs based on the BGP Labeled Unicast (BGP-LU) protocol. Why choose BGP-LU? Because of its proven scalability.

Chapter 2 explains BGP-LU in the context of flat (nonhierarchical) LSPs. Chapter 9 goes one step further by showing hierarchical LSPs; however, for a slightly different use case: interprovider services. Now, let's see how to build hierarchical LSPs in a *single* organization domain, which is partitioned in different areas and/or ASs.

It is important to remember that BGP-LU carries information about *provider infrastructure prefixes*. The label in BGP-LU is a transport (and not a service) label, mapped to the global loopback address of a PE router. In that sense, you can view BGP-LU as a tool to interconnect different routing domains.

In contrast, a PE router is typically the endpoint of an MPLS service such as L3VPN, L2VPN, and so on. This is the service context of BGP, implemented through other NLRIs such as IP VPN and L2VPN, as already discussed in Chapter 3 through Chapter 8.

If you read Chapter 9, this paradigm might sound familiar to you. Indeed, Seamless MPLS has much in common with Inter-AS Option C.

Let's use a bigger example topology to discuss the Seamless MPLS architecture, as illustrated in Figure 16-6.

In Figure 16-6, the network is divided in two ASs: 65001 and 65002. Moreover, AS 65002 is further divided in two IS-IS domains: an L2 domain with area ID 49.000, and an L1 domain with area ID 49.0001. There is no IS-IS route exchange between the two domains: both L1 to L2 leaking and L2 to L1 leaking are blocked. The L1 routers are explicitly configured to ignore the attached bit of the ABR's L1 Link State PDUs. This example uses different MPLS protocols inside the different domains to show that they are completely independent from one another. Thus, there is plain LDP in IS-IS L1 area 49.0001, LDP tunneling–over–RSVP in IS-IS L2 domain, and plain RSVP in OSPF area 0.0.0.0. In some sense, you can look at this architecture from different angles.

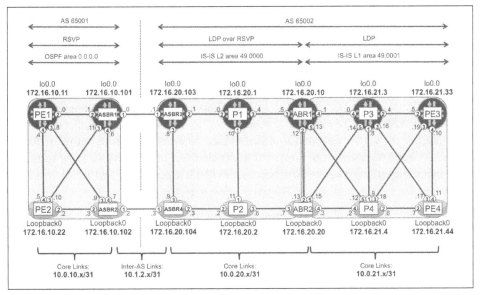

Figure 16-6. Seamless MPLS topology

OSPF, IS-IS, LDP, and RSVP use standard configurations, so let's concentrate on configuring interdomain LSPs based on BGP-LU.

Going back to the description of LDP tunneling over RSVP (previously in this chapter), a targeted LDP session was established between the endpoints of a RSVP LSP. This targeted LDP session served an important role in facilitating the creation of the end-to-end LDP LSP. It exchanged label bindings in order to "glue" together other LDP LSP segments. These other segments were signaled with hop-by-hop LDP sessions outside the RSVP domain.

There is a powerful analogy between LDP tunneling over RSVP and the Seamless MPLS scenario. BGP-LU also glues together different LSP segments that are built on top of a different underlying technology. There are several types of BGP-LU sessions:

- BGP-LU sessions established between the endpoints of an underlying intradomain (LDP, RSVP, etc.) LSP. Let's think of these as *targeted* sessions.

- BGP-LU sessions established between directly connected neighbors, if there is no underlying LSP available for tunneling; for example, at the inter-AS border between AS 65001 and AS 65002. Let's think of these as *single-hop* (hop-by-hop) sessions.

One major difference compared to LDP tunneling is that you need to configure the BGP-LU sessions manually, whereas targeted LDP sessions were created automatically as a result of the LDP tunneling configuration. On the other hand, LDP tunneling works exclusively over RSVP-TE tunnels, whereas multihop BGP-LU is totally agnostic of the specific intradomain MPLS protocol—it can be LDP, RSVP-TE, SPRING, and so on.

Similar to the LDP tunneling case, in every BGP-LU session, a new MPLS label is allocated and stitched to the label of the previous segment. Whereas in LDP this is automatic, there is a pitfall to avoid in BGP. Very often, the border routers (such as ABR1 and ABR2 in the example topology) act as BGP-LU Route Reflectors (RRs) between domains. It is essential to ensure that every time a border router reflects a BGP-LU route, the BGP next-hop attribute is changed to *self*: this, in turn, triggers a new label allocation. This is fine because BGP-LU's purpose is to build transport LSPs.

Note that this recommendation does *not* apply to *service* RRs, where changing the BGP next hop is a bad idea. Changing the next-hop on service RRs forces all the upstream traffic in the domain to traverse the RR instead of using the optimal path.

The architecture, showing BGP-LU session structure and hierarchical LSPs in Seamless MPLS designs, is illustrated in Figure 16-7.

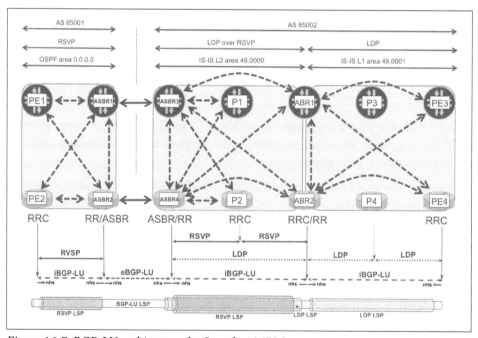

Figure 16-7. BGP-LU architecture for Seamless MPLS

In general, not all the routers participate in the BGP-LU route distribution. For example, routers P3 and P4 do not have any BGP-LU sessions. This illustrates an important fact: the only labeled loopbacks that need to be distributed with BGP-LU correspond to the routers that instantiate the end services (L3VPN, L2VPN, etc.). It also illustrates another fact: routers with limited service capabilities but with sufficient label stack depth can be used as transit nodes. Other loopbacks are not necessarily mapped to labels, unless the administrator wants to run MPLS ping between any two loopbacks in the network for troubleshooting purposes. That having been said, P1 and P2 are included in the BGP-LU distribution; we'll explain the reason later.

The BGP-LU design is similar to a classical hierarchical RR infrastructure. Four ASBR routers are connected with four BGP sessions in a square: two multihop iBGP sessions between intradomain loopbacks, and two single-hop eBGP sessions between physical link addresses. These ASBRs are at the same time the main BGP-LU RR inside each AS. In AS 65001, there are only two RR clients (RRCs). In AS 65002, however, ASBR3 and ASBR4 have four RRCs: two of them (ABR1 and ABR2) build a second level of RR hierarchy, whose clients are PE3 and PE4. As mentioned earlier, every time a BGP-LU prefix is advertised across a domain (area or AS) boundary, the advertising border router performs a BGP next-hop *self* action. This is the default behavior on eBGP sessions, but you need to configure it explicitly on iBGP sessions.

The end result, as shown at the bottom of Figure 16-7, is an end-to-end BGP-LU LSP established between PE routers of remote domains. This BGP-LU LSP is tunneled inside the respective intradomain LSPs of each domain, and it is native (not tunneled) on ASBR-ASBR links.

Seamless MPLS—BGP-LU path selection

One important topic related to BGP-LU is the handling of cumulative IGP link metrics. In the case of a MPLS network with a single IGP domain, it's easy: the IGP calculates end-to-end costs accurately, so the lowest-cost path is selected automatically. In the case of interdomain BGP-LU LSPs, finding the shortest path relies on BGP metric attributes because the IGP cost between IGP domains is not shared across domains.

The standard BGP metric is Multi Exit Discriminator (MED). In principle, one could use MED as the end-to-end cost metric across domains. However, MED has certain limitations that could make large deployments (with many interconnected domains) quite challenging:

- MED is sent only to a neighboring AS (RFC 4271, Section 5.1.4 - *The MULTI_EXIT_DISC attribute received from a neighboring AS MUST NOT be propagated to other neighboring ASes*). In a large-scale design with multiple interconnected ASs, the MED might be lost at some place, so the ultimate goal of measuring end-to-end costs in an entire network might be difficult.

- In the BGP path selection process (RFC 4271, Section 9.1.2.2), the MED is used as a standalone tie-breaking criterion at Step C. The MED takes strict precedence over the IGP metric comparison at Step E. In a BGP-LU–based Seamless MPLS architecture, this is not a good idea.

Let's illustrate the second bullet point with the example topology. For simplicity, all links have cost 1000, with the exception of three links (as outlined in Figure 16-8), whose IGP metric is temporarily increased to 1500. Also, the diagonal links (PE1-ASBR2, PE2-ASBR1, ABR1-P4, ABR2-P3, P3-PE4, and P4-PE3) are temporarily disabled.

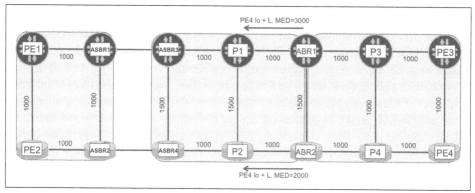

Figure 16-8. BGP-LU MED propagation

Taking into account the cumulative IGP metric, there are multiple possible shortest paths from PE1 to PE4, including these two:

- PE1→ASBR1→ASBR3→P1→ABR1→P3→PE3→PE4
- PE1→PE2→ASBR2→ASBR4→P2→ABR2→P4→PE4

The IGP costs in the L1 IS-IS domain are 3000 from ABR1 to PE4, and 2000 from ABR2 to PE4. When the ABRs advertise PE4's loopback address to the higher-level RRs (ASBR3 and ASBR4), a common practice is to copy the IGP metric into the MED attribute of the BGP-LU route. As a result, ABR1 and ABR2 announce PE4's loopback with MED values 3000 and 2000, respectively. Following BGP selection rules, both ASBR3 and ASBR4 select the route advertised by ABR2 due to its lower MED value. This makes sense for ASBR4, whose shortest path to PE4 is via ABR2. But it's not the best option for ASBR3, whose best cumulative IGP metric path is via ABR1.

Even such a simple example shows that using MED in Seamless MPLS scenarios might not be the best choice. To overcome this limitation, RFC 7311 - *The Accumulated IGP Metric Attribute for BGP* introduces a new BGP attribute called *Accumulated IGP cost*, or in short, *AIGP*. This extension to BGP introduces the following behavior:

- Every time that the BGP next hop (NH) changes, the Accumulated IGP (AIGP) attribute is automatically updated to the value of *current_AIGP* + *IGP_cost_to_current_BGP_NH*. This ensures that the total IGP cost across multiple IGP domains is automatically tracked in the AIGP attribute.

- In the BGP path selection process, among the multiple paths available, the one with a lowest value of *current_AIGP* + *IGP_cost_to_current_BGP_NH* wins. This check is performed at the very beginning of the process, even before comparing the AS_PATH attribute length.

Figure 16-9 illustrates the basic principles of AIGP. The BGP-LU prefix (PE4 loopback) is injected initially with AIGP=0. Because the ABR routers change the BGP next hop, they also update the AIGP: ABR1 sets it to 3000, whereas ABR2 sets it to 2000. When ASBR3 receives the updates from ABR1 and ABR2, it performs a path selection using the AIGP logic. ASBR3 compares the value of *current_AIGP* + *IGP_cost_to_current_BGP_NH*, chooses the route advertised by ABR1, and propagates it with an updated AIGP value. ASBR4, on the other hand, selects the route advertised by ABR2—again, due to AIGP logic.

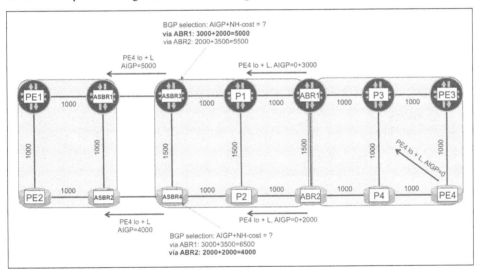

Figure 16-9. BGP-LU AIGP propagation

Seamless MPLS—BGP-LU configuration on edge routers (PE1, PE2, PE3, and PE4)

This is the third BGP-LU example in the book. There is a detailed example in Chapter 2 and one more in Chapter 9. For brevity, this section only shows the configuration that is specific to Seamless MPLS as compared to inter-AS Option C.

The first difference is that in the Seamless MPLS architecture some domains are ASs and other domains are IGP areas within a larger AS. BGP is used as a loop-prevention mechanism based on the AS path—*if I receive a route with my AS in the AS path, I reject it.* Inside an AS there is a similar mechanism based on the cluster list attribute: every iBGP RR adds its cluster ID when it reflects a route and rejects the received routes whose cluster list contains the local cluster ID. Despite the existence of these mechanisms, it is better from a scaling and operational perspective to deploy policies that control the route advertisement flow on the domain borders.

Such policies rely on a geographical community that will eventually help to filter the prefixes based on where the prefix is originally injected.

Example 16-11. Geographical communities

```
65000:11XYY
    X - autonomous system (1 - 65001, 2 - 65002)
    YY - area (00 - area 0.0.0.0 or 49.0000, 01 - area 49.0001)
```

For example, PE1 leaks its own loopback from `inet.0` to `inet.3` with a community called CM-LOOPBACKS-100 (65000:11100). PE1 then announces its local loopback via BGP-LU with this community.

The second difference with respect to inter-AS Option C is that Seamless MPLS uses the AIGP metric attribute in BGP. Putting it all together, following is the delta configuration at PE1:

Example 16-12. Advertising local loopback via BGP-LU on PE1 (Junos)

```
1    protocols {
2        bgp {
3            group iBGP-RR {
4                family inet {
5                    labeled-unicast {
6                        aigp;
7                    }
8                }
9                export PL-BGP-LU-UP-EXP;
10   }}}
11   policy-options {
12       policy-statement PL-BGP-LU-UP-EXP {
13           term LOCAL-LOOPBACK {
14               from {
15                   protocol direct;
16                   rib inet.3;
17                   community CM-LOOPBACKS-100;
18               }
19               then {
20                   aigp-originate;
21   }}}}
```

A similar configuration is required on PE3, with the appropriate community.

In the IOS XR configuration shown in Example 16-13, the AIGP attribute is initialized to zero for consistency with Junos. This is the delta configuration for PE2.

Example 16-13. Advertising local loopback via BGP-LU on PE2 (IOS XR)

```
route-policy PL-BGP-LU-UP-EXP
  if community matches-any CM-LOOPBACKS-100 then
    set aigp-metric 0
    pass
  endif
end-policy
!
router bgp 65001
 neighbor-group iBGP-RR
  address-family ipv4 labeled-unicast
   route-policy PL-BGP-LU-UP-EXP out
!
```

Let's look at the receiving side (ASBR2) and verify that the AIGP is correctly set by PE2.

Example 16-14. Received neighbor loopback on ASBR2 (IOS XR)

```
RP/0/0/CPU0:ASBR2#show bgp 172.16.10.22/32 | begin "Path #1"
 Path #1: Received by speaker 0
 Advertised to peers (in unique update groups):
    10.1.2.3        172.16.10.101
 Local, (Received from a RR-client), (received & used)
   172.16.10.22 (metric 1001) from 172.16.10.22 (172.16.10.22)
     Received Label 3
     Origin incomplete, metric 0, localpref 100, aigp metric 0, [...]
     Community: 65000:11100
     Total AIGP metric 1001
(...)
```

The *Total AIGP metric* is 1001, which is the value of the current AIGP (zero) plus the IGP cost (1001) to the next hop (172.16.10.22). The default OSPF metric for a loopback in IOS XR is 1, plus the configured link cost (1000) yields 1001. The Total AIGP metric is used in the BGP path selection process, as discussed earlier. For the sake of completeness, let's also look at PE2's BGP-LU route on ASBR1 (Junos).

Example 16-15. Received neighbor loopback on ASBR1 (Junos)

```
1    juniper@ASBR1> show route receive-protocol bgp 172.16.10.22
2                   table inet.3 detail
3    inet.3: 12 destinations, 25 routes (12 active, 0 holddown, 0 hidden)
4      172.16.10.22/32 (3 entries, 2 announced)
5        Accepted
6        Route Label: 3
```

```
7          Nexthop: 172.16.10.22
8          MED: 0
9          Localpref: 100
10         AS path: ?
11         Communities: 65000:11100
12         AIGP: 0
```

This looks fine, too, although the Total AIGP metric (sum of current AIGP + IGP cost to next hop) is not explicitly displayed in Junos.

Seamless MPLS—BGP-LU configuration on border routers (ASBRs and ABRs)

As already discussed, the ASBR and ABR routers play the role of RRs for BGP-LU prefixes. They perform *next-hop self* and automatically update the AIGP attribute by taking into account the IGP cost toward the current next hop.

The following design optimizes BGP-LU loopback distribution. This optimization is important in large-scale deployments; otherwise, you can skip it for simplicity.

ASBR1 and ASBR2 have three BGP-LU peer groups, each with a different route policy applied:

1. ASBR1/2 to BGP-LU RRCs (PE1 and PE2) → "DOWN" direction

   - Don't advertise local loopbacks via BGP-LU, and don't reflect the loopbacks learned from the local domain back to PE1 and PE2. These prefixes are reachable anyway thanks to the local domain's IGP/LDP/RSVP protocols.

   - Reflect the BGP-LU loopbacks learned from upstream (eBGP) peers, changing the next hop (configured action) and updating the AIGP (default action).

   - These peers are configured as RR clients (Junos: cluster, IOS XR: route-reflector-client).

2. ASBR1/2 to BGP-LU RR peers (ASBR2 to ASBR1, and the opposite: ASBR1 to ASBR2) → "RR peer" direction

   - Advertise local loopbacks with initial AIGP value ("0").

   - Reflect the BGP-LU loopbacks learned from upstream (eBGP) peers, changing the next hop (configured action) and updating the AIGP (default action).

   - Reflect other BGP-LU loopbacks, like the ones received from downstream iBGP peers PE1 and PE2, with no attribute (next hop or AIGP) change.

3. ASBR1/2 to BGP-LU external peers (ASBR1 to ASBR3, and ASBR2 to ASBR4) → "UP" direction

   - Advertise local loopbacks with initial AIGP value ("0")

- Propagate the BGP-LU loopbacks learned from iBGP (downstream or RR) peers, explicitly changing the next hop and updating the AIGP (default action).

The configuration is long but has nothing special, just BGP business as usual. Routes can be matched on community, protocol, RIB (Junos), route type (Junos: route-type external, IOS XR: path-type is ebgp), and so on.

The main caveat to be aware of is an implementation difference between Junos and IOS XR in the way the AIGP is handled at the domain border.

Example 16-16 shows the specific BGP-LU configuration at Junos ASBR1.

Example 16-16. BGP-LU policies on ASBR1 (Junos)

```
1    protocols {
2        bgp {
3            group iBGP-DOWN:LU+VPN {          ## towards PE1 and PE2 (RRC)
4                family inet {
5                    labeled-unicast { ... }  ## similar config to PE1's
6                }
7                export PL-BGP-LU-DOWN-EXP;
8                cluster 172.16.10.101;
9            }
10           group iBGP-RR:LU+VPN {            ## towards ASBR2 (RR)
11               family inet {
12                   labeled-unicast { ... }
13               }
14               export PL-BGP-LU-RR-EXP;
15           }
16           group eBGP-UP:LU {                ## towards ASBR3 (eBGP)
17               family inet {
18                   labeled-unicast { ... }
19               }
20               export PL-BGP-LU-UP-EXP;
21    }}}
22    policy-options {
23        policy-statement PL-BGP-LU-DOWN-EXP {
24            term 100-LOOPBACKS {
25                from {
26                    protocol [ bgp direct ];
27                    rib inet.3;
28                    community CM-LOOPBACKS-100;
29                }
30                then reject;
31            }
32            term eBGP-LOOPBACKS {
33                from {
34                    protocol bgp;
35                    rib inet.3;
36                    community CM-LOOPBACKS-ALL;
```

```
37                    route-type external;
38                }
39            then {
40                next-hop self;
41                accept;
42            }
43        }
44        from rib inet.3;
45        then reject;
46    }
47    policy-statement PL-BGP-LU-RR-EXP {
48        term LOCAL-LOOPBACK {
49            from {
50                protocol direct;
51                rib inet.3;
52                community CM-LOOPBACKS-100;
53            }
54            then {
55                metric 0;
56                aigp-originate;
57                next-hop self;
58                accept;
59            }
60        }
61        term eBGP-LOOPBACKS {
62            from {
63                protocol bgp;
64                rib inet.3;
65                community CM-LOOPBACKS-ALL;
66                route-type external;
67            }
68            then {
69                next-hop self;
70                accept;
71            }
72        }
73        term ALL-LOOPBACKS {
74            from {
75                protocol [ bgp direct ];
76                rib inet.3;
77                community CM-LOOPBACKS-ALL;
78            }
79            then accept;
80        }
81        from rib inet.3;
82        then reject;
83    }
84    policy-statement PL-BGP-LU-UP-EXP {
85        term LOCAL-LOOPBACK {
86            from {
87                protocol direct;
88                rib inet.3;
```

```
89                        community CM-LOOPBACKS-100;
90                    }
91                    then {
92                        metric 0;
93                        aigp-originate;
94                        next-hop self;
95                        accept;
96                    }
97                }
98                term ALL-LOOPBACKS {
99                    from {
100                       protocol bgp;
101                       rib inet.3;
102                       community CM-LOOPBACKS-ALL;
103                   }
104                   then {
105                       metric 0;
106                       next-hop self;
107                       accept;
108                   }
109               }
110               from rib inet.3;
111               then reject;
112           }
113           community CM-LOOPBACKS-100 members 65000:11100;
114           community CM-LOOPBACKS-ALL members 65000:11...;
115       }
```

Example 16-17 shows the relevant BGP-LU configuration applied to ASBR2.

Example 16-17. BGP-LU policies on ASBR2 (IOS XR)

```
1     community-set CM-LOOPBACKS-100
2       65000:11100
3     end-set
4     !
5     route-policy PL-BGP-LU-DOWN-EXP
6       if community matches-any (65000:11100) then
7         drop
8       endif
9       if community matches-any (65000:[11000..11999]) then
10        if path-type is ebgp then
11          set next-hop self
12          set aigp-metric + 1
13        done
14      endif
15      endif
16    end-policy
17    !
18    route-policy PL-BGP-LU-RR-EXP
19      if destination in (172.16.10.102/32) then
20        set community CM-LOOPBACKS-100
```

```
21        set aigp-metric 0
22      done
23    endif
24    if community matches-any (65000:[11000..11999]) then
25      if path-type is ebgp then
26        set next-hop self
27        set aigp-metric + 1
28        done
29      endif
30      if path-type is ibgp then
31        done
32      endif
33    endif
34  end-policy
35  !
36  route-policy PL-BGP-LU-UP-EXP
37    if destination in (172.16.10.102/32) then
38      set community CM-LOOPBACKS-100
39      set aigp-metric 0
40      set med 0
41      done
42    endif
43    if community matches-any (65000:[11000..11999]) then
44      set med 0
45      done
46    endif
47  end-policy
48  !
49  router bgp 65001
50   bgp router-id 172.16.10.102
51   mpls activate
52    interface GigabitEthernet0/0/0/1
53    !
54   bgp unsafe-ebgp-policy
55   ibgp policy out enforce-modifications
56   address-family ipv4 unicast
57    redistribute connected
58    allocate-label all
59    !
60   neighbor-group iBGP-DOWN:LU_VPN              !! towards PE1 and PE2 (RRC)
61    address-family ipv4 labeled-unicast
62     route-reflector-client
63     route-policy PL-BGP-LU-DOWN-EXP out
64    !
65   !
66   neighbor-group iBGP-RR:LU_VPN                !! towards ASBR1 (RR)
67    address-family ipv4 labeled-unicast
68     route-policy PL-BGP-LU-RR-EXP out
69    !
70   !
71   neighbor-group eBGP-UP:LU                    !! towards ASBR4 (eBGP)
72    address-family ipv4 labeled-unicast
```

```
73      aigp
74      send-community-ebgp
75      route-policy PL-BGP-LU-UP-EXP out
76    !
77    !
78  !
79  router static
80    address-family ipv4 unicast
81      10.1.2.3/32 GigabitEthernet0/0/0/1
82    !
83  !
```

The BGP and policy configurations of ASBR3, ASBR4, ABR1, and ABR2 follow the same principles.

There are some small differences between the default behavior of Junos and IOS XR when it comes to BGP-LU configuration. To unify the overall network behavior, the following measures are taken (in addition to those already mentioned in Chapter 2):

- AIGP support needs to be explicitly configured for both iBGP and eBGP sessions in Junos (see the syntax in Example 16-12, line 6). In IOS XR, AIGP is enabled by default for iBGP and you need to explicitly configure it for eBGP sessions only (see the syntax on Example 16-17, line 73).

- An ASBR-to-ASBR link does not have an IGP running. How does the AIGP metric take this link into account? The answer varies across vendors: Junos increases AIGP by default by a value of 1, whereas IOS XR does not alter AIGP when sending BGP updates over such link. To achieve a uniform metric scheme across vendors, the configuration in IOS XR is set to increase the AIGP metric of reflected eBGP prefixes by a value of 1 (see Example 16-17, lines 12 and 27).

- The manipulation of attributes via outbound route-policies on iBGP sessions is disabled by default in IOS XR, and you need to explicitly enable it (see Example 6-17, line 55).

Seamless MPLS—IPv4 intradomain connectivity between PEs

Now that all the configurations are in place, let's verify end-to-end LSP connectivity. First, from PE1 to PE4, as demonstrated here:

Example 16-18. BGP-LU Ping from PE1 (Junos) to PE4 (IOS XR)

```
juniper@PE1> ping mpls bgp 172.16.21.44/32 source 172.16.10.11
!!!!!
--- lsping statistics ---
5 packets transmitted, 5 packets received, 0% packet loss
```

And now from PE2 to PE3:

Example 16-19. BGP-LU Ping from PE2 (IOS XR) to PE3 (Junos)

```
RP/0/0/CPU0:PE2#ping mpls ipv4 172.16.21.33/32 fec-type
                bgp source 172.16.10.22
(...)
.....
Success rate is 0 percent (0/5)
```

Hmm. The MPLS (BGP-LU) ping from Junos to IOS XR across the Seamless MPLS network is fine, but it fails from IOS XR to Junos. This is because the MPLS Echo Reply is a standard UDP over IPv4 packet, and PE3 does not have a route to reach PE2 on its global routing table, as illustrated here:

Example 16-20. Route from PE3 (Junos) to PE2 (IOS XR)

```
juniper@PE3> show route 172.16.10.22 active-path

inet.3: 14 destinations, 24 routes (14 active, 0 holddown, 0 hidden)
+ = Active Route, - = Last Active, * = Both

172.16.10.22/32
      *[BGP/170] 00:16:15, MED 0, localpref 100, from 172.16.20.10
        AS path: 65001 ?, validation-state: unverified
```

The route is present, but only in the inet.3 table. As already discussed, the inet.3 table provides BGP next-hop resolution for MPLS-based services, but it is not used for normal packet forwarding. There is no entry in the FIB to forward the IPv4 UDP packet toward PE2, and as a result the forwarding lookup hits the default "reject" entry in the FIB.

Example 16-21. Forwarding entry from PE3 (Junos) to PE2 (IOS XR)

```
juniper@PE3> show route forwarding-table destination 172.16.10.22/32
                table default
(...)
Destination    Type RtRef Next hop      Type Index    NhRef Netif
default        perm   0                 rjct    36      1
```

To solve the interdomain connectivity problem for regular IP packets in a Seamless MPLS topology, there are two alternative generic solutions:

- Copying the remote PE's BGP-LU routes from inet.3 to inet.0. This technique is explained in Chapter 2.

- Alternatively, ABRs can inject into the L1 49.0001 area a default route, or a summary route including the loopbacks of remote PEs. Currently, there is no redistribution or leaking in that sense and the baseline IS-IS configuration in this example is set to explicitly ignore the attached bit.

In large Seamless MPLS networks with up to approximately 100,000 loopbacks, the first option might be applied to devices for which installing all the loopbacks in the FIB is not an issue; the second option should be used for devices with limited FIB capacity.

Let's see how to configure the second option. The assumption is that PE3 and PE4 are low FIB scale devices, so ABR1 and ABR2 conditionally inject a default route into the 49.0001 area. All the other Junos routers are assumed to be high FIB scale devices that install all the received BGP-LU loopbacks into both inet.3 and inet.0. Example 16-22 and Example 16-23 provide the configuration at ABR1 and ABR2, respectively.

Example 16-22. Conditional default route advertisement on ABR1 (Junos)

```
routing-options {
    aggregate {
        route 0.0.0.0/0 {
            policy PL-DEFAULT-ROUTE-CONDITION;
            metric 0;
            preference 9;
            discard;
}}}
protocols {
    isis {
        export PL-ISIS-EXP;
}}
policy-options {
    policy-statement PL-DEFAULT-ROUTE-CONDITION {
        term 100-LOOPBACKS {
            from {
                protocol bgp;
                community CM-LOOPBACKS-100;
            }
            then accept;
        }
        then reject;
    }
    policy-statement PL-ISIS-EXP {
        term DEFAULT-ROUTE {
            from {
                protocol aggregate;
                route-filter 0.0.0.0/0 exact;
            }
            to level 1;
            then {
                metric 0;
```

```
        accept;
}}}}
```

Example 16-23. Conditional default route advertisement on ABR2 (IOS XR)

```
route-policy PL-DEFAULT-ROUTE-CONDITION
  if rib-has-route in (172.16.10.11/32, 172.16.10.22/32) then
    set level level-1
  endif
end-policy
!
router static
 address-family ipv4 unicast
  0.0.0.0/0 Null0
  !
!
router isis core
 address-family ipv4 unicast
  default-information originate route-policy PL-DEFAULT-ROUTE-CONDITION
```

In Example 16-22 and Example 16-23, the condition on ABR1 (Junos) is the existence of routes with a specific community, whereas on ABR2 (IOS XR), there is an exact prefix match. In both cases, the ABRs only generate the default route if they have at least one route to one of the loopbacks in AS 65001. For consistency, the Junos configuration explicitly advertises the default route with metric 0, which is the default in IOS XR. The preference of ABR1's aggregate default route is set to 9, which is lower than the preference of IS-IS routes. Otherwise, the default route from ABR2 would suppress the advertisement from ABR1.

With this configuration in place, PE3 should be able to reach PE2's loopback via a default route installed both in the inet.0 RIB and in the FIB.

Example 16-24. Route in the RIB of PE3 (Junos) toward PE2 (IOS XR)

```
juniper@PE3> show route 172.16.10.22 table inet.0

inet.0: 23 destinations, 23 routes (23 active, 0 holddown, 0 hidden)
+ = Active Route, - = Last Active, * = Both

0.0.0.0/0          *[IS-IS/15] 01:20:57, metric 2000
                      to 10.0.21.4 via ge-0/0/2.0
                    > to 10.0.21.18 via ge-0/0/3.0
```

And, as shown in Example 16-25, the MPLS ping between PE2 and PE3 now works without any problems.

Example 16-25. BGP-LU ping from PE2 (IOS XR) to PE3 (Junos)

```
RP/0/0/CPU0:PE2#ping mpls ipv4 172.16.21.33/32 fec-type bgp
                source 172.16.10.22
(...)
!!!!!
Success rate is 100 percent (5/5), round-trip min/avg/max = 1/12/30 ms
```

Services in Seamless MPLS architecture

Now that BGP-LU has built end-to-end transport LSPs through the example topology, it's time to focus on the end services. Let's choose IPv4 VPN for illustration purposes. Actually, there are already some BGP sessions established for the exchange of
IPv4 labeled unicast prefixes, but can these sessions be reused to signal the IPv4 VPN
unicast routes, too? The answer is yes, they can, and if two routers exchange prefixes
of both address families directly, there is one BGP session only. But the BGP session
layout is different for each address family. To get the complete picture, look at both
Figure 16-7 (BGP-LU) and Figure 16-10 (IPv4 VPN).

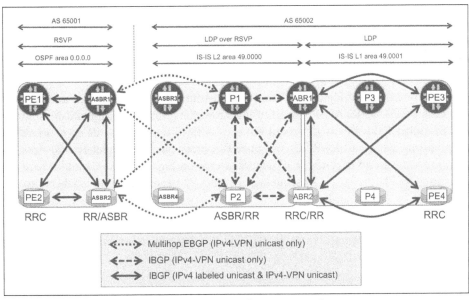

Figure 16-10. BGP IPv4 VPN unicast in Seamless MPLS architecture

The session layout and the BGP next-hop manipulation for each address family are
completely different. This is for a reason: MPLS transport and VPN services are two
different worlds, even if the same protocol (BGP) can signal both. The RRs in the IS-
IS L2 domain are different for each address family: ASBR3/4 for IPv4 labeled unicast,
and P1/2 for IPv4 VPN unicast.

L3VPN in the Seamless MPLS architecture is similar to inter-AS Option C. The most critical aspect is the BGP next-hop handling for each address family:

- For IPv4 labeled unicast (SAFI=4), the BGP next-hop attribute changes at the border of each domain (area or AS). This provides transport hierarchy, using the local tunneling mechanism of each domain.

- For IPv4 VPN unicast (SAFI=128), the BGP next hop *never* changes, as expected with inter-AS Option C. This is the default behavior on iBGP RRs, but it requires a specific configuration on eBGP to preserve the original next-hop value.

No inbound or outbound BGP policies are required for IPv4 VPN. Here are some special configuration requirements:

- Enabling eBGP multihop between RRs in different ASs

- Disabling next-hop change on eBGP sessions

- Disabling the "reject all" default policy of eBGP sessions in IOS XR

- For BGP sessions that signal both the IPv4 LU and the IPv4 VPN Unicast NLRI (like those represented by double-arrow *solid* lines in Figure 16-10), ensure that the BGP policy terms treat each address family independently. We discuss this topic in "Multiprotocol BGP policies" on page 629.

There is one detail of Figure 16-7 that requires further explanation. P1 and P2 peer with the BGP-LU RRs ASBR3 and ASBR4. From the point of view of end-to-end PE-PE transport LSPs, this is not required: the L2 IS-IS domain has its own tunneling mechanism that is not BGP-LU, and pure P-routers can be completely BGP-free. So why are these sessions configured? The answer is on Figure 16-10: P1 and P2 are the RRs for L3VPN prefixes. Consequently, P1 and P2 need to have reachability to the loopbacks of ASBR1 and ASBR2, and that is why Figure 16-7 shows P1 and P2 as BGP-LU peers.

If P1 and P2 did not participate in BGP-LU distribution, other options would be as follows:

- Redistributing ASBR1 and ASBR2 loopbacks from BGP-LU into IS-IS at routers ASBR3 and ASBR4

- ASBR3 and ASBR4 injecting a default route (or a summary route covering ASBR1 and ASBR2 loopbacks) into IS-IS

RRs are a crucial component of the network infrastructure. Using default or summary routes (which suppress more specific routes) to reach these crucial components is considered a bad practice. Redistribution from BGP-LU to IGP is slightly better, but it defeats part of the purpose of using BGP. Thus, the best recommended practice is to include RRs in the BGP-LU delivery mechanism, even if they do not provide VPN services themselves.

The service design model used in this chapter results in all the PE routers receiving all the service prefixes. This approach might not scale for micro-PE (low-scale PE) devices, so Chapter 17 spends more time on optimizing the design.

Multiprotocol BGP policies

In Junos, the following policies evaluate, filter, and modify IP VPN (Unicast) prefixes. It is not mandatory to have all of the policies in place. For example, if there is no local VRF, then there is no vrf-[export|import].

- For prefix export, the VRF's vrf-export policy chain is executed before the *global* export policy chain applied to the BGP session (see Example 16-12, line 9, and Example 16-16, lines 7, 14, and 20). You need the vpn-apply-export knob in order to evaluate the global policy chain. Otherwise, only the vrf-export policy chain (if any) is executed.

- For prefix import, the global *import* policy chain applied at the BGP session (if any) is executed before the VRF's vrf-import policy chain (if any).

A policy chain is an ordered sequence of policies. Very often, it consists of one single policy.

- The IP LU case is simpler: only the global BGP policy chains (applied to the BGP session) evaluate IP LU prefixes.

Here comes the tricky aspect. The same global (import and export) policy chains evaluate both IP LU and IP VPN prefixes. Therefore, you need to carefully define the policy terms so that each term only evaluates prefixes of one address family.

You can select IP LU prefixes with the condition from rib inet.3. Selecting IP VPN prefixes is trickier, as several RIBs are involved (see Chapter 3 and Chapter 17).

In this Seamless MPLS scenario, the global BGP policies only have to process the IP LU prefixes (in order to change the MED, AIGP, and NH). For this reason, only the from `rib inet.3` condition becomes handy. In Chapter 17, you will see an example in which IP VPN prefixes are matched, too.

In IOS XR, policies are applied separately for each address family. Thus, it is easy to keep track of distinct rules that need to be applied to prefixes from different address families. As a result, when multiple address families are deployed, you always need separate policies.

Seamless MPLS—end-to-end forwarding path

Now, after achieving basic connectivity, let's look at Figure 16-11 and Example 16-26 to understand the label states and operations performed on the IPv4 VPN packets. Note that multiple equal-cost paths exist; therefore, multiple traceroute outputs are possible. ASBR1 was temporarily disabled to reduce the available paths and ensure that the traffic traverses both Junos and IOS XR devices.

Example 16-26. Traceroute from VRF on PE1 (Junos) to PE4 (IOS XR)

```
juniper@PE1> traceroute routing-instance VRF-A 192.168.1.44
traceroute to 192.168.1.44 (192.168.1.44), 30 hops max, ...
 1  10.0.10.9 (10.0.10.9)  6.919 ms  7.274 ms  5.375 ms
     MPLS Label=16010 CoS=0 TTL=1 S=0
     MPLS Label=16006 CoS=0 TTL=1 S=1
 2  10.1.2.3 (10.1.2.3)  5.781 ms  17.325 ms  6.071 ms
     MPLS Label=16010 CoS=0 TTL=1 S=0
     MPLS Label=16006 CoS=0 TTL=2 S=1
 3  10.0.20.2 (10.0.20.2)  5.988 ms  5.712 ms  5.417 ms
     MPLS Label=16012 CoS=0 TTL=1 S=0
     MPLS Label=16004 CoS=0 TTL=1 S=0
     MPLS Label=16006 CoS=0 TTL=3 S=1
 4  10.0.20.7 (10.0.20.7)  6.037 ms  5.723 ms  5.503 ms
     MPLS Label=16004 CoS=0 TTL=1 S=0
     MPLS Label=16006 CoS=0 TTL=4 S=1
 5  10.0.21.14 (10.0.21.14)  7.514 ms  6.142 ms  7.800 ms
     MPLS Label=301776 CoS=0 TTL=1 S=0
     MPLS Label=16006 CoS=0 TTL=5 S=1
 6  10.0.21.17 (10.0.21.17)  6.020 ms  *  7.052 ms
```

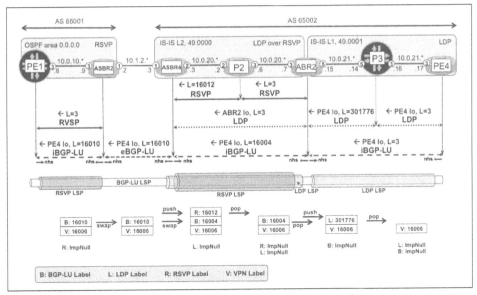

Figure 16-11. MPLS label operations in a Seamless MPLS network

There is label swap operation 16010→16010 at ASBR2. This is totally fine: labels are locally significant and they can have different or the same values.

From the perspective of LDP, the LSP in IS-IS L2 domain of AS 65002 is single hop. If it were multihop, you would see four MPLS labels at this point of the path.

IGP-Less Transport Scaling

Imagine a large-scale data center with more than 100,000 servers in an IGP-less topology (such as the one described in Chapter 2). This data center would require more than 100,000 transport labels to be programmed on the FIB of each device. This is definitely feasible for high-end LSRs, but how about switches with forwarding engines based on merchant silicon? In any case, regardless of the hardware capacity, it is clear that reducing this amount of state would be beneficial. There are at least two complementary strategies to achieve such optimization:

- Implement a hierarchy between different BGP-LU layers.
- Take the servers *off* BGP-LU and use a lighter control plane to program their forwarding plane.

Let's discuss these two strategies separately.

BGP-LU Hierarchy

As of this writing, this model is not defined in any drafts. It is an original idea by Kaliraj Vairavakkalai, who happens to be one of the key contributors of this book.

So far in this chapter, you have seen the following hierarchical LSP examples: RSVP in RSVP, LDP in RSVP, SPRING in RSVP, and BGP-LU in LDP/RSVP/SPRING. Now it's the turn of *BGP-LU in BGP-LU*. Or *BGP-LU in BGP-LU in BGP-LU*. You can add as many layers as you want to this hierarchy, which is based on a clever manipulation of the BGP-LU routes' next-hop attribute.

Figure 16-12 is a real lab scenario based on the simplified data center topology from Chapter 2. However, the solution also works on Seamless MPLS scenarios.

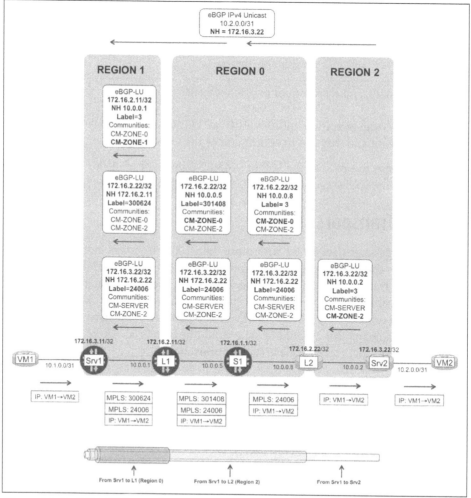

Figure 16-12. BGP-LU hierarchy in IGP-less MPLS network

The key concept is *region*. A region is basically a part of the network. It can be an IGP area, or an AS, or an AS set.

Indeed, in the IGP-less eBGP scenario illustrated in Figure 16-12 and fully explained in Chapter 2, each router *is* a different AS. Thus, in this example, any router set is an AS set, and regions typically identify parts of the data center. As you might remember from Chapter 10, modern data center topologies are hierarchical, and it is quite feasible to partition them in regions (e.g., a collection of PODs).

BGP-LU Hierarchy—control plane

With this generalized region concept in mind, the BGP-LU next-hop rewrite rules are as follows:

- The network is partitioned in regions, and a unique BGP standard community identifies each region.
- Each router R belongs to a *region set*, which consists of one or more regions. For example, Srv1's region set is {1}, whereas L1's region set is {0,1}.
- Each region set has an associated *regional community set*. For example, L1's regional community set is {CM-ZONE-0, CM-ZONE-1}.
- When R advertises a non-BGP route (e.g., its own loopback address) into BGP-LU, R is considered to be the originator of the route. R adds to the route all the communities from R's regional community set.
- If R has to (re)advertise a BGP-LU route that has at least one community matching R's regional community set, R considers the route as intraregion. So, R rewrites the route's BGP next hop of the route to a local address. Which one? It depends on whether the peer is inside or outside the route's region set. You can extract the rule from Figure 16-12.
- If R has to (re)advertise a BGP-LU route that has no single community matching R's regional community set, R considers this route to be interregion. So R does *not* rewrite the route's BGP NH.

In summary, only if the route is intraregion, the BGP next hop is rewritten.

Let's analyze the routes in Figure 16-12 one by one:

*eBGP-LU route **172.16.3.22***

The route is originated by Srv2, whose region set is {2}. Hence, the route has one regional community only: CM-ZONE-2. L2 also belongs to region 2 (and region 0, but this is not important here); hence, it rewrites the BGP next hop of the route to its own loopback address (**172.16.2.22**) and allocates a locally significant label. Neither of the other routers (S1, L1, Srv1) belongs to region 2, so neither of them touches the BGP next hop or the label.

*eBGP-LU route **172.16.2.22***

The route is originated by L2, whose region set is {0, 2}. As a result, the route has two regional communities: CM-ZONE-0 and CM-ZONE-2. S1 also belongs to region 0; hence, it rewrites the BGP next hop of the route to the eBGP peering address and allocates a locally significant label. L1 also belongs to region 0; hence, it rewrites the BGP of the route to its own loopback address (**172.16.2.11**) and allocates a new label. As you can see, S1 and L1 followed a different BGP next hop rewrite logic. Indeed, L1 is advertising the route to a peer that, from L1's perspective, is in region 1. And the route's region set being {0, 2} does not contain 1 so the route is becoming inter-region.

*eBGP-LU route **172.16.2.11***

Srv1 and L1 are directly connected so this intraregion LSP is very short and has no label due to Penultimate Hop Popping (PHP). If there were another LSR between Srv1 and L1, Srv1 would push a three-label stack just for transport.

 The number of BGP routes handled at the control plane is still the same (you could achieve a reduction by using similar techniques to those discussed in Chapter 17).

The scaling benefit of this model is at the FIB or forwarding-plane level. Neither L1 nor S1 need to allocate a label for Srv2's loopback. In other words, LSRs only allocate labels for prefixes originated in their own region set. So a large-scale data center with more than 100,000 servers no longer requires LSRs to allocate more than 100,000 labels. Allocating a label requires one FIB entry, so the fewer labels that are allocated, the thinner the FIB is.

This example topology is too small to appreciate the real benefits. Think of a network with 1,000 different regions!

Example 16-27 shows the three recursive routes from the perspective of Srv1.

Example 16-27. Hierarchical BGP-LU signaling—Srv1 (Junos)

```
juniper@Srv1> show route receive-protocol bgp 10.0.0.1
               table inet.3 detail

inet.3: 12 destinations, 12 routes (11 active, ...)
[...]
* 172.16.2.11/32 (1 entry, 1 announced)
      Accepted
      Route Label: 3
      Nexthop: 10.0.0.1
      AS path: 65201 I
      Communities: 65000:1000 65000:1001

* 172.16.2.22/32 (1 entry, 1 announced)
      Accepted
      Route Label: 300624
      Nexthop: 172.16.2.11
      AS path: 65201 65101 65202 ?
      Communities: 65000:1000

* 172.16.3.22/32 (1 entry, 1 announced)
      Accepted
      Route Label: 24006
      Nexthop: 172.16.2.22
      AS path: 65201 65101 65202 65302 ?
      Communities: 65000:3 65000:1002
```

You can match the routes, next hops, and labels, from Figure 16-12 to Example 16-27. Here are the standard communities in the example:

- Regional communities: CM-ZONE-X (65000:100X), where X is the region number.
- Other communities (see Chapter 2): CM-SERVER (65000:3) identifies server loopbacks and CM-VM (65000:100) identifies the end-user virtual machines (VMs).

BGP-LU hierarchy—forwarding plane

As you can see, the hierarchical transport LSP is ready at the ingress PE (Srv1).

Example 16-28. Forwarding next-hop in Hierarchical BGP-LU—Srv1 (Junos)

```
juniper@Srv1> show route 172.16.3.22 table inet.3

inet.3: 12 destinations, 12 routes (11 active, ...)
[...]
172.16.3.22/32    *[BGP/170] 02:01:28, localpref 10
                    AS path: 65201 65101 65202 65302 ?
```

```
                    > to 10.0.0.1 via ge-2/0/2.0,
                            Push 24006, Push 300624(top)
```

The MPLS service in this example is global (no VPN) IPv4 unicast. Of course, it could be VPN and that would require yet another (service) label. The service IPv4 unicast route is 10.2.0.0/31, and its BGP next hop (172.16.3.22) has already been resolved, so VM2 is now reachable from VM1. This prefix exchange is depicted on top of Figure 16-12. Please refer to Example 2-11 from Chapter 2 for the layout of BGP sessions distributing service prefixes.

Example 16-29. Forwarding next-hop in Hierarchical BGP-LU—Srv1 (Junos)

```
juniper@Srv1> show route receive-protocol bgp 172.16.1.1 detail

inet.0: 11 destinations, 11 routes (10 active, ...)
* 10.2.0.0/31 (1 entry, 1 announced)
     Accepted
     Nexthop: 172.16.3.22
     AS path: 65101 65302 ?
     Communities: 65000:100

juniper@Srv1> show route 10.2.0.0/31 table inet.0

inet.0: 11 destinations, 11 routes (10 active, ...)

10.2.0.0/31  *[BGP/170] 00:32:11, localpref 100, from 172.16.1.1
                AS path: 65101 65302 ?
              > to 10.0.0.1 via ge-2/0/2.0,
                       Push 24006, Push 300624(top)

RP/0/0/CPU0:VM#traceroute vrf VM1 10.2.0.1
[...]
 1  10.1.0.0 0 msec  0 msec  0 msec
 2  10.0.0.1 [MPLS: Labels 300624/24006 Exp 0] 29 msec  ...
 3  10.0.0.5 [MPLS: Labels 301408/24006 Exp 0] 0 msec  ...
 4  10.0.0.8 [MPLS: Label 24006 Exp 0] 9 msec  0 msec  ...
 5  10.0.0.2 9 msec  ...
 6  10.2.0.1 9 msec  ...
```

BGP-LU hierarchy—configuration

You can configure Hierarchical BGP-LU LSPs with plain BGP-LU: no extensions are required. Example 16-30 shows an example of how one eBGP-LU session is configured at L1.

Example 16-30. Hierarchical BGP-LU configuration—L1 (Junos)

```
1    protocols {
2        bgp {
```

```
3                 group eBGP-LU-65301 {
4                     multihop {
5                         no-nexthop-change;
6                     }
7                     export PL-eBGP-LU-OUT-REGION-1;
8       }}}
9       policy-options {
10          policy-statement PL-eBGP-LU-OUT-REGION-1 {
11              term LOCAL-LOOPBACK {
12                  from interface lo0.0;
13                  then {
14                      community add CM-REGION-0;
15                      community add CM-REGION-1;
16                      accept;
17                  }
18              }
19              term REGION-0 {
20                  from community CM-REGION-0;
21                  then {
22                      next-hop 172.16.2.11;
23      }}}
24          community CM-REGION-0 members 65000:1000;
25          community CM-REGION-1 members 65000:1001;
26      }
```

Junos default BGP policies accept BGP prefixes not already accepted or rejected by any term in the explicit policy (chain) shown in Example 16-30.

The key configuration is on lines 4 and 5:

- Even if the actual eBGP session is single hop, Junos needs the multihop statement in order to set (or accept) the BGP next hop to anything different from the single-hop eBGP peering address. In this example, L1 needs to rewrite the BGP next hop of the 172.16.2.22/32 route to L1's loopback address 172.16.2.11 before advertising the route to Srv1.

- The no-nexthop-change Junos knob means: *do not change the BGP NH unless the export policy explicitly changes it*. Because this solution requires a mix of rewrites and non-rewrites, the configuration is absolutely required.

As for IOS XR, ebgp-multihop is also required to accept prefixes with a BGP next hop different from the single-hop eBGP peering address. On the other hand, as of this writing, you can configure one single eBGP session in IOS XR in one of these modes: rewrite the next hop of all the prefixes (default) or rewrite the next hop of *no* prefixes (next-hop-unchanged). The Hierarchical eBGP-LU solution requires a mix of rewrite and non-rewrites, and the authors did not manage to make it work in IOS XR with one single session. IOS XR still supports this solution if you configure two IPv4 addresses on the peering interfaces, establish two parallel eBGP-LU sessions, and carefully use the communities.

MPLS-Capable Servers and Static Labels

Srv1, an MPLS-capable server (acting as a PE) is performing a relatively complex task. Even with hierarchical LSPs, Srv1 still needs to process the eBGP-LU routes of all the remote servers, not to mention the service BGP (IP Unicast, IP VPN, etc.) routes.

Although BGP has many mechanisms to reduce the state (communities, policies RTC, etc.), some large-scale data center administrators prefer to use central controllers that directly program static label stacks on the servers' FIB.

> Of course, eBGP remains the preferred option for the data center *fabric* (L1, S1, L2, S2, etc.).

For example, if Srv1 does not run eBGP-LU, applying this static configuration to Srv1 would work fine, too, as demonstrated here:

Example 16-31. Static label stack configuration—Srv1 (Junos)

```
protocols {
    mpls {
        static-label-switched-path Srv1--->Srv2 {
            label-stack;
            ingress {
                to 172.16.3.22;
                next-hop 10.0.0.1;
                push [ 24006 300624 ];
}}}}
```

The problem is that label values are dynamic and can change at any time. If the controller needs to react every time that a dynamic label value changes in the network, the overall solution does not scale.

There are two alternative ways to solve this challenge:

- Deterministic labels with BGP-LU Prefix SID extensions (discussed in Chapter 2)
- Assigning a static label at L1, map it to the FEC 172.16.3.22/32, and push it from Srv1

Static label stitching

Static LSPs like those described in Chapter 1 do not scale, because they require assigning and programming labels at every hop. The following model is better in that the label only needs to be statically allocated at L1. Let's see how it works.

Example 16-32. Static label stitching configuration at the ingress PE—L1 (Junos)

```
protocols {
    mpls {
        static-label-switched-path ANY-to-Srv2 {
            transit 1000000 {
                next-hop 172.16.3.22;
                stitch;
}}}}
```

With this configuration, if L1 receives a MPLS packet with topmost label 1000000, it processes the packet according to how 172.16.3.22 resolves in L1's inet.3 table. More precisely, the Label Forwarding Information Base (LFIB) entry is: 1000000 → Swap 24006, Push 301408, send to 10.0.0.5.

And if the dynamic labels change, L1 automatically updates the LFIB entry accordingly.

Now suppose that L2 has the following configuration:

Example 16-33. Static label stitching configuration at the egress PE—L2 (IOS XR)

```
mpls static
 address-family ipv4 unicast
  local-label 1000111 allocate
   forward
    path 1 nexthop GigabitEthernet0/0/0/0 10.0.0.2 out-label pop
 !
```

All that Srv1 needs to do is push label 1000111, then label 1000000, and send the packet to L1. When the packet arrives to L2, it has only one label (1000111) and it is safely delivered to the Srv2.

## CHAPTER 17

Scaling MPLS Services

Chapter 16 discusses different methods for scaling IP/MPLS transport. Unfortunately, in order to design large, scalable networks, it is often not enough to scale the transport. As the next step, you will learn about different design models to scale MPLS services.

The general problem with MPLS service scaling is that you can have a network device, which supports a limited number of routes (in L3VPN deployments), limited number of MAC addresses (in VPLS or EVPN deployments), limited number of features supported (e.g., no support for L3VPN, no support for VPLS/EVPN), and so on. To alleviate all of those problems, the MPLS service itself must be designed in a scalable manner.

This chapter presents some typical architectural models to scale L3 MPLS services. More specifically, the two examples used here are: Default Route Hierarchical L3VPN and PWHE-based Hierarchical L3VPN. However, you can port many of the ideas presented here to other MPLS services. These examples are inspired on the Mobile Backhaul (MBH) use case.

Hierarchical L3VPN

The network topology used for the discussion of service scaling will be basically the same as the multidomain topology described in Chapter 16. For reference, this topology is presented in Figure 17-1.

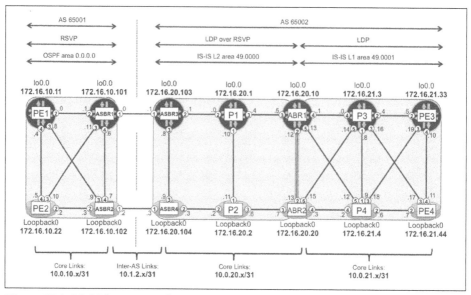

Figure 17-1. Multidomain topology

To create a meaningful basis for a discussion on service scaling, in addition to CE-less VPN-A (built in Chapter 16), VPN-B (with CE) extends the topology. CEs are connected to PE routers as outlined in Figure 17-2. Different CEs use various PE-CE protocols (eBGP, IS-IS, OSPF, VRRP) to connect to PE. The details of PE-CE configurations, however, are not discussed here. The basics of L3VPN and VPLS service are covered in Chapter 3 and Chapter 7.

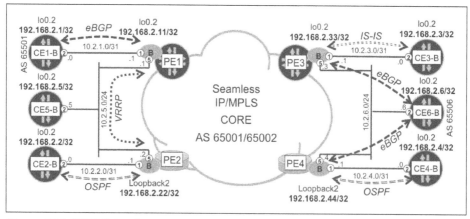

Figure 17-2. VPN-B topology

As in many of the earlier chapters, the physical CE devices are virtualized with routing instances (virtual routers, so-called VRF lite) to create one virtual CE per [physical CE, VPN] pair. In this sense, throughout this chapter there will be further virtual CE devices in addition to those shown in Figure 17-2, as new L3VPN instances are added to the architectural model.

Let's capture the current state of the network by examining the total number of prefixes in VRF-B, as shown in Example 17-1 and Example 17-2.

Example 17-1. VRF-B prefix state on PE1 (Junos)

```
juniper@PE1> show route summary
(...)
VRF-B.inet.0: 19 destinations, 39 routes (19 active, ...)
              Direct:     3 routes,     3 active
               Local:     3 routes,     3 active
                 BGP:    32 routes,    12 active
              Static:     1 routes,     1 active
(...)
```

Example 17-2. VRF-B prefix state on PE2 (IOS XR)

```
RP/0/0/CPU0:PE2#show route vrf VRF-B summary
Route Source      Routes      Backup    Deleted    Memory(bytes)
connected         2           1         0          420
local             3           0         0          420
local VRRP        0           0         0          0
ospf VRF-B        1           0         0          140
bgp 65001         11          0         0          1540
dagr              0           0         0          0
static            1           0         0          140
Total             18          1         0          2660
```

On PE1, VRF-B contains routes to 19 destinations, whereas on all other PEs, there are routes to only 18 (PE3 and PE4 are omitted here to save space). This small difference is caused by the fact that PE1 is a Virtual Router Redundancy Protocol (VRRP) master, thus the additional route (VIP address) is present in VRF-B on that PE. However, as it relates to the overall discussion about L3VPN service scaling, this small discrepancy is irrelevant.

You can imagine that in large-scale deployments, the number of prefixes in VRF-B could be very large, not just the 18 or 19 shown in the example. Depending on the platform used as the PE, the number could be too large. In the subsequent sections of this chapter, architectural models to minimize that number are presented.

To make a meaningful comparison between different architectural models, for each model discussed, additional service instances (L3VPN) will be created. Multiple models running in parallel will give you the opportunity to directly compare advantages and disadvantages of each model. Because, unfortunately, nothing is for free, to make the design more scalable, you might need to give up some other aspects. For example, you might need to choose between design complexity and failover behavior during various network failures.

Default Route L3VPN Model

The idea behind the *Default Route L3VPN* model is very simple:

- Create VRFs somewhere higher in the network hierarchy on more powerful routers. Let's call these routers *Virtual Hub PEs* (V-hubs). These are somewhere deeper in the network infrastructure. V-hubs should be capable of holding all VPN routes for selected VPNs. Depending on the required scale, *selected* VPNs could mean all VPNs, or just a subset of all VPNs. Typically V-hubs are routers sitting in the aggregation layer in the overall network design.

- Within each VPN, advertise the default route from each VRF on the V-hub toward less powerful routers farther down in the network hierarchy. Let's call such routers *Virtual Spoke PEs* (V-spokes). They are closer to the end user. V-spokes do not scale well, thus, within each locally configured VPN, it will receive only default route with the next hop pointing to a V-hub. The advantage of a V-spoke in such a mode is usually low price, small form factor, low power consumption, and so on, which makes it the preferred choice for mass deployment in large quantities. Typically, V-spokes are routers sitting in the access layer in the overall network design.

The idea is not new. If you look carefully, you'll see that a similar idea was demonstrated in Chapter 16. For example, ABR1 and ABR2 routers advertise the default route (in a global routing table) toward lower-layer routers (P3, P4, PE3, and PE4) using IS-IS protocol and suppress all other (IS-IS L2) prefixes. The main difference is that previously this model was applied to a global routing table, whereas now it is applied to multiple VPN routing tables. So, the concept is very similar, but the implementation details, of course, differ. The concept is described in RFC 7024 - *Virtual Hub-and-Spoke in BGP/MPLS VPNs*.

An example of Default Route L3VPN topology is presented in Figure 17-3.

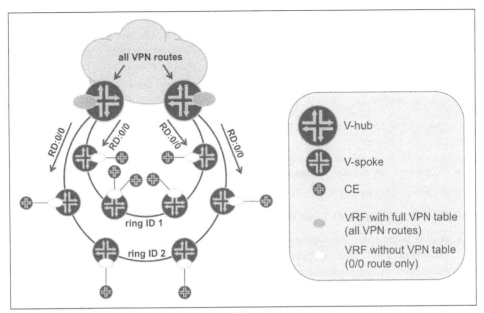

Figure 17-3. The default route L3VPN model

As mentioned previously, you typically could use such a design when a large number of low-end devices (feature-rich but with low scale) are deployed. One typical example could be a Mobile Backhaul (MBH) network, especially in 4G or 5G deployments. In those deployments, the size of the cells (the area covered by a single eNodeB) is relatively small, which naturally increases the overall number of required eNodeBs. This, in turn, is reflected in the large number of access ports (and thus the number of access devices) required from a networking perspective to connect all of those eNodeBs.

As outlined in Figure 17-3, V-spokes (access devices) are typically attached to V-hubs (aggregation devices) via semiclosed rings. Depending on the actual design, multiple VRFs can be created on each V-spoke (Figure 17-3 shows only one). In turn, you could connect multiple CE devices (e.g., eNodeBs) to each V-spoke. V-spokes advertise their locally learned (from locally connected CE devices) VPN prefixes to the V-hubs. In the opposite direction, V-hubs advertise only the default route for each VPN. The end result is that each VRF on V-spoke contains only local CE prefixes and the default route from the V-hubs. For redundancy, both V-hubs terminating access semi-rings are injecting the default route in each VPN. That should result in significantly fewer prefixes in each VRF, compared to nonhierarchical VPN design.

It is important to mention that on V-hubs the VRFs don't need to be attached to any CE. Thus, it's possible that no interfaces will be included in those VRFs. The main purpose of VRFs created on V-hubs is to collect all VPN prefixes for each VRF as well as to aggregate prefixes in each VRF via the default route advertised to V-spokes. Later, V-spokes will send packets using the default route. Those packets will arrive to VRFs on V-hubs, where IP lookup (within the VRF) must take place in order to determine further the forwarding path. As is discussed in Chapter 3, IP lookup inside the VRF is not the default behavior (neither for Junos, nor for IOS XR), and you need to explicitly enable it.

You might also see some similarities with the *Inter-AS Option B + Local VRF* model described in Chapter 9:

- VRFs typically do not necessarily have local CEs attached.
- Packets arrive to the VRF as labeled packets.
- IP lookup is performed inside the VRF for those labeled packets.
- ASBR in the Inter-AS Option B + Local VRF model acts as *kind of* an inline RR, reflecting VPN prefixes between multiprotocol iBGP and multiprotocol eBGP neighbors. In a hierarchical L3VPN model, the V-hub reflects prefixes between two multiprotocol iBGP neighbors.
- Next-hop self is performed when VPN routes are reflected by ASBR in an Inter-AS Option B + Local VRF model. In a hierarchical L3VPN model, a similar result is achieved by advertising the VPN default route, which also uses a next hop that is local to V-hub.

Detailed routing model

To verify this theory in practice, OSPF area 0 (ASBR1, ASBR2, PE1, and PE2) and IS-IS area 49.0001 (ABR1, ABR2, PE3, and PE4) in Figure 17-1 are each functionally—even if not topologically—equivalent to one of the rings in Figure 17-3.

To illustrate the hierarchical L3VPN model, let's create a new VPN-C in the sample interdomain topology used previously. ASBR1 and ASBR2 are acting as V-hubs for PE1 and PE2, which are deployed in a V-spoke role. Similarly, on the other side of the topology, ABR1 and ABR2 are V-hubs, whereas PE3 and PE4 are V-spokes. The overall design for VRF-C is illustrated in Figure 17-4.

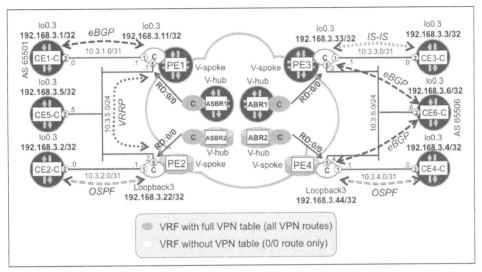

Figure 17-4. VPN-C topology

The configuration of the VRF-Cs on V-spokes is standard; there is nothing specific here. On the V-hubs (ASBR1, ASBR2, ABR1, and ABR2), however, you do not need to configure the PE-CE interfaces in VRF-C. Additionally, within VRF-C on V-hubs, you configure aggregate default discard route with standard community attached. The community will be used to restrict advertisement of this default route to V-spokes only. For reference, Example 17-3 and Example 17-4 present sample Junos and IOS XR configurations, respectively. ABR1 and ABR2 have similar configurations.

Example 17-3. VRF-C configuration on V-hub—ASBR1 (Junos)

```
routing-instances {
    VRF-C {
        instance-type vrf;
        route-distinguisher 172.16.10.101:103;
        vrf-target target:65000:1003;
        routing-options {
            aggregate {
                route 0.0.0.0/0 {
                    community 65000:41999;
                    discard;
}}}}}
```

Example 17-4. VRF-C configuration on V-hub—ASBR2 (IOS XR)

```
vrf VRF-C
 address-family ipv4 unicast
  import route-target
   65000:1003
```

```
    !
    export route-target
      65000:1003
  !
  community-set CM-VPN-DEFAULT-ROUTE
    65000:41999
  end-set
  !
  route-policy PL-VPN-DEFAULT-ROUTE
    set community CM-VPN-DEFAULT-ROUTE
    set origin incomplete
  end-policy
  !
  router bgp 65001
   vrf VRF-C
    rd 172.16.10.102:103
    address-family ipv4 unicast
     aggregate-address 0.0.0.0/0 as-set route-policy PL-VPN-DEFAULT-ROUTE
  !
```

To maintain consistency, in IOS XR, you set the origin attribute explicitly to *incomplete* (this is the default in Junos). Additionally, you configure the IOS XR V-hub to attach a full AS_SET to the advertised aggregated default route (which, again, is the default in Junos).

V-hubs act as VPN RRs. Until now, there was no inbound or outbound BGP policy attached for IPv4 VPN address families. This must change, because the V-hub role is to advertise the default route only to V-spokes, not reflect routes. In the other direction, upstream (as well as between two V-hubs), routes received from V-spokes should be reflected, but the default route should not be sent.

Thus, you must implement the VPN downstream, VPN upstream, and VPN RR BGP outbound policy on V-hubs. To make it possible to compare between standard VPN (VPN-B) and the default route VPN (VPN-C), those policies will affect only VPN route distribution for VPN-C, as demonstrated in Example 17-5. Typically, on real-life *small*-scale V-spokes, all VPNs would be implemented in the default route L3VPN model.

Example 17-5. IPv4 VPN outbound BGP policies on ASBR1 (Junos)

```
protocols {
    bgp {
        group iBGP-DOWN:LU+VPN {
            export [ PL-BGP-LU-DOWN-EXP PL-BGP-VPN-DOWN-EXP ];
        }
        group eBGP-UP:VPN {
            export [ PL-BGP-LU-UP-EXP PL-BGP-VPN-UP-EXP ];
        }
        group iBGP-RR:LU+VPN {
```

```
                export [ PL-BGP-LU-RR-EXP PL-BGP-VPN-RR-EXP ];
}}}
policy-options {
    policy-statement PL-BGP-VPN-DOWN-EXP {
        term LOCAL-DEFAULT-ROUTE {
            from {
                family inet-vpn;
                community CM-VPN-DEFAULT-ROUTE;
            }
            then accept;
        }
        term VRF-C {
            from {
                family inet-vpn;
                community RT-VPN-C;
            }
            then reject;
        }
        from family inet-vpn;
        then accept;
    }
    policy-statement PL-BGP-VPN-UP-EXP {
        term LOCAL-DEFAULT-ROUTE {
            from {
                family inet-vpn;
                community CM-VPN-DEFAULT-ROUTE;
            }
            then reject;
        }
        from family inet-vpn;
        then accept;
    }
    policy-statement PL-BGP-VPN-RR-EXP {
        term LOCAL-DEFAULT-ROUTE {
            from {
                family inet-vpn;
                community CM-VPN-DEFAULT-ROUTE;
            }
            then reject;
        }
        from family inet-vpn;
        then accept;
    }
    community CM-VPN-DEFAULT-ROUTE members 65000:41999;
    community RT-VPN-C members target:65000:1003;
}
```

You can see the definition of the PL-BGP-LU-*-EXP policies in Example 16-16.

Example 17-6. IPv4 VPN outbound BGP policies on ASBR2 (IOS XR)

```
extcommunity-set rt RT-VPN-C
  65000:1003
end-set
!
route-policy PL-BGP-VPN-DOWN-EXP
  if community matches-any CM-VPN-DEFAULT-ROUTE then
    done
  elseif extcommunity rt matches-any RT-VPN-C then
    drop
  endif
  pass
end-policy
!
route-policy PL-BGP-VPN-UP-EXP
  if community matches-any CM-VPN-DEFAULT-ROUTE then
    drop
  endif
  pass
end-policy
!
route-policy PL-BGP-VPN-RR-EXP
  if community matches-any CM-VPN-DEFAULT-ROUTE then
    drop
  endif
  pass
end-policy
!
router bgp 65001
 !
 neighbor-group iBGP-DOWN:LU_VPN
  address-family vpnv4 unicast
   route-policy PL-BGP-VPN-DOWN-EXP out
 !
 neighbor-group eBGP-UP:VPN
  address-family vpnv4 unicast
   route-policy PL-BGP-VPN-UP-EXP out
 !
 neighbor-group iBGP-RR:LU_VPN
  address-family vpnv4 unicast
   route-policy PL-BGP-VPN-RR-EXP out
!
```

There is one important difference between applying BGP policies in Junos and IOS XR, as discussed in "Multiprotocol BGP policies" on page 629.

- In IOS XR, policies are applied separately for each address family.

- In Junos, one single BGP policy chain applies to all the address families signaled in the session. That's why the policies defined in Example 17-5 use the `from family inet-vpn` clause; this way, the IP LU prefixes are unaffected.

Now, it is time for verification. Let's look at the sizes of VRF routing tables.

Example 17-7. VRF-C prefix state on PE1 (Junos)

```
juniper@PE1> show route summary
(...)
VRF-C.inet.0: 9 destinations, 11 routes (9 active, ...)
            Direct:      3 routes,      3 active
            Local:       3 routes,      3 active
              BGP:       4 routes,      2 active
            Static:      1 routes,      1 active
```

Example 17-8. VRF-C prefix state on PE2 (IOS XR)

```
RP/0/0/CPU0:PE2#show route vrf VRF-C summary
Route Source      Routes    Backup    Deleted    Memory(bytes)
connected         2         1         0          420
local             3         0         0          420
ospf VRF-C        1         0         0          140
static            1         0         0          140
bgp 65001         1         0         0          140
dagr              0         0         0          0
Total             8         1         0          1260
```

If you compare these to Example 17-1 and Example 17-2, which show that state for nonoptimized VPN, you can see the decrease in the number of prefixes. Now, there are 10 fewer prefixes. Note that PE1 has more BGP prefixes due to the access eBGP PE-CE session. Let's have a look at the actual routing tables.

Example 17-9. VRF-C routing table on PE1 (Junos)

```
juniper@PE1> show route table VRF-C.inet.0 active-path terse
VRF-C.inet.0: 9 destinations, 11 routes (9 active, ...)
+ = Active Route, - = Last Active, * = Both

A V Destination        P Prf  Metric 1    Next hop     AS path
* ? 0.0.0.0/0          B 170      100                  65002 {65506} ?
* ? 10.3.1.0/31        D   0              >ge-2/0/1.3
* ? 10.3.1.1/32        L   0               Local
* ? 10.3.5.0/24        D   0              >ge-2/0/5.3
* ? 10.3.5.1/32        L   0               Local
* ? 10.3.5.254/32      L   0               Local
* ? 192.168.3.1/32     B 170      100                  65501 I
* ? 192.168.3.5/32     S   5              >10.3.5.5
* ? 192.168.3.11/32    D   0              >lo0.3
```

Example 17-10. VRF-C routing table on PE2 (IOS XR)

```
RP/0/0/CPU0:PE2#show route vrf VRF-C
(...)
B*   0.0.0.0/0 [200/0] via 172.16.10.101 (nexthop in vrf default)
C    10.3.2.0/31 is directly connected, 1w0d, Gi0/0/0/1.3
L    10.3.2.1/32 is directly connected, 1w0d, Gi0/0/0/1.3
C    10.3.5.0/24 is directly connected, 1w0d, Gi0/0/0/5.3
L    10.3.5.2/32 is directly connected, 1w0d, Gi0/0/0/5.3
O    192.168.3.2/32 [110/1001] via 10.3.2.0, 1d02h, Gi0/0/0/1.3
S    192.168.3.5/32 [1/0] via 10.3.5.5, 1w0d
L    192.168.3.22/32 is directly connected, 1w0d, Loopback3
```

As expected, there is a default route pointing to V-hub (ASBR1) and routes associated with locally connected CE devices (CE1-C, CE5-C) only. Remote VPN-C routes (CE2-C, CE3-C, CE4-C, and CE6-C) are not present. Routing tables on other PE routers look similar.

Full VRF routing tables are now available on V-hubs, as shown in Example 17-11 and Example 17-12. As expected, there is one aggregate (Junos) or BGP generated, based on aggregate-address (IOS XR) default discard route, six PE-CE link routes, six CE loopbacks, and four PE VRF loopbacks. There are no local/connected/direct routes, because no local interface is connected to those VRFs. VRF routing tables on remaining V-hubs look similar.

Example 17-11. VRF-C routing table on ASBR1 (Junos)

```
juniper@ASBR1> show route table VRF-C.inet.0 active-path | match "\*"
+ = Active Route, - = Last Active, * = Both
0.0.0.0/0       *[Aggregate/130] 5d 21:37:39
10.3.1.0/31     *[BGP/170] 10:59:25, from 172.16.10.11
10.3.2.0/31     *[BGP/170] 13:37:36, MED 0, from 172.16.10.22
10.3.3.0/31     *[BGP/170] 23:58:34, from 172.16.20.1
10.3.4.0/31     *[BGP/170] 13:29:16, from 172.16.20.1
10.3.5.0/24     *[BGP/170] 10:59:25, from 172.16.10.11
10.3.6.0/24     *[BGP/170] 23:58:34, from 172.16.20.1
192.168.3.1/32  *[BGP/170] 1d 10:59:25, from 172.16.10.11
192.168.3.2/32  *[BGP/170] 1d 13:37:34, MED 1001, from 172.16.10.22
192.168.3.3/32  *[BGP/170] 23:58:34, from 172.16.20.1
192.168.3.4/32  *[BGP/170] 1d 13:29:16, from 172.16.20.1
192.168.3.5/32  *[BGP/170] 1d 10:59:25, from 172.16.10.11
192.168.3.6/32  *[BGP/170] 23:58:34, from 172.16.20.1
192.168.3.11/32 *[BGP/170] 1d 10:59:25, from 172.16.10.11
192.168.3.22/32 *[BGP/170] 1d 13:37:36, MED 0, from 172.16.10.22
192.168.3.33/32 *[BGP/170] 23:58:34, from 172.16.20.1
192.168.3.44/32 *[BGP/170] 1d 13:29:16, from 172.16.20.1
```

Example 17-12. VRF-C routing table on ASBR2 (IOS XR)

```
RP/0/0/CPU0:ASBR2#show route vrf VRF-C
(...)
B* 0.0.0.0/0 [200/0] via 0.0.0.0, 6d11h, Null0
B 10.3.1.0/31 [200/0] via 172.16.10.11 (nexthop in vrf default)
B 10.3.2.0/31 [200/0] via 172.16.10.22 (nexthop in vrf default)
B 10.3.3.0/31 [20/0] via 172.16.21.33 (nexthop in vrf default)
B 10.3.4.0/31 [20/0] via 172.16.21.44 (nexthop in vrf default)
B 10.3.5.0/24 [200/0] via 172.16.10.11 (nexthop in vrf default)
B 10.3.6.0/24 [20/0] via 172.16.21.33 (nexthop in vrf default)
B 192.168.3.1/32 [200/0] via 172.16.10.11 (nexthop in vrf default)
B 192.168.3.2/32 [200/1001] via 172.16.10.22 (nexthop in vrf default)
B 192.168.3.3/32 [20/0] via 172.16.21.33 (nexthop in vrf default)
B 192.168.3.4/32 [20/0] via 172.16.21.44 (nexthop in vrf default)
B 192.168.3.5/32 [200/0] via 172.16.10.11 (nexthop in vrf default)
B 192.168.3.6/32 [20/0] via 172.16.21.33 (nexthop in vrf default)
B 192.168.3.11/32 [200/0] via 172.16.10.11 (nexthop in vrf default)
B 192.168.3.22/32 [200/0] via 172.16.10.22 (nexthop in vrf default)
B 192.168.3.33/32 [20/0] via 172.16.21.33 (nexthop in vrf default)
B 192.168.3.44/32 [20/0] via 172.16.21.44 (nexthop in vrf default)
```

Achieving end-to-end connectivity in the Junos plane

Routing information seems to be perfect, so now, let's verify the connectivity between CE routers, for example between CE1-C and CE3-C.

Example 17-13. Failed ping from CE1-C to CE3-C (Junos)

```
juniper@CE1> ping routing-instance CE1-C source 192.168.3.1
              192.168.3.3 count 1
PING 192.168.3.3 (192.168.3.3): 56 data bytes
--- 192.168.3.3 ping statistics ---
1 packets transmitted, 0 packets received, 100% packet loss
```

Unfortunately, the connectivity is broken. Quick verification using MPLS (L3VPN) ping originating from PE1 yields the same results.

Example 17-14. Failed MPLS ping from PE1 to CE3-C (Junos)

```
juniper@PE1> ping mpls l3vpn VRF-C prefix 192.168.3.3/32 detail
              count 1
Request for seq 1, to interface 340, label 308416, packet size 88
Timeout for seq 1

--- lsping statistics ---
1 packets transmitted, 0 packets received, 100% packet loss
```

Because the routing information looks correct, there must be some problems with forwarding. Let's check what MPLS labels are used to forward traffic from PE1.

Example 17-15. Label stack used to reach CE3-C on PE1 (Junos)

```
juniper@PE1> show route table VRF-C.inet.0 192.168.3.3 active-path
             detail | match "announced|via|Label"
0.0.0.0/0 (2 entries, 1 announced)
             Next hop: 10.0.10.1 via ge-2/0/2.0, selected
             Label-switched-path PE1--->ASBR1
             Label operation: Push 308416
(...)
```

Example 17-16. VPN label advertised by ASBR1 for 0.0.0.0/0 Route

```
juniper@ASBR1> show route advertising-protocol bgp 172.16.10.11 table
               bgp.l3vpn.0 match-prefix 172.16.10.101:103:* detail |
               match "0.0.0.0/0|Label"
* 172.16.10.101:103:0.0.0.0/0 (1 entry, 1 announced)
    VPN Label: 308416
```

To reach the loopback of CE3-C, traffic uses the default route entry, and traffic is sent to ASBR1 via PE1→ASBR1 LSP. A single MPLS label (308416) is used, which is the same label that you can see in the MPLS ping in Example 17-14. This is the VPN label advertised by ASBR1 and associated with the default route (Example 17-16). LSP is single hop, thus no transport label (implicit null) is used. So, we can find nothing suspicious here.

Upon examining the label on ASBR1, however, we discover some unexpected information.

Example 17-17. MPLS routing entry associated to 0/0 route at ASBR1 (Junos)

```
juniper@ASBR1> show route label 308416
(...)
308416             *[VPN/170] 1d 01:40:59
                     Discard
```

Obviously, traffic is discarded instead of being forwarded based on VRF routing information on ASBR1. What is needed, instead, is the capability to perform IP lookup inside VRF. As is discussed in Chapter 3, in Junos, the default label allocation method for VPN prefixes is per access next hop (per CE). Thus, all VPN prefixes sharing the same next hop will share the same VPN label. Using such an approach, IP lookup inside VRF is not required. Packets arriving from an MPLS backbone can be forwarded to the appropriate next hop based on the label.

In the particular case of the Default Route L3VPN model, the next hop for the VPN default route is *discard*. Thus—based on the label associated with the VPN default route—packets are dropped and no IP lookup inside VRF is performed. For hierarchical L3VPN to function properly, you must enable IP lookup inside VRF on V-hubs.

As Chapter 3 details, there are several ways to achieve this, and one of them is the `vrf-table-label` Junos knob deployed on all Junos V-hubs.

Example 17-18. Per-VRF label configuration on ASBR1 (Junos)

```
routing-instances {
    VRF-C {
        vrf-table-label;
}}
```

With this knob, a single label is assigned to all prefixes from a given VRF. Because the label is no longer correlated with next hop, IP lookup inside VRF will be performed to determine the next hop.

Ping between CE1-C and CE3-C works now (output omitted for brevity). Let's check the label assignment after enabling per-VRF label mode.

Example 17-19. VPN label advertised by ASBR1 for 0.0.0.0/0 route

```
juniper@ASBR1> show route advertising-protocol bgp 172.16.10.11 table
               bgp.l3vpn.0 match-prefix 172.16.10.101:103:* detail |
               match "0.0.0.0/0|Label"
172.16.10.101:103:0.0.0.0/0 (1 entry, 1 announced)
    VPN Label: 16
```

Example 17-20. LFIB entry for a label associated to 0/0 at ASBR1 (Junos)

```
juniper@ASBR1> show route label 16
(...)
16                      *[VPN/0] 01:19:27
                           to table VRF-C.inet.0, Pop
```

Examining outputs from Example 17-19 and Example 17-20, you can observe two differences. First, the VPN label itself is different. Second, the routing entry for that label now shows behavior required for proper operation of hierarchical VPN model. Two lookups are performed on the packets:

MPLS label–based lookup
    This determines the VRF routing table for subsequent lookup.

IP-based lookup inside VRF (the one previously determined by first lookup)
    This determines the actual forwarding next hop.

Achieving end-to-end connectivity in the IOS XR plane

Now, after examining connectivity across a Junos-based IP/MPLS network part, let's verify the connectivity across an IOS XR-based network part.

Example 17-21. Connectivity verification between CE2-C and CE4-C

```
juniper@CE2> ping routing-instance CE2-C source 192.168.3.2
              192.168.3.4 count 1
PING 192.168.3.4 (192.168.3.4): 56 data bytes
ping: sendto: No route to host
```

It seems, the default route, although present in VRF-C on PE2 (Example 17-10), is not present on CE2-C. A quick verification confirms that suspicion.

Example 17-22. Missing default route on CE2-C (Junos)

```
juniper@CE2> show route table CE2-C.inet.0 0.0.0.0/0 exact

juniper@CE2>
```

In IOS XR, the default route redistribution into IGP protocols requires special attention. Thus, the configuration on IOS XR–based V-spoke with IGP as PE-CE protocols (PE2, PE4) needs to be extended, as outlined here:

Example 17-23. Default route origination on PE2 (IOS XR)

```
router ospf VRF-C
 vrf VRF-C
  default-information originate
```

This different treatment is specific to IOS XR and redistribution to IGP. This extra configuration is not required when the PE-CE protocol is BGP, as it can be quickly verified on CE6-C, which uses BGP as the PE-CE protocol. With no specific configuration, CE6-C receives the default route from both Junos and IOS XR–based PEs.

Example 17-24. Sources for the default route on CE6-C

```
juniper@CE6> show route table CE6-C.inet.0 0.0.0.0/0 exact detail |
              match "0.0.0.0/0|Source"
0.0.0.0/0 (2 entries, 1 announced)
              Source: 10.3.6.3
              Source: 10.3.6.4
```

On Junos V-hubs, special attention was needed to enable IP lookup inside VRF. In IOS XR devices, this is enabled by default. Chapter 3 points out that the default label allocation method for VPN prefixes in IOS XR is per-prefix. However, this applies only for the VPN prefixes received from CEs. For local prefixes, IOS XR generates a single per-VRF aggregate label. Such prefixes are, for example, PE-CE LAN prefixes, loopback prefixes inside local VRF, aggregate prefixes, or locally defined static routes with null0 next hop. For packets arriving with an aggregate label, IP lookup is performed inside VRF to further determine the next hop. A quick verification confirms these observations.

Example 17-25. VPN label advertised for 0/0 route by V-hubs

```
RP/0/0/CPU0:PE2#show bgp vpnv4 unicast vrf VRF-C 0.0.0.0/0 |
               include "from|Label"
    172.16.10.101 (metric 1001) from 172.16.10.101 (172.16.10.101)
      Received Label 16
    172.16.10.102 (metric 1001) from 172.16.10.102 (172.16.10.102)
      Received Label 16016
```

Example 17-26. LFIB entry for a label associated to 0/0 at ASBR2 (IOS XR)

```
RP/0/0/CPU0:ASBR2#show mpls forwarding labels 16016
Local  Outgoing    Prefix               Outgoing      Next Hop   Bytes
Label  Label       or ID                Interface                Switched
------ ----------- -------------------- ------------- ---------- --------
16016  Aggregate   VRF-C: Per-VRF Aggr[V]   \
                                        VRF-C                    8146
```

MPLS forwarding in the Junos plane

Let's now take a look at the path between CE1-C and CE3-C by using traceroute (see Example 17-27).

Example 17-27. Traceroute from CE1-C to CE3-C

```
juniper@CE1> traceroute routing-instance CE1-C source 192.168.3.1
             192.168.3.3
traceroute to 192.168.3.3 (192.168.3.3) from 192.168.3.1,
 1  PE1-VRF-C (10.3.1.1)  6.810 ms  3.627 ms  3.125 ms
 2  * * *
 3  ASBR3 (10.1.2.1)  16.881 ms  17.374 ms  19.851 ms
     MPLS Label=303120 CoS=0 TTL=1 S=0
     MPLS Label=22 CoS=0 TTL=1 S=1
 4  P1 (10.0.20.0)  19.883 ms  129.772 ms  30.374 ms
     MPLS Label=299856 CoS=0 TTL=1 S=0
     MPLS Label=300320 CoS=0 TTL=1 S=0
     MPLS Label=22 CoS=0 TTL=2 S=1
 5  ABR1 (10.0.20.5)  19.622 ms  22.494 ms  17.512 ms
     MPLS Label=300320 CoS=0 TTL=1 S=0
     MPLS Label=22 CoS=0 TTL=3 S=1
 6  P4 (10.0.21.12)  14.878 ms P3 (10.0.21.0)  17.384 ms
     MPLS Label=299968 CoS=0 TTL=1 S=0
     MPLS Label=22 CoS=0 TTL=4 S=1
 7  PE3-VRF-C (192.168.3.33)  16.859 ms  15.165 ms  15.675 ms
 8  CE3-C (192.168.3.3)  124.331 ms  81.165 ms  16.002 ms
```

Hmm. With the exception of a second hop (apparently ASBR1), everything looks fine. But why didn't ASBR1 respond to the traceroute packets with an *ICMP Time Exceeded* message?

To send an *ICMP Time Exceeded* message, some source IP address needs to be assigned to the packet. This source IP address is later displayed in traceroute output on the host (CE1-C, in this case) originating the traceroute packets. As already discussed, one of the effects of `vrf-table-label` configuration (Example 17-18) is that received MPLS packets are handed over to the VRF for further processing (IP lookup) after the MPLS label is removed. For a traceroute packet, this implies that the *ICMP Time Exceeded* message must be sourced from within VRF.

And therein lies the problem. In the current configuration, there are no interfaces (and thus no local IP address) at all attached to VRF-C on ASBR1. Consequently, ASBR1 is not able to source any locally generated packets (e.g., previously mentioned *ICMP Time Exceeded message*) in VRF-C. You can also verify it by means of a simple ping from VRF-C on ASBR1.

Example 17-28. Failed ping from ASBR1 to CE1-C (Junos)

```
juniper@ASBR1> ping routing-instance VRF-C 192.168.3.1 count 1
PING 192.168.3.1 (192.168.3.1): 56 data bytes
ping: sendto: Can't assign requested address
(...)
```

Therefore, although transit VPN traffic can flow through ASBR1 without any problems, scenarios in which traffic needs to be sourced from VRF-C on ASBR1 are currently not working. To solve this problem, you must add a loopback interface inside VRF-C on ASBR1.

Example 17-29. Loopback configuration in VRF-C on ASBR1 (Junos)

```
interfaces {
    lo0 {
        unit 3 {
            family inet {
                address 192.168.3.101/32;
}}}}
routing-instances {
    VRF-C {
        interface lo0.3;
}}
```

Similarly, some loopback interface should be added on another Junos V-hub (ABR1). With this modification, the *ICMP Time Exceeded* message is sourced from the loopback placed within VRF-C, configured previously. Now, both ping from VRF-C on ASBR1 (not shown for brevity) and traceroute between CE devices works fine.

Example 17-30. Traceroute from CE1-C to CE3-C

```
juniper@CE1> traceroute routing-instance CE1-C source 192.168.3.1
            192.168.3.3
traceroute to 192.168.3.3 (192.168.3.3) from 192.168.3.1, 30 hops max
 1  PE1-VRF-C (10.3.1.1)  4.565 ms  3.823 ms  5.863 ms
 2  ASBR1-VRF-C (192.168.3.101)  6.203 ms  109.403 ms  8.573 ms
 3  ASBR3 (10.1.2.1)  18.768 ms  16.849 ms  15.705 ms
    MPLS Label=303120 CoS=0 TTL=1 S=0
    MPLS Label=22 CoS=0 TTL=1 S=1
(...)
```

The complete output is provided in Example 17-27. Just for comparison, let's examine the traceroute between CE2-C and CE4-C, forcing it to go via IOS XR plane (IGP on ASBR1 and ABR1 was temporarily disabled, when the output shown in Example 17-31 was captured).

Example 17-31. Traceroute from CE2-C to CE4-C

```
juniper@CE2> traceroute routing-instance CE2-C source 192.168.3.2
            192.168.3.4
traceroute to 192.168.3.4 (192.168.3.4) from 192.168.3.2
 1  PE2-VRF-C (10.3.2.1)  3.484 ms  4.882 ms  3.034 ms
 2  ASBR2 (10.0.10.3)  6.378 ms  9.047 ms  5.198 ms
 3  ASBR4 (10.1.2.3)  122.968 ms  18.226 ms  19.753 ms
    MPLS Label=16008 CoS=0 TTL=1 S=0
    MPLS Label=16021 CoS=0 TTL=1 S=1
 4  P2 (10.0.20.2)  18.502 ms  20.385 ms  18.805 ms
    MPLS Label=16005 CoS=0 TTL=1 S=0
    MPLS Label=16004 CoS=0 TTL=1 S=0
    MPLS Label=16021 CoS=0 TTL=2 S=1
 5  ABR2 (10.0.20.7)  18.034 ms  17.620 ms  20.180 ms
    MPLS Label=16004 CoS=0 TTL=1 S=0
    MPLS Label=16021 CoS=0 TTL=3 S=1
 6  P3 (10.0.21.14)  19.625 ms  43.178 ms  21.516 ms
    MPLS Label=300000 CoS=0 TTL=1 S=0
    MPLS Label=16021 CoS=0 TTL=4 S=1
 7  PE4 (10.0.21.17)  19.817 ms  19.515 ms  19.582 ms
    MPLS Label=16021 CoS=0 TTL=1 S=1
 8  CE4-C (192.168.3.4)  19.735 ms  18.215 ms  21.057 ms
```

The difference is that ASBR2 sources the *ICMP Time Exceeded* message from an MPLS interface address, not from an interface within VRF. Thus, loopback inside VRF-C on ASBR2 is not needed for traceroute to work. The MPLS label, however, is still not reported. In that case (0.0.0.0/0 route inside VRF-C), a per-VRF aggregate label is used, which is similar to the previously discussed ASBR1 case.

Question: why does PE4 (V-spoke) return a label in Example 17-31, whereas ASBR2 (V-hub) doesn't? Here's a hint: check the traceroute to CE4-C physical interface (not loopback), where PE4 doesn't report the label either (Example 17-32).

Example 17-32. Traceroute from CE2-C to CE4-C

```
juniper@CE2> traceroute routing-instance CE2-C source 192.168.3.2
             10.3.4.0
traceroute to 10.3.4.0 (10.3.4.0) from 192.168.3.2, 30 hops max
 1  PE2-VRF-C (10.3.2.1)  4.919 ms  7.055 ms  2.955 ms
 2  ASBR2 (10.0.10.3)  6.162 ms  5.481 ms  6.884 ms
 3  ASBR4 (10.1.2.3)  19.437 ms  19.530 ms  18.572 ms
     MPLS Label=16008 CoS=0 TTL=1 S=0
     MPLS Label=16008 CoS=0 TTL=1 S=1
 4  P2 (10.0.20.2)  16.971 ms  16.314 ms  18.551 ms
     MPLS Label=16005 CoS=0 TTL=1 S=0
     MPLS Label=16004 CoS=0 TTL=1 S=0
     MPLS Label=16008 CoS=0 TTL=2 S=1
 5  ABR2 (10.0.20.7)  17.210 ms  18.515 ms  18.357 ms
     MPLS Label=16004 CoS=0 TTL=1 S=0
     MPLS Label=16008 CoS=0 TTL=3 S=1
 6  P3 (10.0.21.14)  18.364 ms  25.810 ms  21.105 ms
     MPLS Label=300000 CoS=0 TTL=1 S=0
     MPLS Label=16008 CoS=0 TTL=4 S=1
 7  PE4 (10.0.21.17)  17.564 ms  15.521 ms  15.989 ms
 8  CE4-C (10.3.4.0)  19.385 ms  20.609 ms  19.845 ms
```

As Chapter 3 specifies, by default IOS XR uses the following label allocation methods:

- Per-prefix label for VPN prefixes received over PE-CE protocols.

- Per-VRF aggregate label for all remaining (locally defined) prefixes (e.g., PE-CE LAN prefixes, loopback prefixes inside local VRF, locally generated aggregate prefixes, or locally defined static routes with null0 next hop). For packets arriving with aggregate label, IP lookup (and ARP resolution) is performed inside the VRF to further determine the next hop.

Traceroute reports the label for prefixes with a per-prefix label, because packets destined to these prefixes are only label-switched on the PE router. Thus, label information is available when a traceroute packet needs to be dropped due to TTL=0. Packets destined to prefixes with an aggregate label are, on the other hand, handled by two lookups: label lookup, which determines appropriate VRF, and IP lookup inside VRF to further determine where about of the packet. Before the packet is handed over to VRF for further processing, its label is removed. Thus, when the traceroute packet is dropped inside VRF, the label information is no longer available and cannot be reported in an *ICMP Time Exceeded* message.

Handling network failures by using Hierarchical L3VPN

The last issue that you will look at is the difference between plain L3VPN and Hierarchical L3VPN during network failure events. Let's assume for this example that on ASBR1 all BGP sessions (with the exception of two sessions only: toward PE1 and PE2) are down due to some network failure. When checking connectivity during that network state, you can observe the following:

- VPN-B (plain VPN) still works fine, and traffic is forwarded via ASBR2 (Example 17-33)
- VPN-C (Hierarchical VPN) no longer works (Example 17-34)

Example 17-33. Healthy connectivity (VPN-B) during simulated failure

```
juniper@CE1> traceroute routing-instance CE1-B source 192.168.2.1
             192.168.2.3
traceroute to 192.168.2.3 (192.168.2.3) from 192.168.2.1
 1  PE1-VRF-B (10.2.1.1)  14.091 ms  2.925 ms  2.548 ms
 2  ASBR2 (10.0.10.9)  225.348 ms  18.487 ms  19.716 ms
    MPLS Label=16014 CoS=0 TTL=1 S=0
    MPLS Label=21 CoS=0 TTL=1 S=1
 3  ASBR4 (10.1.2.3)  17.498 ms  18.760 ms  19.575 ms
    MPLS Label=16007 CoS=0 TTL=1 S=0
    MPLS Label=21 CoS=0 TTL=2 S=1
(...)
```

Example 17-34. Broken connectivity (VPN-C) during simulated failure

```
juniper@CE1> traceroute routing-instance CE1-C source 192.168.3.1
             192.168.3.3
traceroute to 192.168.3.3 (192.168.3.3) from 192.168.3.1, 30 hops max
 1  PE1-VRF-C (10.3.1.1)  158.941 ms  11.196 ms  5.830 ms
 2  * * *
 3  * * *
(...)
```

ASBR1 is advertising the default route even if it has no reachability to PE3 and PE4. This highlights the problem: the introduction of route aggregation reduces the network visibility, which can lead to traffic *blackholing* in certain failure scenarios. In a Hierarchical L3VPN model, V-hubs (e.g., ASBR1) perform route aggregation. Instead of a large number of VPN routes, V-hubs send only the default route.

Thus, as the last step in Hierarchical VPN design, let's enhance the configuration to minimize the likelihood of blackholing. In any aggregation designs, you should inject the aggregate route conditionally. As a condition, you should use reachability to some remote prefixes (in the test topology, for example, VPN prefixes from CEs connected to remote PEs).

From an operation perspective, the easiest way to achieve the desired results is to introduce a community scheme that encodes the source of prefixes, such as the following:

- VPN prefixes sourced in AS 65001, OSPF area 0.0.0.0 will be marked with some community (e.g., 65000:41100)
- VPN prefixes sourced in AS 65002, IS-IS area 49.0001 will be marked with different community (e.g., 65000:41201)

Subsequently, you can use the presence of a VPN prefixes with specific community as a condition to advertise the VPN default route. ASBR1 and ASBR2 will use prefixes with community 65000:41201 as a condition, whereas ABR1 and ABR2 will use prefixes with community 65000:41100.

Let's begin with Junos V-spokes (PE1 and PE3). Standard community can be attached to local VPN prefixes either via VRF export policies, or via BGP export policies. Manipulating VRF export policies will create the situation that VRF export policies for the same VPN will differ from access region to access region. From an operation perspective, you should attempt a design where VRF export policies for specific VPNs are unified. Thus, this option is not the best one in a scaled environment with many VPNs and many access regions.

Using another option requires the selection of local VPN routes (from any local VRF) in the BGP export policy. Only those routes should be marked with the standard community mentioned previously. A technique of selecting VPN routes was already used in Example 17-5. The `from family inet-vpn` knob was used to select all VPN routes, regardless of the VRF. As Chapter 3 discusses, internal RIB structures on pure PE (PE1 in the topology) versus on combined PE + RR/ASBR (ASBR1 in the topology) routers are slightly different in Junos.

One of the implications of this difference is the fact that the `from family inet-vpn` knob selects on pure PE–only VPN routes received via multiprotocol BGP, because this knob operates on the `bgp.l3vpn.0` RIB. Normally this knob is not effective for VPN routes from local VRFs on a pure PE. To make the `from family inet-vpn` knob work in this case, you first need to explicitly copy VPN prefixes from local VRFs into `bgp.l3vpn.0` RIB by using the `advertise-from-main-vpn-tables` knob. On a combined PE + RR/ASBR router, this is done automatically, thus no special attention is required in Example 17-35.

Example 17-35. Location community attachment on PE1 (Junos)

```
protocols {
    bgp {
        advertise-from-main-vpn-tables;
        group iBGP-RR {
```

```
            export PL-BGP-VPN-UP-EXP;
            vpn-apply-export;
}}}
policy-options {
    policy-statement PL-BGP-VPN-UP-EXP {
        from family inet-vpn;
        then {
            community add CM-IPV4-VPN-100;
            accept;
        }
    }
    community CM-IPV4-VPN-100 members 65000:41100;
}
```

Example 17-36. Location community attachment on PE2 (IOS XR)

```
community-set CM-IPV4-VPN-100
  65000:41100
end-set
!
route-policy PL-BGP-VPN-UP-EXP
  set community CM-IPV4-VPN-100
end-policy
!
router bgp 65001
 neighbor-group iBGP-RR
  address-family vpnv4 unicast
    route-policy PL-BGP-VPN-UP-EXP out
!
```

Now, it's time to configure a condition to generate a default route on V-hub routers. Again, the example configuration for Junos (ASBR1) is shown in Example 17-37 and the one for IOS XR (ASBR2) is shown in Example 17-38. You should perform a similar configuration—but referencing to community CM-IPV4-VPN-100 instead—on ABR1 and ABR2. On ASBR1 (Junos), you create a completely new policy, whereas for ASBR2 (IOS XR) you modify the existing policy (see Example 17-4) to include a condition.

Example 17-37. Conditional VPN default route generation on ASBR1 (Junos)

```
policy-options {
    policy-statement PL-VPN-DEFAULT-ROUTE {
        term REMOTE-VPNS {
            from {
                protocol bgp;
                community CM-IPV4-VPN-201;
            }
            then accept;
        }
        then reject;
```

```
    }
    community CM-IPV4-VPN-201 members 65000:41201;
}
routing-instances {
    VRF-C {
        routing-options {
            aggregate {
                route 0.0.0.0/0 {
                    policy PL-VPN-DEFAULT-ROUTE;
}}}}}
```

Example 17-38. Conditional VPN default route generation on ASBR2 (IOS XR)

```
route-policy PL-VPN-DEFAULT-ROUTE
  if community matches-any CM-IPV4-VPN-201 then
    set community CM-VPN-DEFAULT-ROUTE
    set origin incomplete
    done
  endif
  drop
end-policy
```

Now, when you check the VPN default route, you will see that the *contributing routes* are limited to remote (from PE3 or PE4) VPN routes. A contributing route is an active route that is a more specific match for the aggregated destination. The presence of at least one contributing route is required to activate an aggregate route.

Example 17-39. Contributing routes for VPN default route on ASBR1 (Junos)

```
juniper@ASBR1> show route table VRF-C.inet.0 0.0.0.0/0 exact
               extensive all
(...)
               State: <Active Int Ext>
(...)
               Announcement bits (2): 1-KRT 2-rt-export
(...)
               Contributing Routes (8):
                       10.3.3.0/31 proto BGP
                       10.3.4.0/31 proto BGP
                       10.3.6.0/24 proto BGP
                       192.168.3.3/32 proto BGP
                       192.168.3.4/32 proto BGP
                       192.168.3.6/32 proto BGP
                       192.168.3.33/32 proto BGP
                       192.168.3.44/32 proto BGP
```

In IOS XR, you cannot display contributing routes. However, you can verify which routes are matched by the policy you just configured, as presented here:

Example 17-40. Contributing routes for VPN default route on ASBR2 (IOS XR)

```
RP/0/0/CPU0:ASBR2#show bgp vpnv4 unicast vrf VRF-C
                 route-policy PL-VPN-DEFAULT-ROUTE
(...)
    Network          Next Hop     Metric LocPrf Weight Path
Route Distinguisher: 172.16.10.102:103 (default for vrf VRF-C)
*> 10.3.3.0/31     172.16.21.33               0 65002 i
*> 10.3.4.0/31     172.16.21.44               0 65002 ?
*> 10.3.6.0/24     172.16.21.33               0 65002 i
*                  172.16.21.44               0 65002 ?
*> 192.168.3.3/32  172.16.21.33               0 65002 i
*> 192.168.3.4/32  172.16.21.44               0 65002 ?
*> 192.168.3.6/32  172.16.21.33               0 65002 65506 i
*                  172.16.21.44               0 65002 65506 i
*> 192.168.3.33/32 172.16.21.33               0 65002 i
*> 192.168.3.44/32 172.16.21.44               0 65002 ?
```

In Junos, when at least one contributing route is not present—for example, due to some network failure—the corresponding aggregate route goes to *hidden state*. In hidden state, the route is no longer used for forwarding and no longer advertised. The output in Example 17-41 was taken on ASBR1, when BGP sessions to ASBR2, P1 and P2 were disabled temporarily. No contributing routes are available any longer, thus the VPN default route becomes hidden and is no longer advertised.

Example 17-41. Hidden VPN default route on ASBR1 (Junos)

```
juniper@ASBR1> show route table VRF-C.inet.0 0.0.0.0/0 exact
               extensive all
VRF-C.inet.0: 10 destinations, 12 routes (9 active, ...)
0.0.0.0/0 (1 entry, 0 announced)
    Aggregate
            Next hop type: Discard
            State: <Hidden Int Ext>
            AS path: I
            Communities: 65000:41999
              Flags: Brief ASPathChanged Discard  Depth: 0  Inactive
```

In IOS XR, when all contributing routes disappear, the aggregate route is simply removed from the RIB.

Default Route with Local Routes L3VPN Model

Although the Hierarchical VPN model discussed in the previous section decreases the control-plane load on V-spokes, it introduces some inefficiency in traffic forwarding. Taking traceroute from CE3-C to CE4-C can illustrate this inefficiency.

Example 17-42. Suboptimal traceroute from CE3-C to CE4-C

```
juniper@CE3> traceroute routing-instance CE3-C source 192.168.3.3
             192.168.3.4
traceroute to 192.168.3.4 (192.168.3.4) from 192.168.3.3
 1 PE3-VRF-C (10.3.3.1)  105.974 ms  35.702 ms  87.946 ms
 2 P3 (10.0.21.4) 90.2 ms P4 (10.0.21.18) 58.1 ms P3 (10.0.21.4) ...
    MPLS Label=300032 CoS=0 TTL=1 S=0
    MPLS Label=16 CoS=0 TTL=1 S=1
 3 ABR1-VRF-C (192.168.3.103)  11.567 ms  9.499 ms  10.463 ms
 4 P4 (10.0.21.12)  18.656 ms  14.758 ms  15.753 ms
    MPLS Label=16000 CoS=0 TTL=1 S=0
    MPLS Label=16021 CoS=0 TTL=1 S=1
 5 PE4 (10.0.21.7)  17.451 ms  15.600 ms  12.856 ms
    MPLS Label=16021 CoS=0 TTL=1 S=1
 6 CE4-C (192.168.3.4)  13.882 ms  16.727 ms  15.968 ms
```

Traffic first goes to a V-hub (ABR1) based on the default route. On V-hub, IP lookup is performed inside VRF-C and traffic is sent back to PE4. An extra three hops are visited. Depending on the actual deployment, this can create some problems. For example, if latency of the traffic between CE3-C and CE4-C needs to be minimized, the basic Hierarchical VPN model is not really suitable.

Thus, you must enhance the basic model. Let's see how. As illustrated in Figure 17-5, V-hubs, in addition to the previously discussed default route, reflect VPN prefixes of local access domains (rings in the figure). For example, VPN prefixes from all V-spokes on ring 1 are reflected by V-hubs to all V-spokes in that ring. The same happens to VPN prefixes on ring 2. During prefix reflection, next hop remains unchanged. As the end result, V-spokes have prefixes from local ring (local access domain) and additionally the default route injected by V-hubs to reach remote (outside local ring) destinations.

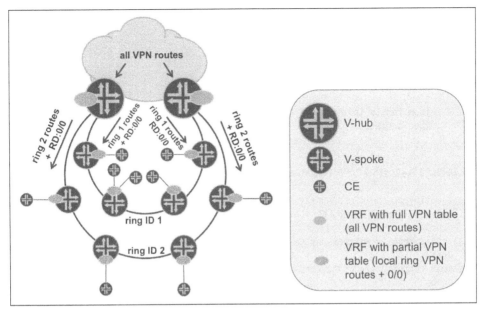

Figure 17-5. Default route with local routes L3VPN model

When communicating between V-spokes on the same ring (access domain), the default route injected by V-hubs is not used. Conversely, when the need arises to communicate between V-spokes in different rings (or with some remote PEs), the default route injected by V-hubs is indeed used. This doesn't cause any huge inefficiency in traffic forwarding, because to reach remote V-spokes, packets must transit V-hubs anyway.

To achieve the desired results, you can use a community scheme introduced into the base model for Hierarchical VPN. Simply, V-hubs will use the community not only as a condition to announce VPN default route, they will also be used to reflect VPN prefixes received from the *local* access domain back to V-spokes in the same local access domain. Example 17-43 and Example 17-44 demonstrate simple extensions to existing `PL-BGP-VPN-DOWN-EXP` policy for ASBR1 (Junos) and ASBR2 (IOS XR), respectively.

Example 17-43. IPv4 VPN outbound BGP policy on ASBR1 (Junos)

```
policy-options {
    policy-statement PL-BGP-VPN-DOWN-EXP {
        term LOCAL-DEFAULT-ROUTE {
(...)
        }
        term ACCESS-DOMAIN-100 {
            from {
                family inet-vpn;
```

```
            community CM-IPV4-VPN-100;
        }
        then accept;
    }
    term VRF-C {
(...)
    }
    from family inet-vpn;
    then accept;
}}
```

Example 17-44. IPv4 VPN outbound BGP policy on ASBR2 (IOS XR)

```
route-policy PL-BGP-VPN-DOWN-EXP
  if community matches-any CM-VPN-DEFAULT-ROUTE then
    done
  elseif community matches-any CM-IPV4-VPN-100 then
    done
  elseif extcommunity rt matches-any RT-VPN-C then
    drop
  endif
  pass
end-policy
```

You can perform similar policy extensions on ABR1 and ABR2. With updated BGP outbound policies on V-hubs, the number of prefixes sent to V-spokes increases slightly (10 additional paths, and out of those, 3 additional active prefixes). You can compare the output in the following examples with that from Example 17-7 and Example 17-8.

Example 17-45. VRF-C prefix state on PE1 (Junos)

```
juniper@PE1> show route summary
(...)
VRF-C.inet.0: 12 destinations, 15 routes (12 active, ...)
            Direct:     3 routes,     3 active
            Local:      3 routes,     3 active
              BGP:     14 routes,     5 active
            Static:     1 routes,     1 active
(...)
```

Example 17-46. VRF-C Prefix State on PE2 (IOS XR)

```
RP/0/0/CPU0:PE2#show route vrf VRF-C summary
Route Source      Routes    Backup    Deleted    Memory(bytes)
connected         2         1         0          444
local             3         0         0          444
static            1         0         0          148
bgp 65001         4         0         0          592
ospf VRF-C        1         0         0          148
```

```
dagr                0          0          0          0
Total              11          1          0       1776
```

If you look at the VPN-C topology (Figure 17-4), three additional active prefixes are actually expected. For example, on PE1 router, the following three additional active BGP prefixes in VRF-C:

- Loopback of CE2-C router
- VRF-C loopback of PE2 router
- LAN prefix from PE2-CE2-C link

There are two additional prefixes (loopback of CE5-C and prefix for LAN connected to CE5-C) advertised to V-hubs from PE2 and reflected back to PE1. However, because for those prefixes there are already better (local/static) prefixes present in the VRF-C table on PE1, BGP prefixes received from V-hubs are not activated.

So, in summary, you see an additional five prefixes (received twice, because there are two V-hubs sending them), of which three are actually actively used for forwarding. If you compare this with Example 17-1 or Example 17-2, it is still a much lower number than with nonhierarchical L3VPN. A similar result occurs in all other PE routers.

Now, when you check the forwarding path between CE3-C and CE4-C routers, based on additional prefixes distributed to local V-spokes, packets are forwarded on the shortest path, as shown here:

Example 17-47. Optimal traceroute from CE3-C to CE4-C

```
juniper@CE3> traceroute routing-instance CE3-C source 192.168.3.3
             192.168.3.4
traceroute to 192.168.3.4 (192.168.3.4) from 192.168.3.3, 30 hops max
 1  PE3-VRF-C (10.3.3.1)  14.720 ms  3.269 ms  2.393 ms
 2  PE4 (10.0.21.11)  58.005 ms  67.934 ms  28.708 ms
    MPLS Label=24003 CoS=0 TTL=1 S=1
 3  CE4-C (192.168.3.4)  8.510 ms  9.473 ms  6.866 ms
```

Pseudowire Head-End Termination L3VPN Model

In previous sections of this chapter, you built a Hierarchical L3VPN service, based on the assumption that V-spokes do support L3VPN, including support for multiprotocol BGP. This is, unfortunately, not always the case. In many designs, you can find V-spokes without BGP support at all. Naturally, with no BGP, there is no L3VPN possible on V-spokes, either.

Therefore, you will need another approach for Hierarchical L3VPN, one which requires only L2 capabilities (including support for MPLS pseudowires to carry L2 traffic) from the V-spoke. The principle is based on a pseudowire (PW) established between V-spoke and V-hubs. Basically, traffic received from a CE is bridged on the V-spoke to the PW terminated on the V-hub. Because you can terminate many PWs from many V-spokes on V-hubs, and from the CE's perspective the L3 segment also terminates at the V-hub, the model is commonly known as the *pseudowire head-end termination* (PWHE) model.

Figure 17-6 presents the overall architecture for this Hierarchical L3VPN model.

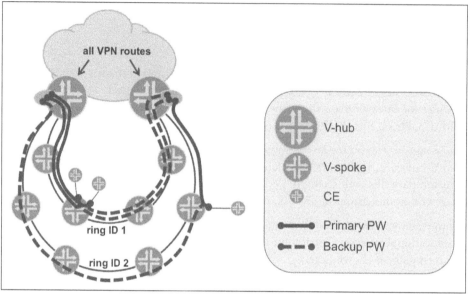

Figure 17-6. The pseudowire head-end termination L3VPN model

Figure 17-6 shows that VRFs are no longer present on the V-spokes—the V-spokes act simply as bridging devices and bridge the traffic between the physical access interface toward the CE, and the PW toward the V-hub. Of course, for redundancy purposes, typically primary/backup PW deployments are recommended, with the primary PW terminated on the primary V-hub, and the backup PW terminated on the backup V-hub. There could be multiple VLANs (corresponding to multiple VPNs) transported inside each PW. At the head-end (V-hub), those VLANs are demultiplexed from the PWs, and each VLAN is placed in appropriate VRF to allow further processing of the packets at L3.

With this architecture, the capability of V-spoke is further "degraded." Prefix scalability is no longer needed at all, because now the only prefixes the V-spoke must deal with are transport network prefixes. Typically, as already discussed in Chapter 16, a large transport network can be divided into multiple smaller IGP domains; thus, the prefix information inside each IGP domain can be quite minimal. Additionally, the only requirement from a protocol-support perspective is some sort of label distribution protocol, IGP, and support for LDP signaled PWs. Thus, Hierarchical L3VPN based on the PWHE model is the primary choice when quite *dummy* (and cheap) V-spokes are deployed.

However, although the possibility to deploy V-spokes without comprehensive L3 service support might sound advantageous, there are, of course, some disadvantages. First, traffic optimization achieved by injecting VPN routes that originated in the local IGP domain, as discussed in previous section, is no longer possible. Consequently, traffic between CE devices connected to V-spokes in the same IGP now always traverses through the V-hub. For some applications, for which latency must be minimized, the Hierarchical L3VPN model based on PWHE might consequently be unsuitable.

Another disadvantage is the increased bandwidth usage in access IGP domains. Whereas in the previously discussed Hierarchical L3VPN model, MPLS-encapsulated IP packets were exchanged between V-spokes and V-hubs in the PWHE model, MPLS encapsulated Ethernet frames carrying IP payload are exchanged. Additional overhead is around 14 to 26 bytes per packet, depending on the number of VLAN tags carried, and whether the control word is used. Although this doesn't look large at the first glance, it might increase bandwidth requirements significantly in some deployments. If the majority of carried traffic uses small IP packets (e.g., VoIP packets using G.729 codec with IP packet sizes as low as 60 bytes) bandwidth usage can increase by 20%–40%. Suboptimal traffic routing (always via V-hub) causes additional bandwidth inefficiency, because traffic exchanged between two V-spokes in the same IGP access domain traverses IGP access domain twice. If your bandwidth resource is limited—for example, limited bandwidth microwave links are used—those disadvantages of the PWHE Hierarchical L3VPN model might be too big to justify deployment of devices without even limited L3VPN support in a V-spoke function. The details are beyond the scope of this book.

## CHAPTER 18

Transit Fast Restoration Based on the IGP

Fast Restoration Concepts

Before starting a detailed discussion about protection and traffic restoration techniques, let's clarify the terminology used in this book.

Ingress/Transit/Egress Transport Protection Concepts

Figure 18-1 presents a generic service model with two dual-homed CE devices connected to a service provider (SP) IP/MPLS network. PE nodes provide the service itself (e.g., L3VPN), whereas Provider (P) nodes are used purely for transmitting packets between PE nodes. Additionally, the figure also shows various failure cases (nine in total) that can affect example traffic flow from *left* CE to *right* CE.

For the purpose of this book, failure categories (and corresponding protection categories) are classified as follows:

Ingress protection
> This is an action performed to minimize traffic loss during failure of an ingress CE-PE link (failure case 1) or ingress PE node (failure case 2). The Point of Local Repair (PLR) is the ingress CE, which after detecting failure (based on Loss of Signal [LoS], or OAM, or BFD, etc.) switches the outgoing traffic to another (bottom) PE node.

Transit protection
> This is an action performed to minimize traffic loss during failure of a transit link (failure case 3, 5, or 7) or transit P node (failure case 4 or 6). The PLR is either the ingress PE node (for failure case 3 or 4) or some transit P node (for failure cases 5, 6, or 7). Different MPLS techniques are available to minimize traffic loss during these failure cases.

Egress protection

This is an action performed to minimize traffic loss during failure of an egress PE (failure case 8) or egress PE-CE link (failure case 9). Depending on the protection techniques deployed, protection action can be performed by the ingress PE node, or by the penultimate P node (to protect against egress PE failure) or by the egress PE node (to protect against egress PE-CE link failure).

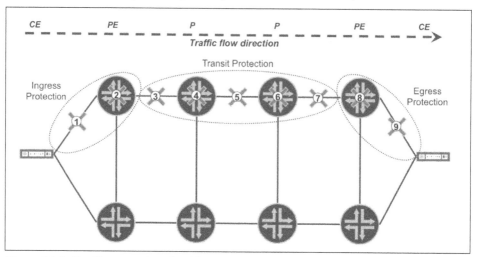

Figure 18-1. Traffic protection classification

Ingress protection isn't typically MPLS-related; instead, it is based purely on the capabilities of some Layer 3 (L3) PE-CE protocols (e.g., BGP, OSPF, RIP, or VRRP) for L3 services, or Layer 2 (L2) protocols (LACP, some variants of Spanning Tree Protocol [STP], or OAM) for L2 services. Thus, ingress protection is not covered in this book.

Techniques that you can deploy for transit protection (LFA, MRT, RSVP-TE protection) are discussed later in this chapter and in Chapter 19, whereas techniques for egress protection are discussed in Chapter 21. Additionally, Chapter 20 covers optimization in FIB data structures allowing for faster FIB reprogramming.

Global Repair Concepts

During network failure events, the following course of actions leads to traffic redirection over a new path, which can avoid a failed link or node:

1. Failure detection

   - Time required to detect the failure

- Various techniques are available, depending on the underlying physical transport technology

2. New state propagation (flooding)

   - Time required to propagate the information about failed link or node through the network
   - Typically involves IGP (IS-IS or OSPF) flooding
   - This time greatly depends on the size of the network, link distances, and so on.

3. Routing database update and new path (and label) computation

   - Time required to compute new paths (next hops)
   - Depends on the IGP database size
   - On modern, high-end routers, this can be approximated with around 1 µs per node (in a network with 1,000 nodes it takes approximately 1 ms to perform Shortest-Path First [SPF] calculation)

4. New next-hops (and labels) installation in Hardware Forwarding Information Base (HW FIB)

   - Time required to program HW FIB in the line cards with newly calculated next-hops (labels)
   - Very hardware dependent
   - Can take a relatively long time (measured in seconds) for large number of next hops in a scaled environment

By optimizing *global* convergence parameters, you can achieve subsecond convergence. However, to achieve sub-100 ms convergence, global (network-wide) convergence is no longer enough, because the state propagation, routing database update, new path calculation, and installation of new next hops in HW FIB cannot really be squeezed below a couple of 100 ms. Thus, for very demanding applications that require sub-100 ms traffic failover times during network failures, tuning global convergence parameters alone is no longer enough. In these cases, *local repair* comes into the picture.

Local Repair Concepts

The idea underpinning local repair is to skip most of the steps that must happen with global repair when a network failure happens. If another next hop was already installed in HW FIB, the only action that needs to be performed during failure events is to detect the failure itself and remove the next hops associated with the failed link or node from the HW FIB. All the other steps are no longer required for local repair. Strictly speaking, local repair is a complement (and not an alternative) to global repair. Indeed, local repair and global repair take place in parallel. Local repair quickly restores data forwarding by using a temporary path while global repair computes the final converged path. As its name implies, local repair is typically a local decision at the PLR and is not negotiated. Rather than on interoperability, we focus on implementation differences.

The most challenging issue with local repair is how to determine potential backup next hops. This chapter and Chapter 19 outline different local-repair techniques that you can deploy in an IP/MPLS network to protect the traffic against transit link or transit node failures, with the goal of providing sub-50 ms traffic restoration times.

 In Junos, ensure that `load-balance per-packet` is applied, as discussed in Chapter 2. This is necessary to enable local-repair next-hop structures.

Loop-Free Alternates

The local-repair mechanism using *Loop-Free Alternates* (LFAs) technique is described in the following RFCs:

- RFC 5714 - *IP Fast Reroute Framework*
- RFC 5715 - *A Framework for Loop-Free Convergence*
- RFC 5286 - *Basic Specification for IP Fast Reroute: Loop-Free Alternates*
- RFC 6571 - *Loop-Free Alternate (LFA) Applicability in SP Networks*

LFA techniques require link-state IGP protocols such as IS-IS or OSPF. When LFA is deployed, in addition to standard SPF calculation, routers perform the SPF calculation from the perspective of each directly connected IGP neighbor. For example, in the topology illustrated in Figure 18-2 (which is a variant of the intradomain topology used in Chapter 16), router PE4, acting as a potential (future) PLR, performs five SPF calculations:

- One *primary* SPF calculation, using the local node (PE4) as the root of the SPF tree. Routers always perform this type of SPF calculations, regardless of whether LFA is enabled, to determine primary next hops due to normal IGP operation.
- Four *backup* SPF calculations, with each calculation using a different direct IGP neighbor node (P2, P5, P6, or PE3) as the root of the SPF tree. Routers perform

this type of SPF calculation to determine backup next-hops only if the LFA feature is enabled.

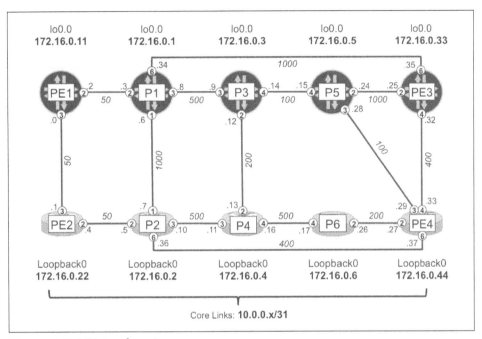

Figure 18-2. LFA topology A

The backup next hop is considered loop-free if the result of a backup SPF calculation does not point back to the node which performs the local repair. In other words, the following condition is checked to determine if the backup next hop is loop-free:

```
Distance(N, D) < Distance(N, S) + Distance(S, D)
```

where:

- S = router performing the local repair
- D = destination under consideration
- N = neighbor node that can be used as a potential backup next hop

For simplicity, and like in other examples of this book, IGP metrics are symmetrically configured, so for any two routers R1 and R2, the R1→R2 and the R2→R1 link metrics are the same.

In the example topology, P2 is the primary next hop to reach P1 from PE4. To verify whether P6 is a feasible backup next hop, you need to test for the following condition:

```
Distance(P6, P1) < Distance(P6, PE4) + Distance(PE4, P1)
750 (P6→PE4→P2→PE2→PE1→P1) < 200 + 550 (PE4→P2→PE2→PE1→P1)
750 < 750 (false)
```

So, P6 cannot be used as backup next hop, because the shortest path to reach P1 from P6 is actually via PE4. When evaluating whether P5 is a feasible backup next hop, you'll get the following:

```
Distance(P5, P1) < Distance(P5, PE4) + Distance(PE4, P1)
600 (P5→P3→P1) < 100 + 550 (PE4→P5→P3→P1)
600 < 650 (true)
```

This makes P5 suitable as a potential backup loop-free next hop for PE4 to reach P1 because the shortest path from P5 to P1 does not traverse PE4.

Only loop-free backup next hops can be installed in the FIB and used as a real backup to forward the traffic during network failures.

There are two types of LFA:

Per-link
> All prefixes originally reachable over a failed link use the same backup next hop. This type of protection is sometimes also called *Per-Next-Hop* LFA.

Per-prefix
> Prefixes originally reachable over a failed link or node may use a different backup next hop on a per-prefix basis.

The next sections of this chapter describe both of these LFA flavors in more detail.

Per-Link LFA

Example 18-1 shows an IOS XR configuration to enable per-link LFA for all IS-IS enabled interfaces. You can simply enhance the existing configuration group (GR-ISIS) used to parameterize ISIS interface configuration.

Example 18-1. Per-Link LFA configuration (IOS XR)

```
group GR-ISIS
 router isis '.*'
  interface 'GigabitEthernet.*'
   address-family ipv4 unicast
    fast-reroute per-link
end-group
router isis core
 apply-group GR-ISIS
```

The first thing to look at is the LFA summary overview, which shows you the backup coverage percentage.

Example 18-2. Backup coverage with per-link LFA on PE4 (IOS XR)

```
RP/0/0/CPU0:PE4#show isis fast-reroute summary
(...)
                             High      Medium    Low       Total
                             Priority  Priority  Priority
Prefixes reachable in L2
  All paths protected        0         0         0         0
  Some paths protected       0         0         0         0
  Unprotected                0         9         15        24
  Protection coverage        0.00%     0.00%     0.00%     0.00%
```

You can see that there are nine medium-priority (loopbacks) and 15 low-priority (links) prefixes for which LFA protection is desired. Based on the topology from Figure 18-2, those numbers are expected. There are 10 loopbacks altogether in the topology but the local loopback is visible only as a directly connected route (not as an IS-IS route). Table 18-1 summarizes the backup coverage results for loopbacks observed on all routers in the topology. On the Junos routers in this topology, LFA is not currently configured; thus, LFA coverage on the Junos plane is not yet available.

Table 18-1. Backup coverage with per-link LFA

P1	P2	P3	P4	P5	P6	PE1	PE2	PE3	PE4
n/a	9	n/a	9	n/a	9	n/a	0	n/a	0
n/a	100%	n/a	100%	n/a	100%	n/a	0%	n/a	0%

Interestingly, for some of the routers, backup coverage is 100%. However, there are some routers for which it seems the LFA is not functioning, because all prefixes are unprotected. Let's have a closer look at one such router (for example, PE4), focusing on the paths toward loopback prefixes.

Example 18-3. Routing table on PE4 (IOS XR)

```
RP/0/0/CPU0:PE4#show route isis | begin /32
i L2 172.16.0.1/32 [115/550] via 10.0.0.36, 00:06:25, Gi0/0/0/6
i L2 172.16.0.2/32 [115/400] via 10.0.0.36, 00:13:02, Gi0/0/0/6
i L2 172.16.0.3/32 [115/200] via 10.0.0.28, 00:13:00, Gi0/0/0/3
i L2 172.16.0.4/32 [115/400] via 10.0.0.28, 00:06:25, Gi0/0/0/3
i L2 172.16.0.5/32 [115/100] via 10.0.0.28, 00:13:00, Gi0/0/0/3
i L2 172.16.0.6/32 [115/200] via 10.0.0.26, 00:13:00, Gi0/0/0/2
i L2 172.16.0.11/32 [115/500] via 10.0.0.36, 00:13:02, Gi0/0/0/6
i L2 172.16.0.22/32 [115/450] via 10.0.0.36, 00:13:02, Gi0/0/0/6
i L2 172.16.0.33/32 [115/400] via 10.0.0.32, 00:13:00, Gi0/0/0/4
```

We can summarize the information from PE4's routing table as such:

- The P6 (172.16.0.6) loopback is reachable via Gi0/0/0/2.
- The PE3 (172.16.0.33) loopback is reachable via Gi0/0/0/4.
- P3, P4, and P5 loopbacks are reachable via Gi0/0/0/3.
- All other loopbacks are reachable via Gi0/0/0/6.

So, if you look carefully at the link metrics, no loop-free backup next hop can be found for most of the loopbacks. Based on the link metrics deployed in the network, all backup SPF calculations for most of the loopbacks will result in the next hop pointing back to PE4. Consequently, these loopbacks do not have LFA backup coverage in this topology. But there are some exceptions; for example, the loopback of P1.

Remember that P5 is a loop-free backup for PE4 to reach P1:

```
Distance(P5, P1) < Distance(P5, PE4) + Distance(PE4, P1)
```

If a feasible backup next hop exists, why is it not used? The answer lies with per-link LFA. As already mentioned, *all* prefixes originally reachable over a failed link must use the same loop-free backup next hop in per-link LFA. And in this example, this is not the case. For P1 (reachable via Gi0/0/0/6 interface), a loop-free backup next hop exists (P5), but for P2, which is normally reachable via Gi0/0/0/6, too, it does not. As a result, in case of Gi0/0/0/6 failure, *all* traffic that originally used Gi0/0/0/6 (P2) as a next hop cannot be redirected over Gi0/0/0/3 (P5), because it would loop for some of the flows—flows destined for P2, for example, given that the shortest path from P5 to P2 is via PE4. Thus, the per-link (per-next-hop) LFA does not install any backup next-hops if the common backup next-hop cannot be used for *each and every* prefix originally reachable over the failed link.

On some other routers, it is better. LFA backup coverage on P2, P4, or P6 is 100%. This means that all IS-IS prefixes are covered by the LFA backup feature. Let's verify the content of the routing table on P4, as well (see Example 18-4).

Example 18-4. Routing table on P4 (IOS XR)

```
RP/0/0/CPU0:P4#show route isis | begin /32
i L2 172.16.0.1/32 [115/650] via 10.0.0.10, 15:24:38, Gi0/0/0/3
                   [115/0] via 10.0.0.12, 15:24:38, Gig0/0/0/2 (!)
i L2 172.16.0.2/32 [115/500] via 10.0.0.10, 02:06:54, Gi0/0/0/3
                   [115/0] via 10.0.0.12, 02:06:54, Gi0/0/0/2 (!)
i L2 172.16.0.3/32 [115/0] via 10.0.0.17, 17:52:11, Gig0/0/0/4 (!)
                   [115/200] via 10.0.0.12, 17:52:11, Gi0/0/0/2
i L2 172.16.0.5/32 [115/0] via 10.0.0.17, 17:52:11, Gi0/0/0/4 (!)
                   [115/300] via 10.0.0.12, 17:52:11, Gi0/0/0/2
i L2 172.16.0.6/32 [115/500] via 10.0.0.17, 17:45:13, Gi0/0/0/4
                   [115/0] via 10.0.0.12, 17:45:13, Gi0/0/0/2 (!)
```

```
i L2 172.16.0.11/32 [115/600] via 10.0.0.10, 15:24:38, Gi0/0/0/3
                    [115/0] via 10.0.0.12, 15:24:38, Gi0/0/0/2 (!)
i L2 172.16.0.22/32 [115/550] via 10.0.0.10, 15:24:38, Gi0/0/0/3
                    [115/0] via 10.0.0.12, 15:24:38, Gi0/0/0/2 (!)
i L2 172.16.0.33/32 [115/0] via 10.0.0.17, 17:50:38, Gi0/0/0/4 (!)
                    [115/800] via 10.0.0.12, 17:50:38, Gi0/0/0/2
i L2 172.16.0.44/32 [115/0] via 10.0.0.17, 17:52:11, Gi0/0/0/4 (!)
                    [115/400] via 10.0.0.12, 17:52:11, Gi0/0/0/2
```

When you compare it to the previous case (Example 18-3), you can see that there are two next hops for each prefix. In each case, one of the next hops is marked with a mysterious (!). A more detailed view of one of the prefixes, shown in the following example, sheds more light on what is actually happening here:

Example 18-5. Detailed RIB entry with per-link LFA backup on P4 (IOS XR)

```
1    RP/0/0/CPU0:P4#show route 172.16.0.33/32 detail | include <pattern>
2    Known via "isis core", distance 115, metric 800, type level-2
3      10.0.0.12, from 172.16.0.33, via GigabitEthernet0/0/0/2, Protected
4        Route metric is 800
5        Path id:1       Path ref count:0
6        Backup path id:33
7      10.0.0.17, from 172.16.0.33, via GigabitEthernet0/0/0/4, Backup
8        Route metric is 0
9        Path id:33              Path ref count:1
```

The primary path (via Gi0/0/0/2) is marked with a Protected tag. This indicates that there must be some backup path, which protects the primary path. Additionally, the primary path contains information about the backup path (line 6), which is expanded in lines 7 through 9. In this particular case, the backup path is via Gi0/0/0/4.

If you look back at the output in Example 18-4, you should see that the primary next-hop and the backup next-hop correlation are always consistent. For example, the Gi0/0/0/2 primary next hop is coupled together with the Gi0/0/0/4 backup next hop for all prefixes that use Gi0/0/0/2 as the primary next hop. This is actually the main characteristic of per-link LFA: failure of the primary link causes redirection of *all* traffic originally flowing via this link over a *single* backup link. If a single backup link that satisfies loop-free criteria cannot be found, the backup next hop is not used at all, as we saw with PE4.

This characteristic of per-link LFA makes it very inefficient in providing high backup coverage in most real deployments. Thus, many router vendors do not implement per-link LFA in their products as more advanced LFA variants provide much better backup coverage. Additionally, per-link LFA does not provide protection against node failure (just link failure), which further reduces its usability. As of this writing, per-link LFA is available in IOS XR but not in Junos or IOS.

In addition to Routing Information Base (RIB) structures investigated previously, let's also have a look at the Forwarding Information Base (FIB) structure.

Example 18-6. IP FIB entry with LFA backup on P4 (IOS XR)

```
RP/0/0/CPU0:P4#show cef 172.16.0.33/32
(...)
 Prefix Len 32, traffic index 0, precedence n/a, priority 3
   via 10.0.0.12, Gi0/0/0/2, 6 dependencies, weight 0, protected
     path-idx 0 bkup-idx 1 NHID 0x0 [0xa14d6d7c 0x0]
     next hop 10.0.0.12
     local label 24005      labels imposed {300400}
   via 10.0.0.17, Gi0/0/0/4, 6 dependencies, weight 0, backup
     path-idx 1 NHID 0x0 [0xa107024c 0x0]
     next hop 10.0.0.17
     local adjacency
     local label 24005      labels imposed {24001}
```

You can see that both the primary and backup next hops use some MPLS labels. In this example topology, the label is exchanged via LDP, as shown in Figure 18-3. The mechanism works fine too if you use SPRING instead of LDP.

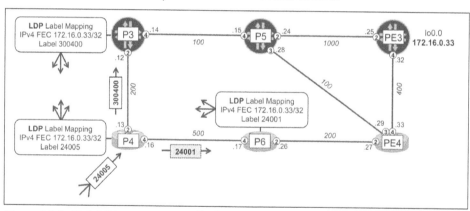

Figure 18-3. Link LFA protecting traffic from P4 to PE3

Label values are different, because P4 receives FECs over different LDP sessions. For the primary and backup next hop, P4 receives the label from P3 and P6, respectively.

The backup next hop is installed not only in the IP FIB, but also in the MPLS FIB (the LFIB). Example 18-7 shows a MPLS FIB entry for the label assigned by P4 to PE3 loopback. The entry is very similar to the IP FIB entry for PE3 loopback discussed previously.

Example 18-7. MPLS FIB entry with LFA backup on P4 (IOS XR)

```
RP/0/0/CPU0:P4#show cef mpls local-label 24005 EOS
(...)
 Prefix Len 21, traffic index 0, precedence n/a, priority 3
   via 40960/0, Gi0/0/0/2, 6 dependencies, weight 0, protected
    path-idx 0 bkup-idx 1 NHID 0x0 [0xa14d6d7c 0x0]
    next hop 10.0.0.12
      local label 24005      labels imposed {300400}
   via 40960/0, Gi0/0/0/4, 6 dependencies, weight 0, backup
    path-idx 1 NHID 0x0 [0xa107024c 0x0]
    next hop 10.0.0.17
    local adjacency
      local label 24005      labels imposed {24001}
```

Now, when the primary interface (Gi0/0/0/2) fails, P5 (depending on how quickly the failure is discovered) removes the primary next hop from FIB structures. Before global convergence completes, traffic can be forwarded based on the backup next hop preprogrammed in the FIB. After global convergence finishes, a new set of primary and backup (if a loop-free backup is found) next hops will be installed in the FIB, overriding the old backup next hop used for temporal traffic forwarding.

Per-Prefix LFA

Per-prefix LFA increases the backup coverage because it allows for different per-prefix backup next hops. Both Junos and IOS XR support it.

Per-prefix LFA in IOS XR

Recall from the discussion about per-link LFA on PE4 that the problem was because different prefixes required different backup next hops. Thus, per-link LFA was not working there. Let's now replace per-link LFA with the per-prefix LFA configuration presented in Example 18-8 and again verify the backup coverage.

Example 18-8. Per-prefix LFA configuration (IOS XR)

```
group GR-ISIS
 router isis '.*'
  interface 'GigabitEthernet.*'
   address-family ipv4 unicast
    fast-reroute per-prefix
```

On two IOS XR routers, there was no backup coverage when per-link LFA was used, but you can now see some increase. Table 18-2 shows that the backup coverage for PE4 in particular has jumped from 0% (with per-link LFA) to 22.2% (with per-prefix LFA).

Table 18-2. Backup coverage with per-prefix LFA

P1	P2	P3	P4	P5	P6	PE1	PE2	PE3	PE4
n/a	9	n/a	9	n/a	9	n/a	**1**	n/a	**2**
n/a	100%	n/a	100%	n/a	100%	n/a	**11.1%**	n/a	**22.2%**

Let's determine which prefixes are actually protected on PE4.

Example 18-9. Prefix-specific LFA information on PE4 (IOS XR)

```
1    RP/0/0/CPU0:PE4#show isis fast-reroute detail | begin "/32"
2    L2 172.16.0.1/32 [550/115] medium priority
3        via 10.0.0.36, Gi0/0/0/6, P2, Weight: 0
4          FRR backup via 10.0.0.28, Gi0/0/0/3, P5, Weight: 0
5          P: No, TM: 700, LC: No, NP: Yes, D: No, SRLG: Yes
6        src P1.00-00, 172.16.0.1
7    (...)
8    L2 172.16.0.4/32 [400/115] medium priority
9        via 10.0.0.28, Gi0/0/0/3, P5, Weight: 0
10         FRR backup via 10.0.0.26, Gi0/0/0/2, P6, Weight: 0
11         P: No, TM: 700, LC: No, NP: Yes, D: No, SRLG: Yes
12       src P4.00-00, 172.16.0.4
13   (...)
```

Now, thanks to the per-prefix LFA feature, you can use the loop-free backup next hops on a per-prefix basis and install them in the FIB. However, there are still some prefixes without a loop-free backup next hop.

Using show command outputs, you can observe the total metric (TM) of the path through the primary next hop (line 2: 550, and line 8: 400) as well as through the backup next hop (line 5: 700, and line 11: 700). Additionally, you get an indication whenever the backup path fulfills node protection (the backup path avoids the neighbor node used as primary next hop) criterion (line 5 and 11: NP: Yes).

Looking at the backup next hop for another prefix on another router (Example 18-10), you can see slightly different flag values.

Example 18-10. Prefix-specific LFA information on P2 (IOS XR)

```
RP/0/0/CPU0:P2#show isis fast-reroute 172.16.0.33/32 detail
L2 172.16.0.33/32 [800/115] medium priority
    via 10.0.0.37, Gi0/0/0/6, PE4, Weight: 0
      FRR backup via 10.0.0.11, Gi0/0/0/3, P4, Weight: 0
      P: No, TM: 1300, LC: No, NP: No, D: No, SRLG: Yes
    src PE3.00-00, 172.16.0.33
```

So, what is the difference between the backup next hops observed in these previous two examples? If you go back to the topology (Figure 18-2), you should see that in

Example 18-9 the backup next hop for the P1 loopback provides protection against primary link (PE4→P2) and primary node (P2) failures. Packets redirected to the backup next hop will reach their final destination without transiting P2. In Example 18-10, however, this is not the case. The packets from P2 destined to PE3 and redirected over the backup next hop (P4) will transit the primary next hop (PE4), because the backup path is P2→P4→P3→P5→*PE4*→PE3. Thus, this backup path provides protection only against primary link failure, not against primary node failure. We'll discuss the other visible flags later, but let's have a look at a few Junos devices first.

Per-prefix LFA in Junos

Let's now enable per-prefix LFA on our Junos devices. Whereas in IOS XR you didn't need to specify what kind of LFA backup next hops are permitted, Junos offers two configuration options:

node-link-protection
> Installs, if possible, loop-free backup next hops, which fulfill both node protection (backup path avoids neighbor node used as primary next hop) and link protection (backup path avoids original link used to reach primary next hop) criteria.

link-protection
> Installs, if possible, loop-free backup next hops, which fulfill at least the link protection (backup path avoids original link used to reach primary next hop) criterion. Node protection criterion (backup path avoids neighbor node used as primary next hop) might be fulfilled as well, but is not verified or enforced.

OK, so you have choices. The first choice looks more promising (protection against both node and link failures), so let's try it first.

Example 18-11. Per-prefix node-link-protection LFA configuration (Junos)

```
groups {
    GR-ISIS {
        protocols {
            isis {
                interface "<*[es]*>" {    # Matches Ethernet and SONET
                    node-link-protection;
}}}}}
protocols {
    isis {
        apply-groups GR-ISIS;
}}
```

If you come from the RSVP-TE world, you will find it surprising the way that [node-]link-protection is interpreted for LFA. This point is discussed in greater detail in Chapter 19.

And again, the first thing you probably want to know is the LFA backup coverage you can achieve. The following example reveals this for you:

Example 18-12. Backup coverage with per-prefix node-link-protection LFA on P5 (Junos)

```
juniper@P5> show isis backup coverage
Backup Coverage:
Topology        Level    Node     IPv4     IPv6    CLNS
IPV4 Unicast      2     55.56%   65.00%   0.00%   0.00%
```

The backup coverage is 55.56% for nodes, and 65.00% for IPv4 prefixes. Because you have a single loopback per node, it basically means five loopback prefixes—out of nine—have LFA backup coverage, whereas four do not. The next column shows backup coverage for all IS-IS prefixes (loopback prefixes + link prefixes). Table 18-3 summarizes LFA backup coverage for loopbacks on all routers with the current LFA feature set enabled.

Table 18-3. Backup coverage with per-prefix node-link-protection LFA

P1	P2	P3	P4	P5	P6	PE1	PE2	PE3	PE4
9	9	8	9	5	9	1	1	8	2
100%	100%	88.9%	100%	55.6%	100%	11.1%	11.1%	88.9%	22.2%

Out of ten routers, only four provide 100% backup coverage. Some of the routers provide backup coverage for a single loopback only. Let's look for destination nodes with no LFA backup next hop from P5.

Example 18-13. Node-specific LFA information on P5 (Junos)

```
1    juniper@P5> show isis backup spf results no-coverage | except item
2    (...)
3    P2.00
4      Primary next-hop: ge-2/0/3.0, IPV4, PE4, SNPA:  0:50:56:8b:4e:c8
5        Root: PE4, Root Metric: 100, Metric: 400, Root Preference: 0x0
6          Not eligible, IPV4, Reason: Primary next-hop link fate sharing
7        Root: P3, Root Metric: 100, Metric: 600, Root Preference: 0x0
8          Not eligible, IPV4, Reason: Path loops
9        Root: PE3, Root Metric: 500, Metric: 800, Root Preference: 0x0
10         Not eligible, IPV4, Reason: Primary next-hop node fate sharing
```

```
11      (...)
12          4 nodes
```

There is a lot of information here. The `no-coverage` keyword was used in the show output; thus, only backup SPF results for destination nodes with no backup coverage from P5 are displayed. They are P2 (lines 3 through 10), as well as P3, P4, and P6 (not listed for brevity). The primary next hop for P2 is PE4 via ge-2/0/3.0 interface (line 4).

For each destination node (in this example, P2), you can see the list of P5's neighbors. These neighbors are evaluated for potential backup next-hop function to reach P2 and thus used as the root of the SPF tree during backup SPF calculations. For every such neighbor, two metrics are displayed. For example, in line 5, `Root Metric` (100) is the metric from the PLR (P5) to the neighbor (PE4), and `Metric` (400) is the metric from the neighbor (PE4) to the destination (P2).

P5 cannot use the primary next hop node (PE4) as a backup next hop (lines 5 and 6), because it is already the primary next-hop node, and there is only a single direct link to the node; therefore, no other link could be used as backup. This is obvious.

P5 cannot use the P3 node as a backup next hop due to a loop (lines 7 and 8). The shortest path from P3 to P2 is via P5 (P3→P5→PE4→P2), so traffic eventually redirected to P3 would come back to P5.

Finally, P5 cannot use the PE3 node due to `primary next-hop node fate sharing`. What does that mean? It means that the shortest path from PE3 to P2 is via the primary next hop PE4 (PE3→PE4→P2); hence, the backup path from P5 to P2 via PE3 (and then via PE4) does not fulfill node protection criterion. Because with `node-link-protection` this criterion is verified and enforced, PE3 cannot be used as backup next hop. Similar analysis can be done for other nodes with no backup coverage.

Before implementing some enhancements in LFA to extend backup coverage, let's explore the Junos RIB and FIB structures (see Example 18-14), similar to what we did for IOS XR in Example 18-6 and Example 18-7.

Example 18-14. Routing table on P5 (Junos)

```
1    juniper@P5> show route protocol isis table inet.0 | find "/32"
2    172.16.0.1/32     *[IS-IS/18] 03:39:20, metric 600
3                       > to 10.0.0.14 via ge-2/0/4.0
4                         to 10.0.0.29 via ge-2/0/3.0
5    172.16.0.2/32     *[IS-IS/18] 00:23:49, metric 500
6                       > to 10.0.0.29 via ge-2/0/3.0
7    172.16.0.3/32     *[IS-IS/18] 03:39:20, metric 100
8                       > to 10.0.0.14 via ge-2/0/4.0
9    172.16.0.4/32     *[IS-IS/18] 03:39:20, metric 300
```

```
10                              > to 10.0.0.14 via ge-2/0/4.0
11       172.16.0.6/32          *[IS-IS/18] 00:23:49, metric 300
12                              > to 10.0.0.29 via ge-2/0/3.0
13       172.16.0.11/32         *[IS-IS/18] 03:39:20, metric 600
14                              > to 10.0.0.29 via ge-2/0/3.0
15                                to 10.0.0.14 via ge-2/0/4.0
16       172.16.0.22/32         *[IS-IS/18] 03:39:20, metric 550
17                              > to 10.0.0.29 via ge-2/0/3.0
18                                to 10.0.0.14 via ge-2/0/4.0
19       172.16.0.33/32         *[IS-IS/18] 03:39:20, metric 500
20                              > to 10.0.0.29 via ge-2/0/3.0
21                                to 10.0.0.25 via ge-2/0/2.0
22       172.16.0.44/32         *[IS-IS/18] 03:39:20, metric 100
23                              > to 10.0.0.29 via ge-2/0/3.0
24                                to 10.0.0.25 via ge-2/0/2.0
```

Some of the prefixes have only a single next hop, whereas some other prefixes—apparently covered by LFA backup—have two next hops. This is to be expected, because for these prefixes, LFA backup next hop is determined and installed. Furthermore the backup next hop for prefixes using the same primary next hop might be different (lines 17 and 18, versus 20 and 21). This confirms that the Junos implementation uses *per-prefix* (and not *per-link*) LFA style. Let's see the available next hops to reach PE2 from P5, by matching Figure 18-4 (IPv4 FECs are signaled with LDP) to Example 18-15.

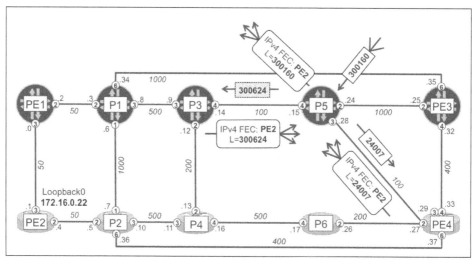

Figure 18-4. Per-prefix LFA protecting traffic from P5 to PE2

Example 18-15. IP/MPLS RIB/FIB entries with LFA backup on P5 (Junos)

```
juniper@P5> show route protocol isis table inet.0 172.16.0.22/32
            detail | match "Prefer|via|Metric"
```

```
*IS-IS    Preference: 18
          Next hop: 10.0.0.29 via ge-2/0/3.0 weight 0x1, selected
          Next hop: 10.0.0.14 via ge-2/0/4.0 weight 0xf000
          Age: 3:42:33   Metric: 550

juniper@P5> show route label 300160 detail | match <pattern>
*LDP      Preference: 9
          Next hop: 10.0.0.29 via ge-2/0/3.0 weight 0x1, selected
          Label operation: Swap 24007
          Next hop: 10.0.0.14 via ge-2/0/4.0 weight 0xf000
          Label operation: Swap 300624
          Age: 3:45:50   Metric: 550

juniper@P5> show route forwarding-table table default destination
            172.16.0.22/32 extensive | match <pattern>
Destination:  172.16.0.22/32
  Next-hop interface: ge-2/0/3.0    Weight: 0x1
  Next-hop interface: ge-2/0/4.0    Weight: 0xf000

juniper@P5> show route forwarding-table table default label 300160
            extensive | match "Dest|interface:|Weight|type"
Destination:  300160
  Next-hop type: Swap 24007         Index: 606   Reference: 1
  Next-hop interface: ge-2/0/3.0    Weight: 0x1
  Next-hop type: Swap 300624        Index: 590   Reference: 1
  Next-hop interface: ge-2/0/4.0    Weight: 0xf000
```

You can see that P3 is a valid backup next hop, because its shortest path to the destination is P3→P1→PE1→PE2 (metric 600), which does not go through P5.

The IP RIB/FIB as well as the MPLS RIB/FIB entries (label 300160 is locally assigned
to prefix 172.16.0.22/32) contain two next hops. The primary next hop has a weight
0x1, whereas the backup next hop has a weight 0xf000. In Junos, only next hops with
the numerically lowest value are actively used for traffic forwarding. If more next
hops have the same (low) value, load-balancing between next hops is performed.
Next hops with higher weight values are true backup next hops only. They are
installed in the FIB but are not used for traffic forwarding in the absence of failures.
When some failure happens, and the primary next hop is removed from the FIB, the
backup next hop is used. And again, if multiple backup next hops exist, the backup
next hop (or next hops) with the lowest weight value will be used for traffic
forwarding.

As observed on P5 (Example 18-13), node and link protection strategy caused some
inefficiency in terms of backup coverage. So let's try using only link protection and
verify backup coverage.

Example 18-16. Per-prefix link-protection LFA configuration (Junos)

```
groups {
    GR-ISIS {
        protocols {
            isis {
                interface "<*[es]*>" {
                    link-protection;
}}}}
```

Table 18-4 shows that on two nodes, backup LFA coverage increased: P5 (from 5 to 7) and PE3 (from 8 to 9). So, the design becomes better and better, but still only five nodes have LFA backup next hops for all loopback prefixes.

Table 18-4. Backup coverage with per-prefix link-protection LFA

P1	P2	P3	P4	P5	P6	PE1	PE2	PE3	PE4
9	9	8	9	**7**	9	1	1	**9**	2
100%	100%	88.9%	100%	**77.8%**	100%	11.1%	11.1%	**100%**	22.2%

Looking back at Example 18-13, it's clear that sometimes backup next hops were rejected due to potential loops. Changing from node and link protection style to link protection style doesn't help in this example, unfortunately, as potential loops remain. You need to deploy some more advanced LFA features to overcome this topology limitation.

But going back to link protection style, when configuring per-prefix link-protection LFA, it seems that you can increase the backup coverage. So, the legitimate question is: *What benefits can node-link protection bring?* Apart from providing a backup path that can protect against primary link and node failure, are there other benefits?

Let's check the forwarding state toward P2 loopback (172.16.0.2/32) on P5 and PE3, when the P1-P3 and P3-P4 links are temporarily disabled in order to slightly change the network topology (or, to simulate multiple failures in the network). The following two examples and Figure 18-5 assume that link (not node-link) protection is configured.

Example 18-17. FIB entry toward P2 loopback on P5 (Junos)

```
juniper@P5> show route forwarding-table table default
            destination 172.16.0.2/32
(...)
Destination    Type RtRef Next hop       Type Index    NhRef Netif
172.16.0.2/32  user    1                 ulst 1048596     15
                            10.0.0.29  ucst      586     29 ge-2/0/3.0
                            10.0.0.25  ucst      581     23 ge-2/0/2.0
```

Example 18-18. FIB entry toward P2 loopback on PE3 (Junos)

```
juniper@PE3> show route forwarding-table table default
             destination 172.16.0.2/32
Routing table: default.inet
Internet:
Destination    Type RtRef Next hop    Type Index    NhRef Netif
172.16.0.2/32  user    0              ulst 1048585   24
                           10.0.0.33  ucst    595    25 ge-2/0/4.0
                           10.0.0.24  ucst    542    26 ge-2/0/2.0
```

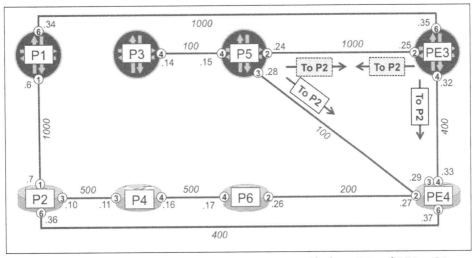

Figure 18-5. Per-prefix link-protection LFA protecting traffic from P5 and PE3 to P2 (potential microloop)

Both P5 and PE3 point to PE4 as the primary next hop. And both P5 and PE3 point to each other as backup next hops. Now, imagine PE4 fails. As discussed already, before global convergence happens, the primary next hop is removed and forwarding is based on the backup next hop. As a result, the FIB entry for 172.16.0.2/32 has the following next hops:

- At P5's FIB, the next hop is 10.0.0.25 (ge-2/0/2.0). In other words, PE3.
- At PE3's FIB, the next hop is 10.0.0.24 (ge-2/0/2.0). In other words, P5.

This is a loop! Both P5 and PE3 have only a single next hop, and they are pointing to each other. Until global convergence happens, which replaces old next hops with newly calculated next hops, there is indeed a loop. You may well ask how is this possible? The technology under discussion is called *Loop-Free* Alternates.

This kind of loop in LFA is called a *microloop*. In this particular case, LFA backup next hop protects only against a single P5-PE4 link failure, but not against PE4's node failure. For single link failure, LFA with link-protection is loop free. However, if the failure is bigger than expected (for example multiple link failures or node failure), then micro-loops might occur if LFA had computed only link-protection backup next hop. This was recognized very early in the LFA development stage (RFC 5286, Section 1.1).

On the other hand, node protection LFA (if available) completely eliminates any chance of micro-loops during multiple link (connected to the same node) failures, at least in those basic LFA deployments where we do not impose any additional path restrictions (like SLRG). Thus, the preferred LFA deployment strategy is to use backup next hops that satisfy node protection criterion (to eliminate microloops), and use backup next hops that satisfy the link protection criterion only as last resort. This logic is implemented by default in IOS XR, whereas in Junos you need to pay extra attention to implement such logic. It is called *node-link-degradation*.

Example 18-19. Node-link protection with link degradation LFA (Junos)

```
groups {
    GR-ISIS {
        protocols {
            isis {
                interface "<*[es]*>" {
                    node-link-protection;
}}}}}
protocols {
    isis {
        apply-groups GR-ISIS;
        backup-spf-options node-link-degradation;
}}
```

LFA backup coverage in Table 18-4 will not change regardless of whether node-link protection with degradation or only link protection is configured. But you gain the benefits of next hops that satisfy node protection requirements (if possible) as well as next hops that otherwise satisfy only link protection requirements. On the other hand, node protection backup paths are typically longer, causing more latency for rerouted traffic during the time the protection is active. However, this typically lasts for a short period of time (few 100 ms up to few seconds in very large networks) until global IGP convergence installs new optimized paths. Before starting the discussion about techniques that can be used to extend LFA backup coverage (remember that in both IOS XR and Junos planes, the LFA backup coverage was still below 100% on some routers), let's review another difference between default IOS XR and Junos LFA implementations. Let's temporarily use a slightly different topology, as illustrated in Figure 18-6.

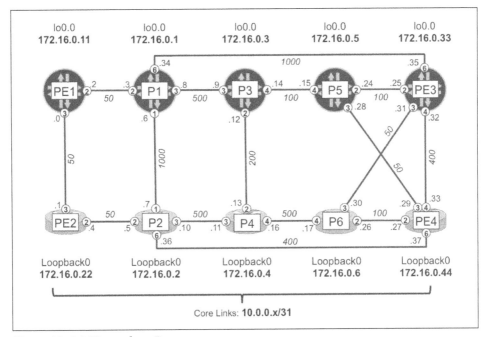

Figure 18-6. LFA topology B

Now, when you check reachability of the PE3-PE4 link prefix on P5 and P6 (see Example 18-20), you will be surprised to find some inconsistency, although P5 and P6 connectivity to PE3 and PE4 is fully symmetrical. In all of the previous cases, loopback prefixes were used to investigate LFA behavior. Loopbacks are injected into the IGP domain by a single router, whereas link prefixes are injected by two routers.

Example 18-20. RIB entry for PE3-PE4 link prefix on P5 and P6

```
juniper@P5> show route 10.0.0.32/31
(...)
10.0.0.32/31       *[IS-IS/18] 00:03:37, metric 450
                    > to 10.0.0.29 via ge-2/0/3.0

RP/0/0/CPU0:P6#show route isis
(...)
i L2 10.0.0.32/31 [115/450] via 10.0.0.31, 00:03:48, Gi0/0/0/3
                  [115/0] via 10.0.0.27, 00:03:48, Gi0/0/0/2 (!)
(...)
```

Whereas P6 (IOS XR) has primary and backup next hops, P5 (Junos) has only a primary next hop; the backup next hop is missing. On P5, the primary next-hop is PE4, so let's see if there is any specific information in the backup SPF results for PE4.

Example 18-21. Backup SPF results for PE4 on P3 (Junos)

```
juniper@P5> show isis backup spf results PE4 | match <pattern>
  Primary next-hop: ge-2/0/3.0, IPV4, PE4, SNPA:  0:50:56:8b:4e:c8
    Root: PE4, Root Metric: 50, Metric: 0, Root Preference: 0x0
      Not eligible, IPV4, Reason: Primary next-hop link fate sharing
    Root: P3, Root Metric: 100, Metric: 150, Root Preference: 0x0
      Not eligible, IPV4, Reason: Path loops
    Root: PE3, Root Metric: 100, Metric: 150, Root Preference: 0x0
      Not eligible, IPV4, Reason: Path loops
```

Neither of P5's neighbors is eligible to be the backup next hop toward PE4. Why is PE3 not considered as a backup next hop? From the perspective of P5, the 10.0.0.32/31 prefix has PE4 as its best originator, therefore that prefix somehow belongs to PE4. Looking at the topology and link metrics, all of P5's neighbors will forward traffic destined for the PE4 node back via P5, causing a loop. So, what is the difference on P6? Let's see.

Example 18-22. Backup SPF results for PE4 on P6 (IOS XR)

```
RP/0/0/CPU0:P6#show isis fast-reroute 10.0.0.32/31 detail
L2 10.0.0.32/31 [450/115] low priority
    via 10.0.0.31, Gi0/0/0/3, PE3, Weight: 0
      FRR backup via 10.0.0.27, Gi0/0/0/2, PE4, Weight: 0
      P: No, TM: 500, LC: No, NP: Yes, D: Yes, SRLG: Yes
    src PE3.00-00, 172.16.0.33
```

As you can see, P6 calculated the backup next hop, which fulfills node protection criterion. It actually means, P6 calculated a backup path that completely avoids the primary next hop PE3; in other words, to reach PE4 as a final destination, and not to reach PE3 (primary next hop) as a final destination. From P6's perspective, PE3 is the *best originator*, whereas PE4 is the *non-best originator* of the 10.0.0.32/31 prefix, and P6 allows redirection to the non-best originator.

In Junos, by default, only the best originator is taken into account for LFA backup next-hop calculations. Thus, P5 tries to find loop-free backup next hops to reach PE4 (best originator) and does not consider the path destined to PE3 (non-best originator) as a possible backup. You can change this default behavior with the following extra configuration knob, to conform with RFC 5286, Section 6.1.

Example 18-23. Enabling non-best originator evaluation (Junos)

```
protocols {
    isis {
        backup-spf-options per-prefix-calculation;
}}
```

The terms used in the configuration knob might be a little misleading. The Junos LFA flavor is per-prefix by default (without any extra configuration), as already verified (Example 18-14)—this knob simply enables calculation of backup next hops for non-best prefix originators.

The following check confirms that after enabling the knob, the backup next hop is properly determined.

Example 18-24. RIB entry for PE3-PE4 link prefix on P3 (Junos)

```
juniper@P5> show route 10.0.0.32/31
(...)
10.0.0.32/31      *[IS-IS/18] 00:01:03, metric 450
                  > to 10.0.0.29 via ge-2/0/3.0
                    to 10.0.0.25 via ge-2/0/2.0
```

Ensuring proper LFA functionality for link prefixes is usually not crucial, because loopback prefixes (not link prefixes) are typically used as next hops for MPLS services (L2VPN, L3VPN, etc.). Proper LFA functionality for prefixes originated by multiple nodes is more important in multiarea deployments, where ABRs redistribute prefixes between adjacent areas. Typically, multiple ABRs are used for redundancy, so prefixes (loopbacks) from another IGP area are originated by multiple ABRs.

Another example is the *anycast* type of architectures. In such architectures, multiple nodes advertise the same *virtual* loopback prefix, which is used as a next hop for VPN services. Chapter 21 presents some examples for such a deployment.

The next sections are based on LFA Topology A (Figure 18-2).

The following LFA sections in this chapter provide incremental configurations. Except where stated otherwise, each section relies on the configuration applied on previous sections.

Extending LFA Backup Coverage

As you discovered from the previous section, native LFA (per-prefix LFA, but especially per-link LFA) does not guarantee 100% backup coverage. The backup coverage is mainly dependent on the link metric costs and overall network topology. Thus, some extensions to native LFA are required to increase—possibly up to 100% in any arbitrary network topology—the backup coverage. Methods to extend the backup LFA coverage include the following architectures:

- LFA with LDP ackup unnels (Remote LFA)

- LFA with RSVP-TE backup tunnels (Topology-Independent Fast ReRoute [TI-FRR])
- LFA with SPRING backup tunnels (Topology-Independent LFA [TI-LFA])

LFA with LDP Backup Tunnels (Remote LFA)

Remote LFA (RLFA) for link protection is specified in RFC 7490. RLFA for node protection is described in *draft-ietf-rtgwg-rlfa-node-protection*. This section assumes that RFC 7490 (and not the node protection draft) is implemented.

RLFA theory of operation

RLFA introduces the concepts of *P-space*, *Q-space*, and *PQ-node* (see Figure 18-7), which must be interpreted in the context of a given PLR and a given protected link:

P-space

This is a set of routers reachable *from* a PLR router (denoted S) using a shortest path and without traversing the protected link. In the case of ECMP, this requirement applies to all the equal-cost shortest paths from S to a node in the P-space. None of these paths can traverse the protected link; otherwise, the node is not in the P-space.

Q-space

This is a set of routers that can reach the primary next hop (denoted E) using a shortest path and without traversing the protected link. In the case of ECMP, this requirement applies to all the equal-cost shortest paths from a node in the Q-space to E. In Q-space calculation, only the primary next hop node, but not the actual destination node, is taken into account. Calculating the Q-space for every destination node would, in the worst case, require an SPF computation rooted on many nodes for each destination, which would be nonscalable in large networks. Therefore, the Q-space of E is used as a proxy for the Q-space of each destination. Conceptually, this is closer to per-link LFA, rather than per-prefix LFA.

PQ-node

This is a node that is a member of both the P-space and the Q-space. Remote LFA uses a PQ-node as a remote backup neighbor and terminates the repair tunnel on the PQ-node. The PQ-node does not need to be directly connected to S (or to E).

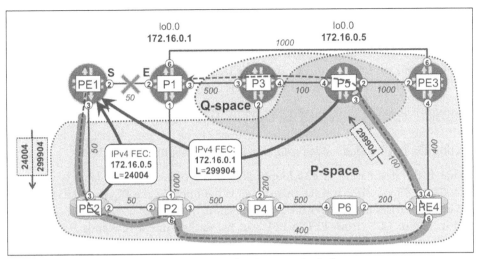

Figure 18-7. Remote LFA P- and Q-spaces for the PE1→P1 link

In the example topology, the PE1→P1 link is not protected with basic LFA. PE2, the only potential backup neighbor of PE1, uses PE1 as the next hop to reach P1, so no loop-free backup next hop is available.

Now, based on RLFA principles, almost all remaining routers (with the exception of the P3 router) belong to P-space. PE1 can reach these routers over the shortest path without crossing the PE1→P1 link. On the other hand, in this particular topology, only P3 and P5 belong to Q-space. Only P3 and P5 can reach P1 over the shortest path without crossing the PE1→P1 link. They will use the P3→P1 link to reach P1.

RLFA functions as follows: PE1 first sends the traffic to some PQ-node (only P5 in the example belongs to both P-space and Q-space). Traffic sent to the PQ-node does not traverse protected links, because this is the definition of P-space. Next, the PQ-node sends the traffic to the destination. Again, based on the definition of Q-space, this traffic does not traverse the protected link.

How does PE1 send packets to destination P1? Simply forwarding packets destined to P1 in the direction of PE2 would cause a loop, because the shortest path from PE2 to P1 is via PE1. Thus, the final destination (P1) of the packet must be invisible to PE2.

To achieve this, PE1 automatically establishes a targeted multihop LDP session to the PQ-node (P5). Over this LDP session, the PQ-Node (P5) sends IPv4 FECs, including the FEC for P1 loopback (172.16.0.1/32). Now, PE1 is able to construct the following label stack for the packets redirected via the PE1→PE2 link toward the PQ-Node.

- In this example, the outer label is 24004. The backup neighbor (PE2) maps it to P5's loopback and advertises it to PE1 over the standard LDP session. (In theory, other MPLS transport flavors might be supported, but that's beyond the scope of this book's tests.) Thanks to this outer label, which is locally significant to PE2, packets can travel from PE1 to P5.

- In this example, the inner label is 299904. The PQ-node (P5) maps it to P1's loopback and advertises it to PE1 over the T-LDP session. Thanks to this inner label, which is locally significant to P5, packets can travel from P5 to P1.

This label stack allows steering the traffic as demonstrated in Figure 18-7, with PHP at PE4 and P3. Because the destination happens to be the E-node (P1), only link protection can be provided; node protection does not even make sense here.

What if the destination is P3's loopback? In this case, the outer label is the same (24004, to P5 via PE2) and the inner label is the one that the PQ-node (P5) maps to P3 and advertises to PE1 over the T-LDP session. The tunnel is exactly the one depicted in Figure 18-7 (from PE1 to P5), and the dashed-line arrow ends at P3. In this case, traffic from the PQ-node (P5) to the final destination does not traverse the E-node (P1). Said differently, node protection is achieved. This is actually a coincidence. In other topologies, traffic from the PQ-node to the final destination may traverse the E-node.

For example, if the destination is PE3's loopback and you temporarily increase the metrics of the P5-PE3 and PE3-PE4 links to 8000, the shortest path from PE1 to reach PE3 is PE1→P1→PE3. The shortest path from the PQ-node (P5) to the destination (PE3) is P5→P3→P1→PE3. In case of P1 node failure, there would be traffic loss until the PQ-node is informed about P1's failure.

In this example, RLFA provides protection for the PE1→P1 link failure. This is a step forward with respect to basic LFA.

RLFA configuration

Now, after discussing the RLFA theory of operation, let's turn to the configuration for both Junos and IOS XR planes, respectively.

Example 18-25. RLFA configuration (Junos)

```
1    protocols {
2        isis {
3            backup-spf-options remote-backup-calculation;
4        }
5        ldp {
6            interface lo0.0;
7            auto-targeted-session;
8    }}
```

Example 18-26. RLFA configuration (IOS XR)

```
1     group GR-ISIS
2      router isis '.*'
3       interface 'GigabitEthernet.*'
4        address-family ipv4 unicast
5         fast-reroute per-prefix level 2
6         fast-reroute per-prefix remote-lfa tunnel mpls-ldp level 2
7      end-group
8     !
9     router isis core
10     apply-group GR-ISIS
11    !
12    mpls ldp
13     address-family ipv4
14      discovery targeted-hello accept
15    !
```

In both cases (Junos and IOS XR), you simply enable RLFA functionality with a keyword (Example 18-25, line 3; Example 18-26, line 6). You also need to ensure that local initiation and acceptance of remotely initiated targeted LDP sessions is enabled. Additionally, if filtering of IPv4 FECs is applied to targeted LDP sessions (as briefly discussed in Chapter 2, Chapter 3, and Chapter 4), these filters need to be removed now.

RLFA in action

RFC 7490 doesn't specify the way to determine the IP address of the remote LFA repair target, referring to it as "out of scope for this document". This caused some small interoperability problems between Junos and IOS XR. Namely, IOS XR determined the IPv4 address used to establish the targeted LDP (TLDP) session using IS-IS TLV 134 (*TE Router ID*), and if not available, the highest /32 prefix advertised via TLV 128 or TLV 135 (*IP Reachability* or *Extended IP Reachability*). Conversely, Junos determined the IPv4 address from IS-IS TLV 134 exclusively. Although TLV 128/135 is included by default in both Junos and IOS XR implementations, TLV 134 is advertised by default in Junos implementation only. This resulted in Junos routers that were not able to establish TLDP sessions to IOS XR routers. As a workaround, enabling full TE database announcements on IOS XR routers was required (see Chapter 2 and Chapter 13 for the exact TE configuration).

OK, after the configuration is done, take a look at Table 18-5 to check the backup coverage again.

Table 18-5. Backup coverage with remote LFA

P1	P2	P3	P4	P5	P6	PE1	PE2	PE3	PE4
9	9	9	9	9	9	9	3	9	8
100%	100%	**100%**	100%	**100%**	100%	**100%**	33.3%	100%	**88.9%**

It's very close to achieving a final design. If you compare Table 18-5 (which shows the current LFA backup coverage) with Table 18-4, you see a considerable increase. This confirms RLFA is useful in increasing backup coverage. However, this also confirms RLFA is still topology dependent because two routers (PE2 and PE4) still do not provide full backup coverage. Later, we'll cover more advanced techniques to finally achieve full backup coverage. But for now, let's verify the routing states.

Example 18-27. RIB/LFA entry toward P1 loopback on PE1 (Junos)

```
juniper@PE1> show isis backup spf results P1 | match <pattern>
   Primary next-hop: ge-2/0/2.0, IPV4, P1, SNPA:  0:50:56:8b:8:f
      Root: P1, Root Metric: 50, Metric: 0, Root Preference: 0x0
        Not eligible, IPV4, Reason: Primary next-hop link fate sharing
      Root: PE2, Root Metric: 50, Metric: 100, Root Preference: 0x0
        Not eligible, IPV4, Reason: Path loops
      Root: P5, Root Metric: 600, Metric: 600, Root Preference: 0x0
         Eligible, Backup next-hop: ge-2/0/3.0, LSP, LDP->P5(172.16.0.5)

juniper@PE1> show isis route 172.16.0.1/32
(...)
Prefix          L Version Metric Interface   NH   Via
172.16.0.1/32 2    1107      50 ge-2/0/2.0  IPV4 P1
                                ge-2/0/3.0  LSP  LDP->P5(172.16.0.5)

juniper@PE1> show route table inet.3 172.16.0.1/32
(...)
172.16.0.1/32 *[LDP/9] 05:17:38, metric 50
          > to 10.0.0.3 via ge-2/0/2.0
            to 10.0.0.1 via ge-2/0/3.0, Push 299904, Push 24004(top)
```

Perfect! You can see that next-hop type for backup next hop is a LDP-based LSP pointing toward P5. Furthermore, the label stack with two labels is associated with the backup next hop. And the verification of received IPv4 FECs confirms that the top label provides reachability to P5 (PQ-node) through PE2 (direct backup next hop), whereas the bottom label provides reachability to P1 (final destination) from P5 (PQ-node).

Example 18-28. IPv4 FECs received on PE1 (Junos)

```
juniper@PE1> show ldp database session 172.16.0.22 | match "Inp|24004"
Input label database, 172.16.0.11:0--172.16.0.22:0
  24004     172.16.0.5/32

juniper@PE1> show ldp database session 172.16.0.5 | match "Inp|299904"
Input label database, 172.16.0.11:0--172.16.0.5:0
 299904     172.16.0.1/32
```

With such a trick, RLFA tunnels the traffic destined for P1 toward P5 through PE2. PE2 looks only at the outer label and politely forwards the traffic to P5. The loop doesn't occur.

After checking the RLFA operation on a Junos device, let's verify it on an IOS XR device. As an example let's have a closer look at the backup for PE2→PE1 link. P-space and Q-space for this case are presented in Figure 18-8.

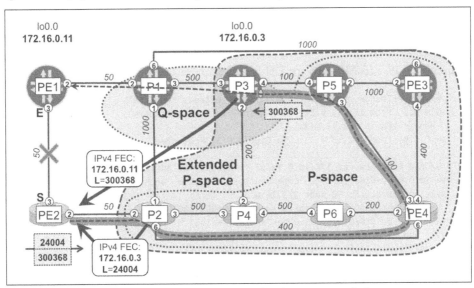

Figure 18-8. Remote LFA P-spaces and Q-space for the PE2→PE1 link

As you can see, there is no overlap between P and Q-space, so no PQ-node. However, even in such situations, there might be cases for which RLFA functionality could still be achieved. When checking protection for the PE2→PE1 link (see the example that follows), you can discover that traffic will be redirected through the LDP tunnel terminated on P3, but going via Gi0/0/0/2 (P2), which is not on the shortest path from PE2 to P3.

Example 18-29. Backup SPF results for PE1 on PE2 (IOS XR)

```
1    RP/0/0/CPU0:PE2#show isis fast-reroute 172.16.0.11/32 detail
2    L2 172.16.0.11/32 [50/115] medium priority
3       via 10.0.0.0, Gi0/0/0/3, PE1, Weight: 0
4        Remote FRR backup via P3 [172.16.0.3], via 10.0.0.5, Gi0/0/0/2 P2
5        P: No, TM: 650, LC: No, NP: No, D: No, SRLG: Yes
6       src PE1.00-00, 172.16.0.11
```

How is this possible? Let's document the trick. PE2 receives IPv4 FECs for P3 loopback (172.16.0.3) from both direct neighbors (PE1 and P2). The shortest path from PE2 to P3 is via PE1 (PE2→PE1→P1→P3, cost 600). So normally, PE2 will send traffic to P3 via PE1, and that is the reason why P3 is not in the P-space. But what about sending the traffic destined to P3 via P2? No loop! The shortest path from P2 to P3 is via P2→P4→P5→P3 (cost 600). Thus, to protect the PE2→PE1 link, PE2 can redirect the traffic via P2, using a standard RLFA label stack (top label: P3; bottom label: PE1). This time, of course, the labels for P3's and PE1's loopbacks are allocated by P2 (direct LDP session) and P3 (targeted LDP session), respectively. And here is what actually happens.

Example 18-30. RIB/FIB entry for PE1 loopback on PE2 (IOS XR)

```
RP/0/0/CPU0:PE2#show route 172.16.0.11/32 | include "from|LFA"
    10.0.0.5, from 172.16.0.11, via Gi0/0/0/2, Backup (remote)
      Remote LFA is 172.16.0.3
    10.0.0.0, from 172.16.0.11, via Gig0/0/0/3, Protected

RP/0/0/CPU0:PE2#show cef 172.16.0.11/32 | include "weight|hop|label"
  via 10.0.0.5, Gi0/0/0/2, 10 dependencies, weight 0, backup
  next hop 10.0.0.5, PQ-node 172.16.0.3
    local label 24001       labels imposed {24004 300368}
  via 10.0.0.0, Gi0/0/0/3, 10 dependencies, weight 0, protected
  next hop 10.0.0.0
    local label 24001       labels imposed {ImplNull}
```

If you're reading this correctly, how can PE2 determine which node it should use to redirect the traffic and terminate the RLFA LDP tunnel? Well, here the RLFA RFC introduces the concept of *Extended P-space*:

Extended P-space

   The union of P-space computed for PLR router (denoted *S*) as well as P-spaces computed for each direct neighbor of *S*, excluding primary next-hop router (denoted *E*). Calculations based on extended P-space are supported by default in IOS XR and Junos.

Thus, in the example topology, you need to check what P-space is computed from P2's point of view, as well. P2's P-space contains all routers with the exception of PE1 and P1. It means P2 can reach all routers (except PE1 and P1) through the shortest path without crossing the PE2→PE1 link. Consequently, P-space is extended with one additional router: P3 (including PE2, the PLR, in the extended P-space does not make sense from the RLFA perspective). P3 belongs to Q-space, fortunately, so it can be used as a PQ-node to terminate the RLFA tunnel.

 Going back to Example 18-29, it's worth mentioning the redefinition of total metric (TM) field. In the case of RLFA, TM means the actual total cost to the PQ-node, not to the destination.

RLFA with RSVP-TE Backup Tunnels

You have seen a lot of configurations already. You have gone through per-link protection, per-prefix protection with various options (node and link protection, link protection, node protection with link protection as fallback), and lastly, remote LFA. All these efforts, although successively increasing LFA backup coverage, did not provide you with the ultimate solution: full backup coverage on all routers. To make things more challenging, you will work on a slightly modified topology now (see Figure 18-9)—without the P2-PE4 direct link—that misses some backup coverage (even with RLFA) for both Junos and IOS XR planes. The following technique takes packets to a Q-node through a non-shortest path, hence extending the effective coverage to 100% (see Table 18-6).

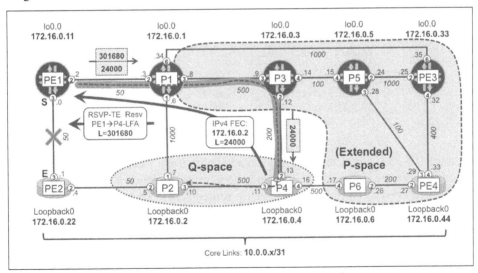

Figure 18-9. LFA topology C—RLFA with RSVP-TE LSP tunnel

Table 18-6. Backup coverage with remote LFA in topology C

P1	P2	P3	P4	P5	P6	PE1	PE2	PE3	PE4
9	9	9	9	9	9	0	3	9	9
100%	100%	100%	100%	100%	100%	0%	33.3%	100%	100%

Unfortunately, as you can see in Figure 18-9, the (extended) P-space and Q-space do not share any common node for the PE1→PE2 link. Consequently, standard LDP-based RLFA does not protect the PE1→PE2 link.

What do you do in such a scenario? You could establish an explicitly (not dynamically) routed tunnel to one of the Q nodes (P2 or P4). Because the tunnel is established via the explicit path from source node (PE1) to Q node (e.g., P4), if you configure the path correctly, there is no loop possibility here. The explicit path must be defined to omit the PE1→PE2 link. LDP does not support explicitly routed tunnels, thus your choice is RSVP-TE (or, *in theory*, SPRING-TE, when available). So, let's configure it! See Example 18-31.

Example 18-31. RLFA configuration with manual RSVP-TE backup (Junos)

```
1     protocols {
2         mpls {
3             label-switched-path PE1-->P4-LFA {
4                 backup;
5                 to 172.16.0.4;
6                 ldp-tunneling;
7                 preference 10;
8                 primary PE1-P1-P3-P4;
9             }
10            path PE1-P1-P3-P4 {
11                10.0.0.3 strict;           ## P1
12                10.0.0.9 strict;           ## P3
13                10.0.0.13 strict;          ## P4
14    }}}
```

Example 18-31 assumes that RLFA is already configured. In addition to enabling TE extensions on the IGP, and RSVP-TE on the interfaces, (which is discussed in Chapter 2), you need to configure an explicitly routed RSVP-TE tunnel to reach the Q-node. Additionally, you must allow the use of this tunnel as a backup tunnel (line 4) in the remote LFA architecture. To prevent the use of this tunnel for normal traffic forwarding, we recommend that you change the route preference to be numerically higher than LDP (line 7) so that the tunnel is less preferred than LDP.

A quick verification, by matching Example 18-32 to Figure 18-9, confirms proper operation. The backup RSVP-TE tunnel is established and LFA uses it as backup next hop toward the loopbacks of three nodes (P2, P4 and PE2). For brevity, the following example shows one destination (P2):

Example 18-32. States for RLFA with manual RSVP-TE backup tunnel (Junos)

```
juniper@PE1> show mpls lsp ingress detail | match <pattern>
From: 172.16.0.11, State: Up, ActiveRoute: 0, LSPname: PE1-->P4-LFA
ActivePath: PE1-P1-P3-P4 (primary)
LSPtype: Static Configured, Penultimate hop popping
 Computed ERO (S [L] denotes strict [loose] hops): (CSPF metric: 750)
 10.0.0.3 S 10.0.0.9 S 10.0.0.13 S
 Received RRO (ProtectionFlag 1=Available 2=InUse 4=B/W 8=Node
              10=SoftPreempt 20=Node-ID):
        10.0.0.3 10.0.0.9 10.0.0.13

juniper@PE1> show route table inet.3 172.16.0.2/32 detail
[...]*LDP    Preference: 9
            Next hop: 10.0.0.1 via ge-2/0/3.0 weight 0x1, selected
            Label operation: Push 24000
            Next hop: 10.0.0.3 via ge-2/0/2.0 weight 0x100
            Label-switched-path PE1-->P4-LFA
            Label operation: Push 24000, Push 301680(top)
            Age: 6:19:29    Metric: 100

juniper@PE1> show isis backup spf results P2 | except item
(...)
P2.00
  Primary next-hop: ge-2/0/3.0, IPV4, PE2, SNPA:  0:50:56:8b:b3:48
    Root: P4, Root Metric: 600, Metric: 500, Root Preference: 0x0
      Eligible, Backup next-hop: ge-2/0/2.0, LSP, PE1-->P4-LFA
    Root: PE2, Root Metric: 50, Metric: 50, Root Preference: 0x0
      Not eligible, IPV4, Reason: Interface is already covered
    Root: P1, Root Metric: 50, Metric: 150, Root Preference: 0x0
      Not eligible, IPV4, Reason: Interface is already covered
  1 nodes
```

Similar to the standard LFA case, the backup next hop has a numerically higher weight (this time it is 0x100), and a two-label stack (301680 is the top label to reach the Q-node via the RSVP-TE tunnel, and 24000 is the bottom label to reach the final destination from the Q-node via LDP) is used. Due to PHP, these labels are popped at P3 and P4, respectively.

After investigating the Junos plane, let's do the same for the IOS XR plane. You can make a detailed analysis again about P- or Q-space for PE2→PE1. But this time let's simply create backup RSVP-TE tunnels using the PE2→P2→P1→PE1 path to avoid the PE2→PE1 link. Again, in addition to the following configuration, you obviously must enable RSVP-TE itself (not shown for brevity):

Example 18-33. RLFA Configuration with manual RSVP-TE backup tunnel (IOS XR)

```
group GR-ISIS            ! This group is applied to isis (not shown)
 router isis '.*'
  interface 'GigabitEthernet.*'
```

```
    address-family ipv4 unicast
     fast-reroute per-prefix level 2
     fast-reroute per-prefix lfa-candidate interface tunnel-te11 level 2
     fast-reroute per-prefix remote-lfa tunnel mpls-ldp level 2
 end-group
 !
 group GR-LSP-LFA
  interface 'tunnel-te.*'
   ipv4 unnumbered Loopback0
   record-route
 end-group
 !
 explicit-path name PE2-P2-P1-PE1
  index 10 next-address strict ipv4 unicast 10.0.0.5
  index 20 next-address strict ipv4 unicast 10.0.0.6
  index 30 next-address strict ipv4 unicast 10.0.0.2
  !
 interface tunnel-te11
  apply-group GR-LSP-LFA
  signalled-name PE2-->PE1-LFA
  destination 172.16.0.11
  path-option 1 explicit name PE2-P2-P1-PE1

 mpls ldp
  interface tunnel-te11
   address-family ipv4
```

The following verification confirms that everything works as expected:

Example 18-34. RLFA states with manual RSVP-TE backup tunnel (IOS XR)

```
RP/0/0/CPU0:PE2#show mpls traffic-eng tunnels | include <pattern>
Name: tunnel-te11  Destination: 172.16.0.11  Ifhandle:0xb80
   Signalled-Name: PE2-->PE1-LFA
     Admin:    up Oper:   up   Path:  valid   Signalling: connected
     path option 1,   type explicit PE2-P2-P1-PE1
                     (Basis for Setup, path weight 1100)

RP/0/0/CPU0:PE2#show route isis | begin /32
i L2 172.16.0.1/32 [115/0] via 172.16.0.11, tunnel-te11 (!)
                   [115/100] via 10.0.0.0, Gi0/0/0/3
i L2 172.16.0.2/32 [115/0] via 10.0.0.0, Gi0/0/0/3 (!)
                   [115/50] via 10.0.0.5, Gi0/0/0/2
i L2 172.16.0.3/32 [115/0] via 172.16.0.11, tunnel-te11 (!)
                   [115/600] via 10.0.0.0, Gi0/0/0/3
i L2 172.16.0.4/32 [115/0] via 10.0.0.0, Gi0/0/0/3 (!)
                   [115/550] via 10.0.0.5, Gi0/0/0/2
i L2 172.16.0.5/32 [115/0] via 172.16.0.11, tunnel-te11 (!)
                   [115/700] via 10.0.0.0, Gi0/0/0/3
i L2 172.16.0.6/32 [115/1000] via 10.0.0.0, Gi0/0/0/3
                   [115/0] via 10.0.0.5, Gi0/0/0/2 (!)
i L2 172.16.0.11/32 [115/0] via 172.16.0.11, tunnel-te11 (!)
```

```
                      [115/50] via 10.0.0.0, Gi0/0/0/3
i L2 172.16.0.33/32 [115/0] via 172.16.0.11, tunnel-te11 (!)
                      [115/1100] via 10.0.0.0, Gi0/0/0/3
i L2 172.16.0.44/32 [115/0] via 172.16.0.11, tunnel-te11 (!)
                      [115/800] via 10.0.0.0, Gi0/0/0/3

RP/0/0/CPU0:PE2#show isis fast-reroute 172.16.0.1/32
L2 172.16.0.1/32 [100/115] medium priority
    via 10.0.0.0, Gi0/0/0/3, PE1, Weight: 0
      FRR backup via 172.16.0.11, tunnel-te11, PE1, Weight: 0
    src P1.00-00, 172.16.0.1
```

It appears, by combining RLFA with the single RSVP-TE tunnel just created, that we've increased the backup coverage to 100 percent on PE2! (Refer back to Table 18-6 for the backup coverage without RSVP-TE tunnel.) However, backup forwarding might be suboptimal in some cases. For example, the LFA backup path to reach P1 loopback from PE2 is PE2→P2→*P1*→PE1→*P1*. First four hops (up to PE1) uses forwarding via RSVP-TE backup tunnel, and the last hop uses forwarding via plain LDP. P1 is visited twice, which is certainly not optimal.

Before moving on to the next LFA flavor, keep in mind the following characteristics of the "RLFA with RSVP-TE Backup Tunnels" on page 703 models that we have just discussed:

- It is an extension of classic RLFA, which only considered LDP backup tunnels, and was originally conceived to provide link protection. In some cases (look back at Figure 18-8), node protection is coincidentally achieved, but that requirement is only considered if node-link-protection is configured and *draft-ietf-rtgwg-rlfa-node-protection* is implemented.
- If protection can be achieved with classic RLFA (without RSVP-TE backup tunnels), then RSVP-TE tunnels, even if configured, are not used.

Neither of these two bullet points hold true in the context of the technology that we'll look at next.

Topology Independent Fast ReRoute

By introducing additional backup RSVP-TE tunnels (for example, a tunnel originated at PE2 and terminated on P1), you could achieve more optimal forwarding over backup paths. However, in complex network topologies, determining and manually configuring backup RSVP-TE tunnels might be a challenging task. Thus, Junos offers an option for automatic creation of RSVP-TE tunnels used for LFA backups: *Topology-Independent Fast ReRoute (TI-FRR)*, which is based on *draft-esale-ldp-node-frr*.

As of this writing, IOS XR doesn't support *TI-FRR*. However, IOS XR already supports *Topology-Independent LFA* (*TI-LFA*), which is based on SPRING tunnels instead of RSVP-TE bypass tunnels. TI-LFA is discussed later in this chapter.

Junos offers two options for automatic bypass RSVP-TE tunnels: tunnels fulfilling link-protection criterion, or tunnels fulfilling node-protection criterion, with fallback to link-protection criterion in case a node-protection tunnel is not possible. Obviously, to provide backup coverage against both node and link failures, we recommend node-link protection bypass RSVP-TE tunnels. So, let's add node and link-protection tunnels to all the routers in the Junos plane. Following is an example for PE1:

Example 18-35. LFA configuration with dynamic RSVP-TE bypass — PE1 (Junos)

```
protocols {
    ldp {
        auto-targeted-session;
        interface lo0.0;
        interface ge-2/0/2.0 {
            node-link-protection {        ## or 'link-protection'
                dynamic-rsvp-lsp;
            }
        }
        interface ge-2/0/3.0 {
            node-link-protection {        ## or 'link-protection'
                dynamic-rsvp-lsp;
}}}}
```

Let's verify the proper operation. For brevity, the example that follows first shows all of the dynamic LSPs originated at the source node (PE1), but it later focuses on one destination node (P3) only. The protected link is PE1→P1, and the protected next-hop node is P1.

Example 18-36. States for MPLS LFA with dynamic RSVP-TE backup tunnel (Junos)

```
1    juniper@PE1> show mpls lsp ingress
2    To          From         LSPname
3    172.16.0.1  172.16.0.11  ge-2/0/2.0:BypassLSP->172.16.0.1
4    172.16.0.2  172.16.0.11  Pnode:172.16.0.1:BypassLSP->172.16.0.2
5    172.16.0.2  172.16.0.11  Pnode:172.16.0.22:BypassLSP->172.16.0.2
6    172.16.0.3  172.16.0.11  Pnode:172.16.0.1:BypassLSP->172.16.0.3
7    172.16.0.22 172.16.0.11  ge-2/0/3.0:BypassLSP->172.16.0.22
8    172.16.0.33 172.16.0.11  Pnode:172.16.0.1:BypassLSP->172.16.0.33
9
10   juniper@PE1> show mpls lsp ingress detail | match <pattern>
11   172.16.0.1
12     From: 172.16.0.11, State: Up, ActiveRoute: 0,
13                     LSPname: ge-2/0/2.0:BypassLSP->172.16.0.1
```

```
14    ActivePath:  (primary)
15    LSPtype: Dynamic Configured, Penultimate hop popping
16     Computed ERO (S [L] denotes strict [loose]): (CSPF metric: 1100)
17    10.0.0.1 S 10.0.0.5 S 10.0.0.6 S
18      Received RRO:
19            10.0.0.1 10.0.0.5 10.0.0.6
20    (...)
21    172.16.0.3
22     From: 172.16.0.11, State: Up, ActiveRoute: 0,
23                    LSPname: Pnode:172.16.0.1:BypassLSP->172.16.0.3
24     ActivePath:  (primary)
25     LSPtype: Dynamic Configured, Penultimate hop popping
26      Computed ERO (S [L] denotes strict [loose] hops): (CSPF metric: 100)
27     10.0.0.1 S 10.0.0.5 10.0.0.11 10.0.0.12 S
28       Received RRO:
29             10.0.0.1 10.0.0.5 10.0.0.11 10.0.0.12
30     (...)
31
32     juniper@PE1> show isis backup spf results P3 | except item
33     (...)
34     P3.00
35       Primary next-hop: ge-2/0/2.0, IPV4, P1, SNPA:  0:50:56:8b:8:76
36         Root: P3, Root Metric: 550, Metric: 0, Root Preference: 0x0
37           Eligible, Backup next-hop: ge-2/0/3.0, LSP,
38                   Pnode:172.16.0.1:BypassLSP->172.16.0.3, Prefixes: 3
39     (...)
40
41     juniper@PE1> show route table inet.3 172.16.0.3/32 detail | match ...
42       *LDP    Preference: 9
43              Next hop: 10.0.0.3 via ge-2/0/2.0 weight 0x1, selected
44              Label operation: Push 299776
45              Next hop: 10.0.0.1 via ge-2/0/3.0 weight 0x100
46              Label-switched-path Pnode:172.16.0.1:BypassLSP->172.16.0.3
47              Label operation: Push 24031
48              Age: 9  Metric: 550
```

The bypass RSVP-TE tunnels are dynamically established, and LFA can use these tunnels as backup next hops for all prefixes that still don't have a backup next hop. You can see the following protection tunnels:

- Two link-protection tunnels (lines 3 and 7), whose name encodes the protected interface name as well as the router ID of the next-hop node, where the LSP is terminated.

- Four node-protection tunnels (lines 4 through 6 and line 8), whose name encodes the next-hop node being protected, and the next-next-hop node, where the LSP is terminated.

Two link-protection tunnels are pretty obvious: PE1 has only two links. But, why do you see four node-protection tunnels for two neighbor nodes? Well, there are four possible ways to reach a next-next-hop:

- PE1→P1→P2 (protected via *Pnode:172.16.0.1:BypassLSP->172.16.0.2*)
- PE1→PE2→P2 (protected via *Pnode:172.16.0.22:BypassLSP->172.16.0.2*)
- PE1→P1→P3 (protected via *Pnode:172.16.0.1:BypassLSP->172.16.0.3*)
- PE1→P1→PE3 (protected via *Pnode:172.16.0.1:BypassLSP->172.16.0.33*)

To put it simply, PE1 can send traffic to one of the following next hops: P1 or PE2. Then, P1 has three possible next hops (excluding the undesirable option of returning the traffic to PE1): P2, P3, and PE3. In turn, PE2 has one single possible next hop: P2.

In the absence of failures, PE1 sends packets destined to P3 via the PE1→P1 link. PE1 can choose between a link-protection bypass (lines 3, and 11 through 19) and a node-protection bypass (lines 6, and 21 through 29). According to the configuration, PE1 prefers the node-protection bypass (lines 38 and 46).

When TI-FRR is enabled, backup LFA or RLFA next hops are no longer used. All backup next hops point to bypass RSVP-TE tunnels. This time the backup next hop has a weight of 0x100 (line 45). As you explore different local-repair techniques used in Junos platforms, you'll see that each of them uses a different weight for backup next hops, therefore it is easy to determine the relative priority of the different next hops.

Let's verify the overall coverage provided by TI-FRR.

Example 18-37. States for TI-FRR (Junos)

```
juniper@PE1> show isis backup coverage
Backup Coverage:
Topology        Level   Node     IPv4     IPv6    CLNS
IPV4 Unicast        2 100.00% 100.00%   0.00%   0.00%
```

Now you have finally achieved 100 percent backup coverage! And, it is completely topology independent. Whatever the topology the backup coverage is always 100 percent.

Modifying the default LFA selection algorithm

In many cases, multiple feasible (*loop-free*) backup next hops might be available. These backup next hops could be direct (for plain per-prefix LFA) or point to a remote PQ-node (when using Remote LFA). A legitimate question would be then: How do you select the best backup next hop among those that are possible? And immediately a second question arises: How do you actually define *best*? Best for one network operator might not be the best for another. Typically, a default algorithm selects the best backup next hop. Just for reference, default tie-breakers in the LFA backup next-hop selection process, for both Junos and IOS XR, are as follows:

Junos

1. Prefer direct (another primary) ECMP next hop.

2. For multihomed prefixes, if PLR is the penultimate router, prefer direct backup next hop to another (non-best) originator if `per-prefix-calculation` is configured.

3. Prefer backup next hop (direct or PQ-node), which provides node protection if `node-link-protection` configured.

4. Prefer backup next hop (direct or PQ-node), which provides link protection, if `link-protection` or `node-link-degradation` configured.

5. Prefer backup next hop (direct or PQ-node) over a link with LDP synchronization enabled and LDP `in-sync` state.

6. Prefer backup next hop (direct or PQ-node) closest to the destination.

7. Prefer backup next hop (direct or PQ-node) closest to PLR.

8. Prefer backup next hop (direct or PQ-node) with lowest System ID.

IOS XR

1. Prefer direct (another primary) ECMP next-hop.

2. Prefer backup next hop with the lowest-total-metric (actually, lowest TM) backup path.

3. Prefer backup next hop reachable using different line card than the primary next hop.

4. Prefer backup next hop, which provides node protection.

 Keep rule 1 in mind. If a backup next hop is not installed, the reason might simply be that another primary next hop (ECMP) is already providing the desired protection.

Even at first sight, the default LFA backup next hop selection process is different. And, of course, it might not suit every operator's needs. Therefore, it should be possible to influence the default LFA backup next-hop selection process. The requirements for this are provided in *draft-ietf-rtgwg-lfa-manageability: Operational management of Loop Free Alternates*.

Both IOS XR and Junos offer a wide range of selection criteria, and provide ways to specify the order in which these criteria should be evaluated:

Junos

Backup path administrative constraints:
- Based on administrative groups (affinity bits)
- Based on Shared Risk Link Group (SRLG)

Bandwidth: For example, the bandwidth over the backup path should be greater or equal to the bandwidth available over primary path.
Protection type:
- Link protection
- Node and link protection
- Node protection with fallback to link protection if node protection not available

Downstream paths only.
Backup neighbors preference:
- Preference list based on IP addresses
- Preference list based on ISIS tags

Metrics:
- Metric from PLR to backup neighbor: highest of lowest
- Metric from backup neighbor to destination: highest or lowest

IOS XR

Backup path administrative constraints:
- Based on SRLG

Protection type:
- Node protection with fallback to link protection if node protection not available

Downstream paths preferred.
Metrics:
- Backup path with lowest total metric (actually, lowest TM) preferred

Line card disjoint backup path preferred
ECMP:
- ECMP path preferred
- Non-ECMP path preferred

Due to the great variety of possible options, this book selects a few in order to introduce policy-based LFA backup next-hop selection. You are encouraged to test the others.

Modifying the default LFA selection algorithm in Junos

In the topology illustrated in Figure 18-10, let's assume that RLFA (without RSVP-TE backup tunnels, and with `node-link-protection`) is configured on PE3. Figure 18-10 illustrates three paths from the source node (PE3) to the destination node (P2):

- The (shortest-path) primary path, which is PE3→P1→PE1→PE2→P2.

- The backup path that PE3 calculates according to the *default* backup next-hop selection algorithm, which chooses P4 as PQ-node. PE3 pushes a bottom (TLDP) label to go from P4 to P2, and a top (LDP) label for the tunnel PE3→P5→P3→P4. This LDP tunnel does *not* follow the shortest path from PE3 to P4. The reason will be explained later in this section.

- The backup path that PE3 calculates according to a *modified* backup next-hop selection algorithm. This modification consists of reversing Step 6 (prefer backup next hop closest to the destination) with Step 7 (prefer backup next hop closest to PLR). PE3 pushes a bottom (TLDP) label to go from P4 to P2, and a top (LDP) label for the tunnel PE3→PE4→P6→P4.

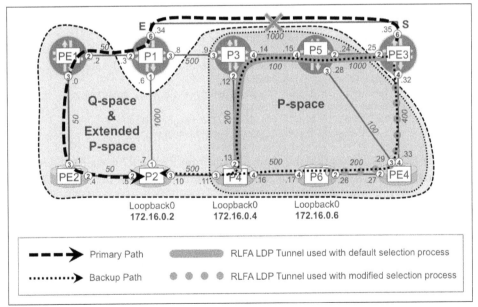

Figure 18-10. Modified LFA next-hop selection process (Junos)

First, let's check at PE3 the backup next hop selected by the default LFA selection process implemented in Junos.

Example 18-38. States toward P2 with default LFA selection process—PE3 (Junos)

```
1    juniper@PE3> show isis backup spf results P2 | except item
2    (...)
3    P2.00
4      Primary next-hop: ge-2/0/6.0, IPV4, P1, SNPA:  0:50:56:8b:16:af
5        Root: P2, Root Metric: 1150, Metric: 0, Root Preference: 0x0
6          Not eligible, LSP, Reason: Primary next-hop node fate sharing
7        Root: PE2, Root Metric: 1100, Metric: 50, Root Preference: 0x0
8          Not eligible, LSP, Reason: Primary next-hop node fate sharing
9        Root: PE1, Root Metric: 1050, Metric: 100, Root Preference: 0x0
10         Not eligible, LSP, Reason: Primary next-hop node fate sharing
11       Root: P1, Root Metric: 1000, Metric: 150, Root Preference: 0x0
12         Not eligible, IPV4, Reason: Primary next-hop link fate sharing
13       Root: P4, Root Metric: 800, Metric: 500, Root Preference: 0x0
14         Eligible, Backup next-hop: ge-2/0/2.0, LSP, LDP->P4(172.16.0.4)
15                                   Prefixes: 1
16       Root: P3, Root Metric: 600, Metric: 650, Root Preference: 0x0
17         Not eligible, IPV4, Reason: Primary next-hop node fate sharing
18         Not eligible, LSP, Reason: Interface is already covered
19       Root: P5, Root Metric: 500, Metric: 750, Root Preference: 0x0
20         Not eligible, IPV4, Reason: Primary next-hop node fate sharing
21       Root: PE4, Root Metric: 400, Metric: 850, Root Preference: 0x0
22         Not eligible, IPV4, Reason: Primary next-hop node fate sharing
23       Root: P6, Root Metric: 600, Metric: 1000, Root Preference: 0x0
24         Not eligible, IPV4, Reason: Missing primary next-hop
25         Not eligible, LSP, Reason: Interface is already covered
26
27   juniper@PE3> show route table inet.3 172.16.0.2/32 detail | match ...
28   172.16.0.2/32 (1 entry, 1 announced)
29           Next hop: 10.0.0.34 via ge-2/0/6.0 weight 0x1, selected
30           Label operation: Push 301168
31           Next hop: 10.0.0.24 via ge-2/0/2.0 weight 0xf100
32           Label operation: Push 24003, Push 300800(top)
```

Example 18-38 illustrates that the shortest path from PE3 to P2 is via P1 (lines 4 and 29). Currently the (remote) backup next hop, selected using the default LFA backup next hop selection process, is P4 (line 14). In most of the other evaluated backup next hops, their reason for noneligibility is `Primary next-hop node fate sharing`. That basically means that the end-to-end backup path through these next hops crosses P1, which is the primary node. Because `node-link-protection` is used in this example, these backup paths do not provide the required node diversity.

The only exception is P6. It says `Missing primary next-hop` (line 24) for IPv4, which means that P6 cannot be used as a direct backup next hop, because it is not directly connected to PE3. It also says `Interface is already covered` (line 25) for

LSP, which means that P6 is not used as remote (PQ-node) backup next-hop, because a better backup next hop has been already selected.

But why exactly has P4 been selected as the best LFA backup next hop? Why not P6? Let's try to evaluate the default LFA backup next-hop selection criteria specified earlier.

1. Prefer direct (another primary) ECMP next hop.

   P2 is reachable via single (no ECMP) primary next-hop, so this verification criterion is invalid for all feasible next hops.

2. For multihomed prefixes, if PLR is the penultimate router, prefer direct backup next hop to another (non-best) originator.

   Loopback of P2 is single-homed, so this verification criterion is invalid for all feasible next hops.

3. Prefer backup next hop (direct or PQ-node), which provides node protection if `node-link-protection` is configured.

   In this example, `node-link-protection` has been configured. It means that at this step only backup next hops that offer node protection are selected. Let's evaluate all feasible next hops:

   P1 P1 is the primary next hop, so it cannot be used as backup next hop

   P2 The shortest path to reach P2 from PE3 is via PE3→P1→PE1→PE2→P2. So, P2 does not belong to PE3 P-space, because the path crosses a primary link (PE3→P1). On the other hand, P2 belongs to extended P-space, because the shortest path from PE3's neighbors (P5→P3→P1→PE1→PE2→P2 and PE4→P5→P3→P1→PE1→PE2→P2) does not use the PE3→P1 link. However, in both cases the path traverses a primary next hop (P1), thus P2 as a backup next hop does not provide node protection, just link protection, and is therefore disqualified as potential backup next hop.

   PE1, PE2 The situation is similar to P2. PE1 or PE2 do not belong to P-space; rather, they belong to extended P-space. And again, the path from PE3's neighbors to PE1 or PE2 traverses P1, so they provide only link protection, but not node protection; therefore they are disqualified as potential backup next hops.

   P4 The shortest path to reach P4 from PE3 is via PE3→PE4→P5→P3→P4. And further, the shortest path from P4 to P2 is via direct link. Thus, you can conclude that P4 belongs to P-space, and neither path from PE3 to P4, nor from P4 to P2, crosses P1. As a result, P4 provides both node and link protection.

   P6 The shortest path to reach P6 from PE3 is via PE3→PE4→P6. And further, the shortest path from P6 to P2 is via P6→P4→P2. Thus, P6 provides both node and link protection.

P3 The shortest path to reach P3 from PE3 is via PE3→PE4→P5→P3, so it does not cross P1. However, the shortest path from P3 to P2 is P3→P1→PE1→PE2→P2. Thus, P3 provides only link protection and therefore is not used as potential backup next-hop.

P5, PE4 Both nodes are direct neighbors of PE3 and feasible backup next hops. The shortest path ([PE4→]P5→P3→P1→PE1→PE2→P2) from either node to P2 crosses P1. Thus, these next hops provide only link protection, so again they are disqualified.

Consequently, you can conclude that the only possible backup next hops in this step of the selection process are **P4** and **P6**.

4. Prefer backup next hop (direct or PQ-node), which provides link protection if `link-protection` or `node-link-degradation` is configured.

   Both previously selected backup next-hops (P4 and P6) provide link protection (in addition to node protection) so this criterion is equal for all selected backup next-hops.

5. Prefer backup next hop (direct or PQ-node) over a link with LDP synchronization enabled and LDP `in-sync` state.

   Network is stable, thus all LDP adjacencies are in `in-sync` state.

6. Prefer backup next hop (direct or PQ-node) closest to the destination.

   The path cost from P4 to P2 is 500 (P4→P2), whereas the path cost from P6 to P2 is 1000 (P6→P4→P2). Therefore, in this step, **P4** is selected as preferred next hop.

7. Prefer backup next hop (direct or PQ-node) closest to PLR

   Single-backup next hop is already selected.

8. Prefer backup next hop (direct or PQ-node) with lowest System ID

   Single backup next hop is already selected.

So, after a detailed analysis of the default LFA backup next hop selection process, you can conclude that the backup path is PE3→P5→P3→P4→P2. Why is PE4 skipped? PE3 is clever enough to realize that the shortest path from PE3 to P4 goes via P5, which is a directly connected neighbor. RLFA makes this exception to the "LDP follows the IGP" rule.

Now, let's make the appropriate configuration changes to influence the selection process.

Example 18-39. Policy LFA (tie-breakers) configuration on PE3 (Junos)

```
1    routing-options {
2        backup-selection {
3            destination 172.16.0.2/32 {
```

```
4                      interface all {
5                          root-metric lowest;
6                          dest-metric lowest;
7                          metric-order [ root dest ];
8                          evaluation-order metric;
9      }}}}
```

In this configuration example, the LFA backup path selection process is changed only for a single prefix (172.16.0.2/32) regardless of what the primary interface for the prefix is (lines 3 and 4). Furthermore, lower metrics are preferred from the PLR to the backup next hop (line 5) and from the backup next hop to the destination (line 6). Next, you specify the order in which the metrics should be evaluated (line 7).

Your choice is to first evaluate the metric from PLR to the backup next hop, and only after that, evaluate the metric from the backup next hop to the destination. If you recall the Junos default LFA selection process, this is just the opposite. And, finally (in line 8), the only specified criterion in the overall LFA backup next-hop selection process is the metric. In this particular case, you don't specify other selection criteria, so the evaluation order consists of a single item. If you specified additional criteria, such as bandwidth requirements, you could indicate if the bandwidth or the metric should be evaluated first in the LFA backup next-hop selection process.

Okay, let's check to see if the selection has changed.

Example 18-40. States toward P2 with modified LFA selection process—PE3 (Junos)

```
1      juniper@PE3> show isis backup spf results P2 | except item
2      (...)
3      P2.00
4        Primary next-hop: ge-2/0/6.0, IPV4, P1, SNPA:  0:50:56:8b:16:af
5      (...)
6          Root: P4, Root Metric: 800, Metric: 500, Root Preference: 0x0
7            Eligible, Backup next-hop: ge-2/0/2.0, LSP, LDP->P4(172.16.0.4)
8                                      Prefixes: 0
9      (...)
10         Root: P6, Root Metric: 600, Metric: 1000, Root Preference: 0x0
11           Eligible, Backup next-hop: ge-2/0/4.0, LSP, LDP->P6(172.16.0.6)
12                                      Prefixes: 1
13
14     juniper@PE3> show route table inet.3 172.16.0.2/32 detail | match ...
15     172.16.0.2/32 (1 entry, 1 announced)
16             Next hop: 10.0.0.34 via ge-2/0/6.0 weight 0x1, selected
17             Label operation: Push 301168
18             Next hop: 10.0.0.33 via ge-2/0/4.0 weight 0x101
19             Label operation: Push 24006, Push 24003(top)
```

Let's compare this output to that of Example 18-38. First, backup SPF results now include all possible backup next hops in the Eligible state. So, the RLFA tunnel to P6 (line 10) is now explicitly mentioned. Second, the remote (PQ-node) backup next hop has changed to P6 as indicated by the nonzero number of protected prefixes (line 12). *Why did the backup next hop change?* Based on the configuration changes in Example 18-39, the path cost from PLR to backup next hop (step 7 in the original selection process) is now evaluated *before* the path cost from the backup next hop to destination (Step 6 in original selection process). The path cost from PE3 to P6 is 600, whereas the path cost from PE3 to P4 is 800. Thus, P6 is selected as the backup next hop.

Because P6 is reachable via PE4, the direct backup next hop changed from P5 to PE4 (line 18). If you compare the outputs carefully, you will also realize that the weight of the backup next hop changed (from 0xf100 to 0x101). In Junos, every type of backup next hop uses a different weight, and now the backup next hop is delivered by the nondefault LFA selection algorithm. Basically, the backup path changed from PE3→P5→P3→P4→P2 to PE3→PE4→P6→P4→P2, successfully modifying the LFA selection!

Let's explore other verification commands related to policy-based LFA.

Example 18-41. Modified LFA selection process verification—PE3 (Junos)

```
juniper@PE3> show backup-selection
Prefix: 172.16.0.2/32
 Interface: all
   Protection Type: Link, Downstream Paths Only: Disabled, SRLG: Loose
   B/w >= Primary: Disabled, Root-metric: lowest, Dest-metric: lowest
   Metric Evaluation Order: Root-metric, Dest-metric
   Policy Evaluation Order: Metric

juniper@PE3> show isis route 172.16.0.2/32
(...)
Prefix          Interface NH   Via                    Backup Score
172.16.0.2/32   ge-2/0/6.0 IPV4 P1
                ge-2/0/4.0 LSP  LDP->P6(172.16.0.6) 0000000000000010
```

The show backup-selection command displays the information about nondefault LFA backup selection elements and reflects the configuration specified in Example 18-39. The show isis route command now displays a Backup Score value. While evaluating the LFA selection policy, each backup path is assigned a *backup score*, which is a composite, 64-bit entity containing 8 blocks of 8 bits. Each of the evaluation criteria contributes to an 8-bit block in the backup score. The evaluation-order (see Example 18-39, line 8) determines the offset of the block. The criterion at the beginning of the evaluation-order list is assigned the biggest offset, such that its block becomes most significant. Because a single evaluation criterion is listed in the example, the offset for that criterion is null, so it occupies the rightmost block. Finally, the result with the biggest score wins.

Modifying the default LFA selection algorithm in IOS XR

After checking the modified LFA selection process in Junos devices, let's verify the feature in the IOS XR plane. The topology depicted in Figure 18-11 shows three different paths from the source node (PE4) to the destination node (P2). You can modify the selection process by introducing SRLG verification, which by default, is not evaluated in the standard LFA selection process. First, let's examine the results of the default selection process.

Example 18-42. States toward P2 with default LFA selection process—PE4 (IOS XR)

```
1    RP/0/0/CPU0:PE4#show isis fast-reroute 172.16.0.2/32 detail
2    L2 172.16.0.2/32 [850/115] medium priority
3      via 10.0.0.28, Gi0/0/0/3, P5, SRGB Base: 0, Weight: 0
4        FRR backup via 10.0.0.26, Gi0/0/0/2, P6, SRGB Base: 0, Weight: 0
5        P: No, TM: 1200, LC: No, NP:Yes, D: No, SRLG: No
6      src P2.00-00, 172.16.0.2
7
8    RP/0/0/CPU0:PE4#show cef 172.16.0.2/32 | include "via|label"
9      via 10.0.0.26, Gi0/0/0/2, 7 dependencies, weight 0, backup
10         local label 24007        labels imposed {24006}
11     via 10.0.0.28, Gi0/0/0/3, 7 dependencies, weight 0, protected
12         local label 24007        labels imposed {300864}
```

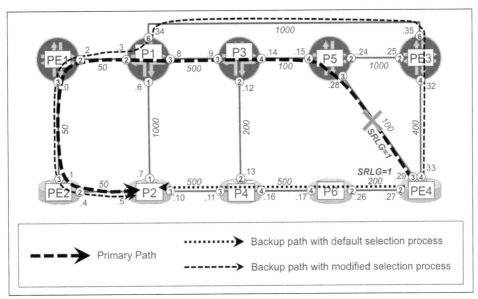

Figure 18-11. Modified LFA next-hop selection process—IOS XR

As you can see in Example 18-42, there is no label stacking. Conversely, if PE4 ran Junos, there would be label stacking by default, because PE4 would select the backup neighbor closest to the destination. In this case, it is PQ-node P4 (instead of the direct neighbor P6) reachable via an LDP tunnel..

Example 18-42 shows that the shortest path from PE4 to P2 is via P5 (lines 3 and 11). Currently the backup next hop (selected using the default LFA backup next hop selection process) is P6 (lines 4 and 9). The end-to-end backup path is PE4→P6→P4→P2 with a cost of 1200 (TM: 1200 statement in line 5). Additionally, the current backup path not only provides link protection, but also node protection (see NP: Yes in line 5), which means the backup path does not cross P5.

Furthermore, for this example, the same SRLG value is assigned to PE4-P5 and PE4-P6 links, by using the configuration discussed in Chapter 13. Therefore, the current backup path via P6 shares the same SRLG value with the primary path via P5. In other words, the primary and backup paths *are not* SRLG disjoint. This is emphasized via the SRLG: No statement (line 5), which is expected, because the default LFA backup next-hop selection algorithm does not take SRLG into consideration.

Let's change this. Obviously, as was discussed in Chapter 13, SRLG is used on purpose —to signify that links with the same SRLG value share the risk. During network failure (for example, a cut fiber) they might fail at the same time. Therefore, there is no point in placing primary and backup paths over links that use the same SRLG value. Let's reflect that into the configuration.

Example 18-43. LFA tie-breakers configuration on PE4 (IOS XR)

```
router isis core
 address-family ipv4 unicast
  fast-reroute per-prefix tiebreaker srlg-disjoint index 1
```

Let's verify and see if any of the changes can be observed.

Example 18-44. States for P2 with modified LFA selection process—PE4 (IOS XR)

```
1    RP/0/0/CPU0:PE4#show isis fast-reroute 172.16.0.2/32 detail
2    L2 172.16.0.2/32 [850/115] medium priority
3      via 10.0.0.28, Gi0/0/0/3, P5, SRGB Base: 0, Weight: 0
4        FRR backup via 10.0.0.32, Gi0/0/0/4, PE3, SRGB Base: 0, Weight: 0
5        P: No, TM: 1550, LC: No, NP: Yes, D: No, SRLG: Yes
6      src P2.00-00, 172.16.0.2
7
8    RP/0/0/CPU0:PE4#show cef 172.16.0.2/32 | include "via|label"
9        via 10.0.0.28, Gi0/0/0/3, 7 dependencies, weight 0, protected
10         local label 24007      labels imposed {300864}
```

```
11      via 10.0.0.32, Gi0/0/0/4, 7 dependencies, weight 0, backup
12        local label 24007    labels imposed {300352}
```

Perfect! The backup next hop changed to PE3 (lines 4 and 11). The total cost of the backup path certainly increased (TM: 1550 in line 5), and now the backup path is completely different (PE4→PE3→P1→PE1→PE2→P2). Node protection is still achieved (P5 is not used by the backup path), and, remarkably, the new backup path is SRLG disjoint with the primary path (SRLG: Yes in line 5).

There are many possible ways to influence the default LFA backup next-hop selection process. Some examples were provided in this section for you to understand the concepts. Again, you should explore more possibilities on your own; the limited space of this book does not allow us to have all the fun we want, so we've only explored the topic in scant detail.

Topology-Independent LFA

Topology-Independent LFA (*TI-LFA*), as the name suggests, is another approach to provide backup coverage independent of the network topology. TI-LFA, as opposed to TI-FRR (which uses RSVP-TE bypass tunnels), is based on the SPRING technology discussed in Chapter 2, and it is defined in *draft-francois-rtgwg-segment-routing-ti-lfa: Topology Independent Fast Reroute using Segment Routing*.

There are two main characteristics of TI-LFA:

1. When calculating the backup path, TI-LFA temporarily removes the protected resource (link or node) from the topology database, and runs standard SPF. Therefore, the backup path calculated by TI-LFA has, among all the paths that skip the protected resource, the lowest total metric to the final destination. This is called the shortest *post-convergence* path.
2. TI-LFA constructs traffic engineered repair tunnel to follow this backup path using SPRING machinery. It uses the repair label list, which is a combination of Node and Adjacency Segment IDs, as already discussed in Chapter 2 (see for example Figure 2-9). Depending on the backup path calculation results, one of the following options are possible:

Option 1: The repair node is a direct neighbor
When the repair node (backup next hop) is a direct neighbor, the outgoing interface is set to that neighbor and the repair label list is *empty* (there is no repair label).
This is comparable to the plain per-prefix LFA local repair discussed earlier.

Option 2: The repair node is a PQ-node
When the repair node (remote backup next hop) is a PQ-node, the repair label list comprises a *single Node Segment ID* to the repair node (PQ-node).

This is comparable to the RLFA architecture discussed previously. Of course, now the backup tunnel to PQ-node is established via SPRING model, rather than LDP.

Option 3: The repair is a Q-node, direct neighbor of the P-node
When the repair node (a Q-node, used as remote backup next hop) is directly connected to the P-node, the repair label list comprises two segments: a *Node Segment ID* to the P-node, *and* an *Adjacency Segment ID* from that P-node to the repair node (Q-node).

This protection method is called *Direct LFA* (DLFA) and it requires the advertisement of a label (Adjacency Segment ID) for each IGP adjacency, which is the default in both Junos and IOS XR.

Option 4: Connecting distant (nondirectly connected) P-nodes and Q-nodes
In some cases, there might not be any adjacent P-nodes and Q-nodes. However, the PLR can perform additional computations to compute a list of segments (combination of Node and Adjacency Segment IDs) that represent a loop-free path from P to Q. The actual computation algorithm is not specified in the TI-LFA draft; it is left to the actual implementation. Furthermore, the computation in this option is CPU intensive.

For link protection, TI-LFA with Options 1 through 3 provides full coverage in any arbitrary redundant network topology with symmetrical link metrics. TI-LFA Option 4 – computationally the most expensive – might be required for link protection only in topologies with asymmetric link metrics. On the other hand, for node or SRLG protection, in order to provide 100% coverage, option 4 might be required even in topologies with symmetrical link metrics. Option 4 was not tested by the authors.

The standard label, based on Node-SID associated with the final destination, is added below the repair label list when sending traffic via the backup next hop (unless the repair label list already takes the packet to the destination node).

As of this writing, TI-LFA was still in early standardization state, therefore the implementation status for both vendors was different, as shown next. IOS XR implemented TI-LFA for link protection only (no node protection) using a backup path computation algorithm that calculated the optimized (lowest total cost) post-convergence path (as specified in TI-LFA draft). After calculating this path, it encoded the repair tunnel via SPRING repair label list according to the options listed previously. Therefore, IOS XR's TI-LFA provided full link-protection coverage in any arbitrary topology with symmetrical IGP metrics, but did not provide node-protection coverage. Junos, on the other hand, didn't use the backup path computation method specified in TI-LFA draft. Instead, Junos used the standard LFA or RLFA backup next-hop selection procedure discussed in the "Modifying the default LFA selection algorithm" section. The resulting repair path uses a SPRING repair list from either Option 1 (direct backup neighbor, no label) or Option 2 (PQ-node as remote backup neighbor, node-SID label), but no Option 3 yet. Therefore, the backup tunnel was not necessarily on the shortest post-convergence path to the destination. In conclusion, Junos SPRING implementation provided protection for both link and node failures, but not for arbitrary topologies. Therefore, to avoid any misunderstanding, we will refer in this book to Junos implementation as simply SPRING-(R)LFA.

 Junos actually implements the shortest post-convergence path logic for a different flavor of local protection. Check the "RSVP-TE one-to-one protection" section in Chapter 19 for more details.

So, let's configure SPRING-(R)LFA/TI-LFA on both Junos and IOS XR planes, exploiting the LFA topology C we already used in the previous section (see Figure 18-9). Both planes are configured for pure SPRING operation (LDP-related configuration parts are removed) with the addition of (TI)-LFA specific configuration. For reference, these configurations are presented in the following two examples.

Example 18-45. TI-LFA configuration on PE4 (IOS XR)

```
group GR-ISIS
 router isis '.*'
  interface 'GigabitEthernet.*'
   address-family ipv4 unicast
    fast-reroute per-prefix level 2
    fast-reroute per-prefix ti-lfa level 2
end-group
!
router isis core
 apply-group GR-ISIS
 address-family ipv4 unicast
  segment-routing mpls
 !
 interface Loopback0
  address-family ipv4 unicast
   prefix-sid index 44
```

Example 18-46. SPRING-(R)LFA configuration on PE3 (Junos)

```
groups {
    GR-ISIS {
        protocols {
            isis {
                interface "<*[es]*>" {
```

```
                  node-link-protection;
}}}}}
protocols {
    isis {
        apply-groups GR-ISIS
        backup-spf-options {
            remote-backup-calculation;
            node-link-degradation;
        }
        source-packet-routing {
            use-mpls-forwarding;
            node-segment {
                ipv4-index 33;
                index-range 256;
}}}}
```

And again, you first check the LFA backup coverage. As Table 18-7 confirms, full backup coverage is achieved on (almost) all routers, so it is truly topology independent. On PE1 (Junos, no support for Option 3 or Option 4), you can extend backup coverage by using the backup RSVP-TE tunnel method, also discussed earlier, in this case for *primary* tunnels based on SPRING instead of LDP.

Table 18-7. Backup coverage with remote LFA in topology C

P1	P2	P3	P4	P5	P6	PE1	PE2	PE3	PE4
9	9	9	9	9	9	**0**	9	9	9
100%	100%	100%	100%	100%	100%	**0%**	100%	100%	100%

 As of this writing, SPRING-(R)LFA on Junos platforms was not truly topology independent, due to missing Option 3 and Option 4 in the Junos implementation. On the other hand, TI-FRR provided topology-independent backup coverage on Junos.

TI-LFA with direct repair node

Our first scenario for the repair tunnel is the situation in which the repair node (backup next hop) is a direct neighbor of PLR, as demonstrated next for IOS XR. In the following example, PE2 is the source node, P6 is the destination node, and P2 is the repair node:

Example 18-47. TI-LFA with direct repair node (IOS XR)

```
1   RP/0/0/CPU0:PE2# show isis fast-reroute 172.16.0.6/32 detail
2   L2 172.16.0.6/32 [1000/115] medium priority
3     via 10.0.0.0, Gi0/0/0/3, PE1, SRGB Base: 800000, Weight: 0
4     FRR backup via 10.0.0.5, Gi0/0/0/2, P2, SRGB Base: 16000, Weight: 0
5       P: No, TM: 1050, LC: No, NP: Yes, D: No, SRLG: Yes
```

```
6       src P6.00-00, 172.16.0.6, prefix-SID index 6, R:0 N:1 P:0 E:0 V:0 L:0
7
8       RP/0/0/CPU0:PE2#show cef 172.16.0.6/32 | include "via|label"
9          via 10.0.0.5, Gi0/0/0/2, 20 dependencies, weight 0, backup
10            local label 24007      labels imposed {16006}
11         via 10.0.0.0, Gi0/0/0/3, 20 dependencies, weight 0, protected
12            local label 24007      labels imposed {800006}
```

Example 18-47 is not illustrated, but it is based on LFA Topology C (see Figure 18-9 or Figure 18-12). On PE2, P6 loopback is reachable via PE1 (lines 3 and 11) as the primary next hop (via PE2→PE1→P1→P3→P5→PE4→P6, with path cost 1000), and a standard LFA selects P2 (lines 4 and 9) as the backup next hop (via PE2→P2→P4→P6, with path cost 1050). Because the standard LFA is able to find a backup next-hop, no repair label list is used. Simply put, for the primary next hop (PE1), PE2 combines P6's Node-SID index 6 (line 6) with PE1's node SRGB 800000 (line 3) to calculate label 800006 (line 12). If the PE2→PE1 link (or the PE1 node) fails, PE2 redirects traffic destined for P6 over the backup next hop (P2), by combining P6's Node-SID index 6 (line 6) with P2's SRGB 16000 (line 4) to calculate label 16006 (line 10).

Now, let's see the feature in Junos. In the following example, PE3 is the source node, P3 is the destination node, and P5 is the repair node:

Example 18-48. SPRING-(R)LFA with direct repair node (Junos)

```
juniper@PE3> show isis backup spf results P3
(...)
P3.00
  Primary next-hop: ge-2/0/4.0, IPV4, PE4, SNPA:  0:50:56:8b:0:43
    Root: P5, Root Metric: 500, Metric: 100, Root Preference: 0x0
      Eligible, Backup next-hop: ge-2/0/2.0, IPV4, P5
(...)
juniper@PE3> show route table inet.3 172.16.0.3/32 detail |
            match "entry|via|oper"
172.16.0.3/32 (1 entry, 1 announced)
        Next hop: 10.0.0.33 via ge-2/0/4.0 weight 0x1, selected
        Label operation: Push 16003
        Next hop: 10.0.0.24 via ge-2/0/2.0 weight 0xf000
        Label operation: Push 800003
```

Similarly, in the Junos plane, the Node-SID index of final destination (P3), coupled with the SRGB of the primary next-hop (PE4: 16000), or the backup next-hop (P5: 800000), is used to determine the outgoing label.

TI-LFA with PQ repair node

The second scenario mentioned in the TI-LFA draft deals with the PQ-node and is similar to the RLFA case discussed previously. This scenario is illustrated in Figure 18-12.

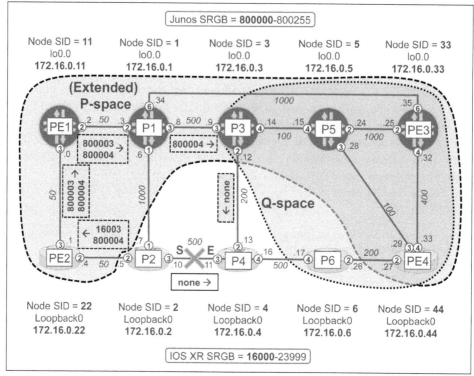

Figure 18-12. TI-LFA with RLFA (PQ-node) Style Repair

Let's see this TI-LFA flavor in IOS XR. In the following example (illustrated in Figure 18-12), P2 is the source node, P4 is the destination node, and P3 is the repair node:

Example 18-49. TI-LFA with PQ-node (IOS XR)

```
1   RP/0/0/CPU0:P2#show isis fast-reroute 172.16.0.4/32 detail
2   L2 172.16.0.4/32 [500/115] medium priority
3     via 10.0.0.11, Gi0/0/0/3, P4, SRGB Base: 16000, Weight: 0
4       TI-LFA backup via P3 (PQ) [172.16.0.3]
5       via 10.0.0.4, Gi0/0/0/2 PE2, SRGB Base: 16000
6       Label stack [16003, 800004]
7       P: No, TM: 850, LC: No, NP: No, D: No, SRLG: Yes
8       src P4.00-00, 172.16.0.4, prefix-SID index 4, R:0 N:1 P:0 E:0 V:0 L:0
9
```

```
10    RP/0/0/CPU0:P2#show cef 172.16.0.4/32 | include "via|label"
11        via 10.0.0.4, Gi0/0/0/2, 10 dependencies, weight 0, backup
12          local label 24006      labels imposed {16003 800004}
13        via 10.0.0.11, Gi0/0/0/3, 10 dependencies, weight 0, protected
14          local label 24006      labels imposed {ImplNull}
```

As with the RLFA case, the label stack associated with the backup next hop ensures delivery to the PQ-node first, and then delivery from the PQ-node to the final destination. The PQ-node is P3 (line 4); thus, the top label is derived from P3's Node-SID: P3's Node-SID index 3 + PE2's (backup next hop) SRGB 16000 (line 5) = 16003 (lines 6 and 12). The second label is derived from P4's (final destination) Node-SID index 4 (line 8) + P3's (PQ-Node) SRGB (800000) = 800004 (lines 6 and 12). When the packet is forwarded on the backup path (P2→PE2→PE1→P1→P3→P4) the first label is swapped to the label derived from P3's Node-SID. The penultimate hop for P3 (P1) removes the first label; consequently, the packet arrives at P3 with a single label only (based on P4's Node-SID). And again, the penultimate hop for P4 (P3) removes that single label, so the packet arrives to P4 without any label.

For the primary next hop, there are no labels (line 14) due to Penultimate Hop Popping (PHP). P4 is directly connected to P2; thus, P2 is the penultimate hop for P4.

In the Junos plane the situation is similar. Let's verify it. In the following example, P5 is the source node, P4 is the destination node, and P2 is the repair node:

Example 18-50. SPRING-(R)LFA with PQ-node (Junos)

```
1     juniper@P5> show isis backup spf results P4
2     (...)
3     P4.00
4      Primary next-hop: ge-2/0/4.0, IPV4, P3, SNPA:  0:50:56:8b:e6:da
5        Root: P2, Root Metric: 750, Metric: 500, Root Preference: 0x0
6         Eligible, Backup next-hop: ge-2/0/2.0, LSP, SPRING->P2(172.16.0.2)
7      (...)
8     juniper@P5> show route table inet.3 172.16.0.4/32 detail | match ...
9     172.16.0.4/32 (1 entry, 1 announced)
10            Next hop: 10.0.0.14 via ge-2/0/4.0 weight 0x1, selected
11            Label operation: Push 800004
12            Next hop: 10.0.0.25 via ge-2/0/2.0 weight 0xf000
13            Label operation: Push 16004, Push 800002(top)
```

For example, to reach P4 from P5, the PQ-node is P2 (line 6). Thus, the top label is derived from P2's Node-SID: P2's Node-SID index 2 + PE3's (backup next hop) SRGB 800000 = 800002 (line 13). The second label is derived from P4's (final destination) Node-SID index 4 + P2's (PQ-Node) SRGB (16000) = 16004 (line 13). For the primary next hop, there is a single label derived from P4's Node-SID coupled with P3's SRGB: 4 + 800000 = 800004 (line 11).

TI-LFA with direct LFA (DLFA) repair

The third scenario describes the situation in which P-node and Q-node are disjointed but directly connected. In this situation, using the *Direct LFA* model, traffic can be forced to flow from the P-node toward the Q-node, despite the fact the IGP shortest path from P-node to Q-node does not necessarily go over the direct link. Let's investigate PE2→PE1 traffic, as illustrated in Figure 18-13.

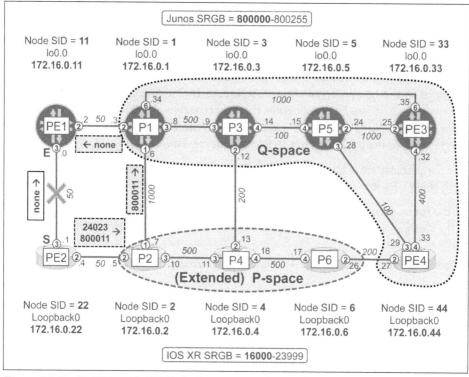

Figure 18-13. TI-LFA with DLFA (adjacent P- and Q-node)–style repair

For the PE2→PE1 link, the P-space (nodes that PE2 can reach over shortest path without going via the PE2→PE1 link) and the Q-space (nodes that can reach PE1 over shortest path without going via the PE2→PE1 link) do not overlap, and therefore there is no PQ-node. RLFA-style protection is consequently not possible.

The good news is that by using Adj-SID, you can force the traffic to go from the P-node via a direct link to the Q-node. And fortunately, there are a couple of adjacent P- and Q-nodes, for example, P1 and P2.

So, let's see how it looks in the network.

Example 18-51. TI-LFA with disjoint but adjacent P-node and Q-node (IOS XR)

```
1    RP/0/0/CPU0:PE2#show isis fast-reroute 172.16.0.11/32 detail
2    L2 172.16.0.11/32 [50/115] medium priority
3         via 10.0.0.0, Gi0/0/0/3, PE1, SRGB Base: 800000, Weight: 0
4            TI-LFA backup via P2 (P) [172.16.0.2], P1 (Q) [172.16.0.1]
5            via 10.0.0.5, GigabitEthernet0/0/0/2 P2, SRGB Base: 16000
6            Label stack [ImplNull, 24023, 800011]
7            P: No, TM: 1100, LC: No, NP: No, D: No, SRLG: Yes
8         src PE1.00-00, 172.16.0.11, prefix-SID index 11, R:0 N:1 ...
9
10   RP/0/0/CPU0:PE2#show cef 172.16.0.11/32 | include "via|label"
11       via 10.0.0.5, Gi0/0/0/2, 18 dependencies, weight 0, backup
12          local label 24003    labels imposed {ImplNull 24023 800011}
13       via 10.0.0.0, Gi0/0/0/3, 18 dependencies, weight 0, protected
14          local label 24003    labels imposed {ImplNull}
15
16   RP/0/0/CPU0:PE2#show isis database P2 verbose | include "IS|SRGB|SID"
17   IS-IS core (Level-2) Link State Database
18       Segment Routing: I:1 V:0, SRGB Base: 16000 Range: 8000
19     Metric: 50         IS-Extended PE2.00
20       ADJ-SID: F:0 B:0 V:1 L:1 S:0 weight:0 Adjacency-sid:24025
21     Metric: 500        IS-Extended P4.00
22       ADJ-SID: F:0 B:0 V:1 L:1 S:0 weight:0 Adjacency-sid:24024
23     Metric: 1000       IS-Extended P1.00
24       ADJ-SID: F:0 B:0 V:1 L:1 S:0 weight:0 Adjacency-sid:24023
25       Prefix-SID Index: 2, R:0 N:1 P:0 E:0 V:0 L:0
```

The primary next hop for PE2→PE1 traffic is PE1 itself, with no label (PHP) associated (line 14). The label stack associated with the backup next hop must ensure three actions:

1. PE2 must send the traffic to P-node (P2).

   This is similar to reaching the PQ-node discussed in the previous case. The label is derived from the Node-SID of the P-node. In the particular case of Figure 18-13, however, the P-node (P2) is directly connected to PE2, thus there is no label associated with this step due to penultimate hop popping (see ImplNull in lines 6 and 12).

2. P-node (P2) must send the traffic to Q-node (P1) over direct link.

   This is a new action, not discussed previously. If the label derived from P1 Node-SID was used for this purpose, traffic would be forwarded from P2 to P1 over the shortest path: P2→PE2→PE1→P1, which isn't good, because the backup path must avoid the PE2→PE1 link. Therefore, instead of Node-SID used in all previous cases, Adj-SID is used. P2 advertises Adj-SID labels for each IGP adjacency: PE2, P1, or P4. The label associated with neighbor P1 is 24023 (line 24). Any packet arriving to P2 with this label will be sent to P1 not using the shortest path, but over a direct link. This is good for the TI-LFA scenario because it allows forcing the traffic to the directly-connected Q-node. Therefore, this label is used as a second label in the label stack (lines 6 and 12). This behavior is called *Direct LFA*.

3. Q-node (P1) must send the traffic to the final destination (PE1).

   There's nothing new here compared to the previous case. PE1's Node-SID index 11 (line 8) is used in combination with SRGB of the Q-node to reach PE1 through the Q-node (P1). P1's SRGB (800000) is used, therefore the resulting label is 800011 (line 6 and line 12).

 In LDP-based RLFA, the TM field in show isis fast-reroute output encodes the path cost to the PQ-node (Example 18-29, line 5). In TI-LFA, however, the TM field retains its original meaning: total cost of the backup path (Example 18-49, line 7; Example 18-51, line 7).

Another example of TI-LFA protection with disjoint but adjacent P-nodes and Q-nodes, is the protection for PE2→PE4 traffic, which uses PE2→PE1→P1→P3→P5→PE4 as a primary path. P4 is P-node and P3 the Q-node, as is shown in the following capture:

Example 18-52. TI-LFA with disjoint but adjacent P-node and Q-node (IOS XR)

```
RP/0/0/CPU0:PE2#show isis fast-reroute 172.16.0.44/32
L2 172.16.0.44/32 [800/115]
     via 10.0.0.0, Gi0/0/0/3, PE1, SRGB Base: 800000, Weight: 0
      TI-LFA backup via P4 (P) [172.16.0.4], P3 (Q) [172.16.0.3]
      via 10.0.0.5, Gi0/0/0/2 P2, SRGB Base: 16000
      Label stack [16004, 24011, 800044]
```

In this example, the following labels are used:

- 16004: Node-SID to reach P4 (P-node) from PE2 via P2
- 24001: Adj-SID to reach P3 (Q-node) via direct link from P4 (P-node)
- 800044: Node-SID to reach PE4 from P3

Theoretically P3 Node-SID could be used to forward traffic between P4 (P-node) and P3 (Q-node), because the shortest path between P4 and P3 is via a direct link. Moreover, the label stack with two labels only—skipping Adj-SID between P4 and P3— would be enough, too, because the shortest path from P4 (P-node) to PE4 (final destination) does not cross the PE2→PE1 link. However, such additional verification of the shortest path between the P-node and the Q-node or final destination node requires additional SPF calculation, where the P-node is placed as the SPF root. In large networks (hundreds of nodes with potentially hundreds or thousands of

P-nodes), that would eventually mean the PLR needs to perform hundreds (if not thousands) of SPF calculations on each IGP topology change. This is very challenging from a performance perspective, and as a result, such additional optimization is typically not implemented in the TI-LFA process.

The last case mentioned in the TI-LFA draft differs from previous cases in that the P-node and the Q-node are not directly connected. Thus, simple Adj-SID to force the traffic from the P-node to the Q-node cannot be used. However, the PLR can perform additional computations to compute a list of segments (combination of Node and Adjacency Segment IDs) from these particular P-nodes. Depending on the network size and the topology, this computation might cause performance challenges.

The resulting list of segments is explicitly path-encoded in the label stack to forward traffic from the P-node to the nonadjacent Q-node. Again, depending on the network topology the list of segments (and corresponding label stack size) might be long. This puts additional requirements on routers to support larger label stacks, which might not be available on all router hardware platforms.

Maximally Redundant Trees

Maximally Redundant Trees (*MRT*) is another approach that provides local-repair-based protection capabilities in LDP-signaled networks. All previously discussed techniques were based on SPF calculations (performed from the perspective of the node in question as well as the node's neighbors, and eventually the node's neighbors' neighbors) to find a loop-free backup next hop. Then, various techniques were discussed to patch the network with some backup tunnels (LDP, RSVP-TE, or SPRING–based) to eventually extend backup coverage.

As of this writing, MRT was still in draft state and defined in several drafts.

MRT provides answers to all of the issues learned during our LFA deployments:

- It provides protection in any arbitrary topology. In other words, MRT is topology independent.
- It provides protection for both unicast and multicast traffic flows from day one (LFA focuses primarily on unicast traffic).
- MRT computation efforts are low (comparable to three SPF computations) in any arbitrary topology (RLFA computation efforts depend on the number of neighbors and neighbors' neighbors).

So, what is MRT? In MRT, three forwarding paths (essentially next hops) are always computed to reach the final destination. One forwarding path (next hop) is computed by using an ordinary SPF algorithm. The other two forwarding paths (next hops) are computed using a newly defined (*draft-ietf-rtgwg-mrt-frr-algorithm*) computation algorithm. This, rather complex to understand, algorithm does not try to optimize the forwarding paths based on metrics, distance, or hop count. Such optimization is the responsibility of standard SPF algorithm. On the other hand, MRT ensures that both MRT forwarding paths (called *MRT-red* and *MRT-blue*) are disjointed (do not share common links or nodes) to the maximum possible degree; hence, the name: *Maximally Redundant Trees*. As a result of such computation, during protection events (lasting few 100 ms up to few seconds) MRT might redirect the traffic over a suboptimal path.

 The details of MRT (or ordinary SPF) computation algorithm are not covered in this book. You are encouraged to study the appropriate drafts for further information on the MRT computation algorithm itself.

Different MPLS labels distinguish all three forwarding paths. Therefore, MRT extensions to the LDP protocol allow allocation of three labels for each IPv4 prefix advertised by LDP.

 As of this writing, MRT was not supported in production routing software, but you can try it in Junosphere. Unlike xLFA solution, MRT is a global solution requiring other IGP nodes to contribute to the protection. Hence it requires global deployment in the IGP, or at least in the context of routing islands.

Now, after this very short overview and introduction, let's verify MRT operation in practice. In addition to standard (node-link protection) LFA (not shown for brevity) you need to enable MRT operation.

Example 18-53. MRT backup configuration (Junos)

```
routing-options mrt;
```

After enabling MRT on all routers in the topology, let's check different LDP traceroutes to the same destination using standard SPF, as well as MRT-red and MRT-blue forwarding paths.

Example 18-54. LDP traceroute to PE1 using SPF, MRT-red, and MRT-blue forwarding —P3 (Junos)

```
juniper@P3> show route table inet.3 172.16.0.11/32 detail | match ...
*LDP  Preference: 9
      Next hop: 10.0.0.8 via ge-0/0/3.0 weight 0x1         ## Primary
      Next hop: 10.0.0.13 via ge-0/0/2.0 weight 0xf000     ## Backup
```

```
juniper@P3> traceroute mpls ldp 172.16.0.11/32
  ttl   Label  Protocol    Address     Previous Hop    Probe Status
    1  300608  LDP         10.0.0.8    (null)          Success
    2       3  LDP         10.0.0.2    10.0.0.8        Egress
(...)
juniper@P3> traceroute mpls ldp 172.16.0.11/32 mrt-red
  ttl   Label  Protocol    Address     Previous Hop    Probe Status
    1  300576  LDP         10.0.0.13   (null)          Success
    2  300144  LDP         10.0.0.10   10.0.0.13       Success
    3  300704  LDP         10.0.0.4    10.0.0.10       Success
    4       3  LDP         10.0.0.0    10.0.0.4        Egress
juniper@P3> traceroute mpls ldp 172.16.0.11/32 mrt-blue
  ttl   Label  Protocol    Address     Previous Hop    Probe Status
    1  300368  LDP         10.0.0.15   (null)          Success
    2  300400  LDP         10.0.0.29   10.0.0.15       Success
    3  300528  LDP         10.0.0.32   10.0.0.29       Success
    4  300688  LDP         10.0.0.34   10.0.0.32       Success
    5       3  LDP         10.0.0.2    10.0.0.34       Egress
(...)
```

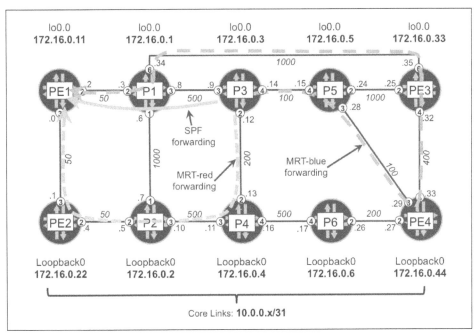

Figure 18-14. Forwarding paths from P3 to PE1 Using SPF, MRT-red, and MRT-blue forwarding topologies

As you can see, MPLS-red and MPLS-blue use disjointed paths to reach PE1 from P3. In this particular case, neither MRT-red nor MRT-blue uses the same path as the SPF path. Depending on the actual topology, though, it may happen that one of the MRT paths equals the SPF path.

But why does forwarding over (nonshortest) MRT paths not cause loops? For example, the shortest paths from P5 to PE1 is via P3; thus, theoretically, the packet destined to PE1 arriving from P3 at P5 should be sent back to P3 causing a loop. The trick that MRT uses, as we've briefly mentioned, is the allocation of three MPLS labels for each loopback. And, of course, implementation of appropriate extensions to LDP to ensure that the three labels for each prefix can be advertised.

Example 18-55. LDP SPF and MRT FECs on P3 (Junos)

```
juniper@P3> show ldp database | match "Input|Output|172.16.0.11/32"
Input label database, 172.16.0.3:0--172.16.0.1:0
 300608       172.16.0.11/32
 300752       172.16.0.11/32, MRT Red
 300688       172.16.0.11/32, MRT Blue
Output label database, 172.16.0.3:0--172.16.0.1:0
 299872       172.16.0.11/32
 300064       172.16.0.11/32, MRT Red
 299968       172.16.0.11/32, MRT Blue
Input label database, 172.16.0.3:0--172.16.0.4:0
 300336       172.16.0.11/32
 300576       172.16.0.11/32, MRT Red
 300848       172.16.0.11/32, MRT Blue
Output label database, 172.16.0.3:0--172.16.0.4:0
 299872       172.16.0.11/32
 300064       172.16.0.11/32, MRT Red
 299968       172.16.0.11/32, MRT Blue
Input label database, 172.16.0.3:0--172.16.0.5:0
 300320       172.16.0.11/32
 300512       172.16.0.11/32, MRT Red
 300368       172.16.0.11/32, MRT Blue
Output label database, 172.16.0.3:0--172.16.0.5:0
 299872       172.16.0.11/32
 300064       172.16.0.11/32, MRT Red
 299968       172.16.0.11/32, MRT Blue
```

The computation algorithms to calculate SPF, MRT-red, and MRT-blue forwarding trees are consistent on all routers. It means that each forwarding topology (SPF, MRT-red, and MRT-blue) is loop-free. Based on the forwarding topology calculation, appropriate forwarding states are configured in the forwarding plane. The forwarding states for SPF topology uses SPF labels, whereas the forwarding states for the MRT-red or MRT-blue topologies use labels allocated for MRT-red or MRT-blue, respectively. As soon as the packet is sent with, for example, an MRT-blue label, it is switched (loop-free) through the network using MRT-blue labels only.

Now, when the standard LFA backup next hop cannot be found, the MRT next hop (either from MRT-red or MRT-blue—whichever is different from SPF next hop) will be used as the backup LFA next hop. Let's have a look for example at PE3.

Example 18-56. MRT—LDP routes on PE3 (Junos)

```
juniper@PE3> show ldp route | find 172.16.0.1/32
172.16.0.1/32  ge-0/0/6.0                    10.0.0.34 IP
               ge-0/0/2.0                    10.0.0.24 IP
               ge-0/0/4.0                    10.0.0.33 MRT Red
               ge-0/0/6.0                    10.0.0.34 MRT Blue
172.16.0.2/32  ge-0/0/6.0                    10.0.0.34 IP
               MRT Backup->10.0.0.33(no LDP tunneling)MRT Backup LSP
               ge-0/0/4.0                    10.0.0.33 MRT Red
               ge-0/0/6.0                    10.0.0.34 MRT Blue
172.16.0.3/32  ge-0/0/4.0                    10.0.0.33 IP
               ge-0/0/2.0                    10.0.0.24 IP
               ge-0/0/4.0                    10.0.0.33 MRT Red
               ge-0/0/6.0                    10.0.0.34 MRT Blue
172.16.0.4/32  ge-0/0/4.0                    10.0.0.33 IP
               ge-0/0/2.0                    10.0.0.24 IP
               ge-0/0/4.0                    10.0.0.33 MRT Red
               ge-0/0/6.0                    10.0.0.34 MRT Blue
172.16.0.5/32  ge-0/0/4.0                    10.0.0.33 IP
               ge-0/0/2.0                    10.0.0.24 IP
               ge-0/0/4.0                    10.0.0.33 MRT Red
               ge-0/0/6.0                    10.0.0.34 MRT Blue
172.16.0.6/32  ge-0/0/4.0                    10.0.0.33 IP
               MRT Backup->10.0.0.34(no LDP tunneling)MRT Backup LSP
               ge-0/0/4.0                    10.0.0.33 MRT Red
               ge-0/0/6.0                    10.0.0.34 MRT Blue
172.16.0.11/32 ge-0/0/6.0                    10.0.0.34 IP
               MRT Backup->10.0.0.33(no LDP tunneling)MRT Backup LSP
               ge-0/0/4.0                    10.0.0.33 MRT Red
               ge-0/0/6.0                    10.0.0.34 MRT Blue
172.16.0.22/32 ge-0/0/6.0                    10.0.0.34 IP
               MRT Backup->10.0.0.33(no LDP tunneling)MRT Backup LSP
               ge-0/0/4.0                    10.0.0.33 MRT Red
               ge-0/0/6.0                    10.0.0.34 MRT Blue
172.16.0.33/32 lo0.0                         IP
172.16.0.44/32 ge-0/0/4.0                    10.0.0.33 IP
               ge-0/0/2.0                    10.0.0.24 IP
               ge-0/0/4.0                    10.0.0.33 MRT Red
               ge-0/0/6.0                    10.0.0.34 MRT Blue
```

As you can see, for the five loopbacks (P1, P3, P4, P5, and PE4) the basic LFA provides backup next hops (you see two IP next hops for each of these loopbacks). For the other four loopbacks (P2, P6, PE1, and PE2), the backup next hop is provided by MRT. The backup next hop for P2, PE1, and PE2 is inherited from MRT-red. MRT-blue cannot be used as a backup next hop, because the MRT-blue next-hop matches the SPF next hop for these loopbacks in this particular topology. For the P6 loopback, it is just the opposite. The SPF next hop matches the MRT-red next hop; thus, the MRT-blue is used as the backup next hop. This is confirmed with the following detailed backup SPF output:

Example 18-57. LFA states for P6 loopback on PE3 (Junos)

```
juniper@PE3> show ospf backup spf 172.16.0.6
(...)
172.16.0.6
  Self to Destination Metric: 600
  Parent Node: 172.16.0.44
  Primary next-hop: ge-0/0/4.0 via 10.0.0.33
  Backup next-hop: Push 300336
  Backup Neighbor: 172.16.0.1
  Alternate Source: MRT Blue
   Neighbor to Destination Metric: 0, Neighbor to Self Metric: 1000
   Self to Neighbor Metric: 1000, Backup preference: 0x0
   Eligible, Reason: Contributes backup next-hop
  Backup Neighbor: 172.16.0.44
  Alternate Source: LFA
   Neighbor to Destination Metric: 200, Neighbor to Self Metric: 400
   Self to Neighbor Metric: 400, Backup preference: 0x0
   Not eligible, Reason: Primary next-hop node fate sharing
  Backup Neighbor: 172.16.0.5
  Alternate Source: LFA
   Neighbor to Destination Metric: 300, Neighbor to Self Metric: 500
   Self to Neighbor Metric: 500, Backup preference: 0x0
   Not eligible, Reason: Primary next-hop node fate sharing
  Backup Neighbor: 172.16.0.1
  Alternate Source: LFA
   Neighbor to Destination Metric: 900, Neighbor to Self Metric: 1000
   Self to Neighbor Metric: 1000, Backup preference: 0x0
   Not eligible, Reason: Primary next-hop node fate sharing

juniper@PE3> show ldp database session 172.16.0.1 | match ...
Input label database, 172.16.0.33:0--172.16.0.1:0
  300384      172.16.0.6/32, MRT Red
  300336      172.16.0.6/32, MRT Blue
Output label database, 172.16.0.33:0--172.16.0.1:0
  300960      172.16.0.6/32, MRT Red
  300752      172.16.0.6/32, MRT Blue
```

In case of the primary link or primary node (PE4) failure, traffic destined for P6 will be switched to the MRT-blue forwarding topology and forwarded with the MRT-blue label over interfaces towards P1. P1, again using the MRT-blue forwarding topology, not SPF forwarding topology, forwards the traffic further over the appropriate interface.

And, what is a very important aspect of MRT, Table 18-8 shows that full backup coverage is always achieved, regardless of the network topology.

Example 18-58. LFA backup coverage with MRT extensions on PE3 (Junos)

```
juniper@PE3> show ospf backup coverage
(...)
Area            Covered  Total  Percent
                  Nodes  Nodes  Covered
0.0.0.0               9      9  100.00%

Route Coverage:

Path Type  Covered   Total  Percent
           Routes   Routes  Covered
Intra          20       24   83.33%
Inter           0        0  100.00%
Ext1            0        0  100.00%
Ext2            0        0  100.00%
All            20       24   83.33%
```

The coverage output for routes does not reach 100 percent, because local prefixes (in the case of the three PE3 link prefixes and one loopback prefix) are always counted as *noncovered*.

Table 18-8. Backup coverage for LFA with MRT extensions

P1	P2	P3	P4	P5	P6	PE1	PE2	PE3	PE4
9	9	9	9	9	9	9	9	9	9
100%	100%	100%	100%	100%	100%	100%	100%	100%	100%

## CHAPTER 19

Transit Fast Restoration Based on RSVP-TE

Until now, the discussion has been about various IP Fast ReRoute (FRR) protection techniques. Let's focus now on protection in RSVP-TE. As in the previous cases, there are a variety of options to provide protection with RSVP transport, just not as many:

- Path protection
- Facility protection (RFC 4090, Section 3.2)
- One-to-one protection (RFC 4090, Section 3.1)

These options are discussed in the three sections of this chapter.

RSVP-TE Path Protection

The concept of path protection is very simple: for each RSVP LSP that requires path protection, an operator defines two (or more) paths. During normal conditions, the primary path is used to forward the traffic for any given LSP. If some failure on the primary path happens, the head-end router can switch the traffic to the secondary path, as illustrated in Figure 19-1.

You can see that the LSP from PE3 to PE1 is configured with two path options. The primary path uses the PE3→P1→PE1 route, whereas the secondary path uses the PE3→PE4→P5→P3→P1→PE1 route. A simple configuration to achieve these desired results is presented Example 19-1.

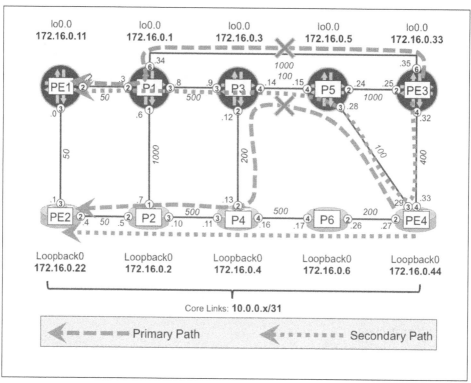

Figure 19-1. RSVP path protection concepts

Example 19-1. RSVP multiple path configuration on PE3 (Junos)

```
protocols {
    mpls {
        label-switched-path PE3--->PE1 {
            to 172.16.0.11;
            primary PE3-P1-PE1;
            secondary PE3-PE4-P5-P3-P1-PE1;
        }
        path PE3-P1-PE1 {
            10.0.0.34 strict;
            10.0.0.2 strict;
        }
        path PE3-PE4-P5-P3-P1-PE1 {
            10.0.0.33 strict;
            10.0.0.28 strict;
            10.0.0.14 strict;
            10.0.0.8 strict;
            10.0.0.2 strict;
        }
}}}
```

The appropriate RIB entries are installed and traffic uses the primary path.

Example 19-2. Primary path forwarding verification on PE3 (Junos)

```
juniper@PE3> show mpls lsp name PE3--->PE1 detail | match <pattern>
  From: 172.16.0.33, State: Up, ActiveRoute: 0, LSPname: PE3--->PE1
  ActivePath: PE3-P1-PE1 (primary)
 *Primary   PE3-P1-PE1      State: Up
  Secondary PE3-PE4-P5-P3-P1-PE1 State: Dn

juniper@PE3> show route table inet.3 172.16.0.11/32
(...)
172.16.0.11/32     *[RSVP/7/1] 00:07:24, metric 1050
                    > to 10.0.0.34 via ge-2/0/6.0,
                                label-switched-path PE3--->PE1

juniper@PE3> traceroute mpls rsvp PE3--->PE1 | match RSVP-TE
  ttl   Label  Protocol  Address    Previous Hop  Probe Status
   1   303440  RSVP-TE   10.0.0.34  (null)        Success
   2        3  RSVP-TE   10.0.0.2   10.0.0.34     Egress
```

Now, as Example 19-3 shows, when a failure occurs (e.g., the link between P1 and PE3 fails), the secondary path is signaled by RSVP, and the new next hop is subsequently used.

Example 19-3. Secondary path forwarding verification on PE3 (Junos)

```
juniper@PE3> show mpls lsp name PE3--->PE1 detail | match <pattern>
  From: 172.16.0.33, State: Up, ActiveRoute: 0, LSPname: PE3--->PE1
  ActivePath: PE3-PE4-P5-P3-P1-PE1 (secondary)
  Primary   PE3-P1-PE1      State: Dn
 *Secondary PE3-PE4-P5-P3-P1-PE1 State: Up

juniper@PE3> show route table inet.3 172.16.0.11/32
(...)
172.16.0.11/32     *[RSVP/7/1] 00:02:22, metric 1150
                    > to 10.0.0.33 via ge-2/0/4.0,
                                label-switched-path PE3--->PE1

juniper@PE3> traceroute mpls rsvp PE3--->PE1 | except "FEC|Hop"

ttl   Label  Protocol  Address      Previous Hop  Probe Status
 1   24032   RSVP-TE   10.0.0.33    (null)        Success
 2  301168   Unknown   10.0.0.28    10.0.0.33     Non-compliant
 3                     172.16.0.3   10.0.0.28     Non-compliant
 4                     172.16.0.1   172.16.0.3    Non-compliant
 5                     172.16.0.11  172.16.0.1    Egress
```

As of this writing, some level of interoperability inconsistency between Junos and IOS XR could be observed in MPLS RSVP-TE LSP Ping (RFC 4379 and RFC 6424). You can see the manifestation of this problem in Label (missing), Protocol (missing or Unknown) and Probe Status (Non-compliant) output fields. Because this issue didn't cause any disturbance to the traffic itself, we didn't dwell on it for a detailed analysis of the problem.

For the sake of completeness, let's configure multiple paths for a RSVP-TE tunnel initiated on an IOS XR device. In this example, we configure an RVSP-TE LSP from PE4 to PE2.

Example 19-4. RSVP multiple path configuration on PE4 (IOS XR)

```
explicit-path name PE4-P6-P4-P2-PE2
 index 10 next-address strict ipv4 unicast 10.0.0.26
 index 20 next-address strict ipv4 unicast 10.0.0.16
 index 30 next-address strict ipv4 unicast 10.0.0.10
 index 40 next-address strict ipv4 unicast 10.0.0.4
!
explicit-path name PE4-P5-P3-P4-P2-PE2
 index 10 next-address strict ipv4 unicast 10.0.0.28
 index 20 next-address strict ipv4 unicast 10.0.0.14
 index 30 next-address strict ipv4 unicast 10.0.0.13
 index 40 next-address strict ipv4 unicast 10.0.0.10
 index 50 next-address strict ipv4 unicast 10.0.0.4
!
interface tunnel-te22
 apply-group GR-LSP
 signalled-name PE4--->PE2
 destination 172.16.0.22
 path-option 1 explicit name PE4-P5-P3-P4-P2-PE2
 path-option 2 explicit name PE4-P6-P4-P2-PE2
```

Based on this configuration, an LSP using the primary path is established and appropriate entries are populated. As is discussed in Chapter 2, the IGP metric for destinations reachable via RSVP-TE tunnels equals the cost of the shortest hop-by-hop path to the destination (in this example, PE4→P5→P3→P1→PE1→PE2; cost: 800). Because this shortest path is not always equal to the path taken by LSP, the reported metric values (line 7, versus 13 and 15 in Example 19-5) might differ. This is true for both Junos and IOS XR devices (with nuances described in the final sections of Chapter 3).

Example 19-5. Primary path forwarding verification on PE4 (IOS XR)

```
1    RP/0/0/CPU0:PE4#show mpls traffic-eng tunnels destination 172.16.0.22
2                   role head detail | include <pattern>
3    Name: tunnel-te22  Destination: 172.16.0.22  Ifhandle:0x1080
4      Signalled-Name: PE4--->PE2
5        Admin:    up Oper:   up   Path:  valid   Signalling: connected
6        path option 1,  type explicit PE4-P5-P3-P4-P2-PE2
7                                       (Basis for Setup, path weight 950)
8        path option 2,  type explicit PE4-P6-P4-P2-PE2
9        Outgoing Interface: Gi0/0/0/3, Outgoing Label: 301360
```

```
10
11    RP/0/0/CPU0:PE4#show route 172.16.0.22/32
12    (...)
13      Known via "isis core", distance 115, metric 800, type level-2
14        172.16.0.22, from 172.16.0.22, via tunnel-te22
15          Route metric is 800
16
17    RP/0/0/CPU0:PE4#traceroute mpls traffic-eng tunnel-te 22
18    (...)
19      0 10.0.0.29 MRU 1500 [Labels: 301584 Exp: 0]
20    L 1 172.16.0.5 MRU 1514 [Labels: 302448 Exp: 7] 30 ms
21    L 2 172.16.0.3 MRU 1514 [Labels: 24010 Exp: 7] 220 ms
22    L 3 10.0.0.13 MRU 1500 [Labels: 24011 Exp: 0] 10 ms
23    L 4 10.0.0.10 MRU 1500 [Labels: implicit-null Exp: 0] 10 ms
24    ! 5 10.0.0.4 10 ms
```

The trace output is as expected. There are some differences, however, in the reported addresses (loopbacks versus link addresses) or Maximum Receive Unit (MRU) sizes (including or excluding the Layer 2 header) depending on whether the reporting node is Junos or IOS XR.

After a network failure occurs (e.g., on the P3-P5 link) traffic shifts to the secondary path, as demonstrated in Example 19-6. This time, the LSP metric (line 7) and the IGP metric (lines 13 and 15) are equal, because after failure of the P3-P5 link, the shortest path to the destination equals the secondary path.

Example 19-6. Secondary path forwarding verification on PE4 (IOS XR)

```
1     RP/0/0/CPU0:PE4#show mpls traffic-eng tunnels destination 172.16.0.22
2                      role head detail | include <pattern>
3     Name: tunnel-te22  Destination: 172.16.0.22  Ifhandle:0x480
4       Signalled-Name: PE4--->PE2
5         Admin:    up Oper:   up   Path: valid   Signalling: connected
6         path option 2,  type explicit PE4-P6-P4-P2-PE2 (Basis for Setup,
7                          path weight 1250)
8         path option 1,  type explicit PE4-P5-P3-P4-P2-PE2
9         Outgoing Interface: Gi0/0/0/2, Outgoing Label: 24012
10
11    RP/0/0/CPU0:PE4#show route 172.16.0.22/32
12    (...)
13      Known via "isis core", distance 115, metric 1250, type level-2
14        172.16.0.22, from 172.16.0.22, via tunnel-te22
15          Route metric is 1250
16
17    RP/0/0/CPU0:PE4#traceroute mpls traffic-eng tunnel-te 22
18    (...)
19      0 10.0.0.27 MRU 1500 [Labels: 24012 Exp: 0]
20    L 1 10.0.0.26 MRU 1500 [Labels: 24010 Exp: 0] 10 ms
21    L 2 10.0.0.16 MRU 1500 [Labels: 24011 Exp: 0] 10 ms
```

```
22    L 3 10.0.0.10 MRU 1500 [Labels: implicit-null Exp: 0] 0 ms
23    ! 4 10.0.0.4 10 ms
```

So far, so good. *But what traffic restoration times could you imagine in your design?* When a failure happens, the following sequence of events are executed:

1. Failure detection

2. The secondary path is signaled via RSVP-TE

3. Installation of a new next hop in the RIB/FIB structures

If the failure occurs close to the head-end router (e.g., the PE3-P1 link fails on the primary path used by LSP from PE3 to PE1), failure detection can be rather quick. Failure of directly connected links or neighbors can be discovered rapidly.

If the failure is farther away from the head-end router (e.g., the P3-P4 link fails on the primary path used by LSP from PE4 to PE2), information about the failure can be propagated to the head-end or tail-end routers (PE4 or PE2) via RSVP-TE signaling messages (PathErr, ResvTear) generated by the router that detects the failure. Alternatively, after IGP global convergence, all the routers in the domain (including head-end and tail-end routers) gain knowledge about the failed link or node. This failure detection can be quite long (several hundred milliseconds), and for certain applications, too long. This problem is discussed a little later in this chapter.

For now, let's check the second and third element of the overall time required for traffic restoration. When a network failure affects the primary path, a secondary path must be signaled and a new next hop installed in RIB/FIB. This certainly takes time, especially in scaled environments with large numbers of LSPs. Therefore you can use the same trick as discussed in the Loop-Free Alternates (LFA) scenarios: preinstalling backup next hops.

Obviously, to preinstall a backup next hop, the secondary path must be presignaled. So, let's do that. You simply designate the secondary path as a *standby* path, as shown in Example 19-7. A standby path is presignaled and corresponds to the next hop preinstalled in the RIB/FIB. But it is only a backup next hop—just like in the LFA case.

Example 19-7. RSVP-TE secondary standby path configuration—PE3 (Junos)

```
protocols{
    mpls {
        label-switched-path PE3--->PE1 {
            secondary PE3-PE4-P5-P3-P1-PE1 {
                standby;
}}}
```

Now let's check what's the difference in the various states related to the PE3--->PE1 LSP.

Example 19-8. Primary/standby path states on PE3 (Junos)

```
juniper@PE3> show mpls lsp name PE3--->PE1 detail | match <pattern>
  From: 172.16.0.33, State: Up, ActiveRoute: 0, LSPname: PE3--->PE1
  ActivePath: PE3-P1-PE1 (primary)
 *Primary   PE3-P1-PE1       State: Up
  Standby   PE3-PE4-P5-P3-P1-PE1 State: Up

juniper@PE3> show route table inet.3 172.16.0.11/32 detail | match ...
   *RSVP   Preference: 7/1
           Next hop: 10.0.0.34 via ge-2/0/6.0 weight 0x1, selected
           Label-switched-path PE3--->PE1
           Next hop: 10.0.0.33 via ge-2/0/4.0 weight 0x2001
           Label-switched-path PE3--->PE1
           Age: 23:15      Metric: 1050
```

You can see the secondary path is presignaled (state is up) and the backup next hop is preinstalled. This time, though, the weight for the backup next hop is 0x2001 (in the LFA case, it was 0xf000, 0x100, or 0x8000, depending on the LFA style used). As long as it is greater than 0x1, it is a backup next hop.

Let's also do the same on the IOS XR device, as shown in Example 19-9. Enabling the path-protection feature and designating one of the path options (e.g., path option 2) to protect the primary path (path option 1) causes the protecting path (path option 2) to be presignaled.

Example 19-9. Primary/standby path configuration and states—PE4 (IOS XR)

```
interface tunnel-te22
 path-protection
 path-option 1 explicit name PE4-P5-P3-P4-P2-PE2 protected-by 2
 path-option 2 explicit name PE4-P6-P4-P2-PE2

RP/0/0/CPU0:PE4#show mpls traffic-eng tunnels destination 172.16.0.22
             role head detail | include <pattern>
Name: tunnel-te22 Destination: 172.16.0.22  Ifhandle:0x480
  Signalled-Name: PE4--->PE2
    Admin:   up Oper:   up  Path: valid  Signalling: connected
    path option 1,  type explicit PE4-P5-P3-P4-P2-PE2
                    (Basis for Setup, path weight 950)
    path option 2,  type explicit PE4-P6-P4-P2-PE2
                    (Basis for Standby, path weight 1250)
    Standby Path: User defined [explicit path option: 2],
    Outgoing Interface: Gi0/0/0/3, Outgoing Label: 301360
    Outgoing Interface: Gi0/0/0/2, Outgoing Label: 24012
```

Manually designing and explicitly configuring primary and secondary path options might be a challenging task, especially in large networks. Furthermore, as your network changes during its lifetime (typically networks grow and sometimes network topologies are modified), keeping track of the most optimal primary and secondary paths could become an operational nightmare. To cope, you can establish primary and secondary paths dynamically.

In typical designs, the primary path is restricted to use only certain links (e.g., links with the smallest delay)—the required techniques for this are discussed in Chapters Chapter 13 and Chapter 15, so they are not covered here.

Let's simply configure two dynamic paths—primary and secondary—without any explicit constraints.

Example 19-10. Dynamic primary/secondary standby path—PE3 (Junos)

```
1     protocols {
2         mpls {
3             label-switched-path PE3--->PE2 {
4                 to 172.16.0.22;
5                 primary PRIMARY;
6                 secondary SECONDARY {
7                     standby;
8                 }
9             }
10            path PRIMARY;
11            path SECONDARY;
12    }}
```

Lines 10 and 11 demonstrate how you can define path options without specifying any next hops. They are basically empty path options. These path options become populated with explicit lists of next hops by a constrained SPF algorithm during the LSP creation time. (This is discussed in Chapter 2.) But what is new here is the way in which these paths are calculated by CSPF.

First, the path options that are designated as primary, named PRIMARY in the example, follow standard CSPF rules, which in the end produce paths based on the lowest total cost to the destination (because no constraints are imposed on the primary path in the example). This cost is 1100, as shown in Figure 19-2 and in Example 19-11, line 5.

Example 19-11. States for primary/standby paths on PE3 (Junos)

```
1     juniper@PE3> show mpls lsp name PE3--->PE2 detail | match <pattern>
2      From: 172.16.0.33, State: Up, ActiveRoute: 0, LSPname: PE3--->PE2
3      ActivePath: PRIMARY (primary)
4     *Primary   PRIMARY          State: Up
5      Computed ERO (S [L] denotes strict [loose]): (CSPF metric: 1100)
6      10.0.0.34 S 10.0.0.2 S 10.0.0.1 S
7      Standby   SECONDARY        State: Up
8      Computed ERO (S [L] denotes strict [loose]): (CSPF metric: 1350)
9      10.0.0.33 S 10.0.0.28 S 10.0.0.14 S 10.0.0.13 S 10.0.0.10 S
10     10.0.0.4 S
```

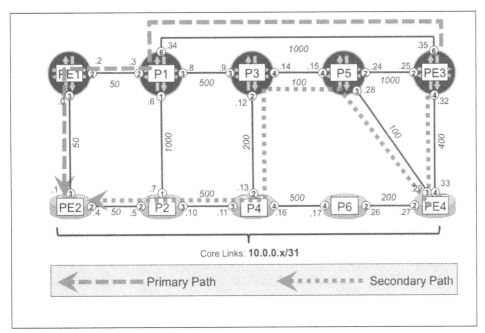

Figure 19-2. RSVP path protection—dynamic PE3--->PE2 LSPs

Conversely, the path option designated as secondary standby (called SECONDARY in the example) is calculated using different rules. You can discover those rules by enabling and monitoring logs for CSPF events, as shown in Example 19-12, and Example 19-13, respectively.

Example 19-12. Enabling logs for CSPF events on PE3 (Junos)

```
protocols {
    mpls {
        traceoptions {
            file cspf size 100m;
            flag cspf;
            flag cspf-link;
            flag cspf-node;
}}}
```

Example 19-13. Monitoring logs for CSPF events on PE3 (Junos)

```
1    juniper@PE3> monitor start cspf
2    (...)
3    <timestamp> CSPF for path PE3--->PE2(secondary SECONDARY)
4    <timestamp> CSPF final destination 172.16.0.22
5    <timestamp> CSPF starting from PE3.00 (172.16.0.33) to 172.16.0.22
6    <timestamp> constraint avoid primary path
```

```
7    <timestamp> Node PE3.00 (172.16.0.33) metric 0, hops 0,
8                      avail 32000 32000 32000 32000
9    <timestamp>   Link 10.0.0.35->10.0.0.34(P1.00/172.16.0.1,
10         Link IDs 338->335) metric 1000 color 0x0 bw 900Mbps
11   <timestamp> link passes constraints
12   <timestamp> Link overlap with primary path, adding cost 8000000
13   (...)
```

When checking the logs, you can spot an entry that indicates the start of CSPF for the secondary path (line 3). CSPF for the secondary path tries to avoid the primary path (line 6), so that the primary and secondary paths are distinct to the highest possible degree. Recall from the discussion about MRTs in Chapter 18, the logic was similar: *MRT-red* and *MRT-blue* forwarding topologies should be distinct, whenever possible. Now, the primary and secondary paths should be diverse, to the highest possible degree. Whereas MRT uses a sophisticated algorithm to find dissimilar paths for MRT-red and MRT-blue forwarding, Junos CSPF for the secondary path uses a more basic approach, as visible in line 12. Put simply, the cost of links used by the primary path is temporarily increased by 8 million. Thus, in this particular example, link PE3→P1 (line 9) is considered by CSPF with a total cost of 8001000: IGP metric 1000 (line 10) + extra cost 8 million (line 12). In this way, CSPF temporarily increases the cost for all the links used by the primary path.

You can see the results of the primary and secondary path computation in Figure 19-2, and in Example 19-11 (line 6 for primary, lines 9 and 10 for secondary). The primary is a path with the smallest total cost (PE3→P1→PE1→PE2; total cost: 1100), whereas the secondary is a completely distinct path (PE4→P5→P3→P4→P2→PE2; total cost: 1350). There are no common links between primary and secondary paths. Also note that the secondary path is not the second shortest path after the primary. The second shortest path in the example topology is PE3→PE4→P5→P3→P1→PE1→PE2, with a total cost of 1200. This path is not chosen for a secondary path option, though, because it shares some links (P1→PE1→PE2) with the primary path. As you can see, the default algorithm to calculate paths for dynamic primary and secondary options provides very good results.

The results with IOS XR are similar. If `path-protection` is configured, you can simply define one dynamic path option. The second dynamic path (to protect the first one) will be automatically presignaled.

Example 19-14. Dynamic primary/secondary standby path—PE4 (IOS XR)

```
interface tunnel-te11
 path-protection
 path-option 1 dynamic
```

Figure 19-3 and Example 19-15 show the path computations. There is, however, a slight difference between Junos and IOS XR behavior when it comes to calculating paths for secondary path options. Junos tries to avoid the links used by the primary path by increasing, temporarily, metrics for these links. It might happen, however, that the secondary path shares some links with the primary path. IOS XR, on the other hand, completely avoids such links (and nodes) by temporarily removing these links (nodes) from the database used as the input for CSPF calculations (see line 7 in Example 19-15). Thus, in IOS XR, the secondary path must be completely distinct from the primary path. If such a path cannot be found, the secondary path is not pre-signaled.

Example 19-15. States for primary/standby paths on PE4 (IOS XR)

```
1    RP/0/0/CPU0:PE4#show mpls traffic-eng tunnels 11 detail
2    Name: tunnel-te11  Destination: 172.16.0.11  Ifhandle:0x680
3     Signalled-Name: PE4--->PE1
4     Admin:    up Oper:   up   Path:  valid   Signalling: connected
5     path option 1,  type dynamic  (Basis for Setup, path weight 750)
6     path option 2,  type dynamic  (Basis for Standby, path weight 1300)
7     Standby Path: Node and Link Diverse [explicit path option: 2]
8     Outgoing Interface: Gi0/0/0/3, Outgoing Label: 301365
9     Outgoing Interface: Gi0/0/0/2, Outgoing Label: 24018
10   (...)
11    Path info (IS-IS core level-2):
12    Node hop count: 4
13    Hop0: 10.0.0.28          ## P5
14    Hop1: 10.0.0.14          ## P3
15    Hop2: 10.0.0.8           ## P1
16    Hop3: 10.0.0.2           ## PE1
17    Hop4: 172.16.0.11        ## PE1
18
19    Standby LSP Path info (IS-IS core level-2), Oper State: Up :
20    Node hop count: 5
21    Hop0: 10.0.0.26          ## P6
22    Hop1: 10.0.0.16          ## P4
23    Hop2: 10.0.0.10          ## P2
24    Hop3: 10.0.0.4           ## PE2
25    Hop4: 10.0.0.0           ## PE1
26    Hop5: 172.16.0.11        ## PE1
```

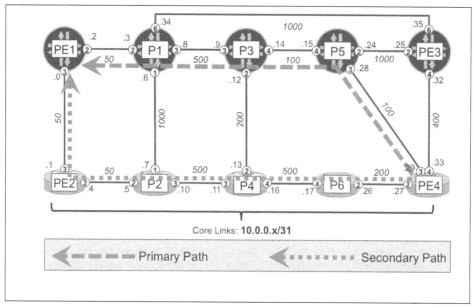

Figure 19-3. RSVP path protection—dynamic PE4--->PE1 LSPs

The last thing you should know about path protection is how RSVP-TE signals different paths belonging to same RSVP-TE tunnel. If you carefully study Chapter 2 and RFC 3209 (*RSVP-TE: Extensions to RSVP for LSP Tunnels*), RSVP-TE maintains a couple of IDs used for identification of tunnels and paths:

Tunnel ID
   A 16-bit identifier used in the SESSION that remains constant over the life of the tunnel.

LSP ID
   A 16-bit identifier used in the SENDER_TEMPLATE and the FILTER_SPEC that can be changed to allow a sender to share resources with itself.

In Junos, you can easily monitor RSVP-TE packet exchange by capturing packets with IP protocol 46 (this is the IP protocol ID assigned to RSVP). If you sniff packets on different interfaces (with Junos command `monitor traffic interface <int> size 2000 no-resolve detail`), you can catch RSVP packets handling primary as well as secondary paths of PE3--->PE2, as shown in Example 19-16.

Example 19-16. RVSP packets monitoring on PE3 (Junos)

```
1    /* Interface ge-2/0/6.0 */
2    RSVPv1 Path Message (1), Flags: [Refresh reduction capable]
3      Session Object (1) Flags: [reject if unknown], Class-Type:
4        Tunnel IPv4 (7), length: 16, IPv4 Tunnel EndPoint: 172.16.0.22,
```

```
 5       Tunnel ID: 0xb14d, Extended Tunnel ID: 172.16.0.33
 6     Session Attribute Object (207) Flags: [ignore and forward if
 7       unknown], Class-Type: Tunnel IPv4 (7), length: 20, Session
 8       Name: PE3--->PE2, Setup Priority: 7, Holding Priority: 0,
 9       Flags: [SE Style desired]
10     Sender Template Object (11) Flags: [reject if unknown],
11       Class-Type: Tunnel IPv4 (7), length: 12, IPv4 Tunnel Sender
12       Address: 172.16.0.33, LSP-ID: 0x0037
13
14     /* Interface ge-2/0/4.0 */
15     RSVPv1 Path Message (1), Flags: [Refresh reduction capable]
16       Session Object (1) Flags: [reject if unknown], Class-Type:
17       Tunnel IPv4 (7), length: 16, IPv4 Tunnel EndPoint: 172.16.0.22,
18       Tunnel ID: 0xb14d, Extended Tunnel ID: 172.16.0.33
19     Session Attribute Object (207) Flags: [ignore and forward if
20       unknown], Class-Type: Tunnel IPv4 (7), length: 20, Session
21       Name: PE3--->PE2, Setup Priority: 7, Holding Priority: 0,
22       Flags: [SE Style desired]
23     Sender Template Object (11) Flags: [reject if unknown],
24       Class-Type: Tunnel IPv4 (7), length: 12,  IPv4 Tunnel Sender
25       Address: 172.16.0.33, LSP-ID: 0x0038
```

The tunnel ID is the same for all paths of the same RSVP-TE tunnel. It is manually assigned in IOS XR (the same as the configured interface tunnel ID) and automatically assigned in Junos. You can see that Tunnel ID 0xb14d (45389 in decimal) is used in the RSVP-TE signaling messages by both the primary (line 5) and the secondary (line 18) paths. The LSP ID, however, is different on both paths. The primary uses 0x0037 (line 12), whereas the secondary uses 0x0038 (line 25). Each time the path is changed (e.g., due to reoptimization) or a new path added, the new LSP ID is automatically generated, maintaining multiple paths belonging to the same RSVP-TE tunnel.

RSVP-TE Facility (Node-Link) Protection

Path protection is based on switchover between the primary and secondary standby paths. The head-end router performs this switchover, so failure information must first be propagated to the head-end router before any repair action can be executed. If the failure happens close to the head-end router (failure of a directly connected link or a directly connected node), failure detection is quite quick. If, however, failure happens farther away from the head-end router, the following failure detection methods can trigger path switchover:

- Notification from the IGP that the topology has changed (e.g., some of the transit routers are no longer available)
- RSVP PathErr or ResvTear messages

- Notification from the Bidirectional Forwarding Detection (BFD) protocol running as the LSP's OAM, which indicates that forwarding over the LSP is broken

Any of these events can result in a relatively slow failure detection, and thus path switchover might by triggered relatively late after failure occurs. For certain loss-sensitive applications this is undesirable.

Thus, RFC 4090 (*Fast Reroute Extensions to RSVP-TE for LSP Tunnels*) introduces two options for protecting traffic flowing via RSVP-TE tunnels using the local-repair paradigm. Similar to the protection cases available for LDP and SPRING (different variants of LFA), traffic is repaired locally; thus, the failure propagation time to head-end router no longer plays a significant role.

Because the terminology used for these two options across vendors can become a bit confusing, Table 19-1 summarizes the terms used by Junos and IOS XR as well as by the RFC (this book uses the RFC terms in all further discussions.)

Table 19-1. RSVP-TE protection terminology

RFC 4090	One-to-one backup	Facility backup
Junos	Fast ReRoute	Link Protection Node-Link Protection
IOS XR	n/a	Fast ReRoute Protection Any Fast ReRoute Protection Node

One of the two options described in RFC 4090 is *facility backup*, whereby "facility" is defined as a link or node. This option shows some similarities to per-link LFA discussed earlier in this chapter. Namely, with facility backup, all eligible traffic flowing through the protected facility (link or node) is rerouted by the means of local repair over the *same* backup next hop when the facility (link or node) fails.

The problem with per-link LFA is its high dependency on topology, which results in no loop-free backup next hop in many situations. This limitation does not affect RSVP-TE protection. Because RSVP-TE has the capability to signal explicit paths, after the path is signaled and states are created on all transit routers, packets do not necessarily use the shortest-path for forwarding any longer. Explicit path specification creates the opportunity to presignal any bypass path, which is completely independent from the network topology or IGP metrics. You used this capability of RSVP-TE in Chapter 18, when you extended LFA backup coverage with manual or dynamic RSVP-TE tunnels. This chapter focuses on pure RSVP-TE scenarios.

So, let's do it. But before getting under way with this section, you must set all RSVP-TE tunnels (full mesh between PE routers) back to their basic state (single, dynamic path option per tunnel.) Then, taking this book's topology as a reference, this is the path followed by each right-to-left tunnels:

- PE3--->PE1 tunnel: PE3→P1→PE1

- PE3--->PE2 tunnel: PE3→PE4→P5→P3→P4→P2→PE2

- PE4--->PE1 tunnel: PE4→P5→P3→P1→PE1

- PE4--->PE2 tunnel: PE4→P5→P3→P4→P2→PE2

Remember that in the IGP and TE worlds, links are seen as two half-links. Let's focus on P5→P3, whose reverse half-link is P3→P5. According to the previous list, the following three LSPs transit the (half-)link P5→P3: PE3--->PE2, PE4--->PE1, and PE4--->PE2.

Manual Link Protection Bypass

Manual bypass LSPs are configured with a strict hop-by-hop ERO. The process is tedious but it provides more control. Automatic bypass LSPs are discussed later in this chapter.

Manual link protection bypass in Junos: P5→P3 link, PE4--->PE2 LSP

Figure 19-4 illustrates a manual bypass LSP, which protects the P5→P3 link. The figure also depicts how this bypass LSP protects the PE4--->PE2 LSP in case of link failure.

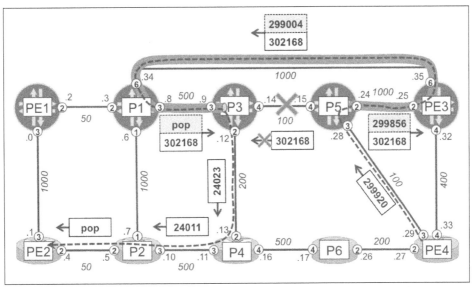

Figure 19-4. Facility (link) protection in Junos (P5→P3 link, PE4--->PE2 LSP)

In the absence of failures, the PE4--->PE2 LSP follows the original path, represented in Figure 19-4 with white labels. The bypass LSP (gray labels on top of the white labels) are used only during local repair after a P5→P3 link failure.

 The PE4--->PE1 LSP, which also transits the P5→P3 link, would be protected by the *same* bypass LSP. Using the color code in Figure 19-4, the PE4--->PE1 LSP would have different *white* labels, but the same *gray* labels for P5→P3 local repair. This is an essential property of facility protection: all the protected LSPs transiting a protected resource rely on the same bypass LSP.

Example 19-17. Manual link protection bypass LSP on P5 (Junos)

```
1    protocols {
2        rsvp {
3            interface ge-2/0/4.0 {
4                link-protection {
5                    bypass P5-PE3-P1-P3 {
6                        to 172.16.0.3;
7                        bandwidth 0;
8                        path {
9                            10.0.0.25 strict;
10                           10.0.0.34 strict;
11                           10.0.0.9 strict;
12   }}}}}}
13
14   juniper@P5> show rsvp interface ge-2/0/[234].0 extensive | match ...
15   ge-2/0/2.0 Index 333, State Ena/Up
16     Authentication, Aggregate, Reliable, NoLinkProtection
17     Protection: Off
18   ge-2/0/3.0 Index 334, State Ena/Up
19     Authentication, Aggregate, Reliable, NoLinkProtection
20     Protection: Off
21   ge-2/0/4.0 Index 335, State Ena/Up
22     Authentication, Aggregate, Reliable, LinkProtection
23     Protection: On, Bypass: 0, LSP: 0, Protected LSP: 0,
24                                       Unprotected LSP: 0
```

A quick verification shows that out of three interfaces for which RSVP is enabled, only one has protection switched on. This is in line with the configuration just committed. However, you also can see in line 23 that no bypass LSP is created and no LSP is currently protected. This is unfortunate, because it means that the efforts are ineffective at the moment.

The problem is that all traffic is considered as *not eligible* for protection by default in RSVP-TE. This is just the opposite of LFA, for which by default all traffic *is eligible* for protection and the system tries to install the backup next hop for as many prefixes/labels as possible. In RSVP-TE, you need to explicitly designate the traffic that requires protection. Let's do it initially for the traffic flowing over PE4--->PE2 and PE3--->PE2 tunnels, following the syntax shown here:

Example 19-18. Local Protection request for PE4--->PE2 on PE4 (IOS XR)

```
interface tunnel-te22
 fast-reroute
```

Example 19-19. Local Protection request for PE3--->PE2 LSP on PE3 (Junos)

```
protocols {
    mpls {
        label-switched-path PE3--->PE2 {
            link-protection;
}}}
```

As illustrated in Example 19-20, the protection states on P5 (it might take some time initially) now look much better.

Example 19-20. Facility (link) protection state on P5 (Junos)

```
1    juniper@P5> show rsvp interface ge-2/0/4.0 extensive | find ...
2    Protection: On, Bypass: 1, LSP: 2, Protected LSP: 2,
3                  Unprotected LSP: 0
4        1 Feb  5 21:36:29 New bypass P5-PE3-P1-P3
5        Bypass: P5-PE3-P1-P3, State: Up, Type: LP, LSP: 1, Backup: 0
6        3 Feb  5 21:36:31 Record Route:  10.0.0.25 10.0.0.34 10.0.0.9
7        2 Feb  5 21:36:31 Up
8        1 Feb  5 21:36:30 CSPF: computation result accepted
```

You can see that bypass LSP is now established. This bypass type (line 5) is LP (link protection), and currently only two regular LSPs can use this bypass for protection (just before, you requested protection for PE4--->PE2 and PE3--->PE2 tunnels only.) You can verify the status of regular LSPs transiting P5 node, as well.

Example 19-21. Protection state of transit LSPs on P5 (Junos)

```
juniper@P5> show mpls lsp detail | match "name|protect"
  LSPname: PE4--->PE1
  LSPname: PE4--->PE2
    Link protection desired
    Type: Link protected LSP
  LSPname: PE3--->PE2, LSPpath: Primary
    Link protection desired
    Type: Link protected LSP
  LSPname: PE2--->PE3
  LSPname: PE2--->PE4
  LSPname: PE1--->PE4, LSPpath: Primary
```

After configuring IOS XR `fast-reroute` option (Example 19-18) for the PE4--->PE2 LSP or Junos `link-protection` option (Example 19-19) for the PE3--->PE2 LSP, these LSPs are signaled using special flags in the RSVP-TE Session Attribute Object.

Make a copy of Figure 19-4 and keep it handy throughout this explanation.

Adding the hidden (and unsupported) knob `write-file` to the packet capturing command from Example 19-16, this time on P5's ge-2/0/3 interface, you can save the RSVP packets into a file for further analysis by external tools (like *Wireshark* or *TShark*). This gives you the option of inspecting RSVP packets in detail, including the aforementioned flags. Let's see a Path message for the PE4--->PE2 LSP (Example 19-22).

Example 19-22. Collected RVSP packets decoding using TShark

```
1    [linux:~/Downloads] juniper% tshark -r rsvp-path-lp.pcap -V
2    (...)
3    Resource ReserVation Protocol (RSVP): PATH Message. SESSION:
4      IPv4-LSP, Destination 172.16.0.22, Short Call ID 0, Tunnel ID 22,
5      Ext ID ac10002c. SENDER TEMPLATE: IPv4-LSP, Tunnel Source:
6      172.16.0.44, Short Call ID: 0, LSP ID: 53.
7    (...)
8       SESSION ATTRIBUTE: SetupPrio 7, HoldPrio 7, Local Protection,
9                          Label Recording, SE Style,  [PE4--->PE2]
10   (...)
11              Flags: 0x07
12                      .... ...1 = Local protection: Desired
13                      .... ..1. = Label recording: Desired
14                      .... .1.. = SE style: Desired
15                      .... 0... = Bandwidth protection: Not Desired
16                      ...0 .... = Node protection: Not Desired
```

PE4 requests local protection for the PE4--->PE2 tunnel (line 12). PE4 requests neither bandwidth nor node protection (lines 15-16), which means the bypass tunnel does not need to satisfy those protection criteria.

Now let's review how the protection is actually achieved.

Example 19-23. Status of PE4--->PE2 RSVP-TE tunnel on PE4 (IOS XR)

```
1    RP/0/0/CPU0:PE4#show mpls traffic-eng tunnels 22 detail
2    [...]
3    Outgoing Interface: GigabitEthernet0/0/0/3, Outgoing Label: 299920
4      Resv Info:
```

```
 5       Record Route:
 6           IPv4 172.16.0.5, flags 0x21 (Node-ID, Protection: available)
 7           IPv4 10.0.0.28, flags 0x1 (Protection: available)
 8           Label 299920, flags 0x1
 9           IPv4 172.16.0.3, flags 0x20 (Node-ID)
10           IPv4 10.0.0.14, flags 0x0
11           Label 306128, flags 0x1
12           IPv4 172.16.0.4, flags 0x20 (Node-ID)
13           Label 24023, flags 0x1
14           IPv4 10.0.0.13, flags 0x0
15           Label 24023, flags 0x1
16           IPv4 172.16.0.2, flags 0x20 (Node-ID)
17           Label 24011, flags 0x1
18           IPv4 10.0.0.10, flags 0x0
19           Label 24011, flags 0x1
20           IPv4 172.16.0.22, flags 0x20 (Node-ID)
21           Label 3, flags 0x1
22           IPv4 10.0.0.4, flags 0x0
23           Label 3, flags 0x1
24
25   [linux:~/Downloads] juniper% tshark -r rsvp-resv-lp.pcap -V
26     Resource ReserVation Protocol (RSVP): RESV Message [...]
27   [...]
28     RECORD ROUTE: IPv4 172.16.0.5 (Node-id), IPv4 10.0.0.28,
29       Label 299920,  (Node-id)... (Node-id) (Node-id) (Node-id)
30       Length: 148
31       Object class: RECORD ROUTE object (21)
32       C-type: 1
33       IPv4 Subobject - 172.16.0.5 (Node-id), Local Protection Avail.
34           Type: 1 (IPv4)
35           Length: 8
36           IPv4 hop: 172.16.0.5 (172.16.0.5)
37           Prefix length: 32
38           Flags: 0x21
39               .... ...1 = Local Protection: Available
40               .... ..0. = Local Protection: Not used
41               .... .0.. = Bandwidth Protection: Not available
42               .... 0... = Node Protection: Not available
43               ..1. .... = Address Specifies a Node-id Address: Yes
44       IPv4 Subobject - 10.0.0.28, Local Protection Available
45           Type: 1 (IPv4)
46           Length: 8
47           IPv4 hop: 10.0.0.28 (10.0.0.28)
48           Prefix length: 32
49           Flags: 0x01
50               .... ...1 = Local Protection: Available
51               .... ..0. = Local Protection: Not used
52               .... .0.. = Bandwidth Protection: Not available
53               .... 0... = Node Protection: Not available
54               ..0. .... = Address Specifies a Node-id Address: No
55       Label Subobject - 299920, The label will be understood if
```

```
56                              received on any interface
57      [...]
```

P5 can act as a PLR for the PE4--->PE2 LSP by providing the requested protection, downstream from its position in the tunnel. For this reason, P5 sets the "Local protection: Available" flag on the two RRO entries that it adds to the Resv message. By looking at these flags, PE4 knows that P5 is able to provide local protection in case failure downstream happens. On the other hand, flag "Local protection: Use" is not set. Therefore, local protection is currently not active.

 It is essential for the head-end PE to be informed of the protection available and active at each of the transit nodes. Otherwise, it would tear down the LSP immediately upon failure detection.

At first glance, it might look strange that some protection capability for the 10.0.0.28 address (address from PE4-P5 link) is being reported. *Did you configure any protection for this link?* No. So far only the simple bypass LSP to protect the P5→P3 link has been configured. But if you carefully read RFC 4090, Section 4.4, you will note that this protection flag *indicates that the link downstream of this node is protected via a local-repair mechanism.* Therefore, it's not that the PE4-P5 link (to which IP address 10.0.0.28 belongs) is protected, but the link downstream of the node with the 10.0.0.28 address is. In essence, we're talking about the link downstream of the P5 node, which is P5→P3.

OK, *so what happens on P5?* Let's check that.

Example 19-24. MPLS RIB entry on P5 (Junos)

```
1      juniper@P5> show route label 299920 detail | match "Pref|via|Label"
2        *RSVP    Preference: 7/1
3                 Next hop: 10.0.0.14 via ge-2/0/4.0 weight 0x1, selected
4                 Label-switched-path PE4--->PE2
5                 Label operation: Swap 306128
6                 Next hop: 10.0.0.25 via ge-2/0/2.0 weight 0x8001
7                 Label-switched-path P5-PE3-P1-P3
8                 Label operation: Swap 306128, Push 299856(top)
```

There are two next hops with different weights. It's similar to the protection cases we discussed previously. The first next hop is the standard one used for normal label switching along the PE4--->PE2 tunnel. You can compare label 306128 (line 5 in the previous example) with the label shown in line 11 of Example 19-23. *Looks similar?* The second next hop, as the weight indicates, is the backup next hop. When P5 sends a packet over the backup next hop, it uses two labels (line 8): the normal label for

PE4--->PE2 tunnel (306128, the same as in line 5), and the additional top label 299856. *What is this label?* Check Figure 19-4 and Example 19-25.

Example 19-25. State for bypass LSP on P5 (Junos)

```
juniper@P5> show rsvp session ingress
To          From        State Rt Style Labelin Labelout LSPname
172.16.0.3  172.16.0.5  Up    0  1 SE     -    299856   P5-PE3-P1-P3
```

> In Junos, ingress (head-end) bypass LSPs are not visible when you use the show mpls lsp command. To display information about ingress (head-end) bypass LSPs, you need to use the show rsvp session command.

This is, in fact, the label for the bypass LSP created previously! So your regular LSP is tunneled inside the bypass LSP in case of P5→P3 link failure. The last segment (P1→P3) of the bypass LSP uses the implicit null label, meaning the traffic will arrive at P3 with the label from the regular LSP (306128). Does the fact that packet arrives at P3 on the *wrong* interface cause any problem (ge-2/0/3.0 instead of ge-2/0/4.0, which is on the path for the regular PE4--->PE1 LSP)? If you look again at lines 8, 11, 13, and 17 of Example 19-23, you will find that all labels on the path are advertised with flag 0x1. What does it mean? Again, lines 55 and 56 of Example 19-23 provide the answer: the label has global (per-node, not per-interface) significance, so packets with this label are properly forwarded regardless of the interface on which they are received. Perfect, you are now set.

If you check more entries in the MPLS RIB, such as in the next example, you can see that out of three tunnels transiting the P5→P3 link, only two tunnels are protected (have a backup next hop). These tunnels are PE3--->PE2 and PE4--->PE2. The PE4--->PE1 tunnel was not configured to request protection, so it is not protected.

> Remember that in RSVP-TE, protection needs to be explicitly requested on a per-tunnel basis.

Example 19-26. MPLS RIB on P5 (Junos)

```
1  juniper@P5> show route table mpls.0 | find RSVP
2  299920 *[RSVP/7/1] 00:34:52, metric 1
3     > to 10.0.0.14 via ge-2/0/4.0, label-switched-path PE4--->PE2
4       to 10.0.0.25 via ge-2/0/2.0, label-switched-path P5-PE3-P1-P3
5  299952 *[RSVP/7/1] 00:10:33, metric 1
6     > to 10.0.0.14 via ge-2/0/4.0, label-switched-path PE3--->PE2
```

```
7          to 10.0.0.25 via ge-2/0/2.0, label-switched-path P5-PE3-P1-P3
8      300000 *[RSVP/7/1] 00:09:20, metric 1
9          > to 10.0.0.14 via ge-2/0/4.0, label-switched-path PE4--->PE1
10     (...)
```

Manual link protection bypass in IOS XR: P4→P2 link, PE3--->PE2 LSP

To understand the complete picture about facility protection on both Junos and IOS XR planes, let's add a bypass LSP in the IOS XR plane (e.g., on router P4 to protect the P4→P2 link), as shown in Figure 19-5.

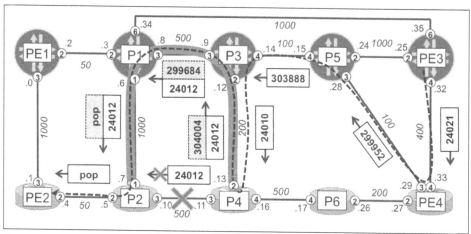

Figure 19-5. Facility (link) protection in IOS XR (P4→P2 link, PE3--->PE2 LSP)

The following IOS XR configuration creates a manual link bypass on P4:

Example 19-27. Manual link protection bypass LSP on P4 (IOS XR)

```
1      explicit-path name P4-P3-P1-P2
2        index 10 next-address strict ipv4 unicast 10.0.0.12
3        index 20 next-address strict ipv4 unicast 10.0.0.8
4        index 30 next-address strict ipv4 unicast 10.0.0.7
5        !
6      interface tunnel-te2
7        ipv4 unnumbered Loopback0
8        signalled-name P4-P3-P1-P2
9        destination 172.16.0.2
10       record-route
11       path-option 1 explicit name P4-P3-P1-P2
12       !
13     mpls traffic-eng
14       interface GigabitEthernet0/0/0/3
15         backup-path tunnel-te 2
```

Now, it's time to verify the link protection status on P4 (IOS XR) by comparing Figure 19-5 to Example 19-28 and Example 19-29.

Example 19-28. PE3--->PE2 RSVP-TE LSP with link-protection—PE3 (Junos)

```
1    juniper@PE3> show mpls lsp name PE3--->PE2 detail
2    (...)
3    172.16.0.22
4     From: 172.16.0.33, State: Up, ActiveRoute: 0, LSPname: PE3--->PE2
5     ActivePath: (primary)
6     Link protection desired
7    *Primary                    State: Up
8      Received RRO (ProtectionFlag 1=Available 2=InUse 4=B/W 8=Node
9                      10=SoftPreempt 20=Node-ID):
10       172.16.0.44(flag=0x20 Label=24021) 10.0.0.33(Label=24021)
11       172.16.0.5(flag=0x21) 10.0.0.28(flag=1 Label=299952)
12       172.16.0.3(flag=0x20) 10.0.0.14(Label=303888)
13       172.16.0.4(flag=0x21 Label=24010) 10.0.0.13(flag=1 Label=24010)
14       172.16.0.2(flag=0x20 Label=24012) 10.0.0.10(Label=24012)
15       172.16.0.22(flag=0x20 Label=3) 10.0.0.4(Label=3)
```

Example 19-29. Facility (link) protection state on P4 (IOS XR)

```
1    RP/0/0/CPU0:P4#show mpls traffic-eng tunnels 2 brief
2                   TUNNEL NAME        DESTINATION     STATUS  STATE
3                   tunnel-te2         172.16.0.2       up    up
4
5    RP/0/0/CPU0:P4#show mpls traffic-eng tunnels role mid | match ...
6      Tunnel Name: PE4--->PE2 Tunnel Role: Mid
7        Session Attributes: Local Prot: Set, Node Prot: Not Set,
8                            BW Prot: Not Set
9      Tunnel Name: PE2--->PE3 Tunnel Role: Mid
10       Session Attributes: Local Prot: Not Set, Node Prot: Not Set,
11                           BW Prot: Not Set
12     Tunnel Name: PE2--->PE4 Tunnel Role: Mid
13       Session Attributes: Local Prot: Not Set, Node Prot: Not Set,
14                           BW Prot: Not Set
15     Tunnel Name: PE3--->PE2 Tunnel Role: Mid
16       Session Attributes: Local Prot: Set, Node Prot: Not Set,
17                           BW Prot: Not Set
18
19   RP/0/0/CPU0:P4#show mpls forwarding labels 24010 detail
20   Local  Outgoing  Prefix      Outgoing     Next Hop     Bytes
21   Label  Label     or ID       Interface                 Switched
22   ------ --------- ----------- ------------ ------------ --------
23   24010  24012     39732          Gi0/0/0/3   10.0.0.10    0
24       Path Flags: 0x400 [ BKUP-IDX:1 (0xa14d64e0) ]
25   (...)
26
27   RP/0/0/CPU0:P4#show mpls traffic-eng fast-reroute database
28   LSP midpoint FRR information:
```

```
29    LSP Identifier          Local  Out Intf/        FRR Intf/  Status
30                            Label  Label            Label
31    --------------------    ------ ----------------  ---------- -------
32    172.16.0.33 39732 [4]   24010  Gi0/0/0/3:24012  tt2:24012  Ready
33    172.16.0.44 22 [29]     24023  Gi0/0/0/3:24012  tt2:24012  Ready
```

Let's analyze Example 19-29. As you can see, the bypass tunnel is up (line 3). Two (out of four) transit (mid point) LSPs request protection, which is signaled via the appropriate flags in Session Attributes Object (lines 7 and 16). Verifying the MPLS forwarding entry (lines 19 through 24) for one of the transit tunnels (Lines 13 and 14 in Example 19-28 determine the incoming and outgoing labels at P4, which are 24010 and 24012, respectively), you can see the normal outgoing label (24012, as in line 23) as well as some reference to the backup path (line 24). You can determine this backup path by using the command in line 27, which shows protection for the PE3--->PE2 (line 32) LSP and the PE4--->PE2 LSP (line 33). Again, you can see the standard primary outgoing interface and label as well as the backup next hop interface in different columns. In essence, incoming packets with the label 24010 are forwarded over Gi0/0/0/3 and the label is swapped to 24012. Or, if this interface is not available, packets are forwarded via bypass tunnel 2 and the label swapped to 24012. Because the bypass tunnel has its own label (see the *gray* labels in Figure 19-5), the end result is a label stack of two labels after P4 performs swap 24012 and push 304004 (bypass label) operations.

Unlike Junos, IOS XR always brings up the manual bypass tunnel, even if there is no single regular LSP that requires protection.

Manual Node-Link Protection Bypass

By now, you should be familiar with how to deploy link protection. So, let's create additional bypass tunnels, but this time to provide protection not simply against link failure, but also against downstream *node failure*, as well.

Manual node-link protection in IOS XR: P2 node, P4→P2 link, PE3--->PE2 LSP

So, for example, if you need a bypass tunnel from P4 to PE2 in order to protect against P2 failure, the following path (see Figure 19-6) meets the requirements: P4→P3→P1→PE1→PE2. The configuration of this bypass tunnel is similar to the one presented in Example 19-27, but the termination point is the neighbor's neighbor (PE2); it is no longer the directly connected neighbor (P2), against whose failure we want to protect. And, of course, the explicit path must not use the node being protected (P2).

Link protection bypass is often referenced as NHOP (next-hop) bypass, whereas node-link protection bypass is often referenced as NNHOP (next-next-hop) bypass.

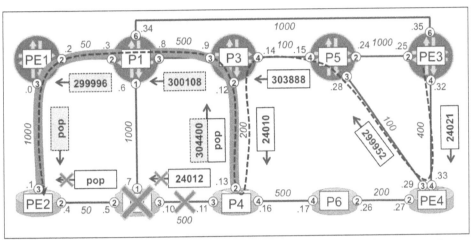

Figure 19-6. Facility (node) protection in IOS XR (P2 node, P4→P2 link, PE3--->PE2 LSP)

After configuring the new bypass LSP (not shown for brevity), let's see if some changes are visible after configuring NNHOP bypasses.

Example 19-30. Facility (node) protection verification on P4 (IOS XR)

```
1   RP/0/0/CPU0:P4#show mpls traffic-eng fast-reroute database
2   LSP midpoint FRR information:
3   LSP Identifier          Local  Out Intf/         FRR Intf/  Status
4                           Label  Label             Label
5   ---------------------   -----  ---------------   ---------  -------
6   172.16.0.33 39732 [1]   24010  Gi0/0/0/3:24012   tt22:Pop   Ready
7   172.16.0.44 22 [53]     24023  Gi0/0/0/3:24012   tt22:Pop   Ready
```

If you carefully compare the output from Example 19-29 and Example 19-30, you will realize that the tunnel used for protection has changed. Instead of tt2 (NHOP bypass terminated on P2), tt22 (NNHOP bypass terminated on PE2) is used.

Figure 19-6 shows the resulting label operations for LSP PE3--->PE2 after P2-P4 link failure, or after P2 node failure. Actually, P4 can protect the link P2-P4 with either a NHOP bypass or a NNHOP bypass. P4 chooses the best option available (and NNHOP is superior to NHOP). When the link P2-P4 fails, P4 does not know at first whether it is a link or a node failure, *so it reacts as if it had been a node failure.*

Before pushing the bypass LSP label, P4 pops the incoming label 24010. If you consider the bypass LSP as one hop, P4 is the penultimate hop and this label pop operation is the result of PHP. But how does P4 know that the packet must arrive unlabeled to PE2, if P4 and PE2 are not directly connected? The RRO included in the Resv messages of the protected LSP (PE3--->PE2) contains a list of next hop, and *also label information* (see Example 19-28). P4 knows that after swapping label 24010 for 24012 and sending a packet to P2, P2 will pop the label (Example 19-28, line 15) and send the packet to PE2. So, when it programs the NNHOP protection for the PE3--->PE2 LSP, P4 programs a backup next hop based on the NHOP's (not its own) label action.

Manual node-link protection in Junos: P3 node, P5→P3 link, PE3--->PE2 LSP

If you need a bypass tunnel from P5 to P4 in order to protect against P3 failure, one option (but not necessarily the shortest one) is to use the P5→PE3→P1→P2→P4 path. The configuration of this bypass tunnel (not shown for brevity) is similar to the one presented in Example 19-17, but the termination point is the neighbor's neighbor (P4).

After configuring the new bypass LSP, let's check the state on P5 (Junos). If you issue the operational commands from Example 19-20 and Example 19-26, you will see no changes. NNHOP bypass is not up, and the two regular transit tunnels (PE3--->PE2 and PE4--->PE2) requesting local protection still use NHOP bypass as a backup next hop. This means that the node (NNHOP) bypass is not working.

So, what is wrong here? Why does it work on P4 (IOS XR) but not on P5 (Junos)? You have just discovered a slightly different interpretation of RFC 4090 as implemented in Junos and IOS XR. In Junos, NNHOP bypass tunnels are used only if one or more regular LSPs request *node protection* in addition to *local protection*—in other words, if the *Node protection desired* flag (RFC 4090, Section 4.3) is set. However, as you can see in line 16 of Example 19-22, this is not currently the case for the PE4--->PE2 LSP (and it is not the case for the PE3--->PE2 LSP either). IOS XR, on the other hand, always attempts to provide the best possible protection (node protection, and if not possible, then link protection), regardless of whether the *Node protection desired* flag is set.

Let's extend the configuration of the PE3--->PE2 tunnel to request node protection (Example 19-31), which results in the *Node protection desired* flag being set in the Session Attribute object, as shown in Example 19-32.

Example 19-31. Node protection request for PE3→PE2 tunnel—PE3 (Junos)

```
protocols {
    mpls {
        label-switched-path PE3--->PE2 {
            node-link-protection;
}}}
```

Example 19-32. Protection state of transit LSPs on P5 (Junos)

```
1    juniper@P5> show mpls lsp detail | match "name|protect"
2      LSPname: PE4--->PE1
3      LSPname: PE4--->PE2
4        Link protection desired
5        Type: Link protected LSP
6      LSPname: PE3--->PE2, LSPpath: Primary
7        Node/Link protection desired
8        Type: Node/Link protected LSP
9      LSPname: PE2--->PE3
10     LSPname: PE2--->PE4
11     LSPname: PE1--->PE4, LSPpath: Primary
12
13   juniper@P5> show rsvp interface ge-2/0/4.0 extensive | find ...
14   Protection: On, Bypass: 2, LSP: 2, Protected LSP: 2,
15                                    Unprotected LSP: 0
16       2 Feb 10 12:52:45 New bypass P5-PE3-P1-P2-P4
17       1 Feb  9 21:15:06 New bypass P5-PE3-P1-P3
18     Bypass: P5-PE3-P1-P3, State: Up, Type: LP, LSP: 1, Backup: 0
19       3 Feb  9 21:15:08 Record Route:  10.0.0.25 10.0.0.34 10.0.0.9
20       2 Feb  9 21:15:08 Up
21       1 Feb  9 21:15:07 CSPF: computation result accepted
22     Bypass: P5-PE3-P1-P2-P4, State: Up, Type: NP, LSP: 1, Backup: 0
23       3 Feb 10 12:52:46 Record Route:  10.0.0.25 10.0.0.34 10.0.0.7
24                                        10.0.0.11
25       2 Feb 10 12:52:46 Up
26       1 Feb 10 12:52:45 CSPF: computation result accepted
27
28   juniper@P5> show route table mpls.0 | find RSVP
29   299920 *[RSVP/7/1] 15:27:11, metric 1
30      > to 10.0.0.14 via ge-2/0/4.0, label-switched-path PE4--->PE2
31        to 10.0.0.25 via ge-2/0/2.0, label-switched-path P5-PE3-P1-P3
32   300048 *[RSVP/7/1] 00:13:07, metric 1
33      > to 10.0.0.14 via ge-2/0/4.0, label-switched-path PE3--->PE2
34        to 10.0.0.25 via ge-2/0/2.0, label-switched-path P5-PE3-P1-P2-P4
35   (...)
```

The NNHOP bypass tunnel (P5-PE3-P1-P2-P4) immediately went up (line 16). Although two LSPs still require protection (line 14), one of the LSPs is now protected by the NHOP bypass (line 18) and another by a NNHOP bypass (line 22). Because the PE3--->PE2 tunnel is now protected via an NNHOP bypass, it is now protected against both the P5→P3 link as well as the P3 node failure.

The configuration change from link-protection to node-link protection causes a new LSP to be signaled. This results, for example, in a label change for the PE3--->PE2 LSP (compare line 5 from Example 19-26 with line 32 from Example 19-32). To avoid traffic interruption when switching from an old LSP (old labels) to a new LSP (new labels), PE3 follows a make-before-break approach. For some period of time, the two LSPs (with different LSP ID) belonging to the

PE3--->PE2 tunnel are up. PE3 later switches traffic from the old LSP to the new LSP, and eventually turns down the old LSP.

Following is the IOS XR configuration to request node protection:

Example 19-33. Node protection request for PE4→PE2 Tunnel—PE4 (IOS XR)

```
interface tunnel-te22
 fast-reroute protect node
```

This causes NNHOP bypass protection for the PE4→PE2 tunnel on P5, too. Because the NHOP bypass is no longer used by any regular LSP, the NHOP bypass will eventually time-out and will be torn down.

Facility Protection in Action

Most of the verifications thus far have been based on operational show commands in the prefailure state. Let's now simulate link failure events.

When a link or node fails, the traffic is locally repaired (redirected over the bypass LSP), and the head-end router of the regular LSP is notified about the failure. While traffic is locally repaired, the head-end router performs CSPF for the regular LSP in order to eventually calculate and signal a new path that avoids the failed facility (link or node). So, seeing a backup path on a traceroute output might be challenging, given that the path might already be resignaled.

If, however, the regular LSP uses an explicit (not dynamic) path, which includes the failed link or node, CSPF fails and it is not possible to resignal the tunnel. In this situation, local repair is in action forever. Even the RSVP-TE Path and Resv messages of the protected LSPs are tunneled through the bypass LSP, which is seen as one hop.

Manual node-link protection in Junos: P3 node, P5→P3 link, PE3--->PE2 LSP

Let's get back to the PE3--->PE2 regular LSP. When the P5→P3 link (or the P3 node) fails, the PLR (P5) removes the primary next hop (via ge-2/0/4 toward P3, label swap 303500), and only the backup next hop (using bypass LSP P5-PE3-P1-P2-P4) remains, as visible in Figure 19-7 and in Example 19-34.

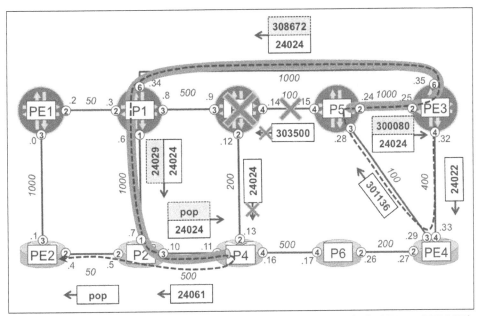

Figure 19-7. Facility (node) protection in Junos (P3 node, P5→P3 link, PE3--->PE2 LSP)

Example 19-34. Routing entry for PE3--->PE2 LSP on P5 (Junos)

```
1    juniper@P5> show route label 301136 detail | match <pattern>
2    301136 (1 entry, 1 announced)
3                    Next hop: 10.0.0.25 via ge-2/0/2.0, selected
4                    Label-switched-path P5-PE3-P1-P2-P4
5                    Label operation: Swap 24024, Push 300080(top)
```

To maintain the local protection state shown in Figure 19-7, the definition of the PE3--->PE2 LSP was changed to a strict ERO, and therefore global protection (new path calculation performed at the head-end router) does not succeed. The following traceroute is targeted to the VPN loopback prefix on PE2; thus, traffic follows the PE3--->PE2 LSP (PE3→PE4→P5→P3→P4→P2→PE2), patched by the NNHOP bypass LSP to avoid the failed P3 node (P5→PE3→P1→P2→P4). The bottom MPLS label corresponds to the VPN service and is not shown in Figure 19-7.

Example 19-35. Facility protection in action (Junos)

```
juniper@PE3> traceroute 192.168.1.22 routing-instance VRF-A
traceroute to 192.168.1.22 (192.168.1.22), 30 hops max ...
 1  PE4 (10.0.0.33)  22.833 ms  ...
      MPLS Label=24022 CoS=0 TTL=1 S=0       ## PE3--->PE2
      MPLS Label=24021 CoS=0 TTL=1 S=1       ## VPN
 2  P5 (10.0.0.28)  14.382 ms  ...
      MPLS Label=301136 CoS=0 TTL=1 S=0      ## PE3--->PE2
```

```
        MPLS Label=24021 CoS=0 TTL=2 S=1          ## VPN
  3  PE3 (10.0.0.25)  13.785 ms  ...
        MPLS Label=300080 CoS=0 TTL=1 S=0         ## NNHOP to avoid P3
        MPLS Label=24024 CoS=0 TTL=1 S=0          ## PE3--->PE2
        MPLS Label=24021 CoS=0 TTL=3 S=1          ## VPN
  4  P1 (10.0.0.34)  15.950 ms  ...
        MPLS Label=308672 CoS=0 TTL=1 S=0         ## NNHOP to avoid P3
        MPLS Label=24024 CoS=0 TTL=2 S=0          ## PE3--->PE2
        MPLS Label=24021 CoS=0 TTL=4 S=1          ## VPN
  5  P2 (10.0.0.7)  14.638 ms  ...
        MPLS Label=24029 CoS=0 TTL=1 S=0          ## NNHOP to avoid P3
        MPLS Label=24024 CoS=0 TTL=3 S=0          ## PE3--->PE2
        MPLS Label=24021 CoS=0 TTL=5 S=1          ## VPN
  6  P4 (10.0.0.11)  13.133 ms  ...
        MPLS Label=24024 CoS=0 TTL=1 S=0          ## PE3--->PE2
        MPLS Label=24021 CoS=0 TTL=6 S=1          ## VPN
  7  P2 (10.0.0.10)  12.445 ms  ...
        MPLS Label=24061 CoS=0 TTL=1 S=0          ## PE3--->PE2
        MPLS Label=24021 CoS=0 TTL=7 S=1          ## VPN
  8  PE2 (10.0.0.4)  13.066 ms  ...
```

The first label (PE3--->PE2) is swapped on each node, whereas the second label (VPN) remains constant. Now, when arriving at P5, traffic is redirected over the NNHOP bypass LSP in order to avoid the P3 node. This bypass LSP terminates on P4, so you can see up to P2 node (the penultimate node for the NNHOP bypass LSP) three labels:

- The first label is the NNHOP bypass LSP label, and it is swapped at each hop.

- The second label is the PE3--->PE2 regular LSP label allocated by NNHOP node, and it remains constant inside the bypass.

- The third label is the VPN label, and it remains constant end to end.

Before P2 sends the traffic to P4 along the NNHOP bypass LSP, it removes the NNHOP label (PHP); thus, traffic arrives to P4 with only two labels (PE3--->PE2 + VPN). From this point, it continues normally along the PE3--->PE2 regular LSP up to PE2.

So, the protection works as expected! However, from what you can see, the path taken during protection (PE3→PE4→P5→PE3→P1→P2→P4→P2→PE2) is certainly suboptimal. Nodes PE3 and P2 are visited twice, for example. Such suboptimal paths are typical in a facility protection scheme, because the bypass LSP simply *patches* the failed facility (link or node). Facility protection does not try to make end-to-end optimal backup paths, but such a suboptimal forwarding state typically takes a relatively short time for regular LSPs with dynamic path option. As already discussed, in the meantime the head-end router performs CSPF for the regular LSP, so this LSP is eventually signaled to a different, more optimal path that avoids failed links.

But how does the head-end router realize that facility protection is active? It gets the information via appropriate flags in the RECORD ROUTE object. Let's check that.

Example 19-36. RECORD ROUTE object with "Local Protection in Use" flag (Junos)

```
1    juniper@PE3> show mpls lsp ingress name PE3--->PE2 detail
2    [...]
3      Received RRO (ProtectionFlag 1=Available 2=InUse 4=B/W 8=Node
4                    10=SoftPreempt 20=Node-ID):
5        172.16.0.44(flag=0x29 Label=24021) 10.0.0.33(flag=9 Label=24021)
6        172.16.0.5(flag=0x2b) 10.0.0.28(flag=0xb Label=301136)
7        172.16.0.3(flag=0x29) 10.0.0.14(flag=9 Label=307424)
8        172.16.0.4(flag=0x29 Label=24024) 10.0.0.13(flag=9 Label=24024)
9        172.16.0.2(flag=0x21 Label=24061) 10.0.0.10(flag=1 Label=24061)
10       172.16.0.22(flag=0x20 Label=3) 10.0.0.4(Label=3)
```

You can see that 172.16.0.5 (loopback of P5) is reported with 0x2b flags. In other words, the following flags are set (see RFC 4090, Section 4.4, and Example 19-23, where meaning of these flags is shown):

0x01
    Local protection available

0x02
    Local protection in use

0x08
    Node protection available

0x20
    Address specifies a Node-ID address

0x01 + 0x02 + 0x08 + 0x20 = 0x2b. Because the flag 0x02 is set by the P5 node, PE3 knows that local protection is used (active) for forwarding at P5. Flag 0x02 is not set at other nodes; thus, other nodes do not use local protection. However, because flag 0x01 is set on all the nodes, local protection is available (ready), and can be immediately used, if downstream failure happens as per the reporting node. In other words, there are bypass LSPs available to protect all the links, and one of these bypass LSPs is currently active.

Manual node-link protection in IOS XR: P3 node, P5→P3 link, PE3--->PE2 LSP

Now, let's examine facility protection in action on the IOS XR plane. For the purposes of this verification, the PE4--->PE2 regular LSP is bound (via an explicit path option) to the PE4→P6→P4→P2→PE1 path prior to simulating the P6→P4 link (or P4 node) failure. To match Figure 19-8 to Example 19-37, remember that for space reasons

Figure 19-8 does not show the VPN label, which remains constant all the way from PE4 to PE2.

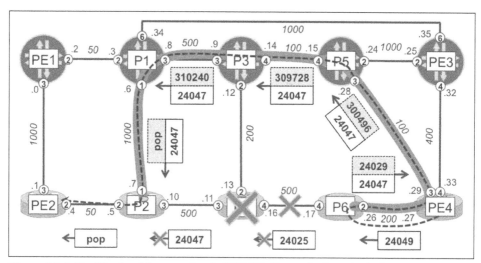

Figure 19-8. Facility (node) protection in IOS XR (P4 node, P6->P4 link, PE4-->PE2 LSP)

Example 19-37. Facility protection in action (IOS XR)

```
1   RP/0/0/CPU0:PE4#traceroute vrf VRF-A 192.168.1.22
2   (...)
3    1  10.0.0.26 [MPLS: Labels 24049/24021 Exp 0]
4    2  10.0.0.27 [MPLS: Labels 24029/24047/24021 Exp 0]
5    3  10.0.0.28 [MPLS: Labels 300496/24047/24021 Exp 0]
6    4  10.0.0.14 [MPLS: Labels 309728/24047/24021 Exp 0]
7    5  10.0.0.8 [MPLS: Labels 310240/24047/24021 Exp 0]
8    6  10.0.0.7 [MPLS: Labels 24047/24021 Exp 0]
9    7  10.0.0.4
10
11  RP/0/0/CPU0:PE4#show mpls traffic-eng tunnels 22 detail
12  [...]
13  Resv Info:
14   Record Route:
15     IPv4 172.16.0.6, flags 0x2b (Node-ID, Protection: available,
16                                 inuse, node)
17     Label 24049, flags 0x1
18     IPv4 10.0.0.26, flags 0xb (Protection: available, inuse, node)
19     Label 24049, flags 0x1
20     IPv4 172.16.0.2, flags 0x21 (Node-ID, Protection: available)
21     Label 24047, flags 0x1
22     IPv4 10.0.0.7, flags 0x1 (Protection: available)
23     Label 24047, flags 0x1
24     IPv4 172.16.0.22, flags 0x20 (Node-ID)
25     Label 3, flags 0x1
```

```
26      IPv4 10.0.0.4, flags 0x0
27      Label 3, flags 0x1
28    Fspec: avg rate=0 kbits, burst=1000 bytes, peak rate=0 kbits
29
30  RP/0/0/CPU0:P6#show mpls traffic-eng fast-reroute database
31  (...)
32  LSP Identifier          Local  Out Intf/       FRR Intf/      Status
33                          Label  Label           Label
34  -------------------- ------ --------------- ------------- -------
35  172.16.0.44 22 [63]     24049  tt111:24047                   Active
```

Similar to the previously observed Junos case, you can see traffic being redirected over the NNHOP bypass LSP, which follows the P6→PE4→P5→P3→P1→P2 path. You can also observe the flag 0x02 (*Local protection in use*) being set (line 15) in addition to some other flags. And, finally, facility protection is now active on P6 router (line 35).

Automatic Protection Bypass

Creating bypass LSPs manually, as done so far in this chapter, might be a very challenging task. Fortunately, both IOS XR and Junos offer the possibility of automatic bypass LSP creation, as configured in Example 19-38 and Example 19-39. This is similar to the automatic bypass tunnels for extending LFA coverage discussed in Chapter 18.

Example 19-38. Automatic bypass tunnel configuration (IOS XR)

```
group GR-MPLS-TE
 mpls traffic-eng
  interface 'GigabitEthernet.*'
   auto-tunnel backup
end-group
!
ipv4 unnumbered mpls traffic-eng Loopback0
!
mpls traffic-eng
 apply-group GR-MPLS-TE
 auto-tunnel backup
  tunnel-id min 101 max 199
```

Example 19-39. Automatic bypass tunnel configuration (Junos)

```
groups {
    GR-RSVP {
        protocols {
            rsvp {
                interface "<*[es]*>" {
                    link-protection;
}}}}}
```

```
protocols {
    rsvp {
        apply-groups GR-RSVP;
}}
```

In both IOS XR and Junos, you enable automatic bypass tunnel creation on an interface basis, using the `auto-tunnel backup` or `link-protection` keywords, respectively. RSVP-TE auto tunneling has been already discussed in Chapter 2 and
Chapter 5. Using groups simplifies the configuration of multiple interfaces, and the
regular expression in Example 19-39 matches both Ethernet and SONET interfaces.

> In IOS XR, manual and automatic bypass tunnel configuration
> cannot coexist on the same interface. In Junos, they can, and man-
> ual bypass tunnel is preferred. If a manual bypass tunnel is not
> operational (not configured or configured but in down state),
> Junos establishes an automatic bypass tunnel.

Additionally, let's request node-link protection (refer to Example 19-31 and
Example 19-33) for all regular tunnels and verify the state of the network, as demonstrated in Example 19-40.

Example 19-40. Bypass LSPs on PE1 (Junos)

```
juniper@PE1> show rsvp session | match <pattern>
Ingress RSVP: 7 sessions
To              From            LSPname
172.16.0.1      172.16.0.11     Bypass->10.0.0.3
172.16.0.3      172.16.0.11     Bypass->10.0.0.3->10.0.0.9
172.16.0.22     172.16.0.11     Bypass->10.0.0.1
172.16.0.33     172.16.0.11     Bypass->10.0.0.3->10.0.0.35
Egress RSVP: 6 sessions
To              From            LSPname
172.16.0.11     172.16.0.22     autob_PE2_t101_Gi0_0_0_3
172.16.0.11     172.16.0.33     Bypass->10.0.0.34->10.0.0.2
172.16.0.11     172.16.0.1      Bypass->10.0.0.2
Transit RSVP: 4 sessions
To              From            LSPname
172.16.0.2      172.16.0.22     autob_PE2_t103_Gi0_0_0_2
172.16.0.4      172.16.0.22     autob_PE2_t102_Gi0_0_0_2_172.16.0.2
172.16.0.22     172.16.0.2      autob_P2_t102_Gi0_0_0_2
```

As you can see, IOS XR and Junos (look at the column labeled `From`) follow different
naming conventions for automatic bypass tunnels. Let's review the terminology:

NHOP (link protection) bypass tunnel
    Junos: `Bypass->`*<NHOP-LINK-IP>*

For example, the NHOP bypass tunnel started on PE1 to protect traffic forwarded via PE1→P1 (ge-2/0/2.0, NHOP-LINK-IP = 10.0.0.3) link:

```
Bypass->10.0.0.3
```

IOS XR: `autob_<S-NODE>_t<ID>_<S-INTF>`

For example, the NHOP bypass tunnel started on PE2 to protect traffic forwarded via PE2→P2 (Gi0/0/0/2, NHOP-LINK-IP = 10.0.0.5) link:

```
autob_PE2_t103_Gi0_0_0_2
```

NNHOP (node and link protection) bypass tunnel

Junos: `Bypass-><NHOP-LINK-IP>-><NNHOP-LINK-IP>`

For example, the NNHOP bypass tunnel started on PE1 to protect traffic forwarded through P1 node (NHOP-LOOPBACK-IP=172.16.0.1) via PE1→P1→P3 path (ge-2//0/2.0, NHOP-LINK-IP = 10.0.0.3, NNHOP-LINK-IP = 10.0.0.9):

```
Bypass->10.0.0.3->10.0.0.9
```

IOS XR: `autob_<S-NODE>_t<ID>_<S-INTF>_<NHOP-LOOPBACK-IP>`

For example, the NNHOP bypass tunnel started on PE2 to protect traffic forwarded through P2 node (NHOP-LOOPBACK-IP=172.16.0.2) via PE2→P2→P4 path (Gi0/0/0/2, NHOP-LINK-IP = 10.0.0.5, NNHOP-LINK-IP = 10.0.0.11):

```
autob_PE2_t102_Gi0_0_0_2_172.16.0.2
```

It's noteworthy that the automatic bypass feature generates a single NHOP bypass tunnel per protected link. However, multiple NNHOP tunnels might be created, depending on the regular LSPs transiting the NHOP node. If in Figure 19-8 you temporarily change the metric of the P1-P2 to 200, regular tunnels from PE1 and PE2 will take following paths:

- PE1--->PE2 tunnel: PE1→P1→**P2**→PE2
- PE1--->PE3 tunnel: PE1→P1→**PE3**
- PE1--->PE4 tunnel: PE1→P1→**P3**→P5→PE4
- PE2--->PE1 tunnel: PE2→P2→**P1**→PE1
- PE2--->PE3 tunnel: PE2→P2→**P1**→PE3
- PE2--->PE4 tunnel: PE2→P2→**P4**→P3→P5→PE4

For all three regular tunnels starting from PE1, the NHOP is the same node (P1). Similarly, for all three regular tunnels starting from PE2, the NHOP is P2. However, three NNHOP automatic bypass tunnels are created on PE1, because NNHOPs are different for each regular LSP started from PE1 (NNHOPs are P2, PE3, and P3, respectively). On PE2, two NNHOP bypass tunnels are required, as two different NNHOPs are used (P1 and P4). Let's verify that in the following two examples:

Example 19-41. NNHOP tunnel status on PE1 (Junos)

```
juniper@PE1> show rsvp interface ge-2/0/2.0 extensive | match ...
Protection: On, Bypass: 3, LSP: 3, Protected LSP: 3,
                                  Unprotected LSP: 0
  Bypass: Bypass->10.0.0.3->10.0.0.7, State: Up, Type: NP, LSP: 1
  Bypass: Bypass->10.0.0.3->10.0.0.9, State: Up, Type: NP, LSP: 1
  Bypass: Bypass->10.0.0.3->10.0.0.35, State: Up, Type: NP, LSP: 1

juniper@PE1> show route table inet.3 protocol rsvp
(...)
172.16.0.22/32 *[RSVP/7/1] 00:53:08, metric 300
    > to 10.0.0.3 via ge-2/0/2.0, LSP PE1--->PE2
      to 10.0.0.1 via ge-2/0/3.0, LSP Bypass->10.0.0.3->10.0.0.7
172.16.0.33/32 *[RSVP/7/1] 03:16:55, metric 1050
    > to 10.0.0.3 via ge-2/0/2.0, LSP PE1--->PE3
      to 10.0.0.1 via ge-2/0/3.0, LSP Bypass->10.0.0.3->10.0.0.35
172.16.0.44/32 *[RSVP/7/1] 03:16:54, metric 750
    > to 10.0.0.3 via ge-2/0/2.0, LSP PE1--->PE4
      to 10.0.0.1 via ge-2/0/3.0, LSP Bypass->10.0.0.3->10.0.0.9
```

Example 19-42. NNHOP tunnel status on PE2 (IOS XR)

```
RP/0/0/CPU0:PE2#show mpls traffic-eng tunnels auto-tunnel
               | include Name
Name: tunnel-te102  Destination: 172.16.0.4   (auto-tunnel backup)
  Signalled-Name: autob_PE2_t102_Gi0_0_0_2_172.16.0.2
Name: tunnel-te104  Destination: 172.16.0.1   (auto-tunnel backup)
  Signalled-Name: autob_PE2_t104_Gi0_0_0_2_172.16.0.2

RP/0/0/CPU0:PE2#show mpls traffic-eng fast-reroute database
Tunnel  Out Intf/        FRR Intf/        Status
        Label            Label
-------  ----------------  ----------------  -------
tt11    Gi0/0/0/2:24041  tt104:307984     Ready
tt33    Gi0/0/0/2:24015  tt104:307968     Ready
tt44    Gi0/0/0/2:24014  tt102:24025      Ready
```

In Junos, you can easily determine for which NNHOP the bypass is established, because NHOP and NNHOP link addresses are encoded in the bypass tunnel name. In IOS XR, you need to execute more commands to find that out.

The RSVP-TE facility protection design is now final. All regular tunnels are protected against transit node and link failures, and appropriate states (primary and backup next hops) are created on all routers. There is 100% backup coverage for both node and link failures. Compared to the much more extensive efforts required to achieve 100% backup coverage with LFA, you can see that RSVP-TE is much simpler. You simply need to enable automatic bypass tunnels, and request node and link protection for regular tunnels, and you are done.

The semantics of the Junos `node-link-protection` keyword used in LFA and RSVP-TE facility protection configurations is slightly different. In LFA, backup next hop is selected only if it fulfills both node and link-protection criteria. In RSVP-TE facility protection, the backup next hop that fulfills node-protection criterion is preferred, but if not found, the backup next hop that fulfills link protection criterion is used. To achieve similar behavior in LFA, you must additionally use the `node-link-degradation` keyword.

RSVP-TE One-to-One Protection

Whereas you can consider facility protection a rough equivalent of per-link LFA, you can view one-to-one protection as a rough equivalent of per-prefix LFA (in the analogy, replace prefixes with protected RSVP-TE LSPs). In one-to-one protection, each eligible regular tunnel is protected independently with separate *detour* LSPs.

Facility backup uses *bypass* LSPs, whereas one-to-one backup uses *detour* LSPs for protection.

With facility backup, during a failure event, traffic belonging to multiple regular tunnels might be forwarded (tunneled) over a single bypass LSP. In one-to-one backup, detour LSPs are associated with a single regular tunnel only; thus, traffic on that single tunnel might use its associated detour LSPs during a failure event. The native merging feature, which will be explained soon, reduces the impact of these detours in terms of scalability.

You can view one-to-one protection as an extension of the RSVP-TE path protection concept discussed earlier in this chapter. In path protection, the head-end router creates the primary and secondary (standby) LSP and performs switchover to the secondary LSP upon failure of the primary LSP. The head-end can detect a failure of the directly connected neighbor relatively fast. However, detecting a failure of transit nodes used by the primary path farther away from the head-end might take some time. Thus, switchover to the secondary standby LSP might be delayed, which is a clear limitation of the path protection scheme.

The one-to-one backup concept overcomes this limitation through automatic creation of secondary standby LSPs at each transit node along the primary path. These secondary standby LSPs are called *detour* LSPs in one-to-one backup architecture. Apart from the name itself, another difference is that detour LSPs don't need to be completely disjointed from the primary path. It is enough if they are disjointed until the NNHOP only, because protection against failure of the NNHOP is handled by the detour LSP initiated at the next hop. This concept is illustrated in Figure 19-9.

 As of this writing, support for one-to-one backup was available in Junos but not in IOS XR.

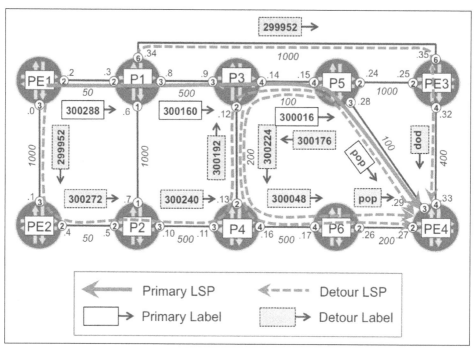

Figure 19-9. One-to-one backup with detour LSPs

From a configuration perspective, you simply need to enable one-to-one protection for each LSP that you want to protect, as demonstrated in Example 19-43.

Before starting this section, all RSVP-TE tunnels (full mesh between PE routers) are set back to their basic state (single, dynamic path option per tunnel) and all the facility protection specific configurations removed.

Example 19-43. One-to-one protection configuration (Junos)

```
protocols {
    mpls {
        label-switched-path PE1--->PE4 {
```

```
          fast-reroute;
}}}
```

 The fast-reroute keyword used in RSVP-TE tunnel configurations in IOS XR and Junos has completely different meanings. In IOS XR, it designates specific RSVP-TE tunnels as eligible for facility (link or node) protection. Exactly the same keyword in Junos results in enabling one-to-one protection for a specific RSVP-TE tunnel. Consult Table 19-1 for the terminology used by RFC 4090. Also check the documentation for both vendors.

The primary LSP for PE1--->PE4 tunnel is established via the shortest path, which is PE1→P1→P3→P5→PE4. Additionally, the head-end router as well as each transit (mid-point) router presignal the detour LSPs. Let's verify, at least on three first nodes from regular LSP, what paths are selected for these detour LSPs (see Example 19-44).

Example 19-44. Detour LSPs for PE1→PE4 LSP

```
1   juniper@PE1> show rsvp session name PE1--->PE4 extensive | match ...
2     Detour is Up
3     Detour Explct route: 10.0.0.1 10.0.0.5 10.0.0.11 10.0.0.12
4                          10.0.0.15 10.0.0.29
5     Detour Record route: <self> 10.0.0.1 10.0.0.5 10.0.0.11 10.0.0.12
6                          10.0.0.15 10.0.0.29
7     Detour Label out: 299952
8
9   juniper@P1> show rsvp session name PE1--->PE4 extensive | match ...
10    Detour is Up
11    Detour Explct route: 10.0.0.35 10.0.0.33
12    Detour Record route: 10.0.0.2 <self> 10.0.0.35 10.0.0.33
13    Detour Label out: 299952
14
15  juniper@P3> show rsvp session name PE1--->PE4 extensive | match ...
16    Detour is Up
17    Detour Explct route: 10.0.0.13 10.0.0.17 10.0.0.27
18    Detour Record route: 10.0.0.2 10.0.0.8 <self> 10.0.0.13 10.0.0.17
19                         10.0.0.27
20    Detour Label out: 300224
21  Detour branch from 10.0.0.0, to skip 172.16.0.1, Up
22    Explct route: 10.0.0.15 10.0.0.29
23    Record route: 10.0.0.0 10.0.0.4 10.0.0.10 10.0.0.13 <self>
24                  10.0.0.15 10.0.0.29
25    Label in: 300192, Label out: 300016
26  Detour branch from 10.0.0.15, to skip 172.16.0.44, Up
27    Explct route: 10.0.0.13 10.0.0.17 10.0.0.27
28    Record route: 10.0.0.2 10.0.0.8 10.0.0.14 10.0.0.15 <self>
29                  10.0.0.13 10.0.0.17 10.0.0.27
30    Label in: 300176, Label out: 300224
```

The path for the detour LSP is by default the shortest path to the destination (PE4), which avoids the primary next-hop node (or link to primary next-hop in case of the penultimate node: P5). That is:

Detour from PE1:
  PE1→PE2→P2→P4→P3→P5→PE4 (avoid P1 node, lines 3 through 6 and 21 through 24)

Detour from P1
  P1→PE3→PE4 (avoid P3 node, lines 11 and 12)

Detour from P3
  P3→P4→P6→PE4 (avoid P5 node, lines 17 and 18)

Detour from P5
  P5→P3→P4→P6→PE4 (avoid P5→PE4 link, lines 26 through 29)

As you can see, the detour LSP to skip the NHOP node doesn't necessarily traverse the NNHOP node (in case of facility backup with node protection, automatic bypass LSP always terminates on the NNHOP node). For example, the detour from P1 to skip node P3 does not traverse P5 (which is the NNHOP node). Put simply, the shortest path from P1 to PE4 that avoids P3 is not via P5.

Another observation is the fact that some detour LSPs use (partially) overlapping paths with another detour LSP or with a primary LSP. For example, the detour LSP from P3 and the detour LSP from P5 have a common P3→P4→P6→PE4 segment (lines 18, 19, 28, and 29). Similarly the detour LSP from PE1 shares the P3→P5→PE4 segment with the primary path.

One-to-one backup architecture is clever enough to realize this and *merge* LSPs (multiple detour LSPs or the detour LSP with the primary LSP) to avoid wasting resources. When the detour LSP from P3 and the detour LSP from P5 are merged together in one LSP at P3 (the *merge node*), P3 uses one single RSVP Path message in the downstream segment. Indeed, downstream from the merge node, there is only one label allocated for the two merged LSPs (lines 20 and 30).

To signal detour LSPs and keep track of merged detour LSPs, RFC 4090 introduces an additional RVSP-TE object: DETOUR object. The DETOUR object is basically a list of [*PLR_ID, Avoid_Node_ID*] pairs. Each pair represents a single detour LSP. For example, [10.0.0.12, 172.16.0.5] represents a detour LSP started at P3 (10.0.0.12) to avoid P5 (172.16.0.5) node. Let's see how a single RSVP-TE Path message, captured on the P4→P6 link, is used for multiple (merged) detour LSPs (from P3, and from P5).

Example 19-45. RSVP-TE Path message with DETOUR object

```
[linux:~/Downloads] juniper% tshark -r rsvp-path-merge.pcap -V
(...)
 Resource ReserVation Protocol (RSVP): PATH Message. SESSION:
   IPv4-LSP, Destination 172.16.0.44, Short Call ID 0,
   Tunnel ID 54692, Ext ID ac10000b. SENDER TEMPLATE: IPv4-LSP,
   Tunnel Source: 172.16.0.11, Short Call ID: 0, LSP ID: 1.
(...)
     DETOUR:
         Length: 20
         Object class: DETOUR object (63)
         C-type: 7
         PLR ID 1: 10.0.0.12
         Avoid Node ID 1: 172.16.0.5
         PLR ID 2: 10.0.0.15
         Avoid Node ID 2: 172.16.0.44
```

Another way to verify the LSP merging operation is to check the MPLS routing entries for incoming labels of different LSPs that are eligible for merging (in this case, the primary path, and the detour from PE1).

Example 19-46. Merging operation at merge node P3

```
1    juniper@P3> show route label 300160 detail | match <pattern>
2    300160 (1 entry, 1 announced)
3          Next hop: 10.0.0.15 via ge-0/0/4.0 weight 0x1, selected
4            Label-switched-path PE1--->PE4
5            Label operation: Swap 300016
6          Next hop: 10.0.0.13 via ge-0/0/2.0 weight 0x4001
7            Label-switched-path PE1--->PE4
8            Label operation: Swap 300224
9
10   juniper@P3> show route label 300192 detail | match <pattern>
11   300192 (1 entry, 1 announced)
12         Next hop: 10.0.0.15 via ge-0/0/4.0 weight 0x1, selected
13           Label-switched-path PE1--->PE4
14           Label-operation: Swap 300016
```

In Example 19-46, the incoming label 300160 (primary LSP) is swapped to label 300016 (line 5) when sent via ge-0/0/4.0 (primary next hop). At the same time, label 300192 (detour LSP from PE1 to avoid P1) is swapped to label 300016 (line 14), too, effectively merging two LSPs (primary + detour from PE1) downstream of the P3 node.

Example 19-47 simulates the P3→P5 link failure and performs traceroute to a PE4's VPN prefix for verification (again, during this verification the primary path was *statically fixed* using an explicit path option). The VPN label is 16 and remains constant.

Example 19-47. One-to-one protection in action (Junos)

```
juniper@PE1> traceroute 192.168.1.44 routing-instance VRF-A
 1  P1 (10.0.0.3)  13.831 ms  7.650 ms  6.315 ms
    MPLS Label=300288 CoS=0 TTL=1 S=0
    MPLS Label=16 CoS=0 TTL=1 S=1
 2  P3 (10.0.0.9)  6.668 ms  5.828 ms  6.962 ms
    MPLS Label=300160 CoS=0 TTL=1 S=0
    MPLS Label=16 CoS=0 TTL=2 S=1
 3  P4 (10.0.0.13)  8.084 ms  5.744 ms  7.895 ms
    MPLS Label=300224 CoS=0 TTL=1 S=0
    MPLS Label=16 CoS=0 TTL=3 S=1
 4  P6 (10.0.0.17)  5.673 ms  6.361 ms  7.924 ms
    MPLS Label=300048 CoS=0 TTL=1 S=0
    MPLS Label=16 CoS=0 TTL=4 S=1
 5 PE4-VRF-A (192.168.1.44) 6.075 ms 6.625 ms 6.421 ms
```

From traceroute, it is obvious that P3 realizes the link failure and uses a backup next hop (lines 6 and 8 in Example 19-46) to forward the traffic via the P3→P4→P6→PE4 detour LSP. If you compare typical traceroute when facility protection is active (Example 19-35 and Example 19-37) with traceroute when one-to-one protection is active, you can spot two major differences:

- Facility protection results in an additional label (bypass LSP) being pushed on the label stack; thus, the resulting label stack is bigger (increased from two to three labels in the examples). One-to-one backup, on the other hand, doesn't cause label stack increase, because the label action on the backup next hop is swap (line 8 in Example 19-46) and not swap/push (line 8 in Example 19-24). In the PHP case, the label action in one-to-one is pop, as compared to swap in facility protection.

- The path taken by traffic during active protection is typically more optimal with one-to-one backup, because one-to-one detour LSPs are established over the shortest post-convergence path to the final destination (avoiding protected node). In facility backup, on the other hand, the bypass LSPs are established only to the NHOP or NNHOP node, resulting typically in suboptimal traffic forwarding during failures.

So, which is better: facility backup or one-to-one backup? The answer is: it depends! One-to-one backup provides more optimal backup paths. Additionally, it has the ability to spread backup paths of multiple regular LSPs using the same resource (link and node), because detour LSPs are separate for each regular LSP. Thus, during failure, traffic originally flowing along the same (failed) link might be forwarded over different paths, minimizing the possible likelihood of intermittent congestion. In facility protection, traffic is forwarded over the same bypass LSP; consequently, intermittent congestion might occur. Conversely, one-to-one protection results in more

RSVP-TE states that need to be maintained in the network, because detours are specific to each regular LSP. Table 19-2 provides a comparison between the total number of RSVP sessions (first row: regular + bypass LSPs, second row: regular + detour LSPs) that need to be maintained at each node using the example topology from this section. The table assumes full mesh of regular LSPs between PE routers, and the desire for both node and link protection.

Table 19-2. Comparison of facility protection and one-to-one protection

Type	P1	P2	P3	P4	P5	P6	PE1	PE2	PE3	PE4
Facility	13	16	15	16	13	5	13	16	12	18
One to One	19	16	20	19	16	8	16	16	15	23

As more and more regular LSPs are added to the network, the differences might be greater.

 One-to-one protection is especially advantageous in ring topologies, for which the suboptimal characteristic of facility backup is quite remarkable, causing a two-stage U-turn effect. Grab a piece of paper and a pencil and do the simulation yourself!

Transit Fast-Restoration Summary

A variety of local protection options to minimize traffic loss during transit link or node failures were discussed in this chapter. *Which is the best?* Again, the answer is: it depends. Each of the options has some advantages and disadvantages, and depending on the focus in the particular deployment, you might choose one or the other. In typical deployments, a mixture of protection technologies is used. For example, RSVP-TE based in the core network, and LFA based in the edge.

Chapter 20 and Chapter 21 discuss additional protection features, this time related to the failure of the egress PE node or egress PE-CE link.

FIB Optimization for Fast Restoration

In Chapter 18 and Chapter 19, you discovered different ways to protect the traffic in case of transit node or transit link failure. All the methods are based on preinstalling a backup next hop in the hardware Forwarding Information Base (HW FIB). Upon network failure, the primary next hop is removed from the HW FIB and traffic uses the preinstalled backup next hop. The difference between each method lies in how the backup next hop is determined and how the backup path is established.

This chapter explores additional FIB optimization techniques that you can implement on the ingress PE to improve failover convergence. PE nodes typically hold a large number of service prefixes. A prefix in this context can be a typical L3 VPN prefix, but it can also be information required to forward traffic using other types of services, such as pseudowires (PWs) signaled by using BGP or LDP. When it comes to optimization of failover times on the ingress PE, there are two main areas requiring special attention:

- Optimization of next-hop structures in the hardware FIB
- Preinstallation of the next hop associated with the backup egress PE

These optimization techniques are explored in the next two sections.

Next-Hop Hierarchy

If you go back and reexamine Figure 18-1 carefully, you probably realize that failure case number 3 is not exactly the same as failure case numbers 5 or 7. Similarly, failure case number 4 is not quite the same as failure case number 6. What makes failure cases 3 or 4 different from failure cases 5, 6, or 7? *The scale!*

In failure cases 5, 6, and 7, the *Point of Local Repair* (PLR) is a pure-P router. The pure-P router typically has a very limited number of prefixes. Only infrastructure prefixes (loopback and link addresses of MPLS transport infrastructure network) are present on the P router. Even in very large MPLS transport networks, with several thousands of nodes, the number of infrastructure prefixes does not exceed 10,000 to 20,000. On PE routers, however, the number of service prefixes can reach several hundred thousand, if not a million routes in very highly scaled designs.

Why is this scaling difference important from a failover perspective? The local repair techniques discussed in previous chapters are based on the following:

- Preinstalling both primary and backup next hops in the HW FIB
- Removing primary next hops from the HW FIB after detecting failure

It's easy to imagine that removing the primary next hops associated with 10,000 routes is much faster than removing the primary next hops associated with one million routes, unless some tricks are in place to ensure that the primary next-hop removal does not depend on the number of prefixes.

And this trick is actually the hierarchical—that is, not flat—structure of next hops installed in the HW FIB. In Junos, such hierarchical next-hop structures are called *indirect next hops* or *chained composite next hops*, whereas in IOS XR, you can find the term *Prefix Independent Convergence (PIC) Core* to describe this. Whatever term is used, it is about next-hop hierarchy.

Topology used in Chapter 20 and in Chapter 21

As of this writing, some of the features discussed in Chapter 20 and Chapter 21 are not implemented on the virtualized x86-based network operating system flavors. For this reason, we used a physical topology, and because we only had one physical ASR 9000, the topology looked like in Figure 20-1. Fortunately, it was enough to test all the features.

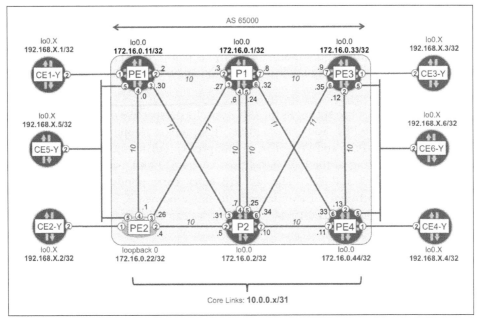

Figure 20-1. Chapter 20 and Chapter 21 topology

In the topology shown in Figure 20-1, various MPLS services are implemented. These are listed in Table 20-1. Configuration of these services is standard, as is discussed in Chapter 3 and Chapter 6, and so the configurations are not covered in this chapter. Additionally, in this topology, LDP with basic LFA (without R-LFA) provides the MPLS transport with local repair style protection.

Table 20-1. Services on egress-protection topology

Service	Customer edge (CE) nodes
L3VPN-B	CE1-B, CE2-B, CE3-B, CE4-B, CE5-B, CE6-B
L3VPN-C	CE1-C, CE2-C, CE3-C, CE4-C, CE5-C, CE6-C
LDP PW 413	CE1-D, CE3-D
LDP PW 424	CE2-D, CE4-D
LDP PW 456	CE5-D (dual-homed), CE6-D (dual-homed)
LDP PW 513	CE1-E, CE3-E
LDP PW 524	CE2-E, CE4-E
LDP PW 556	CE5-E (dual-homed), CE6-E (dual-homed)
BGP L2VPN-F	CE1-F (single-homed), CE6-F (dual-homed)
BGP L2VPN-G	CE2-G (single-homed), CE6-G (dual-homed)

Flat Next-Hop Structures

Before discussing hierarchal next-hop structures, let's first have a look at a simple, flat FIB next-hop structure without any hierarchy, as depicted in Figure 20-2. Such flat FIB structures were typically used in the past on some of the older router hardware platforms.

Figure 20-2 shows some entries in the FIB from the perspective of the PE3 router, all of them pointing to PE1. You can see three VPN prefixes (loopback of CE1-B, loopback of VRF-B on PE1, and PE1→CE1-B link prefix). Furthermore, you can see FIB entries corresponding to the LDP-based pseudowire 413 and pseudowire 513 established between PE3 and PE1. The last FIB entry corresponds to the BGP-based L2VPN-F built between PE1 (attached to single-homed CE1-F) and PE3/PE4 (attached to dual-homed CE6-F). More FIB entries can exist, of course; these are just some examples.

Now, thanks to LDP with LFA protection, each FIB entry has two next-hops: the primary next-hop (with weight 0x0001) and backup next hop (with weight 0xF000). The primary path to reach PE1 from PE3 is via P1 (via interface ge-2/0/7; path cost: 20), and the loop-free backup path via P2 (via interface ge-2/0/6; path cost: 22). So far, the FIB structure still reflects what was previously discussed in Chapter 18 and Chapter 19.

If the PE3→P1 link (or P1 node) fails, the primary next hop (associated with ge-2/0/7 interface) is removed from the FIB, and traffic continues to flow using the preinstalled backup next hop (associated with ge-2/0/6 interface). How long does it take to remove the primary next hop from the HW FIB? For these six example prefixes, you need to remove six next hops, so it is rather quick. However, you can easily imagine that PE1 doesn't advertise only six service prefixes (L3VPN, L2VPN, etc.) to PE3; it might have hundreds of thousands of service prefixes, which is frequently the case in large-scale designs. Now, how long does it take to remove a few hundred thousand next hops from HW FIB? Certainly much longer. Thus, despite the quick failure discovery and the preinstallation of backup next hops in FIB, the recovery time can be very long.

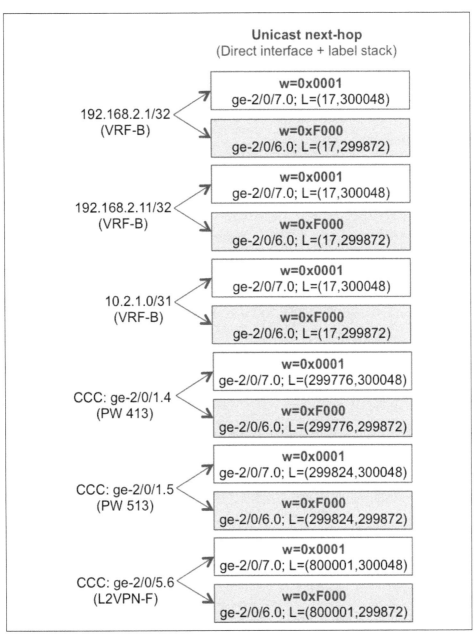

Figure 20-2. Legacy flat FIB next-hop structure on PE3 (Junos)

Indirect Next Hop (Junos)

Here is where designs with hierarchical next-hop structures in the FIB come into play. Similar to the example of the flat FIB in Figure 20-2, you can see an example of hierarchical FIB structure on PE3 in Figure 20-3.

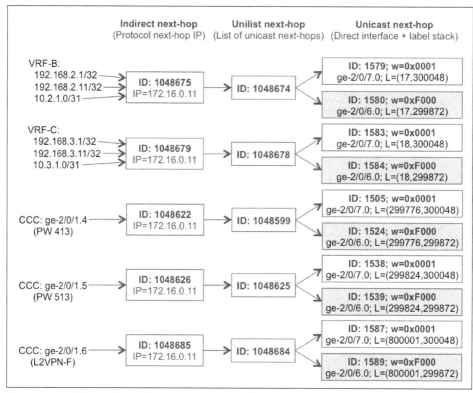

Figure 20-3. Hierarchical (indirect next hop) FIB structure on PE3 (Junos)

 Flat FIB structures are no longer used or recommended. With modern routers, the hierarchical FIB is enabled by default, and in many cases it is not even possible to revert the FIB to a flat next-hop structure.

Depending on the actual hardware, the indirect next hop might not be enabled by default. In that case, it must be explicitly enabled, as demonstrated here:

Example 20-1. Indirect next-hop configuration (Junos)

```
1    routing-options {
2        forwarding-table {
```

```
3              indirect-next-hop;
4    }}
```

This configuration is not required in MX routers with forwarding engines based on the Trio architecture. These do not support flat next-hop structures and they have indirect next-hop enabled by default. Let's have a quick look at PE3's next-hop structure (Example 20-2).

Example 20-2. Indirect next hop of VRF-B routes advertised PE1→PE3 (Junos)

```
1    juniper@PE3> show route forwarding-table destination 192.168.2.1/32
2                  extensive | match "Destination|Index: [1-9]|weight"
3    Destination:  192.168.2.1/32
4      Next-hop type: indirect              Index: 1048675  Reference: 6
5      Next-hop type: unilist               Index: 1048674  Reference: 2
6      Next-hop type: Push 17, Push 300048(top) Index: 1579 Reference: 1
7      Next-hop interface: ge-2/0/7.0  Weight: 0x1
8      Next-hop type: Push 17, Push 299872(top) Index: 1580 Reference: 1
9      Next-hop interface: ge-2/0/6.0  Weight: 0xf000
10
11   juniper@PE3> show route forwarding-table destination 192.168.2.11/32
12                  extensive | match "Destination|Index: [1-9]|weight"
13   Destination:  192.168.2.11/32
14     Next-hop type: indirect              Index: 1048675  Reference: 6
15     Next-hop type: unilist               Index: 1048674  Reference: 2
16     Next-hop type: Push 17, Push 300048(top) Index: 1579 Reference: 1
17     Next-hop interface: ge-2/0/7.0  Weight: 0x1
18     Next-hop type: Push 17, Push 299872(top) Index: 1580 Reference: 1
19     Next-hop interface: ge-2/0/6.0  Weight: 0xf000
20
21   juniper@PE3> show route forwarding-table destination 10.2.1.0/31
22                  extensive | match "Destination|Index: [1-9]|weight"
23   Destination:  10.2.1.0/31
24     Next-hop type: indirect              Index: 1048675  Reference: 6
25     Next-hop type: unilist               Index: 1048674  Reference: 2
26     Next-hop type: Push 17, Push 300048(top) Index: 1579 Reference: 1
27     Next-hop interface: ge-2/0/7.0  Weight: 0x1
28     Next-hop type: Push 17, Push 299872(top) Index: 1580 Reference: 1
29     Next-hop interface: ge-2/0/6.0  Weight: 0xf000
30
31   juniper@PE3> request pfe execute target fpc2 command
32                  "show nhdb id 1048675 recursive"
33   GOT: 1048675(Indirect, IPv4, ifl:361:ge-2/0/7.0, pfe-id:0, i-ifl:0:-)
34   GOT:    1048674(Unilist, IPv4, ifl:0:-, pfe-id:0)
35   GOT:       1579(Unicast, IPv4->MPLS, ifl:361:ge-2/0/7.0, pfe-id:0)
36   GOT:       1580(Unicast, IPv4->MPLS, ifl:381:ge-2/0/6.0, pfe-id:0)
```

In the title for Example 20-2, "Advertised PE1→PE3" stands for routes advertised by PE1, installed on PE3's FIB, and inspected from PE3. This terminology is used for the remaining examples.

The first three commands (lines 1 through 29) show the PE3 FIB structure for three VRF-B prefixes injected by PE1. The last command (lines 31 through 36) is the FPC shell command to display the next-hop hierarchy programmed in the HW FIB itself. As you can see, three levels of hierarchy are created in the FIB:

- First level: *indirect* next hop
- Second level: *unilist* next hop
- Third level: *unicast* next hop

Each next hop has an ID, which represents a next-hop data structure. You can build next-hop hierarchy by appropriately linking next hops using the next hop IDs. You can observe this in lines 31 through 36 back in Example 20-2.

Indirect next hop
Roughly speaking, this is a pseudo next hop representing the BGP protocol next hop. Because PE1 injects all three mentioned VRF-B prefixes (loopback of CE1-B, loopback of VRF-B on PE1, and PE1→CE1-B link prefix), the protocol next hop is a loopback of PE1 for all three prefixes. Thus, these prefixes point to the same indirect next hop, with ID: 1048675 (Example 20-2, lines 4, 14, and 24). The indirect next hop points to a real forwarding next hop (e.g., unilist or unicast next hop).

Unilist next hop
This is simply a container for the list of (possibly multiple) real forwarding next hops. In Example 20-2, indirect next-hop 1048675 points to unilist next-hop 1048674.

Unicast next hop
This is the final direct physical next hop, containing the outgoing interface and full encapsulation (e.g., full MPLS label stack) information. In the example, due to LFA protection, the unilist next hop is a list of the two unicast next hops: primary (ID: 1579, weight: 0x1) and backup (ID: 1580, weight: 0xF000). Now, when failure happens (PE3→P1 link or P1 node fails), removal of only a single next hop (with ID 1579) fixes the failover for the mentioned three VPN prefixes. In the case of flat FIB, removal of the three next hops was required. So, with the hierarchical next-hop structure, you can indeed reduce the number of next hops that need to be removed upon failure detection. This is good, because it improves the failover times.

However, if you check some VPN prefixes in another VRF (VRF-C) or FIB entries for Layer 2 (L2) services (see Example 20-3), you will realize that they use a separate next-hop hierarchy, as presented in Figure 20-3.

Example 20-3. Indirect next hop of VRF-C and L2 routes announced PE1→PE3 (Junos)

```
1    juniper@PE3> show route forwarding-table destination 192.168.3.1/32
2              extensive | match "Destination|Index: [1-9]|weight"
3    Destination:  192.168.3.1/32
4      Next-hop type: indirect              Index: 1048679  Reference: 6
5      Next-hop type: unilist               Index: 1048678  Reference: 2
6      Next-hop type: Push 18, Push 300048(top) Index: 1583 Reference: 1
7      Next-hop interface: ge-2/0/7.0  Weight: 0x1
8      Next-hop type: Push 18, Push 299872(top) Index: 1584 Reference: 1
9      Next-hop interface: ge-2/0/6.0  Weight: 0xf000
10
11   juniper@PE3> show route forwarding-table ccc ge-2/0/1.4 extensive |
12              match "Destination|Index: [1-9]|weight"
13   Destination:  ge-2/0/1.4  (CCC)
14     Next-hop type: indirect              Index: 1048622  Reference: 2
15     Next-hop type: unilist               Index: 1048599  Reference: 2
16     Next-hop type: Push 299776, Push 300048(top) Index: 1505 Ref.: 1
17     Next-hop interface: ge-2/0/7.0  Weight: 0x1
18     Next-hop type: Push 299776, Push 299872(top) Index: 1524 Ref.: 1
19     Next-hop interface: ge-2/0/6.0  Weight: 0xf000
20
21   juniper@PE3> show route forwarding-table ccc ge-2/0/1.6 extensive |
22              match "Destination|Index: [1-9]|weight"
23   Destination:  ge-2/0/1.6  (CCC)
24     Next-hop type: indirect              Index: 1048685  Reference: 2
25     Next-hop type: unilist               Index: 1048684  Reference: 2
26     Next-hop type: Push 800001, Push 300048(top) Index: 1587 Ref.: 1
27     Next-hop interface: ge-2/0/7.0  Weight: 0x1
28     Next-hop type: Push 800001, Push 299872(top) Index: 1589 Ref.: 1
29     Next-hop interface: ge-2/0/6.0  Weight: 0xf000
```

The problem is that the last level in the next-hop hierarchy contains full encapsulation, including a full label stack containing the service label. Thus, despite the fact that the BGP protocol next hop is equal for all service prefixes presented in Figure 20-3, the FIB creates separate next-hop hierarchy structures for service prefixes with different service labels.

Therefore, the *indirect next hop* actually represents the combination of the *BGP protocol next hop* and the *service label*. Each protocol next hop plus service label pair results in separate next-hop hierarchy structures in the FIB. It is also true for L3VPN prefixes that belong to the same VRF but have different VPN labels. If you look at Example 20-4 and some of its VRF-B prefixes advertised by the PE2 (IOS XR) router, you will realize the VPN label (and thus the next-hop hierarchy) are different.

In this configuration example, PE1 (Junos) is configured with vrf-table-label, resulting in a single aggregate VPN label per VRF. PE2 (IOS XR), on the other hand, uses the default label allocation model (per-prefix for prefixes received from CEs plus per-VRF for local VRF prefixes). Therefore, the VPN labels for 192.168.2.2/32 (CE2-B loopback) and 192.168.2.22/32 (loopback inside VRF-B on PE2) are different.

Example 20-4. Indirect next hop of VRF-B routes announced PE2→PE3 (Junos)

```
1    juniper@PE3> show route forwarding-table destination 192.168.2.2/32
2                extensive | match "Destination|Index: [1-9]|weight"
3    Destination:  192.168.2.2/32
4      Next-hop type: indirect              Index: 1048732  Reference: 2
5      Next-hop type: unilist               Index: 1048763  Reference: 2
6      Next-hop type: Push 16089, Push 300304(top) Index: 1617 Ref.: 1
7      Next-hop interface: ge-2/0/7.0  Weight: 0x1
8      Next-hop type: Push 16089, Push 300064(top) Index: 1618 Ref.: 1
9      Next-hop interface: ge-2/0/6.0  Weight: 0x1
10
11   juniper@PE3> show route forwarding-table destination 192.168.2.22/32
12                extensive | match "Destination|Index: [1-9]|weight"
13   Destination:  192.168.2.22/32
14     Next-hop type: indirect              Index: 1048726  Reference: 5
15     Next-hop type: unilist               Index: 1048718  Reference: 2
16     Next-hop type: Push 16088, Push 300304(top) Index: 1612 Ref.: 1
17     Next-hop interface: ge-2/0/7.0  Weight: 0x1
18     Next-hop type: Push 16088, Push 300064(top) Index: 1613 Ref.: 1
19     Next-hop interface: ge-2/0/6.0  Weight: 0x1
```

The weight (lines 7, 9, 17, and 19) of direct, unicast next hops is equal now (0x1), because PE3 can reach PE2 via two equal-cost paths: via P1 and via P2 (both with cost 21). Thus, instead of primary/backup next hops, PE3 performs load balancing.

Generally, you can conclude that the indirect next-hop FIB structure can bring optimization for the following:

- L3VPN prefixes, if per-VRF or per CE (per next hop) label allocation method is used on the egress PE. Per-VRF allocation method results in a single next-hop structure for all VPN prefixes from the same VPN received from the egress PE. Per-CE allocation method results in multiple next-hop structures. However, because the number of CEs connected to the egress PE is typically less than the number of prefixes received from the egress PE, it is still better than a per-prefix label allocation method

- Prefixes from the global routing table (typically Internet prefixes) use the protocol next hop accessible via MPLS transport. This type of traffic does not have a service label; as a result, the single next-hop structure can serve all prefixes reachable over a single egress PE.

However, for other types of deployments (L2 MPLS services, or L3VPNs with per-prefix label allocation) indirect next hop does not improve restoration times. The number of next hops that need to be removed during failure event does not change. Therefore, Junos offers the next generation of hierarchical next-hop structures, chained composite next hop, to address these issues.

Chained Composite Next Hop (Junos)

The problem with indirect next hop is the service label. The fact that it is implemented in the last level of next-hop hierarchy breaks entire next-hop hierarchy concepts. Different service labels advertised by the same egress PE results in completely separate hierarchical next-hop structures being required in the FIB. Chained composite next hop removes that obstacle. Service labels are no longer associated with unicast next hops at the end of the next-hop hierarchy; instead, they are moved to the very top level of the next-hop hierarchy. Figure 20-4 illustrates this concept.

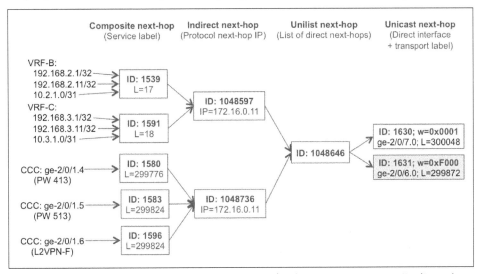

Figure 20-4. Hierarchical (chained composite next hop) FIB Structure on PE3 (Junos)

Chained composite next hop is disabled by default (except for Ethernet VPN [EVPN] where it is enabled by default) and must be explicitly enabled for the required address families, as shown in Example 20-5.

Example 20-5. Chained composite next hop configuration (Junos)

```
routing-options {
    forwarding-table {
        chained-composite-next-hop {
            ingress {
                l2vpn;
                l2ckt;
                l3vpn;
}}}}
```

 To completely reinitialize FIB structures, all BGP sessions are dropped and subsequently reestablished when chained composite next hop is enabled or disabled.

Let's verify the states with operational commands for a couple of prefixes from different L3VPNs and other address families (LDP and BGP-based PWs); see Example 20-6.

Example 20-6. Chained composite next hop of prefixes advertised PE1→PE3 (Junos)

```
1    juniper@PE3> show route forwarding-table destination 192.168.2.1/32
2                  extensive | match "Destination|Index: [1-9]|weight|Push"
3    Destination:  192.168.2.1/32
4      Next-hop type: composite          Index: 1539     Reference: 6
5      Load Balance Label: Push 17, None
6      Next-hop type: indirect           Index: 1048597  Reference: 3
7      Next-hop type: unilist            Index: 1048646  Reference: 3
8      Next-hop type: Push 300048        Index: 1630     Reference: 1
9      Next-hop interface: ge-2/0/7.0  Weight: 0x1
10     Next-hop type: Push 299872        Index: 1631     Reference: 1
11     Next-hop interface: ge-2/0/6.0  Weight: 0xf000
12
13   juniper@PE3> request pfe execute target fpc2 command
14               "show nhdb id 1539 recursive"
15   GOT: 1539(Compst, IPv4->MPLS, ifl:0:-, pfe-id:0, comp-fn:Chain)
16   GOT:  1048597(Indirect, IPv4, ifl:361:ge-2/0/7.0, pfe-id:0, i-ifl:0:)
17   GOT:     1048646(Unilist, IPv4, ifl:0:-, pfe-id:0)
18   GOT:        1630(Unicast, IPv4->MPLS, ifl:361:ge-2/0/7.0, pfe-id:0)
19   GOT:        1631(Unicast, IPv4->MPLS, ifl:381:ge-2/0/6.0, pfe-id:0)
20
21   juniper@PE3> show route forwarding-table destination 192.168.3.1/32
22               extensive | match "Destination|Index: [1-9]|weight|Push"
23   Destination:  192.168.3.1/32
24     Next-hop type: composite          Index: 1591     Reference: 6
25     Load Balance Label: Push 18, None
26     Next-hop type: indirect           Index: 1048597  Reference: 3
27     Next-hop type: unilist            Index: 1048646  Reference: 3
```

```
28   Next-hop type: Push 300048          Index: 1630      Reference: 1
29   Next-hop interface: ge-2/0/7.0  Weight: 0x1
30   Next-hop type: Push 299872          Index: 1631      Reference: 1
31   Next-hop interface: ge-2/0/6.0  Weight: 0xf000
32
33   juniper@PE3> request pfe execute target fpc2 command
34             "show nhdb id 1591 recursive"
35   GOT: 1591(Compst, IPv4->MPLS, ifl:0:-, pfe-id:0, comp-fn:Chain)
36   GOT:  1048597(Indirect, IPv4, ifl:361:ge-2/0/7.0, pfe-id:0, i-ifl:0:)
37   GOT:     1048646(Unilist, IPv4, ifl:0:-, pfe-id:0)
38   GOT:        1630(Unicast, IPv4->MPLS, ifl:361:ge-2/0/7.0, pfe-id:0)
39   GOT:        1631(Unicast, IPv4->MPLS, ifl:381:ge-2/0/6.0, pfe-id:0)
40
41   juniper@PE3> show route forwarding-table ccc ge-2/0/1.4 extensive |
42             match "Destination|Index: [1-9]|weight|Push"
43   Destination:  ge-2/0/1.4  (CCC)
44     Next-hop type: composite          Index: 1580      Reference: 2
45     Load Balance Label: Push 299776, None
46     Next-hop type: indirect           Index: 1048736   Reference: 6
47     Next-hop type: unilist            Index: 1048646   Reference: 3
48     Next-hop type: Push 300048        Index: 1630      Reference: 1
49     Next-hop interface: ge-2/0/7.0  Weight: 0x1
50     Next-hop type: Push 299872        Index: 1631      Reference: 1
51     Next-hop interface: ge-2/0/6.0  Weight: 0xf000
52
53   juniper@PE3> request pfe execute target fpc2 command
54             "show nhdb id 1580 recursive"
55   GOT: 1580(Compst, CCC->MPLS, ifl:0:-, pfe-id:0, comp-fn:Chain)
56   GOT:  1048736(Indirect, IPv4, ifl:361:ge-2/0/7.0, pfe-id:0, i-ifl:0:)
57   GOT:     1048646(Unilist, IPv4, ifl:0:-, pfe-id:0)
58   GOT:        1630(Unicast, IPv4->MPLS, ifl:361:ge-2/0/7.0, pfe-id:0)
59   GOT:        1631(Unicast, IPv4->MPLS, ifl:381:ge-2/0/6.0, pfe-id:0)
60
61   juniper@PE3> show route forwarding-table ccc ge-2/0/1.5 extensive |
62             match "Destination|Index: [1-9]|weight|Push"
63   Destination:  ge-2/0/1.5  (CCC)
64     Next-hop type: composite          Index: 1583      Reference: 2
65     Load Balance Label: Push 299824, None
66     Next-hop type: indirect           Index: 1048736   Reference: 6
67     Next-hop type: unilist            Index: 1048646   Reference: 3
68     Next-hop type: Push 300048        Index: 1630      Reference: 1
69     Next-hop interface: ge-2/0/7.0  Weight: 0x1
70     Next-hop type: Push 299872        Index: 1631      Reference: 1
71     Next-hop interface: ge-2/0/6.0  Weight: 0xf000
72
73   juniper@PE3> request pfe execute target fpc2 command
74             "show nhdb id 1583 recursive"
75   GOT: 1583(Compst, CCC->MPLS, ifl:0:-, pfe-id:0, comp-fn:Chain)
76   GOT:  1048736(Indirect, IPv4, ifl:361:ge-2/0/7.0, pfe-id:0, i-ifl:0:)
77   GOT:     1048646(Unilist, IPv4, ifl:0:-, pfe-id:0)
78   GOT:        1630(Unicast, IPv4->MPLS, ifl:361:ge-2/0/7.0, pfe-id:0)
79   GOT:        1631(Unicast, IPv4->MPLS, ifl:381:ge-2/0/6.0, pfe-id:0)
```

As you can see, the service label is moved out to the top of the next-hop hierarchy structure (lines 5, 25, 45, and 65). Furthermore, indirect next hop now represents the BGP protocol next hop plus address family, because L3VPN (lines 6 and 26) and L2VPN (lines 46 and 66) services are chained to another different indirect next hop. But what is even more important, in the case of PE3→P1 link or P1 node failure, removal of a single next hop (with ID 1630, lines 8, 28, 48, 68) is enough to fix all nine prefixes presented in Figure 20-4. This is especially important in scaled environments, with many hundreds of thousands of service prefixes. The repair action is really prefix-independent; it now depends only on the number of egress PEs reachable via the failed link.

In summary, chained composite next-hop hierarchy contains the following:

Composite next hop
> For each service label, the FIB creates a separate composite next hop. This is true, as well, for L3VPN prefixes belonging to the same VRF but advertised from the egress PE with different VPN labels.

Indirect next hop
> For each egress PE plus address family pair, the FIB creates separate indirect next hops. Indirect next hops are separate per address family, because packet encapsulation requirements might be different for each address family. Composite next hops for service labels from a common address family point to the same indirect next hop, forming the second level of a next-hop hierarchy.

Unilist next hop
> For each egress PE, the FIB creates a single unilist next hop. All indirect next hops for a specific egress PE point to that unilist next hop. This is the third level of the next-hop hierarchy, resulting in a single next hop per egress PE, regardless of service labels and address families advertised by the egress PE.

Unicast next hop
> Depending on the topology (load-balancing, protection) multiple direct unicast next hops might be present.

An additional benefit of using chained composite next-hop structures is more efficient usage of FIB resources. If you calculate next hops used in the indirect and composite next-hop schemes (Figure 20-3 and Figure 20-4), you will find that the number decreased from 20 to 10. Even with such a simple example with very limited number of prefixes, that difference is an impressive 50%.

> Link aggregation (LAG, IEEE 802.3ad) introduces an additional level in the next-hop hierarchy: the unilist next hop points to (multiple) aggregate next hop(s), whereas the aggregate next hop points to its member links as unicast next hops.

BGP PIC Core (IOS XR)

BGP PIC Core is the IOS XR term that describes hierarchical next-hop structures programmed in the HW FIB. In principle, it is similar to the chained composite next-hop structures discussed earlier on the Junos platform; however, the terminology used is slightly different.

In IOS XR, hierarchical next-hop structures are enabled by default, therefore no special configuration is required. So, let's verify the FIB states on PE2 (see Example 20-7).

Example 20-7. BGP PIC next hop for L3VPN routes announced PE4→PE2 (IOS XR)

```
1   RP/0/RSP0/CPU0:PE2#show cef 172.16.0.44/32 | include " via|label"
2    via 10.0.0.27, Gi0/0/0/3, 3 dependencies, weight 0, class 0, backup
3      local label 16002      labels imposed {303200}
4   via 10.0.0.5, Gi0/0/0/2, 3 dependencies, weight 0, class 0, protected
5      local label 16002      labels imposed {302576}
6
7   RP/0/RSP0/CPU0:PE2#show cef vrf VRF-B 192.168.2.4/32 |
8                      include " via|label|path-idx"
9    via 172.16.0.44, 4 dependencies, recursive [flags 0x6000]
10    path-idx 0 NHID 0x0 [0x72747364 0x0]
11     next hop 10.0.0.5/32 Gi0/0/0/2 labels imposed {302576 47}
12
13  RP/0/RSP0/CPU0:PE2# show cef vrf VRF-C 192.168.3.4/32 |
14                      include " via|label|path-idx"
15   via 172.16.0.44, 4 dependencies, recursive [flags 0x6000]
16    path-idx 0 NHID 0x0 [0x72747364 0x0]
17     next hop 10.0.0.5/32 Gi0/0/0/2 labels imposed {302576 48}
18
19  RP/0/RSP0/CPU0:PE2#show cef vrf VRF-B 192.168.2.4/32 internal
20  (...)
21    label_info:[default [o-label:47 l-label:no-label type:0 (...)
22  (...)
23    [nh:172.16.0.44 ifh:NULLIFHNDL tbl:0xe0000000 (...)
24    [depth:2 flags:[recursive,resolved,ldi-preferred] resolves-via:
25     leaf:MPLS::0[0x71945050]:lsd:16002/0[(...)][0x72747364]
26  (...)
27        frr_nhinfo:[BKUP [type:prefix-backup link:link_MPLS
28          nh:10.0.0.27/32ifhandle:Gi0_0_0_3(0xe005640)
29          main-ifhandle:Gi0_0_0_3(0xe000680) tunid:0][0x72f11df0]
30  (...)
31        frr_nhinfo:[PROT [type:prefix-prot link:link_MPLS
32          nh:10.0.0.5/32ifhandle:Gi0_0_0_2(0xe0056c0)
33          main-ifhandle:Gi0_0_0_2(0xe000680) tunid:0][0x72f1268c]
34  (...)
35      0={
36          label_info:[default [o-label:303200 l-label:16002 (...)
37      1={
38          label_info:[default [o-label:302576 l-label:16002 (...)
```

PE2 can reach the PE4 loopback with the primary (lines 4 and 5) and LFA backup (lines 2 and 3) next hops. However, if you check the FIB entry for some VPN prefixes resolved via PE4 loopback, you will see only a single next hop (lines 10 and 11, and lines 16 and 17). At least the index of these next hops (lines 10 and 16) is the same, indicating that VPN prefixes from different VRFs (with different VPN label; lines 11 and 17) actually share the same FIB next-hop structure.

Missing a backup next hop is mysterious, however. Fortunately, this is just a cosmetic display issue. If you use the `internal` knob (line 19) to display FIB structure, you will get much more information, although some of it can be difficult to understand. By carefully reviewing this information, you can nonetheless reverse engineer the hierarchical FIB structure in IOS XR.

First of all, the outgoing service (VPN) label is at the top of the hierarchy (line 21). The prefix resolves via the PE4 loopback (line 23) with the BGP protocol next-hop index (line 25) matching the next-hop index observed previously (line 10 and 16). Next in the hierarchy you can see two IGP next hops: protected primary next hop (lines 31 through 33), and backup next hop (lines 27 through 29). Again, each next hop has an associated next-hop index. Further, you can discover outgoing labels associated with these IGP next hops (lines 36 and 38).

To save a few pages, other VPN prefixes (from VRF-B or VRF-C) reachable via PE4 are not displayed with the `internal` knob. However, the next-hop structures (next-hop indexes) are the same for all such prefixes. This confirms that IOS XR builds hierarchical next-hop FIB structures, as outlined in Figure 20-5.

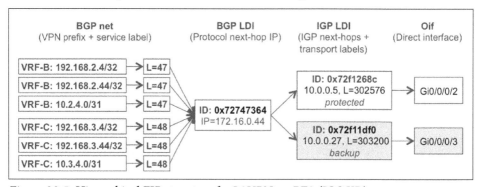

Figure 20-5. Hierarchical FIB structure for L3VPN on PE2 (IOS XR)

Each element in the hierarchy contains *load information* (LDI) with instructions required for proper traffic forwarding.

The next-hop structures for L2 services look similar to the ones for L3 services.

Example 20-8. PIC Core next hop for L2VPN routes advertised PE4→PE2 (IOS XR)

```
1    RP/0/RSP0/CPU0:PE2#show l2vpn forwarding interface Gi0/0/0/5.4
2                        hardware ingress location 0/0/CPU0 |
3                        include "State |--|mpls| ldi"
4    Segment 1                 Segment 2                        State
5    ----------------------  ------------------------------  ------
6    Gi0/0/0/5.4               mpls    172.16.0.44              UP
7     XID: 0xc0008001, bridge: 0, MAC limit: 0, l2vpn ldi index: 0x0054,
8     vc label: 299840,
9
10   RP/0/RSP0/CPU0:PE2#show l2vpn forwarding interface Gi0/0/0/5.6
11                        hardware ingress location 0/0/CPU0 |
12                        include "State |--|mpls| ldi"
13   Segment 1                 Segment 2                        State
14   ----------------------  ------------------------------  ------
15   Gi0/0/0/5.6               mpls    172.16.0.44              UP
16    XID: 0xc0008018, bridge: 0, MAC limit: 0, l2vpn ldi index: 0x0054,
17    vc label: 800003,
```

Now, instead of a BGP LDI index, the L2VPN LDI index is the same (lines 7 and 16), indicating shared a FIB next-hop structure, as illustrated in Figure 20-6.

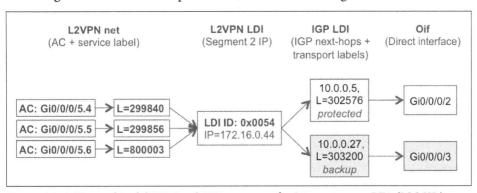

Figure 20-6. Hierarchical (PIC Core) FIB structure for L2 services on PE2 (IOS XR)

Preinstalled Next Hops to Multiple Egress PEs (PIC Edge)

The previous section focused on the optimization of next-hop structures in FIB. During failure of upstream links or upstream nodes, the PE needs to remove only a limited number of primary next hops from its FIB. The number of primary next hops is independent from the number of prefixes. It depends only on the number of egress PEs, thus removal of the primary next hops from the FIB can be executed quite quickly.

In the previous section, all the examples were based on service prefixes (L3VPN, L2VPN) reachable via the single egress PE. However, to increase network resiliency, you can implement services in a redundant way, such that the CE device is dual-homed to two PE devices. If you look at Figure 20-1 again, this is the case for CE5-B/ CE5-C and CE6-B/CE6-C. Prefixes belonging to CE5-B are advertised by both PE1 and PE2. PE3, after receiving these prefixes, performs a selection process and chooses one of them as the best. For example, via PE1, because the IGP cost from PE3 to PE1 is lower than that from PE3 to PE2. Only the best next hop is subsequently installed in the FIB structures discussed previously. Similarly, the CE5-B prefixes advertised by PE3 and PE4 arrive to PE2, but PE2 installs only one next hop in its FIB.

Let's have a look at the RIB and FIB structures on PE3.

Example 20-9. RIB/FIB structures for CE5-B loopback on PE3 (Junos)

```
juniper@PE3> show route table VRF-B 192.168.2.5/32 active-path
(...)
192.168.2.5/32
    *[BGP/170] 00:08:44, MED 0, localpref 100, from 172.16.0.201
        AS path: ?, validation-state: unverified
      > to 10.0.0.8 via ge-2/0/7.0, Push 17, Push 300448(top)
        to 10.0.0.34 via ge-2/0/6.0, Push 17, Push 300144(top)

juniper@PE3> show route forwarding-table destination 192.168.2.5/32
            extensive | match "Destination|Index: [1-9]|weight|Push"
Destination:  192.168.2.5/32
  Next-hop type: composite            Index: 1572     Reference: 6
  Load Balance Label: Push 17, None
  Next-hop type: indirect             Index: 1048626  Reference: 3
  Next-hop type: unilist              Index: 1048703  Reference: 3
  Next-hop type: Push 300448          Index: 1598     Reference: 1
  Next-hop interface: ge-2/0/7.0  Weight: 0x1
  Next-hop type: Push 300144          Index: 1599     Reference: 1
  Next-hop interface: ge-2/0/6.0  Weight: 0xf000

juniper@PE3> request pfe execute target fpc2 command
            "show nhdb id 1572 recursive"
GOT: 1572(Compst, IPv4->MPLS, ifl:0:-, pfe-id:0, comp-fn:Chain)
GOT:  1048626(Indirect, IPv4, ifl:361:ge-2/0/7.0, pfe-id:0, i-ifl:0:)
GOT:    1048703(Unilist, IPv4, ifl:0:-, pfe-id:0)
GOT:      1598(Unicast, IPv4->MPLS, ifl:361:ge-2/0/7.0, pfe-id:0)
GOT:      1599(Unicast, IPv4->MPLS, ifl:381:ge-2/0/6.0, pfe-id:0)
```

Likewise, let's verify that the RIB and FIB structures on PE2 IOS XR look very similar.

Example 20-10. RIB/FIB structures for CE6-B loopback on PE2 (IOS XR)

```
RP/0/RSP0/CPU0:PE2#show bgp vrf VRF-B 192.168.2.6/32 brief
(...)
   Network          Next Hop        Metric LocPrf Weight Path
Route Distinguisher: 172.16.0.22:102 (default for vrf VRF-B)
* i192.168.2.6/32    172.16.0.33          0    100      0 65506 ?
*>i                  172.16.0.44          0    100      0 65506 ?
```

```
RP/0/RSP0/CPU0:PE2#show route vrf VRF-B 192.168.2.6/32
(...)
Routing entry for 192.168.2.6/32
  Known via "bgp 65000", distance 200, metric 0
  Tag 65506, type internal
  Routing Descriptor Blocks
    172.16.0.44, from 172.16.0.201
      Nexthop in Vrf: "default", Table: "default", IPv4 Unicast,
        Table Id: 0xe0000000
      Route metric is 0
  No advertising protos.

RP/0/RSP0/CPU0:PE2#show cef vrf VRF-B 192.168.2.6/32
192.168.2.6/32, version 99, internal 0x5000001 0x0 (ptr 0x72189714)
 Prefix Len 32, traffic index 0, precedence n/a, priority 3
   via 172.16.0.44, 4 dependencies, recursive [flags 0x6000]
   path-idx 0 NHID 0x0 [0x726d2ca4 0x0]
   recursion-via-/32
   next hop VRF - 'default', table - 0xe0000000
   next hop 172.16.0.44 via 16075/0/21
    next hop 10.0.0.5/32 Gi0/0/0/2 labels imposed {300208 47}
```

What failover times can you expect during failure of the primary egress PE? Relatively long ones. Here's why:

IGP convergence

The ingress PE must realize the failure of the primary egress PE. Typically, this is done by IGP. Upon primary egress PE failure, the IGP removes the primary egress PE loopback from the IGP database and the corresponding RIB and FIB structures on the ingress PE. IGP convergence is typically a few hundred milliseconds, and potentially, up to seconds in very large IGP domains.

BGP convergence

This time factor is more critical. After realizing primary egress PE failure, the ingress PE must remove indirect (recursive) next hops associated with the primary egress PE and then install a new, indirect (recursive) next hop associated with the backup egress PE. Again, this can take time. In highly scaled environments, it could take as long as several seconds.

How can you improve this? By preinstalling the next-hop structures associated with backup egress PE in the FIB. This concept has different flavors:

Active/Standby

Both next hops (toward primary and backup egress PE) are installed in the FIB. The next hop associated with the primary egress PE is used actively for forwarding, whereas the next hop associated with the backup egress PE is used only after detection of primary egress PE failure and the removal of primary egress PE next hop from the FIB. IOS XR calls this feature *BGP PIC Edge Unipath*; for Junos, it's simply *BGP PIC Edge*. However, Junos uses `protect core` (not `protect edge`) to configure this feature.

Active/Active

Both next hops (toward primary and backup egress PE) are installed in the FIB, if the BGP path selection considers both BGP updates (from primary and backup egress PE) as equal. This applies to IGP cost toward primary and backup egress PE, as well, which must be equal. The router actively uses both next hops for traffic forwarding, effectively performing load-balancing toward the primary and backup egress PE. IOS XR calls this feature *BGP PIC Edge Multipath*, whereas Junos calls it simply *VPN Multipath*. Optionally, both IOS XR and Junos support unequal-cost multipath, wherein IGP cost to the egress PE is not taken into account by the BGP path selection process.

Active/Standby Next Hops to Egress PEs

Let's first configure Active/Standby next-hops to egress PEs (see Examples Example 20-11 and Example 20-12).

Example 20-11. Configuration of Active/Standby next hops to egress PEs on IOS XR

```
route-policy PL-BGP-BACKUP-PATH
  set path-selection backup 1 install
end-policy
!
router bgp 65000
 vrf VRF-B
  address-family ipv4 unicast
   additional-paths selection route-policy PL-BGP-BACKUP-PATH
```

Example 20-12. Configuration of Active/Standby next hops to egress PEs on Junos

```
routing-instances {
    VRF-B {
        routing-options {
            protect core;
}}}
```

By examining the following FIB next-hop structures, you can confirm that indeed both Junos and IOS XR installed a backup next hop pointing to a backup egress PE in the FIB.

Example 20-13. FIB structures for CE5-B loopback on PE3 (Junos)

```
1    juniper@PE3> show route forwarding-table destination 192.168.2.5/32
2                 extensive | match "Destination|Index: [1-9]|weight|Push"
3    Destination:  192.168.2.5/32
```

```
4     Next-hop type: unilist        Index: 1048685  Reference: 1
5     Next-hop type: composite      Index: 1554     Reference: 6
6     Load Balance Label: Push 17, None
7     Next-hop type: indirect       Index: 1048623  Reference: 3
8                                   Weight: 0x1
9     Next-hop type: unilist        Index: 1048703  Reference: 3
10    Next-hop type: Push 300448    Index: 1598     Reference: 1
11    Next-hop interface: ge-2/0/7.0  Weight: 0x1
12    Next-hop type: Push 300144    Index: 1599     Reference: 1
13    Next-hop interface: ge-2/0/6.0  Weight: 0xf000
14    Next-hop type: composite      Index: 1582     Reference: 2
15    Load Balance Label: Push 16101, None
16    Next-hop type: indirect       Index: 1048621  Reference: 8
17                                  Weight: 0x4000
18    Next-hop type: unilist        Index: 1048707  Reference: 3
19    Next-hop type: Push 300464    Index: 1664     Reference: 1
20    Next-hop interface: ge-2/0/7.0  Weight: 0x1
21    Next-hop type: Push 300160    Index: 1665     Reference: 1
22    Next-hop interface: ge-2/0/6.0  Weight: 0x1
23
24    juniper@PE3> request pfe execute target fpc2 command
25                  "show nhdb id 1048685 recursive"
26    GOT: 1048685(Unilist, IPv4, ifl:0:-, pfe-id:0)
27    GOT:    1554(Compst, IPv4->MPLS, ifl:0:-, pfe-id:0, comp-fn:Chain)
28    GOT:      1048623(Indirect, IPv4, ifl:361:ge-2/0/7.0, pfe-id:0)
29    GOT:        1048703(Unilist, IPv4, ifl:0:-, pfe-id:0)
30    GOT:          1598(Unicast, IPv4->MPLS, ifl:361:ge-2/0/7.0, pfe-id:0)
31    GOT:          1599(Unicast, IPv4->MPLS, ifl:381:ge-2/0/6.0, pfe-id:0)
32    GOT:    1582(Compst, IPv4->MPLS, ifl:0:-, pfe-id:0, comp-fn:Chain)
33    GOT:      1048621(Indirect, IPv4, ifl:361:ge-2/0/6.0, pfe-id:0)
34    GOT:        1048707(Unilist, IPv4, ifl:0:-, pfe-id:0)
35    GOT:          1664(Unicast, IPv4->MPLS, ifl:361:ge-2/0/7.0, pfe-id:0)
36    GOT:          1665(Unicast, IPv4->MPLS, ifl:381:ge-2/0/6.0, pfe-id:0)
```

Example 20-14. FIB structures for CE6-B loopback on PE2 (IOS XR)

```
1     RP/0/RSP0/CPU0:PE2#show route vrf VRF-B 192.168.2.6/32 | include from
2         172.16.0.33, from 172.16.0.201, BGP backup path
3         172.16.0.44, from 172.16.0.201
4
5     RP/0/RSP0/CPU0:PE2#show cef vrf VRF-B 192.168.2.6/32 |
6                       include " via|label|path-idx"
7     (...)
8       via 172.16.0.33, 5 dependencies, recursive, backup [flags 0x6100]
9       path-idx 0 NHID 0x0 [0x726d2d10 0x0]
10       next hop 10.0.0.27/32 Gi0/0/0/3 labels imposed {300432 37}
11       next hop 10.0.0.5/32 Gi0/0/0/2 labels imposed {300128 37}
12      via 172.16.0.44, 6 dependencies, recursive [flags 0x6000]
13       path-idx 1 NHID 0x0 [0x72747364 0x0]
14       next hop 10.0.0.5/32 Gi0/0/0/2 labels imposed {302576 47}
```

Let's use Figure 20-7 to interpret the next-hop structures displayed in Example 20-13.

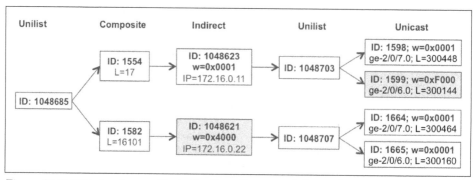

Figure 20-7. FIB structures with Active/Standby egress PE next hops on PE3 (Junos)

In the case of Junos (Example 20-13), you can see the hierarchical next-hop hierarchy with five levels (lines 24 through 36). Junos differentiates between the primary (lines 7, 8, and 28) and the backup (lines 16, 17, and 33) egress PE with different weights (0x0001 versus 0x4000). Furthermore, different weights are applied to the final, direct unicast next hops (0x0001 + 0xF000 versus 0x0001 + 0x0001). Thus, traffic to the primary egress PE (PE1, IGP cost PE3→PE1=20) uses only one link (the second link is simply backup) and—after failure of PE1—traffic to the backup egress PE (PE2, IGP cost PE3→PE2=21) is load-balanced. This is correct, and reflects the IGP metrics used in the topology.

IOS XR (see Example 20-14 and Figure 20-8) behaves in a similar way in principle. However, as already discussed in the BGP PIC Core section, Cisco Express Forwarding (CEF) for VRF prefixes does not display backup LFA next hops. You need to use the `internal` knob with the `show cef vrf` command to see the full picture (it is omitted here, though, to save space).

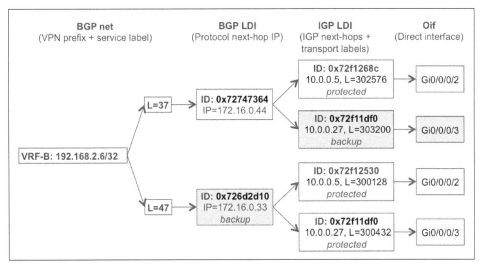

Figure 20-8. FIB structures with Active/Standby egress PE next hops on PE2 (IOS XR)

Active/Active Next Hops to Egress PEs

You can deploy Active/Active next hops to egress PEs in two variants, as mentioned earlier: equal-cost and unequal-cost. From a configuration perspective, multipath must be enabled in the respective VRFs, in both IOS XR and Junos, as presented next.

Example 20-15. Configuration of Active/Active next hops to egress PEs on IOS XR

```
router bgp 65000
  vrf VRF-C
    address-family ipv4 unicast
      maximum-paths ibgp 4 unequal-cost    !! unequal-cost optional
```

Example 20-16. Configuration of Active/Active next hops to egress PEs on Junos

```
routing-instances {
    VRF-C {
        routing-options {
            multipath {
                vpn-unequal-cost;          ## vpn-unequal-cost optional
}}}}
```

 For multipath to work, the BGP selection process must consider BGP updates received from two egress PEs as equal. Specifically, if mixed Junos and IOS XR–based PEs are used, the values of MED and ORIGIN attributes must be unified (the same values advertised by both vendors' PEs), because the default values are different.

Outputs of the verification commands as well as the hierarchical next-hop structures are very similar to those presented in the previous section (see Examples Example 20-13 and Example 20-14). In Junos, the difference is simply in the weights of indirect next hops (the weight is now 0x0000 for both the indirect next hops), which results in load-balancing of traffic toward two egress PEs. In IOS XR, both paths are marked as bgp-multipath instead of one path being marked as backup—again resulting in load-balancing toward the two egress PEs. Let's see that.

Example 20-17. FIB structures for CE5-C loopback on PE3 (Junos)

```
juniper@PE3> show route forwarding-table destination 192.168.3.5/32
             extensive | match "Destination|Index: [1-9]|weight|Push"
(...)
  Next-hop type: indirect              Index: 1048623  Reference: 3
                                       Weight: 0x0
(...)
  Next-hop type: indirect              Index: 1048621  Reference: 8
                                       Weight: 0x0
(...)
```

Example 20-18. FIB structures for CE6-C loopback on PE2 (IOS XR)

```
RP/0/RSP0/CPU0:PE2#show cef vrf VRF-C 192.168.3.6/32 |
                include recursive
   via 172.16.0.33, 6 dependencies, recursive, bgp-multipath
   via 172.16.0.44, 6 dependencies, recursive, bgp-multipath
```

 When Active/Active and Active/Standby mode are configured together, both Junos and IOS XR try first to install multiple next hops in Active/Active mode if possible. For example, if Active/Active mode with equal-cost multipath is configured but IGP cost to egress PEs is not equal, the Active/Standby mode is used.

The traceroutes shown in Example 20-19 and Example 20-20 confirm that in VPN-B (configured for Active/Standby) no load-balancing between the two egress PEs takes place, whereas in VPN-C (configured for Active/Active) traffic is load-balanced toward the two egress PEs:

Example 20-19. Traceroute with Active/Standby next hops to egress PEs

```
juniper@CE5-B> traceroute 192.168.2.6
traceroute to 192.168.2.6 (192.168.2.6), 30 hops max, 40 byte packets
 1  PE2-VRF-B (10.2.5.2)  1.123 ms  0.827 ms  0.847 ms
 2  P1 (10.0.0.5)  0.690 ms  0.688 ms P2 (10.0.0.27)  1.011 ms
    MPLS Label=300496 CoS=0 TTL=1 S=0
    MPLS Label=37 CoS=0 TTL=1 S=1
 3  PE3-VRF-B (192.168.2.33)  0.715 ms  0.618 ms  0.595 ms
```

```
 4  CE6-B (10.2.6.6)  1.415 ms *  1.554 ms

RP/0/RSP0/CPU0:CE6-B#traceroute 192.168.2.5
 1  10.2.6.3 0 msec
    10.2.6.4 0 msec   0 msec
 2  10.0.0.8 [MPLS: Labels 300544/16099 Exp 0] 0 msec   0 msec
    10.0.0.10 0 msec
 3  10.0.0.4 [MPLS: Label 16099 Exp 0] 0 msec   0 msec      ## PE2
    10.0.0.26 0 msec                                        ## PE2
 4  192.168.2.5 0 msec   0 msec   0 msec
```

Example 20-20. Traceroute with Active/Active next hops to egress PEs

```
juniper@CE5-C> traceroute 192.168.3.6
traceroute to 192.168.3.6 (192.168.3.6), 30 hops max, 40 byte packets
 1  PE2-VRF-C (10.3.5.2)  1.366 ms  0.864 ms  1.316 ms
 2  P1 (10.0.0.5)  0.722 ms  0.630 ms P2 (10.0.0.27)  0.645 ms
    MPLS Label=300496 CoS=0 TTL=1 S=0
    MPLS Label=48 CoS=0 TTL=1 S=1
 3  192.168.3.44  0.633 ms  0.602 ms 192.168.3.33  0.645 ms
 4  CE6-C (10.3.6.6)  1.568 ms *  1.462 ms

RP/0/RSP0/CPU0:CE6-C#traceroute 192.168.3.5
 1  10.3.6.3 1 msec
    10.3.6.4 0 msec   0 msec
 2  10.0.0.10 [MPLS: Labels 300288/16102 Exp 0] 0 msec
    10.0.0.32 0 msec
    10.0.0.8 0 msec
 3  10.0.0.26 [MPLS: Label 16102 Exp 0] 0 msec   0 msec      ## PE2
    192.168.3.11 0 msec                                      ## PE1
 4  192.168.3.5 0 msec   0 msec   0 msec
```

BGP Best External Failover

Installing next hops to multiple egress PEs (in Active/Active or Active/Standby mode) requires, obviously, that the ingress PE has information about the prefix from these egress PEs. If, for whatever reason, the ingress PE has updates from the single egress PE, the multiple next hops are not possible.

Now, if you want to deploy the PE3/PE4 router pair in primary/backup fashion, you can, for example, increase local preference for prefixes advertised by PE3 so that prefixes from PE3 are preferred over prefixes from PE4. However, when you verify the routing state in ingress PE, you will realize that the ingress PE (e.g., PE2) no longer has information from the backup egress PE (PE4).

Example 20-21. RIB entry for CE6-B loopback on PE2 (IOS XR)

```
RP/0/RSP0/CPU0:PE2#show route vrf VRF-B 192.168.2.6/32 | include from
    172.16.0.33, from 172.16.0.201
```

If you compare the current RIB state (Example 20-21), with the RIB state observed previously (lines 1 through 3 in Example 20-14), you will clearly see the missing information from PE4. So, what happened? Well, let's check the states on PE4.

Example 20-22. RIB entry for CE6-B loopback on PE4 (Junos)

```
1    juniper@PE4> show route table VRF-B 192.168.2.6/32 detail |
2                 match "Pref|reason|Protocol next hop|Source"
3         *BGP    Preference: 170/-201
4                 Source: 172.16.0.201
5                 Protocol next hop: 172.16.0.33
6                 Localpref: 200
7          BGP    Preference: 170/-201
8                 Source: 172.16.0.202
9                 Protocol next hop: 172.16.0.33
10                Inactive reason: Not Best in its group - Update source
11                Localpref: 200
12         BGP    Preference: 170/-101
13                Source: 10.2.6.6
14                Inactive reason: Local Preference
15                Localpref: 100
```

PE4 receives updates about the CE6-B loopback from three sources, including two updates from the route reflectors (lines 3 through 11), which are reflecting the original update from PE3. It is visible from the protocol next hop, which is the PE3 loopback (lines 5 and 9). These two updates are in principle the same, only the update sources (lines 4 and 8) are different (RR1 and RR2). The third update (lines 12 through 15) is received directly from CE6-B (line 13).

Now, as discussed previously, the configuration for PE3 is temporarily changed so that PE3 advertises the updates with the higher (200) local preference (lines 5 and 10), whereas CE6-B updates inherits the default (100) local preference (line 15). Therefore, the update from PE3 (reflected by two Route Reflectors [RRs]) is preferred over the update received directly from CE6-B (line 14). Consequently, PE4 does not use the update from CE6-B for routing or forwarding—this update remains inactive.

This is the problem. The update from CE6-B is inactive on PE4, therefore PE4 does not send this update to the RRs, and thus PE2 does not receive updates from PE4. So, PE2 cannot install the second next hop in its FIB, as PE2 is not even aware that CE6-B connects not only to PE3, but also to PE4.

Such a scenario is very typical in real deployments, not only in L3VPN designs, but in plain Internet designs as well. Service providers or big enterprises receive Internet feeds over multiple Internet gateways (egress PEs). If the Internet gateways are configured in primary/backup fashion, only prefixes from primary Internet gateways are visible to the rest of the network, preventing the BGP PIC Edge from functioning.

Now, what can you do? You can implement a slight modification to the BGP behavior, as described in *draft-ietf-idr-best-external*. In principle, with this small modification, BGP advertises the best external route, even when that external route is not active; for example, when a BGP internal route is better. This modification does not only allow proper functionality for the BGP PIC Edge in primary/backup PE deployments, it also helps to reduce interdomain churn (Section 9 of the Draft) and persistent IGP route oscillation (Section 10 of the Draft).

Therefore, let's enable this feature on all PEs, including PE4.

Example 20-23. Advertise best external path configuration on Junos

```
protocols {
    bgp {
        group IBGP-RR {
            advertise-external;
}}}
```

Example 20-24. Advertise best external path configuration on IOS XR

```
router bgp 65000
 address-family vpnv4 unicast
  advertise best-external
```

After these configuration changes, nothing changes on PE4 from a forwarding perspective: the update from CE6-B is still inactive. However, PE4 starts to advertise this inactive update toward the route reflectors, so it arrives at PE1 and PE2, making preinstallation of the backup next hop possible.

Example 20-25. RIB entry for CE6-B loopback on PE2 (IOS XR)

```
RP/0/RSP0/CPU0:PE2#show route vrf VRF-B 192.168.2.6/32 | include from
    172.16.0.33, from 172.16.0.201
    172.16.0.44, from 172.16.0.201, BGP backup path
```

Understanding the next-hop structures is a great preparation for the next chapter, which focuses on the egress protection feature set.

## CHAPTER 21

Egress Service Fast Restoration

During failure of a primary egress PE, preinstallation of the next hop associated with the backup egress PE reduces the failover time from seconds to a few hundred milliseconds. BGP convergence is no longer the contributing factor, because the second BGP next hop is preinstalled in the FIB.

However, IGP convergence still contributes to the overall failover time, because the ingress PE must discover failure of the primary egress PE to remove the associated next hop from the FIB. To reduce the detection time to less than a few hundred milliseconds (IGP convergence), you could deploy next-hop tracking or BGP session liveness detection mechanisms (using, for example, multihop Bidirectional Forwarding Detection [BFD]) with very aggressive timers. Very aggressive timers on multihop BFD sessions are, however, a questionable solution from a deployment (scaling) perspective, especially in large-scale networks, where a large number of such BFD sessions would be required.

So, what can you do? The answer is to move the duty of *fixing* the problem from the ingress PE (which is potentially far away from egress PE) to the network node closest to the egress PE. If the network node (let's call it Point of Local Repair [PLR]) directly connects to the egress PE, a failure of the egress PE can be discovered very quickly, without the need for IGP convergence. Upon failure of the primary egress PE, the PLR node redirects the traffic. Therefore, traffic is locally repaired (redirected by the PLR), and the ingress PE has time to detect the primary egress PE failure and make changes in its FIB next-hop structures.

Service Mirroring Protection Concepts

At first sight, the concept of service mirroring protection seems to be easy enough, but there are some challenges that must be solved:

How does the PLR know to which node traffic should be redirected?

The PLR is a typical P node, without any knowledge about VPN prefixes or VPN labels. Thus, based on VPN prefixes or VPN labels, the PLR is not able to correctly determine the proper node to which the traffic should be redirected.

How does the backup egress PE handle traffic originally destined to the primary egress PE?

Even assuming that the traffic is somehow redirected and eventually arrives at the proper backup egress PE, how can such traffic be handled at the backup egress PE? When simply redirecting the traffic, the VPN label of the packets arriving to the backup egress PE is assigned by the primary egress PE. Each label has local significance, so label X assigned by the primary egress PE can have a completely different meaning than label X assigned by the backup egress PE. If the now-redirected packet with label X arrives at the backup egress PE, it might be dropped (the backup egress PE didn't allocated label X at all), or it might be forwarded to wrong destination.

To solve the first problem, both the primary egress PE and node where the traffic is redirected to advertise a shared anycast IP address. This is conceptually similar to anycast rendezvous points in multicast deployments, where the same IP address is injected into IGP by multiple routers acting as rendezvous points. When PLR detects the failure of the primary egress PE, using simple local-repair techniques (LFA or RSVP-TE facility backup), traffic can be redirected because the IP address is the same.

To solve the second problem, the primary egress PE and backup egress PE must send (via a direct BGP session or using a BGP Route Reflector [RR]) their VPN bindings (prefix plus label) to the node where the traffic is redirected to by the PLR. This node protects the primary egress PE by translating VPN labels allocated by the primary egress PE to the corresponding VPN labels allocated by the backup egress PE; therefore, this node is called the *protector* in the overall concept. Because the protector node can protect multiple primary egress PEs, the RIB/FIB structures required for VPN label translation are created separately for each protected primary egress PE. They are built in the *context* of the anycast IP address mentioned previously; consequently, this IP address is called *context ID*.

The entire concept is often called *service mirroring* because the primary egress PE mirrors its VPN information to the protector node. It introduces the following network functions and uses the following terminology:

Ingress PE node

The ingress PE node receives the traffic from the locally connected VPN site, encapsulates the traffic by using the VRF–specific MPLS label stack, and sends it to the egress PE using context-ID anycast IP address.

Primary egress PE node

The primary egress PE is a node that normally receives VPN traffic flows destined to a multihomed (connected to primary and backup egress PE) VPN site. If the ingress PE performs load-balancing toward multiple egress PEs (this is the *Active/Active next hops to egress PEs* model discussed in Chapter 20), it means some of the flows are sent toward one egress PE, whereas the other flows are sent toward the second egress PE. From the egress protection (service mirroring) architecture perspective, the definition of *primary egress PE* is bound to actual traffic flow.

Backup egress PE node

The backup egress PE is a node that normally does not receive VPN traffic flows destined to a multihomed (connected to primary and backup egress PE) VPN site. Again, in the case of load-balancing performed by the ingress PE, the definition of *backup egress PE* is bound to actual flow. Assuming perfect load-balancing, for 50% of the flows, the first egress PE is the primary egress, whereas the second egress PE is the backup egress. For the remaining 50% of flows, it is just the opposite: the second egress PE is the primary egress, whereas the first egress PE is the backup egress.

PLR node

This is the node directly connected to the primary egress PE. Upon failure detection of the primary egress PE (or link toward the primary egress PE), the PLR redirects the traffic toward the protector node. Redirection uses local-repair techniques (LFA or RSVP-TE facility protection), thus failover is very fast (~50 ms).

Protector node

This is the node accepting traffic redirected by the PLR and performing the VPN label translation on received VPN packets. It translates the VPN label allocated by the primary egress PE to the VPN label allocated by the backup egress PE, and then sends the packet with translated VPN label to the backup egress PE. Therefore, the protector must receive appropriate BGP VPN updates from the primary and backup egress PE nodes.

Context-ID

This is the anycast IP address advertised by the primary egress PE and the protector node. Characteristics (e.g., IGP metric) of the anycast IP address advertised by the primary egress PE are better than those advertised by the protector node. Thus, normally the traffic is routed through the network toward the primary egress PE. The primary egress PE uses this anycast IP address as the BGP protocol next hop in outbound BGP updates for NLRIs requiring egress protection. The protector advertises the same anycast IP address in order to attract the traffic in case of primary egress PE failure.

This concept is described in *draft-minto-2547-egress-node-fast-protection* and illustrated in Figure 21-1.

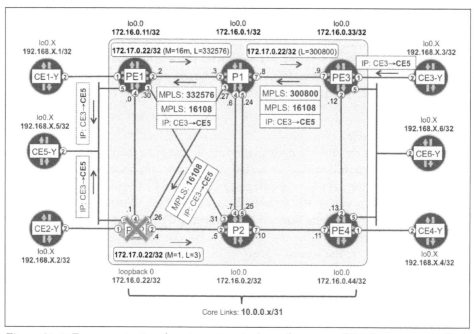

Figure 21-1. Egress protection (service mirroring) topology—combined protector/backup egress PE model

You can deploy egress protection (service mirroring) by using two major architectural models:

Combined protector/backup egress PE model

In the combined model, the protector function and the backup egress PE functions are combined on a single node. Thus, in this model no real translation of VPN labels is required, because the traffic redirected by the PLR to the combined protector/backup egress PE node can be immediately sent to the directly attached multihomed VPN site. However, forwarding of redirected traffic must be based on the VPN labels allocated by the primary egress PE.

Separate (centralized) protector and backup egress PE model

In the centralized protector model, the function of the backup egress PE and the protector are implemented on physically separate nodes. Such a deployment model creates the opportunity to implement egress protection (service mirroring) architecture without any specific support required on the PE nodes. VPN label translation, demanding some sort of support in hardware, is implemented exclusively on the dedicated protector node (or nodes). PEs are standard PEs without any knowledge about egress protection (service mirroring); they simply receive VPN packets with their own VPN labels.

Figure 21-1 shows the combined protector/backup egress PE model only (the centralized protector model is discussed later in this chapter). Traffic flows from right (CE3, CE4, CE6) to left (CE5), flowing normally through the primary egress PE (PE2), are protected by PE1 acting as a combined protector/backup egress PE.

 As of this writing, IOS XR does not support the *protector* function in the overall service mirroring architecture. All other node types used in service mirroring architecture (ingress PE, primary egress PE, backup egress PE, PLR) are supported on IOS XR.

Combined Protector/Backup Egress PE Model

Let's begin this model discussion with the combined protector/backup egress PE model. In this model, PE3 and PE4 are ingress PEs, PE2 (IOS XR) is deployed as the primary egress PE, whereas PE1 is used as the combined protector/backup egress PE. On PE2 (primary egress PE), the following modifications are required:

- BGP VPN NLRI updates advertised by PE2 have MED=0 (lower than on PE1) to ensure that PE2 is the primary egress PE.

- The BGP protocol next hop for these updates is changed by the outbound policy to the secondary address (172.17.0.22) of the loopback interface. This IP address is the context-ID anycast address as mentioned previously.

- The secondary address of the loopback interface is injected into IS-IS (with metric 0) and LDP (with implicit null label).

Example 21-1 summarizes these small configuration changes required on PE2.

Example 21-1. Primary egress PE configuration on PE2 (IOS XR)

```
interface Loopback0
 ipv4 address 172.17.0.22 255.255.255.255 secondary
!
route-policy PL-BGP-UP-VPN-EXP
  set next-hop 172.17.0.22
  done
end-policy
!
router bgp 65000
neighbor-group RR
  address-family vpnv4 unicast
   route-policy PL-BGP-UP-VPN-EXP out
```

Now, PE1 must act as the combined protector/backup egress PE. This results in the following:

- BGP VPN NLRI updates advertised by PE1 have MED=1000 (higher than on PE2), to ensure that the PE1 is backup egress PE
- The BGP protocol next hop remains the default (primary address of loopback interface)
- The protector context-ID (172.17.0.22—the same IP address as used on the primary egress PE) must be defined and injected into IS-IS with high metric (default is 2^{24}-2=16777214) and into LDP (with real, and not implicit null label).
- The BGP sessions toward the RRs are enabled to support egress-protection for the IPv4-VPN address family.

Again, here are the changes required on the combined protector/backup egress PE.

Example 21-2. Combined protector/backup egress PE configuration at PE1 (Junos)

```
protocols {
    mpls {
        egress-protection {
            context-identifier 172.17.0.22 protector;
        }
    }
    bgp {
        group IBGP-RR {
            family inet-vpn unicast {
                egress-protection;
}}}}
policy-options {
    policy-statement PL-VRF-B-EXP {   ## policy for other VRFs similar
        then {
            metric 1000;              ## higher than on PE2
            origin incomplete;        ## the same as on PE2
            community add RT-VPN-B;
            accept;
}}}
routing-instances {
    VRF-B {
        vrf-export PL-VRF-B-EXP;      ## other VRFs similar
}}
```

The context-ID IP address (172.17.0.22/32) is now originated by PE1 and PE2. Thus, on Junos PLR routers (P1 and P2), LFA must be prepared to handle protection of the prefixes originated by multiple routers. You must enable the per-prefix-calculation, as described in Chapter 18.

After implementing the configuration changes, let's verify the states in the network.

Example 21-3. IS-IS and LDP states for PE2 context-ID

```
1    RP/0/RSP0/CPU0:PE2#show isis database detail
2    (...)
3    PE1.00-00      0x0000006c   0xf808        479          0/0/0
4      Metric: 16777214    IP-Extended 172.17.0.22/32
5    (...)
6    PE2.00-00    * 0x00000097   0xaa59        883          0/0/0
7      Metric: 0              IP-Extended 172.17.0.22/32
8
9    RP/0/RSP0/CPU0:PE2#show mpls ldp bindings 172.17.0.22/32
10   172.17.0.22/32, rev 4
11        Local binding: label: ImpNull
12        Remote bindings: (5 peers)
13        Peer                Label
14        ----------------    ---------
15        172.16.0.1:0        300000
16        172.16.0.2:0        300176
17        172.16.0.11:0       332576
18        172.16.0.33:0       300192
19        172.16.0.44:0       300032
```

Verification confirms that the primary egress PE (PE2) advertises the context-ID IP address with a low IGP metric (line 7) and an implicit null label (line 11). The protector (PE1), on the other hand, advertises the same context-ID IP address with a high IGP metric (line 4) and a real label (line 17). Apart from configuring the protector context-ID on PE1, no special configuration is required to achieve this behavior.

The requirements for different IGP metrics are easy to understand: the ingress PEs (PE3 and PE4) should prefer PE2 to reach 172.17.0.22, because in our design PE2 is the primary egress PE. But why does the protector (PE1) advertise a real LDP label, instead of advertising an implicit null, as the primary egress PE (PE2) does?

Let's try to verify routing states on the path from an ingress PE, (e.g., PE3) to reach the loopback of CE5-B (see Example 21-4).

Example 21-4. RIB/FIB states on the path from PE3 (ingress PE) to PE1 (protector)

```
juniper@PE3> show route forwarding-table destination 192.168.2.5/32
            extensive | match "Destination|Index: [1-9]|weight|Push"
Destination:  192.168.2.5/32
  Next-hop type: composite         Index: 1978     Reference: 2
  Load Balance Label: Push 16108, None
  Next-hop type: indirect          Index: 1048717  Reference: 8
  Next-hop type: unilist           Index: 1048657  Reference: 2
  Next-hop type: Push 300800       Index: 1974     Reference: 1
  Next-hop interface: ge-2/0/7.0  Weight: 0x1
```

```
Next-hop type: Push 300112          Index: 1912     Reference: 1
Next-hop interface: ge-2/0/2.0  Weight: 0xf000

juniper@P1> show route label 300800
(...)
299952(S=0)          *[LDP/9] 02:34:57, metric 1
                     > to 10.0.0.26 via ge-2/0/3.0, Pop
                       to 10.0.0.2 via ge-2/0/2.0, Swap 332576
```

The FIB state observed on PE3 is standard, as already discussed in Chapter 18 and Chapter 20. PE3 sends packets with a label stack (16108, 300800) via P1 (the primary next hop to reach 172.17.0.22 used as a BGP next hop) or with a label stack (16108, 300112) via PE4 (the backup LFA next hop to reach 172.17.0.22). When the packet arrives at P1, the top label is removed and the packet is sent via direct link to PE2 (the primary next hop to reach 172.17.0.22), or the top label is swapped and the packet is sent via direct link to PE1 (the backup LFA next hop to reach 172.17.0.22). Thus, when PE2 (the primary PE) fails, P1 redirects the traffic to PE1 (the protector/backup PE) very quickly—based on local repair.

Now, as mentioned earlier, when redirected packets arrive to PE1 (the protector/backup egress PE), they need to be forwarded to the local CE devices based on VPN labels allocated by PE2 (the primary egress PE). P1, which performs redirection, does not alter the VPN label in any way, so the PE2 allocated VPN label is still in the MPLS header of packets redirected to PE1. To achieve that, PE1 needs to do the following:

- Realize that packets arriving from the MPLS core require special treatment, because they are not normal VPN packets, but packets originally destined to PE2 which are just redirected by P1 to PE1.

- Use VPN labels allocated by another PE (PE2) for traffic forwarding.

To achieve the desired functionality, the protector/backup egress PE creates multi-level, multifamily (MPLS and IP) RIB structures, as illustrated in Figure 21-2 as well as the subsequent outputs from several Junos operational commands shown in Example 21-5.

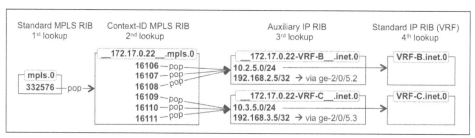

Figure 21-2. RIB structures on combined protector/backup egress PE node—PE1 (Junos)

*Example 21-5. RIB structures on combined protector/backup egress PE node—PE1
(Junos)*

```
1    juniper@PE1> show route table mpls.0 label 332576
2    (...)
3    332576(S=0)        *[LDP/0] 00:07:58
4                          to table __172.17.0.22__.mpls.0
5
6    juniper@PE1> show route table __172.17.0.22__.mpls.0
7    (...)
8    16106              *[Egress-Protection/170] 19:42:05
9                          to table __172.17.0.22-VRF-B__.inet.0
10   16107              *[Egress-Protection/170] 19:42:05
11                         to table __172.17.0.22-VRF-B__.inet.0
12   16108              *[Egress-Protection/170] 19:42:05
13                         to table __172.17.0.22-VRF-B__.inet.0
14   16109              *[Egress-Protection/170] 19:42:05
15                         to table __172.17.0.22-VRF-C__.inet.0
16   16110              *[Egress-Protection/170] 19:42:05
17                         to table __172.17.0.22-VRF-C__.inet.0
18   16111              *[Egress-Protection/170] 19:42:05
19                         to table __172.17.0.22-VRF-C__.inet.0
20
21   juniper@PE1> show route table __172.17.0.22-VRF-B__.inet.0
22   (...)
23   10.2.5.0/24        *[Egress-Protection/170] 19:43:09
24                         to table VRF-B.inet.0
25   192.168.2.5/32     *[Egress-Protection/170] 19:43:09
26                         > to 10.2.5.5 via ge-2/0/5.2
27
28   juniper@PE1> show route table __172.17.0.22-VRF-C__.inet.0
29   (...)
30   10.3.5.0/24        *[Egress-Protection/170] 19:43:15
31                         to table VRF-C.inet.0
32   192.168.3.5/32     *[Egress-Protection/170] 19:43:15
33                         > to 10.3.5.5 via ge-2/0/5.3
```

First, you can see that the label allocated to the protector context-ID is a real label (lines 1 through 4 in Example 21-5, and line 17 from Example 21-3). A real label (and not an implicit null label) is required. Otherwise, PE1 is not able to determine that the arriving packet requires some special treatment. Therefore, for every configured protector context-ID, the protector generates a separate (real) label. In this example, PE1 is configured with the single protector context-ID, but in more complex scenarios, you can configure multiple protector context-IDs. There are some examples of those later in the chapter.

The (real) protector context-ID label is installed in mpls.0 table and points to an auxiliary table called __172.17.0.22__.mpls.0. Therefore, when packets with the label 332576 arrive at PE1, PE1 removes (pops) the label and performs a next lookup in this auxiliary table. But what is this table? This table collects all VPN labels allocated by the primary PE. Accordingly, this auxiliary table is called the *context label table*. If you compare lines 6 through 19 in Example 21-5 with those from Example 21-6, you will see the similarities.

Example 21-6. VPN labels of VRF-B and VRF-C routes received from PE2

```
1       juniper@RR1> show route receive-protocol bgp 172.16.0.22
2                   community target:65000:100[23] detail | match "VPN Label"
3           VPN Label: 16106
4           VPN Label: 16106
5           VPN Label: 16107
6           VPN Label: 16108
7           VPN Label: 16106
8           VPN Label: 16109
9           VPN Label: 16109
10          VPN Label: 16110
11          VPN Label: 16111
12          VPN Label: 16109
```

And that is the reason why the protector node allocates real (not implicit null) labels when advertising protector context-IDs in LDP. Based on this real label, the protector is able to determine that the packet needs special treatment, and performs a second lookup in the context label table, where labels from the primary egress PE are collected. How is this table built? It is based on received BGP NLRIs with the BGP protocol next hop equal to the configured protector context-ID. Because the example's primary egress PE (PE2) uses 172.17.0.22 as a next hop (Example 21-1), the protector (PE1) collects VPN labels of received VPN prefixes with the next hop 172.17.0.22 (protector context-ID) and uses these VPN labels to build a context label table for 172.17.0.22 context-ID.

Entries in the context *label* table (__172.17.0.22__.mpls.0) point to (multiple) context-ID/VRF specific *IP* auxiliary tables: __172.17.0.22-VRF-B__.inet.0 and __172.17.0.22-VRF-C__.inet.0. These auxiliary tables are still built based on IP VPN prefixes received from the primary egress PE. However, as opposed to the case with the context label table, the backup egress PE only installs the prefix in the IP auxiliary table if there is a match between the IP VPN prefix received from the primary egress PE, and the prefix in the local VRF. In this particular case, for example, PE1 installs only two prefixes in each IP auxiliary table (lines 21 through 33 in Example 21-5). What are these two prefixes? They are the loopback of the dual-homed CE5-B (or CE5-C) and the shared LAN prefix for PE1-PE2 connectivity inside VRF-B and VRF-C. Other prefixes advertised by PE2 (e.g., the loopback of CE2-B: 192.168.2.2/32) are not used by PE1 to populate the IP auxiliary tables. Put simply, they cannot be used to protect traffic destined to such prefixes, because PE1 is not connected to the CEs advertising these prefixes. In other words, there is no multihomed CE advertising 192.168.2.2/32 and connected to both the primary egress PE (PE2) and the protector/backup egress PE (PE1).

If you carefully examine the content of the IP auxiliary tables, you should realize that for some prefixes (the loopbacks of directly connected dual-homed CEs) the entry points directly to the outgoing interface. So, this is the final lookup. For some other prefixes (shared LAN prefixes connecting PE1, PE2, and dual-homed CE), the entry points to the next table, which this time is the VRF table presented normally on the (backup) egress PE. Why this difference? If the final destination, including L2 encapsulation (destination MAC address) can be unambiguously determined from the prefix, the IP auxiliary table contains all this information, so no further lookup is needed. If, however, it is not the case (e.g., on 10.2.5.0/24 subnet there could potentially be 254 hosts, each host with a different MAC address, so it is not possible to associate the single destination MAC with the 10.2.5.0/24 prefix), the packet is handed over (next lookup) to normal VRF for further processing. In normal VRF, all features required for packet forwarding are available; for example, ARP machinery for LAN segments to determine the MAC address.

 The protector function in service mirroring architectures require multilevel (up to four levels), multiprotocol (MPLS and IP), lookup implementation in the hardware FIB (HW FIB). This functionality is natively available in Junos in those hardware platforms based on the Trio architecture (all types of MPC line cards for MX Series router). In other Junos platforms, a virtual tunnel (VT) interface implemented in the Packet Forwarding Engine (PFE) is required on routers acting as the protector node.

You are almost done with your first egress protection (service mirroring) design. There is, however, one issue that requires more attention. If you go back to the configuration of the primary egress PE (Example 21-1), you'll see that for all VPN prefixes the next hop is changed to 172.17.0.22. Is this a correct design? What happens to traffic destined to single-homed CEs (e.g., CE2-B) during network failure events?

For the purpose of the discussion, let's temporarily disable the PE2-P1 and PE2-P2 links so that PE2 is reachable only via PE1. Therefore, all traffic from the MPLS core destined for PE2 must flow over PE1. Now let's check how you can reach the loopback of CE2-B from PE3.

Example 21-7. RIB states on the path from PE3 (ingress PE) to PE1 (protector)

```
1    juniper@PE3> show route 192.168.2.2/32 table VRF-B active-path
2    (...)
3    192.168.2.2/32
4        *[BGP/170] 02:18:52, MED 101, localpref 100, from 172.16.0.201
5            AS path: ?, validation-state: unverified
```

```
6               > to 10.0.0.8 via ge-2/0/7.0, Push 16107, Push 300800(top)
7                 to 10.0.0.13 via ge-2/0/2.0, Push 16107, Push 300112(top)
8
9     juniper@P1> show route label 300800
10    (...)
11    300800 (S=0)       *[LDP/9] 00:00:32, metric 21
12                        > to 10.0.0.2 via ge-2/0/2.0, Swap 332576
13
```

PE3 attaches a standard label stack with two labels: VPN label 16107 (allocated by primary PE—PE2) and transport LDP label 300800. Subsequently, PE3 sends the packet toward P1. This time on P1, however, there is only one outgoing interface pointing toward PE1, because due to the previously disabled links, PE2 is reachable only via PE1. P1 uses the same label (332576), as discussed previously, when forwarding the traffic toward PE1.

And what happens now to the traffic, when traffic arrives at PE1? If you go back to the previous discussion (lines 1 through 4 in Example 21-5), you will realize that the traffic is intercepted by PE1. It is not forwarded to PE2. *What does that mean?* It means that the traffic is *blackholed*. Why? As discussed previously, PE1 installs label 16107 (used by PE2 for the loopback of CE2-B) in its context label table (lines 10 and 11 in Example 21-5). But PE1 does not install the loopback of CE2-B in its auxiliary IP table (lines 21 through 26 in Example 21-5). It basically means, the third lookup does not provide any results, and thus traffic is blackholed.

How can you prepare the design to defend the network against such failure scenarios? You change the next hop to context-ID (secondary loopback address) with caution, and only for prefixes advertised by multihomed CEs connected to both primary and protector/egress PE nodes. All other prefixes should use the standard next hop (the primary loopback address). In such a way, if traffic associated with the standard next hop flows through the protector node, the protector node will not intercept it. The protector node will simply forward the traffic toward the primary egress PE.

So, let's slightly modify the configuration (Example 21-1) on the primary egress PE to that shown in Example 21-8.

Example 21-8. Route-policies to support service mirroring on PE2 (IOS XR)

```
1     vrf VRF-B
2       address-family ipv4 unicast
3         export route-policy PL-VRF-B-EXP        ## other VRFs similar
4     !
5     community-set CM-MULTI-HOMED
6       65000:41201
7     end-set
8     !
9     route-policy PL-VRF-B-EXP           ## policy for other VRFs similar
10      if destination in (192.168.2.5/32, 10.2.5.0/24) then
```

```
11        set community CM-MULTI-HOMED
12      endif
13      done
14    end-policy
15    !
16    route-policy PL-BGP-UP-VPN-EXP
17      if community matches-any CM-MULTI-HOMED then
18        set next-hop 172.17.0.22
19        delete community in CM-MULTI-HOMED
20        done
21      endif
22      done
23    end-policy
```

The configuration basically marks multihomed prefixes with a community (lines 5 through 7) using an extra VRF export policy (lines 9 through 14) in an affected VRF (line 3). Then, it modifies the BGP export policy already defined in Example 21-1 to ensure that only multihomed prefixes have their next hop changed to the secondary loopback address (lines 17 through 21). All other VPN prefixes are advertised without next hop modification (line 22), which results in the primary loopback address being used as the BGP next hop.

With this small modification, the protector node, as verified by the outputs presented in Example 21-9, no longer intercepts traffic destined to single-homed prefixes.

Example 21-9. RIB states on the path from PE3 (ingress PE) to PE2

```
1     juniper@PE3> show route 192.168.2.2/32 table VRF-B active-path
2     (...)
3     192.168.2.2/32
4        *[BGP/170] 00:23:17, MED 101, localpref 100, from 172.16.0.201
5          AS path: ?, validation-state: unverified
6        > to 10.0.0.8 via ge-2/0/7.0, Push 16107, Push 300880(top)
7          to 10.0.0.13 via ge-2/0/2.0, Push 16107, Push 300144(top)
8
9     juniper@PE3> show route 192.168.2.5/32 table VRF-B active-path
10    (...)
11    192.168.2.5/32
12       *[BGP/170] 00:23:42, MED 0, localpref 100, from 172.16.0.201
13         AS path: ?, validation-state: unverified
14       > to 10.0.0.8 via ge-2/0/7.0, Push 16108, Push 300800(top)
15         to 10.0.0.13 via ge-2/0/2.0, Push 16108, Push 300112(top)
16
17    juniper@P1> show route label 300880
18    (...)
19    300880(S=0)          *[LDP/9] 07:30:39, metric 20
20                          > to 10.0.0.2 via ge-2/0/2.0, Swap 332752
21
22    juniper@PE1> show route label 332752
23    (...)
```

```
24      332752(S=0)        *[LDP/9] 07:30:49, metric 10
25                          > to 10.0.0.1 via ge-2/0/4.0, Pop
```

PE3 uses a different LDP transport label to reach the single-homed prefix (loopback of CE2-B) and the multihomed prefix (loopback of CE5-B): 300880 (line 6) versus 300800 (line 14). This should be obvious, because the BGP protocol next hop advertised for these prefixes by PE2 is now different: 172.16.0.22 versus 172.17.0.22. Lines 17 through 25 confirm that P1 and PE1 simply forward the traffic to PE2 by performing standard label operations: swap (P1, line 20) and pop (PE1, line 25). Therefore packets arrive at PE2 with a single VPN label and can be forwarded without any problems to the single-homed CE.

Separate (Centralized) Protector and Backup Egress PE Model

The previous section discussed, in detail, the egress protection (service mirroring) model, wherein the protector function and the backup egress PE function was implemented on the same node (PE1). This is not always the case, so let's quickly discuss a deployment model in which these two functions are implemented on different physical nodes, as shown in Figure 21-3.

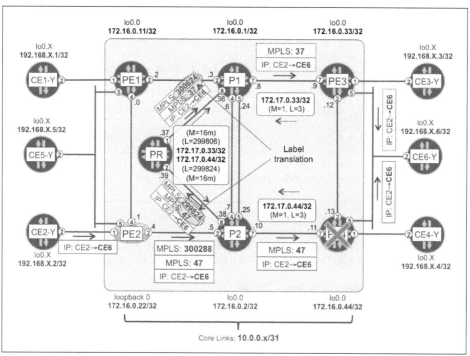

Figure 21-3. Egress protection (service mirroring) topology—centralized protector model

In this scenario, flows from the left side (CE1, CE2, and CE5) to the right side (CE6) are protected by a separate protector node: PR. Both ingress PEs (PE1 and PE2) perform load-balancing (Active/Active next hops to egress PEs) toward both egress PEs (PE3 and PE4). Therefore, for approximately half of the CE6-bound flows, PE3 is the primary egress PE, whereas PE4 is the backup egress PE. For the remaining half of the flows, it's just the opposite: PE3 is the backup egress PE, whereas PE4 is the primary egress PE. Figure 21-3 shows an example flow from PE2 to PE4 only. Both egress PEs inject their context-IDs (172.17.0.33 and 172.17.0.44, respectively) with a low (equal to 1) IGP metric and with an LDP implicit null label. The PR node is now a separate protector node performing translation of VPN labels from the primary egress PE to VPN labels allocated by the backup egress PE.

Let's begin with the configuration adjustments on the PE routers (Example 21-10).

Example 21-10. Primary egress PE configuration on PE3 (Junos)

```
1    protocols {
2        mpls {
3            egress-protection {
4                context-identifier 172.17.0.33 primary;
5            }
6        }
7        bgp {
8            group IBGP-RR {
9                family inet-vpn {
10                   unicast {
11                       egress-protection;
12                   }
13               }
14               export PL-BGP-SET-CONTEXT-ID;
15               vpn-apply-export;
16   }}}
17   policy-options {
18       policy-statement PL-BGP-SET-CONTEXT-ID {
19           term MULTI-HOMED {
20               from tag2 41201;
21               then {
22                   next-hop 172.17.0.33;
23                   accept;
24               }
25           }
26       }
27       policy-statement PL-VRF-B-EXP { ## similar policy for other VRFs
28           term MULTI-HOMED {
29               from interface ge-2/0/5.2;
30               then tag2 41201;
31           }
32           then {
33               community add RT-VPN-B;
```

```
34                    accept;
35              }
36          }
37          community RT-VPN-B members target:65000:1002;
38      }
39      routing-instances {
40          VRF-B {
41              vrf-export PL-VRF-B-EXP;    ## other VRFs similar
42      }}
```

First, the context-ID must be specified. One option is to specify the primary context-ID in the `protocols mpls` section (lines 2 through 6). With this option, the specified context-ID is automatically advertised via IGP and LDP. Another viable option is to specify the primary context-ID as the secondary loopback address—in a similar way as was presented in Example 21-1 for IOS XR.

Next, you must enable egress protection functionality in BGP (line 11). At this configuration level, you can also specify the context-ID address (`set protocols bgp group IBGP-RR family inet-vpn unicast egress-protection context-identifier 172.17.0.33`). However, this is not advisable, if you have single-homed and multihomed CEs connected to the PE. This command results in the BGP protocol next hop being automatically changed to the context-ID for all VPN prefixes. As discussed previously, changing the BGP protocol next hop for single-homed prefixes might lead to traffic blackholing in certain situations.

Thus, you will manipulate the next hop only for multihomed prefixes. One option is to use a special community, in a similar way as discussed in Example 21-8. Another option is to use the interim `tag2` parameter instead of the community. In this way, you don't need to remove the community (like in Example 21-8, line 19), because `tag2` has local significance only—it is not advertised to routing peers. So, you select multihomed prefixes—the simplest way is to use the interface as selection criteria (line 29) in the VRF export policy. All prefixes reachable via the interface connected to the multihomed CE will be marked with some tag2 value (line 30). You don't need to know exactly what the prefixes are, just the interface. Next, on the BGP export policy (line 14), you change next hop to context-ID for tagged prefixes only (lines 22), while keeping the default next hop for other prefixes. The `vpn-apply-export` parameter (line 15), discussed in Chapter 3, is required to ensure that the BGP export policy affects VPN prefixes, as well.

The protector node PR configuration requires special attention. There are no local VRFs on the PR (PR is *not* backup egress PE). Therefore, you need to specify a route policy that will be the basis for egress protection (service mirroring) RIB/FIB structures. The PR builds the RIB/FIB translation table only for VPN prefixes matching the route policy. For scaling, you could, for example, designate the PR as the protector for VPN-B and VPN-C (as in the configuration shown in Example 21-11), while designating some other router as the protector for other VPNs.

Example 21-11. Separate (centralized) protector configuration on PR (Junos)

```
1     protocols {
2         mpls {
3             egress-protection {
4                 context-identifier 172.17.0.33 {
5                     protector;
6                 }
7                 context-identifier 172.17.0.44 {
8                     protector;
9                 }
10            }
11        }
12        bgp {
13            group IBGP-RR {           ## group towards route reflectors
14                family inet-vpn {
15                    unicast {
16                        egress-protection {
17                            keep-import PL-BGP-EGRESS-PROTECTION-RT;
18  }}}}}}
19    policy-options {           ## protection for VPN-B and VPN-C only
20        policy-statement PL-BGP-EGRESS-PROTECTION-RT {
21            from community [ RT-VPN-B RT-VPN-C ];
22            then accept;
23        }
24        community RT-VPN-B members target:65000:1002;
25        community RT-VPN-C members target:65000:1003;
26    }
```

One additional important problem is the configuration of the BGP RR. Or, in general, the configuration of BGP peers sending VPN prefixes to the protector node, if the route reflector design is not used. If constrained route distribution (RFC 4364) is in place (as is discussed in Chapter 3), BGP peers will not send anything to the protector node. Why? Because on pure protector nodes, VRFs are not configured. Therefore the protector node does not advertise toward BGP peers any Route Targets (RTs) inside the RT address family. Thus, based on the constrained route distribution operational model, these BGP peers (RRs) do not advertise any VPN routes to the protector node.

If, on the other hand, the route-target address family is not configured between the protector node and the BGP peers (RRs), these BGP peers send the full VPN table. Whereas the first case prevents proper operation of the protector node (no VPN prefixes received), the second case is not optimal, either. Therefore, let's configure static RT constraints on the RRs (protector's BGP peers) in order to send to the protector only those VPN prefixes with specific RTs—as required by the protector.

Example 21-12. Static RT constraint configuration on RR (Junos)

```
1    protocols {
2        bgp {
3            group IBGP-CLIENTS {
4                neighbor 172.16.0.10 family inet-vpn unicast;    ## PR
5    }}}}
6    routing-options {
7        rib bgp.rtarget.0 {
8            static {          ## matches 65000:1002 and 65000:1003 only
9                route-target-filter 65000:1002/63 neighbor 172.16.0.10;
10   }}}
```

OK, the configuration is complete; let's verify network operation (see Example 21-13).

Example 21-13. RIB/FIB states on egress and ingress PE, and PLR

```
1    juniper@PE3> show route advertising-protocol bgp 172.16.0.201 table V
2
3    VRF-B.inet.0: 18 destinations, 38 routes (18 active, 0 holddown)
4      Prefix              Nexthop          MED    Lclpref    AS path
5    * 10.2.3.0/31         Self                    100        I
6    * 10.2.6.0/24         172.17.0.33             100        I
7    * 192.168.2.3/32      Self             100    100        I
8    * 192.168.2.6/32      172.17.0.33      0      100        65506 ?
9    * 192.168.2.33/32     Self                    100        I
10
11   VRF-C.inet.0: 18 destinations, 40 routes (18 active, 0 holddown)
12     Prefix              Nexthop          MED    Lclpref    AS path
13   * 10.3.3.0/31         Self                    100        I
14   * 10.3.6.0/24         172.17.0.33             100        I
15   * 192.168.3.3/32      Self             100    100        I
16   * 192.168.3.6/32      172.17.0.33      0      100        65506 ?
17   * 192.168.3.33/32     Self                    100        I
18
19   RP/0/RSP0/CPU0:PE2#show cef vrf VRF-B 192.168.2.3/32 | include ...
20      via 172.16.0.33, 4 dependencies, recursive [flags 0x6000]
21        next hop 10.0.0.27/32 Gi/0/0/0/3 labels imposed {301040 37}
22
23   RP/0/RSP0/CPU0:PE2#show cef vrf VRF-B 192.168.2.6/32 | include ...
24      via 172.17.0.33, 3 dependencies, recursive, bgp-multipath (...)
25        next hop 10.0.0.27/32 Gi/0/0/0/3 labels imposed {300624 37}
26      via 172.17.0.44, 3 dependencies, recursive, bgp-multipath (...)
27        next hop 10.0.0.5/32 Gi/0/0/0/2 labels imposed {300288 47}
28
29   juniper@P1> show route label 301040 detail | find ... | match ...
30   301040(S=0) (1 entry, 1 announced)
31           Next hop: 10.0.0.9 via ge-2/0/7.0 weight 0x1, selected
32           Label operation: Pop
33
34   juniper@P1> show route label 300624 detail | find ... | match ...
35   300624(S=0) (1 entry, 1 announced)
```

```
36                    Next hop: 10.0.0.9 via ge-2/0/7.0 weight 0x1, selected
37                    Label operation: Pop
38                    Next hop: 10.0.0.37 via ge-2/0/8.0 weight 0xf000
39                    Label operation: Swap 299808
40
41     juniper@P2> show route label 300288 detail | find ... | match ...
42     300288(S=0) (1 entry, 1 announced)
43                    Next hop: 10.0.0.11 via ge-2/0/7.0 weight 0x1, selected
44                    Label operation: Pop
45                    Next hop: 10.0.0.39 via ge-2/0/8.0 weight 0xf000
46                    Label operation: Swap 299824
```

You can see that the egress PE routers (e.g., PE3) advertise multihomed prefixes with the BGP protocol next hop set to the context-ID (172.17.0.33, in the case of PE3), while using standard next hop (self, which is the address where the BGP session terminates: the primary loopback address) for all other prefixes (lines 1 through 17). On the ingress PE (e.g., PE2) the FIB entry confirms that a different BGP protocol next hop is used (line 20 versus lines 24 and 26), and consequently, a different transport label is used, too (line 21 versus lines 25 and 27). For multihomed prefixes, PE2 load-balances the traffic, because PE2 deploys Active/Active next hops to egress PEs.

On the PLR router (e.g., P1) you can see that the label associated with the primary loopback address of PE3 (lines 20 and 21) is not protected by the LFA backup (lines 29 through 32). Given the network topology (Figure 21-3), this is obvious: there is no loop-free backup path to reach PE3 from P1. You could eventually deploy some more advanced LFA techniques (Remote LFA [RLFA], Topology-Independent Fast ReRoute [TI-FRR]), as discussed in Chapter 18, to enhance backup coverage here.

What is important from this chapter's perspective, however, is the forwarding state for the label associated with the context-ID of PE3. Lines 38 and 39 show that in the case of PE3 failure, P1 will redirect the traffic to the protector node PR performing label swap operation. You can spot similar behavior on P2, with regard to the failure of PE4 (lines 45 and 46).

You can perform similar investigations for other prefixes (e.g., prefixes from VRF-C) as well as from the perspective of another ingress PE (PE1). In all cases, upon failure detection of the directly connected egress PE router, PLR routers (P1 and P2) redirect the traffic destined to the context-ID of PE3 or PE4 toward the PR node based on the preinstalled LFA backup next hop.

And now, it is the task of the PR router to perform VPN label translation and send the traffic to another (not failed) egress PE—the backup egress PE router in service mirroring architecture. So, let's check how it is performed now (see Example 21-14). First, verify if the PR receives the proper NLRIs from the RR. As you remember, you are designing the network to protect traffic only for VRF-B and VRF-C, so you made a configuration (Example 21-12) to ensure that the RR only sends VPN prefixes for these two VPNs to the PR.

Example 21-14. VPN prefix propagation between RR and PR

```
1    juniper@RR1> show route table bgp.rtarget.0
2    (...)
3    65000:65000:1002/95
4                        *[RTarget/5] 2d 18:20:10
5                         Type Static
6                           for 172.16.0.10          ## PR loopback
7                         Local
8
9    juniper@RR1> show route summary table bgp.l3vpn.0
10   (...)
11   bgp.l3vpn.0: 55 destinations, 55 routes (55 active, 0 holddown)
12                   BGP:    55 routes,    55 active
13
14   juniper@RR1> show bgp neighbor 172.16.0.10 | match <pattern>
15     Table bgp.l3vpn.0 Bit: 20001
16       Advertised prefixes:        40
17     Table bgp.l2vpn.0 Bit: 30001
18       Advertised prefixes:         0
19
20   juniper@RR1> show route advertising-protocol bgp 172.16.0.10
21               extensive | match target:65000:1002 | count
22   Count: 20 lines
23
24   juniper@RR1> show route advertising-protocol bgp 172.16.0.10
25               extensive | match target:65000:1003 | count
26   Count: 20 lines
27
28   juniper@PR> show route summary table bgp.l3vpn.0
29   (...)
30   bgp.l3vpn.0: 40 destinations, 80 routes (40 active, 23 holddown)
31                   BGP:    80 routes,    40 active
```

Except where stated otherwise, all of the line numbers in the following two paragraphs refer to Example 21-14. It seems the static RT constraint configuration (Example 21-12) is effective, because the RR installs the appropriate entry in bgp.rtarget.0 RIB (lines 3 through 7). This basically means the RR will send to 172.16.0.10 (PR's loopback) NLRIs that have a route target from the 65000:65000:1002/95 range. This range covers only two RTs—65000:65000:1002 and 65000:65000:1003—which perfectly covers the RTs used for VRF-B and VRF-C. Furthermore, you can see the RR has 55 active routes in bgp.l3vpn.0 RIB (line 11), but only 40 routes are advertised to the PR node (line 16). Additional checks confirm that 20 of those prefixes have the RT for VRF-B (lines 20 through 22) and 20 have the RT for VRF-C (lines 24 through 26). Given the network topology, this is expected because each PE advertises five prefixes in each VPN: three loopbacks (single-homed CE, multihomed CE, and VRF on PE) and two PE-CE links (single-homed CE and multihomed CE).

Therefore, we can conclude that the RR sends only NLRIs associated with VRF-B and VRF-C to the PR. And, because the PR configuration allows reception of NLRIs with these RTs (Example 21-11, lines 17 through 26), you can see the bgp.l3vpn.0 RIB being populated (lines 28 through 31): 40 routes from each RR. So far, so good—the PR has all information required to build VPN translation tables. To enhance scale, you could further restrict the information advertised to the PR. The only information the PR requires are NLRIs from multihomed CEs in VPN-B and VPN-C connected to two egress PEs (PE3 and PE4). Information from single-homed CEs is not required on PR. This optimization, though, is not configured here.

OK, let's now verify (Figure 21-4, Example 21-15) the multilevel, multifamily (MPLS and IP) RIB/FIB structures created on the protector node PR and used for VPN label translation.

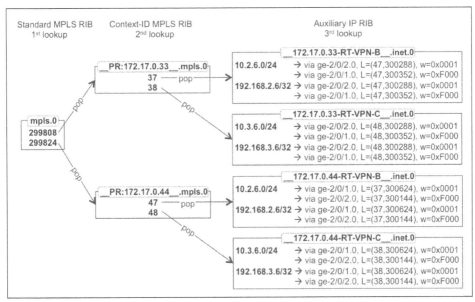

Figure 21-4. RIB structures on a standalone protector node—PR (Junos)

Both egress PEs (PE3 and PE4) advertise two multihomed prefixes within each VRF. PE3 uses label 37 for VRF-B, and label 38 for VRF-C, whereas PE4 uses label 47 and 48, respectively. Therefore, the protector node PR translates VPN label 37 to VPN label 47 (and back) as well as VPN label 38 to VPN label 48 (and back). Labels are allocated dynamically, so it might even happen that VPN labels advertised by both PE3 and PE4 are equal. Nevertheless, the protector node always performs translation, even between numerically equal VPN labels.

We can verify with operational commands if the RIB structure outlined in previous figure is correct.

Example 21-15. RIB structures on standalone protector node—PR (Junos)

```
1    juniper@PR> show ldp database session 172.16.0.1 | find .. | match ..
2      299808       172.17.0.33/32
3      299824       172.17.0.44/32
4
5    juniper@PR> show route table mpls.0
6    (...)
7    299808(S=0)          *[LDP/0] 23:50:07
8                          to table __172.17.0.33__.mpls.0
9    299824(S=0)          *[LDP/0] 3d 02:17:52
10                         to table __172.17.0.44__.mpls.0
11
12   juniper@PR> show route receive-protocol bgp 172.16.0.201
13            next-hop 172.17.0.33 detail | match label
14       VPN Label: 37
15       VPN Label: 37
16       VPN Label: 38
17       VPN Label: 38
18
19   juniper@PR> show route receive-protocol bgp 172.16.0.201
20            next-hop 172.17.0.44 detail | match label
21       VPN Label: 47
22       VPN Label: 47
23       VPN Label: 48
24       VPN Label: 48
25
26   juniper@PR> show route table __172.17.0.
27
28   __172.17.0.33__.mpls.0: 2 destinations, 2 routes (2 active, ...)
29   + = Active Route, - = Last Active, * = Both
30
31   37                   *[Egress-Protection/170] 23:29:45
32                         to table __172.17.0.33-RT-VPN-B__.inet.0
33   38                   *[Egress-Protection/170] 23:29:45
34                         to table __172.17.0.33-RT-VPN-C__.inet.0
35
36   __172.17.0.44__.mpls.0: 2 destinations, 2 routes (2 active, )
37   + = Active Route, - = Last Active, * = Both
38
39   47                   *[Egress-Protection/170] 23:11:43
40                         to table __172.17.0.44-RT-VPN-B__.inet.0
41   48                   *[Egress-Protection/170] 23:11:43
42                         to table __172.17.0.44-RT-VPN-C__.inet.0
43
44   juniper@PR> show route table __172.17.0.33-RT-VPN-B__.inet.0 detail |
45            match "entry|weight|operation|Protocol next hop"
46   10.2.6.0/24 (1 entry, 1 announced)
47            Next hop: 10.0.0.38 via ge-2/0/2.0 weight 0x1, selected
48            Label operation: Push 47, Push 300288(top)
49            Next hop: 10.0.0.36 via ge-2/0/8.0 weight 0xf000
50            Label operation: Push 47, Push 300352(top)
```

```
51                    Protocol next hop: 172.17.0.44
52    192.168.2.6/32 (1 entry, 1 announced)
53                    Next hop: 10.0.0.38 via ge-2/0/2.0 weight 0x1, selected
54                    Label operation: Push 47, Push 300288(top)
55                    Next hop: 10.0.0.36 via ge-2/0/8.0 weight 0xf000
56                    Label operation: Push 47, Push 300352(top)
57                    Protocol next hop: 172.17.0.44
58
59    juniper@PR> show route table __172.17.0.44-RT-VPN-B__.inet.0 detail |
60                    match "entry|weight|operation|Protocol next hop"
61    10.2.6.0/24 (1 entry, 1 announced)
62                    Next hop: 10.0.0.36 via ge-2/0/8.0 weight 0x1, selected
63                    Label operation: Push 37, Push 300624(top)
64                    Next hop: 10.0.0.38 via ge-2/0/2.0 weight 0xf000
65                    Label operation: Push 37, Push 300144(top)
66                    Protocol next hop: 172.17.0.33
67    192.168.2.6/32 (1 entry, 1 announced)
68                    Next hop: 10.0.0.36 via ge-2/0/8.0 weight 0x1, selected
69                    Label operation: Push 37, Push 300624(top)
70                    Next hop: 10.0.0.38 via ge-2/0/2.0 weight 0xf000
71                    Label operation: Push 37, Push 300144(top)
72                    Protocol next hop: 172.17.0.33
```

Unless stated otherwise, all of the line numbers in the following three paragraphs correspond to Example 21-15. The PR node advertises real labels for its locally configured protector context-IDs (lines 2 and 3). And, as expected, these labels match the labels already observed in earlier verifications (Example 21-13, lines 39 and 46). Similar to the combined protector/backup egress PE case, the label associated with the protector context-ID points to a context label table. But in this case, the two protector context-IDs are configured on the PR, and the PR creates two context label tables (lines 8 and 10): one table for each context-ID.

The PR extracts VPN labels from the received NLRIs (lines 12 through 24) and, based on the BGP protocol next hop, places these VPN labels in the appropriate context label table (lines 26 through 42). VPN labels, on the other hand, point to the appropriate auxiliary IP tables, based on the RTs associated with the NLRI. The difference between the previous case (combined protector/backup egress PE) and the current case is that the name (lines 32, 34, 40, and 42) of these auxiliary IP tables is now based on configured route-target names (Example 21-11, lines 24 and 25), and no longer on VRF names. The separate protector node does not contain any VRFs, as already mentioned.

The auxiliary IP tables contain VPN prefixes advertised by the backup egress PE. How is the backup egress PE determined? For example, for NLRIs with BGP protocol next hop 172.17.0.33 (the primary context-ID of PE3), the backup NLRIs have a different BGP protocol next hop. If you look carefully, you will realize that the auxiliary table __172.17.0.33-RT-VPN-B__.inet.0 contains prefixes with the BGP protocol next hop 172.17.0.44 (lines 51 and 57), whereas table __172.17.0.44-RT-VPN-

`B__.inet.0` is just the opposite: with the BGP protocol next hop 172.17.0.33 (lines 66 and 72). Of course, these auxiliary IP tables contain new label stacks, including the VPN label assigned by the backup egress PE, and the transport label to reach the backup egress PE. Additionally, in this particular network topology, the protector node connects to the network in a redundant way (two links); therefore, two direct next hops to reach the backup egress PE can be found in the auxiliary IP tables: the primary and the LFA backup.

Now, when PE3 fails, P1 redirects (using the preinstalled LFA backup next hop) traffic originally flowing via the PE2→P1→PE3 path to the PR. The PR performs label translation based on previously discussed RIB structures. Subsequently, the PR sends the traffic (with the VPN label assigned by PE4) via the PR→P2→PE4 path. PE4 has no clue that anything out of the ordinary has happened on the network. From the perspective of PE4, the received packet (redirected by P1 and translated by the PR) looks like a normal VPN packet with the VPN label assigned by PE4. This confirms that no special feature support is required on the PE nodes in centralized protector designs. All the required intelligence is limited to the protector node.

Context-ID Advertisement Methods

In all the discussions so far about egress protection (service mirroring), IS-IS was distributing context-IDs as some sort of *links*. To be more precise, both primary and protector context-IDs were distributed via TLV 135 (*Extended IP Reachability*), as already verified in lines 4 and 7 in Example 21-3. In addition, label bindings for these context-IDs were distributed via LDP (implicit null label for primary context-ID, and real label for protector context-ID). Therefore, this method of announcing context-IDs in IGP is called *stub-link*. In general, there are three methods of distributing context-ID information:

Stub-Link
> The primary context-ID is advertised as a stub-link in the IS-IS database: *Extended IP Reachability* (TLV type 135). Label binding for primary context-ID (implicit null) is advertised via LDP.
> The protector context-ID is advertised as a stub-link in the IS-IS database: *Extended IP Reachability* (TLV type 135). Label binding for protector context-ID (real label) is advertised via LDP.

Stub-alias
> The primary context-ID is advertised as a stub-link in the IS-IS database: *IP Interface Address* (TLV type 132) and *Extended IP Reachability* (TLV type 135). Label binding for primary context-ID (implicit null label) is advertised via LDP.
> The protector context-ID is advertised as an IPv4 FEC label binding element: *SID/Label Binding* (TLV type 149). Thus, label-binding for protector context-ID (real label) is advertised via IS-IS, not via LDP.

Stub-proxy

The primary context-ID is advertised as a virtual context-ID node in the IS-IS database: *Extended IS Reachability* (TLV type 22) from primary egress PE to virtual context-ID node + virtual context-ID node with a complete set of TLVs (TLV: 1, 14, 129, 132, 134, 135, 137 and two TLVs type 22). Label binding for primary context-ID (implicit null label) is advertised via LDP.

The protector context-ID is advertised as a link to the virtual context-ID node in IS-IS: *Extended IS Reachability* (TLV type 22) from protector to virtual context-ID node. Label binding for protector context-ID (real label) is advertised via LDP.

Note that the stub-link advertisement method has already been discussed in detail in previous sections; therefore, the following section will concentrate on the stub-alias and stub-proxy methods.

 As of this writing, all three methods for advertising context-IDs were supported by IS-IS in Junos. However, OSPF support was limited to the stub-link method only, where the context-ID is advertised as a stub network (Type 3).

Stub-Alias

The stub-link advertisement method has certain limitations, because it greatly depends on the network topology to provide backup coverage for the context-ID. For example, if in the topology outlined in Figure 21-1 the cross-links (PE1-P2 and PE2-P1) are temporarily disabled, P2 has no backup coverage for context-ID 172.17.0.22, as you can see here:

Example 21-16. LFA state for context-ID 172.17.0.22 with stub-link on P2 (Junos)

```
1    juniper@P2> show ldp database session 172.16.0.22 |
2               find Output | match 172.17.0.22
3      299824      172.17.0.22/32
4
5    juniper@P2> show route label 299824 table mpls.0 | find S=0
6    299824(S=0)        *[LDP/9] 00:20:10, metric 20
7                        > to 10.0.0.4 via ge-2/0/2.0, Pop
```

The obvious reason for this situation is the lack of a loop-free backup LFA path. You can, eventually, manipulate the metric of the context-ID advertised by the protector node (PE1), or implement some more advanced LFA extensions (R-LFA, TI-FRR) discussed earlier. Fortunately, there is another option: the protector node (PE1) can advertise the context-ID in stub-alias mode.

You can enable the stub-alias method by using the stub-alias keyword, as shown in Example 21-17. The stub-alias method uses the new IS-IS TLV type 149: *SID/Label*

Binding TLV, as defined in *draft-previdi-isis-segment-routing-extensions*, Section 2.4. This TLV includes the MPLS label that the PLR should use when redirecting the traffic to the protector. However, the transport label the PLR uses to reach the protector is still the traditional LDP label associated with the normal loopback of the protector node.

Example 21-17. Context-ID stub-alias configuration on PE1 (Junos)

```
protocols {
    mpls {
        egress-protection {
            context-identifier 172.17.0.22 {
                protector;
                advertise-mode stub-alias;
}}}}
```

So, let's verify now how it works on the network.

Example 21-18. LFA state for context-ID 172.17.0.22 with stub-alias on P2 (Junos)

```
1    juniper@P2> show isis database PE1 detail | match FEC
2      IP FEC: 172.17.0.22/32              Label:    331776 Mirror
3
4    juniper@P2> show route 172.17.0.22/32 table inet.5
5    (...)
6    172.17.0.22/32
7        *[IS-IS/18] 00:01:32, metric 11, metric2 20
8           to 10.0.0.6 via ge-2/0/4.0, Push 331776, Push 300064(top)
9         > to 10.0.0.24 via ge-2/0/5.0, Push 331776, Push 300064(top)
10
11   juniper@P2> show ldp database session 172.16.0.1 | match <pattern>
12   Input label database, 172.16.0.2:0--172.16.0.1:0
13    300064      172.16.0.11/32
14   Output label database, 172.16.0.2:0--172.16.0.1:0
15    299984      172.16.0.11/32
16
17   juniper@P2> show route 172.17.0.22/32 table inet.0
18   (...)
19   172.17.0.22/32     *[IS-IS/18] 02:51:07, metric 11
20                       > to 10.0.0.4 via ge-2/0/2.0
21
22   juniper@P2> show route 172.17.0.22/32 table inet.3
23   (...)
24   172.17.0.22/32     *[LDP/9] 02:49:45, metric 11
25                       > to 10.0.0.4 via ge-2/0/2.0
26
27   juniper@P2> show route label 299824 table mpls.0 | find S=0
28   299824(S=0) *[LDP/9] 02:34:13, metric 11, metric2 20
29     > to 10.0.0.4 via ge-2/0/2.0, Pop
```

```
30        to 10.0.0.6 via ge-2/0/4.0, Swap 331776, Push 300064(top)
31        to 10.0.0.24 via ge-2/0/5.0, Swap 331776, Push 300064(top)
```

As a result of enabling the stub-alias advertisement mode, PE1 stops advertising the protector context-ID via IS-IS TLV 135 and via LDP. Instead, only IS-IS TLV 149 is used (line 2), which includes both the IP prefix and corresponding label. Based on this information, all routers in the network create routing entries in the new RIB, called inet.5 (lines 4 through 9). The bottom label of this entry is the label advertised in TLV 149, whereas the top label is the transport (LDP) label associated with the originator of TLV 149: the PE1 loopback (line 13). The mirror label is quasi-tunneled inside the LDP tunnel toward PE1.

P2 can reach the PE1 loopback via PE2 or P1 with equal cost (remember, cross-links are temporarily disabled). However, PE2 is the primary node for 172.17.0.22; therefore, P2 installs the path avoiding PE2 to reach 172.17.0.22 in inet.5. Conversely, tables inet.0 and inet.3 have standard entries (lines 17 through 25) not affected by the new TLV 149.

inet.5 is, like inet.3, an auxiliary RIB; therefore, it has no corresponding FIB and its entries are not used (natively) for traffic forwarding.

The trick now is with the entry for the local label bound to the context-ID 172.17.0.22. If you compare lines 5 through 7 in Example 21-16 with lines 27 through 31 in Example 21-18, you can spot the differences. The primary next hop (line 29) is toward PE2, but there are also two backup next hops (parallel links) pointing to P1 (lines 30 and 31). P2 borrows the label stack for these backup next hops from the inet.5 RIB table.

Now when PE2 fails, labeled traffic is protected, whereas native IP traffic is not. P2 redirects the labeled traffic to P1 based on the preinstalled backup next hops found in the mpls.0 RIB (and corresponding FIB) table. P1 removes the top label, and finally, traffic arrives to PE1 with the mirror label (advertised via TLV 149) on the top.

The rest of the story is the same. The protector node uses RIB/FIB structures (similar to those outlined in Figure 21-2) to forward the traffic to the appropriate local CE, based on VPN labels allocated by the primary egress PE. Or, the standalone (centralized) protector node uses RIB/FIB structures similar to those outlined in Figure 21-4 to perform VPN label translation and send the packets to the backup egress PE.

Stub-Proxy

The stub-proxy advertisement method brings a completely new approach. Instead of adding some TLVs here or there, with the stub-proxy method, a completely new IS-IS node is injected into the IS-IS database (Figure 21-5). Of course, it is not a real node, just an emulated one. However, from the point of view of the other routers (e.g., PLR) it looks like a real node, with the IP address equal to the context-ID. This emulated context-ID node is dual-homed, with one emulated link connecting to the primary egress PE, and the second emulated link connecting to the protector node.

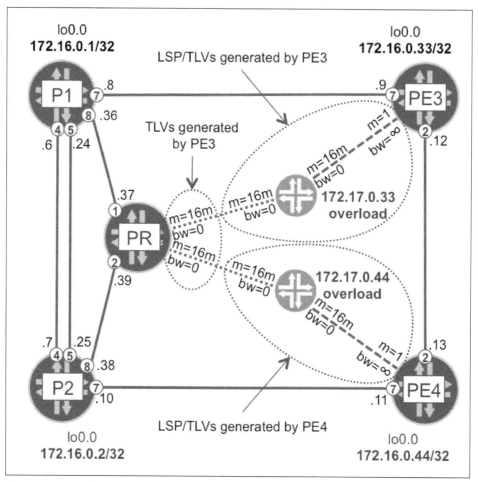

Figure 21-5. Stub-proxy context ID advertisement mode

Therefore, from the view of other nodes in the network topology, the context-ID IP address can either be reached via the primary egress PE or via the protector node. The emulated context-ID node announces the overload bit, thus it cannot be used for transit traffic. This is good, because in reality there is no connection between the primary egress PE and the protector node via context-ID node—it is all just virtual. Furthermore, the path to reach the emulated context-ID node via the primary egress PE is always preferred over the path via the protector node. For the emulated link connected to the emulated context-ID node, the primary egress PE announces *good* link characteristics (low metric, high bandwidth), whereas the protector node announces *bad* link characteristics (high metric, low bandwidth).

Similar to enabling stub-alias mode, you can enable stub-proxy mode on the primary egress PE and on the protector via a single knob, as shown in Example 21-19.

Example 21-19. Context-ID stub-proxy configuration on PE3 (Junos)

```
protocols {
    mpls {
        egress-protection {
            context-identifier 172.17.0.33 {
                primary;                      ##  'protector' on PR
                advertise-mode stub-proxy;
}}}}
```

So, let's check what can be observed in the network now.

Example 21-20. Emulated LSPs/TLVs with stub-proxy (Junos)

```
1    juniper@PE3> show isis database | match 172.17
2    PE3-172.17.0.33.00-00     0x38    0x1453     772 L1 L2 Overload
3    PE4-172.17.0.44.00-00     0x51    0x3b38    1142 L1 L2 Overload
4
5    juniper@PE3> show isis database PE3-172.17.0.33 extensive | find TLVs
6      TLVs:
7        Area address: 49.0000 (3)
8        LSP Buffer Size: 1492
9        Speaks: IP
10       Speaks: IPV6
11       IP router id: 172.17.0.33
12       IP address: 172.17.0.33
13       Hostname: PE3-172.17.0.33
14       IP address: 172.17.0.33
15       IP extended prefix: 172.17.0.33/32 metric 0 up
16       IS extended neighbor: PE3.00, Metric: default 16777214
17         IP address: 172.17.0.33
18         Neighbor's IP address: 172.16.0.33
19         Local interface index: 1, Remote interface index: 2147618817
20         Traffic engineering metric: 16777214
21         Maximum reservable bandwidth: 0bps
22         Maximum bandwidth: 0bps
23       IS extended neighbor: PR.00, Metric: default 16777214
24         IP address: 172.17.0.33
```

```
25        Neighbor's IP address: 172.16.0.10
26        Local interface index: 2, Remote interface index: 2147618818
27        Traffic engineering metric: 16777214
28        Maximum reservable bandwidth: 0bps
29        Maximum bandwidth: 0bps
30
31   juniper@PE3> show isis database PE3 extensive | find TLVs
32   (...)
33      IS extended neighbor: PE3-172.17.0.33.00, Metric: default 1
34        IP address: 172.16.0.33
35        Neighbor's IP address: 172.17.0.33
36        Local interface index: 2147618817, Remote interface index: 1
37        Traffic engineering metric: 1
38        Maximum reservable bandwidth: Infbps
39        Maximum bandwidth: Infbps
40
41   juniper@PR> show isis database PR extensive | find TLVs
42   (...)
43      IS extended neighbor: PE3-172.17.0.33.00, Metric: default 16777214
44        IP address: 172.16.0.10
45        Neighbor's IP address: 172.17.0.33
46        Local interface index: 2147618818, Remote interface index: 2
47        Traffic engineering metric: 16777214
48        Maximum reservable bandwidth: 0bps
49        Maximum bandwidth: 0bps
50   (...)
51      IS extended neighbor: PE4-172.17.0.44.00, Metric: default 16777214
52        IP address: 172.16.0.10
53        Neighbor's IP address: 172.17.0.44
54        Local interface index: 2147618818, Remote interface index: 2
55        Traffic engineering metric: 16777214
56        Maximum reservable bandwidth: 0bps
57        Maximum bandwidth: 0bps
```

After enabling stub-proxy on the primary egress PEs, you will realize that the additional IS-IS nodes appear in the IS-IS database (lines 2 and 3). The names of these nodes are derived from the real node (PE3 or PE4) and corresponding context-ID associated for each real node (172.17.0.33 and 172.17.0.44). In reality, of course, there are no new nodes! PE3 and PE4 are cheating, injecting not only their normal LSP, but also the LSP for the emulated context-ID node, as well. As discussed, the overload bit is set, so the emulated context-ID nodes cannot be used for transit.

Now, if you check the content for one of the emulated context-ID nodes, you'll see plenty of TLVs announced (lines 7 through 16, and 23)—just like in a normal IS-IS node. There are two emulated links (neighbors): the primary egress PE (line 16), and the protector (line 23). In addition to the overload bit, other characteristics (metric and bandwidth) of these emulated links are bad (lines 20 through 22, and 27 through 29): metric high, bandwidth zero. This is just to ensure that no one tries to use this emulated node for transit.

Additionally, the primary egress PEs generate extra *Extended IS Reachability* (TLV type 22) for the emulated link toward the emulated context-ID node. This time the link from the primary egress PE to the emulated context-ID node has good characteristics (lines 37 through 39): low metric and high (infinite) bandwidth.

After enabling stub-proxy mode on the protector, the protector also generates additional *Extended IS Reachability* (TLV type 22) for each emulated link toward each emulated context-ID node. As you can see, the metrics (both default and TE metric) for these links are set to a large value, whereas bandwidth is set to 0 (lines 47 through 49 and 55 through 57). So, basically, these links will be treated as a last resort, when other routers in the network perform CSPF calculations to reach the emulated context-ID node.

> As of this writing, Junos only supported stub-proxy mode with RSVP-TE.

Because stub-proxy mode is not supported with LDP, let's configure the RSVP tunnels from the Junos ingress PE: PE1, as provided in Example 21-21.

> By default, IOS XR does not allow RSVP-TE tunnels destined to an IS-IS node in overload state. Configuring `path-selection ignore overload` under `mpls traffic-eng` stanza disables that check.

Example 21-21. RSVP tunnel configuration on ingress PE (Junos)

```
protocols {
    mpls {
        label-switched-path PE1--->PE3-CTX {
            to 172.17.0.33;
            node-link-protection;
            adaptive;
}}}
```

The RSVP-TE tunnel configuration on ingress PE is pretty standard. The important feature that must be enabled is facility backup (`node-link-protection`), because this feature accommodates local repair–style redirection of traffic at the PLR in case of primary egress PE failure. The destination address this time is actually context-ID, not the loopback of egress PE. Similarly, the tunnel, destined also to the context-ID, must be created on the protector node, too, in order to resolve BGP protocol next-hop addresses.

Let's verify RIB/FIB states on the path from the ingress PE (PE1) to the protector (PR), as illustrated in Example 21-22.

Example 21-22. RIB/FIB states between ingress PE and protector with stub-proxy

```
1    juniper#PE1> show mpls lsp name PE1--->PE3-CTX detail | find RRO
2       Received RRO (ProtectionFlag 1=Available 2=InUse 4=B/W 8=Node
3                      10=SoftPreempt 20=Node-ID):
4           172.16.0.1(flag=0x29) 10.0.0.3(flag=9 Label=300752)
5           172.16.0.33(flag=0x20) 10.0.0.9(Label=3)
6           172.17.0.33(flag=0x20) 172.17.0.33(Label=3)
7
8    juniper#P1> show route label 300752 | find S=0
9    300752(S=0) *[RSVP/7/1] 00:09:05, metric 1
10               > to 10.0.0.9 via ge-2/0/7.0,
11                   label-switched-path PE1--->PE3-CTX
12               to 10.0.0.37 via ge-2/0/8.0,
13                   label-switched-path Bypass->10.0.0.9->172.17.0.33
14
15   juniper#P1> show route forwarding-table label 300752 | find S=0
16   Destination Type  Next hop    Type       Index    Netif
17   300752(S=0) user              ulst       1048578
18                     10.0.0.9    Pop        1644      ge-2/0/7.0
19                     10.0.0.37   Swap 300432 1700     ge-2/0/8.0
20
21   juniper#PR> show route label 300432 | find S=0
22   300432(S=0)        *[MPLS/0] 00:26:35
23                         to table __172.17.0.33__.mpls.0
```

As you can see, verification shows that the RSVP-TE tunnel destined to the context-ID of PE3 is established via the PE1→P1→PE3 path (lines 4 through 6). The label used at the second hop (P1) is 300752. Now, by looking at the forwarding entry on P1, packets arriving with this label use the primary next hop PE3 (line 10) with label action pop (line 18). In case of PE3 failure, packets are forwarded via the node protection bypass (line 13) toward the PR with label action swap (line 19). So far, everything is normal and matches the behavior described in Chapter 19, in which the RSVP-TE facility backup was described in detail.

Now, packets with label 300432 (forwarded via the node protection bypass terminated on context-ID 172.17.0.33) arrive at the PR. And what happens? The PR intercepts these packets using egress protection (service mirroring) RIB/FIB structures (lines 21 through 23)! Why? When the node protection bypass destined to the emulated context-ID node is established via the PR node the PR node actually cheats! As discussed, the emulated context-ID node is not a real node. Therefore, forwarding traffic to that node doesn't make sense. The label from the node protection bypass is actually the context label causing the arriving traffic to perform a lookup on the context label table, as discussed in all the previous cases.

Let's check the details of Explicit Route Object (ERO) and the Record Route object (RRO), as shown in the Example 21-23.

Example 21-23. Node protection bypass ERO and RRO on PLR (Junos)

```
1    juniper#P1> show rsvp session name Bypass->10.0.0.9->172.17.0.33
2             detail | match " route:"
3    Explct route: 10.0.0.37 172.17.0.33 (link-id=2)
4    Record route: <self> 10.0.0.37
```

When you carefully examine the ERO and the RRO information of the node protection bypass, you can actually spot that there is something unusual with this bypass. Namely, whereas the ERO (line 3) contains two links (P1 believes 172.17.0.33 is two links away, based on IS-IS database content), RRO (line 4) lists only a single link, which is, in fact, the only link present.

Junos supports egress protection (service mirroring) with LDP using the stub-link or stub-alias mode, and with RSVP-TE, using all three modes: stub-link, stub-alias, and stub-proxy.

L3VPN PE→CE Egress Link Protection

All discussions so far in this chapter concentrate on fast traffic restoration during failure of the egress PE node. The last failure type is, however, failure of the egress PE→CE link. Link failure is a more likely event than node failure, especially when the AC is connected to a long-distance link. Let's investigate what you can do to optimize failover times during such failures.

Junos calls this type of protection *Link Protection with Host Fast ReRoute* (HFRR) for protecting directly connected prefixes on broadcast interfaces, like Ethernet. Or simply *Provider Edge Link Protection* for other types of PE-CE prefixes (e.g., eBGP). IOS XR calls it *BGP PIC Edge PE-CE Link Protection*. Regardless of the terminology, the goal is the same: to preinstall in the FIB the backup next hop that can be used during failure of a primary PE→CE link.

Looking back at Figure 21-1 you can see dual-homed CEs connected to the PE1/PE2 pair as well as to the PE3/PE4 pair. If traffic destined to the CE5 arrives from the MPLS core at PE2, it is forwarded over the direct PE2→CE5 link. Now, when this link fails, ingress PE (PE3 or PE4) must wait for the BGP update from PE2, which withdraws the CE5 prefix. Only after that can the ingress PE switch to another egress PE (PE1). This process is relatively long (it can take seconds in a scaled environment) because it involves BGP convergence.

You can optimize this behavior if per-VRF aggregated label assignment is enabled on PE2. In that case, PE2 performs IP lookup inside VRF for packets arrived over an MPLS cloud. Therefore, as soon as PE2 updates its RIB (and subsequently FIB) to use the route from PE1 to reach CE5, traffic can be redirected by PE2 to PE1. However, this is still not sub-100 millisecond failover, because a new next hop must be determined and installed in HW FIB after PE→CE link failure.

Previously discussed techniques do not help now, because they rely on egress PE node failure. Here, it is not the egress PE node that fails, but the egress PE→CE link. So, let's enable protection for this type of failure. In IOS XR, you don't need to do anything, if the BGP PIC Edge is already enabled. The configuration shown in Example 20-11 in the previoius chapter actually enables protection against both egress PE node and egress PE→CE link failure. In Junos, however, you need to enable this feature explicitly on a per PE-CE protocol basis. Following shows how you can do it for directly connected hosts and for eBGP routes:

Example 21-24. Link protection with HFRR for direct routes on PE1 (Junos)

```
1    routing-instances {
2        VRF-B {
3            routing-options {
4                interface ge-2/0/5.2 link-protection;
5    }}}
```

Example 21-25. Provider edge link protection for BGP routes on PE3 (Junos)

```
1    routing-instances {
2        VRF-B {
3            protocols {
4                bgp {
5                    group EBGP {
6                        family inet unicast protection;
7    }}}}}
```

In the test topology, PE-CE link protection for only VRF-B has been enabled. Therefore, you will be able to see the differences in the FIB structures for VRF-B (PE-CE link protection enabled) and VRF-C (PE-CE link protection not enabled).

Let's begin verification with PE1.

Example 21-26. HFRR states on PE1 (Junos)

```
1    juniper@PE1> show route table VRF-C 10.3.5.5/32
2
3    juniper@PE1> show route table VRF-B 10.2.5.5/32
4    @ = Routing Use Only, # = Forwarding Use Only
5    10.2.5.5/32 @[ARP/4294967293] 11:12:09, from 10.2.5.0
```

```
6                    Unusable
7            #[FRR/200] 11:12:09, from 10.2.5.0
8            > to 10.2.5.5 via ge-2/0/5.2
9              to 10.0.0.1 via ge-2/0/4.0, Push 16390
10             to 10.0.0.3 via ge-2/0/2.0, Push 16390, Push 299824(top)
11
12   juniper@PE1> show route forwarding-table destination 10.2.5.5/32
13               extensive | match <pattern>
14   Destination:  10.2.5.5/32
15     Next-hop type: unilist          Index: 1048616  Reference: 2
16     Nexthop: 80:71:1f:c0:e9:f0
17     Next-hop type: unicast          Index: 1611     Reference: 5
18     Next-hop interface: ge-2/0/5.2  Weight: 0x1
19     Nexthop:
20     Next-hop type: composite        Index: 1797     Reference: 3
21     Next-hop type: indirect         Index: 1048611  Reference: 2
22                                     Weight: 0x4000
23     Next-hop type: unilist          Index: 1048607  Reference: 2
24     Nexthop: 10.0.0.1
25     Next-hop type: unicast          Index: 1790     Reference: 1
26     Next-hop interface: ge-2/0/4.0  Weight: 0x1
27     Nexthop: 10.0.0.3
28     Next-hop type: Push 299824      Index: 1792     Reference: 1
29     Next-hop interface: ge-2/0/2.0  Weight: 0xf000
30
31   juniper@PE1> request pfe execute target fpc2 command
32               "show nhdb id 1048616 recursive"
33   (...)
34   GOT: 1048616(Unilist, IPv4, ifl:0:-, pfe-id:0)
35   GOT:  1611(Unicast, IPv4, ifl:473:ge-2/0/5.2, pfe-id:0)
36   GOT:  1797(Compst, IPv4->MPLS, ifl:0:-, pfe-id:0, comp-fn:Chain)
37   GOT:   1048611(Indirect, IPv4, ifl:432:ge-2/0/4.0, pfe-id:0, i-ifl:0)
38   GOT:    1048607(Unilist, IPv4, ifl:0:-, pfe-id:0)
39   GOT:     1790(Unicast, IPv4, ifl:432:ge-2/0/4.0, pfe-id:0)
40   GOT:     1792(Unicast, IPv4->MPLS, ifl:433:ge-2/0/2.0, pfe-id:0)
```

Nothing specific happened in the VRF-C (lines 1 and 2). Host route (/32) toward CE5-C is not present in the VRF-C table. The CE5-C host can still be resolved (not shown for brevity) via LAN prefix (10.3.5.0/24), as usual.

Conversely, in the VRF-B, we can observe some interesting things. The CE5-B host is now reachable via two new protocols: Address Resolution Protocol (ARP) (line 5) and Fast ReRoute (FRR) (line 7). The feature name, *Host Fast ReRoute*, is derived from the fact that now the host routes—with corresponding fast reroute backup next-hops—are created in the RIB/FIB structures. The ARP entry is a result of the ARP machinery that discovers MAC addresses for each host (line 16). The router only uses this entry on the control plane, however not for forwarding (observe mark @ and Unusable). Instead, the FRR entry is used for traffic forwarding (observe mark #) and is the basis for next-hop structures created in the FIB.

In the RIB/FIB, you can see that the hierarchical next-hop structure contains primary (weight=0x1, lines 8, 16 through 18, and 35) direct unicast next hop pointing to CE5-B. The unilist backup next hop (weight 0x4000, lines 22, 23, and 38) contains two direct unicast next hops: the direct MPLS link from PE1 to PE2 (lines 9, 24 through 26, and 39) and the link via the MPLS cloud as backup (lines 10, 27 through 29, and 40). Therefore, when the PE1→CE5 link fails, the direct unicast next hop (line 35) is removed, and traffic can be immediately forwarded via the preinstalled backup next hops pointing to the MPLS network.

As of this writing, Junos doesn't support PE-CE link protection for static routes. Hence, CE5-B's loopback address (192.168.2.5) is not protected by the PE-CE link-protection feature on PE1.

After checking PE1 (Junos), let's now verify PE2 (IOS XR).

Example 21-27. BGP PIC Edge PE-CE link protection on PE2 (IOS XR)

```
1    RP/0/RSP0/CPU0:PE2#show cef vrf VRF-C 192.168.3.5/32 |
2                      include "  via|labels"
3       via 10.3.5.5, 3 dependencies, recursive [flags 0x0]
4         next hop 10.3.5.5/32 Gi0/0/0/5.3 labels imposed {None}
5
6    RP/0/RSP0/CPU0:PE2#show cef vrf VRF-B 192.168.2.5/32 |
7                      include "  via|labels"
8       via 10.2.5.5, 3 dependencies, recursive [flags 0x0]
9         next hop 10.2.5.5/32 Gi0/0/0/5.2 labels imposed {None}
10      via 172.16.0.11, 7 dependencies, recursive, backup [flags 0x6100]
11        next hop 10.0.0.0/32 Gi0/0/0/0 labels imposed {ImplNull 17}
```

Similar to the Junos case, VRF-C contains only a single next hop. However, in VRF-B, IOS XR installs the primary next hop pointing to the direct PE2→CE5 link and it also installs the backup next hop pointing to the MPLS cloud. As discussed earlier, PE1 can be reached from PE2 via two next hops: the primary and the LFA backup. However, only the primary is shown in CEF VRF entries. You would need to use the `internal` keyword to display full CEF structure (omitted here for brevity).

As of this writing, IOS XR doesn't support PE-CE link protection for directly connected host routes. Hence, the CE5-B interface address (10.2.5.5) is not protected by PE-CE link-protection feature on PE2.

Verifying PE-CE link protection for the BGP routes on PE3 (see Example 21-28) confirms that hierarchical next-hop structures, similar to structures observed in Example 21-26, are used to provide local repair during PE3→CE6 link failure.

Example 21-28. BGP PE-CE link protection states on PE3 (Junos)

```
1    juniper@PE3> show route table VRF-B 192.168.2.6/32
2    @ = Routing Use Only, # = Forwarding Use Only
3    192.168.2.6/32
4            @[BGP/170] 19:53:29, MED 0, localpref 100
5              AS path: 65506 ?, validation-state: unverified
6            > to 10.2.6.6 via ge-2/0/5.2
7            [BGP/170] 19:53:02, MED 0, localpref 100, from 172.16.0.201
8              AS path: 65506 ?, validation-state: unverified
9            > to 10.0.0.13 via ge-2/0/2.0, Push 17
10           [BGP/170] 19:52:58, MED 0, localpref 100, from 172.16.0.202
11             AS path: 65506 ?, validation-state: unverified
12           > to 10.0.0.13 via ge-2/0/2.0, Push 17
13         #[Multipath/255] 13:42:11, metric 0
14           > to 10.2.6.6 via ge-2/0/5.2
15             to 10.0.0.13 via ge-2/0/2.0, Push 17
16
17   juniper@PE3> show route forwarding-table destination 192.168.2.6/32
18               extensive | match <pattern>
19
20   Destination:  192.168.2.6/32
21     Next-hop type: unilist          Index: 1048743  Reference: 2
22     Nexthop: 10.2.6.6
23     Next-hop type: unicast          Index: 1613     Reference: 5
24     Next-hop interface: ge-2/0/5.2  Weight: 0x1     Uflags: 0x2
25     Nexthop:
26     Next-hop type: composite        Index: 1894     Reference: 2
27     Next-hop type: indirect         Index: 1048742  Reference: 2
28                                     Weight: 0x4000
29     Nexthop: 10.0.0.13
30     Next-hop type: unicast          Index: 1811     Reference: 3
31     Next-hop interface: ge-2/0/2.0  Weight: 0x4000
32
33   juniper@PE3> request pfe execute target fpc2 command
34               "show nhdb id 1048743 recursive"
35   (...)
36   GOT: 1048743(Unilist, IPv4, ifl:0:-, pfe-id:0)
37   GOT:  1613(Unicast, IPv4, ifl:419:ge-2/0/5.2, pfe-id:0)
38   GOT:  1894(Compst, IPv4->MPLS, ifl:0:-, pfe-id:0, comp-fn:Chain)
39   GOT:     1048742(Indirect, IPv4, ifl:413:ge-2/0/2.0, pfe-id:0,i-ifl:0)
40   GOT:        1811(Unicast, IPv4, ifl:413:ge-2/0/2.0, pfe-id:0)
```

OK, it looks like RIB/FIB states are now prepared to handle a PE→CE link failure with local repair–style protection: the backup next hops are preinstalled in the HW FIB. Some attention, however, is required on a loop issue.

With PE-CE link protection deployed on the pair of PEs, a loop can occur during failure of the multihomed CE or during the simultaneous failure of PE-CE links (on both PEs) toward the multihomed CE. This loop is unavoidable. When one PE detects failure of the connected PE→CE link, it removes the corresponding primary next hop and redirects the traffic destined for the multihomed CE toward the second PE. When the traffic arrives at the second PE, the primary next hop is missing, too. Consequently, a second PE redirects the traffic back to the first PE based on a still valid backup next hop. This loop can continue until BGP from both PEs learns that the CE is down and they withdraw their BGP routes.

Layer 2 VPN Service Mirroring

You should have learned by now the general concept of egress protection (service mirroring) with L3VPN services. Similar to L3VPN services, these concepts can be deployed for BGP and LDP-based Layer 2 VPN (L2VPN) services. There are, however, some specific aspects that relate to L2VPN services.

BGP-Based L2VPN Service Mirroring

Let's begin with the BGP-based L2VPN, where BGP is used for autodiscovery and signaling. You should be familiar with basic multihomed BGP L2VPN operations from Chapter 6. Now, you will enhance multihomed BGP L2VPN architecture to ensure fast traffic restoration based on egress-protection (service mirroring) concepts.

Following the topology outlined in Figure 20-1 at the beginning of the Chapter 20, let's create two multihomed point-to-point BGP L2VPNs, using standard configurations discussed in Chapter 6:

L2VPN-F
> This includes CE1-F (connected to PE1) and CE6-F (connected to PE3/PE4 pair, where PE3 is the primary PE, and PE4 is the protector/backup PE)

L2VPN-G
> This includes CE2-G (connected to PE2) and CE6-G (connected to PE3/P4 pair, where PE3 is the protector/backup PE, and PE4 is the primary PE)

 As of this writing, Junos supports BGP L2VPN egress-protection (service mirroring) using only combined protector/backup PE architecture.

So for example, let's extend L2VPN-G for egress-protection to provide fast traffic restoration in the case of primary PE (PE4) failure. On the ingress PE (PE2, IOS XR) no configuration changes are required. Example 21-29 and Example 21-30 present the full configurations with egress-protection extensions for PE4 and PE3, respectively.

Example 21-29. Egress-protected multihomed BGP L2VPN, primary PE4 (Junos)

```
1    protocols {
2        mpls {
3            egress-protection {
4                context-identifier 172.18.0.44 primary;
5            }
6        }
7        bgp {
8            group IBGP-RR {
9                family l2vpn signaling egress-protection;
10           }
11       }
12   }
13   routing-instances {
14       L2VPN-G {
15           instance-type l2vpn;
16           egress-protection context-identifier 172.18.0.44;
17           interface ge-2/0/5.8;
18           route-distinguisher 172.16.0.44:107;
19           vrf-target target:65000:1007;
20           protocols {
21               l2vpn {
22                   encapsulation-type ethernet-vlan;
23                   site CE6-G {
24                       site-identifier 6;
25                       site-preference primary;
26                       mtu 1500;
27                       interface ge-2/0/5.8 remote-site-id 2;
28                   }
29                   pseudowire-status-tlv;
30   }}}}
```

Example 21-30. Egress-protected multihomed BGP L2VPN, protector/backup, PE3 (Junos)

```
1    protocols {
2        mpls {
3            egress-protection {
4                context-identifier 172.18.0.44 protector;
5            }
6        }
7        bgp {
8            group IBGP-RR {
9                family l2vpn signaling egress-protection;
10           }
11       }
12   }
```

```
13    routing-instances {
14        L2VPN-G {
15            instance-type l2vpn;
16            interface ge-2/0/5.8;
17            route-distinguisher 172.16.0.33:107;
18            vrf-target target:65000:1007;
19            protocols {
20                l2vpn {
21                    encapsulation-type ethernet-vlan;
22                    site CE6-G {
23                        site-identifier 6;
24                        site-preference backup;
25                        hot-standby;
26                        mtu 1500;
27                        interface ge-2/0/5.8 remote-site-id 2;
28                    }
29                    pseudowire-status-tlv;
30    }}}}
```

Context-ID must be configured on the primary PE as primary (Example 21-29, lines 2 through 6) and on the protector/backup PE as protector (Example 21-30, lines 2 through 6). Because the previously deployed egress protection for L3VPN used separate (centralized) mode (protector function was not deployed on either PE3 or PE4), you now use a different context-ID. The primary PE uses this context-ID to set the BGP protocol next hop during routing-instance export (Example 21-29, line 16), whereas the protector/backup PE uses this context-ID for egress-protection functions activated by the hot-standby keyword (Example 21-30, line 25).

Note that you can set the BGP protocol next hop to context-ID by using different options:

- Via BGP export policy applied to multiprotocol BGP neighbor or group
- Via routing-instance (L3VPN or L2VPN) egress-protection context-ID configuration
- Via routing-instance (L3VPN or L2VPN) export policy
- Via egress-protection context-ID configuration in BGP address family (inet-vpn unicast or l2vpn signaling)

All options are applicable to both L3VPN and L2VPN deployments. The first option (BGP neighbor export policy) was used in the L3VPN examples in the previous section. It provides more granularity because you can set the BGP protocol next hop only to specific prefixes. In L2VPN deployments, you typically don't need such granularity, so the second option is used in this section's examples. Other options could be used, as well. However, because of limited space in this book, we will leave those to you to explore.

What's next? Similar to the L3VPN case, you need to enable egress-protection functionality in the appropriate address family (lines 7 through 11 in Examples Example 21-29 and Example 21-30). And that's it—you are done! The rest is standard multihomed L2VPN configuration (discussed in Chapter 6), and is repeated here just so you can see the egress-protection configuration from a full multihomed L2VPN perspective (Example 21-31).

Example 21-31. BGP L2VPN verification on ingress PE (IOS XR)

```
1    RP/0/RSP0/CPU0:PE2#show l2vpn xconnect group PE3-PE4
2                       xc-name CE6-G.2:6 detail | include <pattern>
3    PW: neighbor 172.18.0.44, PW ID 131078, state is up ( established )
4        MPLS        Local                        Remote
5        Label       36810                        800003
6        CE-ID       2                            6
7
8    RP/0/RSP0/CPU0:PE2#show cef 172.18.0.44 | include "via|label"
9     via 10.0.0.27, Gi0/0/0/3, 3 dependencies, weight 0,class 0, backup
10       local label 16000      labels imposed {317040}
11    via 10.0.0.5, Gi0/0/0/5, 8 dependencies, weight 0,class 0, protected
12       local label 16000      labels imposed {304384}
```

Verification on the ingress PE shows the expected results. As anticipated, the ingress PE sees the context-ID as next hop (line 3) and therefore uses the LDP transport label associated with that context-ID address to forward frames over this L2VPN. Again, due to the LFA backup, you can see the two direct next hops in the FIB (lines 8 through 12).

The story is the same now with LFA protection for the context-ID as in the case of L3VPN egress protection. In fact, the PLR (P2 router in the topology outlined in Figure 21-3) is not even aware of the type of traffic forwarded using the transport label associated with context-ID 172.18.0.44. The PLR (P2) simply does LFA-style redirection to PE3 during failure of PE4. So, following PE4 failure, traffic arrives at PE3, with some label assigned by PE3 to the protector context-ID 172.18.0.44. Let's check what happens now.

Example 21-32. BGP L2VPN verification on protector/backup egress PE (Junos)

```
1    juniper@PE3> show ldp database session 172.16.0.2 | find .. | match ..
2     300688      172.18.0.44/32
3
4    juniper@PE3> show route label 300688 table mpls.0
5    (...)
6    300688(S=0)        *[MPLS/0] 01:46:47
7                         to table __172.18.0.44__.mpls.0
8
9    juniper@PE3> show route label 800003 table __172.18.0.44__.mpls.0
10   (...)
```

```
11    800003                 *[Egress-Protection/170] 01:48:04
12                            > via ge-2/0/5.8, Pop       Offset: 4
13
14    juniper@PE3> show route receive-protocol bgp 172.16.0.201
15             table L2VPN-G.l2vpn.0 match-prefix 172.16.0.44:107:*
16             detail | match "entries|base|hop|target"
17    *  172.16.0.44:107:6:1/96 (2 entries, 1 announced)
18       Label-base: 800002, range: 2, status-vector: 0x0, offset: 1
19       Nexthop: 172.18.0.44
20       Communities: target:65000:1007 Layer2-info: encaps: VLAN,
21         control flags:[0x2] Control-Word, mtu: 1500,
22         site preference: 65535
```

Unless specified otherwise, line numbers in the following three paragraphs refer to Example 21-32. As you can see, the situation is very similar to the L3VPN case. The protector maintains the label table associated with the protector context-ID (line 7). Within that table, it collects labels from other PEs, just like in the L3VPN case. In this particular example, PE4 (the primary egress PE) announces the NLRI (line 17) with RT 65000:1007 (line 20). The RR reflects this NLRI to PE3 (the protector). PE3 verifies that it is for the protector for this egress PE, because the configured protector context-ID matches the next hop in received NLRI (line 19); therefore, it installs the corresponding label in its context-ID label table.

Just to refresh how the actual label is calculated, the PE3 configuration refers to the remote site with ID = 2 (line 27 in Example 21-30). PE4 announces a label block starting with 800002 and for site IDs starting with 1 (offset=1, line 18). Therefore, for (nonexisting) site 1, the label is 800002, whereas the label for site 2 is 800003. You can see this label being installed in the PE3 context-ID label table (lines 11 and 12). This is also the label used by the ingress PE when sending traffic to PE4 (line 5 in Example 21-31).

RT=65000:1007 (line 20) and site-ID=6 (line 17) advertised by PE4, match the local configuration for L2VPN-G on PE3 (lines 18 and 23 in Example 21-30), and therefore PE3 uses the corresponding PE-CE interface (line 12 in Example 21-32 as well as line 27 in Example 21-30) to send redirected traffic to the locally attached multi-homed device. Thus, confirming that the states required for egress-protection to work are correct.

Now, similar to the L3VPN case, let's extend the protection to cover failure of the PE-CE link, as well. Normally, the PE-CE link is not protected. There is only a single next hop (pointing directly to the connected multihomed CE) installed in the FIB. To have PE-CE link protection you need to have a backup next hop, as well, pointing to the backup PE. What do you need to do? You need to create a special RSVP-TE LSP (called *Edge Protection LSP*) that the primary PE (PE4 in the topology) can use to forward traffic to the backup PE (PE3 in the topology) in case of PE-CE link failure.

Example 21-33. RSVP-TE Edge Protection LSP for PE-CE egress-protection (Junos)

```
1    protocols {
2        mpls {
3            label-switched-path PE4--->PE3-PROTECT {
4                to 172.18.0.44;
5                egress-protection;
6    }}}
```

Configuration of such an LSP on the primary PE is pretty simple: you use context-ID (line 4) as the destination and you use the additional knob `egress-protection` (line 5) to designate this tunnel for egress-protection purposes. That's it! Let's see the outcome using verification from Example 21-34.

Example 21-34. Edge Protection LSP states on backup and primary PE (Junos)

```
1    juniper@PE4> show route label 800003 table mpls.0 detail | match ...
2                    Next hop: via ge-2/0/5.8 weight 0x1, selected
3                    Label operation: Pop        Offset: 4
4                    Next hop: 10.0.0.12 ge-2/0/2.0 weight 0x2
5                    Label-switched-path PE4--->PE3-PROTECT
6                    Label operation: Swap 800003, Push 301136(top)
7
8    juniper@PE3> show route label 301136 | find S=0
9    301136(S=0)         *[MPLS/0] 00:19:30
10                           to table __172.18.0.44__.mpls.0
```

As a result, the tunnel from the primary PE to the backup PE is established. This tunnel is, in turn, used as the backup next hop (lines 4 through 6) on the primary PE for PE-CE link protection. What is special about this tunnel? It's missing the implicit null label. The backup PE (PE3) actually assigns the real label (line 6), which then points to the context-ID label table (lines 8 through 10), and the rest of the story is already familiar.

 As of this writing, Junos supports PE-CE link protection for L2VPNs using RSVP-TE-based edge protection LSPs. LDP-based and SPRING-based edge protection LSPs are not supported.

LDP-Based L2VPN Service Mirroring

In LDP-based L2VPN deployments, there are no BGP protocol next hops. As you might remember, all egress-protection schemes discussed so far are based on manipulating the BGP protocol next hop, and advertising IP addresses corresponding to manipulated BGP protocol next hops into IGP and MPLS transport (LDP or RSVP-TE). Therefore, fast redirection can be done via LFA or RSVP-TE Facility Protection backup next hops. However, another draft (*draft-ietf-pals-endpoint-fast-protection: PW Endpoint Fast Failure Protection*) describes egress-protection (service mirroring) architecture adjusted to LDP-based pseudowire (PW) protection requirements.

The context-ID, and LFA or RSVP-TE Facility Protection–style failover during primary egress PE failure remains the same. However, instead of the BGP protocol next-hop manipulation, the ingress PE must now associate the transport tunnel used for transporting frames of a given PW with the context-ID advertised by the primary and protector/backup egress PE pair. As in previous cases, the transport tunnel itself can be signaled via LDP or RSVP-TE.

 As of this writing, IOS XR supports LDP-signaled PW association only with arbitrary chosen RSVP-TE signaled transport tunnels, but not with arbitrary chosen LDP-signaled transport tunnels. Conversely, in Junos, association with a mix of arbitrary chosen LDP and RSVP-TE–signaled tunnels is supported.

Another difference, when compared to BGP-signaled L2VPN protection, is the fact that LDP-signaled multihomed L2VPNs can be deployed in *revertive* or *nonrevertive* mode. In BGP-based L2VPNs, failover is always revertive: when the primary egress PE restores from failure, traffic always switches back to the primary egress PE. In LDP-based L2VPN, the default behavior is nonrevertive (you can change this default behavior via configuration, if needed). That is, when the primary egress PE restores from failure, the ingress PE still uses the backup egress PE for traffic forwarding until this active PE (the PE that was originally the backup PE) fails.

Why is this difference important? Egress protection is important to protect the active egress PE by redirecting traffic to the available standby egress PE.

- In BGP L2VPNs, if both primary and backup egress PEs are available, the primary is always used as the active egress PE, whereas the backup is used as the standby egress PE. Therefore, there is no need to deploy the egress-protection scheme to protect the backup egress PE.

- In LDP-based L2VPNs, as already mentioned, you might need to protect both the primary and the backup egress PE, because in nonrevertive mode, your active egress PE can be actually the PE originally designated as the backup PE.

Apart from these two differences (no BGP protocol next hop and egress protection for primary and backup egress PE), the overall concepts remain the same.

As of this writing, Junos supports LDP L2VPN egress protection (service mirroring) using combined protector/backup PE architecture only.

So, let's configure egress protection for our LDP-based PW that provides connectivity between the single-homed site CE2-I and the multihomed CE6-I site. As the transport, let's use RSVP-TE tunnels, as IOS XR cannot set arbitrary transport LDP tunnel and this capability is required by the egress protection for LDP signaled PWs. Let's begin with the configuration of PE2 (IOS XR), where the single-homed CE is connected (Example 21-35).

Example 21-35. LDP PW ingress PE configuration on PE2 (IOS XR)

```
1    explicit-path name PE3-LOOSE
2     index 10 next-address loose ipv4 unicast 172.16.0.33
3    !
4    interface tunnel-te1833       !! similar tunnel to PE4 context-ID
5     ipv4 unnumbered Loopback0
6     signalled-name PE2--->PE3-CTX2
7     autoroute announce
8    !
9     destination 172.18.0.33
10    fast-reroute protect node
11    record-route
12    path-option 1 explicit name PE3-LOOSE
13   !
14   l2vpn
15    pw-class PW-L2CKT-ETH-CTX-PE3 !! similar pw-class for PE4 context-ID
16     encapsulation mpls
17      protocol ldp
18      transport-mode ethernet
19      preferred-path interface tunnel-te 1833
20     !
21     backup disable delay 10
22    !
23    xconnect group PE3-PE4
24      p2p CE6-I
25      interface Gi0/0/0/1.9
26      neighbor ipv4 172.16.0.33 pw-id 926
27       pw-class PW-L2CKT-ETH-CTX-PE3
28       backup neighbor 172.16.0.44 pw-id 926
29        pw-class PW-L2CKT-ETH-CTX-PE4
```

On the PE attached to the single-homed CE, you deploy *almost* the same configuration as that used in Chapter 6. However, the difference is that you need to use RSVP-TE tunnels (lines 4 through 12) destined to the context-IDs (line 9) configured on the

PEs connected to the multihomed CE. Because there are two egress PEs, you need to define two such RSVP-TE tunnels (only one is shown here for brevity).

Normally, RSVP-TE tunnels can be established to IP addresses represented by TE Router ID TLVs (TLV type 134). As discussed earlier, the context ID is advertised via Extended IP Reachability (TLV type 135). Therefore, CSPF on your IOS XR device will refuse to initialize the RSVP-TE tunnel. You need to cheat a little! How? By using a path option with a loose next-hop (lines 1, 2, and 12). Your loose next-hop is actually a primary loopback (TE Router ID) of the primary PE. Therefore, Constrained Shortest-Path First (CSPF) is now fully satisfied. It is important to note that the request is for *node protection desired* (line 10), not just for link protection, which is the default in IOS XR with facility protection. Node protection is the key for egress-protection functionality with RSVP-TE as a transport.

You can see a standard LDP-based L2VPN configuration with primary/secondary PWs (lines 23 through 29). The L2VPN, however, refers to special PW-classes (lines 27 and 29) that force the PWs to use specific RSVP-TE tunnels (line 19). Only one of these PW-classes is shown for brevity.

You must extend primary egress PE configuration with specific egress-protection pieces (Example 21-36).

Example 21-36. LDP PW primary egress PE configuration on PE3 (Junos)

```
1      protocols {
2          mpls {
3              egress-protection context-identifier 172.18.0.33 primary;
4          }
5          ldp {
6              upstream-label-assignment;
7          }
8          l2circuit {
9              neighbor 172.16.0.22 {
10                 interface ge-2/0/5.9 {
11                     virtual-circuit-id 926;
12                     encapsulation-type ethernet;
13                     pseudowire-status-tlv hot-standby-vc-on;
14                     egress-protection {
15                         protector-pe 172.16.0.44
16                             context-identifier 172.18.0.33;
17     }}}}}
```

You can see the context-ID configuration (line 3) and some extensions to LDP (lines 5 through 7) (they will be discussed later in this section). In LDP-based L2VPN configurations, you can see egress-protection–specific additions in lines 14 through 16. You must specify the IP address of protector/backup egress PE (in this case, it is PE4) and the context-ID used for protecting this L2VPN. As a result of this configuration,

---

PE3 will try to establish targeted LDP sessions to PE4 in order to exchange additional information required for egress protection functionality.

Optionally, you can enable forwarding (line 13) over a PW reported by the ingress PE as hot-standby (PW Status TLV set to 0x20). Similarly, you can enable forwarding over a hot-standby PW on the backup PE, as well. This provides faster traffic switch-over during PE failures. However, it also can cause multicast or broadcast traffic duplication in the direction from the multihomed CE6-I to the single-homed CE2-I because both PWs (PE3→PE2 and PE4→PE2) now actively forward traffic.

After configuring the primary egress PE, let's turn our attention to the configuration of protector/backup egress PE, outlined in Example 21-37.

Example 21-37. LDP PW protector/backup egress PE on PE4 (Junos)

```
1    protocols {
2        mpls {
3            egress-protection context-identifier 172.18.0.33 protector;
4        }
5        ldp {
6            upstream-label-assignment;
7        }
8        l2circuit {
9            neighbor 172.16.0.22 {
10               interface ge-2/0/5.9 {
11                   virtual-circuit-id 926;
12                   encapsulation-type ethernet;
13                   pseudowire-status-tlv hot-standby-vc-on;
14                   egress-protection {
15                       protected-l2circuit PE2-PE3 ingress-pe 172.16.0.22
16                           egress-pe 172.16.0.33 virtual-circuit-id 926;
17   }}}}}
```

The protector/backup egress PE configuration also contains some egress-protection–related extensions for L2VPN (lines 14 through 16). Specifically, you can list IP addresses of the ingress and primary egress PEs, as well as the VC ID from the ingress to primary egress PE.

OK, that configuration is done, so let's have a look at the states in the network.

Example 21-38. LDP L2VPN egress-protection states

```
1    RP/0/RSP0/CPU0:PE2#show l2vpn xconnect group PE3-PE4 xc-name CE6-I
2                     detail | include "PW: |Local|Label|tunnel"
3      PW: neighbor 172.16.0.33, PW ID 926, state is up ( established )
4        Preferred path tunnel TE 1833, fallback enabled
5          MPLS         Local                      Remote
6          Label        16050                      299936
7      PW: neighbor 172.16.0.44, PW ID 926, state is standby ( all ready )
```

```
8          Preferred path tunnel TE 1844, fallback enabled
9            MPLS         Local                         Remote
10           Label        16051                         299936
11
12     RP/0/RSP0/CPU0:PE2#show mpls traffic-eng tunnels 1833 detail
13     [...] Resv Info:
14       Record Route:
15       IPv4 172.16.0.2, flags 0x29 (Node-ID, Protection: available, node)
16       IPv4 10.0.0.5, flags 0x9 (Protection: available, node)
17       Label 311152, flags 0x1
18       IPv4 172.16.0.33, flags 0x20 (Node-ID)
19       IPv4 10.0.0.35, flags 0x0
20       Label 3, flags 0x1
21       IPv4 172.18.0.33, flags 0x0
22       Label 3, flags 0x1
23
24     juniper@P2> show route label 311152 detail | find S=0 | match ...
25                 Next hop: 10.0.0.35 via ge-2/0/6.0 weight 0x1, selected
26                 Label-switched-path PE2--->PE3-CTX2
27                 Label operation: Pop
28                 Next hop: 10.0.0.11 via ge-2/0/7.0 weight 0x8001
29                 Label-switched-path Bypass->10.0.0.35->172.18.0.33
30                 Label operation: Swap 301648
31
32     juniper@PE4> show rsvp session name Bypass->10.0.0.35->172.18.0.33 |
33                 match "Label|Bypass"
34     To         From        Labelin Labelout LSPname
35     172.18.0.33 172.16.0.2  301648       3 Bypass->10.0.0.35->172.18.0.33
36
37     juniper@PE4> show route label 301648 | find S=0
38     301648(S=0)        *[MPLS/0] 00:02:57
39                          to table __172.18.0.33__.mpls.0
40
41     juniper@PE4> show route table __172.18.0.33__.mpls.0
42     (...)
43     299920             *[L2CKT/7] 01:10:39
44                         > via ge-2/0/5.8, Pop
45     299936             *[L2CKT/7] 01:10:45
46                         > via ge-2/0/5.9, Pop
47     800000             *[Egress-Protection/170] 01:10:00
48                         > via ge-2/0/5.6, Pop      Offset: 4
```

The ingress PE (PE2) establishes two PWs: the PW to primary neighbor (PE3), using tunnel 1833 for transport (lines 3 and 4), and the PW to backup neighbor (PE4), using tunnel 1844 as transport (lines 7 and 8). If you remember, these tunnels are established toward the context-IDs (line 9 in Example 21-35), not to the primary loopback addresses of PE3 or PE4. Looking at one of the tunnels, you can see that P2 provides node protection (line 15). And, indeed, if you check the P2 routing entry for the label announced by P2 (lines 17 and 24) you can see the backup next hop pointing to node-protection bypass (lines 28 through 30).

So far, so good. But why is a node-protection (and not link-protection) bypass LSP established from P2? P2 is only one hop away from PE3, which advertises 172.18.0.33/32, the destination for tunnel 1833. If you carefully check the RRO object (lines 14 through 22), you should spot some unexpected entries. You see there are actually three, not two, links on the path from PE2 to PE3:

- 10.0.0.5, label 311152
- 10.0.0.35, label 3
- 172.18.0.33, label 3

This means that PE3 is cheating. PE3 answered via the RRO object in the RSVP-TE RESV message, that there is an additional hop from PE3 to reach the tunnel destination. Therefore, P2 believes, it can initiate next-next-hop (NNHOP) bypass (to avoid node 172.16.0.33) to protect the tunnel. If you go back to stub-proxy (Figure 21-5), the situation is now slightly different. In stub-proxy context-ID advertising mode, the primary and the protector nodes are cheating even in IS-IS, saying that some additional IS-IS node exists. Now, they are only cheating in RSVP, because in the stub-link context-ID advertising mode, context-IDs are advertised as additional links, not nodes. The allocated label for the second link is 3 (implicit null), so arriving packets will never make it to (nonexistent) hop 172.18.0.33.

Good. So, P2 requests NNHOP bypass to reach 172.18.0.33 and to avoid 10.0.0.35, but to which node? To the protector node (PE4), of course (line 28), because the protector node advertises 172.18.0.33, as well. The protector node completes the bypass establishment, and advertises a real label (lines 30 and 35). This label points to the context-ID table on protector node PE4 (lines 37 through 39).

The context-ID table is populated with labels. Do you remember how it was populated? In previous cases using L3VPN and BGP-based L2VPN services, it was populated via the BGP prefixes received from the primary node. Now, you don't have BGP; you have LDP. So now, the protector needs to receive information required for egress-protection via LDP, not via BGP. As a result of the LDP PW egress-protection configuration (lines 14 through 16 in Example 21-36, and in Example 21-37) the primary PE and the protector/backup PE establish a targeted LDP session. Over this targeted LDP session, the primary PE announces its own label that the primary PE uses for PW being protected.

Example 21-39. Protection FEC element TLV advertised by PE3 (Junos)

```
1    Label Mapping Message (0x0400), length: 60, Message ID: 0x00000254
2      FEC TLV (0x0100), length: 20, Flags: (...)
3        L2 Protection FEC (0x83): Remote PE 172.16.0.22, Group ID 0,
4          PW ID 926, no Control Word, PW-Type: Ethernet
5      Upstream Assigned Label TLV (0x0204), length: 8, Flags: (...)
```

```
6        Label: 299936
7       IPv4 Interface ID TLV (0x082d), length: 16, Flags: (...)
8         IPv4 Next/Previous Hop: 0.0.0.0, Logical Interface 0,
9           context ID: 172.18.0.33
10
11    juniper@PE4> show ldp database session 172.16.0.33 extensive
12    (...)
13     299936    L2PROTEC 172.16.0.22 ETHERNET VC 926
14               Context ID: 172.18.0.33 CtrlWord: No
15               State: Active
```

You can see a couple of new LDP TLVs, which have not been used before:

- **L2 Protection FEC Element** (Type 0x83, lines 3 and 4) introduced by the previously mentioned: *draft-ietf-pals-endpoint-fast-protection*, as an element inside RFC 5036's FEC TLV (TLV 0x0100, line 2).

- **Upstream Assigned Label TLV** (TLV 0x0204, lines 5 and 6) introduced by RFC 6389 - *MPLS Upstream Label Assignment for LDP*, Section 4.

- **IPv4 Interface ID TLV** (TLV 0x082d, lines 7 through 9) introduced by RFC 3472 - *Generalized Multi-Protocol Label Switching (GMPLS) Signaling*.

Now it should be clear why you need to enable upstream label assignment mode (lines 5 through 7 in Example 21-36 and Example 21-37). With a label mapping message that uses a combination of these TLVs, the primary egress PE tells the protector/backup egress PE information required to populate the appropriate egress-protection tables:

- Ingress PE (lines 3 and 13)
- VC ID (lines 4 and 13)
- Label used by primary egress PE (lines 6 and 13)
- Context-ID (lines 9 and 14)

Now, if you go back to the context-ID table, you will recognize the appropriate label used for egress-protection (compare line 45 in Example 21-38 with lines 6 and 13 in Example 21-39). The outgoing interface is the local Attachment Circuit (AC) used on the protector/egress PE for the protected PW (Example 21-37 line 10). Thus, you can confirm that states in the network are ready for egress-protection of your LDP signaled PW.

Just for completeness, Example 21-40 provides the configuration for Junos ingress PE.

Example 21-40. LDP PW ingress PE configuration on PE1 (Junos)

```
1    protocols {
2        mpls {
3            label-switched-path PE1--->PE3-CTX2 {
4                to 172.18.0.33;
5                node-link-protection;
6                inter-domain;
7                adaptive;
8            }
9        }
10       l2circuit {
11           neighbor 172.16.0.33 {
12               interface ge-2/0/1.8 {
13                   psn-tunnel-endpoint 172.18.0.33;
14                   virtual-circuit-id 816;
15                   pseudowire-status-tlv;
16                   revert-time 10;
17                   backup-neighbor 172.16.0.44 {
18                       virtual-circuit-id 816;
19                       psn-tunnel-endpoint 172.18.0.44;
20                       hot-standby;
21   }}}}}
```

In IOS XR, you must trick CSPF into using the path-option with a loose next hop (lines 1, 2, and 12 in Example 21-35). In Junos, the corresponding trick is to specify the `inter-domain` keyword (line 6). Then, you bind the LDP PW to the specific MPLS transport tunnel (signaled via LDP or RSVP-TE) using `psn-tunnel-endpoint` (lines 13 and 19). You also need to ensure that the IP address used as `psn-tunnel-endpoint` is reachable via the appropriate tunnel. Fortunately, Junos creates the routing entry by default, so that the IP address used as the tunnel destination (line 4) is reachable via this tunnel. Therefore, the context-ID used as `psn-tunnel-endpoint` binds the PW to the appropriate tunnel.

Finally, the PE-CE link-protection mechanism (see Example 21-41) is exactly the same as in BGP-based L2VPN. The special egress-protection LSP tunnel redirects traffic to the backup egress PE in case of a PE-CE link failure.

Example 21-41. Egress PE-CE link protection for LDP PW (Junos)

```
juniper@PE3> show route label 299936 table mpls.0 detail |
         match "via|oper|-path"
             Next hop: via ge-2/0/5.9 weight 0x1, selected
             Label operation: Pop
             Next hop: 10.0.0.13 via ge-2/0/2.0 weight 0x2
             Label-switched-path PE3--->PE4-PROTECT
             Label operation: Swap 299936, Push 300160(top)

juniper@PE4> show route label 300160 | find S=0
```

```
(...)
300160(S=0)          *[MPLS/0] 03:14:32
                        to table __172.18.0.33__.mpls.0
```

Egress Peer Engineering Protection

Chapter 13 introduces *Egress Peer Engineering* (EPE), using BGP labeled IPv4 unicast as the next hop. But what happens if your desired egress peer fails? Normally, in EPE architecture, traffic would be *blackholed* until global convergence happens. Traffic arrives with a BGP-LU label, which points to the outgoing interface facing the selected egress peer. The router does not perform IP lookup (just label lookup), therefore if the outgoing interface (peer) fails, there is no backup next hop.

In this section, you will enhance the EPE configuration with a protection mechanism. You have two options from which to choose (or combine):

- Preinstall the backup next hop pointing to another directly connected egress peer (or another link from the same peer)
- Remove the label from received packets and perform normal IP lookup

Figure 21-6 illustrates this scenario for EPE protection. All three peers (PEER1, PEER2, and PEER3) advertise two prefixes: 192.168.20.100/32 and 192.168.20.200/32. Both PE3 and PE4 readvertise these prefixes toward the RRs, without next-hop change, as mandated by EPE architecture.

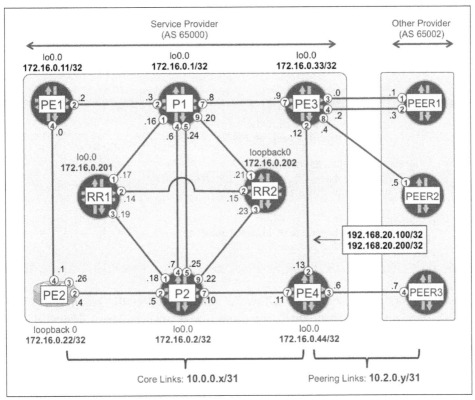

Figure 21-6. Protection in EPE architecture

Let's create a protection scheme on PE3, as follows:

- The upper PE3-PEER1 link should be protected by the bottom PE3-PEER1 link, and IP lookup should be used as a fallback in case of complete PEER1 failure.

- The bottom PE3-PEER1 link should be protected by the PE3-PEER2 link (no IP lookup as fallback).

- The PE3-PEER2 link should be protected with IP lookup only

OK, so let's configure PE3 in order to meet these requirements (Example 21-42).

Example 21-42. EPE protection configuration on PE3 (Junos)

```
1    protocols bgp {
2        egress-te-backup-paths {
3            template BACKUP-FOR-PEER1-UPPER {
4                peer 10.2.0.3;  ## bottom link to PEER1
5                ip-forward;     ## IP lookup as fallback
6            }
```

```
 7              template BACKUP-FOR-PEER1-BOTTOM {
 8                  peer 10.2.0.5;  ## link to PEER2
 9              }
10              template BACKUP-FOR-PEER2 {
11                  ip-forward;    ## IP lookup as fallback
12              }
13          }
14          group eBGP-PEER1-UPPER-LINK {
15              egress-te backup-path BACKUP-FOR-PEER1-UPPER;
16              neighbor 10.2.0.1 peer-as 65002;
17          }
18          group eBGP-PEER1-BOTTOM-LINK {
19              egress-te backup-path BACKUP-FOR-PEER1-BOTTOM;
20              neighbor 10.2.0.3 peer-as 65002;
21          }
22          group eBGP-PEER2 {
23              egress-te backup-path BACKUP-FOR-PEER2;
24              neighbor 10.2.0.5 peer-as 65002;
25          }
26      }
```

This configuration is somewhat self-explanatory. To reflect the requirements discussed previously, you create three EPE protection templates (lines 2 through 13) by using the peer (to specify backup peer) or ip-forward (to specify IP lookup as fallback) keywords. For ip-forward, you can also specify the routing-instance, where the IP lookup should be performed. If not specified, as in the Example 21-42, the default master routing instance is used.

Next, you apply the previously defined EPE protection templates to the appropriate BGP groups (lines 14 through 25). In this particular case, each BGP group has only a single neighbor, but if multiple peers share an EPE protection template, there is a good chance that you will see multiple BGP peers in the same group. Chapter 1 shows how the iBGP-RR group, with two RRs, has the *Add Path* feature enabled for the service NLRI (IPv4 Unicast, in this example). Therefore, any PE router (including PE3) can maintain multiple paths (maximum 6) to the same IP destination. This is crucial in EPE architecture. Without multiple paths to the same destination, the remote PE (e.g., PE1) will not be able to choose the egress link for the specific prefix. The remote PE would receive only a single path. Other paths would be suppressed either by PE3 or by router reflectors.

 This configuration example only covers the protection extension to EPE architecture. For a full EPE configuration, refer to Chapter 13.

OK, let's check the effect of your configuration (Example 21-43).

Example 21-43. Prefixes advertised to RR from PE3 (Junos)

```
1    juniper@PE3> show route advertising-protocol bgp 172.16.201 extensive
2
3    inet.0: 68 destinations, 83 routes (68 active, ...)
4    * 192.168.20.100/32(3 entries, 3 announced)
5     BGP group iBGP-RR type Internal
6         Nexthop: 10.2.0.1
7         Localpref: 100
8         AS path: [65000] 65002 I
9         Addpath Path ID: 1
10    BGP group iBGP-RR type Internal
11        Nexthop: 10.2.0.3
12        Localpref: 100
13        AS path: [65000] 65002 I
14        Addpath Path ID: 2
15    BGP group iBGP-RR type Internal
16        Nexthop: 10.2.0.5
17        Localpref: 100
18        AS path: [65000] 65002 I
19        Addpath Path ID: 3
20   (...)
21   inet.3: 9 destinations, 9 routes (9 active, ...)
22
23   * 10.2.0.1/32 (1 entry, 1 announced)
24    BGP group iBGP-RR type Internal
25        Route Label: 299904
26   (...)
27   * 10.2.0.3/32 (1 entry, 1 announced)
28    BGP group iBGP-RR type Internal
29        Route Label: 299920
30   (...)
31   * 10.2.0.5/32 (1 entry, 1 announced)
32    BGP group iBGP-RR type Internal
33        Route Label: 299936
34   (...)
```

You can see that PE3 advertises to the RRs the prefixes received from the peering routers. To save space, only a single prefix—192.168.20.100/32—is shown (lines 4 through 19). Because Addpath is used, PE3 advertises all different paths. They are different because, based on EPE architecture, the next hop remains unchanged (lines 6, 11, and 16). Additionally, PE3 advertises MPLS labels for these next hops (lines 25, 29, and 33). Therefore, the remote PE (e.g., PE1) can engineer the traffic to the appropriate egress PE by pushing the appropriate label. If PE1 wants to send traffic destined to 192.168.20.100 via the bottom link toward PEER1 (next hop 10.2.0.3), PE1 will encapsulate such packets with label 299920.

So far, so good. This is a typical EPE architecture. But let's now have a closer look at the EPE protection mechanism. So, let's investigate the states associated with the advertised next-hop labels (Example 21-44).

Example 21-44. EPE protection RIB states on PE3 (Junos)

```
1    juniper@PE3> show route table mpls.0 extensive
2    (...)
3    299904 (1 entry, 1 announced)
4    (...)
5            Next hop: 10.2.0.1 via ge-2/0/3.0 weight 0x1, selected
6            Label operation: Pop
7    (...)
8            Next hop: 10.2.0.3 via ge-2/0/4.0 weight 0x2
9            Label operation: Pop
10   (...)
11           Next hop: via lsi.1 (master) weight 0x3
12           Label operation: Pop
13   (...)
14
15   299920 (1 entry, 1 announced)
16   (...)
17           Next hop: 10.2.0.3 via ge-2/0/4.0, weight 0x1, selected
18           Label operation: Pop
19   (...)
20           Next hop: 10.2.0.5 via ge-2/0/8.0 weight 0x2
21           Label operation: Pop
22   (...)
23   299936 (1 entry, 1 announced)
24   (...)
25           Next hop: 10.2.0.5 via ge-2/0/8.0, weight 0x1, selected
26           Label operation: Pop
27   (...)
28           Next hop: via lsi.1 (master) weight 0x3
29           Label operation: Pop
30   (...)
```

You can see in line 3 that label 299904 associated with next hop 10.2.0.1 (the upper link to PEER1) has three next hops, all of them with different weights:

- The primary next hop (weight 0x1) pointing to the upper link to PEER1 (line 5)
- The secondary next hop (weight 0x2) pointing to the bottom link to PEER2 (line 8)
- The tertiary next hop (weight 0x3) pointing to the *label switch interface* (*lsi*) unit 1 (line 11)

This is exactly what you configured (Example 21-42, lines 3 through 6, and 15 and 16)! The label operation on all next hops is *pop* (lines 6, 9, and 12); therefore, packets forwarded over these next hops will have the label removed. Thus, they will arrive to the BGP peer without the label, which matches the peer expectation.

More explanations require the tertiary next hop pointing to lsi.1 interface. As is discussed in Chapter 3, such an interface is used to remove the MPLS label from the received packet (*pop* action in lines 12 and 29), and points to some routing-instance for further lookup. In Chapter 3, it is discussed in the context of L3VPN routing-instances. Now, let's verify to which routing-instance this interface actually belongs.

Example 21-45. Routing table verification for the lsi.1 interface on PE3 (Junos)

```
1    juniper@PE3> show interfaces lsi.1 extensive | match table | last 1
2        Generation: 227, Route table: 0
3
4    juniper@PE3> show route forwarding-table summary extensive |
5                match "Index 0"
6    Routing table: default.inet [Index 0]
7    Routing table: default.iso [Index 0]
8    Routing table: default.inet6 [Index 0]
9    Routing table: default.mpls [Index 0]
```

Bingo! Interface lsi.1 points to the default routing table. If, after removing the label, the remaining packet is an IPv4 one, the lookup will be performed in the default IPv4 (inet) table (line 6). Similarly, if the remaining packet is IPv6, the lookup is performed in the default IPv6 (inet6) table (line 8). So, your IP lookup fallback can work with both IPv4 and IPv6 prefixes received from eBGP peers. If both the primary and the secondary next hops fail (complete failure of PEER1), based on the IP lookup in the global table and depending on the deployed BGP policies, PE3 may decide to send the packet to the direct neighbor, PEER2, or to the remote PEER3 via PE4.

Together with the ip-forward knob, you can specify the routing-instance name where the lookup should be performed. If omitted, the default (master) instance is used, as discussed previously.

The second label (299920), associated with next hop 10.2.0.3 (the bottom link to PEER1) has only two next hops: primary (Example 21-44, lines 17 and 18) pointing to the bottom link to PEER1, and secondary (Example 21-44, lines 20 and 21) pointing to PEER2. This again, reflects the requirements and the configuration. Therefore, in case of PEER1 failure, packets will be sent unconditionally to PEER2 (without IP lookup).

The third label (299936) again has only two next hops, which is in line with the requirements. The backup next hop, similarly to the tertiary next hop in first example, points to the default routing table for lookup.

Protection in Seamless MPLS Architecture

By now, you should be familiar with most of the use cases for fast traffic restoration. You know, for example, how to protect against failure of transit links or transit P nodes. Also, you should have discovered various options to protect the traffic against failure of the egress PE node or the egress PE-CE links.

This section's topic is Seamless MPLS architecture, which you might remember from Chapter 16. If not, quickly have a look at Figure 16-6, which outlines the reference architecture in Seamless MPLS deployments. This figure, along with the final configuration for Seamless MPLS in Chapter 16, is the basis for the tutorial. As you will see, there are some new network components that require protection too: border node (Area Border Router [ABR] or AS Border Router [ASBR]), and ASBR-ASBR link.

Let's begin the discussion with ASBR-ASBR link protection.

Border Link (ASBR-ASBR) Protection

Protection for the ASBR-ASBR link in Seamless MPLS architecture is very similar to protection of egress PE-CE links. The only difference is that on the ASBR you need to enable protection (backup paths) for the IPv4 (labeled) unicast address family in the global routing context, not for the IPv4 VPN unicast address family inside the VRF.

Example 21-46. ASBR-ASBR link protection configuration (Junos)

```
1    protocols {
2        bgp {
3            group EBGP-UP:LU {
4                family inet labeled-unicast protection;
5                multipath;
6    }}}
```

Example 21-47. ASBR-ASBR link protection configuration (IOS XR)

```
1    route-policy PL-BGP-BACKUP-PATH
2      set path-selection backup 1 install
3    end-policy
4    !
5    router bgp 65001
6      address-family ipv4 unicast
7        additional-paths selection route-policy PL-BGP-BACKUP-PATH
```

A quick verification (see Example 21-48 and Example 21-49) confirms that the backup next hops are now present. For example, the route to the loopback of PE1 shows on ASBR3 (Junos) and ASBR4 (IOS XR) with two preinstalled paths: the primary path via the direct ASBR-ASBR link, and the backup path through another ASBR reachable via the MPLS network.

Example 21-48. ASBR-ASBR link protection verification (Junos)

```
1    juniper@ASBR3> show route 172.16.10.11/32 table inet.3 active-path
2    (...)
3    172.16.10.11/32
4     *[BGP/170] 00:05:26, MED 0, localpref 100, from 10.1.2.0
5        AS path: 65001 ?, validation-state: unverified
6      > to 10.1.2.0 via ge-2/0/1.0, Push 300752
7        to 10.0.20.9 via ge-2/0/3.0, label-switched-path ASBR3--->ASBR4
```

Example 21-49. ASBR-ASBR link protection verification (IOS XR)

```
1    RP/0/0/CPU0:ASBR4#show route 172.16.10.11/32 | include from
2        10.1.2.2, from 10.1.2.2, BGP external
3        172.16.20.103, from 172.16.20.103, BGP backup path
```

Border Node (ABR or ASBR) Protection

In case a border node (ABR or ASBR) fails, traffic must be redirected over the remaining border node. As explained in Chapter 16, border nodes are inline RRs for the IPv4 labeled unicast. Additionally, they change the next hop for the reflected IPv4 LU prefixes. Therefore, any failure to the border nodes causes rather long restoration times (seconds) because traffic redirection is based on BGP global convergence.

Unless you perform some optimization. In this section, you will deploy egress protection (service mirroring) concepts, not to protect IPv4 VPN unicast or L2VPN NLRIs, as done previously; this time, you will protect with the service mirroring concept the IPv4 labeled unicast NLRIs.

 As of this writing, the primary border node or protector node function in egress-protection (service mirroring) architecture for IPv4 labeled unicast is not supported in IOS XR. Therefore, the ABR2 node in this chapter's Seamless MPLS topology runs Junos.

The topology for our border node egress-protection discussion is outlined in Figure 21-7, similar to the Seamless MPLS topology used in Chapter 16, with the only difference being that now both ABR1 and ABR2 are both Junos-based devices.

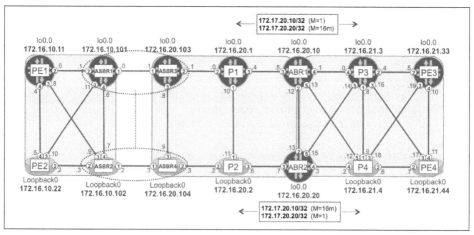

Figure 21-7. ABR egress-protection architecture

You will deploy egress protection using the combined protector/backup border node approach, meaning that ABR1 is the combined protector/backup node for ABR2; vice versa, ABR2 is the combined protector/backup node for ABR1.

The approach to configure this is similar to that used in IPv4 VPN egress protection. You need to do the following:

- Define the primary context-ID on the primary border node
- Define the protector context-ID on the backup border node
- Ensure that the primary border node changes the next hop to its primary context-ID (and no longer to its own primary loopback address) for reflected IPv4 LU prefixes

The base configuration is the same as in Chapter 16. Before configuring egress protection, you must also extend this base configuration with LFA in area 49.0001 and facility (node-link protection) for RSVP-TE in area 49.0002. These techniques were discussed in Chapter 18 and Chapter 19, and are therefore not included in the following configuration, which concentrates only on egress protection specific additions.

Example 21-50. BGP-LU egress-protection configuration on ABR2 (Junos)

```
1    chassis {
2        fpc 2 pic 0 tunnel-services;
3    }
4    protocols {
5        rsvp {
6            tunnel-services;
7        }
8        mpls {
```

```
9           egress-protection {
10              context-identifier 172.17.20.10 protector;
11              context-identifier 172.17.20.20 primary;
12          }
13      }
14      bgp {
15          group iBGP-RR:LU+VPN {
16              family inet labeled-unicast egress-protection;
17              export PL-BGP-RR-LU-EXP;
18          }
19          group iBGP-DOWN:LU+VPN {
20              family inet labeled-unicast egress-protection;
21              export PL-BGP-DOWN-LU-EXP;
22          }
23          group iBGP-UP:LU {
24              family inet labeled-unicast egress-protection;
25              export PL-BGP-UP-LU-EXP;
26          }
27      }
28  }
29  policy-options {
30      policy-statement PL-BGP-DOWN-LU-EXP {
31          term 201-LOOPBACKS {
32              from {
33                  rib inet.3;
34                  community CM-LOOPBACKS-201;
35              }
36              then reject;
37          }
38          term ALL-LOOPBACKS {
39              from {
40                  protocol bgp;
41                  rib inet.3;
42                  community CM-LOOPBACKS-ALL;
43              }
44              then {
45                  next-hop 172.17.20.20;      ## Primary context ID
46                  accept;
47              }
48          }
49          from rib inet.3;
50          then reject;
51      }
52      policy-statement PL-BGP-RR-LU-EXP {
53          term LOCAL-LOOPBACK {
54              from {
55                  protocol direct;
56                  rib inet.3;
57                  interface lo0.0;
58                  community CM-LOOPBACKS-200;
59              }
60              then {
```

```
61              aigp-originate;
62              next-hop self;            ## Loopback
63              accept;
64          }
65      }
66      term 201-LOOPBACKS {
67          from {
68              protocol bgp;
69              rib inet.3;
70              community CM-LOOPBACKS-201;
71          }
72          then {
73              next-hop 172.17.20.20;    ## Primary Context ID
74              accept;
75          }
76      }
77      from rib inet.3;
78      then reject;
79  }
80  policy-statement PL-BGP-UP-LU-EXP {
81      term LOCAL-LOOPBACK {
82          from {
83              protocol direct;
84              rib inet.3;
85              interface lo0.0;
86              community CM-LOOPBACKS-200;
87          }
88          then {
89              aigp-originate;
90              next-hop self;            ## Loopback
91              accept;
92          }
93      }
94      term 201-LOOPBACKS {
95          from {
96              protocol bgp;
97              rib inet.3;
98              community CM-LOOPBACKS-201;
99          }
100         then {
101             next-hop 172.17.20.20;    ## Primary Context ID
102             accept;
103         }
104     }
105     from rib inet.3;
106     then reject;
107 }
108 }
```

Beginning with the configuration of the context-IDs, two additional IP addresses are used as context-IDs (lines 10 and 11):

- 172.17.20.10: the primary context-ID on ABR1 and protector context-ID on ABR2

- 172.17.20.20: the primary context-ID on ABR2 and protector context-ID on ABR1

Next, egress-protection functionality, as mentioned earlier, is enabled this time for the IPv4 labeled unicast address family (lines 16, 20, and 24). The BGP outbound policies deployed earlier (lines 17, 21, and 25) stay there—they are just slightly modified.

Existing policies (shown in full, to avoid any confusion) modify just the next-hop parameter. For locally generated prefixes (local loopback) the next hop can still be the local loopback (lines 62 and 90). Loopback is unique to ABR (no other node injects the same loopback into BGP), so protection for ABR's local loopback, even if ABR fails, cannot be achieved anyway. And, as discussed earlier in the L3VPN egress-protection section, protection for single-homed prefixes might cause blackholing in certain failure scenarios, so it's better not to configure it.

For reflected IPv4 labeled unicast prefixes, however, you change the next hop to the primary context-ID configured at the beginning of the example (lines 45, 73, and 101). Because another ABR reflects the same prefixes and uses the same context-ID in protector mode, these prefixes can be protected by the egress-protection architecture.

The specialty of ABR BGP-LU egress protection that is based on RSVP-TE transport is the requirement for RSVP tunnel services (lines 5 through 7) and is not required in any egress protection schemes discussed earlier (L3VPN or L2VPN). The requirement for tunnel services in ABR BGP-LU protection will be explained later.

The ABR1 configuration is almost the same. You must configure the primary and any protector context IDs (and of course, the next hop set to ABR1's primary context-ID) in the opposite way.

On an IOS XR router initializing a RSVP-TE tunnel (e.g., ASBR4) toward the context-ID shared between ABR1 and ABR2, the configuration follows tricks already discussed in the LDP L2VPN egress-protection section (lines 1 through 12 in Example 21-35). Therefore, you will not see this configuration repeated here. This time, however, you need to assign the traffic to these tunnels, not via some L2VPN configuration statements, but via a simple static route as outlined in the following configuration:

Example 21-51. Associating context-ID with RSVP-TE tunnels (IOS XR)

```
1    router static
2     address-family ipv4 unicast
3      172.17.20.10/32 tunnel-te1710
4      172.17.20.20/32 tunnel-te1720
```

Perfect! The configuration is done, so let's verify states in the network (Example 21-52).

Example 21-52. ABR BGP-LU egress-protection verification

```
1    RP/0/0/CPU0:ASBR4#show cef 172.16.21.33 | include "via |labels"
2     via 172.17.20.10, 4 dependencies, recursive [flags 0x6000]
3      next hop 172.17.20.10 via 24015/0/21
4       next hop 0.0.0.0/32 tt1710      labels imposed {ImplNull 300032}
5     via 172.17.20.20, 4 dependencies, recursive, backup [flags 0x6100]
6      next hop 172.17.20.20 via 24017/0/21
7       next hop 0.0.0.0/32 tt1720      labels imposed {ImplNull 300048}
8
9    RP/0/0/CPU0:ASBR4#show mpls traffic-eng tunnels 1710 detail
10   (...)
11     IPv4 172.16.20.1, flags 0x29 (Node-ID, Protection: available, node)
12     IPv4 10.0.20.10, flags 0x9 (Protection: available, node)
13     Label 303296, flags 0x1
14     IPv4 172.17.20.10, flags 0x0
15     Label 3, flags 0x1
16   (...)
17
18   juniper@P1> show route label 303296 detail | find S=0 | match ...
19           Next hop: 10.0.20.5 via ge-2/0/3.0 weight 0x1, selected
20           Label-switched-path ASBR4--->ABR1-CTX
21           Label operation: Pop
22           Next hop: 10.0.20.11 via ge-2/0/1.0 weight 0x8001 (...)
23           Label-switched-path Bypass->10.0.20.5->172.17.20.10
24           Label operation: Swap 24013
25
26   juniper@ABR2> show rsvp session name Bypass->10.0.20.5->172.17.20.10
27   To         From       Labelin Labelout LSPname
28   172.17.20.10 172.16.20.1 300288       3 Bypass->10.0.20.5->172.17.20.10
29
30   juniper@ABR2> show route label 300288
31   (...)
32   300288   *[RSVP/7/1] 01:43:01, metric 1
33           > via vt-2/0/0.2097155, lsp Bypass->10.0.20.5->172.17.20.10
34   300288(S=0) *[MPLS/0] 01:43:01
35               to table __172.17.20.10__.mpls.0
36
37   juniper@ABR2> show route table __172.17.20.10__.mpls.0
38   (...)
39   300032            *[Egress-Protection/170] 02:31:37
40                   > to 10.0.21.2 via ge-2/0/4.0, Swap 24003
41                     to 10.0.21.14 via ge-2/0/5.0, Swap 299776
42   303600            *[Egress-Protection/170] 02:31:37
43                   > to 10.0.21.2 via ge-2/0/4.0, Swap 24000
44                     to 10.0.21.14 via ge-2/0/5.0, Swap 299856
45
46   juniper@ABR2> show route receive-protocol bgp 172.16.20.10
```

```
47                    table inet.3 detail | match "entries|Label|hop"
48        172.16.20.10/32 (6 entries, 3 announced)
49           Route Label: 3
50           Nexthop: 172.16.20.10
51        172.16.21.33/32 (5 entries, 5 announced)
52           Route Label: 300032
53           Nexthop: 172.17.20.10
54        172.16.21.44/32 (4 entries, 4 announced)
55           Route Label: 303600
56           Nexthop: 172.17.20.10
```

You can see that the PE3 loopback uses the ABR1 primary context-ID as the primary next hop (lines 2 and 3). And, the ABR1 primary context-ID (which is the ABR2 protector context-ID at the same time) uses, in turn, the 1710 RSVP-TE tunnel as the primary next hop (line 4), apparently, as a result of the configuration from Example 21-51. This tunnel is established via a dynamically chosen path that traverses P1 (lines 11 and 12). P1 is directly connected to ABR1 (where the RSVP-TE tunnels terminate), so P1 is the PLR from an egress-protection perspective. The tunnel requested node protection (Example 21-35, line 11); thus, you can see node protection is actually available.

Checking the entries for the label assigned to the tunnel by P1 (lines 13 and 18), you can see the node protection bypass LSP as the backup next hop (lines 22 through 24). ABR2 assigns a label to this bypass LSP (line 28) that points to the context-ID label table (lines 34 and 35), known to us from previous egress-protection discussions for L3VPN and L2VPN. But, you can also see another entry (lines 32 and 33) pointing to a VT (*virtual tunnel*) interface. This is something new.

What's the difference between these two entries? Well, the second entry is for packets with more than one MPLS label (S=0, so there is at least one additional label). Conversely, the first entry is for packets with only a single label. Normally, packets arrive to the protector with multiple labels (e.g., a context-ID label plus a BGP-LU label plus a VPN label). Packets with a single label are packets used eventually for OAM purposes, such as ping or traceroute packets. We will discover later how such packets are handled.

Back to the context-ID label table (lines 37 through 44) that contains currently two labels; apparently these are the labels learned from ABR1 for PE3 and PE4 loopbacks (compare line 39 with line 52, and line 42 with line 55). The outgoing labels are LDP labels to reach PE3 or PE4 loopbacks inside area 49.0001.

Therefore, we can conclude that traffic going from left to right in the topology, destined to the PE3 or PE4 loopback, is protected in case of ABR failure with an egress-protection scheme. If ABR1 fails, P1 redirects the traffic to ABR2. On ABR2, egress-protection RIB/FIB structures ensure that traffic is forwarded appropriately toward PE3 or PE4.

Let's now go back to the case with only the single label (lines 32 and 33), and try to figure out the forwarding status here. The VT interface is an internal tunnel interface connecting a displayed routing table (in this case, the context-ID table) with some other routing table. So, first you need to figure out which table the other end of the VT interface actually belongs to.

Example 21-53. VT loopback verification (Junos)

```
1    juniper@ABR2> show interfaces vt-2/0/0.2097155 detail | match ...
2        Protocol mpls, MTU: Unlimited, Maximum labels: 3,
3            Generation: 182, Route table: 0
4
5    juniper@ABR2> show route forwarding-table summary extensive |
6                    match "inet .*Index 0"
7    Routing table: default.inet [Index 0]
```

The packet goes to a normal global routing table. The label is actually popped, and the router performs normal IP lookup in the global routing table. Therefore, ping or traceroute to the context-ID can be appropriately handled by the protector during the time when the primary node is not available.

So, is the ABR egress protection ready? Not yet! If you go back to lines 37 through 44 in Example 21-52, you'll see two labels received from ABR1 and associated with PE3 and PE4 loopbacks. So, traffic from the left side to the right side across ABRs is protected. What about traffic from the right side to the left side? Unfortunately, this traffic is not protected, because the context-ID table does not contain any labels associated with loopback from the left side of the topology; for example, the loopbacks of PE1 and PE2.

Why are they not there? Let's look again at the route policies deployed on the ABRs for the IPv4 labeled unicast address family (Example 21-50). The ABRs send all BGP-LU loopbacks (lines 38 through 48) downstream (in the direction of PE3 and PE4). However, as of now, the exchange between the two ABRs is limited to local loopbacks, and the loopbacks from area 49.0001, which are marked with the CM-LOOPBACKS-201 community (lines 52 through 79). Both ABRs receive loopbacks of nodes from the left side in the topology from ASBR3 and ASBR4, so it was not really required to exchange these loopbacks again over the direct ABR1-ABR2 session.

But now, the situation is different. To build egress-protection states, ABR1 and ABR2 need to have visibility of the BGP-LU updates advertised downstream. Let's exchange these BGP-LU prefixes between ABRs (Example 21-54).

Example 21-54. BGP-LU policy adjustment between ABRs (Junos)

```
1    policy-options {
2        policy-statement PL-BGP-RR-LU-EXP {
```

```
3          term LOCAL-LOOPBACK {
4              (...)
5          }
6          term 201-LOOPBACKS {
7              (...)
8          }
9          term ALL-LOOPBACKS {
10             from {
11                 protocol bgp;
12                 rib inet.3;
13                 community CM-LOOPBACKS-ALL;
14             }
15             then {
16                 local-preference 90;
17                 community add CM-NO-ADVERTISE;
18                 next-hop 172.17.20.10;              ## Context-ID
19                 accept;
20             }
21         }
22         from rib inet.3;
23         then reject;
24     }
25     community CM-NO-ADVERTISE members no-advertise;
26 }
```

Prefixes exchanged between ABRs are solely for making egress-protection structures possible. To avoid any unexpected forwarding patterns, they should not be readvertised, and should be less preferred than the corresponding prefixes received from upstream neighbors (ASBR3 or ASBR4). Therefore, you use the no-advertise community (lines 17 and 25) and decrease the local preference from 100 to 90 (line 16) when sending these prefixes to the neighboring ABR. Don't forget to set the next hop to the context-ID (line 18) so that the receiving ABR can install received labels in its context-ID label table.

If you check the context-ID label table now, you will see many more labels, as shown in Example 21-55.

Example 21-55. Context-ID label table on ABR2 (Junos)

```
juniper@ABR2> show route table __172.17.20.10__.mpls.0
(...)
300608          *[Egress-Protection/170] 00:44:14
                > to 10.0.21.2 via ge-2/0/4.0, Swap 24005
                  to 10.0.21.14 via ge-2/0/5.0, Swap 299856
300688          *[Egress-Protection/170] 00:43:37
                > to 10.0.20.6 via ge-2/0/3.0, Swap 24029
300704          *[Egress-Protection/170] 00:43:37
                > to 10.0.20.6 via ge-2/0/3.0, Pop
                  to 10.0.20.12 via ge-2/0/2.0, Swap 300640
300720          *[Egress-Protection/170] 00:43:37
```

```
                     > to 10.0.20.6 via ge-2/0/3.0, Swap 24002
                       to 10.0.20.12 via ge-2/0/2.0, Swap 300624
300736               *[Egress-Protection/170] 00:43:37
                     > to 10.0.20.6 via ge-2/0/3.0, Swap 24024
300752               *[Egress-Protection/170] 00:43:37, metric2 3000
                     > to 10.0.20.6 via ge-2/0/3.0, lsp ABR2--->ASBR3
300768               *[Egress-Protection/170] 00:43:37, metric2 2000
                     > to 10.0.20.6 via ge-2/0/3.0, lsp ABR2--->ASBR4
300784               *[Egress-Protection/170] 00:43:37, metric2 2000
                     > to 10.0.20.6 via ge-2/0/3.0, lsp ABR2--->ASBR4
300800               *[Egress-Protection/170] 00:44:15
                       to 10.0.21.2 via ge-2/0/4.0, Swap 24006
                     > to 10.0.21.14 via ge-2/0/5.0, Swap 299872
300992               *[Egress-Protection/170] 00:32:38, metric2 2000
                     > to 10.0.20.6 via ge-2/0/3.0, lsp ABR2--->ASBR4
```

The analysis of the IPv4 labeled unicast protection for the traffic from right side to the left side of the network topology can also be done. Note that it is very similar to the analysis already performed for traffic from left to right, so it will be skipped for the sake of brevity.

How does ASBR node egress protection differ from ABR node egress protection? Not much, actually. You can consider the pair of ASBR nodes (e.g., ASBR1 + ASBR2) as a kind of ABR node for egress-protection perspective. And then, in the left side and in the right side of such a combined node, you simply make the egress-protection configuration similar to the ABR egress configuration done before.

Summary

This chapter covered various egress service fast restoration mechanisms. By combining these mechanisms with those presented in Chapter 18, Chapter 19, and Chapter 20, you can design networks with very low (below 100 milliseconds, or even below 50 milliseconds) failover times, during failure of any network component.

Index

T

targeted LDP session, 46, 307, 603
TCC (Translational Cross-Connect), 278
TCO (total cost of ownership), 491
TDM (Time Division Multiplexing), 277
TE (see Traffic Engineering)
TE auto-bandwidth, 560-568
TE bandwidth reservations, 549-568
TE credibility control preference, 525
TE Metric attribute, 526-530
TE Router ID, 520
TED (see Traffic Engineering Database)
TED Builders (TE protocol), 516
tenants, 126, 371
Time Division Multiplexing (TDM), 277
Time-to-Live (TTL), 23
top transport label, 147
Topology-Independent Fast ReReout (TI-FRR), 707-710
Topology-Independent LFA (TI-LFA), 721-731
ToR (top-of-rack) switches, 106, 370, 438, 449
ToR service nodes (TSN), 480
total cost of ownership (TCO), 491
traffic blackholing (see blackholing)
Traffic Class, 22
Traffic Engineering (TE), 515-547
    bandwidth reservations (see TE bandwidth reservations)
    centralized (see centralized traffic engineering)
Traffic Engineering Database (TED), 525, 549
    and RSVP-TE, 72-75
    and TED builders, 516
traffic polarization, 59
traffic tromboning, 343, 348
transit fast restoration (IGP-based), 673-737
transit fast restoration (RSVP-TE-based), 739-781
Transit P, 21
transit protection, 673
transit SPs, 3
Translational Cross-Connect (TCC), 278
transport addresses, 47, 593
TSN (ToR service nodes), 480
TTL (Time-to-Live), 23

U

UMH (Upstream Multicast Hop), 260
uncertainty, 493

underlay

underlay and overlay architectures, 421-447
unicast frame, 179
unicast IP address, multicast IP address vs., 178
unicast next hop, 790, 796
unilist next hop, 211, 790, 796
universal edge model, 592
unlabeled service, 125
Upstream Multicast Hop (UMH), 260

V

vanilla BGP, 104
    basic configuration, 8-13
    configuration in IGP-less topology, 116
virtual computing entities, 445
Virtual Hub PEs (V-hubs), 644
Virtual Local Area Networks (see VLANs)
virtual machines (VMs), 106, 445
    as IP endpoint, 449-478
    as transit element, 489-513
virtual networks (VNs), 449
Virtual Private LAN Service (see VPLS)
Virtual Private Networks (VPNs) (see specific types, e.g.: Layer 2 VPN)
Virtual Private Wire Service (see VPWS)
Virtual Router Redundancy Protocol (VRRP), 342
virtual routers, 155
virtual routing and forwarding (see VRF)
Virtual Spoke PEs (V-spokes), 644
virtual tunnel (VT) interface, 157, 250, 324, 821, 875
virtual, in context of NFV, 490
VLANs (Virtual Local Area Networks)
    and learning domains in VPLS, 332-337
    EVPN IRB: inter-VLAN forwarding, 360
    in legacy L2 bridged network, 432
    inter-VLAN forwarding, 356-362
    intra-VLAN bridging, 354
    LAN tag translation and manipulation, 300-302, 314
    VLAN tag multiplexing, 298-300, 312-313
VMs (see virtual machines)
VNI (VXLAN Network Identifier), 372
VNs (virtual networks), 449
VPLS (Virtual Private LAN Service), 276, 317-346
    signaled with BGP (see BGP-based VPLS)
    signaled with LDP (see LDP-based VPLS)
VPN forwarders, 433

About the Authors

Antonio "Ato" Sánchez-Monge is a senior engineer at Juniper Networks, transitioning from Advanced Services to the SDN Solutions Engineering team. He holds two master of science degrees in physics and mathematics from Madrid Autonoma University, Spain. He has 16 years of experience in the IP/MPLS Networking industry, first with Hewlett-Packard as a Cisco partner, and then, for the last 11 years, at Juniper Networks, having worked mainly for SP customers. Ato is fluent in three languages and holds certifications for both Cisco (CCIE R&S #13098 Emeritus) and Juniper (JNCIE-SP #222). He has written several books in the Juniper Networks Day One Library, and he led the Junos Cup 2014. MPLS is part of his daily job, from high-level design down to the details, and he is a go-to person inside Juniper for different technologies, including Multicast VPN. Ato lives with his wife and two children near the countryside. In his free time, he enjoys outdoor sports, nature, and fine music.

Krzysztof Grzegorz Szarkowicz is a senior Professional Services consultant at Juniper Networks, holding a master of science degree in electrical engineering from Budapest University of Technology and Economics, Hungary. He has 20 years of experience in the industry, gained with Hewlett-Packard Labs, Telia Research, Ericsson, Cisco, and finally, for the last 9 years, with Juniper Networks; and having performed varied roles as Researcher, Program Manager, Trainer and Consultant. Krzysztof speaks four languages fluently, and he holds certifications for both Cisco (CCIE-SP #14550 Emeritus) and Juniper (JNCIE-SP #400). Inside Juniper, he is a recognized MPLS expert with very extensive field experience on technologies such as Seamless MPLS Mobile Backhaul, including several large-scale deployments. He has strong collaboration links with the Junos MPLS development team. Krzysztof lives with his wife and four children in a house in the countryside. In his free time, he enjoys trekking in the mountains and playing guitar.

Additional Contributors

Lead Technical Reviewer

Harold Ritter is a technical leader at Cisco Systems' Advanced Services. He has been working with SP customers for more than 15 years, helping them to deploy, improve, and troubleshoot large-scale IP4, IPv6, and MPLS networks. Harold holds a master of science in computer engineering and several certifications including two CCIEs (R&S and SP) #4168 and JNCIP. He also enjoys reading and discussing politics.

In addition to deep technical review of all the chapters, Harold's assistance has also been paramount to identify and solve interoperability issues. Many scenarios in this book worked thanks to Harold's technical insight, combined with his humble and fair attitude. Harold, Ato, and Krzysztof played by the rules and cleanly collaborated to make the scenarios work without revealing sensitive or proprietary industrial information of any kind.

Main Contributors

Javier Antich is an experienced networking industry professional with 20 years of experience. He has spent half of his career in Juniper Networks where he has held different positions and is currently a product manager at the JUNOS and MX product line team. He holds a master's degree in telecommunications and an executive MBA. Javier shared some of his sharp technological vision by writing the SDN section within Chapter 1, and the introductory section "NFV in the Software-Defined Networking Era" on page 490 within Chapter 12.

Gonzalo Gómez Herrero (JNCIE-SP #155, CCIE #14068) has been working at Juniper Networks for more than 10 years, where he is currently the core and edge practice architect in the Professional Services Innovation team. He has written a networking book and is actively challenging the technical community with the #TheRouting-Churn blog at *http://forums.juniper.net*. Gonzalo has used his technical expertise to build and document (purposely for this book) Chapter 15's PCE interoperable scenario and case studies.

David Roy (JNCIE SP #703, JNCIE-ENT #305, JNCIE-SEC #144) is a Network Architect with 13 years of experience in Orange, France, first in the R&D division, and currently in the NOC. He is enthusiastic about reverse engineering, keeps the technical blog *http://junosandme.net*, and has also written a book in Juniper Networks Day One Library. David used his multivendor background to write the LDP implementation pages within Chapter 2.

Colophon

The animal on the cover of *MPLS in the SDN Era* is a basket starfish. Basket starfish are a taxon of brittle stars, and the name is broadly applied to many different species.

Like other echinoderms, basket starfish lack blood and "breathe" through gas exchange in their water vascular systems. They generally live in deep-sea habitats and can live up to 35 years in the wild. They are distinguished from other types of starfish by their repeatedly branching arms, which can grow up to 27 inches long.

Each arm has tiny hooks that allow the basket star to capture prey, mainly zooplankton. They can also grow their limbs back if one is pulled off or bitten off by predators. To reproduce, basket starfish can either release eggs and sperm into the water, or they can divide their bodies to regenerate asexually.

Many of the animals on O'Reilly covers are endangered; all of them are important to the world. To learn more about how you can help, go to *animals.oreilly.com*.

The cover image is of unknown origin. The cover fonts are URW Typewriter and Guardian Sans. The text font is Adobe Minion Pro; the heading font is Adobe Myriad Condensed; and the code font is Dalton Maag's Ubuntu Mono.

Get even more for your money.

Join the O'Reilly Community, and register the O'Reilly books you own. It's free, and you'll get:

- $4.99 ebook upgrade offer
- 40% upgrade offer on O'Reilly print books
- Membership discounts on books and events
- Free lifetime updates to ebooks and videos
- Multiple ebook formats, DRM FREE
- Participation in the O'Reilly community
- Newsletters
- Account management
- 100% Satisfaction Guarantee

Signing up is easy:

1. Go to: oreilly.com/go/register
2. Create an O'Reilly login.
3. Provide your address.
4. Register your books.

Note: English-language books only

To order books online:
oreilly.com/store

For questions about products or an order:
orders@oreilly.com

To sign up to get topic-specific email announcements and/or news about upcoming books, conferences, special offers, and new technologies:
elists@oreilly.com

For technical questions about book content:
booktech@oreilly.com

To submit new book proposals to our editors:
proposals@oreilly.com

O'Reilly books are available in multiple DRM-free ebook formats. For more information:
oreilly.com/ebooks

Have it your way.

Milton Keynes UK
Ingram Content Group UK Ltd.
UKHW052351080724
445250UK00004B/10